W9-BTZ-423

West's Law School
Advisory Board

JESSE H. CHOPER
Professor of Law,
University of California, Berkeley

DAVID P. CURRIE
Professor of Law, University of Chicago

YALE KAMISAR
Professor of Law, University of Michigan
Professor of Law, University of San Diego

MARY KAY KANE
Chancellor, Dean and Distinguished Professor of Law,
University of California,
Hastings College of the Law

WAYNE R. LaFAVE
Professor of Law, University of Illinois

ARTHUR R. MILLER
Professor of Law, Harvard University

GRANT S. NELSON
Professor of Law,
University of California, Los Angeles

JAMES J. WHITE
Professor of Law, University of Michigan

TORT AND ACCIDENT LAW

CASES AND MATERIALS

Fourth Edition

By

Robert E. Keeton

Langdell Professor of Law, Emeritus,
Harvard University Law School

Lewis D. Sargentich

Professor of Law,
Harvard University Law School

Gregory C. Keating

Dalessi Professor of Law,
University of Southern California Law School

AMERICAN CASEBOOK SERIES®

THOMSON
＊
WEST

Mat #40043641

West, a Thomson business, has created this publication to provide you with accurate and authoritative information concerning the subject matter covered. However, this publication was not necessarily prepared by persons licensed to practice law in a particular jurisdiction. West is not engaged in rendering legal or other professional advice, and this publication is not a substitute for the advice of an attorney. If you require legal or other expert advice, you should seek the services of a competent attorney or other professional.

American Casebook Series and West Group are trademarks
registered in the U.S. Patent and Trademark Office.

COPYRIGHT © 1983, 1989 WEST PUBLISHING CO.
COPYRIGHT © 1998 WEST GROUP
© 2004 West, a Thomson business
     610 Opperman Drive
     P.O. Box 64526
     St. Paul, MN 55164–0526
     1–800–328–9352

Printed in the United States of America

ISBN 0–314–26379–9

TEXT IS PRINTED ON 10% POST
CONSUMER RECYCLED PAPER

Preface to the Fourth Edition

This edition incorporates a number of substantive changes. We have added textual notes introducing each of the chapters and sections and, within those chapters and sections, we have added textual notes commenting on a variety of topics—restrictions on noneconomic damages, competing conceptions of strict liability, and collective health injury, to name just three. For the most part, these notes comment on materials included in the book and are restrained in their mention of other cases and secondary literature. The predominant aim of these notes is to orient students to the topics at hand and to call their attention to the perplexities of those topics. But these notes often serve other aims as well. Sometimes, they identify major issues and areas of controversy, highlighting the disagreements that divide courts. Other times, they summarize legal developments—such as the Supreme Court's punitive damages jurisprudence—which bear on tort law but which do not warrant treatment in the form of cases.

This edition also expands the casebook's treatment of emerging areas of law—such as "loss of chance" doctrine and primary assumption of risk—and its coverage of accident law in general. The casebook's discussion of "reasonable care" in Chapter 8, for example, includes materials specifically devoted to the issue of "duty" in negligence law. We have also expanded the casebook's coverage of product liability law, an area of particular contemporary ferment. And we have added more than 150 new cases.

We have also made organizational changes. One organizational change is to split the former chapter on product liability law into two chapters. This splitting of the old chapter into two new chapters—19 & 20—is designed to separate the rise of modern product liability law from the present debates which now rage over its contours and character. We hope that this will bring both historic foundation and contemporary controversy into clearer focus.

The addition of a new subpart C—"Tort Liability and Intangible Interests"—to Part I of the book is another organizational change. This new subpart includes two new chapters. Chapter 5, entitled "Defamation and Invasion of Privacy," focuses on "dignitary" torts. Chapter 6, entitled "Misrepresentation: Tort and Contract," focuses on an "economic" tort. These new chapters replace some of the material which appeared at the back of the previous edition. By including these materials in the first part of the book we hope to unify our treatment of intentional torts and to highlight the basic forms of intentional wrongdoing against which the law of torts provides protection. We hope that this new organization invites the exploration of a number of topics, such as the diversity of interests protected by the law of torts; the connections between tort and the adjacent fields of property and contract; and the surprising character of the wrongdoing which tort counts "intentional"—wrongdoing which can often be committed innocently and intentionally at the same time.

We wish to express our appreciation to John Vigil of the class of 2004 at USC Law School and to Sarah Wheatley, of the class of 2005 at USC Law School, for their excellent research assistance.

The Genealogy which follows places this book in the company of its predecessors.

ROBERT E. KEETON
LEWIS D. SARGENTICH
GREGORY C. KEATING

January 2004

A Genealogy of the Casebook

These materials are very much a blend of the old and new. We gratefully acknowledge our intellectual debt to our predecessors in a genealogy of casebook editors on whose work we have drawn freely.

In 1874 Professor James Barr Ames of the Harvard Law Faculty published an 800 page collection of cases upon trespass, conversion and defamation, under the title "Select Cases on Torts." This book formed the nucleus of the first volume of the celebrated "Selection of Cases on the Law of Torts," published in 1893 by Professor Ames and Professor Jeremiah Smith. Professor Smith was responsible for the second volume. In 1904, Smith published a "Supplement" containing recent cases, mostly on labor litigation, and in 1909–10 the same authors brought out another edition of their work. Later editions of Ames and Smith, with new material, were published in 1917 by Dean Roscoe Pound (omitting some of the subject matter, which was at that time allocated to Professor Joseph H. Beale's course on Legal Liability) and in 1929 by Professor Beale (restoring much of the matter omitted in Dean Pound's edition). In 1937 Professors Ned Thurston and Warren A. Seavey published a supplementary pamphlet for use with Beale's edition of Ames and Smith. In 1942 they published a new casebook that drew many of the older cases from Ames and Smith but was substantially different in conception and organization as well as in the addition of new materials.

Page Keeton joined in the casebook published in 1950—Seavey, Keeton & Thurston—which links this history to the more recent succession. Page and Robert Keeton joined Seavey in editing casebooks published in 1957 and 1964. There followed the two editions in 1971 and 1977 of Keeton & Keeton. A supplement to Keeton & Keeton was published in 1981 containing materials which Lewis Sargentich and Henry Steiner had developed in their respective courses.

The first (1983) edition of *Tort and Accident Law* (by Keeton, Keeton, Sargentich and Steiner) drew substantially on its 1977 predecessor, while adopting a new organization of the core topics of "accident law" for which Sargentich and Steiner were responsible. With the third edition (in 1998), the evolving casebook came into the custody of the present editors.

*

Foreword

Lewis Sargentich and Gregory Keating

This casebook divides its subject into two parts. Part I provides a general introduction to tort law. Part II addresses what has become the central concern of a first-year course in torts: how the law responds to physical harm caused by accident.

Part I starts with an overview of different forms of legal liability for physical harming. Then it addresses intentionally caused injury to person or property. It concludes by considering intent-based and other liability for injury to intangible (dignitary, economic) interests. The aims of Part I are to develop understanding of the tort concept of intentionality and other basic tort conceptions; to show the sweep of tort by a selective—not an exhaustive—survey of the field; and to build the groundwork for detailed study of the law of accidents, which ensues.

Part II on accident law divides the tort materials into three segments: the negligence system; passages from fault to strict liability; liability without fault. The subpart on passages to strict liability includes materials on insurance. After an extensive look at tort law of products liability, Part II reaches beyond tort.

The casebook's title "Tort and Accident Law" makes clear that the common law of tort is but one, if the principal, of the categories of law examined. Common law and administrative regulation, tort doctrine and legislation, are seen as alternative ways of handling the same general problem. Part II concludes with three chapters on legal initiatives going "beyond tort" to find satisfactory answers to the modern accident problem. The third-to-last chapter of Part II looks at a number of judicial and legislative innovations that push tort suits away from traditional moorings and toward the approach of no-fault plans. The penultimate chapter investigates a variety of statutory reparation systems, contrasting tort law and no-fault plans as techniques for compensating victims and inducing safety. The final chapter draws methodological comparisons between common law and administrative regulation as means for controlling harmful activities.

Given our concentration upon accident law rather than strictly tort law, it is not surprising that the case materials involve at many points the intersection or overlap of "tort" with "contract" or "property" principles. Relationships among these conventional doctrinal categories as well as between the common law and the regulatory state become an important focus of inquiry.

We should say something about the way we have selected and edited the cases in the book. Our interest is in encouraging students to understand tort doctrine in relationship to its history and to practical moral commitment. Of course the opinions make their doctrinal points. Indeed the basic organization of the materials is doctrinal, and the cases as a whole cover the important doctrinal issues, tensions and contradictions in the historical and contemporary law of accidental harm.

Nonetheless the opinions that we selected go beyond discussion of doctrine and conventional references to "policy." They explore large considerations leading to or indeed forming part of the rule, standard or principle involved. That is, we have been attentive to more broadly ranging judicial rhetoric. For example, many opinions in the casebook set forth extensive justifications for the liability rule selected by the court—perhaps a welfare-maximizing justification involving economic reasoning, or a justification based upon ideas of right or fairness or distributive justice. We have also been partial to opinions which reveal courts' perception or vision of the social, political and historical context in which liability rules are to function. Of course, justifications and visions have changed over time as doctrine has changed. The case materials are designed to illustrate relationships among these changes.

Following the practice of prior editions, we have included both principal cases and "squib" ones. Squib cases selectively extract one or more of the case's points or arguments, and serve a number of different functions in the text. Sometimes they elaborate on the details of doctrine. Other times they illustrate conflicts within doctrine, or among courts. On yet other occasions they develop certain justificatory themes, or connect those themes with particular problems in the pertinent area of the law. More often than not, squib cases pursue issues connected to the principal cases immediately preceding them. Occasionally, however, they anticipate issues raised by the next principal case, or by the next section of the book. When there is a significant shift in topic from one squib case to another, we have sought to mark the transition by inserting a solid line in the center of the page between the cases.

One technical note. We have excised from principal cases numerous citations and footnotes which appeared to serve no purpose in illuminating a doctrinal or theoretical issue. For the most part we have not noted these cuts. Of course many citations, and a few footnotes, have been preserved.

Summary of Contents

D.   BEYOND TORT

Table of Contents

D. BEYOND TORT

Table of Cases

The principal cases are in bold type. Cases cited or discussed in the text are roman type. References are to pages. Cases cited in principal cases and within other quoted materials are not included.

*

TORT AND ACCIDENT LAW
CASES AND MATERIALS
Fourth Edition

*

Part I

INTRODUCTION TO TORT LAW

A. OVERVIEW: TYPES AND THEORIES OF LIABILITY

Chapter 1

FIVE FORMS OF LIABILITY FOR PHYSICAL HARM

Tort law addresses situations in which someone suffers harm on account of the actions of another. The harm suffered may be physical damage to person or property, caused for example by the striking of a blow, the occurrence of an auto accident, or the malfunctioning of a defective product. Or the harm may be nonphysical in character, as when someone's reputation is injured or privacy invaded. In the typical tort situation the victim of an injury comes to court claiming that another person or firm should be held responsible for the harm in question and should be required to repair it. Tort, then, is a body of legal principles aiming to control or regulate harmful behavior; to assign responsibility for injuries that arise in social interaction; and to provide recompense for victims with meritorious claims. It is commonly said that the main concern of tort is redress for harm done, and that the main job of the law of torts is to determine when loss shall be shifted from one to another, and when it shall be allowed to remain where it has fallen.

1

The materials in the present chapter are meant to provide an introductory sketch—an overview—of available forms of legal liability for physical harm. Five forms of liability are represented: battery, negligence, vicarious liability, strict liability, and workers' compensation. All five address situations in which tangible physical injury, to person or property or both, has befallen the complaining victim. While the first—battery—deals with intentional harming, the other four deal with accidents. The focus on physical harm, and in particular on physical accidents, reflects the primary orientation of the casebook as a whole. Hopefully an initial look at the alternative types of liability, side by side, will reveal major points of similarity and contrast and provide a broad framework for further study. Notice, for example, that sometimes liability is predicated on fault, that is, on the wrong-doing or misbehavior of the defendant, while in other forms of liability fault on the part of the defendant is not a prerequisite to recovery. Notice also that the last form of liability—workers' compensation—is different from all the others, and indeed is normally not thought of as a part of tort law proper, but as an alternative to tort.

Tort law in general, and accident law in particular, can be well understood only in light of their history. Immediately following is a note on the very early history of tort. More important are the transformations in legal doctrines wrought over the last 150 years, and the quickening of change and heightening of debate that characterize the last three decades and dominate the present outlook. To study tort is to study an object in motion. Better, it is to study an on-going debate about how a changing society through its legal institutions should respond to harms and misfortunes persistently generated by the clashes and misadventures endemic to social life. The forms of liability portrayed in this chapter are, to a significant extent, in competition with one another. Each must ultimately be grounded in a theory that justifies its own distinctive approach to a common problem. In order to understand the contrasting and alternative forms of liability, and the structure of contemporary debate about tort, and the lines of development of the subject as a whole, it is crucial to look beyond the details of the various liability rules and consider their underlying justifications in moral, economic, and social thought.

TORTS AND WRITS

A primary purpose of primitive law was to preserve the peace and to prevent the use of force by one person against another or another's possession of property. In England immediately after the Conquest the complaint of the King or of the local authority that the peace had been broken was not clearly differentiated from a citizen's complaint of interference with person or property. In the course of time, however, a separation between the two evolved, so that we now have criminal law, dealing with prosecutions by the state, and the law of torts, dealing with suits by individuals seeking redress for interferences with their persons, property, or intangible interests.

An affinity between the criminal law and the law of torts remains. Both deal with wrongs. In a large number of instances an act is a wrong punishable in a prosecution by the state and is also a wrong subject to redress in a suit by an individual. In other cases, however, only one of these forms of redress is available. The same word is sometimes used to designate either a tort or a crime, as in the case of assault, battery, and false imprisonment. But that does not mean that the tort and the crime have the same elements.

The modern law of torts is a product of its history, and an important part of its history is procedural. When, after the Norman Conquest, the King's courts began to take over the administration of justice, new methods of trial were introduced. A person who thought that another had committed a wrong against him could obtain from the King's officer, the Chancellor, a document known as a writ. The writ stated the nature of the complaint and directed the executive officer, the sheriff, to summon the defendant to attend a hearing before a representative of the King. Customary forms of writs gradually developed, and were catalogued in a Register of Writs. The complainant could choose from a number of such "writs of course" that the Chancellor would issue. Those lying within our field are the writs of trespass of various sorts, which became common about the middle of the thirteenth century. Such a writ would allege that the defendant had trespassed upon the person of the plaintiff, or upon the plaintiff's land or chattels. For a time, there was a chance that one could get the Chancellor to invent a writ to fit the needs of a particular case if none of the writs of course would do. By the Provisions of Oxford in 1258, however, the barons, who had become concerned about the power exercised by the Chancellor, exacted an oath that he would seal no writs save writs of course "without the commandment of the King and his council who shall be present." Annulment of the Provisions five years later did not restore the earlier practice, but after a time some writs analogous to writs of course were allowed. A dispute exists as to whether this development originated in the Statute of Westminster II, 1285, or independently of that statute. In any event, a writ of trespass on the case, of great importance in the development of tort law, came to be used for cases in which some requirement of trespass could not be met. This writ was more flexible than trespass, and thus allowed for some growth of the law. But in time various forms of trespass on the case were developed, and they too became rigid.

If able to bring the complaint within the language of some writ, the plaintiff could maintain an action, but not otherwise. The writs limited the actions that could be brought. During the nineteenth century, however, the subservience of substantive law to the terms of writs was formally terminated. The law of torts became recognized as not merely a collection of heterogeneous rules, but a subject responsive to common principles. Nevertheless, the history of the subject has in many cases had a profound effect upon the right of the plaintiff to maintain an action. Categories derived from the writs are still used and sometimes misused in thinking about the law of torts today.

One of the reasons for the success of the King's courts was that they gradually made less and less use of methods of trial such as combat, ordeal and oath taking, and substituted a method by which an attempt was made to ascertain facts rationally. For this purpose the King's courts used the Norman institution of the inquest, a group of people in the neighborhood who would be likely to know the facts. This was the beginning of the modern jury. The specific function of the inquest was to ascertain the facts on which the controversy was based, submitting these facts to the decision of the judge; he would make the application of the rules of law to the facts and decide whether or not the plaintiff had a cause of action. As decisions by rules of law developed, cases came to be reported, the early ones in manuscript. This was a matter of great importance; under the Anglo–American doctrine of stare decisis judges decide cases in the light of principles evolved from earlier decisions.

A note on terminology: Students often find the word and the concept "tort" obscure, and understandably so. What are torts? Torts are civil wrongs—wrongs committed by one person in civil society against another, whose commission entitles the party injured to redress from the party inflicting the injury. That redress usually, but not always, takes the form of money damages.

SMOTHERS v. GRESHAM TRANSFER, INC.
Supreme Court of Oregon, 2001.
332 Or. 83, 23 P.3d 333.

[Terry Smothers, who had been exposed to toxic fumes at his workplace in Oregon, developed severe respiratory problems. Smothers brought a tort suit for damages against his employer, Gresham Transfer. The employer argued that a statute passed by the Oregon legislature in 1995 had the effect of barring Smothers' lawsuit. Smothers rejoined that the statute, when applied to block his civil suit, violated Article 1, Section 10 of the Oregon Constitution. Article 1 of the Oregon Constitution is Oregon's Bill of Rights. Section 10 provides in pertinent part:

> * * * every man shall have remedy by due course of law for injury done
> him in his person, property, or reputation.

The Oregon Supreme Court agreed that the quoted provision, called the "remedy clause," guaranteed Smothers' right to sue in tort, and concluded that the 1995 statute was unconstitutional as applied in Smothers' case.

In a lengthy opinion by Justice Leeson, the unanimous court found the meaning of the remedy clause in its history. The Oregon Constitution was adopted in 1859. The court first turned to mid-nineteenth century dictionaries to define the key terms "remedy" and "injury." A law dictionary of 1839 defined "remedy" as "[t]he means employed to enforce a right or redress an injury"; it defined "injury" as "a wrong or tort." Then the court traced these concepts further back. The excerpts from Justice Leeson's opinion that follow address the writings of two great figures in the history of the common law, Edward Coke (1552–1634) and William Blackstone (1723–1780).]

1. *Edward Coke's Second Institute*

The principle that the law makes available a remedy for injury to person, property, or reputation comes from the common law. The phrasing of remedy clauses that now appear in the Bill of Rights of the Oregon Constitution and 38 other states traces to Edward Coke's commentary, first published in 1642, on the second sentence of Chapter 29 of the Magna Carta of 1225.

The two sentences comprising Chapter 29 of the Magna Carta of 1225 had appeared as separate chapters, 39 and 40, in the original Magna Carta of 1215.[5] *See* A.E. Dick Howard, *Magna Carta: Text and Commentary*, 33–52 (1964) (reprinting complete text of Magna Carta 1215). A 1797 edition of Coke's *Second Institute* translated Chapter 29 of the Magna Carta of 1225 from the original Latin as follows:

> "No freeman shall be taken, or imprisoned, or be disseised of his freehold, or liberties, or free customs, or be outlawed, or exiled, or any otherwise destroyed; nor will we not pass upon him, nor condemn him, but by lawful judgment of his peers, or by the law of the land. We will sell to no man, we will not deny or defer to any man either justice or right."

Edward Coke, *The Second Part of the Institutes of the Laws of England*, 45 (1797). Coke's commentary on the Magna Carta viewed Chapter 29 as a "roote," out of which "many fruitfull branches of the law of England have sprung." * * * Coke used the Magna Carta of 1225, as he had used other ancient texts and reports, as a means to demonstrate how, in his view, the common law protected individuals by placing substantive restraints on both the Crown and Parliament, and by adjusting relations between private individuals. *See* Theodore F.T. Plucknett, *Bonham's Case and Judicial Review*, 40 Harv. L. Rev. 30, 30–31 (1926–27) (discussing Coke's use of history to interpret English law).

The dominant theme in Coke's commentary on the first sentence of Chapter 29 was his explanation that the law protected individuals' rights by prohibiting *official* acts depriving freemen of life, liberty, or property unless done according to "the law of the land" or by judgment of peers. Proceedings "by the law of the land" meant "by the common law, statute law, or custome of England," "by the due course, and process of law," or "by due process of the common law." Coke, *Second Institute* at 45–46, 50. * * *

Coke declared that the second sentence of Chapter 29 had evolved into a different kind of guarantee in English law, *viz.*, one involving the rights of subjects in their *private relations* with one another. The assurance that the king would not sell, deny, or defer justice or right had come to mean that

> " * * * *every subject of this realme, for injury done to him in bonis, terris, vel persona* [in goods, land, or person], *by any other subject,* be

---

5. The only text of the Magna Carta that was available to Coke was the 1225 version. Faith Thompson, *Magna Carta: Its Role in the Making of the English Constitution, 1300–1629*, 5 (1948). However, Coke was aware that King John originally had issued the Magna Carta in 1215, *see* Coke, *Second Institute, A Proeme* at 4 (so stating). King John had done so in response to a list of grievances from his barons. * * *

The Magna Carta of 1215 was law for about only nine weeks, because King John persuaded the Pope to annul it. Theodore F.T. Plucknett, *A Concise History of the Common Law*, 23 (5th ed. 1956). The document was reissued in 1216, 1217, and 1225, each time with many revisions. The reissue of the Magna Carta in 1225 by King Henry III marked the final form of the document. William McKechnie, *Magna Carta*, 183 (1905).

he ecclesiastical, or temporall, free, or bond, man, or woman, old, or young, or be he outlawed, excommunicated, or any other without exception, *may take his remedy by the course of the law, and have justice, and right for the injury done to him, freely without sale, fully without any deniall, and speedily without delay.*"

Coke, *Second Institute* at 55. In other words, Coke asserted that the common law of England had come to guarantee every subject a legal remedy for injury to goods, lands, or person caused by any other subject. The purpose of the remedial branch of the common law was to discover "that which is tort, crooked, or wrong" and restore "right" or "justice." *Id.* at 56. Coke viewed the remedial branch of the law as the best birthright that English subjects had, because it protected their goods, lands, person, life, honor, and estimation from injury and wrong. *Id.* Coke praised the common law, because it guaranteed both justice ("justitiam") and the means to attain it ("rectum"). *Id.*

Coke's commentary on Chapter 29 of the Magna Carta of 1225 thus explained that the common law had evolved to protect individuals in two broad respects. The first was a shield against arbitrary government actions involving a person's life, liberty, or property. The second was a guarantee to every subject that a legal remedy was available for injury to goods, land, or person by any other subject of the realm. As noted, Coke viewed the remedial side of the law as "the best birthright the subject hath." *Id.* at 56.

Coke's *Second Institute* made its way to the American colonies through a variety of sources. Several lawyers had *The Institutes* in their libraries. A.E. Dick Howard, *The Road From Runnymede*, 122–24 (1968). In 1687, William Penn published *The Excellent Priviledge of Liberty & Property Being the Birth–Right of Free–Born Subjects of England,* the first commentary on the Magna Carta of 1225 to be published in the American colonies. Penn had copied his commentary verbatim from Henry Care's *English Liberties,* another commentary on the Magna Carta of 1225 that enjoyed immense popularity in England and in the colonies. Care had paraphrased Coke when writing his commentary on the Magna Carta. To Care, like Coke, the provisions of the Magna Carta of 1225 were not concessions that had been exacted from kings. Rather, the Magna Carta of 1225 affirmed the common law, which the English had claimed as their birthright. Henry Care, *English Liberties,* 6 (American ed. 1721).

* * *

2. *William Blackstone's Commentaries*

Blackstone's *Commentaries on the Laws of England,* the first volume of which was published in 1765, is another important source for understanding what the drafters of state constitutions intended when they included in declarations or bills of rights the guarantee of remedy by due course of law for injury to person, property, reputation and, in some instances, liberty. Blackstone's *Commentaries* updated Coke's accounts of the evolution of the common law. The *Commentaries* sold quickly in the American colonies and became one of the principal means of the colonists' information about the state of English law in general.

* * *

Blackstone described an act that deprives a person of a right as a "wrong." 3 Blackstone, *Commentaries* *116. Wrongs can be public (crimes and misdemeanors) or private (civil injuries). *Id.* Blackstone explained that the remedial part of the law provides a method for recovering for deprivations of rights or for redressing wrongs, be they public or private. 1 Blackstone, *Commentaries* *54. Whenever the common law recognized a right or prohibited an injury, he wrote, it also gave a remedy by legal action initiated by filing the appropriate writ. 3 Blackstone, *Commentaries* *123.

Blackstone echoed Coke in stating that it would be "in vain" for the law to recognize rights, if it were not for the remedial part of the law that provides the methods for restoring those rights when they wrongfully are withheld or invaded. 1 Blackstone, *Commentaries* *56. To Blackstone, the guarantee of legal remedy for injury "is what we mean properly, when we speak of the protection of the law." *Id.* Hence, the maxim of English law, *Ubi jus, ibi remedium:* "for every right, there must be a remedy."

* * *

* * * In *Marbury v. Madison,* 5 U.S. (1 Cranch) 137, 163, 2 L.Ed. 60 (1803), the United States Supreme Court held that the "very essence of civil liberty * * * consists in the right of every individual to claim the protection of the laws, whenever he receives an injury." That rule rested on Blackstone's assertion that " 'it is a general and indisputable rule, that where there is a legal right, there is also a legal remedy by suit or action at law wherever that right is invaded,' " and that " 'every right, when withheld, must have a remedy, and every injury its proper redress.' " *Id.* (quoting Blackstone's *Commentaries*).

SECTION A.   INTENTIONAL HARMING

GARRATT v. DAILEY
Supreme Court of Washington, 1955.
46 Wn.2d 197, 279 P.2d 1091.

HILL, Justice. The liability of an infant for an alleged battery is presented to this court for the first time. Brian Dailey (age five years, nine months) was visiting with Naomi Garratt, an adult and a sister of the plaintiff, Ruth Garratt, likewise an adult, in the back yard of the plaintiff's home, on July 16, 1951. It is plaintiff's contention that she came out into the back yard to talk with Naomi and that, as she started to sit down in a wood and canvas lawn chair, Brian deliberately pulled it out from under her. The only one of the three persons present so testifying was Naomi Garratt. (Ruth Garratt, the plaintiff, did not testify as to how or why she fell.) The trial court, unwilling to accept this testimony, adopted instead Brian Dailey's version of what happened, and made the following findings:

"III. * * * that while Naomi Garratt and Brian Dailey were in the back yard the plaintiff, Ruth Garratt, came out of her house into the back yard. Some time subsequent thereto defendant, Brian Dailey, picked up a lightly built wood and canvas lawn chair which was then and there located in the back yard of the above described premises, moved it sideways a few feet and seated himself therein, at which time he discovered the plaintiff, Ruth Garratt, about to sit down at the place where the lawn chair had formerly been, at which time he hurriedly got up from the chair and attempted to move it toward Ruth Garratt to aid her in sitting down in the chair; that due to the defendant's small size and lack of dexterity he was unable to get the lawn chair under the plaintiff in time to prevent her from falling to the ground. That plaintiff fell to the ground and sustained a fracture of her hip, and other injuries and damages as hereinafter set forth.

"IV. That the preponderance of the evidence in this case establishes that when the defendant, Brian Dailey, moved the chair in question *he did not have any wilful or unlawful purpose* in doing so; that *he did not have any intent to injure the plaintiff, or any intent to bring about any unauthorized or offensive contact with her person* or any objects appurtenant thereto; that the circumstances which immediately preceded the fall of the plaintiff establish that the defendant, *Brian Dailey, did not have purpose, intent or design to perform a prank or to effect an assault and battery upon the person of the plaintiff.*" (Italics ours, for a purpose hereinafter indicated.)

It is conceded that Ruth Garratt's fall resulted in a fractured hip and other painful and serious injuries. To obviate the necessity of a retrial in the event this court determines that she was entitled to a judgment against Brian Dailey, the amount of her damage was found to be $11,000. Plaintiff appeals from a judgment dismissing the action and asks for the entry of a judgment in that amount or a new trial.

The authorities generally, but with certain notable exceptions, see Bohlen, "Liability in Tort of Infants and Insane Persons," 23 Mich.L.Rev. 9, state that when a minor has committed a tort with force he is liable to be proceeded against as any other person would be. * * *

It is urged that Brian's action in moving the chair constituted a battery. A definition (not all-inclusive but sufficient for our purpose) of a battery is the intentional infliction of a harmful bodily contact upon another. The rule that determines liability for battery is given in 1 Restatement, Torts, 29 § 13, as:

"An act which, directly or indirectly, is the legal cause of a harmful contact with another's person makes the actor liable to the other, if

"(a) the act is done with the intention of bringing about a harmful or offensive contact or an apprehension thereof to the other or a third person, and

"(b) the contact is not consented to by the other or the other's consent thereto is procured by fraud or duress, and

"(c) the contact is not otherwise privileged."

We have in this case no question of consent or privilege. We therefore proceed to an immediate consideration of intent and its place in the law of battery. In the comment on clause (a), the Restatement says:

"Character of actor's intention. In order that an act may be done with the intention of bringing about a harmful or offensive contact or an apprehension thereof to a particular person, either the other or a third person, the act must be done for the purpose of causing the contact or apprehension or with knowledge on the part of the actor that such contact or apprehension is substantially certain to be produced." See, also, Prosser on Torts 41, § 8 [p. 30 in 2d ed.].

We have here the conceded volitional act of Brian, i.e., the moving of a chair. Had the plaintiff proved to the satisfaction of the trial court that Brian moved the chair while she was in the act of sitting down, Brian's action would patently have been for the purpose or with the intent of causing the plaintiff's bodily contact with the ground, and she would be entitled to a judgment against him for the resulting damages. Vosburg v. Putney, 1891, 80 Wis. 523, 50 N.W. 403, 14 L.R.A. 226; * * *

* * * After the trial court determined that the plaintiff had not established her theory of a battery (i.e., that Brian had pulled the chair out from under the plaintiff while she was in the act of sitting down), it then became concerned with whether a battery was established under the facts as it found them to be.

In this connection, we quote another portion of the comment on the "character of actor's intention," relating to clause (a) of the rule from the Restatement heretofore set forth:

"It is not enough that the act itself is intentionally done and this, even though the actor realizes or should realize that it contains a very grave risk of bringing about the contact or apprehension. Such realization may make the actor's conduct negligent or even reckless but unless he realizes that to a substantial certainty, the contact or apprehension will result, the actor has not that intention which is necessary to make him liable under the rule stated in this section."

A battery would be established if, in addition to plaintiff's fall, it was proved that, when Brian moved the chair, he knew with substantial certainty that the plaintiff would attempt to sit down where the chair had been. If Brian had any of the intents which the trial court found, in the italicized portions of the findings of fact quoted above, that he did not have, he would of course have had the knowledge to which we have referred. The mere absence of any intent to injure the plaintiff or to play a prank on her or to embarrass her, or to commit an assault and battery on her would not absolve him from liability if in fact he had such knowledge. Mercer v. Corbin, 1889, 117 Ind. 450, 20 N.E. 132, 3 L.R.A. 221. Without such knowledge there would be nothing wrongful about Brian's act in moving the chair and, there being no wrongful act, there would be no liability.

While a finding that Brian had no such knowledge can be inferred from the findings made, we believe that before the plaintiff's action in such a case should be dismissed there should be no question but that the trial court had passed upon that issue; hence, the case should be remanded for clarification of the findings to specifically cover the question of Brian's knowledge, because intent could be inferred therefrom. If the court finds that he had such knowledge the necessary intent will be established and the plaintiff will be entitled to recover, even though there was no purpose to injure or embarrass the plaintiff. Vosburg v. Putney, supra. If Brian did not have such knowledge, there was no wrongful act by him and the basic premise of liability on the theory of a battery was not established.

It will be noted that the law of battery as we have discussed it is the law applicable to adults, and no significance has been attached to the fact that Brian was a child less than six years of age when the alleged battery occurred. The only circumstance where Brian's age is of any consequence is in determining what he knew, and there his experience, capacity, and understanding are of course material. * * *

It is argued that some courts predicate an infant's liability for tort upon the basis of the existence of an estate in the infant; hence it was error for the trial court to refuse to admit as an exhibit a policy of liability insurance as evidence that there was a source from which a judgment might be satisfied. In our opinion the liability of an infant for his tort does not depend upon the size of his estate or even upon the existence of one. That is a matter of concern only to the plaintiff who seeks to enforce a judgment against the infant. * * *

The cause is remanded for clarification, with instructions to make definite findings on the issue of whether Brian Dailey knew with substantial certainty that the plaintiff would attempt to sit down where the chair which he moved had been, and to change the judgment if the findings warrant it.

[On remand, the trial judge concluded that "it was necessary for him to consider carefully the time sequence, as he had not done before; and this resulted in his finding that the arthritic woman had begun the slow process of being seated when the defendant quickly removed the chair and seated himself upon it, and that he knew, with substantial certainty, at that time that she would attempt to sit in the place where the chair had been." Judgment for plaintiff was entered, and was affirmed by the Supreme Court of Washington, 49 Wash.2d 499, 304 P.2d 681 (1956).]

BALDINGER v. BANKS, 26 Misc.2d 1086, 201 N.Y.S.2d 629 (1960). A 6-year-old boy pushed a 4-year-old girl to "take care of" her in an unorganized "game," knowing the contact to be offensive. *Held,* the boy is liable for the girl's broken arm on the theory of battery, even if he had no intent to cause bodily harm.

BALDINGER v. CONSOLIDATED MUTUAL INSURANCE CO., 11 N.Y.2d 1026, 230 N.Y.S.2d 25, 183 N.E.2d 908 (1962). A comprehensive personal liability insurance policy had been issued to the father of the defendant in Baldinger v. Banks, supra. [Coverage of the father, as himself an insured, was not applicable since he was not found to be liable for his son's act.] The policy defined "insured" so as to include the boy as an insured, but it contained a provision excluding from the scope of coverage any "injury * * * caused intentionally by or at the direction of the insured." *Held*, the insurer was liable despite the exclusion clause, since the injury "was not caused intentionally, but was the unintended result of an intentional act."

CONNECTICUT INDEMNITY CO. v. NESTOR, 4 Mich.App. 578, 145 N.W.2d 399 (1966). Eight-year-old child set fire to a house. *Held*, liability insurance coverage applies since the result of damage to the house was not intended though the act was.

ISENHART v. GENERAL CASUALTY CO., 233 Or. 49, 377 P.2d 26 (1962). Liability insurance company refused to defend an action of assault against an insured of a liability insurance policy. The policyholder brought this action to recover his costs of defending. *Held*, the insurance company had no duty to defend. Even if the contract purported to provide for defense against a claim of "intentional conduct in inflicting injury upon another" it would be unenforceable as against public policy.

SECTION B.   NEGLIGENT HARMING

BLYTH v. BIRMINGHAM WATERWORKS CO.

Exchequer, 1856. 11 Exchequer 781.
156 Eng.Rep. 1047.

This was an appeal by the defendants against the decision of the judge of the County Court of Birmingham. The case was tried before a jury, and a verdict found for the plaintiff for the amount claimed by the particulars. The particulars of the claim alleged, that the plaintiff sought to recover for damage sustained by the plaintiff by reason of the negligence of the defendants in not keeping their water-pipes and the apparatus connected therewith in proper order.

The case stated that the defendants were incorporated by stat. 7 Geo. IV, c. cix., for the purpose of supplying Birmingham with water.

By the 84th section of their Act it was enacted, that the company should, upon the laying down of any main-pipe or other pipe in any street, fix, at the time of laying down such pipe, a proper and sufficient fire-plug in each such street, and should deliver the key or keys of such fire-plug to the persons having the care of the engine-house in or near to the said street, and cause another key to be hung up in the watchhouse in or near to the said street. By sec. 87, pipes were to be eighteen inches beneath the surface of the soil. By the 89th section, the mains were at all times to be kept charged with water. The defendants derived no profit from the maintenance of the plugs distinct from the general profits of the whole business, but such maintenance was one of the conditions under which they were permitted to exercise the privileges given by the Act. The main-pipe opposite the house of the plaintiff was more than eighteen inches below the surface. The fire-plug was constructed according to the best known system, and the materials of it were at the time of the accident sound and in good order. The apparatus connected with the fire-plug was as follows:—

The lower part of a wooden plug was inserted in a neck, which projected above and formed part of the main. About the neck there was a bed of brickwork puddled in with clay. The plug was also enclosed in a cast iron tube, which was placed upon and fixed to the brickwork. The tube was closed at the top by a movable iron stopper having a hole in it for the insertion of the key, by which the plug was loosened when occasion required it.

The plug did not fit tight to the tube, but room was left for it to move freely. This space was necessarily left for the purpose of easily and quickly removing the wooden plug to allow the water to flow. On the removal of the wooden plug the pressure upon the main forced the water up through the neck and cap to the surface of the street.

On the 24th of February, a large quantity of water, escaping from the neck of the main, forced its way through the ground into the plaintiff's house. The apparatus had been laid down twenty-five years, and had worked well during that time. The defendants' engineer stated, that the water might have forced its way through the brickwork round the neck of the main, and that the accident might have been caused by the frost, inasmuch as the expansion of the water would force up the plug out of the neck, and the stopper being incrusted with ice would not suffer the plug to ascend. One of the severest frosts on record set in on the 15th of January, 1855, and continued until after the accident in question. An incrustation of ice and snow had gathered about the stopper, and in the street all round, and also for some inches between the stopper and the plug. The ice had been observed on the surface of the ground for a considerable time before the accident. A short time after the accident, the company's turncock removed the ice from the stopper, took out the plug, and replaced it.

The judge left it to the jury to consider whether the company had used proper care to prevent the accident. He thought, that, if the defendants had taken out the ice adhering to the plug, the accident would not have happened, and left it to the jury to say whether they ought to have removed the ice. The jury found a verdict for the plaintiff for the sum claimed.

ALDERSON, B. I am of opinion that there was no evidence to be left to the jury. The case turns upon the question, whether the facts proved show that the defendants were guilty of negligence. Negligence is the omission to do something which a reasonable man, guided upon those considerations which ordinarily regulate the conduct of human affairs, would do or doing something which a prudent and reasonable man would not do. The defendants might have been liable for negligence, if, unintentionally, they omitted to do that which a reasonable person would have done, or did that which a person taking reasonable precautions would not have done. A reasonable man would act with reference to the average circumstances of the temperature in ordinary years. The defendants had provided against such frosts as experience would have led men, acting prudently, to provide against; and they are not guilty of negligence, because their precautions proved insufficient against the effects of the extreme severity of the frost of 1855, which penetrated to a greater depth than any which ordinarily occurs south of the polar regions. Such a state of circumstances constitutes a contingency against which no reasonable man can provide. The result was an accident for which the defendants cannot be held liable.

MARTIN, B. I think that the direction was not correct, and that there was no evidence for the jury. The defendants are not responsible, unless there was negligence on their part. To hold otherwise would be to make the company responsible as insurers.

BRAMWELL, B. The Act of Parliament directed the defendants to lay down pipes, with plugs in them, as safety-valves, to prevent the bursting of the pipes. The plugs were properly made, and of proper material; but there was an accumulation of ice about this plug, which prevented it from acting properly. The defendants were not bound to keep the plugs clear. It appears to me that the plaintiff was under quite as much obligation to remove the ice and snow which had accumulated, as the defendants. However that may be, it appears to me that it would be monstrous to hold the defendants responsible because they did not foresee and prevent an accident, the cause of which was so obscure, that it was not discovered until many months after the accident had happened.

Verdict to be entered for the defendants.

———

STEGGLES v. THE NEW RIVER CO., 11 Weekly Rep. 234 (1863). Pipes of a water company were frozen by an extraordinary frost which caused the plugs in the pipes to "start," letting water escape through the soil, flooding plaintiff's cellar. In an action for the damage thus caused, the plaintiff had a verdict. *Held,* discharging a rule nisi, that the case differed from Blyth v. The Birmingham Waterworks Co., "because here it appeared that it was known that the effect of frost might be to cause the plugs to start, and that some precaution might be taken to prevent the water from escaping through the soil; though what those precautions were did not very distinctly appear. There was, therefore, some evidence for the jury."

THE MAYOR OF THE CITY OF NEW YORK v. BAILEY, 2 Denio 433 (N.Y.1845). The defendant, the corporation of the City of New York, built a dam across the Croton River, as part of its municipal water supply system. Shortly afterwards, in January 1841, a large portion of this dam was carried off by a "high freshet" in the river, damaging the buildings of plaintiff, a lower riparian proprietor. One witness testified that he had seen the river higher "something more than 20 years" previous to 1841. Another testified that the floods of 1839 and 1843 were "nearly as great" as in 1841. In an action for plaintiff's damages, *held,* for plaintiff. The trial court properly declined to nonsuit the plaintiff, since the dam should have been constructed "in such a manner as to resist such extraordinary floods as might have been reasonably expected occasionally to occur."

GENTILE v. PUBLIC SERVICE COORDINATED TRANSPORT, 12 N.J.Super. 45, 78 A.2d 915 (1951). "[I]n examining the early adjudications relating to individual conduct in the field of negligence, we must realize that the hypothetical person of reasonable vigilance, caution, and prudence is our contemporary and not our forefather. What the reasonably prudent individual would do or refrain from doing in our modern environment of hazards cannot rationally be measured today by the probable behavior of our ancestors in the conditions of the age in which they lived."

THE HAND FORMULA

The best known formulation of the idea of reasonable care is that offered by Judge Learned Hand in United States v. Carroll Towing Co., 159 F.2d 169 (2d Cir.1947). The case involved the negligence of the custodian of a barge which broke loose from its mooring. Judge Hand proposed the following formula for determining negligence:

> Since there are occasions when every vessel will break from her moorings, and since, if she does, she becomes a menace to those about her; the owner's duty, as in other similar situations, to provide against resulting injuries is a function of three variables: (1) the probability that she will break away; (2) the gravity of the resulting injury, if she does; (3) the burden of adequate precautions. Possibly it serves to bring this notion into relief to state it in algebraic terms: if the probability be called P; the injury L; and the burden, B; liability depends upon whether B is less than L multiplied by P: i.e., whether $B < PL$. Applied to the situation at bar, the likelihood that a barge will break from her fasts and the damage she will do, vary with the place and time; for example, if a storm threatens, the danger is greater; so it is, if she is in a crowded harbor where moored barges are constantly being shifted about.

Hand's formula—or the "BPL" test—is at the center of a continuing debate about how the law should determine the proper level of safety in social life. The formula prescribes a utilitarian method involving calculation of costs and benefits and choice of the least costly alternative. Safety, it appears, is a matter of economy.

The author of the BPL formula himself noted some obstacles in the way of an algebraic approach. In Moisan v. Loftus, 178 F.2d 148 (2d Cir.1949), Judge Hand points out that the difficulties of determining negligence arise from the necessity of applying a quantitative test to an incommensurable subject matter. Assuming that the equation for negligence is: "$C = P \times D$, in which the C is the care required to avoid risk, D, the possible injuries, and P, the probability that the injuries will occur, if the requisite care is not taken," "of these factors care is the only one ever susceptible of quantitative estimate, and often that is not. The injuries are always a variable within limits, which do not admit of even approximate ascertainment; and, although probability might theoretically be estimated, if any statistics were available, they never are; and, besides, probability varies with the severity of the injuries. It follows that all such attempts are illusory, and, if serviceable at all, are so only to center attention upon which one of the factors may be determinative in any given situation."

SECTION C.   VICARIOUS LIABILITY

RESTATEMENT (SECOND), AGENCY (1958)

§ 2.   Master; Servant; Independent Contractor

(1) A master is a principal who employs an agent to perform service in his affairs and who controls or has the right to control the physical conduct of the other in the performance of the service.

(2) A servant is an agent employed by a master to perform service in his affairs whose physical conduct in the performance of the service is controlled or is subject to the right to control by the master.

(3) An independent contractor is a person who contracts with another to do something for him but who is not controlled by the other nor subject to the other's right to control with respect to his physical conduct in the performance of the undertaking. He may or may not be an agent.

Comment:

a.   Servants and Non-servant Agents. A master is a species of principal, and a servant is a species of agent. The words "master" and "servant" are herein used to indicate the relation from which arises both the liability of an employer for the physical harm caused to third persons by the tort of an employee (see §§ 219–249) and the special duties and immunities of an employer to the employee. See §§ 473–528. Although for brevity the definitions in this Section refer only to the control or right to control the physical conduct of the servant, there are many factors which are considered by the courts in defining the relation. These factors which distinguish a servant from an independent contractor are stated in Section 220. * * *

§ 219.   When Master is Liable for Torts of His Servants

(1) A master is subject to liability for the torts of his servants committed while acting in the scope of their employment.

(2) A master is not subject to liability for the torts of his servants acting outside the scope of their employment, unless:

(a) the master intended the conduct or the consequences, or

(b) the master was negligent or reckless, or

(c) the conduct violated a non-delegable duty of the master, or

(d) the servant purported to act or to speak on behalf of the principal and there was reliance upon apparent authority, or he was aided in accomplishing the tort by the existence of the agency relation.

§ 220.   Definition of Servant

(1) A servant is a person employed to perform services in the affairs of another and who with respect to the physical conduct in the performance of the services is subject to the other's control or right to control.

(2) In determining whether one acting for another is a servant or an independent contractor, the following matters of fact, among others, are considered:

(a) the extent of control which, by the agreement, the master may exercise over the details of the work;

(b) whether or not the one employed is engaged in a distinct occupation or business;

(c) the kind of occupation, with reference to whether, in the locality, the work is usually done under the direction of the employer or by a specialist without supervision;

(d) the skill required in the particular occupation;

(e) whether the employer or the workman supplies the instrumentalities, tools, and the place of work for the person doing the work;

(f) the length of time for which the person is employed;

(g) the method of payment, whether by the time or by the job;

(h) whether or not the work is a part of the regular business of the employer;

(i) whether or not the parties believe they are creating the relation of master and servant; and

(j) whether the principal is or is not in business.

KOHLMAN v. HYLAND

Supreme Court of North Dakota, 1926.
54 N.D. 710, 210 N.W. 643, 50 A.L.R. 1437.

[Action for personal injuries caused by Ludwig, the foreman of the defendant, a contractor engaged in the business of building and repairing telephone lines. The foreman, with other employees, left Hillsboro in a runabout carrying tools to be used in building telephone lines in McKenzie County. He was instructed to proceed due west by way of Mayville, Finley, Cooperstown and Carrington where he was to remain over night. He drove to Finley, then went to the city of McVille, 15 or 20 miles north of Finley, on a personal errand. From there he proceeded west on the road to New Rockford, which was about 18 miles due north of Carrington, intending to go from there to Carrington. Before arriving at New Rockford, he negligently collided with the car in which was the plaintiff. The distance from Hillsboro to Carrington by the prescribed route is about 100 miles; by the route taken, about 136 miles.

At the close of the plaintiff's case, a motion to dismiss was made by the defendant and granted by the trial court.]

JOHNSON, J. [after stating the facts and commenting upon groups of detour cases].

The rule that the master must respond in damages for injuries inflicted by his servant while within the course of the employment has been explained or rested upon a great variety of grounds. It would be neither practically possible nor substantially useful to recanvass territory which has been surveyed many times by nearly every court of last resort in the land. We have heretofore said that the underlying philosophy of the Workmen's Compensation Act is that industry, not the individual, shall bear the risk of injury to the laborers engaged therein. Altman v. Comp. Bur., 50 N.D. 215, 195 N.W. 287. There is always present the possibility of injury to employees, notwithstanding every conceivable precaution may be taken to guard against it. So it is when we look at the situation from the viewpoint of the public. There is an ever-present probability that third persons will suffer injury because somebody's servant is careless, disobedient, or unfaithful to his master. This is a real, not an imaginary risk, to which bear abundant witness the development of the doctrine of respondeat superior and the myriad cases where courts have been lost in the mazes of metaphysical refinement in definition between frolic and detour. This latter risk to the public is clearly one which industry, on the analogy of the Compensation Acts, may well be required to carry, within reasonable bounds. He who employs a servant and puts under his control an automobile must know, as every one knows, that it is not improbable that he will, on occasion, depart from strict instructions. As a fact of practical experience, this is beyond dispute; and that it does result in injury to the public the growing number of cases, involving attempted distinctions between frolic and detour, clearly shows. Such a departure from the path of duty may become so great as to amount to an abandonment of the service in the minds of all reasonable men; it should then be a question of law for the court. On the other hand, there is an area, beyond and around the place within which the strict terms of the employment require the servant to remain, into which common experience with and observation of human nature suggest that he will, as inclination dictates, probably go; that is a risk which properly belongs to the business, and injury to the public by the servant while within this area should ordinarily be accepted as a burden upon the industry itself. Whether the servant is within this permissible "zone" of deviation—permissible only in the sense that he is still within his employment—depends on the facts. The facts may be such that reasonable minds could draw but one conclusion; the question would then be one of law for the court. We are of the opinion, in the case at bar, that reasonable men might well reach different conclusions as to whether the servant was within the area of probable deviation, and therefore within his employment, when the accident occurred. That question should have been submitted to the jury. * * *

* * * It may be conceded, for the sake of the argument only, that had the injury occurred while he was on his way to McVille, and after he left the prescribed route, there would have been no liability, as a matter of law, for the reason that he embarked on an adventure of his own and departed to such an extent from his duties as to terminate or suspend temporarily the employment. The primary question is whether the servant was, at the time of the accident, performing any act in furtherance of his master's business. He was undeniably en route back to the course from which he departed and to the designated place where he and his associates had been directed to remain for the night; in other words, he had resumed his purpose to go to

McKenzie county, and was carrying equipment and passengers in the master's conveyance, and on the master's business: * * *

The judgment is reversed and a new trial ordered.

BURKE, J. (dissenting.) * * * In what way could Ludwig justify the going to McVille to see Sinner's sister? Could he collect pay for extra time employed on the trip? Certainly not. Why not? Because it was no part of his journey. He did not go to McVille for the defendant. The relation of master and servant had ceased to exist between Ludwig and the defendant. Ludwig had become the servant of Sinner, and Ludwig and Sinner are alone responsible, not only to the plaintiff, but to the defendant for the destruction of the automobile. * * *

There is no conflict in the evidence, and no inference can be drawn, except that, at the request of Sinner, Ludwig abandoned his employment, went to McVille, and made such an unusual diversion that the trial court was justified in granting defendant's motion for a directed verdict, and the judgment should be affirmed.

RESTATEMENT (SECOND), AGENCY (1958)

§ 229. Kind of Conduct within Scope of Employment

(1) To be within the scope of the employment, conduct must be of the same general nature as that authorized, or incidental to the conduct authorized.

(2) In determining whether or not the conduct, although not authorized, is nevertheless so similar to or incidental to the conduct authorized as to be within the scope of employment, the following matters of fact are to be considered:

(a) whether or not the act is one commonly done by such servants;

(b) the time, place and purpose of the act;

(c) the previous relations between the master and the servant;

(d) the extent to which the business of the master is apportioned between different servants;

(e) whether or not the act is outside the enterprise of the master or, if within the enterprise, has not been entrusted to any servant;

(f) whether or not the master has reason to expect that such an act will be done;

(g) the similarity in quality of the act done to the act authorized;

(h) whether or not the instrumentality by which the harm is done has been furnished by the master to the servant;

(i) the extent of departure from the normal method of accomplishing an authorized result; and

(j) whether or not the act is seriously criminal.

§ 235. Conduct Not for Purpose of Serving Master

An act of a servant is not within the scope of employment if it is done with no intention to perform it as a part of or incident to a service on account of which he is employed.

HOUSTON TRANSIT CO. v. FELDER, 146 Tex. 428, 208 S.W.2d 880 (1948). Action for damages because of injuries inflicted on plaintiff by Goodson, one of defendant's bus drivers. It was undisputed that a car driven by plaintiff ran into the rear of a transit company bus driven by Goodson, that Goodson left the bus, went to plaintiff's car, and struck plaintiff in the face with a money-changing box. Plaintiff testified that Goodson looked at the bumpers of the two vehicles, shouted something plaintiff did not understand, and struck plaintiff as he was getting out of his car. Goodson testified that he went back to get Felder's name and other information, as it was his duty to do, that Felder refused to give his name and laid his hand on Goodson's shoulder to stop Goodson from going to the rear to get the registration number on the car, and that Goodson hit plaintiff "because of what he called me and laid his hands on me." A jury found that Goodson, while acting in the scope of his employment and not in self-defense, "assaulted" plaintiff. The trial court entered a judgment for defendant notwithstanding the verdict, on the ground that as a matter of law the bus driver was not acting within the scope of his employment in committing the "assault." The intermediate appellate court reversed and rendered judgment for the plaintiff on the verdict, in the amount of $1,000. *Held,* judgment for plaintiff affirmed. "This assault was so closely connected with the performance of Goodson's duties as to prevent the conclusion as a matter of law that when he struck Felder he had ceased to act as the company's agent and had begun to act upon his own responsibility." If the servant commits an assault solely because of his resentment of an insult, the master is not liable. But "what motivated Goodson in striking Felder was for the jury to appraise," and the jury's finding "encompasses the conclusion that it [the assault] was not one committed solely out of resentment or bad feeling."

BIRMINGHAM ELECTRIC CO. v. HAWKINS, 37 Ala.App. 282, 67 So.2d 56 (1953). Defendant's bus driver Wint, apparently angered because he was unable for several blocks to get ahead of the plaintiff's automobile, blew his horn. As the plaintiff turned in front of the bus, Wint told the plaintiff to stop. When the plaintiff did so, he followed him and assaulted him with a revolver. *Held,* judgment for plaintiff reversed. Wint was not acting within the scope of his employment but was performing an act entirely personal to himself.

SECTION D.   STRICT LIABILITY

EXNER v. SHERMAN POWER CONSTRUCTION CO.

United States Circuit Court of Appeals, Second Circuit, 1931.
54 F.2d 510, 80 A.L.R. 686.

[Appeal by the defendant from a judgment entered on a verdict for $28,875 in favor of the plaintiffs.]

AUGUSTUS N. HAND, J. This is an action in tort, brought by Delia H. Exner to recover damages to her person, property, and business which were caused by the explosion of dynamite kept by the defendant company in connection with work upon a hydro-electric development at Bellows Falls, Vt., in which it was engaged. The plaintiff Frederick Exner, the husband of Delia H. Exner, was joined as a plaintiff because he sought to recover damages for injuries to his marital rights.

The defendant kept dynamite in a small hut on the westerly bank of the Connecticut river located conveniently to its work. This hut was approximately 935 feet from the dwelling of the plaintiffs, in which they rented rooms and apartments and carried on a restaurant and lunchroom. The dynamite hut was located close to a thickly settled part of Bellows Falls, and within fifty rods of five dwelling houses, a hotel, several factories, and business buildings belonging to persons other than the plaintiffs.

Mildred Wolfel, one of defendant's witnesses, who observed the explosion from the New Hampshire side of the river, 300 or 400 feet from where it occurred, said that she saw two men coming out of the dynamite hut carrying boxes; that she saw a flash and a ball of fire and then another flash, and experienced an explosion so severe as to throw her across the road. The hut was blown to atoms by the explosions, and three men engaged in getting the cases of dynamite to take down to the place along the river where the blasting was to be done were killed.

There was evidence that Mrs. Exner, the plaintiff, who was in bed in her house at the time of the explosion, was thrown out of bed and received injuries, that her house was so badly shattered as to require extensive repairs, and that her business was damaged. The accident occurred on February 18, 1928.

The principal storehouse of the dynamite was on the eastern or New Hampshire side of the river. From that, dynamite was brought in an automobile across the bridge and placed in the hut to be warmed so as to be in condition for use when needed for blasting. Evidence was introduced that twenty cases of dynamite, weighing fifty pounds each, were sent from the storehouse across the river to the hut the day before the explosion, and that three such cases were still on hand in the hut before the additional twenty cases were brought to it. The morning of the explosion, an order had been given to send fourteen boxes across the river to the hut, but they had not been taken over prior to the explosion. There was evidence that after the explosion one of the witnesses picked up as much as two fifty-pound cases of unexploded dynamite at the scene of the explosion and found four or five more in a tool box thirty to fifty feet from the hut. The general foreman of the defendant testified that about one thousand pounds of dynamite were ordinarily required for daily use in blasting, but on some days when the company was not doing much drilling much less than one thousand pounds would be used.

The defendant's president testified that there was no place where the dynamite hut could be located that would be accessible to the work that would not be within fifty rods from an inhabited dwelling, and, if it had been placed beyond that limit, the dynamite would necessarily have been too cold for use before it reached the job and would have been carried more frequently than was the case through the streets of Bellows Falls, to the greater peril of the inhabitants. He also said that the hut was adopted as a place to store a supply of dynamite for daily use after a hearing before the deputy fire marshal of the state, and with his consent.

There is a statute of Vermont (Rev. Laws 1880, § 4323 [now G.L.7109]), the consideration of which is involved in this case, which reads as follows:

"Keeping explosives. A person who keeps or suffers to be kept upon premises owned or occupied by him, within fifty rods of an inhabited building of another person, more than fifty pounds of gunpowder or nitroglycerine at one time, or more than one pound, unless contained in sound canisters of tin or other metal, or a package containing more than fifty pounds of dynamite, shall be fined twenty-five dollars, and twenty-five dollars additional for each day that it is so kept after notice from an inhabitant of such town to remove the same." * * *

Upon the case as submitted to the jury we must determine whether, under section 4323, or under the common law, the defendant became liable, irrespective of any fault, for the damage arising from the explosion.

The defendant was not, in our opinion, liable to the plaintiffs for a violation of section 4323. It is well established that only members of a class to be benefited can invoke a civil remedy by reason of such a statute as we have here. The plaintiffs inhabited a dwelling more than fifty rods from the dynamite hut, and the act in terms covers only an area within a radius of fifty rods from the place of storage. If there had been no inhabited dwellings within that zone, the plaintiffs would have incurred the same risk as in the present case and would have suffered the same damage from the explosion, yet ex hypothesi the statute would not have been violated. It is impossible to see how the plaintiffs were of the class intended to be benefited by a law forbidding storage of dynamite within an area in which they were not included. It is true that the act contained a provision for fines for continued violation, after notice from an inhabitant of the town to remove the dynamite. But that clause was intended only to afford ample means for informing the storer of the dynamite of his violation of law and to enable inhabitants of the town outside the forbidden area, even busybodies, to benefit those within it by setting penalties in motion. We see no reason to suppose that a general interest in having laws observed or in helping people within the zone extended the protection of the statute to all inhabitants of the town. The plaintiffs were not of the class to be benefited. Any reasoning which would embrace them would be applicable even if they had lived in a corner of the town five miles away. * * *

The question remains whether there was an absolute liability for the damage caused by the explosion at common law. We may say at the outset that we have been referred to nothing relevant as to this in the Vermont decisions, but they would not control in any event, because the matter is one in which we are at liberty to gather the principle to be applied from the general field of jurisprudence.

Dynamite is of the class of elements which one who stores or uses in such a locality, or under such circumstances as to cause likelihood of risk to others, stores or uses at his peril. He is an insurer, and is absolutely liable if damage results to third persons, either from the direct impact of rocks thrown out by the explosion (which would be a common-law trespass) or from concussion.

For the reasons already given in discussing the Vermont statute, we assume that the storage of dynamite in the case at bar was not an act of which the plaintiffs could complain. There was uncontradicted proof that the place of storage and the quantities stored were approved by the deputy fire marshal of the state. While such approval would be no protection against claims of persons inhabiting dwellings within the prescribed zone, the plaintiffs were not of that class and could not have enjoined the storage. The liability of the defendant is not founded on illegal storage or on negligence, which was not proved, but upon the ground that the use of dynamite is so dangerous that it ought to be at the owners' risk.

In Bradford Glycerine Co. v. St. Marys Woolen Mfg. Co., 60 Ohio St. 560, 54 N.E. 528, 45 L.R.A. 658, 71 Am.St.Rep. 740, the defendant manufactured and stored nitroglycerine which exploded and caused damage to the plaintiff. The Supreme Court of Ohio held that the defendant was liable though there was no proof of negligence. To the same effect was the decision in French v. Center Creek Powder Mfg. Co., 173 Mo.App. 220, 158 S.W. 723. These cases followed Rylands v. Fletcher, L.R. 3 H.L. 330, which has found considerable explicit support in this country in the following decisions. [Citations omitted.]

While the rule laid down by BLACKBURN, J., in Rylands v. Fletcher, 1 Exch. at p. 265, and approved by the House of Lords in Fletcher v. Rylands, L.R. 3 H.L. p. 339, has not been followed in America to the full extent of all its implications, and, at the outset its authority was impaired by Brown v. Collins, 53 N.H. 442, 16 Am.Rep. 372, Marshall v. Welwood, 38 N.J.L. 339, 20 Am.Rep. 394, and Losee v. Buchanan, 51 N.Y. 476, 10 Am.Rep. 623, yet in the so-called "blasting" cases an absolute liability, without regard to fault, has uniformly been imposed by the American courts wherever there has been an actual invasion of property by rocks or debris. [Citations omitted.] And the rule of absolute liability for direct injury from blasting has been applied, not only to damage to property, but to the person. [Citations omitted.]

It is true that some courts have distinguished between liability for a common-law trespass, occasioned by blasting, which projects rocks or debris upon the property or the person of the plaintiff, and liability for so-called consequential damages arising from concussion, and have denied liability for the latter where the blasting itself was conducted at a lawful time and place and with due care. [Citations omitted.] Yet in every practical sense there can be no difference between a blasting which projects rocks in such a way as to injure persons or property and a blasting which, by creating a sudden vacuum, shatters buildings or knocks down people. In each case, a force is applied by means of an element likely to do serious damage if it explodes. The distinction is based on historical differences between the actions of trespass and case and, in our opinion, is without logical basis.

We can see no reason for imposing a different liability for the results of an explosion, whether the dynamite explodes when stored or when employed in blasting. To be sure there is a greater likelihood of damage from blasting than from storage, but in each case the explosion arises from an act connected with a business conducted for profit and fraught with substantial risk and possibility of the gravest consequences. As Justice Holmes has said in The Common Law, p. 154: "The possibility of a great danger has the same effect as the probability of a less one, and the law throws the risk of the venture on the person who introduces the peril into the community."

Frequently as much as one thousand pounds of dynamite were stored by the defendant near a group of dwellings, factories, and a hotel. The fact that the explosion was severe enough to kill three men, blow up the hut, unsettle and damage the plaintiff's house, over nine hundred feet away, and that even then, one hundred pounds of dynamite still remained unexploded, shows that there must have been a large amount of dynamite in or about the hut at the time of the accident. When a person engages in such a dangerous activity, useful though it be, he becomes an insurer.

Furthermore, the imposition of absolute liability is not out of accord with any general principles of law. As Professor Holdsworth has said: "The dominant idea of Anglo–Saxon law" was "that man acts at his peril." 2 History of English Law, 52. See, also, Pollock on Torts, 10th Ed., 15. Accordingly the earlier forms of action such as trespass and trespass quare clausum fregit allowed recovery for a direct invasion of person or property without regard to fault. After the later action "sur case" arose, there was a growing tendency to excuse an act causing damage if the defendant was without fault. But, in trespass, fault ordinarily remained a matter of no consequence, and even in cases of damage to the person the early decisions prior to Brown v. Kendall, 6 Cush. 292, 60 Mass. 292, seemed to have imposed liability where there was no negligence. Dickinson v. Watson, T. Jones, 205. Although liability for injury to the person has not in most instances survived except where there has been fault, there still remains absolute liability for trespasses to real estate and for actionable wrongs committed by servants no matter how carefully they are selected by the master. The extent to which one man in the lawful conduct of his business is liable for injuries to another involves an adjustment of conflicting interests. The solution of the problem in each particular case has never been dependent upon any universal criterion of liability (such as "fault") applicable to all situations. If damage is inflicted, there ordinarily is liability, in the absence of excuse. When, as here, the defendant, though without fault, has engaged in the perilous activity of storing large quantities of a dangerous explosive for use in his business, we think there is no justification for relieving it of liability, and that the owner of the business, rather than a third person who has no relation to the explosion, other than that of injury, should bear the loss. The blasting cases seem to afford ample analogies and to justify this conclusion.

Our decision in Actiesselskabet Ingrid v. Central R. R. of N. J., 216 F. 72, L.R.A.1916B, 716, is relied on by the defendant. There a car of dynamite in the New Jersey freightyard of the respondent exploded without negligence on its part and destroyed the libelant's vessel. The libel was dismissed. While the opinion generally disapproved of Fletcher v. Rylands, the decision rested mainly on the ground that the respondent was a common carrier, was obliged to take such freight, and was therefore not liable if it stored it properly and had committed no acts of negligence. See, also, Henry v. Cleveland, C. C. & St. L. Ry. Co., C.C., 67 F. 426.

It is argued that transportation of the dynamite through the town in small quantities would have increased the risk to the public. This seems to be true, and no reason is shown for taking such a course, because it would have added to the danger without relieving the defendant from absolute liability, had an explosion occurred while the dynamite was on the way.

In the case at bar, the court decided that the Vermont statute made the storage illegal and afforded the plaintiffs a remedy. With this we differ, for the reasons already stated. Nevertheless, as we hold that the defendant acted at its own risk in storing a large amount of dynamite at the particular locality chosen, the error was harmless.

Judgment affirmed.

SWAN, J. (Concurring). I concur, although for myself I should have been willing to rest affirmance upon section 4323, Rev.Laws Vt.

––––––––

WALLACE v. A. H. GUION & CO., 237 S.C. 349, 117 S.E.2d 359 (1960). Action for harm to structures on realty caused by concussion and vibration from dynamite used by the defendant contractor in excavating for a sewer line. Demurrer on the ground that the complaint failed to allege (1) negligence, or (2) entry of rocks or debris on plaintiff's property, or (3) use of more explosives than necessary. Demurrer overruled. *Held*, affirmed, citing Exner and Restatement, Torts §§ 519, 520.

RESTATEMENT OF TORTS, SECOND (1977)

§ 519. General Principle

(1) One who carries on an abnormally dangerous activity is subject to liability for harm to the person, land or chattels of another resulting from the activity, although he has exercised the utmost care to prevent the harm.

(2) This strict liability is limited to the kind of harm, the possibility of which makes the activity abnormally dangerous.

§ 520. Abnormally Dangerous Activities

In determining whether an activity is abnormally dangerous, the following factors are to be considered:

(a) existence of a high degree of risk of some harm to the person, land or chattels of others;

(b) likelihood that the harm that results from it will be great;

(c) inability to eliminate the risk by the exercise of reasonable care;

(d) extent to which the activity is not a matter of common usage;

(e) inappropriateness of the activity to the place where it is carried on; and

(f) extent to which its value to the community is outweighed by its dangerous attributes.

SECTION E.   NO–FAULT PLANS

LARSON'S WORKERS' COMPENSATION LAW (NOV. 1996)*

§ 1.10 Typical Compensation Act Summarized

The typical workers' compensation act has these features: (a) the basic operating principle is that an employee is automatically entitled to certain benefits whenever the employee suffers a "personal injury by accident arising out of and in the course of employment" or an occupational disease; (b) negligence and fault are largely immaterial, both in the sense that the employee's contributory negligence does not lessen his or her rights and in the sense that the employer's complete freedom from fault does not lessen its liability; (c) coverage is limited to persons having the status of employee, as distinguished from independent contractor; (d) benefits to the employee include cash-wage benefits, usually around one-half to two-thirds of the employee's average weekly wage, and hospital, medical and rehabilitation expenses; in death cases benefits for dependents are provided; arbitrary maximum and minimum limits are ordinarily imposed; (e) the employee and his or her dependents, in exchange for these modest but assured benefits, give up their common-law right to sue the employer for damages for any injury covered by the act; (f) the right to sue third persons whose negligence caused the injury remains, however, with the proceeds usually being applied first to reimbursement of the employer for the compensation outlay, the balance (or most of it) going to the employee; (g) administration is typically in the hands of administrative commissions; and, as far as possible, rules of procedure, evidence, and conflict of laws are relaxed to facilitate the achievement of the beneficent purposes of the legislation; and (h) the employer is required to secure its liability through private insurance,

* Copyright © 2003 by LexisNexis/Matthew Bender & Co., Inc. Reprinted with permission from *Larson's Workers' Compensation Law*. All rights reserved.

state-fund insurance in some states, or "self-insurance"; thus the burden of compensation liability does not remain upon the employer but passes to the consumer, since compensation premiums, as part of the cost of production, will be reflected in the price of the product.

§ 1.20   Unique Character of American System

The sum total of these ingredients is a unique system which is neither a branch of tort law nor social insurance of the British or continental type, but which has some of the characteristics of each. Like tort, but unlike social insurance, its operative mechanism is unilateral employer liability, with no contribution by the employee or the state; like social insurance, but unlike tort, the right to benefits and amount of benefits are based largely on a social theory of providing support and preventing destitution, rather than settling accounts between two individuals according to their personal deserts or blame.

* * *

§ 2.10   The Test of Liability: Work Connection Versus Fault

The right to compensation benefits depends on one simple test: Was there a work-connected injury? Negligence, and, for the most part, fault, are not in issue and cannot affect the result. Let the employer's conduct be flawless in its perfection, and let the employee's be abysmal in its clumsiness, rashness and ineptitude; if the accident arises out of and in the course of the employment, the employee receives an award. Reverse the positions, with a careless and stupid employer and a wholly innocent employee and the same award issues.

Thus, the test is not the relation of an individual's personal quality (fault) to an event, but the relationship of an event to an employment. The essence of applying the test is not a matter of assessing blame, but of marking out boundaries.

§ 2.20   Underlying Social Philosophy

The ultimate social philosophy behind compensation liability is belief in the wisdom of providing, in the most efficient, most dignified, and most certain form, financial and medical benefits for the victims of work-connected injuries which an enlightened community would feel obliged to provide in any case in some less satisfactory form, and of allocating the burden of these payments to the most appropriate source of payment, the consumer of the product.

* * *

§ 3.20   Allocation of Burden, and Relation of Hazard to Liability

Unlike pure social-insurance plans, the American compensation system does not place the cost on the "public" as such, but on a particular class of consumers, and thus retains a relation between the hazardousness of particular industries and the cost of the system to that industry and consumers of its product.

It is not quite accurate to say, as is often said, that the public ultimately pays the cost of workers' compensation. In the United States it is more precise to say that the consumer of a particular product ultimately pays the cost of compensation protection for the workers engaged in its manufacture. * * * Some employments, like logging and lumbering, are highly dangerous; others, of a clerical and sedentary nature, involve a minimum of hazard. * * *

WHETRO v. AWKERMAN

Supreme Court of Michigan, 1970.
383 Mich. 235, 174 N.W.2d 783.

T. G. KAVANAGH, Justice.

* * *

[These two cases] turn on the same question, for the damages for which workmen's compensation was awarded in each case were caused by the Palm Sunday 1965 tornadoes which devastated parts of Southern Michigan.

Carl Whetro was injured when the tornado destroyed the residence wherein he was working for his employer and seeks reimbursement for his medical expenses. Henry E. Emery was killed when the motel in which he was staying while on a business trip for his employer was destroyed by the tornado, and his widow seeks compensation for his death.

In each case the hearing referee found that the employee's injury arose out of and in the course of his employment. The award was affirmed by the appeal board in each case and by the Court of Appeals in the Whetro case.

The defendant-appellants in both cases base their defense on the assertion that tornadoes are "acts of God" or acts of nature and injuries which are caused by them do not arise "out of" the employment and hence are not compensable under the Workmen's Compensation Act.

For this reason they maintain that the cases were erroneously decided as a matter of law and the awards should be set aside.

The appellants in each case maintain that the injury did not arise "out of" the employment because that phrase as it is used in the act refers to a causal connection between the event which put in motion the forces which caused the injury and the work itself or the conditions under which it is required to be performed.

Employment as a caretaker-gardener or salesman, they argue, does not include tornadoes as incidents or conditions of the work, and the path of injury is determined by the tornado, not the employment.

Appellants cite a series of Michigan decisions involving injury by lightning in which compensation was denied and assert that a tornado is like lightning in that it acts capriciously, leaving its victims and the untouched side by side. The decisions in all of these "lightning cases" denied compensation on the ground that the injury did not arise "out of" the employment because the employment did not expose the workman to any increased risk or to a more hazardous situation than faced by others in the area.

The Court of Appeals was able to distinguish between a tornado and a bolt of lightning as a causative force of injury and base its decision affirming the award for Carl Whetro on the reasoning of the Massachusetts supreme court in Caswell's Case (1940), 305 Mass. 500, 26 N.E.2d 328, wherein recovery was allowed for injuries received when a brick wall of the employer's factory was blown down on workmen during a hurricane. This "contact with the premises" met the requirement that the injury arise "out of" the employment in the mind of the Court of Appeals.

We are unable to accept the distinction drawn between a tornado and bolt of lightning when viewed as the cause of an injury. As we see it, a tornado, no less than a bolt of lightning or an earthquake or flood is an "act of God" and if the phrase "out of" the employment in the Workmen's Compensation Act necessarily entails the notion of proximate causality, no injury received because of an "act of God" should be compensable.

But we are satisfied that it is no longer necessary to establish a relationship of proximate causality between employment and an injury in order to establish compensability. Accordingly we no longer regard an "act of God" whether it be a tornado, lightning, earthquake, or flood as a defense to a claim for a work connected injury. Such a defense retains too much of the idea that an employer should not pay compensation unless he is somehow at fault. This concept from the law of tort is inconsistent with the law of workmen's compensation.

The purpose of the compensation act as set forth in its title, is to promote the welfare of the people of Michigan relating to the liability of employers for injuries or death sustained by their employees. The legislative policy is to provide financial and medical benefits to the victims of work connected injuries in an efficient, dignified and certain form. The act allocates the burden of such payments to the most appropriate source of payment, the consumer of the product.

Fault has nothing to do with whether or not compensation is payable. The economic impact on an injured workman and his family is the same whether the injury was caused by the employer's fault or otherwise.

We hold that the law in Michigan today no longer requires the establishment of a proximately causal connection between the employment and the injury to entitle a claimant to compensation. The cases which have allowed recovery for street risks, increased risks, and on the premises accidents were made without consideration of the proximate causal connection between the nature of the employment and the injury. They have brought the law in Michigan to the point where it can be said today that if the employment is the occasion of the injury, even though not the proximate cause, compensation should be paid.

Such a development of the Michigan law is paralleled by the development of the law in England and Massachusetts—the two jurisdictions which served as Michigan's model in the original legislative drafting and judicial construction of the Workmen's Compensation Act.

* * *

The Massachusetts court said in Baran's Case, [336 Mass. 342, 344, 145 N.E.2d 726, 727 (1957)]: "We think that they [recent cases] disclose the development of a consistent course which is a departure from the earlier view * * *. The injury 'need not arise out of the nature of the employment. * * * The question is whether his employment brought him in contact with the risk that in fact caused his death.' "

* * *

Accordingly, we hold that the employment of Carl Whetro and Henry E. Emery in each case was the occasion of the injury which they suffered and therefore the injuries arose "out of" and in the course of their employment.

The award in each case is affirmed.

* * *

BRENNAN, Chief Justice.

The function of the workmen's compensation act is to place the financial burden of industrial injuries upon the industries themselves, and spread that cost ultimately among the consumers.

This humane legislation was developed because the industrialization of our civilization had left in its wake a trail of broken bodies.

Employers were absolved from general liability for negligence, in exchange for the imposition of more certain liability under the act.

* * *

The workmen's compensation law is society's expression of the moral responsibility of employers and consumers to the workmen whose health and whose lives are sacrificed to industrial and commercial progress and production.

Fault is not the same thing as proximate cause. The compensation law does not use the word *cause*. Rather, it expresses the concept of employer and consumer responsibility in the phrase "arising out of and in the course of" the employment.

The terms "arising out of" and "in the course of" are not redundant. They mean two different things. An adulterous cobbler shot at his last by his jealous wife may be "in the course of" his employment. But the injury does not "arise out of" his job. On what basis of moral responsibility should his injuries be paid for by his employer? By what logic would society decree that his disability should add a farthing to the price of shoes?

The workmen's compensation law is not a utopian attempt to put a price tag on all human suffering and incorporate it into the cost of living.

Lightning, flood, tornados and estranged wives will always be with us, in this vale of tears. They were the occasion of human injury when our forebears were tilling the soil with sharp sticks. They are not a by-product of the industrial revolution, nor are they in any sense the moral responsibility of those who profit by or enjoy the fruits of, our modern industrialized society.

I would reverse without apology for the precedents.

B. BASIC TORT CONCEPTIONS: INTENTIONAL WRONGS

Chapter 2

BATTERY: ANATOMY OF AN INTENTIONAL TORT

The tort of battery, which we examine in detail in this chapter, is only one of a large number of intentional torts. The law of intentional torts as a whole protects a diverse set of interests against various kinds of deliberate interferences.

Battery itself, for example, protects the physical integrity and dignity of the person—but only against harmful or offensive contact, deliberately inflicted. The tort of assault protects peace of mind—but only when it is the fear of intended physical injury that disrupts that peace. The tort of intentional infliction of emotional distress protects emotional tranquility more generally—but only against severe disruption, precipitated by outrageous conduct, aimed at inflicting emotional distress. The tort of conversion protects property rights—but only in personal property, and only against wrongful and deliberate attempts to exercise dominion over that property. The tort of trespass also protects property rights—but only in real property, and only against deliberate affronts to the owner's right of exclusive possession. And so on.

The unity of intentional tort liability thus does not lie in the unity of the interests that it protects—they are enormously varied—but in the fact that it redresses forms of deliberate wrongdoing. The first question of intentional tort law, then, is: What kind of intentionality must be present for the defendant's conduct to count as tortious? Must the defendant have acted from a malicious desire to inflict harm or suffering? Will it do to have intended the harm in the disinterested but fully deliberate spirit that a professional killer intends his killings? Will it do to have intended the act that directly inflicted the injury, thereby inflicting the injury "on purpose"? Or is it enough that the defendant "knew" that the injury would be precipitated by its act? Enough that the defendant realized the injury was likely to happen? Might happen? These are the question with which our study of battery begins.

SECTION A. HARM

GARRATT v. DAILEY

Supreme Court of Washington, 1955.
46 Wn.2d 197, 279 P.2d 1091.

[See p. 7, supra.]

WHITE V. UNIVERSITY OF IDAHO, 797 P.2d 108 (Idaho,1990). Professor Neher "walked up behind [Mrs. White] and touched her back with both of his hands in a movement later described as one a pianist would make in striking and lifting the fingers from a keyboard." He later explained that "his purpose was to demonstrate the sensation of this particular movement by a pianist, not to cause any harm." However, "[t]he resulting contact generated unexpectedly harmful injuries * * * Mrs. White suffered thoracic outlet syndrome on the right side of her body, requiring the removal of the first rib on the right side. She also experienced scarring of the brachial plexus nerve which necessitated the severing of the scalenus anterior muscles." Plaintiff appealed a grant of "partial summary judgment in favor of defendant on the ground that Professor Neher's touching constituted a battery," entitling the defendant to immunity under the Idaho Tort Claims Act. On appeal, all parties stipulated "that Professor Neher intended to touch Mrs. White but did not intend to harm or offend her." *Held*, affirmed.

"The sole issue presented by these facts is whether Professor Neher's contact with Mrs. White constituted a battery. * * * That issue in turn revolves around the question of what type of intent is required to constitute a battery; *i.e.,* must the defendant intend to harm or offend the plaintiff, or must the defendant simply intend to touch the plaintiff? * * *

" * * * Appellants assert that the decisions of this Court, *e.g., Doe v. Durtschi,* 110 Idaho 466, 716 P.2d 1238 (1986), require * * * intent to harm or offend, in order to constitute a battery. While we stated in *Doe* that, 'A battery * * * requires intentional bodily contact which is either harmful or offensive,' 110 Idaho at 471, 716 P.2d at 1243, that does not mean that the person has to intend that the contact be harmful or offensive."

* * *

"The intent element of the tort of battery does not require a desire or purpose to bring about a specific result or injury; it is satisfied if the actor's affirmative act causes an intended contact which is unpermitted and which is harmful or offensive." [citation omitted]

ELLIS v. D'ANGELO
California District Court of Appeal, First District, Division 2, 1953.
116 Cal.App.2d 310, 253 P.2d 675.

DOOLING, Justice. The plaintiff appeals from a judgment for the defendants entered after a demurrer was sustained to her first amended complaint without leave to amend. The complaint is in three counts. Count one alleges a battery by defendant Salvatore D'Angelo, a minor of the age of four years; the second count alleges injuries suffered by the plaintiff as the proximate result of the minor defendant negligently shoving and pushing the plaintiff violently to the floor; the third count seeks a recovery from the parents of the child for their negligence in failing to warn or inform plaintiff of the habit of the child of violently attacking other people. According to the allegation the plaintiff was by the minor defendant "pushed, impelled and knocked * * * violently to the floor" and suffered serious injuries including a fracturing of the bones of both her arms and wrists.

The two counts against the minor will be discussed together. Appellant points to the language of Civil Code, section 41: "A minor, or person of unsound mind, of whatever degree, is civilly liable for a wrong done by him, but is not liable in exemplary damages unless at the time of the act he was capable of knowing that it was wrongful."

This section is based upon sections 23 and 24 of the Field Commission's draft of a Civil Code which was submitted to the New York Legislature in 1865. This may be an anachronistic vestige of earlier common law principles, in other fields now outmoded, of liability without fault for trespass *vi et armis* (see Bohlen, Liability In Tort Of Infants And Insane Persons, 23 Mich.L.Rev. 9) but it remains true that our legislature in Civ.Code, sec. 41 above quoted by providing that a minor or person of unsound mind is civilly liable for wrongs done by him, and particularly by the qualification that he shall not be held for exemplary damages unless he was capable of knowing that the act was wrongful, has indicated clearly that it intended that a minor or person of unsound mind should be liable in compensatory damages for his tortious conduct even though he was not capable of knowing the wrongful character of his act at the time that he committed it. Startling as this idea may be at first blush, we are bound by this legislative declaration and taking it, and the state of the common law with relation to the liability of infants and persons of unsound mind of which it was intended as a codification, it is our duty to determine the legislative intent and to enforce it.

It is generally stated in 27 Am.Jur., Infants, sec. 90, pp. 812–813: "Liability of an infant in a civil action for his torts is imposed as a mode, not of punishment, but of compensation. If property has been destroyed or other loss occasioned by a wrongful act, it is just that the loss should fall upon the estate of the wrongdoer rather than on that of a guiltless person, and that without reference to the question of moral guilt. Consequently, for every tortious act of violence or other pure tort, the infant tort-feasor is liable in a civil action to the injured person in the same manner and to the same extent as an adult. * * * Infancy, being in law a shield and not a sword, cannot be pleaded to avoid liability for frauds, trespasses, or torts. * * *

"A child of tender years may be held liable for acts of violence, and liability has often been imposed for the injuries caused by such acts, although committed in play and without the intent to inflict substantial injury. Of course, if the injury was an accident, or the acts of the child were only the natural activity of friendly play, there is no liability."

So Prosser in his work on Torts, pp. 1085–1086 says:

The law of torts * * * has been more concerned with the compensation of the injured party than with the moral guilt of the wrongdoer, and has refused to hold that an infant is immune from assault and battery, trespass, conversion, defamation, seduction, and negligence. * * *

This general rule denying immunity must, however, be qualified in a number of respects. In many torts, the state of mind of the actor is an important element. For example, an intent to bring about physical contact is necessary to battery, and in most jurisdictions 'scienter,' or intent to deceive, is said to be essential to deceit. It has been recognized that a child may be of such tender years that he is not an intelligent actor and is incapable of the specific intent required, so that the tort has not been committed, and the event is to be classified as an unavoidable accident. Likewise, in the case of negligence, children have been recognized as a special group to whom a more or less subjective standard of conduct is to be applied, which will vary according to their age, intelligence and experience, so that in many cases immunity is conferred in effect by finding merely that there has been no negligence. * * *"

From these authorities and the cases which they cite it may be concluded generally that an infant is liable for his torts even though he lacks the mental development and capacity to recognize the wrongfulness of his conduct so long as he has the mental capacity to have the state of mind necessary to the commission of the particular tort with which he is charged. Thus as between a battery and negligent injury an infant may have the capacity to intend the violent contact which is essential to the commission of battery when the same infant would be incapable of realizing that his heedless conduct might foreseeably lead to injury to another which is the essential capacity of mind to create liability for negligence.

We may take it as settled in the case of infants as stated in the quotation from Am.Jur. above set out that "no different measure (of negligence) is to be applied to their primary than to their contributory faults." In a case involving the question of the liability of an infant for his negligent conduct the court in Hoyt v. Rosenberg, 80 Cal.App.2d 500 at pages 506–507, 182

P.2d 234, at page 238, 173 A.L.R. 883, said: "While the question as to whether a minor has been negligent in certain circumstances is ordinarily one of fact for the jury, an affirmative finding thereon * * * must conform to and be in accordance with the established rule that a minor is expected to use, not the quantum of care expected of an adult, but only that degree or amount of care which is ordinarily used by children of the same age under similar circumstances." This is the same test applied in determining a child's contributory negligence. (19 Cal.Jur., Negligence, sec. 41, pp. 604–605.)

So far as the count charging the infant defendant with negligence is concerned the question presented to the court is whether as a matter of common knowledge we can say that a child four years of age lacks the mental capacity to realize that his conduct which is not intended to bring harm to another may nevertheless be reasonably expected to bring about that result. In the absence of compelling judicial authority to the contrary in the courts of this state we are satisfied that a four year old child does not possess this mental capacity. In the case of Crane v. Smith, 23 Cal.2d 288, 301, 144 P.2d 356, 364, the court said of a three year old child: "And since Janice was too young to be guilty of contributory negligence, the appellant's liability to her is established." In support of this holding the court cited Gonzales v. Davis, 197 Cal. 256, 240 P. 16, which involved a five year old child. * * *

No purpose will be served by reviewing all the authorities. None has been found in this State which we feel compels us to hold that a four year old has the mental capacity for negligent conduct. It is stated in a note collecting the cases from other jurisdictions in 107 A.L.R. 102 et seq.: "In a majority of the cases it seems that the courts have regarded a child between the ages of four and five years as incapable of personal negligence, the rule of conclusive incapacity applying to a child of such an age." (See further cases collected in the supplement to this note in 174 A.L.R. 1119.) We are satisfied from our own common knowledge of the mental development of four year old children that it is proper to hold that they have not at that age developed the mental capacity for foreseeing the possibilities of their inadvertent conduct which would rationally support a finding that they were negligent. The mental development of children from that age forward is so rapid that cases such as Smith v. Harger, 84 Cal.App.2d 361, 191 P.2d 25 dealing with a five year old child are not helpful to us.

When it comes to the count charging battery a very different question is presented. We certainly cannot say that a four year old child is incapable of intending the violent or the harmful striking of another. Whether a four year old child had such intent presents a fact question; and in view of section 41 of the Civil Code which makes the recognition of the wrongful character of the tort immaterial so far as the liability for compensatory damages is concerned, we must hold that the count charging battery states a cause of action.

The third count is without question sufficient to state a cause of action against the defendant parents. It alleges that these defendants employed plaintiff for the first time to act as baby sitter for their son, that the son "habitually engaged in violently attacking and throwing himself forcibly and violently against other people, and violently shoving and knocking them, all of which said defendant parents knew," that said "parents negligently and carelessly failed to warn plaintiff of said child's said traits and disposition and negligently and carelessly failed to inform plaintiff that said child habitually indulged in such violent and furious attacks on others," and that shortly after plaintiff entered on her duties in the home the child attacked her to her resultant injury.

While it is the rule in California, as it is generally at the common law, that there is no vicarious liability on a parent for the torts of a child there is "another rule of law relating to the torts of minors which is somewhat in the nature of an exception, and that is that a parent may become liable for an injury caused by the child, where the parent's negligence made it possible for the child to cause the injury complained of, and probable that it would do so." Buelke v. Levenstadt, 190 Cal. 684, 689, 214 P. 42, 44; Rocca v. Steinmetz, 61 Cal.App. 102, 214 P. 257. * * *

The judgment is reversed with directions to the trial court to overrule the demurrer to the first and third counts of the amended complaint.

NOURSE, P. J., and GOODELL, J., concur.

Respondents' petition for a hearing by the Supreme Court was denied April 27, 1953.

————

WHITE v. PILE, 68 W.N. 176 (D.C. New South Wales 1951). Plaintiff was attacked by defendant, an adult hebephrenic schizophrenic under the delusion plaintiff was his wife. *Held,* for defendant. Either he "did not know what he was doing or did not know that he was doing wrong, so as to bring the case within M'Naghten's rules, as applied in the criminal law." "[I]t is more in accord with reason and the common sense of the thing to allow immunity from the civil consequences of the tort of assault committed by an insane person where the nature and degree of his insanity are such as would establish a defence if the assault were the subject of a criminal charge."

POLMATIER v. RUSS, 206 Conn. 229, 537 A.2d 468 (1988). Defendant, suffering from "a severe case of paranoid schizophrenia" involving delusions of persecution and auditory hallucinations, shot and killed Arthur Polmatier. Tried for murder, defendant was found not guilty by reason of insanity. Polmatier's widow and executrix then brought this civil wrongful death action seeking damages for battery. On appeal from a verdict for plaintiff, *held,* affirmed. "The majority of jurisdictions that have considered this issue have held insane persons liable for their intentional torts." The court invoked the principle that "where one of two innocent persons must suffer loss from an act done, it is just that it should fall on the one who caused the loss rather than upon the other who had no agency in producing it and could not by any means have avoided it." Defendant's acts were not "reflexive" or "convulsive," and the elements of battery, including necessary intention, were present:

Although the trial court found that the defendant could not form a rational choice, it did find that he could make a schizophrenic or crazy choice. Moreover, a rational choice is not required since "[a]n insane person may have an intent to invade the interests of another, even though his reasons and motives for forming that intention may be entirely irrational." 4 Restatement (Second), Torts § 895J, comment c. The following example is given in the Restatement to illustrate the application of comment c: "A, who is insane believes that he is Napoleon Bonaparte, and that B, his nurse, who confines him in his room, is an agent of the Duke of Wellington, who is endeavoring to prevent his arrival on the field of Waterloo in time to win the battle. Seeking to escape, he breaks off the leg of a chair, attacks B with it and fractures her skull. A is subject to liability to B for battery."

BEAUCHAMP v. DOW CHEMICAL CO.
Supreme Court of Michigan, 1986.
427 Mich. 1, 398 N.W.2d 882.

LEVIN, Justice.

* * *

Plaintiff Ronald Beauchamp was employed for two years as a research chemist by defendant Dow Chemical Company. He applied for workers' compensation benefits, alleging impairment of normal bodily functions caused by exposure to tordon, 2, 4–D, and 2, 4, 5–T ("agent orange").

Ronald Beauchamp and his wife, Karen, thereafter commenced this civil action against Dow. The complaint alleged that Ronald Beauchamp had been physically and mentally affected by exposure to "agent orange" and that * * * Dow intentionally assaulted Ronald Beauchamp [by exposing him to the toxic substance]. The circuit court granted summary judgment for Dow * * * on the basis that the complaint failed to state a claim on which relief could be granted. * * *

[Disagreeing with the circuit court, the supreme court held that an employee like Beauchamp may bring a tort suit against his employer if the complaint alleges an "intentional" as opposed to an "accidental" workplace injury. Under Michigan's workers compensation statute, an employee who has suffered on-the-job injury receives statutory benefits without having to prove that the employer was at fault. These benefits are substantially less than the compensatory damages a successful tort suit would bring. The statute includes an "exclusivity provision," which reads: "The right to the recovery of benefits as provided in this act shall be the employee's exclusive remedy against the employer." The court reasoned that this provision abolishes tort suits against employers for accidents on the job, but "actions for intentional torts are not barred." The remaining question is how to define "intentional tort."]

Although a number of courts have agreed that the exclusivity provision of a workers' compensation act does not preclude employees from bringing intentional tort actions against their employers, the courts have not been able to agree on a definition of "intentional" in this context. Some courts have limited the recovery to so called "true intentional torts," that is, when the employer truly intended the injury as well as the act. Other courts have relied on the standard in the Restatement of Torts, 2d, stating that when the employer intended the act that caused the injury and knew that the injury was substantially certain to occur from the act, the employer has committed an intentional tort. The substantial certainty test has apparently been extended by at least one state to cover substantial likelihood of injury.[55]

A

The Court of Appeals in the instant case declared, "In order to allege an intentional tort outside the [workers compensation] act, the plaintiff must allege that the employer intended the injury itself and not merely the activity leading to the injury." A number of states have adopted a similar intentional tort test requiring an actual intent to injure. The case law in Arkansas is illustrative.

In *Heskett v. Fisher Laundry & Cleaners Co.*, 217 Ark. 350, 230 S.W.2d 28 (1950), the Arkansas Supreme Court allowed an employee to bring a civil action for intentional tort against his employer for "a vicious, unprovoked, intentional and violent assault and battery...." In a later case, *Griffin v. George's, Inc.*, 267 Ark. 91, 93, 589 S.W.2d 24 (1979), the court declared that "only if an employer acts with an actual, specific, and deliberate intent to injure may an employee sue the employer in common-law tort." An allegation in *Griffin* that the employer "recognized the substantial certainty that [an unguarded grain auger] would result in injury" did not contain the requisite degree of intent necessary to be classified an intentional tort for the purposes of workers' compensation law.

B

The "substantial certainty" line of cases defines intentional tort more broadly. An intentional tort "is not ... limited to consequences which are desired. If the actor knows that the consequences are certain, or substantially certain, to result from his act, and still goes ahead, he is treated by the law as if he had in fact desired to produce the result." [Bazley v. Tortorich, 397 So.2d 475, 482 (La.1981).] It does not matter whether the employer wishes the injury would not occur or does not care whether it occurs. If the injury is substantially certain to occur as a consequence of actions the employer intended, the employer is deemed to have intended the injuries as well. The substantial certainty test tracks the Restatement definition of an intentional tort.[61]

The distinction between the substantial certainty intentional tort test and the "true" intentional tort tests can become important in cases such as

---

55. *Jones v. VIP Dev. Co.*, 15 Ohio St.3d 90, 472 N.E.2d 1046 (1984).

It has been said, however, that a "high risk or probability of harm is not equivalent to the substantial certainty without which an actor cannot be said to intend the harm in which his act results." [Shearer v. Homestake Mining Co., 557 F.Supp. 549, 559 (D.S.D.1983).] Although a matter of degree, it is generally recognized that at some point, the line has been crossed from intentional to reckless misconduct, and therefore from intentional to accidental injury.

61. Restatement Torts, 2d, § 8.

Griffin in which the facts were assumed, for the purpose of reviewing a trial court decision granting defendant's general demurrer, to be as follows: An employee was mangled when he fell into an auger. The employer had ordered the protective grate removed. The surface near the auger "sloped toward the opening . . . and, since there was usually grain lying upon this surface, one coming near the opening could easily slip . . ." This violation of safety standards was extremely hazardous and the employer "recognized the substantial certainty that it would result in injury to an employee." Nevertheless, the employer placed Griffin "in direct danger of injury . . . in spite of the fact that it was substantially certain that an employee in Griffin's position would be injured by reason thereof." The court, using the true intentional tort test, concluded that the employer did not "desire to bring about the consequences of the act," and, as a result, the tort action was barred by the exclusivity provision of the workers' compensation statute.

Another case that might be decided differently had the standard been substantial certainty rather than true intent was *Serna v. Statewide Contractors*, 6 Ariz.App. 12, 429 P.2d 504 (1967). Two men were killed when a ditch caved in and buried them alive. In the five months preceding the disaster, inspectors had warned that "the sides of the ditch were not sloped properly, the side was sandy, more shoring was needed, and escape ladders should be placed every 25 feet." During that time a cave-in had occurred, burying one of the decedents up to his waist. All warnings were ignored. The court disallowed the action, finding that the act was not "done knowingly and purposely, with the direct object of injuring another."

C

The recent *People v. Film Recovery Systems* case decided in Illinois adds a new perspective to the different intentional tort standards.[66] The facts in the case were as follows: Film Recovery Systems went into the business of recovering silver from film negatives. This was done by placing the negatives into vats of cyanide. Hydrogen cyanide gas would bubble up from the vats and there was inadequate ventilation. The employer knew about the dangers. The labels on the chemicals being used contained adequate warnings; as a result, the employer hired only employees who could not speak or read English. The workers complained about the fumes daily. In 1981, an inspector had warned that the operation had outgrown the plant. The employer's response was to move the executive offices while tripling the size of the operations. Eventually one worker died and several others were seriously injured because of hydrogen cyanide poisoning. The corporate officers were convicted of involuntary manslaughter.

The facts in this case are a good example of the type of employer conduct that would seem to meet the substantial certainty as well as a substantial likelihood of harm standard. It is questionable, however, whether even this outrageous conduct would constitute a "true intentional tort." The employer did not desire to injure or kill the employees, even though the

66. Leviton, "Policy considerations in corporate criminal prosecutions after *People v. Film Recovery Systems, Inc.,*" 1986 ABA National Institute on Workers' Compensation; A Review of Costs, Emerging Developments and Remedies, p. 186.

employer knew with a substantial certainty that his conduct would injure the employees.[67]

D

Selecting the appropriate intentional tort test is difficult. The problem with the substantial certainty test is that it is difficult to draw the line between substantial certainty and substantial risk. In applying the substantial certainty test, some courts have confused intentional, reckless, and even negligent misconduct, and therefore blurred the line between intentional and accidental injuries. The true intentional tort standard keep[s] the distinction clear.[69]

The problem with the true intentional tort test appears to be that it allows employers to injure and even kill employees and suffer only workers' compensation damages so long as the employer did not specifically intend to hurt the worker. The facts in the *Film Recovery System* case are a good example. Prohibiting a civil action in such a case "would allow a corporation to 'cost-out' an investment decision to kill workers." *Blankenship v. Cincinnati Milacron Chemicals,* 69 Ohio St.2d 608, 617, 433 N.E.2d 572 (1982) (Celebrezze, J., concurring).

We adopt the substantial certainty standard. In an effort to avoid the misapplication of that test illustrated by the Ohio line of cases (see n 55), we stress that substantial certainty should not be equated with substantial likelihood. The facts in *Serna* and *Film Recovery System* are examples of what would constitute substantial certainty.

* * *

Remanded to the circuit court for further proceedings consistent with this opinion. * * *

SWOPE v. COLUMBIAN CHEMICALS CO., 281 F.3d 185 (5th Cir.2002). Plaintiff sought damages for permanent, total and disabling lung damage from the chemical company which had employed him. His claim was predicated in part on the theory that the employer committed a battery against him by deliberately exposing him to ozone during his employment as a maintenance worker, causing lung damage. The District Court granted defendant's motion for summary judgment on the battery claim and plaintiff appealed. *Held,* reversed. A genuine issue of material fact existed as to whether employer knew to a substantial certainty that it was continually causing plaintiff bodily harm by exposing him to dangerous amounts of ozone without providing him with any respiratory protection.

---

67. We acknowledge that to convict these employers of involuntary manslaughter under Illinois law, the prosecution did not need to show that the employer intended to injure or kill the employees, or even that there was a substantial certainty that they would be injured or killed; all that needed to be shown was that the employer's acts "create[d] a strong probability of death or great bodily harm to that individual or another." Ill. Ann. Stat., ch. 38, § 9–1.

69. * * * It would be appropriate for the Legislature to address * * * general liability for toxic tort injury which is different in kind from a punch in the nose. The intentional tort standards governing liability for punches in the nose are not readily transferred to toxic torts.

"Many of the principal facts are undisputed. Mr. Claude Swope was employed by Columbian from March 1987 until several days after his final inhalation of ozone on July 10, 1996. Columbian continually required Mr. Swope to breathe ozone without protective respiratory equipment throughout his nine years and some months of employment. Columbian in this manner repeatedly caused him and other employees to breathe levels of ozone high enough to cause them respiratory discomfort, 'choke ups,' nausea, headaches, and chest pains. On at least three occasions, employees other than Mr. Swope had passed out from breathing too much ozone and had been taken to hospital emergency rooms or given oxygen on the plant premises. Many other times, employees had to flee the immediate vicinity in which they were working because the ozone level had become intolerable. * * * [Furthermore,] it is not disputed for purposes of the motion for summary judgment * * * that Columbian's continual exposures of Mr. Swope to ozone caused him to sustain repetitive damage to his lungs. * * * Therefore, the only question presented at this stage of the proceedings is whether there is a genuine issue as to whether Columbian knew to a substantial certainty that its deliberate continual exposures of Mr. Swope to such levels of ozone without respiratory protection were causing him to sustain repetitive physical impairments to his bodily condition."

"A harmful or offensive contact with a person, resulting from an act intended to cause the plaintiff to suffer such a contact, is a battery. The intention need[ed to inflict a battery need] not be malicious nor need it be an intention to inflict actual damage. It is sufficient if the actor intends to inflict either a harmful or offensive contact without the other's consent * * *."

The opinion noted that "from the deposition testimony, it appears that the only safety instruction Columbian ever gave to Mr. Swope and his fellow employees for dealing with such levels of ozone was to vacate the area of excessive concentration of ozone, get some fresh air, and return to work when feeling better."

SECTION B.   OFFENSE

In tort parlance, "intent" is the first "element" of battery as it is of any intentional tort. The second "element" of battery is the substantive interest being protected against deliberate injury. The second set of questions that must be asked, then, is: Why is this kind of deliberate interference with the plaintiff wrong? What interest of the plaintiff's does it injure? Why is that interest worthy of protection?

In the cases considered in Section A, the answer to these questions appears self-evident: People have every reason to want to be protected against physical harm. The cases considered here, by contrast, involve deliberate interferences with the plaintiffs' persons in circumstances where the answer to these questions is not so obvious—circumstances where the contact complained of is "offensive" not "harmful." Are all "offensive" deliberate contacts, no matter how trivial, batteries? Only some "offensive" contacts? Why should any "offensive" contacts count as batteries? What makes those contacts that do count especially wrongful? The cases in this section wrestle with these questions. One of them—*Jones v. Fisher*—ventures beyond these topics to introduce the law of tort damages.

Tort law might answer questions of offensiveness simply by asking if the plaintiff was, in fact, offended. The law declines to do this, and instead asks if the contact in question would offend the sensibilities of a "reasonable person." It thus rejects a "subjective" approach to matters of offensiveness, and adopts an "objective" one. Objectivity here has two dimensions: one is conventional; the other critical, or prescriptive. The conventional dimension asks if the contact in question *would* offend the sensibilities of a normal member of the community. The critical or prescriptive dimension asks if that contact *should* offend the sensibilities of a reasonable person. This leads the law of battery to confront large questions of dignity and equality.

FISHER v. CARROUSEL MOTOR HOTEL, INC.

Supreme Court of Texas, 1967.
424 S.W.2d 627.

GREENHILL, Justice. This is a suit for actual and exemplary damages growing out of an alleged assault and battery. The plaintiff Fisher was a mathematician with the Data Processing Division of the Manned Spacecraft Center, an agency of the National Aeronautics and Space Agency, commonly called NASA, near Houston. The defendants were the Carrousel Motor Hotel, Inc., located in Houston, the Brass Ring Club, which is located in the Carrousel, and Robert W. Flynn, who as an employee of the Carrousel was the manager of the Brass Ring Club. Flynn died before the trial, and the suit proceeded as to the Carrousel and the Brass Ring. Trial was to a jury which found for the plaintiff Fisher. The trial court rendered judgment for the defendants notwithstanding the verdict. The Court of Civil Appeals affirmed. 414 S.W.2d 774. The questions before this Court are whether there was evidence that an actionable battery was committed, and, if so, whether the two corporate defendants must respond in exemplary as well as actual damages for the malicious conduct of Flynn.

The plaintiff Fisher had been invited by Ampex Corporation and Defense Electronics to a one day's meeting regarding telemetry equipment at the Carrousel. The invitation included a luncheon. The guests were asked to reply by telephone whether they could attend the luncheon, and Fisher called in his acceptance. After the morning session, the group of 25 or 30 guests adjourned to the Brass Ring Club for lunch. The luncheon was buffet style, and Fisher stood in line with others and just ahead of a graduate student of Rice University who testified at the trial. As Fisher was about to be served, he was approached by Flynn, who snatched the plate from Fisher's hand and shouted that he, a Negro, could not be served in the club. Fisher testified that he was not actually touched, and did not testify that he suffered fear or apprehension of physical injury; but he did testify that he was highly embarrassed and hurt by Flynn's conduct in the presence of his associates.

The jury found that Flynn "forceably dispossessed plaintiff of his dinner plate" and "shouted in a loud and offensive manner" that Fisher could not be served there, thus subjecting Fisher to humiliation and indignity. It was stipulated that Flynn was an employee of the Carrousel Hotel and, as such, managed the Brass Ring Club. The jury also found that Flynn acted maliciously and awarded Fisher $400 actual damages for his humiliation and indignity and $500 exemplary damages for Flynn's malicious conduct.

The Court of Civil Appeals held that there was no assault because there was no physical contact and no evidence of fear or apprehension of physical contact. However, it has long been settled that there can be a battery without an assault, and that actual physical contact is not necessary to constitute a battery, so long as there is contact with clothing or an object closely identified with the body. 1 Harper & James, The Law of Torts 216 (1956); Restatement of Torts 2d, §§ 18 and 19. In Prosser, Law of Torts 32 (3d Ed. 1964), it is said:

"The interest in freedom from intentional and unpermitted contacts with the plaintiff's person is protected by an action for the tort commonly called battery. The protection extends to any part of the body, or to anything which is attached to it and practically identified with it. Thus contact with the plaintiff's clothing, or with a cane, a paper, or any other object held in his hand will be sufficient; * * * The plaintiff's interest in the integrity of his person includes all those things which are in contact or connected with it."

Under the facts of this case, we have no difficulty in holding that the intentional grabbing of plaintiff's plate constituted a battery. The intentional snatching of an object from one's hand is as clearly an offensive invasion of his person as would be an actual contact with the body. "To constitute an assault and battery, it is not necessary to touch the plaintiff's body or even his clothing; knocking or snatching anything from plaintiff's hand or touching anything connected with his person, when done in an offensive manner, is sufficient." Morgan v. Loyacomo, 190 Miss. 656, 1 So.2d 510 (1941).

* * *

The rationale for holding an offensive contact with such an object to be a battery is explained in 1 Restatement of Torts 2d § 18 (Comment p. 31) as follows:

> Since the essence of the plaintiff's grievance consists in the offense to the dignity involved in the unpermitted and intentional invasion of the inviolability of his person and not in any physical harm done to his body, it is not necessary that the plaintiff's actual body be disturbed. Unpermitted and intentional contacts with anything so connected with the body as to be customarily regarded as part of the other's person and therefore as partaking of its inviolability is actionable as an offensive contact with his person. There are some things such as clothing or a cane or, indeed, anything directly grasped by the hand which are so intimately connected with one's body as to be universally regarded as part of the person.

We hold, therefore, that the forceful dispossession of plaintiff Fisher's plate in an offensive manner was sufficient to constitute a battery, and the trial court erred in granting judgment notwithstanding the verdict on the issue of actual damages.

* * * Damages for mental suffering are recoverable without the necessity for showing actual physical injury in a case of willful battery because the basis of that action is the unpermitted and intentional invasion of the plaintiff's person and not the actual harm done to the plaintiff's body. Restatement of Torts 2d § 18. Personal indignity is the essence of an action for battery; and consequently the defendant is liable not only for contacts which do actual physical harm, but also for those which are offensive and insulting. * * *

* * *

The judgments of the courts below are reversed, and judgment is here rendered for the plaintiff for $900 with interest from the date of the trial court's judgment, and for costs of this suit.

BRZOSKA ET AL., v. OLSON, 668 A.2d 1355 (Del.Sup.Ct.1995). Thirty-eight former dental patients of defendant (who had been HIV-positive during the period that he treated plaintiffs) brought various claims against his estate, including claims for battery. The Superior Court granted defendant's motion for summary judgment on plaintiffs' battery claims, and plaintiffs appealed. The Supreme Court affirmed, holding *"as a matter of law*, that the incidental touching of a patient by an HIV-infected dentist while performing ordinary, consented-to dental procedures is insufficient to sustain a battery claim in the absence of a channel for HIV infection * * *. [S]uch contact is offensive only if it results in actual exposure to the HIV virus." (emphasis in original). The court reasoned that "the performance of dental procedures by an HIV-infected dentist, standing alone" did not "constitute offensive bodily contact for purposes of battery" because it is "unreasonable for a person to fear infection when that person has not been exposed to a disease."

"Although a battery may consist of any unauthorized touching of the person which causes offense or alarm, the test for whether a contact is 'offensive' is not wholly subjective. The law does not permit recovery for the extremely sensitive who become offended at the slightest contact. Rather, for a bodily contact to be offensive, it must offend a reasonable sense of personal dignity. Restatement (Second) of Torts § 19 (1965). In order for a contact be offensive to a reasonable sense of personal dignity, it must be one which would offend the ordinary person and as such one not unduly sensitive as to his personal dignity. It must, therefore, be a contact which is unwarranted by the social usages prevalent at the time and place at which it is inflicted. Restatement (Second) of Torts § 19 cmt. a (1965); Prosser and Keeton, § 9, at 42. The propriety of the contact is therefore assessed by an objective 'reasonableness' standard.

* * *

" * * * Were we to recognize a claim for the fear of contracting AIDS based upon a mere allegation that one may have been exposed to HIV, totally unsupported by any medical evidence or factual proof, we would open a Pandora's Box of 'AIDS-phobia' claims by individuals whose ignorance, unreasonable suspicion or general paranoia cause them apprehension over the slightest of contact with HIV-infected individuals or objects. Such plaintiffs would recover for their fear of AIDS, no matter how irrational. * * * "

STATE v. DAVIS, 1 Hill (19 S.C.L.) 46 (1833). The prosecutor, a deputy sheriff, roped a black slave to himself to prevent escape. The defendant cut the rope and carried off the slave. *Held,* an "assault." "The rope was as much identified with his person, as the hat or coat which he wore, or the stick which he held in his hand."

STEARNS v. SAMPSON, 59 Me. 568 (1871). *Held,* setting aside a verdict for plaintiff, that it was not an assault or battery upon an unlawfully remaining tenant, a woman, to remove the doors and windows of the house in which she lived, causing her to suffer from the cold and to be "embarrassed and distressed."

CARNES v. THOMPSON, 48 S.W.2d 903 (Mo.1932). "If one person intentionally strikes at, throws at, or shoots at another, and unintentionally strikes a third person, he is not excused, on the ground that it was a mere accident, but it is an assault and battery of the third person. Defendant's intention, in such a case, is to strike an unlawful blow, to injure some person by his act, and it is not essential that the injury be to the one intended."

JONES v. FISHER
Supreme Court of Wisconsin, 1969.
42 Wis.2d 209, 166 N.W.2d 175.

This is an assault and battery action brought by the plaintiff-respondent, Aleta I. Jones, for compensatory and punitive damages against Jerome Paul Fisher and Clara Belle Fisher, his wife, defendants-appellants.

The defendants were the owners and operators of a nursing home in Middleton, Wisconsin. The plaintiff, age twenty-six, married but separated, started to work for the defendants as a nurse's aid in December of 1966. She cared for the home residents during the night hours, set up and gave medication, prepared and served breakfast and had some clean-up duties in the kitchen. Until the incident in question the relationship between the parties had been cordial and friendly. The defendants regarded her as a good employee and were personally fond of her.

In September, 1967, the plaintiff was told by her dentist that her teeth were in bad condition. She needed an upper plate but complained to Mrs. Fisher about the cost of her dental work. The Fishers volunteered and did loan her $200 to apply on her dental expenses. All but $10 of the proceeds of the loan was paid to the dentist.

Shortly after she obtained the upper plate she quit working for the Fishers. About a week or more after she quit, on November 6, 1967, at noon, she returned to the nursing home to get her check in the amount of $48 for her last week's work. Mrs. Fisher tried to convince the plaintiff to return to work at the nursing home. The plaintiff refused. Mr. Fisher entered the conversation and inquired when she was going to repay the $200. She told him he could take $20 out of the $48 check and that she would pay the balance at the rate of $20 per month. He told her that was not satisfactory and that she would have to pay the entire amount in three days or leave the upper plate for security. She refused to agree to these conditions. She was told to leave the teeth and an argument ensued. There is a dispute as to whether the Fishers used profane and indecent language toward her. She attempted to run out of the room. Mr. Fisher seized her arms and forced them in back of her. The evidence is unclear as to whether she was forced onto his lap or into a crouched position; if she kicked at Mr. Fisher; or if she threatened to kill him. In any event, Mrs. Fisher grabbed at her face and mouth and extracted the upper plate. Mr. Fisher released her and she immediately ran out of the house. The affray was less than fifteen minutes. At the trial she testified that her arms and her back hurt while she was being held and that her mouth, which was sore because the teeth did not fit properly, hurt when Mrs. Fisher took her plate out. She had no bruises nor scratches. She testified that she was in fear and was humiliated and embarrassed.

After she left the rest home she walked about a block to a drugstore where she called her subsequent employer and asked him to call his lawyer. She then walked another block to the police station and reported the incident to two police officers. One of the officers went to the Fisher nursing home, obtained the teeth, returned to the station and gave Mrs. Jones her teeth. She testified she suffered humiliation, embarrassment and shame at the drugstore and at the police station and that she had these same emotions for about a week which made it difficult to sleep. She did not see a doctor or take any prescriptive medicine.

The jury found that both defendants had committed an assault and battery on her and awarded compensatory damages of $1,000 and punitive damages of $2,500 as to each defendant.

The trial court denied the defendants' motions after verdict and ordered judgment in the amount of $6,000, plus costs.

Defendants appeal.

BEILFUSS, Justice.

* * *

The defendants do not raise any issue as to the assault and battery finding. Their main thrust is that the damages, both compensatory and punitive, are excessive and [they] ask this court * * * to fix a reasonable amount as an option to a new trial.

* * *

The jury awarded the plaintiff $1,000 compensatory damages. Compensatory damages are to compensate the injured party for his actual damages and not as punishment of the defendant. If there is personal injury the award should include compensation for loss of earnings, pain and suffering, and permanent or future disability if such appears. The award can also include compensation for mental suffering such as humiliation, shame, embarrassment, and fear. Granted, mental suffering is many times difficult to evaluate in terms of monetary awards, nevertheless, it is compensable.

Considering the testimony and other proof in the record most favorable to the plaintiff, we find that plaintiff was subjected to a painful physical assault for a very few minutes at the most. She testified her arms and back hurt while she was held and that the soreness of her mouth was aggravated when the teeth were taken. There was no objective physical evidence of injury. She did not consult a physician, nor use prescriptive medicine. Her physical injury was nominal. She testified that she was nervous, humiliated and scared during the altercation at the nursing home, at the drugstore, the police station, and for about a week thereafter and still (at the time of trial) thinks about it. She was without her teeth for, at the most, an hour. Understandably she could suffer humiliation and shame during this period. Conceivably she could continue to suffer these emotions for some time thereafter, but her symptoms were all subjective and not supported by any medical testimony nor any other corroborating evidence. The lack of medical testimony or other corroborating evidence is not fatal to her claim for past suffering but it would have done much to add credence to her almost minimal testimony of her subjective emotions.

In Makowski v. Ehlenbach (1960), 11 Wis.2d 38, 41–43, 103 N.W.2d 907, 910–911, we stated:

"The problem of achieving fairness in assessing damages for personal injury is fraught with difficulty. Theoretical nicety is impossible. Under our judicial system, we rely primarily upon the good sense of jurors to determine the amount of money which will compensate an individual for whatever loss of well-being he has suffered as a result of injury. The general rule governing the trial judge or appellate court in determining whether damages are excessive on the basis of the amount found is stated in 15 Am.Jur., Damages, p. 621, (p. 622), sec. 205, quoted with approval in Bethke v. Duwe, 1950, 256 Wis. 378, 384, 41 N.W.2d 277, 280, as follows:

" 'In actions sounding in damages merely, where the law furnishes no legal rule for measuring them, the amount to be awarded rests largely in the discretion of the jury, and with their verdict the courts are reluctant to interfere. As shown elsewhere, a verdict may be set aside as excessive by the trial court or on appeal when, and not unless, it is so clearly excessive as to indicate that it was the result of passion, prejudice, or corruption, or it is clear that the jury disregarded the evidence or the rules of law. * * *

" 'Since it is for the jury, and not for the court, to fix the amount of the damages, their verdict in an action for unliquidated damages will not be set aside merely because it is large or because the reviewing court would have awarded less. Full compensation is impossible in the abstract, and different individuals will vary in their estimate of the sum which will be a just pecuniary compensation. Hence, all that the court can do is to see that the jury approximates a sane estimate, or, as it is sometimes said, see that the results attained do not shock the judicial conscience.'

" * * * Where the question is a close one, it should be resolved in favor of the verdict."

The trial court was of the opinion the award for compensatory damages was high but not excessive. "In view of the limited, vague and uncorroborated testimony bearing"[2] upon her mental distress, we are of the opinion the award for compensatory damages of $1,000 does "reflect an allowance for the effects of injury not sufficiently proved" and "reflect a rate of compensation which is beyond reason" and, therefore, excessive. We are of the opinion that $500 is a reasonable award to Mrs. Jones for compensatory damages.

The appellants acknowledge that the court has reaffirmed its adherence to the doctrine of punitive damages.[4] They do, however, propose that the doctrine should be limited to cases of sexual assault and cases where the defendant engages in a course of dangerous conduct after he had had time to reflect upon the deleterious effects of such action. We have said the doctrine is to be retained—we are not convinced that the limitations suggested by the appellants are based on appropriate distinctions.

Punitive damages can be awarded where the defendant's transgressions are activated by a malicious motive.[5] However, punitive damages need not be limited where there is no proof of malice. In Kink v. Combs, supra,[6] we stated at page 79, 135 N.W.2d at page 797:

"The defendant claims that the question of punitive or exemplary damages should not have been submitted to the jury because defendant's acts were not activated by malice or vindictiveness. However, malice or vindictiveness are not the *sine qua non* of punitive damages.

" 'Where the defendant's wrongdoing has been intentional and deliberate, and has the character of outrage frequently associated with crime, all but a few courts have permitted the jury to award in the tort action 'punitive' or 'exemplary' damages, or what is sometimes called 'smart money.' " Prosser, Law of Torts (2d Ed. 1955), p. 9.

"For the award of punitive damages it is sufficient that there be a showing of wanton, willful, or reckless disregard of the plaintiff's rights. 6 C.J.S. Assault and Battery § 55b(3), p. 904."

We are of the opinion that the jury could (they are not required to do so)[7] award punitive damages based upon the facts before them. The conduct of Mr. and Mrs. Fisher was illegal, outrageous and grossly unreasonable. It may be as appellants contend that they erroneously thought they had a right

---

2. Lisowski v. Chenenoff (1968), 37 Wis.2d 610, 633, 155 N.W.2d 619, 631.

4. Kink v. Combs (1965), 28 Wis.2d 65, 135 N.W.2d 789; Lisowski v. Chenenoff, supra.

5. See Meshane v. Second Street Co. (1928), 197 Wis. 382, 222 N.W. 320; Wickhem, The Rule of Exemplary Damages in Wisconsin, 2 Wis. L.Rev. (1923), 129, 144, 145.

6. Footnote 4.

7. Malco, Inc. v. Midwest Aluminum Sales (1961), 14 Wis.2d 57, 63, 109 N.W.2d 516.

to take the teeth as security for their loan. Even so, it was grossly unreasonable to use the tactics they did and subject the plaintiff to this outrage.

The principal problem that confronts us is whether the damages awarded are excessive.

Punitive damages are assessed not to compensate the injured party but as a punishment to the wrongdoer and as a deterrent to others.

The evidence reveals that the defendants' own property was worth approximately $75,000, subject to a mortgage of $41,000, leaving an equity of about $34,000. Their net income for the years 1966 and 1967 was about $24,000 per year. It appears as though the nursing home operation was a joint venture between Mr. and Mrs. Fisher. In contrasting the punitive awards with the wealth of the defendants we must either assume the award was $5,000 or consider that each owned one-half of the wealth of the parties.

In viewing the wealth of the defendants, the character and extent of their acts, and the probable motivation, and then applying the standard of punishment and deterrence, the court is of the unanimous opinion that the assessment of $2,500 as punitive damages to each defendant was excessive.

Having determined the punitive damages are excessive, we * * * give the plaintiff the option of accepting a reduced reasonable amount or a new trial on damages.

In Malco v. Midwest Aluminum Sales, supra, we stated, at page 65, 109 N.W.2d at page 521:

"It seems to us that once the jury has decided in its discretion to award punitive damages, the amount thereof must be subject to the control of the court. True, the jury need not award any punitive damages, but having done so, the amount thereof should be subject to the court's revision in the same manner as compensatory damages. It is not logical to say excessive punitive damages cannot be reduced by the court to a reasonable amount because the jury had the power to deny any amount. In such cases, the fact is the jury exercised its discretion and made an excessive award of punitive damages. We hold that * * * a trial court has the power to reduce the amount of punitive damages to what it determines is a fair and reasonable amount for such kind of damages."

The majority of the court is of the opinion that an assessment of $1,000 as to each defendant is a reasonable amount for punitive damages.

The appellants contend that it was error to allow the plaintiff to introduce the net earnings of the defendants as an aid to the jury in fixing the punitive damages. They contend the only admissible proof is net worth.

Net worth may not in all instances be the best measure of an individual's ability to respond in damages. We believe a more accurate gauge is his financial resources, which include his earnings as well as his net worth. In some instances it may work to the defendant's advantage to show his net earnings.

* * *

Our [decision] requires that the judgment be reversed and cause remanded to the trial court with the direction that the plaintiff have the option to elect to take judgment in the amounts fixed by the court in this opinion, plus taxable costs. * * * In the event the plaintiff refuses or neglects to make such election within * * * twenty days, the trial court shall enter an order for a new trial on the issue of damages.

* * *

───────

ROBERT W. HANSEN, Justice (dissenting). The majority opinion sustains the collecting of punitive damages in a case involving a one hour deprivation of dentures. Next may come the case approving such added damages for the near-identical deed of toupee-snatching. We do not minimize the unpleasantness of an hour spent without newly acquired dentures, nor of an hour spent without the adornment of a substitute headpiece. We agree that compensatory damages for the deprivation and humiliation involved are justified. We do not agree that the added penalty of punitive or vindictive damages is also warranted in such instance. We would hold that the public interest does not require nor ought the public policy permit the awarding of punishment damages in this type of situation.

* * *

WHAT IS THE BASIS?

What is the justification in certain situations for permitting a tort-plaintiff to recover money beyond the compensatory damages established? It has been said that such punitive awards are permitted in most jurisdictions " * * * as a punishment to the defendant and as a warning and example to deter him and others from committing like offenses in the future."[4] Can it seriously be contended that such underlying justification is present in the case before us? Would not the recollection of the compensatory damages paid render very unlikely a repetition by the husband and wife here involved of the offense of denture detention? Would not the $1,000 compensatory damage award, standing alone, be a sufficient deterrent to others who might be tempted to hold dentures as security for an unpaid loan? Are we dealing here with a propensity to grab, and hold upper plates that is marked either by a high rate of recidivism or contagion? Is there here present a situation that justifies the heavy-handed use of punishment to deter? We think not, particularly because we do not deal with a matter of plaintiff's rights,[5] but the question of what the public interest requires and what the public policy should permit.

───────

4. 22 Am.Jur.2d Damages No. 237, p. 323.

5. "Plaintiff is not entitled to punitive damages as a matter of right * * * " recommended instruction to jury in Haberman v. Gasser (1899), 104 Wis. 98, 80 N.W. 105, as quoted in "Exemplary or Punitive Damages in Wisconsin" by Prof. James D. Ghiardi, supra, p. 17.

WHAT ARE THE LIMITS?

While the roadway to punitive awards has been around a long time, it always has had limits since such punishment awards were first approved. It has often been said that to warrant the imposition of punitory damages, it must appear that the wrong was inflicted "under circumstances of aggravation, insult, or cruelty, with vindictiveness and malice."[6] The road was widened with the holding that, where actual malice was not present, it would be enough that there be "wanton or reckless disregard of plaintiff's rights."[7] In [Kink v. Combs, quoted by the majority opinion *supra* p. 42, we broadened the road again] approving, this statement:

"Where the defendant's wrongdoing has been intentional and deliberate, *and* has the character of outrage frequently associated with crime, all but a few courts have permitted the jury to award in the tort action 'punitive' or 'exemplary' damages, or what is sometimes called 'smart money.'" Prosser, Law of Torts, 2d, p. 9, sec. 2. (Emphasis supplied.)[8]

Elsewhere it has been said that punitive damages "are imposed in view of the enormity of the offense." Under any of these tests, can it be fairly concluded that the unfortunate altercation between the parties here involved moves into that category of seriousness that warrants awarding of punishment damages?

Unless malice is equated with momentary loss of temper or is to be presumed from an act of poor judgment, there is no element of malevolence or vindictiveness present here. The bicuspid corpus delicti is present only because of an interest-free loan made by defendants to plaintiff. Granted that they expected her to remain in their employ and to pay them back from her earnings, goodwill, not illwill is evidence by the transaction, the advancing of the $200 to pay the dentist.

Conceding that the taking of the upper plate which belonged to the plaintiff, even if paid for by the defendants, was an invasion of her rights, can it be termed "wanton or reckless?" It is evident that there was a mutually cordial, supportive and agreeable relationship between the old couple and the young lady who worked for them in their nursing home, almost up to the incident here involved. It was the lady's decision, loan unpaid, to go to work for someone else that precipitated a change in the relationship. Is this flareup of emotions, this shift in mood, this disappointment of expectations on the part of the employing couple a foundation for a finding of wanton and reckless disregard of the rights of another? If so, the most trivial of altercations and mildest of scuffles dons the garment of wantonness or recklessness.

Given the unfortunate escalation of unpleasantness in the argument of the parties, can its climax, the grabbing of the dentures, be found to have the "character of outrage frequently associated with crime?" If the police

6. For example, Christensen v. Schwartz (1929), 198 Wis. 222, 222 N.W. 231, 223 N.W. 839.

7. Pickett v. Crook (1866), 20 Wis. 358; Meibus v. Dodge (1875), 38 Wis. 300.

8. Kink v. Combs (1965), 28 Wis.2d 65, 135 N.W.2d 789.

had been called to stop the argument, instead of being called to get the plate back, would they have made an arrest? If they had, would a district attorney have issued a state warrant for battery, or even for disorderly conduct, on the basis of what had taken place? If he had, would a misdemeanor court have considered the situation here to involve violation of a criminal statute or as a falling-out among friends to be settled by an apology and a handshake? Is this the type of situation that Prosser contemplated when he wrote of an "outrage frequently associated with crime?" We think it falls short of being that. Certainly, if punitive damages are to be imposed "in view of the enormity of the crime," this is no situation justifying their imposition. * * *

We have grave doubts about the public policy involved in thus placing in private hands the use of punishment to deter. Some observers challenged the right or efficacy of even the state using punishment as punishment to deter.[10] At least in the public administration of criminal justice there are clearly defined crimes, clearly delineated penalties, constitutional protections and in-built restraints.

However, we need not challenge the whole idea of placing the right to seek retribution, in addition to compensation, in private hands, to challenge the applicability of such concept in the case before us. Whether or not it operates to deter scalpings, it ought not be used in the efforts to deter toupee dislodgings. The concept of punitive damages, it has been said, is "not a favorite of the law," should be "exercised with great caution," and properly be "confined within the narrowest limits."[11] This case, it appears to the writer, is well beyond the limits.

So we would sustain the admittedly high award of $1,000 for compensatory damages, as including every ounce of hurt and humiliation that can be placed upon the scales, and strike the awards for punitive damages as not being warranted by the facts of this case. I am authorized to state that Mr. Justice LEO B. HANLEY joins in this dissent.

———

HODGES v. S.C. TOOF & COMPANY, 833 S.W.2d 896 (Tenn. 1992). Plaintiff brought retaliatory discharge action against defendant, alleging that he was fired because he sat as a juror in a three month trial. The jury returned a verdict for the plaintiff, and awarded him $200,000 compensatory and $375,000 punitive damages. The Court of Appeals upheld the jury finding of retaliatory discharge, but vacated the award of compensatory and punitive damages. The Supreme Court granted plaintiff's application for permission to appeal in part to "reexamine the manner in which punitive damages are awarded in Tennessee." Upon reexamination, the court decided that present Tennessee law was "overbroad" because it allowed punitive damages to be awarded for "gross negligence" and chose "to restrict the

---

10. See "The Crime of Punishment" by Dr. Karl Menninger, New York, The Viking Press, 1966.

11. 22 Am.Jur.2d, Damages, sec. 238, p. 326, and cases cited therein at footnotes 19, 20 and 1.

awarding of punitive damages to cases involving only the most egregious of wrongs." * * * "In Tennessee, therefore, a court may may henceforth award punitive damages only if it finds a defendant has acted either (1) intentionally, (2) fraudulently, (3) maliciously, or (4) recklessly."

"A person acts intentionally when it is the person's conscious objective or desire to engage in the conduct or cause the result. A person acts fraudulently when (1) the person intentionally misrepresents an existing, material fact or produces a false impression, in order to mislead another or to obtain an undue advantage, and (2) another is injured because of reasonable reliance upon that representation. A person acts maliciously when the person is motivated by ill will, hatred, or personal spite. A person acts recklessly when the person is aware of, but consciously disregards, a substantial and unjustifiable risk of such a nature that its disregard constitutes a gross deviation from the standard of care that an ordinary person would exercise under all the circumstances.

"Further, because punitive damages are to be awarded only in the most egregious of cases, a plaintiff must prove the defendant's intentional, fraudulent, malicious, or reckless conduct by clear and convincing evidence. This higher standard of proof is appropriate given the twin purposes of punishment and deterrence: fairness requires that a defendant's wrong be clearly established before punishment, as such, is imposed; awarding punitive damages only in clearly appropriate cases better effects deterrence."

LAZENBY v. UNIVERSAL UNDERWRITERS INSURANCE CO., 214 Tenn. 639, 383 S.W.2d 1 (1964). *Held,* liability insurance covered punitive damages assessed against an intoxicated driver.

NORTHWESTERN NATIONAL CASUALTY CO. v. McNULTY, 307 F.2d 432 (5th Cir.1962). *Held,* public policy prohibits insurance against liability for punitive damages.

MINK v. UNIVERSITY OF CHICAGO

United States District Court, N.D. Illinois, 1978.
460 F.Supp. 713.

GRADY, District Judge.

Plaintiffs have brought this action on behalf of themselves and some 1,000 women who were given diethylstilbestrol ("DES") as part of a medical experiment conducted by the defendants, University of Chicago and Eli Lilly & Company, between September 29, 1950, and November 20, 1952. The drug was administered to the plaintiffs during their prenatal care at the University's Lying–In Hospital as part of a double blind study to determine the value of DES in preventing miscarriages. The women were not told they were part of an experiment, nor were they told that the pills administered to them were DES. Plaintiffs claim that as a result of their taking DES, their daughters have developed abnormal cervical cellular formations and are exposed to an increased risk of vaginal or cervical cancer. Plaintiffs also allege that they and their sons have suffered reproductive tract and other abnormalities and have incurred an increased risk of cancer.

The complaint further alleges that the relationship between DES and cancer was known to the medical community as early as 1971, but that the defendants made no effort to notify the plaintiffs of their participation in the DES experiment until late 1975 or 1976 when the University sent letters to the women in the experiment informing them of the possible relationship between the use of DES in pregnant women and abnormal conditions in the genital tracts of their offspring. The letter asked for information to enable the University to contact the sons and daughters of the plaintiffs for medical examination.

The complaint seeks recovery on three causes of action. The first alleges that the defendants committed a series of batteries on the plaintiffs by conducting a medical experiment on them without their knowledge or consent. The administration of DES to the plaintiffs without their consent is alleged to be an "offensive invasion of their persons" which has caused them "severe mental anxiety and emotional distress due to the increased risk to their children of contracting cancer and other abnormalities." The second count is grounded in products liability and seeks to recover damages from defendant Lilly premised on its manufacture of DES as a defective and unreasonably dangerous drug. Finally, the plaintiffs allege that the defendants breached their duty to notify plaintiffs that they had been given DES while pregnant and that children born from that pregnancy should consult a medical specialist. Throughout the complaint plaintiffs claim the defendants intentionally concealed the fact of the experiment and information concerning the relationship between DES and cancer from the plaintiffs.

Both defendants have moved to dismiss the complaint for failure to state a claim. We will deny the motions as to the first cause of action, and grant the motions as to the second and third causes of action.

BATTERY

We must determine whether the administration of a drug, DES, to the plaintiffs without their knowledge or consent constitutes a battery under Illinois law. The defendants argue that the plaintiffs' first count is really a "lack of informed consent" case premised on negligence. Because the named plaintiffs have not alleged specific physical injury to themselves, the defendants contend they have failed to state a claim for negligence and the count should be dismissed.[2] However, if we find the action to be based on a battery theory, it may stand notwithstanding the lack of an allegation of personal physical injury.

* * *

* * * The distinction between battery and negligence is elucidated in Trogun v. Fruchtman, 58 Wis.2d 569, 596, 207 N.W.2d 297, 311–12 (1973):

---

2. We agree with the defendants that if the first cause of action is characterized as negligence, it fails to state a claim. With the exception of a conclusory statement of reproductive tract abnormalities in paragraph 1, the complaint does not allege any physical injury to the plaintiff class. There is no allegation of specific physical injury to any named plaintiff. The damage alleged in the first count is mental distress to the plaintiffs and an increased risk of cancer to the plaintiffs and their children. These allegations are insufficient to support a claim for negligence.

The courts of this country have recognized essentially two theories of liability for allegedly unauthorized medical treatment or therapy rendered by physicians to their patients. The first of these theories is the traditional intentional tort of battery or assault and battery which is simply defined as the unauthorized touching of the person of another. Underlying this theory of liability is, of course, the general feeling that a person of sound mind has a right to determine, even as against his physician, what is to be done to his body. Under this theory, liability is imposed upon a physician who has performed non-emergency treatment upon a patient without his consent.

* * *

The second theory of liability, permitted by a majority of courts, is grounded upon negligence principles rather than on intentional tort. * * * "[This] doctrine of 'informed consent' * * * concerns the duty of the physician or surgeon to inform the patient of the risk which may be involved in treatment or surgery."

As for the application of the distinction, we find the analysis of the court in Cobbs v. Grant, 8 Cal.3d 229, 104 Cal.Rptr. 505, 512, 502 P.2d 1, 8 (1972), persuasive:

The battery theory should be reserved for those circumstances when a doctor performs an operation to which the patient has not consented. When the patient gives permission to perform one type of treatment and the doctor performs another, the requisite element of deliberate intent to deviate from the consent given is present. * * *

* * *

* * * [Here] plaintiffs did not consent to DES treatment; they were not even aware that the drug was being administered to them. They were the subjects of an experiment whereby non-emergency treatment was performed upon them without their consent or knowledge.

* * * Accordingly, we will analyze the plaintiffs' first cause of action under a battery theory.

Battery is defined as the unauthorized touching of the person of another. To be liable for battery, the defendant must have done some affirmative act, intended to cause an unpermitted contact. "[I]t is enough that the defendant sets a force in motion which ultimately produces the result. * * * Proof of the technical invasion of the integrity of the plaintiff's person by even an entirely harmless, but offensive, contact entitles him to vindication of his legal right by an award of nominal damages, and the establishment of the tort cause of action entitles him also to compensation for the mental disturbance inflicted upon him." W. Prosser, Law of Torts § 9, at 35 (4th ed. 1971).

"The gist of the action for battery is not the hostile intent of the defendant, but rather the absence of consent to the contact on the part of the plaintiff." Id. at 36. "The essence * * * [of the] question in a battery case involving a physician is what did the patient agree with the physician to have done, and was the ultimate contact by the physician within the scope of the patient's consent." Cathemer v. Hunter, 27 Ariz.App. 780, 558 P.2d 975, 978 (1976). In sum, to state a cause of action for battery, the plaintiffs must allege intentional acts by the defendants resulting in offensive contact with the plaintiffs' persons, and the lack of consent to the defendants' conduct.

The administration of DES to the plaintiffs was clearly intentional. It was part of a planned experiment conducted by the defendants. The requisite element of intent is therefore met, since the plaintiffs need show only an intent to bring about the contact; an intent to do harm is not essential to the action.

The act of administering the drug supplies the contact with the plaintiffs' persons. "It is not necessary that the contact with the other's person be directly caused by some act of the actor. All that is necessary is that the actor intend to cause the other, directly or indirectly, to come in contact with a foreign substance in a manner which the other will reasonably regard as offensive." Restatement (Second) of Torts § 18, Comment c at 31 (1965). We find the administration of a drug without the patient's knowledge comports with the meaning of offensive contact. Had the drug been administered by means of a hypodermic needle, the element of physical contact would clearly be sufficient. We believe that causing the patient to physically ingest a pill is indistinguishable in principle.

Finally, there is the question of consent. As previously stated, this is the real crux of the issue in cases involving a physician's treatment of his patient. If the patient has assented to the doctor's treatment, he may not later maintain an action in battery. Cathemer v. Hunter, 558 P.2d at 978. The defendants argue that the plaintiffs consented to treatment when they admitted themselves to the University's Lying–In Hospital for prenatal care. The scope of the plaintiffs' consent is crucial to their ultimate recovery in a battery action. * * * These questions, however, are questions of fact which are to be determined by the jury, not by this court on a motion to dismiss. The plaintiffs have alleged sufficient lack of consent to the treatment involved to state a claim for battery against both defendants.

STRICT LIABILITY

In their second cause of action, plaintiffs allege that the DES ingested by them was "defective and unreasonably dangerous at the time it was manufactured, and Lilly is therefore strictly liable to the plaintiffs for their damages." Complaint ¶ 32. * * *

* * *

Clearly, one of the essential elements in a claim for strict liability is physical injury to the plaintiff. The closest the complaint comes to alleging physical injury is the allegation of a "risk" of cancer. The mere fact of risk without any accompanying physical injury is insufficient to state a claim for strict products liability. Likewise, the plaintiffs may not rely on injury to their children to state a claim for relief for themselves, even though they allege mental anxiety and emotional distress as a consequence of the injury to their children.

The plaintiffs argue that they have alleged personal physical injury in paragraph 1, which states that DES "has or may cause reproductive tract and other abnormalities in themselves." There is no indication that any of the named plaintiffs have suffered any of these "abnormalities." Without more concrete allegations of injury to the named plaintiffs, the second count must be dismissed for failure to state a claim.

[The third count—failure to notify—was likewise dismissed because of lack of allegations of physical injury to the named plaintiffs.]

———

CLAYTON v. NEW DREAMLAND ROLLER SKATING RINK, INC., 14 N.J.Super. 390, 82 A.2d 458 (1951), petition for certification denied, 13 N.J. 527, 100 A.2d 567 (1953). Plaintiff fell at a skating rink and broke her arm. Over the protests of plaintiff and her husband, a skating rink officer allegedly manipulated her broken arm in an attempt to set it. *Held*, the complaint stated a cause of action for assault and battery, "[a]lthough his acts may have been performed with the best of intentions."

SECTION C.   CONSENT

The third and final element of battery is lack of consent. An otherwise harmful or offensive contact, deliberately inflicted, is not a battery if the plaintiff has consented to that contact. The inquiry into actual consent is, at bottom, a subjective one. We are asking if this plaintiff did or did not agree to permit the contact at issue. Like the criteria for determining "offensiveness," however, the criteria for determining the existence and extent of actual consent are "objective". (This preference for objective over subjective criteria is, in fact, a characteristic feature of tort law.) In this context, objectivity has two basic dimensions. First, the *presence* of consent is inferred from the conventional meaning of the plaintiff's conduct. Consent is a matter of outward manifestations—of how the plaintiff's conduct appears to other reasonable persons. This aspect of objectivity takes center stage in *O'Brien*. Second, the *content* of consent is determined objectively. We ask what a "reasonable person" would understand herself to have consented to in the context at hand.

Taking an "objective" view of the content of consent once again introduces two different standards of reasonableness into the law of battery. One of these standards is *conventional*. Reasonableness in this sense is a matter of what people normally know or think when they deliberately enter into some activity. "What kind of contact, for instance, do people normally agree to accept when they play football?" The other standard is *prescriptive*. Reasonableness in this sense is a matter of fairness. We ask: "What kind of contact is legitimate given the character of this activity?" "What kind of contact, for instance, improves the game of football?" "What kind of contact impairs the game?" If a certain kind of contact improves the character of an activity, it is fair to require those engaged in the activity to accept it. If it detracts from the activity, it is unfair to insist that they accept it. This aspect of consent comes to the fore in *Hackbart*.

The structure of the law is thus a delicate blend of objective and subjective concepts. Consent is at bottom subjective because it is a matter of what the party in question did or did not agree to—not a matter of what a reasonable person would or would not agree to. Yet both the presence and the content of actual consent are determined objectively. Presence is determined objectively because it is a matter of external manifestation; content is determined objectively because it is blend of convention and prescription.

O'BRIEN v. CUNARD STEAMSHIP CO.

Supreme Judicial Court of Massachusetts, 1891.
154 Mass. 272, 28 N.E. 266.

[On exceptions to an order directing a verdict for defendant.]

KNOWLTON, J. This case presents two questions: first, whether there was any evidence to warrant the jury in finding that the defendant, by any of its servants or agents, committed an assault on the plaintiff; secondly, whether there was evidence on which the jury could have found that the defendant was guilty of negligence towards the plaintiff. To sustain the first count, which was for an alleged assault, the plaintiff relied on the fact that the surgeon who was employed by the defendant vaccinated her on shipboard, while she was on her passage from Queenstown to Boston. On this branch of the case the question is whether there was any evidence that the surgeon used force upon the plaintiff against her will. In determining whether the act was lawful or unlawful, the surgeon's conduct must be considered in connection with the circumstances. If the plaintiff's behavior was such as to indicate consent on her part, he was justified in his act, whatever her unexpressed feelings may have been. In determining whether she consented, he could be guided only by her overt acts and the manifestations of her feelings.

It is undisputed that at Boston there are strict quarantine regulations in regard to the examination of immigrants, to see that they are protected from smallpox by vaccination, and that only those persons who hold a certificate from the medical officer of the steamship, stating that they are so protected, are permitted to land without detention in quarantine or vaccination by the port physician. It appears that the defendant is accustomed to have its surgeons vaccinate all immigrants who desire it, and who are not protected by previous vaccination, and give them a certificate which is accepted at quarantine as evidence of their protection. Notices of the regulations at quarantine, and of the willingness of the ship's medical officer to vaccinate such as needed vaccination, were posted about the ship, in various languages, and on the day when the operation was performed the surgeon had a right to presume that she and the other women who were vaccinated understood the importance and purpose of vaccination for those who bore no marks to show that they were protected.

By the plaintiff's testimony, which in this particular is undisputed, it appears that about two hundred women passengers were assembled below, and she understood from conversation with them that they were to be vaccinated; that she stood about fifteen feet from the surgeon, and saw them form in a line and pass in turn before him; that he "examined their arms, and, passing some of them by, proceeded to vaccinate those that had no mark"; that she did not hear him say anything to any of them; that upon being passed by they each received a card and went on deck; that when her turn came she showed him her arm, and he looked at it and said there was no mark, and that she should be vaccinated; that she told him she had been vaccinated before and it left no mark; "that he then said nothing, that he should vaccinate her again"; that she held up her arm to be vaccinated; that no one touched her; that she did not tell him that she did not want to be vaccinated; and that she took the ticket which he gave her certifying that he had vaccinated her, and used it at quarantine. She was one of a large number of women who were vaccinated on that occasion, without, so far as appears, a word of objection from any of them. They all indicated by their conduct that they desired to avail themselves of the provisions made for their benefit.

There was nothing in the conduct of the plaintiff to indicate to the surgeon that she did not wish to obtain a card which would save her from detention at quarantine, and to be vaccinated, if necessary, for that purpose. Viewing his conduct in the light of the circumstances, it was lawful; and there was no evidence tending to show that it was not. The ruling of the court on this part of the case was correct. * * * [The court further ruled that the company was not liable for the negligence, if any, of the carefully selected surgeon.]

Exceptions overruled.

————

KIRSCHBAUM v. LOWREY, 174 Minn. 107, 218 N.W. 461 (1928). Action for an assault. Plaintiff invited defendant to her house one evening, saying that her husband would not be at home. Upon defendant's arrival, he put his arm around plaintiff. The husband then stepped out of an adjoining room and grabbed defendant. *Held,* for defendant, reversing judgment. The plaintiff's invitation, under the circumstances, "carried with it the insinuative suggestion that [defendant's] advances would not be offensive." "This invited conduct, to the extent that it may be considered an assault, not having exceeded the bounds of the invitation, cannot be made the basis for the recovery of damages * * *."

WRIGHT v. STARR, 42 Nev. 441, 179 P. 877, 6 A.L.R. 981 (1919). Action for assault and battery. Plaintiff alleged that defendant, her dentist, entered her room and violently seized her throat and wrist, twisted her hand and tore her clothes from her person. Defendant testified that he merely kissed the plaintiff with her consent. *Held,* that the trial court properly charged the jury that it was incumbent on plaintiff to prove that defendant's conduct, such as it was, was without her consent, and that "it was unnecessary to affirmatively plead consent in justification of the acts charged in the complaint, which were denied in the answer."

MARKLEY v. WHITMAN

Supreme Court of Michigan, 1893.
95 Mich. 236, 54 N.W. 763.

LONG, J. Plaintiff and defendant were both students at the Buchannan High School. On February 7, 1890, while the plaintiff was on his way home from school, the defendant and others of the scholars were engaged in what is called a "rush" or "horse game." The practice of the game is to find some one in advance, when the others form in a line, each one in the rear pushing the one in advance of him, and so on through the line until the one to be "rushed," who knows nothing of what is coming, is rushed upon by the one in his rear, and pushed or rushed. On the day in question the plaintiff, while going towards home on the sidewalk, was to be rushed. The defendant was in his immediate rear, and engaged in the game. When pushed, he rushed upon the plaintiff, striking him with his hands between the shoulders with such violence that the plaintiff was thrown nearly to the ground. Immediately thereafter he lost his voice above a whisper, and has never recovered its use. His neck was nearly fractured, and for several months he was compelled to take medical treatment in Chicago. It is claimed that he suffered great pain, and has not fully recovered. This action was brought to recover for the injuries thus occasioned. On the trial in the court below, the plaintiff had verdict and judgment for $2,500. Defendant brings error.

The errors relied upon relate principally to the charge of the court. It was claimed on the trial in the court below:

1. That the push against the plaintiff was not an assault, and therefore not actionable.

2. That it was a pure accident.

3. That it was not a dangerous game, and the results which followed from the push could not have been anticipated.

4. That the defendant only put himself in a position ready to be pushed if the spirit of frolic should be entered into by those behind him, and his rush upon the plaintiff was neither invited nor approved.

5. That there was no unlawful intent to injure the plaintiff.

It is insisted that the court below, in its charge, entirely ignored the claim of the defendant made on the trial; and also that the plaintiff was one of the schoolfellows, and stood in a different position to the defendant than would a stranger. The court instructed the jury substantially that, if the plaintiff was participating in the play, or in any way contributed to the injury, he could not recover; that, to entitle the plaintiff to recover, he must show by a preponderance of evidence that the injury was occasioned by the push given by the defendant, and that the defendant either wilfully pushed the plaintiff, or was voluntarily engaged in the game, which must be found to be dangerous, and one reasonably calculated to be dangerous to innocent persons lawfully traveling along the sidewalk upon which the play was conducted. The court below further instructed the jury as follows:

"If the game in question was a dangerous one to indulge in on the street and at the time in question, and if the defendant was voluntarily engaged in such play at the time of the accident, and if the plaintiff was not participating in such sport, and was not guilty of conduct which in any way contributed to the injury, but, on the contrary, was lawfully traveling on the sidewalk, and in the exercise of reasonable care, and if the defendant, while so playing, pushed the plaintiff and injured him, he is liable; and in such case it is no excuse for him to say that he himself was pushed against the plaintiff by some other boy."

This charge fully protected the rights of the defendant, and was as favorable to him as the facts of the case warranted. In fact, on the trial it was little in dispute that the injury occurred exactly as the plaintiff claimed. He was peaceably walking along the street, and had no intimation that he was to be "rushed." He was not participating in the game, and, if his testimony is true, never had taken part in it, and on that occasion was not anticipating that he was the victim selected to be rushed. It was an assault upon him, and the court correctly stated the rules of law applicable to the case; at least, the defendant had no reason to complain. It is evident that the defendant was one of those engaged in the game, which, upon a bare statement of the manner in which it is to be played, must be regarded as dangerous. He voluntarily engaged in it, and his conduct occasioned the injury. It was unlawful to "rush" the plaintiff under the circumstances shown, and the defendant must be held responsible for the consequences which followed. It may be, and probably is, true that those taking part in it did not anticipate the injurious effects upon the plaintiff; but that does not lessen the plaintiff's pain and suffering, or make the act less unlawful. The plaintiff, while passing along the street, and not engaged in the sport, had the same right to be protected from such an assault as a stranger would have had, and the assault upon him was as unlawful as it would have been upon a stranger.

We find no error in the case, and the judgment must be affirmed, with costs.

———

McADAMS v. WINDHAM, 208 Ala. 492, 94 So. 742, 30 A.L.R. 194 (1922). Defendant and plaintiff's intestate entered into a friendly boxing match with their fists, as they had done previously on numerous occasions. In the course thereof, without unlawful intention or undue use of force or negligence, one of defendant's blows struck the intestate over the heart, which produced his death. A directed verdict for defendant was upheld.

ALLEN v. PAYNE & KELLER CO., INC., 710 So.2d 1138 (La.App.1998.) Employee brought suit against his employer and co-worker for injuries sustained when the co-worker "playfully" bumped plaintiff with his knee while plaintiff was stooped over, injuring plaintiff's head (in which an electrode had been implanted to control chronic pain). The trial court dismissed plaintiff's battery claim (along with other claims) and plaintiff appealed. *Held*, reversed.

" * * * [The Louisiana Supreme Court has stated]: 'The intent with which tort liability is concerned is not necessarily a hostile intent, or a desire to do any harm. Rather it is an intent to bring about a result which will invade the interests of another in a way that the law forbids. The defendant may be liable although intending nothing more than a good-natured practical joke, or honestly believing that the act would not injure the plaintiff, or even though seeking the plaintiff's own good.'

* * *

"[By the co-worker's] own testimony, he intended the contact. Although he may not have had malicious intent, the contact did occur, irrespective of his playful nature. Furthermore, from Stafford's testimony, it is evident Allen did not consent to the contact since he was stooped over and was not engaged in horseplay, as admitted by Stafford. In addition, Stafford hit him from behind. Thus, we find the jury's finding that Stafford did not commit a battery clearly wrong."

STATE v. WILLIAMS, 75 N.C. 134 (1876). Indictment for assault and battery. The defendants and the prosecutrix were members of a benevolent society in Hamilton, N. C., known as the "Good Samaritans," which Society had certain rules and ceremonies known as the ceremonies of initiation into and expulsion from the society. The prosecutrix, having been remiss in some of her obligations, and having been called upon to explain, became violent. The defendants, with others, proceeded to perform the ceremony of expulsion, which consisted in suspending her from the wall by means of a cord fastened around her waist. This ceremony had been performed upon others theretofore, in the presence of the prosecutrix. She resisted to the extent of her ability. A conviction was affirmed. "When the prosecutrix refused to submit to the ceremony of expulsion established by this benevolent Society, it could not be lawfully inflicted."

HACKBART v. CINCINNATI BENGALS, INC., 601 F.2d 516 (10th Cir. 1979). Plaintiff Hackbart and defendant Clark were professional football players on opposing teams. During a game plaintiff blocked defendant and turned to watch the play elsewhere on the field. Defendant, "acting out of anger and frustration," intentionally struck a blow with his forearm to the back of plaintiff's neck, causing serious injury. The trial court ruled that plaintiff had no remedy in tort, since professional football "is basically a business which is violent in nature" and one in which the players assume the risk of injury by violence. In the course of reversing the trial judge, the Court of Appeals said:

" * * * The judge compared football to coal mining and railroading insofar as all are inherently hazardous. Judge Matsch said that in the case of football it was questionable whether social values would be improved by limiting the violence.

"Thus the district court's assumption was that Clark had inflicted an intentional blow which would ordinarily generate civil liability and which might bring about a criminal sanction as well, but that since it had occurred in the course of a football game, it should not be subject to the restraints of the law; that if it were it would place unreasonable impediments and restraints on the activity. The judge also pointed out that courts are ill-suited to decide the different social questions and to administer conflicts on what is much like a battlefield where the restraints of civilization have been left on the sidelines.

* * *

" * * * But it is highly questionable whether a professional football player consents or submits to injuries caused by conduct not within the rules, and there is no evidence which we have seen which shows this. * * *

* * *

"The general customs of football do not approve the intentional punching or striking of others. * * * [T]he intentional striking of a player in the face or from the rear is prohibited by the playing rules as well as the general customs of the game. Punching or hitting with the arms is prohibited. Undoubtedly these restraints are intended to establish reasonable boundaries so that one football player cannot intentionally inflict a serious injury on another. Therefore, the notion is not correct that all reason has been abandoned, whereby the only possible remedy for the person who has been the victim of an unlawful blow is retaliation."

MULLEN v. BRUCE, 168 Cal.App.2d 494, 335 P.2d 945 (1959). The defendant, a sanitarium patient under treatment for delirium tremens, attacked her special duty nurse who was trying to prevent defendant from leaving the facility. The court rejected a defense of "implied consent or assumption of risk on plaintiff's part," and approved the formulation of the defense under discussion:

> First, the person in question must have actual knowledge of the danger. Second, she must have freedom of choice. This freedom of choice must come from circumstances that provide her a reasonable opportunity, without violating any legal or moral duty, to safely refuse to expose herself to the danger in question.

ELKINGTON v. FOUST
Supreme Court of Utah, 1980.
618 P.2d 37.

CROCKETT, Chief Justice:

Defendant Rex Foust appeals from a jury verdict which found that he had engaged in a course of sexually assaulting and abusing his adopted daughter plaintiff C_____ from the time she was nine years old until she left home at age sixteen, for which the jury assessed damages: general $10,000, specials $2,600, and punitive $30,000. On appeal, the defendant challenged the verdict on the grounds that the trial court instructed the jury that the plaintiff's consent, if it existed, was not a defense to the defendant's acts.

* * *

Defendant cites authorities to the effect that generally consent is a defense to a willful tort, with which we have no disagreement. But we do not see them as having any application to the instant situation for two reasons: because the plaintiff was a minor and incapable of giving consent to acts of this nature; and because the defendant is precluded from taking advantage of any consent he seduced or coerced her into giving to engage in such activities. It would be an agreement for him to perpetrate a crime in violation of the protections our statute affords minors by prohibiting contributing to their delinquency; and would be so contrary to commonly accepted standards of decency and morality that any consensual agreement to engage in such conduct would be rejected by the law as against public policy and void. Wherefore, it is our conclusion that the court was justified in refusing defendant's request to instruct the jury that if the plaintiff consented she could not recover.

* * *

Affirmed. Costs to plaintiff (respondent).

KATHLEEN K. v. ROBERT B., 150 Cal.App.3d 992, 198 Cal.Rptr. 273 (1984). Plaintiff seeks damages because she contracted genital herpes, allegedly by way of sexual intercourse with defendant. Plaintiff claims that defendant deliberately misrepresented that he was free from venereal disease and that, relying on such representations, she had sexual intercourse with him, which she would not have done had she known the true state of affairs. On appeal from the trial court's ruling that plaintiff had failed to state a cause of action, *held,* for plaintiff. "The disease which [plaintiff] contracted is serious and (thus far) incurable. * * * Like AIDS it is now known by the public to be a contagious and dreadful disease." The court emphasized "the interest of this state in the prevention and control of contagious and dangerous diseases," and approved the approach taken in Barbara A. v. John G., 145 Cal.App.3d 369, 193 Cal.Rptr. 422 (1983):

" * * * In *Barbara A.,* a woman who suffered an ectopic pregnancy and was forced to undergo surgery to save her life, which rendered her sterile, brought an action against the man who impregnated her (her former attorney), alleging that she consented to sexual intercourse in reliance on the man's knowingly false representation that he was sterile. The court reversed a judgment on the pleadings in favor of the defendant and held that the complaint stated causes of action for battery and for deceit.

* * *

"It should be noted that several out-of-state cases, cited by the court in *Barbara A.,* have held that a woman's consent to sexual intercourse was vitiated by the man's fraudulent concealment of the risk of infection with venereal disease. * * * [Defendant distinguishes two of these cases involving suits by a wife against her husband for damages resulting from contraction of venereal disease] on the basis that a husband and wife occupy a confidential relationship of trust and confidence in one another which does

not exist between non-married persons. However, a certain amount of trust
and confidence exists in any intimate relationship, at least to the extent that
one sexual partner represents to the other that he or she is free from
venereal or other dangerous contagious disease. The basic premise underlying these old cases—consent to sexual intercourse vitiated by one partner's
fraudulent concealment of the risk of infection with venereal disease—is
equally applicable today, whether or not the partners involved are married
to each other."

McPHERSON v. McPHERSON, 712 A.2d 1043 (Me., 1998). Plaintiff sought
damages from her ex-husband who infected her with Human Papilloma
Virus (HPV) when they engaged in sexual relations prior to their divorce.
Plaintiff's complaint rested in part on the allegation that her ex-husband
acquired the disease through a "clandestine extramarital affair" and that his
misrepresentation of his fidelity vitiated her consent to sexual intercourse
with him and gave rise to a battery. The Superior Court denied plaintiff
recovery on her battery claim (and on a separate negligence claim) and she
appealed. *Held*, affirmed.

"The [Superior] Court found that no assault and battery occurred
because the sexual intercourse between Steven and Nancy was consensual.
She argues that her consent to have sexual intercourse with Steven was
vitiated by the fact that he failed to inform her of his extramarital affair. 'One
who effectively consents to conduct of another intended to invade his
interests cannot recover in an action of tort for the conduct or for harm
resulting from it.' Restatement (Second) of Torts § 892A(1) (1977). Consent
may be vitiated, however by misrepresentation; If the person consenting to
the conduct of another is induced to consent by a substantial mistake
concerning the nature of the invasion of his interests or the extent of the
harm to be expected from it and the mistake is known to the other or is
induced by the other's misrepresentation, the consent is not effective for the
unexpected invasion or harm. Id. § 892B(2) . By way of illustration, the
Restatement provides: 'A consents to sexual intercourse with B, who knows
that A is ignorant of the fact that B has a venereal disease. B is subject to
liability to A for battery.' Id. § 892B(2) cmt. e, illus. 5."

"Nancy argues only that Steven misled her concerning his fidelity. Given
the court's finding that Steven neither knew nor should have known of his
infection with HPV, however, Nancy cannot argue that Steven misled her
'concerning the nature of the invasion of [her] interest or the extent of the
harm to be expected' therefrom. If the defendant, ignorant of the fact that
he was infected with a sexually transmitted disease, has sexual intercourse
with the plaintiff, 'the defendant will not be liable, because the plaintiff
consented to the kind of touch intended by the defendant, and both were
ignorant of the harmful nature of the invasion.' PROSSER & KEETON, THE
LAW OF TORTS § 18 at 1047, (5th Ed.1984); see Hogan v. Tavzel, 660 So.2d
350 (Fla.Dist.Ct.App.1995). Thus, Steven may not be held liable for assault
and battery."

TEOLIS v. MOSCATELLI, 44 R.I. 494, 119 A. 161 (1923). In the course of
a dispute between them, relative to a division fence, plaintiff accepted the

challenge of defendant to go into the highway and fight. Plaintiff went to the highway and removed his coat, whereupon defendant immediately stabbed him with a knife. Suing for his injury, defendant set up that plaintiff's agreement to fight was such consent as to bar recovery. *Held,* for plaintiff. He agreed to engage in a fist fight; he never consented to being assaulted with a knife. A verdict of $750 was not excessive.

MOHR v. WILLIAMS, 95 Minn. 261, 104 N.W. 12 (1905). Action for battery. Defendant, an ear specialist, examined plaintiff and advised an operation on plaintiff's right ear. Defendant made a more complete examination after plaintiff was anesthetized and discovered a condition of the left ear far more serious than that of the right. After consultation with plaintiff's family physician, he operated on the left ear. The operation was skillfully performed and beneficial. Judgment was for plaintiff. *Held,* (though affirming the granting of a new trial because the verdict was excessive in amount), the jury properly found that there was no consent and hence a battery. [Overruled on another point in Genzel v. Halvorson, 248 Minn. 527, 80 N.W.2d 854 (1957)].

KENNEDY v. PARROTT

Supreme Court of North Carolina, 1956.
243 N.C. 355, 90 S.E.2d 754.

[Action against surgeon on theories of negligence and battery. Plaintiff suffered phlebitis allegedly resulting from deliberate and unauthorized puncturing of cysts on her left ovary during performance of an authorized appendectomy. Appeal from judgment of involuntary nonsuit at the close of the evidence.]

BARNHILL, Chief Justice [After holding the evidence insufficient to support the allegation of negligence].

Prior to the advent of the modern hospital and before anesthesia had appeared on the horizon of the medical world, the courts formulated and applied a rule in respect to operations which may now be justly considered unreasonable and unrealistic. During the period when our common law was being formulated and applied, even a major operation was performed in the home of the patient, and the patient ordinarily was conscious, so that the physician could consult him in respect to conditions which required or made advisable an extension of the operation. And even if the shock of the operation rendered the patient unconscious, immediate members of his family were usually available. Hence the courts formulated the rule that any extension of the operation by the physician without the consent of the patient or someone authorized to speak for him constituted a battery or trespass upon the person of the patient for which the physician was liable in damages.

However, now that hospitals are available to most people in need of major surgery; anesthesia is in common use; operations are performed in the operating rooms of such hospitals while the patient is under the influence of an anesthetic; the surgeon is bedecked with operating gown, mask, and gloves; and the attending relatives, if any, are in some other part of the hospital, sometimes many floors away, the law is in a state of flux. More and more courts are beginning to realize that ordinarily a surgeon is employed to remedy conditions without any express limitation on his authority in respect thereto, and that in view of these conditions which make consent impractical, it is unreasonable to hold the physician to the exact operation—particularly when it is internal—that his preliminary examination indicated was necessary. We know that now complete diagnosis of an internal ailment is not effectuated until after the patient is under the influence of the anesthetic and the incision has been made.

These courts act upon the concept that the philosophy of the law is embodied in the ancient Latin maxim: *Ratio est legis anima; mutata legis ratione mutatur et lex.* Reason is the soul of the law; the reason of the law being changed, the law is also changed.

Some of the courts which realize that in view of modern conditions there should be some modification of the strict common law rule still limit the right of surgeons to extend an operation without the express consent of the patient to cases where an emergency arises calling for immediate action for the preservation of the life or health of the patient, and it is impracticable to obtain his consent or the consent of someone authorized to speak for him.

Other courts, though adhering to the fetish of consent, express or implied, realize that "The law should encourage self-reliant surgeons to whom patients may safely entrust their bodies, and not men who may be tempted to shirk from duty for fear of a law suit." They recognize that "The law does not insist that a surgeon shall perform every operation according to plans and specifications approved in advance by the patient, and carefully tucked away in his office-safe for courtroom purposes." Barnett v. Bachrach, D.C. Mun.App., 34 A.2d 626, 629 * * *.

In major internal operations, both the patient and the surgeon know that the exact condition of the patient cannot be finally and definitely diagnosed until after the patient is completely anesthetized and the incision has been made. In such case the consent—in the absence of proof to the contrary—will be construed as general in nature and the surgeon may extend the operation to remedy any abnormal or diseased condition in the area of the original incision whenever he, in the exercise of his sound professional judgment, determines that correct surgical procedure dictates and requires such an extension of the operation originally contemplated. This rule applies when the patient is at the time incapable of giving consent, and no one with authority to consent for him is immediately available.

In short, where an internal operation is indicated, a surgeon may lawfully perform, and it is his duty to perform, such operation as good surgery demands, even when it means an extension of the operation further than was originally contemplated, and for so doing he is not to be held in damages as for an unauthorized operation. * * *

Here plaintiff submitted her body to the care of the defendant for an appendectomy. When the defendant made the necessary incision he discovered some enlarged follicle cysts on her ovaries. He, as a skilled surgeon, knew that when a cyst on an ovary grows beyond the normal size, it may continue to grow until it is large enough to hold six to eight quarts of liquid and become dangerous by reason of its size. The plaintiff does not say that the defendant exercised bad judgment or that the extended operation was not dictated by sound surgical procedure. She now asserts only that it was unauthorized, and she makes no real showing of resulting injury or damage.

In this connection it is not amiss to note that the expert witnesses testified that the puncture of the cysts was in accord with sound surgical procedure, and that if they had performed the appendectomy they would have also punctured any enlarged cysts found on the ovaries. "That is the accepted practice in the course of general surgery."

What was the surgeon to do when he found abnormal cysts on the ovaries of plaintiff that were potentially dangerous? Was it his duty to leave her unconscious on the operating table, doff his operating habiliments, and go forth to find someone with authority to consent to the extended operation, and then return, go through the process of disinfecting, don again his operating habiliments, and then puncture the cysts; or was he compelled, against his best judgment, to close the incision and then, after plaintiff had fully recovered from the effects of the anesthesia, inform her as to what he had found and advise her that these cysts might cause her serious trouble in the future? The operation was simple, the incision had been made, the potential danger was evident to a skilled surgeon. Reason and sound common sense dictated that he should do just what he did do. So all the expert witnesses testified. * * *

Affirmed.

———

ROGERS v. LUMBERMENS MUTUAL CASUALTY CO., 119 So.2d 649 (La.App. 2d Cir.1960). Action by a patient and her husband against physicians and their insurer for unauthorized removal of the patient's reproductive organs when she had intended to submit to a simple appendectomy. The patient's husband, daughter, and son-in-law were present in the hospital during the entire time of the operation, but no attempt was made by defendants to secure their permission for enlarging the scope of the operation. On admission to the hospital the patient signed a document in the following form: "I hereby authorize the Physician or Physicians in charge to administer such treatment and the surgeon to have administered such anesthetics as found necessary to perform this operation which is advisable in the treatment of this patient." *Held,* the evidence sustained a finding that no consent, express or implied, was given by the patient or anyone authorized in her behalf. "[T]he alleged defenses of emergency, or of the necessity of the operations performed in the interest of the health of the patient, are completely demolished by the testimony of Dr. Mason that no emergency existed and that he removed the female organs as a precautionary measure and because he felt it was good surgical procedure. Conceding, and we have no doubt as to the absolute good faith of Dr. Mason in this evaluation, the desirability, from the standpoint of surgical judgment, of carrying out the drastic operative procedure, this can have no possible effect upon the legal issue of consent * * *." The consent form was "so ambiguous as to be almost completely worthless" and of "no possible weight under the factual circumstances."

MOSS v. RISHWORTH, 222 S.W. 225 (Tex.Com.App.1920); noted, 30 Yale L.J. 92. Plaintiff's 11–year–old daughter, while on a week's visit to her two adult sisters (one of whom was a trained nurse, the other being in training for that calling) at San Antonio, sixty miles from her home, was taken by them to defendant, who, at their request, administered a general anaesthetic and removed her adenoids and tonsils. Shortly after the operation the child died from the combined effects of the anaesthetic and the shock. The operation was performed without the consent of the parents, although defendant believed such consent had been obtained by the child's sisters. In an action under the death statute, *held*, for plaintiff. "The evidence shows that there was an absolute necessity for a prompt operation, but not emergent in the sense that death would likely result immediately upon failure to perform it. In fact, it is not contended that any real danger would have resulted to the child had time been taken to consult the parent with reference to the operation. Therefore the operation was not justified upon the ground that an emergency existed."

ASHCRAFT v. KING, 228 Cal.App.3d 604, 278 Cal.Rptr. 900 (1991). During surgery in 1983, the plaintiff, who was 16 years old at the time, received an HIV contaminated blood transfusion. She brought suit for negligence and battery against the surgeon who performed the operation, predicating her battery claim on the allegation that the defendant used blood from the hospital's general supply, even though she and her family had conditioned their consent to the operation on the defendant's use of family-donated blood. The trial court entered judgment on a jury verdict in favor of the defendant on the negligence claim, and nonsuited plaintiff on her battery cause of action. The Court of Appeals reversed the nonsuit on the battery claim.

"As a general rule, one who consents to a touching cannot recover in an action for battery. (Rest. 2d Torts, § 892A.) Thus, one who gives informed consent to a surgery cannot recover for resulting harm under a theory of battery. However, it is well-recognized a person may place conditions on the consent. If the actor exceeds the terms or conditions of the consent, the consent does not protect the actor from liability for the excessive act. (Rest.2d Torts, § 89A(3), (4), comment h, p. 369.)

"The rule of conditional consent has been applied in battery actions against physicians and surgeons in California and many other jurisdictions.

"In the present case, Ms. Ashcraft's claim of battery rested on the theory that although the operation was consented to, the consent was subject to a specific condition: only family donated blood would be used. If Ms. Ashcraft could establish the existence of this condition and its breach by Dr. King, she would establish a battery. * * *

* * *

"Defendant responds that even if Ms. Ashcraft's consent to surgery was conditioned on the use of family donated blood his violation of that condition did not result in a battery because the condition related only to a 'collateral matter'. * * *

* * *

"Where, as here, the patient has expressly conditioned her consent on certain acts being performed by the doctor, the patient has made that condition or event a matter of primary importance. To label such a condition merely 'collateral' is to ignore the patient's 'right, in the exercise of control over his own body to determine whether or not to submit to lawful medical treatment.' (Cobbs v. Grant, supra, 8 Cal.3d at p. 242, 104 Cal.Rptr. 505, 502 P.2d 1 and see Rest.2d Torts, § 892A and comments following.)"

SECTION D.   SELF–DEFENSE

There are two basic approaches to organizing the factors that bear upon the tortiousness of the defendant's conduct. One approach considers those factors that tend to inculpate the defendant, and those that tend to exculpate her, in a single step. Negligence analysis of the adequacy of the care exercised by a party proceeds in this way. It balances the benefits of exercising more care than the party exercised against the burdens of doing so, in order to decide if reasonable care was exercised.

The tort of battery, like most intentional torts, takes a different approach. It sorts the factors bearing on a claim into those that support liability and those that counsel against the imposition of liability and considers them sequentially. The factors supporting liability—intent, harmful or offensive contact, and lack of consent, in the case of battery—are slotted into the plaintiff's *prima facie* case. Those that counsel against liability are slotted into "defenses" or "privileges." The plaintiff bears the burden of establishing the elements of its *prima facie* case; the defendant bears the burden of establishing the elements of any defense or privilege to that case. In this section, we take up the principal defense to liability for battery, namely, self-defense.

The basic principle of self-defense, as we shall see shortly, is one of proportionality: The party claiming self-defense may use force proportional to that she claims to be defending against. The standing tension between subjectivity and objectivity is, however, particularly acute when the use of proportional force in connection with self-defense is at issue. Do we assess the degree of force necessary from the point of view of an impartial spectator? Or from the perspective of the party asserting the right? If the latter, how much impartial objectivity and accuracy in the calculation of proportionality can we expect from a party under attack? How much do we take into account the particular physical capacities and psychological make-up of the party asserting the right? Do we take into account the relative physical sizes and strengths of the parties involved? Do we take into account the timidity or physical courage of the party asserting the right? If someone's perceptions of the force necessary to repel a battery are skewed by a history of abuse by her spouse do we take that into account? Only when she exercises force against her abuser? If someone's perceptions of the danger that they face is skewed by a racial phobia, do we take that phobia into account? Or do we condemn that phobia as unreasonable and deny that it counts as any kind of justification at all?

These difficult questions cannot be avoided by the law of self-defense. They become even more difficult when the force involved is deadly—when it is sufficient to kill. The use of deadly force presents its own special problem. May it be used whenever it is proportional to the force that it is repelling? Or only when it is impossible to escape the attack by fleeing?

FRAGUGLIA v. SALA

District Court of Appeal of California, First District, Division 2, 1936.
17 Cal.App.2d 738, 62 P.2d 783.

[Action for assault and battery. The plaintiff, a fellow employee of the defendant, became incensed with insulting language used by the defendant, seized a pitchfork and advanced upon the defendant, who grappled with the plaintiff and knocked him down, causing severe injuries. Verdict for plaintiff. Appeal by defendant.]

STURTEVANT, J. [after stating the facts and discussing another part of the charge to the jury].

The defendant contends that instruction XVII, given at the request of the plaintiff, was also a prejudicial error. It was as follows:

"(1) Whenever a person is assaulted by another, he has a right to defend himself, and may use sufficient force to repel the assault in order to protect himself from bodily harm. And when necessary to protect himself from bodily harm at the hands of an assailant, the person assaulted may use sufficient force in repelling the assault, even before the assailant actually commits a battery upon him. But the resistance must be no more than is necessary to accomplish this. If it be greater than is required for such purpose, it becomes in law excessive and without excuse or justification, making the party an aggressor; (2) nor can a person after an assault, follow up his assailant and attack him when in the act of retiring or retreating from the scene of the affray or while helpless upon the ground. Such a course would not be in self defense nor justifiable on any grounds. (3) The fact, if you find it to be a fact, that plaintiff was not free from fault, will not prevent you from rendering a verdict in favor of the plaintiff, if you further find that the resulting assault and battery on plaintiff by defendant was accompanied by greater force than was reasonably necessary for the purpose of self defense."

Nearly all of the instruction comprised in division 1 was addressed to the right of defendant to defend himself. It makes no reference to the facts as they appeared to him. On the contrary it holds the defendant bound by the actual facts without regard to appearances. The defendant's objection to that portion of the instruction is well founded. * * *

The third division of the instruction is addressed to the subject of the use of excessive force. It fails to take into consideration "all the circumstances of the case." In 4 American Jurisprudence, page 152, the author says: "Generally stated, the force which one may use in self-defense is that which reasonably appears necessary, in view of all the circumstances of the case, to prevent the impending injury." The instruction is to the effect [that] if the defendant used some force that was necessary and some that was unnecessary, then he was a trespasser ab initio. That is a misconception of the law. We quote again from 4 American Jurisprudence, p. 153: "One who, in acting in self-defense, uses force in excess of that which he is privileged to use, is liable for so much of the force used as is excessive, and the other person has the normal privilege of defending himself against the use or attempted use of excessive force. In other words, to the extent that excessive violence and unnecessary force is used in repelling an assault, one becomes liable as a trespasser and subject to an action for assault and battery. In determining whether the particular means used is or is not excessive, the amount of force exerted, the means or instrument by which it is applied, the manner or method of applying it, and the circumstances under which it is applied are factors to be considered."

From what we have said it is apparent instructions XVI [the court's discussion of which is omitted] and XVII operated to deprive the defendant Sala of the sole defense which he attempted to prove. It follows that both were prejudicial. In this connection the plaintiff relies on the rule that all of the instructions are to be read together. He does not call to our attention any instruction given which tended to cure the errors complained of. We have not noted any that had such an effect. * * *

The judgment is reversed.

FIXICO v. STATE, 39 Okl.Cr. 95, 263 P. 171 (1928); noted in 13 Corn.L.Q. 623. The defendant, convicted of manslaughter, sought reversal on the ground that the evidence showed that he honestly believed that his life was in danger from an attack by the deceased. *Held*, affirming the conviction, that "Assuming that the deceased was the aggressor, the rule is well settled that the bare belief of one assaulted that he is about to suffer death or great personal injury will not, in itself, justify him in taking the life of his adversary. There must exist reasonable ground for such belief at the time of the killing, and the existence of such ground is a question of fact for the jury."

FAMBROUGH v. WAGLEY, 140 Tex. 577, 169 S.W.2d 478 (1943): "It is settled by our decisions that, with the exception of the rule of evidence which gives to a person accused of crime the benefit of a reasonable doubt, the law of self-defense is the same in both civil and criminal cases."

CHAPMAN v. HARGROVE, 204 S.W. 379 (Tex.Civ.App.1918). Action for battery. The defendant pleaded self-defense and argued that he was not liable if he acted in the reasonable belief that the plaintiff was about to assault him, although the plaintiff had no such unlawful intent. *Held*, verdict for plaintiff upheld. "[I]n a civil action for damages resulting from an assault the purpose is compensation for an injury, and the aggressor cannot escape upon a plea of self-defense by merely proving that he thought he was about to be attacked, when no attack was contemplated by the injured party. To justify a defensive assault provoked by deceptive appearances the defendant must show, not only a situation which creates a reasonable apprehension of danger to himself, but one for which the assaulted party is culpably responsible. Otherwise the injured party might be made to suffer for conditions over which he had no control."

NELSON v. STATE, 42 Ohio App. 252, 181 N.E. 448 (1932). The defendant was convicted of manslaughter. The defendant, who claimed that he was acting in self-defense, complained of an instruction by the trial court to the jury that, "a bare fear, however, of being killed, or of receiving bodily harm, is not sufficient to justify one in inflicting serious injury or death upon another. It must appear that the circumstances were sufficient to excite the fear of a reasonable person similarly situated, and that the defendant acted in good faith." *Held*, reversing the conviction, that a person "may act in self-defense, not only when a reasonable person would so act, but when one with the particular qualities that the individual himself has would so do. A nervous, timid, easily frightened individual is not measured by the same standard that a stronger, calmer, and braver man might be."

DUPRE v. MARYLAND MANAGEMENT CORP.

Supreme Court of New York, Appellate Division, First Department, 1954.
283 App.Div. 701, 127 N.Y.S.2d 615.

PER CURIAM. Plaintiff was a guest in the hotel of the corporate defendant. He has recovered damages for an assault committed by one Jones, a bell-boy. The trial court found that plaintiff initiated the encounter in which he received his injuries, but that Jones used more than sufficient force to repel an attack by plaintiff, and, therefore, found defendant liable to plaintiff in damages.

We agree with the basic findings of the trial court in all respects except the finding that an excess of force was used by Jones in self defense. We find from the record that Jones struck plaintiff after he had twice tried to avoid a physical encounter and after he had been assaulted and threatened with further assault. He struck plaintiff with his fist in self defense fracturing plaintiff's jaw. There is no credible evidence that Jones persisted in an attack after plaintiff was incapacitated. That the blow or blows in retaliation resulted in more serious injury than might have been sufficient to stall the attack is not the test of use of excessive force. One must know that what he does will be excessive—an intent to inflict unnecessary injury must be established. "Detached reflection cannot be demanded" of one facing a dangerous attack. Brown v. U. S., 256 U.S. 335, 343, 41 S.Ct. 501, 502, 65 L.Ed. 961. At least, he is not to be held liable in damages if he fails to anticipate the precise effect of a blow with the fist.

The judgment should be reversed and the complaint dismissed on the merits as to appellant with costs to appellant, * * *.

MORRIS v. PLATT, 32 Conn. 75 (1864). Trespass for an assault by shooting the plaintiff. The defendant's evidence was that he shot in self-defense, to protect himself from an attack by plaintiff and others. The plaintiff's evidence was that he was a mere bystander and did not participate in the contest. The trial judge refused defendant's request to charge that the defendant would not be liable if, while lawfully defending himself against those attacking him, he accidentally shot plaintiff, a bystander; and at plaintiff's request charged that "if the plaintiff was not a party to the assault, but was a mere bystander, he [the defendant] would be liable to the plaintiff for all actual damage caused by the pistol shots, though he had no intention of shooting the plaintiff, and did so accidentally while lawfully exercising his right of self-defense against his assailants." Plaintiff had a verdict. *Held*, defendant's motion for a new trial granted. "It is well settled in this court that a man is not liable, in an action of trespass on the case, for any unintentional consequential injury resulting from a lawful act, where neither negligence nor folly can be imputed to him, and that the burden of proving the negligence or folly, where the act is lawful, is upon the plaintiff;" and upon principle and by authority the rule is the same where "the injury was direct and immediate and the form of action is trespass."

COMMONWEALTH v. DRUM
Court of Oyer and Terminer of Pennsylvania, 1868.
58 Pa. 9.

[Indictment for murder. The evidence disclosed that the deceased was striking defendant with his fists when defendant drew a knife and cut his assailant in the side, making a wound which caused death.]

AGNEW, J. charged the jury. * * * To excuse homicide by the plea of self-defence, it must appear that the slayer had no other possible, or at least probable, means of escaping, and that his act was one of necessity. The act of the slayer must be such as is necessary to protect the person from death or great bodily harm; and must not be entirely disproportioned to the assault made upon him. If the slayer use a deadly weapon, and under such circumstances as the slayer must be aware that death will be likely to ensue, the necessity must be great, and must arise from imminent peril of life, or great bodily injury. If there be nothing in the circumstances indicating to the slayer at the time of his act that his assailant is about to take his life, or do him great bodily harm, but his object appears to be only to commit an ordinary assault and battery, it will not excuse a man of equal, or nearly equal strength in taking his assailant's life with a deadly weapon. In such a case it requires a great disparity of size and strength on the part of the slayer, and a very violent assault on part of his assailant, to excuse it. The disparity on the one hand, and the violence on the other, must be such as to convince the jury that great bodily harm, if not death, might have been suffered, unless the slayer had thus defended himself, or that the slayer had a reasonable ground to think it would be so. The burden lies on the prisoner, in such a case, of proving that there was an actual necessity for taking life, or a seeming one so reasonably apparent and convincing to the slayer, as to lead him to believe he could only defend himself in that way. The jury will remember I am speaking of wilful killing with a deadly weapon. If this intent to kill existed in the mind of the prisoner at the time of giving the blow, two difficulties arise in the case upon the plea of self-defence, which the jury must pass upon and decide. The attack of Mohigan was made with his fists, no weapon appears to have been used by him; the blows appear to have taken no great effect, and at the time Mohigan was alone, while two persons not unfriendly to the prisoner, were interfering on his behalf. Under these circumstances (if you so believe them), was there any real or apparent necessity to take life for the purpose of defence? Did Mohigan do, or try to do, more than beat the prisoner with his fists? Was the disparity of size and strength of the prisoner so great as to require him to take Mohigan's life to prevent great bodily harm to himself, in such a case where no weapon was used against him? The other difficulty arising upon the plea of self-defence, is, whether the prisoner had not an opportunity of escaping, down into the saloon, or down the street, when Riley Miskelly and Robert Miskelly interfered in his behalf. Taking their testimony, was there anything to prevent his escape when Mohigan was diverted in his attack from him? * * *

* * * The true criterion of self-defence * * * is, whether there existed such a necessity for killing the adversary as required the slayer to do it in defence of his life or in the preservation of his person from great bodily harm. If a man approaches another with an evident intention of fighting him with his fists only, and where, under the circumstances, nothing would be likely to eventuate from the attack but an ordinary beating, the law cannot recognize the necessity of taking life with a deadly weapon. In such a case it would be manslaughter; and if the deadly weapon was evidently used with a murderous and badhearted intent, it would even be murder. But a blow or blows are just cause of provocation, and if the circumstances indicated to the slayer a plain necessity of protecting himself from great bodily injury, he is excusable if he slays his assailant in an honest purpose of saving himself from this great harm.

The right to stand in self-defence without fleeing has been strongly asserted by the defence. It is certainly true that every citizen may rightfully traverse the street, or may stand in all proper places, and need not flee from every one who chooses to assail him. Without this freedom our liberties would be worthless. But the law does not apply this right to homicide. The question here does not involve the right of merely ordinary defence, or the right to stand wherever he may rightfully be, but it concerns the right of one man to take the life of another. Ordinary defence and the killing of another evidently stand upon different footing. When it comes to a question whether one man shall flee or another shall live, the law decides that the former shall rather flee than that the latter shall die. * * *

HOOVER v. STATE, 35 Tex.Cr.R. 342, 33 S.W. 337 (1895): "But why did appellant kill deceased? He answers this question by deliberately stating that he did not kill deceased because of the insulting language towards his female relative, but because he (deceased) had threatened to kill him. If this be true, all that deceased did ceases to be a factor in self-defense. Why? Because the acts of deceased did not induce appellant to kill him, he being killed because he had threatened to kill appellant. We have therefore this simple proposition: A. threatens to kill B. B. arms himself, goes into the house of A., and kills him, because he had threatened his (B.'s) life. There is neither manslaughter, self-defense, nor anything else short of murder, in this state of case."

FAMBRO v. STATE, 142 Tex.Crim. 473, 154 S.W.2d 840 (1941). *Held,* conviction affirmed. It must be shown that the life of the person attacked was in danger and that he had resorted to all other means for the prevention of such injury, save retreat, before he would be justified in taking the life of his adversary.

STATE v. FRIZZELLE, 243 N.C. 49, 89 S.E.2d 725 (1955). Defendant was convicted of manslaughter. The incident occurred near the edge of her yard. *Held,* reversed for error in instructing that retreat was required if there was an opportunity to retreat in safety. One need not retreat when assaulted in his own home or place of business. The rule extends to the curtilage of the home, which ordinarily means at least the yard around the dwelling house as well as the area occupied by outbuildings.

LOUISIANA REVISED STATUTES, TITLE 14, CH. 1 § 20. Justifiable homicide

A homicide is justifiable:

(1) When committed in self-defense by one who reasonably believes that he is in imminent danger of losing his life or receiving great bodily harm and that the killing is necessary to save himself from that danger.

(2) When committed for the purpose of preventing a violent or forcible felony involving danger to life or of great bodily harm by one who reasonably believes that such an offense is about to be committed and that such action is necessary for its prevention. The circumstances must be sufficient to excite the fear of a reasonable person that there would be serious danger to his own life or person if he attempted to prevent the felony without the killing.

(3) When committed against a person whom one reasonably believes to be likely to use any unlawful force against a person present in a dwelling or a place of business, or when committed against a person whom one reasonably believes is attempting to use any unlawful force against a person present in a motor vehicle as defined in R.S. 32:1(40), while committing or attempting to commit a burglary or robbery of such dwelling, business, or motor vehicle. The homicide shall be justifiable even though the person does not retreat from the encounter.

(4) When committed by a person lawfully inside a dwelling, a place of business, or a motor vehicle as defined in R.S. 32:1(40), against a person who is attempting to make an unlawful entry into the dwelling, place of business, or motor vehicle, or who has made an unlawful entry into the dwelling, place of business, or motor vehicle, and the person committing the homicide reasonably believes that the use of deadly force is necessary to prevent the entry or to compel the intruder to leave the premises or motor vehicle. The homicide shall be justifiable even though the person committing the homicide does not retreat from the encounter.*

HATTORI v. PEAIRS AND LOUISIANA FARM BUREAU MUTUAL INSURANCE COMPANY
Court of Appeal of Louisiana, First Circuit, 1995.
662 So.2d 509.

LOTTINGER, Chief Justice.

[In this wrongful death and survival action, the parents of a 16-year-old Japanese exchange student brought suit against the homeowner who shot and killed their son (Yoshi Hattori) when he and the sixteen year old son of his host family (Webb Haymaker) mistakenly knocked on the wrong door in search of a Halloween party to which they had been invited.]

As this was to have been a costume party, the boys were dressed up. Because Webb wore a soft cervical collar as a result of an earlier diving accident, his costume was that of an accident victim. Dressed in shorts and tennis shoes, Webb had a bandage around his head, a hand splint and an ace bandage around his knee. He wore no makeup or fake blood. Yoshi loved to dance and had decided to go as John Travolta's character from the movie "Saturday Night Fever." He rented a white tuxedo jacket, black pants and a ruffled white shirt of which he had unbuttoned the top three buttons. He also carried a camera. Neither boy wore a mask.

At approximately 8:15 P.M., the boys walked up the driveway, and rang the front doorbell. No one answered the front door; however, the boys heard the clinking of window blinds emanating from the rear of the carport area to the left of where they stood. Webb, followed by Yoshi to his left, proceeded around the corner, under the carport, toward the carport door. As the boys turned the corner, Webb observed a small boy, approximately eight or nine years of age, peering through the blinds of the carport door. A moment later, the door was opened by a woman wearing a bathrobe and glasses. As Webb attempted to speak to the woman, she slammed the door.

At this point, the boys turned around and walked down the driveway towards the sidewalk. Webb was fairly certain they had stopped at the wrong house, and attempted to communicate this fact to Yoshi. As they stood on the sidewalk near a streetlamp, the carport door opened again, and Webb observed a man standing in the doorway with a large handgun. At that point,

* Part (3) of this statute—known by the nickname "shoot the carjacker"—was enacted by the Louisiana legislature in 1997.—Eds.

Yoshi moved towards the house exclaiming enthusiastically, "We're here for the party!"

Webb, immediately grasping the seriousness of the situation, pleaded with his friend to come back; however, Yoshi, who was not wearing his contact lenses that evening, continued towards the man smiling and explaining several times that he had come for the party. As Yoshi reached the carport, Webb heard the man in the doorway yell, "Freeze"; however, Yoshi continued to move towards the man. From Webb's vantage point, Yoshi was adjacent to the rear-view mirror of the Toyota station wagon parked on the right of the double carport, when the man in the doorway fired. The bullet struck Yoshi in the chest, causing him to fall to the ground on his back, with his head about a foot from the carport door.

* * *

* * * E.M.S. technicians arrived on the scene a short while later at 8:39 P.M. Sometime between 8:48 and 8:49 P.M., while en route to the hospital, Yoshi stopped breathing.

The homeowners, Rodney and Bonnie Peairs, testified that upon hearing the doorbell that evening, Rodney sent his stepson to answer the carport door. Not wanting her son to answer the door after dark, Bonnie Peairs stopped him and answered the door herself. Upon opening the door, she observed a person in bandages standing near a pillar of the porch at the end of the carport. A moment later, she observed an oriental person taller than she, with a small build, come quickly around the corner toward the door. Startled, Bonnie slammed the door, locked it, and yelled for her husband to, "Get the gun." * * *

* * *

ACTION OF THE TRIAL COURT

The shooting attracted national, as well as international attention. Following a four-day trial on September 12–15, 1994, the trial judge rendered judgment in favor of Yoshi's parents, Masaichi and Mieko Hattori (the Hattoris) finding Rodney Peairs to be solidarily liable with his homeowner's insurer, Louisiana Farm Bureau Mutual Insurance Company (Farm Bureau), in the amount of $653,077.85 together with legal interest and costs. Farm Bureau's liability was subject to the $100,000.00 coverage limitations of its policy.

Farm Bureau subsequently tendered its policy limits plus interest; Rodney Peairs has appealed.

* * *

The second assignment of error raised by Rodney Peairs is that the trial court was manifestly erroneous in determining that the shooting was not justified under the circumstances presented by this case. * * * The jurisprudence in Louisiana is well-settled that resort to the use of a dangerous weapon to repel an attack is not justified except in exceptional cases where the actor's fear of danger is not only genuine but is founded upon facts that would likely produce similar emotions in men of reasonable prudence. There was absolutely no need to resort to the use of a dangerous weapon to repel an attack, as, in fact there would have been no fear of an attack if Rodney had summoned help or simply stayed within his home. [We can see no reason why Rodney "was scared to death."—No reason except that] he heard his wife slam a door and say, "Get the gun." The court believes very sincerely that a reasonable person would have responded with "Why do I need [a] gun? What did you see, Bonnie?" * * * We know that when Rodney Peairs first saw Yoshi, he was further away than when Bonnie had seen him, and she was able to shut the door. Self defense is not acceptable. There was no justification whatsoever that a killing was necessary for Rodney Peairs to save himself and/or to protect his family.

        * * * Peairs * * * cites a number of other cases for the proposition that the danger itself need not be real, if the actor reasonably believes that the threat of great bodily harm or death is imminent. Upon review of the cases cited by Rodney Peairs, we find same to be inapposite as the intruders were either armed or engaged in surreptitious activity on the defendant's property.

                                    * * *

        While we do not doubt that Rodney Peairs' fear of impending bodily harm was genuine, we nevertheless find nothing within the record to support his assertion that such fear was reasonable. Prior to the shooting, Yoshi and Webb had announced their presence by ringing the doorbell of the Peairs' home. Testifying that he believed Yoshi to be armed, Rodney Peairs conceded that he did not see a gun, a knife, a stick, or a club—only an object which he later ascertained to be a camera. In the well-lit carport, Rodney Peairs stated that he observed an oriental person proceeding towards him and that he appeared to be laughing. We have no idea why Yoshi failed to heed Rodney Peairs' order to "Freeze," or grasp the danger posed by the gun, but can only speculate that the answer stems from cultural differences and an unfamiliarity with American slang. Under the circumstances of this case, we cannot say that it was either reasonable or necessary for Rodney Peairs to resort to the use of deadly force in order to protect himself and his family. This assignment of error is without merit.

                                    * * *

        For the above reasons, the judgment of the trial court is affirmed at defendant—appellants' costs.

STATE v. LEIDHOLM

Supreme Court of North Dakota, 1983.
334 N.W.2d 811.

VANDE WALLE, Justice.

        Janice Leidholm was charged with murder for the stabbing death of her husband, Chester Leidholm, in the early morning hours of August 7, 1981, at their farm home near Washburn. She was found guilty by a McLean County jury of manslaughter and was sentenced to five years' imprisonment in the State Penitentiary with three years of the sentence suspended. Leidholm appealed from the judgment of conviction. We reverse and remand the case for a new trial.

According to the testimony, the Leidholm marriage relationship in the end was an unhappy one, filled with a mixture of alcohol abuse, moments of kindness toward one another, and moments of violence. The alcohol abuse and violence was exhibited by both parties on the night of Chester's death.

Early in the evening of August 6, 1981, Chester and Janice attended a gun club party in the city of Washburn where they both consumed a large amount of alcohol. On the return trip to the farm, an argument developed between Janice and Chester which continued after their arrival home just after midnight. Once inside the home, the arguing did not stop; Chester was shouting, and Janice was crying.

At one point in the fighting, Janice tried to telephone Dave Vollan, a deputy sheriff of McLean County, but Chester prevented her from using the phone by shoving her away and pushing her down. At another point, the argument moved outside the house, and Chester once again was pushing Janice to the ground. Each time Janice attempted to get up, Chester would push her back again.

A short time later, Janice and Chester re-entered their home and went to bed. When Chester fell asleep, Janice got out of bed, went to the kitchen, and got a butcher knife. She then went back into the bedroom and stabbed Chester. In a matter of minutes Chester died from shock and loss of blood.

* * *

The first, and controlling, issue we consider is whether or not the trial court correctly instructed the jury on self-defense. * * *

* * *

* * * [T]he critical issue which a jury must decide in a case involving a claim of self-defense is whether or not the accused's belief that force is necessary to protect himself against imminent unlawful harm was reasonable. However, before the jury can make this determination, it must have a standard of reasonableness against which it can measure the accused's belief.

Courts have traditionally distinguished between standards of reasonableness by characterizing them as either "objective" or "subjective." An objective standard of reasonableness requires the factfinder to view the circumstances surrounding the accused at the time he used force from the standpoint of a hypothetical reasonable and prudent person. Ordinarily, under such a view, the unique physical and psychological characteristics of the accused are not taken into consideration in judging the reasonableness of the accused's belief.

This is not the case, however, where a subjective standard of reasonableness is employed. Under the subjective standard the issue is not whether the circumstances attending the accused's use of force would be sufficient to create in the mind of a reasonable and prudent person the belief that the use of force is necessary to protect himself against immediate unlawful harm, but rather whether the circumstances are sufficient to induce in *the accused* an honest and reasonable belief that he must use force to defend himself against imminent harm.

* * *

Because (1) the law of self-defense as developed in past decisions of this court has been interpreted to require the use of a subjective standard of reasonableness, and (2) we agree * * * that a subjective standard is the more just, * * * we now decide that the finder of fact must view the circumstances attending an accused's use of force from the standpoint of the accused to determine if they are sufficient to create in the accused's mind an honest and reasonable belief that the use of force is necessary to protect himself from imminent harm.

* * * For example, if the accused is a timid, diminutive male, the factfinder must consider these characteristics in assessing the reasonableness of his belief. If, on the other hand, the accused is a strong, courageous, and capable female, the factfinder must consider these characteristics in judging the reasonableness of her belief.

In its statement of the law of self-defense, the trial court instructed the jury:

> The circumstances under which she acted must have been such as to produce in the mind of reasonably prudent persons, regardless of their sex, similarly situated, the reasonable belief that the other person was then about to kill her or do serious bodily harm to her.

In view of our decision today, the court's instruction was a misstatement of the law of self-defense. A correct statement of the law to be applied in a case of self-defense is:

> [A] defendant's conduct is not to be judged by what a reasonably cautious person might or might not do or consider necessary to do under the like circumstances, but what he himself in good faith honestly believed and had reasonable ground to believe was necessary for him to do to protect himself from apprehended death or great bodily injury. [State v. Hazlett, 16 N.D. 426, 113 N.W. 374, 380 (1907).]

* * *

Hence, a correct statement of the law of self-defense is one in which the court directs the jury to assume the physical and psychological properties peculiar to the accused, viz., to place itself as best it can in the shoes of the accused, and then decide whether or not the particular circumstances surrounding the accused at the time he used force were sufficient to create in his mind a sincere and reasonable belief that the use of force was necessary to protect himself from imminent and unlawful harm.

Leidholm argued strongly at trial that her stabbing of Chester was done in self-defense and in reaction to the severe mistreatment she received from him over the years. Because the court's instruction in question is an improper statement of the law concerning a vital issue in Leidholm's defense, we conclude it amounts to reversible error requiring a new trial.

* * *

The judgment of conviction is reversed and the case is remanded to the district court of McLean County for a new trial.

———

CUSSEAUX v. PICKETT, 279 N.J.Super. 335, 652 A.2d 789 (1994). *Held,* in a case of first impression, "the 'battered woman's syndrome' is now a cause of action under the laws of New Jersey." The elements of the cause of action are: "1) involvement in a marital or marital-like intimate relationship; and 2) physical or psychological abuse perpetrated by the dominant partner to the relationship over an extended period of time; and 3) ... recurring physical or psychological injury over the course of the relationship; and 4) a past or present inability to take any action to improve or alter the situation unilaterally."

"Because the battered-woman's syndrome is the result of a continuing pattern of abuse and violent behavior that causes continuing damage, it must be treated the same way as a continuing tort. It would be contrary to the public policy of this State ... to limit recovery to only those individual incidents of assault and battery for which the applicable statute of limitations has not yet run. The mate who is responsible for creating the condition suffered by the battered victim must be made to account for his actions—all of his actions. Failure to allow affirmative recovery under these circumstances would be tantamount to the courts condoning the continued abusive treatment of women in the domestic sphere."

STATE v. WANROW, 88 Wash.2d 221, 559 P.2d 548 (1977). Defendant Yvonne Wanrow was convicted of second-degree murder for shooting decedent Wesler. She and another woman had recently discovered good reason to believe that Wesler, a neighbor, had sexually molested their children. Wesler came into the house where the frightened and angry women were staying. A large man, Wesler was visibly intoxicated and refused to leave the house when instructed to. Defendant testified that, after shouting for aid of a male relative waiting outside, she turned around and suddenly "found Wesler standing directly behind her. She testified to being gravely startled by this situation and to having then shot Wesler in what amounted to a reflex action." On review by the Washington Supreme Court, *held,* conviction reversed and case remanded for a new trial. The court (per Utter, A.J.) found the trial judge's instructions on self-defense to be erroneous. First, the instructions mistakenly directed the jury to focus only on overt acts or circumstances occurring "at or immediately before the killing" in assessing the defendant's conduct:

> * * * This is not now, and never has been, the law of self-defense in Washington. On the contrary, the justification of self-defense is to be evaluated in light of *all* the facts and circumstances known to the defendant, including those known substantially before the killing.

* * * [T]he limitation to circumstances "at or immediately before the killing" was of crucial importance in the present case. [Defendant's] knowledge of the victim's reputation for aggressive acts was gained many hours before the killing and was based upon events which occurred over a period of years. Under the law of this state, the jury should have been allowed to consider this information in making the critical determination of the " 'degree of force which ... a reasonable person in the same situation ... seeing what [s]he sees and knowing what [s]he knows, then would believe to be necessary.' " *State v. Dunning,* 8 Wash.App. 340, 342, 506 P.2d 321, 322 (1973).

Second, the instructions erred in posing an objective rather than a subjective test for judging defendant's conduct, and this error was compounded as described below:

The second paragraph of instruction No. 10 contains an equally erroneous and prejudicial statement of the law. That portion of the instruction reads:

> However, when there is no reasonable ground for the person attacked to believe that *his* person is in imminent danger of death or great bodily harm, and it appears to *him* that only an ordinary battery is all that is intended, and all that *he* has reasonable grounds to fear from *his* assailant, *he* has a right to stand *his* ground and repel such threatened assault, yet *he* has no right to repel a threatened assault with naked hands, by the use of a deadly weapon in a deadly manner, unless *he* believes, *and has reasonable grounds* to believe, that *he* is in imminent danger of death or great bodily harm.

(Italics ours.) In our society women suffer from a conspicuous lack of access to training in and the means of developing those skills necessary to effectively repel a male assailant without resorting to the use of deadly weapons. * * *

The second paragraph of instruction No. 10 not only establishes an objective standard, but through the persistent use of the masculine gender leaves the jury with the impression the objective standard to be applied is that applicable to an altercation between two men. The impression created—that a 5'4" woman with a cast on her leg and using a crutch must, under the law, somehow repel an assault by a 6'2" intoxicated man without employing weapons in her defense, unless the jury finds her determination of the degree of danger to be objectively reasonable—constitutes a separate and distinct misstatement of the law and, in the context of this case, violates [defendant's] right to equal protection of the law. [Defendant] was entitled to have the jury consider her actions in the light of her own perceptions of the situation, including those perceptions which were the product of our nation's "long and unfortunate history of sex discrimination." *Frontiero v. Richardson,* 411 U.S. 677, 684, 93 S.Ct. 1764, 1769, 36 L.Ed.2d 583 (1973). Until such time as the effects of that history are eradicated, care must be taken to assure that our self-defense instructions afford women the right to have their conduct judged in light of the individual physical handicaps which are the product of sex discrimination. To fail to do so is to deny the right of the individual woman involved to trial by the same rules which are applicable to male defendants.

SECTION E. OTHER PRIVILEGES

Is conduct that would otherwise constitute battery "privileged," and therefore permissible, when done in defense of a third party? When done in defense of one's employee? One's home when one is absent from it? To retrieve property wrongfully seized? These are questions of "other privilege" that the cases in this section address. Conceptually, these "other privileges" radiate out from the core privilege of self-defense. The privilege to use a "mechanical device," for example, adapts the privilege of self-defense to the special circumstance where the party defending itself through the use of force is absent from the scene of its use, and is using that force in defense of real property, not bodily integrity.

These "other privileges" radiate out in diverse directions, and raise correspondingly diverse questions. The use of "mechanical devices" to defend real property leads us to ask: Does the right to stand one's ground and repel an attack on one's home apply when the owner of the home is absent? What does the principle of proportionality call for in this special case? The privilege to come to the aid of another raises the questions: Should we expect intervening bystanders to assess the threat at hand more accurately than those they are attempting to assist? Do we have reason to encourage courageous acts of intervention of this sort? Or do we have more reason to fear expanding the range of cases in which the private use of violence is legally permissible? The "right of recapture" invites the questions: Compared to the interest protected by the privilege of self-defense, how urgent is the interest protected by the privilege to recapture property wrongfully seized? How compelling is the case for the private use of violence in light of this interest?

PEOPLE v. YOUNG
Court of Appeals of New York, 1962.
11 N.Y.2d 274, 229 N.Y.S.2d 1, 183 N.E.2d 319.

PER CURIAM. Whether one, who in good faith aggressively intervenes in a struggle between another person and a police officer in civilian dress attempting to effect the lawful arrest of the third person, may be properly convicted of assault in the third degree is a question of law of first impression here.

The opinions in the court below in the absence of precedents in this State carefully expound the opposing views found in other jurisdictions. The majority in the Appellate Division have adopted the minority rule in the other States that one who intervenes in a struggle between strangers under the mistaken but reasonable belief that he is protecting another who he assumes is being unlawfully beaten is thereby exonerated from criminal liability. The weight of authority holds with the dissenters below that one who goes to the aid of a third person does so at his own peril.

While the doctrine espoused by the majority of the court below may have support in some States, we feel that such a policy would not be conducive to an orderly society. We agree with the settled policy of law in most jurisdictions that the right of a person to defend another ordinarily should not be greater than such person's right to defend himself. * * *

In this case there can be no doubt that the defendant intended to assault the police officer in civilian dress. The resulting assault was forceful. * * * To be guilty of third degree assault "It is sufficient that the defendant voluntarily intended to commit the unlawful act of touching" (1 Wharton's Criminal Law and Procedure [1957].) Since in these circumstances the aggression was inexcusable the defendant was properly convicted.

Accordingly, the order of the Appellate Division should be reversed and the information reinstated.

FROESSEL, Judge (dissenting). * * *

Briefly, the relevant facts are these: On a Friday afternoon at about 3:40, Detectives Driscoll and Murphy, not in uniform, observed an argument taking place between a motorist and one McGriff in the street in front of premises 64 West 54th Street, in midtown Manhattan. Driscoll attempted to chase McGriff out of the roadway in order to allow traffic to pass, but McGriff refused to move back; his actions caused a crowd to collect. After identifying himself to McGriff, Driscoll placed him under arrest. As McGriff resisted, defendant "came out of the crowd" from Driscoll's rear and struck Murphy about the head with his fist. In the ensuing struggle Driscoll's right kneecap was injured when defendant fell on top of him. At the station house, defendant said he had not known or thought Driscoll and Murphy were police officers.

Defendant testified that while he was proceeding on 54th Street he observed two white men, who appeared to be 45 or 50 years old, pulling on a "colored boy" (McGriff), who appeared to be a lad about 18, whom he did not know. The men had nearly pulled McGriff's pants off, and he was crying. Defendant admitted he knew nothing of what had transpired between the officers and McGriff, and made no inquiry of anyone; he just came there and pulled the officer away from McGriff.

Defendant was convicted of assault third degree. In reversing upon the law and dismissing the information, the Appellate Division held that one is not "criminally liable for assault in the third degree if he goes to the aid of another who he mistakenly, but *reasonably*, believes is being unlawfully beaten, and thereby injures one of the apparent assaulters" (emphasis supplied). * * *

* * *

Criminal intent requires an awareness of wrongdoing. When conduct is based upon mistake of fact reasonably entertained, there can be no such awareness and, therefore, no criminal culpability. * * *

It is undisputed that defendant did not know that Driscoll and Murphy were detectives in plain clothes engaged in lawfully apprehending an alleged disorderly person. If, therefore, defendant *reasonably* believed he was lawfully assisting another, he would not have been guilty of a crime. Subdivision 3 of section 246 of the Penal Law provides that it is not unlawful to use force "When committed either by the party about to be injured or by *another person in his aid or defense, in preventing or attempting to prevent an offense against his person,* * * * if the force or violence used is not more than sufficient to prevent such offense" (emphasis supplied). The law is thus clear that if defendant entertained an "honest and reasonable belief" (People ex rel. Hegeman v. Corrigan, 195 N.Y. 1, 12, 87 N.E. 792, supra) that the facts were as he perceived them to be, he would be exonerated from criminal liability.

By ignoring one of the most basic principles of criminal law—that crimes *mala in se* require proof of at least general criminal intent—the majority now hold that the defense in mistake of fact is "of no significance".
* * *

* * *

Although the majority of our courts are now purporting to fashion a policy "conducive to an orderly society," by their decision they have defeated their avowed purpose. What public interest is promoted by a principle which would deter one from coming to the aid of a fellow citizen who he has reasonable ground to apprehend is in imminent danger of personal injury at the hands of assailants? * * * Logic * * * dictates that the rule and policy expressed by our Legislature in the case of homicide, which is an assault resulting in death, should likewise be applicable to a much less serious assault not resulting in death.

* * *

[Order reversed.]

———

FREW v. TEAGARDEN, 111 Kan. 107, 205 P. 1023 (1922). Defendant struck the plaintiff on the arm with the broadside of a pitchfork, doing this to prevent plaintiff from unjustifiably continuing to beat a relative and employee of defendant then working on defendant's farm. The trial judge instructed the jury that defendant would be justified only if his act was necessary to prevent great personal injury to his employee and verdict was given for plaintiff. *Held,* judgment reversed. Defendant was privileged to use such force as reasonably seemed necessary in the protection of his employee.

STATE v. YOUNG, 52 Or. 227, 96 P. 1067, 18 L.R.A.N.S. 688, 132 Am.St.Rep. 689 (1908). The defendant was convicted of assault with a dangerous weapon. *Held,* that it was not a defense that the defendant shot in the belief that his victim and defendant's wife were intending to commit adultery. "[H]omicide in defense of the chastity of a wife, to be justifiable, must be to prevent a present and impending violation thereof, and reasonably necessary to prevent it, not a past offense or future attempt."

KATKO v. BRINEY

Supreme Court of Iowa, 1971.
183 N.W.2d 657, 47 A.L.R.3d 624.

MOORE, Chief Justice.

The primary issue presented here is whether an owner may protect personal property in an unoccupied boarded-up farm house against trespassers and thieves by a spring gun capable of inflicting death or serious injury.

We are not here concerned with a man's right to protect his home and members of his family. Defendants' home was several miles from the scene of the incident to which we refer * * *.

Plaintiff's action is for damages resulting from serious injury caused by a shot from a 20–gauge spring shotgun set by defendants in a bedroom of an old farm house which had been uninhabited for several years. Plaintiff and his companion, Marvin McDonough, had broken and entered the house to find and steal old bottles and dated fruit jars which they considered antiques.

* * * The jury returned a verdict for plaintiff and against defendants for $20,000 actual and $10,000 punitive damages.

* * *

IV. The main thrust of defendants' defense in the trial court and on this appeal is that "the law permits use of a spring gun in a dwelling or warehouse for the purpose of preventing the unlawful entry of a burglar or thief." They repeated this contention in their exceptions to the trial court's instructions 2, 5 and 6. They took no exception to the trial court's statement of the issues or to other instructions.

In the statement of issues the trial court stated plaintiff and his companion committed a felony when they broke and entered defendants' house. In instruction 2 the court referred to the early case history of the use of spring guns and stated under the law their use was prohibited except to prevent the commission of felonies of violence and where human life is in danger. The instruction included a statement breaking and entering is not a felony of violence.

Instruction 5 stated: "You are hereby instructed that one may use reasonable force in the protection of his property, but such right is subject to the qualification that one may not use such means of force as will take human life or inflict great bodily injury. Such is the rule even though the injured party is a trespasser and is in violation of the law himself."

Instruction 6 stated: "An owner of premises is prohibited from willfully or intentionally injuring a trespasser by means of force that either takes life or inflicts great bodily injury; and therefore a person owning a premise is prohibited from setting out 'spring guns' and like dangerous devices which will likely take life or inflict great bodily injury, for the purpose of harming trespassers. The fact that the trespasser may be acting in violation of the law does not change the rule. The only time when such conduct of setting a 'spring gun' or a like dangerous device is justified would be when the trespasser was committing a felony of violence or a felony punishable by death, or where the trespasser was endangering human life by his act."

* * *

The overwhelming weight of authority, both textbook and case law, supports the trial court's statement of the applicable principles of law.

* * *

Restatement of Torts, section 85, page 180, states: "The value of human life and limb, not only to the individual concerned but also to society, so outweighs the interest of a possessor of land in excluding from it those whom he is not willing to admit thereto that a possessor of land has * * * no privilege to use force intended or likely to cause death or serious harm against another whom the possessor sees about to enter his premises or meddle with his chattel, unless the intrusion threatens death or serious bodily harm to the occupiers or users of the premises. * * * A possessor of land cannot do indirectly and by a mechanical device that which, were he present, he could not do immediately and in person. Therefore, he cannot gain a privilege to install, for the purpose of protecting his land from intrusions harmless to the lives and limbs of the occupiers or users of it, a mechanical device whose only purpose is to inflict death or serious harm upon such as may intrude, by giving notice of his intention to inflict, by mechanical means and indirectly, harm which he could not, even after request, inflict directly were he present."

* * *

In Hooker v. Miller, 37 Iowa 613, we held defendant vineyard owner liable for damages resulting from a spring gun shot although plaintiff was a trespasser and there to steal grapes. At pages 614, 615, this statement is made: "This court has held that a mere trespass against property other than a dwelling is not a sufficient justification to authorize the use of a deadly weapon by the owner in its defense; and that if death results in such a case it will be murder, though the killing be actually necessary to prevent the trespass. The State v. Vance, 17 Iowa 138." At page 617 this court said: "[T]respassers and other inconsiderable violators of the law are not to be visited by barbarous punishments or prevented by inhuman inflictions of bodily injuries."

* * *

In addition to civil liability many jurisdictions hold a land owner criminally liable for serious injuries or homicide caused by spring guns or other set devices. * * *

* * *

The legal principles stated by the trial court in instructions 2, 5 and 6 are well established and supported by the authorities cited and quoted supra. There is no merit in defendants' objections and exceptions thereto. Defendants' various motions based on the same reasons stated in exceptions to instructions were properly overruled.

We express no opinion as to whether punitive damages are allowable in this type of case. If defendants' attorneys wanted that issue decided it was their duty to raise it in the trial court.

* * *

Affirmed.

All Justices concur except LARSON, J., who dissents.

LARSON, Justice.

I respectfully dissent, first, because the majority wrongfully assumes that by installing a spring gun in the bedroom of their unoccupied house the defendants intended to shoot any intruder who attempted to enter the room. Under the record presented here, that was a fact question. * * *

* * *

* * * I would hold there is no absolute liability for injury to a criminal intruder by setting up such a device on [one's] property, and unless done with an intent to kill or seriously injure the intruder, I would absolve the owner from liability other than for negligence. I would also hold the court had no jurisdiction to allow punitive damages when the intruder was engaged in a serious criminal offense such as breaking and entering with intent to steal.

* * *

Although the court told the jury the plaintiff had the burden to prove "That the force used by defendants was in excess of that force reasonably necessary and which persons are entitled to use in the protection of their property," it utterly failed to tell the jury it could find the installation was not made with the intent or purpose of striking or injuring the plaintiff. There was considerable evidence to that effect. * * * [B]oth defendants stated the installation was made for the purpose of scaring or frightening away any intruder, not to seriously injure him. It may be that the evidence would support a finding of an intent to injure the intruder, but obviously that important issue was never adequately or clearly submitted to the jury.

* * *

Although I am aware of the often-repeated statement that personal rights are more important than property rights, where the owner has stored his valuables representing his life's accumulations, his livelihood business, his tools and implements, and his treasured antiques as appears in the case at bar, and where the evidence is sufficient to sustain a finding that the installation was intended only as a warning to ward off thieves and criminals, I can see no compelling reason why the use of such a device alone would create liability as a matter of law.

* * *

In the case at bar the plaintiff was guilty of serious criminal conduct, which event gave rise to his claim against defendants. Even so, he may be eligible for an award of compensatory damages which so far as the law is concerned redresses him and places him in the position he was prior to sustaining the injury. The windfall he would receive in the form of punitive damages is bothersome to the principle of damages, because it is a response to the conduct of the defendants rather than any reaction to the loss suffered by plaintiff or any measurement of his worthiness for the award.

When such a windfall comes to a criminal as a result of his indulgence in serious criminal conduct, the result is intolerable and indeed shocks the conscience. If we find the law upholds such a result, the criminal would be permitted by operation of law to profit from his own crime.

Furthermore, if our civil courts are to sustain such a result, it would in principle interfere with the purposes and policies of the criminal law. This would certainly be ironic since punitive damages have been thought to assist and promote those purposes, at least so far as the conduct of the defendant is concerned.

* * *

The majority seem to ignore the evident issue of punitive policy involved herein and uphold the punitive damage award on a mere technical rule of civil procedure.

REGAINING POSSESSION OF REAL PROPERTY

One who has been forcibly dispossessed of real property can properly use force, not involving serious bodily harm, to regain it. One who was dispossessed in his absence can likewise use force against one who entered without a claim of right. If, however, the one entering believed he had a right to enter, force cannot properly be used to regain possession, until the other realizes that he has no right. Where a tenant knowingly overstayed his tenancy, the landlord formerly had a right to use force to eject him. Under modern statutes, however, which provide a speedy means for regaining possession, in most states the landlord has no right to use force. The older rule is stated in Low v. Elwell, 121 Mass. 309 (1876); the modern rule in Bristor v. Burr, 120 N.Y. 427, 24 N.E. 937 (1890), and Fults v. Munro, 202 N.Y. 34, 95 N.E. 23 (1911).

KIRBY v. FOSTER

Supreme Court of Rhode Island, 1891.
17 R.I. 437, 22 A. 1111.

STINESS, J. The plaintiff was in the employ of the Providence Warehouse Co., of which the defendant, Samuel J. Foster, was the agent, and his son, the other defendant, an employee. A sum of fifty dollars belonging to the corporation had been lost, for which the plaintiff, a bookkeeper, was held responsible, and the amount was deducted from his pay. On January 20, 1888, Mr. Foster handed the plaintiff some money to pay the help. The plaintiff, acting under the advice of counsel, took from this money the amount due him at the time, including what had been deducted from his pay, put it into his pocket, and returned the balance to Mr. Foster, saying he had received his pay and was going to leave, and that he did this under advice of counsel. The defendants then seized the plaintiff and attempted to take the money from him. A struggle ensued, in which the plaintiff claims to have received injury, for which this suit is brought. The jury having returned a verdict for the plaintiff, the defendants petition for a new trial * * *. [Their petition raises] but one question, * * * whether the defendants were justified in the use of force upon the plaintiff to retake the money from him. * * *

The defendants contend that * * * the money having been delivered to the plaintiff for the specific purpose of paying the help, his conversion of it to his own use was a wrongful conversion amounting to embezzlement, which justified the defendants in using force in defense of the property under their charge. Unquestionably, if one takes another's property from his possession without right and against his will, the owner or person in charge may protect his possession, or retake the property, by the use of necessary force. * * * But this right of defense and recapture involves two things: first, possession by the owner, and, second, a purely wrongful taking or conversion, without a claim of right. If one has intrusted his property to another, who afterwards, honestly though erroneously claims it as his own, the owner has no right to retake it by personal force. * * * The law does not permit parties to take the settlement of conflicting claims into their own hands. It gives the right of defense, but not of redress. The circumstances may be exasperating; the remedy at law may seem to be inadequate; but still the injured party can not be arbiter of his own claim. Public order and the public peace are of greater consequence than a private right or an occasional hardship. Inadequacy of remedy is of frequent occurrence, but it can not find its complement in personal violence. Upon these grounds the doctrine contended for by the defendants is limited to the defense of one's possession and the right of recapture as against a mere wrongdoer. It is therefore to be noted in this case that the money was in the actual possession of the plaintiff, to whom it had been intrusted for the purpose of paying help, who thereupon claimed the right to appropriate it to his own payment, supposing he might lawfully do so. Conceding that the advice was bad, nevertheless, upon such appropriation the plaintiff held the money [under a claim of

right, and had obtained it without "misrepresentations, trickery, or fraud."]
* * *

* * *

Exceptions overruled.

————

HODGEDEN v. HUBBARD, 18 Vt. 504 (1846). Plaintiff bought a stove from defendants at a warehouse in Montpelier and carried it away. Discovering soon after the sale, on the same day, that plaintiff had misrepresented his assets, defendants pursued and overtook him about two miles from Montpelier and recaptured the stove, using force against plaintiff's person when plaintiff resisted. The trial court charged the jury that, if plaintiff obtained the stove by fraud, defendants would have been privileged to take back the stove if they could have done so peaceably, but they had no privilege to use the force necessary to reacquire it. *Held,* judgment for plaintiff reversed. The trial court should have given defendants' requested charge that if plaintiff obtained the stove by fraud, defendants were justified in pursuing him and using such force as was necessary to take the stove.

LAMB v. WOODRY, 154 Or. 30, 58 P.2d 1257, 105 A.L.R. 914 (1936). The defendant sold a stove to the plaintiff under a conditional sale agreement by which the defendant was privileged to retake the stove if the plaintiff should fail to make the payments. The plaintiff having defaulted, the defendant entered the plaintiff's house and, against the resistance of the plaintiff, forcibly took possession of the stove. *Held,* affirming judgment for plaintiff, that such a conditional seller, although entitled to repossess the property if he can do so peacefully, "is not entitled to use force to retake possession of such property and if he does and in so doing touches the resisting person he is guilty of assault and battery." The "legal right" of the seller to repossess the property sold "may be exercised without the aid of legal process only when the purchaser consents thereto."

ARREST FOR CRIME

The privilege of arrest is essential for the preservation of a lawful society. Nevertheless it is a dangerous one and in Anglo–American society has been narrowly limited. It is less dangerous when the arrest is part of a judicial proceeding already begun—that is, when a complaint has been filed with a magistrate and a warrant has been issued. In general, arrests without a warrant are justified only for the prevention of a crime or because there may be difficulty in apprehending, and later punishing, the offender. It is for this reason that, unless authorized by statute, there can be no arrest without a warrant for minor misdemeanors not involving breach of the peace. As in all cases of privilege, the arrest is proper only if it is made to carry out the purpose for which the privilege is created, that is, to cause the one arrested to be brought before a proper court to be tried. Further, when it is without a warrant, the arrest of even a guilty person is improper unless the arresting person reasonably believes that the one arrested has committed a crime of serious magnitude, affecting public safety. The danger of permitting private persons freely to arrest is reflected in the limited privileges given them. A full statement of the common law privilege of arrest for crime appears in Restatement (Second) of Torts, §§ 112–144 (1965). A summary is presented here.

Arrest With a Warrant. When a valid warrant, or one fair on its face, has been issued by a court having jurisdiction directing a peace officer (rarely a private person) to arrest a named or adequately described person for a crime, an arrest of that person by virtue of the warrant is privileged, if the person arrested is given notice of the reasons for the arrest or notice is not feasible. Normally the arresting person should have the warrant in possession.

Arrest Without a Warrant. A peace officer is privileged to arrest one who has committed, is committing or is attempting to commit a felony, or one whom the officer reasonably suspects of having committed a felony. A peace officer is also privileged to arrest one who has committed or is committing a breach of the peace in the officer's presence; the officer's reasonable belief in the existence of a breach of the peace does not, however, give the officer a privilege to arrest.

A private citizen is privileged to arrest one who has committed, is committing or is attempting to commit a felony. Unlike the police officer, however, the private citizen who reasonably but erroneously believes another to have committed a felony is not privileged to arrest the other unless the felony for which the arrest was made has in fact been committed by someone. The privilege of the private citizen to make arrests for breaches of the peace is the same as that of the peace officer and is limited to the commission of actual breaches of the peace in the presence of the person making the arrest. A private citizen who is called upon by a peace officer to make an arrest or to assist in making an arrest is privileged unless having reason to believe that the peace officer is not privileged; this is true although in fact the peace officer was not privileged to make the arrest.

In making a lawful arrest for any crime, an officer or private person can meet force with force, not being required to retreat. One can use even deadly force if apparently necessary in self-defense. However, deadly force, or weapons involving deadly force, cannot properly be used to prevent the flight of another who has not committed a dangerous felony such as murder, arson, burglary, robbery or rape. See Moreland, The Use of Force in Effecting or Resisting Arrest, 33 Neb.L.Rev. 408 (1954); Schumann v. McGinn, 307 Minn. 446, 240 N.W.2d 525 (1976).

In all cases the privilege of arrest exists only when it is exercised for the purpose of bringing the arrested person before a court. After making the arrest the arresting person has a duty promptly to take the prisoner before a magistrate for committal; the failure so to do is sometimes held to make the arresting person liable as a "trespasser ab initio."

The privilege to arrest should be distinguished from the use of force to prevent crime, or to prevent harm to a third person or to property, whether or not the conduct prevented would involve a crime. Likewise it should be distinguished from the privilege to detain for questioning without an arrest. See Muniz v. Mehlman, 327 Mass. 353, 99 N.E.2d 37 (1951).

Arrest in relation to civil proceedings is privileged in only very limited circumstances and only by one having a warrant; private persons called upon to assist have no greater privilege than the one holding the warrant.

Chapter 3

PERSONAL HARM WITHOUT
PHYSICAL IMPACT

Torts discussed so far in the casebook have to do with physical impact and physical harm. Battery involves physical contact with the person of another. Other tort situations canvassed in the introductory chapter (and the workers' compensation situation there as well) all involve physical accidents: physical risk, through physical cause and effect, leads to physical harm. As seen so far, tort law seems preoccupied with tangible interferences and injuries.

To be sure, battery includes situations where the chief harm is offense, or indignity, a species of mental suffering; and the typical personal injury lawsuit, arising out of physical accident, looks to recovery of damages for injury to feelings and emotions, called pain and suffering. Still, the predicate of recovery in either case is some sort of physical touching.

In the present chapter, we see tort law moving beyond its traditional preoccupation with matters physicalistic. The main topic is the rise and development of a modern tort, intentional infliction of emotional distress. Here injury of a nonphysical—mental or emotional—character comes to the center of tort concern.

SECTION A.   ASSAULT

Assault is a two-sided tort. The elements of assault liability look in two directions, toward the bad conduct of an actor and toward the bad experience of a victim. This two-sidedness is contained within a rather technical, narrowly defined tort.

On the one hand, the definition of assault focuses on bad conduct by a defendant, defendant's intentional breach of the peace. In this respect assault seems an appendage to battery; like battery, liability for assault works to deter antisocial conduct.

The bad conduct may be of two different kinds, corresponding to two definitions of assaultive intent formulated by Section 21 of the Second Restatement of Torts (which appears in full below). (1) The defendant "acts intending to cause a harmful or offensive contact with the person of [another].'' Here defendant intends to commit a battery, but ensuing liability is for assault (given other elements), not battery, when contact in fact does not come about. (2) The defendant ''acts intending to cause ... an imminent apprehension of such a contact.'' Here defendant intends to frighten plaintiff by making it seem that a battery is impending. In short, assault is (1) a miscarried battery or (2) a seeming battery.

On the other hand, the definition of assault also focuses on a particular sort of bad experience suffered by plaintiff, the experience of apprehension. In this respect assault liability works to redress mental harm, and seems to point well beyond battery.

According to the Restatement, a necessary element of assault, in addition to defendant's intentional misconduct, is that ''the other is thereby put in such imminent apprehension.'' The plaintiff must experience apprehension—fear—of imminent invasive contact, a specific distressful mental state. Recovery for this specific sort of mental distress looks, from our present standpoint, to be the augury of something much larger. It seems a preface to liability for intentional infliction of emotional distress—as indeed, in the casebook, it is.

I. DE S. AND WIFE v. W. DE S.
At the Assizes, coram Thorpe, C. J., 1348 or 1349.
Year Book, Liber Assisarum, folio 99, placitum 60.

John of Somerton and M. [Mary?] his wife, complain of W. [Will?] of S. on the ground that W. in the year, etc., by force and arms, etc., at S. did commit an assault upon M., and beat her, etc. And W. pleaded not guilty. And it was found by verdict of the inquest that the said W. came in the night to the house of the said I., and would have bought some wine, but the door of the tavern was closed; and he struck on the door with a hatchet, which he had in his hand, and the woman plaintiff put her head out at a window and ordered him to stop; and he perceived her and struck with the hatchet, but did not touch the woman. Whereupon the inquest said that it seemed to them that there was no trespass, since there was no harm done. THORPE, C. J. There is harm, and a trespass for which they shall recover damages, since he made an assault upon the woman, as it is found although he did no other harm. Wherefore tax their damages, & c. And they taxed the damages at half a mark. THORPE, C. J., awarded that they should recover their damages, & c., and that the other should be taken. Et sic nota, that for an assault a man shall recover damages, & c.

———

WEBB v. PORTLAND MFG. CO., Fed.Cas.No.17,322, 3 Sumn. 189 (Cir. Ct.D.Me.1838). Bill in equity to restrain defendant from using water to which plaintiff was entitled, but for which he had no immediate need. STORY, J. [Associate Justice of the Supreme Court, sitting as circuit justice.] '' * * * I can very well understand that no action lies in a case where there is damnum absque injuria; that is, where there is a damage done without any wrong or violation of any right of the plaintiff. But I am not able to understand, how it can be correctly said, in a legal sense, that an action will not lie, even in case of a wrong or violation of a right, unless it is followed by some perceptible damage, which can be established as a matter of fact; in other words, that injuria sine damno is not actionable. On the contrary, from my earliest reading, I have considered it laid up among the very elements of the common law, that, wherever there is a wrong there is a remedy to redress it; * * * and, if no other damage is established, the party injured is entitled to a verdict for nominal damages."

BEACH v. HANCOCK, 27 N.H. 223 (1853). Trespass, for an assault. Over defendant's exceptions, the trial court (1) ruled that the pointing of a gun in an angry and threatening manner at a person three or four rods distant, who was ignorant whether the gun was loaded or not, was an assault, though the gun was not loaded, and (2) instructed the jury that in assessing damages, it was their right and duty to consider the effect light damages would have in encouraging disregard of law and disturbances of the peace. *Held*, judgment on the verdict for plaintiff.

"One of the most important objects to be attained by the enactment of laws and the institutions of civilized society is, each of us shall feel secure against unlawful assaults. Without such security society loses most of its value. Peace and order and domestic happiness, inexpressibly more precious than mere forms of government, cannot be enjoyed without the sense of perfect security. We have a right to live in society without being put in fear of personal harm. But it must be a reasonable fear of which we complain. And it surely is not unreasonable for a person to entertain a fear of personal injury, when a pistol is pointed at him in a threatening manner, when, for aught he knows, it may be loaded, and may occasion his immediate death. The business of the world could not be carried on with comfort, if such things could be done with impunity.

"We think the defendant guilty of an assault, and we perceive no reason for taking any exception to the remarks of the court. Finding trivial damages for breaches of the peace, damages incommensurate with the injury sustained, would certainly lead the ill-disposed to consider an assault as a thing that might be committed with impunity. But, at all events, it was proper for the jury to consider whether such a result would or would not be produced."

READ v. COKER

Common Pleas, 1853.

13 C.B. 850, 138 Eng.Rep. 1437.

[The first count charged an assault committed by the defendant on the plaintiff on the 24th of March, 1853, by thrusting him out of a certain workshop. Issue was joined on a plea of not guilty. The plaintiff, a paper stainer, being in arrears for rent, on February 23, 1852, induced the defendant to pay off the landlord and carry on the business for their mutual benefit, defendant to pay the rent and other outgoings and to allow the plaintiff a certain sum weekly.*]

The defendant, becoming dissatisfied with the speculation, dismissed the plaintiff on the 22d of March. On the 24th, the plaintiff came to the premises, and, refusing to leave when ordered by the defendant, the latter collected together some of his workmen, who mustered round the plaintiff, tucking up their sleeves and aprons, and threatened to break his neck if he did not go out; and, fearing that the men would strike him if he did not do so, the plaintiff went out. This was the assault complained of in the first count. Upon this evidence the learned judge left it to the jury to say whether there was an intention on the part of the defendant to assault the plaintiff, and whether the plaintiff was apprehensive of personal violence if he did not retire. The jury found for the plaintiff on this count. Damages, one farthing.

[The paragraph below summarizes the argument of defendant's lawyer, Byles, a "serjeant" or barrister, on the question of assault. Within brackets are two interruptions made from the bench by Chief Justice Jervis. The opinion delivered by Jervis follows.]

Byles, Serjt., on a former day in this term, moved for a rule nisi for a new trial, on the ground of misdirection, and that the verdict was not warranted by the evidence. That which was proved as to the first count clearly did not amount to an assault. [JERVIS, C. J. It was as much an assault as a sheriff's officer being in a room with a man against whom he has a writ, and saying to him, "You are my prisoner," is an arrest.] To constitute an assault, there must be something more than a threat of violence. An assault is thus defined in Buller's Nisi Prius, p. 15: "An assault is an attempt or offer, by force or violence, to do a corporal hurt to another, as by pointing a pitchfork at him, when standing within reach; presenting a gun at him, within shooting distance; drawing a sword, and waving it in a menacing manner, & c. The Queen v. Ingram, 1 Salk. 384. But no words can amount to an assault, though perhaps they may in some cases serve to explain a doubtful action: 1 Hawk.P.C. 133; as if a man were to lay his hand upon his sword, and say, 'If it were not assizetime, he would not take such language,'—the words would prevent the action from being construed to be an assault, because they show he had no intent to do him any corporal hurt at that time: Tuberville v. Savage, 1 Mod. 3." * * * So, in 3 Bl.Comm. 120, an assault is said to be "an attempt or offer to beat another, without touching him; as if one lifts up his cane or his fist in a threatening manner at another, or strikes at him but misses him: this is an assault, insultus, which Finch (L. 202) describes to be 'an unlawful setting upon one's person.'" [JERVIS, C. J. If a man comes into a room, and lays his cane on the table, and says to another, "If you don't go out I will knock you on the head," would not that be an assault?] Clearly not: it is a mere threat, unaccompanied by any gesture or action towards carrying it into effect. The direction of the learned judge as to this point was erroneous. He should have told the jury that to constitute an assault there must be an attempt, coupled with a present ability, to do personal violence to the party; instead of leaving it to them, as

---

* Ed. note: According to another report of the same case, the jury found that under this arrangement plaintiff and defendant became joint owners of the machinery and defendant replaced plaintiff as sole tenant of the premises. 22 L.J.C.P. 201.

he did, to say what the plaintiff thought, and not what they (the jury) thought was the defendant's intention. There must be some act done denoting a present ability and an intention to assault.

A rule nisi having been granted.

JERVIS, C. J. I am of opinion that this rule cannot be made absolute to its full extent; but that, so far as regards the first count of the declaration, it must be discharged. If anything short of actual striking will in law constitute an assault, the facts here clearly showed that the defendant was guilty of an assault. There was a threat of violence exhibiting an intention to assault, and a present ability to carry the threat into execution.

MAULE, J., CRESSWELL, J., and TALFOURD, J., concurring.

Rule discharged as to the first count.

———

TROGDEN v. TERRY, 172 N.C. 540, 90 S.E. 583 (1916). Defendant approached plaintiff in a hotel dining room, stood with a walking stick on his arm, and threatened to "whip hell out of" plaintiff unless plaintiff signed "an apology and retraction" which defendant had prepared. Plaintiff signed. *Held*, an assault. "[W]here one person, by a show of violence and force, puts another in fear and forces him to leave a place where he has a right to be, or to commit some act which he otherwise would not perform, he is guilty of an assault."

CULLISON v. MEDLEY, 570 N.E.2d 27 (Ind.1991). "The facts alleged and testified to by Cullison could, if believed, entitle him to recover for an assault against the Medleys. A jury could reasonably conclude that the Medleys intended to frighten Cullison by surrounding him in his trailer and threatening him with bodily harm while one of them was armed with a revolver, even if that revolver was not removed from its holster. Cullison testified that Ernest [Medley] kept grabbing at the pistol as if he were going to take it out, and that Cullison thought Ernest was going to shoot him. It is for the jury to determine whether Cullison's apprehension of being shot or otherwise injured was one which would normally be aroused in the mind of a reasonable person."

STATE v. INGRAM, 237 N.C. 197, 74 S.E.2d 532 (1953); noted, 29 N.Y.U.L.Rev. 219, 32 N.C.L.Rev. 423. The prosecuting witness testified as follows: As she walked away from the highway on a plantation road, defendant drove along the highway very slowly, "leering at me a curious look." He stopped the car. She ran through a small body of woods and, coming into the open, saw him walking fast 65 or 70 feet from her. He stopped at some plum bushes, watched her, and did not speak. She continued to walk to the field where her relatives were, and he turned back. Having reached her relatives, she cried because she was frightened. *Held*, nonsuit should have been entered below because the evidence was insufficient to show assault. There must be "an overt act or an attempt, or the unequivocal appearance of an attempt, with force and violence, to do some immediate physical injury to the person of another. * * * The display of force or menace of violence must be such as to cause the reasonable apprehension of immediate bodily harm."

BROWER v. ACKERLEY, 88 Wash.App. 87, 943 P.2d 1141 (1997). Brower received a series of menacing telephone calls at his home at night. The anonymous calls were traced to defendant's residence. Brower's claim of assault was dismissed by the trial court. *Held*, affirmed. "To constitute civil assault, the threat must be of imminent harm." "The telephone calls received by Brower * * * contained two explicit threats: 'I'm going to find out where you live and I'm going to kick your ass'; and later, 'you're finished; [I'll] cut you in your sleep'. The words threatened action in the near future, but not the imminent future. * * * Because the threats, however frightening, were not accompanied by circumstances indicating that the caller was in a position to reach Brower and inflict physical violence 'almost at once,' we affirm the dismissal of the assault claim."

RESTATEMENT OF TORTS, SECOND (1965)

§ 21. Assault

(1) An actor is subject to liability to another for assault if

(a) he acts intending to cause a harmful or offensive contact with the person of the other or a third person, or an imminent apprehension of such a contact, and

(b) the other is thereby put in such imminent apprehension.

––––––––

STATE v. BARRY, 45 Mont. 598, 124 P. 775 (1912). Defendant leveled a rifle (not shown to have been loaded) at the prosecutor, who did not see defendant until after he had been practically disarmed. *Held*, not an assault, since the prosecutor, not knowing of defendant's conduct, could not have been put in fear for his safety.

WILSON v. BELLAMY, 105 N.C.App. 446, 414 S.E.2d 347 (1992). Plaintiff, a female college student, alleged that she went to a party at a fraternity house, became extremely intoxicated, and was raped by two members of the fraternity in an upstairs room. The two defendants testified that they had consensual sexual contact with plaintiff. Plaintiff testified that after she went upstairs she lost consciousness. The trial court directed a verdict for defendants. On appeal, *held*, that plaintiff's evidence shows no liability for assault, but does show battery. No assault is made out, given plaintiff's testimony that she was unconscious at the relevant time, an admission that "she did not have any apprehension of harmful or offensive contact." On the other hand, "a person who is unconscious or insensibly drunk cannot give consent to physical contact," so plaintiff's battery claim should have been submitted to the jury.

MANNING v. GRIMSLEY, 643 F.2d 20 (1st Cir.1981). Plaintiff, spectator at a baseball game, sued defendant pitcher for battery. While warming up in the bullpen, defendant became irritated because of heckling by nearby spectators. He faced the bleachers and threw the ball at a 90 degree angle from the catcher, at over 80 m.p.h., towards the hecklers. The ball passed through a wire mesh fence and hit plaintiff. In reversing a directed verdict for defendant and remanding for a new trial, the court of appeals concluded from the evidence that a jury could reasonably have inferred that defendant intended "to throw the ball in the direction of the hecklers" and "to cause them immediate apprehension of being hit." Thus the case fell within Restatement Torts, 2d § 13, subjecting an actor to liability for battery if he intends "to cause a harmful or offensive contact with the person of the other or a third person, or an imminent apprehension of such a contact", and a harmful contact results.

SECTION B.   INFLICTION OF EMOTIONAL DISTRESS

This section addresses the tort often called simply "IIED": intentional infliction of emotional distress. The main cases and their accompanying squibs examine the initial evolution and the contemporary operation of independent tort liability for IIED.

The advent of IIED is a noteworthy legal development. The drama of this development may be shown by juxtaposing two pronouncements of the Restatement of Torts, quoted by Justice Traynor in his opinion in *State Rubbish Collectors Assn. v. Siliznoff*, infra. Each pronouncement is a rather large generalization about the nature of tort liability for personal injury; each is asserted in the confident manner of "restatement"; the two, 13 years apart, are flatly contradictory.

In 1934 the Restatement laid down a general limit of tort liability for injurious impacts upon persons. Based on a survey of the various interests protected by tort, the Restatement's commentary said:

> The interest in mental and emotional tranquility and, therefore, in freedom from mental and emotional disturbance is not, as a thing in itself, regarded [by tort law] as of sufficient importance to require others to refrain from conduct intended or recognizably likely to cause such a disturbance.

In other words, though in various situations tort liability may lead to award of damages for emotional distress, the basis of liability is not the occurrence of the emotional distress, but rather the occurrence of some physical interference or physical injury (or another type of actionable interference, such as reputational harm or unwanted publicity). By light of the 1934 generalization, the tort of assault is "an historical anomaly" (per the *Siliznoff* opinion).

In 1947 the Restatement was amended in relevant part, so that its commentary said:

> The interest in freedom from severe emotional distress is regarded [by tort law] as of sufficient importance to require others to refrain from conduct intended to invade it.

In line with this countergeneralization, it is "anomalous" (as Traynor says in *Siliznoff*) to deny recovery for emotional distress just because some element of physical injury is lacking.

What accounts for the Restatement's about-face? What happened in the 13–year interval between generalization and countergeneralization? An interesting answer is offered by legal historian G. Edward White, in his book *Tort Law in America* (1980):

> ... In 1939 [legal scholar] William Prosser announced that "the courts" had "created a new tort," the intentional infliction of emotional distress. ... Prosser's statement had an element of accuracy. But it was also unnecessarily modest. A major contribution to the "creation" of the "new tort" had been made by Prosser himself. He organized the diverse cases where recovery for emotional distress had been granted, criticized the existing rationales employed to avoid liability for emotional distress, and generally sought to treat emotional injuries in terms of the emergent theoretical framework of tort law in the 1930's, which suggested that tort liability be assessed through a "common sense" balancing of social interests. ...

> The contribution of Prosser and other tort scholars ... was ... not to invent the principle of compensation for emotional distress, but to expand the locus of that principle from isolated "exceptional" cases to an established doctrine of tort law.

Id. at 102, 104. White says that this scholarly advocacy of IIED "can be linked" to the general jurisprudential outlook of American Legal Realism:

> Several features common to the climate of educated opinion in which Realism came to prominence had interacted in the "discovery" that tort law could compensate persons for emotional discomfort inflicted by others. The "speculative" nature of emotional injuries had been purportedly eliminated by the insights of the behavioral sciences. ... [T]he possibilities for using tort law as a means of protecting various social interests had emerged as a source of intellectual excitement. Finally, scholars of the 1920's and 1930's had shown a willingness ... to concede that the doctrinal state of an area of tort law was indeterminate and capable of dramatic change.

Id. at 103, 105.

STATE RUBBISH COLLECTORS ASSOCIATION v. SILIZNOFF
Supreme Court of California, in Bank, 1952.
38 Cal.2d 330, 240 P.2d 282.

[Kobzeff signed a contract with Acme Brewing Co. to collect rubbish from the latter's brewery. It was understood that the work would be done by defendant Siliznoff, Kobzeff's son-in-law, whom Kobzeff wished to assist in establishing a rubbish collection business. Both Kobzeff and Abramoff, who formerly had the account but with whose services Acme was dissatisfied, were members of plaintiff association; defendant Siliznoff was not a member. The by-laws of the association provided that one member should not take an account from another member without compensation. Abramoff complained about the loss of the Acme account, and after certain negotiations and incidents, Siliznoff agreed to pay $1850 to Abramoff through the association, and to join the association. No payment was made and the association brought suit on the series of promissory notes, totaling $1850, that Siliznoff had executed. Defendant Siliznoff "cross-complained", asking that the notes be cancelled because of duress and want of consideration, and further praying for general and exemplary damages for assaults by plaintiffs and its agents to compel him to join the association and pay Abramoff for the Acme account. Defendant testified that on the day when he finally agreed to pay for the account he was told he would have "up till tonight to get down to the board meeting and make some kind of arrangements" or they would beat him up, cut up his truck tires, and burn his truck, or otherwise put him out of business; he testified further that the only reason they let him go that night was that he promised to come back the next day and sign. The jury returned a verdict for defendant, and on the cross-complaint found $1250 compensatory and $7500 exemplary damages. After remittitur reducing the exemplary damages to $4000, judgment was entered for defendant Siliznoff, and plaintiff association appealed.]

TRAYNOR, J. * * * Plaintiff contends that the evidence does not establish an assault against defendant because the threats made all related to action that might take place in the future; that neither Andikian nor members of the board of directors threatened immediate physical harm to defendant. We have concluded, however, that a cause of action is established when it is shown that one, in the absence of any privilege, intentionally subjects another to the mental suffering incident to serious threats to his physical well-being, whether or not the threats are made under such circumstances as to constitute a technical assault.

In the past it has frequently been stated that the interest in emotional and mental tranquility is not one that the law will protect from invasion in its own right. [Citations omitted.] As late as 1934 the Restatement of Torts took the position that "The interest in mental and emotional tranquility and, therefore, in freedom from mental and emotional disturbance is not, as a thing in itself, regarded as of sufficient importance to require others to refrain from conduct intended or recognizably likely to cause such a disturbance." Restatement, Torts, § 46, comment c. The Restatement explained the rule allowing recovery for the mere apprehension of bodily harm in traditional assault cases as an historical anomaly, § 24, comment c, and the rule allowing recovery for insulting conduct by an employee of a common carrier as justified by the necessity of securing for the public comfortable as well as safe service. § 48, comment c.

The Restatement recognized, however, that in many cases mental distress could be so intense that it could reasonably be foreseen that illness or other bodily harm might result. If the defendant intentionally subjected the plaintiff to such distress and bodily harm resulted, the defendant would be liable for negligently causing the plaintiff bodily harm. Restatement, Torts, §§ 306, 312. Under this theory the cause of action was not founded on a right to be free from intentional interference with mental tranquility, but on the right to be free from negligent interference with physical wellbeing. A defendant who intentionally subjected another to mental distress without intending to cause bodily harm would nevertheless be liable for resulting bodily harm if he should have foreseen that the mental distress might cause such harm.

The California cases have been in accord with the Restatement in allowing recovery where physical injury resulted from intentionally subjecting the plaintiff to serious mental distress. [Citations omitted.]

The view has been forcefully advocated that the law should protect emotional and mental tranquility as such against serious and intentional invasions, see Goodrich, Emotional Disturbance as Legal Damages, 20 Mich. L.Rev. 497, 508–513; Magruder, Mental and Emotional Disturbance in the Law of Torts, 49 Harv.L.Rev. 1033, 1064–1067; Wade, Tort Liability for Abusive and Insulting Language, 4 Vanderbilt L.Rev. 63, 81–82, and there is a growing body of case law supporting this position. [Citations omitted.] In recognition of this development the American Law Institute amended section 46 of the Restatement of Torts in 1947 to provide: "One who, without a privilege to do so, intentionally causes severe emotional distress to another is liable (a) for such emotional distress, and (b) for bodily harm resulting from it."

In explanation it stated that "The interest in freedom from severe emotional distress is regarded as of sufficient importance to require others to refrain from conduct intended to invade it. Such conduct is tortious. The injury suffered by the one whose interest is invaded is frequently far more serious to him than certain tortious invasions of the interest in bodily integrity and other legally protected interests. In the absence of a privilege, the actor's conduct has no social utility; indeed it is anti-social. No reason or policy requires such an actor to be protected from the liability which usually attaches to the wilful wrongdoer whose efforts are successful." Restatement of the Law, 1948 Supplement, Torts, § 46, comment d.

There are persuasive arguments and analogies that support the recognition of a right to be free from serious, intentional, and unprivileged invasions of mental and emotional tranquility. If a cause of action is otherwise established, it is settled that damages may be given for mental suffering naturally ensuing from the acts complained of [citations omitted] and in the case of many torts, such as assault, battery, false imprisonment, and defamation, mental suffering will frequently constitute the principal element of damages [citation omitted]. In cases where mental suffering constitutes a major element of damages it is anomalous to deny recovery because the defendant's intentional misconduct fell short of producing some physical injury.

It may be contended that to allow recovery in the absence of physical injury will open the door to unfounded claims and a flood of litigation, and that the requirement that there be physical injury is necessary to insure that serious mental suffering actually occurred. The jury is ordinarily in a better position, however, to determine whether outrageous conduct results in mental distress than whether that distress in turn results in physical injury.

From their own experience jurors are aware of the extent and character of the disagreeable emotions that may result from the defendant's conduct, but a difficult medical question is presented when it must be determined if emotional distress resulted in physical injury. See, Smith, Relation of Emotions to Injury and Disease, 30 Va.L.Rev. 193, 303–306. Greater proof that mental suffering occurred is found in the defendant's conduct designed to bring it about than in physical injury that may or may not have resulted therefrom.

That administrative difficulties do not justify the denial of relief for serious invasions of mental and emotional tranquility is demonstrated by the cases recognizing the right of privacy. Recognition of that right protects mental tranquility from invasion by unwarranted and undesired publicity. Melvin v. Reid, 112 Cal.App. 285, 289, 297 P. 91; Restatement, Torts, § 867, comments c and d. As in the case of the protection of mental tranquility from other forms of invasion, difficult problems in determining the kind and extent of invasions that are sufficiently serious to be actionable are presented. Also the public interest in the free dissemination of news must be considered. Nevertheless courts have concluded that the problems presented are not so insuperable that they warrant the denial of relief altogether.

In the present case plaintiff caused defendant to suffer extreme fright. By intentionally producing such fright it endeavored to compel him either to give up the Acme account or pay for it, and it had no right or privilege to adopt such coercive methods in competing for business. In these circumstances liability is clear. * * *

The judgment is affirmed.

———

WALLACE v. SHOREHAM HOTEL CORP., 49 A.2d 81 (D.C.Mun.Ct.App. 1946). Plaintiff was a guest at defendant's cocktail lounge in the company of his wife and friends. He alleged that a waiter gave him incorrect change for the $20 bill given by him to pay the check. When he requested correct change, the waiter stated publicly, for all to hear, that plaintiff had given him a $10 bill and that "we have had people try this before." Disavowing any claim to an action for slander, plaintiff sought damages for humiliation and embarrassment from the waiter's insult. In affirming the lower court's dismissal of the complaint for failure to state a cause of action, the court drew upon a prior decision, Clark v. Associated Retail Credit Men, 70 App.D.C. 183, 105 F.2d 62, 66 (1939). Commenting on liability for mental distress unaccompanied by physical injury, the court had there said:

"The law does not, and doubtless should not, impose a general duty of care to avoid causing mental distress. For the sake of reasonable freedom of action, in our own interest and that of society, we need the privilege of being careless whether we inflict mental distress on our neighbors. It is perhaps less clear that we need the privilege of distressing them intentionally and without excuse. Yet there is, and probably should be, no general principle that mental distress purposely caused is actionable unless justified.

Such a principle would raise awkward questions of de minimis and of excuse. 'He intentionally hurt my feelings' does not yet sound in tort, though it may in a more civilized time."

SAMMS v. ECCLES, 11 Utah 2d 289, 358 P.2d 344 (1961). Complaint alleged that plaintiff, a married woman, suffered severe emotional distress because of defendant's persistent solicitations to sexual intercourse. *Held*, the complaint was good as against a motion for summary judgment, even though under usual circumstances a solicitation to sexual intercourse would not be actionable. The opinion noted that courts have been reluctant to allow a cause of action for emotional distress "unless the emotional distress was suffered as a result of some other overt tort. Nevertheless, recognizing the reality of such injuries and the injustice of permitting them to go unrequited, in many cases courts have strained to find the other tort as a peg upon which to hang the right of recovery."

"Some of these have been unrealistic, or even flimsy. For instance, a technical battery was found where an insurance adjuster derisively tossed a coin on the bed of a woman who was in a hospital with a heart condition, and because of this tort she was allowed to recover for distress caused by his other attempts at intimidation in accusing her of gold-bricking and attempting to defraud his company; courts have also dealt with trespass where hotel employees have invaded rooms occupied by married couples and imputed to them immoral conduct; and other similar torts have been used as a basis for such recovery. [Citations omitted.] But a realistic analysis of many of these cases will show that the recognized tort is but incidental and that the real basis of recovery is the outraged feelings and emotional distress resulting from some aggravated conduct of the defendant."

ECKENRODE v. LIFE OF AMERICA INSURANCE CO.
United States Court of Appeals, Seventh Circuit, 1972.
470 F.2d 1.

KILEY, Circuit Judge.

Plaintiff, a resident of Pennsylvania, filed this three count diversity complaint to recover damages for severe emotional injury suffered as a result of the deliberate refusal of Life of America Insurance Company (Insurer), of Chicago, to pay her the proceeds of Insurer's policy covering the life of her husband. The district court dismissed the suit. Plaintiff has appealed. We reverse.

In Count I plaintiff sought recovery of the face amount of the policy. In Count II she sought compensatory damage for Insurer's "outrageous conduct" in refusing to pay her the policy proceeds when its duty was clear and when it knew of plaintiff's and her family's financial distress. In Count III she sought compensatory and punitive damages 1) because Insurer allegedly defrauded decedent into the insurance contract by its promise of payment of benefits immediately upon proof of the insured's death from "accidental causes," while at the time its practice was not to pay meritorious claims; and 2) because Insurer allegedly sought by "economic coercion" to compel plaintiff—so increasingly financially distressed—to accept less than the face value of the policy or be forced to sue for payment of the proceeds.

The district court dismissed Counts II and III as stating no claim on which relief could be granted, and then dismissed "without prejudice" Count I. After the complaint was dismissed plaintiff filed an action in the Circuit Court of Cook County based on Count I to recover the face amount of the policy and attorney's fees under Ch. 73, § 767, Ill.Rev.Stats. That case was settled. Only Counts II and III, therefore, are before us on this appeal.

I.

Taking the allegations, properly pleaded in Counts II and III, as true, the following facts are stated: Defendant's life insurance policy covering plaintiff's husband issued September 22, 1967. Under the policy Insurer agreed to pay plaintiff $5,000 immediately upon due proof of death from "accidental causes." On December 17, 1967, insured was an accidental victim of a homicide. Plaintiff met all conditions of the policy and repeatedly demanded payment, but Insurer refused to pay. Decedent left plaintiff with several children, but no property of value. She had no money, none even for the funeral expenses. Denied payment by Insurer, she was required to borrow money to support her family, while her financial condition worsened. The family was required to live with, and accept charity from, relatives.

Further: Insurer knew or should have known of the death of decedent from accidental causes and of plaintiff's dire need of the policy proceeds. Yet Insurer repeatedly and deliberately refused her demands for payment, and as a proximate result she was caused to suffer "severe distress and disturbance of [her] mental tranquility." Instead of paying her the proceeds of the policy, and being fully aware of the accidental cause of decedent's death and of plaintiff's financial distress, Insurer breached the policy promise to pay immediately upon proof of death. Insurer, knowing full well that plaintiff needed the proceeds of the policy to provide necessaries for her children, applied "economic coercion" in refusing to make payment on the policy, and in "inviting" plaintiff to "compromise" her claim by implying it (Insurer) had a valid defense to the claim.[2]

II.

The issue before us with respect to Counts II and III is whether plaintiff—beneficiary of her husband's life insurance policy—may on the foregoing "facts" recover damages for severe mental distress allegedly suffered as a result of Insurer's conduct. Illinois law controls our decision, and, in anticipation that the Illinois Supreme Court would hold as we do, we decide the issue in favor of plaintiff.

We have no doubt, in view of Knierim v. Izzo, 22 Ill.2d 73, 174 N.E.2d 157 (1961), that the Illinois Supreme Court would sustain plaintiff's complaint against Insurer's motion to dismiss.

---

2. Attached to the complaint is a copy of Insurer's letter of January 12, 1968. The letter suggests that in view of a police investigation not likely to be completed until the "very dis-tant future," plaintiff might like to suggest an offer to "settle" rather than wait for the police report.

In *Knierim*, plaintiff filed a wrongful death action alleging, inter alia, that defendant Izzo threatened her with the murder of her husband, carried out the threat, and thereby proximately caused her severe emotional distress. The trial court dismissed her complaint, but the Illinois Supreme Court reversed and held that plaintiff had stated a cause of action for an intentional causing of severe emotional distress by Izzo's "outrageous conduct."

The court recognized the "new tort" of intentional infliction of severe emotional distress, following similar recognition by an "increasing number of courts," and cited several state decisions. 174 N.E.2d at 163. The court rejected reasons given by other courts not recognizing the "new tort." As to the reason that mental disturbance is incapable of financial measurement, the court pointed out that "pain and suffering" and "mental suffering" are elements of damage, respectively, in personal injury and malicious prosecution cases. 174 N.E.2d at 163. As to the reason that mental consequences are too evanescent for the law to deal with, the court noted that psychosomatic medicine had learned much in the past "thirty years" about the bodily effects of man's emotions, and that symptoms produced by "stronger emotions" are now visible to the professional eye. 174 N.E.2d at 164. As to the reason that recognizing the "new tort" would lead to frivolous claims, the court observed that triers of fact from their own experiences would be able to draw a line between "slight hurts" and "outrageous conduct." Id. And finally, as to the reason that mental consequences vary greatly with the individual so as to pose difficulties too great for the law, the court adopted an objective standard against which emotional distress could be measured. The court thought that the standard of "severe emotional distress to a person of ordinary sensibilities, in the absence of special knowledge or notice" would be a sufficient limit * * *.

* * *

In *Knierim* the court, inter alia, relied upon State Rubbish Collectors Association v. Siliznoff, 38 Cal.2d 330, 240 P.2d 282 (1952). * * * Later, the California Supreme Court *en banc* affirmed a trial court judgment against an insurance company, including $25,000 for mental suffering caused by the insurance company's earlier unreasonable refusal to accept a settlement within the limits of the liability policy. Crisci v. Security Ins. Co. of New Haven, 66 Cal.2d 425, 58 Cal.Rptr. 13, 426 P.2d 173 (1967). * * * Subsequently in Fletcher v. Western National Life Ins. Co., 10 Cal.App.3d 376, 89 Cal.Rptr. 78 (1970), an appellate court relying upon *Siliznoff* and *Crisci*, held that the defendant insurance company's threatened and actual bad faith refusals to make payments under the disability policy were essentially tortious in nature and could legally be the basis for an action against the company for intentional infliction of emotional distress. * * *

We think that the California court in *Fletcher*, supra, set out correctly the elements of a prima facie case for the tort of "intentional infliction of severe emotional distress":

(1) Outrageous conduct by the defendant;

(2) The defendant's intention of causing, or reckless disregard of the probability of causing emotional distress;

(3) The plaintiff's suffering severe or extreme emotional distress; and

(4) Actual and proximate causation of the emotional distress by the defendant's outrageous conduct.

See *Knierim*, supra; Restatement 2d Torts, § 46(1); Prosser, Torts § 11 (3d Ed. 1964).

* * *

It is recognized that the outrageous character of a person's conduct may arise from an abuse by that person of a position which gives him power to affect the interests of another; and that in this sense extreme "bullying tactics" and other "high pressure" methods of insurance adjusters seeking to force compromises or settlements may constitute outrageous conduct. Restatement 2d Torts § 46 Comment (e); Prosser, Torts § 11 at 49–50. It is also recognized that the extreme character of a person's conduct may arise from that person's knowledge that the other is peculiarly susceptible to emotional distress by reason of some physical or mental condition or peculiarity.

Here Insurer's alleged bad faith refusal to make payment on the policy, coupled with its deliberate use of "economic coercion" (i.e., by delaying and refusing payment it increased plaintiff's financial distress thereby coercing her to compromise and settle) to force a settlement, clearly rises to the level of "outrageous conduct" to a person of "ordinary sensibilities."

Furthermore, it is common knowledge that one of the most frequent considerations in procuring life insurance is to ensure the continued economic and mental welfare of the beneficiaries upon the death of the insured. See *Crisci*, 66 Cal.2d 425, 58 Cal.Rptr. at 19, 426 P.2d at 179. The very risks insured against presuppose that upon the death of the insured the beneficiary might be in difficult circumstances and thus particularly susceptible and vulnerable to high pressure tactics by an economically powerful entity. *Fletcher*, 89 Cal.Rptr. at 95. In the case before us Insurer's alleged high pressure methods (economic coercion) were aimed at the very thing insured against, and we think that the insurance company was on notice that plaintiff would be particularly vulnerable to mental distress by reason of her financial plight.

In deciding as we do, we note that insurance business affects a great many people, is subject to substantial governmental regulation and is stamped with a public interest. *Crisci*, supra; *Fletcher*, supra. We also note that insurance contracts[4] are subject to the same implied conditions of good faith and fair dealing as are other contracts.

---

4. We think it is clear that an action of the type involved here sounds both in contract and   in tort.

It is true that settlement tactics may be privileged under circumstances where an insurer has done no more than insist upon his legal rights in a permissible way. But we do not think that a refusal to make payments based on a bad faith insistence on a non-existent defense is privileged conduct against the complaint here.

* * *

For the reasons given, the judgment of the district court dismissing Counts II and III of plaintiff's complaint is hereby reversed.

DAVIS v. CURRIER, 704 A.2d 1207 (Maine 1997). "[A] party cannot be liable for intentional infliction of emotional distress for insisting on his or her rights in a permissible manner. * * * *See FDIC v. S. Prawer & Co.*, 829 F.Supp. 439, 449 (D.Me. 1993) (noting that the tort of intentional infliction of emotional distress is not designed to protect parties 'from the vicissitudes of the litigation process')."

JACKSON v. BROWN, 904 P.2d 685 (Utah 1995). Plaintiff (Jackson) brought suit against former fiancé (Brown) who, after proposing to Jackson and obtaining a marriage license, called off the announced wedding hours before the ceremony. Jackson asserted breach of promise to marry and intentional infliction of emotional distress (IIED). The court first held that, by itself, "breach of a promise to marry no longer has any legal significance." With respect to the IIED claim, the court observed: "the mere decision to withdraw from a planned marriage is an insufficient basis for this cause of action. * * * Although such a decision may frequently cause some amount of pain for all parties involved, it is not the kind of pain which is susceptible to remedy in the courts."

However, the court went on to note additional facts relevant to the IIED claim. As Jackson discovered after the wedding was called off, Brown was already married; "at no time during his relationship with Jackson was he able, legally, to marry her." Whether Brown's conduct in this context was "outrageous" is "a question for the trier of fact."

WHELAN v. WHELAN, 41 Conn.Supp. 519, 588 A.2d 251 (Conn.Super.Ct.1991). Plaintiff sued her former husband alleging that, when they were still married and living together, defendant falsely told her that he had contracted AIDS (acquired immune deficiency syndrome), and that he wanted her to take their son and go live with relatives in Canada (which she did) so she and the child would not see defendant suffer and die. Plaintiff alleges the false assertion caused her severe distress as she contemplated defendant's impending death, her own likelihood of developing AIDS, and the possibility that their child would become an orphan. In upholding the sufficiency of the complaint, the court said:

"The defendant was undoubtedly correct when he pointed out at oral argument that virtually all dissolutions of marriage involve the infliction of emotional distress. For the tort of intentional infliction of emotional distress to be established, however, the plaintiff must allege and prove conduct considerably more egregious than that experienced in the rough and tumble of everyday life or, for that matter, the everyday dissolution of marriage. * * *

" * * * [T]he court is satisfied that the plaintiff has pleaded a recognizable claim. The court does not doubt that insult, indignity and genuine distress are part and parcel of most, if not all, marital breakups, but there is an enormous difference between these unfortunately routine indignities and a false statement to one's spouse that one has AIDS. The former will doubtless cause sadness and grief, but the latter is likely to cause shock and fright of enormous proportions. The former may now be commonplace in our society, but the latter would, nevertheless, in the language of the Restatement, 'be regarded as atrocious and utterly intolerable in a civilized community.' [Restatement (Second), Torts § 46, comment d.]"

SCHIEFFER v. CATHOLIC ARCHDIOCESE OF OMAHA, 244 Neb. 715, 508 N.W.2d 907 (1993). The complaint alleged that plaintiff, a married woman, entered counseling with her parish priest, defendant Lange, concerning family matters; that Lange made "numerous sexual advances" during pastoral counseling; that he "succeeded in seducing the Plaintiff, and a sexual relationship developed" that went on for seven years; and as a result plaintiff suffered severe and permanent emotional injury and "lost faith in the Catholic Church and in God." The trial court dismissed the suit for failure to state a cause of action.

On appeal the Nebraska Supreme Court held (4–3) that "[a] sexual relationship between two consenting adults is not outrageous conduct such as to give rise to a claim for intentional infliction of emotional distress." The court said "it is a fundamental principle of common law that 'to one who is willing, no wrong is done.' " "What is involved in this case is conduct between consenting adults. * * * The amended petition does allege that the plaintiff was 'vulnerable because of prior emotional problems.' This allegation falls far short of alleging that the plaintiff was incapable of consenting to what took place."

The dissenting opinion argued that plaintiff's consent should not bar her suit as a matter of law. Lange occupied a position of trust; the priest's "duty to plaintiff, given the nature of the counseling relationship, was to help her with family matters"; seduction of plaintiff "would be an obvious breach of that duty." The jury should decide how much weight should be given to consent obtained "by the actions of a fiduciary which constitute overreaching." "Certainly, the fact that the plaintiff here is an adult does not mean that Lange's conduct could not be outrageous."

The dissent added that "here there has been no assertion that Lange's conduct falls within the practices or beliefs of the Catholic Church. Thus, there is no difficult First Amendment issue [of religious freedom] to confront."

PAUL v. WATCHTOWER BIBLE AND TRACT SOCIETY, 819 F.2d 875 (9th Cir.1987). Plaintiff Janice Paul, who had been a devout and active member of the Jehovah's Witness Church, withdrew from the Church in 1975. In Church terminology she became a "disassociated person." In 1981 the

Church's governing body issued a new interpretation of the religion's rules which said that disassociated persons were to be treated the same as persons who had been excommunicated: they should be subjected to "shunning." Thereafter plaintiff's former friends and acquaintances who were Jehovah's Witnesses would not speak to her, have social contact with her, even greet her. Plaintiff brought suit in tort against the governing body alleging that its intentional and "outrageous" conduct—in requiring her to be ostracized—caused her to suffer emotional distress. The trial court granted summary judgment against plaintiff. On appeal, *held*, affirmed. The Jehovah's Witnesses' practice of shunning is "privileged" conduct, "protected under the first amendment of the United States Constitution." "The constitutional guarantee of the free exercise of religion requires that society tolerate the type of harms suffered by Paul as a price well worth paying to safeguard the right of religious difference that all citizens enjoy."

GTE SOUTHWEST, INC. v. BRUCE

Supreme Court of Texas, 1999.
998 S.W.2d 605.

[ABBOTT, Justice.]

In this case we determine whether three GTE Southwest, Incorporated employees may recover damages for intentional infliction of emotional distress based on the workplace conduct of their supervisor. The trial court rendered judgment for the employees on the jury verdict, and the court of appeals affirmed. * * *

Three GTE employees, Rhonda Bruce, Linda Davis, and Joyce Poelstra, sued GTE for intentional infliction of emotional distress premised on the constant humiliating and abusive behavior of their supervisor, Morris Shields. Shields is a former U.S. Army supply sergeant who began working for GTE in 1971. * * *

In May 1991, GTE transferred Shields * * * to Nash, Texas, where he became the supply operations supervisor. The supply department at Nash was small, consisting of two offices and a store room. There were approximately eight employees other than Shields. Bruce, Davis, and Poelstra ("the employees") worked under Shields at the Nash facility. * * * Bruce, Davis, and Poelstra complained to GTE of Shields's conduct, alleging that Shields constantly harassed and intimidated them. The employees complained about Shields's daily use of profanity, short temper, and his abusive and vulgar dictatorial manner. The employees complained that, among other offensive acts, Shields repeatedly yelled, screamed, cursed, and even "charged" at them. In addition, he intentionally humiliated and embarrassed the employees.

GTE investigated these complaints in April 1992, after which GTE issued Shields a "letter of reprimand." After the reprimand, Shields discontinued some of his egregious conduct, but did not end it completely.

Eventually, Bruce, Davis, and Poelstra sought medical treatment for emotional distress caused by Shields's conduct. In March 1994, the employees filed suit, alleging that GTE intentionally inflicted emotional distress on them through Shields. The employees asserted no causes of action other than intentional infliction of emotional distress. The jury awarded $100,000.00 plus prejudgment interest to Bruce, $100,000.00 plus interest to Davis, and $75,000.00 plus interest to Poelstra.

* * *

In determining whether certain conduct is extreme and outrageous, courts consider the context and the relationship between the parties. * * *

In the employment context, some courts have held that a plaintiff's status as an employee should entitle him to a greater degree of protection from insult and outrage by a supervisor with authority over him than if he were a stranger. This approach is based partly on the rationale that, as opposed to most casual and temporary relationships, the workplace environment provides a captive victim and the opportunity for prolonged abuse. [Citations from California, Georgia, Louisiana, and West Virginia omitted.]

In contrast, several courts, including Texas courts, have adopted a strict approach to intentional infliction of emotional distress claims arising in the workplace. These courts rely on the fact that, to properly manage its business, an employer must be able to supervise, review, criticize, demote, transfer, and discipline employees. Although many of these acts are necessarily unpleasant for the employee, an employer must have latitude to exercise these rights in a permissible way, even though emotional distress results. We agree with the approach taken by these courts. [Citations from Arkansas and Texas omitted.]

* * * Thus, to establish a cause of action for intentional infliction of emotional distress in the workplace, an employee must prove the existence of some conduct that brings the dispute outside the scope of an ordinary employment dispute and into the realm of extreme and outrageous conduct. Such extreme conduct exists only in the most unusual of circumstances.

GTE contends that the evidence establishes nothing more than an ordinary employment dispute. To the contrary, the employees produced evidence that, over a period of more than two years, Shields engaged in a pattern of grossly abusive, threatening, and degrading conduct. Shields began regularly using the harshest vulgarity shortly after his arrival at the Nash facility. * * *

More importantly, the employees testified that Shields repeatedly physically and verbally threatened and terrorized them. There was evidence that Shields was continuously in a rage, and that Shields would frequently assault each of the employees by physically charging at them. When doing so, Shields would bend his head down, put his arms straight down by his sides, ball his hands into fists, and walk quickly toward or ''lunge'' at the employees, stopping uncomfortably close to their faces while screaming and yelling. * * *

Bruce also told of an occasion when Shields entered Bruce's office and went into a rage because Davis had left her purse on a chair and Bruce had placed her umbrella on a filing cabinet in the office. Shields yelled and screamed for Bruce to clean up her office. Shields yelled, "If you don't get things picked up in this office, you will not be working for me." He later said that Bruce and Davis would be sent to the unemployment line and "could be replaced by two Kelly girls" that were twenty years old. * * *

Bruce also testified that Shields called her into his office every day and would have her stand in front of him, sometimes for as long as thirty minutes, while Shields simply stared at her. * * *

Shields required Bruce and Davis, both general clerks at GTE, to purchase vacuum cleaners with company funds and to vacuum their offices daily, despite the fact that the company had a cleaning service that performed janitorial services such as vacuuming. The purpose of this seemed not to clean, but to humiliate. * * * Poelstra testified that, after she forgot her paperwork for a driving test, Shields ordered her to wear a post-it note on her shirt that said, "Don't forget your paperwork." * * *

* * *

* * * It is well recognized outside of the employment context that a course of harassing conduct may support liability for intentional infliction of emotional distress. *See, e.g., Duty v. General Fin. Co.,* 154 Tex. 16, 273 S.W.2d 64, 65–66 (1954) (debt collection). In such cases, courts consider the totality of the conduct in determining whether it is extreme and outrageous. *See id.* (analyzing creditor's entire course of conduct, including repetitive threatening phone calls and letters).

Similarly, in the employment context, courts and commentators have almost unanimously recognized that liability may arise when one in a position of authority engages in repeated or ongoing harassment of an employee, if the cumulative quality and quantity of the harassment is extreme and outrageous. * * *

* * *

* * * An employer certainly has much leeway in its chosen methods of supervising and disciplining employees, but terrorizing them is simply not acceptable. If GTE or Shields was dissatisfied with the employees' performance, GTE could have terminated them, disciplined them, or taken some other more appropriate approach to the problem instead of fostering the abuse, humiliation, and intimidation that was heaped on the employees. Accordingly, the trial court properly submitted the issue to the jury, and there was some evidence to support the jury's conclusion that Shields's conduct was extreme and outrageous.

* * *

Generally, a master is vicariously liable for the torts of its servants committed in the course and scope of their employment. This is true even though the employee's tort is intentional when the act, although not specifically authorized by the employer, is closely connected with the servant's authorized duties. * * * Shields's acts, although inappropriate, involved conduct within the scope of his position as the employees' supervisor. GTE admitted as much when it argued that Shields's acts were "mere employment disputes." * * * The jury concluded that Shields's acts were committed in the scope of his employment, and there is some evidence to support this finding. Thus, GTE is liable for Shields's conduct.

* * *

Last, GTE complains about the trial court's admission of expert testimony that Shields's conduct was extreme and outrageous. The employees obtained opinion evidence from three different expert witnesses that Shields's conduct was extreme and outrageous. * * *

The court of appeals held that the trial court's admission of expert testimony on the issue of whether Shields's conduct was extreme and outrageous was error. We agree. * * * [T]o be admissible, expert testimony must generally involve "scientific, technical, or other specialized knowledge" as to which a witness could be qualified as an expert * * * . Where, as here, the issue involves only general knowledge and experience rather than expertise, it is within the province of the jury to decide, and admission of expert testimony on the issue is error.

Nevertheless, the court of appeals correctly concluded that the error was harmless. * * *

[Affirmed.]

Justice OWEN, concurring.

I agree that there is more than a scintilla of evidence to support the jury's finding that Shields intentionally inflicted emotional distress on the plaintiffs. I cannot join the Court's opinion because most of the testimony that the Court recounts is legally insufficient to support the verdict in this case.

* * *

* * * The following conduct is not a basis for sustaining a cause of action for intentional infliction of emotional distress, even when the employees who are upset by the conduct are women:

— cursing, profanity, or "yelling and screaming" when it was not simultaneously accompanied by sexual harassment or physically threatening behavior

— pounding fists on a table when requesting employees "to do things"

— going into "a rage" when employees leave an umbrella or purse on a chair or filing cabinet

— screaming at employees that if they do not "get things picked up" they will be fired

— telling an employee that she would be sent to the unemployment line

— telling an employee that she could be replaced by two Kelly girls * * *

— requiring employees to vacuum their offices daily even though a janitorial service vacuums as well * * *

— telling an employee that she must wear a post-it note that says "don't forget your paperwork."

Most of the foregoing conduct would be offensive and degrading in most circumstances. But it is not " 'so outrageous in character, and so extreme in degree, as to go beyond all possible bounds of decency, and to be regarded as atrocious, and utterly intolerable in a civilized community.' " *Twyman v. Twyman,* 855 S.W.2d 619, 621 (Tex.1993) (quoting Restatement (Second) of Torts § 46 cmt. d (1965)). * * *

The Court's conclusion that there is evidence of intentional infliction of emotional distress because Shields suggested to and even threatened the plaintiffs that they may be discharged or replaced is particularly inconsistent with our prior decisions. We have held that discharging an employee, even when it amounted to wrongful discharge under our laws, did not amount to intentional infliction of emotional distress. *See Southwestern Bell Mobile Sys., Inc. v. Franco,* 971 S.W.2d 52, 54–55 (Tex.1998); *see also Wornick Co. v. Casas,* 856 S.W.2d 732, 735–36 (Tex.1993). We have said that firing an employee in front of her co-workers and then having her escorted off the premises by a security guard was not the type of conduct that could support a finding of intentional infliction of emotional distress. *See Wornick Co.,* 856 S.W.2d at 736. I fail to see how screaming at a plaintiff that she may be fired is conduct of a degree and character that is actionable when actually firing an employee in the presence of her co-workers and physically escorting her off the premises with uniformed security guards is not.

————

MEYERS v. HOT BAGELS FACTORY, INC., 131 Ohio App.3d 82, 721 N.E.2d 1068 (1999). Plaintiff, Kathleen Meyers, met friends for a sandwich at a local restaurant. The proprietor, John Marx, came over and asked Meyers, in a loud voice, "Are you a good fuck?" As Meyers prepared to leave, Marx said, "I can see you have a nice firm ass. You must really be a good fuck." The jury found intentional infliction of emotional distress (IIED), and awarded $15,000 in compensatory damages and $50,000 in punitive damages. On appeal, *held,* affirmed. "Ohio recognizes two types of actions for intentional or willful misconduct resulting in emotional distress," and the conditions of both types of liability are met here. The first type is general liability for IIED, which is established when "the case is one in which the recitation of facts to an average member of the community would arouse his resentment against the actor, and lead him to exclaim, 'Outrageous!' " (quoting from Restatement (Second) of Torts § 46 comment d).

"Ohio also recognizes an actionable form of emotional distress in cases where the business relationship of the plaintiff and defendant creates a situation where the plaintiff is entitled to protection by the defendant. * * * Cases that have recognized this type of willful or intentional infliction of emotional distress date from 1911 to the present and include the removal of a ten-year-old child from a streetcar at night because the only coin he had for the fare was mutilated [1911] and a hotel's refusal to provide a guest access to his room because he had HIV [1994].

"Liability is premised on public policy. The defendant, by 'carrying on a business of a public nature, is by law charged with the duty of extending to his guests "respectful and decent treatment" * * *.' Magruder, Mental and Emotional Disturbance in the Law of Torts (1936), 49 Harv.L.Rev. 1033, 1051–1052. In this situation, the insults may amount to less than extreme outrage in that the special relationship compels a higher than normal duty of care. Further it is the willful conduct of the defendant and not necessarily the seriousness of the emotional distress that gives rise to liability under this type of case."

BROWER v. ACKERLEY, 88 Wash.App. 87, 943 P.2d 1141 (1997). Claiming intentional infliction of emotional distress (IIED), Brower alleged that a series of harassing telephone calls made by defendants caused him to experience feelings of fear and insecurity, as well as sleeplessness and inability to concentrate. Defendants sought dismissal on the ground that Brower's alleged distress was not sufficiently "severe." *Held*, for plaintiff. The court first defined the tort of IIED in terms of three elements: "(1) extreme and outrageous conduct; (2) intentional or reckless infliction of emotional distress; and (3) actual result to the plaintiff of severe emotional distress." Then the court said:

" * * * When the conduct offered to establish the tort's first element is not extreme, a court must withhold the case from a jury notwithstanding proof of intense emotional suffering. The situation is different when the alleged conduct sufficiently satisfies the first two elements, outrageous and extreme conduct, and intentional or reckless infliction of emotional harm. * * * [W]e hold a case of outrage should ordinarily go to a jury so long as the court determines the plaintiff's alleged damages are more than 'mere annoyance, inconvenience, or normal embarrassment' that is an ordinary fact of life.

"Our holding is consistent * * * with the Restatement. According to comment j in the Restatement, severe distress 'must be proved; but in many cases the extreme and outrageous character of the defendant's conduct is in itself important evidence that the distress has existed.' [Restatement (Second) of Torts § 46 Comment *j*.]"

MILLER v. WILLBANKS, 8 S.W.3d 607 (Tenn. 1999). The Millers, parents of a newborn infant, were told that their baby girl, who remained in the hospital for postnatal care, had been diagnosed as suffering from "drug withdrawal syndrome." Mrs. Miller insisted that she had taken no drugs, and submitted to a drug test, which came back negative. But the pediatrician in charge reaffirmed his unsubstantiated suspicion of drug use. False rumors that the infant was a "drug baby" circulated through the hospital; social workers questioned the Millers about their nonexistent drug use. The Millers brought suit against the pediatrician and the hospital asserting intentional infliction of emotional distress (IIED). The IIED action was dismissed by the trial judge "due to the plaintiffs' lack of expert evidence to support their claims of serious mental injury." On appeal to the Tennessee Supreme Court, *held*, for plaintiffs. The court said that, for IIED to be made out, the conduct complained of must be (1) intentional or reckless, (2) outrageous, and (3) "must result in serious mental injury to the plaintiff."

"A majority of courts * * * have concluded that expert proof is generally not necessary to establish the existence of a serious mental injury. The flagrant and outrageous nature of the defendant's conduct, according to these courts, adds weight to a plaintiff's claim and affords more assurance that the claim is serious. Moreover, expert testimony is not essential because other reliable forms of evidence, including physical manifestations of distress and subjective testimony, are available."

" * * * The kinds of emotional distress that may be remedied include 'fright, horror, grief, shame, humiliation, embarrassment, anger, chagrin, disappointment, worry, and nausea.' Restatement (Second) of Torts § 46 cmt. j (1965). Such emotional responses are not so esoteric that they occupy a dimension beyond the cognitive grasp of the average layperson and are therefore accessible only to the expert."

RESTATEMENT OF TORTS, THIRD: LIABILITY FOR PHYSICAL HARM (BASIC PRINCIPLES)
Tent. Draft No. 1 (March 28, 2001).

§ 5. Liability For Intentional Physical Harms

An actor who intentionally causes physical harm is subject to liability for that harm.

Comment:

a. An umbrella rule. The rule of liability in § 5 provides a framework that encompasses many of the specific torts described in much more detail in the Restatement Second of Torts. Among these specific torts in the Restatement Second are harmful battery (§ 13), trespass on land (§ 158), trespass to chattels (§ 217), and conversion by destruction or alteration (§ 226).

The general statement of liability in this section highlights the point that tort law treats the intentional infliction of physical harm differently than it treats the intentional causation of economic loss or the intentional infliction of emotional distress. In cases involving physical harm, proof of intent provides a basic case for liability, although various affirmative defenses may be available. However, as the focus shifts from physical harm to other forms of harm, the intent to cause harm may be an important but not a sufficient condition for liability. * * * When the defendant either intentionally or recklessly causes the plaintiff to suffer emotional distress, to justify a recovery the plaintiff must further establish that the defendant's conduct is "extreme and outrageous" and that the plaintiff's emotional distress is "severe." See Restatement Second, Torts § 46.

* * * Tort law [also] recognizes a broad rule of negligence liability in cases involving physical harm. See § 6. [The text of § 6 appears below.]

c. The continuing authoritativeness of the Restatement Second of Torts. Each of the specific torts recognized in the Restatement Second is developed in that Restatement in considerable detail. * * * [T]he Restatement Second remains largely authoritative in explaining the details of the specific torts encompassed by § 5 and in specifying the elements and limitations of the various affirmative defenses that might be available.

§ 6. Liability For Negligent Physical Harms

An actor who negligently causes physical harm is subject to liability for that harm.

Chapter 4

INTERFERENCE WITH PROPERTY

The three sections of this chapter look briefly at a cluster of doctrinal topics: liability for conversion of personal property; the land-related torts of trespass and nuisance; privileges of public and private necessity. The first topic introduces the idea of proprietary dominion. The second section throws light on the basic tort conception of "intent," as it shows the sense in which trespass to land and nuisance are "intentional" torts. The third segment examines possible justifications for otherwise tortious interferences with property entitlement. All three bring to the fore the connection between tort and property right, a deep connection that runs through tort law concerning physical harm, and comes into central focus again in Chapter 18.

SECTION A.   CONVERSION

The materials of this brief section, on the tort of conversion, begin to develop a vocabulary for thinking about interferences with interests in property. A clear case of conversion involves wrongful appropriation of the personal property of another. While the rest of the chapter concentrates mainly on interferences with possession or use of land, rather than chattels, the basic proprietary conceptions that underlie liability for conversion are pertinent throughout.

ZASLOW v. KROENERT
Supreme Court of California, in Bank, 1946.
29 Cal.2d 541, 176 P.2d 1.

[Action for trespass and conversion by one cotenant against another cotenant and her agent, for taking possession of the house owned in common, excluding the plaintiff from the house and putting his furniture in storage. Plaintiff had judgment for the full value of the furniture and defendants appeal.]

EDMONDS, J. [after stating the facts and dealing with the question of damages for the ouster from the building]. Stated generally, "Conversion is any act of dominion wrongfully exerted over another's personal property in denial of or inconsistent with his rights therein." [Citations omitted.] The liability of one in possession of real property for the conversion of personal property which he finds upon it, depends, in most cases, upon a determination of whether the conduct of the defendant indicates an assumption of control or ownership over the goods. It is clear that, under some circumstances, refusal of one in possession of real property to permit, upon demand, the owner of chattels which were left there to remove his goods, constitutes conversion. And if the possessor of the real estate appropriates the chattels to his own use in obvious defiance of the owner's rights, he is liable to the owner for the conversion of them.

However, every failure to deliver is not such a serious interference with the owner's dominion that the defendant should be required to pay the full value of the goods. (See Prosser on Torts, p. 106). And the act of taking possession of a building and locking it does not, of itself, constitute a conversion of the personal property therein. Nor does the permission of the possessor of the realty by which personal property is allowed to remain upon the premises make him liable for the goods.

In the present case, the court found only that Mrs. Kroenert and Chapman "took and carried away all the personal property and effects" of Zaslow, such taking being without his consent, express or implied. Admittedly, what Chapman did in this regard was to place the goods in storage: there is no evidence tending to prove that either he or Mrs. Kroenert otherwise exerted any dominion over Zaslow's personal property in denial of or inconsistent with his rights. If, upon demand for the return of the chattels, they had prevented the removal of the goods, such acts would have constituted evidence of a conversion. But here the controversy between the parties concerned the occupancy of the house; no demand was made for the return of the personal property. While there is no evidence showing any conduct amounting to conversion, there is proof that Chapman, as the agent of Mrs. Kroenert, acted as custodian of the goods, recognizing Zaslow's complete title and right to them. The defendants did not use the goods. About a month and one-half after Mrs. Kroenert, by Chapman, took possession of the realty, she stated in a letter either received by or shown to Zaslow, that he could secure possession of his personal property by applying at the attorney's office. Zaslow neither said nor did anything in response thereto.

Where the conduct complained of does not amount to a substantial interference with possession or the right thereto, but consists of intermeddling with or use of or damages to the personal property, the owner has a cause of action for trespass or case, and may recover only the actual damages suffered by reason of the impairment of the property or the loss of its use. See Prosser on Torts, p. 102. As Zaslow was a cotenant and had the right of possession of the realty, which included the right to keep his personal property thereon, Chapman's act of placing the goods in storage, although not constituting the assertion of ownership and a substantial interference with possession to the extent of a conversion, amounted to an intermeddling. Therefore, Zaslow is entitled to actual damages in an amount sufficient to compensate him for any impairment of the property or loss of its use. But as the evidence shows $3,500 as the highest value placed upon the goods and it is undisputed that they were not damaged while in storage for about four months, the amount awarded by the judgment has no support in the evidence.

For these reasons, the judgment is reversed with directions to the trial court to redetermine the amount of damages caused by the ouster and the trespass to the personal property.

PEARSON v. DODD, 410 F.2d 701 (D.C.Cir.1969). Plaintiff-appellee, a United States senator, sued defendants-appellants, newspaper columnists, for invasion of privacy and conversion stemming from their exposure of his alleged misdeeds. On interlocutory appeal, the court affirmed the district court's denial of summary judgment for invasion of privacy and reversed the grant of summary judgment for conversion. With respect to the latter issue, it said:

"The District Court ruled that appellants' receipt and subsequent use of photocopies of documents which appellants knew had been removed from appellee's files without authorization established appellants' liability for conversion. We conclude that appellants are not guilty of conversion on the facts shown.

* * *

"The most distinctive feature of conversion is its measure of damages, which is the value of the goods converted. The theory is that the 'converting' defendant has in some way treated the goods as if they were his own, so that the plaintiff can properly ask the court to decree a forced sale of the property from the rightful possessor to the converter.

"Because of this stringent measure of damages, it has long been recognized that not every wrongful interference with the personal property of another is a conversion. Where the intermeddling falls short of the complete or very substantial deprivation of possessory rights in the property, the tort committed is not conversion, but the lesser wrong of trespass to chattels.

"The Second Restatement of Torts has marked the distinction by defining conversion as: ' * * * [A]n intentional exercise of dominion or control over a chattel which so seriously interferes with the right of another to control it that the actor may justly be required to pay the other the full value of the chattel.'[29] Less serious interferences fall under the Restatement's definition of trespass.[30]

"The difference is more than a semantic one. The measure of damages in trespass is not the whole value of the property interfered with, but rather the actual diminution in its value caused by the interference. More impor-

---

29. Restatement (Second) of Torts § 222A(1) (1965).

30. Id., § 217: "A trespass to a chattel may be committed by intentionally (a) dispossessing another of the chattel, or (b) using or intermeddling with a chattel in the possession of another."

tant for this case, a judgment for conversion can be obtained with only nominal damages, whereas liability for trespass to chattels exists only on a showing of actual damage to the property interfered with. * * *

"It is clear that on the agreed facts appellants committed no conversion of the physical documents taken from appellee's files. Those documents were removed from the files at night, photocopied, and returned to the files undamaged before office operations resumed in the morning. Insofar as the documents' value to appellee resided in their usefulness as records of the business of his office, appellee was clearly not substantially deprived of his use of them."

[The court then held that the ideas and information taken by copying the files did not constitute property subject to protection by a suit in conversion.]

MOORE v. REGENTS OF THE UNIVERSITY OF CALIFORNIA, 51 Cal.3d 120, 271 Cal.Rptr. 146, 793 P.2d 479 (1990). Moore's leukemia was treated at a university medical center. His doctor removed blood and tissue for diagnostic purposes; his enlarged spleen was removed surgically; after the operation, on several occasions, more blood and tissue were withdrawn. Later Moore discovered that, all the while, his doctor, in collaboration with a researcher at the center, had been using cells from his body in a project of their own. Moore's cells had abnormal properties which the doctor and the researcher exploited in order to develop a "cell line." They succeeded and, together with the Regents of the university, obtained a patent on a cell line based on Moore's white blood cells. The cell line is able to produce large quantities of a type of protein that has potential therapeutic value.

Moore brought suit against the doctor, the researcher, the Regents, and two companies with which agreements for commercial development of the cell line had been reached. Plaintiff claims that "defendants' unauthorized use of his cells constitutes a conversion," and he asserts "a proprietary interest in each of the products that any of the defendants might ever create from his cells or the patented cell line." The trial court found no cause of action for conversion. The Court of Appeal reversed. In the California Supreme Court, *held*, no conversion. The court explained:

"[Moore's claim,] which would affect medical research of importance to all of society, implicates policy concerns far removed from the traditional, two-party ownership disputes in which the law of conversion arose. Invoking a tort theory originally used to determine whether the loser or the finder of a horse had the better title, Moore claims ownership of the results of socially important medical research * * *.

"Since Moore clearly did not expect to retain possession of his cells following their removal, to sue for their conversion he must have retained an ownership interest in them. But * * * [n]either the Court of Appeal's opinion, the parties' briefs, nor our research discloses a case holding that a person retains a sufficient interest in excised cells to support a cause of action for conversion. We do not find this surprising, since the laws governing such things as human tissues, transplantable organs, blood, fetuses, pituitary glands, corneal tissue, and dead bodies deal with human biological materials as objects sui generis, regulating their disposition to achieve policy goals rather than abandoning them to the general law of personal property. * * *

"Finally, the subject matter of the Regents' patent—the patented cell line and the products derived from it—cannot be Moore's property. * * * Federal law permits the patenting of organisms that represent the product of 'human ingenuity,' but not naturally occurring organisms. Human cell lines are patentable because '[l]ong-term adaptation and growth of human tissues and cells in culture is difficult' * * * and the probability of success is low. * * * Thus, Moore's allegations that he owns the cell line and the products derived from it are inconsistent with the patent, which constitutes an authoritative determination that the cell line is the product of invention."

SECTION B.   TRESPASS AND NUISANCE

This section introduces the land-related torts of trespass to land and nuisance. The materials show the nature of the interests protected by the two torts. Trespass is an offense to ownership rights; in the conventional statement, it is interference with the interest in exclusive possession of land. The usual nuisance is detrimental fallout, arising from defendant's activity, which causes harm to a nearby occupant; it is interference with the interest in use and enjoyment of land. (The latter characterization pertains to "private" nuisance, the focus below; "public" nuisance is addressed in Section B of Chapter 18.)

What follows is an initial look at the two torts—they are revisited in Chapter 18, which examines nuisance doctrine and policy in some detail. The object of the present section is to show the basic elements of trespass and of nuisance, and in particular to show the sense in which each is an "intentional" tort. What sort of intent—what state of mind—on the part of a defendant is a necessary condition of trespass liability? What sort of intentionality is involved in nuisance? These inquiries lead to the conceptual discovery that the two torts are both "intentional" and, in some applications, "strict." The notion of strict liability for intentional interference seems paradoxical, since torts may be either fault-based or strict, and intent seems an index of fault. The present section deepens understanding of both intentionality and strictness.

The section closes with discussion of injunctions in nuisance situations. This is the first time in the casebook that the important remedy of injunction is encountered.

SMITH v. STONE
King's Bench, 1648. Style, 65.

Smith brought an action of trespass against Stone, pedibus ambulando. The defendant pleads this special plea in justification, viz., that he was carried upon the land of the plaintiff by force and violence of others, and was not there voluntarily, which is the same trespass for which the plaintiff brings his action. The plaintiff demurs to this plea.

In this case, ROLL, J., said, that it is the trespass of the party that carried the defendant upon the land, and not the trespass of the defendant: as he that drives my cattle into another man's land is the trespasser against him, and not I, who am owner of the cattle.

GILBERT v. STONE
King's Bench, 1648. Style, 72.

Gilbert brought an action of trespass quare clausum fregit, and taking of a gelding against Stone. The defendant pleads that he for fear of his life, and wounding of twelve armed men, who threatened to kill him if he did not the fact, went into the house of the plaintiff, and took the gelding. The plaintiff demurred to this plea. ROLL, J. This is no plea to justifie the defendant; for I may not do a trespass to one for fear of threatenings of another, for by this means the party injured shall have no satisfaction, for he cannot have it of the party that threatened. Therefore let the plaintiff have his judgment.

———

RAGER v. McCLOSKEY, 305 N.Y. 75, 111 N.E.2d 214 (1953); noted, 20 Brooklyn L.Rev. 122. The complaint alleged that the deputy sheriff, having lawfully entered plaintiff's law office to serve process on plaintiff, remained though repeatedly told to leave. *Held*, complaint stated a cause of action. "A trespass may consist, not only in making an unauthorized entry upon private property, but in refusing to leave after permission to remain has been withdrawn."

CARTAN v. CRUZ CONSTRUCTION CO., 89 N.J.Super. 414, 215 A.2d 356 (1965). One who has permission to be on land becomes a trespasser by doing something that he was not authorized to do.

COPELAND v. HUBBARD BROADCASTING, INC., 526 N.W.2d 402 (Minn.Ct.App.1995). KSTP television aired an investigative report about local veterinarians. "One of the veterinarians, Dr. Sam Ulland, treated Greg and Betty Copeland's cat. Before [a] visit to the Copeland home, Dr. Ulland received the Copelands' permission to bring along a student interested in a career in veterinary medicine. The student, Patty Johnson, did not tell the Copelands or Dr. Ulland that, in addition to being a part-time student * * *, she was also an employee of KSTP and was videotaping Dr. Ulland's practice methods." The broadcast report included two brief video segments filmed inside the Copelands' house. The Copelands sued KSTP for trespass. The district court granted KSTP's motion for summary judgment. On appeal, *held*, reversed. "Courts in other jurisdictions have recognized trespass as a remedy when broadcasters use secret cameras for newsgathering."

"A trespass is committed when a person enters the land of another without consent. * * * Consent may be geographically or temporally restricted." "Minnesota case law establishes that an entrant may become a trespasser by moving beyond the possessor's invitation or permission."

CLEVELAND PARK CLUB v. PERRY

Municipal Court of Appeals for the District of Columbia, 1960.
165 A.2d 485.

ROVER, Chief Judge. [Footnotes omitted.]

The Cleveland Park Club, a private social club which operates a swimming pool for the benefit of its members, sued a nine-year-old boy for damages caused by him. While playing in the water the child swam to the bottom of the pool, a depth of seven feet, and according to his own testimony raised a metal cover over a drain opening and thinking that there was no suction at the time, inserted a tennis ball into the pipe, then replaced the cover. When he returned to get the ball it was gone. As it developed, the ball passed into a critical part of the pipe and caused failure of proper drainage, forcing the club to close the pool and make repairs. The club sued for the cost of these repairs, and from an adverse judgment brings this appeal.

The suit was based on the theory of trespass and the club requested a directed verdict, maintaining that from the child's own admissions a trespass had been committed and that he should be held liable without regard to his age. Counsel for the child resisted that contention by stating he was not willing to concede the right of the club to proceed on a willful tort theory as distinguished from negligence where the age of the child would have a direct bearing on the applicable law. The court ruled that it believed the age of the child was a factor to be considered in the case and denied the club's motion for a directed verdict.

It was also the position of the child's counsel that the boy could not have been a trespasser because the club's lifeguards had on occasion seen boys playing with the drain cover and had failed to take adequate steps to prevent this. The argument advanced was that failure to keep children away from the drain constituted an implied consent to the child's act, and if the child did not act beyond the scope of the club's invitation then he could not be classified a trespasser.

In submitting the case to the jury the court stated that the issue was whether or not the child was a trespasser. The instructions given to the jury were primarily concerned with the scope of the invitation and whether the club had consented to the purported trespass, except that in discussing the question of trespass it used the following language:

"In determining whether or not the defendant is a trespasser, you shall also keep in mind the rule that in cases of tort, * * * liability attaches regardless of age, where the nature of the act is such that children of like age would realize its injurious consequences."

Before commenting on the sufficiency of the instructions we believe that the applicable law, supported by the authorities, is that a child is liable for his torts as if he were an adult, except where his tender years preclude him from framing the mental attitudes necessary to complete the tort in question. In cases of tort which require malice as an essential element, for example, a very young child may be considered as a matter of law incapable of entertaining the requisite evil intent and no liability would attach to his act. Also, in the broad area of negligent torts, the age of a child may prove to be a mitigating factor for he is there held liable only where he has failed to exercise a degree of care equal to that which governs the ordinary child of comparable age, knowledge and experience.

Where, however, the cause of action is based on trespass the cases hold unequivocally that since recovery under that theory is based on force and resultant damage regardless of the intent to injure, a child of the most tender years is absolutely liable to the full extent of the injuries inflicted. The rationale of this position is that the purpose of civil law looks to compensation for the injured party regardless of the intent on the part of the trespasser. While the age of the child will not protect him from liability if his act is denominated a trespass, yet as trespass is an intentional tort an initial determination must be made whether the child concerned formed the intent to do the physical act which released the harmful force. It cannot be said as a matter of law that a child of any age is incapable of intending to do a physical act, and whether he had such intent or whether his action was the result of negligence is a factual question where the child's age, experience and knowledge may also be taken into consideration.

Returning to the instructions given in this case, we believe that two distinct factual issues were intended to be submitted to the jury. The first was whether the child was capable of forming the necessary intent to perform the physical act that released the harmful force, and thus be classified as a trespasser. According to the authorities, this question, which is basically a determination of whether the tort was intentional or negligent, takes into account the child's age. The second factual question, assuming that the first was resolved by a finding that the tort was intentional, was whether the consent of the club vitiated the effect of the intentional act; and the outcome of this issue cannot depend in any way on the age of the child. We are of the opinion that the instructions of the court did not distinguish for the benefit of the jury the duality of these issues, and when age may be considered in one and not the other. The instructions began with a definition of a trespasser and the effect of consent, continued with the quoted instruction which is erroneous in itself as it does not point out to the jury that they are merely to ascertain if the child possessed the capability to perform the physical act intentionally without regard to knowledge of possible injurious consequences, and blended back to instructions concerning the scope of the invitation.

On the ambiguity and error in the instructions alone we believe that the club is entitled to a new trial, but we think an additional comment must be made in view of the circumstances of this case. In a case where plaintiff relies on a theory of intentional tort in order to avoid the age factor of the child which would weigh heavily in a negligence case, we have noted that the courts refuse to find as a matter of law that a child of tender years is incapable of committing the physical act which caused the injury, and generally leave the presence or absence of such intent to be resolved by the jury. Such cases usually involve a simple, uncomplicated act on the part of the child. We do not think the converse of the rule necessarily follows, that is, we do not think that it could never be held as a matter of law that a particular child was not fully capable of entertaining the requisite intent where the evidence was overwhelming. Where, as here, the act of the child is comprised of several rather difficult interrelated steps, having but one obvious objective in mind we think it unrealistic to suppose such behavior could be the result of negligence. Again we should point out that the intent controlling is the intent to complete the physical act and not the intent to produce injurious consequences, for in relying on the intentional tort of trespass the latter is irrelevant.

We conclude that the court was correct in not directing a verdict for the club as the issue of consent was properly a jury question. But insofar as the nature of the child's act is concerned we hold it was clearly intentional, and this issue should not have been submitted to the jury at all. Therefore, retrial of this cause should be confined to the issue of consent. We approve of the disposition made by the court on other issues assigned by the club as error.

Reversed for further proceedings not inconsistent with this opinion.

———

SOUTHERN COUNTIES ICE CO. v. RKO RADIO PICTURES, INC., 39 F.Supp. 157 (S.D.Cal.1941). Action for the loss by fire of plaintiff's building during the time when defendant had taken possession of it, mistakenly believing it to be property on which it had permission to erect a set. The trial judge found that the defendant's employees smoked on the set, that they departed and left the building unguarded at five o'clock, that it was destroyed between seven thirty and eight o'clock, and that "defendant's acts were the proximate cause of loss." *Held*, judgment for plaintiff, alternate grounds for decision being (1) negligence and (2) liability without negligence. "Where one exercises complete dominion over the land or personal property of another, however unwittingly, and during the period of his use thereof a loss or damage occurs, he should be held to act, because of the invasion, at his peril and to be responsible for any loss or damage, even though due to an irresistible or extraordinary force, and even though the event was entirely unexpected." In cases of loss by fire, "[t]he language of causation is used but the result of the unlawful use may have been entirely unexpected and unanticipated since no direct proof of the relation of the fire lighted by a trespasser to that which caused the loss, is required."

LONGENECKER v. ZIMMERMAN, 175 Kan. 719, 267 P.2d 543 (1954). Action for trespass. Defendant, believing that cedar trees near the property line were on her side of the line, had them topped, trimmed and cleaned of bagworms. The trial court instructed the jury that defendant's motive was immaterial and that she was liable for such damages, if any, as plaintiff had sustained. Upon a general verdict for defendant, judgment was entered and plaintiff appealed. *Held*, reversed for new trial. "From every direct invasion of the person or property of another, the law infers some damage, without proof of actual injury. In an action of trespass the plaintiff is always entitled to at least nominal damages, even though he was actually benefited by the act of the defendant."

RANDALL v. SHELTON, 293 S.W.2d 559 (Ky.1956). Plaintiff, while walking in her front yard, was hit by a stone thrown from the highway by a passing truck of the defendant. *Held*, citing Restatement of Torts, Sec. 166, that except where an actor is engaged in extrahazardous activity, an unintentional and non-negligent entry on land in the possession of another or causing a thing or third person to enter the land does not subject actor to liability.

MARGOSIAN v. UNITED STATES AIRLINES, INC., 127 F.Supp. 464 (E.D.N.Y.1955). Owner of property on which airline crashed brought action against airline company. *Held*, for plaintiff on a summary judgment as to the issue of liability, leaving the amount of damages to be determined by jury. Court concluded that where there is no intentional act there can be no trespass, but the intent with which an act is done is by no means the exclusive test of liability.

SCRIBNER v. SUMMERS, 84 F.3d 554 (2d Cir.1996). For many years, up to 1990, defendant operated a steel-treating facility on a site bordering plaintiffs' property. The facility used furnaces which leave a sludge residue containing barium chloride. Defendant periodically took the furnaces outside the building and washed them down. Residue flowed into a drainage ditch that ran downhill to an area adjacent to plaintiffs' property. In 1986 barium was declared a hazardous waste by New York environmental authorities. In the early 1990's plaintiffs discovered that their property was contaminated with defendant's barium. They brought suit for damages alleging that defendant "trespassed on their property because of the migration or leaching of barium particles across" the property line. The trial court found no trespass because "[t]here is no evidence [that defendant] intended the water used in [the] cleaning process to enter plaintiffs' land." On appeal, *held*, reversed. Citing Phillips v. Sun Oil Co., 307 N.Y. 328, 121 N.E.2d 249 (1954), the court said:

"In determining whether [defendant] had the requisite intent for trespass under New York law, * * * the appropriate standard is whether [defendant]: (i) 'intended the act which amounts to or produces the unlawful invasion,' and (ii) 'had good reason to know or expect that subterranean and other conditions were such that there would be passage [of the contaminated water] from defendant's to plaintiff's land.' Phillips, 307 N.Y. at 331."

The appellate court concluded that defendant "is liable in trespass for the damage caused." Defendant "knew that contamination was 'substantially certain to result' from its conduct," given the lay of the plaintiffs' land, "located at a lower elevation level."

Robert Frost counseled that "good fences make good neighbors." [Robert Frost, "Mending Wall."] Alas, if only Mr. Frost had fashioned a solution to migrating barium.

WHEAT v. FREEMAN COAL MINING CORP.

Appellate Court of Illinois, Fifth District, 1974.
23 Ill.App.3d 14, 319 N.E.2d 290.

[Action for damages for interference with use and enjoyment of a 37½ acre farm owned by plaintiffs, Leon and Helen Wheat, resulting from defendant's operation of a coal mine. Plaintiffs' home was a four-room frame house without plumbing. They raised popcorn on the farm, having owned the tract since 1952 and having lived on it until 1966. This action concerned damages for the years 1963–66. The defendant began operating its Orient #5 mine on land west of plaintiffs' home "around 1962." Defendant constructed a pond for use in separating impurities from saleable coal, building a wall around the pond by piling up refuse from its mining operations. Plaintiffs claim that defendant's operations caused large amounts of coal dust and smoke to enter their property; that the dust interfered with their water supply, infested their food, clothing and furniture, and damaged the exterior of their house; that the combustible materials in the retaining wall burned, emitting noxious gases that interfered with the use of plaintiffs' home. The trial court entered judgment for plaintiffs for $12,000 upon a jury verdict, and defendant appealed.]

EBERSPACHER, Justice.

* * *

At the outset, it should be emphasized that this was not a suit for an injunction restraining defendant's activities. In such cases, a stronger showing will be required of plaintiffs with regard to the unreasonableness of defendant's activities and the harm suffered by plaintiffs. (Restatement of the Law of Torts, Section 822.) Our courts have adopted the Restatement approach to the law of nuisance.

Defendant contends that there was no evidence that indicated that its conduct was intentional and unreasonable under the test embraced in Section 822 of the Restatement of the Law of Torts. "Intentional" for purposes of liability under Section 822 is defined as including knowledge that the invasion of another's interest is resulting or substantially certain to result. There is support in the record that defendant would know that some dust and smoke would be carried over to neighboring lands. Defendant's witness, Harry Treadwell, testified that the defendant had been informed of the damage being done to plaintiffs by the operations of the mine.

The determination of whether defendant's conduct has been unreasonable is a question particularly suited for a jury, especially where there is evidence that damage has occurred. Plaintiffs' witnesses testified that some smoke and coal dust were constantly emitted from the mine and entered into plaintiffs' house. * * *

* * *

It is apparent from this evidence elicited from disinterested witnesses that plaintiffs suffered certain unreasonable harm. It is proof which, when viewed in its aspects most favorable to the plaintiffs, tends to prove the charge of their complaint. * * *

Defendant relies heavily on Gardner v. International Shoe Company, 319 Ill.App. 416, 49 N.E.2d 328, aff'd 386 Ill. 418, 54 N.E.2d 482. In that case, judgment for the plaintiffs was reversed where it appeared that the odors emanating from defendant's tannery were necessarily incident to its operation, that the tannery was properly operated, and that plaintiffs were not substantially injured. It appeared that disinterested witnesses had not found the odors particularly offensive. The Appellate Court said, "In the instant case, we have nothing more than unpleasant and disagreeable odors, and those only occasionally perhaps sickening to a few who seem to be unduly sensitive or might we say allergic to such smells." (319 Ill.App. at 428, 49 N.E.2d at 332.) This situation is distinguished from the instant case where plaintiffs' evidence amply supported allegations of continuing offensive odors and physical damage to their home.

The instant case is similar to Patterson v. Peabody Coal Co., 3 Ill.App.2d 311, 122 N.E.2d 48. This was an action by a farmer based on private nuisance in the operation of a coal washer and drier in a mining community. The washer and drier were located about one quarter of a mile from plaintiff's premises. The court there held that where evidence established a substantial deposit of coal dust on plaintiff's premises, the trial court was correct in submitting the question of nuisance to the jury.

The court in *Patterson* said,

"Turning now to the case at bar we think it is distinguished from the *Gardner* case on the issue of the substantiality of the invasion. Here we have a physical substance deposited on plaintiffs' premises in quantity and with frequency. On the other hand we have no doubt of the suitability of the location of defendant's business. It is in a mining community and the refining of the product is necessary to market it. Nor do we have any question of the utility and importance to the public of coal mining and processing. The deposit of dust on plaintiff's premises however seems to be in sufficient quantity, as well as duration, to justify submission of the case to the jury." (3 Ill.App.2d at 317, 122 N.E.2d at 52).

It appears that these circumstances are indistinguishable from those of the present case. The court in *Patterson* apparently laid great stress on the fact of physical injury to plaintiff's premises. The same type of physical injury is present here and makes this case proper for jury determination. The fact of physical injury, amply attested to by disinterested witnesses, makes the issue of whether or not the invasion was unreasonable a jury question.

Defendant cites *Patterson* as holding that a burning gob pile is not "intentional" as a matter of law. The court in *Patterson* found this was not "intentional" because it was caused by spontaneous combustion, and, therefore, was not certain to occur. The evidence showed that defendant had done all in its power to stop the burning and that such burning was an occasional occurrence, causing no substantial injury to plaintiff. (3 Ill.App.2d 311 at 317, 122 N.E.2d 48.) It does not appear that the *Patterson* case was holding, as a matter of law, that a burning gob pile may never constitute a nuisance. The court seems to be holding, that, under the conditions there present, it was not an intentional nuisance. Therefore, a similar holding is not required where, as in the instant case, defendant knew of the burning and did nothing to stop it or where injury was more substantial to plaintiff. Witnesses for plaintiffs here testified that the burning was constant and the odors emitted were severe. It may be noted that defendant's engineer testified that defendant knew spontaneous combustion is likely to result from a gob pile, and, nevertheless, placed gob near plaintiffs' home. The issue of whether defendant's actions constituted an intentional and unreasonable invasion of plaintiffs' enjoyment of their home was properly left to the jury.

In Feder v. Perry Coal Co. (1935), 279 Ill.App. 314, the court held that one has a natural right to have the air over his premises reasonably free from impurities and while defendant has a right to use his property in such a way as he may choose, he has no right to substantially injure plaintiff by casting gas, fumes, dust on his premises.

The issue, as defendant correctly points out, is whether the injury caused to plaintiffs by the alleged nuisance is intentional and unreasonable, weighing the gravity of the injury to plaintiffs against the utility of defendant's conduct. In its opening statement, defendant admitted that some smoke and dust are natural incidents of coal mining and that they are certain to occur. This would seem to indicate that defendant's conduct was intentional within the meaning of the Restatement rule. Since plaintiffs introduced evidence of substantial injury, it became a jury question as to whether or not the injury was unreasonable. There was ample proof to sustain the jury's finding for plaintiffs. Therefore, a judgment notwithstanding the verdict was improper and defendant's motion was properly denied.

* * *

Defendant objects to the exclusion of its evidence regarding the value of plaintiffs' premises. The measure of damages for nuisance is not the fair market value of plaintiffs' land, but rather the damages are measured by the discomfort and the deprivation of the healthful use and comforts of the plaintiffs' home. There is no fixed rule as to damages in such an action. The amount awarded must be left to the sound discretion of the jury in view of the fact of a particular case. Market value is not the proper measure of damages in such an action. Since the measure of damages was not the fair market value of the land, the court did not err in excluding such damages. [Citations omitted.]

* * *

Accordingly, the judgment of the trial court is affirmed.

————

WASHINGTON SUBURBAN SANITARY COMMN. v. CAE–LINK CORP., 330 Md. 115, 622 A.2d 745 (1993). In a nuisance case involving noxious odors emitted by a sewage treatment facility, *held*, that neighboring landowners do not have to prove unreasonable operation of the facility in order to recover damages. "Maryland has long adhered to the rule that proof of nuisance focuses not on the possible negligence of the defendant but on whether there has been unreasonable interference with the plaintiff's use and enjoyment of his or her property." The court (Robt. M. Bell, J.) approved prior decisions holding that "whether an interference is unreasonable is determined by the injury caused by the [offensive] condition and not by the conduct of the party creating the condition."

"Virtually any disturbance of the enjoyment of the property may amount to a nuisance so long as the interference is substantial and unreasonable and such as would be offensive or inconvenient to the normal person." "To prove the existence of a nuisance, therefore, the complained of interference must cause actual physical discomfort and annoyance to those of ordinary sensibilities, tastes and habits; it must interfere seriously with the ordinary comfort and enjoyment of the property."

JENKINS v. CSX TRANSPORTATION, INC., 906 S.W.2d 460 (Tenn.Ct. App.1995). Railroad ties soaked with creosote were regularly transported to defendant's railroad yard in Nashville. Sometimes rail cars loaded with the ties were parked in front of plaintiff's house, adjacent to the yard. Plaintiff developed a severe allergic reaction to creosote fumes which reached her house. Twice she required hospitalization. Defendant was notified of the problem, but the problem continued. Plaintiff brought suit alleging nuisance. The trial court granted summary judgment in favor of defendant on the ground that allergic reaction to creosote was "extremely rare" and "not experienced by persons of normal sensibilities." *Held*, affirmed. "[W]hat constitutes a nuisance is not measured by its effect on the hypersensitive * * *." The appellate court quoted the Second Restatment of Torts: "If normal persons in that locality would not be substantially annoyed or disturbed by the situation, then the invasion is not [actionable], even though the idiosyncrasies of the particular plaintiff may make it unendurable to him."

RESTATEMENT OF TORTS, SECOND (1979)

§ 826. Unreasonableness of Intentional Invasion

An intentional invasion of another's interest in the use and enjoyment of land is unreasonable if

(a) the gravity of the harm outweighs the utility of the actor's conduct, or

(b) the harm caused by the conduct is serious and the financial burden of compensating for this and similar harm to others would not make the continuation of the conduct not feasible.

* * *

Comment on Clause (b):

f. It may sometimes be reasonable to operate an important activity if payment is made for the harm it is causing, but unreasonable to continue it without paying. * * * The process of comparing the general utility of the activity with the harm suffered as a result is adequate if the suit is for an injunction prohibiting the activity. But it may sometimes be incomplete and therefore inappropriate when the suit is for compensation for the harm imposed. The action for damages does not seek to stop the activity; it seeks instead to place on the activity the cost of compensating for the harm it causes. * * *

In a damage action for an intentional invasion of another's interest in the use and enjoyment of land, therefore, the invasion is unreasonable not only when the gravity of the harm outweighs the utility of the conduct, but also when the utility outweighs the gravity—provided the financial burden of compensating for the harms caused by the activity would not render it unfeasible to continue conducting the activity. If imposition of this financial burden would make continuation of the activity not feasible, the weighing process for determining unreasonableness is similar to that in a suit for injunction. * * *

§ 829A. Gravity vs. Utility—Severe Harm

An intentional invasion of another's interest in the use and enjoyment of land is unreasonable if the harm resulting from the invasion is severe and greater than the other should be required to bear without compensation.

Comment:

* * *

b. The rule stated in this Section is a specific application of the general rule stated in § 826. * * * [C]ertain types of harm may be so severe as to require a holding of unreasonableness as a matter of law, regardless of the utility of the conduct. This is particularly true if the harm resulting from the invasion is physical in character. * * *

O'CAIN v. O'CAIN

Court of Appeals of South Carolina, 1996.
322 S.C. 551, 473 S.E.2d 460.

[Plaintiffs, members of "the Harold O'Cain family," brought suit against members of "the Lever O'Cain family." Plaintiffs sued for an injunction to abate a nuisance, described below. The case was tried to a Master–In–Equity, who denied the injunction. This appeal followed.]

HUFF, J.

* * *

All of the parties to this action are the direct descendants of the late Henry H. O'Cain. Henry H. O'Cain devised a tract of land known as Forest Place to his son Harold O'Cain. He further left an adjoining tract of land known as the Old Heirs Place to another son, Lever H. O'Cain. The designated boundary line between the two tracts was an old creek. A public road was built between the two tracts and was later paved by the Highway

Department. While the road runs along the old creek bed, it does not exactly follow the boundary line and, at some points, crosses over the line so that the boundary line runs on both sides of the public road. As a result, the Lever O'Cain family owns a small strip of land between the road and land owned by the Harold O'Cain family. Specifically, this small strip runs in front of the Harold O'Cain home, built over 50 years prior to the institution of this suit, and the home of [Harold's son,] Jerry O'Cain, which was placed on the property around 1986. * * *

* * *

[The Lever O'Cain family raises hogs. Before 1986, their hogs had been kept on the small strip of land. Around 1986 the hogs were moved to another part of their property. But in 1994, the Lever O'Cains—defendants—enclosed the small strip with a fence and brought their hogs back, placing the hogs "directly in front of" the Jerry O'Cain residence. Plaintiffs seek an injunction ordering that the hogs be moved.]

The Harold O'Cain family appeals from the master's finding that the placing of hogs in front of Jerry O'Cain's residence did not constitute a nuisance. * * *

An action for an injunction is equitable. Blanks v. Rawson, 296 S.C. 110, 370 S.E.2d 890 (Ct.App.1988). Since this is an action in equity tried by a single judge, this court has jurisdiction to find facts in accordance with our own view of the preponderance of the evidence. Id.

In resolving issues relating to a private nuisance, we must deal with the conflicting interests of land owners. Winget v. Winn–Dixie Stores, Inc., 242 S.C. 152, 130 S.E.2d 363 (1963). To establish the line beyond which one's exercise of his property rights becomes a legal infringement upon the property rights of another requires the delicate balancing of the correlative rights of the parties; the right of one generally to make such lawful use of his property as he may desire and the right of the other to be protected in the reasonable enjoyment of his property. DeBorde v. St. Michael and All Angels Episcopal Church, 272 S.C. 490, 252 S.E.2d 876 (1979). In cases where an injunction is sought to abate an alleged private nuisance, the court must deal with the conflicting interests of the landowners by balancing the benefits of an injunction to the plaintiff against the inconvenience and damage to the defendant, and grant or deny an injunction as seems most consistent with justice and equity under the circumstances of the case. LeFurgy v. Long Cove Club Owners Association, Inc., 313 S.C. 555, 443 S.E.2d 577 (Ct.App.1994).

An owner of property, even in the conduct of lawful business thereon, is subject to reasonable limitations and, in the operation of such business, must not unreasonably interfere with the health or comfort of neighbors or their right to the enjoyment of their property. Winget, supra. * * * On the other hand, every annoyance or disturbance of a landowner from the use made of property by a neighbor does not constitute a nuisance. * * * [P]eople who live in organized communities must of necessity suffer some inconvenience and annoyance from their neighbors and must submit to annoyances consequent upon the reasonable use of property by others. Id.

Resort must always be had to sound common sense and due regard should be given to the notions of comfort and convenience entertained by persons generally of ordinary tastes and susceptibilities. DeBorde, supra. A lawful business should not be enjoined on account of every trifling or imaginary annoyance, such as may offend the taste or disturb the nerves of a fastidious or overly sensitive person, but on the other hand, no one, whatever his circumstances or condition may be, should be compelled to leave his home or live in mental discomfort, although caused by a lawful and useful business carried on in his vicinity. * * *

Generally, a private nuisance is that class of wrongs that arises from the unreasonable, unwarrantable, or unlawful use by a person of his own property, personal or real. Clark v. Greenville County, 313 S.C. 205, 437 S.E.2d 117 (1993). Nuisance law is based on the premise that every citizen holds his property subject to the implied obligation that he will use it in such a way as not to prevent others from enjoying the use of their property. Id. The traditional concept of private nuisance requires the plaintiff to demonstrate that the defendants unreasonably interfered with their owner-ship or possession of the land. Ravan v. Greenville County, 315 S.C. 447, 434 S.E.2d 296 (Ct.App.1993). A nuisance is a substantial and unreasonable interference with the plaintiff's use and enjoyment of his property. Id. It is anything which hurts, inconveniences, or damages; anything which essential-ly interferes with the enjoyment of life or property. * * *

* * *

Turning to the facts of this case, we find the preponderance of the evidence shows the Lever O'Cain family's use of the small strip of land in front of the Harold O'Cain family property to raise hogs constitutes a private nuisance and should be enjoined. Although the master found the odor and the flies were no worse once the hogs were moved in front of Jerry O'Cain's home, there is testimony from Jerry that the odor and the flies were indeed worse. Further, his wife, Tonya O'Cain, testified having the hogs in front of their house had caused them a lot of stress, the odor and the flies have gotten worse since the hogs have been there, the odor and the flies have affected the use of their decks, and she is embarrassed and ashamed to bring friends and family to her home. She testified the odor was pungent and the flies so bad that she did not even want to be in her home anymore. Based on our review of the record, we do not find this to be the reaction of an overly sensitive person. Further, both Jerry and Tonya testified the situation with the hogs was making it difficult, if not impossible, to sell their home. A person of ordinary tastes and susceptibilities would clearly find such a situation objectionable. Even though the general area of the property is rural, and the business of raising hogs is a legitimate business and likely to occur in such an area, we find the location of the hogs on a small strip of land, between the plaintiffs' property and the road and directly in front of the plaintiffs' residence, is an unreasonable and unwarranted use of the defendants' property and constitutes a private nuisance. The defendants are preventing plaintiffs from enjoying the use of their property by the improper location of the hogs directly in front of the residence. The evidence is clear the defendants had other, more suitable land in the area on which to raise hogs, but chose an area which unreasonably interferes with the plaintiffs' enjoyment of their land. * * * The defendants have, indeed, placed "the pig in the parlor instead of the barnyard."

Balancing the benefits of an injunction to the plaintiffs against the inconvenience and damage to the defendants, we hold that justice and equity dictate the grant of an injunction. * * *

McCOMBS v. JOPLIN 66 FAIRGROUNDS, INC., 925 S.W.2d 946 (Mo.Ct. App.1996). Defendant operates an automobile racetrack on a 100–acre tract outside city limits of Joplin, Missouri. Plaintiffs are 28 homeowners who live near the racetrack. They claim that noise from racing is a nuisance, and ask for an injunction restraining defendant from operating a racetrack on its premises. At trial plaintiffs' expert witness testified that measured sound levels in yards and inside houses during racing sessions exceeded appropriate limits.

The trial judge found that racing noise was a nuisance, and issued an injunction which restricts, but does not prohibit, racing. The injunction requires use of mufflers on all race cars, and limits both the yearly number of races and the length and ending time of each race program. On appeal plaintiffs claim the trial court "erroneously failed to grant a complete injunction." *Held*, affirmed.

The appellate court said that "we believe the court-ordered noise restrictions properly balance the utility of the racetrack's operation against the gravity of Plaintiffs' harm." The utility of the track, which cost over two million dollars, "consists of recreation for thousands of fans" and "businesses and jobs revolving around race track activity." The trial court's injunction "restricted the racetrack's operation to a level which" would avoid "a substantial impairment of Plaintiffs' peaceful enjoyment of their property."

The court found support for its decision in Massey v. Long, 608 S.W.2d 547 (Mo.Ct.App.1980). "In Massey, plaintiff's home was adjacent to defendants' six apartment air-conditioning units. The trial court found the operation of the air-conditioning units was a nuisance and enjoined defendants from operating [them] between the hours of 10 p.m. to 7 a.m." This limited injunction subjected apartment-dwellers to a degree of discomfort not "disproportionate" to the annoyance caused by emitted noise, thus achieving "a proper balancing of the equities."

ALDRIDGE v. SAXEY, 242 Or. 238, 409 P.2d 184 (1965). Suit to enjoin defendants in a semi-rural area from keeping and maintaining German shepherds on his premises. Plaintiff suffered from emphysema and was home during the day. Injunction denied.

SECTION C.   PRIVILEGE

This section investigates situations in which purposeful invasion of someone's property entitlement, ordinarily a tortious wrong, is held to be legally justified or "privileged." Three relevant bodies of doctrine are introduced: (1) law of "public takings," whereby government is empowered to take property for public use; (2) the privilege of "public necessity," authorizing destruction of property to safeguard the public good; (3) the privilege of "private necessity," which permits a private actor to enter and use another's property, without consent, in certain circumstances. Consideration of these doctrines leads to two broad questions of policy, which are framed in dramatic fashion by the last two main cases below.

In the celebrated case of *Vincent* v. *Lake Erie Transportation Co.*, a private actor damages another's property, by engaging in conduct which is held to be fully justified because in the circumstances it serves the greater good, and the actor is made to pay for harm done. The broad question is this: should an actor whose reasonably conducted activity does more good than harm be required to pay for injury imposed on another? A positive answer to this question is an affirmation of strict liability.

In the disquieting case of *Crescent Mining Co.* v. *Silver King Mining Co.*, a private actor enters and uses another's property without permission, and is held liable to pay for any harm done, but an injunction against the actor is denied, because the conduct in question serves the greater good. The broad question is this: should an actor be allowed to impose injury on another so long as the actor's conduct does more good than harm and provided payment for injury is made? A negative answer—willingness to grant an injunction—denies that utilitarian considerations always trump entitlement.

MONONGAHELA NAVIGATION CO. v. UNITED STATES
Supreme Court of the United States, 1893.
148 U.S. 312, 13 S.Ct. 622, 37 L.Ed. 463.

[Pursuant to statute, the United States initiated proceedings to condemn a lock and dam of Monongahela Navigation Co. The company had constructed the lock and dam to make the Monongahela navigable pursuant to a charter from the State of Pennsylvania, and exacted tolls on the river's commerce for use of these improvements pursuant to a state franchise. On appeal from a lower federal court, the Supreme Court held that the company was entitled, under the takings clause of the Fifth Amendment (" * * * nor shall private property be taken for public use, without just compensation"), to compensation for the value of both the tangible property and the franchise to exact tolls. In exploring the meaning of the takings clause, the opinion for the Court of Justice Brewer said:]

* * * The question presented is not whether the United States has the power to condemn and appropriate this property of the Monongahela Company, for that is conceded, but how much it must pay as compensation therefor. Obviously, this question, as all others which run along the line of the extent of the protection the individual has under the Constitution

against the demands of the government, is of importance; for in any society the fullness and sufficiency of the securities which surround the individual in the use and enjoyment of his property constitute one of the most certain tests of the character and value of the government. The first ten amendments to the Constitution, adopted as they were soon after the adoption of the Constitution, are in the nature of a bill of rights, and were adopted in order to quiet the apprehension of many, that without some such declaration of rights the government would assume, and might be held to possess, the power to trespass upon those rights of persons and property which by the Declaration of Independence were affirmed to be unalienable rights.

In the case of Sinnickson v. Johnson, 17 N.J.L. (2 Harr.) 129, 145, cited in the case of Pumpelly v. Green Bay Company, 13 Wall. 166, 178, it was said that "this power to take private property reaches back of all constitutional provisions; and it seems to have been considered a settled principle of universal law that the right to compensation is an incident to the exercise of that power; that the one is so inseparably connected with the other, that they may be said to exist not as separate and distinct principles, but as parts of one and the same principle." And in Gardner v. Newburgh, 2 Johns. Ch. 162, Chancellor Kent affirmed substantially the same doctrine. And in this there is a natural equity which commends it to every one. It in no wise detracts from the power of the public to take whatever may be necessary for its uses; while, on the other hand, it prevents the public from loading upon one individual more than his just share of the burdens of government, and says that when he surrenders to the public something more and different from that which is exacted from other members of the public, a full and just equivalent shall be returned to him.

But we need not have recourse to this natural equity, nor is it necessary to look through the Constitution to the affirmations lying behind it in the Declaration of Independence, for, in this Fifth Amendment, there is stated the exact limitation on the power of the government to take private property for public uses. * * *

* * *

* * * [I]f the property is held and improved under a franchise from the State, with power to take tolls, that franchise must be paid for, because it is a substantial element in the value of the property taken. So, coming to the case before us, while the power of Congress to take this property is unquestionable, yet the power to take is subject to the constitutional limitation of just compensation. It should be noticed that here there is unquestionably a taking of the property, and not a mere destruction. It is not a case in which the government requires the removal of an obstruction. What differences would exist between the two cases, if any, it is unnecessary here to inquire. All that we need consider is the measure of compensation when the government, in the exercise of its sovereign power, takes the property. * * *

HARRISON v. WISDOM
Supreme Court of Tennessee, 1872.
54 Tenn. (7 Heisk.) 99.

[The defendants were citizens of Clarkesville, Tenn., who participated in the destruction of all the liquor in the town prior to the entry into the town of the Federal army. The purpose of the destruction was to prevent the Federal troops from becoming intoxicated, and doing harm to the property and citizens of the town. The plaintiff was one whose liquor was thus destroyed. Plaintiff appealed from a judgment for defendants.]

SNEED, J. * * * The defendants insist that at the time of the alleged trespass upon the plaintiff's property there existed an absolute public necessity for its destruction. The right of defense and self-preservation is a right inherent in communities as well as individuals. Whether an imminent and absolute necessity exists to destroy private property for the common good, is a question to be determined by a jury upon the facts of each particular case. An individual may take life to preserve his own, if he be in danger of death or great bodily harm, or think himself so upon reasonable grounds. But the grounds of his apprehension must be founded upon such facts as will acquit him of acting upon a mere fancied peril or with reckless incaution. The law is jealous in the protection it throws around human life and property, and the right to take either as a measure of self-preservation is to be exercised in a moment of extraordinary exigency when the private or public necessity absolutely demands it. The right to destroy property in cases of extreme emergency, as to prevent the spread of a conflagration, or as in the case now under consideration, is not the exercise of the right of eminent domain, nor the taking of property for public use, but a right existing at common law, founded on necessity, and it may be exercised by individuals in any proper case, free from all liability for the value of the property destroyed: [Citations omitted.]

* * * There are many cases, says Chancellor Kent, in which the rights of property must be made subservient to the public welfare. The maxim is that a private mischief is to be endured rather than a public inconvenience. On this ground rest the rights of public necessity. * * *

* * * An unsubstantial panic is not such a necessity, but such a state of facts must be shown as to leave no doubt of an impending and imminent peril, or that a reasonable ground existed for the apprehension of such a peril, to justify the act * * * Necessity, says Lord Coke, makes that lawful which would be otherwise unlawful: 8 Coke, 69. It is the law of a particular time and place: Hale P.C., 54. It overcomes the law: Hob., 144; and it defends what it compels: Hale P.C., 54. In these brief maxims is written the whole reason of the law that justifies the destruction of private property for the public good.

We are unable to discover where his honor the Circuit Judge has made any material departure from the principles herein announced, either in his general or supplemental charge. But, for the errors in his rulings upon questions of evidence, the judgment will be reversed and a new trial awarded.

———

UNITED STATES v. CALTEX (Philippines), INC., 344 U.S. 149, 73 S.Ct. 200, 97 L.Ed. 157 (1952). Proceedings to recover compensation for demolition of oil companies' terminal facilities in Manila, the claim being asserted under the Fifth Amendment. *Held* (7–2), that destruction of property of strategic value to prevent its falling into enemy hands in wartime did not constitute a compensable taking for public use.

SUROCCO v. GEARY, 3 Cal. 69, 58 Am.Dec. 385 (1853). Action against the Alcalde of San Francisco for ordering the plaintiff's house blown up to stop a conflagration, thereby preventing the plaintiff from removing chattels which would have been saved, although the conflagration spread beyond the house. *Held*, reversing judgment for the plaintiff, that "The right to destroy property, to prevent the spread of a conflagration, has been traced to the highest law of necessity, and the natural rights of man, independent of society or civil government. * * * A house on fire or those in the immediate vicinity which serve to communicate the flames, becomes a nuisance, which it is lawful to abate. * * * If a building should be torn down without apparent or actual necessity, the parties concerned would undoubtedly be liable in an action of trespass."

WEGNER v. MILWAUKEE MUTUAL INS. CO.
Supreme Court of Minnesota, 1991.
479 N.W.2d 38.

TOMLJANOVICH, Justice.

The Minneapolis police department severely damaged a house owned by Harriet G. Wegner while attempting to apprehend an armed suspect. Wegner sought compensation from the City of Minneapolis on trespass and constitutional "taking" theories. * * *

The salient facts are not in dispute. * * * Minneapolis police were staking out an address in Northeast Minneapolis in the hope of apprehending two suspected felons * * *. Before arrests could be made, however, the suspects spotted the police and fled in their car at a high rate of speed with the police in pursuit. Eventually, the suspects abandoned their vehicle, separated and fled on foot. The police exchanged gunfire with one suspect as he fled. This suspect later entered the house of Harriet G. Wegner (Wegner) and hid in the front closet. Wegner's granddaughter, who was living at the house, and her fiance then fled the premises and notified the police.

The police immediately surrounded the house * * *. The police fired at least 25 rounds of chemical munitions or "tear gas" into the house in an attempt to expel the suspect. The police delivered the tear gas to every level of the house, breaking virtually every window in the process. In addition to the tear gas, the police cast three concussion or "flash-bang" grenades into the house to confuse the suspect. The police then entered the home and apprehended the suspect crawling out of a basement window.

The tear gas and flash-bang grenades caused extensive damage to the Wegner house. * * * Wegner alleges damages of $71,000. The City denied Wegner's request for reimbursement, so she turned to her insurance carrier, Milwaukee Mutual Insurance Company (Milwaukee Mutual) for coverage. Milwaukee Mutual paid Wegner $26,595.88 for structural damage, $1,410.06 for emergency board and glass repair and denied coverage for the rest of the claim. * * *

Wegner commenced an action against both the City of Minneapolis and Milwaukee Mutual to recover the remaining damages. In conjunction with a trespass claim against the City, Wegner asserted that the police department's actions constituted a compensable taking under Minn. Const. art. I, § 13. * * *

* * * The district court granted partial summary judgment in favor of the City on the "taking" issue, holding that "Eminent domain is not intended as a limitation on [the] police power." Both Wegner and Milwaukee Mutual appealed the trial court's determination.

The court of appeals affirmed the trial court, reasoning that although there was a "taking" within the meaning of Minn. Const. art. I, § 13, the "taking" was noncompensable under the doctrine of public necessity.

I.

Article I, section 13, of the Minnesota Constitution provides: "Private property shall not be taken, destroyed or damaged for public use without just compensation, first paid or secured." This provision "imposes a condition on the exercise of the state's inherent supremacy over private property rights." *Johnson v. City of Plymouth,* 263 N.W.2d 603, 605 (Minn.1978). This type of constitutional inhibition "was designed to bar Government from forcing some people alone to bear public burdens which, in all fairness and justice, should be borne by the public as a whole." *Armstrong v. United States,* 364 U.S. 40, 49, 80 S.Ct. 1563, 1569, 4 L.Ed.2d 1554 (1960).

* * *

The City contends there was no taking for a public use because the actions of the police constituted a legitimate exercise of the police power. The police power in its nature is indefinable.[2] However, simply labeling the actions of the police as an exercise of the police power "cannot justify the disregard of the constitutional inhibitions." *Petition of Dreosch,* 233 Minn. 274, 282, 47 N.W.2d 106, 111 (1951).

---

2. One commentator explained:

"[The police power] is used by the court to identify those state and local governmental restrictions and prohibitions which are valid and which may be invoked without payment of compensation. In its best known and most traditional uses, the police power is employed to protect the health, safety, and morals of the community in the form of such things as fire regulations, garbage disposal control, and restrictions upon prostitution and liquor. But it has never been thought that government authority under the police power was limited to those narrow uses." Sax, *Takings and the Police Power,* 74 Yale L.J. 36, n. 6 (1966).

* * * This action is based on the plain meaning of the language of Minn. Const. art I, § 13, which requires compensation when property is damaged for a public use. Consequently, the issue in this case is not the reasonableness of the use of chemical munitions to extricate the barricaded suspect but rather whether the exercise of the city's admittedly legitimate police power resulted in a "taking".

In resolving this case of first impression, the well-reasoned decision of *Steele v. City of Houston*, 603 S.W.2d 786 (Tex.1980) provides guidance. In *Steele*, the Texas Supreme Court addressed a constitutional taking claim involving facts strikingly similar to the present case. There, a group of escaped prisoners had taken refuge in a house apparently selected at random. After discovering the prisoners in the house, the Houston police discharged incendiary material into the house * * *. The court, interpreting the taking provision of the Texas Constitution, which is virtually identical to the Minnesota taking provision, stated, "this court has moved beyond the earlier notion that the government's duty to pay for taking property rights is excused by labeling the taking as an exercise of police powers." * * * The court further stated:

> The City argues that the destruction of the property as a means to apprehend escapees is a classic instance of police power exercised for the safety of the public. We do not hold that the police officers wrongfully ordered the destruction of the dwelling; we hold that the innocent third parties are entitled by the Constitution to compensation for their property. * * *

* * * It is undisputed the police intentionally fired tear gas and concussion grenades into the Wegner house. Similarly, it is clear that the damage inflicted by the police in the course of capturing a dangerous suspect was for a public use within the meaning of the constitution.

* * *

II.

We briefly address the application of the doctrine of public necessity to these facts. The Restatement (Second) of Torts § 196 describes the doctrine as follows:

> One is privileged to enter land in the possession of another if it is, or if the actor reasonably believes it to be, necessary for the purpose of averting an imminent public disaster.

See McDonald v. City of Red Wing, 13 Minn. 38 (Gil. 25) (1868) (city excused from paying compensation under the doctrine of "public safety" where city officers destroyed building to prevent the spread of fire). Prosser, apparently somewhat troubled by the potential harsh outcomes of this doctrine, states:

> It would seem that the moral obligation upon the group affected to make compensation in such a case should be recognized by the law, but recovery usually has been denied.

Prosser and Keeton, *The Law of Torts,* § 24 (5th ed. 1984); *see also Restatement (Second) of Torts* § 196 comment h. Here, the police were attempting to apprehend a dangerous felon who had fired shots at pursuing officers. The capture of this individual most certainly was beneficial to the whole community. In such circumstances, an individual in Wegner's position should not be forced to bear the entire cost of a benefit conferred on the community as a whole.

Although the court of appeals found there to be a "taking" under Minn. Const. art. I, § 13, the court ruled the "taking" was noncompensable based on the doctrine of public necessity. We do not agree. Once a "taking" is found, compensation is required by operation of law. * * *

We are not inclined to allow the city to defend its actions on the grounds of public necessity under the facts of this case. We believe the better rule, in situations where an innocent third party's property is taken, damaged or destroyed by the police in the course of apprehending a suspect, is for the municipality to compensate the innocent party for the resulting damages. The policy considerations in this case center around the basic notions of fairness and justice. At its most basic level, the issue is whether it is fair to allocate the entire risk of loss to an innocent home-owner for the good of the public. We do not believe the imposition of such a burden on the innocent citizens of this state would square with the underlying principles of our system of justice. Therefore, the City must reimburse Wegner for the losses sustained.

As a final note, we hold that the individual police officers, who were acting in the public interest, cannot be held personally liable. Instead, the citizens of the City should all bear the cost of the benefit conferred.

The judgments of the courts below are reversed and the cause remanded for trial on the issue of damages.

———

CUSTOMER COMPANY v. CITY OF SACRAMENTO, 10 Cal.4th 368, 41 Cal.Rptr.2d 658, 895 P.2d 900 (1995). Police trapped a suspected felon inside plaintiff's store, and fired numerous tear gas canisters into the store before capturing their suspect. Plaintiff sued to recover for the resulting $275,000 property damage, but does not allege negligence. Plaintiff claims under a provision of the state constitution that requires "just compensation" when property is taken or damaged for public use. *Held* (4–3), that the constitutional provision does not apply. "Any doubt * * * in the present case is dispelled by consideration of those cases applying the so-called emergency exception to the just compensation requirement. The emergency exception has had a long and consistent history in both state and federal courts. [It says that] damage to, or even destruction of, property pursuant to a valid exercise of the police power often requires no compensation under the just compensation clause."

The dissenting opinion (Baxter, J.) said that "given the broad cost-spreading purposes of the just compensation clause," any emergency exception must be kept within narrow bounds. The clause means to ensure that "the adversely affected owner will not absorb alone a cost which the benefitted community should share."

When a deliberate law enforcement action physically invades, destroys, or damages unoffending property, a "public use" has arisen by every logical measure. * * * The damage is inflicted on behalf of the "whole community," by its representatives, for a public purpose. * * * Failure to compensate the owner under these circumstances may thus single him out for a burden which, under the Constitution, should be distributed throughout the benefitted society at large.

PLOOF v. PUTNAM
Supreme Court of Vermont, 1908.
81 Vt. 471, 71 A. 188.

[A general demurrer to the declaration having been overruled, the defendant excepted.]

MUNSON, J. It is alleged as the ground of recovery that on the 13th day of November, 1904, the defendant was the owner of a certain island in Lake Champlain, and of a certain dock attached thereto, which island and dock were then in charge of the defendant's servant; that the plaintiff was then possessed of and sailing upon said lake a certain loaded sloop, on which were the plaintiff and his wife and two minor children; that there then arose a sudden and violent tempest, whereby the sloop and the property and persons therein were placed in great danger of destruction; that to save these from destruction or injury the plaintiff was compelled to, and did, moor the sloop to defendant's dock; that the defendant by his servant unmoored the sloop, whereupon it was driven upon the shore by the tempest, without the plaintiff's fault; and that the sloop and its contents were thereby destroyed, and the plaintiff and his wife and children cast into the lake and upon the shore, receiving injuries.

This claim is set forth in two counts; one in trespass, charging that the defendant by his servant with force and arms willfully and designedly unmoored the sloop; the other in case, alleging that it was the duty of the defendant by his servant to permit the plaintiff to moor his sloop to the dock, and to permit it to remain so moored during the continuance of the tempest, but that the defendant by his servant, in disregard of this duty, negligently, carelessly and wrongfully unmoored the sloop. Both counts are demurred to generally.

There are many cases in the books which hold that necessity, and an inability to control movements inaugurated in the proper exercise of a strict right, will justify entries upon land and interferences with personal property that would otherwise have been trespasses. * * *

* * * In Proctor v. Adams, 113 Mass. 376, 18 Am.Rep. 500, the defendant went upon the plaintiff's beach for the purpose of saving and restoring to the lawful owner a boat which had been driven ashore and was

in danger of being carried off by the sea; and it was held no trespass. See also Dunwich v. Sterry, 1 B. & Ad. 831.

This doctrine of necessity applies with special force to the preservation of human life. One assaulted and in peril of his life may run through the close of another to escape from his assailant. 37 Hen. VII, pl. 26. One may sacrifice the personal property of another to save his life or the lives of his fellows. In Mouse's Case, 12 Co. 63, the defendant was sued for taking and carrying away the plaintiff's casket and its contents. It appeared that the ferryman of Gravesend took forty-seven passengers into his barge to pass to London, among whom were the plaintiff and defendant; and the barge being upon the water a great tempest happened, and a strong wind, so that the barge and all the passengers were in danger of being lost if certain ponderous things were not cast out, and the defendant thereupon cast out the plaintiff's casket. It was resolved that in case of necessity, to save the lives of the passengers, it was lawful for the defendant, being a passenger, to cast the plaintiff's casket out of the barge; that if the ferryman surcharge the barge the owner shall have his remedy upon the surcharge against the ferryman, but that if there be no surcharge, and the danger accrue only by the act of God, as by tempest, without fault of the ferryman, every one ought to bear his loss, to safeguard the life of a man.

* * *

Judgment affirmed and cause remanded.

POLEBITZKE v. JOHN WEEK LUMBER CO., 173 Wis. 509, 181 N.W. 730 (1921). Trespass to recover damages for harms caused by defendant's logs floating upon plaintiff's land and by defendant in entering and removing them. The jury found that plaintiff suffered no actual damage by reason of defendant's entry to remove the logs. *Held*, that the trial court properly gave judgment for defendant. "While there is a conflict of authority, we think it is the better rule that where the property of a person has been carried upon the land of another by flood he has a right to recover its possession and for that purpose to go upon the land where it lies and remove it, and under such circumstances is not liable for nominal damages. * * * Nominal damages are awarded because a party has sustained an invasion of his rights. Here the plaintiff's rights were not invaded. The defendant had a right to remove the property."

VINCENT v. LAKE ERIE TRANSPORTATION CO.
Supreme Court of Minnesota, 1910.
109 Minn. 456, 124 N.W. 221.

[Appeal from an order denying defendant's motion for judgment notwithstanding the verdict or for a new trial.]

O'BRIEN, J. The steamship Reynolds, owned by the defendant, was for the purpose of discharging her cargo on November 27, 1905, moored to plaintiffs' dock in Duluth. While the unloading of the boat was taking place a storm from the northeast developed, which at about ten o'clock P.M., when the unloading was completed, had so grown in violence that the wind was then moving at fifty miles per hour and continued to increase during the night. There is some evidence that one, and perhaps two boats were able to enter the harbor that night, but it is plain that navigation was practically suspended from the hour mentioned until the morning of the twenty-ninth, when the storm abated, and during the time no master would have been justified in attempting to navigate his vessel, if he could avoid doing so. After the discharge of the cargo the Reynolds signaled for a tug to tow her from the dock, but none could be obtained because of the severity of the storm. If the lines holding the ship to the dock had been cast off, she would doubtless have drifted away; but, instead, the lines were kept fast, and as soon as one parted or chafed it was replaced, sometimes with a larger one. The vessel lay upon the outside of the dock, her bow to the east, the wind and waves striking her starboard quarter with such force that she was constantly being lifted and thrown against the dock, resulting in its damage, as found by the jury, to the amount of $500.

We are satisfied that the character of the storm was such that it would have been highly imprudent for the master of the Reynolds to have attempted to leave the dock or to have permitted his vessel to drift away from it. One witness testified upon the trial that the vessel could have been warped into a slip, and that, if the attempt to bring the ship into the slip had failed, the worst that could have happened would be that the vessel would have been blown ashore upon a soft and muddy bank. The witness was not present in Duluth at the time of the storm, and, while he may have been right in his conclusions, those in charge of the dock and the vessel at the time of the storm were not required to use the highest human intelligence, nor were they required to resort to every possible experiment which could be suggested for the preservation of their property. Nothing more was demanded of them than ordinary prudence and care, and the record in this case fully sustains the contention of the appellant that, in holding the vessel fast to the dock, those in charge of her exercised good judgment and prudent seamanship.

It is claimed by the respondent that it was negligence to moor the boat at an exposed part of the wharf, and to continue in that position after it became apparent that the storm was to be more than usually severe. We do not agree with this position. The part of the wharf where the vessel was moored appears to have been commonly used for that purpose. It was situated within the harbor at Duluth, and must, we think, be considered a proper and safe place, and would undoubtedly have been such during what would be considered a very severe storm. The storm which made it unsafe was one which surpassed in violence any which might have reasonably been anticipated.

The appellant contends by ample assignments of error that, because its conduct during the storm was rendered necessary by prudence and good seamanship under conditions over which it had no control, it cannot be held liable for any injury resulting to the property of others, and claims that the jury should have been so instructed. An analysis of the charge given by the trial court is not necessary, as in our opinion the only question for the jury was the amount of damages which the plaintiffs were entitled to recover, and no complaint is made upon that score.

The situation was one in which the ordinary rules regulating property rights were suspended by forces beyond human control, and if, without the direct intervention of some act by the one sought to be held liable, the property of another was injured, such injury must be attributed to the act of God, and not to the wrongful act of the person sought to be charged. If during the storm the Reynolds had entered the harbor, and while there had become disabled and been thrown against the plaintiffs' dock, the plaintiffs could not have recovered. Again, if while attempting to hold fast to the dock the lines had parted, without any negligence, and the vessel carried against some other boat or dock in the harbor, there would be no liability upon her owner. But here those in charge of the vessel deliberately and by their direct efforts held her in such a position that the damage to the dock resulted, and, having thus preserved the ship at the expense of the dock, it seems to us that her owners are responsible to the dock owners to the extent of the injury inflicted.

In Depue v. Flateau, 100 Minn. 299, 111 N.W. 1, 8 L.R.A.,N.S., 485, this court held that where the plaintiff, while lawfully in the defendants' house, became so ill that he was incapable of traveling with safety, the defendants were responsible to him in damages for compelling him to leave the premises. If, however, the owner of the premises had furnished the traveler with proper accommodations and medical attendance, would he have been able to defeat an action brought against him for their reasonable worth?

In Ploof v. Putnam, 81 Vt. 471, 71 A. 188, 20 L.R.A.,N.S., 152, 130 Am.St.Rep. 1072, 15 Am.Ann.Cas. 1151, the Supreme Court of Vermont held that where, under stress of weather, a vessel was without permission moored to a private dock at an island in Lake Champlain owned by the defendant, the plaintiff was not guilty of trespass, and that the defendant was responsible in damages because his representative upon the island unmoored the vessel, permitting it to drift upon the shore, with resultant injuries to it. If, in that case, the vessel had been permitted to remain, and the dock had suffered an injury, we believe the shipowner would have been held liable for the injury done.

Theologians hold that a starving man may, without moral guilt, take what is necessary to sustain life; but it could hardly be said that the obligation would not be upon such person to pay the value of the property so taken when he became able to do so. And so public necessity, in times of war or peace, may require the taking of private property for public purposes; but under our system of jurisprudence compensation must be made.

Let us imagine in this case that for the better mooring of the vessel those in charge of her had appropriated a valuable cable lying upon the dock. No matter how justifiable such appropriation might have been, it would not be claimed that, because of the overwhelming necessity of the situation, the owner of the cable could not recover its value.

This is not a case where life or property was menaced by any object or thing belonging to the plaintiffs, the destruction of which became necessary to prevent the threatened disaster. Nor is it a case where, because of the act of God, or unavoidable accident, the infliction of the injury was beyond the control of the defendant, but is one where the defendant prudently and advisedly availed itself of the plaintiffs' property for the purpose of preserving its own more valuable property, and the plaintiffs are entitled to compensation for the injury done.

Order affirmed.

LEWIS, J. (dissenting). I dissent. It was assumed on the trial before the lower court that appellant's liability depended on whether the master of the ship might, in the exercise of reasonable care, have sought a place of safety before the storm made it impossible to leave the dock. The majority opinion assumes that the evidence is conclusive that appellant moored its boat at respondents' dock pursuant to contract, and that the vessel was lawfully in position at the time the additional cables were fastened to the dock, and the reasoning of the opinion is that, because appellant made use of the stronger cables to hold the boat in position, it became liable under the rule that it had voluntarily made use of the property of another for the purpose of saving its own.

In my judgment, if the boat was lawfully in position at the time the storm broke, and the master could not, in the exercise of due care, have left that position without subjecting his vessel to the hazards of the storm, then the damage to the dock, caused by the pounding of the boat, was the result of an inevitable accident. If the master was in the exercise of due care, he was not at fault. The reasoning of the opinion admits that if the ropes, or cables, first attached to the dock had not parted, or if, in the first instance, the master had used the stronger cables, there would be no liability. If the master could not, in the exercise of reasonable care, have anticipated the severity of the storm and sought a place of safety before it became impossible, why should he be required to anticipate the severity of the storm, and, in the first instance, use the stronger cables?

I am of the opinion that one who constructs a dock to the navigable line of waters, and enters into contractual relations with the owner of a vessel to moor the same, takes the risk of damage to his dock by a boat caught there by a storm, which event could not have been avoided in the exercise of due care, and further, that the legal status of the parties in such a case is not changed by renewal of cables to keep the boat from being cast adrift at the mercy of the tempest.

JAGGARD, J. I concur with LEWIS, J.

WHALLEY v. LANCASHIRE & YORKSHIRE RAILWAY CO., 13 Q.B.D. 131 (1884). Unprecedented rainfall caused water to accumulate against the defendant's embankment. In order to protect the embankment the defendant cut trenches in it, through which the water ran upon the land of the plaintiff on the opposite side of the embankment causing damage. *Held*, that, although the defendant was not responsible for the water on its land, it had no privilege to protect its property at the expense of the plaintiff.

COMMERCIAL UNION ASSURANCE CO. v. PACIFIC GAS & ELECTRIC CO., 220 Cal. 515, 31 P.2d 793 (1934). Action for destruction of a warehouse in which defendant had goods stored and which he entered during a fire to remove his goods, thereby, plaintiff claims, impeding the efforts to extinguish the flames. *Held*, verdict and judgment for defendant affirmed. One is privileged to act reasonably in the protection of his property although increasing the hazard to others' property.

CRESCENT MINING CO. v. SILVER KING MINING CO.

Supreme Court of Utah, 1898.
17 Utah 444, 54 P. 244.

[Silver King built a pipeline across land owned by Crescent. Crescent, the plaintiff, sought an injunction forbidding Silver King's trespass. The trial court refused injunctive relief. Plaintiff appeals.]

MINER, J.:

* * *

The second question for consideration is, did the court err in its conclusions of law and decree rendered in this action, wherein it found and decreed that the plaintiff was not entitled to an injunction against the defendant for the digging of the trench and laying and maintaining the pipe line across the barren, rocky, and worthless mining claims of the plaintiff, mentioned in the complaint and findings herein, but is remitted to its action at law for said acts and damages therefor? In this case the court found that the defendant did not remove the earth, rock or soil of the plaintiff's mining claim, but simply dug a trench, and laid a pipe line therein, and covered it with the material taken out in digging the trench, and that neither the soil nor anything else was removed from the mining claim, and that said mining claim across which the trench was dug was barren, rocky, worthless, uncultivated, not used or worked, and that the pipe line and the digging of the trench did not injure said claim in any manner whatever, and that plaintiff suffered no injury, and was not damaged in any manner, except nominally, for such trespass, and that plaintiff had an adequate remedy at law for the alleged injury. Defendant owned water necessary to run his plant, located several miles away, between which water and its mine the plaintiff owned a strip of barren, rocky, worthless, uncultivated, unused land, on a barren hillside, over which, as claimed, it refused to sell a right of way, or permit the defendant to run its pipe line to its mine. It does not appear that there was any other way of reaching the mine with the water, or that any water was obtainable. Without the water, one of the largest mining industries in the state, employing hundreds of laborers, and producing hundreds of thousands of dollars' worth of mineral annually, must be closed down and cease operation. The laying of the pipe line across this barren, valueless land caused no appreciable injury to the plaintiff. The court found the damages to be nominal. No easement could be acquired by the defendant in the land without the consent of the plaintiff. To restrain the laying of the pipe line would cause defendant irreparable damage, and destroy and lay waste a mining industry of incalculable value, throw out of employment hundreds of laborers, and seriously retard and injure the people of the community and state in which the mine is located. To grant the injunction asked for would work a great and irreparable injury to the defendant, without corresponding or any benefit to the plaintiff; while to refuse it would injure neither, but leave the plaintiff to its remedy at law, where it could obtain such redress as the law should award it. * * * No peculiar, present, speculative, or other value is attached to the land crossed by the line. * * * In section 697, High Inj., it is said that the foundation of the jurisdiction of courts of equity to grant injunctions rests in the probability of irreparable injury, the inadequacy of pecuniary compensation, and the prevention of a multiplicity of suits; and, when facts are not shown to bring the case within these conditions, the relief will be refused. Equity will not, therefore, enjoin a mere trespass to realty, as such, in the absence of any element of irreparable injury. * * *

* * * In the case of McGregor v. Mining Co., this court held that, " * * * When injuries shall be regarded as irreparable at law must depend upon the circumstances of the particular case. If the injury be trivial, as by * * * raising the water of the river a few inches upon its rocky shore, doing him no appreciable or serious damage, equity would not ordinarily interfere by injunction, even in cases where the right has been established at law; for the power is extraordinary in its character, and is to be exercised in general, only in cases of necessity, and when the court can see that other remedies are inadequate to do justice between the parties, and even then it is to be exercised with great care and discretion. If the granting of an injunction would necessarily cause great loss to the defendant,—a loss altogether disproportionate to the injuries sustained by the plaintiff,—that fact should be considered in determining whether the application should be granted; and in some cases it would justly have great weight. * * * "

* * *

* * * The case of Pappenheim v. Railroad Co., 128 N.Y. 436, was brought to restrain the defendant from operating an elevated railroad in front of plaintiff's premises in the city of New York, and to recover damages therefor. The case of Wheelock v. Noonan, 108 N.Y. 179, was brought to compel defendant to remove from six lots belonging to plaintiff stone and heavy boulders which defendant had placed upon the surface thereof, from 14 to 18 feet in height, causing plaintiff great and irreparable damage and injury, and destroying the rental value and use of the premises. These and other cases cited, present a state of facts entirely different from those shown in this case. It is plain that the object of the defendant was not to destroy or injure the plaintiff's property that could not readily be compensated in damages. Its acts were not to destroy or injure the plaintiff's property, but to preserve its own from destruction, without injury, except nominal, to the

plaintiff; and it is claimed that any damages arising therefrom were offered to be paid.

* * *

We find no error in the record. The findings and judgment of the trial court are correct. The judgment of the district court is affirmed, with costs.

McCARTY, District Judge, dissenting.

I * * * dissent from that part of the decision holding that plaintiff is not entitled to equitable relief restraining defendant from maintaining its pipe line across and through plaintiff's mining claims. The trial court found that plaintiff is the owner, in possession, and entitled to the possession, of the mining property across and through which defendant's pipe line is maintained, and was such owner, in possession, and entitled to the possession, of the same at the time said pipe line was constructed, and that defendant's entry and occupation of the property was and is unlawful. In addition to the facts found by the court, the complaint alleges, and the answer admits, the defendant employed a force of armed men, who, against the will and protest of plaintiff, patrolled the pipe line where the same is maintained across and through plaintiff's premises, in order to protect defendant in the commission of the trespass complained of; and it is apparent, as shown by the record, that defendant intends, and, unless plaintiff is awarded injunctive relief, will continue to maintain its pipe line across and through plaintiff's premises, and make use of whatever force it may deem necessary to accomplish its purpose. * * *.

To deny the plaintiff equitable relief would force it to bring a succession and perhaps an indefinite number of suits against the defendant, or abandon that part of its mining property now occupied by the defendant. As shown by the record in this case, the plaintiff, in each action so brought, would be entitled to recover nominal damages only; therefore it would be compelled, if remitted to its legal remedy, to pursue a course of expensive, vexatious, and interminable litigation, or submit to what, in effect, would be a confiscation of its property by defendant. * * *

* * *

The contention that plaintiff should be left to its remedy at law, because that portion of its mining claim over and across which defendant has laid and now maintains its pipe line is barren, rocky, and of no appreciable value, and the damage done the property only nominal, in my opinion ought not to prevail. The plaintiff's right to protection in the quiet, uninterrupted, and peaceable possession of those mining claims, barren, rocky, and apparently worthless though they may be in the estimation of the court, is just as sacred in the eyes of the law as though they were of great value; and it is plain, as shown by the record, that this right cannot be enforced, and the plaintiff protected in the exercise thereof, by an action at law. * * *

* * *

I am of the opinion that the cause should be remanded to the lower court, with directions to enter judgment perpetually restraining defendant from continuing the trespass by maintaining its pipe line across and through plaintiff's premises.

———

JACQUE v. STEENBERG HOMES, INC., 209 Wis.2d 605, 563 N.W.2d 154 (1997). Steenberg Homes, Inc. sold a mobile home to a neighbor of Lois and Harvey Jacque, "an elderly couple, now retired from farming, who own roughly 170 acres" in rural Wisconsin. "Steenberg determined that the easiest route to deliver the mobile home was across the Jacques' land. Steenberg preferred transporting the home across the Jacques' land because the only alternative was a private road which was covered in up to seven feet of snow and contained a sharp curve which would require sets of 'rollers' to be used when maneuvering the home around the curve. Steenberg asked the Jacques on several separate occasions whether it could move the home across the Jacques' farm field. The Jacques refused." Nonetheless, Steenberg proceeded to plow a path through the Jacques' snow-covered field, and then hauled the home across the Jacques' land to the neighbor's lot. Summoned by Mr. Jacque, the sheriff's department issued a $30 "citation for trespass to land" to Steenberg. The Jacques subsequently sued Steenberg Homes for intentional trespass. In the tort suit, the jury found no compensable injury and awarded the Jacques $1 in nominal damages plus $100,000 in punitive damages. On appeal, *held*, the punitive award was appropriate. "[W]e see no reason why the legislative penalty for simple trespass will deter future conduct by Steenberg. Without punitive damages, Steenberg has a financial incentive to trespass again."

"* * * Felix Cohen offers the following analysis summarizing the relationship between the individual and the state regarding property rights:

> [Private property] is property to which the following label can be attached:
>
> > To the world:
> >
> > Keep off X unless you have my permission, which I may grant or withhold.
> >
> > Signed: Private Citizen
> >
> > Endorsed: The State

Felix S. Cohen, Dialogue on Private Property, IX Rutgers Law Review 357, 374 (1954). Harvey and Lois Jacque have the right to tell Steenberg Homes and any other trespasser, " 'No, you cannot cross our land.' But that right has no practical meaning unless protected by the State."

"Punitive damages, by removing the profit from illegal activity, can help to deter such conduct. In order to effectively do this, punitive damages must be in excess of the profit created by the misconduct so that the defendant recognizes a loss. It can hardly be said that the $30 [criminal fine] paid by Steenberg significantly affected its profit for delivery of the mobile home. One hundred thousand dollars will."

C. TORT LIABILITY AND INTANGIBLE INTERESTS

———

In this section we explore the principal forms of tort protection against intangible—nonphysical—harm. Tort law has generally accorded greater protection against physical injury—against harm to the physical integrity of the person and to property—than it has against nonphysical injury, even when nonphysical injury is intentionally inflicted. The late blossoming of intentional infliction of emotional distress, explored in Chapter Three, is a primary case in point. But protection of intangible interests remains an important part of tort law. The next two chapters explore tort protection for intangible "dignitary" and "economic" interests, respectively.

Chapter 5
DEFAMATION AND INVASION OF PRIVACY

Defamation protects the interest in reputation—the individual's interest in the way in which he or she is perceived by others. The law of defamation is one of the oldest branches of tort law and, lately, one of the most suspect. Where most of the rest of the law of torts has expanded over the past hundred years, the law of defamation has been sharply cut back, and by a Constitutional assault, launched under the auspices of the First Amendment and the values that it protects. That assault is the subject of Section B of this Chapter. Before we even reach the assault on tort law's protection of reputation, however, we must explore that law and ask what might be said in defense of according legal protection to reputation.

Iago in *Othello*, has this to say:

Who steals my purse steals trash, 'tis something, nothing
'Twas mine, 'tis his, and has been slave to thousands;
But he that filches from me my good name
Robs me of that which not enriches him
And makes me poor indeed.

Only to contradict that defense almost immediately:

I thought you had received some bodily wound;
There is more sense in that than in reputation,
Reputation is an idle and most false imposition;
Oft got without merit and lost without deserving.

William Shakespeare, The Tragedy of Othello, The Moor of Venice III:iii

Ambivalence about the importance of reputation and the merits of granting that interest legal protection has been pronounced even within the legal literature. In America, the tort of defamation has been faulted as an anachronism, rooted in an utterly alien—anciently European—world of status:

The Englishman is born into a definite status where he tends to stick for life. What he *is* has at least as much importance as what he *does* * * * A slur on his reputation, if not challenged, may cause him to drop several rungs down the social ladder. A man moves within a circle of friends and associates and feels bound to preserve his standing in their eyes. Consequently, not to sue for libel is taken as an admission of truth.

An able American has too much else to do to waste time on an expensive libel suit. * * *

Zecharia Chafee, Government and Mass Communications, 106–07 (1947).

It is, however, possible to muster a strong defense of defamation in modern and American terms. Justice Stewart does so eloquently in his concurring opinion in Rosenblatt v. Baer 383 U.S. 75, 92–93, 86 S.Ct. 669, 679 (1966).

The right of a man to the protection of his own reputation from unjustified invasion and wrongful hurt reflects no more than our basic concept of the essential dignity and worth of every human being—a concept at the root of any decent system of ordered liberty. The protection of private personality, like the protection of life itself, is left primarily to the individual States under the Ninth and Tenth Amendments. But this does not mean that the right is entitled to any less recognition by this Court as a basic of our constitutional system.

* * *

* * * The destruction that defamatory falsehood can bring is, to be sure, often beyond the capacity of the law to redeem. Yet, imperfect though it is, an action for damages is the only hope for vindication or redress the law gives to a man whose reputation has been falsely dishonored.

Moreover, the preventive effect of liability for defamation serves an important public purpose. For the rights and values of private personality far transcend mere personal interests. Surely if the 1950's taught us anything, they taught us that the poisonous atmosphere of the easy lie can infect and degrade a whole society.

Even so, as we shall see, the interest in reputation receives less protection in modern American common law than it did under the traditional common law of England.

SECTION A.   THE PRIMA FACIE CASE

The traditional prima facie case for defamation at common law required only the "publication" of defamatory words and, in certain circumstances, proof of "special damage." Anything else—the truth of the statement published, privilege to publish it—had to be raised as a defense. Defamation at common law was thus a "strict liability" tort, a point illustrated by the following case.

CASSIDY v. DAILY MIRROR NEWSPAPERS, LTD.
Court of Appeal, 1929.
2 K.B. 331, 69 A.L.R. 720.

SCRUTTON L.J.

The facts in this case are simple. A man named Cassidy, who for some reason also called himself Corrigan and described himself as a General in the Mexican Army, was married to a lady who also called herself Mrs. Cassidy or Mrs. Corrigan. Her husband occasionally came and stayed with her at her flat, and her acquaintances met him. Cassidy achieved some notoriety in racing circles and in indiscriminate relations with women, and at a race meeting he posed, in company with a lady, to a racing photographer, to whom he said he was engaged to marry the lady and the photographer might announce it. The photographer, without any further inquiry, sent the photograph to the Daily Mirror with an inscription: 'Mr. M. Corrigan, the race horse owner, and Miss X'—I omit the name—'whose engagement has been announced,' and the Daily Mirror published the photograph and inscription. This paper was read by the female acquaintances of Mrs. Cassidy or Mrs. Corrigan, who gave evidence that they understood from it that that lady was not married to Mr. M. Corrigan and had no legal right to take his name, and that they formed a bad opinion of her in consequence. Mrs. Cassidy accordingly brought an action for libel against the newspaper setting out these words with an innuendo, meaning thereby that the plaintiff was an immoral woman who had cohabited with Corrigan without being married to him.

At the trial counsel for the defendants objected that the words were not capable of a defamatory meaning. McCardie J. held that they were; the jury found that they did reasonably bear a defamatory meaning and awarded the plaintiff 500l. damages. The damages were high, but the plaintiff called considerable evidence of damage to social reputation, and the defendants' solicitors suggested, when the plaintiff alleged she was married to Mr. Corrigan, that there must be some mistake; and even after she had produced her marriage certificate, did not admit the marriage. It is not possible to interfere with the damages, and some allegations of misdirection and wrongful admission of evidence came to nothing.

The real questions involved were: (1.) Was the alleged libel capable of a defamatory meaning? (2.) As the defendants did not know the facts which caused the friends of Mrs. Cassidy to whom they published the words to draw defamatory inferences from them about the plaintiff, were they liable for those inferences?

Now the alleged libel does not mention the plaintiff, but I think it is clear that words published about A may indirectly be defamatory of B. For instance, 'A is illegitimate.' To persons who know the parents those words may be defamatory of the parents. Or again, 'A has given way to drink; it is unfortunately hereditary'; to persons who know A's parents these words may be defamatory. Or 'A holds a D. Litt. degree of the University at X, the only one awarded.' To persons who know B, who habitually describes himself (and rightly so) as 'D. Litt. of X,' these words may be capable of a defamatory meaning. Similarly, to say that A is a single man or a bachelor may be capable of a defamatory meaning if published to persons who know a lady who passes as Mrs. A and whom A visits. * * * [A]s Cotton L.J. said in [Henty's case, citation omitted] the same case in the Court of Appeal: 'One must consider, not what the words are, but what conclusion could reasonably be drawn from it, as a man who issues such a document is answerable not only for the terms of it but also for the conclusion and meaning which persons will reasonably draw from and put upon the document.' * * *

In my view the words published were capable of the meaning 'Corrigan is a single man,' and were published to people who knew the plaintiff professed to be married to Corrigan; it was for the jury to say whether those people could reasonably draw the inference that the so-called Mrs. Corrigan was in fact living in immoral cohabitation with Corrigan, and I do not think their finding should be interfered with.

But the second point taken was that the defendants could not be liable for the inference drawn, because they did not know the facts which enabled some persons to whom the libel was published, to draw an inference defamatory of the plaintiff. * * * 'In my view, since E. Hulton & Co. v. Jones [citation omitted], it is impossible for the person publishing a statement which, to those who know certain facts, is capable of a defamatory meaning in regard to A, to defend himself by saying: 'I never heard of A and did not mean to injure him.' If he publishes words reasonably capable of being read as relating directly or indirectly to A and, to those who know the facts about A, capable of a defamatory meaning, he must take the consequences of the defamatory inferences reasonably drawn from his words.'

It is said that this decision would seriously interfere with the reasonable conduct of newspapers. I do not agree. If publishers of newspapers, who have no more rights than private persons, publish statements which may be defamatory of other people, without inquiry as to their truth, in order to make their paper attractive, they must take the consequences, if on subsequent inquiry, their statements are found to be untrue or capable of defamatory and unjustifiable inferences. * * * .

[Judgment for plaintiff affirmed.]

ELEMENTS OF DEFAMATION

Contemporary American law (as represented, for example, by § 558 of the Second Restatement of Torts) tends to depart from the traditional formulation of the elements of defamation in one respect. It is increasingly common—although not probably not constitutionally compelled*—to require fault, at least in the form of negligence on the part of the party "publishing" the defamatory utterance. In other respects, contemporary American law develops and refines the elements of traditional defamation, but does not substantially revise them. Setting fault aside for the moment, we may formulate the elements of the prima facie case defamation in contemporary American law to be:

* See Dun & Bradstreet, Inc. v. Greenmoss
Builders, Inc., infra p. 199.

(1) A false and defamatory statement

(2) "Of and concerning" another

(3) Unprivileged "publication" to a third party,

(4) Actionability of the statement irrespective of "special harm" or special harm caused by the publication.

DEFAMATORY STATEMENTS AND HARM

The traditional common law formula for determining whether a statement was defamatory, asked if the statement held the plaintiff up to "public ridicule, obloquy or contempt." The materials that follow attempt more contemporary determinations, and explore the relation between types of defamatory statements and types of damages—"presumed" and "actual."

RESTATEMENT OF TORTS, SECOND (1977)

§ 559. Defamatory Communication Defined

A communication is defamatory if it tends so to harm the reputation of another as to lower him in the estimation of the community or to deter third persons from associating or dealing with him.

Comment:

d. Actual harm to reputation is not necessary to make communication defamatory. To be defamatory, it is not necessary that the communication actually cause harm to another's reputation or deter third persons from associating or dealing with him. Its character depends upon its general tendency to have such an effect. In a particular case it may not do so either because the other's reputation is so hopelessly bad or so unassailable that no words can affect it harmfully, or because of the lack of credibility of the defamer. There is a difference in this respect between determining whether a communication is defamatory and determining whether damages can be recovered.

DAVIS v. COSTA–GAVRAS, 619 F.Supp. 1372 (S.D.N.Y.1985). "A statement is defamatory if it tends to diminish the esteem, respect, goodwill, or confidence in which the plaintiff is held, or if it tends to excite adverse, derogatory, or unpleasant feelings or opinions about the plaintiff."

KERNICK v. DARDANELL, 428 Pa. 288, 236 A.2d 191 (1967). "The law stands as a guardian to protect a man's good name earned in the heat of battle, in the sweat of work, and in the laboratory of conscience, but it cannot prescribe hospitalization for abrasions or order surgery for hiccough."

BRYSON v. NEWS AMERICA PUBLICATIONS, INC.
Supreme Court of Illinois, 1996.
174 Ill.2d 77, 220 Ill.Dec. 195, 672 N.E.2d 1207.

Chief Justice BILANDIC delivered the opinion of the court:

The plaintiff, Kimberly Bryson, brought an action against the defendants, News America Publications, Inc., and Lucy Logsdon. The plaintiff's two-count complaint alleged that she was defamed by the publication of an article entitled *Bryson*, which was written by defendant Logsdon and published by defendant News America in the March 1991 edition of Seventeen magazine.

* * *

[The plaintiff's complaint alleged in part that she was defamed by "an article [which] appeared in the March 1991 edition of Seventeen magazine that referred to the plaintiff as a 'slut' and implied that she was an unchaste individual." The trial court granted defendant's motion to dismiss the defamation counts 'for failure to state a cause of action for defamation.' * * * The appellate court affirmed. We granted the plaintiff's petition for leave to appeal.]

* * *

FACTS

A short story entitled *Bryson*, written by defendant Logsdon, was published by the defendant News America in the March 1991 issue of Seventeen magazine as part of a group of stories entitled *New Voices in Fiction*. The story, written in the style of a first-person narrative, recounts a conflict between the unidentified speaker and her high school classmate, Bryson. According to the speaker, Bryson, "[a] platinum-blond, blue-eye-shadowed, faded-blue-jeaned, black polyester-topped shriek" who lives "on the other side of town" was "after" her. In the course of describing events that led up to an after-school fight between Bryson and the speaker, the speaker discusses an incident that occurred two months earlier:

> About two months ago Bryson was at a bonfire with these two guys that nobody knew. One had a tattoo, and they were all drinking. Lots. Who knows what guys like that made Bryson do. The next day she came into school with a black eye. Beth Harper looked at her too long, and Bryson slammed her up against a glass door and cracked her one clean in the mouth.

> Later that afternoon, as Bryson shouted down the hallways like always, I remembered what a slut she was and forgot about the sorriness I'd been holding onto for her.

The story continues as the speaker describes the fight that ensues between the speaker and Bryson. A footnote at the end of the story identifies the author, Lucy Logsdon, as a "native of southern Illinois."

* * *

I. DEFAMATION

* * * A statement is considered defamatory if it tends to cause such harm to the reputation of another that it lowers that person in the eyes of the community or deters third persons from associating with her. [citations omitted] A statement or publication may be defamatory on its face. However, even a statement that is not defamatory on its face may support a cause of action for defamation if the plaintiff has pled extrinsic facts that demonstrate that the statement has a defamatory meaning. See, *e.g., Morrison v. Ritchie & Co.,* 4 Fraser, Sess. Cas., 645, 39 Scot.L.Rep. 432 (1902) (report that plaintiff gave birth to twins considered defamatory, where plaintiff proved, as extrinsic fact, that some readers knew that the plaintiff had been married only one month).

Here, counts I and II of the plaintiff's complaint attempt to state a cause of action for defamation *per se.* Only certain limited categories of defamatory statements are deemed actionable *per se.* If a defamatory statement is actionable *per se,* the plaintiff need not plead or prove actual damage to her reputation to recover. Rather, statements that fall within these actionable *per se* categories are thought to be so obviously and materially harmful to the plaintiff that injury to her reputation may be presumed. If a defamatory statement does not fall within one of the limited categories of statements that are actionable *per se,* the plaintiff must plead and prove that she sustained actual damage of a pecuniary nature ("special damages") to recover.

The defendants raise three arguments in support of the trial court's dismissal of the defamation *per se* counts. They first claim that the statements do not fall within any of the limited categories of statements that are considered actionable *per se.* Second, they argue that the statements may not be considered actionable *per se* because they are reasonably susceptible to an innocent construction. Finally, the defendants claim that, even if the statements may be considered actionable *per se,* they are nevertheless expressions of opinion, protected under the first amendment to the United States Constitution. U.S. Const., amend. I. We consider each of these arguments in turn.

A. Defamation Per Se Counts

We first consider whether the disputed statements may be considered actionable *per se.* The plaintiff alleges that the article is actionable *per se* because it referred to her as a "slut" and implied that she was an "unchaste" individual.

Under our common law, four categories of statements are considered actionable *per se* and give rise to a cause of action for defamation without a showing of special damages. They are: (1) words that impute the commission of a criminal offense; (2) words that impute infection with a loathsome communicable disease; (3) words that impute an inability to perform or want of integrity in the discharge of duties of office or employment; or (4) words that prejudice a party, or impute lack of ability, in his or her trade, profession or business. These common law categories continue to exist except where changed by statute. The Slander and Libel Act (740 ILCS 145/1 *et seq.* (West 1992)) has enlarged the classifications enumerated above by providing that false accusations of fornication and adultery are actionable as a matter of law. * * *

The defendants initially claim that this statute has no application here because it applies only to words that are *spoken* and not in circumstances, such as those here, where the words are written. We reject the defendants' attempt to so limit the statute. We note initially that the defendants' argument relies upon a distinction between spoken and written defamation (slander and libel) that existed at common law, but was abandoned long ago by our courts. At common law, libel and slander were analyzed under different sets of standards, with libel recognized as the more serious wrong. Illinois law evolved, however, and rejected this bifurcated approach in favor of a single set of rules for slander and libel. Libel and slander are now treated alike and the same rules apply to a defamatory statement regardless of whether the statement is written or oral. Given the merger of libel and slander, we reject the defendants' claim that the statute providing for an action where false accusations of fornication are made is not applicable here simply because the alleged defamation was in writing.

Further, after considering the plaintiff's allegations, as stated in the complaint, we find that they fall within this statute's category of statements that are actionable *per se.* As previously stated, the statute applies when persons *use, utter or publish* words which amount to a charge of fornication or adultery. Here, the plaintiff's complaint alleges that the defendants, by using the word "slut," implied that she was "unchaste." The complaint thus alleged, in effect, that the defendants published words that falsely accused the plaintiff of fornication. The defendants' statements fall within this statutorily created category of statements that are considered actionable *per se.*

B.　*Innocent Construction Rule*

Even if a statement falls into one of the recognized categories of words that are actionable *per se,* it will not be found actionable *per se* if it is reasonably capable of an innocent construction. The innocent construction rule requires courts to consider a written or oral statement in context, giving the words, and their implications, their natural and obvious meaning. If, so construed, a statement "may reasonably be innocently interpreted or reasonably be interpreted as referring to someone other than the plaintiff, it cannot be actionable *per se.*" *Chapski v. Copley Press,* 92 Ill.2d 344, 352, 65 Ill.Dec. 884, 442 N.E.2d 195 (1982); [further citation omitted]. Only *reasonable* innocent constructions will remove an allegedly defamatory statement from the *per se* category. [citations omitted] Whether a statement is reasonably susceptible to an innocent interpretation is a question of law for the court to decide. [citations omitted] The defendants offer two arguments in support of their position that the statement alleged to be actionable *per se* is reasonably susceptible to an innocent construction. * * *

* * *

2.   INNOCENT CONSTRUCTION OF "SLUT"

The defendants first claim that the assertion that Bryson is a "slut" is not actionable *per se* because the word "slut" may reasonably be innocently construed as describing Bryson as a "bully." They note that the American Heritage Dictionary includes a number of different definitions for the word "slut," including a "slovenly, dirty woman," "a woman of loose morals," "prostitute," "a bold, brazen girl," or "a female dog." American Heritage Dictionary 1153 (2d Coll. ed. 1985). They argue that, because "a bold, brazen girl" may be considered synonymous with "bully," the court must innocently construe the word "slut."

The defendants apparently believe that the innocent construction rule applies whenever a word has more than one dictionary definition, one of which is not defamatory. The innocent construction rule does not apply, however, simply because allegedly defamatory words are "capable" of an innocent construction. See *Chapski,* 92 Ill.2d at 351–52, 65 Ill.Dec. 884, 442 N.E.2d 195 (modifying the innocent construction rule announced in John v. Tribune Co., 24 Ill.2d 437, 442, 181 N.E.2d 105 (1962)). In applying the innocent construction rule, courts must give the allegedly defamatory words their natural and obvious meaning. *Chapski,* 92 Ill.2d at 351–52, 65 Ill.Dec. 884, 442 N.E.2d 195; 33A Ill.L. & Prac. *Slander & Libel* § 12 (1970). Courts must therefore interpret the allegedly defamatory words as they appeared to have been used and according to the idea they were intended to convey to the reasonable reader. 33A Ill.L. & Prac. *Slander & Libel* § 12, at 25 (1970). When a defamatory meaning was clearly intended and conveyed, this court will not strain to interpret allegedly defamatory words in their mildest and most inoffensive sense in order to hold them nonlibellous under the innocent construction rule.

Here, we need not determine whether the word "slut" always implies unchastity or is always defamatory. When we consider the allegedly defamatory language in context, and give the words and implications their natural and obvious meaning, it is evident that the word "slut" was intended to describe Bryson's sexual proclivities. Immediately preceding the sentence in which Bryson is called a "slut," the author describes an incident that occurred two months earlier. The author states that Bryson appeared at a bonfire with "two guys that nobody knew. One had a tattoo, and they were all drinking. Lots. Who knows what guys like that made Bryson do." The sexual implication underlying the use of "slut" is intensified with the commentary, "Who knows what guys like that made Bryson do." The defendants suggest that this latter statement did not necessarily have sexual undertones, since the author could have been implying that the two men made Bryson engage in conduct of a nonsexual nature, such as shop-lifting. The defendants basically ask this court to construe the words used, not in the plain and popular sense in which they are naturally understood, but in their best possible sense.

The innocent construction rule, however, does not require courts to strain to find an unnatural but possibly innocent meaning for words where the defamatory meaning is far more reasonable. *Chapski*, 92 Ill.2d at 350–

51, 65 Ill.Dec. 884, 442 N.E.2d 195. Nor does it require this court to espouse a naivete unwarranted under the circumstances. Reading the words in the context presented, and giving the words their "natural and obvious" meaning, it is obvious that the word "slut" was used to describe Bryson's sexual proclivities. See *Tonsmeire v. Tonsmeire,* 281 Ala. 102, 106, 199 So.2d 645, 648 (1967) (statement that the plaintiff "had two affairs" could not be innocently construed as referring to platonic associations; statement charged the plaintiff with unchastity and was libelous *per se*); *Jordan v. Lewis,* 20 A.D.2d 773, 774, 247 N.Y.S.2d 650, 653 (1964) (stating that the plaintiff "slept with his secretary" is not susceptible of an innocent construction and, as ordinarily used, charges the plaintiff with sexual promiscuity). Accordingly, we reject the defendant's contention that the defamatory language at issue must be innocently construed as a matter of law.

The defendants finally note that our appellate court has held that it is not defamatory *per se* to call a woman a slut. *Roby v. Murphy,* 27 Ill.App. 394 (1888). We note initially that *Roby* is an 1888 appellate court decision. Appellate court decisions issued prior to 1935 had no binding authority. *Chicago Title & Trust Co. v. Vance,* 175 Ill.App.3d 600, 606, 125 Ill.Dec. 58, 529 N.E.2d 1134 (1988). We also conclude that *Roby* is not persuasive for another reason as well.

Roby was decided more than 100 years ago. It is evident that neither the law of defamation nor our use of language has remained stagnant for the last century. Terms that had innocuous or only nondefamatory meanings in 1888 may be considered defamatory today.

At the time *Roby* was decided, Webster's dictionary defined the term "slut" as "an untidy woman," "a slattern" or "a female dog," and stated that the term was "the same as 'bitch.' " *Roby,* 27 Ill.App. at 398. Apparently, when *Roby* was decided, none of the dictionary definitions of "slut" implied sexual promiscuity. Moreover, the *Roby* court found that, even in its "common acceptance," the term "slut" did not amount to a charge of unchastity. *Roby,* 27 Ill.App. at 398.

We cannot simply assume that the term "slut" means the same thing today as it did a century ago. Many modern dictionaries include the definitions of the term "slut" cited in *Roby,* but add new definitions that imply sexual promiscuity. See, *e.g.,* Webster's New World Dictionary (2d Coll. ed. 1975) ("a sexually immoral woman"); American Heritage Dictionary 1153 (2d Coll. ed. 1985) ("[a] woman of loose morals" "prostitute"). Moreover, in the present age, the term "slut" is commonly used and understood to refer to sexual promiscuity. See *Smith v. Atkins,* 622 So.2d 795 (La.App.1993) (law professor called a female student a "slut" in class; appellate court found that term was libelous *per se*). Thus, for this additional reason, we find *Roby* to be of no value here.

* * *

C. First Amendment

The defendants finally claim that, even if the statements may be considered actionable *per se* and are not susceptible to an innocent construction, they are nevertheless expressions of opinion, protected under the first amendment to the United States Constitution.

Prior to 1990, this court and others perceived a fundamental distinction between statements of fact and statements of opinion for first amendment purposes. Statements of opinion were held to be protected by the first amendment and not actionable in a defamation action. *Owen v. Carr*, 113 Ill.2d 273, 100 Ill.Dec. 783, 497 N.E.2d 1145 (1986); *Mittelman v. Witous*, 135 Ill.2d 220, 142 Ill.Dec. 232, 552 N.E.2d 973 (1989). This rule was grounded primarily on *dictum* contained in *Gertz v. Robert Welch, Inc.*, 418 U.S. 323, 339–40, 94 S.Ct. 2997, 3006–07, 41 L.Ed.2d 789, 805 (1974): "Under the First Amendment there is no such thing as a false idea. However pernicious an opinion may seem, we depend for its correction not on the conscience of judges and juries but on the competition of other ideas."

Recently, however, the United States Supreme Court reexamined the law of defamation within the context of the first amendment and rejected what it called "the creation of an artificial dichotomy between 'opinion' and fact." *Milkovich v. Lorain Journal Co.*, 497 U.S. 1, 19, 110 S.Ct. 2695, 2706, 111 L.Ed.2d 1, 18 (1990). * * * The Court held that there is no *separate* first amendment privilege for statements of opinion and that a false assertion of fact can be libelous even though couched in terms of an opinion. *Milkovich*, 497 U.S. at 18, 110 S.Ct. at 2706, 111 L.Ed.2d at 17–18 (simply couching the statement "Jones is a liar" in terms of opinion—"In my opinion Jones is a liar"—does not dispel the factual implications contained in the statement).

Thus, the test to determine whether a defamatory statement is constitutionally protected is a restrictive one. Under *Milkovich*, a statement is constitutionally protected under the first amendment only if it cannot be "reasonably interpreted as stating actual facts." *Milkovich*, 497 U.S. at 20, 110 S.Ct. at 2706, 111 L.Ed.2d at 19; see, *e.g.*, *Hustler Magazine v. Falwell*, 485 U.S. 46, 50, 57, 108 S.Ct. 876, 879, 883, 99 L.Ed.2d 41, 48, 53 (1988) (parody); *Old Dominion Branch No. 496 v. Austin*, 418 U.S. 264, 284–86, 94 S.Ct. 2770, 2781–82, 41 L.Ed.2d 745, 761–63 (1974) (hyperbole and imaginative expression).

In applying this test we first consider whether a reasonable fact finder could conclude that the allegedly defamatory statement, *i.e.*, that Bryson was a "slut," was an assertion of fact. We answer this question in the affirmative. The clear impact of the statement was that Bryson was, in fact, sexually promiscuous. This was not the sort of loose, figurative or hyperbolic language that would negate the impression that the writer was seriously maintaining that the character depicted in the story was unchaste. The assertion is sufficiently factual to be susceptible to being proven true or false. Whether the statement was *actually* true or false is a question of fact for the jury. We simply hold, as a matter of law, that the allegation of sexual promiscuity in this case contains a provably false factual assertion. Thus, we do not find that the allegedly defamatory statement here was constitutionally protected under the first amendment.

* * *

II.   Defamation *Per Quod*

We next consider whether the trial court properly dismissed counts III and IV of the plaintiff's complaint, which attempt to state a cause of action for defamation *per quod*. The allegations in counts III and IV of the complaint are identical to those found in counts I and II, except that the plaintiff has alleged that she sustained pecuniary loss ("special damages") as a result of the defendant's publication of the allegedly defamatory statements. The defendants argue that the trial court properly dismissed these *per quod* counts because they failed to allege any extrinsic facts to show that the statements are defamatory in character. We disagree.

A cause of action for defamation *per quod* may be brought in two circumstances. First, a *per quod* claim is appropriate where the defamatory character of the statement is not apparent on its face, and resort to extrinsic circumstances is necessary to demonstrate its injurious meaning. To pursue a *per quod* action in such circumstances, a plaintiff must plead and prove extrinsic facts to explain the defamatory meaning of the statement.

A *per quod* action is also appropriate, however, where a statement is defamatory on its face, but does not fall within one of the limited categories of statements that are actionable *per se*. In such *per quod* actions, the plaintiff need not plead extrinsic facts, because the defamatory character of the statement is apparent on its face and resort to additional facts to discern its defamatory meaning is unnecessary. The action is one for defamation *per quod* simply because the statement does not fall into one of the actionable *per se* categories. In other words, the statement is defamatory on its face, but damage to the plaintiff's reputation will not be presumed. As with any defamation *per quod* action, the plaintiff must plead and prove special damages to recover.

Counts III and IV of the plaintiff's complaint attempt to assert this second type of *per quod* action. The plaintiff claims that the statement that Bryson is a "slut" is defamatory *on its face*. Thus, the fact that the plaintiff failed to plead extrinsic facts to explain the defamatory character of the statement is not an adequate or appropriate basis for dismissing counts III and IV. The trial court improperly dismissed them on that ground.

The defendants alternatively argue that counts III and IV were properly dismissed because the plaintiff failed to adequately allege special damages. In any defamation *per quod* action, the plaintiff must plead and prove actual damage to her reputation and pecuniary loss resulting from the defamatory statement ("special damages") to recover. As stated above, we have found that the statement that Bryson is a "slut" falls within the class of statements deemed actionable *per se* under the Libel and Slander Act, because it amounted to a charge of fornication. Because the defamatory statement is actionable *per se*, the plaintiff need not plead or prove special damages to establish a cause of action for defamation. Counts III and IV, which simply restate the allegations found in counts I and II of the complaint, are therefore redundant and unnecessary. We therefore affirm the dismissal of those counts, with the modification that the dismissal is without prejudice.

* * *

Appellate court judgment affirmed in part and reversed in part; circuit court judgment affirmed in part and reversed in part; cause remanded.

———

KAELIN v. GLOBE COMMUNICATIONS CORP., 162 F.3d 1036 (9th Cir.1998). One week after O.J. Simpson was acquitted of murdering his ex-wife, a tabloid newspaper ran a front page headline which read "COPS THINK KATO DID IT! . . . he fears they want him for perjury, say pals." A nondefamatory story on Kato Kaelin appeared within the paper, 17 pages later. Kato Kaelin, a key witness in the trial and (because of it) a public figure, sued the paper for libel, claiming that the headline implied that he was a suspect in the murders. The trial court granted the paper summary judgment, but the Ninth Circuit reversed. The Ninth Circuit held, in part, that reasonable jurors could find (by clear and convincing evidence) that the headline falsely insinuated that Kaelin was a murder suspect, an insinuation which the subheading about perjury and the nondefamtory story inside the paper, did not necessarily dispel.

"California courts in libel cases have emphasized that 'the publication is to be measured, not so much by its effect when subjected to the critical analysis of a mind trained in the law, but by the natural and probable effect upon the mind of the average reader.' Since the publication occurred just one week after O.J. Simpson's highly publicized acquittal for murder, we believe that a reasonable person, at that time, might well have concluded that the ' "it" ' in the first sentence of the cover and internal headlines referred to the murders. Such a reading of the first sentence is not negated by or inconsistent with the second sentence as a matter of logic, grammar, or otherwise. In our view, an ordinary reader reasonably could have read the headline to mean that the cops think that Kato committed the murders *and* that Kato fears that he is wanted for perjury."

———

RESTATEMENT OF TORTS, SECOND (1977)

§ 570. Liability Without Proof of Special Harm

One who publishes matter defamatory to another in such a manner as to make the publication a slander is subject to liability to the other although no special harm results if the publication imputes to the other.

    (a) a criminal offense, * * * or

    (b) a loathsome disease, * * * or

    (c) matter incompatible with his business, trade, profession, or office, * * * or

    (d) serious sexual misconduct * * *

———

CINQUANTA v. BURDETT, 154 Colo. 37, 388 P.2d 779 (1963). Plaintiff alleged that the defendant "had uttered slanderous statements concerning him [which] amounted to slander *per se*. Plaintiff ran a restaurant in Boulder. Defendant had performed work on the restaurant's neon sign. Defendant had not been paid for the work, because of a dispute as to whether plaintiff or plaintiff's insurer should pay defendant. Defendant came to plaintiff's restaurant with some friends and ordered an expensive meal. He insisted on signing the check rather than paying for the dinner. A loud argument ensued in which defendant said to plaintiff: 'I don't like doing business with crooks. You're a dead beat. You've owed me $155.00 for three or four months. You're crooks.'" The trial court held, as a matter of law that these words did not constitute slander per se. No special damages were proven and the trial court granted the defendant's motion to dismiss. *Held*, affirmed.

"We must first consider whether the words 'crook' or 'crooks' impute a crime or a criminal offense to the plaintiff. In determining this question we cannot isolate the offending words from their context and we must examine the words in the light of the total attendant circumstances.

"To come within the exception permitting recovery in an action for slander without proof of special damage because the words spoken impute a crime, it is the general rule that such words must impute conduct constituting a criminal offense chargeable by indictment or by information either at common law or by statute *and* of such kind as to involve infamous punishment or moral turpitude conveying the idea of major social disgrace. Restatement, Torts, § 571, pp. 171–175; Prosser, Torts, 2d Ed., § 93, p. 588. Mere words of abuse spoken in outbursts of excitement or passion do not constitute slander *per se*. The fact that the language is offensive to the plaintiff does not in itself make the words used *slander per se*. It is true that the word 'crook' is derogatory, but the word does not in and of itself impute the commission of a crime. In view of the popular use of the word 'crook' in common language to denote conduct with which the speaker is displeased and with so many dictionary definitions of the word which refer to matters not chargeable as a crime, it is clear to us that the naked use of the word 'crook' does not constitute slander *per se*. Moreover, the context in which the words were uttered in the instant case show that their use was in reference to the refusal of the plaintiff to pay for fixing the sign, conduct which is obviously not criminal in nature. One cannot be charged with a crime either at common law or by any statute of this state because he refused to pay a disputed bill.

"Nor was the language used here such as to constitute slander *per se* as imputing insolvency or mercantile dishonesty to the plaintiff. * * * The words were not spoken to fellow tradesmen * * * where they would be calculated to injure the reputation and credit of the plaintiff. The appellation of 'crook' and 'dead beat' is explained away by the remainder of the words spoken in the oral affray which clearly show that the charge was made in reference to one disputed bill and could in no way imply a general charge of dishonesty or an attack on a mercantile reputation.

HALLS v. MITCHELL [1927] 1 Dom.L.R. 163. *Held,* reversing judgment, that an oral imputation that a person has in the past suffered from a venereal disease is not slanderous per se.

JOANNES v. BURT, 88 Mass. (6 Allen) 236, 83 Am.Dec. 625 (1863). The defendant said that the plaintiff was insane. *Held,* on demurrer, that "no action lies for orally imputing insanity to the plaintiff, without the averment of special damage."

———

FAWCETT PUBLICATIONS, INC. v. MORRIS, 377 P.2d 42 (Okl.1962). In an article in defendant's magazine entitled "The Pill That Can Kill Sports," the statement was made that a drug called "amphetamine" was being used extensively to stimulate athletes and added that during the 1956 season while Oklahoma was having a sensational victory stretch several physicians indicated that Oklahoma players were being sprayed in the nostrils with an atomizer. The article also stated that " * * * if players need therapy, they should not be on the field." Plaintiff was a member of the football team and that the article imputed to him a crime against the laws of Oklahoma. *Held,* that the article was libelous of each member of the football team even though there was no reference to plaintiff personally. Size alone of a group should not be conclusive. The article was regarded as libelous on its face and libelous per se even though plaintiff was not mentioned.

———

RESTATEMENT OF TORTS, SECOND (1977)

§ 575. Slander Creating Liability Because of Special Harm

One who publishes a slander that, although not actionable *per se*, is the legal cause of special harm to the person defamed, is subject to liability to him.

Comment:

b. Special Harm. Special harm * * * is the loss of something having economic or pecuniary value. In its origin, this goes back to ancient conflict of jurisdiction between the royal and the ecclesiastical courts, in which the former acquired jurisdiction over some kinds of defamation only because the could be found to have resulted in "temporal" rather than "spiritual" damage. The limitation has persisted in the requirement that special harm, to serve as the foundation of an action for slander that is not actionable per se, must be "temporal," "material," pecuniary or economic in character.

The more modern decisions have shown some tendency to liberalize the old rule, and to find pecuniary loss when the plaintiff had been deprived of benefit which has a more or less indirect financial value to him. Thus the loss of the society, companionship and association of friends may be sufficient when their hospitality or assistance has been such that it can be found to have a money value. The tendency has been in the direction of finding an indirect benefit to be sufficient.

TERWILLIGER v. WANDS
Court of Appeals of New York, 1858.
17 N.Y. 54, 72 Am. Dec. 420.

[Action for slander charging the plaintiff with "lewd and unchaste conduct" and "alleging special damage." At the trial the plaintiff's evidence tended to show that the defendant had stated to a number of persons that the plaintiff had committed adultery, that the story was all over the country and that when the plaintiff learned of this, and because of it, he became ill, took to his bed and was unable to labor on his farm. At the end of the plaintiff's case, the trial judge granted a nonsuit. The general term sustained this ruling, and the plaintiff appealed.]

STRONG, J.

The words spoken by the defendant not being actionable of themselves, it was necessary in order to maintain the action to prove that they occasioned special damages to the plaintiff. The special damages must have been the natural, immediate and legal consequence of the words. [citation omitted.] [The opinion goes on to note that, in general, it is wrong for a third person to repeat slander and that harm caused by such repetition is usually attributed not to the "original speaking of the words by the defendant," but to the person wrongfully repeating the slander. This principle bars plaintiff's claim.]

* * *

But there is another ground upon which the judgment must be affirmed. The special damages relied upon are not of such a nature as will support the action. The action for slander is given by the law as a remedy for "injuries affecting a man's reputation or good name by malicious, scandalous and slanderous words, tending to his damage and derogation." (3 Bl. Com., 123; Stark. on Sland., Prelim. Obs., 22–29; 1 id., 17, 18.) It is injuries affecting the reputation only which are the subject of the action. In the case of slanderous words actionable per se, the law, from their natural and immediate tendency to produce injury, adjudges them to be injurious, though no special loss or damage can be proved. "But with regard to words that do not apparently and upon the face of them import such defamation as will of course be injurious, it is necessary that the plaintiff should aver some particular damage to have happened." (3 Bl. Com., 124.) As to what constitutes special damages, Starkie mentions the loss of a marriage, loss of hospitable gratuitous entertainment, preventing a servant or bailiff from getting a place, the loss of customers by a tradesman; and says that in general whenever a person is prevented by the slander from receiving that which would otherwise be conferred upon him, though gratuitously, it is sufficient. (1 Stark. on Sland., 195, 202; Cooks Law of Def., 22–24.) In Olmsted v. Miller (1 Wend., 506), it was held that the refusal of civil entertainment at a public house was sufficient special damage. So in

Williams v. Hill, (19 Wend., 305), was the fact that the plaintiff was turned away from the house of her uncle and charged not to return until she had cleared up her character. So in Beach v. Ranney, was the circumstance that persons, who had been in the habit of doing so, refused longer to provide fuel, clothing, & c. (2 Stark. on Ev., 872, 873.) These instances are sufficient to illustrate the kind of special damage that must result from defamatory words not otherwise actionable to make them so; they are damages produced by, or through, impairing the reputation.

It would be highly impolitic to hold all language, wounding the feelings and affecting unfavorably the health and ability to labor, of another, a ground of action; for that would be to make the right of action depend often upon whether the sensibilities of a person spoken of are easily excited or otherwise; his strength of mind to disregard abusive, insulting remarks concerning him; and his physical strength and ability to bear them. Words which would make hardly an impression on most persons, and would be thought by them, and should be by all, undeserving of notice, might be exceedingly painful to some, occasioning sickness and an interruption of ability to attend to their ordinary avocations. There must be some limit to liability for words not actionable per se, both as to the words and the kind of damages; and a clear and wise one has been fixed by the law. The words must be defamatory in their nature; and must in fact disparage the character; and this disparagement must be evidenced by some positive loss arising therefrom directly and legitimately as a fair and natural result. * * * In the present case the words were defamatory, and the illness and physical prostration of the plaintiff may be assumed, so far as this part of the case is concerned, to have been actually produced by the slander, but this consequence was not, in a legal view, a natural, ordinary one, as it does not prove that the plaintiff's character was injured. The slander may not have been credited by or had the slightest influence upon any one unfavorable to the plaintiff; and it does not appear that anybody believed it or treated the plaintiff any different from what they would otherwise have done on account of it. The cause was not adapted to produce the result which is claimed to be special damages. Such an effect may and sometimes does follow from such a cause but not ordinarily; and the rule of law was framed in reference to common and usual effects and not those which are accidental and occasional.

* * *

Where there is no proof that the character has suffered from the words, if sickness results it must be attributed to apprehension of loss of character, and such fear of harm to character, with resulting sickness and bodily prostration, cannot be such special damage as the law requires for the action. The loss of character must be a substantive loss, one which has actually taken place.

It is not necessary to decide whether the doctrine which has some support in the books, that a husband may maintain an action for the slander of his wife producing sickness which prevents her attending to her ordinary business, if it conflicts with the principle now advanced, may be maintained upon some ground of exception to the general rule. It is doubtless true that in such cases the law regards more the loss of the wife's services, which alone entitles the husband to sue, than the influence of the words upon her character, and the husband has no control over the effect of the words; * * *. Still, the objection that special damages of that nature are not a fair, ordinary, natural result of such a wrong remains, and this objection appears to be alike applicable and entitled to the same force whether the action be brought by the husband or the party slandered. (Olmstead v. Brown, 12 Barb., 657; Keenholts v. Becker, 3 Denio, 346.)

Judgment affirmed.

————

GARRISON v. SUN PRINTING & PUBLISHING ASS'N, 207 N.Y. 1, 100 N.E. 430 (1912). Action by a husband for loss of services caused by the mental distress and physical illness of his wife induced by the defendant's publication of defamatory statements concerning her, which were actionable without proof of special damage. *Held,* on demurrer that, although mental distress and consequent illness on the part of the one defamed do not constitute such special damage as to render actionable the publication of defamatory words which are not actionable per se, yet where, as here, the words are actionable in themselves (because "the law presumes an injury to character which of itself will sustain an action"), proof of mental or physical suffering may be presented "as an element of additional or special damages accompanying or resulting from the injury to character thus presumed."

LIBEL AND SLANDER

The distinction between presumed and special (or actual) damages and its importance have their origins in the traditional common law distinction between "libel" and "slander." Libel involved the expression of defamation in a permanent form, such as a writing. Slander, by contrast, involved defamation in an impermanent form, such as speech. The basic idea behind the distinction was that the permanency of libel made it more harmful. Libels, therefore, were ordinarily actionable per se without proof of special damages, whereas slander was generally actionable only upon proof of special (or actual) damages, unless the slander fell into one of the per se categories, discussed in the preceding materials.

The importance of the libel/slander distinction has diminished greatly *Bryson,* supra p. 159, for example, speaks of their "merger" in modern Illinois law. Among other things, once new forms of communication such as television and radio undermined the traditional distinction. But it is worth noting that it is possible to express defamatory ideas in distinctively impermanent ways.

————

BENNETT v. NORBAN, 396 Pa. 94, 151 A.2d 476 (1959). Defendant's employee, suspecting plaintiff of shoplifting, overtook plaintiff as she was leaving store. In an angry manner, the defendant's employee put his hand on plaintiff's shoulder, put himself in a position to block her path, and ordered her to take off her coat, etc. Passers-by stopped to watch to plaintiff's distress. *Held,* the conduct formed a dramatic pantomime suggesting to the assembled crowd that plaintiff was a thief and this, therefore, was slander.

SCHULTZ v. FRANKFORT MARINE, ACCIDENT & PLATE GLASS INSURANCE CO., 152 Wis. 537, 139 N.W. 386 (1913); noted in 26 Harv.L.Rev. 658, 13 Col.L.Rev. 336. The defendants employed detectives who followed the plaintiff openly and persistently, calling it to the attention of his neighbors that he was being watched. *Held,* for plaintiff, setting aside a directed verdict. This constituted "an actionable wrong" to the plaintiff's reputation, analogous to libel because of the "public, notorious and continued character of the surveillance."

"OF AND CONCERNING" THE PLAINTIFF

NEW ENGLAND TRACTOR–TRAILER TRAINING OF CONNECTICUT, INC. v. GLOBE NEWSPAPER COMPANY

Supreme Judicial Court of Massachusetts, Suffolk, 1985.
395 Mass. 471, 480 N.E.2d 1005.

Before HENNESSEY, C.J., and LIACOS, ABRAMS, LYNCH and O'CONNOR, JJ.

LIACOS, Justice.

The plaintiff, New England Tractor–Trailer Training of Connecticut, Inc. (NETTT–Conn), and New England Tractor–Trailer Training of Mass., Inc. (NETTT–Mass), sued the Globe Newspaper Company (Globe) alleging that a series of articles published by the Globe on career training schools defamed NETTT–Mass and NETTT–Conn. [Count one of the complaint] alleged defamation of NETTT–Mass, and count two alleged defamation of NETTT–Conn. The Globe filed a motion for summary judgment on count two and on part of count one. * * * [The trial court] granted the Globe's motion. Subsequently, NETTT–Mass and the Globe stipulated to the dismissal with prejudice of count one of the complaint. NETTT–Conn appealed the allowance of summary judgment on count two. The Appeals Court reversed. 18 Mass.App. 906, 462 N.E.2d 1134 (1984). We granted the Globe's application for further appellate review. We reverse the trial judge's entry of summary judgment for the Globe on count two.

The record reveals the following facts. Commencing on March 25, 1974, the Globe published a series of articles pertaining to the private vocational training industry. NETTT–Conn claimed in its complaint that it was defamed by six of the articles in the series. [The first three articles did not name the plaintiffs, or discuss private vocational instruction for operating tractor-trailers.]

On March 29, 1974, the Globe published a set of articles on the private vocational training industry including one entitled, "Dead-end trip on rattletrap trucks." This article described the "New England Tractor–Trailer School" and quoted Arlan Greenberg, who was described as "N.E. Tractor president." The school was referred to variously as "New England Tractor–Trailer School," "New England," "N.E. Tractor Trailer," and "N.E. Tractor." This article was highly critical of "New England Tractor–Trailer School." It stated, inter alia, that several instructors at the school had been teaching without required certificates; that the trucks were "run-down," "decrepit, sometimes unsafe"; that Arlan Greenberg, "N.E. Tractor president," "made a number of demonstrably false statements and misrepresentations about the school"; and that the school's contracts with its students "violate[d] the laws of at least two states." The last two articles, published on April 12, 1974, and June 6, 1974, referred to "New England Tractor–Trailer School," and concerned investigations of the school by the Massachusetts Registry of Motor Vehicles, the office of the Attorney General of Massachusetts, and the New Hampshire Attorney General's Consumer Protection Division. These last two articles repeated many of the critical statements about "New England Tractor–Trailer School" which were contained in the March 29, 1974, article.

The plaintiff claims that it was defamed by these articles. The defendant, Globe, argues that the articles did not defame the plaintiff because they were not written "of and concerning" the plaintiff. *Hanson v. Globe Newspaper Co.*, 159 Mass. 293, 294, 34 N.E. 462 (1893). The Globe argues that the articles published on March 25, 26, and 27, 1974, contained only generalized statements about the private vocational training industry or referred to particular schools, none of which was, or could be confused with, NETTT–Conn. The Globe further argues that the articles published on March 29, April 12, and June 6, 1974, concerned NETTT–Mass exclusively and were not of and concerning NETTT–Conn. The plaintiff contests the Globe's assertions. It argues that while NETTT–Conn and NETTT–Mass are distinct corporations (the former incorporated under the laws of Connecticut, the latter under the laws of Massachusetts), they hold themselves out to be one school with two locations. The plaintiff argues that there is a genuine issue of material fact, i.e., whether the articles were of and concerning NETTT–Conn, and that summary judgment should not have been granted for the Globe. Mass.R.Civ.P. 56(c), 365 Mass. 824 (1974).

It is a fundamental principle of the law of defamation that a plaintiff must show, inter alia, that the allegedly defamatory words published by a defendant were of and concerning the plaintiff. This requirement is described at length in *Hanson v. Globe Newspaper Co., supra,* ("In a suit for libel or slander, it is always necessary for the plaintiff to allege and prove that the words were spoken or written of and concerning the plaintiff"). The Globe argues that, since an affidavit of the author of these articles shows, without contradiction, that there was no subjective intent to defame NETTT–Conn, it must prevail as matter of law. The Globe relies primarily on *Hanson* to sustain its position.

It is true that in *Hanson v. Globe Newspaper Co., supra*, the majority opinion adopted essentially a subjective test for the determination whether a defendant's words are of and concerning the plaintiff. * * * Compare, however, the dissent of Holmes, J. (in which Morton and Barker, JJ., joined), *id.* at 299, 303, 34 N.E. 462: "Of course it does not matter that the defendant did not intend to injure the plaintiff, if that was the manifest tendency of his words."

Two points need be made about *Hanson.* First, *Hanson* bears close scrutiny today from the twin perspectives of tort law and constitutional law. Written nearly 100 years ago, it represents an historical view of tort law largely rejected by later cases, and it fails to accommodate the profound changes in defamation law brought about by *New York Times Co. v. Sullivan,* and *Gertz v. Robert Welch, Inc..* Second, the issue of negligent defamation of an entity in the position of NETT–Conn was not before the court. *Hanson, supra* 159 Mass. at 299, 34 N.E. 462.

We believe that a purely subjective test for determining whether a defendant's words are of and concerning the plaintiff represents an outmoded historical conception of tort law. See 2 F. Harper & F. James, Torts § 16.2 (1956). As stated by Justice Holmes, an awkward person's "slips are no less troublesome to his neighbors than if they sprang from guilty neglect." O.W. Holmes, Jr., The Common Law 108 (1881). Tort law generally deems those injured by a person's unintentional slips deserving of compensation if the slips could have been avoided through the use of ordinary care.

A purely subjective test for determining whether a defendant's words are of and concerning the plaintiff unduly narrows the potential for liability in defamation cases and leaves deserving plaintiffs uncompensated. In determining the proper test, however, we affirm the "profound national commitment to the principle that debate on public issues should be uninhibited, robust, and wide-open," *New York Times Co. v. Sullivan, supra* 376 U.S. at 270, 84 S.Ct. at 721, and the constitutional rule which follows that courts may not impose liability without fault in defamation cases. *Gertz v. Robert Welch, Inc.,* 418 U.S. [323] at 347, 94 S.Ct.[2997] at 3010. * * * In *Stone v. Essex County Newspapers, Inc.,* 367 Mass. 849, 855, 330 N.E.2d 161 (1975), we resolved the conflict between the "right of redress to one who suffers injury to his reputation by the publishing of a defamatory falsehood" and the "freedom of expression . . . guaranteed by the First Amendment," by holding that "private persons . . . may recover compensation on proof of *negligent* publication of a defamatory falsehood" (emphasis in original). *Id.* at 858, 330 N.E.2d 161. In the present case, we similarly hold that private persons or entities may recover compensation (assuming proof of all other elements of a claim for defamation) on proof that the defendant was negligent in publishing defamatory words which reasonably could be interpreted to refer to the plaintiff. * * *

To the extent that *Hanson* requires proof that the alleged defamatory matter was of and concerning the plaintiff, we adhere to that rule. However, to the extent that *Hanson* appears to require a plaintiff to prove that the defendant actually intended to refer to the plaintiff before liability may attach, we decline to follow it. Rather, we adopt the view that "[t]he question is not so much who was aimed at, as who was hit," *Corrigan v. Bobbs–Merrill Co.,* 228 N.Y. 58, 63–64, 126 N.E. 260 (1920), with one all-important proviso. While the plaintiff need not prove that the defendant "aimed" at the plaintiff, he or she must prove that the defendant was negligent in writing or saying words which reasonably could be understood to "hit" the plaintiff. * * *

It is arguable that our later opinions have already moved away from the *Hanson* subjective test and have adopted this rule of negligent defamation. In any event, we take this opportunity to make clear that a plaintiff may establish that the defendant's words were of and concerning the plaintiff by proving at least that the defendant was negligent in publishing words which reasonably could be interpreted to refer to the plaintiff. This position brings the proof of this aspect of a defamation claim into line with the proof of other aspects of a defamation claim: "As to defamatory impact, the issue is whether in the circumstances of this case a reasonably prudent person, writing an article for publication, would realize that attribution of the racial reference [to the plaintiff] would discredit the plaintiff in the minds of a 'considerable and respectable segment in the community.' " *Schrottman v. Barnicle,* 386 Mass. 627, 641, 437 N.E.2d 205 (1982), quoting *Stone v. Essex County Newspapers, Inc., supra* 367 Mass. at 853, 330 N.E.2d 161. Also, in determining whether an allegedly defamatory statement is fact or opinion, "the test is whether the challenged language can reasonably be read as stating a fact." *Myers v. Boston Magazine Co.,* 380 Mass. 336, 340, 403 N.E.2d 376 (1980). Moreover, an objective test—i.e., inquiry into a reasonable recipient's understanding of the words rather than the speaker's intent—has been used over the years to prove that words are defamatory. *Rue v. Mitchell,* 2 U.S. (2 Dall.) 58, 59, 1 L.Ed. 288 (1790) ("The sense in which words are received by the world, is the sense which Courts of Justice ought to ascribe to them, on the trial of actions for slander").

In holding that a plaintiff must prove that a defendant negligently wrote and published words which reasonably could be interpreted to refer to the plaintiff, we in no way depart from the rule that the plaintiff may plead and prove extrinsic facts tending to show that the words could be so interpreted. "[I]f the person is not referred to by name or in such manner as to be readily identifiable from the descriptive matter in the publication, extrinsic facts must be alleged and proved showing that a third person other than the person libeled understood it to refer to him." *Brauer v. Globe Newspaper Co., supra* 351 Mass. at 56, 217 N.E.2d 736.

While we favor the use of summary judgment procedures in defamation cases, * * * we hold in this case that the trial judge erred in granting summary judgment for the Globe. The affidavits presented several genuine issues of material fact relating to the question whether the Globe articles were of and concerning NETTT–Conn. These issues are (1) whether the Globe intended to refer to NETTT–Conn and was so understood, and (2) if it did not so intend, whether it was negligent in publishing articles which reasonably could be understood to refer to NETTT–Conn.

* * * [With respect to the first of these two issues] we conclude that it is an unresolved question of fact whether the Globe actually intended to refer to NETTT–Mass and NETTT–Conn, or simply to NETTT–Mass.

Moreover, even if a fact finder should conclude that the Globe did not intend to refer to NETTT–Conn, there is a material issue of fact as to whether the Globe was negligent in publishing articles which reasonably could be interpreted to refer to NETTT–Conn. This issue breaks into two distinct components. The first is whether the Globe articles reasonably could be interpreted to refer to NETTT–Conn. The second is, if the articles reasonably could be so understood, whether the Globe was negligent in publishing them. Of course, "[i]f the recipient reasonably understood the communication to be made concerning the plaintiff, it may be inferred that the defamer was negligent in failing to realize that the communication would be so understood.... [However,] [i]t is ... necessary for the plaintiff to prove that a reasonable understanding on the part of the recipient that the communication referred to the plaintiff was one that the defamer was negligent in failing to anticipate." Restatement (Second) of Torts § 564 comment f.

* * *

If a jury were to find that the Globe articles reasonably could be interpreted to refer to NETTT–Conn, it would then be presented with another issue of material fact: Whether the Globe was negligent in writing and publishing articles which could be so interpreted. Pertinent to this issue are the questions whether NETTT–Mass and NETTT–Conn hold themselves out to be one school with two locations; if so, whether the Globe knew, or reasonably should have known, that they did so. * * *

Judgment reversed.

RESTATEMENT OF TORTS, SECOND (1977)

§ 564. Applicability of Defamatory Communication to Plaintiff

A defamatory communication is made concerning that person to whom its recipient correctly, or mistakenly but reasonably, understands that its was intended to refer.

DAVIS v. COSTA–GAVRAS, 619 F.Supp. 1372 (S.D.N.Y. 1985). "The test is whether a reasonable person, viewing the motion picture, would understand that the character portrayed in the film was, in actual fact, the plaintiff acting as described."

MARR v. PUTNAM, 196 Or. 1, 246 P.2d 509 (1952); noted, 41 Cal.L.Rev. 144; 28 N.Y.U.L.Rev. 220 (1952). Plaintiffs operated and advertised a pick-up and delivery radio and repair service. Defendant published an article entitled "Slickers Work Radio Racket." Plaintiffs presented evidence to show that they were the only persons engaged in the business in Salem who operated in the manner described and there was testimony by friends of plaintiff that they understood it to refer to plaintiff. *Held,* that since the article was ambiguous in respect of its application to the plaintiff, the question as to whether the article applied to plaintiff was a question of fact.

PUBLICATION

WESTERN UNION TEL. CO. v. LESESNE
United States Court of Appeals, Fourth Circuit, 1952.
198 F.2d 154.

SOPER, Circuit Judge. This case against the Western Union Telegraph Company comprises two causes of action for libel based on two telegrams containing statements reflecting upon certain conduct of Thomas P. Lesesne, Jr., which were transmitted by the Telegraph Company at the instance of H. G. Willingham. The first telegram, which was addressed to Lesesne, was filed by Willingham with the company on Saturday evening, October 26, 1946, at Columbia, South Carolina, and was delivered by the company the next day in a sealed envelope to the residence of Lesesne in Columbia, South Carolina. When received it was opened and read by his wife since he was sick in bed at the time. A short time before the telegram was sent, a woman had been killed on the streets of Columbia by an automobile driven by Lesesne and the telegram referring to this circumstance was in the following words:

"Although you are an administrative Assistant of the South Carolina State Board of Health and a new deal tick that does not give you a license to run through the streets of Columbia and kill women turn over in bed and regret your wrong doings. Although you have tried to kill the case with political pull we are determined to pull you out into the spot light." * * *

* * *

* * * The contents of the first telegram became known to the agents of the company when it was filed in the company's office and placed in the hands of an agent of the company for transmission to the addressee; and it also became known to the wife of the plaintiff when she opened it upon its delivery to the plaintiff's residence. The instructions of the court on these two circumstances are the subject of objections on the part of the appellant.

As to the communication of the contents of the telegram to the wife, the District Judge told the jury that the transmission and delivery of a libelous telegram to the person defamed does not constitute publication in the meaning of the law, even though the matter actually reached the hands of a third person, unless the Telegraph Company intended or should have reasonably expected that the telegram would be opened and read by a third person. The court, in addition, commented strongly upon the probability that a telegram addressed to a man at his residence might be read in his absence by his wife.

Insofar as these instructions left the determination of the matter to the jury, we find no departure from the prevailing rule in South Carolina. In Riley v. Askin & Marine Co., 134 S.C. 198, 132 S.E. 584, 46 A.L.R. 558, the defendant mailed a letter containing a libelous statement to a 17 year old girl which was opened and read by her parents and it was held that there was no publication in law since it was not reasonable for the company to assume that the parents of such a girl would open and read her mail without her consent. The company cites this decision as ground for a directed verdict in its favor as to the first telegram, since the evidence shows that the message was delivered to the plaintiff's residence in a sealed envelope on a Sunday morning when he would probably be and was in fact at home, and since the wife testified that she would not have opened the telegram except for the fact, unknown to the defendant company, that her husband was sick in bed. We think, however, that the question was for the jury, * * *. [Because] the instant case involves a telegram with its implications of emergency and haste, we are of opinion that the facts did not justify a binding instruction either way upon the question of publication, but required its submission to the jury.

With respect to the communication of the message to the agents of the Telegraph Company who handled it, the court instructed the jury that although the reception, handling and delivery of a libelous telegram by agents of a telegraph company does not of itself constitute publication, provided the contents of the message are not disclosed to any one else, yet if the telegram is not privileged, communication thereof to the agents of the company is a publication which entitles the addressee of the message to recover. * * *

We think this instruction was erroneous under the law of South Carolina. In Rodgers v. Wise, 193 S.C. 5, 7 S.E.2d 517, the Supreme Court of South Carolina said that in the older cases the dictation of a libelous statement by a business man to a stenographer has been held to be a publication, but that the more recent and better considered cases hold that such a communication does not constitute publication in the sense of the law of libel. There was reference in the decision to the authorities holding that when a communication is made by an officer or agent of a corporation to an associate in the ordinary course of business, there is no publication and no actionable libel. The principle of this case was reaffirmed in Watson v. Wannamaker, 216 S.C. 295, 57 S.E.2d 477. * * *

The verdict in this case was a general one and it is therefore uncertain on what ground the jury based its conclusion that the necessary publication of the message had taken place. It may well be that the jury were influenced by the erroneous instructions that the handling of the libelous telegram by the agents of the company was enough to constitute publication in the sense of the law.

The judgment of the District Court * * * will be reversed as to the first cause of action, and the case remanded for a new trial.

———

JONES v. GOLDEN SPIKE CORP., 97 Nev. 24, 623 P.2d 970 (1981). Wally Jones was employed as the head bartender by Golden Spike Corporation. The Golden Spike Corporation owned and operated a casino in Carson

City, Nevada. The president of Golden Spike—Charles Paul Leonard, Jr.—received a report on the performance of the casino's bartenders. After reviewing the report with the company's general manager, Leonard summoned Jones and four other bartenders to his private office. Leonard gave each bartender a typewritten copy of the report to read. Jones alleged that, in the course of the subsequent discussion, "Leonard stated to the group, 'You are all no-good, _____, _____, thieves.' " Jones sued for slander. Golden Spike moved for summary judgment on the ground that, even if the statement was defamatory, it had not been "published." The trial court granted the motion and Jones appealed. *Held*, affirmed.

"Appellant first contends that since the general manager was present, there was a publication. Jurisdictions that have followed the Restatement of Torts have taken that position. We choose to follow the majority rule as set forth in Prins v. Holland–North America Mortgage Co., 107 Wash. 206, 181 P. 680[–81] (1919):

> Publication of a libel is the communication of the defamatory matter to some third person or persons. Here the communication was sent from the main office of the company to its branch office. * * * Agents and employes of this character are not third persons in their relations to the corporation, within the meaning of the laws pertaining to the publication of libels. For the time being, they are a part and parcel of the corporation itself, so much so, indeed, that their acts within the limits of their employment are the acts of the corporation. For a corporation, therefore, acting through one of its agents or representatives, to send a libelous communication to another of its agents or representatives, cannot be a publication of the libel on the part of the corporation. It is but communicating with itself.

* * *

"Appellant also contends there was a publication as to the other four bartenders. We disagree. All five individuals were addressed as a group and the defamatory statement made to them as such. In Pate v. Tyee Motor Inn, 77 Wash.2d 819, 467 P.2d 301, 302 (1970), the court stated: 'Tort liability for slander requires that the defamation be communicated to someone other than the person or *persons* defamed.' (Emphasis added.) Therefore, there was no publication as to the other parties who were defamed."

HEDGPETH v. COLEMAN, 183 N.C. 309, 111 S.E. 517, 24 A.L.R. 232 (1922); noted, 21 Mich.L.Rev. 602, 32 Yale L. Jour. 90. The defendant sent an anonymous letter to a fourteen year old boy, charging him with crime and threatening prosecution. The boy showed it to his older brother who showed it to their father. *Held*, for plaintiff. The jury could find that the defendant "had reasonable ground to know that the letter would necessarily be seen by third persons," since the threat of a prosecution and imprisonment coerced the immature plaintiff into showing it to obtain advice.

LYLE v. WADDLE, 144 Tex. 90, 188 S.W.2d 770 (1945). Defendant, a physician, wrote a letter to the plaintiff to be shown to her physician in another city, the letter making it clear that the defendant had been treating the plaintiff for a venereal disease. Plaintiff showed the letter to her physician and it was alleged that the defendant's diagnosis was improper. *Held*, in answer to a certified question, that since plaintiff voluntarily disclosed the contents of the letter, it was her publication and not the defendant's.

OSTRO v. SAFIR, 165 Misc. 647, 1 N.Y.S.2d 377 (1937). The defendant mailed a postcard to the plaintiff containing the words, "Please send us a check in return for the rubber check sent us." *Held*, that sending a postcard through the mail "is a publication as a matter of law."

DISSEMINATION OF DEFAMATION

BOTTOMLEY v. F.W. WOOLWORTH & CO., LTD., Court of Appeal, 1932, 48 T.L.R. 521. (Scrutton, L.J.) Action for libel. The plaintiff complained that among the "remainders" bought by the defendants and sold by them at their various stores in England were copies of an issue of the "Detective Story Magazine," which contained an article headed "Swindlers and Scoundrels. Horatio Bottomley, Editor and Embezzler." The jury found that the defendants were negligent in not knowing that the magazine contained a libel, "owing to the absence of periodical examination of specimen magazines"; and assessed the damages at £250. The trial judge entered judgment not withstand the verdict for the defendants. Plaintiff appealed. *Held*, affirmed.

To "escape liability" for disseminating a libel, a defendant must show three things:

(1) that he was innocent of any knowledge of the libel contained in the work disseminated by him. In the present case the jury had found that the defendants were innocent of any knowledge of the libel contained in the magazine.

(2) * * * that there was nothing in the work or the circumstances in which it came to him or was disseminated by him which ought to have led him to suppose that it contained a libel. In this case there was no evidence to justify the jury's finding that there was anything in the magazine which ought to have led the defendants to suppose that it contained a libel.

(3) * * * that when the work was disseminated by him it was not by any negligence on his part that he did not know that it contained the libel.

Defendant was entitled to judgment because "the jury had found that something which had no possible connexion with the knowledge of the defendants constituted negligence."

SEXTON v. THE AMERICAN NEWS CO., 133 F.Supp. 591 (N.D.Fla. 1955). Plaintiff brought action against the American News Co. for publishing and circulating a libel contained in an issue of Everybody's Digest. The defendant purchased all copies of this magazine, with certain unimportant exceptions, and then resold the copies to the trade. The testimony was uncontradicted that defendant neither knew, nor was anything done by publisher to put defendant on notice, that the issue contained libelous matter. *Held*, for defendant. A distributor is not liable in the absence of negligence and there was no duty on the part of the defendant to familiarize itself with the contents of the publication in question.

SECTION B. CONSTITUTIONAL CONSTRAINTS

In *Curtis Publishing Co. v. Butts*, excerpted later in this section, Justice Harlan remarked eloquently on a deep conflict between the animating values of the First Amendment and those of the law of defamation:

It is significant that the guarantee of freedom of speech and press falls between the religious guarantees and the guarantee of the right to petition for redress of grievances in the text of the First Amendment, the principles of which are carried to the States by the Fourteenth Amendment. It partakes of the nature of both, for it is as much a guarantee to individuals of their personal right to make their thoughts public and put them before the community, as it is a social necessity required for the "maintenance of our political system and an open society." It is because of the personal nature of this right that we have rejected all manner of prior restraint on publication, * * * The dissemination of the individual's opinions on matters of public interest is for us, in the historic words of the Declaration of Independence, an "unalienable right" that "governments are instituted among men to secure." History shows us that the Founders were not always convinced that unlimited discussion of public issues would be "for the benefit of all of us" but that they firmly adhered to the proposition that the "true liberty of the press" permitted "every man to publish his opinion."

* * *

The history of libel law leaves little doubt that it originated in soil entirely different from that which nurtured these constitutional values. Early libel was primarily a criminal remedy, the function of which was to make punishable any writing which tended to bring into disrepute the state, established religion, or any individual likely to be provoked to a breach of the peace because of the words. Truth was no defense in such actions and while a proof of truth might prevent recovery in a civil action, this limitation is more readily explained as a manifestation of judicial reluctance to enrich an undeserving plaintiff than by the supposition that the defendant was protected by the truth of the publication. The same truthful statement might be the basis of a criminal libel action. See Commonwealth v. Clap, 4 Mass. 163; see generally Veeder, The History and Theory of the Law of Defamation, 3 Col.L.Rev. 546, 4 Cal.L.Rev. 33.

The law of libel has, of course, changed substantially since the early days of the Republic, and this change is 'the direct consequence of the friction between it * * * and the highly cherished right of free speech.' The emphasis has shifted from criminal to civil remedies, from the protection of absolute social values to the safeguarding of valid personal interests. Truth has become an absolute defense in almost all cases, and privileges designed to foster free communication are almost universally recognized. But the basic theory of libel has not changed, and words defamatory of another are still placed 'in the same class with the use of explosives or the keeping of dangerous animals.' Prosser, The Law of Torts s 108, at 792. Thus some antithesis between freedom of speech and press and libel actions persists, for libel remains premised on the content of speech and limits the freedom of the publisher to express certain sentiments, at least without guaranteeing legal proof of their substantial accuracy.

In light of the fact that the law of libel and the First Amendment were nurtured in different soils, yet grow in the same garden and compete for control of common ground, it is, perhaps, surprising that they did not tangle until relatively late in our legal history. Until New York Times v. Sullivan, however, accepted constitutional doctrine took libelous words, along with "fighting words" and obscenity to fall within the "well-defined and narrowly limited classes of speech, the prevention and punishment of which have never been thought to raise any Constitutional problem." Chaplinsky v. New Hampshire, 315 U.S. 568, 62 S.Ct. 766, 86 L.Ed. 1031 (1942).

When constitutionalization came, however, it came with the full force of an explosion long pent-up.

PUBLIC OFFICIALS AND PUBLIC FIGURES

NEW YORK TIMES CO. v. SULLIVAN
Supreme Court of the United States, 1964.
376 U.S. 254, 84 S.Ct. 710, 11 L.Ed.2d 686.

Mr. Justice BRENNAN delivered the opinion of the Court.

We are required for the first time in this case to determine the extent to which the constitutional protections for speech and press limit a State's power to award damages in a libel action brought by a public official against critics of his official conduct.

Respondent L.B. Sullivan is one of the three elected Commissioners of the City of Montgomery, Alabama. He testified that he was "Commissioner of Public Affairs and the duties are supervision of the Police Department, Fire Department, Department of Cemetery and Department of Scales." He brought this civil libel action against the four individual petitioners, who are Negroes and Alabama clergymen, and against petitioner the New York Times Company, a New York corporation which publishes the New York Times, a daily newspaper. A jury in the Circuit Court of Montgomery County awarded him damages of $500,000, the full amount claimed, against all the petitioners, and the Supreme Court of Alabama affirmed. 273 Ala. 656, 144 So.2d 25.

Respondent's complaint alleged that he had been libeled by statements in a full-page advertisement that was carried in the New York Times on March 29, 1960. * * *

Of the 10 paragraphs of text in the advertisement, the third and a portion of the sixth were the basis of respondent's claim of libel. They read as follows:

Third paragraph:

"In Montgomery, Alabama, after students sang, 'My Country, 'Tis of Thee' on the State Capitol steps, their leaders were expelled from school, and truckloads of police armed with shotguns and tear-gas ringed the Alabama State College Campus. When the entire student body protested to state authorities by refusing to re-register, their dining hall was padlocked in an attempt to starve them into submission."

Sixth paragraph:

"Again and again the Southern violators have answered Dr. King's peaceful protests with intimidation and violence. They have bombed his home almost killing his wife and child. They have assaulted his person. They have arrested him seven times—for 'speeding,' 'loitering' and similar 'offenses.' And now they have charged him with 'perjury'—a *felony* under which they would imprison him for *ten years.* * * * "

Although neither of these statements mentions respondent by name, he contended that the word "police" in the third paragraph referred to him as the Montgomery Commissioner who supervised the Police Department, so that he was being accused of "ringing" the campus with police. He further claimed that the paragraph would be read as imputing to the police, and hence to him, the padlocking of the dining hall in order to starve the students into submission. As to the sixth paragraph, he contended that since arrests are ordinarily made by the police, the statement "They have arrested [Dr. King] seven times" would be read as referring to him; he further contended that the "They" who did the arresting would be equated with the "They" who committed the other described acts and with the "Southern violators." Thus, he argued, the paragraph would be read as accusing the Montgomery police, and hence him, of answering Dr. King's protests with "intimidation and violence," bombing his home, assaulting his person, and charging him with perjury. Respondent and six other Montgomery residents testified that they read some or all of the statements as referring to him in his capacity as Commissioner.

It is uncontroverted that some of the statements contained in the two paragraphs were not accurate descriptions of events which occurred in Montgomery. Although Negro students staged a demonstration on the State Capitol steps, they sang the National Anthem and not "My Country, 'Tis of Thee." Although nine students were expelled by the State Board of Education, this was not for leading the demonstration at the Capitol, but for demanding service at a lunch counter in the Montgomery County Courthouse on another day. Not the entire student body, but most of it, had protested the expulsion, not by refusing to register, but by boycotting classes on a single day; virtually all the students did register for the ensuing semester. The campus dining hall was not padlocked on any occasion, and the only students who may have been barred from eating there were the few who had neither signed a preregistration application nor requested temporary meal tickets. Although the police were deployed near the campus in large numbers on three occasions, they did not at any time "ring" the campus, and they were not called to the campus in connection with the demonstration on the State Capitol steps, as the third paragraph implied. Dr. King had not been arrested seven times, but only four; and although he claimed to have been assaulted some years earlier in connection with his arrest for loitering outside a courtroom, one of the officers who made the arrest denied that there was such an assault.

On the premise that the charges in the sixth paragraph could be read as referring to him, respondent was allowed to prove that he had not participated in the events described. Although Dr. King's home had in fact been bombed twice when his wife and child were there, both of these occasions antedated respondent's tenure as Commissioner, and the police were not only not implicated in the bombings, but had made every effort to apprehend those who were. Three of Dr. King's four arrests took place before respondent became Commissioner. Although Dr. King had in fact been indicted (he was subsequently acquitted) on two counts of perjury, each of which carried a possible five-year sentence, respondent had nothing to do with procuring the indictment.

Respondent made no effort to prove that he suffered actual pecuniary loss as a result of the alleged libel. * * *

The cost of the advertisement was approximately $4800, and it was published by the Times upon an order from a New York advertising agency acting for the signatory Committee. * * * [No one] at the Times made an effort to confirm the accuracy of the advertisement, either by checking it against recent Times news stories relating to some of the described events or by some other means.

Alabama law denied a public officer recovery of punitive damages in a libel action brought on account of a publication concerning his official conduct unless he first makes a written demand for a public retraction and the defendant fails or refuses to comply. Alabama Code, Tit. 7, § 914. Respondent served such a demand upon each of the petitioners. * * * The times did not publish a retraction in response to the demand, but wrote respondent a letter stating, among other things, that "we * * * are somewhat puzzled as to how you think the statements in any way reflect on you," and "you might, if you desire, let us know in what respect you claim that the statements in the advertisement reflect on you." Respondent filed this suit a few days later without answering the letter. The Times did, however, subsequently publish a retraction of the advertisement upon the demand of Governor John Patterson of Alabama * * *. When asked to explain why there had been a retraction for the Governor but not for respondent, the Secretary of the Times testified: * * * that he did not think that "any of the language in there referred to Mr. Sullivan."

The trial judge submitted the case to the jury under instructions that the statements in the advertisement were "libelous per se" and were not privileged, so that petitioners might be held liable if the jury found that they had published the advertisement and that the statements were made "of and concerning" respondent. The jury was instructed that, because the statements were libelous *per se*, "the law * * * implies legal injury from the bare fact of publication itself," "falsity and malice are presumed," "general damages need not be alleged or proved but are presumed," and "punitive damages may be awarded by the jury even though the amount of actual damages is neither found nor shown." An award of punitive damages—as distinguished from "general" damages, which are compensatory in nature—apparently requires proof of actual malice under Alabama law, and the judge charged that "mere negligence or carelessness is not evidence of actual malice or malice in fact, and does not justify an award of exemplary or punitive damages." He refused to charge, however, that the jury must be "convinced" of malice, in the sense of "actual intent" to harm or "gross negligence and recklessness," to make such an award, and he also refused to require that a verdict for respondent differentiate between compensatory and punitive damages. The judge rejected petitioners' contention that his rulings abridged the freedoms of speech and of the press that are guaranteed by the First and Fourteenth Amendments.

In affirming the judgment, the Supreme Court of Alabama sustained the trial judge's rulings and instructions in all respects. 273 Ala. 656, 144 So.2d 25. * * *

Because of the importance of the constitutional issues involved, we granted the separate petitions for certiorari of the individual petitioners and of the Times. 371 U.S. 946, 83 S.Ct. 510, 9 L.Ed.2d 496. We reverse the judgment. We hold that the rule of law applied by the Alabama courts is constitutionally deficient for failure to provide the safeguards for freedom of speech and of the press that are required by the First and Fourteenth Amendments in a libel action brought by a public official against critics of his official conduct. We further hold that under the proper safeguards the evidence presented in this case is constitutionally insufficient to support the judgment for respondent.

* * *

Under Alabama law as applied in this case, a publication is "libelous per se" if the words "tend to injure a person * * * in his reputation" or to "bring [him] into public contempt"; the trial court stated that the standard was met if the words are such as to "injure him in his public office, or impute misconduct to him in his office, or want of official integrity, or want of fidelity to a public trust * * *." The jury must find that the words were published "of and concerning" the plaintiff, but where the plaintiff is a public official his place in the governmental hierarchy is sufficient evidence to support a finding that his reputation has been affected by statements that reflect upon the agency of which he is in charge. Once "libel per se" has been established, the defendant has no defense as to stated facts unless he can persuade the jury that they were true in all their particulars. [citations omitted] His privilege of "fair comment" for expressions of opinion depends on the truth of the facts upon which the comment is based. [citation omitted] Unless he can discharge the burden of proving truth, general damages are presumed, and may be awarded without proof of pecuniary injury. A showing of actual malice is apparently a prerequisite to recovery of punitive damages, and the defendant may in any event forestall these by a retraction meeting the statutory requirements. Good motives and belief in truth do not negate an inference of malice, but are relevant only in mitigation of punitive damages if the jury chooses to accord them weight. [Citation omitted.]

The question before us is whether this rule of liability, as applied to an action brought by a public official against critics of his official conduct, abridges the freedom of speech and of the press that is guaranteed by the First and Fourteenth Amendments.

* * *

The general proposition that freedom of expression upon public questions is secured by the First Amendment has long been settled by our decisions. * * * Mr. Justice Brandeis, in his concurring opinion in Whitney v. California, 274 U.S. 357, 375–76 (1927) gave the principle its classic formulation:

> Those who won our independence believed * * * that public discussion is a political duty; and that this should be a fundamental principle of American government. * * * Believing in the power of reason as applied through public discussion, they eschewed silence coerced by law—the argument of force in its worst form. Recognizing the occasional tyrannies of governing majorities, they amended the Constitution so that free speech and assembly should be guaranteed.

Thus we consider this case against the background of a profound national commitment to the principle that debate on public issues should be uninhibited, robust, and wide-open, and that it may well include vehement, caustic, and sometimes unpleasantly sharp attacks on government and public officials. The present advertisement, as an expression of grievance and protest on one of the major public issues of our time, would seem clearly to qualify for the constitutional protection. The question is whether it forfeits that protection by the falsity of some of its factual statements and by its alleged defamation of respondent.

Authoritative interpretations of the First Amendment guarantees have consistently refused to recognize an exception for any test of truth, whether administered by judges, juries, or administrative officials—and especially not one that puts the burden of proving truth on the speaker. * * *

Just as factual error affords no warrant for repressing speech that would otherwise be free, the same is true of injury to official reputation. Where judicial officers are involved, this Court has held that concern for the dignity and reputation of the courts does not justify the punishment as criminal contempt of criticism of the judge or his decision. This is true even though the utterance contains "half-truths" and "misinformation." Pennekamp v. Florida, 328 U.S. 331, 342, 343, n. 5, 345, 66 S.Ct. 1029, 90 L.Ed. 1295; such repression can be justified, if at all, only by a clear and present danger of the obstruction of justice. If judges are to be treated as "men of fortitude, able to thrive in a hardy climate," [citation omitted] surely the same must be true of other government officials, such as elected city commissioners. Criticism of their official conduct does not lose its constitutional protection merely because it is effective criticism and hence diminishes their official reputations.

* * *

What a State may not constitutionally bring about by means of a criminal statute is likewise beyond the reach of its civil law of libel. The fear of damage awards under a rule such as that invoked by the Alabama courts here may be markedly more inhibiting than the fear of prosecution under a criminal statute. Alabama, for example, has a criminal libel law which subjects to prosecution "any person who speaks, writes, or prints of and concerning another any accusation falsely and maliciously importing the commission by such person of a felony, or any other indictable offense involving moral turpitude," and which allows as punishment upon conviction a fine not exceeding $500 and a prison sentence of six months. Alabama Code, Tit. 14, § 350. Presumably a person charged with violation of this statute enjoys ordinary criminal-law safeguards such as the requirements of an indictment and of proof beyond a reasonable doubt. These safeguards are not available to the defendant in a civil action. The judgment awarded in this case—without the need for any proof of actual pecuniary loss—was one thousand times greater than the maximum fine provided by the Alabama criminal statute, and one hundred times greater than that provided by the Sedition Act. And since there is no double-jeopardy limitation applicable to civil lawsuits, this is not the only judgment that may be awarded against petitioners for the same publication. Whether or not a newspaper can survive a succession of such judgments, the pall of fear and timidity imposed upon those who would give voice to public criticism is an atmosphere in which the First Amendment freedoms cannot survive. Plainly the Alabama law of civil libel is "a form of regulation that creates hazards to protected freedoms markedly greater than those that attend reliance upon the criminal law." Bantam Books, Inc. v. Sullivan, 372 U.S. 58, 70, 83 S.Ct. 631, 639, 9 L.Ed.2d 584.

The state rule of law is not saved by its allowance of the defense of truth. A defense for erroneous statements honestly made is no less essential here than was the requirement of proof of guilty knowledge which, in Smith v. California, 361 U.S. 147, 80 S.Ct. 215, 4 L.Ed.2d 205, we held indispensable to a valid conviction of a bookseller for possessing obscene writings for sale.

* * *

A rule compelling the critic of official conduct to guarantee the truth of all his factual assertions—and to do so on pain of libel judgments virtually unlimited in amount—leads to a comparable "self-censorship." Allowance of the defense of truth, with the burden of proving it on the defendant, does not mean that only false speech will be deterred. Even courts accepting this defense as an adequate safeguard have recognized the difficulties of adducing legal proofs that the alleged libel was true in all its factual particulars.

Under such a rule, Would-be critics of official conduct may be deterred from voicing their criticism, even though it is believed to be true and even though it is in fact true, because of doubt whether it can be proved in court or fear of the expense of having to do so. They tend to make only statements which "steer far wider of the unlawful zone." [citation omitted] The rule thus dampens the vigor and limits the variety of public debate. It is inconsistent with the First and Fourteenth Amendments.

The constitutional guarantees require, we think, a federal rule that prohibits a public official from recovering damages for a defamatory false-hood relating to his official conduct unless he proves that the statement was made with "actual malice"—that is, with knowledge that it was false or with reckless disregard of whether it was false or not.

* * *

We conclude that such a privilege is required by the First and Four-teenth Amendments.

We hold today that the Constitution delimits a State's power to award damages for libel in actions brought by public officials against critics of their official conduct. Since this is such an action the rule requiring proof of actual malice is applicable. * * *

Since respondent may seek a new trial, we deem that considerations of effective judicial administration require us to review the evidence in the present record to determine whether it could constitutionally support a judgment for respondent. This Court's duty is not limited to the elaboration of constitutional principles; we must also in proper cases review the evidence to make certain that those principles have been constitutionally applied. This is such a case, particularly since the question is one of alleged trespass across "the line between speech unconditionally guaranteed and speech which may legitimately be regulated." Speiser v. Randall, 357 U.S. 513, 525, 78 S.Ct. 1332, 1342, 2 L.Ed.2d 1460. * * *

Applying these standards, we consider that the proof presented to show actual malice lacks the convincing clarity which the constitutional standard demands, and hence that it would not constitutionally sustain the judgment for respondent under the proper rule of law. The case of the individual petitioners requires little discussion. Even assuming that they could constitu-tionally be found to have authorized the use of their names on the advertisement, there was no evidence whatever that they were aware of any erroneous statements or were in any way reckless in that regard. The judgment against them is thus without constitutional support.

* * *

We also think the evidence was constitutionally defective in another respect: it was incapable of supporting the jury's finding that the allegedly libelous statements were made "of and concerning" respondent.

* * *

Mr. Justice BLACK, with whom Mr. Justice DOUGLAS joins (concurring).

I concur in reversing this half-million-dollar judgment against the New York Times and the four individual defendants. * * * I base my vote to reverse on the belief that the First and Fourteenth Amendments not merely "delimit" a State's power to award damages to "a public official against critics of his official conduct" but completely prohibit a State from exercising such a power. The Court goes on to hold that a State can subject such critics to damages if "actual malice" can be proved against them. "Malice," even as defined by the Court, is an elusive, abstract concept, hard to prove and hard to disprove. The requirement that malice be proved provides at best an evanescent protection for the right critically to discuss public affairs and certainly does not measure up to the sturdy safeguard embodied in the First Amendment. Unlike the Court, therefore, I vote to reverse exclusively on the ground that the Times and the individual defendants had an absolute, unconditional constitutional right to publish in the Times advertisement their criticisms of the Montgomery agencies and officials. * * * Nor is my reason for reversal the size of the half-million-dollar judgment, large as it is. If Alabama has constitutional power to use its civil libel law to impose damages on the press for criticizing the way public officials perform or fail to perform their duties, I know of no provision in the Federal Constitution which either expressly or impliedly bars the State from fixing the amount of damages.

The half-million-dollar verdict does give dramatic proof, however, that state libel laws threaten the very existence of an American press virile enough to publish unpopular views on public affairs and bold enough to criticize the conduct of public officials.

* * *

* * * An unconditional right to say what one pleases about public affairs is what I consider to be the minimum guarantee of the First Amendment.

I regret that the Court has stopped short of this holding indispensable to preserve our free press from destruction.

Mr. Justice GOLDBERG, with whom Mr. Justice DOUGLAS joins (concurring in the result).

* * *

In my view, the First and Fourteenth Amendments to the Constitution afford to the citizen and to the press an absolute, unconditional privilege to criticize official conduct despite the harm which may flow from excesses and abuses. The prized American right "to speak one's mind," about public officials and affairs needs "breathing space to survive," [citation omitted] The right should not depend upon a probing by the jury of the motivation of the citizen or press. The theory of our Constitution is that every citizen may speak his mind and every newspaper express its view on matters of public concern and may not be barred from speaking or publishing because those in control of government think that what is said or written is unwise, unfair, false, or malicious. * * *

* * *

The conclusion that the Constitution affords the citizen and the press an absolute privilege for criticism of official conduct does not leave the public official without defenses against unsubstantiated opinions or deliberate misstatements. "Under our system of government, counter argument and education are the weapons available to expose these matters, not abridgement * * * of free speech * * *." Wood v. Georgia, 370 U.S. 375, 389, 82 S.Ct. 1364, 1372, 8 L.Ed.2d 569. The public official certainly has equal if not greater access than most private citizens to media of communication. In any event, despite the possibility that some excesses and abuses may go unremedied, we must recognize that "the people of this nation have ordained in the light of history, that, in spite of the probability of excesses and abuses, [certain] liberties are, in the long view, essential to enlightened opinion and right conduct on the part of the citizens of a democracy." Cantwell v. Connecticut, 310 U.S. 296, 310, 60 S.Ct. 900, 906, 84 L.Ed. 1213. As Mr. Justice Brandeis correctly observed, "sunlight is the most powerful of all disinfectants."

For these reasons, I strongly believe that the Constitution accords citizens and press an unconditional freedom to criticize official conduct. It necessarily follows that in a case such as this, where all agree that the allegedly defamatory statements related to official conduct, the judgments for libel cannot constitutionally be sustained.

ST. AMANT v. THOMPSON, 390 U.S. 727, 88 S.Ct. 1323, 20 L.Ed.2d 262 (1968). Petitioner made a televised political speech in which he charged respondent, deputy sheriff, with criminal conduct, without having checked the charges or investigating the source's reputation for truthfulness. *Held*, failure to investigate, by itself, did not establish "reckless disregard."

"The defendant in a defamation action brought by a public official cannot, however, automatically insure a favorable verdict by testifying that he published with a belief that the statements were true. The finder of fact must determine whether the publication was indeed made in good faith. Professions of good faith will be unlikely to prove persuasive, for example, where a story is fabricated by defendant, is the product of his imagination, or is based wholly on an unverified anonymous telephone call. Nor will they be likely to prevail when the publisher's allegations are so inherently improbable that only a reckless man would have put them in circulation. Likewise, recklessness may be found where there are obvious reasons to doubt the veracity of the informant or the accuracy of his reports."

Justice Fortas dissented, on the ground that the failure to make "a good faith" check into the statement was sufficient to establish "reckless disregard."

HERBERT v. LANDO, 441 U.S. 153, 99 S.Ct. 1635, 60 L.Ed.2d 115 (1979) (White, Justice). Plaintiff a Colonel in the Army brought suit against Lando, the producer of an episode of the television show "60 Minutes" (along with CBS, the network which broadcast the show) because of criticism voiced in the episode about Lando's behavior as an American military officer in Vietnam. During pretrial discovery, Lando refused to answer some questions about why he made certain investigations and not others; what conclusions he had drawn about the honesty of various people he had interviewed; and conversations he had had with Mike Wallace, then a reporter for the program. Lando asserted that these discussions and thought processes were protected from disclosure by the First Amendment. The Supreme Court disagreed.

"In the first place, it is plain enough that the suggested privilege for the editorial process would constitute a substantial interference with the ability of a defamation plaintiff to establish the ingredients of malice as required by *New York Times*. As respondents would have it, the defendant's reckless disregard of the truth, a critical element, could not be shown by direct evidence through inquiry into the thoughts, opinions and conclusions of the publisher but could be proved only by objective evidence from which the ultimate fact could be inferred. It may be that plaintiffs will rarely be successful in proving awareness of falsehood from the mouths of the defendant himself, but the relevance of answers to such inquiries * * * can hardly be doubted. To erect an impenetrable barrier to the plaintiff's use of such evidence on his sided of the case is a matter of some substance, particularly when defendants themselves are prone to assert their good-faith belief in the truth of their publications, and libel plaintiffs are required to prove knowing or reckless falsehood with 'convincing clarity.' "

———

LONG. v. ARCELL, 618 F.2d 1145 (5th Cir.1980). *Held*, JNOV in favor of defendant newspaper, affirmed. The only evidence for the jury involved conflicting accounts of conversations. "If the applicable burden of proof had been a preponderance of the evidence, a jury verdict either way would have to stand. * * * [But] [t]his record simply does not contain *clear and convincing evidence* that the defendants knew that their information was incorrect or had a 'high degree of awareness' of its 'probable falsity.' (emphasis supplied)."

ANDERSON v. LIBERTY LOBBY, 477 U.S. 242, 106 S.Ct. 2505, 91 L.Ed.2d 202 (1986) (White, Justice). The columnist Jack Anderson published several articles about the Liberty Lobby, portraying it as "neo-Nazi, anti-Semitic, racist, and fascist." At the end of discovery, Anderson moved for summary judgment on the basis of affidavits signed by his principal researcher, asserting that the researcher had spent "substantial time" researching the articles. The District Court granted the motion, after holding that *New York Times v. Sullivan* applied to the case. The Court of Appeals reversed in part, holding that for purposes of summary judgment, the requirement that actual malice be proved by clear and convincing evidence, rather than by a preponderance of the evidence was irrelevant. *Held*, on further appeal to the Supreme Court, reversed and remanded. *New York Times v. Sullivan's* "clear-and-convincing evidence" requirement must be considered by a court ruling on a summary judgment motion.

" * * * [W]e are convinced that the inquiry involved in a ruling on a motion for summary judgment or for a directed verdict necessarily implicates the substantive evidentiary standard of proof that would apply at the trial on the merits. If the defendant in a run-of-the-mill civil case moves for summary judgment or for a directed verdict based on the lack of proof of a material fact, the * * * judge's inquiry * * unavoidably asks whether reasonable jurors could find by a preponderance of the evidence, that the plaintiff is entitled to a verdict * * * ''

* * *

"Thus, in ruling on a motion for summary judgment, the judge must view the evidence presented through the prism of the substantive evidentiary burden. This conclusion is mandated by the nature of this determination. The question here is whether a jury could reasonably find *either* that the plaintiff proved his case by the quality and quantity of evidence required by the governing law *or* that he did not. Whether a jury could reasonably find for either party, however, cannot be defined except by the criterial governing what evidence would enable the jury to find for either party without some benchmark as to what standards govern its deliberations and within what boundaries its ultimate decision must fall, and these standards and boundaries are in fact provided by the applicable evidentiary standards."

Justice Brennan dissented on the ground that "whether evidence is 'clear and convincing' or proves a point by a mere preponderance, is for the factfinder to determine." Justice Rhenquist, joined by Chief Justice Burger, dissented complaining that "[t]he primary effect of the Court's opinion today will likely be to cause the decisions of trial judges on summary judgment motions in libel cases to be more erratic and inconsistent than before. This is largely because the Court has created a standard that is different from the standard traditionally applied in summary judgment motions without even hinting as to how its new standard will be applied to particular cases."

BOSE CORP. v. CONSUMERS UNION, 466 U.S. 485, 104 S.Ct. 1949, 80 L.Ed.2d 502 (1984) (Stevens, Justice). Plaintiff brought a "product disparagement" claim against defendant. A federal district judge sitting as the trier of fact found actual malice and entered judgment against the defendant, publisher of the magazine *Consumer Reports*. After undertaking an independent examination of the record—which it believed was required by *New York Times v. Sullivan*—the Court of Appeals reversed. *Held*, affirmed.

"The requirement of independent appellate review reiterated in *New York Times Co. v. Sullivan* is a rule of federal constitutional law. * * * The question whether the evidence in the record in a defamation case is of the convincing clarity required to strip the utterance of First Amendment protection is not merely a question for the trier of fact. Judges, as expositors of the Constitution, must independently decide whether the evidence in the record is sufficient to cross the constitutional threshold that bars the entry of any judgment that is not supported by clear and convincing proof of 'actual malice.' "

PUBLIC FIGURES

CURTIS PUBLISHING CO.V. BUTTS
Supreme Court of the United States, 1967.
388 U.S. 130, 87 S.Ct. 1975, 18 L.Ed.2d 1094.

[An article published in the Saturday Evening Post, which was owned by Curtis Publishing Company, accused Butts, the coach of the University of Georgia football team of conspiring to fix a 1962 Georgia–Alabama game by giving Paul Bryant, coach of the University of Alabama team, crucial information about Georgia's offensive strategy. The evidence tended to exculpate Butts and to show that the Post had "departed greatly from the standards of good investigation and reporting." The case came to the Supreme Court on appeal from a jury verdict against Curtis, affirmed on appeal.

Butts was considered in conjunction with another case, *Associated Press v. Walker*, which arose out of the distribution of a news dispatch by the Associated Press giving an eyewitness account of events on the campus of the University of Mississippi on the night of September 30, 1962, "when a massive riot erupted because of federal efforts to enforce a court decree ordering the enrollment of a Negro, James Meredith, as a student in the University." Among other things, the news dispatcher reported that Edwin Walker had taken command of a crowd resisting integration, and had led a charge against the federal marshals enforcing the decree. *Walker* also came to the Supreme Court on a jury verdict for the plaintiff, affirmed on appeal.]

Mr. Justice HARLAN announced the judgments of the Court and delivered an opinion in which Mr. Justice CLARK, Mr. Justice STEWART, and Mr. Justice FORTAS join

* * *

In New York Times [v. Sullivan] we were adjudicating in an area which lay close to seditious libel, and history dictated extreme caution in imposing liability. The plaintiff in that case was an official whose position in government was such "that the public (had) an independent interest in the qualifications and performance of the person who (held) it." Such officials usually enjoy a privilege against libel actions for their utterances, and there were analogous considerations involved in New York Times. Thus we invoked "the hypothesis that speech can rebut speech, propaganda will answer propaganda, free debate of ideas will result in the wisest governmental policies", Dennis v. United States, 341 U.S. 494, 503, 71 S.Ct. 857, 864, 95 L.Ed. 1137, and limited recovery to those cases where "calculated falsehood" placed the publisher "at odds with the premises of democratic government and with the orderly manner in which economic, social, or political change is to be effected." That is to say, such officials were permitted to recover in libel only when they could prove that the publication involved was deliberately falsified, or published recklessly despite the publisher's awareness of probable falsity. Investigatory failures alone were held insufficient to satisfy this standard.

In the cases we decide today none of the particular considerations involved in New York Times is present. These actions cannot be analogized to prosecutions for seditious libel. Neither plaintiff has any position in government which would permit a recovery by him to be viewed as a vindication of governmental policy. Neither was entitled to a special privilege protecting his utterances against accountability in libel. We are prompted, therefore, to seek guidance from the rules of liability which prevail in our society with respect to compensation of persons injured by the improper performance of a legitimate activity by another. Under these rules, a departure from the kind of care society may expect from a reasonable man performing such activity leaves the actor open to a judicial shifting of loss. In defining these rules, and especially in formulating the standards for determining the degree of care to be expected in the circumstances, courts have consistently given much attention to the importance of defendants' activities. Prosser, The Law of Torts s 31, at 151. The courts have also, especially in libel cases, investigated the plaintiff's position to determine whether he has a legitimate call upon the court for protection in light of his prior activities and means of self-defense. We note that the public interest in the circulation of the materials here involved, and the publisher's interest in circulating them, is not less than that involved in New York Times. And both Butts and Walker commanded a substantial amount of independent public interest at the time of the publications; both, in our opinion, would have been labeled "public figures" under ordinary tort rules. See Spahn v. Julian Messner, Inc., 18 N.Y.2d 324, 274 N.Y.S.2d 877, 221 N.E.2d 543, remanded on other grounds, 387 U.S. 239, 87 S.Ct. 1706, 18 L.Ed.2d 744. Butts may have attained that status by position alone and Walker by his purposeful activity amounting to a thrusting of his personality into the "vortex" of an important public controversy, but both commanded sufficient continuing public interest and had sufficient access to the means of counterargument to be able "to expose through discussion the falsehood and fallacies" of the defamatory statements. Whitney v. People of State of California, 274 U.S. 357, 377, 47 S.Ct. 641, 649, (Brandeis, J., dissenting).

These similarities and differences between libel actions involving persons who are public officials and libel actions involving those circumstanced as were Butts and Walker, viewed in light of the principles of liability which are of general applicability in our society, lead us to the conclusion that libel actions of the present kind cannot be left entirely to state libel laws, unlimited by any overriding constitutional safeguard, but that the rigorous federal requirements of New York Times [v. Sullivan] are not the only appropriate accommodation of the conflicting interests at stake. We consider and would hold that a "public figure" who is not a public official may also recover damages for a defamatory falsehood whose substance makes substantial danger to reputation apparent, on a showing of highly unreasonable conduct constituting an extreme departure from the standards of investigation and reporting ordinarily adhered to by responsible publishers. Cf. Sulzberger, Responsibility and Freedom, in Nelson, Freedom of the Press from Hamilton to the Warren Court 409, 412.

[Judgment in *Butts* affirmed; judgment in *Walker* reversed.]

PRIVATE PARTIES

First Amendment concern with defamation law radiates out from the core of cases involving public officials and matters of deep public importance, through ones involving public figures and on to ones involving private parties, either in connection with public matters or in connection with private matters. Where defamation actions involve only private parties and private matters, the concerns of the First Amendment may be exhausted and states may be free to retain (or return to) the traditional rules of defamation, including strict liability.

GERTZ v. ROBERT WELCH, INC.

Supreme Court of the United States, 1974.
418 U.S. 323, 94 S.Ct. 2997, 41 L.Ed.2d 789.

[The petitioner was an attorney who had been retained to represent the family of a youth killed by a Chicago policeman named Nuccio, in a civil suit against Nuccio. Nuccio had been prosecuted for the homicide and convicted of second degree murder. In his capacity as counsel to family in the civil litigation, Gertz had attended the coroner's inquest into Nelson's death and had initiated the civil damages suit, but he had not discussed Officer Nuccio with the press and had played no role in the criminal case. The respondent published American Opinion, a monthly outlet for the views of the John Birch Society. Early in the 1960's the magazine began to warn of a nationwide conspiracy to discredit local law enforcement agencies and to create in their place a national police force capable of supporting a communist dictatorship. As part of its efforts to alert the public to this danger, the magazine's editor engaged a regular contributor to the magazine to write about the Nuccio episode. The resulting article charged that Nuccio was the victim of a "frame-up" of which Gertz was a "major architect." The article falsely asserted that Gertz had a long police record, was an official of the Marxist League for Industrial Democracy, was a "Leninist" and a "Communist-fronter." The article also described Gertz as an officer of the National Lawyers Guild, which the article described as a communist organization that "probably did more than any other outfit to plan the Communist attack on the Chicago police during the 1968 Democratic Convention." The only truth in this allegation was that Gertz "had been a member and officer of the National Lawyers Guild some fifteen years earlier." The editor of American Opinion "made no effort to verify or substantiate the charges" against Gertz.

Gertz brought suit in federal District Court, on diversity grounds. At first, the trial judge ruled that Gertz was not a public official or public figure and that there was no defense to his defamation suit under Illinois law. The jury awarded Gertz $50,000. The judge then changed his mind and granted the defendant judgment notwithstanding the verdict, on the ground that matters of public concern were being discussed and *New York Times v. Sullivan* therefore applied. The Court of Appeals affirmed, Relying on the intervening decision of the Supreme Court in *Rosenbloom v. Metromedia, Inc.*, 403 U.S. 29, 91 S.Ct. 1811, 29 L.Ed.2d 296 (1971) the Court of Appeals concluded that clear and convincing evidence of actual malice was absent. Relying on *St. Amant v. Thompson*, [supra p. 190] the court concluded that reckless disregard for truth could not be established by mere failure to investigate. Gertz appealed.]

Mr. Justice POWELL delivered the opinion of the Court.

* * *

We begin with the common ground. Under the First Amendment there is no such thing as a false idea. However pernicious an opinion may seem, we depend for its correction not on the conscience of judges and juries but on the competition of other ideas.[2] But there is no constitutional value in false statements of fact. Neither the intentional lie nor the careless error materially advances society's interest in "uninhibited, robust, and wide-open" debate on public issues. New York Times Co. v. Sullivan, 376 U.S., at 270, 84 S.Ct., at 721. They belong to that category of utterances which "are no essential part of any exposition of ideas, and are of such slight social value as a step to truth that any benefit that may be derived from them is clearly outweighed by the social interest in order and morality." Chaplinsky v. New Hampshire, 315 U.S. 568, 572, 62 S.Ct. 766, 769, 86 L.Ed. 1031 (1942).

Although the erroneous statement of fact is not worthy of constitutional protection, it is nevertheless inevitable in free debate. As James Madison pointed out in the Report on the Virginia Resolutions of 1798, "Some degree of abuse is inseparable from the proper use of everything; and in no instance is this more true than that of the press." 4 Elliot's Debates (1876), p. 571. And punishment of error runs the risk of inducing a cautious and restrictive exercise of the constitutionally guaranteed freedoms of speech and press. Our decisions recognize that a rule of strict liability that compels a publisher or broadcaster to guarantee the accuracy of his factual assertions may lead to intolerable self-censorship. Allowing the media to avoid liability only by proving the truth of all injurious statements does not accord adequate protection to First Amendment liberties. As the Court stated in New York Times Co. v. Sullivan, supra, 376 U.S., at 279, 84 S.Ct., at 725, "Allowance of the defense of truth, with the burden of proving it on the defendant, does not mean that only false speech will be deterred." The First Amendment requires that we protect some falsehood in order to protect speech that matters.

The need to avoid self-censorship by the news media is, however, not the only societal value at issue. If it were, this Court would have embraced long ago the view that publishers and broadcasters enjoy an unconditional

---

2. As Thomas Jefferson made the point in his first Inaugural Address: "If there be any among us who wish to dissolve this union or change its republican form of government, let them stand undisturbed as monuments of the safety with which error of opinion may be tolerated where reason is left free to combat it."

and indefeasible immunity from liability for defamation. Such a rule would indeed obviate the fear that the prospect of civil liability for injurious falsehood might dissuade a timorous press from the effective exercise of First Amendment freedoms. Yet absolute protection for the communications media requires a total sacrifice of the competing value served by the law of defamation.

The legitimate state interest underlying the law of libel is the compensation of individuals for the harm inflicted on them by defamatory falsehoods. We would not lightly require the State to abandon this purpose, for, as Mr. Justice Stewart has reminded us, the individual's right to the protection of his own good name "reflects no more than our basic concept of the essential dignity and worth of every human being—a concept at the root of any decent system of ordered liberty. The protection of private personality, like the protection of life itself, is left primarily to the individual states under the Ninth and Tenth Amendments. But this does not mean that the right is entitled to any less recognition by this Court as a basic of our constitutional system." Rosenblatt v. Baer, 383 U.S. 75, 92–93, 86 S.Ct. 669, 679, 15 L.Ed.2d 597 (1966) (opinion of Stewart, J.).

Some tension necessarily exists between the need for a vigorous and uninhibited press and the legitimate interest in redressing wrongful injury. As Mr. Justice Harlan stated, "some antithesis between freedom of speech and press and libel actions persists, for libel remains premised on the content of speech and limits the freedom of the publisher to express certain sentiments, at least without guaranteeing legal proof of their substantial accuracy." Curtis Publishing Co. v. Butts, 388 U.S., at 152, 87 S.Ct., at 1990. In our continuing effort to define the proper accommodation between these competing concerns, we have been especially anxious to assure to the freedoms of speech and press that "breathing space" essential to their fruitful exercise. To that end this Court has extended a measure of strategic protection to defamatory falsehood.

* * *

With that caveat we have no difficulty in distinguishing among defamation plaintiffs. The first remedy of any victim of defamation is self-help—using available opportunities to contradict the lie or correct the error and thereby to minimize its adverse impact on reputation. Public officials and public figures usually enjoy significantly greater access to the channels of effective communication and hence have a more realistic opportunity to counteract false statements than private individuals normally enjoy.[9] Private individuals are therefore more vulnerable to injury, and the state interest in protecting them is correspondingly greater.

More important than the likelihood that private individuals will lack effective opportunities for rebuttal, there is a compelling normative consideration underlying the distinction between public and private defamation

---

9. Of course, an opportunity for rebuttal seldom suffices to undo harm of defamatory falsehood. Indeed, the law of defamation is rooted in our experience that the truth rarely catches up with a lie. But the fact that the self-help remedy of rebuttal, standing alone, is inadequate to its task does not mean that it is irrelevant to our inquiry.

plaintiffs. An individual who decides to seek governmental office must accept certain necessary consequences of that involvement in public affairs. He runs the risk of closer public scrutiny than might otherwise be the case. And society's interest in the officers of government is not strictly limited to the formal discharge of official duties. As the Court pointed out in Garrison v. Louisiana, 379 U.S. 64, 77, 85 S.Ct. 209, 217, 13 L.Ed.2d 125 (1964), the public's interest extends to "anything that might touch on an official's fitness for office. * * * Few personal attributes are more germane to witness for office than dishonesty, malfeasance, or improper motivation, even though these characteristics may also affect the official's private character."

Those classed as public figures stand in a similar position. Hypothetically, it may be possible for someone to become a public figure through no purposeful action of his own, but the instances of truly involuntary public figures must be exceedingly rare. * * * More commonly, those classed as public figures have thrust themselves to the forefront of particular public controversies in order to influence the resolution of the issues involved. In either event, they invite attention and comment.

* * *

We hold that, so long as they do not impose liability without fault, the States may define for themselves the appropriate standard of liability for a publisher or broadcaster of defamatory falsehood injurious to a private individual.[10] This approach provides a more equitable boundary between the competing concerns involved here. It recognizes the strength of the legitimate state interest in compensating private individuals for wrongful injury to reputation, yet shields the press and broadcast media from the rigors of strict liability for defamation. At least this conclusion obtains where, as here, the substance of the defamatory statement makes substantial danger to reputation apparent.[11] This phrase places in perspective the conclusion we announce today. Our inquiry would involve considerations somewhat different from those discussed above if a State purported to condition civil liability on a factual misstatement whose content did not warn a reasonably prudent editor or broadcaster of its defamatory potential. Cf. Time, Inc. v. Hill, 385 U.S. 374, 87 S.Ct. 534, 17 L.Ed.2d 456 (1967). Such a case is not now before us, and we intimate no view as to its proper resolution.

* * *

[Reversed and remanded.]

GERTZ v. ROBERT WELCH, INC., 680 F.2d 527 (7th Cir.1982). On remand, Gertz having amended his complaint to allege both negligence and actual malice, the jury found in favor of Gertz and awarded compensatory damages of $100,000 and punitive damages of $300,000. Held, judgment on the verdict affirmed.

10. Our caveat against strict liability is the prime target of Mr. Justice White's dissent. * * *

11. Curtis Publishing Co. v. Butts, 388 U.S. 130, 155, 87 S.Ct. 1975, 1991, 18 L.Ed.2d 1094 (1967).

PHILADELPHIA NEWSPAPERS, INC. v. HEPPS, 475 U.S. 767, 106 S.Ct. 1558, 89 L.Ed.2d 783 (1986) "To ensure that true speech on matters of public concern is not deterred, we hold that the common-law presumption that defamatory speech is false cannot stand when a plaintiff seeks damages against a media defendant for speech of public concern."

DUN & BRADSTREET, INC. v. GREENMOSS BUILDERS, INC., 472 U.S. 749, 105 S.Ct. 2939, 86 L.Ed.2d 593 (1985). Dun & Bradstreet ("D & B") issued a credit report on the plaintiff to several customers, which stated that the plaintiff had filed for voluntary bankruptcy. The report was inaccurate. Greenmoss learned of the error and asked D & B both to send out an immediate correction and to provide it with a list of clients who had received the report. D & B sent out a correction letter. The letter noted the error in the original report, but did not provide a complete appraisal of Greenmoss's actual financial position. D & B then refused to take any further action. Greenmoss sued in state court ... The jury returned a verdict of $50,000 in presumed damages and $300,000 in punitive damages. The Vermont Supreme Court affirmed, noting that *Gertz* was limited to media defendants.

"In light of the reduced constitutional value of speech involving no matters of public concern, we hold that the state interest adequately supports awards of presumed and punitive damages—even absent a showing of "actual malice."

ROSENBLATT v. BAER, 383 U.S. 75, 86 S.Ct. 669, 15 L.Ed.2d 597 (1966) (Stewart J., concurring) " 'Civil actions for slander and libel developed in early ages as a substitute for the duel and a deterrent to murder. They lie within the genuine orbit of the common law, and in the distribution of American sovereignty they fall exclusively within the jurisdiction of the states. The First Amendment further assures their exclusion from the federal domain. The Fourteenth Amendment, by absorbing the First, unquestionably gives the Supreme Court authority to block state use of civil suits as a substitute for laws of seditious libel. But considering the differences in derivation, in purpose, in value to society, and in the natural location of power, there seems to be no compelling constitutional reason to bar private suits. The most absolute construction of the First Amendment, as applied to the states by the Fourteenth, would permit a line to be drawn between the spurious common law of seditious libel and the genuine common law of civil liability for defamation of private character. It is the misuse of civil liability that offends the Constitution.' [Irving] Brant, The Bill of Rights: Its Origin and Meaning 502—503 (1965)."

MILKOVICH v. LORAIN JOURNAL CO.
Supreme Court of the United States, 1990.
497 U.S. 1, 110 S.Ct. 2695, 111 L.Ed.2d 1.

CHIEF JUSTICE RHENQUIST delivered the Opinion of the Court.

Respondent J. Theodore Diadiun authored an article in an Ohio newspaper implying that petitioner Michael Milkovich, a local high school wrestling coach, lied under oath in a judicial proceeding about an incident involving petitioner and his team which occurred at a wrestling match. Petitioner sued Diadiun and the newspaper for libel, and the Ohio Court of Appeals affirmed a lower court entry of summary judgment against petitioner. This judgment was based in part on the grounds that the article constituted an "opinion" protected from the reach of state defamation law by the First Amendment to the United States Constitution. We hold that the First Amendment does not prohibit the application of Ohio's libel laws to the alleged defamations contained in the article.

* * *

Respondents would have us recognize, * * * [a] First–Amendment-based protection for defamatory statements which are categorized as "opinion" as opposed to "fact." For this proposition they rely principally on the following dictum from our opinion in *Gertz*:

> Under the First Amendment there is no such thing as a false idea. However pernicious an opinion may seem, we depend for its correction not on the conscience of judges and juries but on the competition of other ideas. But there is no constitutional value in false statements of fact.

Judge Friendly appropriately observed that this passage "has become the opening salvo in all arguments for protection from defamation actions on the ground of opinion, even though the case did not remotely concern the question." *Cianci v. New Times Publishing Co.,* 639 F.2d 54, 61 (CA2 1980). Read in context, though, the fair meaning of the passage is to equate the word "opinion" in the second sentence with the word "idea" in the first sentence. Under this view, the language was merely a reiteration of Justice Holmes' classic "marketplace of ideas" concept. See *Abrams v. United States,* 250 U.S. 616, 630, 40 S.Ct. 17, 22, 63 L.Ed. 1173 (1919) (dissenting opinion) ("[T]he ultimate good desired is better reached by free trade in ideas— . . . the best test of truth is the power of the thought to get itself accepted in the competition of the market").

Thus, we do not think this passage from *Gertz* was intended to create a wholesale defamation exemption for anything that might be labeled "opinion." See *Cianci, supra,* at 62, n. 10 (The "marketplace of ideas" origin of this passage "points strongly to the view that the 'opinions' held to be constitutionally protected were the sort of thing that could be corrected by discussion"). Not only would such an interpretation be contrary to the tenor and context of the passage, but it would also ignore the fact that expressions of "opinion" may often imply an assertion of objective fact.

If a speaker says, "In my opinion John Jones is a liar," he implies a knowledge of facts which lead to the conclusion that Jones told an untruth. Even if the speaker states the facts upon which he bases his opinion, if those facts are either incorrect or incomplete, or if his assessment of them is erroneous, the statement may still imply a false assertion of fact. Simply couching such statements in terms of opinion does not dispel these implications. * * * It is worthy of note that at common law, even the privilege of fair comment did not extend to "a false statement of fact, whether it was expressly stated or implied from an expression of opinion." Restatement (Second) of Torts, § 566, Comment *a* (1977).

* * *

* * * [W]e think *Hepps* stands for the proposition that a statement on matters of public concern must be provable as false before there can be liability under state defamation law, at least in situations, like the present, where a media defendant is involved.[7] Thus, unlike the statement, "In my opinion Mayor Jones is a liar," the statement, "In my opinion Mayor Jones shows his abysmal ignorance by accepting the teachings of Marx and Lenin," would not be actionable. *Hepps* ensures that a statement of opinion relating to matters of public concern which does not contain a provably false factual connotation will receive full constitutional protection.[8]

Next, the *Bresler-Letter Carriers–Falwell* line of cases provides protection for statements that cannot "reasonably [be] interpreted as stating actual facts" about an individual. This provides assurance that public debate will not suffer for lack of "imaginative expression" or the "rhetorical hyperbole" which has traditionally added much to the discourse of our Nation.

The *New York Times–Butts-Gertz* culpability requirements further ensure that debate on public issues remains "uninhibited, robust, and wideopen." * * * Finally, the enhanced appellate review required by *Bose Corp.* provides assurance that the foregoing determinations will be made in a manner so as not to "constitute a forbidden intrusion of the field of free expression." *Bose Corp.*, 466 U.S., at 499, 104 S.Ct., at 1959 (quotation omitted).

We are not persuaded that, in addition to these protections, an additional separate constitutional privilege for "opinion" is required to ensure the freedom of expression guaranteed by the First Amendment. The dispositive question in the present case then becomes whether a reasonable factfinder could conclude that the statements in the Diadiun column imply an assertion that petitioner Milkovich perjured himself in a judicial proceed-

---

7. In *Hepps* the Court reserved judgment on cases involving nonmedia defendants, see 475 U.S., at 779, n. 4, 106 S.Ct., at 1565, n. 4, and accordingly we do the same. Prior to *Hepps*, of course, where public-official or public-figure plaintiffs were involved, the *New York Times* rule already required a showing of falsity before liability could result. 475 U.S., at 775, 106 S.Ct., at 1563.

8. We note that the issue of falsity relates to the *defamatory* facts implied by a statement. For

instance, the statement, "I think Jones lied," may be provable as false on two levels. First, that the speaker really did not think Jones had lied but said it anyway, and second that Jones really had not lied. It is, of course, the second level of falsity which would ordinarily serve as the basis for a defamation action, though falsity at the first level may serve to establish malice where that is required for recovery.

ing. We think this question must be answered in the affirmative. As the Ohio Supreme Court itself observed: "[T]he clear impact in some nine sentences and a caption is that [Milkovich] 'lied at the hearing after ... having given his solemn oath to tell the truth.'" This is not the sort of loose, figurative, or hyperbolic language which would negate the impression that the writer was seriously maintaining that petitioner committed the crime of perjury. Nor does the general tenor of the article negate this impression.

We also think the connotation that petitioner committed perjury is sufficiently factual to be susceptible of being proved true or false. * * *

* * *

Reversed.

SECTION C.　PRIVILEGES AND SPECIAL CASES

DEFENSES AND PRIVILEGES

At common law, as *Philadelphia Newspapers v. Hepps*, supra p. 199 makes plain, truth was an affirmative defense—but only an affirmative defense—to a prima facie case of defamation. (Indeed, in an earlier period in English legal history, when the law of criminal libel was used to suppress criticism of the government, truth was not even a defense to charges of criminal libel, because truths critical of the state were even more likely than falsehoods to stir up popular antagonism). *Hepps* constitutionally compels a shift in the burden of proving falsity in defamation suits involving private parties and—or so the prevailing reading has it—matters of "public concern." It is possible, then, that in defamation suits among private parties involving matters of "private concern", truth may still be treated as an affirmative defense which must be proved by the defendant. The squib case following this note explains how this defense operates.

Even so, truth today appears rarely used as a defense. Suits brought against "true" allegations are likely few and far between. When truth appears as an issue in contemporary defamation cases, it is usually the plaintiff who bears the burden of proving it. Plaintiffs in Auvil v. 60 Minutes, 67 F.3d 816 (9th Cir.1995), for example, saw their product disparagement suit fail because they were unable to raise an issue of material fact with respect to the falsity of the claims (about the dangers of spraying the chemical Alar on apples) that they were challenging.

In some circumstances, other defenses not unique to defamation law apply. Consent, for example, can be a defense to the disclosure of otherwise defamatory information, as when a job applicant agrees to release from liability persons who provide confidential information about the applicant to a prospective employer. See e.g., Baker v. Bhajan, 871 P.2d 374 (N.M.1994). For the most part, however, it is privileges distinctively applicable to defamation that relieve defendants of liability for otherwise defamatory statements.

As in trespass, privileges may be either absolute (or unqualified) or conditional (or qualified). Absolute privileges exculpate speakers even if the speaker deliberately lies about the plaintiff. This is a narrow class of privileges, applying to various public officials—legislative, judicial and executive. Qualified or conditional privileges are more common. Most of the privileges included in this section fall into that category.

————

THE DEFENSE OF TRUTH

LAWRENCE v. BAUER PUBLISHING & PRINTING, LTD., 89 N.J. 451, 446 A.2d 469 (1982). President and secretary-treasurer of taxpayers' association sued for libel. Defendants asserted truth as a defense. Plaintiffs moved to strike this defense. On appeal, the Supreme Court of New Jersey stated:

"Defendants assert that the trial court erred in granting plaintiffs' motion to strike truth as a defense. Under the common law, truth, if established, exonerates the publisher of a defamatory statement of fact. See Medico v. Time, Inc., 643 F.2d 134, 137 (3d Cir.1981); Restatement (Second) of Torts § 581A (1977). For the defense to apply, however, the truth must be as broad as the defamatory imputation or 'sting' of the statement. [citations omitted.]

"After hearing argument on plaintiffs' motion to strike the defense of truth, the trial court determined that defendants' publication of the statements that plaintiffs were suspected of and being investigated for committing the crimes of forgery and false swearing imputed to plaintiffs the very commission of those crimes. Therefore, the court ruled that defendants could not assert the justification of truth unless they were prepared to prove not only that the reported investigation was conducted or that 'forgery charges loomed,' but also that plaintiffs did in fact commit forgery and false swearing. See Restatement (Second) of Torts § 581A, comment c, at 236 (1977). When defense counsel conceded that he was unprepared to prove that plaintiffs had in fact committed the criminal offenses imputed to plaintiffs, the trial court ordered the defense of truth stricken from the case."

* * *

"There is considerable authority for the proposition that the fact that defendants accurately reported information obtained from another source will not relieve them of liability. Under that analysis the defense of truth does not refer to the truthful republication of a defamatory statement but to the truth of the statement's contents. Restatement (Second) of Torts § 578, comment b, at 235–36 (1977). Thus, if defendant published that a third person stated that plaintiff has committed a crime, it is no justification that the third party did in fact make that statement. *Rogers,* supra, 2 N.J. at 401–02, 66 A.2d 869. Defendant must prove that in fact plaintiff committed the crime. See L. Eldridge, Law of Defamation § 67 at 331 (1978). Similarly, a statement that criminal charges were imminent would be truthful only if such charges were demonstrably impending.

"The trial court viewed the statement in this case as imputing to plaintiffs the crimes of forgery and false swearing and therefore imposed on defendants the burden of proving that plaintiffs had actually committed those crimes. A more literal reading of the headline indicates that the correct interpretation may have been that charges of forgery and false swearing were forthcoming. Whether the 'truth' defense should be framed in terms of proof that defendants committed the crimes referred to in the article or simply that charges concerning those charges might 'loom' is a provocative question we need not decide today, given our holding that plaintiffs were public figures who have not demonstrated the requisite malicious libel by defendants necessary to sustain a libel judgment."

MEDIA PRIVILEGES: FAIR COMMENT

DAIRY STORES, INC. v. SENTINEL PUBLISHING CO., INC.

Supreme Court of New Jersey, 1986.
104 N.J. 125, 516 A.2d 220.

[During a drought in 1981, two weekly newspapers owned by the defendant published a series of articles on the increased sale of bottled water in a New Jersey municipality. One of these articles concluded, on the basis of laboratory tests, that plaintiff's bottled water was not "pure spring water" as advertised, because it contained choline in excessively high concentration. After defendant refused to retract the article, plaintiff brought a suit for defamation, which the trial court "viewed as including a claim for product disparagement." Defendant sought and obtained summary judgment and plaintiff appealed to the state Supreme Court.]

POLLOCK, J.

This appeal requires that we declare the standard of liability of a newspaper, its reporter, and an independent laboratory retained by them for statements that allegedly defamed the plaintiff corporation's reputation and disparaged its product. Relying on the First Amendment to the United States Constitution, the Law Division granted summary judgment for the defendants, finding that they had not published the statements with reckless disregard for their truth. The Appellate Division affirmed. We granted certification, and now affirm the judgment of the Appellate Division. In reaching that result, we look to federal law for guidance, but we base our decision on the common-law privilege of fair comment.

* * *

At the outset, we must consider the distinction between causes of action for defamation and for product disparagement. The focus of our decision, however, is on the dispute whether the articles were privileged because they treated matters of public interest and, if so, whether the defendants were so careless that they lost the protection of any such privilege. In ruling for defendants, the lower courts looked to federal constitutional law and found that Krauszer's had not established that the defendants published the articles with "actual malice," a test that the United States Supreme Court has developed to measure statements about public officials and public figures.

We find, however, that the characterization of Krauszer's as a public figure is problematic, and that the more appropriate principle is the common-law privilege of fair comment. Before embarking on a more detailed analysis of the principles of defamation law, including fair comment, we must first determine the nature of the cause of action.

* * *

Although the two causes sometimes overlap, actions for defamation and product disparagement stem from different branches of tort law. A defamation action, which encompasses libel and slander, affords a remedy for damage to one's reputation. By comparison, an action for product disparagement is an offshoot of the cause of action for interference with contractual relations, such as sales to a prospective buyer. The two causes may merge when a disparaging statement about a product reflects on the reputation of the business that made, distributed, or sold it. If, for example, a statement about the poor quality of a product implies that the seller is fraudulent, then the statement may be actionable under both theories. Courts generally are reluctant to impute a lack of integrity to a corporation merely from a criticism of its product. On the premise that the reputation of a business is more valuable than any particular product it sells, courts have responded more readily to a claim of damage to one's reputation than to a claim for product disparagement. Semantics contributes to the confusion of the two causes because terms used to describe a product disparagement action, such as "trade libel" and "slander of title," tend to blur the distinction between such an action and one for defamation.

Recent decisions of the United States Supreme Court have further blurred the dividing line between the two causes. Traditionally, a plaintiff in a product disparagement action has borne the burden of establishing that the disparaging statement was both false and injurious. By comparison, in a defamation action, the plaintiff was entitled to a presumption that the defamatory statement was both false and harmful. As a result [of the constitutional developments studied in section B, supra], the difference between product disparagement and defamation has narrowed further when a statement treats a matter of public concern.

Here, Sentinel's article reported the presence of chlorine in Covered Bridge water and stated that Krauszer's kept the source of its bottled water a "well-guarded secret." Arguably, these statements not only disparaged Covered Bridge water by casting doubt on whether it was spring water, but also defamed Krauszer's corporate reputation by implying that it was trying to hide something through non-disclosure of the source of the water, *e.g.*, that the water did not come from a spring or that the spring was contaminated.

* * * [F]or the purposes of this appeal, we assume that the articles were not only disparaging, but also false and defamatory. As a result, the distinction between defamation and product disparagement disappears, and our attention shifts to whether the publications were privileged and whether the defendants abused any such privilege.

* * *

The evolution of the law of defamation reflects the tension between society's competing interests in encouraging the free flow of information about matters of public concern and in protecting an individual's reputation. * * *

Traditionally, the common law has accommodated that need by recognizing that some otherwise defamatory statements should be "privileged," *i.e.,* that their publication does not impose liability on the publisher. Privileges may be "absolute," which means that the statements are completely immune, or "qualified." A qualified privilege may be overcome, with the result that the publisher will be liable, if publication of a defamatory statement was made with "malice." Common-law malice, or malice-in-fact, has meant variously that the statement was published with an improper purpose or ill will, or without belief or reasonable grounds to believe in its truth.

Certain statements, such as those made in judicial, legislative, or administrative proceedings, are absolutely privileged because the need for unfettered expression is crucial to the public weal. Other statements, such as those made outside those forums but for the public welfare, enjoy a qualified privilege. For example, property owners have a qualified privilege to make statements about potential drainage, health, and fiscal problems from a proposed trailer park. Likewise, citizens have a qualified privilege to make statements to authorities for the prevention and detection of crime. We have also recognized a qualified privilege of the press to report statements made in a public municipal council "conference room" meeting. Therefore, a qualified or conditional privilege has emerged as one of the prime means for the common law to balance the interests in reputation with the publication of information in the public interest.

Insofar as defenses to product disparagement are concerned, a qualified privilege should exist wherever it would exist in a defamation action. Prosser & Keeton, *supra,* § 128 at 974; *Restatement (Second), supra,* § 646A. Because the common law historically has held the interest in one's reputation as more worthy of protection than the interest of a business in the products that it makes, it follows that the right to make a statement about a product should exist whenever it is permissible to make such a statement about the reputation of another.

One illustration of a qualified privilege is fair comment, which is sometimes described as rendering a statement non-libelous. No matter how described, the defense is lost upon a showing that the statement was made with malice. F. Harper & F. James, *Law of Torts,* § 5.28 at 457 (1956) (Harper & James). The roots of fair comment are imbedded in the common law, but in recent years, those roots have intertwined with others arising from constitutional law. * * *

* * *

* * * Although constitutional considerations have dominated defamation law in recent years, the common law provides an alternative, and

potentially more stable, framework for analyzing statements about matters of public interest.

Another reason for turning to the common law is that the constitutional concepts do not comfortably fit the activities or products of a corporation. As the Law Division noted, the term "public figure" does not readily apply to corporate enterprises, and "public controversy" is poorly suited to describe the commercial activities of such an enterprise. 191 N.J.Super. at 212–13, 465 A.2d 953. The term "public figure" includes individuals who engage in a public controversy and ill fits a corporation, which ordinarily is interested not in thrusting itself into such a controversy, but in selling its products.

* * *

* * * [T]he "public figure" device provides an awkward and uncertain method of determining whether statements about corporations or their products are actionable. Although the United States Supreme Court has withdrawn constitutional protection from statements on matters of public interest, the Court has left open to state courts the prospect of protecting such statements through common-law privileges, including fair comment. Providing such protection would be consistent with the enhanced protection we have provided to speech in other areas. [citations omitted] Thus, we turn to the analysis of the scope of the fair comment privilege.

* * *

Generally speaking, the doctrine of fair comment extends to virtually all matters of legitimate public interest. Through the principle of fair comment, New Jersey courts have long accorded protection to wide-ranging statements about public officials. The courts have likewise applied the principle to controversial public issues, such as internal security during the McCarthy era, and to criticism of a proposed trailer park that was perceived as posing a threat to drainage, property values, and taxes. Drinking water, the subject of the present litigation, has also been held to be a topic of vital public concern and subject to fair comment. *Mick v. American Dental Ass'n*, 49 N.J.Super. 262, 280, 282–83, 139 A.2d 570 (App.Div.), certif. denied, 27 N.J. 74, 141 A.2d 318 (1958). In *Mick*, the Appellate Division sustained the dismissal of a libel action brought by a member-dentist against the American Dental Association. The dentist had opposed fluoridation of public drinking water. Thereafter, the Association responded to an inquiry about the dentist by stating it believed his views "to be based on complete misinformation and to be totally irresponsible." Observing that fluoridation of drinking water affects the health of citizens, the Appellate Division found the letter to deal with a subject of public interest relating to the general welfare.

* * *

We recognize that not everything that is newsworthy is a matter of legitimate public concern, and that sorting such matters from those of a more private nature may be difficult. In this regard, the assessment of public interest includes a determination whether the person "voluntarily and knowingly engaged in conduct that one in his position should reasonably know would implicate a legitimate public interest, engendering the real possibility of public attention and scrutiny." *Sisler v. Gannett Co., Inc.,* 104 N.J. 256, 274, 516 A.2d 1083, 1092 (1986).

* * *

It would be anomalous to consider food and drink to be a subject of public interest when purchased in a restaurant, but not when purchased in a store. This conclusion applies with particular force to bottled drinking water, which is the subject of state regulation. * * * As an essential of human life, drinking water is a paradigm of legitimate public concern. We leave to the future a more complete definition of matters of legitimate public concern. For this decision, it suffices to conclude that drinking water is such a subject.

Because the present case involves a product that is unquestionably a matter of legitimate public concern, we believe it is more prudent to extend that standard for the time being only to such products, leaving to another day the determination whether the standard should apply to statements about all products no matter how prosaic or innocuous. * * *

* * *

Throughout the country, courts have divided on the issue whether fair comment should be restricted to statements of opinion or should extend to factual statements. Underlying the distinction is the premise that the widest possible latitude should extend to expressions of opinion on matters of public concern, but that factual misstatements should be more narrowly confined.

* * *

The need for the free flow of information and commentary on matters of legitimate public concern leads us to conclude that fair comment should extend beyond opinion to statements of fact. When confronting such a matter, a publisher should not be unduly inhibited in analyzing whether a statement is an immune opinion or a potentially culpable statement of fact. [citation omitted]. We believe we come close to fulfilling the policy considerations that underlie fair comment if we evaluate factual statements as the subject of a qualified privilege. This conclusion leads to further consideration of the facts that will constitute an abuse of the privilege.

* * *

In traditional defamation analysis, one difference between absolute and qualified privileges is that an absolute privilege grants complete immunity to the publisher, but a qualified privilege accords immunity only if the statement is made without malice. *Rainier's Dairies v. Raritan Valley Farms, Inc.,* [19 *N.J.* 552, 558, 117 *A.*2d 889 (1955)]. The defense of fair comment, like other qualified privileges, may be overcome by showing that a statement was made with malice. *Mick v. American Dental Ass'n, supra,* 49 N.J.Super. at 279, 139 A.2d 570. * * *

* * *

As the actual malice standard has evolved, the relevant test is not "whether a reasonably prudent man would have published, or would have investigated before publishing," but "whether the defendant in fact entertained serious doubts as to the truth of his publication." *St. Amant v. Thompson,* 390 U.S. 727, 731, 88 S.Ct. 1323, 1325, 20 L.Ed.2d 262, 267 (1968). That test, which is substantially subjective, is akin to the common-law requirement that to qualify as fair comment, a statement must honestly express the writer's true opinion. *Leers v. Green,* [24 *N.J.* 239, 254, 131 *A.*2d 781 (1957)]; *Coleman v. MacLennan,* [78 *Kan.* 711, 98 *P.* 281, 286 (1908),] (privilege overcome by showing that defendant did not have an honest belief in the truth of the facts); *see also Restatement, supra,* § 600 (1938) (abuse of conditional privilege when the defendant "does not believe in the truth of the defamatory matter").

The bald assertion by the publisher that he believes in the truth of the statement may not be sufficient. *St. Amant v. Thompson, supra,* 390 U.S. at 732, 88 S.Ct. at 1326, 20 L.Ed.2d at 267. Notwithstanding a publisher's denial that it had serious doubts about the truthfulness of the statement, other facts might support an inference that the publisher harbored such doubts. * * *

* * *

[W]e conclude that the actual malice standard should apply to non-media as well as to media defendants.

Even if we did not reach that conclusion, it would be inappropriate to distinguish between the independent expert, Paterson, and the media defendants. In an era when science and technology frequently touch our lives, the media have an increasing need for scientific and technical advice. The preparation of articles on a variety of topics that are the daily fare of newspapers, particularly those describing the quality of products intended for human consumption, may require expert assistance. If an outside expert is held liable on a standard of care lower than that applicable to a media defendant, that expert may decline to conduct tests for reporters investigating important public issues. The effect would be to prevent the media from preparing publications with crucial information, or to preclude publication. This would have a chilling, or even freezing, effect on the dissemination of information that is in the public interest. We would be loathe to foreclose the media from vital sources that they need to speak intelligently on these matters. As a result, we conclude that outside experts that conduct tests and submit reports to the media are so closely related to news gathering that they should be treated like media defendants.

* * *

The dispositive question, then, is whether there is a genuine issue that any of the defendants displayed reckless disregard in publishing the two factual statements. * * *

As to the two defamatory statements, nothing in the record before us creates a genuine issue of material fact that any defendant knew the statements to be false or entertained serious doubts about their truth. Paterson, knowing that the water was supposed to be spring water, confirmed the positive test results through subsequent tests, all of which were reviewed by two other chemists. This procedure does not bespeak a reckless disregard for the truth.

Insofar as Sentinel and its reporter are concerned, Dzielak started out carefully enough by seeking the services of an independent testing laboratory. The first laboratory found that the water did not contain chlorine, but upon learning that Krauszer's was a customer of that laboratory, Dzielak understandably sought confirmation elsewhere. Upon obtaining Paterson's positive test results for chlorine, she consulted still another laboratory, but she did not understand its report. A more careful reporter might have deferred publication until all doubts were finally resolved, but we cannot conclude that Dzielak entertained serious doubts about the truth of her stories.

The judgment of the Appellate Division is affirmed.

MEDIA PRIVILEGES: FAIR REPORT

MARTIN v. WILSON PUBLISHING CO., 497 A.2d 322 (R.I.1985). On October 19, 1977, an article focusing on the plaintiff and on changes that were taking place in Shannock village as a result of his real estate acquisitions was published in the Chariho Times. The article stated:

> "Some residents stretch available facts when they imagine Mr. Martin is connected with the 1974 rash of fires in the village (the abandoned depot, the back of the Shannock Spa, and even that old barn he loved). Local fire officials feel that certain local kids did it for kicks. The same imaginations note that the fire at the old Shannock mill before he bought it made it cheaper (but less valuable), or that the fire there since he bought it might have been profitable (though derelict buildings, such as it was, are customarily uninsurable)."

* * *

"The common-law privilege of fair report protects the publication of fair and accurate reports of public meetings and judicial proceedings, even when an individual is defamed during the proceeding or action. This privilege does not abrogate the policy of protecting one's reputation but rather subordinates this value to the countervailing public interest in the availability of information about official proceedings and public meetings."

* * *

"The defendants argue by analogy that the underlying concept of fair report should similarly protect republishing a rumor already in existence, even in the face of knowledge of its falsity. We are of the opinion, however, that there is little merit to this argument, especially in light of the contours of this case. It is important to observe that the fair-report privilege accommodates the important societal interest in facilitating dissemination of information about judicial and governmental proceedings at which identified and identifiable persons may participate in resolving disputes and advancing the progress of government. In a judicial proceeding if one is defamed through cross-examination, opportunity exists for the one defamed to respond to rebut the defamation. With public meetings those susceptible of defamation may attend such gatherings and defend against attacks. We find no similar countervailing policy to protect repetition of rumors. The spreading of rumors does not give the person defamed by them the opportunity to rebut the underlying allegations of the rumor. To attempt to defend against a rumor is not unlike attempting to joust with a cloud. Publication of a rumor further fuels the continued repetition and does so in an especially egregious way by enshrining it in print. Thus there is little room to deny that the opportunity for abuse of the reporting of the existence of a defamatory rumor is great, and as a result a number of courts (and today we join them) have denied the right to report the existence of rumors when the underlying accusation of the rumor is believed to be false."

* * *

"We [therefore endorse] a rule that republication of false defamatory statements about an individual may be printed only in the extremely limited situation in which the publication accurately attributes such statements to an identified and responsible source. * * * Moreover, we discern no public policy which would be served by immunizing the reporting of false or baseless rumors. The need to report judicial and governmental proceedings is not paralleled by any discernible advantage to be secured to the public by the reporting of rumors. Consequently, publication of such rumors makes the publisher responsible under the "actual malice" test of *New York Times* for ascertaining the truth of the underlying defamatory material in such circumstances."

OFFICIAL PRIVILEGES

McGRANAHAN v. DAHAR

Supreme Court of New Hampshire, 1979.
119 N.H. 758, 408 A.2d 121.

BROOKS, Justice. This action for defamation and "malicious use of process" presents the question of how much protection from civil liability is afforded persons participating in judicial proceedings.

The defendant, Victor W. Dahar, is an attorney who owns real estate in the city of Manchester. The lessee of one of Dahar's properties, American Snacks, Inc., applied for and was granted a tax abatement for the property for 1973. Following its usual procedure, the city issued and sent the abatement check to Dahar, the record owner of the property. Early in 1975, American Snacks brought suit in the Hillsborough County Superior Court alleging that Dahar had wrongfully converted the tax abatement check which American Snacks claimed belonged to it. As part of his defense, Dahar made certain statements to his attorneys and filed pleadings alleging that the disputed money belonged to the city, not to American Snacks, because the tax abatement had been unlawfully granted. In particular, Dahar implied that the plaintiff here, John F. McGranahan, then chairman of the board of assessors for the city of Manchester, had improperly granted a tax abatement to a property in which he held a financial interest. McGranahan was not a party to the civil action of American Snacks, Inc. v. Dahar. At about the same time, members of the Manchester Police Department and the city prosecutor talked with Dahar about his suspicions. On April 10, 1975, McGranahan was arrested and charged with official oppression, RSA 643:1. Dahar testified on behalf of the State at McGranahan's trial, which took place in June 1975 in the Manchester District Court. Reports of the trial appeared in the news media. McGranahan was acquitted on all counts.

McGranahan then brought this action against Dahar, pleading in a single count trespass, libel, slander, and "malicious use of process." * * *

[The trial court denied a motion to dismiss.]

* * *

We reverse.

In the context of this case, determination of the scope of the privilege to be recognized requires a balancing of two important principles: the right of an individual to enjoy an unsullied reputation, and the public interest in free and full disclosure of facts pertinent to judicial proceedings. Discussions with attorneys and investigating officers, and even the filing of pleadings frequently and necessarily occur at a time when the declarant may not have access to information verifying or disproving the statements. The purpose of a judicial proceeding is to test the truth or falsity of allegations of criminal or wrongful conduct. Many of the cases in our courts involve allegations of undesirable conduct by one or more citizens. We cannot envision that these allegations should become the basis for defamation actions each time the alleged wrongdoer prevails in the first action. Under such a rule, our judicial system would be seriously hampered by parties' fears that if they were unable to establish unequivocally the truth of their pleadings they would face the burden of an extended defamation action in addition to the proceeding in which the statements were made. Annot., 38 A.L.R.3d 272, 277 (1971).

On the other hand, pleadings, testimony, and other portions of judicial proceedings are public documents and events. [Citations omitted.] A person's reputation undoubtedly may be harmed as much by allegations contained in pleadings, or spoken from a witness stand, even if ultimately disproven, as by those proclaimed from a soapbox in the village square. There is no reason to protect one who uses the form of a judicial proceeding merely as a pretext for circulating defamatory material. Cf. State v.

Burnham, 9 N.H. 34 (1837) (leaflet cast in form of petition for removal of public officer).

Due to these competing interests, the general rule is that statements made in the course of judicial proceedings are absolutely privileged from civil actions, provided they are pertinent to the subject of the proceeding. The requirement of pertinence eliminates protection for statements made needlessly and wholly in bad faith. McLaughlin v. Cowley, 127 Mass. 316, 319 (1879). The rule reflects a determination that the potential harm to an individual is far outweighed by the need to encourage participants in litigation, parties, attorneys, and witnesses, to speak freely in the course of judicial proceedings. This rule does not assume that all persons who participate in judicial proceedings are free from malice. Rather, it reflects a determination that the need to protect honest participants from vexatious litigation to vindicate themselves is so important that the law will not risk subjecting them to defamation suits merely in order that the occasional malicious participant may be penalized in damages.

This court has previously indicated adoption of the general rule affording an absolute privilege or immunity to statements made in the course of judicial proceedings. * * *

We next consider the specific statements that the plaintiff alleges were defamatory of him, to determine whether they are included in the absolute privilege.

* * *

* * * Subjecting a client to liability, or indeed to the burden of defending against a defamation action, for statements made to his attorney pertinent to and during the course of legal representation would seriously impair the full and frank discussions that the attorney-client privilege is designed to protect. * * *

Affording a party to litigation or a witness absolute immunity for pleadings filed and statements made in court would come to little if they were to be subjected to potential liability for preliminary conversations with their attorney in which they have an opportunity to test their knowledge and the basis for their opinions. On balance, the plaintiff's desire for civil damages in defamation is not sufficiently compelling to warrant abrogation of the attorney-client privilege. * * *

There is little question here of pertinency. The plaintiff himself alleges that the statements were all made "for the ulterior purpose of creating a plausible defense to the suit by American Snacks." Whether the privilege in this instance exists cannot turn on the ultimate success of the defense propounded by the defendant with the advice of counsel. In order to further full and open disclosure and exploration between attorney and client, immunity must be afforded for all statements that bear on the subject matter of the legal representation. A client seeking legal advice cannot be expected to anticipate those facts that will ultimately give rise to a successful legal argument. We hold that the defendant's statements to his attorneys concerning the American Snacks suit are privileged and cannot be the basis for this action in defamation. Restatement (Second) of Torts § 587, Comment *b* (1977).

* * *

The plaintiff's final argument concerning the civil pleadings is that they should not be privileged because he was not a party to the civil action and therefore he was unable to protect himself against defamatory statements. We disagree. Whether the privilege attaches depends on the nature of the proceedings in which the statements were made; it makes no difference whether the person allegedly defamed was a participant in those proceedings. * * * We hold that all statements contained in the civil pleadings in this matter are privileged and cannot be the basis for any action for defamation.

* * *

Plaintiff also seeks damages in defamation for statements the defendant made to members of the Manchester Police Department, the city solicitor, and city prosecutor, during the investigation that led to the plaintiff's arrest. It is not specified in the complaint whether the defendant is alleged to have initiated those conversations by making a complaint, formal or informal, or merely to have cooperated in response to questioning from those investigating the incident. The question before us is whether statements made, as here, in the prearrest investigatory process were sufficiently connected with the subsequent judicial proceeding to be covered by the absolute privilege.

In an action for defamation, unlike an action for *malicious prosecution,* it is immaterial whether the statements led to the institution of criminal charges against the person accused of a crime; the harm would be deemed to stem from the accusations alone, even if they were not republished outside of the police station. In a case where no criminal charges result from the complaint or statements made, the harm suffered by the person thus accused is minimal. That potential harm to a person's reputation is far outweighed by the substantial interests of society in encouraging citizens to report suspected criminal activity to the appropriate legal authorities, and to cooperate fully in investigations. * * *

[In the omitted portions of the opinion the court discusses the limited circumstances in which the provision of false information to law enforcement personnel might give rise to either a tort claim for "abuse of process" or a tort claim for "malicious prosecution." * * *

* * *

We think the investigation alleged in the complaint was sufficiently connected to the criminal proceeding itself to be included within the privilege. Cf. Ritchey v. Maksin, 71 Ill.2d 470, 17 Ill.Dec. 662, 376 N.E.2d 991 (1978) (complaint from State department of agriculture); Vasquez v. Courtney, 276 Or. 1053, 557 P.2d 672 (1976) (presentencing investigation). For this reason, we adopt the rule that treats both formal and informal complaints and statements to a prosecuting authority as part of the initial steps in a judicial proceeding, and as such entitled to absolute immunity from an action for defamation. W. Prosser, Torts § 114 at 781 (4th ed. 1971). The same absolute immunity or privilege applies to statements made to the city or county attorney or those investigating a suspected crime. Vogel v. Gruaz, 110 U.S. 311, 4 S.Ct. 12, 28 L.Ed. 158 (1884); Bergman v. Hupy, 64 Wis.2d 747, 221 N.W.2d 898 (1974).

* * *

In this case there is no serious contention that Dahar's testimony was not relevant to the criminal trial in which it occurred. In fact, the basis of McGranahan's complaint is that it was Dahar's testimony, and that alone, which was responsible for the entire proceeding. Under these circumstances, we hold that Dahar is immune from suit for defamation stemming from his testimony.

* * *

FLANAGAN v. McLANE, 87 Conn. 220, 87 A. 727, 88 A. 96 (1913). The defendant, suspecting plaintiff of having stolen money while working at defendant's house, wrote of her suspicion to a constable, asking him to investigate. Subsequently she wrote again saying that the money had been found in a place where she had never put it, adding that she still believed that plaintiff had taken it. *Held* (3–2), for defendant, upholding a verdict in her favor. "The defendant was in a way bound to let the officer know that the money had been found," and, under the circumstances, "was legally entitled, if acting honestly and without malice, to reaffirm her belief in the plaintiff's guilt for the guidance of the officer in case it was or might become his duty to pursue the investigation with a view to criminal proceedings." The dissenting judges considered the second letter unprivileged. "It was written primarily to have the peace officer desist from the investigation of the theft of which the defendant had complained to him over three weeks previously. Belief in the charge did not justify her in its reiteration upon withdrawal of it from the officers."

METHODIST FEDERATION FOR SOCIAL ACTION v. EASTLAND, 141 F.Supp. 729 (D.D.C.1956); noted, 4 U.C.L.A.L.Rev. 466 (1957). Subcommittee of Congress issued a pamphlet in which the plaintiff association was cited as a front for the Communist Party. 75,000 additional copies were ordered printed by a Congressional resolution. Plaintiff sought an injunction to prohibit publication and distribution of the pamphlet. *Held*, (2–1) that the complaint failed to state a cause of action on the basis, among other reasons, of Congressional immunity.

FRANKFURTER, J., in TENNEY v. BRANDHOVE, 341 U.S. 367, 71 S.Ct. 783, 95 L.Ed. 1019 (1951): "The holding of this court in Fletcher v. Peck, 6 Cranch 87, 10 U.S. 87, 3 L.Ed. 162, that it was not consonant with our scheme of government for a court to inquire into the motives of legislators, has remained unquestioned. * * * Investigations, whether by standing or special committees, are an established part of representative government. * * * Self-discipline and the voters must be the ultimate reliance for discouraging or correcting such abuses. The courts should not go beyond the narrow confines of determining that a committee's inquiry may fairly be deemed within its province. To find that a committee's investigation has exceeded the bounds of legislative power it must be obvious that there was a usurpation of functions exclusively vested in the Judiciary or the Executive."

CHAMBERLAIN v. MATHIS, 151 Ariz. 551, 729 P.2d 905 (1986). Plaintiffs were the internal audit staff of the Arizona Health Care Cost Containment System (AHCCCS). In that capacity, they prepared an audit report and delivered it to the defendant, the Director of the Arizona Department of Health Services (ADHS). Mathis refused to grant public access to the report. In the presence of several people including a newspaper reporter, Mathis made several allegedly defamatory comments regarding the audit, calling plaintiffs "incompetent and unqualified as auditors," among other things. Mathis's comments were published in *The Arizona Republic*.

Plaintiffs sued for defamation. The trial court dismissed their complaint on the ground that Mathis enjoyed an absolute privilege. The court of appeals reversed, holding that there was no absolute privilege and that whether Mathis was entitled to "high-level executive immunity" was a question of fact for the jury. Mathis appealed to the Arizona Supreme Court.

Held, "Mathis is entitled to qualified immunity from liability for his allegedly defamatory statements concerning plaintiffs. He forfeits his immunity if, and only if, he (1) acted outside the outer perimeter of his required or discretionary functions, or (2) acted with malice in that he knew his statements regarding plaintiffs were false or acted in reckless disregard of the truth. The reasonableness of Mathis's conduct should be measured by an objective standard. * * * "

"The rationale for granting executive government officials immunity for conduct within the scope of their employment is that government must be allowed to govern. If executive officials are denied immunity, they may elevate personal interest above official duty. Public servants would be obligated to spend their time in court justifying their past actions, instead of performing their official duties. Ultimately, government, including good government, may be hampered and qualified individuals may be hesitant to serve in positions that require great responsibility."

"The arguments favoring official immunity are countered by the legitimate complaints of those injured by government officials. * * * One's reputation is a significant, intensely personal possession that the law strives to protect. The entire common law of defamation attests to the importance we attach to an individual's right to seek compensation for damage to his reputation. * * * Not even the critical need for open and robust public debate on issues of public concern is sufficient to completely shield malicious defamations. *New York Times v. Sullivan,* 376 U.S. 254, 280, 84 S.Ct. 710, 726, 11 L.Ed.2d 686 (1964).

"The interests furthered by absolute official immunity are also countered by basic principles of equal justice. 'Our system of jurisprudence rests on the assumption that all individuals, whatever their position in government, are subject to [the] law.' *Butz v. Economou,* 438 U.S. 478, 506, 98 S.Ct. 2894, 2910, 57 L.Ed.2d 895 (1978) (federal executive officials entitled only to qualified immunity when "constitutional tort" is alleged). As we stated in *Grimm,* "[t]he more power bureaucrats exercise over our lives, the more ... some sort of ultimate responsibility [should] lie for their most outrageous conduct." *Grimm [v. Arizona Bd. of Pardons and Paroles,* 115 Ariz. 260, 266, 564 P.2d 1227, 1233 (1977) * * * "

* * *

"Although there may be some government offices that require absolute immunity, *e.g., Nixon v. Fitzgerald,* 457 U.S. 731, 102 S.Ct. 2690, 73 L.Ed.2d 349 (1982), we believe the general rule of qualified immunity announced in *Grimm* should govern the case before us. Qualified immunity protects government officials from liability for acts within the scope of their public duties unless the official knew or should have known that he was acting in violation of established law or acted in reckless disregard of whether his activities would deprive another person of their rights. [citations omitted]. We believe this to be the better rule for several reasons.

"We explained in *Grimm* that because immunity 'deprives individuals of a remedy for wrongdoing, [it] should be bestowed only when and at the level necessary.' *Grimm,* 115 Ariz. at 265, 564 P.2d at 1232. Thus, although we have recognized an absolute immunity for persons participating in judicial proceedings, we have narrowly construed the requirement that the act raising the privilege have a close, direct relationship to such proceedings. * * *

"The case for absolute official immunity is premised on the *assumption* that the possibility of inquiry into official motives or conduct will deter proper and necessary official action. * * * However, after we limited government immunity and granted police officers and members of the parole board qualified, rather than absolute, immunity, neither government, law enforcement, nor the parole system came to a standstill. We are therefore reluctant to base a rule that eliminates both deterrence of public officials and compensation of victims on such speculative grounds. We believe that in the vast majority of cases, qualified immunity will adequately protect state executive officials. W. PROSSER & W. KEETON, [THE LAW OF TORTS, 4th ed. 1984] § 114, at 822 ("It does not appear" that government has been hindered "in those states where only the qualified privilege is recognized....").

"We recognize, however, that qualified immunity may offer executive public officials insufficient protection if plaintiffs, by merely alleging malice, can force public officials to engage in intensive discovery and cumbersome, time-consuming trials. * * *

"We believe the negative aspects of suits against public officials will be minimized if plaintiffs, instead of merely alleging subjective malice, are required to establish proof of *objective* malice. Thus, in a defamation case, qualified immunity will protect a public official if the facts establish that a reasonable person, with the information available to the official, "could have formed a reasonable belief that the defamatory statement in question was true and that the publication was an appropriate means for serving the interests which justified the privilege." Handler & Klein, *The Defense of Privilege in Defamation Suits Against Government Executive Officials,* 74 HARV.L.REV. 44, 68 (1960); *see also Harlow v. Fitzgerald,* 457 U.S. at 816–17, 102 S.Ct. at 2737–39.[6]

" * * * The use of an objective test for public officials is not a favor bestowed upon such officials. Instead, it flows from the need to keep public officials available to perform their duties and from recognition that lawsuits are filed against the innocent as well as the guilty. *Halperin v. Kissinger,* 606 F.2d at 1214–15 (Gesell, J., concurring)."

OTHER PRIVILEGES

RETAIL CREDIT CO. v. RUSSELL
Supreme Court of Georgia, 1975.
234 Ga. 765, 218 S.E.2d 54.

[Retail Credit Co., a commercial credit reporting agency, issued a credit report on Russell which reported, falsely, that a former employer had "dismissed him for dishonesty" and would not rehire him, and that Russell had "admitted to taking money over a period of time." After repeated attempts to get the report retracted and the mistaken information corrected, the report still circulated. Russell sued for libel. A jury awarded him $15,000 in damages. Retail Credit appealed.]

HALL, Justice. * * *

* * *

II.   The Claim of Privilege

The heart of Retail Credit's defense to this suit is its claim that in providing consumer reports pursuant to its contracts with its subscribers (customers), it is protected by a conditional privilege which may be overcome only by plaintiff's showing that false and defamatory matter was published with malice.

Correctly, Retail Credit does not bottom this claim on the First Amendment, as federal decisions have made plain that no First Amendment privilege is available for false and defamatory credit or other consumer reports. * * *

Rather than a First Amendment claim, Retail Credit urges a statutory conditional privilege grounded in Code Ann. § 105–709. That statute recognizes certain privileges including those claimed here, namely, a privilege for

---

6. Of course, this objective standard does not shield a public official who *knew* his statements were false, even though a reasonable person in the official's situation may have had reasonable grounds for believing the statements were true.

statements made in the performance of a legal or moral public or private duty, (Code Ann. § 105–709(2)), and statements made with the speaker's bona fide intent to protect his own interest (Code Ann. § 105–709(3)). Retail Credit urges that the information here was provided pursuant to contracts with its customers, and for that reason fell within the scope of these privileges. Though we find this argument circular—Retail Credit claims the privilege exists because it has contracted to do something in the doing of which the privilege would be beneficial to it—it is not necessary to consider these Code sections as if they existed in a vacuum, because they have already been construed in a manner adverse to Retail Credit's contentions here.

* * *

We are convinced that our law should not be changed [to recognize a conditional privilege for credit reporting agencies.] Apparently, 48 of the 50 states, excluding only Georgia and Idaho, recognize a conditional privilege in these circumstances. In the face of a conditional privilege, which requires that he prove malice to prevail, a falsely maligned consumer is virtually helpless to protect or avenge his reputation. The conditional privilege recognized almost nationwide would appear to have contributed to the evils which led to passage of the Fair Credit Reporting Act. The pre-Act woes of the consumer are well detailed in Note, The Fair Credit Reporting Act, 56 Minn.L.Rev. 819, 821–824 (1972) which noted that

> Aggravating this situation [of inaccurate reports] was the inability of a person injured by a false or misleading report to recover damages in a defamation action. Virtually every jurisdiction recognized the doctrine that reports furnished in good faith to parties having a legitimate interest in the information reported possess a qualified privilege which is not lost simply because the report contains some inaccurate or defamatory matter. The consumer injured by such a report could defeat the privilege only by showing that the report had been furnished out of malice or supplied to persons with no legitimate interest in the information. Since these facts were usually absent, the agencies were effectively insulated from liability for defamation.

Id. p. 823 (footnotes omitted.) We cannot agree to this weighting of the scales against the individual who stands alone facing a commercial Goliath with the power to destroy—not necessarily through malice but perhaps merely from carelessness—his credit rating, commercial advantages, insurance protection and employment, all through the publication of erroneous reports concerning his affairs. In weighing the policy factors inhering in conditional privilege, "Immunity is granted or withheld on the principle of the residuum of social convenience deriving from the protection of one interest at the expense of another." 1 Harper & James, Torts, p. 435, Defamation § 5.25 (1956). An individual living in a world more and more dominated by large commercial entities is less able to bear the burden of the consequences of a false credit or character report than the agency in the business of selling these reports. * * * "We hereby reaffirm the *Johnson* and *Pritchett* results and the policy of this state, that such reports do not enjoy a conditional privilege." See also Southeast Bankcard Assn. v. Woodruff, 124 Ga.App. 478, 480, 184 S.E.2d 191.

We endorse the reasoning of the Fifth Circuit in Hood v. Dun & Bradstreet, Inc., supra, in which that court considered whether this court, presented with a proper case, would adhere to *Johnson* and its progeny or would reject them. The Fifth Circuit, reversing the district court which had come to the opposite conclusion, wrote that sound reasons existed for maintaining the Georgia law as it has traditionally existed:

> * * * We find at least two reasons why a Georgia court would adhere to its earlier Supreme Court decisions.

> First, this case demonstrates that in one of the states that has refused to grant the privilege, credit reporting agencies exist and are thriving on the credit reporting business. If the basic assumption underlying the rule was correct, presumably there would be no credit reporting agencies in Georgia or Idaho. Additionally, we find that Dun & Bradstreet is not the only credit reporting agency doing a thriving business in Georgia, but there are at least twenty others, one of which is Retail Credit Co., one of the largest such organizations in the United States. Moreover, an empirical study that was prepared comparing credit transactions in Boise, Idaho, where there is no privilege with a city in its neighboring state, Spokane, Washington, where the privilege exists, also lends support to the assertion that in those states where no conditional privilege is recognized, credit information is readily available and thus does not inhibit commercial credit transactions. Irresistible logic and the absence of empirical verification compel this court to conclude that the privilege should not be blindly applied to credit reporting agencies in this case.

> A second reason for our decision is that in recent years there has been an apparent shift in emphasis from the protection of the credit reporting agency to the protection of the individual or business enterprise being investigated. The growth in consumer protection in regard to credit reporting is obvious from legislation such as the Fair Credit Reporting Act (FCRA). 15 U.S.C.A. §§ 1681–1681t (Supp.1971). Pursuant to the FCRA, the credit agency must disclose to the consumer the substance and sources of information upon its demand, id. § 1681d, the consumer has a right to correct and explain information contained in the report, id., § 1681i, and it may limit access to those who have a 'legitimate business need.' Id. § 1681b(3)(E). Furthermore, the Act does not preclude an action at common law except where information that would give rise to a cause of action is obtained by the complainant pursuant to the provisions of the Act. Id. § 1681h(e). * * *

The Georgia rule accords, we think, far better than the conditional privilege recognized elsewhere, with the trend of modern authority to recognize that credit reporting agencies should be held to a fairly high standard of accuracy. * * *

* * *

In conclusion, the publication here in issue was entitled to no privilege under Georgia law, and the trial court's refusal to charge the jury concerning privilege was correct. Retail Credit's enumerations of error numbers 1 through 4 are without merit.

* * *

Judgment affirmed.

MacINTOSH v. DUN, 1908 A.C. 390, 2 B.R.C. 203 (Privy Council 1908). In holding a mercantile agency strictly accountable, the court said:

> If, then, the proprietors of the Mercantile Agency are to be regarded as volunteers in supplying the information which they profess to have at their disposal, what is their motive? Is it a sense of duty? Certainly not. It is a matter of business with them. Their motive is self-interest. They carry on their trade, just as other traders do, in the hope and expectation of making a profit.
>
> Then comes the real question: Is it in the interest of the community, is it for the welfare of society, that the protection which the law throws around communications made in legitimate self-defence, or from a bona fide sense of duty, should be extended to communications made from motives of self-interest by persons who trade for profit in the characters of other people? The trade is a peculiar one; still there seems to be much competition for it; and in this trade, as in most others, success will attend the exertions of those who give the best value for money and probe most thoroughly the matter placed in their hands. * * * [I]nformation such as that which [credit agencies] offer for sale may be obtained in many ways, not all of them deserving of commendation. It may be extorted from the person whose character is in question through fear of misrepresentation or misconstruction if he remains silent. It may be gathered from gossip. It may be picked up from discharged servants. It may be betrayed by disloyal employees. It is only right that those who engage in such a business, touching so closely very dangerous ground, should take the consequences if they overstep the law. * * *

SLOCINSKI v. RADWAN, 83 N.H. 501, 144 A. 787, 63 A.L.R. 643 (1929). Plaintiff was the pastor of a church. The three defendants, members of his congregation, circulated to fellow members of the congregation reports, now conceded to be false but received by them in documentary form from apparently reliable sources, that plaintiff had been guilty of criminal conduct with women and girls in other places. Plaintiff brought separate actions of slander which were tried together. *Held,* for defendants, setting aside verdicts for plaintiff and ordering a new trial. Private communications between church members in regard to the qualifications of their minister are qualifiedly privileged. "It is hard to imagine a more obvious example of common interest than that which is shared by the members of a church in the character and conduct of the minister, since these factors determine his capacity for spiritual leadership. * * * Charges against clergymen publicly made before church bodies are happily the exception rather than the rule. * * * Any rule designed to penalize the formation of public sentiment in such cases by arresting the preliminary sifting of reports through private discussion, free from the taint of malice and for a proper purpose, is without justification and would be foredoomed to practical failure as an attempt to decree that men and women shall not act like human beings."

SIMONSEN v. SWENSON, 104 Neb. 224, 177 N.W. 831, 9 A.L.R. 1250 (1920); noted, 20 Col.L.Rev. 890, 34 Harv.L.Rev. 312, 30 Yale L.J. 289. The defendant, a physician, employed by the plaintiff to give him a physical examination, told the plaintiff that probably his disease was syphilis, but that definite information could be obtained only by making certain Wasserman tests for which he (defendant) had no equipment. The defendant, who was also the physician to the owner of the small hotel in which the plaintiff lived, told the owner to be careful with reference to the plaintiff's bed clothing in order to prevent contagion. Further tests revealed that it was extremely unlikely that plaintiff had syphilis, but the symptoms, and information upon which defendant acted were "reasonably sufficient to cause the defendant to believe as he did." *Held,* for defendant, upholding a directed verdict.

SECTION D. INVASION OF PRIVACY

Unlike defamation, which is one of the oldest of torts, privacy is one of the most modern. Tort law's protection of privacy is modern both in spirit and in fact. It is modern in spirit because, whereas defamation is concerned with the protection of our standing in the eyes of others, privacy is concerned with the protection of our inner selves. The space that it seeks to protect is the space in which we can choose how, and how much of ourselves, to reveal to others. Whereas defamation is rooted in a pre-modern world of ascribed status, the privacy torts are rooted in a modern sense of individual dignity. Tort law's protection of privacy is modern in fact, because the idea that tort law should protect privacy as an independent interest does not catch fire until very late in the nineteenth century, and actual protection of privacy as an independent interest by the law of torts does not reach full bloom until the twentieth century.

Tort law's protection of privacy is customarily traced to a famous article—*The Right to Privacy*, 4 Harv. L. Rev. 193 (1890)—written by Louis Brandeis and his law partner, Samuel Warren. Famously and controversially, *The Right to Privacy* develops the argument that diverse strands of law apparently concerned to protect interests other than the interest in privacy should be woven together to create a "right to privacy." The animus of Warren and Brandeis's article was directed against the proliferating publication by newspapers and magazines of private information about socially prominent persons. "Gossip," they complain, "is no longer the resource of the idle and of the vicious, but has become a trade, which is pursued with industry as well as effrontery." The harm done was both to the persons so exposed and to the public at large, whose sensibility was coarsened by explosion of such gossip: "Triviality destroys at once robustness of thought and delicacy of feelings."

Even after the publication of Warren & Brandeis's famous article, the tort law of privacy was relatively slow to develop. That law had both to work its way free of property conceptions—some cases which prefigured a general "right to privacy" actually protected against the commercial appropriation of a person's private life—and to avoid absorption by the emerging tort of Intentional Infliction of Emotional Distress. Warren & Brandeis conceived invasion of privacy to be an essentially dignitary harm. To many courts, however, it appeared that the harm done by invasion of privacy was either essentially commercial or essentially emotional. It seemed, therefore, that invasion of privacy as a distinct, dignitary wrong might pull free of traditional property conceptions only to be sucked into newly fashioned conceptions of emotional injury. The privacy torts did not pull free of both these gravitational pulls and blossom in their own right until the middle of the twentieth century.*

The tort law of privacy which emerged consisted of four torts: (1) wrongfully intruding into the private life of another person; (2) unjustifiably appropriating or exploiting another's personality for gain; (3) publicizing the private affairs of another to persons who have no legitimate interest in knowing about those affairs; and (4) publicizing private facts about another that unreasonably places another in a false light before the public. The materials that follow explore these four torts.

LAKE v. WAL–MART STORES, INC.
Supreme Court of Minnesota, 1998.
582 N.W.2d 23, 26 Media L. Rep. 2175.

BLATZ, Chief Justice.

Elli Lake and Melissa Weber appeal from a dismissal of their complaint for failure to state a claim upon which relief may be granted. The district court and court of appeals held that Lake and Weber's complaint alleging intrusion upon seclusion, appropriation, publication of private facts, and false light publicity could not proceed because Minnesota does not recognize a common law tort action for invasion of privacy. We reverse as to the claims of intrusion upon seclusion, appropriation, and publication of private facts, but affirm as to false light publicity.

Nineteen-year-old Elli Lake and 20–year-old Melissa Weber vacationed in Mexico in March 1995 with Weber's sister. During the vacation, Weber's sister took a photograph of Lake and Weber naked in the shower together. After their vacation, Lake and Weber brought five rolls of film to the Dilworth, Minnesota Wal–Mart store and photo lab. When they received their developed photographs along with the negatives, an enclosed written

---

* For a brief history of the emergence of the "privacy torts" see G. Edward White, <u>Tort Law in America</u>, 173–76 (1980).

notice stated that one or more of the photographs had not been printed because of their "nature."

In July 1995, an acquaintance of Lake and Weber alluded to the photograph and questioned their sexual orientation. Again, in December 1995, another friend told Lake and Weber that a Wal–Mart employee had shown her a copy of the photograph. By February 1996, Lake was informed that one or more copies of the photograph were circulating in the community.

Lake and Weber filed a complaint against Wal–Mart Stores, Inc. and one or more as-yet unidentified Wal–Mart employees on February 23, 1996, alleging the four traditional invasion of privacy torts—intrusion upon seclusion, appropriation, publication of private facts, and false light publicity. Wal–Mart denied the allegations and made a motion to dismiss the complaint under Minn. R. Civ. P. 12.02, for failure to state a claim upon which relief may be granted. The district court granted Wal–Mart's motion to dismiss, explaining that Minnesota has not recognized any of the four invasion of privacy torts. The court of appeals affirmed.

Whether Minnesota should recognize any or all of the invasion of privacy causes of action is a question of first impression in Minnesota. The Restatement (Second) of Torts outlines the four causes of action that comprise the tort generally referred to as invasion of privacy. Intrusion upon seclusion occurs when one "intentionally intrudes, physically or otherwise, upon the solitude or seclusion of another or his private affairs or concerns * * * if the intrusion would be highly offensive to a reasonable person." Appropriation protects an individual's identity and is committed when one "appropriates to his own use or benefit the name or likeness of another." Publication of private facts is an invasion of privacy when one "gives publicity to a matter concerning the private life of another * * * if the matter publicized is of a kind that (a) would be highly offensive to a reasonable person, and (b) is not of legitimate concern to the public." False light publicity occurs when one "gives publicity to a matter concerning another that places the other before the public in a false light * * * if (a) the false light in which the other was placed would be highly offensive to a reasonable person, and (b) the actor had knowledge of or acted in reckless disregard as to the falsity of the publicized matter and the false light in which the other would be placed."

I

This court has the power to recognize and abolish common law doctrines. The common law is not composed of firmly fixed rules. Rather, as we have long recognized, the common law:

> is the embodiment of broad and comprehensive unwritten principles, inspired by natural reason, an innate sense of justice, adopted by common consent for the regulation and government of the affairs of men. It is the growth of ages, and an examination of many of its principles, as enunciated and discussed in the books, discloses a constant improvement and development in keeping with advancing civiliza-

tion and new conditions of society. Its guiding star has always been the rule of right and wrong, and in this country its principles demonstrate that there is in fact, as well as in theory, a remedy for all wrongs.

As society changes over time, the common law must also evolve:

* * *

The tort of invasion of privacy is rooted in a common law right to privacy first described in an 1890 law review article by Samuel Warren and Louis Brandeis.[10] The article posited that the common law has always protected an individual's person and property, with the extent and nature of that protection changing over time. The fundamental right to privacy is both reflected in those protections and grows out of them:

> Thus, in the very early times, the law gave a remedy only for physical interference with life and property, for trespass *vi et armis*. Then the "right to life" served only to protect the subject from battery in its various forms; liberty meant freedom from actual restraint; and the right to property secured to the individual his lands and his cattle. Later, there came a recognition of a man's spiritual nature, of his feelings and his intellect. Gradually the scope of these legal rights broadened; and now the right to life has come to mean the right to enjoy life,—the right to be let alone; the right to liberty secures the exercise of extensive civil privileges; and the term "property" has grown to comprise every form of possession—intangible, as well as tangible.[11]

Although no English cases explicitly articulated a "right to privacy," several cases decided under theories of property, contract, or breach of confidence also included invasion of privacy as a basis for protecting personal violations.[12] The article encouraged recognition of the common law right to privacy, as the strength of our legal system lies in its elasticity, adaptability, capacity for growth, and ability "to meet the wants of an ever changing society and to apply immediate relief for every recognized wrong."

The first jurisdiction to recognize the common law right to privacy was Georgia. 122 Ga. 190, 50 S.E. 68 (1905) In *Pavesich v. New England Life Ins. Co.,* the Georgia Supreme Court determined that the "right of privacy has its foundation in the instincts of nature," and is therefore an "immutable" and "absolute" right "derived from natural law." *Id.* 50 S.E. at 69–70. The court emphasized that the right of privacy was not new to Georgia law, as it was encompassed by the well-established right to personal liberty. *Id.* at 70.

Many other jurisdictions followed Georgia in recognizing the tort of invasion of privacy, citing Warren and Brandeis' article and *Pavesich*. Today, the vast majority of jurisdictions now recognize some form of the right to privacy. Only Minnesota, North Dakota, and Wyoming have not yet recognized any of the four privacy torts. Although New York and Nebraska courts have declined to recognize a common law basis for the right to privacy and instead provide statutory protection, we reject the proposition that only the

---

10. Samuel D. Warren and Louis D. Brandeis, *The Right to Privacy,* 4 Harv. L.Rev. 193 (1890).

11. *Id.* at 193.

12. *Id.* at 203–10.

legislature may establish new causes of action. The right to privacy is inherent in the English protections of individual property and contract rights and the "right to be let alone" is recognized as part of the common law across this country. Thus, it is within the province of the judiciary to establish privacy torts in this jurisdiction.

Today we join the majority of jurisdictions and recognize the tort of invasion of privacy. The right to privacy is an integral part of our humanity; one has a public persona, exposed and active, and a private persona, guarded and preserved. The heart of our liberty is choosing which parts of our lives shall become public and which parts we shall hold close.

Here Lake and Weber allege in their complaint that a photograph of their nude bodies has been publicized. One's naked body is a very private part of one's person and generally known to others only by choice. This is a type of privacy interest worthy of protection. Therefore, without consideration of the merits of Lake and Weber's claims, we recognize the torts of intrusion upon seclusion, appropriation, and publication of private facts. Accordingly, we reverse the court of appeals and the district court and hold that Lake and Weber have stated a claim upon which relief may be granted and their lawsuit may proceed.

II.

We decline to recognize the tort of false light publicity at this time. We are concerned that claims under false light are similar to claims of defamation, and to the extent that false light is more expansive than defamation, tension between this tort and the First Amendment is increased.

False light is the most widely criticized of the four privacy torts and has been rejected by several jurisdictions. Most recently, the Texas Supreme Court refused to recognize the tort of false light invasion of privacy because defamation encompasses most false light claims and false light "lacks many of the procedural limitations that accompany actions for defamation, thus unacceptably increasing the tension that already exists between free speech constitutional guarantees and tort law." *Cain v. Hearst Corp.*, 878 S.W.2d 577, 579–80 (Tex.1994). * * *

We agree * * * The primary difference between defamation and false light is that defamation addresses harm to reputation in the external world, while false light protects harm to one's inner self. Most false light claims are actionable as defamation claims; because of the overlap with defamation and the other privacy torts, a case has rarely succeeded squarely on a false light claim.[26]

Additionally, unlike the tort of defamation, which over the years has become subject to numerous restrictions to protect the interest in a free press and discourage trivial litigation, the tort of false light is not so restricted. Although many jurisdictions have imposed restrictions on false light actions identical to those for defamation, we are not persuaded that a

26. J. Clark Kelso, *False Light Privacy: A*   (1992).
Requiem, 32 Santa Clara L.Rev. 783, 785–86

new cause of action should be recognized if little additional protection is afforded plaintiffs.

Thus we recognize a right to privacy present in the common law of Minnesota, including causes of action in tort for intrusion upon seclusion, appropriation, and publication of private facts, but we decline to recognize the tort of false light publicity. This case is remanded to the district court for further proceedings consistent with this opinion.

Affirmed in part, reversed in part.

TOMLJANOVICH, Justice (dissenting).

I respectfully dissent. If the allegations against Wal–Mart are proven to be true, the conduct of the Wal–Mart employees is indeed offensive and reprehensible. As much as we deplore such conduct, not every contemptible act in our society is actionable.

* * *

We have become a much more litigious society since 1975 when we acknowledged that we have never recognized a cause of action for invasion of privacy. We should be even more reluctant now to recognize a new tort.

RUSH v. MAINE SAVINGS BANK, 387 A.2d 1127 (Me.1978). Mortgagors brought action against bank for invasion of privacy alleging that bank violated duty of confidentiality by complying with Internal Revenue Service summons seeking information about the mortgage loan agreement, the original amount, the balance, and any delinquency. *Held*, summary judgment for defendants affirmed. Plaintiff's complaint did not allege any of the four tortious kinds of "invasions of privacy."

FROELICH v. WERBIN, 219 Kan. 461, 548 P.2d 482 (1976). Burneta Adair's former husband had previously sued her seeking to recover a million dollars for defamation because she had stated that he was homosexual and William Froelich was his lover. Mrs. Adair was interested in proving the truth of the statement and she asked Syd Werbin, deputy sheriff and friend, to get a sample of Froelich's hair for purpose of comparing it with hair from her former husband's bed. While Froelich was in hospital, Werbin paid an orderly to get a sample, which he did. But evidence at trial indicated that the hair was not taken from the person of plaintiff or from the hospital room, but from a piece of adhesive tape which was thrown into a trash container in a utility room. *Held*, that since there had been no intrusion into the secluded hospital room and since plaintiff did not even know that the hair had been obtained until several months after it happened, this was not the kind of highly offensive intrusion that would be actionable.

SHULMAN v. GROUP W PRODUCTIONS, 18 Cal.4th 200, 74 Cal.Rptr.2d 843, 955 P.2d 469 (1998). Plaintiffs, mother and son, were injured in a severe automobile accident. They had to be cut from the car by "the jaws of life" and flown to a hospital by helicopter. The accident left plaintiff Ruth Shulman paraplegic. A video camera operator employed by defendant "roamed the accident scene, videotaping the rescue" and then accompanied the victims to the hospital in the rescue helicopter. Plaintiffs were videotaped until they were inside the hospital. Portions of the video were broadcast as a segment of "On Scene: Emergency Response."

Plaintiffs sued defendants for invasion of privacy under two of the privacy torts: (1) "unlawful intrusion"—by videotaping the rescue in the first place—and (2) "public disclosure of private facts"—by broadcasting the videotape. The trial court granted defendant's motion for summary judgment "on the ground that the events depicted in the broadcast were newsworthy and the producers' activities were therefore protected under the First Amendment to the United States Constitution. The Court of Appeal reversed, finding triable issues of fact exist as to one plaintiff's claim for publication of private facts and legal error on the trial court's part as to both plaintiffs' intrusion claims."

Held, as to the "disclosure of private facts" claim: Summary judgment reinstated. "[T]he material broadcast was newsworthy as a matter of law, and, therefore, cannot be the basis for tort liability under a private facts claim." *Held*, as to the unlawful intrusion claim: Reversal of summary judgment for the defendant affirmed: Triable issues existed "as to whether defendants invaded plaintiff's privacy by accompanying plaintiffs in the helicopter" and "as to whether defendants tortiously intruded by listening to Ruth's confidential conversations with [the nurse] at the rescue scene, without Ruth's consent." "Moreover, we hold defendants had no constitutional privilege so as to intrude on plaintiff's seclusion and private communications."

CANTRELL v. FOREST CITY PUBLISHING CO.

Supreme Court of the United States, 1974.
419 U.S. 245, 95 S.Ct. 465, 42 L.Ed.2d 419.

Mr. Justice STEWART delivered the opinion of the Court.

Margaret Cantrell and four of her minor children brought this diversity action in a federal district court for invasion of privacy against the Forest City Publishing Company, publisher of a Cleveland newspaper, The Plain Dealer, and against Joseph Eszterhas, a reporter formerly employed by The Plain Dealer, and Richard Conway, a Plain Dealer photographer. The Cantrells alleged that an article published in The Plain Dealer Sunday Magazine unreasonably placed their family in a false light before the public through its many inaccuracies and untruths. The District Judge struck the claims relating to punitive damages as to all the plaintiffs and dismissed the actions of three of the Cantrell children in their entirety, but allowed the case to go to the jury as to Mrs. Cantrell and her oldest son, William. The jury returned a verdict against all three of the respondents for compensatory money damages in favor of these two plaintiffs.

The Court of Appeals for the Sixth Circuit reversed, holding that, in the light of the First and Fourteenth Amendments, the District Judge should have granted the respondents' motion for a directed verdict as to all the

Cantrells. Cantrell v. Forest City Publishing Co., 484 F.2d 150. We granted certiorari, 418 U.S. 909, 94 S.Ct. 3202, 41 L.Ed.2d 1156.

I

In December 1967, Margaret Cantrell's husband Melvin was killed along with 43 other people when the Silver Bridge across the Ohio River at Point Pleasant, West Virginia, collapsed. The respondent Eszterhas was assigned by The Plain Dealer to cover the story of the disaster. He wrote a "news feature" story focusing on the funeral of Melvin Cantrell and the impact of his death on the Cantrell family.

Five months later, after conferring with the Sunday Magazine editor of The Plain Dealer, Eszterhas and photographer Conway returned to the Point Pleasant area to write a follow-up feature. The two men went to the Cantrell residence, where Eszterhas talked with the children and Conway took 50 pictures. Mrs. Cantrell was not at home at any time during the 60 to 90 minutes that the men were at the Cantrell residence.

Eszterhas' story appeared as the lead feature in the August 4, 1968, edition of The Plain Dealer Sunday Magazine. The article stressed the family's abject poverty; the children's old, ill-fitting clothes and the deteriorating condition of their home were detailed in both the text and accompanying photographs. As he had done in his original, prizewinning article on the Silver Bridge disaster, Eszterhas used the Cantrell family to illustrate the impact of the bridge collapse on the lives of the people in the Point Pleasant area.

It is conceded that the story contained a number of inaccuracies and false statements. Most conspicuously, although Mrs. Cantrell was not present at any time during the reporter's visit to her home, Eszterhas wrote, "Margaret Cantrell will talk neither about what happened nor about how they are doing. She wears the same mask of non-expression she wore at the funeral. She is a proud woman. She says that after it happened, the people in town offered to help them out with money and they refused to take it." Other significant misrepresentations were contained in details of Eszterhas' descriptions of the poverty in which the Cantrells were living and the dirty and dilapidated conditions of the Cantrell home.

The case went to the jury on a so-called "false light" theory of invasion of privacy. In essence, the theory of the case was that by publishing the false feature story about the Cantrells and thereby making them the objects of pity and ridicule, the respondents damaged Mrs. Cantrell and her son William by causing them to suffer outrage, mental distress, shame, and humiliation.

II

In Time, Inc. v. Hill, 385 U.S. 374, 87 S.Ct. 534, 17 L.Ed.2d 456, the Court considered a similar false light, invasion of privacy action. * * * This Court, guided by its decision in New York Times Co. v. Sullivan, 376 U.S. 254, 84 S.Ct. 710, 11 L.Ed.2d 686, which recognized constitutional limits on a State's power to award damages for libel in actions brought by public officials, held that the constitutional protections for speech and press precluded the application of the New York statute to allow recovery for "false reports of matters of public interest in the absence of proof that the defendant published the report with knowledge of its falsity or in reckless disregard of the truth." Id., 385 U.S. at 388, 87 S.Ct. at 542.

* * *

* * * [T]he District Judge was clearly correct in believing that the evidence introduced at trial was sufficient to support a jury finding that the respondents Joseph Eszterhas and Forest City Publishing Company had published knowing or reckless falsehoods about the Cantrells.[5] There was no dispute during the trial that Eszterhas, who did not testify, must have known that a number of the statements in the feature story were untrue. In particular, his article plainly implied that Mrs. Cantrell had been present during his visit to her home and that Eszterhas had observed her "wear[ing] the same mask of nonexpression she wore [at her husband's] funeral." These were "calculated falsehoods," and the jury was plainly justified in finding that Eszterhas had portrayed the Cantrells in a false light through knowing or reckless untruth.

The Court of Appeals concluded that there was no evidence that Forest City Publishing Company had knowledge of any of the inaccuracies contained in Eszterhas' article. However, there was sufficient evidence for the jury to find that Eszterhas' writing of the feature was within the scope of his employment at The Plain Dealer and that Forest City Publishing Company was therefore liable under traditional doctrines of *respondeat superior.* * * *

For the foregoing reasons, the judgment of the Court of Appeals is reversed and the case is remanded to that court with directions to enter a judgment affirming the judgment of the District Court as to the respondents Forest City Publishing Company and Joseph Eszterhas.

———

VOGEL v. W. T. GRANT CO., 458 Pa. 124, 327 A.2d 133 (1974). Vogel and Smith, plaintiffs, alleged that W. T. Grant, a firm with which they had credit accounts, had violated their rights to privacy by contacting third parties—their employers and various relatives—and discussing Vogel's and Smith's debts with these third parties, in order to harass Vogel and Smith into paying the debts. The trial court agreed and enjoined Grant from contacting any third parties, except to locate a debtor who has concealed his whereabouts. *Held*, reversed. "We cannot agree that Grant's conduct rises to the level of an invasion of privacy."

5. Although we conclude that the jury verdicts should have been sustained as to Eszterhas and Forest City Publishing Company, we agree with the Court of Appeals' conclusion that there was insufficient evidence to support the jury's verdict against the photographer Conway. Conway testified that the photographs he took were fair and accurate depictions of the people and scenes he found at the Cantrell residence. This testimony was not contradicted by any other evidence introduced at the trial. Nor was there any evidence that Conway was in any way responsible for the inaccuracies and misstatements contained in the text of the article written by Eszterhas. In short, Conway simply was not shown to have participated in portraying the Cantrells in a false light.

"Unreasonable publicity given to the existence of a debt has often been held to constitute an invasion of privacy.

"The Restatement (Second) of Torts has parsed the holdings of these and other cases and arrived at an accurate formulation of the tort of invasion of privacy. Section 652D, titled Publicity Given to Private Life, states:

> One who gives publicity to matters concerning the private life of another, of a kind highly offensive to a reasonable man, is subject to liability to the other for invasion of his privacy.

Restatement (Second) of Torts § 652D (Tent.Draft No. 13, 1967).

"We find this articulation, advocated by Dean Prosser and adopted by the Restatement (Second) tentative draft, to be both logical and precise. It is in accord with the common-law development of the tort of invasion of privacy in Pennsylvania. * * *

"The crux of the tort developed in these cases and described in section 652D is publicity. Without it there is no actionable wrong. The classic example of unreasonable publicity given to a lawful debt is found in Brents v. Morgan, 221 Ky. 765, 299 S.W. 967 (1927). There an automobile repairman placed in a show window of his garage a five by eight foot notice calling attention to a customer's overdue account. The court concluded that despite the truth of the notice's assertion, publication of the debt could constitute an actionable invasion of plaintiff's right to privacy. And publication, the court found, had been accomplished by disclosing the existence of the debt to the public at large. Compare Household Finance Corp. v. Bridge, 252 Md. 531, 250 A.2d 878 (1969).

"In *Brents*, as in many later debt collection cases, the court applied a three-part test in determining whether the right to privacy had been violated: *publicity* which is *unreasonable* must be given to a *private fact*. If there is no publicity, or if it is only what would normally be considered reasonable, or if the fact publicized is not a private one, there has been no actionable invasion of privacy.

* * *

"We conclude that here there has been no such publicity. The only persons notified of the arrearage in the Smith account were Smith's employer and mother. While four persons, three relatives and one employer, were contacted in connection with the Vogel account, even notification of this small group does not, in this case, constitute publication. We need not now determine how many outside parties must be notified to make a creditor's disclosures rise to the level of publication. We hold only that in these circumstances notification of two or four third parties is not sufficient to constitute publication. Without proof of publication, appellees have not established an actionable invasion of privacy."

NORRIS v. MOSKIN STORES, INC., 272 Ala. 174, 132 So.2d 321 (1961); noted, 15 Ala.L.Rev. 304. The defendant creditor's agent made three telephone calls to members of the plaintiff debtor's family suggesting that plaintiff had been having illicit relations with her. This was done in an attempt to coerce payment of a debt. *Held*, that the complaint stated a cause of action and the jury could find activities beyond the realm of reasonable action from oral communications as well as from written communications.

Chapter 6

MISREPRESENTATION: CONTRACT AND TORT

Tortious conduct leading to physical injury often involves a representational element. Misrepresentations are capable of vitiating plaintiff's consent to physical contact in battery cases, as we have seen in Chapter 2. Some affirmative duties to rescue plaintiffs in peril arise from the representations implicit in actions—undertaking a rescue may signal to other would-be rescuers that their assistance is not needed. Actions which induce detrimental reliance in this way thus bind those who take them to the rescues they have begun, as we shall see in Chapter 10. In the law of products liability, studied in Chapters 19 and 20, misrepresentations serve both as an independent basis of liability and figure in product defects which involve the disappointment of consumer expectations. Other examples of the role of representation in tortious conduct leading to physical injury could be added to this list. The tort law of misrepresentation studied in this chapter, however, operates in a different context, a context where economic loss, not physical injury, is the normal and expected harm. That loss is usually connected with a commercial transaction, and usually arises because the plaintiff was either induced to make a promise to perform an unfavorable contract or induced to give up more than was received in exchange. In these cases, the wrong (if there is any) involves words not actions, saying not doing.

It is tempting to suppose that, because it addresses merely economic losses, the tort of misrepresentation is less important than those intentional torts which protect the physical integrity of the person. This is an attractive, but questionable, supposition. Physical harm is a central topic for the law of intentional torts because physical aggression against other people is a fundamental form of wrongdoing. Misrepresentation is an equally central topic for the law of intentional torts because the deliberate infliction of injury through deception is an equally fundamental form of wrongdoing. Knowing misrepresentation—the core case of misrepresentation—is generally called "fraud" outside of professional legal discourse. In moral and political theory, fraud is often paired with force as one of the two fundamental forms of harmful conduct.

Because the economic losses with which the tort of misrepresentation is concerned generally arise in connection with commercial transactions, the tort of misrepresentation operates in a domain saturated by the law of contract. Just as the interests protected by the torts of trespass, conversion, trespass to chattels and nuisance are bound up with the law of property, so too the interests protected by the tort of misrepresentation are bound up with the law of contract. Obtaining the benefits of contract by deceit is as harmful and as wrongful as taking property by force. Misrepresentation protects the integrity of contract in the way that trespass and conversion protect the integrity of property.

Misrepresentation is presumptively thought of as an intentional tort, and deliberate misrepresentation—knowing misrepresentation—is taken to be the core instance of the tort. In some circumstances, however, liability may be imposed for misrepresentations which are not known to be false, but which the exercise of reasonable care would have shown to be false. This is negligent misrepresentation. In yet other circumstances, plaintiffs may prevail without proving either knowledge or fault in the making of the false representation. This form of liability is said to be strict.

SECTION A.   INTENTIONAL MISREPRESENTATION

We begin our study of misrepresentation with intentional misrepresentation. The simplest way to understand the relation among the various forms of misrepresentation—intentional, negligent and strict—is to suppose that they share all the same elements except one. They all, that is, involve false representations which are reasonably relied upon by the plaintiff and cause economic loss. They differ only in the state of mind or "scienter" that they require. In the case of intentional misrepresentation, the representation is known to be false; in the case of negligent misrepresentation, the representation would have been known to be false had the defendant exercised reasonable care; and in the case of strict liability recovery can be had without proving either that the defendant knew the representation to be false, or that the defendant should have known the representation to be false.

There is much to be said for this understanding. The elements of misrepresentation, reasonable reliance, and economic loss are, in fact, common to all three forms of the tort, and the states of mind required to establish liability do indeed vary. These commonalities and variations are essential to understanding the different forms of misrepresentation. Conceiving the torts solely in these terms, however, tends to obscure the fact that these forms of misrepresentation relate in different ways to the law of contract. Grasping these different relations is especially important to understanding the two older forms of misrepresentation—intentional and strict. The relation between tort and contract is not only the topic of a later section of this chapter, it is also a fundamental issue in *Pasley v. Freeman*, the case which follows this note and which is generally thought to have given birth to the tort of intentional misrepresentation.

PASLEY v. FREEMAN

King's Bench, 1789. 3 T.R. 51.

[This was an action in the nature of a writ of deceit, to which the defendant pleaded the general issue. The third count of the declaration stated that the defendant, intending to deceive and defraud the plaintiffs, persuaded them to sell and deliver goods to one Falch upon trust and credit, by falsely, deceitfully and fraudulently asserting that Falch was a person safely to be given credit, whereas Falch was not such a person, as the defendant well knew; that plaintiffs, believing defendant's statement to be true and relying thereon, sold and delivered to Falch on credit goods of the value of £2,634, 16s. 1d., and have never been able to collect the said sum of money or any part thereof. After a verdict for the plaintiffs on the third count, a motion was made in arrest of judgment.]

ASHHURST, J. The objection in this case, which is to the third count in the declaration, is that it contains only a bare assertion, and does not state that the defendant had any interest, or that he colluded with the other party who had. But I am of opinion that the action lies notwithstanding this objection. It seems to me that the rule laid down by CROKE, J., in Bayly v. Merrel, 3 Bulstr. 95, is a sound and solid principle, namely, that fraud without damage, or damage without fraud, will not found an action; but where both concur an action will lie. The principle is not denied by the other judges, but only the application of it, because the party injured there, who was the carrier, had the means of attaining certain knowledge in his own power, namely, by weighing the goods; and therefore it was a foolish credulity, against which the law will not relieve. But that is not the case here, for it is expressly charged that the defendant knew the falsity of the allegation, and which the jury have found to be true; but *non constat* that the plaintiffs knew it, or had any means of knowing it, but trusted to the veracity of the defendant. And many reasons may occur why the defendant might know that fact better than the plaintiffs; as if there had before this event subsisted a partnership between him and Falch which had been dissolved; but at any rate it is stated as a fact that he knew it.

It is admitted that a fraudulent affirmation, when the party making it has an interest, is a ground of action, as in Risney v. Selby, which was a false affirmation made to a purchaser as to the rent of a farm which the defendant was in treaty to sell to him. But it was argued that the action lies not unless where the party making it has an interest, or colludes with one who has. I do not recollect that any case was cited which proves such a position; but if there were any such to be found, I should not hesitate to say that it could not be law, for I have so great a veneration for the law as to suppose that nothing can be law which is not founded in common sense or common honesty. For the gist of the action is the injury done to the plaintiff, and not whether the defendant meant to be a gainer by it; what is it to the plaintiff whether the defendant was or was not to gain by it? The injury to him is the same. And it should seem that it ought more emphatically to lie against him, as the malice is more diabolical if he had not the temptation of gain. For the same reason, it cannot be necessary that the defendant should collude with one who has an interest. But if collusion were necessary, there seems all the reason in the world to suppose both interest and collusion from the nature of the act; for it is to be hoped that there is not to be found a disposition so diabolical as to prompt any man to injure another without benefiting himself. But it is said that if this be determined to be law, any man may have an action brought against him for telling a lie, by the crediting of which another happens eventually to be injured. But this consequence by no means follows; for in order to make it actionable it must be accompanied with the circumstances averred in this count, namely, that the defendant, "intending to deceive and defraud the plaintiffs, did deceitfully encourage and persuade them to do the act, and for that purpose made the false affirmation, in consequence of which they did the act." Any lie accompanied with those circumstances I should clearly hold to be the subject of an action; but not a mere lie thrown out at random without any intention of hurting anybody, but which some person was foolish enough to act upon; for the *quo animo* is a great part of the gist of the action.

Another argument which has been made use of is, that is a new case, and that there is no precedent of such an action. Where cases are new in their principle, there I admit that it is necessary to have recourse to legislative interposition in order to remedy the grievance; but where the case is only new in the instance, and the only question is upon the application of a principle recognized in the law to such new case, it will be just as competent to courts of justice to apply the principle to any case which may arise two centuries hence, as it was two centuries ago; if it were not, we ought to blot out of our law-books one fourth part of the cases that are to be found in them. The same objection might, in my opinion, have been made with much greater reason in the case of Coggs v. Barnard; for there the defendant, so far from meaning an injury, meant a kindness, though he was not so careful as he should have been in the execution of what he undertook. And indeed the principle of the case does not, in my opinion, seem so clear as that of the case now before us, and yet that case has always been received as law. Indeed, one great reason, perhaps, why this action has never occurred may be that it is not likely that such a species of fraud should be practised unless the party is in some way interested. Therefore I think the rule for arresting the judgment ought to be discharged.

[Judgment affirmed]

RESTATEMENT OF TORTS, SECOND (1977)

§ 525   Liability for Fraudulent Misrepresentation

One who fraudulently makes a misrepresentation of fact, opinion, intention or law for the purpose of inducing another to act or to refrain from action in reliance upon it, is subject to liability to the other in deceit for pecuniary loss caused to him by his justifiable reliance upon the misrepresentation.

INTENT OR "SCIENTER"

DERRY v. PEEK

House of Lords, 1889. 14 App.Cas. 337.

[The action was brought by Peek against Derry, the chairman, and Messrs. Wakefield, Moore, Pethick, and Wilde, four of the directors of the Plymouth, Devonport and District Tramways Company, claiming damages for the fraudulent misrepresentations of the defendants whereby the plaintiff was induced to take shares in the company. By a special Act (45 & 46 Vict. c. clix.) the Plymouth, Devonport and District Tramways Company was authorized to make certain tramways.

By sect. 35 the carriages used on the tramways might be moved by animal power and, with the consent of the Board of Trade, by steam or any mechanical power for fixed periods and subject to the regulations of the Board.

By sect. 34 of the Tramways Act 1870 (33 & 34 Vict. c. 78) which section was incorporated in the special Act, "all carriages used on any tramway shall be moved by the power prescribed by the special Act, and where no such power is prescribed, by animal power only."

In February 1883 the appellants as directors of the company issued a prospectus containing the following paragraph:

"One great feature of this undertaking, to which considerable importance should be attached, is, that by the special Act of Parliament obtained, the company has the right to use steam or mechanical motive power, instead of horses, and it is fully expected that by means of this a considerable saving will result in the working expenses of the line as compared with other tramways worked by horses."

Soon after the issue of the prospectus the respondent, relying, as he alleged, upon the representations in this paragraph and believing that the company had an absolute right to use steam and other mechanical power, applied for and obtained shares in the company.

The company proceeded to make tramways, but the Board of Trade refused to consent to the use of steam or mechanical power except on certain portions of the tramways.

In the result the company was wound up, and the respondent in 1885 brought this action. The defendants pleaded (inter alia) that if the statements complained of were untrue, they were made by the defendants in good faith, and that they had reasonable grounds for believing them to be true.

At the trial before STIRLING, J., the defendants testified as follows: Wilde, a member of the bar, said that he knew the consent of the Board of

Trade was necessary but thought that consent had been given practically since the plans had been laid before it and no objections had been raised. Pethick thought the Board of Trade had no more right to refuse their consent than they would in the case of a railroad; that they might have required additions or changes, but that on any reasonable requirement being complied with they could not refuse their consent. Moore said that he thought that consent had been obtained and that they were starting as a tramway company with full power to use steam as other companies were doing. Wakefield said it never occurred to him to say anything about the consent of the Board of Trade because as they had got the Act of Parliament for steam he presumed at once that they would get consent. Derry said that he was aware that the consent of the Board of Trade was necessary but he thought that as the company had obtained their act the Board's consent would follow as a matter of course and that the question of such consent being necessary never crossed his mind at the time the prospectus was issued.

STIRLING, J., came to the conclusion that the directors all believed that the company had the right stated in the prospectus; and that their belief was not so unreasonable, and their proceedings so reckless or careless, that they ought to be fixed with the consequences of deceit. He ordered the action to be dismissed.

On appeal by plaintiff to the Court of Appeal, the judgment of STIRLING, J., was reversed by COTTON, HANNEN, and LOPES, L. JJ. They held the directors liable in this action for deceit, on the ground that they made the statement without any reasonable ground for believing it to be true. L.R., 37 Ch.Div. 541.

The defendants, Derry, et al., appealed from the decision of the Court of Appeal to the House of Lords.]

LORD HERSCHELL. My Lords, in the statement of claim in this action the respondent, who is the plaintiff, alleges that the appellants made in a prospectus issued by them certain statements which were untrue, that they well knew that the facts were not as stated in the prospectus, and made the representations fraudulently, and with the view to induce the plaintiff to take shares in the company.

"This action is one which is commonly called an action of deceit, a mere common-law action." This is the description of it given by COTTON, L. J., in delivering judgment. * * * In an action of deceit * * * it is not enough to establish misrepresentation alone; it is conceded on all hands that something more must be proved to cast liability upon the defendant, though it has been a matter of controversy what additional elements are requisite. * * *

* * * I think the authorities establish the following propositions: First, in order to sustain an action of deceit there must be proof of fraud, and nothing short of that will suffice. Secondly, fraud is proved when it is shown that a false representation has been made (1) knowingly, or (2) without belief in its truth, or (3) recklessly, careless whether it be true or false. Although I have treated the second and third as distinct cases, I think the

third is but an instance of the second, for one who makes a statement under such circumstances can have no real belief in the truth of what he states. To prevent a false statement being fraudulent there must, I think, always be an honest belief in its truth. And this probably covers the whole ground, for one who knowingly alleges that which is false has obviously no such honest belief. Thirdly, if fraud be proved, the motive of the person guilty of it is immaterial. It matters not that there was no intention to cheat or injure the person to whom the statement was made. * * *

In my opinion making a false statement through want of care falls far short of, and is a very different thing from, fraud, and the same may be said of a false representation honestly believed though on insufficient grounds. Indeed COTTON, L. J., himself indicated, in the words I have already quoted, that he should not call it fraud. But the whole current of authorities, with which I have so long detained your Lordships, shows to my mind conclusively that fraud is essential to found an action of deceit, and that it cannot be maintained where the acts proved cannot properly be so termed. And the case of Taylor v. Ashton, 11 M. & W. 401, appears to me to be in direct conflict with the dictum of Sir George Jessel [in Smith v. Chadwick, 20 Ch.Div. 27, to the effect that a false statement honestly believed but carelessly made would sustain an action of deceit], and inconsistent with the view taken by the learned judges in the Court below. I observe that Sir Frederick Pollock, in his able work on Torts (p. 243, note), referring, I presume, to the dicta of COTTON, L. J., and Sir George Jessel, M. R., says that the actual decision in Taylor v. Ashton, 11 M. & W. 401, is not consistent with the modern cases on the duty of directors of companies. I think he is right. But for the reasons I have given I am unable to hold that anything less than fraud will render directors or any other persons liable to an action of deceit.

At the same time I desire to say distinctly that when a false statement has been made the questions whether there were reasonable grounds for believing it, and what were the means of knowledge in the possession of the person making it, are most weighty matters for consideration. The ground upon which an alleged belief was founded is a most important test of its reality. I can conceive many cases where the fact that an alleged belief was destitute of all reasonable foundation would suffice of itself to convince the Court that it was not really entertained, and that the representation was a fraudulent one. So, too, although means of knowledge are, as was pointed out by Lord Blackburn in Brownlie v. Campbell, 5 App.Cas. p. 952, a very different thing from knowledge, if I thought that a person making a false statement had shut his eyes to the facts, or purposely abstained from inquiring into them I should hold that honest belief was absent, and that he was just as fraudulent as if he had knowingly stated that which was false. * * *

I quite admit that the statements of witnesses as to their belief are by no means to be accepted blindfold. The probabilities must be considered. Whenever it is necessary to arrive at a conclusion as to the state of mind of another person, and to determine whether his belief under given circumstances was such as he alleges, we can only do so by applying the standard of conduct which our own experience of the ways of men has enabled us to form; by asking ourselves whether a reasonable man would be likely under the circumstances so to believe. I have applied this test, with the result that I have a strong conviction that a reasonable man situated as the defendants were, with their knowledge and means of knowledge, might well believe what they state they did believe, and consider that the representation made was substantially true. * * *

I think the judgment of the Court of Appeal should be reversed. [LORD HALSBURY, L. C., LORD WATSON, LORD BRAMWELL, and LORD FITZGER- ALD delivered concurring opinions.]

Order of the Court of Appeal reversed; order of STIRLING, J., restored.

————

RENO v. BULL, 226 N.Y. 546, 124 N.E. 144 (1919). Action of deceit by the purchaser of corporate shares against the directors of a corporation who had approved a prospectus containing untrue statements as to the assets and prospects of the corporation. The trial court instructed the jury that if the defendants had "authorized a false statement to be made, when by common prudence and the exercise of ordinary care, they could have discovered that these representations were false, then they are just as liable as if they had actual personal knowledge that they were false." *Held*, charge was erroneous.

CHATHAM FURNACE CO. v. MOFFATT, 147 Mass. 403, 18 N.E. 168 (1888). Action for deceit. In leasing a mine to the plaintiff, the defendant erroneously stated, as of his own knowledge, that a tract containing several thousand tons of iron ore was included in the leased land. His error was due to a survey which had been based on an erroneous assumption that the main shaft of the mine ran due north. When the map was made, the defendant had been notified that this course had been assumed and not verified. At the time the defendant showed the map to the plaintiff, he had forgotten this fact. *Held*, for plaintiff.

"[T]he charge of fraudulent intent, in an action for deceit, may be maintained by proof of a statement made as to the party's own knowledge, which is false; provided the thing stated is not merely a matter of opinion, estimate or judgment, but is susceptible of actual knowledge; and in such a case it is not necessary to make any further proof of an actual intent to deceive. The fraud consists in stating that the party knows the thing to exist, when he does not know it to exist; and if he does not know it to exist, he must ordinarily be deemed to know that he does not. Forgetfulness of its existence after a former knowledge, or a mere belief in its existence, will not warrant or excuse a statement of actual knowledge."

NASH v. MINNESOTA TITLE INSURANCE & TRUST CO., 163 Mass. 574, 586, 40 N.E. 1039, 1042, 28 L.R.A. 753 (1895) (Holmes, J., dissenting). When a man makes a representation, not "in casual talk, but in a business matter, for the very purpose of inducing others to lay out their money on the faith of it, * * * he knows that others will understand his words according to their usual and proper meaning, and not by the accident of what he happens to have in his head, and it seems to me one of the first principles of social intercourse that he is bound at his peril to know what that meaning is. * * * Of course, if the words are technical, or have a peculiar meaning in the place where they were used this can be shown."

ACTIONABILITY AND RELIANCE

The elements of intentional misrepresentation are commonly said to require that the representation be "material" and "reasonably" relied. These two aspects of the tort are closely intertwined. Some kinds of representations are actionable because they are appropriately relied on, whereas others are not. (Representations of existing fact are the clearest example of representations on which it is appropriate to rely.) But the law proceeds on the supposition that there are subtle distinctions between the two concepts. So it seems appropriate both to link and to distinguish them.

VULCAN METALS CO. v. SIMMONS MANUFACTURING CO.
United States Circuit Court of Appeals, Second Circuit, 1918.
248 Fed. 853.

[Two actions tried together. The first, brought by the Vulcan Metals Company against the Simmons Manufacturing Company, was for deceit because of misrepresentations in connection with the sale, by the Simmons Company to the Vulcan Company of certain machinery for the manufacture of vacuum cleaners, together with the patents covering their manufacture; the second was brought by the Simmons Company against the Vulcan Company upon some of the notes given for the purchase price, in which action the Vulcan Company filed a counterclaim based on the seller's alleged misrepresentations.

The defendant had made misrepresentations which were "substantially the same as those contained in a booklet issued by the Simmons Manufacturing Company for the general sale of the vacuum cleaners. They include commendations of the cleanliness, economy and efficiency of the machine; that it was absolutely perfect in even the smallest detail; that water power, by which it worked, marked the most economical means of operating a vacuum cleaner with the greatest efficiency; that the cleaning was more thoroughly done than by beating or brushing; that, having been perfected, it was a necessity which every one could afford; that it was so simple that a child of six could use it; that it worked completely and thoroughly; that it was simple, long-lived, easily operated and effective; that it was the only sanitary portable cleaner on the market; that perfect satisfaction would result from its use; that it would last a lifetime; that it was the only practical jet machine on the market; and that perfect satisfaction would result from its use if properly adjusted. The booklet is in general the ordinary compilation, puffing the excellence and power of the vacuum cleaner, and asserting its superiority over all others of a similar sort." The defendant's salesman made a demonstration of the cleaner to the plaintiff's purchasing agent with borax sprinkled upon a carpet and allowed the plaintiff's agent to take one for experiment, this being retained for some time. There were also representations that the cleaners had never been put on the market.

The district court directed a verdict in favor of the Simmons Company in each action. The Vulcan Company appeals.]

LEARNED HAND, J. The first question is of the misrepresentations touching the quality and powers of the patented machine. These were general commendations or in so far as they included any specific facts, were not disproved; e.g., that the cleaner would produce 18 inches of vacuum with 25 pounds water pressure. They raise, therefore, the question of law how far general "puffing" or "dealers' talk" can be the basis of an action for deceit.

The conceded exception in such cases has generally rested upon the distinction between "opinion" and "fact"; but that distinction has not escaped the criticism it deserves. An opinion is a fact, and it may be a very relevant fact; the expression of an opinion is the assertion of a belief, and any rule which condones the expression of a consciously false opinion condones a consciously false statement of fact. When the parties are so situated that the buyer may reasonably rely upon the expression of the seller's opinion, it is no excuse to give a false one. Bigler v. Flickinger, 55 Pa. 279. And so it makes much difference whether the parties stand "on an equality." For example, we should treat very differently the expressed opinion of a chemist to a layman about the properties of a composition from the same opinion between chemist and chemist, when the buyer had full opportunity to examine. The reason of the rule lies, we think, in this: There are some kinds of talk which no sensible man takes seriously, and if he does he suffers from his credulity. If we were all scrupulously honest, it would not be so; but, as it is, neither party usually believes what the seller says about his own opinions, and each knows it. Such statements, like the claims of campaign managers before election, are rather designed to allay the suspicion which would attend their absence than to be understood as having any relation to objective truth. It is quite true that they induce a compliant temper in the buyer, but it is by a much more subtle process than through the acceptance of his claims for his wares.

So far as concerns statements of value, the rule is pretty well fixed against the buyer. It has been applied more generally to statements of quality and serviceability. But this is not always so. As respects the validity of patents it also obtains. Cases of warranty present the same question and have been answered in the same way.

In the case at bar, since the buyer was allowed full opportunity to examine the cleaner and to test it out, we put the parties upon an equality. It seems to us that general statements as to what the cleaner would do, even though consciously false, were not of a kind to be taken literally by the buyer. As between manufacturer and customer, it may not be so; but this was the case of taking over a business, after ample chance to investigate. Such a buyer, who the seller rightly expects will undertake an independent and adequate inquiry into the actual merits of what he gets, has no right to treat as material in his determination statements like these. The standard of honesty permitted by the rule may not be the best; but, as Holmes, J., says in Deming v. Darling, 148 Mass. 504, 20 N.E. 107, 2 L.R.A. 743, the chance that the higgling preparatory to a bargain may be afterwards translated into assurances of quality may perhaps be a set-off to the actual wrong allowed by the rule as it stands. We therefore think that the District Court was right in disregarding all these misrepresentations.

[The court then found that the representations that the cleaners had never been put on the market were material and relied upon, and directed a new trial in the action of deceit, but (after a rehearing in which the court divided 2–1) not upon the counterclaim, which, the majority of the court concluded, was not available as a defense to the second action.]

———

DEMING v. DARLING, 148 Mass. 504, 20 N.E. 107 (1889). Action for deceit. The defendant sold the plaintiff a railroad bond, representing that it was "of the very best and safest and was an A No. 1 bond," and that the railroad, situated in Ohio, was good security for the bonds. The court declined to charge the jury that such statements "are expressions of opinion of value and even though false" will not sustain the action, but did charge that such expressions of opinion, "if made in good faith, * * * would not support an action of deceit." Verdict for plaintiff. *Held*, for defendant, sustaining exceptions for plaintiff. "The law does not exact good faith from a seller in those vague commendations of his wares which manifestly are open to difference of opinion, which do not imply untrue assertions concerning matters of direct observation. * * * The rule is not changed by the mere fact that the property is at a distance and is not seen by the buyer. Moreover, in this case, market prices at least were easily accessible to the plaintiff."

EDGINGTON v. FITZMAURICE, L.R. 29 Ch.Div. 459 (C.A.1885). Action for damages against the directors of a corporation. Plaintiff purchased debenture bonds of corporation in reliance on statement made in prospectus that debentures were being issued to enable the corporation to make improvements in the physical plant. Actually, the object of the issuance was to provide funds with which to pay off existing liabilities. *Held*, for plaintiff, the statement being regarded as a misrepresentation of a material fact, i.e., the state of mind of the directors.

SIMPSON v. WIDGER et al., 311 N.J.Super. 379, 709 A.2d 1366 (1998). Plaintiff purchased a horse from defendants. Four years later, the horse became lame and unfit for use as a show horse. The lameness was caused by "ringbone" a condition involving calcification of the horse's bones. Veterinary examinations undertaken at the time of purchase indicated that the horse suffered from bone abnormalities which had the potential to develop into "ringbone, with resulting lameness." The purchaser brought suit against the sellers, alleging in part that they committed fraud by misrepresenting the "serviceability" of the horse and the risk of the horse becoming subsequently "unserviceable" because of ringworm. The trial court entered summary judgment in favor of defendants on this claim. *Held* affirmed. The horse was "serviceable" at the time of sale.

" 'A misrepresentation amounting to actual legal fraud consists of a material representation of a presently existing or past fact, made with knowledge of its falsity and with the intention that the other party rely thereon, resulting in reliance by that party to his detriment.' [citation omitted].

"Viewing the evidence most favorably for plaintiffs, the most that can be inferred is that Scher knew that the presence of ringbone was a *possibility* which *might* affect the horse's serviceability and resale value. Possibilities are not 'presently existing' facts. Nor should we lose sight of the rule that fraud must be proven by clear and convincing evidence." [citation omitted]

RELIANCE: REASONABLE AND ACTUAL

The "actionability" of the alleged misrepresentation is closely connected to—but not quite the same as—the justifiability of plaintiff's reliance. Fraud claims sometimes fail because the plaintiff either did not rely, or did not reasonably rely. The following cases emphasize the reliance and its reasonableness—or the lack of either of these—more than the actionability of the representations at issue. Inquiry into the reasonableness of the plaintiff's reliance leads to a focus on the plaintiff's conduct as well as the defendant's. In some circumstances, the reasonableness of the plaintiff's reliance may be in question because the plaintiff's conduct appears too gullible. Traditional ideas of *caveat emptor* make their presence felt here, demanding vigilance on the part of buyers. In other circumstances, the reasonableness of plaintiff's reliance may be in question because reasonableness may require an investigation into the factual predicates of the representations relied upon. At some point, the placing of demands on plaintiffs becomes problematic, crossing into the imposition of an affirmative duty of reasonable care on the part of potential victims of fraud.

———

HYMA v. LEE, 338 Mich. 31, 60 N.W.2d 920 (1953). Action of deceit. Plaintiff alleged that he was a believer in spiritualism and was led to believe by defendant that the latter was a medium; that defendant represented to plaintiff that he had received information through the "voices" that there was an oil pool under land that the plaintiffs owned, and that in reliance thereon plaintiff had invested $4,200 in an oil well which failed to produce. *Held*, that a cause of action was stated. By inducing plaintiff to believe that he was a medium, a relation of trust and confidence was established and plaintiff thus established his right to rely.

ENFIELD v. COLBURN, 63 N.H. 218 (1884). Plaintiff alleged that defendant fraudulently represented that he had a valid claim for damages against the plaintiff and that plaintiff in reliance thereon investigated the claim at large expense and found it to be false. *Held*, for defendant. If plaintiff investigated, he did not rely.

LEWIS v. WHITE, 2 Utah 2d 101, 269 P.2d 865 (1954). Purchaser of motel sought damages for fraud. The fraud on which they relied was based on certain alleged false representations as to insulation, sewage disposal, and that property produced an income of $1,000 per month whereas in fact the income was about $225 per month. *Held*, the trial court should have charged jury that purchasers must have *reasonably* relied upon the representations and such investigation and inquiry should have been made as reasonable care would dictate.

BISHOP v. E. A. STROUT REALTY AGENCY
United States Court of Appeals, Fourth Circuit, 1950.
182 F.2d 503.

PARKER, Chief Judge. This is an appeal by plaintiffs from a judgment for defendant on a directed verdict in an action to recover damages for deceit. Plaintiffs are husband and wife who purchased a tract of land with water frontage for the purpose of using it as an angler's camp. The defendant is the real estate agency that is alleged to have sold the property acting through its local representative or "associate", one Oscar C. Davis, who was not joined in the action. The complaint alleges that plaintiffs were induced to purchase the land through the false and fraudulent representations of Davis as to the depth of the adjacent water and that they suffered damage as a result. The case was heard before a jury and the trial judge directed verdict for defendant on the ground that the falsity of the representations could have been discovered by plaintiffs by an examination of the property purchased. Defendant contends that the direction of the verdict should be sustained on the ground given by the trial judge and also on the additional grounds that no fraudulent intent was shown, that there was no proof of damage and that it was not shown that Davis was acting for defendant in the sale of the property.

As the case must be tried again it is not desirable to discuss the evidence in detail. It is sufficient to say that when taken in the light most favorable to plaintiffs, as it must be on motion for directed verdict, it was amply sufficient to take the case to the jury. There was evidence tending to show that the property was listed with defendant for sale, that Davis handled business for defendant in the locality where the land was situated and that defendant afterwards recognized the sale as having been made through its agency. There was evidence that plaintiffs notified Davis of the purpose for which they desired the property and of the necessity of having deep water adjacent to it so that boats could be brought in, and that they were assured by him that this property would suit them to a "T" and that the water adjacent was not less than six feet deep at low tide and nine feet or more deep at high tide. They testified that they were shown the property at high tide and relied upon these statements of Davis without making soundings because they trusted him and had no reason to believe that he was not telling the truth. Plaintiffs paid $3,000 down, giving a $4,000 mortgage for the remainder of the purchase price, and entered into possession and made certain expenditures for improvements. Shortly thereafter they discovered that the water adjacent to the property was very shallow. Because of this, it was not at all suited for the purpose for which it had been purchased and plaintiffs had to abandon it. When they attempted to see Davis, they were unable to get him to meet with them to discuss the matter. The mortgage given by plaintiffs was foreclosed and the property was bought in at the foreclosure sale for the amount of the mortgage debt. * * *

We do not think that plaintiffs are precluded of recovery because they accepted and relied upon the representations of Davis as to the depth of the water without making soundings or taking other steps to ascertain their truth or falsity. The depth of the water was not a matter that was apparent to ordinary observation; Davis professed to know whereof he was speaking; and there was nothing to put plaintiffs on notice that he was not speaking the truth. There is nothing in law or in reason which requires one to deal as though dealing with a liar or a scoundrel, or that denies the protection of the law to the trustful who have been victimized by fraud. The principle underlying the caveat emptor rule was more highly regarded in former times than it is today; but it was never any credit to the law to allow one who had defrauded another to defend on the ground that his own word should not have been believed. The modern and more sensible rule is that applied by the Court of Appeals of Maryland in Standard Motor Co. v. Peltzer, 147 Md. 509, 510, 128 A. 451, where it was held not to be negligence or folly for a buyer to rely on what had been told him. This is in accord with the modern trend in all jurisdictions which is summed up in A.L.I.Restatement of Torts, sec. 540 as follows:

> The recipient in a business transaction of a fraudulent misrepresentation of fact is justified in relying upon its truth, although he might have ascertained the falsity of the representation had he made an investigation.

The rule is thus stated with citation of the pertinent authorities in 55 Am.Jur. p. 539:

> The tendency of the courts, however, is not to deny relief to a defrauded purchaser on the ground that he was negligent in relying on the vendor's representations, and the mere fact that he could have ascertained by inquiry and investigation the falsity of express representations of existing facts, the truth of which was known to the vendor and unknown to the purchaser, will not necessarily bar him from relief. In this connection it has been said that the unmistakable drift is toward the doctrine that the vendor cannot shield himself from liability by asking the law to condemn the credulity of the purchaser.

Defendant places particular reliance upon the old case of Buschman v. Codd, 52 Md. 202, where the rule is stated: "Where the real quality of the thing is an object of sense, obvious to a person of ordinary intelligence, and the parties have equal knowledge or means of acquiring information by the exercise of ordinary inquiry and diligence, and nothing is said for the purpose of preventing such inquiries as every prudent person ought to make, under such circumstances there is no warranty of the seller's knowledge of the truth of his representations, or of the fact being as it is stated to be." We do not think that this indicates that the law of Maryland differs from the law prevailing in other jurisdictions. See A.L.I. Restatement of Torts sec. 541. The case here, however, is not one of a representation obviously false but of a representation of fact which plaintiffs had no reason to doubt, made by one who professed to know whereof he was speaking and who made it for the purpose of influencing their judgment and bringing about a sale of the property. The rule applicable in such a situation is the general rule as set forth in the Restatement, which was applied by the Court of Appeals of Maryland in Standard Motor Company v. Peltzer, supra, where the false representation was that a 1917 model truck offered for sale was a 1920 model and had been used for only a very short while. In answer to an argument based on Buschman v. Codd, supra, that the plaintiff was not justified in relying upon the representation, the court said:

> The evidence showed that the buyer here had some experience as an owner and user of a truck, and that the truck was displayed for his inspection without restriction. On some of his visits to the salesrooms he remained an hour and more. He testified, however, that his illiteracy rendered him unable to read marks or names on the truck and its engine, and that, having the statements of the selling agents to depend upon, he did not undertake to determine any of the facts for himself. He was not an expert in motor vehicles; he was a farmer. The selling agents, on the other hand, were presumably experts with exact information as to the truck they were selling. And the court could not say that it was negligence and folly for this buyer to accept and rely on whatever had been told him.

[147 Md. 509, 128 A. 453.]

* * *

The judgment appealed from will be reversed and the case will be remanded for a new trial.

Reversed and remanded.

TAYLOR v. ARNEILL, 129 Colo. 185, 268 P.2d 695 (1954); noted, 27 Rocky Mt.L.Rev. 115. A, a real estate agent, negotiated a sale of hotel property between V and P. Before signing the contract P inspected the property, at which time A, although his company had surveyed the land only two years before, innocently represented to P that the boundary line was a retaining wall and abutment, which was in fact 20 feet past the boundary and on land owned by V. This 20 foot space was a parking lot and a major inducement to the purchase. *Held*, reversing trial court judgment for plaintiff ordering conveyance of the 20 foot space, that "if a purchaser of land does not avail himself of the means and opportunities which are afforded him for acquainting himself with the character and value of the land, he will not be heard to say that he has been deceived by the vendor's representations."

STARKWEATHER v. BENJAMIN, 32 Mich. 305 (1875). Action for damages, based on misrepresentations concerning the quantity of land in a parcel purchased from defendant, and which was purchased by the acre. *Held*, for plaintiff, distinguishing the case from one where falsity is apparent simply from casual observation.

DICE v. AKRON, CANTON & YOUNGSTOWN RAILROAD CO., 342 U.S. 359, 72 S.Ct. 312, 96 L.Ed. 398 (1952); noted, 37 Corn.L.Q. 799, 66 Harv.L.Rev. 162, 31 Tex.L.Rev. 218, 13 Ohio St.L.J. 416. Plaintiff, a railroad fireman, brought suit for damages under F.E.L.A. as a result of being seriously injured when an engine in which he was riding jumped the track. Defense was a release signed in payment of the sum of $924.63. Plaintiff alleged release invalid because he had signed it relying upon deliberately false statement that document was only a receipt. Trial judge entered judgment for defendant notwithstanding jury verdict for $25,000 on the ground that plaintiff had been "guilty of supine negligence." *Held*, for plaintiff, reversing trial court. The view that negligence in failing to read release should defeat recovery by injured party was regarded as being out of harmony with modern practice to relieve injured persons from the effect of releases fraudulently obtained.

MISREPRESENTATION BY OMISSION

The outer perimeter of misrepresentation is defined by failure to disclose a material fact. The problems with which the law must grapple in this domain parallel those which arise as the law presses further and further into the reasonableness of plaintiff's behavior. Imposing liability for a straightforward failure to disclose appears to cross two important boundaries. The first of these is the boundary between misfeasance and nonfeasance. In core cases, misfeasance involves acting in a way which inflicts injury, whereas nonfeasance involves failing to confer a benefit on someone. Negative duties not to harm others are generally thought to lie at the center of tort law; affirmative duties to benefit others are generally taken to be exceptional and peripheral. The second boundary transgressed is the boundary between intentional and negligent wrongdoing. Imposing a duty to disclose appears to some courts and commentators to involve introducing a duty of care into a tort whose "scienter" element has long been deliberately defined to exclude merely careless conduct. Complicating the problem—and in some way undercutting these apparently sharp, categorical distinctions— is the fact that the line between committing and omitting is not always sharp and can, in fact, be blurred by parties intent on engaging in "sharp" dealing. It is not surprising, then, that cases involving nondisclosure have been on the cutting edge of modern misrepresentation law.

JOHNSON v. DAVIS
Supreme Court of Florida, 1985.
480 So.2d 625.

ADKINS, Justice.

We have before us a petition to review the decision in *Johnson v. Davis*, 449 So.2d 344 (Fla. 3d DCA 1984), which expressly and directly conflicts with *Banks v. Salina,* 413 So.2d 851 (Fla. 4th DCA 1982), and *Ramel v. Chasebrook Construction Co.,* 135 So.2d 876 (Fla. 2d DCA 1961). We have jurisdiction, article V, section 3(b)(3), Florida Constitution, and approve the decision of the district court.

In May of 1982, the Davises entered into a contract to buy for $310,000 the Johnsons' home, which at the time was three years old. The contract required a $5,000 deposit payment, an additional $26,000 deposit payment within five days and a closing by June 21, 1982. The crucial provision of the contract, for the purposes of the case at bar, is Paragraph F which provided:

> F.   *Roof Inspection:* Prior to closing at Buyer's expense, Buyer shall have the right to obtain a written report from a licensed roofer stating that the roof is in a watertight condition. In the event repairs are required either to correct leaks or to replace damage to facia or soffit, seller shall pay for said repairs which shall be performed by a licensed roofing contractor.

The contract further provided for payment to the "prevailing party" of all costs and reasonable fees in any contract litigation.

Before the Davises made the additional $26,000 deposit payment, Mrs. Davis noticed some buckling and peeling plaster around the corner of a window frame in the family room and stains on the ceilings in the family room and kitchen of the home. Upon inquiring, Mrs. Davis was told by Mr. Johnson that the window had had a minor problem that had long since been corrected and that the stains were wallpaper glue and the result of ceiling beams being moved. There is disagreement among the parties as to whether Mr. Johnson also told Mrs. Davis at this time that there had never been any problems with the roof or ceilings. The Davises thereafter paid the remainder of their deposit and the Johnsons vacated the home. Several days later, following a heavy rain, Mrs. Davis entered the home and discovered water "gushing" in from around the window frame, the ceiling of the family room, the light fixtures, the glass doors, and the stove in the kitchen.

Two roofers hired by the Johnsons' broker concluded that for under $1,000 they could "fix" certain leaks in the roof and by doing so make the roof "watertight." Three roofers hired by the Davises found that the roof was inherently defective, that any repairs would be temporary because the roof was "slipping," and that only a new $15,000 roof could be "watertight."

The Davises filed a complaint alleging breach of contract, fraud and misrepresentation, and sought recission of the contract and return of their deposit. The Johnsons counterclaimed seeking the deposit as liquidated damages.

The trial court entered its final judgment on May 27, 1983. The court made no findings of fact, but awarded the Davises $26,000 plus interest and awarded the Johnsons $5,000 plus interest. Each party was to bear their own attorneys' fees.

The Johnsons appealed and the Davises cross-appealed from the final judgment. The Third District found for the Davises affirming the trial court's return of the majority of the deposit to the Davises ($26,000), and reversing the award of $5,000 to the Johnsons as well as the court's failure to award the Davises costs and fees. Accordingly, the court remanded with directions to return to the Davises the balance of their deposit and to award them costs and fees.

* * *

[We agree with the district court's conclusion that the Johnson's did not breach the contract, entitling the Davis's to the remedy of recission.] The contract contemplated the possibility that the roof may not be watertight at the time of inspection and provided a remedy if it was not in such a condition. The roof inspection provision of the contract did not impose any obligation beyond the seller correcting the leaks and replacing damage to the facia or soffit. The record is devoid of any evidence that the seller refused to make needed repairs to the roof. * * *

We also agree with the district court's conclusions under a theory of fraud and find that the Johnsons' statements to the Davises regarding the condition of the roof constituted a fraudulent misrepresentation entitling respondents to the return of their $26,000 deposit payment. In the state of Florida, relief for a fraudulent misrepresentation may be granted only when the following elements are present: (1) a false statement concerning a material fact; (2) the representor's knowledge that the representation is false; (3) an intention that the representation induce another to act on it; and, (4) consequent injury by the party acting in reliance on the representation. *See Huffstetler v. Our Home Life Ins. Co.*, 67 Fla. 324, 65 So. 1 (1914).

The evidence adduced at trial shows that after the buyer and the seller signed the purchase and sales agreement and after receiving the $5,000 initial deposit payment the Johnsons affirmatively repeated to the Davises that there were no problems with the roof. The Johnsons subsequently received the additional $26,000 deposit payment from the Davises. The record reflects that the statement made by the Johnsons was a false representation of material fact, made with knowledge of its falsity, upon which the Davises relied to their detriment as evidenced by the $26,000 paid to the Johnsons.

The doctrine of caveat emptor does not exempt a seller from responsibility for the statements and representations which he makes to induce the buyer to act, when under the circumstances these amount to fraud in the legal sense. To be grounds for relief, the false representations need not have been made at the time of the signing of the purchase and sales agreement in order for the element of reliance to be present. The fact that the false statements as to the quality of the roof were made after the signing of the purchase and sales agreement does not excuse the seller from liability when the misrepresentations were made prior to the execution of the contract by conveyance of the property. It would be contrary to all notions of fairness and justice for this Court to place its stamp of approval on an affirmative misrepresentation by a wrongdoer just because it was made after the signing of the executory contract when all of the necessary elements for actionable fraud are present. Furthermore, the Davises' reliance on the truth of the

Johnsons' representation was justified and is supported by this Court's decision in *Besett v. Basnett*, 389 So.2d 995 (1980), where we held "that a recipient may rely on the truth of a representation, even though its falsity could have been ascertained had he made an investigation, unless he knows the representation to be false or its falsity is obvious to him." *Id.* at 998.

In determining whether a seller of a home has a duty to disclose latent material defects to a buyer, the established tort law distinction between misfeasance and nonfeasance, action and inaction must carefully be analyzed. The highly individualistic philosophy of the earlier common law consistently imposed liability upon the commission of affirmative acts of harm, but shrank from converting the courts into an institution for forcing men to help one another. This distinction is deeply rooted in our case law. Liability for nonfeasance has therefore been slow to receive recognition in the evolution of tort law.

In theory, the difference between misfeasance and nonfeasance, action and inaction is quite simple and obvious; however, in practice it is not always easy to draw the line and determine whether conduct is active or passive. That is, where failure to disclose a material fact is calculated to induce a false belief, the distinction between concealment and affirmative representations is tenuous. Both proceed from the same motives and are attended with the same consequences; both are violative of the principles of fair dealing and good faith; both are calculated to produce the same result; and, in fact, both essentially have the same effect.

Still there exists in much of our case law the old tort notion that there can be no liability for nonfeasance. The courts in some jurisdictions, including Florida, hold that where the parties are dealing at arms's length and the facts lie equally open to both parties, with equal opportunity of examination, mere nondisclosure does not constitute a fraudulent concealment. *See Ramel v. Chasebrook Construction Co.*, 135 So.2d 876 (Fla. 2d DCA 1961). The Fourth District affirmed that rule of law in *Banks v. Salina*, 413 So.2d 851 (Fla. 4th DCA 1982), and found that although the sellers had sold a home without disclosing the presence of a defective roof and swimming pool of which the sellers had knowledge, "[i]n Florida, there is no duty to disclose when parties are dealing at arms length." *Id.* at 852.

These unappetizing cases are not in tune with the times and do not conform with current notions of justice, equity and fair dealing. One should not be able to stand behind the impervious shield of caveat emptor and take advantage of another's ignorance. Our courts have taken great strides since the days when the judicial emphasis was on rigid rules and ancient precedents. Modern concepts of justice and fair dealing have given our courts the opportunity and latitude to change legal precepts in order to conform to society's needs. Thus, the tendency of the more recent cases has been to restrict rather than extend the doctrine of caveat emptor. The law appears to be working toward the ultimate conclusion that full disclosure of all material facts must be made whenever elementary fair conduct demands it.

The harness placed on the doctrine of caveat emptor in a number of other jurisdictions has resulted in the seller of a home being liable for failing to disclose material defects of which he is aware. This philosophy was succinctly expressed in *Lingsch v. Savage*, 213 Cal.App.2d 729, 29 Cal.Rptr. 201 (1963):

> It is now settled in California that where the seller knows of facts materially affecting the value or desirability of the property which are known or accessible only to him and also knows that such facts are not known to or within the reach of the diligent attention and observation of the buyer, the seller is under a duty to disclose them to the buyer.

In *Posner v. Davis*, 76 Ill.App.3d 638, 32 Ill.Dec. 186, 395 N.E.2d 133 (1979), buyers brought an action alleging that the sellers of a home fraudulently concealed certain defects in the home which included a leaking roof and basement flooding. Relying on *Lingsch*, the court concluded that the sellers knew of and failed to disclose latent material defects and thus were liable for fraudulent concealment. *Id.* 32 Ill.Dec. at 190, 395 N.E.2d at 137. Numerous other jurisdictions have followed this view in formulating law involving the sale of homes. *See Flakus v. Schug*, 213 Neb. 491, 329 N.W.2d 859 (1983) (basement flooding); *Thacker v. Tyree*, 297 S.E.2d 885 (W.Va.1982) (cracked walls and foundation problems); *Maguire v. Masino*, 325 So.2d 844 (La.Ct.App.1975) (termite infestation); *Weintraub v. Krobatsch*, 64 N.J. 445, 317 A.2d 68 (1974) (roach infestation); *Cohen v. Vivian*, 141 Colo. 443, 349 P.2d 366 (1960) (soil defect).

We are of the opinion, in view of the reasoning and results in *Lingsch*, *Posner* and the aforementioned cases decided in other jurisdictions, that the same philosophy regarding the sale of homes should also be the law in the state of Florida. Accordingly, we hold that where the seller of a home knows of facts materially affecting the value of the property which are not readily observable and are not known to the buyer, the seller is under a duty to disclose them to the buyer. This duty is equally applicable to all forms of real property, new and used.

In the case at bar, the evidence shows that the Johnsons knew of and failed to disclose that there had been problems with the roof of the house. Mr. Johnson admitted during his testimony that the Johnsons were aware of roof problems prior to entering into the contract of sale and receiving the $5,000 deposit payment. Thus, we agree with the district court and find that the Johnsons' fraudulent concealment also entitles the Davises to the return of the $5,000 deposit payment plus interest. We further find that the Davises should be awarded costs and fees.

The decision of the Third District Court of Appeals is hereby approved.

It is so ordered.

BOYD, Chief Justice, dissenting.

I respectfully but strongly dissent to the Court's expansion of the duties of sellers of real property. This ruling will give rise to a flood of litigation and will facilitate unjust outcomes in many cases. If, as a matter of public policy, the well settled law of this state on this question should be changed, the change should come from the legislature. Moreover, I do not find sufficient evidence in the record to justify rescission or a finding of fraud even under present law. I would quash the decision of the district court of appeal.

My review of the record reveals that there is not adequate evidence from which the trier of fact could have found any of the following crucial facts: (a) that at the time Johnson told Mrs. Davis about the previous leaks that had been repaired, he knew that there was a defect in the roof; (b) that at that time or the time of the execution of the contract, there were in fact any defects in the roof; (c) that it was not possible to repair the roof to "watertight" condition before closing.

* * *

Homeowners who attempt to sell their houses are typically in no better position to measure the quality, value, or desirability of their houses than are the prospective purchasers with whom such owners come into contact. Based on this and related considerations, the law of Florida has long been that a seller of real property with improvements is under no duty to disclose all material facts, in the absence of a fiduciary relationship, to a buyer who has an equal opportunity to learn all material information and is not prevented by the seller from doing so. *See, e.g., Ramel v. Chasebrook Construction Co.,* 135 So.2d 876 (Fla. 2d DCA 1961). This rule provides sufficient protection against overreaching by sellers, as the wise and progressive ruling in the *Ramel* case shows. The *Ramel* decision is not the least bit "unappetizing."

I do not agree with the Court's belief that the distinction between nondisclosure and affirmative statement is weak or nonexistent. It is a distinction that we should take special care to emphasize and preserve. Imposition of liability for seller's nondisclosure of the condition of improvements to real property is the first step toward making the seller a guarantor of the good condition of the property. Ultimately this trend will significantly burden the alienability of property because sellers will have to worry about the possibility of catastrophic post-sale judgments for damages sought to pay for repairs. The trend will proceed somewhat as follows. At first, the cause of action will require proof of actual knowledge of the undisclosed defect on the part of the seller. But in many cases the courts will allow it to be shown by circumstantial evidence. Then a rule of constructive knowledge will develop based on the reasoning that if the seller did not know of the defect, he should have known about it before attempting to sell the property. Thus the burden of inspection will shift from the buyer to the seller. Ultimately the courts will be in the position of imposing implied warranties and guaranties on all sellers of real property.

* * *

I would quash the decision of the district court of appeal. This case should be remanded for findings by the trial court based on the evidence already heard. The action for rescission based on fraud should be dismissed.

The only issue is whether the Johnsons were in compliance with the contract at the time of the breach by the Davises. Resolving this issue requires a finding of whether the roof could have been put in watertight condition by spot repairs or by re-roofing and in either case whether the sellers were willing to fulfill their obligation by paying for the necessary work. If so, the Johnsons should keep the entire $31,000 deposit.

———

TURNBULL v. LAROSE, 702 P.2d 1331 (Alaska 1985). Plaintiffs agreed to purchase a commercial office building from defendant on condition that one of the building's tenants, a state agency, exercise its option to extend its lease of space in the building by another year. Plaintiff alleged that defendant had represented that, "if the state took the [one year] lease option, the state 'would more than likely stay in the building for many years to come.' " Plaintiff would thus acquire both a building and a long-term tenant. After plaintiff had entered into a purchase agreement with the defendant—but before that purchase agreement had been consummated—the state agency exercised its option to renew the lease for another year, but "on the condition that it could assign the lease to another party in the middle of the one-year lease period." The defendant conveyed to the plaintiff the information that the agency had exercised its option, but not that the agency had conditioned that exercise on obtaining a right to assign the lease to another party. After the sale of the building was consummated, the state agency assigned the lease and vacated the premises. Plaintiff was unable to find a new tenant and was forced to sell the vacant building.

At trial, plaintiff contended: (1) that defendant "knew before the purchase agreement was consummated that the state intended to assign the lease * * * and thus had no long-term desire" to occupy the building, and (2) that plaintiff would not have consummated the transaction "had it known that the state had definitely decided to vacate the building." The trial court entered summary judgment in favor of defendant, on the ground that plaintiff "did not reasonably rely upon any alleged misrepresentations made" by defendant. *Held* reversed and remanded. Under § 551 of the Restatement (Second) of Torts (1977), the defendant had a duty to disclose "subsequently acquired information" that defendant knew made its previous representation "untrue or misleading."

Defendants arguments that plaintiff "could not, as a matter of law, justifiably rely on [its] alleged remarks" about the intent of the state agency "because they were mere opinions, as distinguished from statements of fact," was "unpersuasive." "Salespersons cannot immunize themselves from liability when conducting risky transactions simply by phrasing their representations as to the extent of the risk in the form of opinions or predictions. While we have noted that some sales talk or 'puffing' should be discounted by the reasonable buyer, [footnote citation omitted] we decline to adopt a rule which 'amounts to a seller's privilege to lie his head off.' Prosser, Law of Torts, § 109 at 723 (4th ed. 1971)."

EXTENT OF LIABILITY AND DAMAGES

LABORERS LOCAL 17 HEALTH AND BENEFIT FUND ET AL. v. PHILIP MORRIS, INC.
United States Circuit Court of Appeals, Second Circuit, 1999.
191 F.3d 229.

CARDAMONE, J. [The opinion first explains that the plaintiff funds were organized under ERISA to provide health care to members of their various unions.]

BACKGROUND

A. *Plaintiffs' Complaint*

Plaintiffs' complaint sets forth the following factual allegations, which we assume, for purposes of the motion to dismiss, are true. Over the past several decades, in response to medical indictments of smoking, the defendant tobacco companies engaged in an advertising campaign designed to mislead the public, and plaintiffs specifically, as to the true extent of the dangers that smoking poses to good health. Defendants actively concealed information that would have demonstrated the actual health risks, the addictiveness of nicotine, the effectiveness of various treatments for smoking addiction, and defendants' own ability to manufacture less addictive products. Moreover, plaintiffs and plan participants had no knowledge—until very recently—of defendants' wrongdoing. As a result, thousands of participants in plaintiffs' health care Funds became ill and/or died from smoking cigarettes produced and sold by defendant tobacco companies. Plaintiffs spent tens of millions of dollars to provide medical services for participants suffering from cigarette smoking-related diseases.

On the basis of these allegations, plaintiffs' complaint asserts ten causes of action (I to X) * * * [These causes include ones alleging common law fraud. The common law fraud claim was said, later in the opinion to present the same proof and proximate cause requirements as the RICO claim.] * * * [T]he complaint seeks past and future damages to recover for "money expended . . . to provide medical treatment to [plaintiffs'] participants and beneficiaries who have suffered and are suffering from tobacco-related illnesses." As interpreted by the district court, the complaint also seeks damages inflicted on the Funds' infrastructure independent of the harm suffered by plan participants. These latter damages, alleged to be separate and wholly distinct from participants' medical costs, consist of losses suffered due to the Funds' inability to control costs, to promote the use of safer alternative products, and to establish programs to educate their participants not to use tobacco products.

Ordinarily, plaintiffs' right to sue for damages would be subrogated to the rights of those individual smokers for whom they provided health care benefits. In other words, plaintiffs would stand in the shoes of the injured participants and recoup damages from defendants, as tortfeasors, only to the extent defendants were liable to the participants themselves. But the Funds have not asserted such a subrogation action in this complaint. Instead, they have sued in their own right for the money spent for plan participants and, in addition, for injuries and damages they insist were separate from the injuries to plan participants and that harmed plaintiffs, the welfare benefit funds themselves.

B. Prior Proceedings

* * * [D]efendants moved to dismiss the complaint for failure to state a claim under Fed.R.Civ.P. 12(b)(6). * * * [The court granted the motion in part and denied it in part leaving four causes of action intact, including the federal RICO claims and the state common-law claims of fraud, misrepresentation, and concealment.]

In denying defendants' motion to dismiss with respect to these latter causes of action, the district court found proximate causation linking plaintiffs' injuries to defendants' asserted unlawful conduct * * * . It held that a rational trier of fact could find that defendants' alleged wrongdoing proximately caused plaintiffs' alleged injuries, reasoning that the injuries were arguably (a) foreseeable and (b) not too remote as a matter of law, in light of the policy factors articulated in *Holmes v. Securities Investor Protection Corp.*, 503 U.S. 258, 269–70, 112 S.Ct. 1311, 117 L.Ed.2d 532 (1992). The district court also determined that the possible availability of a subrogation remedy was no bar to the maintenance of the RICO, fraud, and breach of special duty claims. * * *

Defendants then sought interlocutory appeal of those portions of the order denying their Rule 12(b)(6) motion to dismiss. [The district court certified two questions for appeal. The first of these was:]

Whether, under the circumstances alleged in plaintiffs' complaint, economic injuries incurred by a union health care trust fund are purely derivative of the physical injuries which its participants suffered, and are therefore too remote to permit recovery as a matter of law.

[The second question involved possible preemption of plaintiff's state law claims.]

* * * [W]e granted leave to appeal these certified questions * * * and now reverse.

* * *

DISCUSSION

* * *

Proximate Cause

The first certified question we are called upon to answer raises a question of proximate cause, namely, whether the chain of causation linking defendants' alleged wrongdoing to plaintiffs' alleged injuries is too remote to permit recovery as a matter of law. We begin by analyzing this subject in the context of plaintiffs' RICO claims.

* * *

* * * In *Holmes*, 503 U.S. at 268, 112 S.Ct. 1311, the Supreme Court stated that a plaintiff's standing to sue under RICO requires a showing that the defendant's violation not only was a "but for" cause of his injury, but was the proximate cause as well. To determine in a given case whether proximate cause is present, common law principles are applied. *See id.* at 267–68, 112 S.Ct. 1311 (explaining that statutory standing under RICO encompasses common law principles of proximate cause because Congress implicitly incorporated those principles into the RICO statute) (citing *Associated Gen. Contractors, Inc. v. Carpenters,* 459 U.S. 519, 532–33, 103 S.Ct. 897, 74 L.Ed.2d 723 (1983) (*AGC*) (plaintiff unions barred from bringing antitrust suit to challenge allegedly coerced business relationship of third parties with nonunion firms)).

A. The Concept In General

Any discussion of proximate cause should be approached with some trepidation because, as a scholarly treatise teaches, no topic is subject to more disagreement or such confusion. Proximate cause is an elusive concept, one "always to be determined on the facts of each case upon mixed considerations of logic, common sense, justice, policy and precedent." W. Page Keeton et al., *Prosser & Keeton on The Law of Torts,* § 42, at 279 (5th ed.1984) (quoting 1 Street, *Foundations of Legal Liability,* 110 (1906)). In everyday terms, the concept might be explained as follows: Because the consequences of an act go endlessly forward in time and its causes stretch back to the dawn of human history, proximate cause is used essentially as a legal tool for limiting a wrongdoer's liability only to those harms that have a reasonable connection to his actions. The law has wisely determined that it is futile to trace the consequences of a wrongdoer's actions to their ultimate end, if end there is.

* * *

B. Direct Injury as a Requirement of Proximate Cause

Over the passage of time, however, courts have somewhat clarified the definition of proximate cause by identifying several traditional common law principles limiting liability whose application, in aggregate, formulates the proximate cause analysis. As noted in *Holmes,* " 'proximate cause' [is used] to label generically the judicial tools used to limit a person's responsibility for the consequences of that person's own acts." 503 U.S. at 268, 112 S.Ct. 1311.

Among these "judicial tools," one notion traditionally included in the concept of proximate causation is the requirement that there be "some direct relation between the injury asserted and the injurious conduct alleged." *Holmes,* 503 U.S. at 268, 112 S.Ct. 1311. For this reason, "a plaintiff who complain[s] of harm flowing merely from the misfortunes visited upon a third person by the defendant's acts [is] generally said to stand at too remote a distance to recover." *Id.* at 268–69, 112 S.Ct. 1311.

* * *

II. THE DIRECT INJURY TEST: EXPLANATION AND APPLICATION

As Justice Holmes writing for the Court observed in *Southern Pac. Co. v. Darnell–Taenzer Lumber Co.,* 245 U.S. 531, 533, 38 S.Ct. 186, 62 L.Ed. 451 (1918), "[t]he general tendency of the law, in regard to damages at least, is not to go beyond the first step." *Accord Holmes,* 503 U.S. at 271–72, 112 S.Ct. 1311 (quoting *AGC,* 459 U.S. at 534, 103 S.Ct. 897). For that reason, where a plaintiff complains of injuries that are wholly derivative of harm to a third party, plaintiff's injuries are generally deemed indirect and as a consequence too remote, as a matter of law, to support recovery. *See Holmes,* 503 U.S. at 268–69, 112 S.Ct. 1311. At the same time, the Supreme Court noted the impossibility of articulating a black-letter rule capable of dictating a result in every case. *See id.* at 272 n. 20, 112 S.Ct. 1311. Accordingly, it identified three policy factors to guide courts in their application of the general principle that plaintiffs with indirect injuries lack standing to sue under RICO. *See id.* at 269–70, 112 S.Ct. 1311. First, the more indirect an injury is, the more difficult it becomes to determine the amount of plaintiff's damages attributable to the wrongdoing as opposed to other, independent factors. Second, recognizing claims by the indirectly injured would require courts to adopt complicated rules apportioning damages among plaintiffs removed at different levels of injury from the violative acts, in order to avoid the risk of multiple recoveries. Third, struggling with the first two problems is unnecessary where there are directly injured parties who can remedy the harm without these attendant problems. *See Holmes,* 503 U.S. at 269–70, 112 S.Ct. 1311.

* * *

C. *Applying the Direct Injury Test to Instant Case*

1.   Parties' Contentions

The defendants' principal point on appeal is that the plaintiffs' damages are entirely derivative of the harm suffered by individual smokers as a result of defendants' acts. Hence, defendants believe that plaintiffs' alleged injuries are indirect, since they flow from the misfortunes visited upon third persons, and that plaintiffs therefore stand at too remote a distance to recover.

In response, plaintiffs declare that their complaint alleges a direct injury brought about by defendants' misconduct towards the Funds themselves. Plaintiffs allege that defendants misrepresented the health risks of smoking and the addictiveness of nicotine, causing the Funds to fail to implement smoking cessation programs, and deliberately shifting the costs of health care for tobacco related illnesses from the tobacco companies to the Funds. In turn, this led to what the district court termed "harm to [plaintiffs'] infrastructure, financial stability, [and] ability to project costs." *Laborers Local 17,* 7 F.Supp.2d at 285. Plaintiffs insist that these injuries were direct, since the "activities of the Funds themselves were affected by defendants' misconduct."

Ultimately, however, whether plaintiffs' injuries are labeled as "infrastructure harm" or "harm to financial stability," their damages are entirely derivative of the harm suffered by plan participants as a result of using tobacco products. Without injury to the individual smokers, the Funds would not have incurred any increased costs in the form of the payment of benefits, nor would they have experienced the difficulties of cost prediction and control that constituted the crux of their infrastructure harms. Being purely contingent on harm to third parties, these injuries are indirect. Consequently, because defendants' alleged misconduct did not proximately cause the injuries alleged, plaintiffs lack standing to bring RICO claims against defendants.

2. Policy Considerations

Further, this conclusion is consistent with the three policy factors addressed by *Holmes,* which buttress the principle that plaintiffs with indirect injuries lack standing to sue under RICO. 503 U.S. at 269–70. "First, the less direct an injury is, the more difficult it becomes to ascertain the amount of a plaintiff's damages attributable to the violation, as distinct from other, independent, factors." Id. at 269, 112 S.Ct. 1311 [citation omitted]. * * * [T]he damage claims here are incredibly speculative. It will be virtually impossible for plaintiffs to prove with any certainty: (1) the effect any smoking cessation programs or incentives would have had on the number of smokers among the plan beneficiaries; (2) the countereffect that the tobacco companies' direct fraud would have had on the smokers, despite the best efforts of the Funds; and (3) other reasons why individual smokers would continue smoking, even after having been informed of the dangers of smoking and having been offered smoking cessation programs. On a fundamental level, these difficulties of proving damages stem from the agency of the individual smokers in deciding whether, and how frequently, to smoke. In this light, the direct injury test can be seen as wisely limiting standing to sue to those situations where the chain of causation leading to damages is not complicated by the intervening agency of third parties (here, the smokers) from whom the plaintiffs' injuries derive.

These concerns become particularly pointed in a case, like the present one, where the injuries are alleged to derive not simply from defendants' affirmative misconduct but also from plaintiffs' fraudulently induced inaction. That is, it is often easier to ascertain the damages that flow from actual, affirmative conduct, than to speculate what damages arose from a party's failure to act. In the latter situation, as in the case at hand, it becomes difficult to distinguish among the multitude of factors that might have affected the damages. Here, for example, plaintiffs' alleged damages might have derived from inefficiencies in the Funds' own management, as well as from non-smoking related health problems suffered by the smokers, and it would be the sheerest sort of speculation to determine how these damages might have been lessened had the Funds adopted the measures defendants allegedly induced them not to adopt.

The complexity of these calculations makes the ultimate question of damages suffered by the Funds virtually impossible to determine. Indeed, this case seems to present precisely the type of large, complicated damages claims that *Holmes* * * * sought to avoid. Moreover, for us to rule otherwise could lead to a potential explosion in the scope of tort liability, which, while perhaps well-intentioned, is a subject best left to the legislature.

The second policy factor addressed in *Holmes* focuses on the possibility that "recognizing claims of the indirectly injured would force courts to adopt complicated rules apportioning damages among plaintiffs removed at different levels of injury from the violative acts, to obviate the risk of multiple recoveries." 503 U.S. at 269, 112 S.Ct. 1311 (citing *AGC,* 459 U.S. at 543–44, 103 S.Ct. 897). Under New York law, the smokers are prohibited from recovering medical costs paid to them by insurers. New York law dictates that "where the plaintiff seeks to recover the cost of medical care" and the court finds that such costs were reimbursed by an insurance company, the court "shall reduce the amount of award by such a finding." N.Y. C.P.L.R. § 4545(c) (McKinney 1992). As a result, the district court believed the suit presented no risk of multiple recoveries. *See Laborers Local 17,* 7 F.Supp.2d at 285. [Futhermore, under New York's "single satisfaction rule" plaintiffs are barred from "recovering damages several times over from multiple defendants."]

* * *

* * * But, even were we to assume that the single satisfaction rule would prohibit duplicative recoveries by multiple plaintiffs against a single defendant, it would not cure the ultimate problem set forth in *Holmes,* that is, that courts would be forced to "adopt complicated rules apportioning damages among" the Funds, the employers, and perhaps even the unions, each of which is "removed at [a] different level[ ] of injury." *Holmes,* 503 U.S. at 269, 112 S.Ct. 1311.

In the third policy factor discussed by *Holmes,* the Supreme Court concluded that the need to grapple with the problems of calculating and apportioning damages was unjustified where "directly injured victims can generally be counted on to vindicate the law as private attorneys general, without any of the problems attendant upon suits by plaintiffs injured more remotely." *Id.* * * *

* * * [In the present case] the smokers themselves have sufficient independent incentive to pursue their own causes of action for such additional types of injuries as pain and suffering. Although these will not be RICO claims, they will remedy the harm done by defendants' alleged misconduct. Moreover, these actions will promote "the general interest in deterring injurious conduct," which *Holmes* noted as the objective of this policy factor. 503 U.S. at 269, 112 S.Ct. 1311. * * *

In sum, the policy considerations highlighted in *Holmes* support our conclusion that the Funds have failed to establish proximate causation and that, accordingly, they lack standing to sue the defendants under RICO.

IV. COMMON LAW FRAUD AND SPECIAL DUTY CLAIMS

Our inquiry into RICO standing began with the Supreme Court's holding in *Holmes* that the statute requires that at least the proximate causation principles found generally in the common law, including the direct injury requirement discussed above, be met. These principles also apply in general terms to the fraud and special duty causes of action asserted by plaintiffs under New York common law. [citations omitted] Hence, analogous principles to those that doomed plaintiffs' RICO causes of action also bar plaintiffs' common law fraud and special duty actions.

* * *

Accordingly, we hereby reverse the district court's March 25, 1998 order with respect to causes of action I and II (the RICO claims), V (the fraud claim), and VI (the special duty claim). The case is remanded to the district court with directions to dismiss plaintiffs' complaint.

———

CLARK v. McDANIEL, 546 N.W.2d 590 (Iowa, 1996). In 1992, plaintiffs purchased a Ford Taurus station wagon "from a couple named Peirce." The Pierces represented the car to be a 1989 model. It turned out, however, "that the car had been "clipped," *i.e.,* the rear half of a 1986 Taurus had been welded to the front half of a 1989 model." When the Clarks confronted the Pierces, the Clarks discovered that the Pierces were themselves unaware that the car had been clipped. They had merely relayed representations made to them by McDaniel, the used car salesman who sold the wagon to the Pierces. The Clarks brought suit against both the Pierces and McDaniel. After a bench trial, the court dismissed the claim against the Pierces and entered judgment against McDaniel. McDaniel appealed, contending that he could not be liable to the Clarks for any misrepresentations, because there was no "direct contact between him and the Clarks." *Held*, affirmed. The court adopted Restatement § 533, and imposed liability under it.

Under § 533 "persons who fraudulently misrepresent the truth can be held liable to third parties if they have a 'reason to expect' their misrepresentation will be communicated to third parties." "The maker's liability 'includes those whom he has reason to expect [the misrepresentation] to reach and influence, although he does not make the misrepresentation with that intent or purpose.' Restatement § 533 cmt. d." It was "reasonable to charge a seller, especially a dealer in vehicles, with knowledge that his buyer will pass along information to a second buyer that has been provided by the original seller concerning such significant matters as 'clipping' and * * * the model year of the vehicle."

CONNOR v. GREAT WESTERN SAVINGS AND LOAN ASSOCIATION, 69 Cal.2d 850, 73 Cal.Rptr. 369, 447 P.2d 609 (1968). This was an action by purchasers of single-family homes in a residential development tract against a savings and loan association. The purchasers of a home sustained damage from an ill-designed foundation. Defendant knew that persons in charge of the construction companies were operating on their capitalization. The defendant was not only a lender to those engaged in the development but had the right to exercise considerable control over the developer. *Held*, that the defendant was subject to liability for negligence to home owners in failing to prevent the construction of unsound homes.

SELMAN v. SHIRLEY, 161 Or. 582, 85 P.2d 384 (Oregon, 1938). Defendant fraudulently induced plaintiffs, a seaman in the United States Navy and his wife who lived in southern California, to purchase 160 acres of land in Oregon by falsely representing that the land contained 4,000 cords of wood worth 50 cents a cord, as well as a stream which flowed through the property "throughout the year and supplied enough water to irrigate ten acres." In fact, there were only 200 cords of wood on the property, and the stream dried up during the summer months. It did "not flow sufficient water to irrigate even a small garden patch."

The only issue before the court was the measure of damages. The findings in the case stated "that the property was 'of the fair market value of $2,000 at the time said contract was entered into' " and that plaintiffs had " 'suffered no damages, having agreed to pay $2,000 for said premises.' " The plaintiffs contended that they were "entitled to the benefit of their bargain which contemplated that they should have, not only 160 acres of land, but also a growth of timber upon the land aggregating 4000 cords and a good irrigating stream; and that the rule which measures their damages should be based upon that premise." The defendants contended that—in tort actions for fraud as distinguished from contract actions for breach of warranty—Oregon case law had "rejected the benefit-of-the-bargain rule in favor of the rule which grants damages equal only to the out-of-pocket loss." No warranty cause of action was available the plaintiffs. *Held*, plaintiffs are entitled to the benefit-of-the-bargain. Damages should be "awarded upon the basis of 50 cents per cord for the difference between the represented 4,000 cords and the actual 200 cords."

"[We reconcile our prior decisions as follows.] First of all, it is evident that the party guilty of fraud is liable for such damages as naturally and proximately resulted from the fraud. This is the universal rule. Next, our decisions warrant the conclusions: (1) If the defrauded party is content with the recovery of only the amount that he actually lost, his damages will be measured under that rule; (2) if the fraudulent representation also amounted to a warranty, recovery may be had for loss of the bargain because a fraud accompanied by a broken promise should cost the wrongdoer as much as the latter alone; (3) where the circumstances disclosed by the proof are so vague as to cast virtually no light upon the value of the property had it conformed to the representations, the court will award damages equal only to the loss sustained; and (4) where, * * * the damages under the benefit-of-the-bargain rule are proved with sufficient certainty, that rule will be employed."

RESTATEMENT OF TORTS SECOND (1977)

§ 549. Measure of Damages for Fraudulent Misrepresentation

(1) The recipient of a fraudulent misrepresentation is entitled to recover as damages in an action of deceit against the maker the pecuniary loss to him of which the misrepresentation is a legal cause, including

(a) the difference between the value of what he has received in the transaction and its purchase price or other value given for it; and

(b) pecuniary loss suffered otherwise as a consequence of the recipient's reliance upon the misrepresentation.

(2) The recipient of a fraudulent misrepresentation in a business transaction is also entitled to recover additional damages sufficient to give him the benefit of his contract with the maker, if these damages are proved with reasonable certainty.

[The Reporter's Note to this section describes it as "a compromise position, between the 'out-of-pocket' and the 'benefit-of-the-bargain' rules as the normal measure of damages in an action of deceit." According to the Note, this compromise position was supported by eight states, including Oregon. Seven states applied the "out of pocket" measure alone and another thirty-two applied the "benefit of the bargain" measure alone.— Eds.]

———

PEOPLE v. S. W. STRAUS & CO., INC., 156 Misc. 642, 282 N.Y.S. 972 (1935). A claim in fraud was filed against a receiver of a bankrupt corporation by bond holders. It was asserted that a false representation was made, inducing sale of the bonds, that the bonds were first mortgage bonds, whereas the security was inferior. It was not claimed that the properties which secured the bonds, at the time of the claimant's purchases, were not of a value substantially in excess of all liens. Plaintiff asserted as a rule of damages, however, that in all cases of fraud practiced in the sale of bonds the measure of damages should be the difference between what was paid and the value at the time of discovery of the fraud. Held, for defendant on the issue of damages. The evidence warranted the conclusion that the collapse in the value of bonds was due to economic conditions and not to the misrepresentation. The court distinguished the case from one where the value of a bond declined because of the failure of a company attributable to a misrepresentation about the financial condition of the company.

FOTTLER v. MOSELEY, 185 Mass. 563, 70 N.E. 1040 (1904). Relying upon the false and fraudulent representations of the defendant, a broker, the plaintiff revoked an order for the sale of certain shares of stock. Subsequently, an officer and director of the company embezzled nearly $100,000 of the company and the stock fell in price. The plaintiff later sold his stock at a loss. The plaintiff sought recovery for loss resulting from the fall in price of the stock due to the embezzlement. Held, for the plaintiff. "If the defendant fraudulently induced the plaintiff to refrain from selling his stock when he was about to sell it, he did him a wrong, and a natural consequence of the wrong for which he is liable was the possibility of loss from diminution in the value of the stock, from any one of numerous causes."

SECTION B.   NEGLIGENT MISREPRESENTATION

GREYCAS, INC. v. PROUD

United States Circuit Court of Appeals, Seventh Circuit, 1987.
826 F.2d 1560.

POSNER, C. J.,

Theodore S. Proud, Jr., a member of the Illinois bar who practices law in a suburb of Chicago, appeals from a judgment against him for $833,760, entered after a bench trial. The tale of malpractice and misrepresentation that led to the judgment begins with Proud's brother-in-law, Wayne Crawford, like Proud a lawyer but one who devoted most of his attention to a large farm that he owned in downstate Illinois. The farm fell on hard times and by 1981 Crawford was in dire financial straits. He had pledged most of his farm machinery to lenders, yet now desperately needed more money. He approached Greycas, Inc., the plaintiff in this case, a large financial company headquartered in Arizona, seeking a large loan that he offered to secure with the farm machinery. He did not tell Greycas about his financial difficulties or that he had pledged the machinery to other lenders, but he did make clear that he needed the loan in a hurry. Greycas obtained several appraisals of Crawford's farm machinery but did not investigate Crawford's financial position or discover that he had pledged the collateral to other lenders, who had perfected their liens in the collateral. Greycas agreed to lend Crawford $1,367,966.50, which was less than the appraised value of the machinery.

The loan was subject, however, to an important condition, which is at the heart of this case: Crawford was required to submit a letter to Greycas, from counsel whom he would retain, assuring Greycas that there were no prior liens on the machinery that was to secure the loan. Crawford asked Proud to prepare the letter, and he did so, and mailed it to Greycas, and within 20 days of the first contact between Crawford and Greycas the loan closed and the money was disbursed. A year later Crawford defaulted on the loan; shortly afterward he committed suicide. Greycas then learned that most of the farm machinery that Crawford had pledged to it had previously been pledged to other lenders.

The machinery was sold at auction. The Illinois state court that determined the creditors' priorities in the proceeds of the sale held that Greycas did not have a first priority on most of the machinery that secured its loan; as a result Greycas has been able to recover only a small part of the loan. The judgment it obtained in the present suit is the district judge's estimate of the value that it would have realized on its collateral had there been no prior liens, as Proud represented in his letter.

That letter is the centerpiece of the litigation. Typed on the stationery of Proud's firm and addressed to Greycas, it identifies Proud as Crawford's lawyer and states that, "in such capacity, I have been asked to render my opinion in connection with" the proposed loan to Crawford. It also states that "this opinion is being delivered in accordance with the requirements of the Loan Agreement" and that

I have conducted a U.C.C., tax, and judgment search with respect to the Company [i.e., Crawford's farm] as of March 19, 1981, and except as hereinafter noted all units listed on the attached Exhibit A ("Equipment") are free and clear of all liens or encumbrances other than Lender's perfected security interest therein which was recorded March 19, 1981 at the Office of the Recorder of Deeds of Fayette County, Illinois.

The reference to the lender's security interest is to Greycas's interest; Crawford, pursuant to the loan agreement, had filed a notice of that interest with the recorder. The excepted units to which the letter refers are four vehicles. Exhibit A is a long list of farm machinery—the collateral that Greycas thought it was getting to secure the loan, free of any other liens. Attached to the loan agreement itself, however, as Exhibit B, is another list of farm machinery constituting the collateral for the loan, and there are discrepancies between the two lists; more on this later.

Proud never conducted a search for prior liens on the machinery listed in Exhibit A. His brother-in-law gave him the list and told him there were no liens other than the one that Crawford had just filed for Greycas. Proud made no effort to verify Crawford's statement. The theory of the complaint is that Proud was negligent in representing that there were no prior liens, merely on his brother-in-law's say-so. No doubt Proud *was* negligent in failing to conduct a search, but we are not clear why the *misrepresentation* is alleged to be negligent rather than deliberate and hence fraudulent, in which event Greycas's alleged contributory negligence would not be an issue (as it is, we shall see), since there is no defense of contributory or comparative negligence to a deliberate tort, such as fraud. Proud did not merely say, "There are no liens"; he said, "I have conducted a U.C.C., tax, and judgment search"; and not only is this statement, too, a false one, but its falsehood cannot have been inadvertent, for Proud knew he had not conducted such a search. The concealment of his relationship with Crawford might also support a charge of fraud. But Greycas decided, for whatever reason, to argue negligent misrepresentation rather than fraud. It may have feared that Proud's insurance policy for professional malpractice excluded deliberate wrongdoing from its coverage, or may not have wanted to bear the higher burden of proving fraud[1], or may have feared that an accusation of fraud would make it harder to settle the case—for most cases, of course, are settled, though this one has not been. In any event, Proud does not argue that either he is liable for fraud or he is liable for nothing.

He also does not, and could not, deny or justify the misrepresentation; but he argues that it is not actionable under the tort law of Illinois, because he had no duty of care to Greycas. (This is a diversity case and the parties agree that Illinois tort law governs the substantive issues.) [The opinion then discusses and rejects Proud's claim that Greycas is bringing suit for legal malpractice and cannot sustain this claim because, as a nonclient, Greycas is not owed a duty of care under Illinois law. After concluding that the Greycas

---

1. Many jurisdictions require that fraud be proved by "clear-and-convincing evidence." See e.g., Simpson v. Widger, supra p. 243.—Eds.

is owed a duty of care under Illinois' legal malpractice law, the court shifts gears and analyzes Greycas's claim as one for negligent misrepresentation, observing that "nothing is more common in American jurisprudence than overlapping torts."[2]]

* * *

The claim of negligent misrepresentation might seem utterly straightforward. It might seem that by addressing a letter to Greycas intended (as Proud's counsel admitted at argument) to induce reliance on the statements in it, Proud made himself *prima facie* liable for any material misrepresentations, careless or deliberate, in the letter, whether or not Proud was Crawford's lawyer or for that matter anyone's lawyer. Knowing that Greycas was relying on him to determine whether the collateral for the loan was encumbered and to advise Greycas of the results of his determination, Proud negligently misrepresented the situation, to Greycas's detriment. But merely labeling a suit as one for negligent misrepresentation rather than professional malpractice will not make the problem of indefinite and perhaps excessive liability, which [has led the Illinois courts] to place limitations on the duty of care [owed by lawyers to nonclients], go away * **

The absence of a contract between the lender and the accountant defeated the suit in *Ultramares[Corp. v. Touche, Niven & Co.*, 255 N.Y. 170, 174 N.E. 441 (1931) (Cardozo, J.) (holding that an accountant's negligent misrepresentation was not actionable at the suit of a lender who had relied on the accountant's certified audit of the borrower)]—yet why should privity of contract have been required for liability just because the negligence lay in disseminating information rather than in designing or manufacturing a product? The privity limitation in products cases had been rejected, in another famous Cardozo opinion, years earlier. See *MacPherson v. Buick Motor Co.*, 217 N.Y. 382, 111 N.E. 1050 (1916). Professor Bishop suggests that courts were worried that imposing heavy liabilities on producers of information might cause socially valuable information to be underproduced. See *Negligent Misrepresentation Through Economists' Eyes*, 96 L.Q.Rev. 360 (1980). Many producers of information have difficulty appropriating its benefits to society. The property-rights system in information is incomplete; someone who comes up with a new idea that the law of intellectual property does not protect cannot prevent others from using the idea without reimbursing his costs of invention or discovery. So the law must be careful not to weigh these producers down too heavily with tort liabilities. For example, information produced by securities analysts, the news media, academicians, and so forth is socially valuable, but as its producers can't capture the full value of the information in their fees and other remuneration the information may be underproduced. Maybe it is right, therefore—or at least efficient—that none of these producers should have to bear the full costs * * *

2. The overlap between professional malpractice and negligent misrepresentation is not peculiar to cases involving lawyers. There is a general tendency for these two kinds of torts to overlap. Professionals such as lawyers, accountants and surveyors are prominent members of the class of persons whose representations fall within the purview of the tort of negligent misrepresentation, because they provide financial information for the guidance of others in commercial transactions.—Eds.

At least that was once the view; and while *Ultramares* has now been rejected, in Illinois as elsewhere—maybe because providers of information are deemed more robust today than they once were or maybe because it is now believed that auditors, surveyors, and other providers of professional services were always able to capture the social value of even the information component of those services in the fees they charged their clients—a residuum of concern remains. So when in *Rozny v. Marnul,* 43 Ill.2d 54, 250 N.E.2d 656 (1969), the Supreme Court of Illinois, joining the march away from *Ultramares,* held for the first time that negligent misrepresentation was actionable despite the absence of a contract, and thus cast aside the same "privity of contract" limitation later overruled with regard to professional malpractice in *Pelham v. Griesheimer,* 92 Ill.2d 13, 64 Ill.Dec. 544, 440 N.E.2d 96 (1982]), the court was careful to emphasize facts in the particular case before it that limited the scope of its holding—facts such as that the defendant, a surveyor, had placed his "absolute guarantee for accuracy" on the plat and that only a few persons would receive and rely on it, thus limiting the potential scope of liability. See *id.* at 67–68, 250 N.E.2d at 663.

Later Illinois cases, however, influenced by section 552 of the Second Restatement of Torts (1977), state the limitation on liability for negligent misrepresentation in more compact terms—as well as in narrower scope—than *Rozny.* These are cases in the intermediate appellate court, but, as we have no reason to think the Supreme Court of Illinois would reject them, we are bound to follow them. See *Williams, McCarthy, Kinley, Rudy & Picha v. Northwestern National Ins. Group,* 750 F.2d 619, 624 (7th Cir.1984). They hold that "one who in the course of his business or profession supplies information for the guidance of others in their business transactions" is liable for negligent misrepresentations that induce detrimental reliance. *Penrod v. Merrill Lynch, Pierce, Fenner & Smith,* 68 Ill.App.3d 75, 81–82, 24 Ill.Dec. 464, 469, 385 N.E.2d 376, 381 (1979); see also *Perschall v. Raney,* 137 Ill.App.3d 978, 983, 92 Ill.Dec. 431, 434, 484 N.E.2d 1286, 1289 (1985); Prosser and Keeton on the Law of Torts § 107, at p. 747 (5th ed. 1984). Whether there is a practical as distinct from a merely semantic difference between this formulation of the duty limitation and that of *Pelham* may be doubted but cannot change the outcome of this case. Proud, in the practice of his profession, supplied information (or rather misinformation) to Greycas that was intended to guide Greycas in commercial dealings with Crawford. Proud therefore had a duty to use due care to see that the information was correct. He used no care.

Proud must lose on the issue of liability even if the narrower, *ad hoc* approach of *Rozny* is used instead of the approach of section 552 of the Restatement. Information about the existence of previous liens on particular items of property is of limited social as distinct from private value, by which we mean simply that the information is not likely to be disseminated widely. There is consequently no reason to give it special encouragement by overlooking carelessness in its collection and expression. Where as in this case the defendant makes the negligent misrepresentation directly to the plaintiff in the course of the defendant's business or profession, the courts have little difficulty in finding a duty of care. Prosser and Keeton on the Law of Torts, *supra,* § 107, at p. 747.

There is no serious doubt about the existence of a causal relationship between the misrepresentation and the loan. Greycas would not have made the loan without Proud's letter. Nor would it have made the loan had Proud advised it that the collateral was so heavily encumbered that the loan was as if unsecured, for then Greycas would have known that the probability of repayment was slight. Merely to charge a higher interest rate would not have been an attractive alternative to security; it would have made default virtually inevitable by saddling Crawford with a huge fixed debt. * * *

Proud argues, however, that his damages should be reduced in recognition of Greycas's own contributory negligence, which, though no longer a complete defense in Illinois, is a partial defense, renamed "comparative negligence." It is as much a defense to negligent misrepresentation as to any other tort of negligence. On the issue of comparative negligence the district court said only that "defendant may have proved negligence upon the part of plaintiff but that negligence, if any, had no causal relationship to the malpractice of the defendant or the damages to the plaintiff." This comment is not easy to fathom. If Greycas was careless in deciding whether to make the loan, this implies that a reasonable investigation by Greycas would have shown that the collateral for the loan was already heavily encumbered; knowing this, Greycas would not have made the loan and therefore would not have suffered any damages.

But we think it too clear to require a remand for further proceedings that Proud failed to prove a want of due care by Greycas. Due care is the care that is optimal given that the other party is exercising due care. It is not the higher level of care that would be optimal if potential tort victims were required to assume that the rest of the world was negligent. A pedestrian is not required to exercise a level of care (e.g., wearing a helmet or a shin guard) that would be optimal if there were no sanctions against reckless driving. Otherwise drivers would be encouraged to drive recklessly, and knowing this pedestrians would be encouraged to wear helmets and shin guards. The result would be a shift from a superior method of accident avoidance (not driving recklessly) to an inferior one (pedestrian armor).

So we must ask whether Greycas would have been careless not to conduct its own UCC search had Proud done what he had said he did— conduct his own UCC search. The answer is no. The law normally does not require duplicative precautions unless one is likely to fail or the consequences of failure (slight though the likelihood may be) would be catastrophic. One UCC search is enough to disclose prior liens, and Greycas acted reasonably in relying on Proud to conduct it. Although Greycas had much warning that Crawford was in financial trouble and that the loan might not be repaid, that was a reason for charging a hefty interest rate and insisting that the loan be secured; it was not a reason for duplicating Proud's work. It is not hard to conduct a UCC lien search; it just requires checking the records in the recorder's office for the county where the debtor lives. See Ill.Rev.Stat. ch. 26, ¶ 9–401. So the only reason to backstop Proud was if

Greycas should have assumed he was careless or dishonest; and we have just said that the duty of care does not require such an assumption. * * *

[AFFIRMED.]

RESTATEMENT OF TORTS, SECOND (1976)

§ 552.   Information Negligently Supplied for the Guidance of Others

(1) One who, in the course of his business, profession or employment, or in any other transaction in which he has a pecuniary interest, supplies false information for the guidance of others in their business transactions, is subject to liability for pecuniary loss caused to them by their justifiable reliance upon the information, if he fails to exercise reasonable care or competence in obtaining or communicating the information.

(2) Except as stated in Subsection (3), the liability stated in Subsection (1) is limited to loss suffered

(a) by the person or one of a limited group of persons for whose benefit and guidance he intends to supply the information or knows that the recipient intends to supply it; and

(b) through reliance upon it in a transaction that he intends the information to influence or knows that the recipient so intends or in a substantially similar transaction.

(3) The liability of one who is under a public duty to give the information extends to loss suffered by any of the class of persons for whose benefit the duty is created, in any of the transactions in which it is intended to protect them.

RESTATEMENT OF TORTS, SECOND (1976)

§ 552B. Damages for Negligent Misrepresentation

(1) The damages recoverable for a negligent misrepresentation are those necessary to compensate the plaintiff for the pecuniary loss to him of which the misrepresentation is a legal cause, including

(a) the difference between the value of what he has received in the transaction and its purchase price or other value given for it; and (b) pecuniary loss suffered otherwise as a consequence of the plaintiff's reliance upon the misrepresentation.

(2) the damages recoverable for a negligent misrepresentation do not include the benefit of the plaintiff's contract with the defendant.

Comment:

* * *

b.   This Section rejects, as to negligent misrepresentation, the possibility that, in a proper case, the plaintiff may also recover damages that will give him the benefit of his contract with the defendant, * * * The considerations of policy that have led the courts to compensate the plaintiff for the loss of his bargain in order to make the deception of a deliberate defrauder unprofitable to him, do not apply when the defendant has had honest intentions but has merely failed to exercise reasonable care in what he says or does.

SECTION C.   CONTRACT AND TORT

The tort of misrepresentation operates in a domain where contract is also pervasively in play. Indeed, the interests protected by the tort are often said to be "contractual." We noted this at the outset of the chapter, remarking that misrepresentation protects the institution of contract from being subverted by deception, just as trespass and conversion protect the institution of property from being subverted by force. Here we consider more specific relations between contract and tort.

Perhaps the most salient effect of contract on the law of misrepresentation is that it makes available a kind of strict liability—liability for misrepresentations which are neither known to be false nor negligently believed not to be false, but "innocent," made without any moral culpability. This is an old feature of the law of misrepresentation, tied to the contract remedy of recission. Both the liability and the remedy are grounded in the intuition that one who procures an advantage by a misrepresentation, however innocently, is not entitled to the advantage procured thereby and must return it. The availability of contract as a legal instrument also enables buyers and sellers to single out certain representations as especially important—as warranties—and to attempt to exclude other representations as superseded by the contract.

The tort law of misrepresentation and the law of contract thus interact harmoniously in a variety of ways. But the relations between the two bodies of law are not always felicitous and, in some ways, are surprisingly unsettled. The remedy available for misrepresentations predicated on "contractual" theories is not always recission and recisssion alone. The appropriateness of other remedies is a matter of enduring debate. More generally, the degree of deference that tort should show to contract, when contract terms, rules and remedies are available as an alternative to tort, is a matter of recurring debate, raised both by particular questions such as the enforceability of contractual and integration clauses, and by the far more general question of the role of the economic loss rule in this area of law.

LIABILITY FOR INNOCENT MISREPRESENTATION

DERRY v. PEEK
House of Lords, 1889. 14 App.Cas. 337.

[The facts of this case are summarized a p. ___ supra, with a substantial excerpt from Lord Herschell's opinion following that summary. In a portion of his opinion which was not included in the earlier excerpt Lord Herschell has the following to say about an "action of deceit" at "common-law."]

* * * I think it important that it should be borne in mind that [an action for deceit] differs essentially from one brought to obtain rescission of a contract on the ground of misrepresentation of a material fact. The principles which govern the two actions differ widely. Where rescission is claimed it is only necessary to prove that there was misrepresentation; then, however honestly it may have been made, however free from blame the person who made it, the contract, having been obtained by misrepresentation, cannot stand. * * * I lay stress upon this because observations made by learned judges in actions for rescission have been cited and much relied upon at the bar by counsel for the respondent. Care must obviously be observed in applying the language used in relation to such actions to an action of deceit. Even if the scope of the language used extend beyond the particular action which was being dealt with, it must be remembered that the learned judges were not engaged in determining what is necessary to support an action of deceit, or in discriminating with nicety the elements which enter into it.* * *

ALDRICH v. SCRIBNER

Supreme Court of Michigan, 1908.
154 Mich. 23, 117 N.W. 581.

[Action for fraud alleged to have been committed by the defendant in an exchange of land with the plaintiffs. The plaintiffs claimed that the defendant's agent had represented the land as having "175 fruit trees in good bearing condition" and that the defendant had stated to the plaintiffs that the statements made by the agent were true. Neither party had seen the land and the defendant claimed that whatever statements were made were made honestly. Judgment was entered for defendant on a verdict directed by the court, and plaintiffs bring error.]

CARPENTER, J. [after discussing Busch v. Wilcox, 82 Mich. 315, 46 N.W. 940, Holcomb v. Noble, 69 Mich. 396, 37 N.W. 497, actions of deceit by buyer against seller, and Krause v. Cook, 144 Mich. 365, 108 N.W. 81, an action of deceit by the buyer against the seller's agent who had made misrepresentations]. In Michigan we have held (see cases cited in the opinion of Justice Morse in the Holcomb case, supra) that, in order to constitute a fraud, it is not necessary that the person making the statement should either know that it is untrue or be recklessly and consciously ignorant whether it be true or not. It is sufficient if it be false in fact. It must be said, however, that in the cases in which this principle has been applied, the defendant obtained what the false representations caused the plaintiff to lose. Applied in such cases, the principle is a just and salutary one. This may be illustrated by the Holcomb case—which is a typical case. There, because plaintiff, Holcomb, credited a certain false statement of fact, he paid defendant, Noble, more for land purchased than otherwise he would have paid. The false statement of fact was an agency whereby the property of the plaintiff was transferred to defendant. The law would be justly subject to reproach if it afforded no redress in such a case. In Michigan the law does give redress in such a case, and that redress may be obtained in an action for fraud. It may seem somewhat unjust to characterize such conduct as fraudulent, but the court was apparently placed in the dilemma of either so characterizing it or of altogether denying compensation, and it chose the least objectionable of these two alternatives. This principle, which is altogether just in its application to cases where the loss of the plaintiff has inured to the profit of the defendant, would be most unjust if it applied to cases where the defendant has obtained no such profit. This may be illustrated by taking a concrete case, and I take a case even plainer in its facts than the Krause case. Let us suppose that, with commendable motives and in the best of faith, one friend communicates to another with all amplitude of detail certain information he has received respecting a mine, which it is known that neither of them has ever visited. The object of this communication is to induce the one to whom it is made to purchase stock, but not from the one making the communication, but from a third person having no relation to him. The stock is purchased accordingly, without any profit resulting to the friend making the communication; the information proves to be false and the stock worthless. Did the friend who communicated the information which proved to be false commit a fraud? He did no moral wrong. Indeed, from a moral point of view, his conduct was commendable, and, unless compelled to do so, the court should not announce a rule of law which penalizes commendable conduct. Are we compelled to declare that there exists a rule of law which makes such conduct fraudulent? Manifestly not, unless we are bound to declare that the doctrine of the Holcomb and Busch cases applies. Must we so declare? As already pointed out, the case differs materially from the Holcomb and the Busch cases, and this difference is such that the doctrine of those cases has no just application. That doctrine was designed to accomplish justice; as applied in the Holcomb and Busch cases and in similar cases it does accomplish justice. As applied to cases where the loss of the plaintiff has not inured to the profit of the defendant, it accomplishes an injustice, and it therefore has no application to such cases. It is true that the Krause case differs from the supposed illustrative case stated in this opinion in this: That the defendant Cook did profit to the extent of 10 per cent. of the loss sustained by plaintiff. If there were any rule of law by which we could hold a wrongdoer responsible for 10 per cent. of the damages, and relieve him of responsibility for 90 per cent. of the damages, it might have been just to have applied the principle of the Holcomb and Busch cases to the Krause case. But there is no such rule, and therefore we held, and were bound to hold, that the principle was inapplicable. The Krause case was not, therefore, within the rule of the Holcomb and Busch cases, and is not inconsistent with that rule.

* * * For the purpose of determining whether the principle of the Holcomb and Busch Cases is applicable I draw a distinction between the suits brought against a party to the contract and the suits brought against those who are not parties to the contract. If it is brought against a party to the contract, that principle is applicable. If it is not brought against a party to the contract, that principle is not applicable. When one is fraudulently induced to enter into a contract, it is quite correct, in a general sense, to say that his loss inures to the profit of the other party to the contract. In a legal sense the other party to the contract is the beneficiary of the fraud, and,

speaking generally, his profits equal the losses of the defrauded party. I concede, however, that, under the well-settled rule that the measure of damages is the difference between the actual value of the property and its value as represented, cases will arise where the losses of the defrauded party will exceed the profits of the other party to the contract. Such a case will arise whenever the defrauded party has paid less for property than it would be worth if the false representations had been true. I have no hesitation in saying that such cases are within the principle of the Holcomb and Busch Cases. The party to the contract is in such a case the legal beneficiary of the fraud. The defrauded party paid him what he himself regarded and accepted as the equivalent of the value of the property as it was represented to be. In such case I think it would be quite correct to say that the defendant, in consideration of what he did receive, understood that he should make good any loss caused plaintiff by relying upon the false representation. I think there is no injustice in holding him responsible for that loss. * * *

I vote, therefore, for the reversal of the judgment.

[Four other judges concurring, judgment was reversed.]

———

HAM v. HART, 58 N.M. 550, 273 P.2d 748 (1954); noted, 28 So.Cal. L.Rev. 193, 33 Tex.L.Rev. 524. Alleging that the vendor had fraudulently misrepresented the amount of water that a certain well would deliver, the purchaser sought damages measured by the expenses incurred in making up the deficiency. The trial court found that the misrepresentations were innocently made and dismissed the complaint. *Held*, reversing trial court, that there is no essential difference between the principle involved in an action for damages and a suit for rescission, consequently an innocent misrepresentation is actionable. The court apparently means to approve a benefit-of-the-bargain measure of damages.

RESTATEMENT, SECOND, TORTS (1976)

§ 552C. Misrepresentation in Sale, Rental or Exchange Transaction

(1) One who, in a sale, rental or exchange transaction with another, makes a misrepresentation of a material fact for the purpose of inducing the other to act or to refrain from acting in reliance upon it, is subject to liability to the other for pecuniary loss caused to him by his justifiable reliance upon the misrepresentation, even though it is not made fraudulently or negligently.

(2) Damages recoverable under the rule stated in this section are limited to the difference between the value of what the other has parted with and the value of what he has received in the transaction.

Caveat:

The Institute expresses no opinion as to whether there may be other types of business transactions, in addition to those of sale, rental and exchange, in which strict liability may be imposed for innocent misrepresentation under the conditions stated in this Section.

———

WILSON v. JONES, 45 S.W.2d 572 (Tex.Com.App.1932). Action against Jones, a banker, for damages because of a representation that he was banker of a certain person and that her signature on a note was genuine. The signature was a forgery. Jones was receiving a commission from the sale of the note. In holding for the plaintiff the court said that in Texas the rule was firmly established that where affirmative representations of fact are made and designed to be acted upon by another and he does so believing them to be true when they are false, one making the representation is liable regardless of his knowledge of the falsity or intent to deceive. Moreover, "an expert's opinion as to a matter susceptible of actual knowledge" was regarded as a statement of fact. It is well to observe that the cases the court cited to support its position were cases on the remedy of rescission.

WARRANTIES

CHANDELOR v. LOPUS
Exchequer Chamber, 1603. Cro.Jac. 4.

Action upon the case. Whereas the defendant being a goldsmith, and having skill in jewels and precious stones, had a stone which he affirmed to Lopus to be a bezar-stone, and sold it to him for one hundred pounds; ubi revera it was not a bezar-stone: the defendant pleaded not guilty, and verdict was given and judgment entered for the plaintiff in the King's Bench.

But error was thereof brought in the Exchequer Chamber; because the declaration contains not matter sufficient to charge the defendant, viz. that he warranted it to be a bezar-stone, or that he knew that it was not a bezar-stone; for it may be, he himself was ignorant whether it were a bezar-stone or not.

And all the Justices and Barons (except ANDERSON) held, that for this cause it was error: for the bare affirmation that it was a bezar-stone, without warranting it to be so, is no cause of action: and although he knew it to be no bezar-stone, it is not material; for every one in selling his wares will affirm that his wares are good, or the horse which he sells is sound; yet if he does not warrant them to be so, it is no cause of action, and the warranty ought to be made at the same time of the sale; as F.N.B. 94, c, and 98, b; 5 Hen. 7, pl. 41; 9 Hen. 6, pl. 53; 12 Hen. 4, pl. 1, 42 Ass. 8; 7 Hen. 4, pl. 15. Wherefore, forasmuch as no warrant is alleged, they held the declaration to be ill.

ANDERSON to the contrary; for the deceit in selling it for a bezar, whereas it was not so, is cause of action.

But, notwithstanding, it was adjudged to be no cause, and the judgment reversed.

[In 1 Dyer 75a, note 23, it is stated, as to the principal case, "There the opinion of POPHAM [C. J.] was, that if I have any commodities which are damaged (whether victuals or otherwise), and I, knowing them to be so, sell them for good, and affirm them to be so, an action upon the case lies for the deceit; but although they be damaged, if I, knowing not that, affirm them to be good, still no action lies, without I warrant them to be good."]

OXFORD ENGLISH REFERENCE DICTIONARY (2002).[3] "Bezoar /'bi:zo:(r), 'bezeu,a:(r)/ *n.* a small stone which may form in the stomachs of certain animals, esp. ruminants, and which was once used as an antidote for various ailments. [ult. F. Pers. *padzahr* antidote, Arab. *bazahr*]"

THE UNIFORM COMMERCIAL CODE

A number of sections of the Uniform Commercial Code bear on the formation of warranties. The single most pertinent provision is reprinted here. Other pertinent provisions of the UCC, including §§ 2–314 (Implied Warranty: Merchantability; Usage of Trade); 2–315 (Implied Warranty; Fitness for a Particular Purpose); and 2–316 (Exclusion or Modification of Warranties) are included in the products liability materials in Chapter 19 and pp. 937–938, infra.

——————

2–313. Express Warranties by Affirmation, Promise, Description, Sample

(1) Express warranties by the seller are created as follows:

(a) Any affirmation of fact or promise made by the seller to the buyer which relates to the goods and becomes part of the basis of the bargain creates an express warranty that the goods shall conform to the affirmation or promise.

(b) Any description of the goods which is made part of the basis of the bargain creates an express warranty that the goods shall conform to the description.

(c) Any sample or model which is made part of the basis of the bargain creates an express warranty that the whole of the goods shall conform to the sample or model.

(2) It is not necessary to the creation of an express warranty that the seller use formal words such as "warrant" or "guarantee" or that he have a specific intention to make a warranty, but an affirmation merely of the value of the goods or a statement purporting to be merely the seller's opinion or commendation of the goods does not create a warranty.

SIMPSON v. WIDGER et al., 311 N.J.Super. 379, 709 A.2d 1366 (1998). The facts of this case are described supra, p. 243. Plaintiff brought a claim for breach of warranty, in addition to his claim of fraud, alleging that a number of the seller's representations' constituted express warranties under

---

3. Reprinted by permission of Oxford University Press.

§ 2–313 of the UCC, which is in force in New Jersey. The court analyzed the warranty claim as follows:

"In his deposition, Simpson said Scher used these phrases in describing The Mighty Quinn: 'good horse,' 'sound horse,' 'appropriate for [him] to buy.' He also testified that 'the substance of our conversation was that this was a good horse and was worth the money.' In a certification, he added that he told Scher he wanted to be sure he would be able to resell the horse after Catherine went to college.

"To the extent that Scher affirmed the value of the horse, it is clear that no warranty was created under *N.J.S.A.* 12A:2–313(2), *supra,* since that section expressly excludes affirmation of value from the concept of express warranty. The words 'good' or 'appropriate for purchase' added nothing to what was clearly the essence of the seller's representation, which was that The Mighty Quinn was sound." The term "sound" by contrast was a term with a particular meaning "in the context of horse dealing" and thus capable of being warranted. In horse dealing, "sound" means "serviceably sound" and "serviceably sound" means a horse "capable of doing his job although he may have some minor unsoundness or blemish not serious enough to incapacitate him." Defendant did not breach its warranty of soundness, however, because its representation that The Mighty Quinn was "sound" was true.

THE ECONOMIC LOSS RULE

ALL-TECH TELECOM, INC. v. AMWAY CORPORATION

United States Circuit Court of Appeals, Seventh Circuit, 1999.
174 F.3d 862.

POSNER, C. J.,

A disappointed plaintiff, All–Tech Telecom, appeals frrom the district court's grant of summary judgment to the defendant, Amway, on All–Tech's claims of intentional and negligent misrepresentation and promissory estoppel. All-Tech was allowed to get to the jury on claims of breach of warranty, and the jury found a breach but awarded no damages. There is no challenge to the jury's verdict, only to the grant of summary judgment on the other claims. * * *

In 1987, Amway had offered distributors a new product (really a product plus a service), the "TeleCharge" phone. The phone was intended for the use of customers of hotels and restaurants. The customer would use a credit card or telephone calling card to pay for a long-distance call. The hotel or restaurant, along with the distributor, Amway, and the long-distance phone companies involved in the calls, would divide the line charges. Beginning in 1988, All-Tech, which was created for the very purpose of being an Amway distributor of TeleCharge phones and the associated telephone service, bought a large number of the phones. For a variety of reasons beyond All–Tech's control, including equipment problems, regulatory impediments to the provision of the TeleCharge program, and finally the obsolescence of the phones, which caused Amway to withdraw the product from the market in 1992, TeleCharge was a flop. All–Tech claims to have been lured into and kept in this losing venture by a series of misrepresentations, such as that Amway had done extensive research before offering the service, that the service would be the "best" in the nation, that any business telephone line could be used with the TeleCharge phone, that the service had been approved in all 50 states and did not require the approval of any telephone company, that each phone could be expected to generate an annual revenue for the distributor of $750, that the carrier that Amway had retained to handle the calls and billings for the TeleCharge phones (International Tele–Charge, Inc. (ITI)) was the largest company of its kind in the nation, and that the purchaser of a TeleCharge phone would have to deal with ITI—the phone could not be reprogrammed to work with any other carrier.

The district court threw out All–Tech's claims of misrepresentation on the basis of the "economic loss" doctrine of the common law. * * *

One explanation for [the economic loss doctrine] * * * is the desirability of confining remedies for contract-type losses to contract law. Suppliers injured in their pocketbook because of a fire at the shop of a retailer who buys and distributes their goods sustain the kind of purely business loss familiarly encountered in contract law, rather than the physical harm, whether to person or to property, with which tort law is centrally concerned. These suppliers can protect themselves from the loss caused them by the fire by buying business-loss insurance, by charging a higher price, or by including in their contract with the retailer a requirement that he buy a minimum quantity of goods from the supplier, regardless. The suppliers thus don't need a tort remedy.

This point has implications for commercial fraud * * * . Where there are well-developed contractual remedies, such as the remedies that the Uniform Commercial Code (in force in all U.S. states) provides for breach of warranty of the quality, fitness, or specifications of goods, there is no need to provide tort remedies for misrepresentation. The tort remedies would duplicate the contract remedies, adding unnecessary complexity to the law. Worse, the provision of these duplicative tort remedies would undermine contract law. That law has been shaped by a tension between a policy of making the jury the normal body for resolving factual disputes and the desire of parties to contracts to be able to rely on the written word and not be exposed to the unpredictable reactions of lay factfinders to witnesses who testify that the contract means something different from what it says. Many doctrines of contract law, such as the parol evidence and "four corners" rules, are designed to limit the scope of jury trial of contract disputes (another example is the statute of frauds). Tort law does not have these screens against the vagaries of the jury. In recognition of this omission, the "economic loss" doctrine in the form invoked by the district judge in this case on the authority of a growing body of case law * * * forbids commercial contracting parties (as distinct from consumers, and other individuals not engaged in business) to escalate their contract dispute into a charge of tortious misrepresentation if they could easily have protected themselves from the misrepresentation of which they now complain. * * *.

The function of the economic-loss doctrine in confining contract parties to their contractual remedies is particularly well illustrated by cases involving product warranties. If the seller makes an oral representation that is important to the buyer, the latter has only to insist that the seller embody that representation in a written warranty. The warranty will protect the buyer, who will have an adequate remedy under the Uniform Commercial Code if the seller reneges. To allow him to use tort law in effect to enforce an oral warranty would unsettle contracts by exposing sellers to the risk of being held liable by a jury on the basis of self-interested oral testimony and perhaps made to pay punitive as well as compensatory damages. This menace is averted by channeling disputes into warranty (contract) law, where oral warranties can be expressly disclaimed, or extinguished by operation of the parol evidence rule. UCC §§ 2–202, 2–316(1) and comment 2. It is true that, in principle, the cheapest way to prevent fraud is to punish the fraudfeasor; but in practice, owing to the ever-present possibility of legal error, the really cheapest way in some cases may be to place a burden of taking precautions on the potential victim.

Some of our cases describe the economic-loss doctrine in words that might seem to imply the abolition of the tort of misrepresentation (including deliberate fraud) in all cases in which the plaintiff and the defendant are business firms having a preexisting contractual relationship that had given rise to the fraud or other misrepresentation. But it is a disservice to courts, as well as a common source of erroneous predictions concerning the scope and direction of the law, to treat a judicial opinion as if it were a statute, every clause of which was Law. It is difficult to write a judicial opinion without making some general statements by way of background and explanation. But in a system of case law such statements can be misleading if carelessly lifted from the case-specific contexts in which they were originally uttered. * * *

If commercial fraud is to go completely by the boards, as a literal reading of some of the economic-loss cases might suggest, then prospective parties to contracts will be able to obtain legal protection against fraud only by insisting that the other party to the contract reduce all representations to writing, and so there will be additional contractual negotiations, contracts will be longer, and, in short, transaction costs will be higher. And the additional costs will be incurred in the making of *every* commercial contract, not just the tiny fraction that end up in litigation. Granted, there are costs of uncertainty from the possibility of falsely charging fraud when a contractual relationship sours, as it did in this case. But the fraud tort comes with safeguards against false claims, such as the requirement of pleading fraud with particularity and (in many though not all jurisdictions) a heightened burden of proof—clear and convincing evidence versus a bare preponderance of the evidence, the standard civil burden.

But the representations challenged in this case do not press against the boundaries of the economic-loss doctrine. For they are in the nature of warranties (remember that the plaintiff made warranty claims, which the judge sent to the jury), and we cannot think of a reason why the fact that the "product" warranted was a hybrid of a product and a service should affect the application of the doctrine. A genuine stumbling block to affirming on its basis, however, is the fact that its application to cases of *intentional* misrepresentation is uncertain. *Daanen & Janssen, Inc. v. Cedarapids, Inc.*, *supra*, 573 N.W.2d [842] at 851, ducks the issue, and we haven't a clue as to how Wisconsin will resolve it. Other jurisdictions have divided over it * * * and the balance of the competing considerations is, as we have suggested, close. We need not choose. Amway has a solid alternative ground for affirmance: All–Tech failed to present any evidence of actionable misrepresentation. * * *

AFFIRMED.

———

GIFFORD v. WICHITA FALLS & S. RY. CO., 211 F.2d 494 (5th Cir.1954). In a personal injury suit, the plaintiff sought to avoid a release which he executed for the sum of $6,000, on the ground that it was procured by fraud. The alleged fraud was an oral promise, unenforceable as such because of the parol evidence rule, made by defendant, to give plaintiff a lifetime job. Plaintiff sought to show by testimony that the promise was made without any intention of performing it. *Held*, reversing a directed verdict for the defendant, that if the jury believed plaintiff's testimony there would be actionable fraud.

DANANN REALTY CO. v. HARRIS, 5 N.Y.2d 317, 184 N.Y.S.2d 599, 157 N.E.2d 597 (1959). The purchaser of a leasehold interest in a building alleged that the seller had fraudulently misrepresented post-operating expenses and profits. With the contract before it, trial court dismissed the action apparently on the ground that it was barred by an exculpatory clause in the contract as follows: "the Purchaser has examined the premises agreed to be sold and is familiar with the physical condition thereof. The Seller has not made and does not make any representations as to the physical condition, rents, leases, expenses, operation, or any other matter or thing related to the aforesaid premises * * * and the Purchaser hereby expressly acknowledges that no such representations have been made and the Purchaser further acknowledges that it has inspected the premises and agrees to take the premises 'as is.' " *Held*, affirmed. Where there is a specific disclaimer clause as to be distinguished from a general omnibus type of statement, plaintiff will not be heard to say that the agreement was executed in reliance upon contradictory oral representations. To hold otherwise would say that it is impossible for two businessmen dealing at arm's length to agree that the buyer is not buying in reliance on any representations of the seller as to a particular fact.

WISCONSIN LOAN & FINANCE CORP. v. GOODNOUGH, 201 Wis. 101, 228 N.W. 484, 67 A.L.R. 1259 (1930). The infant defendant misrepresented age when signing a note, thereby inducing plaintiff to make a loan. *Held*, that he would be liable in an action for deceit. Court made a distinction between a representation such as this which induces the unenforceable contract and a representation or promise which is a part of the contract such as a warranty. As the latter there would be no liability in tort.

Part II

ACCIDENT LAW: IN TORT AND BEYOND

Our law of accidents is generally thought to have emerged in the latter half of the nineteenth century, with the demise of the old forms of action and the rise of a rational system of procedure. In understanding our law of accidents as it exists today, it helps to distinguish, in broad sweep, between two periods in its history. The first period, which we call "classical" runs from the middle of the nineteenth century to the early 20th century. This period sees the emergence of tort accident law as a coherent body of law organized around general principles of responsibility for harm done. In this period, fault liability reigned supreme within tort law, and tort law itself was hemmed in by property and contract. "Modern" tort law emerges in the early 20th century. Modern tort law is characterized by an erosion in the primacy of the fault principle within tort accident law, and by a reshaping of the relations between tort and contract, so that tort takes hold of areas it had previously ceded to contract and property.

We begin our study of accident law with faulty liability, and our study of fault liability with the emergence of fault and the rise of classical tort accident law.

A. THE NEGLIGENCE SYSTEM

In one important respect, the tort law of accidents is discontinuous with the law of intentional wrongdoing that we have studied so far. When intentional injury is inflicted on purpose, the standard instance of intentional injury is very different from the standard instance of accidental injury. When, for example, a battery is committed *on purpose,* a harmful or offensive contact with the plaintiff's person is the aim of the defendant's action. Except in special circumstances—such as self-defense—deliberately using physical violence against another person is unjustified conduct. The same is true of deliberately inflicting severe emotional distress by outrageous conduct, of purposefully seizing or occupying other people's property, of knowingly deceiving them, and so on. The fewer purposeful batteries, conversions, trespasses and knowing frauds there are, the better. Accidental injuries, by contrast, are the byproduct of activities whose point or purpose is something quite different from the harm inflicted on the plaintiff. The activity which gives rise to accidental injury is, moreover, generally valuable and desirable, even though the injury itself is undesirable.

In the following chapter, for instance, the injury in the first case, *The Case of the Thorns,* is the unintended consequence of the defendant's trimming of his hedge. The injury in *Rylands v. Fletcher,* a later case in the chapter, is the unintended result of the defendant's operation of a cotton mill. Trimming one's hedge and milling cotton are, in general, productive and mutually beneficial activities, even though they create risks of physical injury which sometimes materialize into harm. When tort law addresses accidents, therefore, it addresses activities which are generally valuable, and it generally seeks to reap the benefits of the activities which breed accidental harm while reducing the incidence and mitigating the effects of accidental harm itself.

In another important respect, the tort law of accidents is *continuous* with the tort law of intentional wrongdoing. Both bodies of law sometimes take culpable conduct as the trigger for liability, and other times take the failure to make reparation for harm reasonably inflicted as the trigger for liability. In our study of trespass and nuisance we have seen—surprisingly, since it is natural to take "intent" to be an index of culpability—that the intent necessary to commit many intentional torts need not involve conduct that is culpable or blameworthy. In the case of intentional nuisance, for example, we have seen that liability may be predicated simply on the existence of knowing and unreasonable harm to the plaintiff's interest in the use and enjoyment of his or her land. (*Wheat v. Freeman, supra,* p. 129 is a case in point.) Liability imposed on this basis is "strict." The only criticism that the law lodges against the defendant is that the defendant failed to compensate the plaintiff for having inflicted more harm on the plaintiff than the plaintiff should have been asked to bear *without compensation.* No criticism is lodged against the conduct giving rise to the nuisance. In other cases of intentional nuisance—*O'Cain v. O'Cain, supra,* p. 133 is one instance—we have seen the underlying conduct itself criticized as unreasonable, and injunctions issued to reshape that conduct.

The distinction between liability predicated on unreasonable conduct and liability predicated on unreasonable failure to make reparation for harm done is even clearer in the case of the doctrine of conditional privilege, illustrated by *Vincent v. Lake Erie, supra,* p. 145. The defendant's conduct in *Vincent*—saving its ship at the cost of smashing plaintiff's dock—was eminently reasonable. Defendant behaved unreasonably only in so far as it failed to make reparation for the harm that it inflicted.

This distinction between liability predicated on unreasonable conduct and liability predicated on the unreasonable failure to make reparation is fundamental to the tort law of accidents. That law is split between two competing principles of responsibility for harm unintentionally inflicted—negligence and strict liability. Negligence holds injurers accountable only for harms arising out of risks that they have unreasonably imposed. Strict liability holds injurers accountable for certain harms arising out of reasonable risk impositions, on the ground that it would be unreasonable to ask the victims harmed to bear the costs of the injurers' activities. Both of these principles have their roots in the emergence of classical accident law in the latter half of the nineteenth century.

Chapter 7

THE RISE OF CLASSICAL ACCIDENT LAW

SECTION A.   THE EMERGENCE OF FAULT

The tort law of accidents is generally thought to take shape as a field in the middle of the nineteenth century, around the time that the common law worked its way free of the forms of action and coalesced around general principles of liability, the fault principle in particular. But the tort law of accidents has ancient antecedents. We begin our study of accident law with a brief look at those antecedents and the subsequent emergence of the fault principle.

It is sometimes said that early accident law (epitomized here by *The Case of the Thorns* and *Weaver v. Ward*) embodied an "act at your peril" conception of strict liability. The "act at your peril" conception has much in common with intentional tort liability. The "act at your peril" conception predicates liability on invasion of the plaintiff's person or property by the defendant's action, exonerating the defendant only in cases of "unavoidable accident." An "unavoidable accident" is one that, upon close examination, proves not to have issued from the defendant's *voluntary* "act." In other words, early accident law is a system in which absence of agency is the only category of *excuse*, understanding excuse to be a reason that relieves someone of responsibility for having inflicted an impermissible harm. Within this system, the question of *justification*—the question of selecting or specifying the norm to which the defendant must conform her conduct— barely arises. The defendant is responsible for violating the plaintiff's personal integrity, or intruding uninvited upon his property, unless the defendant didn't "act" or the harm arose from the "act" of another.

By the middle of the nineteenth century, the concept of "unavoidable accident" has undergone a metamorphosis, coming to mean an accident that was not precipitated by *wrongful* conduct on the part of the defendant, rather than an accident that was not precipitated by the voluntary conduct of the defendant. This metamorphosis unfolds in *Vincent v. Stinebour* and *Brown v. Kendall*, in a process where obligations of care of various stringency are also entertained. With the transformation in the meaning of "unavoidable accident," the question of excuse recedes, and the question of justification comes to the fore. What kind of care must a defendant exercise—what standard of conduct must a defendant conform his or her conduct to—in order to be free of fault? This is the central question of a "fault" regime, and the focus of *Brown v. Kendall* and *The Nitro–Glycerine Case*. *Butterfield v. Forrester* introduces one other basic element of the classical fault system: the absence of "contributory fault" on the part of the plaintiff.

Procedurally, the emergence of fault liability is entangled with the distinction between two of the forms of action: trespass and case, and the decline of those forms in the nineteenth century. You may therefore wish to review the note on "Torts and Writs" in Chapter One.

THE CASE OF THE THORNS
1466. Y.B. 6 Ed. 4, 7a, pl. 18.

[The case is summarized as follows in Lambert v. Bessey, T. Raym. 421 (1679).] Trespass quare vi & armis clausum fregit, & herbam suam pedibus conculcando consumpsit in six acres. The defendant pleads, that he hath an acre lying next the said six acres, and upon it a hedge of thorns, and he cut the thorns, and they ipso invito fell upon the plaintiff's land, and the defendant took them off as soon as he could, which is the same trespass; and the plaintiff demurred; and adjudged for the plaintiff; for though a man doth a lawful thing, yet if any damage do thereby befall another, he shall answer for it, if he could have avoided it. As if a man lop a tree, and the boughs fall upon another ipso invito, yet an action lies. If a man shoot at butts, and hurt another unawares, an action lies. I have land through which a river runs to your mill, and I lop the sallows growing upon the riverside, which accidentally stop the water, so as your mill is hindered, an action lies. If I am building my own house, and a piece of timber falls on my neighbour's house and breaks part of it, an action lies. If a man assault me, and I lift up my staff to defend myself, and in lifting it up hit another, an action lies by that person, and yet I did a lawful thing. And the reason of all these cases is, because he that is damaged ought to be recompensed. But otherwise it is in criminal cases, for there actus non facit reum nisi mens sit rea.

WEAVER v. WARD
King's Bench, 1616. Hobart 134.

Weaver brought an action of trespass of assault and battery against Ward. The defendant pleaded that he was, amongst others, by the commandment of the lords of the council, a trained soldier in London, of the band of one Andrews, captain, and so was the plaintiff: and that they were skirmishing with their muskets charged with powder for their exercise in re militari against another captain and his band; and as they were so skirmishing, the defendant, casualiter et per infortunium et contra voluntatem suam, in discharging his piece, did hurt and wound the plaintiff; which is the same, etc., absque hoc, that he was guilty aliter sive alio modo.

And, upon demurrer by the plaintiff, judgment was given for him; for, though it were agreed that if men tilt or tourney in the presence of the king, or if two masters of defense, playing their prizes kill one another, that this shall be no felony, or if a lunatic kill a man, or the like, because felony must be done animo felonico; yet, in trespass, which tends only to give damages according to hurt or loss, it is not so; and, therefore, no man shall be excused of a trespass (for this is the nature of an excuse, and not of a justification, prout ei bene licuit), except it may be judged utterly without his fault; as if a man by force take my hand and strike you, or if here the defendant had said that the plaintiff ran across his piece when it was discharging, or had set forth the case with the circumstances so as it had appeared to the court that it had been inevitable, and that the defendant had committed no negligence to give occasion to the hurt.*

———

VINCENT v. STINEHOUR, 7 Vt. 62 (1835). Action of trespass, the declaration alleging that the defendant had driven against and over the plaintiff with his horse and sulkey, while the plaintiff was walking on the road. The trial court, after refusing to charge that the plaintiff, if run upon by defendant, "must recover, though there was no fault, neglect, or want of prudence on the part of the defendant," told the jury that "every man in pursuing his lawful business, must use the prudence of the most prudent kind of men. * * * If, however, there was no such neglect or want of prudence, but that it [the event] was the result of accident, unavoidable on the part of the defendant, they would find for the defendant." In affirming a judgment for defendant the court said: "The principle of law which is laid down by all the writers upon this subject, and which is gathered from and confirmed by the whole series of reported cases, is, that no one can be made responsible, in an action of trespass, for consequences, where he could not have prevented those consequences by prudence and care. Thus it has been laid down, that if a horse, upon a sudden surprise, run away with his rider, and runs against a man and hurts him, this is no battery. Where a person, in doing an act which it is his duty to perform, hurts another, he is not guilty of battery. A man falling out of a window, without any imprudence, injures another—there is no trespass. A soldier, in exercise, hurts his companion— no recovery can be had against him. In the case of Gibbons v. Pepper, 4 Mod. 405, it was distinctly decided, that if a horse runs away with his rider, against his will, and he could not have avoided it, and runs against another, it is no battery in the rider, and he can defend under the general issue. * * * To prevent any abuse of this protection, a person is accounted negligent or careless, and blame is imputed to him, if he does not use an extraordinary degree of circumspection and prudence, greater than is commonly practiced, and if he might have prevented the accident. Therefore, where a person is doing a voluntary act, which he is under no obligation to do, he is held answerable for any injury which may happen to another,

* Editor's Note: "The dominant understanding of negligence at the beginning of the nineteenth century meant neglect or failure fully to perform a preexisting duty, whether imposed by contract, statute, or common law status." MORTON HORWITZ, THE TRANSFORMATION OF AMERICAN LAW 1780–1860, 87 (1977). In our terms "fault" meant "default"—the "failure to do" something that the defendant was required to do, keep his cattle penned in, for example. John H. Wigmore, *Responsibility for Tortious Acts: Its History.—* III, 7 HARV. L. REV. 441, 453–54 (1894).

either by carelessness or accident. On this principle, the case of Underwood v. Hewson, 1 Str. 596, was decided. The act of uncocking the gun was voluntary, not unavoidable; a greater degree of prudence was therefore required. The case of a man turning round, and knocking down another, whom he did not see—the shooting an arrow at a mark, which glanced— were of this class. The act was purely voluntary, not one which the person was required to do."

BROWN v. KENDALL

Supreme Judicial Court of Massachusetts, 1850.
60 Mass. (6 Cush.) 292.

[Trespass for assault and battery, originally commenced against George K. Kendall, the defendant, who died pending the suit, and his executrix was summoned in.

It appeared in evidence, on the trial, that two dogs, belonging to the plaintiff and the defendant, respectively, were fighting in the presence of their masters; that the defendant took a stick about four feet long, and commenced beating the dogs in order to separate them; that the plaintiff was looking on, at the distance of about a rod, and that he advanced a step or two toward the dogs. In their struggle, the dogs approached the place where the plaintiff was standing. The defendant retreated backward from before the dogs, striking them as he retreated; and as he approached the plaintiff, with his back toward him, in raising his stick over his shoulder, in order to strike the dogs, he accidentally hit the plaintiff in the eye, inflicting upon him a severe injury.

Whether it was necessary or proper for the defendant to interfere in the fight between the dogs; whether the interference, if called for, was in a proper manner; and what degree of care was exercised by each party on the occasion; were the subject of controversy between the parties, upon all the evidence in the case, of which the foregoing is an outline.

Acting under instructions, the nature of which appears in the opinion of the court, the jury returned a verdict for the plaintiff. The defendant alleged exceptions.]

SHAW, C. J. This is an action of trespass, vi et armis, brought by George Brown against George K. Kendall, for an assault and battery; and the original defendant having died pending the action, his executrix has been summoned in. The rule of the common law, by which this action would abate by the death of either party, is reversed in this commonwealth by statute, which provides that actions of trespass for assault and battery shall survive. Rev.Stats., ch. 93, § 7.

The facts set forth in the bill of exceptions preclude the supposition, that the blow, inflicted by the hand of the defendant upon the person of the plaintiff, was intentional. The whole case proceeds on the assumption, that the damage sustained by the plaintiff, from the stick held by the defendant, was inadvertent and unintentional; and the case involves the question how far and under what qualifications, the party by whose unconscious act the damage was done is responsible for it. We use the term "unintentional" rather than involuntary, because in some of the cases, it is stated, that the act of holding and using a weapon or instrument, the movement of which is the immediate cause of hurt to another, is a voluntary act, although its particular effect in hitting and hurting another is not within the purpose or intention of the party doing the act.

It appears to us, that some of the confusion in the cases on this subject has grown out of the long-vexed question, under the rule of the common law, whether a party's remedy, where he has one, should be sought in an action of the case, or of trespass. This is very distinguishable from the question, whether in a given case, any action will lie. The result of these cases is, that if the damage complained of is the immediate effect of the act of the defendant, trespass vi et armis lies; if consequential only, and not immediate, case is the proper remedy. Leame v. Bray, 3 East 593; Huggett v. Montgomery, 2 B. & P.N.R. 446, Day's Ed., and notes.

In these discussions, it is frequently stated by judges, that when one receives injury from the direct act of another, trespass will lie. But we think this is said in reference to the question, whether trespass and not case will lie, assuming that the facts are such, that some action will lie. These dicta are no authority, we think, for holding, that damage received by a direct act of force from another will be sufficient to maintain an action of trespass, whether the act was lawful or unlawful, and neither wilful, intentional, or careless. In the principal case cited, Leame v. Bray, the damage arose from the act of the defendant, in driving on the wrong side of the road, in a dark night, which was clearly negligent, if not unlawful. In the course of the argument of that case (p. 595), Lawrence, J., said: "There certainly are cases in the books, where, the injury being direct and immediate, trespass has been holden to lie, though the injury was not intentional." The term "injury" implies something more than damage; but, independently of that consideration, the proposition may be true, because though the injury was unintentional, the act may have been unlawful or negligent, and the cases cited by him are perfectly consistent with that supposition. So the same learned judge in the same case says (p. 597), "No doubt trespass lies against one who drives a carriage against another, whether done wilfully or not." But he immediately adds, "Suppose one who is driving a carriage is negligently and heedlessly looking about him, without attending to the road when persons are passing, and thereby runs over a child and kills him, is it not manslaughter? and if so, it must be trespass; for every manslaughter includes trespass;" showing what he understood by a case not wilful.

We think, as the result of all the authorities, the rule is correctly stated by Mr. Greenleaf, that the plaintiff must come prepared with evidence to show either that the intention was unlawful, or that the defendant was in fault; for if the injury was unavoidable, and the conduct of the defendant was free from blame, he will not be liable. 2 Greenl.Ev. §§ 85–92. Wakeman v. Robinson, 1 Bing. 213. If, in the prosecution of a lawful act, a casualty purely accidental arises, no action can be supported for an injury arising therefrom. Davis v. Saunders, 2 Chit.R. 639; Com.Dig.Battery, A., Day's Ed., and notes; Vincent v. Stinehour, 7 Vt. 62. In applying these rules to the present case, we can perceive no reason why the instructions asked for by the defendant ought not to have been given; to this effect, that if both plaintiff and defendant at the time of the blow were using ordinary care, or if at that time the defendant was using ordinary care, and the plaintiff was not, or if at that time, both the plaintiff and defendant were not using ordinary care, then the plaintiff could not recover.

In using this term, ordinary care, it may be proper to state, that what constitutes ordinary care will vary with the circumstances of cases. In general, it means that kind and degree of care, which prudent and cautious men would use, such as is required by the exigency of the case, and such as is necessary to guard against probable danger. A man, who should have occasion to discharge a gun, on an open and extensive marsh, or in a forest, would be required to use less circumspection and care, than if he were to do the same thing in an inhabited town, village or city. To make an accident, or casualty, or, as the law sometimes states it, inevitable accident, it must be such an accident as the defendant could not have avoided by the use of the kind and degree of care necessary to the exigency, and in the circumstances in which he was placed.

We are not aware of any circumstances in this case, requiring a distinction between acts which it was lawful and proper to do, and acts of legal duty. There are cases, undoubtedly, in which officers are bound to act under process, for the legality of which they are not responsible, and perhaps some others in which this distinction would be important. We can have no doubt that the act of the defendant in attempting to part the fighting dogs, one of which was his own, and for the injurious acts of which he might be responsible, was a lawful and proper act, which he might do by proper and safe means. If, then, in doing this act, using due care and all proper precautions necessary to the exigency of the case, to avoid hurt to others, in raising his stick for that purpose, he accidentally hit the plaintiff in his eye, and wounded him, this was the result of pure accident, or was involuntary and unavoidable, and therefore the action would not lie. Or if the defendant was chargeable with some negligence, and if the plaintiff was also chargeable with negligence, we think the plaintiff can not recover without showing that the damage was caused wholly by the act of the defendant, and that the plaintiff's own negligence did not contribute as an efficient cause to produce it.

The court instructed the jury, that if it was not a necessary act, and the defendant was not in duty bound to part the dogs, but might with propriety interfere or not as he chose, the defendant was responsible for the consequences of the blow, unless it appeared that he was in the exercise of extraordinary care, so that the accident was inevitable, using the word not in a strict but a popular sense. This is to be taken in connection with the charge afterward given, that if the jury believed, that the act of interference in the fight was unnecessary (that is, as before explained, not a duty incumbent on the defendant), then the burden of proving extraordinary care on the part of the defendant, or want of ordinary care on the part of the plaintiff, was on the defendant.

The court are of the opinion that these directions were not conformable to law. If the act of hitting the plaintiff was unintentional, on the part of the defendant, and done in the doing of a lawful act, then the defendant was not liable, unless it was done in the want of exercise of due care, adapted to the exigency of the case, and therefore such want of due care became part of the plaintiff's case, and the burden of proof was on the plaintiff to establish it.

* * * [W]e are of opinion, that the other part of the charge, that the burden of proof was on the defendant, was incorrect. Those facts which are essential to enable the plaintiff to recover, he takes the burden of proving. The evidence may be offered by the plaintiff or by the defendant; the question of due care, or want of care, may be essentially connected with the main facts, and arise from the same proof; but the effect of the rule, as to the burden of proof, is this, that when the proof is all in, and before the jury, from whatever side it comes, and whether directly proved, or inferred from circumstances, if it appears that the defendant was doing a lawful act, and unintentionally hit and hurt the plaintiff, then unless it also appears to the satisfaction of the jury, that the defendant is chargeable with some fault, negligence, carelessness, or want of prudence, the plaintiff fails to sustain the burden of proof, and is not entitled to recover.

New trial ordered.

STANLEY v. POWELL, [1891] 1 Q.B. 86; noted, 5 Harv.L.Rev. 36. Action under reformed procedure, the statement of claim alleging that the defendant had negligently, wrongfully and unskilfully fired his gun and wounded the plaintiff in the eye. The defendant denied the negligence. The defendant, a member of a party shooting pheasants, fired at a bird. One of the shots glanced off the bough of an oak at a considerable angle and struck the plaintiff, who was engaged in carrying cartridges and the game which was shot. The jury found specially that the defendant was not negligent in firing the gun. *Held*, for defendant [after discussing, the earlier cases]: "If the case is regarded as an action on the case for an injury by negligence the plaintiff has failed to establish that which is the very gist of such an action; if, on the other hand, it is turned into an action for trespass, and the defendant is (as he must be) supposed to have pleaded a plea denying negligence and establishing that the injury was accidental in the sense above explained, the verdict of the jury is equally fatal to the action."

FOWLER v. LANNING, [1959] 1 Q.B. 426, 1 All E.R. 290; noted in 1959 Camb.L.J. 33, 75 L.Q.Rev. 161. In an action "for trespass to the person," the plaintiff alleged simply that on a certain date and at a certain time "the defendant shot the plaintiff," and that by reason thereof the plaintiff sustained personal injuries, particulars of which were given. The defendant objected that the statement of claim was bad in law, disclosing no cause of action, because it did not allege that the shooting was either intentional or negligent. *Held*, for defendant. The defense, which is the modern equivalent of demurrer, raises the practical issue whether "the onus lies upon the plaintiff to prove the defendant was negligent, in which case, under the modern system of pleading, he must so plead and give particulars of negligence * * *." "It is fashionable today to regard trespass to the person as representing the historic principle that every man acts at his peril and is liable for all the consequences of his acts; negligence as representing the more modern view that a man's freedom of action is subject only to the obligation not to infringe any duty of care which he owes to others * * *. But however true this may have been of trespass in medieval times—and I respectfully doubt whether it ever was—the strict principle that every man acts at his peril was not applied in the case of trespass to the person even as long ago as 1617. It is true that in that year, in the much-cited case of Weaver v. Ward, which arose out of a shooting accident during an exercise of trained bands, the Court of King's Bench held that a plea that the defendant 'casualiter et per infortuniam et contra voluntatem suam, in discharging of his piece did hurt and wound the plaintiff' was demurrable. But it would seem that this was because the plea, which was a special plea, was insufficient because, although it denied intention, it did not negative negligence on the part of the defendant." "In trespass on the case the onus of proof of the defendant's negligence undoubtedly lay upon the plaintiff. Where it lay in trespass is much more difficult to determine." A "formidable body of academic opinion" maintains "that the onus of proof of absence of negligence on the part of a defendant in a case founded on trespass to the person lies upon the defendant himself," highway cases having become an exception. But it seems a more supportable view that "[t]he onus of proving negligence, where the trespass is not intentional, lies upon the plaintiff, whether the action be framed in trespass or in negligence." This is the law of highway cases, "and there is no reason in principle, nor any suggestion in the decided authorities, why it should be any different in other cases." Thus, the plaintiff "must state the facts which he alleges constitute negligence." This requirement is not merely an "academic pleading point" but rather "serves to secure justice between the parties." It would offend the underlying principle of modern pleading "that a plaintiff, by calling his grievance 'trespass to the person' instead of 'negligence,' should force a defendant to come to trial blindfold; * * *." Leave to amend the statement of claim granted.

THE NITRO–GLYCERINE CASE
Supreme Court of the United States, 1872.
82 U.S. (15 Wall.) 524, 21 L.Ed. 206.

[The defendant—Wells, Fargo & Co.—was an express carrier engaged in transporting packages between New York and California. It received at New York a box about two and a half feet square and weighing three hundred and twenty nine pounds, to be carried to California. There was nothing about it to indicate that its contents were dangerous and the defendant made no inquiries. It was carried by steamer and the Panama Railway to San Francisco, where a substance resembling sweet oil was found to be leaking from the box. Two days later, according to defendant's practice, it was taken to the defendant's office for examination. There, in the presence of an officer of the steamship company and others an employee of the defendant with mallet and chisel proceeded to open it. An explosion immediately occurred, killing the bystanders and damaging the building, owned by the plaintiff and in which the defendant's office was situated. It was then discovered that the contents had been nitroglycerine. Nitroglycerine had been discovered in 1847; in 1864 it was first suggested by Nobel, a European, that it could be used for blasting. A few weeks previously a case from Nobel had arrived at San Francisco and the consignees were then trying to interest people in the explosive qualities of the substance. It was not generally an article of commerce and its properties were little known.

By stipulation, the case was tried by the court, which found that the defendant had no reason to know of the nature of the shipment or to suspect its dangerous character, and held that the defendant was not liable for harm to any part of the building not leased by it. To review the judgment, the plaintiff sued out a writ of error.]

FIELD J. [after holding that the defendant was under no duty to inquire as to the contents of the box].

The defendants, being innocently ignorant of the contents of the case, received in the regular course of their business, were not guilty of negligence in introducing it into their place of business and handling it in the same manner as other packages of similar outward appearance were usually handled. "Negligence" has been defined to be "the omission to do something which a reasonable man, guided by those considerations which ordinarily regulate the conduct of human affairs, would do, or doing something which a prudent and reasonable man would not do."** It must be determined in all cases by reference to the situation and knowledge of the parties and all the attendant circumstances. What would be extreme care under one condition of knowledge, and one state of circumstances, would be gross negligence with different knowledge and in changed circumstances. The law is reasonable in its judgments in this respect. It does not charge culpable negligence upon any one who takes the usual precautions against accident, which careful and prudent men are accustomed to take under similar circumstances.

* * *

This action is not brought upon the covenants of the lease; it is in trespass for injuries to the buildings of the plaintiff, and the gist of the action is the negligence of the defendants; unless that be established, they are not liable. The mere fact that injury has been caused is not sufficient to hold them. No one is responsible for injuries resulting from unavoidable accident, whilst engaged in a lawful business. A party charging negligence as a ground of action must prove it. He must show that the defendant, by his act or by his omission, has violated some duty incumbent upon him, which has caused the injury complained of.

The cases between passengers and carriers for injuries stand upon a different footing. The contract of the carrier being to carry safely, the proof

** Blyth v. Birmington Water Works, 11 Ex-   chequer, 784.

of the injury usually establishes a *prima facie* case, which the carrier must overcome. His contract is shown, *prima facie* at least, to have been violated by the injury. Outside of these cases, in which a positive obligation is cast upon the carrier to perform safely a special service, the presumption is that the party has exercised such care as men of ordinary prudence and caution would exercise under similar circumstances, and if he has not, the plaintiff must prove it.

Here no such proof was made, and the case stands as one of unavoidable accident, for the consequences of which the defendants are not responsible. The consequences of all such accidents must be borne by the sufferer as his misfortune.

This principle is recognized and affirmed in a great variety of cases—in cases where fire originating in one man's building has extended to and destroyed the property of others; in cases where injuries have been caused by fire ignited by sparks from steamboats or locomotives, or caused by horses running away, or by blasting rocks, and in numerous other cases which will readily occur to every one. The rule deducible from them is, that the measure of care against accident, which one must take to avoid responsibility, is that which a person of ordinary prudence and caution would use if his own interests were to be affected, and the whole risk were his own.

And the principle is not changed whether the injury complained of follows directly or remotely from the act or conduct of the party. The direct or remote consequences of the act or conduct may determine the form of the action, whether it shall be case or trespass, where the forms of the common law are in use, but cannot alter the principle upon which liability is enforced or avoided. * * * In Harvey v. Dunlop,*** which was before the Supreme Court of New York, the action was trespass for throwing a stone at the plaintiff's daughter, by which her eye was put out. It did not appear that the injury was inflicted by design or carelessness, but on the contrary that it was accidental, and it was held that the plaintiff could not recover. "No case or principle can be found," said Mr. Justice Nelson, in denying a new trial, "or, if found, can be maintained, subjecting an individual to liability for an act done without fault on his part;" and in this conclusion we all agree.

Judgment affirmed.

Butterfield v. Forrester, 11 East 60, 103 Eng.Rep. 926 (King's Bench, 1809). The "defendant, for the purpose of making some repairs to his house, which was close by the roadside at one end of the town, had put up a pole across this part of the road, a free passage being left by another branch or street in the same direction. That the plaintiff left a public house not far distant from the place in question at 8 o'clock in the evening in August, when they were just beginning to light candles, but while there was light enough left to discern the obstruction at one hundred yards distance; and the witness who proved this, said that if the plaintiff had not been riding very hard he might have observed and avoided it; the plaintiff, however, who was riding violently, did not observe it, but rode against it, and fell with his

*** Lalor's Reports, 193.

horse and was much hurt in consequence of the accident." There was no evidence that the plaintiff was "intoxicated at the time."

Held, verdict for defendant affirmed. The accident "appeared to happen entirely from [plaintiff's] own fault." Plaintiff would have seen the obstacle had he exercised ordinary care. "One person being in fault will not dispense with another's using ordinary care for himself. Two things must concur to support this action: an obstruction in the road by the fault of the defendant, and no want of ordinary care to avoid it on the part of the plaintiff."

SECTION B.   THE CONTEST BETWEEN NEGLIGENCE AND STRICT LIABILITY

Fault liability emerges out of a background of "act at your peril" strict liability. But, although the emergence of fault liability eclipses the "act at your peril" conception of strict liability, the emergence of fault does not mark the disappearance of strict liability. Instead strict liability itself is freed from the constraints of the forms of actions and recast as a competing principle of responsibility for accidental injury. Whereas the basic principle of fault liability is that people should be held accountable for harms which flow from their wrongful agency, the basic principle of strict liability is that people should be held accountable for harms which flow from their purposeful activity—from their agency, wrongful or not. The generalization of strict liability as a competing principle to fault liability is identified with the famous English case of *Rylands v. Fletcher*, and with the subsequent debate over that case and the merits of strict liability in American case law.

The conflict between fault and strict liability is a conflict between two competing, highly general, principles of responsibility. Each principle has powerful intuitive appeal. Fault liability appeals to the moral intuition that it is wrong to hold people responsible for harms they have caused when they have acted justifiably. Strict liability replies, as Judge Blackburn puts it his *Rylands* opinion [infra p. 296], that fault liability "damnifies" victims "without any fault of [their] own." People who undertake purposeful, profitable activity for their own benefit should not be allowed to foist the costs of their actions, activities and choices onto others simply because they have proceeded carefully. Strict liability appeals to the moral intuition that I should bear the costs of my activities and you should bear the costs of yours.

The specific facts of the case are set out below. But some more general background is also worth mentioning. The events which gave rise to Fletcher's suit against Rylands took place near Lancashire, in the north of England, in 1862. The industrial revolution was in its first full bloom, and both Fletcher and Rylands were full participants in this early blossoming of industrial activity. Fletcher was mining coal and Rylands was milling cotton. These two industries were the backbone of the economy of England's industrial north, and critical to the economy of the entire country. They were on the cutting edge of the industrial revolution; they coexisted in close proximity to each other; and they clashed over water. (The flooding of Fletcher's mine by water which escaped from a reservoir Rylands had constructed to supply his cotton mill occasioned the lawsuit.) Water was a resource needed by cotton mills, a hazard to mines, and a standing source of friction between the two enterprises.

FLETCHER v. RYLANDS

Exchequer Chamber, 1866. L.R. 1 Exch. 265.

RYLANDS v. FLETCHER

House of Lords, 1868. L.R. 3 H.L. 330.

[In November, 1861, Fletcher brought an action against Rylands and Horrocks to recover damages for an injury caused to his mines by water flowing into them from a reservoir which defendants had constructed. The declaration (set out in L.R. 1 Exch. 265, 266) contained three counts, each count alleging negligence on the part of the defendants. The case came on for trial at the Liverpool Summer Assizes, 1862, when a verdict was entered for the plaintiff, subject to an award to be thereafter made by an arbitrator. Subsequently the arbitrator was directed, instead of making an award, to state a special case for the consideration of the Court of Exchequer.

The material facts in the special case stated by the arbitrator were as follows:—Fletcher, under a lease from Lord Wilton, and under arrangements with other landowners, was working coal mines under certain lands. He had worked the mines up to a spot where he came upon old horizontal passages of disused mines, and also upon vertical shafts which seemed filled with marl and rubbish.

Rylands and Horrocks owned a mill standing on land near that under which Fletcher's mines were worked. With permission of Lord Wilton, they constructed on Lord Wilton's land a reservoir to supply water to their mill. They employed a competent engineer and competent contractors to construct the reservoir. It was not known to Rylands and Horrocks, nor to any of the persons employed by them, that any coal had ever been worked under or near the site of the reservoir; but in point of fact the coal under the site of the reservoir had been partially worked at some time or other beyond living memory, and there were old coal workings under the site of the reservoir communicating by means of other and intervening old underground workings with the recent workings of Fletcher.

In the course of constructing and excavating for the bed of the said reservoir, five old shafts, running vertically downwards, were met with in the portion of land selected for the site of the said reservoir. At the time they were so met with the sides or walls of at least three of them were constructed of timber, and were still in existence, but the shafts themselves were filled up with marl, or soil of the same kind as the marl or soil which immediately surrounded them, and it was not known to, or suspected by, the defendants, or any of the persons employed by them in or about the planning or constructing of the said reservoir, that they were (as they afterwards proved to be) shafts which had been made for the purpose of getting the coal under the land in which the said reservoir was made, or that they led down to coal workings under the site of the said reservoir.

For the selection of the site of the said reservoir, and for the planning and constructing thereof, it was necessary that the defendants should employ an engineer and contractors, and they did employ for those purposes a competent engineer and competent contractors, by and under whom the said site was selected and the said reservoir was planned and constructed, and on the part of the defendants themselves there was no personal negligence or default whatever in or about or in relation to the selection of the said site, or in or about the planning or construction of the said reservoir; but in point of fact reasonable and proper care and skill were not exercised by or on the part of the persons so employed by them, with reference to the shafts so met with as aforesaid, to provide for the sufficiency of the said reservoir to bear the pressure of water which, when filled to the height proposed, it would have to bear.

The reservoir was completed about the beginning of December, 1860, when the defendants caused the same to be partially filled with water, and on the morning of the 11th December in the same year, whilst the reservoir was so partially filled, one of the shafts which had been so met with as aforesaid gave way and burst downwards; in consequence of which the water of the reservoir flowed into the old workings underneath, and by means of the underground communications so then existing between those old coal workings and the plaintiff's coal workings in the plaintiff's colliery, as above described, large quantities of the water so flowing from the said reservoir as aforesaid found their way into the said coal workings in the plaintiff's colliery, and by reason thereof the said colliery became and was flooded, and the working thereof was obliged to be and was for a time necessarily suspended.

The question for the opinion of the Court was whether the plaintiff was entitled to recover damages from the defendants by reason of the matters thus stated by the arbitrator.

The Court of Exchequer, POLLOCK, C. B., and MARTIN, B., concurring; BRAMWELL, B., dissenting [(1865, 3 H. & C. 774) gave judgment for the defendants.]

Plaintiff brought error in the Exchequer Chamber.

BLACKBURN, J. This was a special case stated by an arbitrator, under an order of nisi prius, in which the question for the Court is stated to be, whether the plaintiff is entitled to recover any and, if any, what damages from the defendants by reason of the matters thereinbefore stated. * * *

The plaintiff, though free from all blame on his part, must bear the loss, unless he can establish that it was the consequence of some default for which the defendants are responsible. The question of law therefore arises, what is the obligation which the law casts on a person who, like the defendants, lawfully brings on his land something which, though harmless whilst it remains there, will naturally do mischief if it escape out of his land. It is agreed on all hands that he must take care to keep in that which he has brought on the land and keeps there, in order that it may not escape and damage his neighbors; but the question arises whether the duty which the law casts upon him, under such circumstances, is an absolute duty to keep it in at his peril, or is, as the majority of the Court of Exchequer have thought, merely a duty to take all reasonable and prudent precautions in order to keep it in, but no more. If the first be the law, the person who has brought on his land and kept there something dangerous, and failed to keep it in, is responsible for all the natural consequences of its escape. If the second be the limit of his duty, he would not be answerable except on proof of negligence, and consequently would not be answerable for escape arising from any latent defect which ordinary prudence and skill could not detect.

Supposing the second to be the correct view of the law, a further question arises subsidiary to the first, viz., whether the defendants are not so far identified with the contractors whom they employed as to be responsible for the consequences of their want of care and skill in making the reservoir in fact insufficient with reference to the old shafts, of the existence of which they were aware, though they had not ascertained where the shafts went to.

We think that the true rule of law is that the person who for his own purposes brings on his lands and collects and keeps there anything likely to do mischief if it escapes, must keep it in at his peril, and if he does not do so, is prima facie answerable for all the damage which is the natural consequence of its escape. He can excuse himself by showing that the escape was owing to the plaintiff's default; or perhaps that the escape was the consequence of vis major, or the act of God; but as nothing of this sort exists here, it is unnecessary to inquire what excuse would be sufficient. The general rule, as above stated, seems on principle just. The person whose grass or corn is eaten down by the escaping cattle of his neighbor, or whose mine is flooded by the water from his neighbor's reservoir, or whose cellar is invaded by the filth of his neighbor's privy, or whose habitation is made unhealthy by the fumes and noisome vapors of his neighbor's alkali works, is damnified without any fault of his own; and it seems but reasonable and just that the neighbor, who has brought something on his own property which was not naturally there, harmless to others so long as it is confined to his own property, but which he knows to be mischievous if it gets on his neighbor's, should be obliged to make good the damage which ensues if he does not succeed in confining it to his own property. But for his act in bringing it there no mischief could have accrued, and it seems but just that he should at his peril keep it there, so that no mischief may accrue, or answer for the natural and anticipated consequences. And upon authority, this we think is established to be the law, whether the things so brought be beasts, or water, or filth, or stenches.

The case that has most commonly occurred and which is most frequently to be found in the books is as to the obligation of the owner of cattle which he has brought on his land to prevent their escaping and doing mischief. The law as to them seems to be perfectly settled from early times; the owner must keep them in at his peril, or he will be answerable for the natural consequences of their escape; that is, with regard to tame beasts, for the grass they eat and trample upon, though not for any injury to the person of others, for our ancestors have settled that it is not the general nature of horses to kick, or bulls to gore; but if the owner knows that the beast has a vicious propensity to attack man, he will be answerable for that too. [The court here discussed the rules with reference to the liability for trespasses of cattle and for harm done by animals.]

As has been already said, there does not appear to be any difference in principle between the extent of the duty cast on him who brings cattle on his land to keep them in, and the extent of the duty imposed on him who brings on his land water, filth, or stenches, or any other thing which will, if it escape, naturally do damage, to prevent their escaping and injuring his neighbor; and the case of Tenant v. Goldwin [1 Salk. 21, 360; 2 Ld.Raym. 1089], is an express authority that the duty is the same and, is, to keep them in at his peril. [The court here discussed Tenant v. Goldwin in which case it was held that the defendant was liable for harm caused by the seepage of filth from the defendant's privy through a wall to the plaintiff's premises, on the analogy of the animal trespass cases.]

No case has been found in which the question as to the liability for noxious vapors escaping from a man's works by inevitable accident has been discussed, but the following case will illustrate it. Some years ago several actions were brought against the occupiers of some alkali works at Liverpool for the damage alleged to be caused by the chlorine fumes of their works. The defendants proved that they at great expense erected contrivances by which the fumes of chlorine were condensed and sold as muriatic acid, and they called a great body of scientific evidence to prove that this apparatus was so perfect that no fumes possibly could escape from the defendants' chimneys. On this evidence it was pressed upon the jury that the plaintiff's damage must have been due to some of the numerous other chimneys in the neighborhood; the jury, however, being satisfied that the mischief was occasioned by chlorine, drew the conclusion that it had escaped from the defendants' works somehow, and in each case found for the plaintiff. No attempt was made to disturb these verdicts on the ground that the defendants had taken every precaution which prudence or skill could suggest to keep those fumes in, and that they could not be responsible unless negligence were shown; yet, if the law be as laid down by the majority of the Court of Exchequer, it would have been a very obvious defense. If it had been raised the answer would probably have been that the uniform course of pleading in actions on such nuisances is to say that the defendant caused the noisome vapors to arise on his premises, and suffered them to come on the plaintiff's, without stating that there was any want of care or skill in the defendant, and that the case of Tenant v. Goldwin, supra, showed that this was founded on the general rule of law, that he whose stuff it is must keep it that it may not trespass. There is no difference in this respect between chlorine and water; both will if they escape do damage, the one by scorching and the other by drowning, and he who brings them there must at his peril see that they do not escape and do that mischief. What is said by Gibbs, C. J., in Sutton v. Clarke, 6 Taunt. 44, though not necessary for the decision of the case, shows that that very learned judge took the same view of the law that was taken by Lord Holt.

But it was further said by Martin, B., [in the Court of Exchequer] that when damage is done to personal property, or even to the person, by collision, either upon land or at sea, there must be negligence in the party doing the damage to render him legally responsible; and this is no doubt true, and as was pointed out by Mr. Mellish during his argument before us, this is not confined to cases of collision, for there are many cases in which proof of negligence is essential, as, for instance, where an unruly horse gets on the footpath of a public street and kills a passenger, Hammack v. White, 11 C.B.,N.S., 588, 31 L.J.,C.P., 129; or where a person in a dock is struck by the falling of a bale of cotton which the defendant's servants are lowering: Scott v. London Dock Company, 3 H. & C. 596, 35 L.J.Ex., 17,220; and many other similar cases may be found. But we think these cases distinguishable from the present. Traffic on the highways, whether by land or sea, cannot be conducted without exposing those whose persons or property are near it to some inevitable risk; and that being so, those who go on the highway, or have their property adjacent to it, may well be held to do so subject to their taking upon themselves the risk of injury from that inevitable danger; and persons who by the license of the owner pass near to warehouses where goods are being raised or lowered, certainly do so subject to the inevitable risk of accident. In neither case, therefore, can they recover without proof of want of care or skill occasioning the accident; and it is believed that all the cases in which inevitable accident has been held an excuse for what prima facie was a trespass, can be explained on the same principle, viz., that the circumstances were such as to show that the plaintiff had taken that risk upon himself. But there is no ground for saying that the plaintiff here took upon himself any risk arising from the uses to which the defendants should choose to apply their land. He neither knew what these might be, nor could he in any way control the defendants, or hinder their building what reservoirs they liked, and storing up in them what water they pleased, so long as the defendants succeeded in preventing the water which they there brought from interfering with the plaintiff's property.

The view which we take of the first point renders it unnecessary to consider whether the defendants would or would not be responsible for the want of care and skill in the persons employed by them, under the circumstances stated in the case.

We are of opinion that the plaintiff is entitled to recover, but as we have not heard any argument as to the amount, we are not able to give judgment for what damages. The parties probably will empower their counsel to agree on the amount of damages; should they differ on the principle the case may be mentioned again.

Judgment for the plaintiff.

[Rylands and Horrocks brought error in the House of Lords against the judgment of the Exchequer Chamber.]

THE LORD CHANCELLOR (LORD CAIRNS) [after stating the facts]. My Lords, the principles on which this case must be determined appear to me to be extremely simple. The defendants, treating them as the owners or occupiers of the close on which the reservoir was constructed, might lawfully have used that close for any purpose for which it might in the ordinary course of the enjoyment of land be used; and if, in what I may term the natural user of that land, there had been any accumulation of water, either on the surface or under ground, and if, by the operation of the laws of nature, that accumulation of water had passed off into the close occupied by the plaintiff, the plaintiff could not have complained that that result had taken place. If he had desired to guard himself against it, it would have lain upon him to have done so by leaving, or by interposing, some barrier between his close and the close of the defendants in order to have prevented that operation of the laws of nature. * * *

On the other hand, if the defendants, not stopping at the natural use of their close, had desired to use it for any purpose which I may term a non-natural use for the purpose of introducing into the close that which in its natural condition was not in or upon it, for the purpose of introducing water either above or below ground in quantities and in a manner not the result of any work or operation on or under the land; and if in consequence of their doing so, or in consequence of any imperfection in the mode of their doing so, the water came to escape and to pass off into the close of the plaintiff, then it appears to me that that which the defendants were doing they were doing at their own peril; and if in the course of their doing it the evil arose to which I have referred, the evil, namely, of the escape of the water and its passing away to the close of the plaintiff and injuring the plaintiff, then for the consequence of that, in my opinion, the defendants would be liable. * * *

My Lords, these simple principles, if they are well founded, as it appears to me they are, really dispose of this case.

[LORD CAIRNS here quotes BLACKBURN, J.'s., opinion in the Exchequer Chamber]. My Lords, in that opinion I must say I entirely concur. Therefore, I have to move your Lordships that the judgment of the Court of Exchequer Chamber be affirmed, and that the present appeal be dismissed with costs.

LORD CRANWORTH. My Lords, I concur with my noble and learned friend in thinking that the rule of law was correctly stated by Mr. Justice BLACKBURN in delivering the opinion of the Exchequer Chamber. If a person brings, or accumulates, on his land anything which, if it should escape, may cause damage to his neighbor, he does so at his peril. If it does escape and cause damage, he is responsible, however careful he may have been, and whatever precautions he may have taken to prevent the damage.

In considering whether a defendant is liable to a plaintiff for damage which the plaintiff may have sustained, the question in general is not whether the defendant has acted with due care and caution, but whether his acts have occasioned the damage. This is all well explained in the old case of Lambert v. Bessey, reported by Sir Thomas Raymond (Sir T. Raym. 421).* And the doctrine is founded on good sense. For when one person, in managing his own affairs, causes, however innocently, damage to another, it

---

* [Eds.] The case mentioned by Lord Cranworth had been emphasized by Fletcher's counsel, who used it to establish the proposition that "if a man doeth a lawful act, yet if injury to another ariseth from it, the man who does the act shall be answerable." L.R. 3 H.L. at 337. The quoted language states the holding of the fifteenth century Case of the Thorns (see p. 284 supra), which was summarized by Sir Thomas Raymond in his report of the seventeenth century Lambert v. Bessey decision.

is obviously only just that he should be the party to suffer. He is bound sic uti suo ut non loedat alienum. This is the principle of law applicable to cases like the present, and I do not discover in the authorities which were cited anything conflicting with it. * * *

[Lord Cranworth here discusses Smith v. Kenrick, 7 C.B. 515, 137 Eng.Rep. 205 (1849), and Baird v. Williamson, 15 C.B.,N.S., 376, 143 Eng.Rep. 831 (1863). In Smith, the owner of a coal mine, in working it, left no barrier between it and a mine on a lower level. The water percolating through the upper mine flowed into the lower mine. The owner of the lower mine was held to have no ground of complaint, the damage being occasioned by natural flow. In Baird, on the other hand, the owner of an upper mine pumped up quantities of water, which passed into the plaintiff's mine in addition to the natural flow. Though this was done without negligence, he was held liable.]

Applying the principle of these decisions to the case now before the House, I come without hesitation to the conclusion that the judgment of the Exchequer Chamber was right. The plaintiff had a right to work his coal through the lands of Mr. Whitehead and up to the old workings. If water naturally rising in the defendants' land (we may treat the land as the land of the defendants for the purpose of this case) had by percolation found its way down to the plaintiff's mine through the old workings, and so had impeded his operations, that would not have afforded him any ground of complaint. Even if all the old workings had been made by the plaintiff, he would have done no more than he was entitled to do; for, according to the principle acted on in Smith v. Kenrick, [7 C.B. 515] the person working the mine under the close in which the reservoir was made had a right to win and carry away all the coal without leaving any wall or barrier against Whitehead's land. But that is not the real state of the case. The defendants, in order to effect an object of their own, brought on to their land, or on to land which for this purpose may be treated as being theirs, a large accumulated mass of water, and stored it up in a reservoir. The consequence of this was damage to the plaintiff, and for that damage, however skilfully and carefully the accumulation was made, the defendants, according to the principles and authorities to which I have adverted, were certainly responsible.

I concur, therefore, with my noble and learned friend in thinking that the judgment below must be affirmed, and that there must be judgment for the defendant in error.

Judgment of the Court of Exchequer Chamber affirmed.

LOSEE v. BUCHANAN
Commission of Appeals of New York, 1873.
51 N.Y. 476.

[This action was for damages caused by the explosion of a steam boiler used at a paper mill. The explosion projected parts of the boiler on to plaintiff's premises, injuring buildings and personal property. The appellate opinion below of the Commission, a special tribunal created by the New

York legislature in this period to clear up a backlog in appeals, follows an original trial, a reversal and remand, and a second trial.]

EARL, C. * * * The plaintiff claimed, as he did upon the first trial, that the defendants were liable without the proof of any negligence, and requested the justice so to rule, and the refusal of the justice to comply with this request raises the principal question for our consideration upon this appeal.

* * *

The claim on the part of the plaintiff is, that the casting of the boiler upon his premises by the explosion was a direct trespass upon his right to the undisturbed possession and occupation of his premises, and that the defendants are liable just as they would have been for any other wrongful entry and trespass upon his premises.

I do not believe this claim to be well founded, and I will briefly examine the authorities upon which mainly an attempt is made to sustain it.

* * * In Hay v. The Cohoes Company (2 Comst., 159), the defendant, a corporation, dug a canal upon its own land for the purposes authorized by its charter. In so doing it was necessary to blast rocks with gunpowder, and the fragments were thrown against and injured the plaintiff's dwelling upon lands adjoining. It was held that the defendant was liable for the injury, although no negligence or want of skill in executing the work was alleged or proved. This decision was well supported by the clearest principles. The acts of the defendant in casting the rocks upon plaintiff's premises were direct and immediate. The damage was the necessary consequence of just what the defendant was doing, and it was just as much liable as if it had caused the rocks to be taken by hand, or any other means, and thrown directly upon plaintiff's land. This is far from an authority for holding that the defendants, who placed a steam boiler upon their lands, and operated the same with care and skill, should be liable for the damages caused by the explosion, without their fault or any direct or immediate act of theirs. It is true that Judge Gardner, in writing the opinion of the court, lays down broadly the principle that "every individual is entitled to the undisturbed possession and lawful enjoyment of his own property," citing the maxim *sic utere tuo*,* etc. But this principle, as well as the maxim, as will be seen, has many exceptions and limitations, made necessary by the exigencies of business and society.

* * *

In the case of McKeon v. Lee (4 Rob. Superior Court R., 449) it was held, that the defendant had no right to operate a steam engine and other machinery upon his premises so as to cause the vibration and shaking of plaintiff's adjoining buildings to such an extent as to endanger and injure them. This case was decided upon the law of nuisances. It was held that the engine and machinery, in the mode in which they were operated, were a nuisance, and the decision has been affirmed at this term of this court. The

---

* [Eds.] Sic utere tuo ut alienum non laedas   to injure that of another).
(Use your own property in such a manner as not

decision in this case, and in scores of similar cases to be found in the books, is far from an authority that one should be held liable for the accidental explosion of a steam boiler which was in no sense a nuisance. * * *

Blackstone (vol. 3, p. 209) says, "that whenever an act is directly and immediately injurious to the person or property of another, and therefore necessarily accompanied with some force, an action of trespass *vi et armis* will lie;" for "the right of *meum* and *tuum* or property in lands being once established, it follows as a necessary consequence that this right must be exclusive; that is, that the owner may retain to himself the sole use and occupation of his soil. Every entry, therefore, thereon without the owner's leave, and especially contrary to his express order, is a trespass or transgression." The learned author was here laying down the distinction between an action of trespass and trespass on the case, and asserting the rule that in the former action the injury must be direct and immediate, and accompanied with some force, whereas in the latter action it could be indirect and consequential. He was also manifestly speaking of a direct entrance by one upon the lands of another. He was laying down a general rule that every unauthorized entrance upon the land of another is a trespass. This was sufficiently accurate for the enunciation of a general rule. Judges and legal writers do not always find it convenient, practicable or important, in laying down general rules, to specify all the limitations and exceptions to such rules. The rule, as thus announced, has many exceptions, even when one makes a personal entry upon the lands of another. I may enter my neighbor's close to succor his beast whose life is in danger; to prevent his beasts from being stolen or to prevent his grain from being consumed or spoiled by cattle; or to carry away my tree which has been blown down upon his land, or to pick up my apples which have fallen from my trees upon his land, or to take my personal property which another has wrongfully taken and placed there, or to escape from one who threatens my life. (Bacon's Abridgment, Trespass, F.) Other illustrations will be given hereafter.

By becoming a member of civilized society, I am compelled to give up many of my natural rights, but I receive more than a compensation from the surrender by every other man of the same rights, and the security, advantage and protection which the laws give me. So, too, the general rules that I may have the exclusive and undisturbed use and possession of my real estate, and that I must so use my real estate as not to injure my neighbor, are much modified by the exigencies of the social state. We must have factories, machinery, dams, canals and railroads. They are demanded by the manifold wants of mankind, and lay at the basis of all our civilization. If I have any of these upon my lands, and they are not a nuisance and are not so managed as to become such, I am not responsible for any damage they accidentally and unavoidably do my neighbor. He receives his compensation for such damage by the general good, in which he shares, and the right which he has to place the same things upon his lands. I may not place or keep a nuisance upon my land to the damage of my neighbor, and I have my compensation for the surrender of this right to use my own as I will by the similar restriction imposed upon my neighbor for my benefit. I hold my property subject to the risk that it may be unavoidably or accidentally injured by those who live near me; and as I move about upon the public highways and in all places where other persons may lawfully be, I take the risk of being accidentally injured in my person by them without fault on their part. Most of the rights of property, as well as of person, in the social state, are not absolute but relative, and they must be so arranged and modified, not unnecessarily infringing upon natural rights, as upon the whole to promote the general welfare.

I have so far found no authorities and no principles which fairly sustain the broad claim made by the plaintiff, that the defendants are liable in this action without fault or negligence on their part to which the explosion of the boiler could be attributed.

But our attention is called to a recent English case, decided in the Exchequer Chamber, which seems to uphold the claim made. In the case of Fletcher v. Rylands (1 Exchequer, 265, Law Reports) the defendants constructed a reservoir on land separated from the plaintiff's colliery by intervening land. * * * That case was appealed to the House of Lords and affirmed (3 H.L. [Law Rep.], 330), and was followed in Smith v. Fletcher (20 W.R., 987).

It is sufficient, however, to say that the law, as laid down in those cases, is in direct conflict with the law as settled in this country. Here, if one builds a dam upon his own premises and thus holds back and accumulates the water for his benefit, or if he brings water upon his premises into a reservoir, in case the dam or the banks of the reservoir give away and the lands of a neighbor are thus flooded, he is not liable for the damage without proof of some fault or negligence on his part.

* * *

In conflict with the rule as laid down in the English cases is a class of cases in reference to damage from fire communicated from the adjoining premises. Fire, like water or steam, is likely to produce mischief if it escapes and goes beyond control; and yet it has never been held in this country that one building a fire upon his own premises can be made liable if it escapes upon his neighbor's premises and does him damage without proof of negligence. The rule, as laid down in Clark v. Foot, is as follows: "If A. sets fire to his own fallow ground, as he may lawfully do, which communicates to and fires the woodland of B., his neighbor, no action lies against A. unless there was some negligence or misconduct in him or his servant." And this is the rule throughout this country except where it has been modified by statute. * * *

* * * All these cases and the class of cases to which they belong are in conflict with the rule as claimed by the plaintiff. A man may build a fire in his house or his steam boiler, and he does not become liable without proof of negligence if sparks accidentally pass directly from his chimney or smokestack to the buildings of his neighbor. The maxim of *sic utere tuo*, etc., only requires, in such a case the exercise of adequate skill and care.

The same rule applies to injuries to the person. No one in such case is made liable without some fault or negligence on his part, however serious the injury may be which he may accidentally cause; and there can be no reason for holding one liable for accidental injuries to property when he is exempt from liability for such injuries to the person. It is settled in numerous cases that if one driving along a highway accidentally injures another he is not liable without proof of negligence.

In Hussey v. Dunlap, (Lalor's Supplement, 193), the action was for throwing a stone at the plaintiff's daughter and putting out her eye. It did not appear that the injury was inflicted by design or carelessness, but did appear that it was accidental, and the court held that the plaintiff could not recover, laying down the broad rule that no liability results from the commission of an act arising from inevitable accident, or which ordinary human care and foresight could not guard against. * * *

[The court here describes Brown v. Kendall, 60 Mass. (6 Cush.) 292 (1850), and includes excerpts from Chief Justice Shaw's opinion in that case.]

In support of the plaintiff's claim in this action the rule has been invoked that, where one of two innocent parties must suffer, he who puts in motion the cause of the injury must bear the loss. But, as will be seen by the numerous cases above cited, it has no application whatever to a case like this.

This examination has gone far enough to show that the rule is, at least in this country, a universal one, which, so far as I can discern, has no exceptions or limitations, that no one can be made liable for injuries to the person or property of another without some fault or negligence on his part.

In this case the defendants had the right to place the steam boiler upon their premises. It was in no sense a nuisance, and the jury have found that they were not guilty of any negligence. The judgment in their favor should, therefore, have been affirmed at the General Term * * *.

* * *

BROWN v. COLLINS, 53 N.H. 442, 16 Am.Rep. 372 (1873). Defendant was driving his horses with due care on a public highway when they became frightened by a locomotive and unmanageable. They ran upon plaintiff's land and broke a post there. Plaintiff sued in trespass to recover the post's value. The court, in an opinion by DOE, J., held that defendant was not liable.

In criticizing such principles of a liability without negligence as may have existed in the English common law, the court stated:

"It would seem that some of the early English decisions were based on a view as narrow as that which regards nothing but the hardship 'of the party suffering;' disregards the question whether, by transferring the hardship to the other party, any thing more will be done than substitute one suffering party for another; and does not consider what legal reason can be given for relieving the party who has suffered, by making another suffer the expense of his relief. For some of those decisions, better reasons may now be given than were thought of when the decisions were announced: but whether a satisfactory test of an actionable tort can be extracted from the ancient authorities, and whether the few modern cases that carry out the doctrine of those authorities as far as it is carried in [Rylands v. Fletcher] can be sustained, is very doubtful. The current of American authority is very strongly against some of the leading English cases.''

[In its extended criticism of the opinions in Rylands v. Fletcher, the court observed:]

"Every thing that a man can bring on his land is capable of escaping, against his will, and without his fault, with or without assistance, in some form, solid, liquid, or gaseous, changed or unchanged by the transforming processes of nature or art, and of doing damage after its escape. * * * This is going back a long way for a standard of legal rights, and adopting an arbitrary test of responsibility that confounds all degrees of danger, pays no heed to the essential elements of actual fault, puts a clog upon natural and reasonably necessary uses of matter, and tends to embarrass and obstruct much of the work which it seems to be man's duty carefully to do. The distinction made by Lord CAIRNS, Rylands v. Fletcher, L.R., 3 H.L. 330, between a natural and a non-natural use of land, if he meant any thing more than the difference between a reasonable use and an unreasonable one, is not established in the law. Even if the arbitrary test were applied only to things which a man brings on his land, it would still recognize the peculiar rights of savage life in the wilderness, ignore the rights growing out of a civilized state of society, and makes a distinction not warranted by the enlightened spirit of the common law: it would impose a penalty upon efforts, made in a reasonable, skillful, and careful manner, to rise above a condition of barbarism. It is impossible that legal principle can throw so serious an obstacle in the way of progress and improvement. * * *

* * *

"It is not improbable that the rules of liability [without negligence] for damage done by brutes or by fire, found in the early English cases, were introduced, by sacerdotal influence, from what was supposed to be the Roman or the Hebrew law. It would not be singular if these rules should be spontaneously produced at a certain period in the life of any community. Where they first appeared is of little consequence in the present inquiry. They were certainly introduced in England at an immature stage of English jurisprudence, and an undeveloped state of agriculture, manufactures, and commerce, when the nation had not settled down to those modern, progressive, industrial pursuits which the spirit of the common law, adapted to all conditions of society, encourages and defends. They were introduced when the development of many of the rational rules now universally recognized as principles of the common law had not been demanded by the growth of intelligence, trade and productive enterprise, when the common law had not been set forth in the precedents, as a coherent and logical system on many subjects other than the tenures of real estate. At all events, whatever may be said of the origin of those rules, to extend them, as they were extended in Rylands v. Fletcher, seems to us contrary to the analogies and the general principles of the common law, as now established. * * * ''

———

ROBB v. CARNEGIE BROS & CO., 22 A. 649, 145 Pa. 324 (1891). Plaintiff brought suit to recover damages for injuries to his farm inflicted by smoke and gases emanating from coke-ovens erected and operated by defendants on adjoining land. Plaintiff prevailed in the trial court, and defendants appealed. *Held*, reversed. Plaintiff may recover "for his actual loss in the products of his farm or the destruction of his soil," but "shall not be allowed exemplary damages * * * so that the defendants shall not be treated as wrongdoers in the establishment of their plant on a well-selected and secluded tract of land belonging to themselves."

"The coal company was using its own land in the only manner practicable to it. The harm done thereby to others was the least in amount consistent with the natural and lawful use of its own. If this use was to be denied to the coal company, because some injury or inconvenience to others was unavoidable, then the result would be practical confiscation of the coal lands for the benefit of householders living on lower ground. But the defendants are not developing the minerals in their land, or cultivating its surface. They have erected coke-ovens upon it, and are engaged in the manufacture of coke. Their selection of this site, rather than some other, is due to its location, and to their convenience, and has no relation to the character of the soil, or to the presence or absence of underlying minerals. The selection was no doubt a wise one, quite secluded, and quite convenient to the several mines from which the material was to be obtained for the making of coke; but it was the selection of a manufacturing site, and is subject to the same considerations as though glass or lumber or iron had been the commodity to be produced instead of coke. * * * The injury, if any, resulting from the manufacture of coke at this site, is in no sense the natural and necessary consequence of the exercise of the legal rights of the owner to develop the resources of his property, but is the consequence of his election to devote his land to the establishment of a particular sort of manufacturing, having no natural connection with the soil or the subjacent strata. * * * "

"The plaintiff in this case is therefore in the right court, and, if he is substantially hurt by the use to which the defendants have seen fit to devote their land, we see no reason why he may not recover, * * *. It is a fundamental principle of our system of government that the interest of the public is higher than that of the individual, so that when these interests are in conflict the latter must give way. If the individual is thereby deprived of his property without fault on his part, he is entitled to compensation; but if he is affected only in his tastes, his personal comfort, or pleasure, or preferences, these he must surrender for the comfort and preferences of the many. Thus highways are necessary to the public business and comfort. Some noise and dust are necessarily occasioned by the legitimate use of them. This may be disagreeable, perhaps in some cases positively harmful, to some one or more of the persons living along them; but for this there is no remedy, at law or in equity. It is one of the necessary consequences of subjecting the individual to the public in those things as to which their interests are in conflict. Railroads have become the great highways of travel and commerce. The turnpike and canal have been superseded * * *. The law recognizes the public character of these highways. Their presence is necessary to the prosperity and comfort of the public. To some persons who live near them, as to some persons who live upon a busy city street, the incessant roar of business and the dust of passing vehicles or trains may be unpleasant or painful; but whether such persons live upon a country road, a paved street, or a railroad they are alike remediless. No action will lie against the municipality, the turnpike, or the railroad company for the noise and dust caused by the legitimate use or operation of the highway in either case. For negligence or malice the wrong-doer is liable to the party injured, but for the lawful use of the road, in the customary manner, no liability attaches to the traveler or owner. * * * "

"But the production of iron or steel or glass or coke, while of great public importance, stands on no different ground from any other branch of manufacturing, or from the cultivation of agricultural products. They are needed for use and consumption by the public, but they are the results of private enterprise, conducted for private profit and under the absolute control of the producer. He may increase his business at will, or diminish it. He may transfer it to another person, or place, or state, or abandon it. He may sell to whom he pleases, at such price as he pleases, or he may hoard his productions, and refuse to sell to any person or at any price. He is serving himself in his own way, and has no right to claim exemption from the natural consequences of his own act. The interests in conflict in this case are therefore not those of the public and of an individual, but those of two private owners who stand on equal ground as engaged in their own private business. * * * "

Chapter 8

REASONABLE CARE: GENERAL
CONSIDERATIONS

In this chapter we start our close, sustained look at negligence doctrine. The topic at hand is the general meaning of reasonable care. Here it is, for the most part, a useful simplification to assume that the duty to take reasonable care exists, and to ask what it amounts to. The tort obligation to use reasonable care to avoid causing accidental injury is, indeed, a very highly general legal duty.

What sort of analysis tells us whether an actor's conduct is unreasonable or reasonable, negligent or not negligent? This is the question pursued in the first and third sections of the chapter, which show negligence analysis at work. The intervening–second–section briefly introduces the possibility that, for special reasons, the general legal duty of due care might be modified or cut back. Special doctrines limiting and shaping the duty of due care are the central subject matter of Chapter 10.

The first and third sections of the chapter pursue the same general question—what is reasonable care?—but they focus on different kinds of situations where different types of analysis come to the fore.

In the three main cases of Section A, defendants are actors in charge of specific sorts of risk. "Risk" refers to the chance that someone might be physically injured by accident on account of the actor's activity. Here the actors' risky activities, in one line of business or another, are on-going. Risks are recurrent, not one-shot in character. The actors charged with negligence have time to plan ahead, and the capacity to plan. Their ability to control risk is not at issue. The question is: what to do? Which of possible precautions should be adopted?

In most of the eight main cases of Section C, actors charged with negligence are human individuals confronting the sorts of situations we all encounter in everyday life. In these cases risks are highly situational; they come up on the spot, in fast-moving circumstances. (Five of the cases involve traffic accidents.) It's pretty clear on reflection what these actors ought to have done, what "safety rule" should have been followed. The question is, not what to do, but how much to expect. How much acumen and self-discipline, for the sake of safety, should be expected from fallible humans? From persons of limited capacity?

SECTION A.   COSTS AND BENEFITS

What is "reasonable care" or "due care"? We know that negligence is the lack of it. In a negligence case, the actor creates an unreasonable risk of harm to another, whom harm befalls. What makes the actor's risk "unreasonable"? We might personify the issue, and ask what a reasonable person would have done. This approach seems question-begging—"Q: What is reasonable care? A: It's the care a reasonable person would use." But actually, it is a helpful start; it stimulates the right set of tacit understandings.

To become more definite, we need to be able to say something about the ethical nature of a reasonable person. The following passage from *The Nitro–Glycerine Case* (1872) of Chapter 7 is instructive:

> ... the measure of care against accident, which one must take to avoid responsibility, is that which a person of ordinary prudence and caution would use if his own interests were to be affected, and the whole risk were his own.

On this view, the reasonable person combines prudential capacity, skill and good judgment in the use of resources to advance ends over time, and an ethical commitment, not to disregard the interests of others, but to regard self and others as on a par. The reasonable person is not an egoist, one who devalues and exploits others; nor an altruist, prepared always to sacrifice self.

Reasonable care requires, then, striking a balance between one's own interests and the interests of others. Negligence analysis involves unbiased appraisal and comparison of conflicting interests, those in favor of running a risk, and those in favor of not running it. All explications of the idea of reasonable care emphasize, at some level, such weighing and balancing.

One particular formulation of the idea of negligence has been very influential. This is the "Hand formula"—or the "BPL" formula—introduced in Chapter 1, Section 2. According to the Hand formula, in every negligence case one must weigh "B" against "PL." The term "PL" refers to a risk, or a probability of loss; this notation calls attention to the fact that risks vary in two dimensions, degree of likelihood that harm will happen ("P") and gravity of harm threatened ("L"). The term "B," meaning burden, refers to a costly precaution which might be taken in order to avoid or reduce risk; that is, it refers to a possible safety precaution, and to the cost of it. In negligence analysis, "B" and "PL" are causally related; attention centers on a particular "B" which would avoid a particular "PL"; the question is whether the identified "B" ought to be borne in order to avert the corresponding "PL."

THE HAND FORMULA

[See p. 14, supra]

CHICAGO, BURLINGTON AND QUINCY
RAILROAD CO. v. KRAYENBUHL
Supreme Court of Nebraska, 1902.
65 Neb. 889, 91 N.W. 880.

[Plaintiff, a four-year-old, was playing with other children on and near defendant's railroad track. The children found defendant's turntable unlocked and unguarded, and set it in motion. Plaintiff's foot was caught between rails and severed at the ankle. In the course of reversing a judgment for plaintiff and remanding for further proceedings, the court addressed the principle that a landowner may expect trespassing young children to use potentially dangerous facilities on its land and should take reasonable precautions to prevent such use. It continued:]

* * * At first sight, it would seem that the principle, thus stated, is too broad, and that its application would impose unreasonable burdens on owners, and intolerable restrictions on the use and enjoyment of property. But it must be kept in mind that it requires nothing of the owner that a man of ordinary care and prudence would not do of his own volition, under like circumstances. Such a man would not willingly take up unreasonable burdens, nor vex himself with intolerable restrictions.

It is true, as said in Loomis v. Terry, 17 Wend. 497, 31 Am.Dec. 306, "the business of life must go forward"; the means by which it is carried forward cannot be rendered absolutely safe. Ordinarily, it can be best carried forward by the unrestricted use of private property by the owner; therefore the law favors such use to the fullest extent consistent with the main purpose for which, from a social standpoint, such business is carried forward, namely, the public good. Hence, in order to determine the extent to which such use may be enjoyed, its bearing on such main purpose must be taken into account, and a balance struck between its advantages and disadvantages. If, on the whole, such use defeats, rather than promotes, the main purpose, it should not be permitted; on the other hand, if the restrictions proposed would so operate, they should not be imposed. The business of life is better carried forward by the use of dangerous machinery; hence the public good demands its use, although occasionally such use results in the loss of life or limb. It does so because the danger is insignificant, when weighed against the benefits resulting from the use of such machinery, and for the same reason demands its reasonable, most effective, and unrestricted use, up to the point where the benefits resulting from such use no longer outweigh the danger to be anticipated from it. At that point the public good demands restrictions. For example, a turntable is a dangerous contrivance, which facilitates railroading; the general benefits resulting from its use outweigh the occasional injuries inflicted by it; hence the public good demands its use. We may conceive of means by which it might be rendered absolutely safe, but such means would so interfere with its beneficial use that the danger to be anticipated would not justify their adoption; therefore the public good demands its use without them. But the danger incident to its use may be lessened by the use of a lock which would prevent children, attracted to it, from moving it; the interference with the proper use of the turntable occasioned by the use of such lock is so slight that it is outweighed by the danger to be anticipated from an omission to use it; therefore the public good, we think, demands the use of the lock. The public good would not require the owner of a vacant lot on which there is a pond to fill up the pond or inclose the lot with an impassable wall to insure the safety of children resorting to it, because the burden of doing so is out of proportion to the danger to be anticipated from leaving it undone. But where there is an open well on a vacant lot, which is frequented by children, of which the owner of the lot has knowledge, he is liable for injuries sustained by children falling into the well, because the danger to be anticipated from the open well, under the circumstances, outweighs the slight expense or inconvenience that would be entailed in making it safe.

Hence, in all cases of this kind in the determination of the question of negligence, regard must be had to the character and location of the premises, the purpose for which they are used, the probability of injury therefrom, the precautions necessary to prevent such injury, and the relations such precautions bear to the beneficial use of the premises. The nature of the precautions would depend on the particular facts in each case. In some cases a warning to the children or the parents might be sufficient; in others, more active measures might be required. But in every case they should be such as a man of ordinary care and prudence would observe under like circumstances. If, under all the circumstances, the owner omits such precautions as a man of ordinary care and prudence, under like circumstances, would observe, he is guilty of negligence. * * *

OSBORNE v. MONTGOMERY, 203 Wis. 223, 234 N.W. 372 (1931). Action for personal injuries caused by defendant's opening, without looking back or giving any warning, the left hand door of a parked automobile at the moment when the plaintiff was passing on his bicycle. *Held*, although reversing the judgment and ordering a new trial because the verdict was excessive, that the plaintiff had made out a cause of action. In upholding the charge to the jury, ROSENBERRY, C. J., said: "The fundamental idea of liability for wrongful acts is that upon a balancing of the social interests involved in each case, the law determines that under the circumstances of a particular case an actor should or should not become liable for the natural consequences of his conduct. One driving a car in a thickly populated district, on a rainy day, slowly and in the most careful manner, may do injury to the person of another by throwing muddy or infected water upon that person. Society does not hold the actor responsible because the benefit of allowing people to travel under such circumstances so far outweighs the probable injury to bystanders that such conduct is not disapproved. Circumstances may require the driver of a fire truck to take his truck through a thickly populated district at a high rate of speed, but if he exercises that degree of care which such drivers ordinarily exercise under the same or similar circumstances, society, weighing the benefits against the probabilities of damage, in spite of the fact that as a reasonably prudent and intelligent man he should foresee that harm may result, justifies the risk and holds him not liable."

RESTATEMENT OF TORTS, THIRD: LIABILITY FOR PHYSICAL HARM (BASIC PRINCIPLES)

Tent. Draft No. 1 (March 28, 2001).

§ 3. Negligence

A person acts with negligence if the person does not exercise reasonable care under all the circumstances. Primary factors to consider in ascertaining whether the person's conduct lacks reasonable care are the foreseeable likelihood that it will result in harm, the foreseeable severity of the harm that may ensue, and the burden that would be borne by the person and others if the person takes precautions that eliminate or reduce the possibility of harm.

Comment:

a. Terminology. Conduct that displays reasonable care is the same as conduct that is reasonable, conduct that shows "ordinary care," conduct that avoids creating an "unreasonable risk of harm," and conduct that shows "reasonable prudence." Because a "reasonably careful person" (or a "reasonably prudent person") is one who acts with reasonable care, the "reasonable care" standard for negligence is basically the same as a standard expressed in terms of the "reasonably careful person" (or the "reasonably prudent person").

b. Negligence and contributory negligence. The definition of negligence set forth in this section applies whether the issue is the negligence of the defendant or the contributory negligence of the plaintiff. There are, however, certain differences in emphasis between negligence and contributory negligence. A defendant is held liable for negligent conduct primarily because that conduct creates a risk of harm to a third party; the plaintiff's contributory negligence serves as at least a partial affirmative defense primarily because it exposes the plaintiff to a risk of harm. * * *

e. Balancing risks and benefits. Insofar as this section identifies primary factors for ascertaining negligence, it can be said to suggest a "risk-benefit test" for negligence, where the "risk" is the overall level of the foreseeable risk created by the actor's conduct and the "benefit" is the advantages that the actor or others gain if the actor refrains from taking precautions. (Hence this benefit is the same as the burdens which the precautions, if adopted, would entail.) The test can also be called a "cost-benefit test," where "cost" signifies the cost of precautions and the "benefit" is the reduction in risk those precautions would achieve. Overall, this section can be referred to as supporting a "balancing approach" to negligence.

The balancing approach rests on and expresses a simple idea. Conduct is negligent if its disadvantages outweigh its advantages, while conduct is not negligent if its advantages outweigh its disadvantages. The disadvantage in question is the magnitude of risk that the conduct occasions: as noted, the phrase "magnitude of the risk" includes both the foreseeable likelihood of harm and the foreseeable severity of harm, should an incident ensue. The "advantages" of the conduct relate to the burdens of risk prevention that are avoided when the actor declines to incorporate some precaution. The actor's conduct is hence negligent if the magnitude of the risk outweighs the burden of risk prevention. * * *

———

TWOHIG v. BRINER, 168 Cal.App.3d 1102, 214 Cal.Rptr. 729 (1985). Candace Twohig, a passenger in the front seat of a car owned and driven by Janet Briner, was injured in a two-car collision. There were no seatbelts in the car for a passenger to use at the time of the accident. Twohig sued Briner alleging that Briner had created an unreasonable risk of harm to her passengers even if not at fault in the accident itself, because seatbelts for occupants had been removed with Briner's knowledge while she owned the car. The trial court granted summary judgment in favor of defendant. On appeal, *held,* for plaintiff. Injury from lack of a seatbelt is foreseeable, since "foreseeability is not to be measured by what is more probable than not, but includes whatever is likely enough in the setting of modern life that a reasonably thoughtful [person] would take account of it in guiding practical conduct." One may be held negligent for creating even "the risk of a slight possibility of injury if a reasonably prudent [person] would not do so."

> [R]emoving the seatbelts [exposes] passengers to increased danger by eliminating their option to "buckle up" so as to reduce the probability of suffering personal injuries resulting from "second collisions." It is entirely foreseeable, indeed likely, an owner/operator of an automobile will be involved in vehicle accidents resulting in "second collision" injuries to passengers even when driving with due care. In light of the circumstances of modern life, Briner should have foreseen the probability of the very type of accident occurring here, with "second collision" injuries to her passenger. Moreover, it is of no consequence the accident was caused solely by the fault of a third party, because the likelihood a third person may so act constitutes a hazard underscoring Briner's negligence, if in fact it is established she removed manufacturer-installed seat belts from her [car], and thus does not sever liability for the resulting harm.

DAVIS v. CONSOLIDATED RAIL CORP.

United States Court of Appeals, Seventh Circuit, 1986.
788 F.2d 1260.

POSNER, Circuit Judge.

This is a personal injury suit under the diversity jurisdiction; the substantive issues are governed by the tort law of Illinois. The suit arises from an accident that occurred in 1983. The plaintiff, Davis, was 33 years old at the time, an experienced railroad worker who for the past six years had been employed as an inspector of cars by the Trailer Train Company, a lessor of piggyback cars to railroads. He made the inspections in railroad yards, among them Conrail's marshaling yard in East St. Louis. On the day of the accident, Davis, driving an unmarked van * * *, arrived at the yard and saw a train coming in from east to west. He noticed that several of the cars in the train were Trailer Train cars that he was required to inspect. The train halted, and was decoupled near the front; the locomotive, followed by several cars, pulled away to the west. The remainder of the train was stretched out for three-quarters of a mile to the east; and because it lay on a curved section of the track, its rear end was not visible from the point of decoupling. An employee of Conrail named Lundy saw Davis sitting in his van, didn't know who he was, thought it was queer he was there, but did nothing.

Shortly afterward Davis began to conduct the inspections. This required him to crawl underneath the cars to look for cracks. One of the cars was the third from the end (that is, from the point where the train had been decoupled). Unbeknownst to Davis, a locomotive had just coupled with the other (eastern) end of the train. It had a crew of four. * * * [The locomotive crew] was ordered to move the train several car lengths to the east because it was blocking a switch. The crew made the movement, but without blowing the train's horn or ringing its bell. The only warning Davis had of the impending movement was the sudden rush of air as the air brakes were activated. He tried to scramble to safety before the train started up but his legs were caught beneath the wheels of the car as he crawled out from under it. One leg was severed just below the knee; most of the foot on the other leg was also sliced off. The train had not been "blue flagged." It is law (49 C.F.R. § 218) as well as custom in the railroad industry that whenever work is being done on a train a blue metal flag be placed at either end to warn employees not to move the train. Though well aware of the custom, Davis had neither blue flagged the train before crawling under it nor asked an employee of Conrail to blue flag it.

Davis brought this suit against Conrail, charging negligence. * * * A jury found for Davis, assessed damages at $3 million, but found that Davis's own negligence had been one-third responsible for the accident, and therefore awarded damages of $2 million [pursuant to Illinois' "comparative negligence" scheme]. * * * Conrail argues that it was not negligent at all (which if correct would mean that Davis was entitled to zero damages) * * *.

* * *

In the famous negligence formula of Judge Learned Hand, which is recognized to encapsulate the more conventional verbal formulations of the negligence standard, see Prosser and Keeton on the Law of Torts 173 and n. 46 (5th ed. 1984), a defendant is negligent only if B<PL, meaning, only if the burden of precautions is less than the magnitude of the loss if an accident that the precautions would have prevented occurs discounted (multiplied) by the probability of the accident. See *United States v. Carroll Towing Co.*, 159 F.2d 169, 173 (2d Cir.1947). If P is very low, elaborate precautions are unlikely to be required even if L is large * * *.

[Guided by the Hand formula, the court rejected one theory of Conrail's negligence offered by Davis.] It is that before the train was moved, a member of the crew should have walked its length, looking under the cars. The probability that someone was under a car was too slight, as it reasonably would have appeared to the crew, to warrant the considerable delay in moving the train that would have been caused by having a crew member walk its entire length and then walk back, a total distance of a mile and a half. It might have taken an hour, since the crew member would have had to look under each one of the train's 50 cars, and since the cars were only 12 inches off the ground, so that he would have had to get down on all fours to see under them.

Davis's [remaining] theory is more plausible. He argues that it was negligent for the crew to move the train without first blowing its horn (also referred to as the whistle) or ringing its bell. Since no member of the crew was in a position where he could see the train's western end, which was now its rear end, a reasonable jury could find * * * that it was imprudent to move the train without a signal in advance. Although the crew had no reason to think that Davis was under a car, someone—whether an employee of Conrail or some other business invitee to the yard (such as Davis)—might have been standing in or on a car or between cars, for purposes of making repairs or conducting an inspection; and any such person could be severely, even fatally, injured if the train pulled away without any warning or even just moved a few feet. Regarding the application of the Hand formula to such a theory of negligence, not only was B vanishingly small—for what would it cost to blow the train's horn?—but P was significant, though not large, once all the possible accidents that blowing the horn would have averted are added together. For in determining the benefits of a precaution—and PL, the expected accident costs that the precaution would avert, is a measure of the benefits of the precaution—the trier of fact must consider not only the expected cost of this accident but also the expected cost of any other, similar accidents that the precaution would have prevented. Blowing the horn would have saved not only an inspector who had crawled under the car (low P), but also an inspector leaning on a car, a railroad employee doing repairs on the top of a car, a brakeman straddling two cars, and anyone else who might have business in or on (as well as under) a car. The train was three-quarters of a mile long. It was not so unlikely that somewhere in that stretch a person was in a position of potential peril to excuse the crew from taking the inexpensive precaution of blowing the train's horn. Or so at least the jury could conclude * * *.

Against this conclusion Conrail [has put forward] a number of arguments. * * *

* * *

[The] strongest argument is that Conrail had no duty to warn persons who might be in or on or under the train—given the blue flag rule. There is in general no duty to anticipate and take precautions against the negligence of another person. Such a requirement would tend to induce potential injurers to take excessive safety precautions relative to those taken by potential victims; the cost of safety would rise. Thus, "If the motorist on the through highway had to travel at such a speed that he could stop his car in time to avoid collisions with vehicles which ignore stop signs on intersecting roads, the purpose of having a through highway in the first place would be entirely thwarted." Hession v. Liberty Asphalt Products, Inc., 93 Ill.App.2d 65, 74, 235 N.E.2d 17, 22 (1968). * * *

[Conrail argues] that the rule regarding blue flagging excuses the crew from any duty of care to persons who might be injured by a sudden starting of the train, because all such persons can protect themselves by blue flagging and are careless if they fail to do so. There is some evidence, however, that the rule was honored in the breach. Davis inspected cars at the yard three or four times a week, never posted or requested the posting of a blue flag, and was seen by many employees of Conrail without remonstrance from them. Maybe all these people were careless but maybe the rule of blue flagging is not so universal as the defendants claim. * * *

* * * [D]espite the blue flag rule there was some probability that an employee or invitee was working in or dangerously near the train, reasonably believing that he would receive some warning before the train pulled away. * * *

Moreover, we were careful to qualify our statement of the rule that a potential injurer is entitled to assume that potential victims will exercise due care, by saying that this was true "in general." A certain amount of negligence is unavoidable * * *. Potential injurers may therefore be required to take some care for the protection of the negligent, especially when the probability of negligence is high or the costs of care very low. See Prosser and Keeton on the Law of Torts, supra, § 33, at pp. 198–99. You cannot close your eyes while driving through an intersection, merely because you have a green light. If, as the jury could have found, Conrail could have avoided this accident by the essentially costless step of blowing the train's horn, it may have been duty-bound to do so even if only a careless person would have been endangered by a sudden movement of the train.

* * *

[The court went on to note that Davis' employer, Trailer Train, had no safety rules for its employees.] Since blue flagging takes some time, the absence of a work rule put Davis in a potential dilemma. If he was too meticulous about safety, this might slow down his inspections too much and jeopardize his job. * * * It strikes us (and more important must have struck the jury) as unusual that a worker in such a dangerous job should be allowed to go about his work without receiving any instructions with regard to safety. * * *

Affirmed.

BROTHERHOOD SHIPPING CO. v. ST. PAUL FIRE & MARINE INS. CO., 985 F.2d 323 (7th Cir.1993). Plaintiff's ship, a freighter, was damaged during a fierce storm on Lake Michigan. At the time the ship was berthed in the Port of Milwaukee. The shipowner brought suit in admiralty against the City of Milwaukee, which owns the port. Plaintiff alleges negligence by defendant, and estimates its total loss (cost of the ship's repairs plus revenue lost during repair) at $4.5 million. Plaintiff says that its ship was damaged because of a perilous condition in the part of the port where the ship was berthed, and because of the port's failure to give timely warning of the peril. The district court granted the city's motion for summary judgment. On appeal, *held*, for plaintiff.

Writing for the appellate court, Circuit Judge Posner said that the issue was whether the evidence gathered in pretrial discovery, viewed in a light favorable to plaintiff, would warrant a finding that the city was negligent. "In answering that question, we apply the standard of negligence laid down by Judge Hand in the famous admiralty case of United States v. Carroll Towing Co., 159 F.2d 169, 173 (2d Cir.1947)." Judge Posner described the peril at the port as follows:

"The Port of Milwaukee has a breakwater, with, of course, a gap in it to allow ships to go in and out of the harbor. Two of the slips in the harbor, where ships berth, are directly opposite the gap in the breakwater. As a result of this geometry, * * * a northeast gale—and such gales are common on Lake Michigan—can afflict these slips with two severe patterns of wave action, which the parties refer to as 'cross-slapping' and 'over-topping.' Waves from the open water surge through the gap in the breakwater, strike the wall on the other side, recoil, and collide with the next surge, creating a wave twice as high as the other waves stirred up in the harbor by the gale. This is cross-slapping. Overtopping occurs when waves in this area of the harbor become so violent that they spill over the wall of the slip at which a ship is berthed."

In December 1987 plaintiff's ship entered the harbor and was berthed in one of the two slips opposite the gap in the breakwater. At noon the next day the ship's captain learned a northeaster was brewing, made inquiries, and was reassured that he could ride out the storm. At 5:30 p.m. the captain received a "weather notice" from the city's harbor master, which warned of "very severe" wave action. The captain then decided to move the ship to a safer berth, but found that the harbor's pilot had already left for the day; also, there were no tugs or linesmen available at that hour. Conditions worsened and at 6:15 a.m. "the stern ropes broke and the stern of the ship was dashed against the wall of the slip." Thus plaintiff's ship "became the tenth victim [since 1964] of cross-slapping and over-topping." Judge Posner continued:

"Evaluating these facts with the aid of the Hand formula, we note first that L in the formula—the magnitude or gravity of the loss [from an accident that the precautions not taken would have averted]—was substantial. * * * As for the likelihood of such an accident (P), it could not be reckoned small, given the history of accidents to ships at the two exposed slips in the outer harbor. So PL, the expected accident cost, was substantial and therefore imposed on the defendant a duty of taking substantial precautions.

"At least three types of precaution were possible. One was a structural alteration to the harbor that would have eliminated the problem once and for all * * *. The second possible precaution was to have pilots, tugs, and linesmen available round the clock in the winter to remove endangered ships from the slips at short notice. The third was to give the masters of the ships berthed at the 'bad' slips * * * sufficient early warning to enable them to obtain a pilot, tugs, and linesmen before the close of business on the day of a storm. The city did none of these things. It did not build a baffle or other device that would have prevented cross-slapping and over-topping. It did not arrange for pilots, tugs, and linesmen to stand by after 5 p.m. during the winter in case there was a storm. [And it did not provide timely, effective notice or warning of the peril.] * * *

"Given the unpredictability of Lake Michigan storms and the vagaries of a notice system, sole reliance on such a system to protect mariners * * * might not suffice to fulfill the city's duty of care, provided one of the alternatives—a structural alteration to the harbor or the provision of stand-by rescue services—would be less costly than the expected accident cost that would remain once the notice system was in place. * * * But we need not get into any of these issues. * * * For purposes of this appeal it is enough that the plaintiff has raised a genuine issue of material fact concerning the adequacy of the precautions that the City of Milwaukee took to prevent the type of serious, and by no means remotely unlikely, accident that occurred."

SNYDER v. AMERICAN ASSOCIATION OF BLOOD BANKS

Superior Court of New Jersey, Appellate Division, 1995.
282 N.J.Super. 23, 659 A.2d 482.
Affirmed, 144 N.J. 269, 676 A.2d 1036 (1996).

PRESSLER, P.J.A.D.

In August 1984 plaintiff William Snyder underwent coronary bypass surgery at St. Joseph's Hospital in Paterson, New Jersey. As a result of being transfused with contaminated blood supplied to the hospital by the Bergen Community Blood Center (BCBC), he was infected with the AIDS virus (HIV). He and his wife Roslyn, who sues per quod, brought this action against, among others, the hospital, his physicians, the BCBC and its personnel, and the American Association of Blood Banks (AABB), of which BCBC is an institutional member. Following pretrial settlements with some defendants and dismissals of others, trial proceeded only against defendant

AABB. The jury, by way of its answers to special interrogatories, found that the AABB was negligent in not having recommended surrogate testing for AIDS to its institutional members prior to August 1984. The jury further found that that negligence substantially enhanced plaintiff's risk of contracting AIDS by transfusion and constituted a thirty percent causative factor in his having actually contracted the disease. Finally, the jury found that plaintiff's total damages were $1,000,000 and his wife's $350,000. Judgment was accordingly entered in their favor in the amount of thirty percent of total damages, a total of $405,000, plus prejudgment interest. Defendant appeals. We affirm.

* * *

[The evidence presented at trial below] dealt with AABB's internal structure, its general role in the blood-banking industry, and its specific role in determining the response of the voluntary blood-banking community to the AIDS threat between 1981, when the first AIDS cases were reported by the Centers for Disease Control (CDC), and March 1985, when the first test for HIV was in place.

Both parties relied on the testimony of distinguished experts, most of whom were involved during the critical time period either in AIDS research, AIDS epidemiology, AIDS treatment, or blood-banking on the highest levels. From their testimony, the following history of those years emerges. * * *

[In 1981 the CDC, an agency of the federal Public Health Service, began reporting to the medical community unusual cases of illnesses associated with immunosuppression. "By June 1982, it had become clear that a new immunodeficiency disease of epidemic proportion" had arisen "primarily among young homosexual men, although cases were also reported among IV drug users and Haitians, particularly recent immigrants." In July 1982 a "red flag" was raised by "three cases of the disease among hemophiliac men who had no other risk factors."] At least from that time forward, the CDC and others working in the field assumed as a working hypothesis that AIDS was caused by a blood-transmissible infectious agent. * * * [F]rom the point of view of CDC, the assumption that AIDS was caused by a blood-transmissible virus became a matter of high probability when it reported, in December 1982, that an infant had died of AIDS in California after having been transfused at birth with blood from a donor who had himself subsequently died of AIDS.

The CDC regarded that piece of information as so critical in terms of protection of the nation's blood supply that it called an emergency workshop meeting in Atlanta for January 4, 1983, attended by many of the scientists and physicians responsible for formulating and implementing the nation's blood supply policy, including, among others, representatives of government, the AABB, the National Hemophilia Foundation, and the National Gay Task Force. By that time the CDC had an AIDS Task Force in place consisting of CDC scientists who had special expertise in various facets of the disease. * * * The Task Force was convinced that AIDS was blood-transmissible. It was also convinced that epidemiologically the disease mirrored hepatitis B, involving exactly the same high-risk groups and in the same proportions. What came to be known as the Spira data, presented at the meeting, showed that among those patients having AIDS, about ninety percent of gay men, one hundred percent of IV drug users, and ninety-eight percent of Haitians also tested positive on the hepatitis B core antibody test (core test). * * * The recommendation of these physicians was that all persons belonging to the high-risk groups should be screened out of the blood-donation system. Three modes of screening were recommended: direct questioning of prospective donors to determine if they belonged to a high-risk group; careful taking of medical histories from donors including questions regarding such early AIDS symptoms as night sweats and weight loss; and, most significantly, surrogate testing. That is to say, since the AIDS-causing agent had not yet been identified, the effort was to find a test of both high sensitivity and high specificity that would enable identification of persons suffering from or at risk of AIDS. At least three such surrogate tests were suggested: the core test, a lymphocyte count test, and a T4/T8 cell test. Since the T4/T8 cell test required sophisticated equipment and specially trained personnel and the lymphocyte test appeared to lack adequate specificity, the core test appeared most promising.

As testified to by those of the witnesses at trial who attended the January 4, 1983, meeting, it was highly emotional, contentious, and fractious. According to plaintiff's witnesses, the chief source of obstruction was the blood bankers and particularly AABB's representative, the chairman of its Transfusion–Transmitted Disease Committee, who declined to subscribe to the view of a blood-transmissible infectious agent as the cause of AIDS.[1] Accordingly no real consensus and no recommendations immediately resulted. The meeting, however, marked a turning point in the saga of the nation's blood supply over the next two years. A few blood bankers then acted in accordance with the CDC's views in respect of surrogate testing. Most, including the AABB and almost all of its institutional members, the American Red Cross, and the Council of Community Blood Banks did not. According to plaintiff's experts, reasonably prompt action by the AABB following the January 4, 1983, meeting would have significantly promoted the safety of the blood supply and saved it from much of its consequent contamination.

Thus in January 1983, Dr. Thomas Asher, the operator of a substantial commercial blood fractionating facility, instituted total lymphocyte testing, rejecting all blood under a 1500 count. No case of AIDS, he testified,

---

1. The meeting was described by Dr. [Donald] Francis [of the CDC] as follows:

"The reactions of the blood bankers led, really, by the representative Dr. [Joseph] Bove, from the AABB, * * * [were] remarkably obstructive. * * *

"[The] reluctance and the inertia that we at CDC faced with the blood banks in that meeting was * * * so ridiculous and so alarming that it got to the point of me literally pounding on the table and shouting to these individuals as to how many deaths it's going to take before you will act.

"And I was saying, do you need ten, do you need twenty, do you need forty, when we get to that level, then are you going to act? * * *

"And this, the initial negativism, accepting such a thing as transfusion associated AIDS, and then the real hostility towards moving ahead and doing something, saying it was going to cost too much, it was going to cause too much trouble, was just a most unfortunate expression of AABB policy."

resulted from any blood so collected, tested, and distributed by his company. Dr. Edward Engleman, chief of the Stanford University Hospital blood bank, instituted T-cell testing, and by the beginning of 1984, refused to accept supplemental blood from other sources that had not been either T–Cell or core tested. A group of voluntary blood banks in northern California instituted core testing early in 1984. Most of the rest of the blood-supply collectors, however, followed the AABB recommendation not to implement surrogate testing or direct questioning of donors, but only to implement donor self-deferral based on a written brochure explaining the high-risk groups. The heart of plaintiff's case against the AABB is the opinion of his experts * * * that the AABB's failure to have recommended surrogate testing to its institutional members, as well as its affirmative recommendation not to so test was, based on what it then knew and understood, unreasonable, imprudent, and, in the end, negligent.

We review the evidence of the AABB's course of action following the January CDC meeting in the context of the proofs, virtually undisputed, of its position in American blood banking. To begin with, the AABB is a non-profit corporation organized in 1947 under the laws of Illinois. Its certificate of incorporation describes it as "a trade association of local and regional blood banks" whose purposes, among others, are to "foster the exchange of ideas and information" relating to blood banks and transfusion services, to promote standards of performance and service by blood banks, to "function as a clearing house" for the exchange of blood and blood-credits, to encourage the development of blood banks, and to "plan for cooperation amongst blood banks at times of disaster."

Those statements may well understate its actual influence and preeminence in the voluntary blood-banking industry. According to the evidence, its institutional membership includes almost every voluntary blood bank in the country, nearly 2,400 in 1992. * * * The AABB publishes a periodically updated technical manual, entitled "Standards for Blood Banks and Transfusion Services," covering all aspects of blood banking, including donor screening and blood testing, with which its institutional members are required to comply. It inspects and accredits its members' facilities. Some states defer entirely to AABB inspection and accreditation. Others, like New Jersey, defer only in some respects. It is clear that its role in prescribing procedures and policies for the conduct of voluntary blood banks is quasi-governmental. Indeed, the testimony from the BCBC officials was that had surrogate testing been recommended by the AABB, even if not required, the BCBC surely would have done so. Consequently, plaintiff's experts directly attributed the almost total failure of the American voluntary blood banks to engage in any surrogate testing to the AABB's failure to make such a recommendation and its recommendation that such testing not be done.

We note further that the AABB was also described by several of the expert witnesses as inordinately influential in setting national blood policy in the first half of the 1980's, a primary responsibility of the FDA [Food and Drug Administration], by reason of AABB's participation in the FDA's Blood Products Advisory Council and other agencies, councils, and committees charged with formulating national blood policy, and by reason, apparently, of its acknowledged expertise. Indeed, the Report of the Presidential Commission on the Human Immunodeficiency Virus Epidemic (June 1988) (HIV Report) concluded that one of the obstacles to progress during the early years of the epidemic was the extent of governmental deference to industry views. * * * Finally, the evidence shows that AABB is an effective lobbyer for the perceived interests of the blood-banking community. Certainly the evidence permits the inference that the AABB is the national blood-banking establishment. It has written the rules. It has set the standards. It speaks for it.

Against this background, we consider the evidence of the AABB's response to the CDC Task Force's January 4, 1983, presentation. We note first that the Chairman of its Transfusion–Transmitted Disease Committee certainly acknowledged in private communications and internal memoranda to the AABB Board his belief, even before the January 4, 1983, meeting that AIDS was caused by a blood-transmissible agent, a belief most experts had come to share when the hemophiliac cases were reported the previous July. The early public statements of AABB however, notably those it made jointly with the American Red Cross and the Council of Community Blood Centers, were at best equivocal. Thus, the joint statement of January 13, 1983, stressed that the "possibility" that AIDS was spread by "blood borne transmission" was "still unproven" and that "evidence of transmission by blood transfusion is inconclusive." Nevertheless, because of the possibility, the joint statement recommended caution in the use of blood products and "reasonable attempts to limit blood donation from individuals or groups that may have an unacceptably high risk of AIDS." Laboratory screening was specifically not recommended.

That joint statement set the tone for the AABB's position even after Dr. [Luc] Montagnier's work [in identifying the HIV virus] was duplicated in this country by Dr. Robert Gallo in the spring of 1984 and continuing until a specific AIDS test was in place in the spring of 1985. In short, it continued to recommend against surrogate testing, direct questioning of donors, and directed donations. * * *

The general tenor of the evidence as a whole justifies the inference that every responsible expert in the United States was convinced well before the end of 1983, and most before the end of 1982, that AIDS was caused by an infectious, blood-transmitted agent. A New England Journal of Medicine article published in January 1984 was regarded by the medical community as entirely persuasive. The AABB nevertheless continued to express skepticism until Dr. Gallo's work was announced and even then, although it conceded the dangers posed by the high-risk groups, it resisted surrogate testing and direct questioning, procedures that, according to the HIV Report, supra, at 78, are now matters of standard operating procedure in the protection of the blood supply.

The testimony of AABB's impressive array of experts in blood banking, most of whom hold or have held important positions in the AABB, supported its approach during the critical time period. Foremost among their reasons was their opinion that no then available surrogate test, and certainly not the core test, was effective in identifying substantial numbers of persons at risk of AIDS, i.e., that the tests lacked adequate sensitivity, and that the surrogate tests would result in an untoward percentage of false positives requiring the deferral of too many healthy donors and the consequent diminution of the blood supply, i.e., that the tests lacked adequate specificity. * * * Defendant's experts were also concerned with the bioethical problem of what to tell prospective donors who tested positive on the core test vis-a-vis the possibility of their having AIDS. They were concerned about creating panic. They were concerned with at-risk persons coming to blood banks for the sole purpose of being tested for the possibility of AIDS. The risk of transfusion-related AIDS was apparently underestimated.[6] There was some belief that self-deferral was "working." There were tensions created by the gay politics of the time. Defendant's experts consequently took the position that the blood supply was best protected by not implementing surrogate testing during the critical period.

The question that this jury had to resolve, based on the sharply conflicting expert testimony, was whether AABB, the policy-setter, knowing what it knew from 1981 to 1985, had made a reasonable and prudent decision in recommending to its 2,400 institutional members that they not conduct surrogate testing of blood in order to help identify prospective donors belonging to high-risk groups. The HIV Report, supra, at 78, concludes that "the initial response of the nation's blood banking industry to the possibility of contamination of the nation's blood by a new infectious agent was unnecessarily slow." The evidence at this trial supports the jury's finding that the response was not only "unnecessarily slow" but also that it was clearly imprudent and unreasonable, resulting in unnecessary contamination of the blood supply.

Turning from the broad issues implicated and explicated at this trial to the specific situation of plaintiff, we note the following evidence. In [an earlier appeal], we permitted confidential discovery under court supervision of the HIV-infected donor whose blood resulted in plaintiff's contraction of AIDS. That discovery took place. Insofar as relevant to the surrogate testing issue with which we must be exclusively concerned because of the jury's verdict, this much is plain. That donor tested positive on the hepatitis B core test in 1994. Plaintiff's experts concluded, based on the characteristic relationship between the occurrences of hepatitis B and AIDS in homosexual men, that the donor, as a matter of reasonable medical probability, would also have tested positive ten years earlier. Defendant's experts disputed that opinion. But clearly then, there was adequate evidence in this record to support the finding that had the core test been recommended by AABB for use at any time up to the middle of 1984, BCBC would have been using it and this donor's blood would have been deferred.

---

6. According to the HIV Report, supra, at 78, as of June 1988, there were 2,399 cases of transfusion-caused AIDS in this country. As of 1992, there were 6,311 cases of transfusion-caused AIDS. Since HIV testing of blood began in March of [1985], however, only 29 such cases have arisen. See Linda M. Dorney, Comment, Culpable Conduct With Impunity: The Blood Industry and the FDA's Responsibility for the Spread of AIDS Through Blood Products, 3 J.Pharm. & Law 129 (1994) * * *.

[Having upheld the jury's finding of negligence, the court went on to reject AABB's claim of charitable immunity, and its claim that it owed no duty of care to Snyder. On the issue of causation, the court said: "The question before the jury was whether the risk that plaintiff would be infected by HIV in August 1984 was enhanced because BCBC did not perform core testing." It approved the "enhanced-risk theory" of Restatement (Second) of Torts § 323 (discussed at p. 571, infra). The court concluded:]

In reviewing the sorry history of this nation's response to the AIDS epidemic during its first three years, and particularly the contamination of the blood supply by HIV that could have been avoided, Dr. Francis opined that there was enough blame to go around. We are persuaded that plaintiff adequately proved the portion of blame fairly attributable to AABB.

The judgment appealed from is affirmed.

———

N.N.V. v. AMERICAN ASSOCIATION OF BLOOD BANKS, 75 Cal.App.4th 1358, 89 Cal.Rptr.2d 885 (1999). This case, like the foregoing *Snyder v. American Association of Blood Banks*, involves a claim that the American Association of Blood Banks (AABB) was negligent in failing to recommend that member blood banks adopt "surrogate testing" in order to screen donated blood for AIDS infection prior to the development of a specific test for the AIDS virus in March 1985. Here the trial court granted summary judgment in favor of AABB, and the intermediate appellate court affirmed. The California appellate court (Kremer, P.J.) made several objections to the approach taken by the New Jersey Supreme Court in its opinion affirming the judgment against AABB in *Snyder*.

" * * * [W]e disagree with the *Snyder* majority's decision. We find it flawed in many aspects. * * * The issue before the court was whether the AABB was negligent in failing to recommend surrogate testing. The *Snyder* majority, however, focused on a different issue, i.e., whether the AABB was negligent in failing to realize AIDS could be transmitted through blood transfusion. * * *

"We further note the *Snyder* majority's 'foreseeability' analysis is flawed because it is a hindsight analysis; it focuses on the 'devastating' consequences resulting from contaminated blood rather than looking to the circumstances, including the state of knowledge and recommendations of other relevant organizations, as they existed at the time the AABB adopted its standards. * * *

" * * * Contrary to the *Snyder* majority, we believe imposition of liability in these circumstances would not further the goals of preventing future harm * * *.

* * *

" * * * We believe deference should be given to professional associations that are making these sorts of policy decisions based on evolving medical and scientific knowledge. We believe public policy and the needs of the community are best served by encouraging free scientific and medical debate unhindered by threats of liability * * *. As long as a professional medical association acts in good faith in setting standards when medical and scientific knowledge is in a state of debate, we believe, as a matter of public policy, liability should not be imposed."

RESTATEMENT OF TORTS, SECOND (1965)

§ 282. Negligence Defined

In the Restatement of this Subject, negligence is conduct which falls below the standard established by law for the protection of others against unreasonable risk of harm. * * *

Comment:

* * *

d. Negligence Contrasted With Intended Harm. The definition of negligence given in this Section includes only such conduct as creates liability for the reason that it involves a risk and not a certainty of invading the interest of another. It therefore excludes conduct which creates liability because of the actor's intention to invade a legally protected interest of the person injured or of a third person (see 8A, Comment *b*, which defines "intent" as including knowledge that the conduct will invade the interest, as well as a purpose to invade it). * * *

* * *

f. Negligence Contrasted With Liability Without Fault. The fact that negligence as here defined is conduct which falls below the standard of behavior established by law for the protection of others carries with it the idea of social fault. Therefore it does not include acts which, although done with every precaution which it is practicable to demand, involve an irreducible minimum of danger to others, but which are so far justified by their utility or by traditional usage that even the most perfect system of preventive law would not forbid them. * * *

g. The word "risk" standing by itself denotes a chance of harm. In so far as risk is of importance in determining the existence of negligence, it is a chance of harm to others which the actor should recognize at the time of his action or inaction.

* * *

§ 283. Conduct of a Reasonable Man: The Standard

Unless the actor is a child, the standard of conduct to which he must conform to avoid being negligent is that of a reasonable man under like circumstances.

Comment:

* * *

e. Weighing Interests. The judgment which is necessary to decide whether the risk so realized is unreasonable, is that which is necessary to determine whether the magnitude of the risk outweighs the value which the law attaches to the conduct which involves it. This requires not only that the actor give to the respective interests concerned the value which the law attaches to them, but also that he give an impartial consideration to the harm likely to be done the interests of the other as compared with the advantages likely to accrue to his own interests, free from the natural tendency of the actor, as a party concerned, to prefer his own interests to those of others.

f. Reasonable Consideration for Others and Reasonable Prudence. In so far as the conduct of the reasonable man furnishes a standard by which negligence is to be determined, the standard is one which is fixed for the protection of persons other than the defendant. In so far as the contributory negligence of the actor is concerned, the standard is one to which the actor is required to conform for his own protection * * *. When a plaintiff's contributory negligence is in question, the "reasonable man" is a man of reasonable "prudence." Where a defendant's negligence is to be determined, the "reasonable man" is a man who is reasonably "considerate" of the safety of others and does not look primarily to his own advantage.

* * *

§ 291. Unreasonableness; How Determined; Magnitude of Risk and Utility of Conduct

Where an act is one which a reasonable man would recognize as involving a risk of harm to another, the risk is unreasonable and the act is negligent if the risk is of such magnitude as to outweigh what the law regards as the utility of the act or of the particular manner in which it is done.

Comment:

a. The problem involved may be expressed in homely terms by asking whether "the game is worth the candle."

b. * * * Conduct is not negligent unless the magnitude of the risk involved therein so outweighs its utility as to make the risk unreasonable. * * *

* * *

d. Weighing Risk Against Utility of Conduct Which Creates It. The magnitude of the risk is to be compared with what the law regards as the utility of the act. If legal and popular opinion differ, it is the legal opinion which prevails. The point upon which there is likely to be such divergence between the two is usually in respect to the social value of the respective interests concerned. * * *

e. The law attaches utility to general types or classes of acts as appropriate to the advancement of certain interests rather than to the purpose for which a particular act is done, except in the case in which the purpose is of itself of such public utility as to justify an otherwise impermissible risk. Thus, the law regards the free use of the highway for travel as of sufficient utility to outweigh the risk of carefully conducted traffic, and does not ordinarily concern itself with the good, bad, or indifferent purpose of a particular journey. It may, however, permit a particular method of travel which is normally not permitted if it is necessary to protect some interest to which the law attaches a pre-eminent value, as where the legal rate of speed is exceeded in the pursuit of a felon or in conveying a desperately wounded patient to a hospital.

* * *

§ 292. Factors Considered in Determining Utility of Actor's Conduct

In determining what the law regards as the utility of the actor's conduct for the purpose of determining whether the actor is negligent, the following factors are important:

(a) the social value which the law attaches to the interest which is to be advanced or protected by the conduct;

(b) the extent of the chance that this interest will be advanced or protected by the particular course of conduct;

(c) the extent of the chance that such interest can be adequately advanced or protected by another and less dangerous course of conduct.

Comment on Clause (a):

a. Legal Valuation of Actor's Interests. The most important factor in determining the utility of the actor's conduct is the value which the law attaches to the interest which the conduct is intended and appropriate to advance or protect. The interest may be exclusively public, as in the case of the apprehension of an actual or reasonably supposed criminal. It may be a purely private interest of the actor or a third person. It may be an interest which is primarily of private advantage, but the public may nonetheless be interested, not merely as the protector of the private interest, but also because the general public good is advanced by the protection and advancement of such private interests. Thus, the idea that the interest of the public as a group can best be served by permitting the utmost freedom of individual initiative is inherent in both legal and popular thought. The irreducible minimum of risk both to employees and outsiders which is inherent in manufacture is not regarded as unreasonable, not so much because manufacture is profitable to those who carry it on, but because it is believed that the whole community benefits by it. The operation of railways and other public utilities, no matter how carefully carried on, produces accidents which kill or harm many people but the risk involved in the operation is more than counterbalanced by the service which they render the public.

* * *

Comment on Clause (c):

   c.   Alternative Opportunity for Actor to Advance His Interest. If the actor can advance or protect his interest as adequately by other conduct which involves less risk of harm to others, the risk contained in his conduct is clearly unreasonable. If any other practicable course of conduct is clearly likely to give his interest a less adequate advancement or protection the question whether the risk is or is not unreasonable depends upon whether the additional risk involved in the particular course of conduct outweighs the additional advancement or protection which it is likely to secure. * * *

§ 293.   Factors Considered in Determining Magnitude of Risk

   In determining the magnitude of the risk for the purpose of determining whether the actor is negligent, the following factors are important:

   (a) the social value which the law attaches to the interests which are imperiled;

   (b) the extent of the chance that the actor's conduct will cause an invasion of any interest of the other or of one of a class of which the other is a member;

   (c) the extent of the harm likely to be caused to the interests imperiled;

   (d) the number of persons whose interests are likely to be invaded if the risk takes effect in harm.

* * *

SECTION B.   DETERMINING DUTY

   The duty to use reasonable care to avoid causing physical harm to others is a very highly general legal obligation. It is the foundation of the tort law of negligence. In the normal negligence case, the existence of a legally binding duty of due care is not an open question. Rather the issue is whether the generally applicable duty of due care has been breached in the given case—that is, the issue is whether or not casual negligence has occurred.

   Why should courts make rulings on "duty" when the duty to use reasonable care is so long and well established in the law? There are two main reasons. First, in some cases there may be special considerations of policy which counsel that the general obligation of due care should be cut back. A duty inquiry may conclude that the general rule of negligence liability ought not apply in a particular area of life. Second, with respect to some types of conduct, it may be possible and desirable for courts to spell out the general duty of due care in more specific terms. A duty inquiry may lead to the formulation of a specific tort rule saying that such-and-such conduct (for example, not wearing a seatbelt) always amounts to negligence. Notice that the first way of modifying the general duty—cutting it back—produces particular rules of nonliability, while the second way—spelling it out—produces particular rules of liability.

The present section provides an introductory look at how courts go about deciding duty questions that arise in negligence lawsuits. Mainly the materials that follow focus on the determining of duty in situations where the question is whether law's general obligation of reasonable care should be cut back. Also included are cases holding that certain kinds of risky activity should achieve a higher level of care than the law generally requires.

The matter of legal duty is the central concern of Chapter 10, "The Duty of Care: Special Relations and Statuses." Chapter 10 addresses two major doctrines of duty worked out by common-law courts: the traditional precept that there is no duty to act in aid of someone in peril, which has many exceptions, and doctrine defining the duty of landowners to entrants upon their land. Duty determinations in particular contexts also appear at other points in the chapters on negligence law—for example, the duty of care incumbent on servers of alcohol is discussed in Chapter 13.

RESTATEMENT OF TORTS, THIRD: LIABILITY FOR PHYSICAL HARM (BASIC PRINCIPLES)

Tent. Draft No. 1 (March 28, 2001).

§ 7. Duty

Even if the defendant's conduct can be found negligent * * * and is the legal cause of the plaintiff's physical harm, the defendant is not liable for that harm if the court determines the defendant owes no duty to the plaintiff, either in general or relative to the particular negligence claim. Determinations of no duty are unusual and are based on judicial recognition of special problems of principle or policy that justify the withholding of liability.

Comment:

a. The proper role for duty. * * * [I]in cases involving negligent conduct that causes physical harm courts have recognized a general duty of reasonable care that operates on the defendant. This general duty is incorporated into the standard of negligence liability for physical harm * * *. In cases involving negligent conduct that causes physical harm, courts * * * are not obliged to refer to the general duty on a case-by-case basis.

There are, however, particular situations involving conduct that causes physical harm in which the requirements of negligence and legal causation are or may be satisfied, but in which, for reasons of principle or policy, the imposition of liability is plainly troublesome. In such cases, judicial screening of the plaintiff's claim, under the heading of duty, is appropriate. For example, * * * [m]any modern [duty] cases concern bartenders and social hosts who serve alcoholic beverages to inebriated customers or guests, who themselves later drive their cars negligently, injuring innocent third parties. In such cases, reasonable juries could plausibly find negligence on the part of the drink-dispenser, and could also find that the negligence is a legal cause of the resulting injury. Nevertheless, recognizing liability is bold and potentially problematic. Accordingly, courts have assumed the responsibility of reviewing plaintiffs' claims by undertaking a duty analysis. In doing so, most courts have decided that liability is appropriate for the bartender, while not appropriate for the social host.* * *

b.　Anticipating third-party tortious misconduct. As the examples of bartender and social-host liability suggest, duty can become an issue in cases in which the only negligent conduct of the defendant involves the defendant setting the stage or creating the opportunity for the tortious misconduct of some third party. * * *

c.　Administrability. A duty analysis can be proper when the issue is whether a new category of tort claims will be sufficiently capable of judicial administration. The particular issue might be whether courts will be able fairly and reliably to draw the lines that would need to be drawn if a new extension of tort liability is to prove acceptable. Or—when for example the plaintiff is contending that the defendant's entire activity is negligent—the particular issue might be whether a courtroom trial of the seemingly relevant factual claims would prove to be manageable.

f.　Duty and negligence. In cases in which reasonable minds cannot differ, * * * courts take negligence claims away from the jury and determine that the party was, or was not, negligent as a matter of law. Having done so, the court may express its result in terms of whether there is a duty to behave in a certain way. These expressions inaccurately convey the idea of a duty issue that is separate from and antecedent to the negligence issue. In fact, these are merely cases in which the one-sidedness of the evidence permits the court itself to specify the content of the negligence standard.

In other situations, reasonable minds can differ as to the application of the negligence standard to the case's particular facts, yet the case presents a recurring problem that leads courts to conclude * * * that the negligence determination should be rendered by the court rather than by the jury. It is common for courts to express the conclusions they reach in such cases in terms of "duty." When conducting such a duty analysis, the court primarily considers, as would the jury in dealing with the issue of negligence, the magnitude of the foreseeable risk and the burden of risk prevention. In a duty case, however, the court considers those factors from the perspective not of the individual plaintiff and defendant but rather of the entire categories of plaintiffs and defendants whose liability situation is being considered. In conducting such an analysis, the court can take into account factors that might elude the attention of the jury in a particular case, such as the overall social impact of imposing some significant precaution burden on a category of actors.

The duty reviews identified in previous Comments have involved placing limits on what otherwise might be the reach of ordinary negligence principles. The duty analysis identified in this Comment is more balanced: it can favor defendants when the analysis results in a holding of no duty, or it can favor plaintiffs when the analysis yields an affirmative finding on the duty issue, and in doing so takes the issue away from juries in subsequent cases. * * *

MILLER v. WAL–MART STORES, INC., 219 Wis.2d 250, 580 N.W.2d 233 (1998). "This court has, on several occasions, expounded on Wisconsin's common law of negligence. 'In order to maintain a cause of action for negligence in this state, there must exist: (1) A duty of care on the part of the defendant; (2) a breach of that duty; (3) a causal connection between the conduct and the injury; and (4) an actual loss or damage as a result of the injury.' *Rockweit v. Senecal*, 197 Wis.2d 409, 418, 541 N.W.2d 742 (1995). Even if these elements are met, public policy considerations may nevertheless preclude imposing liability on the defendant. *See Morgan v. Pennsylvania Gen. Ins. Co.*, 87 Wis.2d 723, 737, 275 N.W.2d 660 (1979).

"* * * In Wisconsin, everyone has a duty of care to the whole world. *See Morgan*, 87 Wis.2d at 732, 275 N.W.2d 660.

[T]he proper analysis of duty in Wisconsin is as follows: 'The duty of any person is the obligation of due care to refrain from any act which will cause foreseeable harm to others even though the nature of that harm and the identity of the harmed person or harmed interest is unknown at the time of the act....'

Rockweit, 197 Wis.2d at 419–20, 541 N.W.2d 742. 'A defendant's duty is established when it can be said that it was foreseeable that his act or omission to act may cause harm to someone.' *Rolph v. EBI Cos.*, 159 Wis.2d 518, 532, 464 N.W.2d 667 (1991). The duty is to refrain from such act or omission.

* * *

"Even when negligence and negligence as a cause-in-fact are present, liability does not necessarily follow. If the jury determines that the defendant has a duty to the plaintiff, the defendant breaches that duty and the breach causes injury in fact, public policy considerations may nevertheless preclude imposing liability on the defendant. *See Morgan*, 87 Wis.2d at 737, 275 N.W.2d 660. This is solely a judicial determination."

RANDI W. v. MUROC JOINT UNIFIED SCHOOL DIST., 14 Cal.4th 1066, 929 P.2d 582, 60 Cal.Rptr.2d 263 (1997). The California Supreme Court summed up its approach to the question of duty:

In this state, the general rule is that all persons have a duty to use ordinary care to prevent others from being injured as the result of their conduct. (*Rowland v. Christian* (1968) 69 Cal.2d 108, 112, 70 Cal.Rptr. 97, 443 P.2d 561.) As we have observed, "*Rowland* enumerates a number of considerations ... that have been taken into account by courts in various contexts to determine whether a departure from the general rule is appropriate: 'the major [considerations] are *the foreseeability of harm to the plaintiff*, the degree of certainty that the plaintiff suffered injury, the closeness of the connection between the defendant's conduct and the injury suffered, the moral blame attached to the defendant's conduct, the policy of preventing future harm, the extent of the burden to the defendant and consequences to the community of imposing a duty to exercise care with resulting liability for breach, and the availability, cost, and prevalence of insurance for the risk involved.' (Italics added.) (69 Cal.2d at p. 113, 70 Cal.Rptr. 97, 443 P.2d 561.) The foreseeability of a particular kind of harm plays a very significant role in this calculus, but a court's task—in determining 'duty'—is not to decide whether a *particular* plaintiff's injury was reasonably foreseeable in light of a *particular* defendant's conduct, but rather to evaluate more generally whether the category of negligent conduct at issue is sufficiently likely to result in the kind of harm experienced that liability may appropriately be imposed on the negligent party." (*Ballard v. Uribe* (1986) 41 Cal.3d 564, 572–573, fn. 6, 224 Cal.Rptr. 664, 715 P.2d 624.)

VAN SKIKE v. ZUSSMAN

Appellate Court of Illinois, First District, 1974.
22 Ill.App.3d 1039, 318 N.E.2d 244.

[Action by minor and his mother for injuries caused by fire. The minor plaintiff obtained a toy cigarette lighter as a prize from a gumball machine operated by defendant Zussman in Defendant Rivera's store, immediately purchased lighter fluid from defendant Rivera, and "set himself on fire" when he attempted to fill the toy lighter with the lighter fluid. The trial court dismissed the complaint for failure to state a cause of action against either defendant, and plaintiff appealed.]

STAMOS, Justice.

* * *

A complaint for negligence must set out: the existence of a duty owed by the defendant to the plaintiff, a breach of that duty, and an injury proximately resulting from the breach. (Mieher v. Brown, 54 Ill.2d 539, 301 N.E.2d 307.) The existence of a duty is a question of law to be determined by the court.

As to defendant Zussman, plaintiff alleges that he knew or should have known that he had placed his cigarette lighter dispensing machines in a store that sold flammable fluids. It is conceded by plaintiff that the lighter was a toy rather than a functional lighter; but plaintiff argues, the fact that the miniature lighter was nonfunctional is of no consequence, for a toy lighter, as in the present case, can cause injury in the same way that a functional lighter might. The argument runs that it is not the name or label of the object which is determinative, but rather the use which the object itself suggests be made of it. The minor plaintiff thought the toy was functional, and defendant Zussman is negligent for failure to foresee a young boy's lack of judgment.

Although foreseeability is generally accepted as the test to be applied by a jury in determining if a duty has been violated in defining the scope of the duty there are many factors other than foreseeability that may condition a judge's imposing or not imposing a duty in the particular case. (Mieher v. Brown, supra.) Not only will the court consider the likelihood of the injury, the magnitude of the burden of guarding against it, and the consequences of placing that burden upon defendant (Lance v. Senior, 36 Ill.2d 516, 224 N.E.2d 231.), but considerations of public policy are important as well. (Mieher v. Brown, supra.) In addition, in determining whether there was a legal duty, the occurrence involved must not have been simply foreseeable, as the plaintiff contends; it must have been reasonably foreseeable. The creation of a legal duty requires more than a mere possibility of occurrence. Cunis v. Brennan, 56 Ill.2d 372, 308 N.E.2d 617.

Tested by these general principles, we conclude that the complaint failed to state a cause of action against defendant Zussman. We initially note that the lighter which defendant dispensed in his gumball machines was merely a nonfunctional toy; it did not produce the spark or emit the flame which, in the words of the complaint, "caused plaintiff to set himself on fire." Plaintiff's theory must therefore be that it is reasonably foreseeable that a child who purchases a toy similitude will (1) perceive the object to be an actual fire producing mechanism; (2) and purchase a flammable liquid with which to operate the mechanism; and yet (3) will obtain some external source of fire which ignites the flammable liquid.

Plaintiff provides no authority in support of his theory and we are of the opinion that the events upon which plaintiff seeks to state a cause of action against defendant Zussman do not, in contemplation of law, establish a duty. Viewing the concept of duty from a foreseeability perspective alone, we cannot say the dispensing of miniature toy lighters in an establishment which sells lighter fluid creates a reasonably foreseeable risk of harm.

We turn next to the contention that the complaint stated a cause of action against defendant Rivera. Although not clearly delineated, plaintiff apparently alleges the following alternative theories of recovery: (1) that lighter fluid is an inherently dangerous substance and therefore within the doctrine that one who places a dangerous implement in the hands of a person incompetent to use it is chargeable with knowledge of the consequences; (2) the sale of lighter fluid to a minor is actionable on general principles of negligence; and (3) the sale of lighter fluid to a minor on the same premises on which miniature toy lighters are dispensed is sufficient to impose liability.

At common law the legal principle is established that if one sells a dangerous article or instrumentality such as firearms or explosives to a child whom he knows or ought to know to be, by reason of youth and inexperience, unfit to be trusted with it, and might innocently and ignorantly play with it to his injury, and injury does result, he may be found guilty of negligence and consequently liable in damages. Annot., 20 A.L.R.2d 119, 124.

In Mondt v. Ehrenwerth, 251 Ill.App. 226, defendant had sold ten cents worth of benzine to a boy of thirteen who subsequently, while demonstrating to a five-year-old child how the substance would burn, ignited the benzine, causing the can to explode and resulting in the infant's death. The court held that the benzine, in the small quantity so sold, could not be considered an imminently dangerous article. Directly on point is Traynor v.

United Cigar–Whelan Stores Corp., 274 App.Div. 800, 79 N.Y.S.2d 329, where a closed bottle of cigarette lighter fluid sold by the defendant to an eleven-year-old child who uncorked the bottle, applied a match thereto, and was burned by the ensuing flame, was held not to be a dangerous instrumentality within the doctrine that one who puts a dangerous implement in the hands of a person incompetent to use it is chargeable with knowledge of the consequences.

Upon the basis of the foregoing authority, we conclude that lighter fluid is not inherently dangerous, with the result that the selling of it to minors does not impute to the vendor a knowledge of the consequences. The possibility always exists that a child purchasing lighter fluid, paint, glue, hairspray, or like products, will improperly ignite the product to his injury; however, the creation of a legal duty requires more than the mere possibility of occurrence. (Cunis v. Brennan, supra.) In this regard, we note the language of the *Traynor* decision in holding that a complaint, alleging the sale of lighter fluid to an eleven-year-old minor who sustained injuries when he subsequently ignited the substance, failed to state a cause of action:

> The fluid was an article in common use, not inherently dangerous, and the occurrence was not of such a character that reasonable prudence and foresight would forecast its happening. 79 N.Y.S.2d 329, 330.

The mere possibility that a minor purchasing lighter fluid might place a match or some other external source of fire thereto, resulting in uncontrolled ignition, does not justify the imposition of a prohibition against the sale of such products to minors. Apart from the likelihood of injury, the court must also consider the magnitude of the burden of guarding against it and the consequences of placing that burden upon the defendant. (Lance v. Senior, supra.) The burden of liability for self-inflicted injuries sustained by minors who purchase household flammables, absent something which would give notice of the likelihood of such misuse in a given case, would render retail trade extremely hazardous. (See Mondt v. Ehrenwerth, supra.) Accordingly, we hold that the sale of lighter fluid to a six-year-old child, in and of itself, does not state a cause of action against the vendor when the minor sustains injuries resulting from the ignition of the substance by an external source of fire.

Although not actionable in itself, the sale of lighter fluid to a minor may be actionable if coupled with circumstances from which injuries may be reasonably anticipated. (See Driscoll v. Rasmussen Corp., 35 Ill.2d 74, 219 N.E.2d 483; Compare Clark v. Ticehurst, 176 Kan. 544, 271 P.2d 295 with Tharp v. Monsees, (Mo.), 327 S.W.2d 889.) The remaining question is whether the allegations of the complaint sufficiently establish that defendant was placed on notice that an improper use of the lighter fluid was contemplated. In this respect plaintiff bears the burden of pleading the facts necessary to his cause of action, and failure to do so cannot be remedied by liberal construction or argument. Plaintiff had ample time in which to file an amended complaint, yet he failed to avail himself of the opportunity. The present complaint alleges that the minor plaintiff obtained the miniature cigarette lighter from a gumball machine on the same premises on which he immediately thereafter purchased lighter fluid, and that subsequently "the minor plaintiff attempted to fill said lighter with fluid and was caused to set himself on fire." As earlier stated, the miniature toy lighter was nonfunctional, and therefore, was not the source of the spark or flame which ignited the lighter fluid. For the reasons that the complaint against defendant Zussman failed to state a cause of action, a complaint against defendant Rivera for selling lighter fluid to a minor is not augmented by an allegation that miniature toy lighters were also periodically dispensed in a gumball machine located on the premises. The mere presence of miniature toy lighters on the premises, as to the sale of lighter fluid, was not reasonably foreseeable as a causative factor in the harm alleged. The judgment of the trial court is affirmed.

Judgment affirmed.

———————

LUGO v. LJN TOYS, 146 A.D.2d 168, 539 N.Y.S.2d 922 (1989), aff'd mem., 75 N.Y.2d 850, 552 N.Y.S.2d 914, 552 N.E.2d 162 (1990). The six-year-old plaintiff "sustained serious and permanent eye injuries when a detachable part of a toy, flung in her direction by an eight-year-old neighbor, Brian Franks, struck her left eye." The toy, manufactured by defendant, was a robot-like plastic figure called "Voltron—Defender of the Universe." Voltron was the hero of a popular animated cartoon series, a favorite television program of Brian's. On television Voltron fought enemies with his "spinning laser blade," a star-shaped weapon with eight sharp points. "The cartoons depicted Voltron calling upon the spinning blade, which would appear in his hand, and then spinning it toward his opponent, who would be sliced or cut upon contact. * * * It was this weapon, designed to detach from the hand of the Voltron toy, that Brian threw, causing [plaintiff's] injuries."

The injured child, by her parents, sued the defendant manufacturer for damages, alleging that defendant's toy product was negligently designed. Plaintiffs say it was foreseeable that children might throw the toy's detachable sharp-pointed part. Defendant moved for summary judgment, which was denied. On appeal, *held*, for plaintiffs. The appellate court reviewed evidence plaintiffs planned to present at trial:

"Plaintiffs' experts assert that the television shows and video cassettes depicting Voltron's use of the spinning blade as an offensive weapon could influence a child, consciously or unconsciously, to emulate such behavior. These experts have also expressed the view that the design of the toy, which permitted the spinning blade to be readily detached from Voltron's hand— indeed, such detachability was intended—posed unreasonable risks and dangers to the children for which it was marketed."

The court concluded: "we * * * relegate this controversy to the proper forum, the jury." A dissenting opinion objected: "even if plaintiffs' theory of liability and foreseeability could be factually supported and were upheld, its logical conclusion would hold the manufacturer of a Spiderman costume liable for the injury inflicted by a misguided child who, emulating the cartoon, unsuccessfully tried to scale a building."

CLINTON v. COMMONWEALTH EDISON CO., 36 Ill.App.3d 1064, 344 N.E.2d 509 (1st Dist. 1976). Fifteen-year-old boy was electrocuted in yard of family residence when he came in contact with 7200–volt electrical line. Action by his mother against the power company and an electrician. The trial court granted defendants' motions for directed verdicts, and plaintiff appealed. *Held*, affirmed.

"We feel that to require defendants under the facts of this case to have used an insulated line over the Clintons' property would in effect be tantamount to requiring defendants and all who are engaged in the business of supplying electrical service to insulate all of their lines. Factors in addition to the foreseeability of occurrences must be taken into consideration in determining defendants' legal duty; the likelihood of the injury, the magnitude of the burden of guarding against it and the consequences of placing that burden upon defendants (Lance v. Senior, 36 Ill.2d 516, 518, 224 N.E.2d 231), as well as public policy and social requirements. (Mieher v. Brown, 54 Ill.2d 539, 545, 301 N.E.2d 307.) The minimal risk of injury does not justify the imposition of such a heavy burden on the electrical business nor on the public who will undoubtedly bear the ultimate cost."

KIMBAR v. ESTIS, 1 N.Y.2d 399, 153 N.Y.S.2d 197, 135 N.E.2d 708 (1956). Action by a boy and his father against the operators of a summer camp for injuries sustained by the boy when he stepped off a camp path at night and broke his nose on a tree. Plaintiffs asserted that among other things the path should have been lighted. *Held*, defendant's motion to dismiss made at the end of plaintiffs' case should have been granted. "To hold summer camps to a duty of floodlighting woods would not only impose upon them a condition almost impracticable under many circumstances—but would be unfair, as well, to the youth who seek the adventure of living closer to nature. * * * "

GRACE & CO. v. CITY OF LOS ANGELES, 168 F.Supp. 344 (S.D.Cal. 1958). Action for water damage to coffee stored in a shed at a berth maintained by the city and a dock-and-wharf company. The water escaped from a pipe because of graphitic corrosion. The pipe had not been inspected for forty years. *Held*, for defendant. "Graphitic corrosion may occur in one spot and then may not occur for many feet along the line. * * * To make complete inspection it would be necessary to remove the earth from beneath the line. The removal of the earth from beneath the pipe would remove its support, putting a strain upon the pipe itself, and might cause a sinking or bending of the pipe, occasioning damage more extensive than the corrosion itself. * * * Although it might have been desirable to make an inspection of the water lines every two or three years, such inspection would be prohibitively expensive and economically unfeasible. The City, like individuals, is required to take only reasonable precautions."

STAGL v. DELTA AIRLINES

United States Court of Appeals, Second Circuit, 1995.
52 F.3d 463.

CALABRESI, Circuit Judge:

If a man chooses to leave a cart standing in the street, he must take the risk of any mischief that may be done. *Illidge v. Goodwin,* 5 Carrington & Payne's Reports 190 (1831).

In the one hundred and sixty-four years since Chief Justice Tindal of the English Court of Common Pleas first set down this rule of tort liability, our means of transportation have advanced considerably. Nevertheless, the rule's basic premise, that a tortfeasor is liable for the foreseeable acts of an intervening party, remains sound in our modern age of aeronautics. Indeed, as this case in part demonstrates, the concept of intervening causation may apply equally well to the "mischief" engendered by an unattended airport baggage carousel as it does to a neglected horse and wagon.

Plaintiff, Eleanor M. Stagl, appeals from a judgment of the United States District Court for the Eastern District of New York (the Honorable John R. Bartels, *Senior District Judge*), granting summary judgment to defendant, Delta Air Lines, Inc., and dismissing her personal injury action against Delta which was based upon the airline's alleged negligent supervision and management of its baggage retrieval system. * * * Because we agree with Mrs. Stagl that the district judge erroneously granted Delta's motion * * *, we reverse the judgment and remand the case for further proceedings.

* * *

On May 1, 1993, Mrs. Stagl, then 77 years old, was a passenger on a Delta flight from Orlando, Florida to LaGuardia Airport in New York City. The plane was delayed for approximately one-half hour, and Mrs. Stagl noted that upon its arrival in New York the passengers were visibly upset. After disembarking from the aircraft, Mrs. Stagl proceeded to a designated baggage carousel located in Delta's terminal in order to retrieve her luggage.

In her affidavit in opposition to Delta's motion for summary judgment, Mrs. Stagl describes the Delta terminal as "bedlam." According to her, "[p]eople were crowded around the baggage carousel and everyone seemed in a hurry to get out of the airport." Moreover, they were "rowdy and unruly, pushing and shoving each other, grabbing their luggage from the moving carousel by whatever means possible." She further claims that Delta did not provide any personnel, or make any cautionary announcement to quell the turmoil; nor did the airline cordon-off a separate area in which elderly and disabled passengers could safely obtain their luggage.

In an attempt to reclaim her own belongings, Mrs. Stagl made her way to the "front rank" of the throng surrounding the baggage carousel. Apparently, an unidentified man to one side of her reached across the conveyor belt, grabbed his satchel with great force, and unwittingly triggered a domino effect. His bag collided with another's suitcase, which, in turn, fell off the carousel, toppling Mrs. Stagl. As a result, she suffered a broken hip.

Mrs. Stagl brought this diversity action in the district court, claiming that Delta did not exercise reasonable care to ensure her safety. She complained that the airline negligently failed to take any crowd-control measures or to provide a safe method by which elderly and disabled people could retrieve their luggage. Mrs. Stagl alleged that her physical injuries were the proximate result of Delta's inaction.

* * *

A. Delta's Duty of Reasonable Care

The district court ruled that "Delta owed no duty to protect [Mrs. Stagl] from the particular injury involved here." * * * [T]he district court concluded that Delta had no obligation "to protect against or warn of potential negligent conduct by third persons within the terminal building." This was error.

There is no question that Delta, as an owner or occupier of the premises, owed a duty to take reasonable steps in maintaining the safety of its baggage retrieval area. *See Basso v. Miller,* 40 N.Y.2d 233, 241, 386 N.Y.S.2d 564, 568, 352 N.E.2d 868, 872 (1976) ("A landowner must act as a reasonable [person] in maintaining his property in a reasonably safe condition in view of all the circumstances, including the likelihood of injury to others, the seriousness of the injury, and the burden of avoiding the risk.").

This duty is a broad one, and it includes the obligation "to take reasonable precautions to protect [patrons] from dangers which are foreseeable from the arrangement or use of the property," W. Page Keeton, Dan B. Dobbs, Robert E. Keeton, David G. Owen, Prosser and Keeton on Torts, § 61 at 425–26 (5th ed. 1984) [hereinafter "Prosser & Keeton"], as well as to exercise reasonable care in protecting visitors from the foreseeable, injurious actions of third parties. *See Nallan v. Helmsley–Spear, Inc.,* 50 N.Y.2d 507, 518–19, 429 N.Y.S.2d 606, 613, 407 N.E.2d 451, 457 (1980) (landlord has duty to take reasonable precautionary measures to minimize risk of foreseeable criminal activity and make premises safe for visiting public).

* * *

* * * Here * * * Mrs. Stagl was injured in Delta's own baggage terminal, over which Delta had full dominion and control. Under these circumstances, we think that New York law would apply the traditional landowner's duty of reasonable care to Delta. As the occupier of these premises, Delta was required to take all reasonable measures to ensure that Mrs. Stagl's trip to the baggage carousel was a safe one.[1]

In the present case, the district judge refused to impose an obligation upon Delta to safeguard passengers against the foreseeable risks created by its concentration of allegedly unruly travelers around a congested baggage

---

1. In addition to the traditional landowner's duty, we note that New York law imposes a duty of reasonable care on Delta, as a common carrier, "to protect its passengers from other travelers." *Pulka v. Edelman,* 40 N.Y.2d 781, 784, 390 N.Y.S.2d 393, 396, 358 N.E.2d 1019, 1022 (1976). * * *

carousel. In the district court's opinion, such a duty would "offer little if any real public benefit, and yet would impose upon the airline burdensome and costly obligations." Although we appreciate that, under New York law, the "existence and scope of an alleged tortfeasor's duty is usually a policy-laden declaration reserved for Judges" that, in part, weighs competing socioeconomic factors in an attempt to distribute "burdens of loss and reparation on a fair, prudent basis," *Palka v. Servicemaster Management Servs. Corp.*, 83N.Y.2d 579, 585, 611 N.Y.S.2d 817, 820, 634 N.E.2d 189, 192 (1994), we also note that New York courts do not exercise this authority on an *ad hoc* basis.

> To the contrary, the judicial power to modify the general rule that
>
> > [w]henever one person is by circumstances placed in such a position with regard to another that every one of ordinary sense who did think would at once recognize that if he did not use ordinary care and skill in his own conduct with regard to the circumstances he would cause danger of injury to the person or property of the other, a duty arises to use ordinary care and skill to avoid such danger,

Havas v. Victory Paper Stock Co., 49 N.Y.2d 381, 386, 426 N.Y.S.2d 233, 236, 402 N.E.2d 1136, 1138 (1980) (quoting *Heaven v. Pender*, 11 Q.B.D. 503, 509 (1883)), is reserved for very limited situations. Thus, for example, in determining that a tort duty to third parties may arise out of a contractual assumption of responsibilities, *see Palka*, 83 N.Y.2d at 587, 611 N.Y.S.2d at 821, 634 N.E.2d at 193, and in recognizing that concepts underlying the former assumption of risk doctrine survive in a very limited area, and may serve to bar some sports-related negligence claims despite the passage of a comparative negligence statute, *see Turcotte v. Fell*, 68 N.Y.2d 432, 437–39, 510 N.Y.S.2d 49, 52–53, 502 N.E.2d 964, 967–68 (1986), New York courts have conducted fact-specific duty analyses. But where, as here, the applicable duty relationship is well established, we do not believe New York law condones the limitation of a familiar liability rule simply to avoid placing a disproportionate burden on a defendant in a particular case. The law deals with that problem not by redefining the defendant's duties in each case, but by asking whether—considering all the circumstances of the particular case—the defendant breached its duty of care.

B.   *Delta's Alleged Breach of Duty*

Apparently as an alternative basis for its decision, the district court determined that "Delta fulfilled its duty to act reasonably under the circumstances." This, of course, raises the age-old debate as to when it is appropriate for a court to decide the question of a defendant's due care as a matter of law, rather than allowing a jury to resolve it as an issue of fact. The problem was perhaps best presented in *Lorenzo v. Wirth*, 170 Mass. 596, 49 N.E. 1010 (1898), the noted case that posed the burning question of whether a court may rule that an open coalhole in the sidewalk, with a pile of recently delivered coal upon it, is so obviously hazardous to all pedestrians that the exercise of ordinary care does not require the placement of additional warnings.

Answering in the affirmative, then-Judge Holmes stated that "[i]n simple cases of this sort, courts have felt able to determine what, in every case, however complex, defendants are bound at their peril to know, namely, whether the given situation is on one or the other side of the line [of the defendant's duty of care]." 170 Mass. at 600, 49 N.E. at 1101. Judge Knowlton took the opposite view in *Lorenzo,* and insisted that the

> kind of conduct ... required under complex conditions, to reach the usual standard of due care, namely, the ordinary care of persons of common prudence, is a question of fact, to be determined according to the observation and experience of common men. Even when there is no conflict in testimony, if there are acts and omissions, of which some tend to show negligence, and others do not, the question whether there was negligence or not is, in my judgment, a question for the jury.

170 Mass. at 604, 49 N.E. at 1101–02 (Knowlton, J., dissenting).

Although vestiges of this polemic survive, *see, e.g., Akins v. Glens Falls City School Dist.,* 53 N.Y.2d 325, 441 N.Y.S.2d 644, 424 N.E.2d 531 (1981) (concluding, over strong dissent, that the installation of a standard backstop fence fulfills a baseball park owner's duty of reasonable care to protect spectators from foul balls as a matter of law), Holmes' view—" 'that standards of conduct ought increasingly to be fixed by the court for the sake of certainty—has been largely rejected.' " *See* Fowler V. Harper, Fleming James, Jr., Oscar S. Gray, The Law of Torts § 15.3, at 358–59 n. 16 & n. 4 (2d ed. 1986) [hereinafter "Harper & James"] (quoting *Nuckoles v. F.W. Woolworth Co.,* 372 F.2d 286, 289 (4th Cir.1967)); Richard M. Nixon, *Changing Rules of Liability In Automobile Accident Litigation,* 3 Law & Contemp.Probs. 476, 477 (1936).[4] Indeed, the New York Court of Appeals has concluded that it is

> particularly appropriate to leave [a finding of negligence] to the jury, not only because of the idiosyncratic nature of most tort cases ... , or because there was room for a difference of view as to whether [the defendant's] conduct in the particular circumstances of this case did or did not evidence a lack of due care, but, perhaps above all, because in the determination of issues revolving about the reasonableness of conduct, the values inherent in the jury system are rightfully believed an important instrument in the adjudicative process. ...

Havas, 49 N.Y.2d at 388, 426 N.Y.S.2d at 237, 402 N.E.2d at 1139 (citations omitted); *see also Nallan,* 50 N.Y.2d at 520 n. 8, 429 N.Y.S.2d at 614 n. 8, 407 N.E.2d at 458 n. 8; ("[w]hat safety precautions may reasonably be required of a landowner is almost always a question of fact for the jury").[5]

* * *

4. It may be worth noting that Mr. Nixon wrote this article when he was a law student at Duke University Law School. Long before he became a significant political figure, Mr. Nixon's article was recognized as a leading piece on the Holmes–Knowlton controversy because it was one of the first to apply "legal realism" to the debate. Nixon suggested the desirability of the Holmes position because of the per-

ceived tendencies of juries to be biased in favor of plaintiffs. *See* 3 Law & Contemp.Probs. at 477. Despite his own viewpoint, however, Nixon recognized that, by and large, Holmes had lost out. *See id.* at 479.

5. * * * Among the * * * considerations that may be relevant in determining whether Delta met its basic obligation to maintain its

In support of her contention that Delta was careless in managing its baggage carousel and the crowd around it, Mrs. Stagl submitted the affidavit of an engineer named Grahme Fischer. Mr. Fischer enumerated several ways in which, in his opinion, Delta could have made the baggage carousel area safer for passengers like Mrs. Stagl. Without expressing any views regarding the reasonableness of the proposed measures contained in this affidavit, we conclude that, when read in the light most favorable to Mrs. Stagl, Mr. Fischer's statement clearly raises issues of fact as to whether Delta sufficiently discharged its duty of care.[6]

[Summary judgment vacated; case remanded.]

———

LUGTU v. CALIFORNIA HIGHWAY PATROL, 26 Cal.4th 703, 110 Cal. Rptr.2d 528, 28 P.3d 249 (2001). The car in which plaintiffs were riding was travelling at an excessive speed in the westbound portion of Highway 78. Highway 78 has a total of six lanes, three in each direction, separated by a 10–foot-wide median strip. An officer of the California Highway Patrol (CHP) pulled his motorcycle alongside the speeding car, sounded his siren, and motioned the driver to stop in the center median area of the highway. The driver stopped and received a speeding citation. A truck travelling in the fast westbound lane (nearest the median) drifted onto the median strip and slammed into the rear of the stopped car, seriously injuring the occupants. Plaintiffs sued the truck driver (who had not kept his eyes on the road) and also the motorcycle officer and his employer, the CHP. They alleged that the CHP officer was negligent in ordering their car to stop on the median strip rather than on the right-side shoulder of the highway. The trial court granted summary judgment in favor of the CHP officer and the CHP, ruling that the officer "had no duty to stop plaintiffs on the right shoulder as a matter of law." On review in the California Supreme Court, *held*, a legal duty of due care on the part of the officer does exist.

"Under general negligence principles, of course, a person ordinarily is obligated to exercise due care in his or her own actions so as not to create an unreasonable risk of injury to others * * *. It is well established, moreover, that one's general duty to exercise due care includes the duty not to place another person in a situation in which the other person is exposed to an unreasonable risk of harm through the reasonably foreseeable conduct (including the reasonably foreseeable negligent conduct) of a third person. * * *

* * *

premises in a reasonably safe condition are "such variables as the seriousness of the risk and the cost of the various safety measures." *Nallan,* 50 N.Y.2d at 520 n. 8, 429 N.Y.S.2d at 614 n. 8, 407 N.E.2d at 458 n. 8. And the fact-specific nature of these considerations, of course, militates even more strongly in favor of allowing a jury to resolve the matter. * * *

6. We do not mean to suggest that Mrs. Stagl necessarily had to submit expert evidence in order for her claim to survive summary judgment. Other evidence could have done as well. Mr. Fischer's statement was merely one way to raise a triable issue of fact in this case.

"Consistent with the basic tort principle recognizing that the general duty of due care includes a duty not to expose others to an unreasonable risk of injury at the hands of third parties, past California cases uniformly hold that a police officer who exercises his or her authority to direct another person to proceed to—or to stop at—a particular location, owes such a person a duty to use reasonable care in giving that direction, so as not to place the person in danger * * *.

* * *

"Accordingly, we conclude that, under California law, a law enforcement officer has a duty to exercise reasonable care for the safety of those persons whom the officer stops, and that this duty includes the obligation not to expose such persons to an unreasonable risk of injury by third parties. The summary judgment in favor of [the CHP officer and the CHP] cannot be sustained on the ground that [the officer] owed no legal duty of care to plaintiffs.

* * *

"[Moreover,] the evidence before the trial court on the summary judgment motion clearly raised a triable issue for the jury's determination on the question of negligence. * * * [W]e conclude that the trial court erred in finding that the undisputed evidence established, as a matter of law, that [the officer] was not negligent."

RESTATEMENT OF TORTS, THIRD: LIABILITY FOR PHYSICAL HARM (BASIC PRINCIPLES), Tent. Draft No. 1 (March 28, 2001). Under the title "Judge and Jury," Section 8(b) provides: "When, in light of all the facts relating to the actor's conduct, reasonable minds can differ as to whether the conduct lacks reasonable care, it is the function of the jury to make that determination." The Comment on this subsection explains:

" * * * The longstanding American practice has been to treat the negligence question as one that is assigned to the jury * * *. [S]o long as reasonable minds can differ in evaluating whether the actor's conduct lacks reasonable care, the responsibility for making this evaluation rests with the jury. To be sure, in some cases reasonable minds can reach only one conclusion. Accordingly, the rule recognized in this section permits a significant number of directed verdicts—that the actor's conduct must be found negligent, or free of negligence. Yet most of the time, the rule set forth in this section calls for a jury decision on the negligence issue. * * * "

FOSTER v. CITY OF KEYSER
Supreme Court of Appeals of West Virginia, 1997.
202 W.Va. 1, 501 S.E.2d 165.

[An explosion resulted when natural gas escaped from an underground transmission line of Mountaineer Gas Company. Plaintiffs claimed that strict liability should apply. The court said that "cogent arguments exist both for and against" strict liability. It noted a prior case "in a related area," *Peneschi v. National Steel Corp.*, 170 W.Va. 511, 295 S.E.2d 1 (1982), which held that the activity of accumulating and using combustible gas is "an abnormally dangerous activity that gives rise to strict liability." But the court decided not to impose strict liability on transmission—as opposed to accumulation—of natural gas. Instead it affirmed that "the dangerous activity of transmitting natural gas" should be subject to "an extremely high standard of care."]

In our opinion in *Peneschi*, we discussed and analyzed a number of our past cases in which strict liability was or was not imposed upon dangerous activities and instrumentalities. We noted that in cases where strict liability was not imposed, a party engaged in such activities or employing a dangerous instrumentality was held to "the highest degree of care, a standard commensurate with the dangerousness to be avoided." 170 W.Va. at 517, 295 S.E.2d at 7. * * *

* * *

The properties of natural gas which make it useful and valuable also make it dangerous. Natural gas contains a great deal of energy—which partially accounts for its utility, and for its ability to do a lot of damage if it explodes. When escaped natural gas mixes with the atmosphere in certain concentrations, the mixture is explosive and easily ignited by a flame or spark.

Natural gas is often transmitted under substantial pressure, so a leak in a gas transmission line can result in the escape of a large volume of gas in a short time. Gas transmission lines are often buried, sometimes quite deeply (in the instant case, it appears that the gas transmission line in question may have been six feet under the surface)—so inspection, maintenance and repair is not simple. Escaping gas can flow easily and quickly through a path of least resistance, which in populated areas is often along or through other utility pipes or drains into buildings.

It is a tribute to human ingenuity generally and to the people who work in gas transmission particularly that in spite of this combination of factors which renders transmitting natural gas a particularly and inherently dangerous activity, relatively few natural gas explosions occur, considering how widely gas is transmitted and used.

Nevertheless, explosions do occur, and law books in every jurisdiction are amply stocked with cases involving the sorting out of who should pay for the injuries and damages caused by explosions of gas which leaks from gas transmission lines. This is such a case.

In many such cases, this Court (and others) have recognized and discussed the high duty of care to which an enterprise which is transmitting natural gas through transmission lines must adhere.

Like other states, we "recognize the dangerous character of natural gas and the correlative duty of utility companies that furnish it." *Reed v. Smith Lumber Co.*, 165 W.Va. 415, 418, 268 S.E.2d 70, 71 (1980). It has been said that the installation of natural gas lines is an inherently dangerous activity. *Noack v. B. L. Watters, Inc.*, 410 So.2d 1375, 1376 n.1 (Fla.App.1982). "[I]n view of the highly dangerous character of gas and its tendency to escape, a gas company must use a degree of care to prevent the escape of gas from its pipes proportionate to the level of danger." 27A Am.Jur.2d Energy & Power Sources, § 373.

* * *

We therefore hold that natural gas is a dangerous substance and a distributor of natural gas is required to exercise a high degree of care and diligence to prevent injury and damage to the public from the escape of gas. A distributor of natural gas is required to exercise a degree of care commensurate to the danger involved in the transaction of its business. The duty to use due care which a distributor of natural gas owes to the public is a continuing one and one which cannot be delegated to another.

In analogous circumstances, we have held that because electricity is inherently dangerous, its management requires a "peculiarly high level of care." *Miller v. Monongahela Power*, 184 W.Va. 663, 668, 403 S.E.2d 406, 411 (1991). "[A]lthough we have never gone so far as to make electric companies insurers, we have come reasonably close by making it clear that any deviation from the highest possible standard of care is sufficient to impose liability." *Id.*

———

BRILLHART v. EDISON LIGHT & POWER CO., 368 Pa. 307, 82 A.2d 44 (1951). A supplier of electric current is bound to use the "very highest degree of care practicable" to avoid injury. "[T]he general public is not bound to the high degree of foresight in respect of danger from electric wires as is the company maintaining them."

BAYER v. CRESTED BUTTE MOUNTAIN RESORT, 960 P.2d 70 (Colo. 1998). Plaintiff, who was riding in a ski lift chair without a restraining device, became unconscious, slid from the chair, and fell to the ground below, suffering severe injuries. Plaintiff argued that, according to Colorado common law, a ski lift operator is held to "the highest degree of care" in the design of its conveyance. Defendant rejoined that the Colorado legislature had done away with the "highest care" standard by enacting a statute declaring that ski lifts are not "common carriers." On certification to the Colorado Supreme Court, *held*, that the statute in question does not change "the common law standard requiring a ski lift operator to exercise the highest degree of care."

The court (Hobbs, J.) noted that other jurisdictions "imposed on ski lift operators a common carrier status in requiring the higher duty of care," but said that in Colorado common carrier status makes "no difference in this regard." "[W]hile common carriers may be required to exercise the highest degree of care towards their passengers, it does not follow that transport device operators who are not classified as common carriers are dispensed from exercising the highest degree of care when the attendant circumstances warrant such caution." Ski lift operators should be held to the higher duty because of "the degree of control they exercise over passengers, the relative powerlessness of a passenger to secure his or her own safety * * *, and the consequent state of dependence and trust which a passenger must place in the lift operators." "[T]he attendant circumstances of ski lift operation, like amusement rides, demand the highest degree of care."

The court went on to rule that the duty of highest care applies to the design of a ski lift, including its safety devices, as well as to the construction, maintenance, and running of the lift. "Ordinary care is not applicable * * *. [W]e hold that the standard of care applicable to ski lift operators in Colorado for the design, construction, maintenance, operation, and inspection of a ski lift, is the highest degree of care commensurate with the practical operation of the lift."

BETHEL v. NEW YORK CITY TRANSIT AUTHORITY, 92 N.Y.2d 348, 681 N.Y.S.2d 201, 703 N.E.2d 1214 (1998). "We granted leave to appeal in this case to confront directly whether a duty of highest care should continue to be applied, as a matter of law, to common carriers and conclude that it should not. We thus realign the standard of care required of common carriers with the traditional, basic negligence standard of reasonable care under the circumstances. Under that standard, there is no stratification of degrees of care as a matter of law (*see*, Prosser and Keeton, Torts § 34, at 210 [5th ed.]). Rather, 'there are only different amounts of care, as a matter of fact' (*id.*, at 211)."

The court emphasized that "the single, reasonable person standard" when applied in different cases will produce "a sliding scale of due care *factually*," with different magnitudes of care required depending on the circumstances, and thus by itself will "permit courts and juries to take fully into account the ultrahazardous nature of a tortfeasor's activity." "The objective, reasonable person standard in basic traditional negligence theory * * * necessarily takes into account the circumstances with which the actor was actually confronted when the accident occurred, including the reasonably perceivable risk and gravity of harm to others and any special relationship of dependency between the victim and the actor."

SECTION C. OBJECTIVE OR SUBJECTIVE ASSESSMENT

Due care is the level of safety that a reasonable person, in the circumstances, would attain. So the conduct of a reasonable person is the standard by which negligence is assessed. What are the characteristics—traits, capacities—of the imagined "reasonable person"? There are two basic alternatives. First, we may imagine an abstract being who is ordinary in all respects and always acts the same in like circumstances. The result is the so-called "objective," or impersonal, standard for assessing negligence. Or we might imagine a being who is "reasonable" but also has some of the particular capacities and traits of the particular individual whose conduct is being judged. The result is a more "subjective," or personalized, standard of judgment.

The law's test for negligence is certainly standardized—"objective"—to a significant degree. The fact that an actor meant well does not automatically block a finding of negligence—so the test is not wholly "subjective." The materials below explore the degree of variability of the law's yardstick for negligence. They explicate the criterion of a reasonable person's conduct under the circumstances.

A major issue is how negligence doctrine deals with physical and mental incapacities that limit the performance of actors being judged. Will a particular incapacity be taken into account? If so, legal assessment is in line with moral assessment of fault, which takes capacity to be crucial. Or will the incapacity be ignored by law, left out of account, and the actor be held to a standard of performance that the actor is incapable of attaining? Is so, law blind to incapacity will find negligence, in some cases, though moral assessment would exculpate. Liability imposed on innocent conduct, without moral culpability or blame, is strict in nature. Materials that follow show how negligence doctrine may lead, paradoxically, to strict liability.

The section focusses on law's expectations for performances by human individuals, not performances of corporate entities like railroads or blood banks. Note that in four of the eight main cases, the actor whose conduct is being assessed is the plaintiff; the question is whether contributory negligence has occurred; and the assumption is that contributory negligence, if established, is a bar to recovery. These cases state doctrines of "the reasonable person" which are broadly applicable and operative today. However, in a modern regime of (pure) comparative fault, while the *existence* of contributory negligence would be determined in line with the doctrines stated herein, the *effect* would be to reduce (not bar) recovery.

VAUGHAN v. MENLOVE
Common Pleas, 1837.
3 Bing., N.C., 468.

[The declaration alleged, in substance, that plaintiff was the owner of two cottages; that defendant owned land near to the said cottages; that defendant had a rick or stack of hay near the boundary of his land which was likely to ignite by spontaneous combustion, and thereby was dangerous to the plaintiff's cottages; that the defendant, well knowing the premises, wrongfully and negligently kept and continued the rick in the aforesaid dangerous condition; that the rick did ignite, and that plaintiff's cottages were burned by fire communicated from the rick or from certain buildings of defendant's which were set on fire by flames from the rick. The defendant pleaded not guilty, and that there was no negligence.]

At the trial it appeared that the rick in question had been made by the defendant near the boundary of his own premises; that the hay was in such a state when put together, as to give rise to discussions on the probability of fire; that though there were conflicting opinions on the subject, yet during a period of five weeks the defendant was repeatedly warned of his peril; that his stock was insured; and that upon one occasion, being advised to take the rick down to avoid all danger, he said "he would chance it." He made an aperture or chimney through the rick; but in spite, or perhaps in consequence of this precaution, the rick at length burst into flames from the spontaneous heating of its materials; the flames communicated to the defendant's barn and stables, and thence to the plaintiff's cottages, which were entirely destroyed.

PATTESON, J., before whom the cause was tried, told the jury that the question for them to consider was, whether the fire had been occasioned by gross negligence on the part of the defendant; adding, that he was bound to proceed with such reasonable caution as a prudent man would have exercised under such circumstances.

A verdict having been found for the plaintiff, a rule nisi for a new trial was obtained, on the ground that the jury should have been directed to consider, not whether the defendant had been guilty of a gross negligence with reference to the standard of ordinary prudence, a standard too uncertain to afford any criterion, but whether he had acted bona fide to the best of his judgment; if he had, he ought not to be responsible for the misfortune of not possessing the highest order of intelligence. * * *

TINDAL, C. J. I agree that this is a case primae impressionis; but I feel no difficulty in applying to it the principles of law as laid down in other cases of a similar kind. Undoubtedly this is not a case of contract, such as a bailment or the like, where the bailee is responsible in consequence of the remuneration he is to receive: but there is a rule of law which says you must so enjoy your own property as not to injure that of another; and according to that rule the defendant is liable for the consequence of his own neglect: and though the defendant did not himself light the fire, yet mediately he is as much the cause of it as if he had himself put a candle to the rick; for it is well known that hay will ferment and take fire if it be not carefully stacked. It has been decided that if an occupier burns weeds so near the boundary of his own land that damage ensues to the property of his neighbor, he is liable to an action for the amount of injury done, unless the accident were occasioned by a sudden blast which he could not foresee. Turberville v. Stamp, 1 Salk. 13. But put the case of a chemist making experiments with ingredients, singly innocent, but when combined liable to ignite; if he leaves them together, and injury is thereby occasioned to the property of his neighbor, can any one doubt that an action on the case would lie?

It is contended, however, that the learned judge was wrong in leaving this to the jury as a case of gross negligence, and that the question of negligence was so mixed up with reference to what would be the conduct of a man of ordinary prudence that the jury might have thought the latter the rule by which they were to decide; that such a rule would be too uncertain to act upon; and that the question ought to have been whether the defendant had acted honestly and bonâ fide to the best of his own judgment. That, however, would leave so vague a line as to afford no rule at all, the degree of judgment belonging to each individual being infinitely various: and though it has been urged that the care which a prudent man would take, is not an intelligible proposition as a rule of law, yet such has always been the rule adopted in cases of bailment, as laid down in Coggs v. Bernard, 2 Ld.Raym. 909. * * * The care taken by a prudent man has always been the rule laid down; and as to the supposed difficulty of applying it, a jury has always been able to say, whether, taking that rule as their guide, there has been negligence on the occasion in question.

Instead, therefore, of saying that the liability for negligence should be coextensive with the judgment of each individual, which would be as variable as the length of the foot of each individual, we ought rather to adhere to the rule, which requires in all cases a regard to caution such as a man of ordinary prudence would observe. That was in substance the criterion presented to the jury in this case, and therefore the present rule must be discharged.

[Concurring opinions were delivered by PARK and VAUGHAN, JJ. GASELEE, J., concurred in the result.]

Rule discharged.

LA MARRA v. ADAM

Superior Court of Pennsylvania, 1949.
164 Pa.Super. 268, 63 A.2d 497.

[Actions and cross actions resulting from a collision at an intersection between two automobiles, which damaged both cars and the passengers. One of the cars was a police car which at 1 A.M., while carrying a prematurely born baby to a hospital, drove through a red light at 45 miles per hour. At the trial the jury found the civilians not negligent and that the police car was being driven recklessly. From the resulting judgments in favor of the civilians and against the police and the city, appeals are taken to this court.]

FINE, J. [after stating the facts and dealing with contributory negligence]. Was the police car operated in reckless disregard for the safety of others? A police car operated in chase or apprehension of law violators or suspects or an ambulance when traveling in emergency is exempt from The Motor Vehicle Code of May 1, 1929, P.L. 905, as amended by the Act of June 5, 1937, P.L. 1718, regarding speed, § 1002(f), 75 P.S. § 501, traffic signals, § 1026(d), 75 P.S. § 635, entries upon through highways and stop intersections, § 1016(d), 75 P.S. § 591; and when operated upon official business with audible signal, the exemption applies to the right of way rule, § 1014(b), 75 P.S. § 573. These exemptions are conditional upon the vehicle being operated "with due regard for the safety of all persons using the highway"; they do not protect the operator "from the consequences of a reckless disregard of the safety of others," or "from the consequence of an arbitrary exercise of [the] right of way." The municipality is jointly and severally liable with the operator for damages caused where such negligence is of a reckless nature. Reilly v. Philadelphia, 328 Pa. 563, 195 A. 897. As stated by Mr. Justice LINN while on the Superior Court: "Recklessness implies conscious appreciation of the probable extent of danger or risk incident to contemplated action, while negligence in the legal sense implies knowledge only of a probable source of danger in the act": Lloyd v. Noakes, 96 Pa.Super. 164, 168. In the Restatement, Torts, § 500 (p. 1293), it is set forth that a person has acted in reckless disregard for the safety of others "if he intentionally does an act or fails to do an act which it is his duty to the other to do, knowing or having reason to know of facts which would lead a reasonable man to realize that the actor's conduct not only creates an unreasonable risk of bodily harm to the other but also involves a high degree of probability that substantial harm will result to him." Neither the speed at which the car was traveling nor the operation of the car through a red light are enough to make out a case against appellants provided there was no "reckless disregard for the safety of others." * * *

* * * While the hour of the accident militates against recklessness, we cannot say as a matter of law that it was not recklessness to drive a police car or ambulance at forty-five miles per hour through a red light, particularly where another car was committed to the intersection, plainly to be seen and to whose operator no audible or cautionary signal was given of the emergency mission of the oncoming car. The essential elements of recklessness are present in this case, viz., the operation of the police car at a high rate of speed through a red signal without audible warning to a car, proceeding through the intersection on a green light and plainly visible on a broad well lighted thoroughfare, created a situation of grave peril and unreasonable risk of bodily harm to other users of the highway, which the operator of the police car knew or should have known would arise from his conduct. The fact that the police officer was engaged in the performance of his duties did not relieve him of the duty of care at intersections, nor absolve the city from liability for his negligence in the course of duty. * * *

The judgments are affirmed.

ALTMAN v. ARONSON, 231 Mass. 588, 121 N.E. 505, 4 A.L.R. 1185 (1919). Tort for damages resulting from the alleged negligence of defendants, gratuitous bailees of plaintiff's goods, whereby the goods were lost to plaintiff. *Held,* that defendants, being gratuitous bailees, were liable only for gross negligence. "Gross negligence is substantially and appreciably higher in magnitude than ordinary negligence. It is materially more want of care than constitutes simple inadvertence. It is an act or omission respecting legal duty of an aggravated character as distinguished from a mere failure to exercise ordinary care. It is very great negligence, or the absence of slight diligence, or the want of even scant care. * * * The element of culpability which characterizes all negligence is in gross negligence magnified to a high degree as compared with that present in ordinary negligence. * * * But it is something less than wilful, wanton and reckless conduct * * *. It falls short of being such reckless disregard of probable consequences as is equivalent to a wilful and intentional wrong. Ordinary and gross negligence differ in degree of inattention, while both differ in kind from wilful and intentional conduct which is or ought to be known to have a tendency to injure."

MYHAVER v. KNUTSON

Supreme Court of Arizona, 1997.
189 Ariz. 286, 942 P.2d 445.

FELDMAN, Justice.

Plaintiffs Bruce and Barbara Myhaver sought review of a court of appeals' decision holding that the "sudden emergency" instruction was properly given in a case arising out of an automobile collision. We granted review to determine whether a sudden emergency instruction is ever appropriate * * *.

In November 1990, Elmo Knutson was driving north on 43rd Avenue * * * in Phoenix when Theresa Magnusson entered 43rd Avenue from a shopping center driveway and headed south in Knutson's lane. Seeing Magnusson's car in his lane, Knutson accelerated and swerved left, avoiding what he perceived to be an impending head-on collision. In doing this, he crossed the double yellow line into oncoming traffic and collided with Bruce Myhaver's pickup. Magnusson continued south not realizing she was involved. A police officer who saw the accident stopped her a short distance away and asked her to return to the scene.

Myhaver was seriously injured as a result of the collision and brought a damage action against both Knutson and Magnusson. Magnusson settled and was named as a non-party at fault, and the Myhavers proceeded to trial against Knutson.

* * *

At trial, [the] judge ruled that the [sudden emergency] instruction was appropriate under the facts and instructed the jury as follows:

> In determining whether a person acted with reasonable care under the circumstances, you may consider whether such conduct was affected by an emergency.

> An "emergency" is defined as a sudden and unexpected encounter with a danger which is either real or reasonably seems to be real. If a person, without negligence on his or her part, encountered such an emergency and acted reasonably to avoid harm to self or others, you may find that the person was not negligent. This is so even though, in hindsight, you feel that under normal conditions some other or better course of conduct could and should have been followed.

[The jury found Knutson not liable.]

* * *

* * * [T]he sudden emergency instruction tells the jury that in the absence of antecedent negligence, a person confronted with a sudden emergency that deprives him of time to contemplate the best reaction cannot be held to the same standard of care and accuracy of choice as one who has time to deliberate. See Jeffrey F. Ghent, Annotation, *Modern Status of Sudden Emergency Doctrine*, 10 A.L.R.5th 680, 687 (1993). Criticism of

this doctrine has focused on its ability to confuse a jury as to (1) whether the reasonable person standard of care, or some lower standard, applies in an emergency; and (2) how it affects the application of comparative negligence principles.[2] *Id.* The annotation's author notes that a few jurisdictions have abolished sudden emergency instructions, either generally or just in automobile accident cases, while others have discouraged their use, sometimes placing specific restrictions on which cases are appropriate for their use. *Id.* at 688. However, several jurisdictions still explicitly retain the sudden emergency doctrine, either generally or with the qualification that sudden emergency instructions are allowed but not required.

* * *

Commentators on Arizona's negligence law have described the problem and the present state of our law as follows:

> Conceptually, the emergency doctrine is not an independent rule. It is merely an application of the general standard of reasonable care; the emergency is simply one of the circumstances faced. Arguably, giving a separate instruction on sudden emergency focuses the jury's attention unduly on that aspect of a case. * * *

JEFFERSON L. LANKFORD & DOUGLAS A. BLAZE, THE LAW OF NEGLIGENCE IN ARIZONA § 3.5(1), at 43 (1992).

* * *

A similar [point] is made by the leading commentators on negligence law, noting that a

> further qualification which must be made is that some "emergencies" must be anticipated, and the actor must be prepared to meet them when he engages in an activity in which they are likely to arise. Thus, under present day traffic conditions, any driver of an automobile must be prepared for the sudden appearance of obstacles and persons in the highway, and of other vehicles at intersections, just as one who sees a child on the curb may be required to anticipate its sudden dash into the street, and his failure to act properly when they appear may be found to amount to negligence.

W. PAGE KEETON ET AL., PROSSER AND KEETON ON THE LAW OF TORTS § 33, at 197 (5th ed. 1984). * * *

* * *

Knapp [*v. Stanford*, 392 So.2d 196 (Miss.1980),] is a good example of those cases abandoning the sudden emergency instruction. The defendant, faced with an oncoming car in his lane of travel, swerved to his right and went off the shoulder of the road. After the other car passed him, he swerved back to his left and lost control of his car. The Mississippi Supreme Court held that the emergency instruction was inappropriate because the emergency was over at the time the accident occurred, the two cars having

---

2. The doctrine evidently had its origins as a defense to contributory negligence, so it is of less consequence in states like Arizona that have adopted comparative negligence.

passed each other and defendant having undertaken to return to the road. It further concluded that the instruction should not be given in the future because a sudden emergency was simply a factor to be considered in determining reasonable conduct and a separate instruction might overemphasize that factor as well as confuse the jury on comparative negligence issues.

Although criticizing the instruction and holding that it need not be given, other states leave it to the judge's discretion. * * *

* * *

Having noted that the instruction is but a factor to be considered in determining reasonable care, is subsumed within the general concept of negligence, is a matter of argument rather than a principle of law, and can single out and unduly emphasize one factor and thus mislead a jury, we join those courts that have discouraged use of the instruction and urge our trial judges to give it only in the rare case. The instruction should be confined to the case in which the emergency * * * arises from events the driver could not be expected to anticipate.

We do not, however, join those courts that absolutely forbid use of the instruction. There are cases in which the instruction may be useful * * *. We believe, however, that in those few cases in which the instruction is given, it would be important to explain that the existence of a sudden emergency and reaction to it are only some of the factors to be considered in determining what is reasonable conduct under the circumstances. Even though a judge may exercise his discretion and give a sudden emergency instruction in a particular case, it will rarely, if ever, be error to refuse to give it.

Applying these principles to the case at bench, we conclude that the trial judge did not abuse his discretion in giving the instruction. This is a case in which there was no evidence of antecedent negligence by Knutson, in whose favor the instruction was given. In light of the testimony of the various witnesses, there was no question about the existence of an emergency. Knutson was faced with a situation not ordinarily to be anticipated and one of imminent peril when Magnusson pulled out of the shopping center and suddenly turned toward him in the wrong lane of traffic. Finally, Knutson's reaction—swerving across the center line into the path of Myhaver's oncoming vehicle—was probably both reflexive in nature and the type of conduct that absent a sudden emergency would almost automatically be found as negligence, if not negligence per se. Given these facts, the real and only issue was whether Knutson's conduct was reasonable under the circumstances of the emergency. We believe, therefore, the trial judge had discretion to instruct on the sudden emergency as a factor in the determination of negligence.

[Affirmed.]

ZLAKET, Chief Justice, specially concurring.

I am puzzled by the majority's desire to perpetuate a jury instruction that is admittedly of marginal value but has such enormous potential for harm. In my opinion, today's decision prolongs a decades-old controversy surrounding the "sudden emergency" doctrine and provides little added guidance to Arizona's trial judges. * * *

* * *

Moreover, today's resolution fails to address the essential flaw in the instruction—that it overemphasizes and tends to accord independent status to what is but one of many elements in every negligence analysis. If drivers cannot "be expected to anticipate" certain events, they are by definition free from negligence. * * *

* * *

However, because the instruction in question has not yet been specifically disapproved in Arizona, and appears to have been harmless under the particular facts of this case, I am unwilling to say that the trial judge abused his discretion. I therefore concur in the result.

FRUEHAUF TRAILER CO. v. GUSEWELLE, 190 F.2d 248 (8th Cir.1951), certiorari denied 342 U.S. 866, 72 S.Ct. 105, 96 L.Ed. 651 (1951). "The sudden emergency doctrine is not an exception to the general rule that one must act at all times as a reasonably prudent man would act under the same circumstances. An emergency is merely one of the circumstances to be considered by the jury."

NORTHLAND INSURANCE CO. v. AVIS RENT–A–CAR, 62 Wis.2d 643, 215 N.W.2d 439 (1974). Balistreri was "tailgating" a large semi truck. The semi swerved to avoid a disabled vehicle parked partly on the travelled portion of the highway. Balistreri collided with the disabled vehicle. The court said:

"In the present case, Balistreri could not see the disabled truck until he was 40 feet from it and after the semi turned to the left. Balistreri's completely blocked view of the road ahead was caused by tailgating the eight-foot wide, 12–foot high semi-truck some 55 to 60 [feet] behind. * * *

"Under this view, Balistreri placed himself in a position which precludes the application of the emergency doctrine. The three requirements for the emergency doctrine were set out in Cook v. Thomas (1964), 25 Wis.2d 467, 471, 131 N.W.2d 299, and approved in Geis v. Hirth (1966), 32 Wis.2d 580, 146 N.W.2d 459. These three requirements included freedom from negligence contributing to the creation of the emergency, a short-time interval, and a question of the driver's management and control after he becomes aware of the situation. Since Balistreri was negligent in respect to creating the situation, he was not entitled to the emergency-doctrine instruction."

MORAN v. ATHA TRUCKING, 208 W.Va. 379, 540 S.E.2d 903 (1997). "Having recognized the problems surrounding the sudden emergency doctrine * * *, however, we do not choose to abandon it. Instead, we believe that the doctrine can be clarified so as to mitigate its dangers while still providing a useful tool for juries in allocating fault in our comparative negligence scheme."

"We believe * * * that a jury instruction concerning a sudden emergency must state that the existence of an emergency requiring a rapid decision is *one factor* in the total comparative fault analysis. Such an instruction should be included in the instruction on determining the comparative negligence of the parties and should not be a separate instruction. This will avoid placing undue emphasis on the existence of the sudden emergency."

PUBLIC SERVICE OF NEW HAMPSHIRE v. ELLIOTT
United States Circuit Court of Appeals, First Circuit, 1941.
123 F.2d 2.

[Plaintiff, a nineteen-year-old boy, in the second year of a course on electrical construction, was injured by coming too close to a high tension wire while he was a member of a group invited to inspect defendant's electrical substation at Manchester, N. H. From a judgment for the plaintiff, defendant appeals.]

MAGRUDER, C. J. [after holding that New Hampshire law requires a land owner to use care in the control of dynamic forces with respect to licensees and known trespassers]. On the issue of contributory negligence we cannot say that the trial judge was in error in concluding that a reasonable jury might find the plaintiff free from contributory negligence. It may be that the plaintiff knew more than the ordinary uninstructed layman about the properties of electricity; hence the plaintiff's conduct must be judged in the light of that superior knowledge. Torts Restatement, § 289, and comment n. But while the plaintiff may have had some theoretical instruction on the destructive force of high voltage electricity, the jury might conclude, not unreasonably, that an ordinary prudent man in the plaintiff's position would not have been on the lookout for exposed parts so close to the aisle, especially in the absence of any warning signs in the high tension room and in the absence of any cautionary remarks by the chief operator as he led the visitors into the room.

Perhaps the plaintiff, if he had focused his attention on the construction of the current transformer, might, with the knowledge he had, have come to a realization that he was in dangerous proximity to unguarded parts above the bushing. But the "reasonable man," that standardized man to whose assumed conduct in like circumstances the plaintiff's conduct must conform, is not altogether devoid of human frailties. This "reasonable man" may, for instance, make an error of judgment in an emergency. [Citations omitted.] So, too, his standardized mind may be inadvertent to conditions indicative of danger, where adequate diverting circumstances are present. [Citations omitted.] On the facts of the case at bar we cannot say that the plaintiff was guilty of contributory negligence as a matter of law in failing to direct his attention to a careful study of the details of the current transformer unit before making the spontaneous and wholly natural gesture of pointing toward the glass jar mounted on top of it.

[Judgment affirmed.]

REYNOLDS v. LOS ANGELES GAS & ELECTRIC CO., 162 Cal. 327, 122 P. 962 (1912). The plaintiff, an elderly woman, during the day saw a ditch being dug across the usual approach to her premises. In the evening she went out and, remembering the open ditch, to avoid it, took an unaccustomed route. Upon returning a few moments later, being in a hurry and having forgotten about the ditch, she took her accustomed path, fell into the ditch and suffered harm. *Held,* reversing a judgment for plaintiff and remanding the cause, that plaintiff, who was subjected to no peril, stress, strain, or haste which would excuse her forgetfulness, having known of the dangerous defect, was bound at her peril to remember it.

WAND v. CITY OF SHELBINA, 420 S.W.2d 348 (Mo.1967). Action by pedestrian against city for injuries sustained in fall on a cracked sidewalk step. *Held,* directed verdict for city reversed for new trial. Plaintiff contended that a car horn, which she thought was her daughter's, attracted her attention and that under controlling precedent this was a sufficient diversion to support a jury finding that she was not contributorily negligent.

"Defendant, of course, contends that the sounding of the automobile horn was only a trivial diversion which could not excuse plaintiff in the process of taking a step in close proximity to the defect in the sidewalk step. However, under the above authorities, we consider its triviality and effect to be for the jury to determine in deciding the issue of contributory negligence."

See Seavey, Negligence—Subjective or Objective, 41 Harv.L.Rev. 1 (1927); Edgerton, Negligence, Inadvertence and Indifference, 39 Harv.L.Rev. 849 (1926).

RESTATEMENT OF TORTS, THIRD: LIABILITY FOR PHYSICAL HARM (BASIC PRINCIPLES), Tent. Draft No. 1 (March 28, 2001). Section 12, titled "Knowledge and Skills," provides:

> If an actor has skills or knowledge that exceed those possessed by most others, these skills or knowledge are circumstances to be taken into account in determining whether the actor has behaved as a reasonably careful person.

DELAIR v. McADOO, 324 Pa. 392, 188 A. 181 (1936). The plaintiff was injured when the defendant lost control of his automobile due to a blow out of a rear tire while he was passing plaintiff's car, proceeding in the same direction. The plaintiff charged negligence, in that the tire was worn through to and into the fabric over its entire area. *Held,* for plaintiff. "We have in this state more than a million automobiles and trucks, approximately two for every three families. * * * Any ordinary individual, whether a car owner or not, knows that when a tire is worn through to the fabric, its further use is dangerous and it should be removed. When worn through several plys, it is very dangerous for further use. All drivers must be held to a knowledge of these facts. An owner or operator cannot escape simply because he says he does not know. He must know. The hazard is too great to permit cars in this condition to be on the highway."

RESTATEMENT OF TORTS, THIRD: LIABILITY FOR PHYSICAL HARM (BASIC PRINCIPLES)
Tent. Draft No. 1 (March 28, 2001).

§ 11. Disability

(a) If an actor has a physical disability, the actor's conduct is negligent if it does not conform to that of a reasonably careful person with the same disability.

(b) If an actor engages in substandard conduct because of sudden incapacitation or loss of consciousness brought about by physical illness, this conduct constitutes negligence only if the sudden incapacitation or loss of consciousness was reasonably foreseeable to the actor.

(c) Unless the actor is a child, the actor's mental or emotional disability is not considered in determining whether conduct is negligent.

Comment:

a. Disabilities considered. The physical disabilities this section takes into account generally need to be significant and objectively verifiable. For reasons relating to convenience of administration, it is not worthwhile to attempt to take into account disabilities that are minor or not susceptible to objective verification. Thus, a person's claim of being born clumsy would not be regarded as relevant.

b. Implications. * * * [T]he section recognizes that * * * a person's significant physical disability should be taken into account in determining whether the person's conduct lacks reasonable care. * * * Accordingly, the test is whether the individual has acted as a reasonably careful person with the particular disability. With physical disabilities, then—just as with childhood—tort law tailors the negligence standard to acknowledge the individual situation of the actor. To this extent, tort law employs what can be called a subjective rather than a fully objective standard of care. * * *

c. Old age. Old age, as such, is not taken into account in assessing the negligence of a person's conduct. * * *

e. Mental and emotional disability. When the actor is a child, the quite subjective rules concerning children * * * apply, and any mental or emotional disability suffered by the child is taken into account in determining whether the child has behaved reasonably. For adults, however, such a disability is typically disregarded in considering whether the person has exercised reasonable care. This is the position taken by the Restatement Second of Torts (§ 283B), and the position is supported by a consistent line of modern cases. * * *

* * *

Just as the rules concerning children * * * and the physical-disability rules in this section apply equally to the issues of negligence and contributory negligence, the rule in Subsection (c) that a person's mental disabilities shall be disregarded applies in the context of the person's contributory negligence as well as the context of the person's negligence. Restatement Third, Torts: Apportionment of Liability § 3, Comment *a*, concludes that the "[s]tandard for plaintiff's negligence [is the] same as [the] standard for defendant's negligence." The shift in tort doctrine from contributory negligence as a full defense to comparative responsibility as a partial defense weakens [arguments that] otherwise might favor a dual standard that would treat the mentally disabled plaintiff more leniently than the mentally disabled defendant. Under comparative [fault], * * * even though the plaintiff's mental disability is ignored in considering whether the plaintiff is contributorily negligent at all * * *, that disability can be considered in the course of the more open-ended process of apportioning percentages of responsibility between the plaintiff and the defendant. * * * Indeed, if the evidence shows that the plaintiff is largely unable to appreciate risks or largely unable to control conduct in light of risk, the jury is likely to assign to the plaintiff only a small share of the overall responsibility. Here, as elsewhere, the flexibility of comparative negligence permits intermediate accommodations that were not available under the traditional all-or-nothing defense of contributory negligence.

SMITH v. SNELLER

Superior Court of Pennsylvania, 1942.
147 Pa.Super. 231, 24 A.2d 61.
Affirmed in 345 Pa. 68, 26 A.2d 452.

[Action for negligence. Defendants dug a trench across a sidewalk, protecting it only by the earth thrown up from it. Plaintiff, a house to house canvasser with impaired eyesight, fell into it. Verdict for plaintiff. Defendant appeals from a refusal to enter judgment for defendant notwithstanding verdict.]

HIRT, J. [after stating the facts]. Sympathetic as we are to the plaintiff in his effort to make a living in spite of his physical handicap, we think it clear that he did not present a case free from contributory negligence and is barred from recovery on that ground. This question is raised by the refusal of the lower court to enter judgment for defendants n.o.v.

There is no doubt as to the degree of impairment of plaintiff's vision. He could perceive light and, under favorable conditions, objects, but could not distinguish them. His sight was so impaired that his reference to himself in his statement of claim as a "blind person" is an accurate appraisal, for all practical purposes, of his ability to see. He was somewhat familiar with the neighborhood and he managed to go about without an attendant, guided by the sky line of the buildings and was able to keep on the sidewalk by means of the poles and trees along the curb or hedges marking the property lines. These, under favorable light conditions, he was able to see dimly. When on the witness stand on the trial of this case, however, he could not see the trial judge nor an examiner who was within five feet of him nor the foreman of the jury six feet away.

Describing what occurred just before his injury, plaintiff said: "I was walking along very carefully there; there was a hedge and of course some trees that I use as markers, and I felt a break in the paving, and felt some dirt, and my foot started to go down a little bit and then gave way and I could not hold my balance and fell in there. I didn't get directly into the hole but stepped on the edge of the dirt embankment there, and that gave away and I went in." He did not carry a cane and, because he was unable to see, did not have notice of the break in the pavement, the pile of earth on the sidewalk, nor the open trench in front of him. The injury occurred in the early afternoon of July 1, 1940, a bright summer day. But for his blindness he also would have seen a barricade along the north side of the trench.
* * *

It is not negligence for a blind person to walk unattended upon the sidewalks of a city but, in so doing there is a heavy burden upon him; he must conform with the standard of care "established by law for all persons alike, whether they be sound or deficient." Plaintiff's conduct failed to meet that standard. The fact that plaintiff did not anticipate the existence of an unguarded ditch, in itself, does not charge him with negligence. But it is common knowledge, chargeable to plaintiff, that obstructions and defects of one kind or another are not uncommon in the sidewalks of a city, any one of which may be the source of injury to the blind. Plaintiff's vision was so defective that he could not depend upon it to warn him of a dangerous condition immediately in front of him. A cane, the blind man's "long arm" is a poor substitute for sight but can be made useful in determining whether the road before him is clear. It is especially serviceable on a hard surface pavement. Its skillful use in this case, in all probability, would have warned plaintiff that a section of the concrete pavement had been removed, or that the excavated material had been thrown upon the walk, in time to avoid falling into the trench. A blind man may not rely wholly upon his other senses to warn him of danger but must use the devices usually employed, to compensate for his blindness. Only by so doing can he go about with comparative safety to himself.

Judgment reversed and directed to be entered for defendant appellant n.o.v.

———

WILSON v. CLARK, 238 Or. 126, 393 P.2d 659 (1964). Jury question whether involuntary sneeze was an excusing distraction; directed verdict for plaintiff reversed.

REEG v. HODGSON, 1 Ohio App.2d 272, 202 N.E.2d 310 (1964). Instruction properly given that if defendant suffered sudden unforeseeable cramp causing foot to slip off brake, he could not be found negligent.

WILLIAMSON v. GARLAND

Court of Appeals of Kentucky, 1966.
402 S.W.2d 80.

DAVIS, Commissioner. Dennis Neal Williamson, a minor nearly 12 years old, was injured when he was riding a bicycle which collided with the automobile of appellee Raymond Garland. In this damage suit the trial court directed a verdict for appellee; in announcing its decision, the trial court expressed the view that there was no showing of appellee's negligence and appellant was guilty of contributory negligence as a matter of law. This appeal challenges each of these rulings as erroneous.

The accident occurred on a clear day in August, on Jackson Street at or near its intersection with 29th Street in Paducah. Jackson Street is the preferred street. Jackson is a four lane street, running in an east-west direction; 29th Street runs north-south.

Appellant was riding a bicycle northwardly on 29th Street just before the accident. He was "ahead" in a bicycle race being engaged in between Bruce Johnson, also 11, and himself. Appellee was driving his car eastwardly on Jackson at about 20–25 mph; he was driving in the lane nearest the right curb of Jackson. A hedge and slight embankment on the west side of 29th Street partially obstructed the views for travelers going north on 29th and east on Jackson.

According to Bruce Johnson, who was trailing appellant on his bicycle, appellant applied his brake as he approached Jackson Street, but skidded in some loose gravel, entered Jackson Street, turned eastwardly on Jackson, and started "pumping" the bike down Jackson. Bruce expressed the opinion that appellant "tried to outrun" the approaching car of appellee. The boy said that he thought the collision occurred "by a telephone pole."

* * *

The appellant sustained a fractured skull and brain injury in the collision; he was unable to recall the details of the accident with any degree of certainty. The appellee was called to testify briefly on cross-examination, and said that he did not see appellant before the impact. * * *

During the trial appellant was not able to recall details of the accident, although appellee's counsel elicited answers from him in which he stated that he knew traffic was heavy along Jackson Street, that he should have stopped before entering Jackson, he should have looked to his left but did not think he had, and the accident would not have occurred if he had stopped and looked for traffic. * * *

We examine the question of contributory negligence. Appellant's counsel concedes that the act of appellant would constitute contributory negligence as a matter of law if done by an adult, but asserts that the same rule is not applicable here because of appellant's age. The litigants recognize that our cases have uniformly followed the rule that children ranging from seven through 14 years of age are presumed incapable of contributory negligence, although the presumption is a rebuttable one. * * *

* * *

It seems to us that the better rule would be to impose on the child-plaintiff the duty to exercise that degree of care reasonably to be expected from the ordinary child of like age, intelligence and experience under like or similar circumstances. It is quite obvious that the normal seven-year-old child should not be charged with the same degree of care to be expected of the normal 14-year-old child, so the blanket rule of rebuttable presumption as to all children encompassed within these age limits lacks basis in reason.[1]

* * * This is not to say that no case could arise in which it would be proper to find a child in the 7–14 age group guilty or free of contributory negligence as a matter of law, but it is to say that the case at bar is not such a one. Our earlier decisions to the contrary shall no longer be authoritative as to the presumption against capacity as it relates to children seven to 14, inclusive. Henceforth, when an issue is presented respecting the contributory negligence of a minor plaintiff seven or more years of age, unless the contributory negligence (or lack of it) is established as a matter of law, the jury shall be instructed that the minor is charged with the duty to exercise care for his own safety, commensurate with that degree of care usually exercised by an ordinarily prudent minor of the same age, intelligence and experience of the plaintiff.

This brings us to the question of whether any negligence of the appellee appears in this record. We conclude that the physical facts, considered with the testimony of Bruce Johnson and the appellee, are sufficient to create a jury issue whether appellee was negligent. It will be recalled that appellee said he did not see appellant until the moment of impact—the injured boy and his damaged bicycle were found about 60 feet past the intersection—Bruce Johnson thought the collision occurred by the pole, and that appellant had made his turn and started pumping his pedals as if to "beat" the oncoming car. The marks on the car are not incompatible with the appellant's theory that the car sideswiped the bicycle after the latter had taken its course in the stream of Jackson Street traffic. This leaves the question of appellee's lookout and whether he exercised ordinary care to avoid colliding with the appellant under the circumstances. The jury might well have believed that the car necessarily overtook the bicycle, and that its driver had ample opportunity to avoid the collision in the exercise of ordinary care. In this state of record we hold that it was error to adjudge that the appellee was as a matter of law free of negligence.

* * *

The judgment is reversed for further proceedings consistent with this opinion.

MONTGOMERY and STEWART, JJ., dissenting.

———

MASTLAND, INC. v. EVANS FURNITURE, INC., 498 N.W.2d 682 (Iowa 1993). A landlord brought suit alleging that negligence of the tenant's very

---

1. These multiples of seven are criticized by Prosser, who says that the great majority of courts have rejected such fixed and arbitrary rules of delimitation. Prosser on Torts, 3d ed., p. 158.

young child, in playing with a cigarette lighter, caused a fire that destroyed the leased premises. In the course of ruling against the plaintiff, the Iowa Supreme Court said that the inquiry concerning a child's negligence involves a "subjective" step followed by an "objective" step:

"The jury's first inquiry is a subjective one: What was the capacity of this particular child—given what the evidence shows about his age, intelligence and experience—to perceive and avoid the particular risk involved in this case? Once this has been determined, the focus becomes objective: How would a reasonable child of like capacity have acted under similar circumstances? The particular child in question can be found negligent only if his actions fall short of what may reasonably be expected of children of similar capacity."

DELLWO v. PEARSON, 259 Minn. 452, 107 N.W.2d 859, 97 A.L.R.2d 866 (1961). The 12–year-old defendant, operating a motorboat, crossed over plaintiff's fishing line, entangling the line in the propeller of defendant's boat and causing a pull on plaintiff's reel that jerked it against the side of her boat, forcing the reel to come apart. Part of it struck her glasses and injured her eye. The trial court instructed the jury that a child is not held to the same standard as an adult, but is required only to exercise the care ordinarily exercised by children of like age, mental capacity and experience under the same or similar circumstances. The jury returned a verdict for defendant. From judgment on the verdict, plaintiff appeals, alleging error in the instruction on proximate cause. *Held,* reversed because of error in the instruction on proximate cause. [That part of the opinion is reprinted infra, p. 626] For guidance on retrial, the court observed that, while the standard of care described in the trial court's instruction is appropriate for the issue of contributory negligence, on the issue of negligence as a basis of liability "we hold that in the operation of an automobile, airplane or powerboat, a minor is to be held to the same standard of care as an adult."

WRIGHT v. TATE
Supreme Court of Appeals of Virginia, 1967.
208 Va. 291, 156 S.E.2d 562.

SNEAD, Justice. Leslie Robinson Wright, a guest passenger in an automobile operated by Homer Neal Wright, defendant, was fatally injured when the vehicle ran off Route 606 in Bland county and struck a tree. Fred B. Tate, Jr., Administrator of the estate of Leslie Robinson Wright, plaintiff, brought an action against defendant to recover damages for the wrongful death of his decedent.

* * *

[The plaintiff's decedent, Leslie Wright, was 22 years old, single, and resided with and supported his parents.]

In Restatement, (Second), Torts, (1965) § 464, p. 507, the standard of conduct relating to contributory negligence is defined thus: "Unless the actor is a child or an insane person, the standard of conduct to which he must conform for his own protection is that of a reasonable man under like circumstances." Under Comment g. of § 464, p. 509, it is stated: "Mental deficiency which falls short of insanity, however, does not excuse conduct which is otherwise contributory negligence."

Under these principles, which we adopt, an adult who is of low mentality but not insane is held to the same standard of care as a person of greater intellect. If the rule were otherwise, there would be a different standard for each level of intelligence resulting in confusion and uncertainty in the law.

Here, the evidence shows that plaintiff's decedent was a person of low mentality who was capable of performing only the simplest of tasks, could not be trusted around machinery because "he might get hurt", and lacked initiative. There was no showing that he was insane or that a guardian had ever been appointed to care for either his person or property. There was no medical testimony with regard to his mental status. Moreover, plaintiff's decedent was regularly employed as a farm worker and supported the family. His sister testified that he could "read and write to an extent, and some things he could learn." He was able to cash his pay checks and to purchase provisions for the family. According to his brother-in-law, "[h]e was strong and * * * proud to work." Since insanity was not shown, plaintiff's decedent was bound by the standard of conduct "of a reasonable man under like circumstances."

"* * * We have several times said that a guest may be guilty of contributory negligence if he knows or reasonably should know that his driver had been drinking intoxicating liquor to an extent likely to affect the manner of his driving and voluntarily continues as a passenger after a reasonable opportunity to leave the automobile.

"However, in Yorke v. Maynard, supra, we pointed out that the fact that the host had been drinking and the guest had knowledge of this fact is not sufficient to establish contributory negligence as a matter of law. The evidence must go beyond this and show that because of his drinking the driver's ability to drive was impaired, that the guest knew, or in the exercise of ordinary care should have known this and yet entered or continued to ride in the car. Whether the guest knew or should have known that the intoxicated condition of the driver impaired his ability to drive is ordinarily a question for the jury. 8 Am.Jur.2d, Automobiles, etc., §§ 537, 538, pp. 94–96." Meade, Adm'r v. Meade, Adm'r, 206 Va. 823, 827, 147 S.E.2d 171, 174.

Here, there was no conflict in the evidence as to whether defendant was in an intoxicated condition from the time the group left Blankenship's store at Hollybrook until the time of the mishap. All of the evidence showed that defendant was in such a condition. Under the circumstances that existed, a reasonable man should have known, as a matter of law, that the intoxicated condition of defendant impaired his ability to drive. Thus, there was no jury question on this point.

Plaintiff's decedent voluntarily entered the car at Hollybrook which was driven by defendant at high speeds and in a very reckless manner. When the group reached the restaurant on Cloyd's mountain and stopped for beer, Kermit Gussler requested that he be permitted to drive back to Hollybrook, but his request was denied. He then asked the occupants to "hitchhike" back to Hollybrook with him. No one accepted his invitation and they started on the return trip, with defendant driving the vehicle. But before they left the mountain, plaintiff's decedent told Kermit Gussler that he should drive the car. This fact is uncontradicted. Hence, plaintiff's decedent recognized his safety was in jeopardy with defendant driving.

On the return trip defendant continued to drive the car in a reckless manner. When they stopped at Latha Spangler's home to put water in the radiator, plaintiff's decedent had another opportunity to alight from the automobile and avoid exposure to further recklessness of the driver. There, Kermit Gussler renewed his invitation to "hitchhike", but plaintiff's decedent elected to continue on the ride. After further reckless driving by defendant, the fatal crash occurred.

We hold that plaintiff's decedent was, as a matter of law, contributorily negligent. He entered defendant's car when he knew or in the exercise of ordinary care should have known that defendant's driving ability was impaired. Further, upon witnessing defendant's careless operation of the vehicle, he continued to ride after having had a reasonable opportunity to alight from the car. Thus, the trial court erred in overruling defendant's motion to strike plaintiff's evidence.

In view of this conclusion, it becomes unnecessary to discuss other errors assigned.

Accordingly, the verdict of the jury is set aside; the judgment appealed from is reversed; and final judgment is entered here for defendant.

BREUNIG v. AMERICAN FAMILY INSURANCE CO.
Supreme Court of Wisconsin, 1970.
45 Wis.2d 536, 173 N.W.2d 619, 49 A.L.R.3d 179.

[Action by truck driver against insurer of car and driver, Erma Veith. The defense was that Veith was not negligent because just before the collision she suddenly and without warning was seized with a mental aberration or delusion that rendered her unable to operate the car with her conscious mind. A psychiatrist testified that she was suffering from "schizophrenic reaction, paranoid type, acute." Verdict for plaintiff, and judgment for plaintiff after plaintiff accepted a reduction in damages and filed a remittitur. The defendant appealed.]

HALLOWS, Chief Justice.

* * *

The Insurance Company argues Erma Veith was not negligent as a matter of law because there is no evidence upon which the jury could find that she had knowledge or warning or should have reasonably foreseen that she might be subject to a mental delusion which would suddenly cause her to lose control of the car. Plaintiff argues there was such evidence of forewarning and also suggests Erma Veith should be liable because insanity should not be a defense in negligence cases.

The case was tried on the theory that some forms of insanity are a defense to and preclude liability for negligence under the doctrine of Theisen v. Milwaukee Automobile Mut. Ins. Co. (1962), 18 Wis.2d 91, 118 N.W.2d 140, 119 N.W.2d 393. We agree. Not all types of insanity vitiate responsibility for a negligent tort. The question of liability in every case must depend upon the kind and nature of the insanity. The effect of the mental illness or mental hallucinations or disorder must be such as to affect the person's ability to understand and appreciate the duty which rests upon him to drive his car with ordinary care, or if the insanity does not affect such understanding and appreciation, it must affect his ability to control his car in an ordinarily prudent manner. And in addition, there must be an absence of notice of forewarning to the person that he may be suddenly subject to such a type of insanity or mental illness.

In *Theisen* we recognized one was not negligent if he was unable to conform his conduct through no fault of his own but held a sleeping driver negligent as a matter of law because one is always given conscious warnings of drowsiness and if a person does not heed such warnings and continues to drive his car, he is negligent for continuing to drive under such conditions. But we distinguished those exceptional cases of loss of consciousness resulting from injury inflicted by an outside force, or fainting, or heart attack, or epileptic seizure, or other illness which suddenly incapacitates the driver of an automobile when the occurrence of such disability is not attended with sufficient warning or should not have been reasonably foreseen.

Theisen followed Eleason v. Western Casualty & Surety Co. (1948), 254 Wis. 134, 35 N.W.2d 301 * * *. In *Eleason* we held the driver, an epileptic, possessed knowledge that he was likely to have a seizure and therefore was negligent in driving a car and responsible for the accident occurring while he had an epileptic seizure. * * *

There are authorities which generally hold insanity is not a defense in tort cases except for intentional torts. Restatement of Torts, 2d Ed., p. 16, sec. 283B, and appendix (1966) and cases cited therein. These cases rest on the historical view of strict liability without regard to the fault of the individual. Prosser, in his Law of Torts, 3d Ed. p. 1028, states this view is a historical survival which originated in the dictum in Weaver v. Ward (1616), Hob. 134, 80 English Reports 284, when the action of trespass still rested upon strict liability. He points out that when the modern law developed to the point of holding the defendant liable for negligence, the dictum was repeated in some cases.

The policy basis of holding a permanently insane person liable for his tort is: (1) Where one of two innocent persons must suffer a loss it should be borne by the one who occasioned it; (2) to induce those interested in the estate of the insane person (if he has one) to restrain and control him; and (3) the fear an insanity defense would lead to false claims of insanity to avoid liability. These three grounds were mentioned in the In re Guardianship of Meyer (1935), 218 Wis. 381, 261 N.W. 211, where a farm hand who was insane set fire to his employer's barn. The insurance company paid the loss and filed a claim against the estate of the insane person and was allowed to recover.

* * * The plaintiff cites * * * Johnson v. Lombotte (1961) 147 Colo. 203, 363 P.2d 165, for holding insanity is not a defense in negligence cases. * * * In *Johnson,* the defendant was under observation by order of the county court and was being treated in a hospital for "chronic schizophrenic state of paranoid type." On the day in question, she wanted to leave the hospital and escaped therefrom and found an automobile standing on a street with its motor running a few blocks from the hospital. She got into the car and drove off, having little or no control of the car. She soon collided with the plaintiff. Later she was adjudged mentally incompetent and committed to a state hospital. *Johnson* is not a case of sudden mental seizure with no forewarning. The defendant knew she was being treated for a mental disorder and hence would not have come under the nonliability rule herein stated.

We think the statement that insanity is no defense is too broad when it is applied to a negligence case where the driver is suddenly overcome without forewarning by a mental disability or disorder which incapacitates him from conforming his conduct to the standards of a reasonable man under like circumstances. These are rare cases indeed, but their rarity is no reason for overlooking their existence and the justification which is the basis of the whole doctrine of liability for negligence, i.e., that it is unjust to hold a man responsible for his conduct which he is incapable of avoiding and which incapability was unknown to him prior to the accident.

We need not reach the question of contributory negligence of an insane person or the question of comparative negligence as those problems are not now presented. All we hold is that a sudden mental incapacity equivalent in its effect to such physical causes as a sudden heart attack, epileptic seizure, stroke, or fainting should be treated alike and not under the general rule of insanity.

An interesting case holding this view in Canada is Buckley & Toronto Transp. Comm'n v. Smith Transport, Ltd., 1946 Ont.Rep. 798, 4 Dom.L.Rep. 721 * * *. There, the court found no negligence when a truck driver was overcome by a sudden insane delusion that his truck was being operated by remote control of his employer and as a result he was in fact helpless to avert a collision.

[In the present case, a psychiatrist testified that Mrs. Veith's] mental illness appeared in August, 1965, prior to the accident. In that month Mrs. Veith visited the Necedah Shrine where she was told the Blessed Virgin had sent her to the shrine. She was told to pray for survival. Since that time she felt it had been revealed to her the end of the world was coming and that she was picked by God to survive. Later she had visions of God judging people and sentencing them to Heaven or Hell; she thought Batman was good and was trying to help save the world and her husband was possessed of the devil. Mrs. Veith told her daughter about her visions.

The question is whether she had warning or knowledge which would reasonably lead her to believe that hallucinations would occur and be such as to affect her driving an automobile. * * * It is for the jury to decide * * *. The jury could find that a woman, who believed she had a special relationship to God and was the chosen one to survive the end of the world, could believe that God would take over the direction of her life to the extent of driving her car. Since these mental aberrations were not constant, the jury could infer she had knowledge of her condition and the likelihood of a hallucination just as one who has knowledge of a heart condition knows the possibility of an attack. While the evidence may not be strong upon which to base an inference, especially in view of the fact that two jurors dissented on this verdict and expressly stated they could find no evidence of forewarning, nevertheless, the evidence to sustain the verdict of the jury need not constitute the great weight and clear preponderance.

* * *

C.T.W. v. B.C.G. & D.T.G., 809 S.W.2d 788 (Tex.Ct.App.1991). Suit was brought on behalf of two boys who had been subjected to "various sexual encounters" by their stepgrandfather, a pedophile. The claim was that defendant "was negligent in not avoiding situations in which he would be alone with one of the boys when he knew he had strong sexual urges toward them." On appeal, *held*, judgment for plaintiffs affirmed. The court said:

"Dr. Gripon [plaintiffs' expert] testified that pedophiles know that their sexual urges are not as they should be and that they will lead to trouble. He also testified that there is nothing that would prohibit pedophiles from refraining from such conduct, from getting help, or from seeing that they don't get around young boys. * * *

"From such evidence, the jury could have found that an ordinary, prudent person, under similar circumstances, would have at least avoided situations in which he would have been alone with either of the two boys. The evidence as a whole indicated that it would have been difficult for [defendant] to remove himself from such situations, but Dr. Gripon's testimony justified an inference that a reasonable person would do so under the circumstances."

JOLLEY v. POWELL, 299 So.2d 647 (Fla.App., 2d Dist., 1974), certiorari denied, 309 So.2d 7 (Fla.1975). Certified question whether in an action for wrongful death there is available to the defendant the affirmative defense of insanity at the time of the act causing the alleged wrongful death. It was alleged that defendant James Powell shot and killed Karen Ann Jolley "under most bizarre circumstances." He was acquitted of homicide "by reason of insanity." This action followed. Excerpts from the court's opinion follow:

"At the outset, we restrict the scope of the question. We do so because, while Florida has not answered the precise question, the general rule in jurisdictions which have considered it make a distinction between insanity as a defense to an unintentional tort and as a defense to those torts requiring a specific state of mind which a defendant may be incapable of forming. These latter would include, for example, actions based on deceit, malice or defamation. Therefore, since this action is based on a 'wrongful act' or 'negligence,' as circumscribed by Florida's wrongful death act[3], we limit the scope of the question as relating to unintentional tort actions and answer the question in the negative.

"It is surely not unusual in tort law nor indeed is it unfair that persons may be held responsible for failing to live up to a standard which, as a matter of fact, they cannot meet. As Justice Holmes observed:[4]

"The standards of the law are standards of general application * * * It does not attempt to see men as God sees them, for more than one sufficient reason * * * [The awkward man's] slips are no less troublesome to his neighbors than if they sprang from guilty neglect."

And who would deny that the victim of a nuisance may have it abated regardless of the intent of the offending party.

"So liability without subjective fault, under some circumstances, is one price men pay for membership in society. The sane and the insane, the awkward and the coordinated are equally liable for their acts or omissions. In such cases we do not decide fault, rather we determine upon whom our society imposes the burden of redress for a given injury. As Holmes implied in his 'awkward man' parable, a principle at least co-equal with that of the fault principle in the law of torts is that the innocent victim should have redress.

"Accordingly, most jurisdictions faced with the question here presented have decided that the insanity of a tortfeasor does not justify an exception to the general rule which holds a tortfeasor ordinarily to the objective, 'reasonable man' standard. In doing so, those courts have generally refused to recognize such an exception because other principles inherent in the law of torts would be violated by relieving an insane person of his liability simply because he is incapable of 'subjective fault.' Among these other principles are that 'where one of two innocent persons must suffer a loss, it should be borne by the one who occasioned it,'[6] and that the burden of injury should be borne by that class of persons who had some power initially to prevent the injury suffered. This latter 'class' would include, it has been held, those interested in an insane person's estate who would be in a position to gain economically by taking steps to protect society from such insane persons.[7] We agree with these cases.

"In addition to the foregoing reasoning, we are also of the view that practical considerations in the administration of justice militate against unnecessarily injecting all of the confusion and potential for false claims inherent in the unsatisfactory tests of insanity in criminal cases into civil actions. We therefore reiterate, when the predicate for a wrongful death action is unintentional tort the standard against which such tort is measured

3. Section 768.16 et seq., F.S.1972.

4. Holmes, The Common Law 108 (1881).

6. See, Seals v. Snow (1927) 123 Kan. 88, 90, 254 P. 348, 349. See, also Kuhn v. Zabotsky (1967) 9 Ohio St.2d 129, 224 N.E.2d 137.

7. See, McGuire v. Almy (1937) 297 Mass. 323, 8 N.E.2d 760; Prosser, Law of Torts, 3d ed. § 129 p. 37.

is the objective, 'reasonable man standard' and the subjective state of mind of the tortfeasor is irrelevant.

"In passing, we point out that we do not mean to say here that insanity would not be a defense to a claim for punitive damages. Our rationale would seem to suggest that such a defense would indeed be available in such cases. We need not decide the point now, however, since punitive damages are not sought herein."

BERBERIAN v. LYNN, 355 N.J.Super. 210, 809 A.2d 865 (2002). Gernannt suffered advanced Alzheimer's disease and was hospitalized. One night he tried to leave the hospital by the fire door exit. Berberian, a nurse, tried to redirect Gernannt back to his room. Gernannt pushed Berberian, causing her to fall and break her leg. The jury found Gernannt was not negligent.

The court acknowledged "the Restatement of Torts principle that mental disability does not generally excuse a person from [negligence] liability," but went on:

" * * * [A] similar issue was addressed in Cowan v. Doering, 111 N.J. 451, 459–460, 545 A.2d 159 (1988), where a patient being treated for an overdose of sleeping pills in an earlier suicide attempt, jumped from a second story hospital room window in another suicide attempt. The court adopted a flexible capacity-based standard for the contributory negligence of mentally disturbed plaintiffs which measures the conduct of such a plaintiff in light of his or her mental capacity and is similar to that used for infant plaintiffs. * * *

" * * * In our view, the flexible capacity-based standard is appropriate when considering the potential negligence liability of Alzheimer's patients, such as Gernannt, towards their care-givers, and we conclude such relaxation of the reasonable person standard was appropriate here. Thus, the trial judge properly instructed the jury to consider Gernannt's mental disability when determining his liability, and explained that Gernannt could not be found negligent if the jury determined that he lacked the capacity to understand the consequences of his actions."

The court added: "What occurred could also be viewed as an intentional act by defendant, but it is questionable that the requisite intent could be established."

Chapter 9

STANDARD OF CARE AND
PROOF OF FAULT

The prior chapter considered the general tort conception of reasonable care, and ways in which the standard of reasonable care is brought to bear on particular situations. We've seen that negligence analysis—say, BPL analysis—involves considerable rigor, and that the doctrines defining the reasonable person are somewhat detailed. Still, the standard of reasonable care remains, in jurisprudential jargon, a broad "standard" and not a precise "rule." The conventional distinction between a "rule" and a "standard" is this: a rule is a fairly definite legal precept which requires for its application just findings of fact; a standard is a more open-ended norm which requires an evaluative appraisal of the facts found. To apply a standard in case after case is to work out, anew in each factual context, a highly circumstantial "rule" to be followed there.

Can the abstract idea of reasonable care be made more definite and concrete? Be spelled out so that it operates more like a preexisting "rule"? This chapter explores two possibilities. First, reasonable care might be equated with the level of care established by a specific custom, or by the practice of a particular profession. Second, reasonable care might be defined as the care specifically required by a relevant safety statute. Spelling out reasonable care in terms of a prevailing custom, or an available statute, would, at least in certain respects, simplify negligence assessment, making it more like routine rule-application.

The chapter ends with a look at a special method of proving negligence, by use of the doctrine of res ipsa loquitur (the thing speaks for itself). This doctrine, when applicable, does greatly simplify matters, at least for the party asserting it.

SECTION A.   CUSTOMARY AND PROFESSIONAL
STANDARDS

Suppose the defendant in a negligence case shows that the conduct attacked as negligent in fact conformed to a customary or a professional safety norm. Does compliance with custom shield defendant's conduct from negligence criticism? What about compliance with a professional standard of care?

Modern law treats customary norms and professional norms—or non-professional custom and professional custom—differently: the one, somewhat skeptically; the other, rather deferentially. In a nutshell: customary standards have weight, but are not conclusive, while professional standards are usually conclusive.

Defendant's conformance to a relevant custom is evidence of due care, which counts in defendant's favor, but is normally not conclusive proof of no negligence. An actor's adherence to standards of safety generally prevailing in some area of social practice is a factor to be taken into account, in deciding whether the actor used due care. But despite such adherence by defendant, plaintiff may recover if the basic criteria of negligence analysis—those, say, of BPL assessment—show the customary care taken to be inadequate.

Defendant's conformance to a relevant professional standard is normally sufficient to defeat a claim of malpractice. "Malpractice" refers to negligence of a professional. Reasonable care for a professional is, in general, that degree of care and skill ordinarily exercised by qualified members of the profession. In a malpractice case, the plaintiff is normally required to use the pertinent professional standard as a sword: plaintiff must present expert testimony to prove what the applicable professional standard is, and that the defendant fell short of it.

The first main case below, decided in 1890, comes from the classical—not the modern—period of American tort law. It displays an approach to custom at variance with the modern skepticism just described. But the 1890 decision presents a question that keeps coming up: why not treat this or that customary practice with the same sort of deference that the law accords to professional practice?

TITUS v. BRADFORD, BORDELL AND KINZUA RAILROAD CO.
Supreme Court of Pennsylvania, 1890.
136 Pa. 618, 20 A. 517.

[Defendant operated a narrow-gauge railroad that connected with various standard-gauge lines. It received loaded broad-gauge box-cars, removed them from their "trucks" or wheel assemblies, and set them on narrow-gauge trucks for transport on its own line. One type of box-car—used by the New York, Pennsylvania and Ohio Railroad—was so constructed that it would rock unduly when set upon the type of truck used by defendant. Blocks or wedges of wood were used to eliminate rocking. While moving along defendant's line such a car tipped off its truck, a securing block having become loose, and James Titus, a brakeman riding the car, was killed.]

OPINION, Mr. Justice MITCHELL:

We have examined all the testimony carefully, and fail to find any evidence of defendant's negligence. The negligence declared upon is the placing of a broad-gauge car upon a narrow-gauge truck, * * * and particularly the New York, Pennsylvania & Ohio car body described by the witnesses. But the whole evidence, of plaintiff's witnesses as well as of defendant's, shows that the shifting of broad-gauge or standard car bodies on to narrow-gauge trucks for transportation, is a regular part of the business of narrow-gauge railroads, and the plaintiff's evidence makes no attempt to show that the way in which it was done here was either dangerous or unusual. * * *

But, even if the practice had been shown to be dangerous, that would not show it to be negligent. Some employments are essentially hazardous, as said by our Brother Green, in North. C. Ry. Co. v. Husson, 101 Pa. 1, of coupling railway cars; and it by no means follows that an employer is liable "because a particular accident might have been prevented by some special device or precaution not in common use." All the cases agree that the master is not bound to use the newest and best appliances. He performs his duty when he furnishes those of ordinary character and reasonable safety, and the former is the test of the latter; for, in regard to the style of implement or nature of the mode of performance of any work, "reasonably safe" means safe according to the usages, habits, and ordinary risks of the business. Absolute safety is unattainable, and employers are not insurers. They are liable for the consequences, not of danger but of negligence; and the unbending test of negligence in methods, machinery, and appliances is the ordinary usage of the business. No man is held by law to a higher degree of skill than the fair average of his profession or trade, and the standard of due care is the conduct of the average prudent man. The test of negligence in employers is the same, and however strongly they may be convinced that there is a better or less dangerous way, no jury can be permitted to say that the usual and ordinary way, commonly adopted by those in the same business, is a negligent way for which liability shall be imposed. Juries must necessarily determine the responsibility of individual conduct, but they cannot be allowed to set up a standard which shall, in effect, dictate the customs or control the business of the community.

In Ship–Building Works v. Nuttall, 119 Pa. 149, our Brother Williams said: "The testimony shows that such an attachment is not in general use. * * * It is not enough that some persons regard it as a valuable safeguard. The test is, general use. Tried by this test, the saw of the defendant was such a one as the company had a right to use, because it is such as is commonly used by mill owners, and it was error to leave to the jury any question of negligence based on the failure to provide a spreader."

As already seen, the testimony of plaintiff's own witnesses showed the custom of the appellant company to perform this part of its work in the way complained of. The defendant's witnesses showed the custom of at least two other narrow-gauge roads to use the same way. There was no countervailing evidence on part of plaintiff, though, as was said in the closely analogous case of North C. Ry. Co. v. Husson, 101 Pa. 1, "it was certainly a part of the duty of the plaintiff to affirmatively establish that the loading of cars in the manner complained of was an unusual occurrence." In the absence of such evidence, * * * a verdict [should have been] directed for the defendant.

It is also entirely clear that defendant's third point [that decedent assumed the risk] should have been affirmed. The deceased had been a brakeman on this train for five or six months, during which this mode of carrying broad-gauge cars had been used; cars similar to the one on which the accident occurred had been frequently carried, and that very car at least once, about ten days before. He not only thus had ample opportunity to know the risks of such trains, but he had his attention specially called to the alleged source of the accident, by having worked, just before becoming a brakeman, on the hoist by which the car bodies were transferred to the trucks. It was a perfectly plain case of acceptance of an employment, with full knowledge of the risks.

PITTSBURGH, S. & N. RAILROAD CO. v. LAMPHERE, 137 Fed. 20 (3d Cir.1905). Plaintiff, a railroad brakeman, was working atop a freight car when the train passed under a low bridge. Plaintiff was struck by the bridge and injured. He argued that his employer was negligent in failing to use customary warning devices. Defendant objected to evidence about the practices of "well-regulated railroads." Said the court:

" * * * [I]t would seem that no more appropriate or relevant testimony could be adduced by a plaintiff in such a case as the present, than that which would tend to show what were the ordinary or customary means used by other persons engaged in a like business, to safeguard an admittedly dangerous situation. Undoubtedly it was the right of the plaintiff to show, by testimony, how the approaches to such bridges were usually guarded in the operation of railroads. If the court below had persisted in excluding all such testimony, then the jury would have been left to form its own opinion of what, under all the circumstances, was a reasonably safe place and conditions, in which and under which the railroad's servants should work, and to apply its own standard of what would be the exercise of ordinary care * * *. To deprive the jury of the benefit of such testimony, in cases where the work to be done requires a high degree of technical knowledge and experience, would oftentimes leave employers at the mercy of the variant or, perhaps, capricious judgment of a jury. Of course, to show what was customary in the practice of other railroads in this respect, testimony as to the practice on more than one railroad is necessary, and it is reasonable to require such testimony as to a sufficient number, to establish what might properly be called a custom in the business of railroading. It would, of course, be unreasonable to require testimony as to all railroads, or as to more than would be fairly within the power of parties to produce in the ordinary conduct of a suit. * * * Nor do we see why a witness, who has qualified himself as an expert in railroad management, cannot testify what good railroading in his opinion requires, in the respect under consideration, nor do we think if defendant had shown that upon another railroad no such warning signals were given on the approach to a low bridge, objection could be made to testimony that such railroad was not a well-regulated one, but on the contrary was notoriously badly equipped and managed. * * * "

McCOMISH v. DeSOI, 42 N.J. 274, 200 A.2d 116 (1964). Defendant constructed a machine—a sling—designed to hoist equipment weighing about a ton. The sling gave way and caused a serious accident. In attacking the design of the sling plaintiffs relied on "the following recognized manuals or codes specifying standard or prevailing safety practices in the field under discussion: American Tiger Brand Wire Rope, United States Steel, United States Army Corps of Engineers, United States Navy Safety Precautions, United States Air Force Manual and United States Army Harbor Craft Crewman's Handbook." The court upheld use of such safety codes or manuals as "pertinent and valuable aids in the resolution of the issue of negligence." Prevailing safety practices are not "of themselves the absolute measure of due care," but do have "probative force as evidence" of what reasonable care requires in a particular area. The court cited with approval a number of other cases in which "generally recognized and accepted" safety criteria were given evidentiary weight: for example, the National Electrical Safety Code, the Standard Automobile Engineers Handbook, specifications of the National Fire Protection organization, a booklet of the National Safety Council, standards of the Labelling Committee of the Manufacturing Chemists Association, and the National Safety Code of the U.S. Bureau of Standards.

RAIM v. VENTURA, 16 Wis.2d 67, 113 N.W.2d 827 (1962). Action for personal injuries sustained by a minor when a plate glass entrance door of defendant's cheese market shattered as she struck it with her head. The minor plaintiff, 10 years old and 55 pounds in weight, bumped into the door when running or walking rapidly toward it in order to get out of the rain. The door contained a single panel of ¼-inch plate glass, 3 feet 2 inches wide by 6 feet 7 inches high. There was a metallic center strip across the width of the glass. A white metallic pull bar was attached to the outside and the word "Pull" was lettered on the glass above the center strip. Plaintiffs alleged that defendant violated a "safe-place statute." The defendant impleaded the supplier of the door. After the jury returned its verdict for the plaintiffs the court granted both the defendant's and the impleaded defendant's motions for directed verdict and dismissed the complaint and cross-complaint on the merits. Plaintiffs appeal. *Held,* affirmed. A usage that is patently unsafe is not controlling on the court. "However, where there is an avalanche of acceptability of a custom or usage, and where such general practice contravenes no established law, public policy or common sense, it may be persuasive as to what is a rule of reason in a safe-place case. * * * In the case at bar there was evidence that more than two thousand doors like the respondent's have been installed in the Kenosha area during the past eight years; 98% of all the glass doors in such area are like the one in question in that they employ ¼-inch plate glass. In our opinion the existence of such one-sided usage was properly considered by the trial judge * * *."

THE T. J. HOOPER

United States Circuit Court of Appeals, Second Circuit, 1932.
60 F.2d 737.
Noted in 19 Va.L.Rev. 526.

Appeal from the District Court of the United States for the Southern District of New York.

L. HAND, J. The barges No. 17 and No. 30, belonging to the Northern Barge Company, had lifted cargoes of coal at Norfolk, Virginia, for New York in March, 1928. They were towed by two tugs of the petitioner, the "Montrose" and the "Hooper," and were lost off the Jersey Coast on March tenth, in an easterly gale. The cargo owners sued the barges under the contracts of carriage; the owner of the barges sued the tugs under the towing contract, both for its own loss and as bailee of the cargoes; the owner of the tugs filed a petition to limit its liability. All the suits were joined and heard together, and the judge found that all the vessels were unseaworthy; the tugs, because they did not carry radio receiving sets by which they could have seasonably got warnings of a change in the weather which should have caused them to seek shelter in the Delaware Breakwater en route. He therefore entered an interlocutory decree holding each tug and barge jointly liable to each cargo owner, and each tug for half damages for the loss of its barge. The petitioner appealed, and the barge owner appealed and filed assignments of error.

Each tug had three ocean going coal barges in tow, the lost barge being at the end. The "Montrose," which had the No. 17, took an outside course; the "Hooper" with the No. 30, inside. The weather was fair without ominous symptoms, as the tows passed the Delaware Breakwater about midnight of March eighth, and the barges did not get into serious trouble until they were about opposite Atlantic City some sixty or seventy miles to the north. The wind began to freshen in the morning of the ninth and rose to a gale before noon; by afternoon the second barge of the Hooper's tow was out of hand and signalled the tug, which found that not only this barge needed help but that the No. 30 was aleak. Both barges anchored and the crew of the No. 30 rode out the storm until the afternoon of the tenth, when she sank, her crew having been meanwhile taken off. The No. 17 sprang a leak about the same time; she too anchored at the Montrose's command and sank on the next morning after her crew also had been rescued. The cargoes and the tugs maintain that the barges were not fit for their service; the cargoes and the barges that the tugs should have gone into the Delaware Breakwater, and besides, did not handle their tows properly. [The court confirmed the findings of the court below that the barges were not seaworthy in fact and that had the masters of the tugs received radio broadcasts from the weather bureau at Arlington indicating an approaching storm they would not have proceeded to sea, since "prudent masters * * * would have found the risk more than the exigency warranted."]

To be sure the barges would, as we have said, probably have withstood the gale, had they been well found; but a master is not justified in putting his tow to every test which she will survive, if she be fit. There is a zone in which proper caution will avoid putting her capacity to the proof; a coefficient of prudence that he should not disregard. Taking the situation as a whole, it seems to us that these masters would have taken undue chances, had they got the broadcasts.

They did not, because their private radio receiving sets, which were on board, were not in working order. These belonged to them personally, and were partly a toy, partly a part of the equipment, but neither furnished by the owner, nor supervised by it. It is not fair to say that there was a general custom among coastwise carriers so to equip their tugs. One line alone did it; as for the rest, they relied upon their crews, so far as they can be said to have relied at all. An adequate receiving set suitable for a coastwise tug can now be got at small cost and is reasonably reliable if kept up; obviously it is a source of great protection to their tows. Twice every day they can receive these predictions, based upon the widest possible information, available to every vessel within two or three hundred miles and more. Such a set is the ears of the tug to catch the spoken word, just as the master's binoculars are her eyes to see a storm signal ashore. Whatever may be said as to other vessels, tugs towing heavy coal laden barges, strung out for half a mile, have little power to maneuver, and do not, as this case proves, expose themselves to weather which would not turn back stauncher craft. They can have at hand protection against dangers of which they can learn in no other way.

Is it then a final answer that the business had not yet generally adopted receiving sets? There are, no doubt, cases where courts seem to make the general practice of the calling the standard of proper diligence; we have indeed given some currency to the notion ourselves [citations omitted]. Indeed in most cases reasonable prudence is in fact common prudence; but strictly it is never its measure; a whole calling may have unduly lagged in the adoption of new and available devices. It never may set its own tests, however persuasive be its usages. Courts must in the end say what is required; there are precautions so imperative that even their universal disregard will not excuse their omission. But here there was no custom at all as to receiving sets; some had them, some did not; the most that can be urged is that they had not yet become general. Certainly in such a case we need not pause; when some have thought a device necessary, at least we may say that they were right, and the others too slack. The statute (section 484, title 46, U.S.Code [46 U.S.C.A. § 484]) does not bear on this situation at all. It prescribes not a receiving, but a transmitting set, and for a very different purpose; to call for help, not to get news. We hold the tugs liable therefore because, had they been properly equipped, they would have got the Arlington reports. The injury was a direct consequence of this unseaworthiness.

Decree affirmed.

SAGLIMBENI v. WEST END BREWING CO., 274 App.Div. 201, 80 N.Y.S.2d 635 (1948), affirmed 298 N.Y. 875, 84 N.E.2d 638 (1949). Plaintiff was injured when one of defendant's beer bottles exploded. Defendant used old—returned—bottles rather than new ones, and plaintiff argued that the practice of refilling old bottles was unduly dangerous since they might contain weaknesses or defects. Defendant rejoined that its methods "followed the customary practice and usage of all breweries" that use of old bottles was "a standard practice"; and that its quality controls (four pressure tests plus three inspections) were "identical with the practice of all modern breweries." In upholding a jury verdict for plaintiff the court said:

"It was for the jury to say, even though usage and custom were shown, whether the use of old bottles under the circumstances disclosed was hazardous to the public and therefore negligent. If the hazard remained after standard tests were made the jury was not bound to find that such tests were conclusive proof of due care. It would be a strange doctrine indeed to admit the hazard, created for economic reasons, and then say as a matter of law that the public must bear the risk."

NORTHWEST AIRLINES v. GLENN L. MARTIN CO., 224 F.2d 120 (6th Cir.1955), certiorari denied 350 U.S. 937, 76 S.Ct. 308, 100 L.Ed. 818 (1956), rehearing denied 350 U.S. 976, 76 S.Ct. 431, 100 L.Ed. 846 (1956). The Airlines sued the aircraft manufacturer for damages allegedly caused by negligence in design and manufacture of airplanes, wing splices of which were vulnerable to metal fatigue. Instructions to the jury submitted, among other defenses, an issue of contributory negligence of the Airlines in failing to have radar, which might have aided the pilot to avoid a thunderstorm in which one of the planes crashed. In August, 1948, when the plane was lost, no airline had airborne radar in operational use. Verdict and judgment for defendant. *Held* (2–1), reversed, one ground of error being the submission of contributory negligence in not having radar. Customary practice is not ordinary care, but only evidence of ordinary care. Nevertheless, there is no evidence in the record that in August, 1948, satisfactory airborne radar was commercially available. The evidence indicated, as construed most favorably to defendant's contention of contributory negligence, that airborne radar was likely to become feasible after further development.

LOW v. PARK PRICE CO., 95 Idaho 91, 503 P.2d 291 (1972). Action by owner of car for conversion and negligence. While the car was in storage with the defendant garage owner, awaiting repairs, the transmission disappeared. Defendant introduced evidence of the prevailing custom and usage regularly observed by other service garages in the area, with respect to protection of cars in their custody, and evidence that defendant had "done what others do under like circumstances." In a nonjury trial, the district court entered judgment for defendant, and plaintiff appealed. *Held,* affirmed.

" * * * The appellant-bailor failed to introduce any evidence to overcome the inference of reasonable care arising from the respondent-bailee's evidence; and there is nothing in common experience to lead to the conclusion that the respondent's conduct was negligent. Therefore, even though the burden of persuasion is on the respondent-bailee, in this case the bailee proved, by a preponderance of the evidence, its freedom from negligence.

"The appellant's remaining assignment of error—to the effect that the court erred in refusing to allow the appellant to ask one of the garage-owner witnesses what his profits amounted to for the preceding year—is without merit. In making this inquiry, the appellant sought to disprove the witness's assertion that he could not afford to hire a night watchman. The district court correctly concluded that the information sought to be elicited was immaterial. Whether the garage owner could afford to hire a night watchman is immaterial to the question of whether ordinary care requires a night watchman. Of course, the cost of the suggested precaution would be relevant in determining whether the reasonable man would employ it. But in this case, the appellant did not seek to establish the cost of employing a night watchman; rather, the appellant sought to show that the witness's profits were such as to indicate that he could currently afford to take such a precaution against theft."

PROFESSIONAL MALPRACTICE

Malpractice is negligence of a professional, measured by a special standard. The usual test for assessing negligence of a professional, such as a physician, is the standard of care and skill practiced by a qualified member of the relevant profession. In a routine medical malpractice case, plaintiff must prove by expert testimony what the medical profession's standard is, and also must prove, again by expert testimony, breach of that standard. The jury is instructed to apply the profession's standard, not its own independent judgment about reasonable care under the circumstances.

What constitutes a profession? This is the threshold question. If a group of social actors is deemed to be a profession, then the group in effect sets the standard used by the courts in deciding negligence of group members. Otherwise, the group's own standard of care is merely a "custom," and adherence to custom is not a conclusive defense against an allegation of negligence. Not every group of experts or specialists in society is accorded professional status. Moreover, not every performance by a member of a recognized profession is so bound up with special knowledge and experience that it must be judged by a special standard. Sometimes the conduct of a professional is, like the conduct of everyone else, suitably judged by the law's general test of reasonable care.

In a malpractice action where it is conceded that plaintiff must prove the professional standard and breach of it by expert testimony, a number of subordinate disputes may break out. The requirement of expert testimony leads to debate about whether plaintiff's expert is sufficiently knowledgeable to state the standard pertinent to the case—whether the standard espoused by plaintiff's expert is the right one. Often the decisive question is which set of practitioners should serve as the reference group in defining malpractice. Should defendant's conduct be measured by a local or a national standard? With reference to the care used by a general practitioner or the care used by a particular type of specialist?

Can a professional standard be overridden? Suppose the plaintiff concedes that the defendant adhered to a relevant professional standard, but says that the professional standard is too low. Can general negligence analysis—the law's general method of balancing costs and benefits—be employed to show that the professional standard itself is unreasonable? The answer is that attacking a professional standard as unreasonably deficient is an uphill battle, but it is possible for such a frontal attack to succeed.

———

STEPAKOFF v. KANTAR, 393 Mass. 836, 473 N.E.2d 1131 (1985). Defendant, a psychiatrist, was sued for negligence on account of the suicide of his patient, Gerald Stepakoff. Stepakoff's widow alleged that defendant, having diagnosed Stepakoff as "manic-depressive psychotic" and "potentially suicidal," and knowing Stepakoff was undergoing an episode of unusual stress, failed to take reasonable steps to protect his patient from self-inflicted harm, including involuntary hospitalization. On review of a jury verdict for defendant, *held*, affirmed. The trial judge properly refused to instruct the jury that defendant had a duty to use "reasonable care under the circumstances." The Supreme Judicial Court explained:

The judge instructed the jury: "[I]f you find that the care and treatment given by Dr. Kantar to Gerald Stepakoff from December of 1973 to February of 1975 was not in accordance with good medical practice and in violation or breach of the standard of care and skill of the average member of the medical profession practicing his specialty of psychiatry between December '73 and February of 1975, and that, if as a direct and proximate result of that negligence, Gerald Stepakoff died, the plaintiff, Helen Stepakoff, would be entitled to recover. . . ." That instruction fully and accurately stated the law. The plaintiff was not entitled to further instructions relative to the reasonableness of the defendant's acts or failures to act. The plaintiff has not directed our attention to any case in which a court has bifurcated the duty owed by a psychiatrist to a suicidal patient by declaring that, when diagnosing a patient, the psychiatrist must exercise the care and skill customarily exercised by an average qualified psychiatrist, while, after diagnosing a patient as suicidal, the psychiatrist's duty to take preventive measures becomes one of "reasonableness." We are unwilling to disturb our longstanding rule that a physician, practicing a specialty, owes to his or her patient a duty to comply in all respects with the standard set by the average physician practicing that specialty.

We are not moved to a different conclusion by *Tarasoff v. Regents of the Univ. of Cal.*, 17 Cal.3d 425, 439, 131 Cal.Rptr. 14, 551 P.2d 334 (1976), in which the California Supreme Court imposed on psychiatrists a duty of reasonable care to foreseeable victims of the psychiatrists' patients. The instant case involves a psychiatrist's duty to his patient, not to third parties. * * *

POWELL v. CATHOLIC MEDICAL CENTER, 145 N.H. 7, 749 A.2d 301 (2000). Plaintiff, employed to draw blood samples from hospital patients, was injured when a patient suddenly attacked her. She sued the hospital and the patient's attending physician alleging that defendants "breached their duty to warn her of the patient's potentially assaultive behavior about which the defendants knew or should have known." Defendants argued that their conduct should be measured by a "reasonable professional" standard rather than a "reasonable person" standard. *Held*, for plaintiff. "The case before us is an ordinary duty of care case. * * * Specialized training and experience do not excuse a physician from exercising the reasonable care of an ordinary person. In this case, the progress notes of the patient detail numerous prior events that served to put [defendants] on notice that the patient may have been a threat. * * * Specialized training and experience were not required to make that determination."

ROSSELL v. VOLKSWAGEN OF AMERICA

Supreme Court of Arizona, 1985.
147 Ariz. 160, 709 P.2d 517.

FELDMAN, Justice.

This is a product liability action brought by Phyllis A. Rossell, as guardian ad litem on behalf of her daughter, Julie Ann Kennon (plaintiff), against the manufacturer and the North American distributor of Volkswagen automobiles. The defendants will be referred to collectively as "Volkswagen." The case involves the design of the battery system in the model of the Volkswagen automobile popularly known as the "Beetle" or "Bug." The jury found for the plaintiff and awarded damages in the sum of $1,500,000. The court of appeals held that the plaintiff had failed to establish a prima facie case [of negligence liability] and that the trial judge had erred in denying Volkswagen's motion for judgment n.o.v. Believing that the court of appeals had incorrectly stated the applicable law * * *, we granted review. * * *

* * * This action arises from a 1970, one-vehicle accident. At the time of the accident Julie, then eleven months old, was sleeping in the front passenger seat of a 1958 Volkswagen driven by her mother. At approximately 11:00 p.m., on State Route 93, Ms. Rossell fell asleep and the vehicle drifted to the right, off the paved roadway. The sound of the car hitting a sign awakened Rossell, and she attempted to correct the path of the car, but oversteered. The car flipped over, skidded off the road and landed on its roof at the bottom of a cement culvert. The force of the accident dislodged and fractured the battery which was located inside the passenger compartment. In the seven hours it took Rossell to regain full consciousness and then extract herself and her daughter from the car, the broken battery slowly dripped sulfuric acid on Julie. The acid severely burned her face, chest, arm, neck, part of her back and shoulder, and both hands. Since the accident Julie has undergone extensive corrective surgery but remains seriously disfigured and in need of additional surgery.

Plaintiff filed the complaint in May, 1978. * * * [T]he case was submitted to the jury only on the question of Volkswagen's negligence in locating the battery inside the passenger compartment.

Plaintiff argued at trial that battery placement within the passenger compartment created an unreasonable risk of harm and that alternative designs were available and practicable. In their trial motions and later motion for judgment n.o.v., Volkswagen argued that plaintiff had failed to make a prima facie case. * * *

* * *

We turn, then, to the central issue presented. What type of proof must plaintiff produce in order to make a prima facie case of negligent design against a product manufacturer? What is the standard of care? In the ordinary negligence case, tried under the familiar rubric of "reasonable care," plaintiff's proof must provide facts from which the jury may conclude that defendant's behavior fell below the "reasonable man" standard. This question is ordinarily decided without providing the jury with any direct evidence about the details of what may or may not comply with the standard of care. The risk/benefit analysis involved in deciding what is reasonable care under the circumstances is generally left to the jury * * *.

Thus, in the usual negligence case the jury is left to reach its own conclusion on whether defendant's conduct complied with the legal standard of reasonable care. There need be no opinion testimony on the subject; the jury is encouraged, under proper instruction, to consider the circumstances, use its own experience and apply community standards in deciding what is or is not negligence.

Volkswagen claims that negligent design cases are an exception. They contend that product manufacturers are held to an expert's standard of care, as are professionals such as lawyers, doctors and accountants. In professional malpractice cases the reasonable man standard has been replaced with the standard of "what is customary and usual in the profession." [W. Prosser & P. Keeton, The Law of Torts (5th ed. 1984)] § 32, at 189. This, of course, requires plaintiff to establish by expert testimony the usual conduct of other practitioners of defendant's profession and to prove, further, that defendant deviated from that standard.

> It has been pointed out often enough that this gives the medical profession, and also the [other professions], the privilege, *which is usually emphatically denied to other groups,* of setting their own legal standards of conduct, merely by adopting their own practices.

Id. (emphasis supplied).

Should we adopt for manufacturers in negligent design cases a rule "emphatically denied to other groups" but similar to those applied to defendants in professional malpractice cases? Such a rule, of course, would require—not just permit—plaintiff to present explicit evidence of the usual conduct of other persons in the field of design by offering expert evidence of what constitutes "good design practice." Plaintiff would also be required to establish that the design adopted by the defendant deviated from such "good practice." We believe that such a rule is inappropriate.

The malpractice requirement that plaintiff show the details of conduct practiced by others in defendant's profession is not some special favor which the law gives to professionals who may be sued by their clients. It is, instead, a method of holding such defendants to an even higher standard of care than that of an ordinary, prudent person. Prosser, *supra* § 32 at 185. Such a technique has not been applied in commercial settings, probably because the danger of allowing a commercial group to set its own standard of what is reasonable is not offset by professional obligations which tend to prevent the group from setting standards at a low level in order to accommodate other interests. Thus, it is the general law that industries are not permitted to establish their own standard of conduct because they may be influenced by motives of saving "time, effort or money." Prosser, *supra* § 33 at 194. Long ago, Judge Learned Hand expressed the rule in a case in which the defendant claimed that it had not been negligent in failing to put Mr. Marconi's invention on its tugboats * * *. *The T.J. Hooper,* 60 F.2d 737, 740 (2d Cir.1932). This, of course, is not to say that evidence of custom and usage is inadmissible.

> What usually is done may be evidence of what ought to be done, but what ought to be done is fixed by a standard of reasonable prudence, whether it usually is complied with or not.

Texas & Pacific Railway Co. v. Behymer, 189 U.S. 468, 470, 23 S.Ct. 622, 623, 47 L.Ed. 905 (1903) (Holmes, J.). Holmes' view has been previously considered and approved by this court. *Atchison, Topeka & Santa Fe Railway Co. v. Parr,* 96 Ariz. 13, 17, 391 P.2d 575, 578 (1964).

Volkswagen argues that case law already recognizes that in negligent design cases a manufacturer is not liable absent a showing that he failed to conform to the standard of care in design followed by other manufacturers. We do not agree. [The court distinguished prior cases involving professionals—insurance broker, professional engineer, physicians—sued by clients or patients.] None of these cases consider[s] the liability of a manufacturer for defects in mass-produced products. They do involve, instead, the liability of professionals who generally work in close relationship with their clients or patients. * * * [Volkswagen's argument] would, of course, tend to permit commercial defendants to prevail as a matter of law if their conduct complied with a general, negligent practice prevailing in their industry. This is exactly the rule criticized in Prosser, rejected by both Justice Holmes and Judge Hand, and rejected by this court in *Parr, supra.*

In view of public policy and existing law, we decline to transform defective design cases into malpractice cases. We believe the law is best left as it is in this field. Special groups will be allowed to create their own standards of reasonably prudent conduct only when the nature of the group and its special relationship with its clients assure society that those standards will be set with primary regard to protection of the public rather than to such considerations as increased profitability. We do not believe that automobile manufacturers fit into this category. This is no reflection upon automobile manufacturers, but merely a recognition that the necessities of the marketplace permit manufacturers neither the working relationship nor the concern about the welfare of their customers that the professions generally permit and require from their practitioners.

Therefore, in Arizona the rule in negligence cases shall continue to be that evidence of industry custom and practice is generally admissible as evidence relevant to whether defendant's conduct was reasonable under the circumstances. In determining what is reasonable care for manufacturers, the plaintiff need only prove the defendant's conduct presented a foreseeable, unreasonable risk of harm. As in all other negligence cases, the jury is permitted to decide what is reasonable from the common experience of mankind. We do not disturb the rule that in determining what is "reasonable care," expert evidence may be required in those cases in which factual issues are outside the common understanding of jurors. However, unlike most malpractice cases, there need not be explicit expert testimony establishing the standard of care and the manner in which defendant deviated from that standard. M. Udall & J. Livermore, LAW OF EVIDENCE § 25 at 43–44 (2d ed. 1982). With these principles in mind, we now turn to a consideration of the evidence in order to determine whether plaintiff did prove a prima facie case.

Plaintiff presented two experts, Jon McKibben, an automotive engineer, and Charles Turnbow, a safety engineer. * * * There was evidence from which the jury could find that from both an engineering and practical standpoint the 1958 Volkswagen could have been designed with the battery outside the passenger compartment, as was the Karmann Ghia, an upscale model which used the same chassis as the Beetle. There was further testimony that placement of the battery inside the passenger compartment was unreasonably dangerous because "batteries do fracture in crashes, not infrequently." According to McKibben,

> the degree to which the battery inside the compartment is a hazard depends to some extent on how likely it is that that battery is going to become dislodged or fractured or somehow spill acid. And certainly in a roll-over type crash, a battery in that location is more likely to be a hazard to the occupants. So the fact that this model Volkswagen tends to turn over with relatively high frequency makes the battery placement inside the car a more serious hazard than it might be in other types of vehicles.

* * *

We conclude that the plaintiff did present expert evidence that the battery design location presented a foreseeable, unreasonable risk of harm, that alternative designs were available and that they were feasible from a technological and practical standpoint. We reject Volkswagen's contention that in addition to the evidence outlined above, plaintiff was compelled to produce expert opinion evidence that the standard of "good design practice" required Volkswagen to design the car so that the battery system was located outside the passenger compartment. Unlike a malpractice case, the jury was free to reach or reject this conclusion on the basis of its own experience and knowledge of what is "reasonable," with the assistance of expert opinion describing only the dangers, hazards and factors of design involved.[5]

[The court then rejected Volkswagen's contentions concerning other matters.]

* * *

The opinion of the court of appeals is vacated. The judgment is affirmed.

———————

RAKOWSKI v. RAYBESTOS–MANHATTAN, INC., 5 N.J.Super. 203, 68 A.2d 641 (App.Div.1949). Plaintiff, employee of defendant, was harmed by constant attendance upon an X–ray machine. It was conceded that defendant used the greatest precautions prescribed by a group of recognized scientists and satisfied the standards adopted in that line of industrial activity. *Held,* directed verdict for defendant affirmed. The fact that experts for the plaintiff testified that defendant should have taken added precautions is immaterial.

BROWN v. UNITED BLOOD SERVICES, 109 Nev. 758, 858 P.2d 391 (1993). In June 1984 plaintiff had major surgery requiring blood transfusion. He contracted AIDS from transfused blood supplied by the defendant United Blood Services (UBS), a blood bank. The infected blood, from a person identified as "John Donor," was given to UBS in May 1984. Plaintiff brought this negligence suit alleging that UBS failed to employ adequate measures to screen donated blood for AIDS infection. At trial plaintiff's two expert witnesses testified that while a specific test for the AIDS virus was not available until March 1985, it was possible at the time of plaintiff's surgery to engage in "surrogate testing" for AIDS. A surrogate test is used to detect a disease which is commonly associated with the target disease. Plaintiff's experts testified that a surrogate test not used by UBS, the "core antibody test" (which tests for hepatitis B, present in a large percentage of AIDS carriers), could have been used in 1984, and that "John Donor's blood would have tested positive * * * had the core antibody test been used, and thus would have been rejected." The jury returned a verdict for plaintiff. Appeal was made to the Nevada Supreme Court. (Plaintiff died while the appeal was pending; his mother appeared as his personal representative.) *Held*, for defendant.

The court said the issue was whether UBS's conduct should be measured by "an ordinary negligence standard, which permitted the jury to determine how a reasonably prudent blood bank should have performed," or instead by "a professional standard of care defined by the prevailing customs and practices" of blood banks. The court ruled that "the production and safeguarding of the nation's blood supply" is "a professional activity, entitled to a professional standard of care." Therefore "UBS could have been held liable in the instant case only by proof that [its conduct] fell

———————

5. We need not concern ourselves with whether any of these issues could have been submitted to the jury without expert evidence. The evidence was presented; there is no need to go beyond that.

below the standards promulgated and practiced by the industry" at the time. But even plaintiff's experts agreed that "the vast majority of blood banks in 1984 were not doing surrogate testing," because "the AABB [American Association of Blood Banks] did not require it," and that "AABB standards are the standard of practice for blood banks." "[W]e conclude as a matter of law" that lack of surrogate testing by UBS "conformed to the industry-wide standard."

In footnotes the court added that "a plaintiff * * * would be entitled to attempt to demonstrate" that "the national blood banking community's standard of care was unreasonably deficient in view of the knowledge then available." However, plaintiff here "elected to focus on UBS's procedures compared against an ordinary standard of care rather than attack the adequacy of the prevailing industry standard."

SANDERS v. CASA VIEW BAPTIST CHURCH, 134 F.3d 331 (5th Cir. 1998). The plaintiffs, Robyn Sanders and Lisa Mullanix, sued a minister of their church who had undertaken to counsel each plaintiff about her marital problems. They alleged that the minister, one Baucum, committed malpractice and breached his fiduciary duty as a marriage counselor by encouraging and consummating a sexual relationship with each plaintiff. The jury found for plaintiffs and awarded punitive damages. On appeal Baucum argued that his counseling activities were religious in nature and therefore shielded from judicial scrutiny by the First Amendment's guarantee of free exercise of religion. *Held*, judgment affirmed. It is true that courts have "rejected uniformly" claims of "clergy malpractice." "The First Amendment difficulties posed by a claim for clergy malpractice are not, however, present in this case because the duties underlying the plaintiffs' claims for malpractice by a marriage counselor and breach of fiduciary duties are not derived from religious doctrine. That is, because the jury found that Baucum held himself out as possessing the education and experience of a professional marriage counselor, his counseling activities with the plaintiffs were judged, not by a standard of care defined by religious teachings, but by a professional standard of care developed through expert testimony describing what a reasonably prudent counselor would have done under the same or similar circumstances."

VERGARA v. DOAN
Supreme Court of Indiana, 1992.
593 N.E.2d 185.

SHEPARD, Chief Justice.

Javier Vergara was born on May 31, 1979, at the Adams Memorial Hospital in Decatur, Indiana. His parents, Jose and Concepcion, claimed that negligence on the part of Dr. John Doan during Javier's delivery caused him severe and permanent injuries. A jury returned a verdict for Dr. Doan and the plaintiffs appealed. The Court of Appeals affirmed. Plaintiffs seek transfer, asking us to abandon Indiana's modified locality rule. We grant transfer to examine the standard of care appropriate for medical malpractice cases.

In most negligence cases, the defendant's conduct is tested against the hypothetical reasonable and prudent person acting under the same or similar circumstances. Miller v. Griesel (1974), 261 Ind. 604, 308 N.E.2d 701. In medical malpractice cases, however, Indiana has applied a more specific articulation of this standard. It has become known as the modified locality rule: "The standard of care . . . is that degree of care, skill, and proficiency which is commonly exercised by ordinarily careful, skillful, and prudent [physicians], at the time of the operation and *in similar localities*." Burke v. Capello (1988), Ind., 520 N.E.2d 439, 441 (emphasis added). Appellants have urged us to abandon this standard, arguing that the reasons for the modified locality rule are no longer applicable in today's society. We agree.

The modified locality rule is a less stringent version of the strict locality rule, which measured the defendant's conduct against that of other doctors in the same community. When the strict locality rule originated in the late 19th century, there was great disparity between the medical opportunities, equipment, facilities, and training in rural and urban communities. Travel and communication between rural and urban communities were difficult. The locality rule was intended to prevent the inequity that would result from holding rural doctors to the same standards as doctors in large cities. * * *

With advances in communication, travel, and medical education, the disparity between rural and urban health care diminished and justification for the locality rule waned. The strict locality rule also had two major drawbacks, especially as applied to smaller communities. First, there was a scarcity of local doctors to serve as expert witnesses against other local doctors. Second, there was the possibility that practices among a small group of doctors would establish a local standard of care below that which the law required. Pederson v. Dumouchel, 72 Wash.2d 73, 431 P.2d 973, 977 (1967). In response to these changes and criticisms, many courts adopted a modified locality rule, expanding the area of comparison to similar localities. This is the standard applied in Indiana. * * *

Use of a modified locality rule has not quelled the criticism. See Jon R. Waltz, The Rise and Gradual Fall of the Locality Rule in Medical Malpractice Litigation, 18 DePaul L.Rev. 408 (1969) (predicting eventual disappearance of locality rule); Brent R. Cohen, The Locality Rule in Colorado: Updating the Standard of Care, 51 U.Colo.L.Rev. 587 (1980) (urging a standard based on medical resources available to the doctor under the circumstances in which patient was treated). Many of the common criticisms seem valid. The modified locality rule still permits a lower standard of care to be exercised in smaller communities because other similar communities are likely to have the same care. Shilkret v. Annapolis Emergency Hosp., 276 Md. 187, 349 A.2d 245 (1975). We also spend time and money on the difficulty of defining what is a similar community. Cf. Id. The rule also seems inconsistent with the reality of modern medical practice. The disparity between small town and urban medicine continues to lessen with advances in communication, transportation, and education. In addition, widespread insurance coverage has provided patients with more choice of doctors and hospitals by reducing the financial constraints on the consumer in selecting caregivers. These reasons and others have led our Court of Appeals to observe that the modified locality rule has fallen into disfavor. * * * Many states describe the care a physician owes without emphasizing the locality of practice. [Here a footnote cites cases from 18 states.] Today we join these states and adopt the following: a physician must exercise that degree of care, skill, and proficiency exercised by reasonably careful, skillful, and prudent practitioners in the same class to which he belongs, acting under the same or similar circumstances. Rather than focusing on different standards for different communities, this standard uses locality as but one of the factors to be considered in determining whether the doctor acted reasonably. Other relevant considerations would include advances in the profession, availability of facilities, and whether the doctor is a specialist or general practitioner. * * *

[The court went on to rule that the trial judge's instruction to the jury, which spoke of the standard of medical care in "Decatur, Indiana or similar localities," was erroneous, but that the error in this case "was harmless and does not require reversal."]

* * * [T]he standard we have adopted today hardly prohibits consideration of the locality of practice. Locality of practice remains a proper subject for evidence and argument because it may be relevant to the circumstances in which the doctor acted.

* * *

We affirm the judgment of the trial court.

DeBRULER, DICKSON and KRAHULIK, JJ., concur.

GIVAN, Justice, concurring in result.

Although the majority opinion states that it is abandoning the modified locality rule, they claim the rule now to be that the physician must exercise the care and skill of practitioners in the same class to which he belongs and "acting in the same or similar circumstances." * * *

I do not perceive this "new standard" to differ materially from the modified locality rule. The ability of a physician to perform may well be vastly different in a small rural community hospital than that same physician might be able to perform in a large well-equipped metropolitan hospital.

I believe the majority has articulated a distinction without a difference. I would not confuse the issue by purporting to do away with the modified locality rule.

———

RIGGINS v. MAURIELLO, 603 A.2d 827 (Del.1992). In a medical malpractice case, part of the instruction to the jury charged that "a physician cannot be liable for a mere error of judgment in deciding what to do or what not to do for the patient provided that he has done what he thinks is best in the exercise of reasonable care." *Held*, by the Delaware Supreme Court, that the "mere error of judgment" charge "is undesirable and should be abandoned." "A proper instruction should state that, when a physician chooses between appropriate alternative medical treatments, harm which results from the physician's good faith choice of one proper alternative over the other is not malpractice."

MOZINGO v. PITT COUNTY MEMORIAL HOSPITAL, 331 N.C. 182, 415 S.E.2d 341 (1992). A baby was severely injured during childbirth at a teaching hospital. At the time, by contract with the hospital, defendant was the designated "on-call" physician (reachable by telephone at home) responsible for supervision of obstetrics residents at the hospital. When defendant's coverage shift began, the baby's mother, who had "known risk factors," had already been admitted; she gave birth about five hours into defendant's shift. Defendant never called in to the hospital to find out about admitted patients and plan for their care. A second-year resident provided treatment at the birth. The issue was whether defendant owed a duty of active care to mother and child though his status "did not fit traditional notions of the doctor-patient relationship." *Held*, for plaintiffs. "[I]n the increasingly complex modern delivery of health care, a physician who undertakes to provide on-call supervision of residents actually treating a patient may be held accountable to that patient." The North Carolina Supreme Court quoted with approval as follows:

"The health care environment requires cooperation and teamwork. Physicians are dependent upon many other health care professionals in a health care institution to ensure good patient care.... The health care professional is obligated to take actions to protect the interest of patients, who are innocent parties in the health care environment. A failure to act in the interest of good patient care or in the protection of the public welfare creates liability."

WELSH v. BULGER, 548 Pa. 504, 698 A.2d 581 (1997). Bobbi Jo Welsh's baby died because of injuries received in childbirth at Nason Hospital. A caesarean (surgical) delivery was needed, but Welsh's physician was not qualified as a surgeon, and he delivered the child vaginally with forceps. Welsh sued Nason Hospital alleging "corporate negligence." According to her expert witness, Dr. Warner, "If * * * the hospital had arranged for an appropriate cesarean section with the nurses' input on this, there is every reason to believe that Kyle Allan Welsh would be an absolutely normal child today." The hospital's motion for summary judgment was granted by the trial court. On review by the Pennsylvania Supreme Court, *held*, reversed. Plaintiff's allegations and evidence are sufficient to sustain her claim of "corporate negligence." "[C]orporate negligence is based on the negligent acts of the institution. A cause of action for corporate negligence arises from the policies, actions or inaction of the institution itself rather than the specific acts of individual hospital employees."

The court said that the report of Dr. Warner, plaintiff's expert witness, "indicates that the hospital breached the standard of care by not arranging for a qualified surgeon to perform a cesarean section. * * * Dr. Warner's report is * * * sufficient to establish a *prima facie* claim of corporate negligence against the hospital for failure to retain only competent physicians and for failure to formulate and enforce policies to ensure quality care." " * * * Dr. Warner opined that the nurses * * * must have known that there was a problem with the delivery but failed to act on that knowledge. Dr. Warner concluded that * * * if the nurses had notified the hospital of the need for a cesarean section, then the injury would not have occurred. Thus, Dr. Warner's report is sufficient to support a *prima facie* claim of corporate negligence for Nason Hospital's failure to oversee all persons who practice medicine within its walls as to patient care."

"[I]t is well established that a hospital staff member or employee has a duty to recognize and report abnormalities in the treatment and condition of [the hospital's] patients. If the attending physician fails to act after being informed of such abnormalities, it is then incumbent upon the hospital staff member or employee to so advise the hospital authorities so that appropriate action might be taken. When there is a failure * * * to question a physician's order which is not in accord with standard medical practice and the patient is injured as a result, the hospital will be liable for such negligence."

PETROVICH v. SHARE HEALTH PLAN, 188 Ill.2d 17, 241 Ill.Dec. 627, 719 N.E.2d 756 (1999). Plaintiff alleged negligence by her primary care physician in failing to diagnose her oral cancer in a timely manner. She also asserted a vicarious liability claim against Share Health Plan, the health maintenance organization (HMO) chosen by her employer to provide health care coverage to employees. The trial court granted summary judgment in favor of Share Health. On appeal to the Illinois Supreme Court, *held*, plaintiff "is entitled to a trial" on her vicarious liability claim, under each of two theories. First, Share Health's member handbook said that the HMO will provide for "all your healthcare needs" and spoke of participating physicians as "our staff"; such statements might "lead a reasonable person to conclude that the physician who was alleged to be negligent was an agent or employee of the HMO," not an independent contractor. Second, plaintiff presented "adequate evidence to support a finding that Share exerted such sufficient control over its participating physicians so as to negate their status as independent contractors." The court (Bilandic, J.) made the following general observations on HMO liability for physician malpractice:

" * * * Traditionally, physicians treated patients on demand, while insurers merely paid the physicians their fee for the services provided. Today, managed care organizations * * * have stepped into the insurer's shoes, and often attempt to reduce the price and quantity of health care services provided to patients through a system of health care cost containment. * * *

"This court has never addressed a question of whether an HMO may be held liable for medical malpractice. Share asserts that holding HMOs liable for medical malpractice will cause health care costs to increase and make health care inaccessible to large numbers of people. * * * We disagree with Share that the cost-containment role of HMOs entitles them to special consideration. The principle that organizations are accountable for their tortious actions and those of their agents is fundamental to our justice system. * * * Moreover, HMO accountability is essential to counterbalance the HMO goal of cost-containment. To the extent that HMOs are profit-making entities, accountability is also needed to counterbalance the inherent drive to achieve a large and ever-increasing profit margin. * * *

"Indeed, the national trend of courts is to hold HMOs accountable for medical malpractice under a variety of legal theories, including vicarious liability on the basis of apparent authority, vicarious liability on the basis of *respondeat superior*, direct corporate negligence, breach of contract and breach of warranty."

INFORMED CONSENT

Two different tort theories protect a patient's interest in controlling health care decisions made in the patient's own case. The traditional theory is battery. When a medical professional intentionally brings about contact with the person of a patient without the patient's consent, the unauthorized touching may amount to a battery, since bodily contact without consent is offensive. Battery liability in a medical context is addressed in Chapter 2, and again briefly below. When the medical professional has obtained consent to contact from the patient, no battery occurs, but the professional—say, a surgeon—may be liable for negligence if the patient's consent was not "informed." The modern theory of informed consent has to a considerable extent superceded battery, and has also gone beyond battery, in protecting the patient's right to medical self-determination.

The cases that follow show an evolution: from the starting point of "medical battery," to establishment of the modern legal doctrine of informed consent, and its acceptance by the medical profession; then to expansion of informed consent liability well beyond the traditional realm of battery (to include noninvasive treatment not involving any "touching"). The sequence ends with a decision that heads back toward the beginning, an informed consent judgment awarding a type of recovery (damages for offense to dignity without physical harm) more at home in the realm of battery than the field of negligence.

———

BLANCHARD v. KELLUM, 975 S.W.2d 522 (Tenn.1998). Plaintiff, who had gum disease, needed to have her teeth extracted. She consulted defendant, a dental surgeon, who proceeded to anesthetize plaintiff's entire mouth "and began a full extraction of all thirty-two of the plaintiff's teeth." In unbearable pain, plaintiff demanded a halt to the procedure. By that time sixteen teeth had been extracted. Plaintiff brought suit alleging that defendant "never informed her that all thirty-two teeth would be simultaneously extracted during a single office visit." The trial court granted summary judgment for defendant. The court of appeals affirmed because plaintiff had not offered an expert's opinion that defendant deviated from the professional standard of care. *Held*, reversed. This is a claim of "medical battery," not lack of informed consent. A battery claim "does not require the testimony of an expert witness." The court explained:

"We believe that there is a distinction between: (1) cases in which a doctor performs an unauthorized procedure; and (2) cases in which the procedure is authorized but the patient claims that the doctor failed to inform the patient of any or all the risks inherent in the procedure. Performance of an unauthorized procedure constitutes a medical battery. A simple inquiry can be used to determine whether a case constitutes a medical battery: (1) was the patient aware that the doctor was going to perform the procedure (i.e., did the patient know that the dentist was going to perform a root canal on a specified tooth or that the doctor was going to perform surgery on the specified knee?); and, if so (2) did the patient authorize performance of the procedure? A plaintiff's cause of action may be classified as a medical battery * * * when answers to either of the above questions are in the negative. * * * "

COBBS v. GRANT, 8 Cal.3d 229, 104 Cal.Rptr. 505, 502 P.2d 1 (1972). Plaintiff underwent surgery for treatment of a duodenal ulcer. The immediate surgical purpose was achieved, but two "inherent risks" of such surgery came to pass: injury to plaintiff's spleen, necessitating its removal; development of a gastric ulcer, necessitating removal of half of plaintiff's stomach. Plaintiff sued his surgeon for malpractice *inter alia* on the ground that he had not been informed of the risks of the initial surgery. While reversing a judgment for plaintiff and remanding the case for retrial a unanimous court (per Mosk, J.) said the following about informed consent:

" * * * [W]e employ several postulates. The first is that patients are generally persons unlearned in the medical sciences and therefore, except in rare cases, courts may safely assume the knowledge of patient and physician are not in parity. The second is that a person of adult years and in sound mind has the right, in the exercise of control over his own body, to determine whether or not to submit to lawful medical treatment. The third is that the patient's consent to treatment, to be effective, must be an informed consent. And the fourth is that the patient, being unlearned in medical sciences, has an abject dependence upon and trust in his physician for the information upon which he relies during the decisional process, thus raising an obligation in the physician that transcends arms-length transactions.

"From the foregoing axiomatic ingredients emerges a necessity, and a resultant requirement, for divulgence by the physician to his patient of all information relevant to a meaningful decisional process. * * *

* * *

"A concomitant issue is the yardstick to be applied in determining reasonableness of disclosure. This defendant and the majority of courts have related the duty to the custom of physicians practicing in the community. The majority rule is needlessly overbroad. Even if there can be said to be a medical community standard as to the disclosure requirement for any prescribed treatment, it appears so nebulous that doctors become, in effect, vested with virtual absolute discretion. * * * Unlimited discretion in the physician is irreconcilable with the basic right of the patient to make the ultimate informed decision regarding the course of treatment to which he knowledgeably consents to be subjected.

"A medical doctor, being the expert, appreciates the risks inherent in the procedure he is prescribing, the risks of a decision not to undergo the treatment, and the probability of a successful outcome of the treatment. But once this information has been disclosed, that aspect of the doctor's expert function has been performed. The weighing of these risks against the individual subjective fears and hopes of the patient is not an expert skill. Such evaluation and decision is a nonmedical judgment reserved to the patient alone. A patient should be denied the opportunity to weigh the risks only where it is evident he cannot evaluate the data, as for example, where there is an emergency or the patient is a child or incompetent. * * *

* * *

"In sum, the patient's right of self-decision is the measure of the physician's duty to reveal. That right can be effectively exercised only if the patient possesses adequate information to enable an intelligent choice. The scope of the physician's communications to the patient, then, must be measured by the patient's need, and that need is whatever information is material to the decision. * * *

"We point out, for guidance on retrial, an additional problem which suggests itself. There must be a causal relationship between the physician's failure to inform and the injury to the plaintiff. Such causal connection arises only if it is established that had revelation been made consent to treatment would not have been given. * * *

" * * * [In determining causation] an objective test is preferable: i.e., what would a prudent person in the patient's position have decided if adequately informed of all significant perils."

ASHE v. RADIATION ONCOLOGY ASSOCIATES, 9 S.W.3d 119 (Tenn. 1999). Here the Tennessee Supreme Court (Holder, J.) decided to join "the majority of jurisdictions" which have adopted "the objective standard" for causation in informed consent cases. "We * * * are of the opinion that the objective test appropriately respects a patient's right to self-determination. The finder of fact may consider and give weight to the patient's testimony as to whether the patient would have consented to the procedure upon full disclosure of the risks. When applying the objective standard, the finder of fact may also take into account the characteristics of the plaintiff including the plaintiff's idiosyncrasies, fears, age, medical condition, and religious beliefs. Accordingly, the objective standard affords the ease of applying a uniform standard and yet maintains the flexibility of allowing the finder of fact to make appropriate adjustments to accommodate the individual characteristics and idiosyncrasies of an individual patient. We, therefore, hold that the standard to be applied in informed consent cases is whether a reasonable person in the patient's position would have consented to the procedure or treatment in question if adequately informed of all significant perils."

CULBERTSON v. MERNITZ, 602 N.E.2d 98 (Ind.1992). Plaintiff claimed lack of informed consent to surgery because certain risks were not disclosed. *Held* (3–2), that "expert medical testimony is necessary to establish whether a physician's disclosure of risks comports with what a reasonably prudent physician would have disclosed." The court acknowledged that "the patient does not want the medical profession to determine in a paternalistic manner what the patient should or should not be told," but said that "a review of medical ethics standards of care in 1992 should assuage this fear." It quoted from the 1992 Code of Medical Ethics, of the American Medical Association, as follows:

> The patient's right of self-decision can be effectively exercised only if the patient possesses enough information to enable an intelligent choice. The patient should make his own determination on treatment. * * * The physician has an ethical obligation to help the patient make choices from among the therapeutic alternatives consistent with good medical practice. Informed consent is a basic social policy for which exceptions are permitted (1) where the patient is unconscious or otherwise incapable of consenting and harm from failure to treat is imminent; or (2) when risk-disclosure poses such a serious psychological threat of detriment to the patient as to be medically contraindicated. Social policy does not accept the paternalistic view that the physician may remain silent because divulgence might prompt the patient to forego needed therapy. Rational, informed patients should not be expected to act uniformly, even under similar circumstances, in agreeing to or refusing treatment.

MATTHIES v. MASTROMONACO, 160 N.J. 26, 733 A.2d 456 (1999). Jean Matthies, age 81, broke her hip. Her physician, Dr. Mastromonaco, considered two treatment alternatives: surgery, which was risky given Matthies' age and frailty; and "bed rest" to allow the fracture to heal. He recommended bed rest. Matthies followed this recommendation, and never regained her ability to walk. Matthies brought suit alleging lack of informed consent. "Matthies asserts that she would not have consented to bed rest if Dr. Mastromonaco had told her of the probable effect of the treatment on the quality of her life. She claims that Dr. Mastromonaco knew that without surgery, she never would walk again. He did not provide her, however, with the opportunity to choose between bed rest and the riskier, but potentially more successful, alternative of surgery." Defendant argued that there was no duty of informed consent in this case, because a physician must secure a patient's informed consent only to invasive procedures involving bodily touching. *Held*, that the doctrine of informed consent "is based not on battery, but on negligence," and it "applies to noninvasive, as well as invasive, procedures." "The rationale for basing an informed consent action on negligence rather than battery principles is that the physician's failure is better viewed as a breach of professional responsibility than as a nonconsensual touching."

"Physicians may neither impose their values on their patients nor substitute their level of risk aversion for that of their patients. One patient may prefer to undergo a potentially risky procedure, such as surgery, to enjoy a better quality of life. Another patient may choose a more conservative course of treatment to secure reduced risk at the cost of a diminished lifestyle. The choice is not for the physician, but the patient in consultation with the physician. By not telling the patient of all medically reasonable alternatives, the physician breaches the patient's right to make an informed choice."

LUGENBUHL v. DOWLING, 701 So.2d 447 (La.1997). Plaintiff had a history of hernia problems. Years ago he underwent three unsuccessful hernia operations until, in 1975, a successful hernia repair was performed using surgical mesh. When he needed another hernia operation in 1987, he told his new surgeon, Dr. Dowling, the defendant in the present case, that he wanted surgical mesh to be used. Defendant agreed to use mesh, or appeared to agree, but he had mental reservations. During the operation the surgeon decided, based on his intraoperative assessment of plaintiff's condition, not to use mesh. Plaintiff brought suit against Dr. Dowling claiming lack of informed consent. At trial plaintiff was unable to prove that Dr. Dowling's failure to use mesh was a cause of any physical or financial harm. *Held*, plaintiff is entitled to damages for "injury to the personality," fixed by the Supreme Court at $5,000. The court (per Lemmon, J.) said:

" * * *[I]t was incumbent upon the doctor to explain to the patient the advantages and disadvantages in the use of mesh, the attendant risks, and the necessity of reserving the decision on the use of mesh to the surgeon during the course of the operation. The doctor * * * failed to discharge that duty in this case. Accordingly, the doctor failed to obtain adequate informed consent to the surgery * * *.

" * * * While we have herein rejected battery as the basis for analyzing liability in lack of informed consent cases, some of the damages generally awarded in battery cases are applicable * * * in this case.

"[Here] the doctor failed to provide adequate information in response to the patient's request [that mesh be used], thereby causing damages to plaintiff's dignity, privacy and emotional well-being. The doctor, rather than explaining the advantages and disadvantages of the patient's express request, patronized his patient and mentally reserved the right to decide to disregard the patient's expressed wishes. * * *

" * * * While plaintiff failed to prove physical damages or pecuniary loss, he is still entitled to an award of general compensatory damages caused by the doctor's breach of duty. In this type of case, damages for deprivation of self-determination, insult to personal integrity, invasion of privacy, anxiety, worry and mental distress are actual and compensatory."

HELLING v. CAREY

Supreme Court of Washington, En Banc, 1974.
83 Wn.2d 514, 519 P.2d 981.

[Malpractice action against ophthalmologists. The patient claimed that she suffered permanent visual damage due to open angle glaucoma as a result of defendants' failure to diagnose and treat the condition. Testimony of the medical experts for both the plaintiff and the defendants established that the standards of the specialty do not require routine pressure tests for glaucoma upon patients under 40 years of age. Plaintiff appeals from a judgment upon a verdict for defendants.]

HUNTER, Associate Justice.

* * *

We find this to be a unique case. The testimony of the medical experts is undisputed concerning the standards of the profession for the specialty of ophthalmology. It is not a question in this case of the defendants having any greater special ability, knowledge and information than other ophthalmologists which would require the defendants to comply with a higher duty of care than that "degree of care and skill which is expected of the average practitioner in the class to which he belongs, acting in the same or similar circumstances." Pederson v. Dumouchel, 72 Wash.2d 73, 79, 431 P.2d 973 (1967). The issue is whether the defendants' compliance with the standard of the profession of ophthalmology, which does not require the giving of a routine pressure test to persons under 40 years of age, should insulate them from liability under the facts in this case where the plaintiff has lost a substantial amount of her vision due to the failure of the defendants to timely give the pressure test to the plaintiff.

The defendants argue that the standard of the profession, which does not require the giving of a routine pressure test to persons under the age of 40, is adequate to insulate the defendants from liability for negligence because the risk of glaucoma is so rare in this age group. The testimony of the defendant, Dr. Carey, however, is revealing as follows:

Q. Now, when was it, actually, the first time any complaint was made to you by her of any field or visual field problem? A. Really, the first time that she really complained of a visual field problem was the August 30th date. [1968] Q. And how soon before the diagnosis was that? A. That was 30 days. We made it on October 1st. Q. And in your opinion, how long, as you now have the whole history and analysis and the diagnosis, how long had she had this glaucoma? A. I would think she probably had it ten years or longer. Q. Now, Doctor, there's been some reference to the matter of taking pressure checks of persons over 40. What is the incidence of glaucoma, the statistics, with persons under 40? A. In the instance of glaucoma under the age of 40, is less than 100 to one per cent. The younger you get, the less the incidence. It is thought to be in the neighborhood of one in 25,000 people or less. Q. How about the incidence of glaucoma in people over 40? A. Incidence of glaucoma over 40 gets into the two to three per cent category, and hence, that's where there is this great big difference and that's why the standard around the world has been to check pressures from 40 on.

The incidence of glaucoma in one out of 25,000 persons under the age of 40 may appear quite minimal. However, that one person, the plaintiff in this instance, is entitled to the same protection, as afforded persons over 40, essential for timely detection of the evidence of glaucoma where it can be arrested to avoid the grave and devastating result of this disease. The test is a simple pressure test, relatively inexpensive. There is no judgment factor involved, and there is no doubt that by giving the test the evidence of glaucoma can be detected. The giving of the test is harmless if the physical condition of the eye permits. The testimony indicates that although the condition of the plaintiff's eyes might have at times prevented the defendants from administering the pressure test, there is an absence of evidence in the record that the test could not have been timely given.

Justice Holmes stated in Texas & Pac. Ry. v. Behymer, 189 U.S. 468, 470, 23 S.Ct. 622, 623, 47 L.Ed. 905 (1903):

> What usually is done may be evidence of what ought to be done, but what ought to be done is fixed by a standard of reasonable prudence, whether it usually is complied with or not.

In The T. J. Hooper, 60 F.2d 737, on page 740 (2d Cir.1932), Justice Hand stated:

> [I]n most cases reasonable prudence is in fact common prudence; but strictly it is never its measure; a whole calling may have unduly lagged in the adoption of new and available devices. It never may set its own tests, however persuasive be its usages. *Courts must in the end say what is required; there are precautions so imperative that even their universal disregard will not excuse their omission.*

(Italics ours.)

Under the facts of this case reasonable prudence required the timely giving of the pressure test to this plaintiff. The precaution of giving this test to detect the incidence of glaucoma to patients under 40 years of age is so imperative that irrespective of its disregard by the standards of the ophthalmology profession, it is the duty of the courts to say what is required to protect patients under 40 from the damaging results of glaucoma.

We therefore hold, as a matter of law, that the reasonable standard that should have been followed under the undisputed facts of this case was the timely giving of this simple, harmless pressure test to this plaintiff and that, in failing to do so, the defendants were negligent, which proximately resulted in the blindness sustained by the plaintiff for which the defendants are liable.

There are no disputed facts to submit to the jury on the issue of the defendants' liability. Hence, a discussion of the plaintiff's proposed instructions would be inconsequential in view of our disposition of the case.

The judgment of the trial court and the decision of the Court of Appeals is reversed, and the case is remanded for a new trial on the issue of damages only.

HALE, C. J., and ROSELLINI, STAFFORD, WRIGHT and BRACHTEN-BACH, JJ., concur.

UTTER, Associate Justice (concurring).

I concur in the result reached by the majority. I believe a greater duty of care could be imposed on the defendants than was established by their profession. The duty could be imposed when a disease, such as glaucoma, can be detected by a simple, well-known harmless test whose results are definitive and the disease can be successfully arrested by early detection, but where the effects of the disease are irreversible if undetected over a substantial period of time.

The difficulty with this approach is that we as judges, by using a negligence analysis, seem to be imposing a stigma of moral blame upon the doctors who, in this case, used all the precautions commonly prescribed by their profession in diagnosis and treatment. Lacking their training in this highly sophisticated profession, it seems illogical for this court to say they failed to exercise a reasonable standard of care. It seems to me we are, in reality, imposing liability, because, in choosing between an innocent plaintiff and a doctor, who acted reasonably according to his specialty but who could have prevented the full effects of this disease by administering a simple, harmless test and treatment, the plaintiff should not have to bear the risk of loss. As such, imposition of liability approaches that of strict liability.

Strict liability or liability without fault is not new to the law. Historically, it predates our concepts of fault or moral responsibility as a basis of the remedy.

* * *

When types of problems rather than numbers of cases are examined, strict liability is applied more often than negligence as a principle which determines liability. Peck, Negligence and Liability Without Fault in Tort Law, 46 Wash.L.Rev. 225, 239 (1971). There are many similarities in this case to other cases of strict liability. Problems of proof have been a common feature in situations where strict liability is applied. Where events are not matters of common experience, a juror's ability to comprehend whether reasonable care has been followed diminishes. There are few areas as difficult for jurors to intelligently comprehend as the intricate questions of proof and standards in medical malpractice cases.

In applying strict liability there are many situations where it is imposed for conduct which can be defined with sufficient precision to insure that application of a strict liability principle will not produce miscarriages of justice in a substantial number of cases. If the activity involved is one which can be defined with sufficient precision, that definition can serve as an accounting unit to which the costs of the activity may be allocated with some certainty and precision. With this possible, strict liability serves a compensatory function in situations where the defendant is, through the use of insurance, the financially more responsible person. Peck, Negligence and Liability Without Fault in Tort Law, supra at 240, 241.

If the standard of a reasonably prudent specialist is, in fact, inadequate to offer reasonable protection to the plaintiff, then liability can be imposed without fault. To do so under the narrow facts of this case does not offend my sense of justice. The pressure test to measure intraocular pressure with the Schiotz tonometer and the Goldman applanometer takes a short time, involves no damage to the patient, and consists of placing the instrument against the eyeball. An abnormally high pressure requires other tests which would either confirm or deny the existence of glaucoma. It is generally believed that from 5 to 10 years of detectable increased pressure must exist before there is permanent damage to the optic nerves.

Although the incidence of glaucoma in the age range of the plaintiff is approximately one in 25,000, this alone should not be enough to deny her a claim. Where its presence can be detected by a simple, well-known harmless test, where the results of the test are definitive, where the disease can be successfully arrested by early detection and where its effects are irreversible if undetected over a substantial period of time, liability should be imposed upon defendants even though they did not violate the standard existing within the profession of ophthalmology.

* * *

FINLEY and HAMILTON, JJ., concur.

———

GATES v. JENSEN, 92 Wn.2d 246, 595 P.2d 919 (1979). In this medical malpractice case the court en banc reaffirmed "the rule of Helling v. Carey, that reasonable prudence may require a standard of practice which is higher than that exercised by the relevant professional community." It did so despite defendants' argument that the Washington legislature had abrogated *Helling* by enacting the following provision:

In any civil action for damages based on professional negligence against * * * a member of the healing arts * * * the plaintiff in order to prevail shall be required to prove * * * that the defendant or defendants failed to exercise that degree of skill, care and learning possessed by other persons in the same profession * * *.

According to the court, the provision as originally drafted required only the skill, care and learning "practiced" by others in the medical profession, but the bill was amended to require the skill, care and learning "possessed" by others. The enacted standard "is much broader" and "allows ample scope" for *Helling*. Two judges dissented on the ground that the express purpose of the statute was to overturn the *Helling* decision.

UNITED BLOOD SERVICES v. QUINTANA, 827 P.2d 509 (Colo.1992). The Colorado Supreme Court summed up its approach to professional negligence:

" * * * If the standard adopted by a practicing profession were to be deemed conclusive proof of due care, the profession itself would be permitted to set the measure of its own legal liability, even though that measure might be far below a level of care readily attainable through the adoption of practices and procedures substantially more effective in protecting others against harm than the self-decreed standard of the profession. * * *

"To be sure, there is a presumption that adherence to the applicable standard of care adopted by a profession constitutes due care for those practicing that profession. The presumption, however, is a rebuttable one, and the burden is on the one challenging the standard of care to rebut the presumption by competent evidence. In a professional negligence case, therefore, a plaintiff should be permitted to present expert opinion testimony that the standard of care adopted by the school of practice to which the defendant adheres is unreasonably deficient by not incorporating readily available practices and procedures substantially more protective against the harm caused to the plaintiff * * *.

"If * * * the jury is not convinced by a preponderance of the evidence that the standard of care adopted by the defendant's school is unreasonably deficient, the jury must accept the standard of the defendant's school of practice as conclusive evidence of reasonable care and must determine the issue of negligence on the basis of the defendant's compliance or noncompliance with that standard."

ADVINCULA v. UNITED BLOOD SERVICES, 176 Ill.2d 1, 223 Ill.Dec. 1, 678 N.E.2d 1009 (1996). In a case involving AIDS virus in the blood supply, the Illinois Supreme Court affirmed the primacy of law's reasonable care standard over a profession's own standard of performance: "In Illinois negligence law, while custom and practice can assist in determining what is proper conduct, they are not conclusive necessarily of it. This precept holds true even in the area of medical professional negligence. In a professional malpractice case, where expert testimony is required to establish the requisite professional standard of care, evidence that a defendant's conduct conformed with local usage or general custom indicates due care, but may not be conclusive of it. Such evidence may be overcome by contrary expert testimony (or its equivalent) that the prevailing professional standard of care, itself, constitutes negligence."

SECTION B.   STATUTORY STANDARDS:
NEGLIGENCE PER SE

A large majority of states embrace the doctrine of negligence per se, which is affirmed by Benjamin Cardozo's well-known opinion in Martin v. Herzog, immediately below. In a nutshell, the doctrine says that if an actor violates a pertinent safety statute, and the violation results in injury, the fact of the violation by itself—"per se"—conclusively establishes the actor's negligence. Cases that follow discuss applications, limits, and possible expansions, of this basic idea.

Notice that the statutes used in the cases below to establish negligence per se all have something in common. They are statutes which do not themselves authorize private civil lawsuits to recover damages for injury caused by noncompliance. For example, the statutes involved in Martin v. Herzog are traffic laws enforcible by public-law sanctions (mainly fines); the traffic laws themselves make no mention of private civil lawsuits.

What the tort doctrine of negligence per se does is this: in a typical case, it takes a legislated rule which is enforced by regulatory penalties, and incorporates the rule into a tort lawsuit for damages. It makes use of public-law statutes for tort's own common-law purposes.

MARTIN v. HERZOG

Court of Appeals of New York, 1920.
228 N.Y. 164, 126 N.E. 814.

CARDOZO, J. The action is one to recover damages for injuries resulting in death. Plaintiff and her husband, while driving toward Tarrytown in a buggy on the night of August 21, 1915, were struck by the defendant's automobile coming in the opposite direction. They were thrown to the ground, and the man was killed. At the point of the collision the highway makes a curve. The car was rounding the curve, when suddenly it came upon the buggy, emerging, the defendant tells us, from the gloom. Negligence is charged against the defendant, the driver of the car, in that he did not keep to the right of the center of the highway. Highway Law, § 286, subd. 3, and section 332 (Consol.Laws, c. 25). Negligence is charged against the plaintiff's intestate, the driver of the wagon, in that he was traveling without lights. Highway Law, § 329a, as amended by Laws 1915, c. 367. There is no evidence that the defendant was moving at an excessive speed. There is none of any defect in the equipment of his car. The beam of light from his lamps pointed to the right as the wheels of his car turned along the curve toward the left; and, looking in the direction of the plaintiff's approach, he was peering into the shadow. The case against him must stand, therefore, if at all, upon the divergence of his course from the center of the highway. The jury found him delinquent and his victim blameless. The Appellate Division reversed, and ordered a new trial.

We agree with the Appellate Division that the charge to the jury was erroneous and misleading. The case was tried on the assumption that the hour had arrived when lights were due. It was argued on the same assumption in this court. In such circumstances, it is not important whether the hour might have been made a question for the jury. A controversy put out of the case by the parties is not to be put into it by us. We say this by way of preface to our review of the contested rulings. In the body of the charge the trial judge said that the jury could consider the absence of light "in determining whether the plaintiff's intestate was guilty of contributory negligence in failing to have a light upon the buggy as provided by law. I do not mean to say that the absence of light necessarily makes him negligent, but it is a fact for your consideration." The defendant requested a ruling that the absence of a light on the plaintiff's vehicle was "prima facie evidence of contributory negligence." This request was refused, and the jury were again instructed that they might consider the absence of lights as some evidence of negligence, but that it was not conclusive evidence. The plaintiff then requested a charge that "the fact that the plaintiff's intestate was driving without a light is not negligence in itself," and to this the court acceded. The defendant saved his rights by appropriate exceptions.

We think the unexcused omission of the statutory signals is more than some evidence of negligence. It *is* negligence in itself. Lights are intended for the guidance and protection of other travelers on the highway. Highway Law, § 329a. By the very terms of the hypothesis, to omit, willfully or heedlessly, the safeguards prescribed by law for the benefit of another that he may be preserved in life or limb, is to fall short of the standard of diligence to which those who live in organized society are under a duty to conform. That, we think, is now the established rule in this state. Whether the omission of an absolute duty, not willfully or heedlessly, but through unavoidable accident, is also to be characterized as negligence, is a question of nomenclature into which we need not enter, for it does not touch the case before us. There may be times, when, if jural niceties are to be preserved, the two wrongs, negligence and breach of statutory duty, must be kept distinct in speech and thought.

In the conditions here present they come together and coalesce. A rule less rigid has been applied where the one who complains of the omission is not a member of the class for whose protection the safeguard is designed. [Citations omitted.] Courts have been reluctant to hold that the police regulations of boards and councils and other subordinate officials create rights of action beyond the specific penalties imposed. This has led them to say that the violation of a statute is negligence, and the violation of a like ordinance is only evidence of negligence. An ordinance, however, like a statute, is a law within its sphere of operation, and so the distinction has not escaped criticism. Whether it has become too deeply rooted to be abandoned, even if it be thought illogical, is a question not now before us. What concerns us at this time is that, even in the ordinance cases, the omission of a safeguard prescribed by statute is put upon a different plane, and is held not merely some evidence of negligence, but negligence in itself. [Citations omitted.]

In the case at hand, we have an instance of the admitted violation of a statute intended for the protection of travelers on the highway, of whom the defendant at the time was one. Yet the jurors were instructed in effect that they were at liberty in their discretion to treat the omission of lights either as innocent or as culpable. They were allowed to "consider the default as lightly or gravely" as they would (Thomas, J., in the court below). They might as well have been told that they could use a like discretion in holding a master at fault for the omission of a safety appliance prescribed by positive law for the protection of a workman. Jurors have no dispensing power, by which they may relax the duty that one traveler on the highway owes under the statute to another. It is error to tell them that they have. The omission of these lights was a wrong, and being wholly unexcused, was also a negligent wrong. No license should have been conceded to the triers of the facts to find it anything else.

We must be on our guard, however, against confusing the question of negligence with that of the causal connection between the negligence and the injury. A defendant who travels without lights is not to pay damages for his fault, unless the absence of lights is the cause of the disaster. A plaintiff who travels without them is not to forfeit the right to damages, unless the absence of lights is at least a contributing cause of the disaster. To say that conduct is negligence is not to say that it is always contributory negligence. "Proof of negligence in the air, so to speak, will not do." Pollock, Torts (10th Ed.) p. 472.

[The court then held that the absence of lights could have been found to be a cause of the accident and affirmed the order of the Appellate Division, granting a new trial. HOGAN, J., gave a dissenting opinion.]

————

SCHOOLEY v. PINCH'S DELI MARKET, 134 Wash.2d 468, 951 P.2d 749 (1998). In violation of a statute, defendant sold liquor to a minor, who shared the liquor with plaintiff, also a minor. Intoxicated, plaintiff dove into a shallow pool, receiving injuries that rendered her a quadriplegic. *Held*, that plaintiff, though not the minor to whom the alcohol was illegally sold, is "within the class of persons the statute was enacted to protect." "The recognized purpose of legislation prohibiting the sale of alcohol to minors is to protect minors' health and safety interests from their 'own inability to drink responsibly' * * *. Because minors who drink commonly do so with other minors, protecting all those injured as a result of the illegal sale of alcohol to minors is the best way to serve the purpose for which the legislation was created, to prevent minors from drinking."

PELKEY v. BRENNAN, 12 A.D.2d 215, 209 N.Y.S.2d 691 (3d Dept.1961). A 13–year-old girl was injured by a fall at defendant's skating rink while there after 7 p.m. unaccompanied by an adult. A statute made it a misdemeanor for the operator of the rink to permit the presence of a child under 16 unaccompanied by a parent or authorized adult during specified hours, including the time when this accident occurred. The trial court's charge permitted a verdict for plaintiffs if the jury found that violation of the statute was a proximate cause of the accident. Verdict and judgment for plaintiffs. *Held*, reversed and new trial ordered. The statute, setting prohibitory hours for minors at such places as dance houses and billiard halls as well as skating rinks, was enacted to protect the children's morals and conduct, and not to protect children from physical injury.

DI PONZIO v. RIORDAN, 89 N.Y.2d 578, 657 N.Y.S.2d 377, 679 N.E.2d 616 (1997). A customer at defendant's gas station left his motor running when he went into the station's storefront area to pay for fuel. The customer's car began moving and pinned plaintiff, who was pumping gas, against his own car. Plaintiff alleged that defendant failed to comply with a regulation requiring that gas station customers be warned to turn off their engines when fueling their vehicles. *Held*, that violation of the regulation "does not give rise to liability" in this case. The purpose of the regulation is to safeguard against "the hazards of fire and explosions." "The occurrence that led to plaintiff's injury was clearly outside this limited class of hazards."

SNAPP v. HARRISON, 699 So.2d 567 (Miss.1997). A fire broke out on Harrison's premises and spread to premises occupied by the Snapp brothers. The Snapps claimed Harrison was negligent. Harrison rejoined that the plaintiffs had themselves violated the fire code. The trial court instructed the jury that such violation was contributory negligence per se. *Held*, it was error to give the instruction, but the error was harmless.

"To prevail in an action for negligence *per se*, a party must prove that he was a member of the class sought to be protected under the statute, that his injuries were of a type sought to be avoided, and that violation of the statute proximately caused his injuries." Here Harrison was not within the class protected by the fire code provision in question, and he "should not have gotten the benefit" of a negligence per se instruction.

However, the jury was merely instructed to consider the Snapps' noncompliance with the fire code when making a determination of comparative fault. "The comparative negligence instruction given, while erroneously acknowledging negligence *per se* on the part of the Snapps, does not dictate a verdict for Harrison. Instead, it directs the jury to reduce the damages awarded to the plaintiff" in the event the defendant was found liable. Here the jury did not find the defendant liable. "Therefore, we find that the giving of this negligence *per se* instruction under the facts of this case was harmless error."

TEDLA v. ELLMAN
Court of Appeals of New York, 1939.
280 N.Y. 124, 19 N.E.2d 987.

[Plaintiffs were wheeling a baby carriage filled with junk on the right hand side of the Sunrise Highway on Sunday evening after dark, when they were struck by defendants' automobile as it was passing them. One of them carried a lighted lantern. The jury found that the accident was due solely to the negligence of the driver and judgments were entered for plaintiffs and affirmed in the Appellate Division (253 App.Div. 764, 300 N.Y.S. 1051). Defendants appeal on the ground that plaintiffs were guilty of contributory negligence because of violation of the Vehicle and Traffic Law (Consol.Laws c. 71) which provides that "pedestrians walking or remaining on the paved portion, or traveled part of a roadway shall be subject to, and comply with, the rules governing vehicles, with respect to meeting and turning out, except that such pedestrians shall keep to the left of the center line thereof, and turn to their left instead of right side thereof, so as to permit all vehicles passing them in either direction to pass on their right. Such pedestrians shall not be subject to the rules governing vehicles as to giving signals." Section 85, subd. 6.]

LEHMAN, J. The plaintiffs showed by the testimony of a State policeman that "there were very few cars going east" at the time of the accident, but that going west there was "very heavy Sunday night traffic." Until the recent adoption of the new statutory rule for pedestrians, ordinary prudence would have dictated that pedestrians should not expose themselves to the danger of walking along the roadway upon which the "very heavy Sunday night traffic" was proceeding when they could walk in comparative safety along a roadway used by very few cars. It is said that now, by force of the statutory rule, pedestrians are guilty of contributory negligence as matter of law when they use the safer roadway, unless that roadway is left of the center of the road. Disregard of the statutory rule of the road and observance of a rule based on immemorial custom, it is said, is negligence which as matter of law is a proximate cause of the accident, though observance of the statutory rule might, under the circumstances of the particular case, expose a pedestrian to serious danger from which he would be free if he followed the rule that had been established by custom. If that be true, then the Legislature has decreed that pedestrians must observe the general rule of conduct which it has prescribed for their safety even under circumstances where observance would subject them to unusual risk; that pedestrians are to be charged with negligence as matter of law for acting as prudence dictates. It is unreasonable to ascribe to the Legislature an intention that the statute should have so extraordinary a result, and the courts may not give to a statute an effect not intended by the Legislature.

The Legislature, when it enacted the statute, presumably knew that this court and the courts of other jurisdictions had established the general principle that omission by a plaintiff of a safeguard, prescribed by statute, against a recognized danger, constitutes negligence as matter of law which bars recovery for damages caused by incidence of the danger for which the safeguard was prescribed. The principle has been formulated in the Restatement of the Law of Torts: "A plaintiff who has violated a legislative enactment designed to prevent a certain type of dangerous situation is barred from recovery for a harm caused by a violation of the statute if, but only if, the harm was sustained by reason of a situation of that type." § 469. So where a plaintiff failed to place lights upon a vehicle, as required by statute, this court has said: "we think the unexcused omission of the statutory signals is more than some evidence of negligence. It is negligence in itself. Lights are intended for the guidance and protection of other travelers on the highway. Highway Law [Consol.Laws, c. 25] § 329–a. By the very terms of the hypothesis, to omit, willfully or heedlessly, the safeguards prescribed by law for the benefit of another that he may be preserved in life or limb, is to fall short of the standard of diligence to which those who live in organized society are under a duty to conform. That, we think, is now the established rule in this State." Martin v. Herzog, 228 N.Y. 164, 168, 126 N.E. 814, 815, per Cardozo, J. The appellants lean heavily upon that and kindred cases and the principle established by them.

The analogy is, however, incomplete. The "established rule" should not be weakened either by subtle distinctions or by extension beyond its letter or spirit into a field where "by the very terms of the hypothesis" it can have no proper application. At times the indefinite and flexible standard of care of the traditional reasonably prudent man may be, in the opinion of the Legislature, an insufficient measure of the care which should be exercised to guard against a recognized danger; at times, the duty, imposed by custom, that no man shall use what is his to the harm of others provides insufficient safeguard for the preservation of the life or limb or property of others. Then the Legislature may by statute prescribe additional safeguards and may define duty and standard of care in rigid terms; and when the Legislature has spoken, the standard of the care required is no longer what the reasonably prudent man would do under the circumstances but what the Legislature has commanded. That is the rule established by the courts and "by the very terms of the hypothesis" the rule applies where the Legislature has prescribed safeguards "for the benefit of another that he may be preserved in life or limb." In that field debate as to whether the safeguards so prescribed are reasonably necessary is ended by the legislative fiat. Obedience to that fiat cannot add to the danger, even assuming that the prescribed safeguards are not reasonably necessary and where the legislative anticipation of dangers is realized and harm results through heedless or willful omission of the prescribed safeguard, injury flows from wrong and the wrongdoer is properly held responsible for the consequent damages.

The statute upon which the defendants rely is of different character. It does not prescribe additional safeguards which pedestrians must provide for the preservation of the life or limb or property of others, or even of themselves, nor does it impose upon pedestrians a higher standard of care. What the statute does provide is rules of the road to be observed by pedestrians and by vehicles, so that all those who use the road may know how they and others should proceed, at least under usual circumstances. A general rule of conduct—and, specifically, a rule of the road—may accomplish its intended purpose under usual conditions, but, when the unusual occurs, strict observance may defeat the purpose of the rule and produce catastrophic results.

Negligence is failure to exercise the care required by law. Where a statute defines the standard of care and the safeguards required to meet a recognized danger, then, as we have said, no other measure may be applied in determining whether a person has carried out the duty of care imposed by law. Failure to observe the standard imposed by statute is negligence, as matter of law. On the other hand, where a statutory general rule of conduct fixes no definite standard of care which would under all circumstances tend to protect life, limb or property but merely codifies or supplements a common-law rule, which has always been subject to limitations and exceptions; or where the statutory rule of conduct regulates conflicting rights and obligations in manner calculated to promote public convenience and safety, then the statute, in the absence of clear language to the contrary should not be construed as intended to wipe out the limitations and exceptions which judicial decisions have attached to the common-law duty; nor should it be construed as an inflexible command that the general rule of conduct intended to prevent accidents must be followed even under conditions when observance might cause accidents. We may assume reasonably that the Legislature directed pedestrians to keep to the left of the center of the road because that would cause them to face traffic approaching in that lane and would enable them to care for their own safety better than if the traffic approached them from the rear. We cannot assume reasonably that the Legislature intended that a statute enacted for the preservation of the life and limb of pedestrians must be observed when observance would subject them to more imminent danger. * * * The generally accepted rule and the reasons for it are set forth in the comment to section 286 of the Restatement of the Law of Torts: "Many statutes and ordinances are so worded as apparently to express a universally obligatory rule of conduct. Such enactments, however, may in view of their purpose and spirit be properly construed as intended to apply only to ordinary situations and to be subject to the qualification that the conduct prohibited thereby is not wrongful if, because of an emergency or the like, the circumstances justify an apparent disobedience to the letter of the enactment. * * * The provisions of statutes intended to codify and supplement the rules of conduct which are established by a course of judicial decision or by custom, are often construed as subject to the same limitations and exceptions as the rules which they supersede. Thus, a statute or ordinance requiring all persons to drive on the right side of the road may be construed as subject to an exception permitting travelers to drive upon the other side, if so doing is likely to prevent rather than cause the accidents which it is the purpose of the statute or ordinance to prevent."

Even under that construction of the statute, a pedestrian is, of course, at fault if he fails without good reason to observe the statutory rule of conduct. The general duty is established by the statute, and deviation from it without good cause is a wrong and the wrongdoer is responsible for the damages resulting from his wrong. * * *

Judgment affirmed.

———

WALKER v. MISSOURI PACIFIC RAILWAY, 95 Kan. 702, 149 P. 677 (1915). A local ordinance prohibited the blocking of any street by a train for longer than 5 minutes, and another ordinance prohibited stopping trains for any length of time on Central Avenue. A state statute prohibited blocking of certain roads for longer than 10 minutes. The defendant's train was stopped across Central Avenue for a disputed length of time for the repair of the locomotive's brake rigging, which was dragging on the track. As a result of this blockade, the fire department was delayed 3 to 4 minutes on its way to extinguish a fire in the plaintiff's house, which allegedly was destroyed by reason of the delay. *Held*, for defendant, reversing a judgment for plaintiff and ordering a new trial. The trial court erred in charging that this obstruction was a violation of the ordinance "without regard to whether the obstruction was reasonable or unreasonable, accidental or intentional." "This statute must be so construed as to permit trains to stop anywhere to prevent accidents. The question of the necessity for stopping the train to prevent an accident should have been submitted to the jury."

MUSSIVAND v. DAVID, 45 Ohio St.3d 314, 544 N.E.2d 265 (1989). Defendant, infected with a venereal disease, had sexual relations with plaintiff's wife, and infected her with the disease; she in turn infected plaintiff. An Ohio statute provides that a person who knows or has reasonable cause to believe "he is suffering from a dangerous, contagious disease" shall not "knowingly fail to take reasonable measures to prevent exposing himself to other persons." *Held*, plaintiff has valid claim of negligence, but not negligence per se. This statute speaks "only in abstract or general terms." "What measures would be reasonable will depend, in part, on the type of disease and how it is transmitted * * *. [The statute is the same as] a standard of due care which should be exercised by a reasonably prudent person under the circumstances."

BAUMAN v. CRAWFORD

Supreme Court of Washington, 1985.
104 Wash.2d 241, 704 P.2d 1181.

PEARSON, Justice.

This appeal requires us to decide whether the negligence per se doctrine should be applicable to minors, or whether minors should instead be judged only by the special child's standard of care in a civil negligence action. We hold that a minor's violation of a statute does not constitute proof of negligence per se, but may, in proper cases, be introduced as evidence of a minor's negligence. Accordingly, we reverse the decision [below]. * * *

[Here a plaintiff of 14, riding his bicycle after dark, was injured in an intersection collision with defendant's automobile. The bicycle had no headlight, in violation of a city ordinance and a state statute. This omission, according to the trial court's instructions, was negligence per se.]

Washington has long recognized the special standard of care applicable to children: a child's conduct is measured by the conduct of a reasonably careful child of the same age, intelligence, maturity, training and experience. * * *

A majority of courts in states which apply the negligence per se doctrine to adults have recognized a fundamental conflict between that doctrine and the special child's standard of care. Scholarly commentary also overwhelmingly supports the view that negligence per se is inapplicable to children.

* * * These courts and commentators also recognize that refusal to consider a child's minority in effect substitutes a standard of strict liability for the criterion of the reasonable child.

* * *

A significant number of the courts which decline to apply negligence per se to minors have determined that violation of a statute by a minor may be introduced as evidence of negligence, as long as the jury is clearly instructed that the minor's behavior is ultimately to be judged by the special child's standard of care.

We agree with these courts that allowing a statutory violation to be introduced simply as one factor to be considered by the trier of fact is an equitable resolution of the dilemma created by a minor's violation of law. We therefore remand for a new trial on the issue of liability under proper instructions. At that trial the jury must be instructed as to the special child's standard of care. The jury may then be instructed that violation of a relevant statute[1] may be considered as evidence of negligence only if the jury finds that a reasonable child of the same age, intelligence, maturity and experi-

---

1. A statute must still be shown to be applicable under the negligence per se test before its violation may be introduced even as mere evidence of negligence. That is, the statute must be designed to protect the proper class of persons, to protect the particular interest involved, and to protect against the harm which results. Thus, only relevant statutory violations will be admitted.

ence as petitioner would not have acted in violation of the statute under the same circumstances.

* * *

BRACHTENBACH, Justice (concurring).

I concur in the rationale and result of the majority but I am convinced that in the appropriate case this court should reexamine the entire theory of negligence per se arising from the alleged violation of a statute, an ordinance or an administrative regulation.

This court has long been committed to the rule that violation of a positive statute constitutes negligence per se. In *Engelker v. Seattle Elec. Co.*, 50 Wash. 196, 96 P. 1039 (1908), the court noted that some jurisdictions follow the rule that a violation of a statute is mere evidence of negligence but it adopted the doctrine "that a thing which is done in violation of positive law is in itself negligence." This rule has been applied to violations of statutes, ordinances and regulations, in determining both the liability of defendants and the contributory negligence of the plaintiffs. * * *

The rule, however, has not been applied with relentless indifference to actual fault. A violation of statute has been held not to constitute negligence per se where the violation is due to some cause beyond the violator's control, and which reasonable prudence could not have guarded against; where the violation is due to an emergency; where the violation is merely technical; where the violation is perpetuated out of necessity; or where the violator is not given notice that his actions were in violation of the law. [Citations omitted.]

* * *

Currently, the majority of American jurisdictions follow the negligence per se doctrine and find that a breach of statutory duty is a breach of standard of care for civil negligence cases. Seven states follow the theory that a breach of a statutory duty is evidence of negligence in civil action, while five states hold that a violation of a statute is prima facie negligence which may be rebutted by competent evidence. In addition, some of the courts which follow the majority rule as to statutes have held that the breach of ordinances, or traffic laws, or the regulations of administrative bodies is only evidence for the jury. Such cases seem to indicate a desire to leave some leeway for cases where a violation may not be necessarily unreasonable. 2 F. Harper & F. James, *Torts* § 17.6 (1956).

* * * [C]riticism of the negligence per se doctrine is mounting in the courts. Authors of treatises and journal articles are also increasingly critical of the doctrine and write favorably of the evidence-of-negligence doctrine. Objection is made to the court's inferring a legislative intent to create a standard of care in civil cases where the Legislature is silent. * * * The Legislature has not considered the policy problems peculiar to civil liability nor has it composed the legislation in terms of a standard of due care in damage suits or for judging negligence. Reliance on the Legislature for a standard of reasonableness under these circumstances would not make for the wisest decision.

* * *

Criticism is also made because of the imposition of liability without fault. As noted above, the Washington courts have joined in this criticism and produced multiple exceptions in order to avoid this aspect of the doctrine. This exception-finding approach produces a weakened doctrine and ultimately places the jury's task of determining negligence with the court under all circumstances. Such an approach also leads to distorted statutory construction which affects the criminal law as well.

The defect in our prior reasoning is that the negligence per se doctrine removes the determination of negligence from the fact-finding function of the jury, or the court sitting as a fact finder. While it is a convenient method to affix liability, it runs counter to the basic notion of determining tort liability. I would prospectively limit the doctrine to an evidence of negligence standard.

JAROSH v. VAN METER, 171 Neb. 61, 105 N.W.2d 531, 82 A.L.R.2d 714 (1960), quoting Doan v. Hoppe, 133 Neb. 767, 277 N.W. 64 (1938): "This court has held many times that the violation of a statute or an ordinance regulating traffic does not constitute negligence as a matter of law but is evidence of negligence to be considered by the jury in connection with other circumstances in evidence. The mere fact that a pedestrian walks across a street between intersections contrary to ordinance is not of itself negligence. But, one who does so must necessarily be required to exercise a greater degree of care than one who walks across a street at a crosswalk where protection is afforded by giving the pedestrian the right of way."

STATUTORY CLAIMS DISTINGUISHED

A statute, state or federal, might expressly provide that someone injured by a violation of the statute may sue the violator for damages caused by noncompliance. A plaintiff who exercises the statutory right to sue is claiming recovery under the statute itself, not under the common law of tort. If the statute is federal, the claim for damages is federal. For example, the federal Consumer Product Safety Act (CPSA), excerpted below, sets up a commission which issues safety standards for consumer products. The commission enforces its standards through regulatory sanctions (fines, recall orders, and the like). In addition, the CPSA expressly authorizes private civil suits for damages (§ 2072) and also for injunctions (§ 2073).

When a statute does not in so many words make provision for private suits against violators, interpretation of the statute by the courts may nonetheless conclude that the statute should be read to authorize a private right of action. In other words, the right of injured persons to recover damages from violators may be established by implication of statutory meaning, using ordinary canons of statutory interpretation. Again, as in the case of an express right of action, a plaintiff who exercises an implied statutory right to sue is claiming recovery under the statute itself, not under the common law of tort.

The tort doctrine of negligence per se comes into play when a safety statute does not itself, either explicitly or impliedly, establish a right to sue for damages. Then the right to sue comes from the common law—the tort law—of a particular state. The statute incorporated within a tort lawsuit may be federal, but the suit for damages retains its state-law character. Most states that employ the doctrine of negligence per se apply it to violations of administrative regulations as well as violations of statutes.

CONSUMER PRODUCT SAFETY ACT
15 U.S.C. §§ 2051 et seq.
(enacted in 1972).

§ 2053. Consumer Product Safety Commission

(a) An independent regulatory commission is hereby established, to be known as the Consumer Product Safety Commission, consisting of five Commissioners who shall be appointed by the President, by and with the advice and consent of the Senate. * * *

§ 2056. Consumer Product Safety Standards

(a) The Commission may promulgate consumer product safety standards * * *. A consumer product safety standard shall consist of one or more of any of the following types of requirements:

(1) Requirements expressed in terms of performance requirements.

(2) Requirements that a consumer product be marked with or accompanied by clear and adequate warnings or instructions, or requirements respecting the form of warnings or instructions.

Any requirement of such a standard shall be reasonably necessary to prevent or reduce an unreasonable risk of injury associated with such product.

§ 2072. Suits for Damages

(a) Any person who shall sustain injury by reason of any knowing (including willful) violation of a consumer product safety rule, or any other rule or order issued by the Commission may sue any person who knowingly (including willfully) violated any such rule or order in any district court of the United States in the district in which the defendant resides or is found or has an agent, [and] shall recover damages sustained, and may, if the court determines it to be in the interest of justice, recover the costs of suit, including reasonable attorneys' fees * * *.

(c) The remedies provided for in this section shall be in addition to and not in lieu of any other remedies provided by common law or under Federal or State law.

§ 2073. Private Enforcement

Any interested person * * * may bring an action in any United States district court for the district in which the defendant is found or transacts business to enforce a consumer product safety rule * * *, and to obtain appropriate injunctive relief. * * *

§ 2074. Private Remedies

(a) Compliance with consumer product safety rules * * * shall not relieve any person from liability at common law or under State statutory law to any other person.

———

BREITWIESER v. KMS INDUSTRIES, INC., 467 F.2d 1391 (5th Cir.1972). Employees under the age of 18 may not be assigned to "particularly hazardous" jobs defined in regulations issued by the Secretary of Labor pursuant to the federal Fair Labor Standards Act. Defendant's 16–year-old employee had a fatal accident when assigned to such a job. The boy's parents brought a wrongful death action in federal court. (A state tort action was barred because workers compensation benefits—$750—were available.) Plaintiffs sought civil damages as a remedy for the employer's FLSA violation. *Held,* for defendant. The FLSA "does not provide for damages in child labor cases," but rather "explicitly provides for criminal penalties of up to six months in prison and a $10,000 fine." There is no basis for "implying" a private cause of action for damages, since the legislature did not intend to create such a remedy and since criminal sanctions "are substantial enough to serve as an adequate deterrent to violations." Judge Wisdom said in dissent:

" * * * [C]ivil suits for violations of the FLSA serve as a necessary or appropriate supplement in the nature of an action by a private attorney general to effectuate congressional policy in favor of protecting child labor from an employer's abuses.

" * * * The effect of the Act is to impose on employers the duty of assigning minors only to non-hazardous tasks. Correlatively, working minors have a right to be free from assignment to hazardous tasks. An employer's violation of his statutory duty imposes civil liability in this as in any other case where the violation of a duty causes injury to an individual to whom the duty is owed. For every right there is a remedy. If the right is created by a federal statute, the federal courts have the power to fashion an appropriate remedy. As Mr. Justice Black said in Bell v. Hood, [327 U.S. 678, 684, 66 S.Ct. 773, 777 (1946)] * * *: 'where federally protected rights have been invaded, it has been the rule from the beginning that courts will be alert to adjust their remedies so as to grant the necessary relief.' "

SMITH v. WAL–MART STORES, 167 F.3d 286 (1999). Plaintiff, age 74, walked only with the assistance of a walker. While shopping at defendant's store, she used the restroom, where she fell and broke her neck. She alleged negligence per se. The restroom stall was too narrow for her walker and lacked grab bars, and so was not in compliance with requirements for handicapped accessibility of the federal Americans With Disabilities Act (ADA). In this diversity suit, the parties agreed that Georgia law controls. *Held*, for plaintiff. "A state can incorporate requirements of federal law into its law * * *." The ADA itself "does not grant a private cause of action" to redress physical injury caused by an ADA violation; at the same time, "ADA contains no provision barring application of it as the basis for a state cause of action." Plaintiff's claim of "negligence per se under Georgia law" may be based on defendant's violation of the federal ADA.

COMPLIANCE WITH STATUTE

A party who asserts negligence per se is using a statutory norm as a sword. The assertion is that the opposing party's failure to comply with the statute amounts, in and of itself, to actionable negligence. A statutory standard may also be put to use as a shield. Suppose the plaintiff claims that defendant's conduct was negligent according to the ordinary tort criterion of reasonable care, but defendant shows that the conduct in question was in compliance with a relevant safety statute. Does the showing of statutory compliance automatically defeat plaintiff's claim?

The answer is that in negligence lawsuits statutes work better as tools of attack than as means of protection. Compliance with a pertinent statute is a factor to be considered in deciding whether conduct is negligent, but in most cases compliance is not a "per se" defense against an allegation of negligence.

————

McGETTIGAN v. NEW YORK CENTRAL RAILROAD, 268 N.Y. 66, 196 N.E. 745, 99 A.L.R. 283 (1935); noted in 49 Harv.L.Rev. 843. The defendant railroad, in accordance with a rule of the Public Service Commission, installed a flashing signal in the center of a road crossing, having obtained the approval of its location from the Public Service Commission. The plaintiff was injured when the automobile in which he was riding struck the base of the signal. *Held*, for plaintiff. The jury might find the defendant negligent. The permission of the Commission could give no immunity from liability for doing a negligent act.

MITCHELL v. HOTEL BERRY CO., 34 Ohio App. 259, 171 N.E. 39 (1929). Action against a hotel keeper for harm caused to a guest by fire, claimed to be due to insufficient exits or means of information as to exits. The defendant had complied with the provisions of the statute with reference to hotels. *Held*, reversing judgment on a verdict directed for the defendant, that the jury could find the defendant guilty of negligence, since the statute fixed only the minimum requirements and it may have been negligent for the defendant to have done no more than was required by the statute.

WILSON v. PIPER AIRCRAFT CORP., 282 Or. 61, 577 P.2d 1322 (1978). Two passengers died in the crash of a small airplane manufactured by defendant. In this wrongful death action plaintiffs claimed that the design of the aircraft was "dangerously defective" in certain respects, including the engine's susceptibility to icing. Defendant rejoined "that the design of this model of airplane was specifically approved by the Federal Aviation Administration (FAA) under its statutory authority to set safety standards for aircraft, and that this particular airplane had been issued an FAA certificate of airworthiness." The court held that FAA approval, while "appropriate for consideration by the trier of fact," does not amount to a "complete defense." "We have * * * refused to hold compliance with statutory or administrative safety standards to be conclusive on the question of tort liability * * *." However, the court went on to say that "[t]aking into account all of the evidence, including the FAA determination," plaintiffs' proof of defective design was insufficient. In a concurring opinion Justice Linde wrote:

"It is true that compliance with government safety standards will generally not be held to negate a claim of 'dangerously defective' design, but it would equally be an oversimplification to say that it can never do so. The role of such compliance should logically depend on whether the goal to be achieved by the particular government standards, the balance struck between safety and its costs, has been set higher or lower than that set by the rules governing the producer's civil liability. It may well be that when government intervenes in the product market to set safety standards, it often confines itself to demanding only minimum safeguards against the most flagrant hazards, well below the contemporary standards for civil liability. But that was not necessarily the case when the first safety standards were legislated, and it is not necessarily so for all products today.

"In the design of aircraft, government regulation obviously places a much greater weight on the side of safety than it does for most products. The FAA not only sets detailed performance standards for the operational aspects of the design, it also requires that the design be tested for compliance with these standards by the producer and ultimately by the agency itself before a certificate is issued. * * * FAA certification of a design represents a more deliberate, technically intensive program to set and control a given level of safety in priority to competing considerations than is true of many run-of-the-mill safety regulations.

* * *

" * * * [O]nce the common-law premise of liability is expressed as a balance of social utility so closely the same as the judgment made in administering safety legislation, it becomes very problematic to assume that one or a sequence of law courts and juries are to repeat that underlying social judgment de novo as each sees fit. Rather, when the design of a product is subject not only to prescribed performance standards but to government supervised testing and specific approval or disapproval on safety grounds, no further balance whether the product design is 'unreasonably dangerous' for its intended or foreseeable use under the conditions for which it is approved needs to be struck by a court or a jury *unless* one of two things can be shown: either that the standards of safety and utility assigned to the regulatory scheme are less inclusive or demanding than the premises of the law of products liability, or that the regulatory agency did not address the allegedly defective element of the design or in some way fell short of its assigned task."

GORE v. PEOPLE'S SAVINGS BANK
Supreme Court of Connecticut, 1995.
235 Conn. 360, 665 A.2d 1341.

KATZ, J.

The primary question on this certified appeal is whether the Appellate Court properly concluded that a landlord of a residential dwelling may be held strictly liable pursuant to General Statutes (Rev. to 1985) §§ 47a–7, 47a–8 and 47a–54f(b)[1] for personal injuries sustained by a minor tenant due to the minor's exposure to lead-based paint in the landlord's dwelling. The plaintiffs, Thomas Gore and Wanda Copeland, brought an action on behalf of their minor son, Kendall Copeland, claiming, inter alia, that the defendants, People's Savings Bank and M.S.B. Real Estate Corporation, were strictly liable for the damages caused by their son's exposure to lead-based paint in the defendants' dwelling. The trial court, Thim, J., granted the defendants' motion for a directed verdict on the strict liability count * * *. The Appellate Court reversed the decision of the trial court, concluding that "§§ 47a–7 and 47a–8, when read together, and § 47a–54f provide for civil damages pursuant to a claim of strict liability" * * *.

[In 1984, the child Kendall and his parents moved into an apartment in Bridgeport owned by defendants. Kendall ingested chips of sweet-tasting paint in the apartment and, in 1985, was diagnosed as having a high level of lead in his blood. High lead levels in children cause, among other injuries, decreased intelligence, impaired development, hearing loss, kidney ailments, and blood disorders including anemia. Upon notification of Kendall's medical status, an official from Bridgeport's lead poisoning prevention program conducted tests at the apartment utilizing a lead-paint analyzer, a portable X-ray machine. In the living room of the apartment, where chips of paint were found on a window sill, the analyzer measured lead concentrations in excess of the level allowed under the federal lead-paint standard. Defendants were notified of the results of the inspection, and they subsequently abated the lead hazard in plaintiffs' apartment.]

By amended complaint dated October 1, 1992, the plaintiffs brought an action against the defendants for injuries that Kendall had suffered due to

---

1. General Statutes (Rev. to 1985) § 47a–7 provides in relevant part: "Landlord's responsibilities. (a) A landlord shall: * * * (2) make all repairs and do whatever is necessary to put and keep the premises in a fit and habitable condition * * *."

General Statutes (Rev. to 1985) § 47a–8 provides: "Paint not conforming to standards renders property unfit. The presence of paint which does not conform to federal standards as required in accordance with the Lead–Based Paint Poisoning Prevention Act, Chapter 63 of the Social Security Act, * * * shall constitute a noncompliance with subdivision (2) of subsection (a) of section 47a–7." * * *

General Statutes (Rev. to 1985) § 47a–54f(b) provides: "Paint on the accessible surfaces of a tenement house shall not be cracked, chipped, blistered, flaking, loose, or peeling so as to constitute a health hazard." * * *

[Ed. note: Violation of these provisions is a defense in an action for nonpayment of rent.]

his exposure to the lead-based paint. * * * [The plaintiffs claimed, inter alia,] that the defendants were strictly liable for the damages caused by the lead-based paint violations. On October 20, 1992, after the close of evidence, the trial court granted the defendants' motion for a directed verdict on the strict liability count against each defendant.

* * *

The Appellate Court reversed * * *. In doing so, the Appellate Court first determined that violations of §§ 47a–7(a)(2), 47a–8 and 47a–54f(b) constitute negligence per se for the purposes of a claim brought on behalf of a minor injured by lead-based paint in the landlord's apartment. In particular, the Appellate Court determined, on the basis of the language of these statutory provisions and their legislative history, that the provisions satisfied the two-prong test for negligence per se: (1) that the plaintiffs were within the class of persons protected by the statute; and (2) that the injury suffered is of the type that the statute was intended to prevent. * * *

* * *

* * * The Appellate Court concluded that a violation of §§ 47a–8 and 47a–54f constitutes negligence per se, and that, because these statutory provisions do not expressly provide landlords the opportunity for proving the "excuse" of lack of notice, landlords are strictly liable for damages resulting from the violations upon proof of proximate causation. * * *

We conclude that, although the Appellate Court properly determined that the presence of lead paint in violation of §§ 47a–8 and 47a–54f constitutes negligence per se, these sections do not impose strict liability on landlords. * * *

[The following analysis focusses on § 47a–8, the most specific provision; it applies equally to the other provisions.]

In determining whether a violation of § 47a–8 constitutes negligence per se or provides a basis to subject the landlord to strict liability, we must first discuss traditional principles of landlord premises liability [for personal injury]. We have recognized that, under the common law, landlords have a duty to use reasonable care to maintain in a reasonably safe condition those areas of their premises over which they exercise control. Cruz v. Drezek, 175 Conn. 230, 234, 397 A.2d 1335 (1978) * * *. We stated in Cruz v. Drezek, supra at 235: "There could be no breach of the duty resting upon the [landlords] unless they knew of the defective condition or were chargeable with notice of it because, had they exercised a reasonable inspection of their premises, they would have discovered it * * *."

* * *

Although the common law imposes on landlords only a duty to maintain in a reasonably safe condition those areas of their premises over which they exercise control, statutes may impose on landlords additional duties or obligations. * * * Indeed, under general principles of tort law, a requirement imposed by statute may establish the applicable standard of care to be applied in a particular action. * * *

"Negligence per se operates to engraft a particular legislative standard onto the general standard of care imposed by traditional tort law principles, i.e., that standard of care to which an ordinarily prudent person would conform his conduct. To establish negligence, the jury in a negligence per se case need not decide whether the defendant acted as an ordinarily prudent person would have acted under the circumstances. They merely decide whether the relevant statute or regulation has been violated. If it has, the defendant was negligent as a matter of law." Wendland v. Ridgefield Construction Services, Inc., 184 Conn. 173, 178, 439 A.2d 954 (1981).

In cases involving the doctrine of negligence per se, however, the defendant ordinarily may avoid liability upon proof of a valid excuse or justification. 2 Restatement (Second), Torts § 288A (1965); see also Sanderson v. Steve Snyder Enterprises, Inc., 196 Conn. 134, 150, 491 A.2d 389 (1985). In particular, even if a defendant has contravened a statute the violation of which constitutes negligence per se, that defendant usually may avoid liability by showing that "he neither knows nor should know of the occasion for compliance." 2 Restatement (Second), Torts § 288A. The commentary to the Restatement explains that "where the actor neither knows nor should know of any occasion or necessity for action in compliance with the legislation or regulation, his violation of it will ordinarily be excused." Id., comment (f). The Restatement provides the following example: "A statute provides that no vehicle shall be driven on the public highway at night without front and rear lights. While A is driving on the highway at night his rear light goes out because of the failure of an electric bulb. A has used all reasonable diligence and care in the inspection of his car, and is unaware that the light has gone out. Before he has had any reasonable opportunity to discover it, the absence of the light causes a collision with B's car, approaching from the rear, in which B is injured. A is not liable to B on the basis of the violation of the statute." Id., illustration (3).

On the other hand, some statutes that create a standard of care the violation of which constitutes negligence per se do not permit a defendant to avoid liability on the basis of an excuse. "Such statutes in reality result in strict liability, although the courts have continued to speak of liability for negligence. When they are adopted by the court as defining a standard of conduct for a tort action, the standard adopted is one of strict liability, and the statute is still construed to permit no excuse." Id., comment (c). Nonetheless, "most legislative enactments ... receive no such strict construction." Id., comment (d).

* * *

In the specific circumstances of a case such as this, in which the plaintiffs claim that the landlord's violation of § 47a–8 caused damages resulting from their minor son's ingestion of lead-based paint in the apartment, we believe that the policies underlying the negligence per se doctrine apply and, therefore, we agree with the Appellate Court's conclusion that

§ 47a–8 imposes on landlords a standard of care the violation of which constitutes negligence per se. * * *

* * *

We disagree, however, with the Appellate Court's further conclusion that the legislature intended not to permit excuses or justifications for such a per se violation. * * * The Appellate Court, after first concluding that the defendants' violation of § 47a–8 constituted negligence per se for the purposes of the plaintiffs' action, determined that it provided for strict liability because the statutory provision was "lacking any provision for an excuse for the violation. . . ." This analysis presumes that, if a statute is construed as providing for negligence per se, then that statute should be further construed as providing for no excuses unless the statute itself expressly provides for such excuses. The Appellate Court cited no authority for such a presumption in this context. A court's interpretation that a statute provides for negligence per se ordinarily does not lead to the further conclusion that the statute prohibits excuses. See 2 Restatement (Second), Torts § 288A, comment (d). * * *

Examining § 47a–8 under this framework, we are unpersuaded that the legislature intended to create a standard the violation of which establishes a landlord's strict liability for injuries sustained by a minor plaintiff due to exposure to lead-based paint. * * * We agree that the language and histories of these sections indicate the legislature's intent to prohibit the use of lead-based paints and to prevent the existence of chipped or otherwise dilapidated paint for the protection of children, but the plaintiffs have shown us nothing to indicate that the legislature intended the extraordinary result of holding a landlord liable for injuries sustained by a minor due to exposure to lead-based paint regardless of a valid excuse or justification, such as lack of notice, for the violation. * * *

* * *

The judgment of the Appellate Court is reversed and the case is remanded to that court for consideration of the plaintiffs' other claims.

In this opinion the other justices concurred.

————

ANTWAUN A. v. HERITAGE MUTUAL INS. CO., 228 Wis.2d 44, 596 N.W.2d 456 (1999). Suit was brought on behalf of a 3-year-old child who ingested flakes of lead paint present in apartments occupied by his family. It is conceded that, during the time of the child's exposure to lead paint, the landlords "had notice of deteriorating paint in the apartments," but they "did not have any actual knowledge of lead paint on their properties." *Held*, that facts alleged by plaintiff are sufficient to establish breach of the landlords' common law duty "to avoid exposing persons lawfully on the property [to] an unreasonable risk of harm."

The court noted that lead paint was banned for residential use by the federal Consumer Product Safety Commission in 1978. The buildings in the present case were constructed prior to 1978. The court emphasized that by the 1990's, when the child in this case suffered lead poisoning, the dangers of lead paint in older residential housing had been widely publicized and were "extensively known."

" * * * [W]e conclude that a duty to test for lead paint arises whenever the landlord of a residential property constructed before 1978 either knows or in the use of ordinary care should know that there is peeling or chipping paint on the rental property. Where peeling or chipping paint is present in a pre–1978 residential structure, it is foreseeable that lead paint may be present which, if accurate, would expose the inhabitants to an unreasonable risk of harm."

KREBS v. RUBSAM, 91 N.J.L. 426, 104 A. 83 (1918). The defendants, owners of a tenement house, were under a statutory duty "to keep a proper light burning in the public hallways near the stairs, upon every floor, between sunset and ten o'clock each evening." Plaintiff alleges that because of a negligent failure to perform this duty deceased fell while descending the stairs before ten o'clock in the evening, and sustained fatal injuries. The light had just been extinguished by an unauthorized person without the knowledge of the defendant's janitor. *Held,* affirming judgment entered on a verdict directed for defendant, that a civil action does not lie in the absence of negligence.

HETHERTON v. SEARS, ROEBUCK & CO., 445 F.Supp. 294 (D.Del. 1978). The federal Gun Control Act of 1968 prohibits sale of firearms in violation of state law. A state statute prohibits convicted felons from purchasing firearms. Defendant Sears sold a .22 caliber rifle to one Fullman, unaware that he had two felony convictions. Fullman used the rifle to shoot and wound plaintiff. According to plaintiff Sears might have discovered the felony convictions "merely by making one phone call" to the local police station, and was negligent "because it failed to use reasonable caution in attempting to ascertain whether Fullman was prohibited from possessing a deadly weapon." *Held,* for defendant. Sears had no "actual knowledge" of the buyer's criminal record, and the court declined to recognize "a duty of investigation," saying "it is difficult to define the limits of a possible duty to investigate on the part of firearms sellers."

SPALDING v. WAXLER, 2 Ohio St.2d 1, 205 N.E.2d 890 (1965). An Ohio statute requires motor vehicle operators to maintain effective brakes. The foot brake on a truck driven by defendant suddenly failed, causing a collision. Defendant showed "that the truck was regularly serviced, that the brakes had been inspected and adjusted less than six months prior to the collision, and that he had no warning that his foot brake would fail." *Held,* for plaintiff. Defendant's evidence "falls short of what is required to constitute a legal excuse" sufficient to negate negligence per se. The brake failure was not "a circumstance over which he had no control."

> One who operates a motor vehicle has a mandatory duty to maintain * * * brakes in good working order at all times. Proof that he exercised ordinary care in maintaining the brakes is not sufficient to constitute compliance. If the operator has not maintained the brakes in

such a condition that they are adequate to control the movement of and to stop and hold his vehicle, he has failed to comply with the brake-equipment statute.

CHICAGO, INDIANAPOLIS & LOUISVILLE RAILWAY v. STIERWALT, 87 Ind.App. 478, 153 N.E. 807 (1926). Action for damages under the Federal Employers' Liability Act. The plaintiff, a brakeman, was hurt because of a freight car coupler which was defective, in violation of the Federal Safety Appliance Act. Trying to release the coupler, he went between the cars, which started while he was there. *Held,* for plaintiff. The Federal Safety Appliance Act "imposes an absolute duty on public carriers of interstate commerce. No cars loaded or unloaded can be used in interstate traffic that do not comply with the standard prescribed by the statute. This duty is not discharged by showing the use of reasonable care in equipping cars with the required safety appliances."

SECTION C.   PROOF: RES IPSA LOQUITUR

The Latin phrase *res ipsa loquitur* means "the thing speaks for itself." The tort doctrine of res ipsa loquitur allows a plaintiff to establish defendant's negligence by pointing to the general type of situation out of which harm arose. Plaintiff may prevail without proving specific facts from which a detailed narrative of culpability may be inferred. An accident situation "speaks for itself" when, according to common experience, accidents of that type ordinarily occur only if there is negligence by someone in the position of the defendant.

The traditional statement of the doctrine formulates three conditions for its application: (1) the accident is of a type that ordinarily doesn't happen in the absence of negligence; (2) the defendant was in exclusive control of the instrumentality that caused the accident; (3) the plaintiff was not responsible for causing the accident. Modern cases tend to downplay the traditional element of "exclusive control," holding that res ipsa loquitur may apply in situations where "control" is shared by multiple defendants or where the precise "instrumentality" of injury is unknown. One recent formulation of res ipsa loquitur would boil down the three traditional conditions into a single requirement: "the accident * * * is a type of accident that ordinarily happens because of the negligence of the class of actors of which the defendant is the relevant member." See Section 17 of Restatement of Torts, Third: Liability for Physical Harm (Basic Principles), Tent. Draft No. 1 (2001).

Res ipsa loquitur is a doctrine of evidence. It allows the plaintiff to make out a prima facie case of defendant's negligence based on evidence which is in nature "circumstantial" rather than direct. Still, the proof involved in a res ipsa loquitur case is different from garden-variety circumstantial proof. When res ipsa loquitur prevails, defendant's liability rests on the overall probability of negligence for a general type of situation. Defendant is deemed negligent though no conclusion is ever reached about what actually happened in the individual situation. By contrast, run-of-the-mill circumstantial proof focusses on a specific situation in order to establish in detail what happened there.

In the first main case of this section, the plaintiff does not rely on the special doctrine of res ipsa loquitur, but rather on the generally applicable methodology of circumstantial proof and rational inference. The rest of the section considers what the special doctrine adds.

THOMPSON v. FRANKUS
Supreme Judicial Court of Maine, 1955.
151 Me. 54, 115 A.2d 718.

[Action by plaintiffs, husband and wife, against a landlord whose tenant the wife was visiting, for injuries suffered by the wife when she tripped and fell on a stairway maintained for the common use of the tenants of the building. At the close of evidence the trial judge directed verdicts for the defendant, and plaintiffs appealed.]

WEBBER, Justice.

* * * Briefly stated, the evidence now before us, viewed in the light most favorable to plaintiffs, would have justified jury findings that the plaintiff wife was injured while attempting to descend an unlighted stairway controlled by the defendant landlord and maintained for the common use of her tenants; that this plaintiff was an invitee of a tenant; that the linoleum stair covering was badly torn, loose and full of holes, which condition was known to the defendant; that the plaintiff lighted a match before stepping from a stair covered with the defective linoleum and stumbled or tripped and fell to the foot of the stairway; and that there was no other means of egress available to the plaintiff who sought to leave the premises to return to her home. Both plaintiffs showed resulting damages.

It is almost universally held that a landlord who has retained control of common stairways owes to his tenants and their invitees the duty of exercising ordinary care to keep such stairways reasonably safe for their intended use. * * *

There is evidence in the record before us upon which the jury could have found that the defendant had negligently failed to repair the worn and torn linoleum stair covering which had become dangerously defective by reason of "wear, breaking or decay." The evidence would have further supported a jury finding that the dangerous condition thus created by the negligence of the landlord was so enhanced and aggravated by a complete absence of lighting as to give rise to a further duty owed by the defendant to the tenant's invitees to light the stairway. The defendant's negligence, or lack of it, was therefore a jury question upon this evidence.

Likewise the issue of the contributory negligence of plaintiff wife was a jury question. She was under some urgency to return home. No other means of egress was available. She lighted a match which enabled her to look where she was going before taking the step which resulted in her fall. She did not wait for the tenant to bring a light. She proceeded over an unlighted stairway. It is for the jury to say whether she used that care and caution which an ordinarily prudent person would have exercised under the same circumstances and having the same urgency to leave the premises. We cannot say that she was guilty of contributory negligence as a matter of law. * * *

The defendant contends that there is no evidence upon which the jury could have found that any negligence of hers was the proximate cause of the plaintiff's fall. Plaintiffs' counsel suggests that in directing a verdict for defendant the presiding Justice below was persuaded to that action by the failure of the plaintiff wife to state specifically what caused her to stumble as, for example, that she slipped on loose linoleum or caught her foot on torn linoleum or in a hole in the stair covering. The record is silent as to the reasons which weighed in the mind of the Justice below. However, defendant's counsel contend that "if the plaintiff, who knew and could see what she was doing, cannot tell the jury what caused her to fall, how can a jury answer this question without speculation, conjecture or guessing?" The fallacy of this argument is readily apparent. A plaintiff may under many circumstances be completely unable to remember or recount or explain an accident, but may nevertheless recover if the deficiency is met by other reliable evidence. Such evidence may be direct or circumstantial. It may come from eye witnesses or known physical facts. It may raise reasonable inferences which satisfy the burden of proof. "There was no direct evidence as to the cause of decedent's fall. The sole claim of the defendant is that in the absence of other evidence than that stated, the jury could not find that the fall of the deceased was caused by the defective condition of the stairway. A jury cannot base their conclusions upon guess or speculation, but they are entitled to draw reasonable inferences and their verdict must stand if the evidence is such as to justify in their minds 'a reasonable belief of the probability of the existence of the material facts.'" White v. Herbst, 128 Conn. 659, 25 A.2d 68. To hold otherwise would be but to invite perjury on the part of plaintiffs who in all honesty do not know or cannot recall exactly what did happen. An examination of cases where the plaintiff's inability by his own testimony to make out a case has defeated recovery will disclose that the deficiencies in proof were not supplied by other independent evidence. So here there was evidence of stair covering upon the stair where plaintiff tripped (as well as other stairs) which by reason of tears and holes might, especially in darkness, cause one to trip. There is evidence that the plaintiff, proceeding slowly and cautiously by the light of a match, did stumble and trip and fall. The jury might reasonably infer that she stumbled or tripped *over* the defective covering and *because* of the defects. In a legal sense, the consequences of such a hazardous condition were readily foreseeable. * * *

It remains only to examine some of the cases on which the defendant relies.

* * *

Deojay v. Lyford, 139 Me. 234, 29 A.2d 111, was a case in which no affirmative acts of negligence of the defendant were shown and it was held that res ipsa loquitur could not be applied to airplanes while landing merely because they deviated somewhat in course.

* * *

In Alling v. Northwestern Bell Tel. Co., 156 Minn. 60, 194 N.W. 313, plaintiff advanced the theory that lightning had hit a tree, jumped to a car and thence to a wire and thence to the decedent. The wire remained intact. Several experts testified that it was impossible for the wire to have carried the charge. The plaintiff's expert admitted that no one could say what lightning would do or where it would go. The court properly held that plaintiff's claim advanced no further than speculation or conjecture. The court well stated the rule at page 314 of 194 N.W., which we believe is applicable: "The burden is on plaintiff to show that it is more probable that the harm resulted in consequence of something for which the defendant was responsible than in consequence of something for which he was not responsible. If the facts furnish no sufficient basis for *inferring* which of several possible causes produced the injury, a defendant who is responsible for only one of such possible causes cannot be held liable." (Emphasis supplied.) In the case now before us, an inference drawn by a jury that plaintiff's fall resulted directly from a defective stair covering coupled with the absence of lighting would rest upon credible evidence rather than upon mere conjecture, surmise and speculation.

We therefore conclude that there was evidence which, if believed by the jury, would have sustained plaintiffs' burden of proof on each essential issue. The cases should have been submitted to jury determination under proper instructions.

Exceptions sustained.

NEWING v. CHEATHAM

Supreme Court of California, in Bank, 1975.
15 Cal.3d 351, 124 Cal.Rptr. 193, 540 P.2d 33.

[Action for wrongful death of Newing against the administration of the estate of Cheatham, pilot-owner of private aircraft that crashed, killing Newing, Cheatham and Bird, the only other occupant. The trial court directed a verdict for plaintiffs on the issue of liability, the jury found damages in the amount of $125,000, and judgment in that amount was entered for the plaintiff. Defendant appealed.]

SULLIVAN, Justice.

* * *

About 1 p.m. on Sunday, October 25, 1970, Richard Newing, Harold Cheatham, and Ronald Bird departed from Brown Field at Chula Vista, California, aboard a single-engine Cessna 172 aircraft owned and piloted by Cheatham. Neither Newing nor Bird was a licensed pilot. At the time of take-off the weather was clear and the visibility unrestricted. There was no evidence that the plane landed at any other field that afternoon, or that it sent any radio messages. When it failed to return, a search was commenced.

On the following day the plane's wreckage was located by a search aircraft in mountainous terrain about 13 miles east of Tijuana, Mexico, and an equal distance southeast of Brown Field. A rescue party found all occupants of the airplane dead. The clock on the instrument panel was stopped at 5:18.

Plaintiffs brought this action for wrongful death alleging that the crash had been caused by Cheatham's negligence. At trial, [two] theories were advanced in support of plaintiffs' case. [The first, based on circumstantial evidence,] was that Cheatham had negligently permitted the airplane to run out of fuel while in flight. * * * [Also,] Cheatham's negligence was said to be established by the doctrine of res ipsa loquitur.

[THE CIRCUMSTANTIAL CASE]

In support of the first of these theories, plaintiffs offered the testimony of Jorge Areizaga Rojo, then Commandante of the Tijuana Airport, and of Jesus Leon an airport mechanic. Rojo, who testified as an expert witness, had been a member of the rescue party that first reached the wreckage of the aircraft. Accompanied by Leon, he returned to the site on the second day after the crash in order to gather information for a report to the Mexican authorities. Rojo testified that he visually inspected the fuel tanks of the aircraft, which were carried on its wings, but saw no fuel. He also attempted, but without success, to drain fuel from the bottom of each tank by removing drain plugs.

Leon testified that he had inspected the aircraft's fuel system, although he had not dismantled it, but had found no trace of fuel. Both men visually inspected the ground beneath the aircraft, but saw no indication of fuel spillage. They also attempted to measure the fuel in one of the wing tanks; Leon estimated the level of the fuel to be $\frac{3}{16}$ of an inch. Rojo indicated that whatever fuel remained in the tanks was probably "unusable," in the sense that it was not a sufficient quantity to reach the engine. Rojo also testified concerning the general structural condition of the aircraft, the appearance of the propeller and control surfaces, the upright position in which the plane had come to rest, and the general description of the accident site. All of these factors, he said, indicated that the crash had been caused by fuel exhaustion.

On cross-examination, however, Rojo conceded that the appearance and condition of the plane would have been the same if the crash had been caused by engine failure or some similar mechanical malfunction resulting in loss of power. He also indicated that since the aircraft had not been brought to a level position before he had attempted to drain fuel from the tanks, a useable amount of fuel might have remained within. He admitted that there had been no very thorough investigation of other potential causes of the crash. Despite the foregoing, however, he remained of the opinion that the plane had crashed because it had run out of fuel.

Plaintiffs also called as an expert witness Michael Potter, an airline pilot who had logged some 1,200 hours of flight time in small aircraft, including 200 hours in a Cessna 172. Potter testified at length concerning the training received by student pilots with respect to fuel management and emergencies in flight. He stated that a prudent pilot maintains at the minimum a 45–minute reserve of fuel, and ordinarily flies high enough above surrounding terrain to permit his aircraft to glide to a safe landing in the event of a power failure. Potter also testified that, according to the operator's manual, a Cessna 172 has sufficient fuel capacity to fly for 4.3 hours when operated at the usual power settings and with a "lean" fuel mixture. Thus, he said, the Cheatham plane, if operated in the usual manner with respect to power settings, fuel mixture, and altitude, should have run out of fuel at just the time indicated on its damaged clock.[2] However, he indicated on cross-examination that the endurance of a Cessna 172 can be greater or less than 4.3 hours depending upon the manner in which it is operated. Despite this, Potter said that the crash had probably been caused by fuel exhaustion and the pilot's failure to maintain proper terrain clearance. This opinion was based upon his examination of photographs of the wreckage, his observations made during overflights of the crash site, the testimony of Rojo and Leon, and an experiment in which he ran the engine of a stationary Cessna 172 until its fuel supply was exhausted. From such experiment Potter found that $\frac{5}{16}$ of an inch of fuel remained in the tanks after the engine had stopped.

Defendant called as an expert witness Robert Rudich, an experienced air traffic controller who had written widely on the subject of air crash investigations and had participated in many such investigations, though chiefly as an analyst of cockpit recording devices and as an editor of final reports. Rudich expressed no opinion as to the cause of the crash, but testified instead about the procedures that must be employed in a sound air crash investigation. According to Rudich, such an inquiry must consist of a progressive "ruling out" of the whole gamut of potential causes ranging from human error to mechanical or structural failure. Where fuel exhaustion is suspected, the entire fuel system must be dismantled and painstakingly inspected from end to end in order to eliminate the possibility that one of its components has malfunctioned. In addition, the plane's other systems must be checked for signs of similar mechanical failure. The court did not permit Rudich to express an opinion as to the quality of the investigation conducted by Rojo and Leon, although the implication of his testimony was that their investigation had been rudimentary at best. However, Rudich was allowed to testify about an experiment he performed on a detached Cessna 172 wing arranged at an angle approximating that of the wing of the downed plane as shown in photographs of the wreckage. Rudich found that it required 7.5 gallons of gasoline to raise the fuel level in the wing tank to $\frac{3}{16}$ of an inch. This was said to constitute a usable amount of fuel.

In addition to this expert testimony, defendant introduced evidence that the three dead men had been drinking beer together on the day of the crash. The owner of a National City tavern testified that Newing, a man named "Harold," and another man had drunk draft beer in his establish-

---

2. According to Rojo, the clock probably had been stopped by the impact of the crash. Thus, a crash at 5:18, the time at which the clock stopped, would have occurred just 4.3 hours after the take-off at 1 p.m. However, there was no evidence that the clock had been properly set. Nor was there any evidence as to the altitude, power settings, or fuel mixture at which the plane had been operated.

ment for about an hour that morning, although he was unable to say how much beer they had consumed. A member of the rescue party testified that eight or nine empty beer cans had been found in the wreckage of the Cheatham plane. Evidence was also produced that the Mexican physicians who had performed autopsies on the bodies of the three men, had noted a strong odor of alcohol emanating from the remains of Cheatham and Bird, but not from Newing's.

* * *

[THE RES IPSA CASE]

It is settled law in this state that the "doctrine of res ipsa loquitur is applicable where the accident is of such a nature that it can be said, in the light of past experience, that it probably was the result of negligence by someone and that the defendant is probably the one responsible." (Di Mare v. Cresci (1962) 58 Cal.2d 292, 298–299, 23 Cal.Rptr. 772, 776, 373 P.2d 860, 864.) According to the classic and oft-repeated statement, there are three conditions for the application of the doctrine: "(1) the accident must be of a kind which ordinarily does not occur in the absence of someone's negligence; (2) it must be caused by an agency or instrumentality within the exclusive control of the defendant; (3) it must not have been due to any voluntary action or contribution on the part of the plaintiff." (Ybarra v. Spangard (1944) 25 Cal.2d 486, 489, 154 P.2d 687, 689; see Wolfsmith v. Marsh (1959) 51 Cal.2d 832, 835, 337 P.2d 70.) The existence of one or more of these conditions is usually a question of fact for the jury. In a proper case, however, they all may exist as a matter of law. The question to be answered here is whether, as the trial judge determined, this is such a case.

Turning to consider the foregoing three conditions for the application of the doctrine, we direct our attention to the first condition, namely that the accident must be of a kind which ordinarily does not occur in the absence of negligence. In determining whether this condition is satisfied, a court may consider common knowledge, the testimony of expert witnesses, and the circumstances relating to the particular accident at issue. (Zentz v. Coca Cola Bottling Co. (1952) 39 Cal.2d 436, 446, 247 P.2d 344.) It need not be concluded that negligence is the only explanation of the accident, but merely the most probable one. We deal here in probabilities, not certainties.

Whether aircraft accidents are more often than not the result of negligence is a question that has vexed the courts of many jurisdictions for decades. According to Prosser, many early cases took the position that not enough was known about the hazards of flight to permit an inference of negligence to arise from the mere fact of a plane crash. (Prosser, Law of Torts (4th ed. 1971) p. 216.) Advances in the safety and frequency of air travel, however, have led to a trend in the opposite direction. Thus, while judicial opinion on the subject is by no means unanimous, res ipsa loquitur, over the years, has been applied to an increasing variety of aircraft mishaps. [Citations omitted.]

* * *

As we previously noted, the first condition for invocation of the res ipsa doctrine is satisfied if under the facts of the case, common experience indicates that the accident would not have occurred unless there had been negligence on the part of someone. In the instant case, it seems reasonably clear in light of the circumstances surrounding the crash that the accident ordinarily would not have taken place in the absence of negligence. The evidence is uncontradicted that the airplane took off from Chula Vista in clear weather with no restrictions on visibility. There is no evidence that weather conditions contributed in any way to the crash of the plane. Nor was there any evidence that the plane had collided with other aircraft while in flight. Indeed the condition of the plane after the crash was such as to eliminate an air collision. It thus fell to the ground, apparently unaffected by external factors, only a few miles from the airport whence it had departed some hours earlier. Under the circumstances of the present case, "it seems reasonably clear that the accident probably would not have occurred without negligence by someone." (Zentz v. Coca Cola Bottling Co., supra, 39 Cal.2d 436, 447, 247 P.2d 344, 350.) The evidence bearing on these circumstances is not only uncontradicted but of such a nature that no issue of fact is raised as to the existence of the first condition for the application of the doctrine of res ipsa loquitur. (Roddiscraft, Inc. v. Skelton Logging Co., 212 Cal.App.2d 784, 794, 28 Cal.Rptr. 277.) We conclude that the first condition is established as a matter of law.

The doctrine's second condition, as traditionally formulated, is that the agency or instrumentality causing the accident must have been within the exclusive control or management of the defendant. The purpose of this requirement is to link the defendant with the probability, already established, that the accident was negligently caused.

The facts of this case are such as to satisfy this condition, like the first, as a matter of law. Cheatham was the owner of the aircraft, and there is no dispute that he was at the controls when the plane took off on its final flight. Since neither of his passengers seems to have been a licensed pilot, there is no reason to suppose that anyone other than he operated the plane at any time before the crash. Moreover, Cheatham's ultimate responsibility for all decisions concerning the aircraft's operation was established by an applicable federal air regulation.[5] * * *

Defendant argues, however, that plaintiffs have not negated the possibility that the crash was caused by something other than the manner in which the plane was operated. He states that such crashes commonly occur because of mechanical failures of one kind or another, and cites a considerable array of cases in which such failures were said to have occurred. The short answer is that the record is devoid of evidence of such kind of mechanical failure. * * * With respect to the operation and maintenance of the aircraft, the control exercised by Cheatham as owner-pilot was complete. There thus can be no doubt that this element of the doctrine exists as a matter of law.

5. 14 Code of Federal Regulations, section 91.3(a) provides: "The pilot in command of an aircraft is directly responsible for, and is the final authority as to, the operation of that aircraft."

The third of the traditional conditions for the application of res ipsa loquitur is that the accident must not have been caused by any voluntary action or contribution on the part of the plaintiff. The purpose of this requirement, like that of control by the defendant is to establish that the defendant is the one probably responsible for the accident. The plaintiff need not show that he was entirely inactive at the time of the accident in order to satisfy this requirement, so long as the evidence is such as to eliminate his conduct as a factor contributing to the occurrence. (Shahinian v. McCormick (1963) 59 Cal.2d 554, 560, 30 Cal.Rptr. 521, 381 P.2d 377.)

* * * [T]he uncontradicted evidence shows that the body of plaintiffs' decedent was found by the rescue party in one of the rear seats of the four-seater aircraft. From that position, it is difficult to imagine how he could have interfered physically with the operation of the aircraft in any way. (Cf. Guerra v. Handlery Hotels, Inc. (1959) 53 Cal.2d 266, 271, 1 Cal.Rptr. 330, 347 P.2d 674.) Moreover, as noted above, there is no dispute that Cheatham was the pilot in command of the aircraft, and it must be presumed that he made all decisions concerning its operation and preparation for flight. There is no basis for supposing that Newing exerted any influence with respect to the making of these decisions. Thus the evidence concerning the basic operation of the aircraft is such as to conclusively eliminate Newing's conduct as a potential cause of the accident.

A separate question in this respect, however, is said to arise from the evidence that the three men drank beer together on the day of the crash. Defendant argues that Newing's conduct in drinking with Cheatham may have contributed to the happening of the accident, and that plaintiffs have not carried their burden with respect to negating this possibility. * * * [But the] evidence concerning the beer drinking was too vague to support a finding that Newing contributed by means of it to the happening of the crash. Plaintiffs are not obligated to eliminate entirely speculative causal possibilities involving the conduct of their decedent. It is enough if they rebut those inferences of their decedent's responsibility which are reasonably supported by the evidence. Plaintiffs discharged this burden by introducing evidence from which it must be inferred that Newing did not interfere with Cheatham's operation or command of the aircraft.

The evidence presented in the trial court, therefore, was such as to satisfy all three conditions for the applicability of res ipsa loquitur as a matter of law. Since the facts giving rise to the doctrine were undisputed, the inference of negligence arose as a matter of law; to put it another way, the conclusion is compelled that there is a balance of probabilities pointing to the decedent's negligence. (See Zentz v. Coca Cola Bottling Co., supra, 39 Cal.2d 436, 449, 247 P.2d 344; Prosser, Res Ipsa Loquitur in California (1949) 37 Cal.L.Rev. 183, 194–195.) This gave rise to a presumption affecting the burden of producing evidence pursuant to Evidence Code section 646.[6] It then became defendant's obligation to introduce sufficient evidence

6. Evidence Code section 646 provides: "(a) As used in this section, 'defendant' includes any party against whom the res ipsa loquitur presumption operates.

to sustain a finding either that the accident resulted from some cause other than Cheatham's negligence, or, else, that Cheatham exercised due care in all possible respects wherein he might have been negligent. (See Cal.Law Revision Com. comment to Evid. Code, § 646.) Defendant introduced no such evidence. He has at most argued that the crash *could* have resulted from causes other than the negligence of his decedent. Mere speculation of this sort is insufficient to discharge defendant's burden of explanation. (Dierman v. Providence Hospital (1947) 31 Cal.2d 290, 295–296, 188 P.2d 12; Roberts v. Trans World Airlines, 225 Cal.App.2d 344, 354–355, 37 Cal.Rptr. 291.) Consequently, the trial court was correct in concluding that res ipsa loquitur established Cheatham's negligence as a matter of law.

* * *

[In the omitted parts of the opinion, the court approved the trial court's conclusion that as a matter of law Newing was not contributorily negligent and did not assume the risk of "Cheatham's allegedly alcoholic condition."]

The judgment is affirmed.

UNITED STATES v. KESINGER, 190 F.2d 529 (10th Cir.1951). An Army Air Force B–17 crashed on plaintiffs' farm, destroying their barn and milk house. Plaintiffs sued the United States for damages under the Federal Tort Claims Act. The appellate court affirmed a judgment for plaintiffs on the ground of res ipsa loquitur, thus making it unnecessary to rule on plaintiffs' alternative ground of strict liability for trespass "in the pursuit of an extra-hazardous activity." Said the court:

"An airplane of a proven safe type of design taking off for an ordinary routine flight under normal weather conditions does not crash in the ordinary course of things, unless there has been a failure to properly inspect, service and maintain it, or unless it is not operated with due care.

* * *

"The rule of res ipsa loquitur is applicable when the thing which caused the injury was, at the time of the injury, in the custody and under the exclusive control of the defendant, and the occurrence was one which in the ordinary course of things does not happen if the one having such exclusive

"(b) The judicial doctrine of res ipsa loquitur is a presumption affecting the burden of producing evidence.

"(c) If the evidence, or facts otherwise established, would support a res ipsa loquitur presumption and the defendant has introduced evidence which would support a finding that he was not negligent or that any negligence on his part was not a proximate cause of the occurrence, the court may, and upon request shall, instruct the jury to the effect that:

"(1) If the facts which would give rise to res ipsa loquitur presumption are found or otherwise established, the jury may draw the inference from such facts that a proximate cause of the occurrence was some negligent conduct on the part of the defendant; and

"(2) The jury shall not find that a proximate cause of the occurrence was some negligent conduct on the part of the defendant unless the jury believes, after weighing all the evidence in the case and drawing such inferences therefrom as the jury believes are warranted, that it is more probable than not that the occurrence was caused by some negligent conduct on the part of the defendant."

control uses proper care. It will take the case to the jury unless the entire evidence is such that the presumption cannot stand against it. It is not enough that the evidence of the defendant would, if true, be sufficient to rebut the presumption, because it is for the trier of facts to pass upon the credibility of the witnesses and the truth of their testimony.

"The rule is based in part upon the theory that the defendant, having custody and exclusive control of the instrumentality which caused the injury, has the best opportunity of ascertaining the cause of the accident, and that the plaintiff has no such knowledge and is compelled to allege negligence in general terms and to rely upon the proof of the happening of the accident in order to establish negligence.

* * *

"The evidence adduced by the United States established that the airplane had been properly inspected, serviced and maintained; that it was free from mechanical defects and was aerodynamically sound; that it was a particularly safe type of aircraft and was regarded as a perfect flying airplane; that the weather conditions were better than normal, and that the air was free from turbulence, and that 68 per cent of airplane accidents are the result of pilot failure."

McDOUGALD v. PERRY, 716 So.2d 783 (Fla.1998). Plaintiff was injured when his car was struck by a 130–pound spare tire that came loose from a tractor-trailer ahead of him on the highway. He sued the truck's driver and the driver's employer. *Held*, res ipsa loquitur applies, since "common sense dictates" that a spare tire will stay with the truck carrying it "unless there is a failure of reasonable care by the person or entity in control of the truck." "[T]he doctrine of *res ipsa loquitur* is particularly applicable in wayward wheel cases." Justice Anstead, concurring "fully," had this to say:

" * * * The thread of common sense in human experience ties today's decision to an opinion voiced by Baron Pollock in the 1863 decision in *Byrne v. Boadle*, 2 Hurlet & C. 722, 159 Eng.Rep. 299 (Ex. 1863). In *Byrne* * * * Pollock declared for the Court:

* * * [I]f an article calculated to cause damage is put in a wrong place and does mischief, I think that those whose duty it was to put it in the right place are prima facie responsible * * *. The present case upon the evidence comes to this, a man is passing in front of the premises of a dealer in flour, and there falls down upon him a barrel of flour. I think it apparent that the barrel was in the custody of the defendant who occupied the premises, and who is responsible for the acts of his servants who had the control of it; and in my opinion the fact of its falling is prima facie evidence of negligence, and the plaintiff who was injured by it is not bound to shew that it could not fall without negligence, but if there are any facts inconsistent with negligence it is for the defendant to prove them.

"We can hardly improve upon this explanation for our decision today. The common law tradition is alive and well."

INFERENCE OR PRESUMPTION?

Proof of the elements of res ipsa loquitur may be thought to give rise to an "inference" of defendant's negligence, which a jury may or may not embrace, or to a full "presumption." The California court in Newing v. Cheatham, supra, said that plaintiff's proof of res ipsa elements creates "a presumption affecting the burden of producing evidence," and so, when defendant fails to produce specific evidence tending to overcome the presumption, a verdict should be directed in plaintiff's favor. Other courts are not so hard on a defendant.

SULLIVAN v. CRABTREE, 36 Tenn.App. 469, 258 S.W.2d 782 (1953). Plaintiffs' son was killed when a truck in which he was a passenger suddenly swerved off the highway and overturned. In affirming a judgment in favor of the surviving driver, the court said:

"[W]here a motor vehicle, without apparent cause, runs off the road and causes harm, the normal inference is that the driver was negligent, and *res ipsa loquitur* is usually held to apply.

* * *

"It is true there has been confusion in the cases as to the procedural effect of *res ipsa loquitur,* some cases giving it one and some another of these * * * different effects:

"(1) It warrants an *inference* of negligence which the jury may draw or not, as their judgment dictates.

"(2) It raises a *presumption* of negligence which requires the jury to find negligence if defendant does not produce evidence sufficient to rebut the presumption.

* * *

"In exceptional cases the inference may be so strong as to require a directed verdict for plaintiff, as in cases of objects falling from defendant's premises on persons in the highway * * *.

"In the ordinary case, however, *res ipsa loquitur* merely makes a case for the jury—merely permits the jury to choose the inference of defendant's negligence in preference to other permissible or reasonable inferences.

"We think this is true in the case before us. * * * Since * * * conflicting inferences might be reasonably drawn from the evidence, it was for the jury to choose the inference they thought most probable * * *."

GEORGE FOLTIS, INC. v. CITY OF NEW YORK, 287 N.Y. 108, 38 N.E.2d 455, 153 A.L.R. 1122 (1941). The plaintiff's premises were damaged by water from a water main in which a longitudinal split in the "flange part" had developed. The plaintiff introduced no other evidence. The defendant introduced evidence to the effect that the pipe was of cast iron, new when laid nine years before at the approved depth of four feet, that field inspectors had tested it carefully before it was laid and that it was their duty to see it was properly laid. It was undisputed that cast iron pipes do not become defective for decades, but that their length of life may be affected by chemicals in the ground or in the water. The defendant offered no opinion as to the cause of the break. The trial judge reserved decision on plaintiff's motion for directed verdict at the close of the evidence and submitted five questions to the jury, in response to which they found that the defendant was not negligent in the construction of the main, in its supervision, or in shutting off the water after notice. The trial judge then granted plaintiff's motion for directed verdict. The Appellate Division by a divided court sustained the judgment. The defendant appealed. *Held* (by divided court), reversed for new trial.

"The direction of a verdict in favor of the plaintiff might be justified if the rule of res ipsa loquitur created a full presumption in favor of the plaintiff. It is without logical foundation if res ipsa loquitur is only a common-sense rule for the appraisal of the probative force of evidence which enables an injured person, in proper case, to establish prima facie that the injury was caused by the defendant's negligence, though the injured person may be unable to produce direct evidence of want of care in any particular. See Wigmore on Evidence, 3d Ed., § 2509. It has been said by the Supreme Court of the United States that: 'Res ipsa loquitur means that the facts of the occurrence warrant the inference of negligence, not that they compel such an inference; that they furnish circumstantial evidence of negligence where direct evidence of it may be lacking, but it is evidence to be weighed, not necessarily to be accepted as sufficient; that they call for explanation or rebuttal, not necessarily that they require it; that they make a case to be decided by the jury, not that they forestall the verdict. * * *' Sweeney v. Erving, 228 U.S. 233, 240, 33 S.Ct. 416, 418, 57 L.Ed. 815, Ann.Cas.1914D, 905. * * *

"Where a plaintiff establishes prima facie by direct evidence that injury was caused by negligence of the defendant the court may seldom direct a verdict, though the plaintiff's evidence is not contradicted or rebutted by the defendant. In such cases the question of whether the defendant was in fault in what he did or failed to do is ordinarily one of fact to be determined by the jury unless the jury is waived. The practice should be the same where under the rule of res ipsa loquitur the plaintiff establishes prima facie by circumstantial evidence a right to recover. * * * "

GROVES v. FLORIDA COCA–COLA BOTTLING CO., 40 So.2d 128 (Fla. 1949). Plaintiff, a waitress, was hurt by the explosion of a carbonated beverage bottled by defendant. The evidence was that the bottle had been delivered by defendant's employees, that no one had thereafter touched it except the waitress, who had handled it carefully, and that it had been subjected to no unusual changes in temperature. *Held,* judgment for defendant on nonsuit, reversed. A prima facie case of negligence is shown, under the doctrine of res ipsa loquitur.

BOYD v. MARION COCA–COLA BOTTLING CO., 240 S.C. 383, 126 S.E.2d 178 (1962). Action against bottler for injuries sustained when a bottle exploded in a storekeeper's face as he was in the act of filling his cold drink box. Evidence was offered that two bottles from the same crate exploded and that two weeks later another bottle exploded while undisturbed in a crate. Defendant "introduced considerable testimony tending to show the improbability of bottles exploding or breaking in such fashion * * *."

Verdict and judgment for the plaintiff. *Held,* affirmed. "The doctrine of res ipsa loquitur does not prevail in South Carolina * * *. In order for Respondent to prevail, therefore, there must be some showing of negligence on the part of Appellant, and such negligence may be established by circumstantial as well as direct evidence."

FOSTER v. CITY OF KEYSER

Supreme Court of Appeals of West Virginia, 1997.
202 W.Va. 1, 501 S.E.2d 165.

STARCHER, Justice:

This case arose out of a natural gas explosion in Keyser, West Virginia. Gas apparently leaked from an underground gas transmission line that runs along Beacon Street, and flowed through a sewer line into a house, where the gas ignited and exploded. * * *

* * *

In the consolidated cases, the plaintiffs, alleging personal and/or property damages as a result of the explosion, sued: (1) Mountaineer Gas Company ("Mountaineer"), which provided natural gas service to the residence from a buried natural gas transmission line running along the public street on which the residence is located; (2) the City of Keyser ("Keyser"), which provides sewage service to the residence through a buried sewer pipe that runs along the same street and near the gas transmission line; and (3) Parks Excavating Company ("Parks"), which was employed by Keyser to do excavation and repair of Keyser's sewer line in the area of the residence.

* * *

How did the explosion occur? From the limited record before us, it appears (we note that our factual discussion is not determinative in subsequent proceedings in this case) that about six weeks before the explosion, Parks, while working on the sewer line, uncovered and then backfilled around Mountaineer's gas transmission line. Parks contends that he requested from Mountaineer constant surveillance of his work during the portion of the excavation when the gas transmission line would be uncovered or exposed. Parks also claims that Mountaineer refused the request for help and explained that Mountaineer was short-staffed and could not spare the manpower to survey the project. Mountaineer apparently did perform some inspection of the excavation.

A West Virginia Public Service Commission ("PSC") investigation of the explosion concluded that movement and strain on the gas transmission line from Parks' excavation activities contributed to the failure of a compression coupling joining two sections of the gas line, which in turn led to the line's separation. Gas under pressure then apparently flowed through a nearby sewer line into the residence, after which the gas was ignited in an unknown fashion.

[The trial judge granted partial summary judgment in favor of plaintiffs, holding the gas company strictly liable. The gas company appealed. The Supreme Court of Appeals decided against strict liability. "[O]ur decision not to uphold the circuit court's application of strict liability is largely predicated upon our conclusion that other principles of law—a high standard of care and *res ipsa loquitur*—can sufficiently address the concerns that argue for strict liability in gas transmission line leak/explosion cases." The supreme court went on to discuss the approach to *res ipsa loquitur* which should be taken upon remand of the case.]

The availability of the evidentiary rule of *res ipsa loquitur* is an important method of proof, where appropriate, in permitting the fair adjudication of responsibility for injuries caused by dangerous activities and instrumentalities, short of imposing strict liability on parties engaged in such activities or employing such instrumentalities. * * *

* * *

In many of our cases involving *res ipsa loquitur*, including cases arising out of gas leak explosions, we have stated that showing "control" or "exclusive control" by the party charged with negligence—over the activity or instrumentality which led to damages—is a prerequisite of invoking the rule of *res ipsa loquitur*.

* * *

We stated a three-part test for the invoking of *res ipsa loquitur*, containing the element of "exclusive control," in Syllabus Point 2 of *Royal Furniture Co. v. City of Morgantown*, 164 W.Va. 400, 263 S.E.2d 878 (1980) * * *:

> Before the doctrine of *res ipsa loquitur* is applicable, three essentials must exist: (1) the instrumentality which causes the injury must be under the exclusive control and management of the defendant; (2) the plaintiff must be without fault; and, (3) the injury must be such that in the ordinary course of events it would not have happened had the one in control of the instrumentality used due care.

* * *

[Subsequently,] in *Bronz v. St. Jude's Hosp. Clinic*, 184 W.Va. 594, 402 S.E.2d 263 (1991), we recognized that an "exclusive control" requirement of *res ipsa loquitur* does not connote that such control must be individual * * *, and we stated that *res ipsa loquitur* can be applicable to multiple defendants. * * *

In *Bronz*, we also quoted with approval *Gilbert v. Korvette's, Inc.*, 457 Pa. 602, 327 A.2d 94 (1974), one of several decisions which have explicitly adopted the American Law Institute's formulation of *res ipsa loquitur,* set forth in the *Restatement of Torts 2d* [1965] § 328D.

> The Restatement rule, however, disavows the requirement of exclusive control. A party's negligence may be inferred when "other responsible causes ... are sufficiently eliminated by the evidence...." Exclusive control may eliminate other causes, but the critical inquiry is not control but whether a particular defendant is the *responsible cause* of the injury. Responsibility, of course, may be shared by two or more defendants. Consequently, if *responsibility* is vested in and shared by two or more parties, each may be subjected to liability [under *res ipsa loquitur*].

The *Restatement of Torts 2d* [1965] § 328D, entitled "Res Ipsa Loquitur," provides:

> (1) It may be inferred that harm suffered by the plaintiff is caused by negligence of the defendant when
>
> (a) the event is of a kind which ordinarily does not occur in the absence of negligence;
>
> (b) other responsible causes, including the conduct of the plaintiff and third persons, are sufficiently eliminated by the evidence; and
>
> (c) the indicated negligence is within the scope of the defendant's duty to the plaintiff.
>
> (2) It is the function of the court to determine whether the inference may reasonably be drawn by the jury, or whether it must necessarily be drawn.
>
> (3) It is the function of the jury to determine whether the inference is to be drawn in any case where different conclusions may reasonably be reached.

The comments to Section 328D state in pertinent part:

> g. *Defendant's exclusive control....* It is not, however, necessary to the inference that the defendant have such exclusive control; and exclusive control is merely one way of proving his responsibility. He may be responsible, and the inference may be drawn against him, where he shares the control with another, as in the case of the fall of a party wall which each of two landowners is under a duty to inspect and maintain. * * * He may be responsible where he is under a duty to control the conduct of a third person, as in the case of a host whose guests throw objects from his windows. * * * Exclusive control is merely one fact which establishes the responsibility of the defendant; and if it can be established otherwise, exclusive control is not essential to a res ipsa loquitur case. The essential question becomes one of whether the probable cause is one which the defendant was under a duty to the plaintiff to anticipate or guard against.

Many courts have ignored or rejected a strict or literal application of a "control" or "exclusive control" test for *res ipsa loquitur,* finding * * * that a focus on a party's actual "control" of a dangerous instrumentality can be a misleading and unhelpful approach to ascertaining whether the rule of *res ipsa loquitur* may be applied to the party to create a permissible inference of the party's negligence.

* * *

In *Worden v. Union Gas System, Inc.,* 182 Kan. 686, 324 P.2d 501 (1958), the court held that a plaintiff was entitled to use *res ipsa loquitur* against a contractor defendant who engaged in excavation near a gas transmission line, and against the defendant company that owned and operated the gas transmission line.

In another gas explosion case, *Phillips v. Delaware Power & Light Co.,* 57 Del. 466, 202 A.2d 131 (1964), the court stated that there was no longer a requirement of actual exclusive control for *res ipsa loquitur* to apply. Furthermore, while a paving company might have caused the break, the gas company knew of the paving and had the responsibility to make sure that the paving was not affecting the gas transmission line. As to other causes, such as traffic or weathering, the gas company was required to have knowledge of those possibilities and act accordingly. * * *

* * * *See also Koppinger v. Cullen–Schiltz & Associates,* 513 F.2d 901, 907 (8th Cir.1975) (*res ipsa loquitur* was properly submitted as to multiple defendants, including city engineer, excavation company, and gas transmission company.)

Compared with cases like the foregoing, and with our more recent cases * * *, the holdings and language in many of our older cases dealing with explosions from gas transmission line leaks—and the availability of *res ipsa loquitur* in such cases—manifest a notably more tolerant, "these things happen" approach, and impose stricter burdens upon parties seeking to use *res ipsa.* This difference can probably be explained by improvements in society's ability to use dangerous technology safely and resulting changes in the expectations which society has of people and entities that manage and profit from such technology. *Cf. Morningstar v. Black and Decker Mfg. Co.,* 162 W.Va. 857, 253 S.E.2d 666 (1979) (adopting strict liability for defective products).

* * *

In summary, these older West Virginia cases provide additional evidence that a requirement of "exclusive control" in *res ipsa loquitur* cases can lead to rather harsh results, inconsistent with the purpose of the rule—to allow negligence in certain cases to be proved circumstantially.

Additionally, it should be noted that our past formulations of the requirements for the invocation of the rule of *res ipsa loquitur* have another apparent flaw—because they in effect implement the doctrine of contributory negligence, which we discarded in *Bradley v. Appalachian Power,* 163 W.Va. 332, 256 S.E.2d 879 (1979), when we adopted [a form of] comparative negligence.

* * *

It [is] not surprising that the great majority of jurisdictions which have adopted some form of comparative negligence (and the scholarly commentators) hold that a party seeking to utilize *res ipsa loquitur* need not be entirely free of fault with respect to the accident in question.

While the issue is not directly presented by the facts of the instant case, we believe that the reasoning of these cases is sound, and that therefore the above-quoted *Royal Furniture res ipsa loquitur* test is an erroneous statement of what our law is, insofar as it implies that a plaintiff who is to any degree at fault in causing an accident is barred from proving the superior negligence of a tortfeasor using *res ipsa loquitur*.[11]

From the foregoing discussion, it appears that past formulations in our law of the rule of *res ipsa loquitur* are unsatisfactory. For example, the *Royal Furniture* test is clearly inadequate in part (1), which mandates "exclusive control" by the party to be charged with negligence—and in part (2), which requires that a plaintiff be faultless. And in the particular context of the instant case, this *Royal Furniture res ipsa loquitur* test would be inadequate for the circuit court of Mineral County to use upon remand.

* * *

* * * [W]e conclude that the formulation of the rule of *res ipsa loquitur* which is stated in the *Restatement of Torts 2d*, Sec. 328D [1965] should ordinarily provide a fairer, broader, and more generally applicable and useful formulation of the rule, and we therefore adopt it. Syllabus Point 2 of *Royal Furniture Co. v. City of Morgantown*, 164 W.Va. 400, 263 S.E.2d 878 (1980) is hereby overruled. * * *

[Reversed and remanded.]

———

WARD v. FORRESTER DAY CARE, INC., 547 So.2d 410 (Ala.1989). Evidence showed an 11-week-old child received a broken arm while he was in a day care center. Employees testified no injurious incident and no negligence occurred at the center. "The plaintiffs' position is that the defendant's employees have adopted a 'conspiracy of silence.'" *Held*, that res ipsa loquitur applies. The court pointed to "a small, but growing, body of law" applying res ipsa loquitur "to institutions such as hospitals, nursing homes, and child care centers where the 'instrumentality' causing the injury is not known." Usually the doctrine is applied to "injury by machinery and instrumentalities under the exclusive control" of the defendant; "as a doctrine of necessity it should apply with equal force in cases wherein medical and nursing staffs take the place of machinery."

11. It appears that in [West Virginia's] comparative negligence context, the language of the *Restatement* formulation of the *res ipsa loquitur* prerequisites, which *inter alia* requires that "other responsible causes, including the conduct of the plaintiff and third persons, are *sufficiently eliminated* by the evidence" (emphasis added) means that to invoke *res ipsa loquitur*, a party must present evidence from which the jury could find that the plaintiff was less negligent than any other parties whose negligence, however shown, caused or contributed to the accident—and this showing would be "sufficient elimination" of the plaintiff's responsibility. *Cf. Turk v. H.C. Prange Co.*, 18 Wis.2d 547, 558 n. 2, 119 N.W.2d 365, 372 n. 2 (1963) (*res ipsa loquitur* available if plaintiff can be found less than fifty percent negligent).

YBARRA v. SPANGARD

Supreme Court of California, 1944.
25 Cal.2d 486, 154 P.2d 687, 162 A.L.R. 1258.

[In 1939, plaintiff's physician, Dr. Tilley, diagnosed the plaintiff's ailment and arranged for an appendectomy to be performed by Dr. Spangard at a hospital owned and managed by Dr. Swift. The plaintiff was given a hypodermic injection and later was awakened by Dr. Tilley and Dr. Spangard and wheeled into the operating room by a nurse, Miss Gisler, one of Dr. Swift's employees. Dr. Reser, an anesthetist employed by Dr. Swift, adjusted the plaintiff for the operation, pushing his body to the head of the operating table and, according to plaintiff's testimony, placed him back against two hard objects at the top of his shoulders about one inch below his neck. Dr. Reser administered the anaesthetic and the next morning plaintiff was in his hospital room attended by a special nurse, Miss Thompson. Plaintiff joined all the doctors and nurses in an action for negligence.

The plaintiff's testimony was that before the operation he had never experienced any pain in his right arm or shoulder; but that when he awoke he felt a sharp pain between the neck and the point of the right shoulder; that the pain spread down the lower part of his arm and continued to grow worse after he left the hospital. One of plaintiff's expert witnesses testified that from X-ray pictures there was a wasting away of the muscle above the shoulder and that that condition was due to injury by pressure or strain applied between the plaintiff's right shoulder and neck. Another testified that the plaintiff's injury was paralysis of traumatic origin. The defendants introduced no evidence. The trial court entered judgment of nonsuit as to all defendants from which plaintiff appeals.]

GIBSON, C. J. [after stating the facts]. The doctrine of res ipsa loquitur has three conditions: "(1) the accident must be of a kind which ordinarily does not occur in the absence of someone's negligence; (2) it must be caused by an agency or instrumentality within the exclusive control of the defendant; (3) it must not have been due to any voluntary action or contribution on the part of the plaintiff." Prosser, Torts, p. 295. It is applied in a wide variety of situations, including cases of medical or dental treatment and hospital care. * * *

The present case is of a type which comes within the reason and spirit of the doctrine more fully perhaps than any other. The passenger sitting awake in a railroad car at the time of a collision, the pedestrian walking along the street and struck by a falling object or the debris of an explosion, are surely not more entitled to an explanation than the unconscious patient on the operating table. Viewed from this aspect, it is difficult to see how the doctrine can, with any justification, be so restricted in its statement as to become inapplicable to a patient who submits himself to the care and custody of doctors and nurses, is rendered unconscious, and receives some injury from instrumentalities used in his treatment. Without the aid of the doctrine a patient who received permanent injuries of a serious character, obviously the result of some one's negligence, would be entirely unable to recover unless the doctors and nurses in attendance voluntarily chose to disclose the identity of the negligent person and the facts establishing liability. If this were the state of the law of negligence, the courts, to avoid gross injustice, would be forced to invoke the principles of absolute liability, irrespective of negligence, in actions by persons suffering injuries during the course of treatment under anesthesia. But we think this juncture has not yet been reached, and that the doctrine of res ipsa loquitur is properly applicable to the case before us.

The condition that the injury must not have been due to the plaintiff's voluntary action is of course fully satisfied under the evidence produced herein; and the same is true of the condition that the accident must be one which ordinarily does not occur unless some one was negligent. We have here no problem of negligence in treatment, but of distinct injury to a healthy part of the body not the subject of treatment, nor within the area covered by the operation. The decisions in this state make it clear that such circumstances raise the inference of negligence and call upon the defendant to explain the unusual result. * * *

The argument of defendants is simply that plaintiff has not shown an injury caused by an instrumentality under a defendant's control, because he has not shown which of the several instrumentalities that he came in contact with while in the hospital caused the injury; and he has not shown that any one defendant or his servants had exclusive control over any particular instrumentality. Defendants assert that some of them were not the employees of other defendants, that some did not stand in any permanent relationship from which liability in tort would follow, and that in view of the nature of the injury, the number of defendants and the different functions performed by each, they could not all be liable for the wrong, if any.

We have no doubt that in a modern hospital a patient is quite likely to come under the care of a number of persons in different types of contractual and other relationships with each other. For example, in the present case it appears that [plaintiff's physician, Dr. Tilley, and the surgeon, Dr. Spangard,] were physicians or surgeons commonly placed in the legal category of independent contractors; and Dr. Reser, the anesthetist, and defendant Thompson, the special nurse, were employees of Dr. Swift [the hospital owner] and not of the other doctors. But we do not believe that either the number or relationship of the defendants alone determines whether the doctrine of res ipsa loquitur applies. Every defendant in whose custody the plaintiff was placed for any period was bound to exercise ordinary care to see that no unnecessary harm came to him and each would be liable for failure in this regard. Any defendant who negligently injured him, and any defendant charged with his care who so neglected him as to allow injury to occur, would be liable. The defendant employers would be liable for the neglect of their employees; and the doctor in charge of the operation would be liable for the negligence of those who became his temporary servants for the purpose of assisting in the operation. * * *

It may appear at the trial that, consistent with the principles outlined above, one or more defendants will be found liable and others absolved, but this should not preclude the application of the rule of res ipsa loquitur. The control at one time or another, of one or more of the various agencies or instrumentalities which might have harmed the plaintiff was in the hands of every defendant or of his employees or temporary servants. This, we think, places upon them the burden of initial explanation. Plaintiff was rendered unconscious for the purpose of undergoing surgical treatment by the defendants; it is manifestly unreasonable for them to insist that he identify any one of them as the person who did the alleged negligent act.

The other aspect of the case which defendants so strongly emphasize is that plaintiff has not identified the instrumentality any more than he has the particular guilty defendant. Here, again, there is a misconception which, if carried to the extreme for which defendants contend, would unreasonably limit the application of the res ipsa loquitur rule. It should be enough that the plaintiff can show an injury resulting from an external force applied while he lay unconscious in the hospital; this is as clear a case of identification of the instrumentality as the plaintiff may ever be able to make. * * *

We do not at this time undertake to state the extent to which the reasoning of this case may be applied to other situations in which the doctrine of res ipsa loquitur is invoked. We merely hold that where a plaintiff receives unusual injuries while unconscious and in the course of medical treatment, all those defendants who had any control over his body or the instrumentalities which might have caused the injuries may properly be called upon to meet the inference of negligence by giving an explanation of their conduct.

The judgment is reversed.

Rehearing denied; TRAYNOR, J., dissenting.

[At the trial without a jury which followed this decision, each defendant, except the hospital owner, testified that he had not observed any incident which could have caused the harm. The judge held that this did not overcome the inference of negligence and found against all of them. In 93 Cal.App.2d 43, 208 P.2d 445, the Court of Appeal affirmed the judgment, the court quoting the remark of Justice Holmes that law does not always keep step with logic. See comment in 63 Harv.L.Rev. 643 (1950). The court does not mention evidence, which appears in the record, that plaintiff's teeth were diseased and that there was expert testimony to the effect that such disease may have caused harm to the arm.]

———

ESTATE OF CHIN v. ST. BARNABAS MEDICAL CENTER, 160 N.J. 454, 734 A.2d 778 (1999). Angelina Chin died while undergoing a diagnostic procedure which normally involves minimal risk. The incorrect hook-up of tubes attached to the diagnostic device (an hysteroscope) caused noxious gas to enter her body. Decedent's husband brought a wrongful death lawsuit asserting negligence on the part of the physician who performed the procedure, three nurses who assisted, and the hospital in question. At trial plaintiff's evidence did not identify the person who performed the incorrect hook-up, and each defendant "simply insisted that he or she was not the party individually responsible." The trial judge's instructions to the jury embraced the theory of "collective *res ipsa loquitur*" established by a prior New Jersey case. The trial judge instructed that the entire burden of proof shifted to the defendants, and that "there must be a verdict against at least one defendant in this case because obviously somebody did something wrong." The jury exonerated the one nurse who "did not connect any tubing," and found all the other defendants liable. On review in the New Jersey Supreme Court, *held*, instructions and jury verdict approved.

"Angelina Chin, who was unconscious, helpless, and utterly blameless, suffered a fatal injury that bespeaks negligence on the part of one or more of the defendants." " * * * [I]n a case in which the plaintiff was unconscious and is clearly blameless, and all potential defendants are before the court, then only the putative defendants can be at fault and at least one defendant must be culpable. In that setting, * * * defendants must not only come forward to explain the cause of plaintiff's injuries, but also must convince the jury that they individually are not responsible."

NEVADA STATUTE RELATING TO MEDICAL MALPRACTICE
Nev.Rev.Stat. 41A.100.1

Liability for personal injury or death is not imposed upon any provider of medical care based on alleged negligence in the performance of that care unless evidence consisting of expert medical testimony, material from recognized medical texts or treatises or the regulations of the licensed medical facility wherein the alleged negligence occurred is presented to demonstrate the alleged deviation from the accepted standard of care in the specific circumstances of the case and to prove causation of the alleged personal injury or death, except that such evidence is not required and a rebuttable presumption that the personal injury or death was caused by negligence arises where evidence is presented that the personal injury or death occurred in any one or more of the following circumstances:

(a) A foreign substance other than medication or a prosthetic device was unintentionally left within the body of a patient following surgery;

(b) An explosion or fire originating in a substance used in treatment occurred in the course of treatment;

(c) An unintended burn caused by heat, radiation or chemicals was suffered in the course of medical care;

(d) An injury was suffered during the course of treatment to a part of the body not directly involved in the treatment or proximate thereto; or

(e) A surgical procedure was performed on the wrong patient or the wrong organ, limb or part of a patient's body.

MAYOR v. DOWSETT, 240 Or. 196, 400 P.2d 234 (1965). Plaintiff, a 34-year-old woman in good health, was paralyzed after anaesthetic for childbirth. *Held,* res ipsa loquitur applied. It was unnecessary to determine whether there is common knowledge among laymen that paralysis of a healthy woman following childbirth with use of spinal anaesthesia would not happen without negligence in administration of the anaesthesia, since there was expert testimony that such injury is not expected if due care is exercised.

WASHINGTON HOSPITAL CENTER v. BUTLER, 127 U.S.App.D.C. 379, 384 F.2d 331 (1967). Diabetic sustained injuries in a fall from an x-ray table when vertical irradiation was attempted. Judgment was entered against a hospital and radiologists, although neither side adduced evidence of medical practice in the community.

Chapter 10

THE DUTY OF CARE: SPECIAL RELATIONS AND STATUSES

We saw in Chapter 8 that duty in negligence law is usually presumed to exist. The materials in this chapter explore circumstances where this presumption does not hold. The first section, in fact, explores a body of tort law which stands this presumption on its head. "No duty to act" is the general rule of the classical doctrine examined in Section A.

The cases commonly thought to be at the core of the "no duty to act" doctrine are often called "Good Samaritan" cases. Implicit in this name is the belief that these are cases where the objection to the defendant's conduct is that the defendant could have rescued the plaintiff from peril, but did not. The flip side of this coin is the belief that these are cases where the defendant is *not* to be faulted for having acted in a way which created the peril the plaintiff faces. The premise of classical doctrine—explored in Section A—is that natural and legal persons who are not legally responsible for putting a victim in peril, have "no duty to act" to protect the victim from that peril. We have a general duty not to put strangers at unreasonable risk of injury, but no general duty to protect strangers from perils for which we are not legally responsible.

These cases get much of their edge from the fact that defendants typically might prevent the harms at issue at little cost to themselves. If duty were recognized, breach would be easy to find. Under classical doctrine: "If A saw that B was about to be struck on the head by a flowerpot thrown from a tenth-story window, and A knew that B was unaware of the impending catastrophe and also knew that he could save B with a shout, yet he did nothing and as a result B was killed, still, A's inaction, though gratuitous (there was no risk or other nontrivial cost to A) and even reprehensible, would not be actionable." *Stockberger v. U.S.*, 332 F.3d 479 (7th Cir.2003) (Posner, J.).

As you make your way through the cases in Section A you should ask yourself just how far their factual circumstances fit our intuitive conception of a case where the defendant's actions are not responsible for putting the plaintiff in peril. Classical doctrine is notable in part for its aggressive interpretation of the reach of this paradigm.

SECTION A. CLASSICAL CONCEPTIONS: NO DUTY TO ACT

UNION PACIFIC RAILWAY v. CAPPIER

Supreme Court of Kansas, 1903.
66 Kan. 649, 72 P. 281.

SMITH, J. This was an action brought by Adeline Cappier, the mother of Irvin Ezelle, to recover damages resulting to her by reason of the loss of her son, who was run over by a car of plaintiff in error, and died from the injuries received. The trial court, at the close of the evidence introduced to support a recovery by plaintiff below, held that no careless act of the railway company's servants in the operation of the car was shown, and refused to permit the case to be considered by the jury on the allegations and attempted proof of such negligence. The petition, however, contained an averment that the injured person had one leg and an arm cut off by the carwheels, and that the servants of the railway company failed to call a surgeon, or to render him any assistance after the accident, but permitted him to remain by the side of the tracks and bleed to death. Under this charge of negligence a recovery was had.

While attempting to cross the railway tracks Ezelle was struck by a moving freight car pushed by an engine. A yardmaster in charge of the switching operations was riding on the end of the car nearest to the deceased and gave warning by shouting to him. The warning was either too late or no heed was given to it. The engine was stopped. After the injured man was clear of the track, the yardmaster signalled the engineer to move ahead, fearing, as he testified, that a passenger train then about due would come upon them. The locomotive and car went forward over a bridge, where the general yardmaster was informed of the accident and an ambulance was summoned by telephone. The yardmaster then went back where the injured man was lying and found three Union Pacific switchmen binding up the wounded limbs and doing what they could to stop the flow of blood. The ambulance arrived about thirty minutes later and Ezelle was taken to a hospital, where he died a few hours afterward.

In answer to particular questions of fact, the jury found that the accident occurred at 5:35 P.M.; that immediately one of the railway employees telephoned to police headquarters for help for the injured man; that the ambulance started at 6:05 P.M. and reached the nearest hospital with Ezelle at 6:20 P.M., where he received proper medical and surgical treatment. Judgment against the railway company was based on the following question and answer:

"Ques. Did not defendant's employees bind up Ezelle's wounds and try to stop the flow of blood as soon as they could after the accident happened? Ans. No."

* * *

After the trespasser on the track of a railway company has been injured in collision with a train, and the servants of the company have assumed to take charge of him, the duty arises to exercise such care in his treatment as the circumstances will allow. We are unable, however, to approve the doctrine that when the acts of a trespasser himself result in his injury, where his own negligent conduct is alone the cause, those in charge of the instrument which inflicted the hurt, being innocent of wrong-doing, are nevertheless blameable in law if they neglect to administer to the sufferings of him whose wounds we might say were self-imposed. With the humane side of the question courts are not concerned. It is the omission or negligent discharge of legal duties only which come within the sphere of judicial cognizance. For withholding relief from the suffering, for failing to respond to the calls of worthy charity, or for faltering in the bestowment of brotherly love on the unfortunate, penalties are found not in the laws of men, but in that higher law, the violation of which is condemned by the voice of conscience, whose sentence of punishment for the recreant act is swift and sure. In the law of contracts it is now well understood that a promise founded on a moral obligation will not be enforced in the courts. Bishop states that some of the older authorities recognize a moral obligation as valid, and says:

Such a doctrine, carried to its legitimate results, would release the tribunals from the duty to administer the law of the land; and put, in the place of law, the varying ideas of morals which the changing incumbents of the bench might from time to time entertain. Bish.Cont. § 44.

Ezelle's injuries were inflicted, as the court below held, without the fault of the yardmaster, engineer, or fireman in charge of the car and locomotive. The railway company was no more responsible than it would have been had the deceased been run down by the cars of another railroad company on a track parallel with that of plaintiff in error. If no duty was imposed on the servants of defendant below to take charge of, and care for, the wounded man in such a case, how could a duty arise under the circumstances of the case at bar? In Barrows on Negligence, page 4, it is said:

The duty must be owing from the defendant to the plaintiff, otherwise there can be no negligence, so far as the plaintiff is concerned; * * * and the duty must be owing to plaintiff in an individual capacity, and not merely as one of the general public.

This excludes from actionable negligence all failures to observe the obligations imposed by charity, gratitude, generosity, and the kindred virtues. The moral law would obligate an attempt to rescue a person in a perilous position,—as a drowning child,—but the law of the land does not require it, no matter how little personal risk it might involve, provided that the person who declines to act is not responsible for the peril.

In the several cases cited in the brief of counsel for defendant in error to sustain the judgment of the trial court, it will be found that the negligence on which recoveries were based occurred after the time when the person injured was in the custody and care of those who were at fault in failing to give him proper treatment.

[Judgment reversed.]

HURLEY v. EDDINGFIELD, 156 Ind. 416, 59 N.E. 1058 (1901). BAKER, J. The appellant sued appellee for $10,000 damages for wrongfully causing the death of his intestate. The court sustained appellee's demurrer to the complaint, and this ruling is assigned as error.

"The material facts alleged may be summarized thus: At and for years before decedent's death appellee was a practicing physician at Mace, in Montgomery county, duly licensed under the laws of the state. He held himself out to the public as a general practitioner of medicine. He had been decedent's family physician. Decedent became dangerously ill, and sent for appellee. The messenger informed appellee of decedent's violent sickness, tendered him his fee for his services, and stated to him that no other physician was procurable in time, and that decedent relied on him for attention. No other physician was procurable in time to be of any use, and decedent did rely on appellee for medical assistance. Without any reason whatever, appellee refused to render aid to decedent. No other patients were requiring appellee's immediate service, and he could have gone to the relief of decedent if he had been willing to do so. Death ensued, without decedent's fault, and wholly from appellee's wrongful act. The alleged wrongful act was appellee's refusal to enter into a contract of employment. Counsel do not contend that, before the enactment of the law regulating the practice of medicine, physicians were bound to render professional service to every one who applied. Whart.Neg. § 731. The act regulating the practice of medicine provides for a board of examiners, standards of qualification, examinations, licenses to those found qualified, and penalties for practicing without license. Acts 1897, p. 255; Acts 1899, p. 247. The act is a preventive, not a compulsive, measure. In obtaining the state's license (permission) to practice medicine, the state does not require, and the licensee does not engage, that he will practice at all or on other terms than he may choose to accept. Counsel's analogies, drawn from the obligations to the public on the part of innkeepers, common carriers, and the like, are beside the mark. Judgment affirmed."

BUCH v. ARMORY MANUFACTURING CO., 69 N.H. 257, 44 A. 809 (1898). The 8-year-old plaintiff was taken by his 13-year-old brother, employed by defendant as a back boy in a mill, into the mill to learn the work. The elder brother acted without explicit authority, though there was an informal practice of such training of younger brothers. Plaintiff, ignorant of English, was directed to leave by the overseer after a day and a half of openly assisting the back boys. It was unclear whether he correctly understood these directions. Soon thereafter plaintiff was injured when his hand was caught in machinery that was in good order and properly maintained. After a jury trial, plaintiff had a verdict. In setting the verdict aside and ordering judgment for defendant, the appellate court stated:

"Assuming, then, that the plaintiff was incapable either of appreciating the danger or of exercising the care necessary to avoid it, is he, upon the facts stated, entitled to recover? He was a trespasser in a place dangerous to children of his age. In the conduct of their business and management of their machinery the defendants were without fault. The only negligence charged upon, or attributed to, them is that, inasmuch as they could not make the plaintiff understand a command to leave the premises, and ought to have known that they could not, they did not forcibly eject him. Actionable negligence is the neglect of a legal duty. The defendants are not liable unless they owed to the plaintiff a legal duty which they neglected to perform. With purely moral obligations the law does not deal. For example, the priest and Levite who passed by on the other side were not, it is supposed, liable at law for the continued suffering of the man who fell among thieves, which they might, and morally ought to have, prevented or relieved. Suppose A., standing close by a railroad, sees a two year old babe on the track, and a car approaching. He can easily rescue the child, with entire safety to himself, and the instincts of humanity require him to do so. If he does not, he may, perhaps, justly be styled a ruthless savage and a moral monster; but he is not liable in damages for the child's injury, or indictable under the statute for its death. Pub.St. c. 278, § 8. 'In dealing with cases which involve injuries to children, courts * * * have sometimes strangely confounded legal obligation with sentiments that are independent of law.' Indianapolis v. Emmelman, 108 Ind. 530, 9 N.E. 155. * * * 'No action will lie against a spiteful man, who, seeing another running into danger, merely omits to warn him. To bring the case within the category of actionable negligence, some wrongful act must be shown, or a breach of some positive duty; otherwise, a man who allows strangers to roam over his property would be held answerable for not protecting them against any danger they might encounter while using the license.' Gautret v. Egerton, L.R.2 C.P. 371, 375.''

YANIA v. BIGAN, 397 Pa. 316, 155 A.2d 343 (1959). The complaint alleged that Bigan, a coal strip-mine operator, by taunting caused Yania, another coal strip-mine operator and a business visitor on Bigan's premises, to jump into a water-filled trench, without having warned him of the danger, and that Bigan then neglected to take reasonable steps to aid Yania, with the result that Yania drowned. *Held,* for the defendant, Bigan, sustaining preliminary objections in the nature of demurrers. "The mere fact that Bigan saw Yania in a position of peril in the water imposed upon him no legal, although a moral, obligation or duty to go to his rescue unless Bigan was legally responsible, in whole or in part, for placing Yania in the perilous position." We find no such legal responsibility here.

SECTION B. MODERN CONCEPTIONS

Modern doctrine is typically thought to accept the same general rule as classical doctrine—no "duty to act"—but to recognize a large number of distinct circumstances in which exceptions to that general duty take hold. In *Stockberger v. U.S.*, 332 F.3d 479 (7th Cir.2003) Judge Posner offers one version of the conventional understanding of the three categories into which most of these exceptions fit:

The first type of case is where the rescuer had either assumed, explicitly or implicitly, a contractual duty to rescue the victim; *Folsom v. Burger King*, 135 Wash.2d 658, 958 P.2d 301, 311 (Wash.1998); or had created in the victim a reasonable expectation that he had assumed such a duty. * * * 3 Fowler V. Harper, Fleming James, Jr. & Oscar S. Gray, *The Law of Torts* § 18.6, p. 717 (2d ed.1986).

In the second type of case, the victim was in the rescuer's custody and thus without access to alternative rescuers. [citations omitted] Typical cases of this type are ones in which the victim is a prison inmate or a patient in a mental hospital. E.g., *Overall v. State*, 525 N.E.2d 1275 (Ind.App.1988); *Iglesias v. Wells*, 441 N.E.2d 1017 (Ind.App.1982); *Murdock v. City of Keene*, 137 N.H. 70, 623 A.2d 755, 756–57 (N.H. 1993); *Salazar v. City of Chicago*, 940 F.2d 233, 237 (7th Cir.1991); *Clements v. Swedish Hospital*, 252 Minn. 1, 89 N.W.2d 162, 165–66 (Minn.1958). These cases are readily assimilated to cases of the first type through the concept of an implicit contractual duty.

The third class consists of cases in which the victim's peril had been caused by the putative rescuer himself—even if he had caused it nonnegligently, e.g., * * * *L.S. Ayres & Co. v. Hicks*, 220 Ind. 86, 40 N.E.2d 334 (Ind.1942); * * * but *a fortiori* if he had caused it negligently or otherwise culpably. E.g., *Carlisle v. Kanaywer*, 24 Cal.App.3d 587, 101 Cal.Rptr. 246 (App.1972).

* * *

In short * * * when the rescuer either has assumed explicitly or implicitly a duty of rescue, or has caused the injury, the reasons behind the common law rule fall away and the rule is bent.

Our organization of the cases in this section follows this conventional understanding, for the most part. But many of the cases themselves, we think, evidence an ambivalent relation to this doctrinal organization, even when they purport to instantiate it. In a significant number of cases, the justifications advanced in support of a particular duty to act are far-reaching, enough so to challenge the dominance of the general rule and to put pressure on the doctrinal cubbyholes themselves. The principle "no duty to act" seems to be warring with a counter-principle, which counsels imposing duties to act whenever it is reasonable to do so and the duty can be articulated in a workable way.

PRINCIPLE AND COUNTER–PRINCIPLE

L. S. AYRES & CO. v. HICKS
Supreme Court of Indiana, 1942.
220 Ind. 86, 40 N.E.2d 334.

[Plaintiff, a six-year-old boy, caught his fingers in a moving escalator in defendant's store where his mother was shopping. He alleges that the escalator was so constructed as to be dangerous to children and that after his fingers were caught, defendant negligently delayed in stopping the escalator. Judgment was for the plaintiff and a motion for a new trial, on various grounds, was denied.]

SHAKE, C. J. [after stating the facts and findings of no negligence in the construction of the escalator, turning to the matter of aggravation of the existing harm to the fingers]: It may be observed, on the outset, that there is no general duty to go to the rescue of a person who is in peril. * * *

There may be principles of social conduct so universally recognized as to be demanded that they be observed as a legal duty, and the relationship of the parties may impose obligations that would not otherwise exist. Thus, it has been said that, under some circumstances, moral and humanitarian considerations may require one to render assistance to another who has been injured, even though the injury was not due to negligence on his part and may have been caused by the negligence of the injured person. Failure to render assistance in such a situation may constitute actionable negligence if the injury is aggravated through lack of due care. Am.Jr.Negligence, § 16; 69 L.R.A. 533. The case of Depue v. Flateau, 1907, 100 Minn. 299, 111 N.W. 1, 8 L.R.A.,N.S., 485, lends support to this rule. It was there held that one who invited into his house a cattle buyer who called to inspect cattle which were for sale owed him the duty, upon discovering that he had been taken severely ill, not to expose him to danger on a cold winter night by sending him away unattended while he was in a fainting and helpless condition.

After holding that a railroad company was liable for failing to provide medical and surgical assistance to an employee who was injured without fault but who was rendered helpless, by reason of which the employee's injuries were aggravated, it was said with the subsequent approval of this court in Tippecanoe Loan, etc., Co. v. Cleveland, etc. R. Co., 1915, 57 Ind. App. 644, 649, 650, 104 N.E. 866, 868, 106 N.E. 739:

> In some jurisdictions the doctrine * * * has been held to apply to cases where one party has been so injured as to render him helpless by an instrumentality under the control of another, even though no relation of master and servant, or carrier and passenger, existed at the time. It has been said that the mere happening of an accident of this kind creates a relation which gives rise to a legal duty to render such aid to the injured party as may be reasonable necessary to save his life, or to prevent a serious aggravation of his injuries, and that this subsequent duty does not depend upon the negligence of the one party, or the freedom of the other party from contributory negligence, but it exists irrespective of any legal responsibility for the original injury.

From the above cases it may be deduced that there may be a legal obligation to take positive or affirmative steps to effect the rescue of a person who is helpless and in a situation of peril, when the one proceeded against is a master or an invitor or when the injury resulted from use of an instrumentality under the control of the defendant. Such an obligation may exist although the accident or original injury was caused by the negligence of the plaintiff or through that of a third person and without any fault on the part of the defendant. Other relationships may impose a like obligation, but it is not necessary to pursue that inquiry further at this time.

In the case at bar the appellee was an invitee and he received his initial injury in using an instrumentality provided by the appellant and under its control. Under the rule stated above and on the authority of the cases cited this was a sufficient relationship to impose a duty upon the appellant. * * *

———

SZABO v. PENNSYLVANIA RAILROAD, 132 N.J.L. 331, 40 A.2d 562 (1945). [Plaintiff's decedent, a member of the track crew of the defendant, was overcome by the heat. Plaintiff alleged that knowing this, defendant failed to render the required assistance and, after taking charge of the decedent, failed to use due care. Judgment for the plaintiff was reversed by the Supreme Court, 131 N.J.L. 238, 36 A.2d 8, on the ground that a verdict should have been directed for defendant. The plaintiff appeals.]

Held, there is an exception to the rule "that in the absence of a contract or a statute, there rests no duty upon an employer to provide medical service or other means of cure to an ill, diseased or injured employee, even though it result from the negligence of the master. * * *

"That exception is, that where one engaged in the work of his master receives injuries, whether or not due to the negligence of the master, rendering him helpless to provide for his own care, dictates of humanity, duty and fair dealing require that the master put in the reach of such stricken employee such medical care and other assistance as the emergency, thus created, may in reason require, so that the stricken employee may have his life saved or may avoid further bodily harm. This duty arises out of strict necessity and urgent exigency. It arises with the emergency and expires with it."

VERMONT STATUTE ANN., TITLE 12

§ 519 Emergency Medical Care:

(a) A person who knows that another is exposed to grave physical harm shall, to the extent that the same can be rendered without danger or peril to himself or without interference with important duties owed to others, give reasonable assistance to the exposed person unless that assistance or care is being provided by others.

(b) A person who provides reasonable assistance in compliance with subsection (a) of this section shall not be liable in civil damages unless his acts constitute gross negligence or unless he will receive or expects to receive remuneration. Nothing contained in this subsection shall alter existing law with respect to tort liability of a practitioner of the healing arts for acts committed in the ordinary course of his practice.

(c) A person who willfully violates subsection (a) of this section shall be fined not more than $100.00.

DUTCH PENAL CODE, Art. 450. One who, witnessing the danger of death with which another is suddenly threatened, neglects to give or furnish him such assistance as he can give or procure without reasonable fear of danger to himself or to others, is to be punished, if the death of the person in distress follows, by a detention of three months at most and [a fine].

FRENCH PENAL CODE, Art. 63, paragraph 2 (enacted 1945) provides penalties by fine or imprisonment up to three years against one who abstains voluntarily from giving to a person in peril such aid, by personal action or by calling for help, as he could give without risk to himself or another.

ASSUMING A DUTY

Judge Posner's *Stockberger* opinion speaks of cases where a "contractual" duty to rescue the victim has been "assumed," either "explicitly or implicitly" as a well-recognized category of exceptions to the general rule that there is "no duty to act." The case that follow are the kinds of cases he had in mind. Indeed, the first of them—*Folsom*—is one of the opinions that he cites.

FOLSOM v. BURGER KING

Supreme Court of Washington, 1998.
135 Wash.2d 658, 958 P.2d 301.

JOHNSON, Justice

On May 17, 1992, Blake Pirtle entered a Spokane, Washington Burger King through the back door entrance and murdered employees Dawnya Calbreath and Robert Tod Folsom during a robbery. Pirtle was convicted on two counts of aggravated first degree murder. [citation omitted] This case involves a lawsuit filed by the estates of the two Burger King employees killed by Blake Pirtle while at work (plaintiffs). [Plaintiffs brought suit against the employer of the deceased victims Hatter, Inc., the franchisor, Burger King, and a security firm, Spokane Security System. The employer was held to be immune under the Worker's Compensation law and Burger King was held not to have retained sufficient control for a duty of care towards the victims to have arisen. The following excerpts pertain to their claims against Spokane Security System.]

* * *

DUTY TO RESCUE

Plaintiffs claim a "special relationship" arose between employees and Spokane Security under the voluntary rescue doctrine. To support this theory, plaintiffs allege that until June 30, 1991, Spokane Security had contracted with the former operator of the restaurant to provide and maintain a security alarm system for the restaurant. On June 30, 1991,

Edwin Hatter, the new franchise owner, terminated the contract. Although Spokane Security closed the account, the security alarm equipment was not removed because Spokane Security "didn't get around to it." Clerk's Papers at 1103. The security system included a button in the freezer, which the employees activated during the robbery. Since the security system remained, Spokane Security received a signal from the alarm and telephoned the restaurant, but found the telephone number disconnected. After determining the account was closed and was labeled "disregard signals," the Spokane Security employee took no further action. Throughout this sequence of events, plaintiffs allege three Washington State Patrol troopers were having coffee at a restaurant across the street. Further, they had their radio scanners on and were prepared to respond to dispatch calls. Plaintiffs argue if the troopers had been dispatched, the murders would have been prevented.

Plaintiffs allege a "special relationship" between Spokane Security and the employees arose out of the contract to provide security and the voluntary act of failing to remove the security equipment. Plaintiffs argue this "special relationship" created the duty of Spokane Security to rescue or attempt to rescue the employees. The trial court granted summary judgment to Spokane Security. Finding no "special relationship" between the plaintiffs and Spokane Security, the trial court determined Spokane Security owed no duty of care to the employees. We affirm the trial court; plaintiffs attempted to weave two theories of tort law together in an effort to impose potential liability on Spokane Security.

Under traditional tort law, absent affirmative conduct or a special relationship, no legal duty to come to the aid of a stranger exists. W. Page Keeton et al., *Prosser and Keeton on the Law of Torts* § 56 (5th ed.1984). Further, a private person does not have the duty to protect others from criminal acts of third parties. *Hutchins v. 1001 Fourth Ave. Assocs.*, 116 Wash.2d 217, 223, 802 P.2d 1360 (1991). There are exceptions to these traditional rules.[1] An exception may create an affirmative duty to protect another from harm. *Hutchins*, 116 Wash.2d at 227–28, 802 P.2d 1360. If an exception applies, liability may be imposed despite the absence of negligence. These special relationships typically arise when one party is entrusted with the well-being of the other party. [citations omitted]

Plaintiffs * * * fail to explain "which ['special relationship'] exception applies. Spokane Security contracted to provide security monitoring for the Burger King restaurant; however, the contract was terminated by Hatter, Inc. [plaintiff's employer] 10 months prior to the murders. While the facts indicate the equipment remained in place and was functional, Spokane Security was not contractually obligated to provide security services and plaintiffs have not [shown that Spokane Security had] a[nother previously] established special relationship with the employees. * * *."

---

1. Restatement (Second) of Torts §§ 314A and 314B (1965) identify five relationships that give rise to an affirmative duty to act: (1) common carrier to passengers; (2) innkeeper to guests; (3) possessor of land open to public to visitors; (4) individuals voluntarily controlling another such that opportunities for protection are removed; and (5) employers to employees acting within the scope of employment.

An additional exception to the traditional no duty to rescue rule may arise if a defendant takes steps to assist a person in need and acts negligently in rendering that assistance. This duty is not based on a previously established relationship as described above; rather, the duty arises when one party voluntarily begins to assist an individual needing help. Plaintiffs argue Spokane Security voluntarily agreed to render aid when Spokane Security failed to remove the security system. In this case, we must determine whether Spokane Security had a duty to protect the employees under the voluntary rescue doctrine.

* * *

Typically, liability for attempting a voluntary rescue has been found when the defendant makes the plaintiff's situation worse by: (1) increasing the danger; (2) misleading the plaintiff into believing the danger had been removed; or (3) depriving the plaintiff of the possibility of help from other sources. W. Page Keeton et al., *Prosser and Keeton on the Law of Torts* § 56 (5th ed.1984)."

* * * [W]e recognize that liability can arise from the negligent performance of a voluntarily undertaken duty. * * *. When a defendant undertakes a rescue, a special relationship develops, giving rise to actionable negligence if a defendant breaches the duty of care by failing to act reasonably. Plaintiffs allege a special relationship arose and argue Spokane Security voluntarily agreed to rescue the employees when it left the security system in place. Plaintiffs allege the act of failing to remove the security system induced reliance and caused harm."

In this case, plaintiffs have failed to establish that the voluntary rescue doctrine applies. The duty to rescue arises when a rescuer knows a danger is present and takes steps to aid an individual in need. *Brown [v. MacPherson's, Inc.,]*, 86 Wash.2d at 298, 545 P.2d 13 [(1975)](summary judgment not granted and duty to rescue doctrine applicable when avalanche danger existed and defendants had opportunity to warn plaintiffs of danger but failed to do so). The act (leaving the system in place) plaintiffs rely on to trigger the voluntary rescue doctrine took place in this case before any danger existed.* * * "

The plaintiffs have not presented any facts showing Spokane Security knew the tragic events would take place or that Spokane Security negligently withdrew from rescuing once the employees were in danger. Spokane Security did not undertake the duty to aid the employees by failing to remove the security system because the danger was not imminent and the threat of harm was not present. In this case, we decline to adopt a rule where the failure to remove the security system creates an ongoing duty to rescue employees from unknown dangers. Further, the failure of Spokane Security to telephone emergency services does not invoke the voluntary rescue doctrine because the failure to call was not an affirmative act creating the harm, making the situation worse, or inducing reliance.

We affirm the trial court. Applying the facts of this case to traditional tort theories, plaintiffs have not shown that Spokane Security had a duty to assist the employees. Spokane Security's inaction did not create the danger to the employees, there was no special relationship between Spokane Security and the employees, and the voluntary rescue doctrine is not so broad as to cover the facts of this case.

––––––

LACEY v. UNITED STATES, 98 F.Supp. 219 (D.Mass.1951). Action for damages arising from Coast Guard's alleged negligent failure to rescue occupants of crashed airplane. *Held,* for the Government on its motions to vacate and dismiss complaints. "It is true that, while the common law imposes no duty to rescue, it does impose on the Good Samaritan the duty to act with due care *once he has undertaken rescue operations.* The rationale is that other would-be rescuers will rest on their oars in the expectation that effective aid is being rendered. * * * That the Government does not come within the Good Samaritan rule is demonstrated by the fact that the complaint does not show that the Coast Guard's rescue attempt reached the stage where other would-be rescuers were induced to cease their efforts in the belief that the Coast Guard had the situation in hand."

ERIE RAILROAD CO. v. STEWART, 40 F.2d 855 (6th Cir.1930). Plaintiff, a passenger in a truck, was injured when the truck was struck by defendant's train at a heavily travelled street crossing in Cleveland. No statute required a railroad to provide a watchman, but defendant voluntarily maintained one. The watchman, nearby at the time of the accident, failed to give timely warning of the approaching train. In affirming a judgment in plaintiff's favor, the court said: "So, in the present case, the evidence conclusively establishes the voluntary employment of a watchman, knowledge of this fact and reliance upon it by the plaintiff, a duty, therefore, that the company, through the watchman, will exercise reasonable care in warning such travelers as plaintiff, the presence of the watchman thereabouts, and no explanation of the failure to warn. Therefore, even though the duty be considered as qualified, rather than absolute, a prima facie case was established by plaintiff, requiring the defendant to go forward with evidence to rebut the presumption of negligence thus raised, or else suffer a verdict against it on this point. * * * "

LE JUENE ROAD HOSPITAL, INC. v. WATSON, 171 So.2d 202 (Fla.App. 1965) Award of $5,000 to 11-year-old boy discharged by defendant hospital, shortly after admission for acute appendicitis, when boy's mother failed to produce $200 to insure payment for treatment. Operation at another hospital several hours later, violent illness prolonged. *Held,* having begun treatment, defendant was liable for failure to continue treatment when it was foreseeable the boy's condition would be aggravated.

CUSTODY

"Custody" cases are also taken to form a well-recognized class of exceptions to the general "no duty to act" rule—an exception justified by the dependence of the person in custody on the care and protection of the party with custody. But, as the principal case in this section shows, "custody" of a dangerous person can also give rise to a duty to protect unnamed third parties from coming to grief at that person's hands. "Custody" cases, in other words, may involve either a duty to protect the person in "custody," or a duty to protect third parties *from* the person in "custody."

The first of the custody cases we consider is instructive for a second reason as well. It illustrates a continuing preoccupation of cases which do recognize affirmative duties to act, namely, defining the *scope* of the duty whose existence is being recognized so that the duty is manageable. This preoccupation with scope tells us much about the distinctive difficulties of institutionalizing duties to act, and pays a kind of backhand tribute to classical doctrine's concern that unbridled duties to protect and rescue others, whenever the benefits of so doing exceed the costs, may become so sweeping and ill-defined as to threaten individual liberty.

DUDLEY v. OFFENDER AID AND RESTORATION
OF RICHMOND, INC.
Supreme Court of Virginia, 1991.
241 Va. 270, 401 S.E.2d 878.

RUSSELL, Justice.

A convicted felon serving a penitentiary sentence was permitted to reside in privately operated "halfway house." While there, he left the premises of the "halfway house", broke and entered the residence of a woman, raped her, and strangled her to death. Her administrator brought this action at law against the operator of the "halfway house" alleging that the decedent's death resulted from the negligence of the operator in failing to exercise reasonable care to control the felon.

The trial court sustained a demurrer and dismissed the case. We awarded the administrator an appeal. The sole question on appeal is whether the operator of the "halfway house" had the duty to exercise reasonable care to control the felon so as to prevent him from causing harm to the decedent. We answer the question in the affirmative. * * *

* * *

The motion for judgment alleges that the "Halfway House" was filthy and ill-kept and that the residents were essentially unsupervised. Three of the four supervising personnel were themselves convicted criminals having histories which included prostitution, burglary, and malicious wounding. Security measures were practically nonexistent. The alarm system was easily disabled by the inmates, permitting them to enter and leave freely during the night. Windows were unsecured. Spencer's room had a window opening onto a fire escape which gave him unrestricted access to the ground outside. Alcohol and drugs were commonly used in the building. Inmates were permitted to leave during the day, and a log was maintained in which they were to "sign out" and "sign in" so that supervisory personnel could monitor their whereabouts. In practice, the system was not enforced.

On September 19, 1987, Spencer was counted present in the "Hospitality House" during a head count at 3:50 p.m. During a later "head count" between 7:00 and 8:00 p.m., he was unaccounted for. At some time during that night, Spencer broke open a kitchen window in the apartment of Debbie Dudley Davis. * * * He entered the apartment, bound Debbie Davis, beat and raped her, and murdered her by strangulation.

* * *

* * * We [have] adopted the principles expressed in the Restatement (Second) of Torts § 319 (1965), and held that they were controlling. That section provides "One who takes charge of a third person whom he knows or should know to be likely to cause bodily harm to others if not controlled is under a duty to exercise reasonable care to control the third person to prevent him from doing such harm." [An agency "assuming custody" of a convicted felon from the Department of Corrections "necessarily" becomes " '[o]ne who takes charge' " of a third person "within the meaning of Restatement § 319".]

The scope of the defendant's duty is commensurate with the scope of the risk created by its breach. In every case, it is for the court to determine, as a question of law, from all the circumstances, if it is controverted, whether the plaintiff falls within the class of those to whom the defendant owes a duty. If that question is answered affirmatively, it is for the jury, properly instructed, to determine as an issue of fact whether the defendant breached the duty.

* * *

* * * [W]e hold that Debbie Dudley Davis, although not foreseeably at risk as an individual, was a member of a class consisting of those persons [within] the area foreseeably accessible to Spencer during his hours at large on the streets of Richmond on the night of September 19, 1987, as a result of OAR's negligent failure to control him.

* * *

Reversed and Remanded.

MIRAND v. CITY OF NEW YORK, 84 N.Y.2d 44, 614 N.Y.S.2d 372, 637 N.E.2d 263 (1994). Two sisters, students at a public high school, brought suit against the board of education to recover damages for injuries sustained when they were assaulted by a fellow student. *Held*, evidence sustained finding that school was liable for negligent supervision. "Schools are under a duty to adequately supervise the students in their charge and they will be held liable for foreseeable injuries proximately related to the absence of adequate supervision."

The court elaborated: " '[A] teacher owes it to his [or her] charges to exercise such care of them as a parent of ordinary prudence would observe in comparable circumstances.' The duty owed derives from the simple fact that a school, in assuming physical custody and control over its students, effectively takes the place of parents and guardians." In order to establish breach of this duty of supervision, "[a]ctual or constructive notice to the school of prior similar conduct is generally required because, obviously, school personnel cannot be expected to guard against all of the sudden, spontaneous acts that take place among students daily."

COGHLAN v. BETA THETA FRATERNITY, 133 Idaho 388, 987 P.2d 300 (Idaho 1999). Plaintiff, an underage sorority member, fell thirty feet from a fire escape and sustained permanent injuries after becoming intoxicated at parties hosted by other fraternities at the University of Idaho. *Held*, "no special relationship exist[s] between the university and its students in light of the adult status of modern college students and the diminished custodial role of modern universities."

REX v. RUSSELL, [1933] Vict.L.R. 59; noted, 47 Harv.L.Rev. 531. The defendant, although offering no encouragement or persuasion to her to do it, nevertheless stood by and watched his wife drown their two infant children and then herself. *Held,* manslaughter.

STATE v. WRIGHT, 66 N.J. 466, 332 A.2d 606 (1975). Conviction of mother for manslaughter of child who died at age of 6½ months due to defendant's knowing failure to provide the child with food adequate to sustain her life.

CONTROL

"Control" is the last, and perhaps the broadest, of the standard categories of modern exceptions to the classical rule. It may also be the category in which the counter-principle counseling the recognition of affirmative duties whenever they are reasonable and can be workably specified surfaces most aggressively. *L. S. Ayres & Co. v. Hicks, supra* p. 446 is a canonical illustration of both the category and the generality of the principle behind it. The cases that follow are contemporary.

J.S. v. R.T.H.
Supreme Court of New Jersey, 1998.
155 N.J. 330, 714 A.2d 924.

HANDLER, J.

In this case, two young girls, ages 12 and 15, spent substantial periods of recreational time with their neighbor at his horse barn, riding and caring for his horses. Betraying the trust this relationship established, the neighbor, an older man, sexually abused both girls for a period of more than a year. Following the man's conviction and imprisonment for these sexual offenses, the girls, along with their parents, brought this action against the man and his wife for damages, contending that the wife's negligence rendered her, as well as her husband, liable for their injuries. The man conceded liability for both the intentional and negligent injuries that he inflicted on the girls by his sexual abuse. His wife, however, denied that, under the circumstances, she could be found negligent for the girls' injuries. [The trial court agreed with her and entered summary judgment on her behalf. The Appellate Division reversed and the New Jersey Supreme Court granted defendant's petition for certification.] This case presents the issue of whether a wife who suspects or should suspect her husband of actual or prospective sexual abuse of their neighbors' children has any duty of care to prevent such abuse. * * *

* * *

The sexual assaults occurred over a period of a year, from 1991 until John's arrest in November 1992. * * * It was not until November 1992, when her son informed her of John's arrest, that Mary first learned that her husband had had any sexual contact with the girls. Mary was shocked by the news; she had believed her husband and the girls were just friends who spent time together because of the horses. * * * Both at the trial level and on appeal, however, Mary conceded for the purposes of argument that "at all relevant times" she "knew or should have known of her husband's proclivities/propensities."

II

A.

In determining whether a duty is to be imposed, courts must engage in a rather complex analysis that weighs and balances several, related factors, including the nature of the underlying risk of harm, that is, its foreseeability and severity, the opportunity and ability to exercise care to prevent the harm, the comparative interests of, and the relationships between or among, the parties, and, ultimately, based on considerations of public policy and fairness, the societal interest in the proposed solution. *See Hopkins v. Fox & Lazo Realtors,* 132 *N.J.* 426, 439, 625 *A.*2d 1110 (1993).

Foreseeability of the risk of harm is the foundational element in the determination of whether a duty exists. *See Williamson v. Waldman,* 150 *N.J.* 232, 239, 696 *A.*2d 14 (1997). The "[a]bility to foresee injury to a potential plaintiff" is "crucial" in determining whether a duty should be imposed. *Carter Lincoln–Mercury, Inc. v. EMAR Group, Inc.,* 135 *N.J.* 182, 194, 638 *A.*2d 1288 (1994).

Foreseeability as a component of a duty to exercise due care is based on the defendant's knowledge of the risk of injury and is susceptible to objective analysis. *Weinberg v. Dinger,* 106 *N.J.* 469, 484–85, 524 *A.*2d 366 (1987). That knowledge may be an actual awareness of risk. *Carvalho v. Toll Bros. & Developers,* 143 *N.J.* 565, 576–77, 675 *A.*2d 209 (1996). Such knowledge may also be constructive; the defendant may be charged with knowledge if she is "in a position" to "discover the risk of harm." *Id.* at 578, 675 *A.*2d 209. In some cases where the nature of the risk or the extent of harm is difficult to ascertain, foreseeability may require that the defendant have a "special reason to know" that a "particular plaintiff" or "identifiable class of plaintiffs" would likely suffer a "particular type" of injury. *See People*

Express Airlines, Inc. v. Consolidated Rail Corp., 100 *N.J.* 246, 262, 263, 495 *A.*2d 107 (1985). Further, when the risk of harm is that posed by third persons, a plaintiff may be required to prove that defendant was in a position to "know or have reason to know, from past experience, that there [was] a likelihood of conduct on the part of [a] third person[ ]" that was "likely to endanger the safety" of another. *Clohesy v. Food Circus Supermarkets, Inc.*, 149 *N.J.* 496, 507, 694 *A.*2d 1017 (1997) (internal quotation and citation omitted).

* * *

The Court, in its determination whether to impose a duty, must also consider the scope or boundaries of that duty. *See Kelly, supra,* 96 *N.J.* at 552, 476 *A.*2d 1219 (observing that determination of the scope of duty in negligence cases "has traditionally been a function of the judiciary"). * * * When the defendant's actions are "relatively easily corrected" and the harm sought to be prevented is "serious," it is fair to impose a duty. *Kelly, supra,* 96 *N.J.* at 549–50, 476 *A.*2d 1219. In the final analysis, the "reasonableness of action" that constitutes such a duty is "an essentially objective determination to be made on the basis of the material facts" of each case. *Weinberg, supra,* 106 *N.J.* at 484, 524 *A.*2d 366.

B.

Here, a man criminally sexually assaulted unrelated, adolescent children whom he had befriended. The defendant is the spouse of the wrongdoer. The abuse occurred on her own property over an extended period of time. The tortious, assaultive conduct is of a type that is extremely difficult to identify, anticipate, and predict. While these considerations bear on all of the factors that are relevant in determining whether a duty of care should be recognized and imposed on the spouse, they bear materially on the primary element of foreseeability. Although conduct involving sexual abuse is often secretive, clandestine, and furtive, a number of factors are relevant when determining whether or not it is foreseeable to a wife that her husband would sexually abuse a child. These include whether the husband had previously committed sexual offenses against children; the number, date, and nature of those prior offenses; the gender of prior victims; the age of prior victims; where the prior offenses occurred; whether the prior offense was against a stranger or a victim known to the husband; the husband's therapeutic history and regimen; the extent to which the wife encouraged or facilitated her husband's unsupervised contact with the current victim; the presence of physical evidence such as pornographic materials depicting children and the unexplained appearance of children's apparel in the marital home; and the extent to which the victims made inappropriate sexual comments or engaged in age-inappropriate behavior in the husband and wife's presence. *See, e.g., Pamela L. v. Farmer,* 112 *Cal.App.*3d 206, 169 *Cal.Rptr.* 282 (1980) (finding that foreseeability of harm is great where the sexual assault occurred in the marital home, the child victims were expressly invited into the home by the wife, the wife knew that the husband had molested children in the past, and the wife left the children in the unsupervised presence of her husband); *Doe v. Franklin,* 930 *S.W.*2d 921 (Tex.Ct.

App.1996) (ruling that foreseeability requirement is met where wife had knowledge that her husband was a pedophile, wife invited child victim into home, child tried to tell the wife of the molestation, and wife left child in the unsupervised presence of the husband); * * * *Doe v. Poritz,* 142 *N.J.* 1, 15, 662 *A.*2d 367 (1995) (noting that there is a 10–29% recidivism rate for offenders who sexually assault little girls and a 13–40% recidivism rate for offenders who sexually assault little boys).

Moreover, there is some empirical support for the conclusion that sexual abuse of a child, while extremely difficult to detect or anticipate, is a risk that can be foreseen by a spouse. This evidence indicates that an extremely high percentage of child sexual molesters are men, many of whom are married. U.S. Dept. of Justice, Bureau of Justice Statistics, *Child Victimizers: Violent Offenders and Their Victims* 5 (March 1996). The vast majority of child victims are female and many child victims fall prey to an immediate relative or a family acquaintance; most of these sexual assaults are committed either in the offender's home or the victim's home. *Id.* at 10–12. Given those factors, the wife of a sexual abuser of children is in a unique position to observe firsthand telltale signs of sexual abuse. A wife may well be the only person with the kind of knowledge or opportunity to know that a particular person or particular class of persons is being sexually abused or is likely to be abused by her husband. *Cf. Franklin, supra,* 930 *S.W.*2d at 928 (concluding that once wife assumed the task of caring for her child and inviting the child into her home, the wife had a duty not to leave the child alone with her pedophiliac husband); [further citation omitted]

These considerations warrant a standard of foreseeability in this case that is based on "particular knowledge" or "special reason to know" that a "[p]articular plaintiff" or "identifiable class of plaintiffs" would suffer a "particular type" of injury. *See People Express, supra,* 100 *N.J.* at 260, 262, 263, 495 *A.*2d 107; * * * *Tarasoff v. Regents of the Univ. of Cal.,* 17 *Cal.*3d 425, 131 *Cal.Rptr.* 14, 551 *P.*2d 334, 340 (1976) (imposing a duty of reasonable care under the circumstances when defendant has a basis for determining that a readily identifiable victim is likely to be harmed by the actions of a third person). "Particularized foreseeability" in this kind of case will conform the standard of foreseeability to the empirical evidence and common experience that indicate a wife may often have actual knowledge or special reason to know that her husband is abusing or is likely to abuse an identifiable victim and will accommodate the concerns over the inherent difficulties in predicting such furtive behavior. That test of foreseeability will also ensure that the wife is not subject to a broad duty that may expose her to liability to every child whom her husband may threaten and harm. Foreseeability under that definitional standard is neither unrealistic nor unfair.

* * *

The Legislature has dealt comprehensively with the subject of child abuse and has enacted a plethora of statutes designed to prevent the sexual abuse of children. For example, *N.J.S.A.* 9:6–8.10 requires any person having reasonable cause to believe that a child has been subject to abuse to report the abuse immediately to the Division of Youth and Family Services. The duty to report is not limited to professionals, such as doctors, psychologists, and teachers, but is required of every citizen. *State v. Hill*, 232 *N.J.Super.* 353, 356, 556 *A.*2d 1325 (Law Div.1989). Indeed, friends or neighbors are often in the best position to fulfill this statutory duty because they are the people "who frequently hear or observe acts of child abuse." *Id.* at 357, 556 *A.*2d 1325. * * *

It is a disorderly persons offense to fail to report an act of child abuse reasonably believed to have been committed. *N.J.S.A.* 9:6–8.14. * * * Another statute, *N.J.S.A.* 2A:61B–1a(1), declares that a person who stands in loco parentis to a child and knowingly permits or acquiesces in sexual abuse of the child by another person in the household is also guilty of sexual abuse. * * * "Megan's Law," *N.J.S.A.* 2C:7–1 to–11, provides yet more evidence of the State's intolerance of sexual abuse of children. In affirming the constitutionality of the community notification and registration requirements of Megan's Law for convicted sex offenders, this Court recognized the enormous public interest in protecting society from the threat of potential molestation, rape, or murder of women and children. *See Poritz, supra,* 142 *N.J.* at 13, 662 *A.*2d 367.

* * *

Moreover, the societal interest in enhancing marital relationships cannot outweigh the societal interest in protecting children from sexual abuse. The child-abuse reporting statute itself has mandated that balance—it applies to every citizen, including a spouse. *Supra* at 343, 714 *A.*2d at 931. As the Appellate Division here described, "the Legislature's adoption of that statute [*i.e.,* "Megan's Law"] is an expression of New Jersey's strong public policy favoring protection of children over the privacy of an offending adult." 301 *N.J.Super.* at 157, 693 *A.*2d 1191. Thus, "[t]he protective privilege ends where the public peril begins." *Tarasoff, supra,* 131 *Cal.Rptr.* 14, 551 *P.*2d at 347; * * * Thus, while the marital relationship is a genuine concern in this case, it is by no means dispositive.

* * *

* * * Defendant contends that the imposition of a duty to prevent her husband from engaging in sexual abuse of another person would be unfair. She argues that sexual offenses are extremely difficult to combat and that she did not necessarily have the power, the ability, or the opportunity to control her husband and should not be expected or required to police his conduct continuously. However, fairness concerns in these circumstances can be accommodated by a flexible duty of care that requires a spouse, when there is particularized foreseeability of harm of sexual abuse to a child, to take reasonable steps to prevent or warn of the harm. *See Franklin, supra,* 930 *S.W.*2d at 928–29 (holding that "a duty exists to not place a child in a situation in which the risk of sexual abuse is heightened and in which the risk is foreseeable" and that therefore a wife who "knew or should have known of her husband's proclivities, [ ] should have taken steps to ensure that [the grandchild] would not be placed in harm's way or to otherwise

ensure that her husband would not be in a position to act on his tempta-tions"); * * *; *Pamela L., supra,* 169 *Cal.Rptr.* 282 (finding that children who suffered sexual abuse stated valid cause of action against pedophile's wife, where the complaint alleged that the wife knew her husband had molested children in the past, she encouraged and invited the children to be alone with her husband in the family pool when she was at work, and she unreasonably exposed the children to harm); * * * *Tarasoff, supra,* 131 *Cal.Rptr.* 14, 551 *P.*2d at 340 (imposing duty [to warn] when defendant knew that a third person posed a risk of harm to the victim).

C.

Considerations of foreseeability, the comparative interests and relation-ships of the parties, and public policy and fairness support the recognition of a duty of care. Based in large measure on the strong public policy of protecting children from sexual abuse, we conclude that there is a sound, indeed, compelling basis for the imposition of a duty on a wife whose husband poses the threat of sexually victimizing young children.

[Judgment of the Appellate Division reversing summary judgment af-firmed.]

THAPAR v. ZEZULKA, 994 S.W.2d 635 (Tex.1999) *Held*, reinstating summary judgment and reversing Court of Appeals, a mental professional does not have a duty "to warn the appropriate third parties when a patient makes specific threats of harm toward a readily identifiable person." The court relied primarily on a Texas statute, classifying "communications be-tween mental-health 'professional[s]' and their 'patient[s]/client[s]' as confi-dential" and prohibiting mental-health professionals from disclosing patient communications to third parties unless an exception applied. No statutory exception allowed disclosure of patient threats against a third party to the party threatened, although a statutory exception did permit—but did not require—mental health care professionals to disclose such threats to law enforcement authorities.

" * * * We are not faced here with the question of whether a doctor owes a duty to third parties to warn a patient of risks from treatment which may endanger third parties.[2] Instead, we are asked whether a mental-health professional owes a duty to directly warn third parties of a patient's threats.

"The California Supreme Court first recognized a mental-health profes-sional's duty to warn third parties of a patient's threats in the seminal case *Tarasoff v. Regents of University of California.* The court of appeals here cited *Tarasoff* in recognizing a cause of action for Thapar's failure to warn of her patient's threats. But we have never recognized the only underlying duty

---

2. *See Gooden v. Tips,* 651 S.W.2d 364, 365–66 (Tex.App.—Tyler 1983, no writ) (holding doctor owed duty to third party to warn patient not to drive after prescribing the drug Quaalude to patient); *see also Flynn v. Houston Emergi-care, Inc.,* 869 S.W.2d 403, 405–06 (Tex.App.— Houston [1st Dist.] 1994, writ denied) (holding doctor owed no duty to third party to warn patient not to drive after patient was treated for cocaine use because doctor did not create im-pairment that resulted in injury).

upon which such a cause of action could be based—a mental-health professional's duty to warn third parties of a patient's threats.* * * * [W]e decline to adopt a duty to warn now because the confidentiality statute governing mental-health professionals in Texas makes it unwise to recognize such common-law duty.

"We consider legislative enactments that evidence the adoption of a particular public policy significant in determining whether to recognize a new common-law duty. For example, in recognizing the existence of a common-law duty to guard children from sexual abuse, we found persuasive the Legislature's strongly avowed policy to protect children from abuse. The statute expressing this policy, however, makes the reporting of sexual abuse mandatory and makes failure to report child abuse a crime. Further, under the statute, those who report child abuse in good faith are immune from civil and criminal liability. Thus, imposing a common law duty to report was consistent with the legislative scheme governing child abuse.

"The same is not true here. The confidentiality statute here does not make disclosure of threats mandatory nor does it penalize mental-health professionals for not disclosing threats. And, perhaps most significantly, the statute does not shield mental-health professionals from civil liability for disclosing threats in good faith. On the contrary, mental-health professionals make disclosures at their peril. [footnote omitted] Thus, if a common-law duty to warn is imposed, mental-health professionals face a Catch–22. They either disclose a confidential communication that later proves to be an idle threat and incur liability to the patient, or they fail to disclose a confidential communication that later proves to be a truthful threat and incur liability to the victim and the victim's family.

"The confidentiality statute here evidences an intent to leave the decision of whether to disclose confidential information in the hands of the mental-health professional. * * * "

SHEPARD v. REDFORD COMMUNITY HOSPITAL, 151 Mich.App. 242, 390 N.W.2d 239 (1986). Hospital had a physician-patient, and thus a special, relationship with plaintiff's mother and so owed a duty of reasonable care to her minor son, who was a foreseeable potential victim of negligent failure to diagnose her spinal meningitis.

SECTION C.   VARIABLE DUTY: LANDOWNERS

The duties owed by owners and occupiers of land present special problems in part because some of the duties at issue are affirmative duties to act—duties to protect entrants onto one's property from harm at the hands of third parties, for instance. But the presence of affirmative duty issues is not the central reason why duty is an especially prominent issue in this

---

* The *Tarasoff* court applied the Restatement (Second) of Torts § 315 (1965) to the facts. Section 315 states: "There is no duty so to control the conduct of a third person as to prevent him from causing physical harm to another unless (a) a special relation exists between the actor and the third person which imposes a duty upon the actor to control the third person's conduct, or (b) a special relation exists between the actor and the other which gives to the other a right to protection."—Eds.

corner of law (sometimes called "premises liability"). Duty is an especially prominent part of premises liability law because the concepts and categories of the law of real property are available as an alternative to the concepts and categories of tort. The property rights of owners and occupiers might—and historically have—determined the duties that they owe to entrants onto their property.

We have already seen two examples of how property conceptions can displace tort ones. *Union Pacific Railway v. Cappier, supra* p. 442, and *Buch v. Amory Manufacturing, supra* p. 444 frame the question before them as whether the defendant landowners had duties to act because they view the facts before them through the lenses of property law. On the face of it, the landowners in both cases seemed to have acted towards the victims, and quite decisively. In *Cappier*, plaintiff's decedent was on the defendant railway's property and he was injured—run over and mortally wounded—by an instrumentality (a train engine) under its control. In *Buch*, plaintiff was injured while engaged in learning how to work in defendant's factory, and he too was injured by an instrumentality (machinery) under defendant's control. Property conceptions are responsible for casting the cases as affirmative duty ones. The defendants were no more legally responsible for the harms which befell the victims than strangers who happened upon the scenes of the accidents would be, because both plaintiffs were on defendants' property without defendants' permission. Classical doctrine held that trespassers were not owed duties of reasonable care. Legally, therefore, defendants were innocent of responsibility for the harms plaintiffs suffered—even though that harm was inflicted by instrumentalities under defendants' control, and even if that harm might have been averted by defendants' exercise of due care.

The following cases explore the determination of duty in accordance with property conceptions, and the modern contest between this approach and the negligence duty of reasonable care.

BASSO v. MILLER

Court of Appeals of New York, 1976.
40 N.Y.2d 233, 386 N.Y.S.2d 564, 352 N.E.2d 868.

COOKE, Judge.

Ice Caves Mountain, Inc., operates a large scenic park as a tourist attraction on property leased from the Village of Ellenville. During the summer months the premises are open to the public from approximately 8 a.m. until a half hour before dark on the payment of an admission fee. Although the witnesses differed on certain points, the record reveals relevant events of the late afternoon and early evening of September 3, 1972.

In the late afternoon of that September day, Jeffrey Shawcross, a patron, walked off the main trail up the hillside and fell into a 40-foot crevice, where he remained until rescued about four and a half hours later. Another customer, 17-year-old Frederick Coutant, after hearing of the accident, went down into the hamlet of Cragsmoor and told "a couple of people" about it, among them the plaintiff and defendant Miller. These two, riding on Miller's motorcycle, proceeded up to Ice Caves Mountain. Miller drove, plaintiff sat behind as passenger on the single seat, with his arms wrapped around Miller's midriff and his feet on the exhaust pipes. It was still daylight when the two arrived at the entrance. Plaintiff testified that Miller stopped the motorcycle, got off, went into the house where tickets were sold, spoke to the girl on duty, returned and the two, plaintiff and Miller, proceeded by motorcycle through the raised barrier along the mountain drive to the parking lot. After waiting about 45 minutes, plaintiff testified that he received instructions pursuant to which he carried first aid equipment and rope down to the fissure into which Shawcross had fallen. On a second trip, plaintiff testified he carried a stretcher and additional equipment, assisted a nurse and eventually helped carry Shawcross, on the stretcher, to the ambulance. Once the rescue was completed, plaintiff and Miller returned to the motorcycle, resumed the riding position as previously described and, following the road traveled on earlier, left the parking area at what plaintiff estimated to be a speed of 20–30 miles per hour. It was now 9:30 or 10:00 p.m. As the motorcycle approached a curve, plaintiff testified that it hit a series of holes, went out of control, slipped from one side of the road to the other and threw both driver and passenger out onto rocks. Plaintiff testified that he had been a summer resident of Cragsmoor for the past 16 years, had been to Ice Caves Mountain several times, that he had a 1972 season's pass but had been there only once before during that summer.

Defendant William Miller's testimony as to the day's events was similar to that of plaintiff. He also testified to having a season's pass, to making frequent trips up the mountain and to knowing the area "like the back of my hand." Miller related his conversation with Annette Ballentine, the girl on duty in the tollhouse, stating that when he told her that he was going up to help with the rescue, she answered, "Don't. They have enough help." To that Miller testified he responded "something like, 'I am going up anyway. I don't think there is enough help. I could help anyway.'"

Annette Ballentine's recollection of the events differed from that of plaintiff and Miller in that, although the substance of the conversation was the same, she testified that Miller had driven his motorcycle through the open doors and into the gift shop where she was on duty. Both Miller and his passenger remained seated on the cycle during the conversation and, at its end, after her admonition not to go up, Miller backed the motorcycle out of the shop and proceeded through the space in the gate, which she testified was not raised to permit vehicles to pass through, but lowered. This witness also testified that after learning of the Shawcross accident and prior to plaintiff's arrival she had telephoned her boss, Fred Grau, as well as the Ellenville Rescue Squad, the Cragsmoor Fire Department and the State Police. As the summoned rescuers arrived, the witness explained that she pushed the button which raised the gate, permitting them into the premises. Although the practice may not have been always followed, there was testimony that visitors with season passes were required to stop and sign in at the gatehouse.

Fred Grau, president of Ice Caves Mountain, Inc., testified that after learning of the accident he came to the scene to direct the rescue operation but permitted the fire department to take over when the fire chief arrived with approximately 20 men. When Miller drove into the parking lot, Grau told him to move as he, Miller, had placed his cycle in the spot reserved for the ambulance.

Ralph Stedner, chief of the Cragsmoor Volunteer Fire Department, testified that of the 13 men who responded to the emergency, 8 were used and the rest sent back to the firehouse as they were not needed. The witness could recall Grau as the only "civilian" helping and, in response to questions by the court, Stedner testified that he tried to keep all of the volunteer civilians back because even though they wanted to help, they did not know what to do.

While there was additional testimony, the foregoing suffices for this review. The court charged the jury to the effect that the plaintiff's status on the mountain was determinative of the duty of care owed to him by the defendant Ice Caves Mountain. The court described the status and commensurate duties in this fashion:

> With respect to the Ice Caves Mountain, now we get into his status on the mountain. You have three options that you can find. You can find that when he was up on that mountain, he was a trespasser. That is, that he had no right to be there. If you find that he was a trespasser without any right to be on that mountain, then the duty of the people who operated Ice Caves Mountain is not to do any willful or wanton or aggressive act with respect to his safety, and I am telling you now that as a matter of law, if you find that Basso was a trespasser on that night, September 3, 1972, he cannot recover against Ice Caves Mountain * * *

> The second thing that he could have been is equivalent to a guest. That is, that he went up to the mountain to watch what was going on and that against the wishes of Miss Ballentine, under instructions from her superiors and that when he got up there, instead of being thrown out, his presence was accepted as a mere watching, as a mere observing of what was going on. In that case, Ice Caves Mountain had a duty to him which was to make sure that if there were any dangerous conditions existing on the roadway that they should let him know. In other words, they owed him some duty not to let him get harmed because of a dangerous condition which existed on the mountain, to advise him of the conditions that may have caused him harm. That is, if he was a mere guest.

> Your third option is that if he was there for the business of the Ice Caves Mountain * * * there are two ways that he could have been there under the business of Ice Caves Mountain; one is that he was there as a patron; he had a season pass and * * * he could have been up there as an observer under the season pass which entitled him to the use of the roadways or he could have been a rescuer helping in the rescue of Mr. Shawcross, which is the business of Ice Caves Mountain. That is, if somebody gets trapped in a crevice on Ice Caves Mountain, getting him

out of there is the business of Ice Caves Mountain, and anybody who is there in assisting in that rescue is doing it for the business of Ice Caves Mountain and in those two circumstances, whether he was legally there as a patron of Ice Caves Mountain or as a rescuer, then the duty owed to him is a little bit more than for the other two. Then the duty is to act—then the duty is to keep the premises in a reasonably safe condition so as to prevent anybody lawfully on the premises from becoming injured. They were under a duty to exercise reasonable care to keep the premises in a reasonably safe condition for the use of a person such as the plaintiff coming on the premises."

Ice Caves Mountain took exception to the charge as to duty owed to a social guest or, as more frequently denominated, a licensee, claiming it placed too great a duty upon it. Ice Caves contends, and correctly so, that the New York standard has been that as a licensee a plaintiff must take the premises as he finds them, and that the owner thereof is liable only if he is found to have committed affirmative acts of negligence or if a trap existed or there was concealed danger not likely to be discovered. There is only a duty to warn of known dangerous defects which the defendant "should know or suspect that the licensee will not discover himself after a reasonable inspection of the premises."

Based on the charge as given, the jury returned a verdict for plaintiff, on the issue of liability, and made an apportionment whereby 60% of the verdict was to be borne by defendant Miller and 40% by defendant Ice Caves Mountain. Both defendants appealed from the interlocutory judgment of liability and apportionment. Although the Appellate Division unanimously affirmed, it granted both defendants leave to appeal, certifying the following question: "Was the order of this court dated March 12, 1975 properly made?"

While several issues are raised, the one of paramount importance relates to the duty of care owed by the owner or occupier of land to one upon his property. In New York, for long, it has been the status of the plaintiff which has been determinative of the duty and, often, the ascribing of status has been a difficult task. In the instant case, for example, much of the testimony in the nearly 1,000–page record was elicited in order to enable the jury to classify the plaintiff as a trespasser, licensee or invitee. As a further complication, not only did the jury have to weigh and evaluate the differing testimony as to status at any particular time, but also had to determine whether the status of the plaintiff shifted as the afternoon turned to evening. As the trial court explained, under one view of the facts, it was possible for the jury to have labeled plaintiff a trespasser when he entered without permission and against the wishes of Ms. Ballentine, a licensee when seen but not ejected by Mr. Grau, the "boss", in the parking lot, and an invitee when assisting in the rescue. This being so, it remains a curiosity of the law that the duty owed to plaintiff on exit may have been many times greater than that owed him on his entrance, though he and the premises all the while remained the same.

Rather than to demand continued attempts to fit a plaintiff into one of the three rigid categories, the court pauses instead to reflect, to reconsider the necessity for such classification and to state today that the distinctions need no longer be made. Taking a broad view, we note that nearly 20 years have passed since the distinctions between licensees and invitees have been abolished by statute in England (Occupiers' Liability Act [1957], 5 & 6 Eliz. 2, ch. 31) and since the United States Supreme Court in Kermarec v. Compagnie Generale, 358 U.S. 625, 630–631, 79 S.Ct. 406, 3 L.Ed.2d 550, leveled direct criticism at this aspect of tort law. In its determination that such categories have no place in admiralty law, the *Kermarec* court made these cogent comments (pp. 630–631, 79 S.Ct. p. 410): "The distinctions which the common law draws between licensee and invitee were inherited from a culture deeply rooted to the land, a culture which traced many of its standards to a heritage of feudalism. In an effort to do justice in an industrialized urban society, with its complex economic and individual relationships, modern common-law courts have found it necessary to formulate increasingly subtle verbal refinements, to create subclassifications among traditional common-law categories, and to delineate fine gradation in the standards of care which the landowner owes to each. Yet even within a single jurisdiction, the classifications and subclassifications bred by the common law have produced confusion and conflict. As new distinctions have been spawned, older ones have become obscured. Through this semantic morass the common law has moved, unevenly and with hesitation, towards 'imposing on owners and occupiers a single duty of reasonable care in all the circumstances.' "

New York courts are not unmindful of the adoption of the single standard of care in several of our sister States. Beginning with the 1968 California Supreme Court decision in Rowland v. Christian, 69 Cal.2d 108, 70 Cal.Rptr. 97, 443 P.2d 561, we have observed the growing number of well-reasoned decisions abandoning the common-law distinctions and adopting the simple rule of reasonable care under the circumstances. While we have demonstrated our inclination to correlate the duty of care owed plaintiff with the risk of harm reasonably to be perceived regardless of status, and concurrently consider the question of foreseeability, we have not, until today, abandoned the classifications entirely and announced our adherence to the single standard of reasonable care under the circumstances whereby foreseeability shall be a measure of liability. To be sure, this standard of reasonable care should be no different than that applied in the usual negligence action. Contributory and, now, comparative negligence, as well as assumption of the risk, all fit into their respective places, to be invoked when appropriate.

Indeed as the duty was so clearly stated in Smith v. Arbaugh's Rest. [469 F.2d 97]: "A landowner must act as a reasonable man in maintaining his property in a reasonably safe condition in view of all the circumstances, including the likelihood of injury to others, the seriousness of the injury, and the burden of avoiding the risk". Application of the single rule in the instant case exemplifies its good sense, for the duty of keeping the roads of Ice Caves Mountain in repair should not vary with the status of the person who uses them but, rather, with the foreseeability of their use and the possibility of injury resulting therefrom. While the likelihood of a plaintiff's presence had been an implicit consideration in the determination of status and the duty commensurate therewith, it now becomes a primary independent factor in determining foreseeability and the duty of the owner or occupier will vary with the likelihood of plaintiff's presence at the particular time and place of the injury. While status is no longer determinative, considerations of who plaintiff is and what his purpose is upon the land are factors which, if known, may be included in arriving at what would be reasonable care under the circumstances.

Of course, before it becomes appropriate for the jury to consider all such questions, the court, as it would in the usual negligence action, must make the threshold determination as to whether the plaintiff, by introducing adequate evidence on each element, has made out a case sufficient in law to support a favorable jury verdict. Only in those cases where there arises a real question as to the landowner's negligence should the jury be permitted to proceed. In all others, where proof of any essential element falls short, the case should go no further. While the rigid status classifications are to be dispensed with, the function of the court and the standard of proof remain the same.

The failure of the court to properly instruct the jury on the duty owed to a licensee coupled with the jury's rendering of a general verdict, the latter making it impossible for this court to determine whether the erroneous charge was significant in the determination, mandates a reversal and new trial as to liability, wherein the standard enunciated today should be applied.

* * *

BREITEL, Chief Judge (concurring).

I concur in the result reached by the majority but for different reasons.

Abandoning all the rules governing liability of a possessor to one injured on his property, rules evolved progressively in the common-law process over the past 200 years, the court substitutes an amorphous "single standard" of "reasonable care under the circumstances" * * *. While still vulnerable to criticism and deserving of modification to adapt to social and economic change, the rules in this State have produced both progressive evolution and a predictive stability. Finally, and perhaps most important, the majority would delegate to the jury the responsibility to determine the applicable social policy, thus abdicating the judicial role where not controlled by legislative primacy in determining public policy.

Under traditional common-law analysis, in actions based on negligence, a possessor's duty to one on his property is measured by the status of that person, namely, by the circumstances under which he came or remained on the property. The injured person is classified as trespasser, licensee or invitee, that is, how did he come there or what was he doing there—burglar, social guest, or one on the possessor's business, or the like.

* * *

As Prosser has noted, the three categories "make out, as a general pattern, a rough sliding scale, by which, as the legal status of the visitor improves, the possessor of the land owes him more of an obligation of protection" (Prosser, [4th ed.], § 58, at p. 357). The sliding scale thus reflects the foreseeability of injuries to others, the obligation of the injured person to foresee the precautions likely to be taken for his benefit, and the varying economic burdens justifiably placed on the possessor to protect those on his property against harm. Because they are elaborations of rules of law they are given to the fact finders to guide them in applying the social policy embraced in the rules to the facts as they find them.

The roots of the common-law principles largely antedate the development of modern negligence law. In nineteenth century England and America, when the economy was largely agrarian and land formed the principal basis of wealth, it was considered socially desirable policy to allow a landowner to use and exploit his land as he saw fit, without need for vigilance or protection for those who came upon the property without privilege or consent. Thus, rigid rules then virtually immunizing the landowner from liability for injuries sustained on his property were formulated to effectuate that policy.

As the economy shifted from an agrarian to an industrial base and personalty replaced realty as the principal basis of wealth, a corresponding change in social policy, one less favorable to the landowner or possessor occurred. No longer does the policy of unrestricted freedom to use one's land, which has usually meant no more than a desire to be free of the burden and expense of taking precautions, inevitably outweigh considerations of human safety.

The law, of course, has not been insensitive to this shift in social policy. Instead, the courts, through the common-law process, have progressively struck a better balance between the competing social policies. This has been done on a case-by-case basis by eliminating the common-law distinctions in the case of children, by broadening the more favored categories to include persons who in the past would not have been included, or by expanding the concept of a "trap" and thereby increasing the possessor's liability for injuries caused by dangerous conditions on his land.

Thus, for example, the "child trespasser" doctrine has been developed to impose, in appropriate circumstances, liability upon a possessor for injuries sustained by children on his property regardless of whether they are trespassers. The "economic benefit" theory which predicated invitee status upon the economic benefit the possessor may derive from the visitor's presence, has been supplanted by the "public invitation" theory, which confers invitee status upon those who come upon the possessor's property at the encouragement of the possessor. In some States, social guests have been elevated from the licensee to the invitee category. Public employees, such as firemen and policemen, have been placed in a sui generis class, to whom is owed a duty of reasonable care to keep in a safe condition those parts of the premises which are used as the ordinary means of access, and to warn such employees, known to be on the property, of unforeseeably dangerous conditions * * *.

* * *

* * * The criticism [of the common-law rules] is partly justified. But it must be seen for what it is—a logomachy over labels and not a disagreement with underlying policy. Thus, the critics have recognized that a person's "status", that is, the purpose for which he has come upon the property, is a significant element in determining foreseeability, and therefore the liability of a possessor (Rowland v. Christian, 69 Cal.2d 108, 117–118, 70 Cal.Rptr. 97, 443 P.2d 561, supra). Other elements, such as the closeness of the connection between the injury and the defendant's conduct, the moral blame attached to the defendant's conduct, and the policy of preventing future harm, despite assertion to the contrary, are in fact subsumed in the status of the party and the duty owed to one of that status.

The "single standard", appealingly simple, is actually deceptively so. It has been observed that abolition of all developed rules and principles in favor of a broad "single" standard of care is an illusory reform. Abolition, it is said, will engender only an evolution of a new set of rules under the "single" standard (see Payne, Occupiers' Liability Act, 21 Mod.L.Rev. 359, 362). If this be true, the single standard, like any monistic methodology, will hardly be a simplification but an enigma masked in an elusive generalization, so broad, that there are no articulated exceptions. The solution offered is that the jury will know and will decide.

Of course, candor compels recognition of the propensity of juries, motivated by sympathy, to allow injured plaintiffs, especially children, to recover even when the law would seem to suggest an opposite result. The "single standard" provides hospitable ground for the play of jury *ad hoc* promulgation of "rules" of law, social policy, and sometimes humane but ungoverned and ungovernable sympathy.

The abolition of the common-law rules regarding deliberate adult trespassers is a good example. Surely a landowner is not obligated, even under the single standard, to make his property safe for adult trespassers entering upon the property to pursue criminal ends. It is no answer to say that the jury will take care of the problem by denying recovery to such a trespasser as a matter of fact. The role of the jury in our system is to find facts and not to make the law. The lawmaking function is the province of the Legislature and the courts. * * *

* * * It may be that further reform in this State is needed. Thus, for example, in the proper cases, many if not all, of the distinctions between licensees and invitees could be modified or should be eliminated.

* * * Indeed, some jurisdictions have placed social guests within the category of invitees * * * In the proper case, therefore, the rule treating invited guests as licensees deserves re-examination.

But such a re-evaluation in the instant case is unnecessary. The jury could properly have found that Basso was a public invitee in that he presented himself to the rescuers and was enlisted in aid of their rescue operation. In such circumstances, the property owner owed Basso a duty to keep the premises reasonably safe for his use. Thus, it was a question of fact, properly resolvable by the jury, whether the road was maintained in a reasonably safe condition. * * *

However, as the majority has stated, the charge, on any view, with respect to the duty owed to a licensee was incorrect, and thus the defendant Ice Caves Mountain, Inc., is entitled to a new trial.

Accordingly, I concur in the result. * * *

PINNELL v. BATES. 838 So.2d 198 (Miss.2002). Plaintiff—a "social guest" in defendant's home, and therefore a licensee under Mississippi's categories—broke her leg and a finger when she fell from the home's concrete steps onto its concrete porch, leaving the house at 9:00 in the evening. The trial court granted homeowner's motion for summary judgment, and plaintiff appealed. *Held*, by the Mississippi Supreme Court, that: (1) common law distinction between licensees and invitees would not be abolished, but (2) genuine issue of material fact regarding whether visitor was an invitee precluded summary judgment.

"We decline to accept Pinnell's invitation to abolish the legal distinctions between licensees and invitees. Eliminating the distinction curtails the right of unbridled use of private property. The concept that "a man's home is his castle" is the shield of protection for the owner of the humblest one-room shack as well as the owner of a large estate.

"Homeowners [defined in a footnote to include "all possessors of land, including those who occupy, lease or own land."] would be exposed to greater liability and would have to shoulder a heavier burden. Worse still, a jury would have the power to decide whether a homeowner has arranged the living room furniture or maintained his yard in a reasonable manner, purchased the correct 'non-slip' flooring or contracted with the correct construction crew to repair the home.

"The distinction between a business visitor, heretofore considered an invitee, and a social visitor, heretofore considered to be a licensee, would be abolished, and the duty owed to a social guest would be identical to the duty owed to a business invitee. Eliminating homeowners' protection from liability for injuries sustained by social guests would impose on the home-owners the same standard and duty a commercial enterprise such as Wal-Mart owes to its customers. However, in reality, there are enormous differences between businesses and residences:

> Businesses extend invitations to prospective customers, clients, etc., to come to their places of business for commercial purposes. Persons so coming are, for the most part, personally unknown to those extending the invitation. It is anticipated these invitees will roam freely about the public areas of businesses, and a part of the cost of doing business is providing reasonably safe premises. These establishments are, ordinari-

ly, professionally designed, built, and equipped. Safety and convenience account for much of their sterile uniformity.

Residences are designed to please the homeowners and meet their needs and wants. A residence reflects the homeowners' individuality and is equipped and operated by the homeowners according to how they want to live. We live in the age of the do-it-yourselfer. Few homes would meet OSHA's standards, and few individuals would desire to live in such a home. Modern businesses do not have polished hardwood floors, throw rugs, extension cords, rough flagstone paths, stairways without handrails, unsupervised small children, toys on the floor, pets and all the clutter of living—homes do. There are good reasons behind the old adage that most accidents occur in the home.

Jones v. Hansen, 254 Kan. 499, 867 P.2d 303, 317–18 (1994) (McFarland, J., dissenting)."

McRae, P.J., dissented, stating that *thirteen* states "have abolished the classifications altogether" while *another fourteen* have either abrogated the licensee/invitee distinction or implemented "the reasonableness standard while while maintaining the trespasser classification."**

"Pinnell should not be classified as either an invitee or a licensee in this case. It is evident that with the passage of time the feudal status classifications have caused much confusion throughout the legal community, especially in light of our comparative negligence standard. * * * Therefore, I would abolish the archaic classifications this Court created and adopt the reasonable person in like circumstances standard which we apply in any other negligence case. * * *

"We require people to behave as reasonably prudent people in almost every other area of tort law. It makes sense to require the same conduct in premises liability. * * * "

BOYETTE v. TRANS WORLD AIRLINES, INC., 954 S.W.2d 350 (Mo.App. 1997). Plaintiff's decedent (Rutherford), who had consumed at least two drinks immediately before his plane flight and six drinks during the flight, disembarked and, when he reached the gate, commandeered an electric golf cart and began driving around the gate area. With airport security personnel in hot pursuit, Rutherford abandoned the cart and fled on foot. He attempted to hide in a trash chute, but slid down the chute and was crushed and killed by the trash compactor into which it fed. *Held*, summary judgment for defendants, *affirmed*.

Under Missouri law, Defendant owed Rutherford the " 'highest degree of care to safely transport its passengers and protect them while in transit,' " but that duty was discharged once "Rutherford safely reached the airport." Thereafter, he was a trespasser, owed no duty to rescue under Missouri law. "Trespassers take the premises, for better or for worse, as they find them,

---

** The majority counted differently. It claimed (1) "that the states are at best evenly divided on whether to continue to recognize the common law distinctions;" (2) that some of the states which had abolished the categories "still look to the traditional status distinctions in deciding cases;" and (3) discerned a "a reversal of "the trend" of states to abandon the distinctions between invitees and licensees."

assuming the risk of injury from their condition, 'the owner being liable only for hidden dangers intentionally placed to injure them or for any willful, illegal force used against them.' [Cite omitted]. This is the rule whether the trespasser is known or unknown. *Politte v. Union Electric Co.*, 899 S.W.2d 590, 592 (Mo.App. E.D.1995). Thus, only if the City put the trash compactor on the premises intentionally to injure Rutherford * * * would a duty arise.''

THE RETREAT OF CONTRACT

Premises liability has expanded substantially over the course of the past thirty or forty years, and not all of this expansion is attributable to the displacement of the categories by the tort duty of reasonable care in many jurisdictions. The demise of contractual limitations on tort liability has also played a prominent role in this expansion. In classical tort law, the reach of duties of care was often restricted by the doctrine of privity of contract. When contract was a live alternative to tort—as it is not in stranger accidents but is in many other settings—privity of contract restricts tort duties to parties with whom the would-be bearer of the duty has contractual relations. The doctrine of privity of contract reflects classical doctrine's preference for contract over tort, just as the categories reflect classical doctrine's preference for property over tort. In the context of real property, the doctrine of privity of contract operated to restrict the duties of owners and occupiers sharply: Owners of real property who leased the property to tenants who then operated business on the premises were not liable to entrants onto that property for injuries occasioned by the owner's failure to maintain the property in a reasonably safe condition.

PUTNAM v. STOUT, 38 N.Y.2d 607, 381 N.Y.S.2d 848, 345 N.E.2d 319 (1976). A supermarket customer sued the lessor of the supermarket and parking lot for injuries when she fell because her shoe caught in a driveway hole. The lease included the lessor's covenant to repair. Judgment below for plaintiff. *Held*: affirmed.

'' * * * Historically, the majority rule has been that upon the landlord's breach of the covenant to repair, the tenant obtained only an action in contract for the breach. It followed that third persons not parties to the contract had no right of action whatever against the landlord, and were relegated to recovery against the tenant, or not at all. The rule was sustained on the rationale that the tenant, as occupier of the land, had control of its safety and if he so desired, could protect himself by excluding people from his property or by discriminating against those whom he believed would not look out for their own safety whereas the landlord had neither control nor possession, and his covenant to repair did not reserve either to him. * * *

"These rationales no longer retain the vitality they may once have had. * * * As the Supreme Court of New Jersey had occasion to comment in the course of overturning its privity of contract precedent in covenant-to-repair cases: 'Under modern social conditions, the precept of privity is sterile and no longer serves the interests of justice. And this apart from other influences, for the obvious reason that it is utterly unrealistic to say that when the head of a family leases premises and bargains for an agreement on the part of the lessor to maintain them in good repair, the parties do not recognize that the pact is in the interest and for the protection of members of his household and others who enter thereon in his right. It is likewise inconsistent with reality to suggest that the parties do not accept their mutual engagements with a full awareness that if the necessary repairs are not made, the safety of such persons will be endangered.' (Faber v. Creswick, 31 N.J. 234, 240, 156 A.2d 252, 255.)

" * * * [T]he Restatement (Second) of Torts has formulated the following rule:

> A lessor of land is subject to liability for physical harm caused to his lessee and others upon the land with the consent of the lessee or his sublessee by a condition of disrepair existing before or arising after the lessee has taken possession if
>
> (a) the lessor, as such, has contracted by a covenant in the lease or otherwise to keep the land in repair, and
>
> (b) the disrepair creates an unreasonable risk to persons upon the land which the performance of the lessor's agreement would have prevented, and
>
> (c) the lessor fails to exercise reasonable care to perform his contract. (Restatement, Torts 2d, § 357.)

"We * * * adopt the Restatement formulation as the law rule to be applied. * * * First, the lessor has agreed, for a consideration, to keep the premises in repair; secondly, the likelihood that the landlord's promise to make repairs will induce the tenant to forego repair efforts which he otherwise might have made; thirdly, the lessor retains a reversionary interest in the land and by his contract may be regarded as retaining and assuming the responsibility of keeping his premises in safe condition; finally, various social policy factors must be considered: (a) tenants may often be financially unable to make repairs; (b) their possession is for a limited term and thus the incentive to make repairs is significantly less than that of a landlord; and (c) in return for his pecuniary benefit from the relationship, the landlord could properly be expected to assume certain obligations with respect to the safety of the others. * * *

"Applying the formulation to this case, it is clear that the landlord is also liable to plaintiff. It is undisputed, of course, that plaintiff was on the land with the permission of Grand Union, that Steigler covenanted to keep the driveway in repair, that the disrepair created an unreasonable risk of harm to plaintiff, which performance of the covenant would have prevented, and that since Steigler had not even attempted to repair the driveway, he failed to exercise reasonable care to perform his contract. We conclude, therefore, that the [lessor is] liable to plaintiff."

"OPEN AND OBVIOUS" RISKS

"Open and obvious" risks present special problems for modern premises liability doctrine. Classical doctrine held that, if a risk was "open and obvious" the owner or occupier of the property had no duty to take further precautions against it. The openness and obviousness of the risk sufficed to warn potential victims of the hazard at issue, shifting the burden of precaution to the entrant onto the property. Whether the doctrine should be retained or discarded by modern negligence law is a topic of dispute. Some courts insists that the doctrine survives untouched by both the adoption of a single standard of care and comparative negligence; other courts insist that these two developments require the abandonment of the doctrine.

———

SCHINDLER v. GALE'S SUPERIOR SUPERMARKET, INC., 142 Ohio App.3d 146, 754 N.E.2d 298 (2001). Plaintiff was injured when she "tripped over a metal rail affixed to the sidewalk for the purpose of keeping shopping carts orderly," as she approached the entrance to defendant's supermarket "to shop for groceries as she had done on numerous occasions." Defendant moved for summary judgment on the ground that the metal rail was "open and obvious" and that the supermarket therefore owed no further duty of care. In support of its motion, defendant included excerpts from plaintiff's deposition conceding that she did not see the rail, but would have, had she looked down while walking. The trial court granted defendant's motion, without opinion. *Held, reversed and remanded.*

"Under the open-and-obvious doctrine, an owner or occupier of property owes no duty to warn invitees of hazardous conditions that are open and obvious. *Simmers v. Bentley Constr. Co.* (1992), 64 Ohio St.3d 642, 644, 597 N.E.2d 504, 506. The rationale behind this doctrine is that the open-and-obvious nature of the hazard itself serves as a warning. Thus, the owner or occupier may reasonably expect that persons entering the premises will discover those dangers and take appropriate measures to protect themselves. *Simmers,* 64 Ohio St.3d at 644, 597 N.E.2d at 506.

"The application of comparative negligence principles, on the other hand, requires the factfinder to apportion the percentage of each party's negligence that proximately caused the plaintiff's damages. See R.C. 2315.19(A)(2). Ordinarily, this is an issue best determined by the jury unless the evidence is so compelling that reasonable minds can reach but one conclusion. In such a case, summary judgment is appropriate if the only conclusion a reasonable trier of fact could reach is that the plaintiff was over fifty percent negligent so as to bar recovery under comparative negligence principles."

* * *

" * * * [W]hen analyzed in terms of the duty owed, I find the [open and obvious] doctrine questionable because it rests on a legal fiction * * *.

To say that a claim is barred because the defendant owed the plaintiff no duty to warn him of the danger is to disregard an express duty on the part of the premises owner to maintain the premises in a reasonably safe condition. [citation omitted] With this in mind, this court is of the opinion that the time has come to analyze the openness and obviousness of a hazard not in terms of the duty owed but rather in terms of causation."

"The issue of a plaintiff's negligence in disregarding or failing to perceive an obvious hazard seems particularly suited to consideration under a comparative negligence standard. * * * Summary judgment, therefore, should be granted * * * on the grounds that the hazard was open and obvious [only] when the plaintiff's negligence in disregarding the hazard is deemed greater than that of the defendant's negligence in creating the hazard. * * * "

" * * * In this case, appellant testified at her deposition that she was walking towards the entrance when she tripped over the metal rail. There was no evidence to support that the rail was covered in any way so as to obstruct her view but rather that she just did not see the metal rail because she was looking straight ahead and not down at the ground. Had she done so, she admits, she would have seen the rail and possibly avoided injury. Appellant's duty to use care, however, does not require her to constantly look downward. See *Grossnickle v. Germantown* (1965), 3 Ohio St.2d 96, 32 O.O.2d 65, 209 N.E.2d 442, paragraph two of the syllabus; see, also, *Texler* [*v. D.O. Summers Cleaners & Shirt Laundry Co.*], 81 Ohio St.3d at 681, 693 N.E.2d at 274–275 [Ohio Supreme Court, 1998]. Visibility of the metal rail, while important, is only one of several attendant circumstances to be considered [in apportioning fault between plaintiff and defendant]."

ARMSTRONG v. BEST BUY CO., INC., 2001 WL 1581568 (Ohio App. 9 Dist. 2001) (not reported in N.E.2d). "Armstrong filed a negligence suit against Best Buy for injuries he sustained when he tripped over a shopping cart corral guardrail in the entranceway to the store. Best Buy moved for summary judgment, asserting that it is not liable for Armstrong's injuries because the guardrail was an open and obvious danger. Finding that the guardrail 'was open and obvious to anyone walking into the building[,]' the trial court granted summary judgment in favor of Best Buy." *Held, affirmed.*

"Armstrong has argued that the open and obvious doctrine is no longer viable as an absolute bar to recovery * * *. The doctrine, he has contended, has been replaced by comparative negligence. In support, Armstrong has cited the Eighth Appellate District's decision in *Schindler v. Gale's Superior Supermarket Inc.* (2001), 142 Ohio App.3d 146, in which the court, interpreting *Texler*, determined that 'the time has come to analyze the openness and obviousness of a hazard not in terms of the duty owed but rather in terms of causation.' *Id.* at 153."

"We reject the Eighth District's interpretation of *Texler*. * * * [A] careful reading of *Texler* reveals that the issue of whether the open and obvious doctrine operated to negate an element of the defendant's duty was not before the court; the narrow issue before the court was the plaintiff's contributory negligence, which concerns the proximate cause component of negligence, not the duty element. * * * "

* * *

Since the Ohio Supreme Court's decision in *Texler*, this Court has continued to analyze the open and obvious doctrine under the duty element of negligence. [citations omitted] Furthermore, this Court finds that the doctrine is not inconsistent with the principles of comparative negligence. This is because the analyses are separate: the open and obvious doctrine relates to the duty element, which must be established before the comparative negligence issue is ever reached. [citations omitted] * * * "

KLOPP v. WACKENHUT CORP., 113 N.M. 153, 824 P.2d 293 (1992). " * * * If we were to accept that no duty is owed to invitees foreseeably injured only through contributory negligence, we would vitiate the ameliorating effect of comparative fault. While we fully understand that, absent a breach of duty, in logic there can be no fault to compare, the fallacy in that argument is that it is premised not on the foreseeable behavior of business visitors, but on the foreseeable behavior of reasonably careful visitors. On that premise, the negligence of a particular visitor is preclusive if outside the ambit of the foreseeable behavior of reasonably careful visitors.

"Simply by making hazards obvious to reasonably prudent persons, the occupier of premises cannot avoid liability to a business visitor for injuries caused by dangers that otherwise may be made safe through reasonable means. A risk is not made reasonable simply because it is made open and obvious to persons exercising ordinary care. * * * [W]e think that some degree of negligence on the part of all persons is foreseeable, just like the inquisitive propensities of children, and thus, should be taken into account by the occupant in the exercise of ordinary care."

THE DUTY TO PROTECT

Entrants onto real property may be attacked by third persons who are also on the premises. Landlord-tenant and invitor-invitee are frequently cited "special relationships," which trigger affirmative duties. The existence and scope of a duty to protect entrants onto their land from harm at the hands of other entrants, persists as an issue—and may well become more salient—when the categories are abandoned.

———

SMITH V. LAGOW, 642 N.W.2d 187 (S.D.2002). Tenant lost her key and was subsequently stabbed to death in her apartment by paid killers, hired by a man who blamed her for his marital troubles. *Held*, summary judgment for landlord *reversed*. "If landlords insist on the exclusive right to change locks, then they should have some duty to change those locks when they are no longer effective against foreseeable criminal activity."

KNOLL v. BOARD OF REGENTS, 258 Neb. 1, 601 N.W.2d 757 (1999). During pledge week, plaintiff was abducted from a room on the University of Nebraska campus by members of a fraternity, handcuffed to a radiator and made to drink 15 shots of liquor and 3 to 6 beers. After becoming ill, he was taken to a restroom on the third floor and handcuffed to the toilet. He broke loose and fell from a third floor window while attempting to escape. *Held*, "the University owes a landowner-invitee duty to students to take reasonable steps to protect against foreseeable acts of hazing, including student abduction on the University's property, and the harm that naturally flows therefrom."

STEWART v. ALDRICH, 788 A.2d 603 (Me.2002). *Held*, landlords are not responsible for tenant's dangerous dogs, which attacked a seven-year-old child, even if landlords were aware of the danger. Landlords will be liable only if they retain "control" over the premises, similar to the control they retain over the common areas of an apartment builiding. "We have never held, however, that the landlord retains control over the premises merely because he has the power to coerce tenants through the power of eviction or nonrenewal of a lease."

———

DUDAS v. GLENWOOD GOLF CLUB, INC., 261 Va. 133, 540 S.E.2d 129 (2001). "In Wright [v. Webb, 234 Va. 527, 533, 362 S.E.2d 919, 922 (1987)], we said that '[o]rdinarily, the owner or possessor of land is under no duty to protect invitees from assaults by third parties while the invitee is upon the premises ... [unless] there is a special relationship between [the] possessor of land and his invitee giving rise to a duty to protect the invitee from such assaults.' We recognized that one such special relationship is that of business invitor and its business invitee. However, we declined to find inherent in that bare relationship an absolute duty of the business invitor to protect its invitees from criminal assaults by unknown third parties on its premises. We observed that:

> In ordinary circumstances, it would be difficult to anticipate when, where, and how a criminal might attack a business invitee. Experience demonstrates that the most effective deterrent to criminal acts of violence is the posting of a security force in the area of potential assaults. In most cases, that cost would be prohibitive. Where invitor and invitee are both innocent victims of assaultive criminals, it is unfair to place that burden on the invitor.

Accordingly, we limited the duty owed by the business invitor to protect its invitee against criminal assaults to those instances where it 'knows that criminal assaults against persons are occurring, or are about to occur, on the premises which indicate an *imminent probability of harm* to [its] invitee.' (Emphasis added [by the *Dudas* court, citation omitted]).

* * *

" * * * Our decision in *Wright* fashioned a narrow exception to the general rule [of no duty]. In applying that exception, careful analysis of particular factual patterns * * * must be used to avoid permitting the narrow exception to swallow the general rule. Dudas' contention in the present case would [swallow the rule]. * * * Dudas' theory of liability is premised solely upon the foreseeability of the danger of injury to a business invitee.

" * * * in *Thompson v. Skate America, Inc.*, 261 Va. 121, ___, 540 S.E.2d 123, 127 (2001) (decided today), we have recognized that when a business invitor has knowledge that a particular individual has a history of violent, criminal behavior while on its premises, and thereby poses an imminent probability of harm to an invitee, the business invitor has a duty of care to protect its other invitee from assault by that person."

CLOHESY v. FOOD CIRCUS SUPERMARKETS, 694 A.2d 1017 (N.J.1997). "This Court has previously held that business owners and landlords have a duty to protect patrons and tenants from foreseeable criminal acts of third parties occurring on their premises. * * * Consequently, the focus on the duty question in the present case is primarily on foreseeability." To "guard against making a shopkeeper liable for *all* crimes occurring on the shopkeeper's premises," prior New Jersey decisions have adopted a test of foreseeability tantamount to the "totality of the circumstances" test:

> Under the totality of the circumstances approach, the actual knowledge of criminal acts on the property and constructive notice based on the total circumstances are relevant to foreseeability. As in this case, foreseeability can stem from prior criminal acts that are lesser in degree than the one committed against a plaintiff. It can also arise from prior criminal acts that did not occur on the defendant's property, but instead occurred in close proximity to the defendant's premises. In determining that a criminal assault was foreseeable in the parking lot, we have considered all the criminal acts that have occurred on Foodtown's property and those that occurred in close proximity to its property; the property's size and location; the absence of any security; the architectural design of the building in relation to the area of the parking lot where the crime occurred; the size of the parking lot; the type of business defendant operates; the nature and circumstances of nearby businesses; and the increasing level of crime in the general neighborhood.

TRESPASSERS

Concurring in *Basso*, Judge Breitel drew attention to the problems of extending the single standard of care to trespassers, or at least to felony criminal ones. Trespassers come in a wide variety of configurations: child and adult, innocent, recreational, and felony criminal, at the least. Jurisdictions which have adopted the single standard must decide if *all* of these kinds of trespassers receive the benefits of the single standard. Jurisdictions which retain the categories must decide if *any* of these trespassers should receive the benefit of a duty of care.

CALIFORNIA STATUTE ON FELONY TRESPASSERS
(CA CIVIL CODE § 847)

§ 847. Immunity from liability; injuries or death occurring on property during or after commission of certain felonies

(a) An owner, including, but not limited to, a public entity, as defined in Section 811.2 of the Government Code, of any estate or any other interest in real property, whether possessory or nonpossessory, shall not be liable to any person for any injury or death that occurs upon that property during the course of or after the commission of any of the felonies set forth in subdivision (b) by the injured or deceased person.

(b) The felonies to which the provisions of this section apply are the following: (1) Murder or voluntary manslaughter; (2) mayhem; (3) rape; (4) sodomy by force, violence, duress, menace, or threat of great bodily harm; (5) oral copulation by force, violence, duress, menace, or threat of great bodily harm; (6) lewd acts on a child under the age of 14 years; (7) any felony punishable by death or imprisonment in the state prison for life; (8) any other felony in which the defendant inflicts great bodily injury on any person, other than an accomplice, or any felony in which the defendant uses a firearm; (9) attempted murder; (10) assault with intent to commit rape or robbery; (11) assault with a deadly weapon or instrument on a peace officer; (12) assault by a life prisoner on a noninmate; (13) assault with a deadly weapon by an inmate; (14) arson; (15) exploding a destructive device or any explosive with intent to injure; (16) exploding a destructive device or any explosive causing great bodily injury; (17) exploding a destructive device or any explosive with intent to murder; (18) burglary; (19) robbery; (20) kidnapping; (21) taking of a hostage by an inmate of a state prison; (22) any felony in which the defendant personally used dangerous or deadly weapon; (23) selling, furnishing, administering, or providing heroin, cocaine, or phencyclidine (PCP) to a minor, (24) grand theft as defined in Sections 487 and 487a of the Penal Code; and (25) any attempt to commit a crime listed in this subdivision other than an assault.

(c) The limitation on liability conferred by this section arises at the moment the injured or deceased person commences the felony or attempted felony and extends to the moment the injured or deceased person is no longer upon the property.

(d) The limitation on liability conferred by this section applies only when the injured or deceased person's conduct in furtherance of the commission of a felony specified in subdivision (b) proximately or legally causes the injury or death.

* * *

(f) This section does not limit the liability of an owner or an owner;s agent which otherwise exists for willful, wanton, or criminal conduct, or for willful or malicious failure to guard or warn against a dangerous condition, use, structure, or activity.

MOODY v. MANNY'S AUTO REPAIR, 110 Nev. 320, 871 P.2d 935 (1994). "Plaintiff, an on-duty police officer observed a vehicle proceed through a red traffic signal. To avoid traffic in front of him and promptly give chase, Moody turned his motorcycle into the entrance of a parking lot leased by Manny's and owned by Peress. Moody collided with a steel cable strung across the entrance to the parking lot. Moody alleges that the cable was unlit and unmarked." *Held,* henceforth, owners and occupiers of land, "must exercise reasonable care not to subject others to an unreasonable risk of harm." "In the instant case, Moody's recovery should depend on the reasonableness of the use of the cable barrier under the circumstances rather than the status of Moody as a trespasser, licensee, or invitee at the time of the injury."

In support of its decision the court quoted Rowland v. Christian: " 'A man's life or limb does not become less worthy of compensation under the law because he has come upon the land of another without permission or with permission but without a business purpose. Reasonable people do not ordinarily vary their conduct depending upon such matters * * *.' "

PRIDGEN v. BOSTON HOUSING AUTHORITY, 364 Mass. 696, 308 N.E.2d 467, 70 A.L.R.3d 1106 (1974). Action against housing authority and others by boy and his mother seeking damages for injuries boy sustained. He and friends entered the elevator, climbed up through an escape hatch in the ceiling, and got onto the platform roof of the elevator. One of the friends caused the car to move up and down by pressing a button located on top of the car. The plaintiff slipped from the roof into the elevator shaft and was caught on metal brackets. The elevator moved down and struck him, causing severe injuries. There was evidence that, after the mother had learned of the boy's position in the elevator shaft, she had asked an employee of the authority for help, and had not received it. She then heard the elevator move and her son scream. *Held,* jury finding of negligence against the housing authority sustained.

"This is not a case of an intruder who is cut during the act of pushing his fist through the glass in a door which the owner has no duty to open for him; rather, we are dealing with one who is injured after his original trespass is effectively frustrated by virtual physical entrapment in a position of peril. We hold that as to the latter trespasser the owner owes a duty to exercise reasonable care to prevent injury or further injury to him, including, if necessary, the duty to take reasonable affirmative action. We reject any notion that this is a duty which can never be violated by nonfeasance. The owner in such a situation is required to act if, in the same circumstances, an ordinary and reasonably prudent person would have acted, and, in doing so, he must exercise the degree and standard of care which would have been exercised by an ordinary and reasonably prudent person in those circumstances.

"The rule which we have stated is in part a recognition by the law of the ever changing concepts of each individual's rights and duties in relation to all other members of our society, and it reflects current standards of concern for the personal safety and well being of each individual. It is also consistent with a number of judicial precedents, both in this Commonwealth and elsewhere, indicating a trend toward the imposition of a single duty of reasonable care by owners or occupiers of premises to all persons coming thereon.''

———

BENNETT v. STANLEY, 92 Ohio St.3d 35, 748 N.E.2d 41 (2001). Estate and survivors of a mother and her five-year-old son who had drowned in their next door neighbor's pool—the mother, apparently, in an attempt to rescue her child—brought suit against the neighbor. When the neighbors— the Stanleys—had purchased the property the pool was surrounded by a brick wall and a fence. The Stanleys had drained the pool, removed the tarp that had covered it, and taken down the fence which surrounded the pool on two sides. Rainwater subsequently filled the pool to a depth of six feet and the pool became "pond-like," containing "tadpoles and frogs." Its sides, which had no ladders, were "slimy with algae." The trial court granted defendant's motion for summary judgment, and the intermediate appellate court affirmed: The victims were either trespassers, in which case they were owed only a duty "to refrain from wanton and willful misconduct" or, if the mother entered the property in an attempt to rescue her child, she was a licensee, "who is owed no greater duty of care than a trespasser."

Held, reversed and remanded. Although Ohio has "consistently held that children have a special status in tort law;" that the "amount of care required to discharge a duty owed to a child of tender years is necessarily greater than that required to discharge a duty owed to an adult under the same circumstances;" and "has even accorded special protection to child trespassers by adopting the 'dangerous instrumentality' doctrine;" it "is one of only three states that have not either created a special duty for trespassing children or done away with distinctions of duty based upon a person's status as an invitee, licensee, or trespasser." Henceforth, Ohio will apply the doctrine of "attractive nuisance" as "set forth in Restatement of the Law 2d, Torts (1965), Section 339:

A possessor of land is subject to liability for physical harm to children trespassing thereon caused by an artificial condition upon land if:

      (a) the place where the condition exists is one upon which the possessor knows or has reason to know that children are likely to trespass, and

      (b) the condition is one of which the possessor knows or has reason to know and which he realizes or should realize will involve an unreasonable risk of death or serious bodily harm to such children, and

      (c) the children because of their youth do not discover the condition or realize the risk involved in intermeddling with it or in coming within the area made dangerous by it, and

      (d) the utility to the possessor of maintaining the condition and the burden of eliminating the danger are slight as compared with the risk to children involved, and

(e) the possessor fails to exercise reasonable care to eliminate the danger or otherwise to protect the children."

* * *

"Adopting the attractive nuisance doctrine would be merely an incremental change in Ohio law, not out of line with the law that has developed over time. It is an appropriate evolution of the common law. While the present case is by no means a guaranteed winner for the plaintiff, it does present a factual scenario that would allow a jury to consider whether the elements of the cause of action have been fulfilled.

* * *

"The Restatement's version of the attractive nuisance doctrine balances society's interest in protecting children with the rights of landowners to enjoy their property. Even when a landowner is found to have an attractive nuisance on his or her land, the landowner is left merely with the burden of acting with ordinary care. A landowner does not automatically become liable for any injury a child trespasser may suffer on that land."

TEXAS UTILITIES ELEC. CO. v. TIMMONS, 947 S.W.2d 191 (Tex.1997). Plaintiff's decedent, a 14-year-old boy, was killed when a lethal jolt of electricity arced into his body from the lines of the electrical tower he had climbed and was now descending. The victim was less intelligent than the average teenager of his age and was a poor student, even in the special education classes which he had attended for three years. He was aware of the general dangers associated with touching power lines but neither he, nor anyone else with him the night of his death, was aware of the phenomenon of electrical arcing.*** While climbing, he had avoided touching the power lines. *Held*, summary judgment for defendant reinstated. As a matter of law, a 90–foot electrical transmission tower is not an attractive nuisance to a 14-year-old boy. He "knew that it was dangerous to touch the wires" even if he "did not know that the current would jump from the wire to his body" if he got too close to it.

"We are also of the opinion that the injured boy was not of such tender age as to bring him within the attractive nuisance doctrine. * * * We are of the opinion that he was not so immature in judgment, experience, and intelligence as to be overpowered by childish impulses and led to believe, by the mere attractiveness of the tower, that he had a right to play on the tower and that he could do so without fear of danger."

Gonzales and Spector, JJ, dissenting, would have held "that the attractive-nuisance doctrine applies to this case and that Timmons has raised fact issues about whether Texas Utilities Electric Company breached its duty of reasonable care to the child." Their dissent observed that, "[s]ince 1922,

---

*** The opinion quoted the Texas Commission of Appeals commenting on the state of public knowledge about the dangers of electrical arcing in 1992:

The public knows that it is dangerous to touch a live wire, but very few know that there exists danger of death from this powerful current by near approach to the wire so charged, without actually coming in contact with the wire. Only those who are engaged in the business, and those who have stood beside some inanimate form whose scorched and burned flesh bears mute evidence to its tremendous power, know this.

Texas courts have applied the attractive-nuisance doctrine to a fourteen-year-old child injured by electrical arcing while climbing an electric transmission tower" and quoted from a prior decision by The Texas Commission of Appeals, which had been approved by the Texas Supreme Court:

> The public knows that it is dangerous to touch a live wire, but very few know that there exists danger of death from this powerful current by near approach to the wire so charged, without actually coming in contact with the wire. Only those who are engaged in the business, and those who have stood beside some inanimate form whose scorched and burned flesh bears mute evidence to its tremendous power, know this.

SECTION D.   IMMUNITIES

The materials in Section D address circumstances where special immunities block or limit the operation of otherwise applicable tort duties. Some of these immunities pertain to the exercise of governmental power. These have their origin in pre-modern conceptions of the absolute power of the sovereign, and find their modern justification in policies pertaining to the proper division of authority among legislatures, administrative agencies and courts with respect to supervising the provision of public services, such as police protection. Others pertain to "private" relationships or institutions, such as spousal parent-child relationships and charitable institutions. Here the question is whether the law should place certain relationships, or institutions, beyond the reach of tort law and, if so, to what extent.

FRIEDMAN v. STATE OF NEW YORK, ET AL.
Court of Appeals of New York, 1986.
67 N.Y.2d 271, 502 N.Y.S.2d 669, 493 N.E.2d 893.

[Three personal injury accidents were consolidated for purposes of appeal. All three involved "crossover" automobile accidents, "in which a vehicle crossed the median dividing opposing lanes of traffic." In all three cases, a "common issue [was] presented: whether the state breached its duty to alleviate a known hazardous highway condition."

Dena Friedman's car was traveling east on an elevated roadway when it was hit by a car cutting into her lane. The collision forced Friedman across the median and into westbound traffic, where her car was struck again and pushed over a curb and into a 50 foot deep ravine. Five years earlier, the New York Department of Transportation had decided, after studying the roadway, that a median barrier should be constructed. Prior to Friedman's accident, no steps had been taken to implement this decision. Under the Court of Claims Act, the case was tried before a judge who decided in Friedman's favor. The Appellate Division affirmed the judgment.

Cataldo's and Muller's accidents both took place on the Tappan Zee Bridge, a three mile long six-lane suspension bridge crossing the Hudson River north of New York City. Both Cataldo's and Muller's accidents were caused by cars crossing over into their lanes, and they, too, argued that their accidents would have been prevented by the installation of a median barrier.

However, a New York State Thruway Authority (the "Thruway Authority") study in 1962 had concluded that "while barriers eliminate most crossover accidents, they tend to increase other types of accidents because they often bounce cars back into the flow of traffic, causing rear end and 'pile on' collisions when traffic is heavy in one direction." Another study by the Thruway Authority conducted in 1972 "reiterated the fears expressed ten years ago" about "bounce-back" collisions, and expressed further fears that a median divider would also increase "rear end collisions resulting from disabled cars that would have to remain in the traffic lanes because of the loss of the median as a refuge." In 1973 a third study concluded that a partial barrier should be constructed.

Cataldo was injured in 1972. The Appellate Division reversed a judgment in her favor on the ground that, at the time of her accident, the Thruway Authority "was acting pursuant to a reasonable public safety plan." Muller was injured in 1977, more than three years after the Thruway Authority concluded that a partial median barrier should be constructed. The Appellate Division nonetheless reversed a judgment in favor of Muller, ruling "that the delay in installing the barrier once the decision to do so was made was not unreasonable."]

* * *

We now affirm the orders of the Appellate Division in Friedman and Cataldo, and reverse the order appealed from in Muller.

It has long been held that a municipality " 'owe[s] to the public the absolute duty of keeping its streets in a reasonably safe condition' " * * * While this duty is nondelegable, it is measured by the courts with consideration given to the proper limits on intrusion into the municipality's planning and decision-making functions. Thus, in the field of traffic design engineering, the State is accorded a qualified immunity from liability arising out of a highway planning decision. In the seminal Weiss case, we recognized that "[t]o accept a jury's verdict as to the reasonableness and safety of a plan of governmental services and prefer it over the judgment of the governmental body which originally considered and passed on the matter would be to obstruct normal governmental operations and to place in inexpert hands what the Legislature has seen fit to entrust to experts" * * *. The Weiss court examined a municipality's decision to design a traffic light with a four-second interval between changing signals, and concluded that there was no indication that "due care was not exercised in the preparation of the design or that no reasonable official could have adopted it." * * * We went on to note that "something more than a mere choice between conflicting opinions of experts is required before the State or one of its subdivisions may be charged with a failure to discharge its duty to plan highways for the safety of the traveling public." * * *

Under this doctrine of qualified immunity, a governmental body may be held liable when its study of a traffic condition is plainly inadequate or there is no reasonable basis for its traffic plan. Once the State is made aware of a dangerous traffic condition it must undertake reasonable * * * study thereof with an eye toward alleviating the danger * * *. Moreover, after the State implements a traffic plan it is "under a continuing duty to review its plan in the light of its actual operation." * * *

In Cataldo and Muller it is clear that no liability can flow from the Authority's initial decision in 1962 not to construct median barriers on the tangent section of the bridge. This decision was consistent with the opinions that were expressed by experts in the Authority's employ and was a rational response to valid safety concerns. The claimants argue, however, that by failing to reevaluate the barrier issue between 1962 and 1972 the Authority breached its "continuing duty to review its plan in the light of its actual operation" * * *. They contend that this inactivity was inexcusable given the changes in the state of the art of highway design occurring during that time. While this position might have some force if urged with respect to an accident occurring during the 10–year period of inactivity, such is not the case at bar. Here, both accidents occurred after the Authority reviewed its plan in 1972 and again reached the conclusion that the public's safety would be better served by not installing median barriers.

Claimants argue, however, that the 1972 engineer's reports upon which the Authority's decision was made were the product of inadequate study of the issue * * *. The gravamen of this assertion is that the reports failed to consider the history of the west curve barrier since its installation in 1962 and attached inordinate importance to operational difficulties that would be incurred while downplaying safety concerns to an inappropriate degree. * * * Appellants would have us examine the criteria that were considered by the State's professional staff, emphasize factors allegedly overlooked, and, with the benefit of hindsight, rule that the studies were inadequate as a matter of law. We decline this invitation, for to do so, as the Appellate Division correctly concluded, "would constitute the type of judgment substitution that Weiss v. Fote prohibits" * * *.

Because the Authority's decisions prior to the Cataldo accident in 1973 not to install median barriers were based on reasonable public safety considerations the Appellate Division properly dismissed the claim in that case. The Authority fulfilled its duty under Weiss by studying the dangerous condition, determining that design changes were not advisable and later reaching the same conclusion upon reevaluation of its decision.

In Friedman and Muller, however, a further basis upon which the defendants may be held liable is tendered: that once a decision has been reached to go forward with a plan intended to remedy a dangerous condition, liability may result from a failure to effectuate the plan within a reasonable period of time. Although this precise question has not been specifically addressed by this court, several Appellate Division decisions have held that when the State is made aware of a dangerous highway condition and does not take action to remedy it, the State can be held liable for resulting injuries * * *. This conclusion flows logically from the premise that the State has a nondelegable duty to maintain its roads in a reasonably safe condition * * * and it applies even if the design in question complied with reasonable safety standards at the time of construction. * * * When * * * analysis of a hazardous condition by the municipality results in the formulation of a remedial plan, an unjustifiable delay in implementing the plan constitutes a breach of the municipality's duty to the public just as surely as if it had totally failed to study the known condition in the first instance.

In Friedman, there is evidence to support the affirmed finding that the State unreasonably delayed its remedial action.

Similarly, in Muller, we conclude that the record evidence more nearly comports with the trial court's finding that the three-year delay between the Authority's decision in 1974 to construct median barriers and the Muller accident in 1977 was unreasonable.

* * *

We conclude, therefore, that the order of the Appellate Division in Cataldo should be affirmed, with costs. The order appealed from in Muller should be reversed, with costs, and the judgment of the Court of Claims reinstated. In Friedman, the order of the Appellate Division should be affirmed, with costs, and the certified question answered in the affirmative.

———

HICKS v. STATE, 88 N.M. 588, 544 P.2d 1153 (1975). *Held,* "[c]ommon law sovereign immunity may no longer be interposed as a defense by the State, or any of its political subdivisions, in tort actions." The doctrine "is one of common law, judicially created." New Mexico joins "the growing number of states which have judicially abolished it." According to an appendix to the opinion, thirty-three states had generally (most of these states) or partially abolished governmental immunity. Eight other states had abolished or waived immunity where there was insurance coverage. Eleven of the abolitions had been by judicial decision.

"The original justification for the doctrine of sovereign immunity was the archaic view that 'the sovereign can do no wrong.' It is hardly necessary for this court to spend time to refute this feudalistic contention. * * * The argument has been presented that the elimination of sovereign immunity will result in an intolerable burden upon the State. We believe it is safe to say that adequate insurance can be secured to eliminate that burden in a satisfactory manner. In addition, it would appear that placing the financial burden upon the State, which is able to distribute its losses throughout the populace, is more just and equitable than forcing the individual who is injured to bear the entire burden alone."

NIESE v. CITY OF ALEXANDRIA, 264 Va. 230, 564 S.E.2d 127 (2002). Plaintiff alleged that she was raped twice by a police officer employed by the City of Alexandria—the second time after she had reported the first rape to the city. The trial court granted the city's motion to dismiss plaintiff's complaint. *Held, affirmed.* A city is immune from liability for intentional torts committed by an employee during the performance of a governmental function.

"[T]he doctrine of sovereign immunity is 'alive and well' in Virginia."
Messina v. Burden, 228 Va. 301, 307, 321 S.E.2d 657, 660 (1984). It is well
established that the doctrine of sovereign immunity protects municipalities
from tort liability arising from the exercise of governmental functions.
Hoggard v. City of Richmond, 172 Va. 145, 147–48, 200 S.E. 610, 611
(1939). As we explained in *Hoggard:*

> [A] municipality is clothed with two-fold functions; one governmental,
> and the other private or proprietary. In the performance of a govern-
> mental function, the municipality acts as an agency of the state to
> enable it to better govern that portion of its people residing within its
> corporate limits. To this end there is delegated to, or imposed upon, a
> municipality, by the charter of its creation, powers and duties to be
> performed exclusively for the public. In the exercise of these govern-
> mental powers a municipal corporation is held to be exempt from
> liability for its failure to exercise them, and for the exercise of them in a
> negligent or improper manner. This immunity is based on the theory
> that the sovereign can not [sic] be sued without its consent, and that a
> designated agency of the sovereign is likewise immune."

Plaintiff urged the court to adopt an exception to the rule of sovereign
immunity for the tort of negligent retention, as it "did with respect to the
doctrine of charitable immunity for the tort of negligent hiring." *See J. v.
Victory Tabernacle Baptist Church,* 236 Va. 206, 210, 372 S.E.2d 391, 394
(1988) (holding that the independent tort of negligent hiring "operates as
an exception to the charitable immunity of religious institutions"). In
Messina, 228 Va. at 307–08, 321 S.E.2d at 660, we explained the purpose
behind sovereign immunity as follows:

> One of the most often repeated explanations for the rule of state
> immunity from suits in tort is the necessity to protect the public purse.
> However, protection of the public purse is but one of several purposes
> for the rule.... [S]overeign immunity is a privilege of sovereignty and
> ... without the doctrine there would exist inconvenience and danger to
> the public in the form of officials being fearful and unwilling to carry
> out their public duties.... [I]f the sovereign could be sued at the
> instance of every citizen the State could be 'controlled in the use and
> disposition of the means required for the proper administration of the
> government.'

*241 (Internal citations omitted). The same purposes do not underlie the
doctrine of charitable immunity and we decline to create an exception to the
protection afforded by sovereign immunity for the independent tort of
negligent retention."

IMMUNITY OF "PUBLIC OFFICERS"

A possible source of compensation for the victim of governmental
activity is a claim against an individual who was acting for the government,
as distinguished from a claim against the government itself. Even if governmental immunity exists, the victim often has a cause of action against the

individual wrongdoer though he cannot recover against the government. Here again the victim encounters an immunity. When recognized, the immunity of public officers from liability for harming others in the performance of their duties is supposed to serve the purpose of encouraging fearless and independent public service, motivated by the public interest. Judges, legislators and high executives of government have such immunity, and in varying degrees immunity is extended to many other groups of governmental personnel. A distinction is often made between "discretionary" and "ministerial" functions, immunity extending only to the former. E.g., Mathis v. Nelson, 79 Ga.App. 639, 54 S.E.2d 710 (1949). A further distinction between "misfeasance" and "nonfeasance" is used in a few jurisdictions, no liability being imposed for inaction when this distinction is invoked. E.g., Moynihan v. Todd, 188 Mass. 301, 74 N.E. 367, 108 Am.St.Rep. 473 (1905).

FEDERAL TORT CLAIMS ACT

(Sections below are from Title 28, U.S.C.A.)

§ 1346. United States as Defendant

(b) Subject to the provisions of chapter 171 of this title, the district courts, together with the United States District Court for the District of the Canal Zone and the District Court of the Virgin Islands, shall have exclusive jurisdiction of civil actions on claims against the United States, for money damages, accruing on and after January 1, 1945, for injury or loss of property, or personal injury or death caused by the negligent or wrongful act or omission of any employee of the Government while acting within the scope of his office or employment, under circumstances where the United States, if a private person, would be liable to the claimant in accordance with the law of the place where the act or omission occurred.

§ 2402. [Actions Against the United States Under Section 1346(b) Shall Be Tried by the Court Without a Jury]

Chapter 171, § 2674: The United States shall be liable, respecting the provisions of this title relating to tort claims, in the same manner and to the same extent as a private individual under like circumstances, but shall not be liable for interest prior to judgment or for punitive damages. * * *

§ 2680. Exceptions

The provisions of this chapter and section 1346(b) of this title shall not apply to

(a) Any claim based upon an act or omission of an employee of the Government, exercising due care, in the execution of a statute or regulation, whether or not such statute or regulation be valid, or based upon the exercise or performance or the failure to exercise or perform a discretionary function or duty on the part of a federal agency or an employee of the Government, whether or not the discretion involved be abused.

(b) Any claim arising out of the loss, miscarriage, or negligent transmission of letters or postal matter. * * *

(h) Any claim arising out of assault, battery, false imprisonment, false arrest, malicious prosecution, abuse of process, libel, slander, misrepresentation, deceit, or interference with contract rights: Provided, That, with regard to acts or omissions of investigative or law enforcement officers of the United States Government, the provisions of this chapter and section 1346(b) of this title shall apply to any claim arising, on or after the date of the enactment of this proviso, out of assault, battery, false imprisonment, false arrest, abuse of process, or malicious prosecution. For the purpose of this subsection, "investigative or law enforcement officer" means any officer of the United States who is empowered by law to execute searches, to seize evidence, or to make arrests for violations of Federal law.

C.R.S. ET AL. v. UNITED STATES OF AMERICA
United States Court of Appeals, Eighth Circuit, 1993.
11 F.3d 791.

MAGILL, Circuit Judge.

D.B.S., N.A.S., and their minor child C.R.S.**** (plaintiffs) brought this suit under the Federal Tort Claims Act (FTCA), 28 U.S.C. §§ 1346(b), 2671–2680 (1988), alleging that they all contracted AIDS as a result of the federal government's negligence in providing D.B.S. with contaminated blood when he underwent transfusions at the Martin Army Community Hospital (MACH) in Fort Benning, Georgia, while a member of the Minnesota National Guard. Plaintiffs appeal from the district court's order granting defendant's motion for summary judgment. 820 F.Supp. 449. For the reasons set forth below, we affirm the district court's order.

In August 1983, D.B.S. was ordered to go to Fort Benning for basic training. While in training, D.B.S. required emergency medical care for an intestinal condition. He underwent surgery and blood transfusions at MACH in response to the condition. After recovering from his surgery, D.B.S. completed the training and returned to his home in Minnesota in December 1983. In November 1984, he married N.A.S. and they had three children, including C.R.S., who was born in June 1987.

In late 1987, the Minnesota National Guard discharged D.B.S. In early 1989, all three plaintiffs discovered that they had tested positive for the presence of the human immunodeficiency virus (HIV) after undergoing blood tests. In the summer of 1992, Donor 3903, one of nine donors whose blood MACH had used in D.B.S.'s transfusions, also tested HIV positive.

* * *

Plaintiffs brought suit in the United States District Court for the District of Minnesota in 1990 after four government agencies rejected their administrative claims. They asserted two negligence claims: (1) that the military was negligent in adopting the FDA/AABB [American Association of Blood Banks]

**** Plaintiff C.R.S. died on June 26, 1993.

blood donor screening procedures in 1983, which they allege were unreasonable in the military context, and (2) that the military was negligent in later failing to warn D.B.S. of the risk that he had received contaminated blood at MACH. * * * The government asserted [that] the discretionary function exception to the FTCA, 28 U.S.C. § 2680(a) (1988), barred the claims. The district court granted this motion, finding that § 2680(a) barred all claims. Plaintiffs then filed this appeal.

* * *

Congress waived the sovereign immunity of the United States by enacting the FTCA, under which the federal government is liable for certain torts its agents commit in the course of their employment. See 28 U.S.C. § 2674 (1988). The FTCA, however, does not provide a blanket waiver, but rather retains the government's immunity from suit through several exceptions. One such exception is the discretionary function exception, which prohibits suits "based upon the exercise or performance or the failure to exercise or perform a discretionary function or duty on the part of a federal agency or an employee of the Government, whether or not the discretion involved be abused." *Id.* § 2680(a).

The Supreme Court has announced a two-part test for determining when the discretionary function exception applies. The first requirement is that the conduct at issue indeed be discretionary, that is, it must "involve [ ] an element of judgment or choice." Berkovitz v. United States, 486 U.S. 531, 536, 108 S.Ct. 1954, 1958, 100 L.Ed.2d 531 (1988). Agency decisions exercising delegated authority from Congress to establish programs and policies in implementing the general provisions of a regulatory statute, for example, involve one type of judgment that the exception protects. Decisions made at the operational level, as well as decisions made at the policy-planning level, can involve the exercise of protected discretion. Moreover, "the fact that determinations are made at a relatively low level does not prevent the applicability of the exception." Judgment or choice is absent "when a federal statute, regulation, or policy specifically prescribes a course of action for an employee to follow" because then "the employee has no rightful option but to adhere to the directive." Berkovitz, 486 U.S. at 536, 108 S.Ct. at 1958–59.

The exception's second requirement is that the judgment at issue be "of the kind that the discretionary function exception was designed to shield." *Id.* Because the exception's purpose is to prevent "judicial 'second-guessing' " of government decisions based on public policy considerations, it protects only those judgments "grounded in social, economic, and political policy." A decision, however, need not involve conscious consideration of policy factors by the government agent. The focus of the inquiry, rather, is "on the nature of the actions taken and whether they are susceptible to policy analysis."

Plaintiffs' first claim is that the MBPO [Military Blood Program Office] was negligent in its failure to screen blood donors adequately for HIV. They claim that the defendant's decision to adopt the civilian screening procedures of the FDA and the AABB was unreasonable because of special circumstances prevailing in the military. The FDA/AABB procedures, for instance, relied on donors in groups at high risk for AIDS voluntarily to defer from giving blood, a system which plaintiffs argue was unlikely to work in an environment like the military which punishes those who engage in high-risk behavior such as homosexual contact and drug abuse. The defendant, they allege, should have designed its own more stringent procedures to address the threat of infected blood in light of these special circumstances. In short, plaintiffs challenge only the government's decision, not its implementation of this decision.

Applying the Supreme Court's two-part test, we find that the defendant's decision to adopt civilian screening procedures was a protected exercise of judgment within the discretionary function exception. First, the decision was discretionary because it involved the exercise of judgment and choice. * * * To be sure, Directive 6480.5 directed the MBPO to "develop . . . policies" concerning blood "collection, procurement, processing, storage, distribution, and management." * * * The directive, however, vested the MBPO with broad discretion to choose the type of screening procedures it deemed appropriate, leaving even the choice of how to go about making this decision to the MBPO. * * *

* * *

Moreover, the defendant's decision regarding screening procedures meets the second part of the Supreme Court's test because it was susceptible to a balancing of social, economic, and political policy factors. How to screen those donating blood the military is to use in its hospitals implicates a host of complex policy issues, ranging from the need to keep costs in check given the budget constraints under which government operates to the need to ensure that the blood supply is safe and plentiful. Moreover, the complicated public health issues surrounding AIDS were compounded here because at the time the decision to adopt FDA/AABB screening procedures was made, the medical community still had imperfect knowledge regarding many aspects of the disease. In short, the issue of what screening procedures to adopt is precisely the type of policy-bound decision that Congress intended to insulate from judicial scrutiny through the discretionary function exception.

Plaintiffs' second claim is that the government was negligent in failing to warn D.B.S. of the risk that he had received contaminated blood during his 1983 transfusions. They claim that once the laboratory test for HIV became available in 1985, defendant should have alerted those who had previously undergone transfusions in military hospitals of the possibility they had become infected. Such a warning, they assert, could have prevented transmission of AIDS from D.B.S. to his wife and child.

Our analysis of this claim parallels that which we used for the screening claim. The issue again is whether the defendant is entitled to summary judgment because the government's conduct is protected by the discretionary function exception. Thus, the first question is whether the defendant's failure to warn was discretionary, that is, whether the conduct involved judgment or choice that had not been removed by statute or regulation.

Under Berkovitz, an agency policy strips government employees of discretion when it "specifically prescribes a course of action for an employee to follow." 486 U.S. at 536, 108 S.Ct. at 1958. Indeed, to remove discretion, the policy must constitute a "specific mandatory directive." *Id.* at 544, 108 S.Ct. at 1963.

We conclude that the [applicable] Guidelines [issued by the Army Surgeon General] were not a specific mandatory directive removing discretion from defendant regarding whether to notify people like D.B.S. [Because the pertinent provisions "lacked clarity and specificity" the guidelines "did not remove discretion from Army employees."] * * *

* * *

Although they contained "mandatory" language, the Guidelines had broad and confusing provisions subject to wildly varying interpretations. Far from "specifically prescrib[ing] a course of action," Berkovitz, 486 U.S. at 536, 108 S.Ct. at 1958, or creating "clear duties incumbent upon the governmental actors," Kennewick Irrigation Dist., 880 F.2d at 1026, the Guidelines at best left all relevant details to the discretion of government employees. At worst, the policy did not by its terms require the Army to do anything as to people in D.B.S.'s position. Because the policy was unclear and insufficiently specific, the Army retained discretion whether to identify and warn contacts and persons at risk. Thus, we hold that the Guidelines were not a "specific mandatory directive" requiring defendant to notify D.B.S. of the risk that he had received infected blood. Berkovitz, 486 U.S. at 544, 108 S.Ct. at 1963.

* * *

We hold that § 2680(a) bars both of plaintiffs' claims. We therefore affirm the district court's order granting summary judgment in favor of defendant.

JOHN R. GIBSON, Circuit Judge, concurring in part and dissenting in part.

I agree with the court that appellants' claim that the MBPO negligently failed to screen blood donors for HIV is barred by the discretionary function exception. I part company with the court's conclusion, however, that appellants' failure to warn claim is also barred by the discretionary function exception.

* * *

The court's interpretation of the Guidelines creates ambiguity when none exists. The court adopts an interpretation of the Guidelines that is not even argued by the military. * * *

* * *

The court also makes much of the fact that the precise details of identification and notification are not set forth in the Guidelines. Of course, the regulation or policy must set forth clearly and specifically what the government employee must do, but neither the Supreme Court nor this court have required that the underlying details of the required conduct be set forth in precise detail. * * * Indeed almost all conduct, including mandated conduct, can be broken down at some level into discretionary details.

* * *

There is no doubt that the government's initial decision regarding whether to notify certain people about possible blood contamination is a decision susceptible to policy analysis. * * * Thus, any claim challenging the decision to issue a warning is barred by the discretionary function exception. * * * Nevertheless, once the Army decided to identify and warn high-risk individuals, the policy analysis ceased. * * * The court confuses the distinction between the policy decision and the implementation of the policy decision. The court, in essence, concludes that once the initial policy decision is protected by the discretionary function exception, all acts that follow in implementing that decision are also protected. This is the very rationale the Supreme Court rejected in Berkovitz. * * *

For these reasons I reject the application of the discretionary function exception, and would remand for trial on the merits.

————

INDIAN TOWING CO. v. UNITED STATES, 350 U.S. 61, 76 S.Ct. 122, 100 L.Ed. 48 (1955). Action by a barge charterer and others for damages sustained when a tug went aground, allegedly because Coast Guard personnel, in maintaining a lighthouse near the mouth of the Mississippi, were negligent in failing to check the electrical system and to repair the light or give notice that it was not functioning. *Held*, for plaintiff. "[I]t is hornbook tort law that one who undertakes to warn the public of danger and thereby induces reliance must perform his 'good samaritan' task in a careful manner."

LAIRD v. NELMS, 406 U.S. 797, 92 S.Ct. 1899, 32 L.Ed.2d 499 (1972). The Federal Tort Claims Act authorizes lawsuits against the United States to recover damages for injury "caused by the negligent or wrongful act or omission of any employee of the Government." In this suit involving property damage from a sonic boom created by military aircraft, the Supreme Court (per Rehnquist, J.) held that the statutory language excludes "strict liability of any sort." Accordingly tort suits against the federal government cannot be based "solely on the ultrahazardous nature of an activity undertaken by the Government." Justice Stewart wrote in dissent:

"The rule announced by the Court today seems to me contrary to the whole policy of the Tort Claims Act. * * * Nothing in the language or the legislative history of the Act compels such a result, and we should not lightly conclude that Congress intended to create a situation so much at odds with common sense and the basic rationale of the Act. We recognized that rationale in [Rayonier Inc. v. United States, 352 U.S. 315, 77 S.Ct. 374, 1 L.Ed.2d 354 (1957)], a case involving negligence by employees of the United States in controlling a forest fire:

"Congress was aware that when losses * * * are charged against the public treasury they are in effect spread among all those who contribute financially to the support of the Government and the resulting burden on each taxpayer is relatively slight. But when the entire burden falls on the injured party it may leave him destitute or grievously harmed. Congress could, and apparently did, decide that this would be unfair when the public as a whole benefits from the services performed by Government employees. 352 U.S., at 320, 77 S.Ct., at 377.

ALLEN v. UNITED STATES, 527 F.Supp. 476 (D.Utah 1981), *rev'd*, 816 F.2d 1417 (10th Cir.1987). Nearly 1,000 persons sued under the Tort Claims Act for injuries allegedly sustained as a result of the Government's open-air testing of nuclear weapons at a Nevada test site from 1951–1962. The Government moved to dismiss, relying in part on the discretionary function exception of § 2680(a). The district court denied the motion, stating it would not consider that exception prior to a full trial on the merits, and entered a judgment of liability to plaintiffs in ten of the twenty-four bellwether cases which it tried, the basic issue being causation-in-fact. 588 F.Supp. 247 (1984). The court of appeals reversed, holding that the Atomic Energy Commission, in planning and conducting the program related to open-air testing of atomic bombs, was making policy judgments of the kind within the discretionary function exception. Since decisions at lower levels were also within the exception, it was irrelevant whether the Commission and its employees were negligent in failing to protect the public adequately. All challenged action was immune from suit.

NON–JUDICIAL REMEDIES FOR TORTS OF THE UNITED STATES

28 U.S.C.A. § 2672, part of the Tort Claims Act, provides for administrative adjustment of negligence claims against the United States, provided that awards or settlements exceeding $25,000 require the approval of the Attorney General. Section 2675 gives a claimant the right to bring suit without being prejudiced by an administrative disposition with which he is dissatisfied. By several other Acts, administrative adjustment of claims is provided for independently of the Tort Claims Act, and the annual volume of such claims is substantial. Moreover, many persons unable to obtain compensation through the courts and administrative agencies seek relief from Congress by private claim bill. The volume of such requests is so great that a study reveals a body of decisional principles employed in their disposition. The custom of granting relief by private bill in certain types of cases goes far toward doing away with some of the exceptions written into the Tort Claims Act.

PIERCE v. YAKIMA VALLEY MEMORIAL HOSPITAL ASSOCIATION

Supreme Court of Washington, en Banc, 1953.
43 Wn.2d 162, 260 P.2d 765.

HAMLEY, J. This appeal presents a single question, namely: Where a paying patient of a charitable, non profit hospital sustains injuries by reason of the negligence of a nurse, may such patient recover damages from the hospital?

The alleged negligence consisted of the act of a hospital nurse in injecting a foreign substance into plaintiff's left arm, causing pain and permanent injury. It was not alleged that defendant failed to exercise due care in the selection or retention of the nurse, or that it was guilty of what has been termed "administrative negligence," such as the failure to furnish proper equipment.

The trial court sustained a demurrer to the complaint. * * *

* * *

The almost unanimous view expressed in the recent decisions of our sister states is that, in so far as the rule of immunity was ever justified because of the need of financial encouragement and protection changed conditions have rendered the rule no longer necessary.

In the Haynes case, [Haynes v. Presbyterian Hospital Ass'n 241 Iowa 1269, 45 N.W.2d 151 (1950)] this recognition of a fundamental change in the conditions which prompted formulation of the immunity rule is expressed in these words:

> No doubt, at the outset of the theory, the need for charity in the way of treatment of the suffering, was urgent and the general good of society demanded encouragement thereof. At that time hospitals, being the particular so-called charity which we have before us, were relatively few in number and were created and conducted solely by funds donated by public spirited people. Their doors were open to all alike, irrespective of race, color, creed or ability to pay. There was little, if any, paternal care granted by the state. The granting of immunity from liability for the negligence of their employees may have been proper as a basis for encouraging such charity.

> Today, the situation is vastly different. The business of the hospitals of today has grown into an enormous one. They own and hold large assets, much of it tax free by statute, and employ many persons. The state has become paternal to an astonishing degree, as evidenced by numerous statutes found in our code. Also, we take judicial notice of the extensive use of the many types of hospital insurance, as well as liability insurance by the institutions. Thus it is evident that times have changed and are now changing in the business, social, economic and legal worlds. The basis for, and the need of such encouragement is no longer existent.

The same basic change in conditions which is referred to in Haynes v. Presbyterian Hospital Ass'n, and other cited cases, has unquestionably occurred in this state. * * *

In the instant case it was alleged in the complaint that respondent hospital is fully protected by liability insurance from which any judgment for appellant would be paid. However, the fact that an individual defendant institution has, or does not have, such protection, is wholly immaterial in determining liability. The taking of liability insurance could create no liability where none before existed. Our view in this regard accords with the great weight of authority. See A.L.R.2d 29, 139.

The fact that the protection afforded by liability insurance is now available to charitable institutions generally is nevertheless appropriate for consideration, where the question is whether, as a matter of public policy, such institutions need immunity. As Judge Rutledge pointed out in [a prior] case:

> What is at stake, so far as the charity is concerned, is the cost of reasonable protection, the amount of the insurance premium as an added burden on its finances, not the awarding over in damages of its entire assets. [President and Directors of Georgetown College v. Hughes, 130 F.2d 810, 824 (1942)] * * *

If the roll of other American state and territorial courts was called today on the question of whether a hospital would be immune from suit under the facts of the instant case, we believe that it would show the following: Twenty-six courts would grant immunity; twenty would deny immunity; the result in four states and one territory would be doubtful. * * *

* * * American judicial thinking, which formerly gave "overwhelming" acceptance to the immunity rule, now gives that doctrine a very modest majority. This indicates, of course, that the trend of recent decisions has been away from nonliability. * * *

It is our conclusion that there is today no factual justification for immunity in a case such as this, and that principles of law, logic and intrinsic justice demand that the mantle of immunity be withdrawn. * * *

* * * We closed our courtroom doors without legislative help, and we can likewise open them. * * *

* * *

It is our opinion that a charitable, nonprofit hospital should no longer be held immune from liability for injuries to paying patients caused by the negligence of employees of the hospital. Our previous decisions holding to the contrary are hereby overruled.

The judgment is reversed and remanded, with directions to overrule the demurrer.

GRADY, C. J. (concurring). * * * [E]xperience has demonstrated that when immunity from liability is involved, legislatures are faced with strong opposition to change by those who are the beneficiaries of such rule, and proponents of a change find efforts to secure corrective legislation futile.

When such a situation arises and the courts have become convinced that the rule should no longer exist, there is justification for action to be taken by them. * * *

LANDGRAVER v. EMANUEL LUTHERAN CHARITY BOARD, 203 Or. 489, 280 P.2d 301 (1955). Action against charitable corporation for personal injuries caused by negligence. In the trial court, judgment on the pleadings for defendant. *Held* (5–2), affirmed. Many sound reasons have been given for abrogating the rule of immunity. "Not the least of those reasons is the availability of insurance in this modern age to cover the risks." The rule of immunity was established as a matter of public policy. When ascertained and declared by the courts, such public policy becomes the law of the state and is as binding as legislative enactment. Any change therein should be a matter solely for legislative determination.

BOONE v. BOONE, 345 S.C. 8, 546 S.E.2d 191 (2001). Wife sued husband to recover for personal injuries wife suffered in auto accident in Georgia while riding in car driven by husband. The Circuit Court dismissed her complaint on the ground that Georgia law, which provides interspousal immunity in personal injury actions, applied. *Held, reversed,* "application of the doctrine of interspousal immunity violates the public policy of South Carolina." South Carolina courts will no longer apply lex loci delicti doctrine when law of foreign state recognizes doctrine of interspousal immunity.

"Interspousal immunity is a common law doctrine based on the legal fiction that husband and wife share the same identity in law, namely that of the husband. 92 A.L.R.3d 901 (1979). Accordingly, at common law, it was 'both morally and conceptually objectionable to permit a tort suit between two spouses.' " *Id.* at 906.

With the passage of Married Women's Property Acts in the mid-nineteenth century, married women were given a legal estate in their own property and the capacity to sue and be sued. Under this legislation, a married woman could maintain an action against her husband for any tort against her property interest such as trespass to land or conversion. Since the legislation destroyed the "unity of persons," a husband could also maintain an action against his wife for torts to his property. [citations omitted]

"For a long time, however, the majority of courts held Married Women's Property Acts did not destroy interspousal immunity for personal torts. Courts adopted two inconsistent arguments in favor of continued immunity. First, they theorized suits between spouses would be fictitious and fraudulent, particularly against insurance companies. Second, they claimed interspousal suits would destroy domestic harmony. [citations omitted]

"In the twentieth century, most courts either abrogated or provided exceptions to interspousal immunity. [citations omitted] South Carolina has abolished the doctrine of interspousal immunity from tort liability for personal injury. *Pardue v. Pardue,* 167 S.C. 129, 166 S.E. 101 (1932); *see S.C.Code Ann. § 15–5–170 (1976)* ('[a] married woman may sue and be sued as if she were unmarried. When the action is between herself and her husband she may likewise sue or be sued alone.'). Very few jurisdictions now recognize interspousal tort immunity."

* * *

"It is the public policy of our State to provide married persons with the same legal rights and remedies possessed by unmarried persons. *See Bryant v. Smith,* 187 S.C. 453, 198 S.E. 20 (1938) (recognizing purpose of predecessor to § 15–5–170 is to give married women all rights and remedies possessed by unmarried women); *see also* S.C.Code Ann. § 16–3–615 (Supp.2000) (amending law to provide spouse may be convicted of sexual battery against spouse). Had the parties to this action not been married to each other, Wife could have maintained a personal injury action against Husband. We find it contrary to "natural justice," *see Rauton v. Pullman Co., supra,* to hold that because of their marital status, Wife is precluded from maintaining this action against Husband. Accordingly, we conclude application of the doctrine of interspousal immunity violates the public policy of South Carolina.

"Moreover, the reasons given in support of interspousal immunity are simply not justified in the twenty-first century. There is no reason to presume married couples are more likely than others to engage in a collusive action. Whether or not parties are married, if fraudulent conduct is suspected, insurers can examine and investigate the claim and, at trial, cross-examine the parties as to their financial stakes in the outcome of the suit. Fraudulent claims would be subject to the trial court's contempt powers and to criminal prosecution for perjury and other crimes. It is unjustified to prohibit all personal injury tort suits between spouses simply because some suits may be fraudulent.

"Additionally, we do not agree that precluding spouses from maintaining a personal injury action against each other fosters domestic harmony. Instead, we find marital harmony is promoted by allowing the negligent spouse, who has most likely purchased liability insurance, to provide for his injured spouse. *See Elam v. Elam,* 275 S.C. 132, 268 S.E.2d 109 (1980) (Court considered existence of universal automobile liability insurance a relevant factor in abolishing common law doctrine of parental immunity)."

LUSBY v. LUSBY, 283 Md. 334, 390 A.2d 77 (1978). Wife brought an action for damages against husband. She alleged that husband in a pick-up truck and two other men in another truck forced her to stop her car off the highway. Husband and the other men made her enter a pick-up truck, where husband "did forcefully and violently, despite [her] desperate attempts to protect herself, carnally know [her] against her will." With her husband's assistance, the other two men then attempted to rape her. The lower court granted defendant's motion to dismiss, on the ground that the parties were married on the date of the alleged incident and that hence plaintiff lacked legal capacity to sue husband. The court of appeals reversed and remanded the case. "We can conceive of no sound public policy in the latter half of the 20th–century which would prevent one spouse from recovering from another for the outrageous conduct here alleged. . . . We find nothing in our prior cases or elsewhere to indicate that under the common law of Maryland a wife was not permitted to recover from her husband in tort when she alleged and proved the type of outrageous, intentional conduct here alleged."

———

WINN v. GILROY, 296 Or. 718, 681 P.2d 776 (1984). Two minor children of husband and wife (who were separated and living apart) were killed in an automobile collision while passengers in a car driven by the allegedly intoxicated and negligent husband. Wife, as personal representative of the children's estates, brought a wrongful death action against husband. That action was dismissed by the trial court on ground that a father was immune from liability for negligence toward his children. The court of appeals affirmed, but the supreme court here held that the father was not immune and remanded for further proceedings. In his opinion for the court, Justice Linde stated:

" * * * Summarizing the state of the law in 1977, the Restatement (Second) reported that '[c]onstant criticism of the immunity has led to its erosion by the development of numerous exceptions to it, which have been more or less sporadically recognized by many courts, until there are now very few jurisdictions if any, in which the immunity exists in any complete form.' Restatement (Second) of Torts § 895(G), comment (d) (1979). Instead, the Restatement propounded the rule as follows:

> (1) A parent or child is not immune from tort liability to the other solely by reason of that relationship.

> (2) Repudiation of general tort immunity does not establish liability for an act or omission that, because of the parent-child relationship, is otherwise privileged or is not tortious.

" * * * Subsection (2) recognizes that apart from any immunity, acts or omissions may be privileged or not be tortious between parents and children that might be tortious toward other persons. The distinction between 'immunity' and 'privileged' or nontortious conduct is not merely verbal. It goes far toward clarifying the issue.

* * *

"This confusion of reasons concerning parental duties and privileges with reasons concerning litigation could not withstand analysis when courts began to reexamine parental immunity. The growth of exceptions * * * showed that rejection of intrafamily litigation, expressed as 'immunity,' was replaced by drawing substantive lines for parental liability. If immunity from being sued by one's minor child really rested on the adverse impact of litigation, there was no explanation why it did not bar a child's property or contract claim; and exceptions for tort claims if the parent's tort was intentional or 'wilful,' * * * could be explained only by assuming as a matter of law that this act already had destroyed the 'peace and tranquility of the home.' These exceptions and others showed that the court was concerned more with defining the required quality of parental conduct within the domestic setting than with litigiousness, that is to say, with substantive standards of parental duties and privileges more than with immunity from suit. * * *

"The case before us involves injuries to children resulting from a parent's allegedly intoxicated and negligent driving of an automobile. * * * [W]e do not find it necessary in this case to state a general formula for deciding what acts or omissions of a parent may be privileged or not be tortious toward a child, though the same act or omission might be tortious toward persons in a different position. It is possible to distinguish between those obligations that a parent owes his or her child specifically by virtue of parenthood from the general duty of ordinary care to avoid foreseeable harm that the defendant would owe to other persons, for instance to someone else's child, under the same circumstances. Negligence suffices to make the parent liable for the child's injury in the second kind of case though perhaps not for substandard performance of specifically parental duties, where a more stringent test * * * may remain proper.

" * * * It is evident that the parent's responsibility for physical conditions in the home, for food and medical care, for recreation, sports, toys, and games, and for general supervision involve a range of distinct issues that need not be swept within a single verbal formula before they arise. Even a claim that the family automobile is in some respect in unsafe condition, for instance, may call for a different analysis from a claim based on a parent's negligent driving.

" * * * When the allegations of the present complaint are tested under Restatement (Second) of Torts § 895G by criteria of tortiousness and privilege rather than by a doctrine of parental immunity from a child's legal action, there can be no doubt that the complaint survives a motion to dismiss. A driver can hardly claim a 'privilege' of driving while intoxicated or otherwise contrary to law. Nor is there any doubt that the complaint alleges negligent driving that would be tortious toward any other passenger who was injured."

DOE v. HOLT, 332 N.C. 90, 418 S.E.2d 511 (1992). Minor children sued their father for damages allegedly resulting from his repeated rapes and sexual molestation. The Superior Court, dismissed the complaint on the ground that it was barred by the parent-child immunity doctrine and the intermediate appellate court reversed. *Held,* affirmed. "It would be unconscionable if children who were injured by heinous acts of their parents such as alleged here should have no avenue by which to recover damages in redress of those wrongs. Where a parent has injured his or her child through a willful and malicious act, any concept of family harmony has been destroyed. Thus, the foremost public purpose supporting the parent-child immunity doctrine is absent, and there is no reason to extend the doctrine's protection to such acts."

"We wish to make it clear that no issue involving reasonable chastisement of children by their parents is before us in the present case, and we expressly do not intend to be understood as commenting on situations involving such issues. * * * Furthermore, our opinion in the present case is not intended to permit interference in the proper scope of discretion parents must utilize in rearing their children. As the Supreme Court of New Jersey recognized in Foldi, there is no universally correct philosophy on how to raise one's child. Foldi, 93 N.J. at 546, 461 A.2d at 1152. In no way do we intend to indicate that reasonable parental decisions concerning children should be reviewed in the courts of this state. Such decisions make up the essence of parental discretion, discretion which allows parents to shape the views, beliefs and values their children carry with them into adulthood. These decisions are for the parents to make, and will be protected as such. * * *

"Here, we have addressed a different concern; when a parent steps beyond the bounds of reasonable parental discretion and commits a willful and malicious act which injures his or her child, the parent negates the public policies which led to recognition of the parent-child immunity doctrine in North Carolina, and the doctrine does not shield the parent."

COMMERCE BANK v. AUGSBURGER, 288 Ill.App.3d 510, 223 Ill.Dec. 872, 680 N.E.2d 822 (1997). Estate of a three-year-old child brought a wrongful death action against the child's foster parents, among others, alleging that they negligently supervised and monitored the child and negligently placed her in a closet, where she died of asphyxiation and hyperthermia. *Held*, affirming lower court, foster parents were entitled to parental immunity, and the conduct in question was immune from liability under the Illinois doctrine.

"The binding Illinois case on the subject of parental immunity is the comparatively recent case of *Cates v. Cates*, 156 Ill.2d 76, 189 Ill.Dec. 14, 619 N.E.2d 715 (1993). There, a suit was brought on behalf of a daughter against her father for injuries she received in a collision while riding as a passenger in a motor vehicle driven by him. Negligence was charged and the father claimed parental immunity. The circuit court granted the father's motion to dismiss on parental immunity grounds, the appellate court affirmed, but the supreme court reversed. That court held that no parental immunity existed when the duty to drive carefully was owed by the father, not merely to the daughter, but to the public generally. Thus, the *Cates* court concluded that the negligence of the father did not involve the supervision or discipline of the child and did not bring into play the doctrine of parental immunity.

* * *

"While upholding the right of the daughter to sue her father for negligent driving, the *Cates* court emphasized that parental immunity still existed * * * to offer 'protection to conduct inherent to the parent-child relationship' (*Cates,* 156 Ill.2d at 104, 189 Ill.Dec. at 28, 619 N.E.2d at 729) and further stated:

> The standard we have thus developed focuses primarily on conduct inherent to the parent-child relationship * * * Such a standard is consistent with other jurisdictions which have abrogated the immunity in order to achieve greater clarity in the area of parent-child negligence. The standard we have created is not, however, as extreme because we do not fully abrogate the immunity, but rely on an exception. Our standard also allows a broader area of negligent conduct to remain immunized. Thus, under our standard, parental discretion in the provision of care includes maintenance of the family home, medical treatment, and *supervision of the child.* A child may attempt to sue a parent alleging that the child fell on a wet, freshly mopped floor in the home, but the immunity would bar such an action because the parent was exercising his discretion in providing and maintaining housing for the child." (Emphasis added.)

Cates, 156 Ill.2d at 105, 189 Ill.Dec. 14, 619 N.E.2d at 729.

"The conduct with which the Augsburgers are charged is severe, but plaintiff did not see fit to allege that conduct was willful and wanton. If it was willful and wanton, parental immunity would not be a defense. *Cates,* 156 Ill.2d at 83, 189 Ill.Dec. at 17, 619 N.E.2d at 718; *Nudd,* 7 Ill.2d at 619, 131 N.E.2d at 531. The second-amended complaint describes the Augsburgers' conduct as a failure to supervise and monitor the child and the negligent placement of the child in a closet. This is the very type of conduct for which the *Cates* opinion would still provide for the defense of parental immunity."

HARTMAN v. ARMSTRONG, 821 S.W.2d 852 (Mo.1991). Unemancipated minor children brought personal injury actions against father, grandfather, and mother. *Held,* parental immunity doctrine is abrogated in favor of reasonable parent standard. "Taken to its logical conclusion, the doctrine [of parental immunity] has the effect of causing the parent to owe a greater duty to the general public than to his or her own child."

Chapter 11

BASIC DEFENSES: VICTIM CONDUCT
AND CHOICE

This chapter addresses the two basic defenses to negligence liability, contributory negligence and assumption of risk. Here we should assume that defendant's conduct, which harmed plaintiff, has been found negligent. Now the negligence lawsuit enters a new phase. It is as if, in the first phase, we "look to the defendant" to see if the negligence liability rule applies; and now, we "look to the plaintiff."

Contributory negligence refers to plaintiff conduct–unreasonable conduct which contributed to the accident at issue. Assumption of risk refers to plaintiff choice–knowing choice with respect to the risk that came to pass. The two defenses are like two circles which overlap in part; in the area of overlap is behavior that may be described alternatively as "knowing" contributory negligence or as "unreasonable" assumption of risk.

The chapter has an historical dimension, since there is a classical and a modern rendition of each defense. The categories of contributory negligence and assumption of risk were well defined by classical tort law—that is, by the law extant in the latter part of the nineteenth century and the first third of the twentieth. Basic classical definitions are still serviceable, and in some jurisdictions classical rules remain pretty much intact. But classical doctrine worked out the defenses in a much more liability-restrictive manner than distinctively modern law. In modern tort, contributory negligence is no longer always a bar to any recovery by plaintiff, and the effective scope of assumption of risk has shrunk considerably. The four sections of the chapter trace these evolutions: they present classical contributory negligence, followed by modern comparative fault; then classical assumption of risk, followed by modern remnants.

SECTION A.   CONTRIBUTORY NEGLIGENCE

The defense of contributory negligence turns the spotlight of negligence assessment on the plaintiff, the person injured in an accident. The name "contributory negligence" reminds us that two things must be shown in order for the defense to be made out. First, plaintiff's conduct must be found to be negligent. Second, plaintiff's negligence must be found to have contributed to the causation of the accidental injury at issue. In a case where both the causative negligence of the defendant and the contributory negligence of the plaintiff are made out, the injury might have been avoided in either of two ways: by defendant care or by plaintiff care. Had defendant been careful, the accident probably wouldn't have happened; likewise, had plaintiff been careful, the same accident probably wouldn't have happened.

The cases of the present section take the approach that a plaintiff is barred from any recovery for injury to which the plaintiff's own negligence contributed causally (unless the "last clear chance" doctrine applies). This is the classical approach to contributory negligence: the effect of contributory negligence is to bar recovery altogether. The distinctively modern approach, addressed in the following section, is not to bar recovery by a contributorily negligent plaintiff but rather to reduce recovery in proportion to plaintiff's comparative fault.

While the classical approach is dated, and in some states superseded altogether, it is by no means dead. The classical "bar" still operates today (a) in those few states which have not adopted comparative fault and (b) in those comparative fault regimes (discussed in the next section) which are a blend of the old and the new.

The method for analyzing the reasonableness of a plaintiff's conduct is the same as that for analyzing the reasonableness of a defendant's conduct. In either case, the basic question is: what would a reasonable person, balancing pros and cons, have done in the circumstances? However, there is a conceptual difference between defendant's negligence and plaintiff's contributory negligence which is worth noting. Defendant's negligence is an other-regarding default: it involves failure to take due care to protect others. Plaintiff's contributory negligence is a self-regarding lapse: it involves failure to take care to protect oneself. This difference is usefully framed by the Second Restatement excerpt immediately below (albeit in the gender-laden reasonable "man" terminology of another era).

RESTATEMENT OF TORTS, SECOND (1965)

§ 283. Conduct of a Reasonable Man: The Standard

Unless the actor is a child, the standard of conduct to which he must conform to avoid being negligent is that of a reasonable man under like circumstances.

Comment:

* * *

f. Reasonable Consideration for Others and Reasonable Prudence. In so far as the conduct of the reasonable man furnishes a standard by which negligence is to be determined, the standard is one which is fixed for the protection of persons other than the defendant. In so far as the contributory negligence of the actor is concerned, the standard is one to which the actor is required to conform for his own protection * * *. When a plaintiff's contributory negligence is in question, the "reasonable man" is a man of reasonable "prudence." Where a defendant's negligence is to be determined, the "reasonable man" is a man who is reasonably "considerate" of the safety of others and does not look primarily to his own advantage.

———

DAVIES v. SWAN MOTOR CO., [1949] 2 K.B. 291, 1 All E.R. 620 (C.A.) The deceased, who was assisting in collecting refuse, was riding on steps at the side of the truck, placed there so that he could conveniently empty receptacles into the truck, when the driver of defendant's truck, negligently attempting to pass, ran into the steps, causing death to the rider. *Held,* that the trial court was in error in finding that deceased was not guilty of contributory negligence. BUCKNILL, L. J., adopted the statement that: "Negligence ordinarily means breach of a legal duty to take care, but as used in the expression 'contributory negligence', it does not mean breach of duty. It means the failure of a person to use reasonable care for the safety of himself or his property, so that he becomes 'the author of his own wrong.'"

RAWL v. UNITED STATES, 778 F.2d 1009 (4th Cir.1985). A pilot took his small private airplane aloft in bad weather at night, though he was not qualified to fly in such conditions. Air traffic controllers, in assisting the plane to land, gave mistaken directions which disoriented the pilot and caused the plane to crash. *Held,* under South Carolina law, that the contributory negligence of the pilot bars any recovery for the negligence of the controllers. Said the court:

> The common law doctrine of contributory negligence has deep roots in South Carolina law. [Contributory negligence] has been described as: "a want of ordinary care upon the part of the person injured by the actionable negligence of another, combining and concurring with that negligence, and contributing to the injury as a proximate cause thereof, without which the injury would not have occurred." Easler v. Railway Co., 59 S.C. 311, 322, 37 S.E. 938, 941 (1901). * * * [A] finding of contributory negligence on the part of the plaintiff bars recovery of damages from the defendant. See 57 Am.Jur.2d § 288 ("[T]here can be no recovery of damages for negligence if the injured person, by his own negligence, * * * proximately contributed to the injury.").

KRALL v. ROYAL INNS OF AMERICA, INC., 374 F.Supp. 146 (D.Alaska 1973). Plaintiff, a construction worker, got his hand caught in a hoist that lacked guardrails and other safeguards prescribed by the Alaska General Safety Code. Plaintiff argued that contributory negligence should not be a defense against negligence per se based on violations of the Safety Code. *Held*, for defendant. The court first noted that the state legislature had not abrogated the defense, and distinguished situations involving "dram shop" legislation and sale of firearms to minors where the contributory negligence defense is not available.

"Plaintiff's second reason for eliminating the defense is the worker's limited ability to exercise self-protective care because of economic duress. * * *

" * * * In theory requiring employers to bear the full losses of accidents caused by violations of the safety code should sensitize them to the mandates of the code. Obliging employers to internalize fully costs of violation-accidents would aid in the prevention and deterrence of those accidents. * * * [Since the employee is] subject to economic pressure which inhibits his efforts to promote safety, the employer is clearly the better accident avoider. As such, the argument concludes, the employer should be charged with the costs of all accidents caused by violation of the Safety Code.

"However, * * * the theory proves too much as the rationale would charge all accident costs to employers. Also, the Unions' increased awareness and assertion of power in the name of safety lessens the economic pressure on workers. * * * Thus, the court discerns no compelling reason to deny the defense."

GREYCAS, INC. v. PROUD, 826 F.2d 1560 (7th Cir.1987), cert. denied, 484 U.S. 1043, 108 S.Ct. 775, 98 L.Ed.2d 862 (1988). Posner, Circuit Judge: "Due care is the care that is optimal given that the other party is exercising due care. It is not the higher level of care that would be optimal if potential tort victims were required to assume that the rest of the world was negligent. A pedestrian is not required to exercise a level of care (e.g., wearing a helmet or a shin guard) that would be optimal if there were no sanctions against reckless driving. Otherwise drivers would be encouraged to drive recklessly, and knowing this pedestrians would be encouraged to wear helmets and shin guards. The result would be a shift from a superior method of accident avoidance (not driving recklessly) to an inferior one (pedestrian armor)."

QUANAH, ACME & PACIFIC RAILWAY v. STEARNS, 206 S.W. 857 (Tex. Civ.App.1918). Railroad sparks set fire to grass and timber on plaintiff's grazing land adjacent to defendant's railway. Defendant argued that plaintiff's failure to plough a fireguard on his own land amounted to contributory negligence. On appeal from a judgment against the railroad, *held*, for plaintiff (now appellee).

"No charge of negligent use of his property is made against appellee in this case, unless permitting grass to grow on his pasture lands is such negligence. He had not placed any property near appellant's track, negligently or otherwise; his grass was there before the railroad was constructed, and his act in permitting it to remain and grow does not subject him to the charge of 'rashly or purposely exposing it to the hazard.' The rule is settled that he is not required to anticipate the company's negligence and has the right to the full and free enjoyment of his property for all lawful purposes."

The court concluded by quoting with approval: "The distinction between the cases of the railroad company and that of the contiguous owner is obvious. The company uses a dangerous agent and must provide proper safeguards; the landowner does nothing of the kind and has a right to remain quiescent."

BAUMGARTNER v. STATE FARM MUTUAL AUTOMOBILE INSURANCE CO., 356 So.2d 400 (La.1978). Here a divided Louisiana Supreme Court abolished the defense of contributory negligence in personal injury suits brought by pedestrians against motorists. The majority opinion said:

" * * * [I]n motor vehicle-pedestrian cases there is lacking a 'mutuality of risks.' That is, the operator of a dangerous instrumentality, such as a motor vehicle, creates a great risk of injury to the life and limb of others. Thus he owes a duty to the public to protect it from that danger. The pedestrian, on the other hand, endangers himself only, therefore his duty is owed primarily to himself. The motorist runs small risk of harm, physical or financial, from a pedestrian's negligence.

" * * * The operator of a motor vehicle, a dangerous instrumentality, has the constant duty to watch out for the possible negligent acts of pedestrians and avoid injuring them. A higher standard of care than that required of pedestrians is imposed upon the motorist commensurate with the hazards his conduct inflicts upon the public safety. Therefore, he should not be able to escape responsibility for injury to the pedestrian by pleading the latter's negligence. * * * "

WASHINGTON METRO. AREA TRANSIT AUTHORITY v. JOHNSON

District of Columbia Court of Appeals, 1997.
699 A.2d 404.

RUIZ, Associate Judge:

Eleanor and Franklin Johnson filed wrongful death and survival actions against Washington Metropolitan Area Transit Authority (WMATA) for the death of their daughter, Devora Johnson, who, on March 20, 1986, jumped onto the tracks before an oncoming train. It is undisputed that by jumping onto the tracks Devora Johnson intended to commit suicide. However, her death could have been avoided if the train conductor had not delayed in engaging the emergency brake to stop the train. At issue is whether Devora Johnson's suicidal intention as a matter of law relieved WMATA of responsibility for the train operator's tortious conduct under the doctrine of last clear chance.[1]

[The wrongful death suit, because of diversity of citizenship, was tried in federal court. The applicable law was the local tort law of the District of Columbia. Trial evidence showed that the train operator tested positive for cocaine and marijuana shortly after the collision. The jury found WMATA liable. Defendant appealed the adverse judgment to the United States Court of Appeals for the District of Columbia Circuit.]

1. The question presented by this case is distinguishable from that presented in *District of Columbia v. Peters*, 527 A.2d 1269 (D.C. 1987), which addressed a defendant's liability for a suicide that follows the defendant's negligent conduct. In *Peters*, the decedent committed suicide two years after becoming paralyzed from an injury inflicted by the police during an arrest. *Peters* noted that "suicide generally is considered to be a deliberate, intentional, and intervening act" which precludes recovery for prior negligent acts alleged to have caused the decedent to take his or her own life. There is an exception to this general rule for situations where the defendant's prior negligent conduct causes the decedent "to have an irresistible or uncontrollable impulse to commit suicide." *Peters* is inapplicable because the Johnsons are not alleging that WMATA's actions caused Ms. Johnson to commit suicide or that WMATA failed to prevent Ms. Johnson from jumping on the tracks.

The Circuit Court for the District of Columbia, concluding that a question of District of Columbia law was determinative of the issue and that no controlling precedent existed in the decisions of this court, certified to this court the following question:

> Under District of Columbia law, and upon the facts described below, may a plaintiff who has voluntarily assumed an unreasonable risk of incurring a particular injury recover from a defendant who failed to take the last clear chance to prevent that injury?

The question certified by the Circuit Court is phrased in terms of whether a plaintiff who has "voluntarily assumed an unreasonable risk" can benefit from the last clear chance doctrine. The question involves the two sometimes distinct, sometimes overlapping, theories of contributory negligence and assumption of risk. Before applying them to the facts of this case, we briefly describe their different origins and relevant District of Columbia case law.

Contributory Negligence and the Doctrine of Last Clear Chance

In the District of Columbia, a plaintiff whose negligence contributes to his or her injury may not recover from a negligent defendant unless the defendant had the last clear chance to avoid injuring the plaintiff. *Felton v. Wagner,* 512 A.2d 291, 296 (D.C.1986). [Ed. note: On the page cited, the *Felton* opinion says, "In the District of Columbia contributory negligence is an absolute bar to recovery in a negligence action," though the bar does not apply in a situation of "last clear chance."] The doctrine of last clear chance is well established in our jurisprudence. *See, e.g., Terminal Taxicab Co. v. Blum,* 54 App.D.C. 357, 298 F. 679 (1924). To prevail under the doctrine of last clear chance a plaintiff has the burden of establishing:

> (1) that the plaintiff was in a position of danger caused by the negligence of [the] plaintiff * * *; (2) that the plaintiff was oblivious to the danger, or unable to extricate herself from the position of danger; (3) that the defendant was aware, or by the exercise of reasonable care should have been aware, of the plaintiff's danger and of her oblivion to it or her inability to extricate herself from it; and (4) that the defendant, with means available to him, could have avoided injuring the plaintiff after becoming aware of the danger and the plaintiff's inability to extricate herself from it, but failed to do so.

Felton, supra, 512 A.2d at 296; *see also Robinson v. District of Columbia,* 580 A.2d 1255, 1258 (D.C.1990) (same). The last clear chance doctrine applies to a defendant who "with means available to him, could have avoided injuring the plaintiff after [defendant] became aware of, or reasonably should have become aware of, the danger and the plaintiff's inability to extricate himself from it." *Robinson, supra,* 580 A.2d at 1258–59.

The doctrine of last clear chance has been characterized as a transitional doctrine, preparing the way for a system of comparative negligence. *See* Fleming James, Jr., *Last Clear Chance: A Transitional Doctrine,* 47 YALE L.J. 704 (1938). Various justifications have been offered for the last clear chance doctrine. One common explanation is that the plaintiff's negligence was not the proximate cause of the harm because the defendant had the last opportunity to prevent it. *See* Restatement (Second) of Torts § 479 cmt. a (1965);[4] *but see* W. Page Keeton et al., Prosser and Keeton on the Law of Torts § 66, at 463 (5th ed.1984) (noting that this explanation runs contrary to the "evolving ideas of proximate cause"). Another justification involves an assessment of relative fault where "the later negligence of the defendant involves a higher degree of fault. . . ." Keeton et al., *supra*, at 463. This justification is especially applicable to situations where the defendant acts recklessly or intentionally or where the defendant has discovered a helpless plaintiff. *Id.* (noting that this rationale cannot explain other situations where "the defendant's fault consists merely in a failure to discover the danger at all, or in slowness, clumsiness, inadvertence or an error in judgment in dealing with it"). Perhaps the real justification for the rule is "a fundamental dislike for the harshness of the contributory negligence defense," Keeton et al., *supra*, at 464, which would explain why it seems particularly apt in situations where the defendant's negligence is seen "as the final and decisive factor in producing the injury." Restatement, *supra*, § 479 cmt. a.

Assumption of Risk

Assumption of risk, like contributory negligence, relieves a negligent defendant of liability. It is a complete defense to a claim of negligence "under a theory of 'waiver' or 'consent' " proceeding from the premise that a person, after evaluating a situation, has voluntarily decided to take a known risk. *Sinai v. Polinger Co.,* 498 A.2d 520, 524 (D.C.1985). * * * [T]he elements of the defense are "first, knowledge of the danger and second, a voluntary exposure to that known danger." [*Morrison v. MacNamara*, 407 A.2d 555, 566 (D.C.1979).] * * *

The doctrine of last clear chance is applied in cases where a defense of contributory negligence has been raised, and does not apply if the sole defense is that the injured party assumed the risk. Both defenses, however, may be asserted in the same case arising from a single set of facts * * *.

Suicides

We consider the certified question "upon the facts" of this case, a suicide, that was characterized as constituting both contributory negligence and assumption of risk. Keeping in mind the principles underlying the two doctrines, we turn to consider whether, under District of Columbia law, * * * WMATA may be held liable under the doctrine of last clear chance for its failure to avoid the fatal consequences of Ms. Johnson's suicide. * * * We confirm that District of Columbia law does not except suicides from the last clear chance doctrine.

* * *

---

4. The Restatement (Second) of Torts § 479 comment a states:

"[T]he plaintiff's negligence is not a 'proximate' or legal cause of the harm to him, because the later negligence of the defendant is a superseding cause which relieves the plaintiff of responsibility for it."

* * * Here, Ms. Johnson, the mother of a young child, chose a public venue for a most violent death. Evidence presented at trial in this case showed that Ms. Johnson had a history of serious mental illness, including seven hospitalizations. * * *

We are unpersuaded by the argument that our holding today will provide an incentive for individuals to commit suicide in the hope that their estates will benefit. That policy argument is purely speculative. No study or judicial finding has been offered in support of the proposition that suicides will be encouraged if the last clear chance doctrine is available in cases involving suicides. There is nothing in the record of the case before us indicating that Ms. Johnson sought death in order to benefit her estate. * * *

* * *

We believe that application of the doctrine of last clear chance to the facts before us on this certified question squares with the objective of negligence law * * *. Whether or not a person intends suicide—a fact that may well be unknown to anyone other than the suicidal person at the time of the incident—should not, consistent with the principles underlying the law of negligence, excuse a person who acts unreasonably under the circumstances particularly where, as here, there was virtual certainty that the foreseeable harm would be death. Therefore, it is precisely because the result of suicide is death, that we do not carve out a suicide exception to a doctrine that preserves the incentive for the last actor who has an opportunity to act to prevent the death to do so. The primary focus in applying the last clear chance doctrine is on the actions of the defendant, not the intent of the injured person, and * * * on a determination whether the defendant acted reasonably under the circumstances to prevent injury to a person who has placed himself or herself in harm's way. Our holding herein means that the law does not avert that focus in the case of suicides.

MEYN v. DULANEY–MILLER AUTO CO. et al., 118 W.Va. 545, 191 S.E. 558 (1937). The plaintiff was crossing a street at night, at an angle and between crosswalks, when he was run down and injured by an automobile driven by the defendant's servant. *Held,* for defendant, reversing judgment for the plaintiff. Someone whose escape from a position of peril is barred only by his own careless obliviousness of impending danger is not entitled to recover except where the defendant actually knew of his position of peril, or "knew of the plaintiff's situation, and, under the circumstances, in the exercise of reasonable care should have realized the plaintiff's peril, and, on such realization, could have avoided the injury"; citing Restatement of Torts, §§ 479, 480.

SPIER v. BARKER

Court of Appeals of New York, 1974.

35 N.Y.2d 444, 363 N.Y.S.2d 916, 323 N.E.2d 164.

[While driving her car plaintiff was injured in a collision with defendants' tractor-trailer. Plaintiff was ejected from her car which then rolled over her and pinned her legs. The car was equipped with seat belts, but plaintiff had not been using them. The Court of Appeals addressed the question "what effect, if any, the failure of a plaintiff to wear a seat belt has upon his right to recovery."]

Upon the trial defendants called, as an expert witness, a professor of mechanical and aerospace engineering, who had also been previously employed as a consulting engineer in the field of accident analysis and reconstruction. He testified to an extensive background in the use of seat belts in both the aircraft and automotive industries. Over plaintiff's objection, the expert was permitted to give his opinion that "The seat belt is an extremely effective device in either preventing or alleviating injury." More specifically, he stated that the seat belt is the most effective improvement that has been made in the automobile in the last 20 years. After viewing photographs of the vehicles and the accident scene, the expert opined that had the plaintiff been wearing a seat belt, she would not have been ejected from her automobile; and that had she not been ejected, she probably would not have been seriously injured. When asked on cross-examination if the fact that plaintiff was ejected from her automobile might have saved her life, the engineer stated that "the worst thing that could have happened to her [was] being ejected from the vehicle."

Having permitted the defense expert to testify as to what would have probably happened to the plaintiff had she used the seat belt available to her, the trial court charged the jury as follows: "If you find that a reasonably prudent driver would have used a seat belt, and that she would not have received some or all of her injuries had she used the seat belt, then you may not award any damages for those injuries you find she would not have received had she used the seat belt. The burden of proving that some or all of her injuries would not have been received had she used the seat belt rests upon the [defendants]". Although the plaintiff's counsel took no exception to the trial court's charge, he requested the court to charge the jury "that there isn't any law in the State of New York that requires a person to wear a seat belt or to anticipate the happening of an accident." The trial court so charged.

* * *

Despite the fact that the "seat belt defense", as it is commonly known, has received extensive examination in other jurisdictions as well as several legal periodicals, it is raised as a matter of first impression in this court. We today hold that nonuse of an available seat belt, and expert testimony in regard thereto, is a factor which the jury may consider, in light of all the other facts received in evidence, in arriving at its determination as to whether the plaintiff has exercised due care, not only to avoid injury to himself, but to mitigate any injury he would likely sustain (Mount v. McClellan, 91 Ill.App.2d 1, 234 N.E.2d 329). However, as the trial court observed in its charge, the plaintiff's nonuse of an available seat belt should be strictly limited to the jury's determination of the plaintiff's damages and should not be considered by the triers of fact in resolving the issue of liability. * * *

* * *

Since section 383 of the Vehicle and Traffic Law does not require occupants of a passenger car to make use of available seat belts, we hold that a plaintiff's failure to do so does not constitute negligence per se. * * * Likewise, we do not subscribe to the holdings of those cases in which the plaintiff's failure to fasten his seat belt may be determined by the jury to constitute contributory negligence as a matter of common law. In our view, the doctrine of contributory negligence is applicable only if the plaintiff's failure to exercise due care causes, in whole or in part, *the accident*, rather than when it merely exacerbates or enhances the severity of his injuries. That being the case, holding a nonuser contributorily negligent would be improper since it would impose liability upon the plaintiff for all his injuries though use of a seat belt might have prevented none or only a portion of them. Having disapproved of these two variations of the seat belt defense, we address ourselves to the defendants' contention that nonuse of an available seat belt may be considered by the jury in assessing the plaintiff's damages where it is shown that the seat belt would have prevented at least a portion of the injuries.

As Prosser has indicated, the plaintiff's duty to mitigate his damages is equivalent to the doctrine of avoidable consequences, which precludes recovery for any damages which could have been eliminated by reasonable conduct on the part of the plaintiff (Prosser, Torts [4th ed.], § 65, pp. 422–424). Traditionally both of these concepts have been applied only to postaccident conduct, such as a plaintiff's failure to obtain medical treatment after he has sustained an injury. To do otherwise, it has been argued, would impose a preaccident obligation upon the plaintiff and would deny him the right to assume the due care of others (Kleist, Seat Belt Defense—An Exercise in Sophistry, 18 Hastings L.J. 613, 616). We concede that the opportunity to mitigate damages prior to the occurrence of an accident does not ordinarily arise, and that the chronological distinction, on which the concept of mitigation damages rests, is justified in most cases. However, in our opinion, the seat belt affords the automobile occupant an unusual and ordinarily unavailable means by which he or she may minimize his or her damages *prior* to the accident. Highway safety has become a national concern; we are told to drive defensively and to "watch out for the other driver". When an automobile occupant may readily protect himself, at least partially, from the consequences of a collision, we think that the burden of buckling an available seat belt may, under the facts of the particular case, be found by the jury to be less than the likelihood of injury when multiplied by its accompanying severity.

At this juncture, there can be no doubt whatsoever as to the efficiency of the automobile seat belt in preventing injuries. * * * Furthermore, though it has been repeatedly suggested that the seat belt itself causes injury, to date the device has never been shown to worsen an injury, but, on the contrary, has prevented more serious ones. * * *

Another objection frequently raised is that the jury will be unable to segregate the injuries caused by the initial impact from the injuries caused by the plaintiff's failure to fasten his seat belt. In addition to underestimating the abilities of those trained in the field of accident reconstruction, this argument fails to consider other instances in which the jury is permitted to apportion damages (i.e., as between an original tort-feasor and a physician who negligently treats the original injury). Furthermore, if the defendant is unable to show that the seat belt would have prevented some of the plaintiff's injuries, then the trial court ought not submit the issue to the jury.

HALVORSON v. VOELLER, 336 N.W.2d 118 (N.D.1983). In the case of a motorcyclist who suffered severe brain injury from an intersection collision with an automobile, the North Dakota Supreme Court held that a "motorcycle helmet defense" similar to the "seatbelt defense" should be recognized. "Although the courts which reject the seatbelt defense appear to constitute a clear majority, no small number of courts are in the minority." The reasoning of *Spier v. Barker*—that the burden of buckling a seatbelt may be less than the likelihood of injury when multiplied by its accompanying severity—"applies with equal force to a case in which nonuse of a safety helmet is considered in mitigation of damages." Accordingly the court approved the following jury instruction:

> If you find (1) it was unreasonable for the plaintiff to not wear a helmet, and (2) the plaintiff would not have received some or all of his injuries had he worn a helmet, then (3) the amount of damages awarded the plaintiff for the injuries he sustained must be reduced in proportion to the amount of injury he would have avoided by the use of a helmet. The burden of proof on both (1) and (2) rests with the defendant.

SECTION B. COMPARATIVE FAULT

In a comparative fault regime, the effect of plaintiff's contributory negligence is not to bar plaintiff's recovery altogether, but rather to reduce the amount of damages that plaintiff receives. When defendant is found to have committed causative negligence, and plaintiff to have committed contributory negligence, the jury proceeds to comparison. This means, in a simple two-party case, assigning to the plaintiff and to the defendant respective percentages of fault which, added together, equal 100%. Say the respective percentages are 20% for plaintiff and 80% for defendant. Then plaintiff's damages are reduced by 20%, or plaintiff's percentage of fault—that is, plaintiff recovers a fraction of damages equal to defendant's percentage of fault, or 80%.

How does one go about comparing fault? What are the relevant factors to be weighed? The short answer is that anything relevant in determining the existence of causative negligence and contributory negligence in the first place, will come up again in assessment of the parties' relative degrees of fault. Comparative fault assessment pays particular attention to basic matters addressed by doctrines surveyed in Chapter 8. Comparison of fault assesses the comparative magnitude of a party's B, P, and L (that is, burden of precaution, degree of risk created, gravity of loss threatened); and also assesses the comparative degree of a party's knowledge of risk, attentiveness to danger, and, especially, capacity to control risk. So the present topic is a good occasion for review of the basic elements of negligence analysis, now put to a new use as terms of comparison.

LI v. YELLOW CAB COMPANY OF CALIFORNIA
Supreme Court of California, In Bank, 1975.
13 Cal.3d 804, 119 Cal.Rptr. 858, 532 P.2d 1226.

SULLIVAN, Justice.

In this case we address the grave and recurrent question whether we should judicially declare no longer applicable in California courts the doctrine of contributory negligence, which bars all recovery when the plaintiff's negligent conduct has contributed as a legal cause in any degree to the harm suffered by him, and hold that it must give way to a system of comparative negligence, which assesses liability in direct proportion to fault. As we explain in detail infra, we conclude that we should. * * *

The accident here in question occurred near the intersection of Alvarado Street and Third Street in Los Angeles. At this intersection Third Street runs in a generally east-west direction along the crest of a hill, and Alvarado Street, running generally north and south, rises gently to the crest from either direction. At approximately 9 p.m. on November 21, 1968, plaintiff Nga Li was proceeding northbound on Alvarado in her 1967 Oldsmobile. She was in the inside lane, and about 70 feet before she reached the Third Street intersection she stopped and then began a left turn across the three southbound lanes of Alvarado, intending to enter the driveway of a service station. At this time defendant Robert Phillips, an employee of defendant Yellow Cab Company, was driving a company-owned taxicab southbound in the middle lane on Alvarado. He came over the crest of the hill, passed through the intersection, and collided with the right rear portion of plaintiff's automobile, resulting in personal injuries to plaintiff as well as considerable damage to the automobile.

The court, sitting without a jury, found as facts that defendant Phillips was traveling at approximately 30 miles per hour when he entered the intersection, that such speed was unsafe at that time and place, and that the traffic light controlling southbound traffic at the intersection was yellow when defendant Phillips drove into the intersection. It also found, however, that plaintiff's left turn across the southbound lanes of Alvarado "was made at a time when a vehicle was approaching from the opposite direction so close as to constitute an immediate hazard." The dispositive conclusion of law was as follows: "That the driving of NGA LI was negligent, that such negligence was a proximate cause of the collision, and that she is barred from recovery by reason of such contributory negligence." Judgment for defendants was entered accordingly.

* * *

It is unnecessary for us to catalogue the enormous amount of critical comment that has been directed over the years against the "all-or-nothing" approach of the doctrine of contributory negligence. The essence of that criticism has been constant and clear: the doctrine is inequitable in its operation because it fails to distribute responsibility in proportion to fault. Against this have been raised several arguments in justification, but none have proved even remotely adequate to the task. The basic objection to the doctrine—grounded in the primal concept that in a system in which liability is based on fault, the extent of fault should govern the extent of liability—remains irresistible to reason and all intelligent notions of fairness.

Furthermore, practical experience with the application by juries of the doctrine of contributory negligence has added its weight to analyses of its inherent shortcomings: "Every trial lawyer is well aware that juries often do in fact allow recovery in cases of contributory negligence, and that the compromise in the jury room does result in some diminution of the damages because of the plaintiff's fault. But the process is at best a haphazard and most unsatisfactory one." (Prosser, Comparative Negligence, [41 Cal.L.Rev. 1 (1953)], p. 4; fn. omitted.) (See also Prosser, Torts, § 67, pp. 436–437; Comments of Malone and Wade in Comments on Maki v. Frelk—Comparative v. Contributory Negligence: Should the Court or Legislature Decide? (1968) 21 Vand.L.Rev. 889, at pp. 934, 943; Ulman, A Judge Takes the Stand (1933) pp. 30–34; cf. Comment of Kalven, 21 Vand.L.Rev. 889, 901–904). It is manifest that this state of affairs, viewed from the standpoint of the health and vitality of the legal process, can only detract from public confidence in the ability of law and legal institutions to assign liability on a just and consistent basis. (See Keeton, Creative Continuity in the Law of Torts (1962) 75 Harv.L.Rev. 463, 505; Comment of Keeton in Comments on Maki v. Frelk, supra, 21 Vand.L.Rev. 889, at p. 916, Note (1974) 21 U.C.L.A.L.Rev. 1566, 1596–1597.)

It is in view of these theoretical and practical considerations that to this date 25 states,[6] have abrogated the "all or nothing" rule of contributory negligence and have enacted in its place general apportionment *statutes* calculated in one manner or another to assess liability in proportion to fault. In 1973 these states were joined by Florida, which effected the same result by *judicial* decision. (Hoffman v. Jones (Fla.1973) 280 So.2d 431.) We are

---

6. Arkansas, Colorado, Connecticut, Georgia, Hawaii, Idaho, Maine, Massachusetts, Minnesota, Mississippi, Nebraska, Nevada, New Hampshire, New Jersey, North Dakota, Oklahoma, Oregon, Rhode Island, South Dakota, Texas, Utah, Vermont, Washington, Wisconsin, Wyoming. (Schwartz, Comparative Negligence (1974), Appendix A, pp. 367–369.)

In the federal sphere comparative negligence of the "pure" type (see *infra*) has been the rule since 1908 in cases arising under the Federal Employers' Liability Act (see 45 U.S.C. § 53) and since 1920 in cases arising under the Jones Act (see 46 U.S.C. § 688) and the Death on the High Seas Act (see 46 U.S.C. § 766.)

likewise persuaded that logic, practical experience, and fundamental justice counsel against the retention of the doctrine rendering contributory negligence a complete bar to recovery—and that it should be replaced in this state by a system under which liability for damage will be borne by those whose negligence caused it in direct proportion to their respective fault.

* * *

[The court rejected the argument that "any change in the law of contributory negligence must be made by the Legislature, not by this court." It noted that "the doctrine of contributory negligence is of judicial origin," and said that the doctrine is subject to "continuing judicial evolution." Then the court turned to "considerations of a practical nature."]

A * * * major area of concern involves the administration of the actual process of fact-finding in a comparative negligence system. The assigning of a specific percentage factor to the amount of negligence attributable to a particular party, while in theory a matter of little difficulty, can become a matter of perplexity in the face of hard facts. The temptation for the jury to resort to a quotient verdict in such circumstances can be great. These inherent difficulties are not, however, insurmountable. Guidelines might be provided the jury which will assist it in keeping focussed upon the true inquiry, and the utilization of special verdicts or jury interrogatories can be of invaluable assistance in assuring that the jury has approached its sensitive and often complex task with proper standards and appropriate reverence.

[Another] area of concern, the status of the doctrines of last clear chance and assumption of risk, involves less the practical problems of administering a particular form of comparative negligence than it does a definition of the theoretical outline of the specific form to be adopted. Although several states which apply comparative negligence concepts retain the last clear chance doctrine, the better reasoned position seems to be that when true comparative negligence is adopted, the need for last clear chance as a palliative of the hardships of the "all-or-nothing" rule disappears and its retention results only in a windfall to the plaintiff in direct contravention of the principle of liability in proportion to fault. As for assumption of risk, we have recognized in this state that this defense overlaps that of contributory negligence to some extent and in fact is made up of at least two distinct defenses. "To simplify greatly, it has been observed * * * that in one kind of situation, to wit, where a plaintiff *unreasonably* undertakes to encounter a specific known risk imposed by a defendant's negligence, plaintiff's conduct, although he may encounter that risk in a prudent manner, is in reality a form of contributory negligence * * *. Other kinds of situations within the doctrine of assumption of risk are those, for example, where plaintiff is held to agree to relieve defendant of an obligation of reasonable conduct toward him. Such a situation would not involve contributory negligence, but rather a reduction of defendant's duty of care." (Grey v. Fibreboard Paper Products Co. (1966) 65 Cal.2d 240, 245–246, 53 Cal.Rptr. 545, 548, 418 P.2d 153, 156.) We think it clear that the adoption of a system of comparative negligence should entail the merger of the defense of assumption of risk into the general scheme of assessment of liability in proportion to fault in those particular cases in which the form of assumption of risk involved is no more than a variant of contributory negligence.

* * *

The existence of the foregoing areas of difficulty and uncertainty * * * has not diminished our conviction that the time for a revision of the means for dealing with contributory fault in this state is long past due and that it lies within the province of this court to initiate the needed change by our decision in this case. * * *

Our previous comments [about] two areas of concern (i.e., the status of the doctrines of last clear chance and assumption of risk, and the matter of judicial supervision of the finder of fact) have provided sufficient guidance to enable the trial courts of this state to meet and resolve particular problems in this area as they arise. As we have indicated, last clear chance and assumption of risk (insofar as the latter doctrine is but a variant of contributory negligence) are to be subsumed under the general process of assessing liability in proportion to fault, and the matter of jury supervision we leave for the moment within the broad discretion of the trial courts.

* * *

It remains to identify the precise form of comparative negligence which we now adopt for application in this state. Although there are many variants, only the two basic forms need be considered here. The first of these, the so-called "pure" form of comparative negligence, apportions liability in direct proportion to fault in all cases. This was the form adopted by the Supreme Court of Florida in Hoffman v. Jones, supra, and it applies by statute in Mississippi, Rhode Island, and Washington. Moreover it is the form favored by most scholars and commentators. The second basic form of comparative negligence, of which there are several variants, applies apportionment based on fault *up to the point* at which the plaintiff's negligence is equal to or greater than that of the defendant—when that point is reached, plaintiff is barred from recovery. Nineteen states have adopted this form or one of its variants by statute. The principal argument advanced in its favor is moral in nature: that it is not morally right to permit one more at fault in an accident to recover from one less at fault. Other arguments assert the probability of increased insurance, administrative, and judicial costs if a "pure" rather than a "50 percent" system is adopted, but this has been seriously questioned.

We have concluded that the "pure" form of comparative negligence is that which should be adopted in this state. In our view the "50 percent" system simply shifts the lottery aspect of the contributory negligence rule[21] to a different ground. As Dean Prosser has noted, under such a system "[i]t is obvious that a slight difference in the proportionate fault may permit a

---

21. "The rule that contributory fault bars completely is a curious departure from the central principle of nineteenth century Anglo-American tort law—that wrongdoers should bear the losses they cause. Comparative negligence more faithfully serves that central principle by causing the wrongdoers to share the burden of resulting losses in reasonable relation to their wrongdoing, rather than allocating the heavier burden to the one who, as luck would have it, happened to be more seriously injured." (Comments on Maki v. Frelk, supra, 21 Vand.L.Rev. 889, Comment by Keeton, pp. 912–913.)

recovery; and there has been much justified criticism of a rule under which a plaintiff who is charged with 49 percent of a total negligence recovers 51 percent of his damages, while one who is charged with 50 percent recovers nothing at all." (Prosser, Comparative Negligence, supra, 41 Cal.L.Rev. 1, 25; fns. omitted.) In effect "such a rule distorts the very principle it recognizes, i.e., that persons are responsible for their acts to the extent their fault contributes to an injurious result. The partial rule simply lowers, but does not eliminate, the bar of contributory negligence." (Juenger, Brief for Negligence Law Section of the State Bar of Michigan in Support of Comparative Negligence as Amicus Curiae, Parsonson v. Construction Equipment Company, [1972], 18 Wayne L.Rev. 3, 50.)

We also consider significant the experience of the State of Wisconsin, which until recently was considered the leading exponent of the "50 percent" system. There that system led to numerous appeals on the narrow but crucial issue whether plaintiff's negligence was equal to defendant's. Numerous reversals have resulted on this point, leading to the development of arcane classifications of negligence according to quality and category. * * *

For all of the foregoing reasons we conclude that the "all-or-nothing" rule of contributory negligence as it presently exists in this state should be and is herewith superseded by a system of "pure" comparative negligence, the fundamental purpose of which shall be to assign responsibility and liability for damage in direct proportion to the amount of negligence of each of the parties. Therefore, in all actions for negligence resulting in injury to person or property, the contributory negligence of the person injured in person or property shall not bar recovery, but the damages awarded shall be diminished in proportion to the amount of negligence attributable to the person recovering. The doctrine of last clear chance is abolished, and the defense of assumption of risk is also abolished to the extent that it is merely a variant of the former doctrine of contributory negligence; both of these are to be subsumed under the general process of assessing liability in proportion to negligence. Pending future judicial or legislative developments, the trial courts of this state are to use broad discretion in seeking to assure that the principle stated is applied in the interest of justice and in furtherance of the purposes and objectives set forth in this opinion.

It remains for us to determine the extent to which the rule here announced shall have application to cases other than those which are commenced in the future. It is the rule in this state that determinations of this nature turn upon considerations of fairness and public policy. Upon mature reflection, in view of the very substantial number of cases involving the matter here at issue which are now pending in the trial and appellate courts of this state, and with particular attention to considerations of reliance applicable to individual cases according to the stage of litigation which they have reached, we have concluded that a rule of limited retroactivity should obtain here. Accordingly we hold that the present opinion shall be applicable to all cases in which trial has not begun before the date this decision becomes final in this court, but that it shall not be applicable to any case in which trial began before that date (other than the instant case)—

except that if any judgment be reversed on appeal for other reasons, this opinion shall be applicable to any retrial.

As suggested above, we have concluded that this is a case in which the litigant before the court should be given the benefit of the new rule announced. Here * * * considerations of fairness and public policy do not dictate that a purely prospective operation be given to our decision. To the contrary, sound principles of decision-making compel us to conclude that * * * the new rule here announced should be applied additionally to the case at bench so as to provide incentive in future cases for parties who may have occasion to raise "issues involving renovation of unsound or outmoded legal doctrines." (See Mishkin, Foreword, The Supreme Court 1964 Term (1965) 79 Harv.L.Rev. 56, 60–62.)

* * *

The judgment is reversed.

WRIGHT, C. J., and TOBRINER and BURKE, JJ., concur. [A separate opinion by MOSK, J., is omitted.]

CLARK, Justice (dissenting).

I dissent.

* * * In my view, [the court's] action constitutes a gross departure from established judicial rules and role.

* * *

Contrary to the majority's assertions of judicial adequacy, the courts of other states—with near unanimity—have conceded their inability to determine the best system for replacing contributory negligence, concluding instead that the legislative branch is best able to resolve the issue.

By abolishing this century old doctrine today, the majority seriously erodes our constitutional function. We are again guilty of judicial chauvinism.

McCOMB, J., concurs.

———

SCOTT v. RIZZO, 96 N.M. 682, 634 P.2d 1234 (1981). Here the New Mexico Supreme Court unanimously rejected the "anachronistic 'all-or-nothing' doctrine" of contributory negligence, and embraced a "pure" form of comparative fault embodying "the principle of requiring wrongdoers to share the losses caused, at the ratio of their respective wrongdoing." The court (adopting as its own opinion that of Judge Walters below) said the rule that a plaintiff's negligence bars recovery "flowered during the industrial revolution, with judges protective of the growth of fledgling businesses, and solicitous that material and industrial progress be unhampered by the economic burdens attending liability for negligent injury to others." By the date of its decision, according to the court, 35 states had adhered to some form of comparative fault, reflecting a trend against the contributory negligence rule in "common-law jurisdictions throughout the world, with the exception of fourteen other states in this country."

WILLIAMS v. DELTA INTERNATIONAL MACHINERY CORP., 619 So.2d 1330 (Ala.1993). The Alabama Supreme Court, after "exhaustive study" and "lengthy deliberations," declined (6–2) to adopt comparative fault, and reaffirmed the rule that a plaintiff's contributory negligence bars recovery, "which has been the law in Alabama for approximately 162 years."

Chief Justice Hornsby, in dissent, wrote: "Since [1990], two additional jurisdictions have abandoned the doctrine of contributory negligence in favor of the doctrine of comparative negligence. See McIntyre v. Balentine, 833 S.W.2d 52 (Tenn.1992), and Nelson v. Concrete Supply Co., 303 S.C. 243, 399 S.E.2d 783 (1991). At the time of this dissent, almost every common law jurisdiction in the world and 46 American states have replaced the outmoded doctrine of contributory negligence with some form of the doctrine of comparative negligence. * * * [E]ach jurisdiction adopting the doctrine of comparative negligence * * * has recognized that the doctrine of contributory negligence is inconsistent with the legal logic of the common law tort system and leads to unjust results. That legal reasoning applies with equal force to the law of our state."

COMPARATIVE FAULT PROVISIONS

Below are examples of enacted comparative fault statutes, grouped under two categories. In Li v. Yellow Cab Co., supra, the court noted that there are two basic types of comparative fault schemes: "pure" and "fifty percent."

Under "pure" comparative fault, a plaintiff's contributory negligence never bars all recovery. Rather, no matter what the plaintiff's relative percentage of fault may be, plaintiff's recovery is reduced by that percentage.

In "fifty percent" schemes a line is drawn above which plaintiff is barred altogether, and below which recovery is reduced proportionately. If plaintiff's comparative fault is 51% or more, plaintiff is barred; if 49% or less, recovery is reduced. If exactly 50%, some states permit reduced recovery (e.g. Ohio and Texas); some states deny recovery (e.g. Nebraska).

1. Pure Comparative Fault

New York Civil Practice Law and Rules Section 1411:

In any action to recover damages for personal injury, injury to property, or wrongful death, the culpable conduct attributable to the claimant or to the decedent, including contributory negligence or assumption of risk, shall not bar recovery, but the amount of damages otherwise recoverable shall be diminished in the proportion which the culpable conduct attributable to the claimant or decedent bears to the culpable conduct which caused the damages.

2. "Fifty Percent" Provisions

Nebraska Revised Statutes Section 25–21,185.09:

Any contributory negligence chargeable to the claimant shall diminish proportionately the amount awarded as damages for an injury attributable to the claimant's contributory negligence but shall not bar recovery, except that if the contributory negligence of the claimant is equal to or greater than the total negligence of all persons against whom recovery is sought, the claimant shall be totally barred from recovery. * * *

Ohio Revised Code Annotated Section 2315.19(A)(2):

Contributory negligence or implied assumption of the risk of a person does not bar the person or his legal representative as complainant from recovering damages that have directly and proximately resulted from the negligence of one or more other persons, if the contributory negligence or implied assumption of the risk of the complainant or of the person for whom he is legal representative was no greater than the combined negligence of all other persons from whom the complainant seeks recovery. However, any compensatory damages recoverable by the complainant shall be diminished by an amount that is proportionately equal to the percentage of negligence or implied assumption of the risk of the complainant or of the person for whom he is legal representative * * *.

Texas Civil Practice and Remedies Code Ann. Chapter 33:

§ 33.001. In an action [in tort], a claimant may not recover damages if his percentage of responsibility is greater than 50 percent.

§ 33.011(4). "Percentage of responsibility" means that percentage, stated in whole numbers, attributed by the trier of fact to each claimant, each defendant, each settling person, or each responsible third party with respect to causing or contributing to cause in any way, whether by negligent act or omission, by any defective or unreasonably dangerous product, [or] by other conduct or activity violative of the applicable legal standard * * *, the personal injury, property damage, death, or other harm for which recovery of damages is sought.

§ 33.012(a). If the claimant is not barred from recovery under Section 33.001, the court shall reduce the amount of damages to be recovered by the claimant with respect to a cause of action by a percentage equal to the claimant's percentage of responsibility.

WATERSON v. GENERAL MOTORS CORP., 111 N.J. 238, 544 A.2d 357 (1988). Here the court explained how the seat belt defense (see p. 511 supra) would work in a comparative fault regime. The plaintiff would not bear all the cost of the injury avoidable by use of a seat belt; rather the fault of plaintiff and defendant would be compared as to such injury. The court said:

"After the jury has * * * found (1) that the failure to use a seat belt constituted negligence and (2) that plaintiff sustained avoidable, second-collision injuries, the jury must then determine the percentage of plaintiff's comparative fault for damages arising from those injuries. The total negligence for these second-collision or seat-belt damages consists of (a) defendant's negligence in causing the accident (since without that negligence there would have been no accident and no injuries of any kind), (b) plaintiff's comparative negligence, if any, in causing the accident (since, again, without plaintiff's comparative negligence there would have been no accident and no injuries), and (c) plaintiff's negligence in failing to use a seat belt (since without that negligence there would not have been any second collision injuries). The total fault for these seat-belt damages, as for all damages, is one-hundred percent. Thus, the jury must determine the percentage of plaintiff's fault for these damages that are attributable to plaintiff's failure to wear a seat belt."

VON DER HEIDE v. COMMONWEALTH, 553 Pa. 120, 718 A.2d 286 (1998). Decedent died when the car he was driving struck a guardrail. His wife brought this wrongful death action against the Pennsylvania Department of Transportation (PennDOT) alleging that the guardrail was in a defective condition. The jury found PennDOT 60% negligent and decedent 40% negligent, and decedent's recovery was reduced in accord with Pennsylvania's comparative fault scheme. On appeal PennDOT argued that decedent's negligence amounted to a "superseding cause" of the injury, and therefore there should be no recovery at all. *Held*, that the doctrine of "superseding cause" does not apply to the negligence of a plaintiff. " 'A superseding cause is an act of a third person or other force which, by its intervention, prevents the actor from being liable for harm to another which his antecedent negligence is a substantial factor in bringing about.' Restatement (Second) of Torts § 440." "A superseding cause was not present in this case because there was never a third party or event to be considered beyond the conduct of the defendant and the plaintiff."

A concurring opinion noted that "some comparative negligence jurisdictions have continued to apply superseding cause to a narrow category of cases in which an injured plaintiff's conduct * * * amounts to more than mere negligence * * *. [A]pplication of the doctrine * * * would seem appropriate in a case in which a plaintiff's own intentional, unforeseeable conduct severs the causal connection between the defendant's negligence and the plaintiff's injuries."

HOW TO COMPARE FAULT

A typical statutory provision establishing comparative fault tells what happens once fault is apportioned: plaintiff's recovery is reduced or perhaps, if plaintiff's percentage of fault is too high in a "fifty percent" scheme, barred altogether. But the typical provision does not itself say how to determine relative shares of fault. Some guidance in how to compare fault is given by official comment on the Uniform Comparative Fault Act, 12 Unif. Laws Ann., a model statute put forward by the National Conference of Commissioners on Uniform State Laws in 1977. The Uniform Act's own text on the topic of how to apportion fault—its Section 2(b)—does not say much:

In determining the percentages of fault, the trier of fact shall consider both the nature of the conduct of each party at fault and the extent of the causal relation between the conduct and the damages claimed.

The Commissioners' Comment on this section, however, offers a helpful list of relevant factors, plus an observation about causal responsibility:

Percentages of Fault. In comparing the fault of the several parties for the purpose of obtaining percentages there are a number of implications arising from the concept of fault. The conduct of the claimant or of any defendant may be more or less at fault, depending upon all the circumstances including such matters as (1) whether the conduct was mere inadvertence or engaged in with an awareness of the danger involved, (2) the magnitude of the risk created by the conduct, including the number of persons endangered and the potential seriousness of the injury, (3) the significance of what the actor was seeking to attain by his conduct, (4) the actor's superior or inferior capacities, and (5) the particular circumstances, such as the existence of an emergency requiring a hasty decision.

* * * An error in driving on the part of a bus driver with a load of passengers may properly produce an evaluation of greater fault than the same error on the part of a housewife gratuitously giving her neighbor a ride to the shopping center * * *.

In determining the relative fault of the parties, the fact-finder will also give consideration to the relative closeness of the causal relationship of the negligent conduct of the defendants and the harm to the plaintiff. Degrees of fault and proximity of causation are inextricably mixed, as a study of last clear chance indicates, and that common law doctrine has been absorbed in this Act. * * *

FERGUSON v. NORTHERN STATES POWER CO., 307 Minn. 26, 239 N.W.2d 190 (1976). Plaintiffs, father and son, were trimming tall trees in their back yard when a cut branch came into contact with an uninsulated high-voltage transmission line maintained by defendant power company. The son was seriously injured by escaping electricity. Neither plaintiff was aware that the line in question carried 8000 volts, and was not an ordinary household service line. In a special verdict the jury found all parties negligent and specified the percentage of fault attributable to each party. Since plaintiffs' negligence totalled more than 50 percent, judgment was entered for defendant. The Supreme Court reversed, saying:

"The problem lies in the issue of comparative negligence. In light of the relative risks involved, we have serious doubts about the reasonableness of the jury's apportionment of causal negligence.

"Because of the comparatively greater knowledge possessed by a utility of the extraordinary magnitude of the risk involved in the transmission of high-voltage electricity through residential neighborhoods, the risk to which it subjects the ordinary city dweller is not the equivalent of the risk the residential user subjects himself to by coming in close proximity to the overhead wires. The risks are different in degree. While we cannot hold that they are so different as to be an absolute bar to the defense of contributory negligence, we do rule that in a case such as this, involving a dangerous instrumentality and a great disparity in risks, the jury, in order to fairly and accurately apportion causal negligence, should be instructed to give special consideration to this disparity."

CHAMPAGNE v. UNITED STATES, 513 N.W.2d 75 (N.D.1994). An Indian Health Services hospital admitted an 18-year-old Native American male who had attempted suicide. The patient was discharged three days later, thereafter "received no counseling or other form of treatment," and within a month killed himself. Proper medical care more likely than not would have prevented the suicide. In a wrongful death suit brought by the deceased patient's parents, *held*, that the fault of the suicide victim in causing his own death should be compared with the fault of the medical provider, if the mentally ill patient "retains some capacity to protect himself from harm." "But, if the medical provider, knowing the patient is suicidal and too mentally incapacitated to assume responsibility for his own well-being, undertakes a duty of care to the patient that takes in the patient's duty of self care, then the patient's fault in the act of suicide is greatly reduced."

"In making the fault comparison, the factfinder should always take into account the extent of the patient's diminished mental capacity to care for his own safety. * * * A mentally ill person can only be held to the degree of care that his diminished capacity permits. The worse the suicidal patient's diminished capacity, the greater the medical provider's responsibility."

BLAZOVIC v. ANDRICH
Supreme Court of New Jersey, 1991.
124 N.J. 90, 590 A.2d 222.

The opinion of the Court was delivered by STEIN, J.

* * *

On August 19, 1982, plaintiff, Thomas Blazovic, [and some friends] gathered at the Plantation Restaurant and Lounge (Plantation) in Fairfield. Defendants James Andrich, James Philbin, Dean Angelo, Vincent LaBanca, and Louis Zecchino were also at Plantation that night. The two groups sat at opposite ends of the barroom and had no contact while inside the bar. * * * [D]efendants left Plantation at approximately 11:15 p.m. Approximately fifteen minutes later, plaintiff and his friends also left the bar. The ensuing events are disputed. Plaintiff contends that while in Plantation's parking lot, he observed a group of people, including defendants, throwing stones or rocks at a nearby sign. Plaintiff testified that he politely asked them to stop, at which point the group ran toward him, pushed him to the ground, and proceeded to punch and kick him. * * * [D]efendants claim that on leaving the bar, they remained in Plantation's parking lot, throwing small stones to see who could come closest to a nearby sign. Defendant Andrich testified that a short time later, plaintiff came out of Plantation and began swearing at defendants. Both sides agree that [one] of defendants began the physical confrontation.

[Plaintiff sued for his damages. In answer to special interrogatories, the jury found that defendants "committed an intentional assault and battery against Thomas Blazovic." The jury also found "that plaintiff's own negligence had contributed to his injuries." Thus the case presented the following general question: whether, under New Jersey's Comparative Negligence Act, the fault of a negligent plaintiff should be compared with the fault of an intentional wrongdoer. Should a plaintiff's damages be reduced because of contributory negligence, when a defendant is guilty not just of negligence but rather of intentional misconduct? Excerpts below address this question.]

* * *

The adoption of the Comparative Negligence Act in 1973 reflected a legislative decision to ameliorate the harsh results that accompanied the common-law doctrine of contributory negligence. Ostrowski v. Azzara, 111 N.J. 429, 436 (1988). Under the earlier scheme, a negligent plaintiff was precluded from any recovery even when the plaintiff's negligence was substantially less than the defendant's. * * *

The change to a comparative-negligence system eliminated the "all or nothing" approach to tort recovery in favor of apportionment of liability among all parties to an action in rough equivalence to their causal fault. Under the Act, a plaintiff equally negligent as or less negligent than the defendant is not barred, but recovery is instead diminished by the percentage of negligence attributed to the plaintiff by the trier of fact. N.J.S.A. 2A:15–5.1.

* * *

It is now well-settled that the Act's application is not limited to negligence actions. In Suter v. San Angelo Foundry & Machine Co., 81 N.J. 150 (1979), a sheetmetal worker filed a strict-liability action against the manufacturer of a sheetmetal rolling machine due to injuries sustained by the worker when his hand became caught in the machine. The manufacturer sought to bar any recovery, relying on the alleged contributory negligence of the injured plaintiff and the inapplicability of the Comparative Negligence Act to a strict-liability claim. The Court rejected the contention that the Act was limited to negligence actions, reasoning that that limitation would frustrate the legislative intent to mitigate the unfairness associated with the total bar to recovery posed by common-law contributory negligence. Consequently, we determined that "the Act was intended to cover fault in a broader sense rather than in the narrow negligence concept." Although we found that the plaintiff's conduct did not constitute contributory negligence, we held that fault could be apportioned under the Act between strictly-liable and negligent parties.

Comparative negligence principles have also been applied to conduct characterized as wanton and willful. In McCann v. Lester, 239 N.J.Super. 601 (App.Div.1990), * * * [the court] reasoned that

* * * it serves the interest of justice and our expanded concept of comparative fault for percentages also to be attributed to the conduct of the willful, wanton or reckless party, as well as the party who is merely negligent. As we have been taught by Suter v. San Angelo Foundry, supra, the labels attached by the law to various types of conduct should not thwart the principle that it is the overall fault of the parties which is to be measured.

* * * The McCann holding is in accord with those of several other jurisdictions. * * *

Despite the widespread [application] of comparative-fault principles to cases involving reckless or wanton and willful conduct, most courts that have considered the issue have declined to extend comparative-fault principles to conduct characterized as intentional. See, e.g., * * * Uniform Comparative Fault Act § 1 Comment, 12 U.L.A. 44 (Supp. 1979) (as a general principle, Act does not include intentional torts).

* * * Early cases distinguished between negligent and intentional conduct in order to circumvent the harsh effect of the contributory-negligence bar, reflecting the view that intentional tortfeasors should be deterred and required to pay damages irrespective of plaintiff's negligence. See, e.g., Steinmetz v. Kelly, 72 Ind. 442, 446 (1880) ("An intentional and unlawful assault and unlawful battery, inflicted upon a person, is an invasion of his right to personal security, for which the law gives him redress, and of this redress he cannot be deprived on the ground that he was negligent * * *."). Other courts have reached the same result by theorizing that intentional and negligent conduct are "different in kind" * * *.

Some jurisdictions, however, have permitted apportionment of fault between negligent and intentional tortfeasors. For example, in Comeau v. Lucas, 90 A.D.2d 674, 455 N.Y.S.2d 871 (App.Div.1982), an intoxicated rock-band member hired to play at a private party attacked and beat one of the guests who was also intoxicated and disruptive. The trial court instructed the jury to apportion damages between the negligent plaintiff and the intentionally-tortious defendant. In doing so, the jury reduced plaintiff's recovery by ten percent due to his contributory negligence. * * * [See also] Baugh v. Redmond, 565 So.2d 953 (La.Ct.App.1990) (comparative fault principles should apply in battery action if plaintiff's words or actions are sufficient to establish provocation) * * *.

* * *

We are unpersuaded by the decisions of other jurisdictions that reject apportionment of fault in actions involving intentional tortfeasors. Those decisions derive from an earlier era when courts attempted to avoid the harsh effect of the contributory-negligence defense and sought to punish and deter intentional tortfeasors. * * * Refusal to compare the negligence of a plaintiff whose percentage of fault is no more than fifty percent with the fault of intentional tortfeasors is difficult to justify under a comparative-fault system in which that plaintiff's recovery can be only diminished, not barred. * * *

Moreover, we reject the concept that intentional conduct is "different in kind" from both negligence and wanton and willful conduct, and consequently cannot be compared with them. Instead, we view intentional wrongdoing as "different in degree" from either negligence or wanton and willful conduct. To act intentionally involves knowingly or purposefully engaging in conduct "substantially certain" to result in injury to another. Restatement (Second) of Torts § 8A comment b (1965). In contrast, wanton and willful conduct poses a highly unreasonable risk of harm likely to result in injury. Id. at § 500 comment a. Neither that difference nor the divergence between intentional conduct and negligence precludes comparison by a jury. The different levels of culpability inherent in each type of conduct will merely be reflected in the jury's apportionment of fault. By viewing the various types of tortious conduct in that way, we adhere most closely to the guiding principle of comparative fault—to distribute the loss in proportion to the respective faults of the parties causing that loss. Thus, consistent with the evolution of comparative negligence and joint-tortfeasor liability in this state, we hold that responsibility for a plaintiff's claimed injury is to be apportioned according to each party's relative degree of fault, including the fault attributable to an intentional tortfeasor.

Apportionment of fault between intentional and negligent parties will not eliminate the deterrent or punitive aspects of tort recovery. Where tortious conduct merits punitive as well as compensatory damages, a plaintiff's comparative fault will reduce recovery only of compensatory damages. * * * Because punitive damages are designed to punish the wrongdoer, and not to compensate the injured party, they [cannot] be apportioned * * *. That principle will accomplish the goal of equitably dividing liability for a plaintiff's compensatory damages, while keeping intact the policy of punishing wanton or intentional acts.

––––––

MORGAN v. JOHNSON, 137 Wash.2d 887, 976 P.2d 619 (1999). A night of drinking ended in altercation. The female plaintiff alleged that the male defendant punched and kicked her. The jury found that defendant "intentionally caused bodily harm," but also found that Washington's "intoxication defense" applied, and so no damages were awarded. This defense, established by statute, bars recovery if a plaintiff's intoxication "was a proximate cause of the injuries * * * and the plaintiff was more than 50 percent at fault." *Held*, reversed and remanded for determination of plaintiff's damages. "The very nature of the intoxication defense involves a comparative fault analysis," but "comparative fault is inapplicable in the context of an intentional tort" like assault or battery. " '[I]ntentional torts are part of a wholly different legal realm * * *. ' "

JESS v. HERRMANN, 26 Cal.3d 131, 161 Cal.Rptr. 87, 604 P.2d 208 (1979). Jess and Herrmann were both injured when their two cars collided. Jess sued Herrmann for damages, and Herrmann counterclaimed ("filed a cross-complaint") against Jess. The jury found both parties negligent. It assigned 40 percent of the fault to Jess and 60 percent to Herrmann;

determined that Jess had suffered $100,000 damages and Herrmann $14,000; and concluded that Jess was entitled to recover $60,000 (60% of $100,000) and that Herrmann was entitled to recover $5,600 (40% of $14,000). The trial court offset the two awards and entered a single judgment in favor of Jess for $54,400. The question on appeal in the California Supreme Court was whether two separate judgments should have been entered. Said the court:

" * * * If both Jess and Herrmann carry adequate automobile insurance, in the absence of a mandatory setoff rule Jess would receive $60,000 from defendant Herrmann's insurer * * * and Herrmann would receive $5,600 from Jess' insurer * * *. Under the setoff rule applied by the trial court, however—despite the fact that both Jess' and Herrmann's injuries, financial losses and insurance coverage remained in fact unchanged—Jess' recovery from Herrmann's insurer is reduced to $54,400 and Herrmann is denied any recovery whatsoever from Jess' insurer.

"As these facts demonstrate, a mandatory setoff rule in the typical setting of insured tortfeasors does not serve as an innocuous accounting mechanism or as a beneficial safeguard against an adversary's insolvency but rather operates radically to alter the parties' ultimate financial positions. Such a mandatory rule diminishes *both* injured parties' actual recovery and accords both insurance companies a corresponding fortuitous windfall at their insureds' expense. * * *

" * * * [V]irtually all of the commentators who have analyzed this issue concur in Professor Fleming's conclusion that '[t]he only sensible solution from the point of view of compensation and loss spreading is * * * to proscribe set-off under "pure" comparative negligence law whenever the participants are insured.' Fleming, Foreward: Comparative Negligence at Last—By Judicial Choice (1976) 64 Cal.L.Rev. 239, 247 * * *.

" * * * At least in cases in which both parties to a lawsuit carry adequate insurance to cover the damages found to be payable to an injured party, both the public policy of California's financial responsibility law and considerations of fairness clearly support a rule barring a setoff of one party's recovery against the other. * * * "

SECTION C. ASSUMPTION OF RISK: CLASSICAL DOCTRINE

The defense of assumption of risk marks an abrupt break in the conceptual structure of negligence doctrine. The defenses of contributory and comparative negligence apply basic negligence concepts (duty and breach) to the special circumstance of the plaintiff's exercise of caution for her own protection against the carelessness of others. The defense of assumption of risk, in all of its myriad forms (classical and modern, express and implied, primary, secondary, reasonable and unreasonable), involves the suspension of otherwise applicable tort duties for reasons that sound more in contract than in tort. Indeed, the conceptual unity of the doctrine, in all its diverse forms, stems from its contractual character. The defense of assumption of risk asserts that the victim has, by her choice, voluntarily altered the duties of care owed to her.

Classical doctrine recognized a broad and sweeping—but not unlimited—defense of assumption of risk. The three principal cases which follow illustrate the classical doctrine and its limits. The contrast between the factual circumstances of the first of these cases and the next two is important to understanding both the domain and the logic of the defense. *Clayards* is an accident on a public road, between strangers; *Farwell* and *Lamson* are workplace accidents. *Farwell* and *Lamson* therefore involve parties who have preexisting legal relations. The existence of those relations makes contract a live alternative to tort. The principles, policies and concepts of contract law might be used to determine the rights and duties of the parties.

CLAYARDS v. DETHICK
Queen's Bench, 1848. 12 Q.B. 439.
116 Eng.Rep. 932.

[Action of case for causing the death of the plaintiff's horse. At the trial before Denman, C. J., it appeared that the plaintiff, a cab proprietor, had stables opening upon Gower Mews, a cul-de-sac. The mews communicated with Gower Street by a passage 13½ feet wide and 56½ feet long. It had no other outlet to the street. The defendant, in constructing a drain, acting pursuant to the authority of the Commissioner of Sewers, made an unfenced excavation in the mews 4½ feet from one side and 2½ feet from the other side of the passageway, piling the earth on the wider space between the trench and the side to the height of four feet. The plaintiff brought out a horse from his stables and was about to put down planks over to the narrower space in order to get the horse across, when the defendant said he would not be answerable if the plaintiff did that and told him to lead the horse over the piled up earth. This the plaintiff, with assistance, did successfully. Later in the day, the plaintiff, in the absence of the defendant, led out another horse and attempted to lead it over. There was testimony that the defendant's workmen objected on this occasion and that the plaintiff insisted on continuing. On this occasion the earth gave way and the horse fell in. It was strangled in the attempt to get it out.]

The Lord Chief Justice, in summing up, observed that, if the defendants' witnesses were to be believed, and the plaintiff on the second occasion had, in defiance of warning, incurred an evidently great danger, this was a rashness on his part which would excuse the defendants; but that it could not be the plaintiff's duty to refrain altogether from coming out of the mews merely because the defendants had made the passage in some degree dangerous; that the defendants were not entitled to keep the occupiers of the mews in a state of siege till the passage was declared safe, first creating a nuisance and then excusing themselves by giving notice that there was some danger: though, if the plaintiff had persisted in running upon a great and obvious danger his action could not be maintained. And he left it to the jury to say whether or not the plaintiff had so acted. Verdict for plaintiff: damages £20. The defendant obtained a rule nisi.

PATTESON, J. * * * Now the defendants had clearly no right to leave a trench open in the passage to this mews without a proper fence, and, having done so, to tell the plaintiff "you shall keep your horse in the stable till we inform you that you may remove him." But whether or not the plaintiff contributed to the mischief that happened by want of ordinary caution, is a question of degree. If the danger was so great that no sensible man would have incurred it, the verdict must be for the defendants: and the case was rightly put to the jury as depending on this question. The plaintiff here had passed safely in the afternoon over the place at which the accident happened. According to the evidence for the defendants, he was told, on attempting to pass in the evening, that he could not do it without danger to himself and the men below. The jury, however, do not appear to have believed this statement. The whole question was, whether the danger was so obvious that the plaintiff could not with common prudence make the attempt. That was properly put to the jury; and they have found for the plaintiff.

COLERIDGE, J. The plaintiff was not bound to abstain from pursuing his livelihood because there was some danger. It was necessary for the defendants to shew a clear danger and a precise warning. Whether these facts existed or not, was for the consideration of the jury; and if the jury disbelieved them, the plaintiff was entitled to the verdict.

[LORD DENMAN, C. J., concurred, in a brief opinion.]

Rule discharged.

FARWELL v. THE BOSTON AND WORCESTER RAIL ROAD CORP.

Supreme Judicial Court of Massachusetts, 1842.
45 Mass. (4 Metc.) 49.

In an action of trespass upon the case, the plaintiff alleged in his declaration, that he agreed with the defendants to serve them in the employment of an engineer in the management and care of their engines and cars running on their rail road between Boston and Worcester, and entered on said employment, and continued to perform his duties as engineer till October 30th 1837, when the defendants, at Newton, by their servants, so carelessly, negligently and unskilfully managed and used, and put and placed the iron match rail, called the short switch, across the rail or track of their said rail road, that the engine and cars, upon which the plaintiff was engaged and employed in the discharge of his said duties of engineer, were thrown from the track of said rail road, and the plaintiff, by means thereof, was thrown with great violence upon the ground; by means of which one of the wheels of one of said cars passed over the right hand of the plaintiff, crushing and destroying the same.

The case was submitted to the court on the following facts agreed by the parties: "The plaintiff was employed by the defendants, in 1835, as an engineer, and went at first with the merchandize cars, and afterwards with the passenger cars, and so continued till October 30th 1837, at the wages of two dollars per day; that being the usual wages paid to engine-men, which are higher than the wages paid to a machinist, in which capacity the plaintiff formerly was employed. * * * "

* * *

SHAW, C. J. This is an action of new impression in our courts, and involves a principle of great importance. It presents a case, where two persons are in the service and employment of one company, whose business it is to construct and maintain a rail road, and to employ their trains of cars to carry persons and merchandize for hire. They are appointed and employed by the same company to perform separate duties and services, all tending to the accomplishment of one and the same purpose—that of the safe and rapid transmission of the trains; and they are paid for their respective services according to the nature of their respective duties, and the labor and skill required for their proper performance. The question is, whether, for damages sustained by one of the persons so employed, by means of the carelessness and negligence of another, the party injured has a remedy against the common employer. It is an argument against such an action, though certainly not a decisive one, that no such action has before been maintained.

It is laid down by Blackstone, that if a servant, by his negligence, does any damage to a stranger, the master shall be answerable for his neglect. But the damage must be done while he is actually employed in the master's service; otherwise, the servant shall answer for his own misbehavior. 1 Bl.Com. 431. McManus v. Crickett, 1 East, 106. This rule is obviously founded on the great principle of social duty, that every man, in the management of his own affairs, whether by himself or by his agents or servants, shall so conduct them as not injure another; and if he does not, and another thereby sustains damage, he shall answer for it. If done by a servant, in the course of his employment, and acting within the scope of his authority, it is considered, in contemplation of law, so far the act of the master that the latter shall be answerable *civiliter*. But this presupposes that the parties stand to each other in the relation of strangers, between whom there is no privity; and the action, in such case, is an action sounding in tort. The form is trespass on the case, for the consequential damage. The maxim *respondeat superior* is adopted in that case, from general considerations of policy and security.

But this does not apply to the case of a servant bringing his action against his own employer to recover damages for an injury arising in the course of that employment, where all such risks and perils as the employer and the servant respectively intend to assume and bear may be regulated by the express or implied contract between them, and which, in contemplation of law, must be presumed to be thus regulated.

The same view seems to have been taken by the learned counsel for the plaintiff in the argument; and it was conceded, that the claim could not be placed on the principle indicated by the maxim *respondeat superior*, which binds the master to indemnify a stranger for the damage caused by the careless, negligent or unskilful act of his servant in the conduct of his affairs. The claim, therefore, is placed, and must be maintained, if maintained at all, on the ground of contract. As there is no express contract between the parties, applicable to this point, it is placed on the footing of an implied contract of indemnity, arising out of the relation of master and servant. It would be an implied promise, arising from the duty of the master to be responsible to each person employed by him, in the conduct of every branch of business, where two or more persons are employed, to pay for all damage occasioned by the negligence of every other person employed in the same service. * * *

The general rule, resulting from considerations as well of justice as of policy, is, that he who engages in the employment of another for the performance of specified duties and services, for compensation, takes upon himself the natural and ordinary risks and perils incident to the performance of such services, and in legal presumption, the compensation is adjusted accordingly. And we are not aware of any principle which should except the perils arising from the carelessness and negligence of those who are in the same employment. These are perils which the servant is as likely to know, and against which he can as effectually guard, as the master. They are perils incident to the service, and which can be as distinctly foreseen and provided for in the rate of compensation as any others. To say that the master shall be responsible because the damage is caused by his agents, is assuming the very point which remains to be proved. * * *

If we look from considerations of justice to those of policy, they will strongly lead to the same conclusion. In considering the rights and obligations arising out of particular relations, it is competent for courts of justice to regard considerations of policy and general convenience, and to draw from them such rules as will, in their practical application, best promote the safety and security of all parties concerned. This is, in truth, the basis on which implied promises are raised, being duties legally inferred from a consideration of what is best adapted to promote the benefit of all persons concerned, under given circumstances. * * *

The liability of passenger carriers is founded on similar considerations. They are held to the strictest responsibility for care, vigilance and skill, on the part of themselves and all persons employed by them, and they are paid accordingly. The rule is founded on the expediency of throwing the risk upon those who can best guard against it. Story on Bailments, § 590, & seq.

We are of opinion that these considerations apply strongly to the case in question. Where several persons are employed in the conduct of one common enterprise or undertaking, and the safety of each depends much on the care and skill with which each other shall perform his appropriate duty, each is an observer of the conduct of the others, can give notice of any misconduct, incapacity or neglect of duty, and leave the service, if the common employer will not take such precautions, and employ such agents as the safety of the whole party may require. By these means, the safety of each will be much more effectually secured, than could be done by a resort to the common employer for indemnity in case of loss by the negligence of each other. Regarding it in this light, it is the ordinary case of one sustaining an injury in the course of his own employment, in which he must bear the loss himself, or seek his remedy, if he have any, against the actual wrongdoer.

In applying these principles to the present case, it appears that the plaintiff was employed by the defendants as an engineer, at the rate of wages usually paid in that employment, being a higher rate than the plaintiff had before received as a machinist. It was a voluntary undertaking on his part, with a full knowledge of the risks incident to the employment; and the loss was sustained by means of an ordinary casualty, caused by the negligence of another servant of the company. Under these circumstances, the loss must be deemed to be the result of a pure accident, like those to which all men, in all employments, and at all times, are more or less exposed; and like similar losses from accidental causes, it must rest where it first fell, unless the plaintiff has a remedy against the person actually in default; of which we give no opinion.

It was strongly pressed in the argument, that although this might be so, where two or more servants are employed in the same department of duty, where each can exert some influence over the conduct of the other, and thus to some extent provide for his own security; yet that it could not apply where two or more are employed in different departments of duty, at a distance from each other, and where one can in no degree control or influence the conduct of another. But we think this is founded upon a supposed distinction, on which it would be extremely difficult to establish a practical rule. When the object to be accomplished is one and the same, when the employers are the same, and the several persons employed derive their authority and their compensation from the same source, it would be extremely difficult to distinguish, what constitutes one department and what a distinct department of duty. It would vary with the circumstances of every case. * * *

Besides, it appears to us, that the argument rests upon an assumed principle of responsibility which does not exist. The master, in the case supposed, is not exempt from liability, because the servant has better means of providing for his safety, when he is employed in immediate connexion with those from whose negligence he might suffer; but because the *implied contract* of the master does not extend to indemnify the servant against the negligence of any one but himself; and he is not liable in tort, as for the negligence of his servant, because the person suffering does not stand towards him in the relation of a stranger, but is one whose rights are regulated by contract express or implied. The exemption of the master, therefore, from liability for the negligence of a fellow servant, does not depend exclusively upon the consideration, that the servant has better means to provide for his own safety, but upon other grounds. Hence the separation of the employment into different departments cannot create that liability, when it does not arise from express or implied contract, or from a responsibility created by law to third persons, and strangers, for the negligence of a servant.

A case may be put for the purpose of illustrating this distinction. Suppose the road had been owned by one set of proprietors whose duty it was to keep it in repair and have it at all times ready and in fit condition for the running of engines and cars, taking a toll, and that the engines and cars were owned by another set of proprietors, paying toll to the proprietors of the road, and receiving compensation from passengers for their carriage; and suppose the engineer to suffer a loss from the negligence of the switch-tender. We are inclined to the opinion that the engineer might have a remedy against the railroad corporation; and if so, it must be on the ground, that as between the engineer employed by the proprietors of the engines and cars, and the switch-tender employed by the corporation, the engineer would be a stranger, between whom and the corporation there could be no privity of contract; and not because the engineer would have no means of controlling the conduct of the switch-tender. The responsibility which one is under for the negligence of his servant, in the conduct of his business, towards third persons, is founded on another and distinct principle from that of implied contract, and stands on its own reasons of policy. The same reasons of policy, we think, limit this responsibility to the case of strangers, for whose security alone it is established. Like considerations of policy and general expediency forbid the extension of the principle, so far as to warrant a servant in maintaining an action against his employer for an indemnity which we think was not contemplated in the nature and terms of the employment, and which, if established, would not conduce to the general good.

In coming to the conclusion that the plaintiff, in the present case, is not entitled to recover, considering it as in some measure a nice question, we would add a caution against any hasty conclusion as to the application of this rule to a case not fully within the same principle. It may be varied and modified by circumstances not appearing in the present case, in which it appears, that no wilful wrong or actual negligence was imputed to the corporation, and where suitable means were furnished and suitable persons employed to accomplish the object in view. * * *

ECKERT v. LONG ISLAND RAILROAD, 43 N.Y. 502 (1871). Plaintiff's husband saved a small child from being run over by a negligently operated train, but was himself struck and killed. The Court of Appeals affirmed a judgment against the railroad, holding that decedent's conduct was "not negligent." Allen, J., wrote in dissent:

"The plaintiff's intestate * * * went upon the track of the defendant's road in front of an approaching train, voluntarily, in the exercise of his free will, and while in the full possession of all his faculties, and with capacity to judge of the danger. His action was the result of his own choice, * * * [and] the maxim *volenti non fit injuria* applies. It is a well established rule, that no one can maintain an action for a wrong, when he consents or contributes to the act which occasions his loss. One who with liberty of choice, and knowledge of the hazard of injury, places himself in a position of danger, does so at his own peril, and must take the consequences of his act. * * *

"Whenever there has been notice of the danger, and freedom of action, the injured party has been compelled to bear the consequences of the action irrespective of the character and degree of negligence of other parties. * * *

* * *

"* * * The rescue of the child from apparent imminent danger was a praiseworthy act * * *. But the principles of law cannot yield to particular cases."

LAMSON v. AMERICAN AX & TOOL CO.

Supreme Judicial Court of Massachusetts, 1900.

177 Mass. 144, 58 N.E. 585.

HOLMES, C. J. This is an action for personal injuries caused by the fall of a hatchet from a rack in front of which it was the plaintiff's business to work at painting hatchets, and upon which the hatchets were to be placed to dry when painted. The plaintiff had been in the defendant's employment for many years. About a year before the accident new racks had been substituted for those previously in use, and it may be assumed that they were less safe, and were not proper, but were dangerous, on account of the liability of the hatchets to fall from the pegs upon the plaintiff when the racks were jarred by the motion of machinery near by. The plaintiff complained to the superintendent that the hatchets were more likely to drop off than when the old racks were in use, and that now they might fall upon him, which they could not have done from the old racks. He was answered, in substance, that he would have to use the racks or leave. The accident which he feared happened, and he brought this suit.

The plaintiff, on his own evidence, appreciated the danger more than any one else. He perfectly understood what was likely to happen. That likelihood did not depend upon the doing of some negligent act by people in another branch of employment, but solely on the permanent conditions of the racks and their surroundings and the plaintiff's continuing to work where he did. He complained, and was notified that he could go if he would not face the chance. He stayed, and took the risk. He did so none the less that the fear of losing his place was one of his motives. Exceptions overruled.

MURPHY v. STEEPLECHASE AMUSEMENT CO., 250 N.Y. 479, 166 N.E. 173 (1929); noted in 15 Cornell L.Q. 132. The defendant amusement park operated a "flopper" for those who might be amused by a contest between their reactions and an undulating moving belt. The plaintiff, after watching it operate upon others, stepped upon it and was thrown, fracturing a knee cap. *Held* (6–1), for defendant, reversing the judgment below. "One who takes part in such a sport accepts the dangers that inhere in it so far as they are obvious and necessary, just as a fencer accepts the risk of a thrust by his antagonist or a spectator at a ball game the chance of contact with the ball."

FRED HARVEY CORP. v. MATEAS, 170 F.2d 612 (9th Cir.1948). Plaintiff was one of a party of seven who rented defendant's mules to go from the rim to the bottom of the Grand Canyon, led by defendant's servant. The plaintiff was inexperienced, the mule was fresh from pasture and used to leading, unused to following. Plaintiff was thrown when the mule "bucked".

Held, judgment for plaintiff affirmed. Defendant was negligent and plaintiff assumed only the risk of riding a gentle, well trained and ordinarily safe mule.

HUDSON v. KANSAS CITY BASEBALL CLUB, 349 Mo. 1215, 164 S.W.2d 318, 142 A.L.R. 858 (1942). Action for negligence. The plaintiff, a man of 64, alleged that he attended a professional ball game in defendant's park, as he had occasionally done before, paid for a reserved seat and thought that it was protected by a wire netting; that he was not protected; that he was struck by a foul ball; that defendant was negligent in not informing him of the lack of protection. *Held,* for defendant on demurrer. Defendant was not negligent and even if it were, plaintiff must have seen that he was not sitting behind a wire screen and must have realized the perils incident to the game.

TELEGA v. SECURITY BUREAU, INC., 719 A.2d 372 (Pa.Super.1998). Plaintiff, a Pittsburgh Steelers season ticket holder for several years with seats behind the end zone, "stood up in front of his assigned seat, extended his arms, and cleanly fielded" a football which had just been kicked for a field goal. "When he attempted to sit down, Mr. Telega was thrust from his seat and trampled face first into the cement aisle by aggressive fans who stripped him of the souvenir ball. Mr. Telega suffered numerous injuries from this attack, including facial lacerations, a sprained shoulder and arm resulting in extensive physical therapy, and a broken nose that required surgery." *Held,* reversing summary judgment for defendant, no assumption of risk.

"Although this type of unruly, improper fan conduct may have occurred in Mr. Telega's section of the stadium before, being trampled by displaced fans is not a risk inherent in or so ordinary a part of the spectator sport of football such that it is certain to occur at any and every stadium in the Commonwealth. The trial court's reliance on Mr. Telega's prior knowledge of such 'fan upheaval' and his report of this dangerous behavior to management and security personnel is an attempt improperly to shift the focus of the 'no-duty' inquiry from the risks inherent in the game of football itself to an examination of other risks which may be present in a particular football stadium. By creating the notion that 'if it happened before, it must be customary,' the trial court concludes that if a spectator is injured at a football game, and had prior knowledge of the risk of injury, the risk is automatically an inherent part of the spectator sport and recovery is barred. This broad-sweeping extension of the 'no-duty' rule inappropriately attributes to Mr. Telega the responsibility to ensure his own safety and protect himself from the behavior of aggressive fans despite the presence of Appellee whose primary obligation it was to regulate crowd control. Indeed, such an interpretation of the 'no-duty' rule would permit amusement facility operators to avoid liability for 'universally prevalent negligent conditions,' and would relieve them of all duty to protect against any risk within the facility. This approach is clearly undesirable and defies the well-established principles of negligence."

JOHNSON v. CITY OF NEW YORK, 186 N.Y. 139, 78 N.E. 715 (1906). The defendant city illegally permitted persons to use a highway for an automobile race. The plaintiff went from her house five miles away to see the races. She found a place adjacent to the highway and was there struck when one of the machines going at a rapid rate was deflected from the road against her. *Held,* for defendant, reversing a judgment for plaintiff entered on a directed verdict. "It does not lie in the mouth of the plaintiff to assert as a ground of liability the illegality of an act from which she sought to draw pleasure and enjoyment. * * * The acts of the defendant though illegal were illegal as against the public and travelers on the highway, not as against the plaintiff."

———

RESTATEMENT, SECOND, TORTS (1965), § 496E. Necessity of voluntary assumption

(1) A plaintiff does not assume a risk of harm unless he voluntarily accepts the risk.

(2) The plaintiff's acceptance of a risk is not voluntary if the defendant's tortious conduct has left him no reasonable alternative course of conduct in order to

(a) avert harm to himself or another, or

(b) exercise or protect a right or privilege of which the defendant has no right to deprive him.

———

PATTON v. CITY OF GRAFTON, 116 W.Va. 311, 180 S.E. 267 (1935). Action for harm to plaintiff's wife caused by her fall from an unguarded and slippery public walkway into an adjacent open cellar. She was aware of the danger, but, as she knew, the only alternative route was equally dangerous. *Held,* for plaintiff. "Use of a highway known to have attendant danger does not alone make a traveler negligent, but use wanting reasonable care;" and "[a]s the alternative route becomes less convenient and more circuitous, and particularly when it itself is dangerous, the plaintiff may without negligence use a highway in a proportionately serious state of disrepair. Restatement, Torts, § 473b."

HUNN v. WINDSOR HOTEL CO., 119 W.Va. 215, 193 S.E. 57 (1937). Plaintiff, a guest at defendant's hotel, having two means of exit, one down the ordinary steps, the other down an obviously unstable plank, chose the plank because more convenient. *Held,* directed verdict for defendant, affirmed. Plaintiff assumed the risk.

SECTION D. ASSUMPTION OF RISK: MODERN CONCEPTIONS

The modern defense of assumption of risk is less sweeping in scope than its classical counterpart, but more complex in its architecture. There are "express" and "implied" versions of the defense, "primary" and "secondary" versions of implied assumption of risk, and "reasonable" and "unreasonable" versions of implied secondary assumption of risk. To understand the substance of the doctrine we must first work our way through this tangle of terms.*

"Express" assumption of risk involves an *explicit* agreement—usually written—by the plaintiff to accept the risk of the defendant's wrongdoing. "Implied" assumption of risk involves an *implicit* agreement—an agreement identified and specified by a judge or jury—ostensibly on the basis of the parties' conduct.

"Primary" implied assumption of risk is a defense in name and as a matter of procedure, but not in substance. Procedurally, "primary" assumption of risk is a defense because defendants bear the burden of asserting and proving it. Substantively, "primary" assumption of risk is a doctrine of "no duty" because it holds, in the circumstances to which it applies, that the defendant never owed the plaintiff a duty of care in the first place. Indeed, some jurisdictions dispense with assumption of risk language entirely, and effect the ends of "primary" assumption of risk through a doctrine of "no duty." *Crawn v. Campo, infra* page 546, is an example of this approach.

"Secondary" implied assumption of risk *is* an affirmative defense to a breach of a duty of care. The question that it asks is not whether the defendant owed the plaintiff a duty of care in the first place, but whether the plaintiff implicitly agreed to accept the risk of harm flowing from the defendant's breach of its established duty of care. Mid-twentieth century tort doctrine broke "secondary" implied assumption of risk down further, distinguishing between reasonable and unreasonable decisions to encounter negligently created risks. This conceptualization of the plaintiff's choice in reasonableness terms paved the way for the absorption of "secondary" assumption of risk by negligence law. *Siragusa v. Swedish Hospital, infra* p. 539 illustrates the absorption of secondary assumption of risk by contributory negligence. *Li v. Yellow Cab, supra* p. 514, shows the merger of the defense into comparative negligence.

Only a sliver of "secondary" assumption of risk doctrine has survived this process of absorption. That sliver—called the "firefighter's rule"—applies to encounters between firefighters and the fires they fight. The "firefighter's rule" had its origin in the classical property law doctrine that licensees took the premises as they found them; modern law has recast the rule as a special case of assumption of risk. The "firefighter's rule" is often extended to police officers as well. *Moody v. Delta Western, Inc.*, infra p. 550, addresses this issue

---

* To complicate matters further, modern terminology is not fully standardized. Many jurisdictions dispense with the term "secondary" implied assumption of risk and speak directly about its two forms—"implied reasonable" and "implied unreasonable." *Scott v. Pacific West Mountain Resort, infra* p. 542, takes this approach. This note follows the usage of other jurisdictions, including California, which deploy the general label "secondary" to cover both "implied reasonable" and "implied unreasonable" assumption of risk. Using "secondary" as a general cover term underscores the fundamental difference between "primary" assumption of risk on the one hand, and both "implied reasonable" and "implied unreasonable" assumption of risk on the other hand.—Eds.

A final note: In the cases below involving workplace injuries, common law doctrines are used because Worker's Compensation statutes do not apply.

———

THE EMERGENCE OF MODERN DOCTRINE

The cases that follow trace the demise of the classical doctrine, and the restructuring of concepts from which modern doctrine emerges.

SIRAGUSA v. SWEDISH HOSPITAL

Supreme Court of Washington, 1962.
60 Wash.2d 310, 373 P.2d 767.

[Action by nurse's aid against her employer for injuries sustained while at work. As she was standing at the wash basin in a six-patient ward, a patient in a wheelchair pushed the door inward. On the door was a metal hook placed there to permit persons to open the door from the inside with a forearm. This hook struck the upper part of the plaintiff's back. Plaintiff asserted that defendant was negligent in failing to provide her a safe place to work. Defendant denied negligence and asserted contributory negligence and assumption of risk. At the close of the evidence, the trial court granted defendant's motion challenging the sufficiency of the evidence, ruled that plaintiff had assumed the risk, and dismissed the action. Plaintiff appealed.]

HUNTER, Judge. * * * The trial court applied the doctrine of assumption of risk as it has been stated by this court in many previous cases, and there were no contentions made regarding the propriety of the rule. This latter fact is readily understandable in view of the numerous decisions of this court which set forth the doctrine as it was presented by counsel in the trial court. However, the quantity of litigation in which the defense of assumption of risk has been raised and the current social and economic attitudes toward the master-servant relationship require that we re-examine our previous statements of the assumption of risk doctrine in the master-servant area and subject the bases of the rule to the tests of logic and experience. * * *

The history underlying the development of the doctrine was adroitly summarized in Tiller v. Atlantic Coast Line R. Co., 318 U.S. 54, 63 S.Ct. 444, 87 L.Ed. 610 (1943), by Mr. Justice Black:

> Perhaps the nature of the present problem can best be seen against the background of one hundred years of master-servant tort doctrine. Assumption of risk is a judicially created rule which was developed in response to the general impulse of common law courts at the beginning of this period to insulate the employer as much as possible from bearing the "human overhead" which is an inevitable part of the cost— to someone—of the doing of industrialized business. The general purpose behind this development in the common law seems to have been to give maximum freedom to expanding industry. * * *

In a concurring opinion in the Tiller case, Mr. Justice Frankfurter remarked:

> * * * *The notion of "assumption of risk" as a defense—that is, where the employer concededly failed in his duty of care and nevertheless escaped liability because the employee had "agreed" to "assume the risk" of the employer's fault—rested, in the context of our industrial society, upon a pure fiction. * * ** (Italics ours.)

Our present consideration of the rule only concerns "assumption of risk" where the master is negligent in creating or maintaining the dangerous condition. Where the dangers are ordinarily incident to the work, though it is said that the servant "assumes" these, the true analysis is that the master is under no duty to protect the servant with regard to such risks and any injuries, therefore, are not due to the master's negligence. Jobe v. Spokane Gas & Fuel Co., 73 Wash. 1, 131 P. 235, 48 L.R.A.,N.S., 931 (1913); 2 Harper & James, Law of Torts, § 21.4 (1956). Hence, the point of inquiry here is to re-examine the rule which bars a servant's recovery for injuries due to his master's negligence, although he was not acting unreasonably (contributorily negligent) in exposing himself to a known dangerous condition.

* * * [T]he practical effect of the present operation of the doctrine of assumption of risk is to reduce substantially or strictly limit the asserted duty of care owed by the employer to his employees. It is * * * pure fiction to speak of the employer's duty as one of furnishing a reasonably safe place to work. If an employee is barred from recovery merely because he was aware or should have been aware of the dangerous condition which caused his injury, then it must be because the employer was only under a duty to give warning of the dangerous condition. Only if the employer's duty is relegated to one of providing warning is it fair or just to allow a defense to the employee's action on the ground that the employee "received" warning from his self-acquired knowledge and appreciation of the risk involved. See Keeton, Assumption of Risk and the Landowner, 22 La.L.Rev. 108 (1961); 2 Harper & James, Law of Torts § 21.4 (1956); 3 Labatt, Master & Servant § 953 (2d ed. 1913). On the other hand, if it is true and desirable that the employer has the positive duty to furnish a reasonably safe place to work, it is not just or fair to permit an employer to escape liability for a failure to perform this duty simply because the employee was aware of the danger when he reasonably elected to expose himself to it while in the course of his employment. To do so is to affirm and deny, in the same breath, the employer's duty of care.

* * *

To bar recovery when the employee is acting reasonably in exposing himself to a known and appreciated risk is to indulge in the unrealistic and rigid presumption that, in so exposing himself, the employee "assents" to relieve his employer from his responsibility to furnish a safe place in which to work. Such a presumption has no basis in experience, and is not founded upon any current social policy. The existence of such a notion has been soundly rejected by the courts which have carefully analyzed the matter.
* * *

The time has now come, therefore, to state unqualifiedly that an employer has a duty to his employees to exercise reasonable care to furnish them with a reasonably safe place to work. We now hold that if an employer negligently fails in this duty, he may not assert, as a defense to an action based upon such a breach of duty, that the injured employee is barred from recovery merely because he was aware or should have known of the dangerous condition negligently created or maintained. However, if the employee's voluntary exposure to the risk is unreasonable under the circumstances, he will be barred from recovery because of his contributory negligence. Knowledge and appreciation of the risk of injury, on the part of the employee, are properly important factors which should be given weight in the determination of the issues of whether the employer is *negligent* in maintaining the dangerous condition and whether the employee is *contributorily negligent* in exposing himself to it. * * *

The prior decisions of this court, in so far as they are inconsistent with the reasoning and rule we now express, are hereby overruled.

Applying the rule to the instant case, the trial court erred in dismissing the plaintiff's action on the ground of assumption of risk. * * *

[Reversed and remanded for new trial.]

SALINAS v. VIERSTRA, 107 Idaho 984, 695 P.2d 369 (1985). Bistline, J., for the Idaho Supreme Court: " * * * [T]he 'all-or-nothing' effect of application of the assumption of risk defense is inequitable. It runs counter to all sense of reason and fairness. This is particularly true in today's age of comparative negligence; it would be the ultimate legal inconsistency to reject contributory negligence as an absolute defense yet at the same time allow its effect to continue under the guise of assumption of risk. * * *

" * * * [W]e hold that the use of assumption of risk as a defense shall have no legal effect in this state. The types of issues raised by a plaintiff's non-express assumption of risk are readily handled by resort to contributory negligence principles. Thus, such issues should be discussed in terms of contributory negligence, not assumption of risk, and applied accordingly under our comparative negligence laws.

"The one exception to our holding today involves a situation where a plaintiff, either in writing or orally, expressly assumes the risk involved. * * *

" * * * [W]e acknowledge the validity of a contractual assumption of risk operating as a total bar to recovery. [But we reaffirm] the general contract rule that contracts which violate public policy are not recognized."

SPRINGROSE v. WILLMORE, 292 Minn. 23, 192 N.W.2d 826 (1971). Plaintiff, a sixteen year old passenger, consented to riding with defendant sixteen year old driver, with knowledge of defendant's inexperience as a driver and more importantly, with knowledge that she was engaging with others in drag racing and driving dangerously. Held, that the doctrine of implied assumption of the risk must be recast as an aspect of contributory negligence in the light of the adoption of comparative negligence.

MEISTRICH v. CASINO ARENA ATTRACTIONS, INC., 31 N.J. 44, 155 A.2d 90 (1959). Assumption of risk has "two distinct meanings." First, "it is an alternative expression for the proposition that defendant was not negligent, i.e., either owed no duty or did not breach the duty owed." In this primary sense "plaintiff's knowledge of the risk is crucially involved in the issue of defendant's breach of duty." Second, "assumption of risk is an affirmative defense to an established breach of duty." "[W]e think it clear that assumption of risk in its secondary sense is a mere phase of contributory negligence."

OREGON REVISED STATUTES. Section 18.470 establishes comparative negligence for cases where plaintiff's fault is "not greater" than defendant's. Section 18.475(2), enacted in 1975, provides: "The doctrine of implied assumption of the risk is abolished."

"PRIMARY" ASSUMPTION OF RISK

"Primary" assumption of risk is the preeminent modern form of the doctrine. It is an implied form of the doctrine—the "contract" relieving defendants' of their duties of ordinary care is written by the court, not the parties—and quite tort-like in its character. The content of the "contract"— the risks assumed—is determined not by reference to the subjective understandings of the parties, but by reference to the understandings of reasonable people. Like tort duties, the risks assumed are determined "objectively." The basic premise of the doctrine is that the character of certain activities is incompatible with the imposition of duties of care. Their flourishing depends on the suspension of duties of ordinary care with respect to the activities' "inherent risks." The central task involved in applying the doctrine (once its domain of application is settled) is the identification of an activity's "inherent risks."

SCOTT v. PACIFIC WEST MOUNTAIN RESORT
Supreme Court of Washington, 1992.
119 Wash.2d 484, 834 P.2d 6.

ANDERSEN, Justice.

On March 11, 1989, 12-year-old Justin Scott sustained severe head injuries while skiing at a commercial ski resort owned by Pacific West Mountain Resort (hereafter ski resort). Justin was a student of the privately owned Grayson Connor Ski School (hereafter ski school) which offered lessons at the ski resort.

At the time of his injury, Justin was attempting to ski on a slalom race course which had been laid out by the ski school owner, allegedly according to instructions from an agent of the ski resort.

* * *

Witnesses to the accident agreed Justin was practicing on the race course and that he missed one of the gates and left the course. One witness reported that as Justin left the course, he appeared to be turning uphill to avoid an unused tow-rope shack but was unable to do so and was ejected out of his skis and down into the depression under the shack. He was found unconscious underneath the shack wrapped around one of the shack's 12–by 12–inch supports, and had sustained severe head injuries. * * *

The Scotts sued both the ski resort and the ski school alleging the race course had been improperly prepared and had been negligently placed too close to an unfenced tow-rope shack which was supported by exposed unpadded pillars. The exact distance between the shack and the race course is disputed but there was evidence the shack was approximately 40 feet from the closest gate. * * *

* * *

The ski resort moved for summary judgment on the ground that Justin had "assumed the risk" and was thus barred from recovery in a negligence action against the ski resort. The trial judge granted that motion and dismissed the claims against the ski resort.

* * *

The entire doctrine of "assumption of risk" is surrounded by much confusion, and has been improperly applied in many ski accident cases. This is partially because at common law both assumption of risk and contributory negligence operated as total bars to recovery. Therefore, it was formerly not critical that the two concepts be carefully distinguished. With the enactment of the comparative negligence and comparative fault statutes, it became essential to separate the various kinds of assumption of risk to distinguish between the kinds that shift the defendant's duty to the plaintiff (and hence bar the claim) and the types which are essentially contributory negligence (and hence simply reduce damages). * * *

Under the traditional Prosser and Keeton analysis, the assumption of risk doctrine is divided into four classifications: (1) express; (2) implied primary; (3) implied reasonable; and (4) implied unreasonable. Shorter v. Drury, 103 Wash.2d 645, 655, 695 P.2d 116, cert. denied, 474 U.S. 827, 106 S.Ct. 86, 88 L.Ed.2d 70 (1985).

Express assumption occurs when parties agree in advance that one of them is under no obligation to use reasonable care for the benefit of the other and will not be liable for what would otherwise be negligence. * * * The bar of express assumption is based on contract and survives the enactment of comparative negligence statutes. * * *

* * *

[Implied reasonable and implied unreasonable] assumption of risk * * * involve the plaintiff's voluntary choice to encounter a risk created by the defendant's negligence. [They] retain no independent significance from contributory negligence after the adoption of comparative negligence.

* * *

A number of Washington cases are in agreement with Dean Prosser, that primary implied assumption of the risk [which was the basis of the grant of summary judgment in favor of the ski resort operator] remains a complete bar to recovery. This is because primary assumption occurs when the plaintiff has impliedly consented to assume a duty. If the defendant does not have the duty, there can be no breach and hence no negligence. A classic example of primary assumption of risk occurs in sports cases. One who participates in sports "assumes the risks" which are inherent in the sport. To the extent a plaintiff is injured as a result of a risk inherent in the sport, the defendant has no duty and there is no negligence. Therefore, that type of assumption acts as a complete bar to recovery. The doctrine of primary implied assumption of the risk can perhaps more accurately be described as a way to define a defendant's duty. A defendant simply does not have a duty to protect a sports participant from dangers which are an inherent and normal part of a sport. * * *

* * *

* * * As Dean Prosser explains, primary implied assumption of risk should continue to be an absolute bar after the adoption of comparative fault because in this form it is a principle of "no duty" and hence no negligence, thus negating the existence of any underlying cause of action.

* * *

* * * To determine whether summary judgment was properly granted to the ski resort operator, it is essential to define what duties the ski resort owed to Justin and what risks were assumed by Justin.

* * *

Since Justin assumed the risks inherent in the sport of skiing, the issue is whether all the risks which caused his injuries were inherent in the sport.

There are ski cases in other jurisdictions which reach differing results as to whether a skier assumes the risk of collision with a fixed object in the ski trail. However, the evidence in the instant case was not just that Justin collided with an obvious stationary object because of difficult snow conditions. An accident resulting from such conditions would ordinarily be due to risks "inherent" in the sport of skiing. However, in this case, some of the evidence would support a conclusion that the race course was laid out in an unnecessarily dangerous manner that was not obvious to a young novice ski-racing student. While participants in sports are generally held to have impliedly assumed the risks inherent in the sport, such assumption of risk does not preclude a recovery for negligent acts which unduly enhance such risks. Review of analogous cases is helpful in this situation. * * *

In Marietta v. Cliffs Ridge, Inc., 385 Mich. 364, 373, 189 N.W.2d 208 (1971), the court held that it was a question of fact to be left to the jury whether a ski facility was negligent in using 1½-inch sapling poles as slalom gate markers rather than bamboo or fiber glass poles.

In Ashcroft v. Calder Race Course, Inc., 492 So.2d 1309 (Fla.1986), a jockey was injured when thrown from his horse which had veered across a race course out of control toward an exit gap, the negligent placement of which was found to be the cause of the accident. The court said the jockey's assumption of risk waived only risks inherent in the sport itself. Riding on a race track with a negligently placed exit gap was not an inherent risk in the sport and it was error for the judge to instruct the jury on assumption of risk.

In Jessup v. Mt. Bachelor, Inc., 101 Or.App. 670, 792 P.2d 1232, review denied, 310 Or. 475, 799 P.2d 646 (1990), the Oregon court recently explained that a skier is barred from recovery from a ski area operator for injury caused solely by the inherent risks of skiing, but if the injury was caused by a combination of the inherent risks of skiing and operator negligence, the doctrine of comparative fault applies.

These cases illustrate the proposition that primary assumption of the risk in a sports setting does not include the failure of the operator to provide reasonably safe facilities. Here, there is evidence that could support a finding that the race course for beginning racers was placed dangerously close to an unfenced, unpadded, abandoned shed. [Because "summary judgment should be granted only if, from all the evidence, reasonable persons could reach but one conclusion,"] we conclude that summary judgment was improperly granted. * * *

STIRPE v. T.J. MALONEY & SONS, INC., 252 A.D.2d 871, 675 N.Y.S.2d 709 (1998). "It is well settled that the doctrine of primary assumption of risk which, if applicable, would operate as a complete bar to an injured plaintiff's claim, 'is limited to plaintiffs injured while voluntarily participating in a sporting or entertainment activity.' [citation omitted]"

SANCHEZ v. HILLERICH & BRADSBY CO., et al., 104 Cal.App.4th 703, 128 Cal.Rptr.2d 529 (2002). Plaintiff, a college pitcher, suffered serious head injuries when he was struck by a line drive hit by an aluminum bat. The bat "was a newly designed hollow aluminum alloy bat with a pressurized air bladder which, according to its designer, substantially increases the speed at which the ball leaves the surface of the bat." *Held*, summary judgment for defendant bat manufacturer reversed. "Appellant presented sufficient evidence to establish that use of this particular bat significantly increased the inherent risk that a pitcher would be hit by a line drive and that the unique design properties of this bat were the cause of his injuries."

"A risk is inherent in a sport if its elimination (1) would chill vigorous participation in the sport; and (2) would alter the fundamental nature of the activity. [citation omitted]

"The essence of a baseball game is the contest between the defense, the pitcher and other players in the field, and the batter, for mastery over what happens to the pitched ball. The batter wants to hit the ball safely, usually away from the defense, so that the batter can advance on the bases. The defense wants to get the batter out, either by striking the batter out, or by causing the batter to hit the ball to a spot where one of the defensive players can make a play on it. Inherent in this mix is the risk that the pitcher, or any infielder, may have to catch, or avoid being hit with, a sharply batted ball. Appellant acknowledged he was aware of this risk. Thus, given the foundational facts of this case, a prima facie showing of assumption of the risk has been established. But appellant argued that use of the Air Attack 2 increased the risk above that inherent in the sport, and presented evidence on the issue [thereby raising a triable issue of fact]."

"NO DUTY"

Some courts approach the range of cases addressed by "primary assumption of the risk" through a doctrine of "no duty." This approach places less emphasis on the concept of "inherent risk" and more on whether the conduct complained of can be reasonably classified as "reckless." The last case in this section—*Lestina v. West Bend*—dissents from the trend expressed by both primary assumption of risk doctrine, and "no-duty" doctrine.

———

CRAWN v. CAMPO, 136 N.J. 494, 643 A.2d 600 (1994). Crawn was playing catcher in a pickup softball game. He was injured when Campo, trying to score from second base, slid or ran into him. "The majority of jurisdictions that have considered the issue of a person's duty to exercise care to avoid injury when engaged in a sports activity have concluded that to constitute a tort, conduct must exceed the level of ordinary negligence. Most courts have determined that the appropriate duty players owe to one another is not to engage in [injurious] conduct that is reckless or intentional. * * *

* * *

"The imposition of a recklessness standard is primarily justified by two policy reasons. One is the promotion of vigorous participation in athletic activities. See, e.g., Nazbony [v. Barnhill], 334 N.E.2d at 260 (stating that law should not 'place unreasonable burdens on the free and vigorous participation in sports by our youth').

* * *

"[The second reason is that] [p]articipation in recreational sports activities has unique aspects that separate such sports from other common activities. In many recreational sports, softball included, some amount of physical contact is expected. Physical contact is an inherent or integral part of the game in many sports. See Gauvin [v. Clark], 537 N.E.2d at 96 ('Players, when they engage in sport, agree to undergo some physical contacts which could amount to assault and battery absent the players' consent.') The degree of physical contact allowed varies from sport to sport and even from one group of players to another. In addition, the physicality of sports is accompanied by a high level of emotional intensity. Ross [v. Clouser], 637 S.W.2d at 14 (noting 'proper fervor' of competition); see Lazaroff [Torts & Sports], 7 U. Miami Ent. & Sports L. Rev. at 195 (noting difficulty of distinguishing 'between negligence and recklessness in the context of a game where players are encouraged to play with reckless abandon'); Lestina [v. West Bend Mut. Ins. Co.], 501 N.W.2d at 35 (Wilcox, J., dissenting) (noting that although defendant's conduct 'clearly violated a rule of the game,' conduct occurred in 'heat of the game,' and should not subject defendant to negligence liability).

"Our analysis is further complicated by the wide variation in expectations regarding the physical contact and emotional intensity that are appropriate from sport to sport and from game to game. * * *

* * *

"The reasonableness of conduct that occurs within a consensual relationship can be fairly evaluated only by reference to the nature of the consent and mutual understanding of the persons in the relationship and to the common expectations that serve to identify what conduct is acceptable among those persons. * * *

"Realistically, complete agreement among the eighteen or twenty persons engaged in playing a softball game covering the limitless kinds of physical contact that can occur in the course of the game can rarely, if ever, be found. That consideration indicates that a legal duty of care based on the standard of what, objectively, an average reasonable person would do under the circumstances is illusory, and is not susceptible to sound and consistent application on a case-by-case basis. Accordingly, we hold that the duty of care in establishing liability arising from informal sports activity should be based on a standard that requires, under the circumstances, conduct that is reckless or intentional.

" * * * The heightened standard will more likely result in affixing liability for conduct that is clearly unreasonable and unacceptable from the perspective of those engaged in the sport yet leaving free from the supervision of the law the risk-laden conduct that is inherent in sports and more often than not assumed to be 'part of the game.' "

LEONARD ex rel. MEYER v. BEHRENS, 601 N.W.2d 76 (Iowa 1999). Fifteen-year-old Eric Leonard brought suit against a fellow participant in a game of "paintball" for injuries sustained when he was shot in the eye with a "paintball"—a "gelatin capsule[] filled with colored vegetable oil [and] intended to break on contact." Players fired the "capsules" at one another with slingshots. The game was an informal, unsupervised one, played by a group of teenagers at a farm. Participants in the game had goggles to wear to protect their eyes. The goggles tended to fog up, and Eric's did. He removed them from his eyes, placed them on his head, and was shot in the eye. *Held,* directed verdict for defendant affirmed. The lower court "correctly applied the recklessness standard" to the case.

"Courts analyzing whether a particular activity is a contact sport such that the recklessness standard would be applicable have generally found 'the relevant inquiry is whether the participants were involved in a contact sport, not whether the sport was formally organized or coached.' *Pfister v. Shusta,* 167 Ill.2d 417, 212 Ill.Dec. 668, 657 N.E.2d 1013, 1017 (1995). Thus, the standard has been applied to unorganized, informal, and spontaneous sports activities and games. *See, e.g., Pfister,* 212 Ill.Dec. 668, 657 N.E.2d at 1013 (spontaneous game of kick-the-can in lobby of college dormitory); *Azzano v. Catholic Bishop of Chicago,* 304 Ill.App.3d 713, 237 Ill.Dec. 694, 710 N.E.2d 117 (1999) (school recess activity known as 'killerball'); *Keller v. Mols,* 156 Ill.App.3d 235, 108 Ill.Dec. 888, 509 N.E.2d 584 (1987) (unsupervised game of floor hockey among minors on backyard patio); *Marchetti v. Kalish,* 53 Ohio St.3d 95, 559 N.E.2d 699 (1990) (child's game of kick-the-can).

* * *

" * * * [We] hold that paintball is a contact sport for which a participant's liability is determined under a recklessness standard. In games in which physical contact is inherent, indeed, the very purpose of the game as in paintball, rules infractions and mishaps are virtually inevitable and justify a different standard of care.

"Applying this standard, we conclude the trial court correctly ruled that there was not substantial evidence of Chad's recklessness to support submission of the plaintiffs' claim to the jury. The record does not support a finding that Chad knew Eric was not wearing goggles or that Eric attempted to alert other participants that he was not wearing them. Under these circumstances, the evidence would not support a finding that Chad shot the paint ball at Eric knowing or having reason to know that his conduct created an unreasonable risk of physical harm to Eric, or that harm was highly probable to follow his actions. * * * "

———

LESTINA v. WEST BEND MUT. INS. CO., 176 Wis.2d 901, 501 N.W.2d 28 (1993). "The case comes to this court on certification by the court of appeals pursuant to sec. 809.61, Stats.1991–92. The sole question presented by the certification is 'what is the standard of care in Wisconsin for a [recreational] sports player who is alleged to have caused injury to another player during and as part of the [recreational team contact sports] competition.' The circuit court determined that negligence was the governing legal standard. For the reasons set out below, we conclude that the rules of negligence govern liability for injuries incurred during recreational team contact sports. Accordingly, we affirm the judgment of the circuit court.

"Few sports cases can be found which have allowed a complainant to recover on proof of negligence.** One commentator has concluded that this

---

** While several cases adopt the negligence standard, most of these cases do not involve contact team sports. See, e.g., *Babych v. McRae,* 41 Conn.Sup. 280, 567 A.2d 1269 (Super.Ct.1989) (applying negligence standard to injury in professional hockey game); *LaVine v.*

scarcity results from fear that the imposition of liability in such cases would discourage participation in sports-related activities. Cameron J. Rains, Sports Violence: A Matter of Societal Concern, 55 Notre Dame Lawyer 796, 799 (1980). We do not agree that the application of the negligence standard would have this effect. We believe that the negligence standard, properly understood and applied, accomplishes the objectives sought by the courts adopting the recklessness standard, objectives with which we agree.

"Because it requires only that a person exercise ordinary care under the circumstances, the negligence standard is adaptable to a wide range of situations. An act or omission that is negligent in some circumstances might not be negligent in others. Thus the negligence standard, properly understood and applied, is suitable for cases involving recreational team contact sports. The very fact that an injury is sustained during the course of a game in which the participants voluntarily engaged and in which the likelihood of bodily contact and injury could reasonably be foreseen materially affects the manner in which each player's conduct is to be evaluated under the negligence standard. To determine whether a player's conduct constitutes actionable negligence (or contributory negligence), the fact finder should consider such material factors as the sport involved; the rules and regulations governing the sport; the generally accepted customs and practices of the sport (including the types of contact and the level of violence generally accepted); the risks inherent in the game and those that are outside the realm of anticipation; the presence of protective equipment or uniforms; and the facts and circumstances of the particular case, including the ages and physical attributes of the participants, the participants' respective skills at the game, and the participants' knowledge of the rules and customs. Niemczyk v. Burleson, 538 S.W.2d 737 (Mo.Ct.App.1976).

"Depending as it does on all the surrounding circumstances, the negligence standard can subsume all the factors and considerations presented by recreational team contact sports and is sufficiently flexible to permit the 'vigorous competition' that the defendant urges. [footnote omitted] We see no need for the court to adopt a recklessness standard for recreational team contact sports when the negligence standard, properly understood and applied, is sufficient."

THE FIREFIGHTER'S RULE

The distinctive modern forms of assumption of risk doctrine—"primary," the "firefighter's rule" and "express"—differ in their respective debts to contract and tort. "Express" assumption of risk owes the most to

Clear Creek Skiing Corp., 557 F.2d 730 (10th Cir.1977) (applying negligence standard to injury in collision between snow skiers); *Gray v. Houlton*, 671 P.2d 443 (Colo.Ct.App.1983) (applying negligence standard to injury in collision between snow skiers); *Duke's GMC, Inc. v. Erskine*, 447 N.E.2d 1118 (Ind.Ct.App.1983) (applying negligence standard to golf injury); *Bourque v. Duplechin*, 331 So.2d 40 (La.Ct.App.1976) (applying negligence standard to injury in soft-ball game) (but see *Picou v. Hartford Ins. Co.*, 558 So.2d 787 (La.Ct.App.1990), adopting a reckless standard); *Jenks v. McGranaghan*, 32 A.D.2d 989, 299 N.Y.S.2d 228 (App.Div.1969) (applying negligence standard to golf injury); *Gordon v. Deer Park School District*, 71 Wash.2d 119, 426 P.2d 824 (1967) (applying negligence standard to softball spectator injured when struck on the head with a bat).

contract. The basic issue that it raises is whether and how far an explicit contractual agreement to displace tort duties should be honored. "Primary" assumption of risk owes the most to tort and the least to contract: the "contract" is fashioned by the court and its content is determined by reference to the understandings of a reasonable person. The "firefighter's rule" started its life outside this conceptual framework. It has its origins in the scheme of status categories traditionally applied to entrants onto land, a topic covered in Section C of Chapter 10 of this casebook.

In *Gibson v. Leonard*, 143 Ill. 182, 32 N.E. 182 (1892), the Illinois Supreme Court held that a firefighter who entered private property in the performance of his job duties was a licensee. The property owner therefore owed the firefighter only a duty to "refrain from willful or affirmative acts which are injurious." *Id.* at 189, 32 N.E. 183. This barred firefighters from recovering from property owners whose ordinary negligence caused a fire requiring their response and resulting in their injury. This property based rationale, however, eventually sank under the weight of its own inadequacies. In *Flowers v. Rock Creek Terrace Ltd. Partnership*, 308 Md. 432, 520 A.2d 361, 366–67 (1987), the Maryland Court of Appeals noted several of these. First, a rule based on the premises liability theory could be applied only in the landowner context. Second, the rule created serious anomalies: other public employees, such as postmen and building inspectors—who often enter land pursuant to legal authority rather than express invitation of the landowner—were entitled to due care, while their counterparts in the fire and police departments were not. The ongoing decline of the licensee category only compounds these problems.

The original rationale for the rule, then, has not survived. But the rule itself has, now justified by a mix of public policy and contractual rationales.

MOODY v. DELTA WESTERN, INC.
Supreme Court of Alaska, 2002.
38 P.3d 1139.

MATTHEWS, Justice.

The question in this case is whether the so-called Firefighter's Rule applies in Alaska. The Firefighter's Rule holds that firefighters and police officers who are injured may not recover based on the negligent conduct that required their presence. For public policy reasons we join the overwhelming majority of states that have adopted the rule.

I. FACTS AND PROCEEDINGS

The facts of this case are undisputed. On or around July 25, 1996, a Delta Western employee left a fuel truck owned by Delta Western in a driveway in Dillingham. The keys were in the ignition, the door was unlocked, and the truck contained fuel and weighed over 10,000 pounds. Delta Western had a policy of removing the keys from the ignitions of its trucks. Delta Western enacted this policy because of past incidents involving the theft and unauthorized entry of its trucks.

Joseph Coolidge, who was highly intoxicated, entered the unlocked truck and proceeded to drive around Dillingham. He ran cars off the road, nearly collided with several vehicles, and drove at speeds exceeding seventy miles per hour. Brent Moody, the chief of the Dillingham Police Department, was one of the officers who responded to the reports of the recklessly driven fuel truck. The driver of the van in which Moody was a passenger attempted to stop the truck after moving in front of it, but Coolidge rammed the van, throwing Moody against the dashboard and windshield. Moody suffered permanent injuries.

Moody filed suit against Delta Western, alleging that the company (through its employe) negligently failed to remove the truck's keys from the ignition. In its amended answer, Delta Western argued that the "Firefighter's Rule" barred Moody's cause of action. Delta Western moved for summary judgment based on its Firefighter's Rule defense. The superior court granted Delta Western's motion, holding that the Firefighter's Rule bars police officers from recovering for injuries caused by the "negligence which creates the very occasion for their engagement."

Moody now appeals.

II.   Standard of Review

The question presented is one of law and of first impression: whether Alaska should adopt the Firefighter's Rule. We therefore apply the de novo standard of review, "adopt[ing] the rule of law which is most persuasive in light of precedent, reason and policy."

III.   Discussion

Nearly all of the courts that have considered whether or not to adopt the Firefighter's Rule have in fact adopted it. Only one court has rejected it.***

* * *

Jurisdictions adopting the Firefighter's Rule emphasize its narrowness; the doctrine bars only recovery for the negligence that creates the need for the public safety officer's service. Thus the Firefighter's Rule does not apply to negligent conduct occurring after the police officer or firefighter arrives at the scene or to misconduct other than that which necessitates the officer's presence.

Modern courts stress interrelated reasons, based on public policy, for the rule. The negligent party is said to have no duty to the public safety officer to act without negligence in creating the condition that necessitates the officer's intervention because the officer is employed by the public to respond to such conditions and receives compensation and benefits for the risks inherent in such responses. Requiring members of the public to pay for injuries resulting from such responses effectively imposes a double payment

---

*** *See Christensen v. Murphy,* 296 Or. 610, 678 P.2d 1210, 1218 (1984).

obligation on them. Further, because negligence is at the root of many calls for public safety officers, allowing recovery would compound the growth of litigation.

Courts find an analogy in cases in which a contractor is injured while repairing the condition that necessitated his employment. In these cases, the owner is under no duty to protect the contractor against risks arising from the condition the contractor is hired to repair, and thus is not liable even if the condition was the product of the owner's negligence. *See, e.g., Peters v. Titan Navigation Co.,* 857 F.2d 1342, 1345 (9th Cir.1988) (affirming summary judgment for shipowner regarding claims brought by hydraulic system repairman who was injured after slipping on spilled hydraulic fluid, because owner owes no duty to protect repairman from risks inherent in the very condition he was hired to repair); *see also* 41 Am.Jur.2d, Independent Contractors § 41, n. 74 (1995) and the cases there cited. This "contractor for repairs" exception to the general duty of reasonable care is grounded in necessity and fairness. Property owners should not be deterred by the threat of liability to the contractor from summoning experts to repair their property, regardless of why repairs are needed. Further, owners have paid for the contractor's expertise at confronting the very danger that injured him and should not have to pay again if the contractor is then injured. The same factors are found to apply with respect to the public's need to call for the services of public safety officers.

We agree with the reasoning of the modern courts and with the analogy to contractor cases. The Firefighter's Rule reflects sound public policy. The public pays for emergency responses of public safety officials in the form of salaries and enhanced benefits. Requiring members of the public to pay for injuries incurred by officers in such responses asks an individual to pay again for services the community has collectively purchased. Further, negligence is a common factor in emergencies that require the intervention of public safety officers. Allowing recovery would cause a proliferation of litigation aimed at shifting to individuals or their insurers costs that have already been widely shared. * * *

We thus conclude that the Firefighter's Rule applies in Alaska. We reach this conclusion based on the merits of the rule as accepted by the overwhelming majority of the courts of our sister states. It follows that summary judgment was properly granted.

AFFIRMED.

———

HARRIS–FIELDS v. SYZE, 461 Mich. 188, 600 N.W.2d 611 (1999). *Held,* reversing summary judgment for defendant, the firefighter's rule did not bar wrongful death claim against motorist who negligently struck and killed police officer standing on the shoulder of a road during a traffic stop. "The basic principle of the fireman's rule is that recovery is barred for conduct that draws the officer to the location of the injury to perform the normal duties of the officer's work." Therefore, the rule does not bar plaintiff's claim in a case "in which the officer has stopped one motorist for a traffic violation and then is injured by the allegedly negligent conduct of a second motorist."

DAY v. CASLOWITZ, 713 A.2d 758 (R.I.1998). Police officer brought negligence action against homeowner arising from officer's slip and fall on homeowner's snow and ice-covered walkway while officer was investigating home-security system alarm. *Held*, summary judgment for homeowner, affirmed.

"The plaintiff argues that because the snow-and ice-covered walkway (the condition that caused his injuries) did not create the occasion for his presence at the scene * * * the [firefighter's] rule should not preclude his claim. * * * In our view plaintiff's injuries resulted from a risk inherent in responding to the exigent stimulus created by the activated alarm; the risk of such a fall on snow and ice was a foreseeable consequence of the officer's doing his duty in these circumstances; and defendant, the alleged tortfeasor, was the person who was at least partially responsible for the situation (installation of a home-security alarm that would alert the police after it was triggered) that brought the officer to the scene. Recovery is thus precluded by the rule."

ROSENBLOOM v. HANOUR CORP., 66 Cal.App.4th 1477, 78 Cal.Rptr.2d 686 (1998). Plaintiff, an employee of a company which built and maintained an aquarium for a private club, was bitten while attempting to remove a shark from the aquarium. *Held*, summary judgment in favor of defendant affirmed. Plaintiff assumed the risk as a matter of law. The defendant "recognized expertise was necessary for the dangerous task of handling a shark and accordingly hired a known expert in the field to do the work. Shark bites were the company's occupational hazard, and no duty was owed to protect the shark handler from the very danger that he or she was employed to confront." It "was not relevant that plaintiff himself was not experienced."

MINNICH v. MED–WASTE, INC., 349 S.C. 567, 564 S.E.2d 98 (2002). "South Carolina has never recognized the firefighter's rule, and we find it is not part of this state's common law. * * * We are not persuaded by any of the various rationales advanced by those courts that recognize the firefighter's rule. The more sound public policy—and the one we adopt—is to decline to promulgate a rule singling out police officers and firefighters for discriminatory treatment.

"[C]ourts [have] been unable to agree on a consistent rationale for the rule." The original rationale—that the firefighter was a licensee, owed no duty of reasonable care—has been abandoned as a failure. Modern courts have replaced it with three different rationales. First, they have argued that "firemen and policemen, unlike invitees or licensees, enter at unforeseeable times and at areas not open to the public." This makes it unreasonable "to require the level of care that is owed to invitees or licensees." Second, courts have asserted that "police officers and firefighters, aware of the risks inherent in their chosen profession, have assumed those risks." Third, modern opinions have claimed that, because "injuries to firemen and policemen are compensable through workers' compensation [i]t follows that liability for their on-the-job injuries is properly borne by the public rather than by individual property owners."

Courts have been equally unable "to agree on the proper parameters for the rule." Some courts have limited the rule so that it only bars recovery for the negligence which occasioned the officer's presence, whereas others have interpreted it more broadly. The result of these disagreements is a rule "riddled with exceptions." "[C]riticism of the rule abounds." It rests on "an indulgence in legal fiction" and embodies inequitable distinctions. Applying it leads into a "morass of legal analysis."

Finally, the court noted that "recently, a number of state legislatures have acted to limit or abolish the firefighter's rule." The court cited statutes in Virginia, Nevada, New York, New Jersey, Minnesota, and Florida.

EXPRESS ASSUMPTION OF RISK

The problem of express assumption of risk is whether, and to what extent, express contractual agreements can relieve defendants of liability for breaches of otherwise applicable duties of ordinary care.

———

TUNKL v. REGENTS OF THE UNIVERSITY OF CALIFORNIA
Supreme Court of California, 1963.
60 Cal.2d 92, 32 Cal.Rptr. 33, 383 P.2d 441.

TOBRINER, Justice.

This case concerns the validity of a release from liability for future negligence imposed as a condition for admission to a charitable research hospital. For the reasons we hereinafter specify, we have concluded that an agreement between a hospital and an entering patient affects the public interest and that, in consequence, the exculpatory provision included within it must be invalid under Civil Code section 1668.

* * *

[Hugo Tunkl sued for damages allegedly owing to negligence of two physicians employed by the University of California at Los Angeles Medical Center, a nonprofit research hospital. Upon admission Tunkl signed a document stating that "the patient * * * hereby releases The Regents of the University of California, and the hospital from any and all liability for the negligent or wrongful acts or omissions of its employees." When he signed Tunkl was in great pain and under sedation, but the jury determined that he knew or should have known the significance of the release. Judgment was entered in favor of the Regents.]

We begin with the dictate of the relevant Civil Code section 1668. The section states: "All contracts which have for their object, directly or indirectly, to exempt anyone from responsibility for his own fraud, or willful injury to the person or property of another, or violation of law, whether willful or negligent, are against the policy of the law."

The course of section 1668, however, has been a troubled one. * * * [T]he courts' interpretations of it have been diverse. Some of the cases have applied the statute strictly, invalidating any contract for exemption from liability for negligence. * * * The recent case of Mills v. Ruppert (1959) 167 Cal.App.2d 58, 62–63, 333 P.2d 818; however, apparently limits "[N]egligent * * * violation of law" exclusively to statutory law. Other cases hold that the statute prohibits the exculpation of gross negligence only; still another case states that the section forbids exemption from active as contrasted with passive negligence.

In one respect * * * the decisions are uniform. The cases have consistently held that the exculpatory provision may stand only if it does not involve "the public interest."[6] * * *

* * *

If, then the exculpatory clause which affects the public interest cannot stand, we must ascertain those factors or characteristics which constitute the public interest. The social forces that have led to such characterization are volatile and dynamic. No definition of the concept of public interest can be contained within the four corners of a formula. The concept, always the subject of great debate, has ranged over the whole course of the common law; rather than attempt to prescribe its nature, we can only designate the situations in which it has been applied. We can determine whether the instant contract does or does not manifest the characteristics which have been held to stamp a contract as one affected with a public interest.

In placing particular contracts within or without the category of those affected with a public interest, the courts have revealed a rough outline of that type of transaction in which exculpatory provisions will be held invalid. Thus the attempted but invalid exemption involves a transaction which exhibits some or all of the following characteristics. It concerns a business of a type generally thought suitable for public regulation. The party seeking exculpation is engaged in performing a service of great importance to the public, which is often a matter of practical necessity for some members of the public. The party holds himself out as willing to perform this service for any member of the public who seeks it, or at least for any member coming within certain established standards.[12] As a result of the essential nature of the service, in the economic setting of the transaction, the party invoking exculpation possesses a decisive advantage of bargaining strength against

---

6. The view that the exculpatory contract is valid only if the public interest is not involved represents the majority holding in the United States. * * *

12. See Burdick, The Origin of the Peculiar Duties of Public Service Companies, 11 Colum.L.Rev. (1911) 514, 616, 743. There is a close historical relationship between the duty of common carriers, public warehousemen, innkeepers, etc. to give reasonable service to all persons who apply, and the refusal of courts to permit such businesses to obtain exemption from liability for negligence. * * *

any member of the public who seeks his services. In exercising a superior bargaining power the party confronts the public with a standardized adhesion contract of exculpation, and makes no provision whereby a purchaser may pay additional reasonable fees and obtain protection against negligence. Finally, as a result of the transaction, the person or property of the purchaser is placed under the control of the seller, subject to the risk of carelessness by the seller or his agents.

While obviously no public policy opposes private, voluntary transactions in which one party, for a consideration, agrees to shoulder a risk which the law would otherwise have placed upon the other party, the above circumstances pose a different situation. In this situation the releasing party does not really acquiesce voluntarily in the contractual shifting of the risk, nor can we be reasonably certain that he receives an adequate consideration for the transfer. Since the service is one which each member of the public, presently or potentially, may find essential to him, he faces, despite his economic inability to do so, the prospect of a compulsory assumption of the risk of another's negligence. The public policy of this state has been, in substance, to posit the risk of negligence upon the actor; in instances in which this policy has been abandoned, it has generally been to allow or require that the risk shift to another party better or equally able to bear it, not to shift the risk to the weak bargainer.

In the light of the decisions, we think that the hospital-patient contract clearly falls within the category of agreements affecting the public interest. To meet that test, the agreement need only fulfill some of the characteristics above outlined; here, the relationship fulfills all of them. Thus the contract of exculpation involves an institution suitable for, and a subject of, public regulation. (See Health & Saf.Code, §§ 1400–1421, 32000–32508.) That the services of the hospital to those members of the public who are in special need of the particular skill of its staff and facilities constitute a practical and crucial necessity is hardly open to question.

* * *

In insisting that the patient accept the provision of waiver in the contract, the hospital certainly exercises a decisive advantage in bargaining. The would-be patient is in no position to reject the proffered agreement, to bargain with the hospital, or in lieu of agreement to find another hospital. The admission room of a hospital contains no bargaining table where, as in a private business transaction, the parties can debate the terms of their contract. As a result, we cannot but conclude that the instant agreement manifested the characteristics of the so-called adhesion contract. * * *

In brief, the patient here sought the services which the hospital offered to a selective portion of the public; the patient, as the price of admission and as a result of his inferior bargaining position, accepted a clause in a contract of adhesion waiving the hospital's negligence; the patient thereby subjected himself to control of the hospital and the possible infliction of the negligence which he had thus been compelled to waive. The hospital, under such circumstances, occupied a status different than a mere private party; its contract with the patient affected the public interest. * * *

* * * Defendant * * * contends that while the public interest may possibly invalidate the exculpatory provision as to the paying patient, it certainly cannot do so as to the charitable one. * * *

* * * [W]e see no distinction in the hospital's duty of due care between the paying and nonpaying patient. The duty, emanating not merely from contract but also tort, imports no discrimination based upon economic status. * * * To immunize the hospital from negligence as to the charitable patient because he does not pay would be as abhorrent to medical ethics as it is to legal principle.

* * *

We must note, finally, that the integrated and specialized society of today, structured upon mutual dependency, cannot rigidly narrow the concept of the public interest. From the observance of simple standards of due care in the driving of a car to the performance of the high standards of hospital practice, the individual citizen must be completely dependent upon the responsibility of others. The fabric of this pattern is so closely woven that the snarling of a single thread affects the whole. We cannot lightly accept a sought immunity from careless failure to provide the hospital service upon which many must depend. Even if the hospital's doors are open only to those in a specialized category, the hospital cannot claim isolated immunity in the interdependent community of our time. It, too, is part of the social fabric, and prearranged exculpation from its negligence must partly rend the pattern and necessarily affect the public interest.

The judgment is reversed.

————

SHORTER v. DRURY, 103 Wash.2d 645, 695 P.2d 116 (1985). Doreen Shorter's physician, Dr. Robert Drury, advised that she undergo a dilation and curettage procedure (D and C) after she suffered a failed pregnancy. She and her husband were told there was a small risk this routine procedure could cause a perforated uterus and internal bleeding. The Shorters were Jehovah's Witnesses, prohibited by religious doctrine from receiving blood transfusions. At the hospital Mrs. Shorter and her husband signed the following form (underlining indicates blanks completed in handwriting):

GENERAL HOSPITAL OF EVERETT

REFUSAL TO PERMIT BLOOD TRANSFUSION

Date November 30, 1979 Hour 6:15 a.m. I request that no blood or blood derivatives be administered to Doreen V. Shorter during this hospitalization. I hereby release the hospital, its personnel, and the attending physician from any responsibility whatever for unfavorable reactions or any untoward results due to my refusal to permit the use of blood or its derivatives and I fully understand the possible consequences of such refusal on my part.

[/s/ Doreen Shorter]_____

Patient

[/s/ Elmer Shorter]_____

Patient's Husband or Wife

The operation was negligently performed by Dr. Drury, causing severe laceration of the uterus and profuse bleeding. Mrs. Shorter continued to refuse blood transfusion, as did Mr. Shorter, and Mrs. Shorter bled to death. In a wrongful death action for negligence, *held* (5–4), by the Washington Supreme Court, that while the patient did not assume the risk that the operation would be negligently performed, she and her husband did expressly assume the risk that she might die from bleeding unremedied by a transfusion, including bleeding caused by negligence.

First, the court found the "Refusal To Permit Blood Transfusion" signed by the Shorters to be valid and voluntary. The refusal was not "a release from liability for negligence," and so cases holding "exculpatory clauses" contrary to public policy are inapposite:

> In refusing a blood transfusion, the Shorters were acting under the compulsion of circumstances. The compulsion, however, was created by the religious convictions of the Shorters not by the tortious conduct of defendant.

> * * * Given the particular problems faced when a patient on religious grounds refuses to permit necessary or advisable blood transfusions, we believe the use of a release such as signed here is appropriate. * * * The alternative of physicians or hospitals refusing to care for Jehovah's Witnesses is repugnant in a society which attempts to make medical care available to all its members.

Second, the court held that "the doctrine of express assumption of risk survived the enactment of the comparative negligence statute, and is applicable in Washington." Express assumption of the risk is "merely a form of waiver or consent." In the present case, Mrs. Shorter and her husband expressly assumed a "specific risk":

> The defendants do not argue, nor do we hold, that the Shorters assumed the risk of the "direct consequences" of Dr. Drury's negligence. Those "consequences" would be recoverable [in a negligence action brought for consequences other than the death]. Defendant argues, however, and we agree, that the Shorters * * * assumed the risk of death from an operation which had to be performed without blood transfusions and where blood could not be administered under any circumstances including where the doctor made what would otherwise have been correctable surgical mistake. The risk of death from a failure to receive a transfusion to which the Shorters exposed themselves was created by, and must be allocated to, the Shorters themselves.

CUDNIK v. WILLIAM BEAUMONT HOSPITAL, 207 Mich.App. 378, 525 N.W.2d 891 (1994). "Presenting an issue of first impression in Michigan, this case involves the validity of an exculpatory agreement executed by plaintiff's decedent before receiving radiation therapy at defendant hospital. The trial court granted summary disposition to defendant on the ground that '[p]laintiff's decedent signed a valid release of liability between the parties.' We reverse and remand for further proceedings.

* * *

"As a general proposition, parties are free to enter into any contract at their will, provided that the particular contract does not violate the law or contravene public policy. * * * In a variety of settings, this Court has upheld the validity of exculpatory agreements or releases that absolve a party from liability for damages caused by the party's negligence. See Dombrowski v. Omer, 199 Mich.App. 705, 502 N.W.2d 707 (1993) (festival event); Paterek v. 6600 Ltd., 186 Mich.App. 445, 465 N.W.2d 342 (1990) (softball facility); St. Paul Fire & Marine Ins. Co. v. Guardian Alarm Co., 115 Mich.App. 278, 320 N.W.2d 244 (1982) (security alarm company). In other cases, however, this Court has declared such agreements unenforceable as being contrary to this state's public policy. See Stanek v. Nat'l Bank of Detroit, 171 Mich.App. 734, 430 N.W.2d 819 (1988) (exculpatory clause in a bank's stop payment order held to be invalid on public policy grounds); Allen v. Michigan Bell Telephone Co., 18 Mich.App. 632, 171 N.W.2d 689 (1969) (clause limiting liability for damages resulting from a telephone company's failure to include an ad in its Yellow Pages held invalid, because the parties were not in a position of equal bargaining power).

* * *

"The question whether a hospital may absolve itself from liability for the negligence of its employees via an exculpatory agreement signed by a patient is an issue of first impression in Michigan. The overwhelming majority of other jurisdictions that have addressed this question have held that such agreements are invalid and unenforceable because medical treatment involves a particularly sensitive area of public interest. Tunkl v. Regents of the Univ. of California, 60 Cal.2d 92, 32 Cal.Rptr. 33, 383 P.2d 441 (1963); Ash v. New York Univ. Dental Center, 164 A.D.2d 366, 564 N.Y.S.2d 308 (1990); Smith v. Hosp. Authority of Walker, Dade & Catoosa Cos., 160 Ga.App. 387, 287 S.E.2d 99 (1981); Meiman v. Rehabilitation Center, Inc., 444 S.W.2d 78 (Ky.App.1969). Today we join in the view of these jurisdictions.

* * *

"[W]e find [following the approach of *Tunkl*, the 'leading case on this subject'] that the agreement in this case also fulfills all of the relevant characteristics of a contract affecting the public interest. * * * "

MORGANTEEN v. COWBOY ADVENTURES, INC., 190 Ariz. 463, 949 P.2d 552 (App.1997). Plaintiff sued riding stables for injuries suffered during a trail ride, claiming that the stables gave her negligent instruction. Stable sought and obtained summary judgment in the trial court on the ground that—as a condition of participating in the ride—plaintiff had signed a preprinted exculpatory covenant releasing Cowboy Adventures in advance from liability for any injuries she might sustain. *Held*, reversed. There was a genuine issue of fact "whether 'Mrs. Morganteen "understood and accepted" that she must *both* follow the wrangler's advice *and* release him [from liability] if the advice was negligent.' "

Arizona law " 'disfavors contractual provisions by which one party seeks to immunize himself against the consequences of his own torts.' " Their enforcement is limited by three conditions: "(1) that there 'is no public policy impediment to the limitation'; (2) 'that the parties did, *in fact*, bargain for the limitation'; and (3) that the limiting language be strictly construed against the party seeking to enforce it." Arizona law places "particular emphasis on the second factor." Liability in tort may be bargained away, but tort "remedies may not be waived in an unknowing exchange of forms. . . . An actual bargain must be made by those responsible for the transaction."

COOPER v. ASPEN SKIING COMPANY, 48 P.3d 1229 (Colo.2002). Seventeen-year-old plaintiff lost control and crashed into a tree while training on a ski race course, suffering permanent injuries including blindness. The trial court entered judgment as a matter of law in favor of defendants, on the ground that his mother had signed a release prior to the injury. *Held*, reversed and remanded.

"[W]e agree with the Washington Supreme Court that 'there are instances where public policy reasons for preserving an obligation of care owed by one person to another outweigh our traditional regard for freedom of contract.' *Scott v. Pac. W. Mountain Resort*, 119 Wash.2d 484, 834 P.2d 6, 11, 12 (1992) (holding that 'to the extent a parent's release of a third party's liability for negligence purports to bar a child's own cause of action, it violates public policy and is unenforceable'). Accordingly, we hold that Colorado's public policy affords minors significant protections which preclude parents or guardians from releasing a minor's own prospective claim for negligence. We base our holding on our understanding of Colorado's public policy to protect children as reflected by legislation protecting minors as well as decisions from other jurisdictions, which we find persuasive. * * *

"The General Assembly has demonstrated an on-going commitment to afford minors significant safeguards from harm by passing numerous statutes designed to protect minor children. Most significant of these for purposes of this case are the protections accorded minors in Colorado in the post-injury claim context. Colorado laws do not allow a parent the unilateral right to foreclose a child's existing cause of action to recover for torts committed against him. Rather, * * * the Colorado Probate Code provides significant procedural protections for minors in the post-injury claim context. This legislation creates mechanisms for the appointment of a conservator to protect a minor's settlement rights. § 15–14–403, 5 C.R.S. (2001); § 15–14–425(2)(t), 5 C.R.S. (2001). It also provides minors important protections by creating means by which the court may ratify the settlement of a minor's claims. § 15–14–412(1)(b), 5 C.R.S. (2001). Importantly, a parent may not act as a minor's conservator as a matter of right, but only when appointed by the court. § 15–14–413, 5 C.R.S. (2001).

* * *

"To allow a parent or guardian to execute exculpatory provisions on his minor child's behalf would render meaningless for all practical purposes the special protections historically accorded minors. In the tort context especially, a minor should be afforded protection not only from his own improvident decision to release his possible prospective claims for injury based on another's negligence, but also from unwise decisions made on his behalf by parents who are routinely asked to release their child's claims for liability. In Colorado, it has long been the rule that courts owe a duty to 'exercise a watchful and protecting care over [a minor's] interests, and not permit his rights to be waived, prejudiced or surrendered either by his own acts, or by the admissions or pleadings of those who act for him.' *Seaton v. Tobill,* 11 Colo.App. 211, 216, 53 P. 170, 172 (1898). Nearly one hundred years later we confirmed this steadfast principle: 'Courts are charged with the responsibility to take special care in protecting the rights of minor children.' *Abrams v. Connolly,* 781 P.2d 651, 658 (Colo.1989). Thus, a minor is accorded special protection, and to allow a parent to release a child's possible future claims for injury caused by negligence may as a practical matter leave the minor in an unacceptably precarious position with no recourse, no parental support, and no method to support himself or care for his injury.

* * *

"Our holding that parents may not release a minor's prospective claim for negligence comports with the vast majority of courts that have decided the issue. * ** [By the court's count, the majority position has been taken by ten jurisdictions. Two jurisdictions have taken the opposition position.]

———

DALURY v. S–K–I, LTD., and KILLINGTON, LTD., 164 Vt. 329, 670 A.2d 795 (1995). "While skiing at Killington Ski Area, plaintiff Robert Dalury sustained serious injuries when he collided with a metal pole that formed part of the control maze for a ski lift line. Before the season started, Dalury had purchased a midweek season pass and signed a form releasing the ski area from liability." Killington required skiers to sign the release. *Held,* the release was against public policy, and therefore unenforceable.

"[Many] courts have incorporated the Tunkl factors into their decisions. The Colorado Supreme Court has developed a four-part inquiry to analyze the validity of exculpatory agreements: (1) existence of a duty to the public, (2) the nature of the service performed, (3) whether the contract was fairly entered into, and (4) whether the intention of the parties is expressed in clear and unambiguous language. Jones v. Dressel, 623 P.2d 370, 376 (Colo.1981). In the Jones case, the court concluded, based on the Tunkl factors, that no duty to the public was involved in air service for a parachute jump, because that sort of service does not affect the public interest. Using a similar formula, the Wyoming Supreme Court concluded that a ski resort's sponsorship of an Ironman Decathlon competition did not invoke the public interest. Milligan v. Big Valley Corp., 754 P.2d 1063, 1066–67 (Wyo.1988).

"On the other hand, the Virginia Supreme Court recently concluded, in the context of a 'Teflon Man Triathlon' competition, that a preinjury release from liability for negligence is void as against public policy because it is simply wrong to put one party to a contract at the mercy of the other's negligence. Hiett v. Lake Barcroft Community Ass'n, 244 Va. 191, 418 S.E.2d 894, 897 (1992). The court stated: " '[T]o hold that it was competent for one party to put the other parties to the contract at the mercy of its own misconduct . . . can never be lawfully done where an enlightened system of jurisprudence prevails. Public policy forbids it, and contracts against public policy are void.' " Id.

"Having reviewed these various formulations of the public policy exception, we accept them as relevant considerations, but not as rigid factors that, if met, preclude further analysis. Instead, we recognize that no single formula will reach the relevant public policy issues in every factual context. Like the court in Wolf v. Ford, 335 Md. 525, 644 A.2d 522, 527 (1994), we conclude that ultimately the 'determination of what constitutes the public interest must be made considering the totality of the circumstances of any given case against the backdrop of current societal expectations.'

* * *

"Whether or not defendants provide an essential public service does not resolve the public policy question in the recreational sports context. * * *

* * *

"The policy rationale [for prohibiting releases of liability] is to place responsibility for maintenance of the land on those who own or control it, with the ultimate goal of keeping accidents to the minimum level possible. Defendants, not recreational skiers, have the expertise and opportunity to foresee and control hazards, and to guard against the negligence of their agents and employees. They alone can properly maintain and inspect their premises, and train their employees in risk management. They alone can insure against risks and effectively spread the cost of insurance among their thousands of customers. Skiers, on the other hand, are not in a position to discover and correct risks of harm, and they cannot insure against the ski area's negligence.

"If defendants were permitted to obtain broad waivers of their liability, an important incentive for ski areas to manage risk would be removed with the public bearing the cost of the resulting injuries. * * * "

Chapter 12

CAUSATION OF HARM

Plaintiff's prima facie case is usually described as consisting of injury along with duty, breach, actual causation (or cause in fact) and proximate causation. Actual causation, which we study in this chapter, is concerned with whether the plaintiff's injury was the result of the defendant's breach of its duty of care. Proximate causation, which we study in the next chapter, is concerned with the extent of a defendant's liability for injuries it has caused through breach of a duty of care.

The standard ordering of the plaintiff's case—duty, breach, actual cause, proximate cause—is not just an analytic convenience. Without a duty, there can be no breach, and our inquiry into defendant's possible liability comes to an end. With duty established we can take up breach, and with breach established we can take up actual causation. So the question we are asking is: Did defendant's *breach of its duty of care* cause an injury to the plaintiff? This framing of the question by prior inquiry into duty and breach is important. Injuries have an infinite number of causes: the victim had to get in the way of the injurer, the victim had to get up in the morning, the victim had to have been born, the victim's mother and father had to have been born, had to have met each other, and so on. The general question—What caused the plaintiff's injury?—invites a far-reaching inquiry. The question asked under the rubric of actual causation in the law of negligence is far more specific. Actual causation doctrine asks only if the defendant's breach of its duty of care caused injury to the plaintiff. (When there is more than one defendant, it asks if the defendants' breaches of their duties of care caused injury to the plaintiff.)

The question asked by actual causation doctrine is a straightforward one, but the enterprise of answering it turns out to raise conceptual puzzles. Conceptually, the problem—and the surprise—is that it is not always easy to tell if the defendant's breach of a duty of care has injured the plaintiff. It may be, for example, that the defendant breached its duty of care and the plaintiff suffered the very injury which led to the imposition of the duty in the first place, but the defendant's breach of its duty did not "actually cause" the injury to the plaintiff. We begin our study of actual causation with a case which explores this very possibility.

SECTION A. ACTUAL CAUSE

BARNES v. BOVENMYER

Supreme Court of Iowa, 1963.
255 Iowa 220, 122 N.W.2d 312.

GARFIELD, Chief Justice. * * *

V.   Of course proof of defendant's negligence did not entitle plaintiff to go to the jury. There must also be substantial evidence it was the [actual] cause of plaintiff's damage. * * *

The issue of proximate cause boils down to this: The jury could find defendant was negligent in not discovering and advising removal of the piece of steel from the eyeball before late afternoon July 1, and that with ordinary skill and care he would have done this the morning of the preceding day. It may even be conceded the piece in the eye should have been discovered Sunday evening. Is there any evidence this delay of 36 or 48 hours probably caused loss of the eye? As indicated, we are compelled to hold there is none. Further, the evidence on the question is that the delay probably did not cause loss of the eye.

The matter of causal connection between defendant's negligence and loss of plaintiff's eye is not within the knowledge and experience of ordinary laymen. It is a question upon which only a medical expert can express an intelligent opinion. It is a question essentially within the domain of expert testimony.

This is ordinarily the rule in actions of this kind. Annos. 141 A.L.R. 5, 6–12; 13 A.L.R.2d 11, 31–34. We are fully aware there are exceptions to the rule. See annotations last above. One exception we have recognized several times is where the harmful result of the negligence is so obvious as to lie within common knowledge. This exception cannot be applied here.

The accepted method of proving proximate cause would be by expert testimony that defendant's delay in discovering the piece of steel in the eye was the probable cause of its loss. Some decisions say it is sufficient to furnish substantial evidence upon which a reasonable basis for inference may be had, provided the matter is not left to conjecture and speculation. Ramberg v. Morgan, 209 Iowa 474, 486–487, 218 N.W. 492; Anno. 59 A.L.R. 884, 886–90.

The only expert witness was Dr. Emerson, called by plaintiff. He proved to be a much better witness for defendant than for plaintiff on the issue of proximate cause. Plaintiff's counsel did not question the doctor on this issue but asked some questions on the issue of negligence. On cross-examination Dr. Emerson more than once expresses the opinion [that] failure to remove the foreign body at an earlier time in all probability did not cause loss of the eye, infection entered it when the piece of steel did and removal of the steel would not remove the infection which caused loss of the eye. There may be circumstances to cast doubt on this negative testimony. However, even if it were not accepted, it would not supply the requisite affirmative proof of proximate cause.

An extended annotation in 13 A.L.R.2d 11, 98, on proximate cause in malpractice actions contains this appraisal of those similar to this: "A large proportion of eye injuries arise from the accidental introduction into the eye of foreign objects, and a number of malpractice cases have been based on the doctor's allegedly negligent failure to discover and remove such objects. These cases have frequently turned upon the question whether prompt removal would have been helpful in any event, since, if not, the failure to remove the object creates no liability even if negligent. In most of the instances involving eye injuries from foreign objects causation has been held not to have been established."

See also Anno. 68 A.L.R.2d 426, 430–3, on malpractice in eye treatment and surgery.

Although the question is not argued or suggested, we have considered whether the evidence is sufficient to justify a finding defendant's negligence caused temporary pain and suffering for which some recovery could be had, as in Kosak v. Boyce, 185 Wis. 513, 201 N.W. 757. In our opinion there is no sufficient basis for such an allowance.

Affirmed.

RESTATEMENT OF TORTS, THIRD: LIABILITY FOR PHYSICAL HARM (BASIC PRINCIPLES)
Tent. Draft No. 2 (March 25, 2002).

§ 26. Factual Cause

An actor's tortious conduct must be a factual cause of another's physical harm for liability to be imposed. Conduct is a factual cause of harm when the harm would not have occurred absent the conduct. * **

Comment:

b. "But-for" standard for factual cause. The standard for factual causation in this section is familiarly referred to as the "but-for" test, as well as a sine qua non test. Both express the same concept: an act is a factual cause of an outcome if, in the absence of the act, the outcome would not have occurred. With recognition that there are multiple factual causes of an event * * * a factual cause can also be described as a necessary condition for the outcome. * * *

e. Counterfactual inquiry for factual cause. The requirement that the actor's tortious conduct be necessary for the harm requires a counterfactual inquiry. One must ask what would have occurred if the actor had not engaged in the tortious conduct. In some cases, in which the tortious conduct consists of the entirety of an act, this inquiry may not be difficult. Thus, if an actor's battery is alleged to have broken another's arm, assessing what would have occurred if the actor had not assaulted the other person poses little difficulty. In other cases, especially those in which the tortious conduct consists of marginally more risky conduct or in which the actor failed to take a precaution that would have reduced the risk to another, such as by warning of the danger, the counterfactual inquiry may pose difficult problems of proof.

———————

SOWLES v. MOORE, 65 Vt. 322, 26 A. 629, 21 L.R.A. 723 (1893). A statute required a fence around holes cut in ice on ponds. Plaintiff's horses became frightened, and ran away, into a hole cut in the ice by defendant and left unprotected by a fence. *Held,* for defendant. The trial judge correctly charged that if the fence prescribed by statute would not have prevented the accident, the plaintiff could not recover.

FORD v. TRIDENT FISHERIES CO., 232 Mass. 400, 122 N.E. 389 (1919). Action for negligently causing the drowning of the plaintiff's intestate, while serving as mate of the defendant's steam trawler. As he was walking up a flight of four steps, the vessel rolled and he was thrown overboard. "[N]o cry was heard, no clothing was seen floating in the water, and Ford was not seen by any one from the time he fell overboard." At the close of the plaintiff's evidence the judge ordered a verdict for the defendant and the plaintiff alleged exceptions. *Held,* exceptions overruled. "The plaintiff also contends that the boat which was lowered to pick up the intestate was lashed to the deck instead of being suspended from davits and in order to launch it the lashings had to be cut; that McCue, who manned it, had only one oar and was obliged to scull, instead of rowing as he might have done if he had had two oars. Even if it be assumed that upon these facts it could have been found the defendant was negligent, there is nothing to show they in any way contributed to Ford's death. He disappeared when he fell from the trawler and it does not appear that if the boat had been suspended from davits and a different method of propelling it had been used he could have been rescued."

ZUCHOWICZ v. UNITED STATES, 140 F.3d 381 (2d Cir.1998) (Calabresi, J.) "The problem of linking defendant's negligence to the harm that occurred is one that many courts have addressed in the past. A car is speeding and an accident occurs. That the car was involved and was a cause of the crash is readily shown. The accident, moreover, is of the sort that rules prohibiting speeding are designed to prevent. But is this enough to support a finding of fact, in the individual case, that *speeding* was, in fact, more probably than not, the cause of the accident? The same question can be asked when a car that was driving in violation of a minimum speed requirement on a super-highway is rear-ended. Again, it is clear that the car and its driver were causes of the accident. And the accident is of the sort that minimum speeding rules are designed to prevent. But can a fact finder conclude, without more, that the driver's negligence in *driving too slowly* led to the crash? To put it more precisely—the defendant's negligence was strongly causally linked to the accident, and the defendant was undoubtedly a *but for* cause of the harm, but does this suffice to allow a fact finder to say that the defendant's *negligence* was a *but for* cause?"

"At one time, courts were reluctant to say in such circumstances that the wrong could be deemed to be the cause. They emphasized the logical fallacy of *post hoc, ergo propter hoc,* and demanded some direct evidence connecting the defendant's wrongdoing to the harm. *See, e.g., Wolf v. Kaufmann,* 227 A.D. 281, 282, 237 N.Y.S. 550, 551 (1929) (denying recovery for death of plaintiff's decedent, who was found unconscious at foot of stairway which, in violation of a statute, was unlighted, because the plaintiff had offered no proof of 'any causal connection between the accident and the absence of light')."

"All that has changed, however. And, as is so frequently the case in tort law, Chief Judge Cardozo in New York and Chief Justice Traynor in California led the way. In various opinions, they stated that: if (a) a negligent act was deemed wrongful *because* that act increased the chances that a particular type of accident would occur, and (b) a mishap of that very sort did happen, this was enough to support a finding by the trier of fact that the negligent behavior caused the harm. Where such a strong causal link exists, it is up to the negligent party to bring in evidence denying *but for* cause and suggesting that in the actual case the wrongful conduct had not been a substantial factor."

ALDER v. BAYER CORP., AGFA DIV., 61 P.3d 1068 (Utah 2002). Hospital technicians brought suit against the manufacturer of an x-ray processing machine (the AFGA Divison of Bayer), alleging that they had been made ill through exposure to chemical fumes resulting from AFGA's negligent installation and servicing of an x-ray machine. Under AFGA's supervision, the machine had been installed in a suite of rooms whose air was not exchanged completely at least ten times an hour, the minimum rate required by the machine's installation guidelines. *Held,* summary judgment for defendant on proof of causation reversed.

" * * * The alleged harm occurred in the absence of adequate air exchange. Under the reasoning of *Zuchowicz,* this alone is sufficient to support causation and AGFA bears the burden of refuting the presumption of 'but for' causation.

"Individuals routinely feel the effects of a wide array of common phenomena whose mechanisms remain unexplained by science, including, for example, the law of gravity, the nature of light, the source of personality, and the process of cell differentiation. If a bicyclist falls and breaks his arm, causation is assumed without argument because of the temporal relationship between the accident and the injury. The law does not object that no one measured the exact magnitude and angle of the forces applied to the bone. Courts do not exclude all testimony regarding the fall because the mechanism of gravity remains undiscovered. Legally, an observable sequence of condition—>event—>altered condition, has been found sufficient to establish causation even when the exact mechanism is unknown. Therefore, we hold that Technicians enjoy the same opportunity to prove that which they can, as do the victims of more prosaic injuries."

WHAT HARM HAS THE DEFENDANT CAUSED?

The basic question of causation is: Has the defendant's tortious conduct caused the harm for which the plaintiff seeks recovery? But a second question often arises as well: What harm has the plaintiff caused? This problem is especially acute in the "loss of chance" cases we take up in the next section, but it is not confined to those cases, as the following squib makes clear.

––––––

DILLON v. TWIN STATE GAS & ELECTRIC CO., 85 N.H. 449, 163 A. 111 (1932). Action for negligently causing the death of the plaintiff's intestate, a boy of 15, who fell from a bridge and was electrocuted by coming in contact with the defendant's uninsulated live wire which was dangerously close to the bridge. Irrespective of the defendant's negligence, however, the deceased would undoubtedly have been killed or gravely injured when he struck the surface below. A jury trial resulted in a disagreement. *Held,* that the trial court properly refused to direct a verdict for the defendant. With reference to a new trial, on the issue of damages, the court said: "If it were found that [the deceased] would have thus fallen with death probably resulting, the defendant would not be liable unless for conscious suffering found to have been sustained from the shock. In that situation his life or earning capacity had no value. To constitute actionable negligence there must be damage, and damage is limited to those elements the statute prescribed. If it should be found that but for the current he would have fallen with serious injury then the loss of life or earning capacity resulting from the electrocution would be measured by its value in such injured condition. Evidence that he would be crippled would be taken into account in the same manner as though he had already been crippled."

B. "LOSS OF CHANCE" AND OTHER PROBABILISTIC HARM

The normal tortious injury has its origins in set of circumstances which can be reported in a historical narrative. In *Garratt v. Dailey, supra* p. 7, for instance, we are told that the plaintiff broke her hip when the defendant pulled the chair that plaintiff was about to sit in out from underneath her. In *Davis v. Consolidated Rail Corp., supra* p. 314, we are told that the plaintiff had one leg severed just below the knee and most of the foot on the other leg sliced off when the train that he was inspecting started without warning. In an important class of cases, however, the plaintiff's injury cannot be traced to its source in a narrative history of this sort. This class of cases involves health injuries—cancers, physical traumas and heart conditions, for example—where the plaintiff's injury might have been produced either by the defendant's tortious conduct, or by a source of risk wholly independent of that conduct.

The plaintiff may both have been subject to a preexisting risk of leukemia—the background risk of leukemia that we all are subject to, perhaps—and have been exposed by the defendant to a toxic substance which increases her chances of contracting leukemia. In the litigation made famous by the book and the film A CIVIL ACTION, the plaintiffs claimed that defendant's discharges of toxic materials created just this sort of increased risk of leukemia. Or the plaintiff may have suffered from a preexisting physical condition—say a skull fracture, a heart condition, or premature labor. The medical negligence of the defendant may have diminished her chances (or her fetus's chances) of recovering from that condition, or increased her chances of suffering even greater harm at the hands of this condition. Or the plaintiff may have been suffering from a progressive disease such as breast cancer, and had her prospects of long-term survival diminished by the defendant's failure to make a timely diagnosis of the disease.

In the core "loss of chance" case the victim's chance of some favorable outcome is diminished by defendant's negligence, and the victim then suffers the unfavorable outcome whose chance had been increased by defendant's negligence. For example, the defendant's negligence may have diminished the victim's chance of avoiding the recurrence of a cancer, and the cancer subsequently recurs. Or the defendant's negligence may have diminished the victim's chance of recovering fully from a heart attack or skull fracture, and the victim then fails to recover fully. And so on. The underlying problem of causation that this class of cases presents, however, remains the same: *Either the defendant's tortious conduct or the independent source of risk might have caused the plaintiff's injury.* We may be able to divide the total long run harm caused between the tortious and non-tortious sources of the risk at hand, but we cannot tell in any given case which of the two is responsible for the particular injury that befell the plaintiff. Either source is sufficient to have caused plaintiff's injury; neither is necessary.

In a case of a breast cancer patient whose cancer was negligently misdiagnosed, for example, we may know that the misdiagnosis permitted the patient's tumor to double in size and diminished the plaintiff's chances of long-term survival from 40% to 10%. If the plaintiff dies from the metastasization of her cancer, however, we cannot know if she was one of the ten percent of patients who would have died even if her cancer had been correctly diagnosed at an earlier stage, or if she is one of the thirty percent who would not have died but for the negligent misdiagnosis of her cancer. All that we know is that either the preexisting cancer or the defendant's negligence is sufficient to cause her death, and that each will be responsible for a certain number of deaths in a suitably large population of patients.

What test of causation should we apply in these kinds of cases? How should we conceptualize the harm that the plaintiff suffers? Should we award plaintiffs damages for all of the harm that they have suffered? Or should we discount their total damage by the chance that the defendant's tortious conduct caused it? Consider again the case of a plaintiff who dies from breast cancer in the wake of a negligent misdiagnosis of her condition which diminished her chances of survival by thirty percent. In such a case, should we award the full value of long-term survival or discount the plaintiff's damages by the chance that she would have died anyway? Should we, that is, award thirty percent of the value of long-term survival?

Traditional tort conceptions of harm and causation entitle a plaintiff suffering from breast cancer, who dies from the cancer subsequent to negligent misdiagnosis of it, to the full value of long-term survival if the defendant's negligent treatment of her condition "more likely than not" caused her death. If a plaintiff dies of breast cancer when she had a 90% chance of surviving long-term with proper treatment, and a 75% chance of surviving long-term subsequent to defendant's negligent treatment of her condition, the defendant's negligence "more likely than not" caused her death. After the defendant's negligence, plaintiff's total risk of dying from her cancer was 25%; defendant was responsible for 60% of that total, because his negligence increased her risk of dying from the disease from 10% to 25%. (Fifteen is to twenty-five as sixty is to one hundred.) Defendant's negligence is "more likely than not" the cause of her death, since there is a 60% chance that the negligence is responsible for the fatal recurrence of the cancer.

If, on the other hand, a plaintiff dies of breast cancer when she had a 70% chance of surviving long-term with proper treatment, and a 50% chance of surviving long-term subsequent to defendant's negligent treatment of her condition, the defendant's negligence, "more likely than not," did *not* cause her death. Her total risk of dying from cancer was 50%; defendant was responsible for only 40% of that total, because his negligence increased her risk of dying from the disease from 30% to 50%. (Twenty is to fifty as forty is to one hundred.) "More likely than not" defendant's negligence is not the cause of plaintiff's death, since there is only a 40% chance that the negligence is responsible for the fatal recurrence of the cancer.

The alternative in this circumstance is to award compensation for the "loss of a chance," a practice now followed by a majority of American jurisdictions. The following cases examine this doctrine.

SCAFIDI v. SEILER
Supreme Court of New Jersey, 1990.
119 N.J. 93, 574 A.2d 398.

STEIN, J.

In this medical malpractice case, the proofs presented as a factual issue whether the defendant's failure properly to treat and arrest Jamie Scafidi's early labor proximately caused the premature birth and death of her infant child. The trial court declined plaintiffs' request that it instruct the jury on causation in accordance with the "increased risk" standard authorized by our opinion in Evers v. Dollinger, 95 N.J. 399, 417, 471 A.2d 405 (1984). The court also refused to instruct the jury that it was defendant's burden to prove that damages could be apportioned to reflect the likelihood that plaintiff Jamie Scafidi's preexistent condition was independently responsible for the premature birth and death. See Fosgate v. Corona, 66 N.J. 268, 272–73, 330 A.2d 355 (1974). Although finding that defendant's conduct was negligent, the jury returned a verdict for defendant, determining that his negligence was not a proximate cause of the infant's premature birth and death.

The Appellate Division held that the trial court committed reversible error by refusing to give the jury an Evers v. Dollinger charge, but sustained the trial court's refusal to impose on defendant the burden of proving that damages could be apportioned. We granted certification, and now affirm the judgment of the Appellate Division. We hold, however, that any damages awarded to plaintiffs on retrial, assuming that defendant's proofs include evidence that the infant's premature birth and death might have occurred even if defendant's treatment had been proper, should be apportioned to reflect the likelihood that the premature birth and death would have been avoided by proper treatment. Thus, plaintiffs' damages will be limited to the value of the lost chance for recovery attributable to defendant's negligence.

* * *

In Evers v. Dollinger, we addressed causation in the context of allegations that a defendant's negligence exacerbated a plaintiff's preexistent illness. Defendant had failed to diagnose properly a lump in the plaintiff's right breast, which a second physician determined to be a cancerous growth requiring an extended mastectomy. * * *

In view of the information presented to the Court that the plaintiff's cancer had recurred and metastasized, we addressed in Evers the standard by which causation should be charged to the jury on retrial. In that connection we discussed a series of medical malpractice cases decided in Pennsylvania that applied "a standard of causation that is more flexible than that used in conventional tort claims." Id. at 413, 471 A.2d 405 * * *

Adopting the reasoning of these Pennsylvania decisions, we determined in Evers that the principle set forth in Restatement (Second) of Torts § 323(a)[1] applies to medical malpractice cases. Accordingly, we held that on retrial plaintiff should be permitted to demonstrate, within a reasonable degree of medical probability, that the seven months delay resulting from defendant's failure to have made an accurate diagnosis and to have rendered proper treatment increased the risk of recurrence or of distant spread of plaintiff's cancer, and that such increased risk was a substantial factor in producing the condition from which plaintiff currently suffers.

The legal principle adopted by this Court in Evers reflects the emerging pattern of decisions on this issue in federal and state courts throughout the country. A clear majority of the courts that have considered proximate causation in the context of harm resulting from both a plaintiff's preexistent

---

1. The Restatement (Second) of Torts § 323(a) provides in pertinent part: One who undertakes, gratuitously or for consideration, to render services to another which he should recognize as necessary for the protection of the other's person or things, is subject to liability to the other for physical harm resulting from his failure to exercise reasonable care to perform his undertaking, if (a) his failure to exercise such care increased the risk of such harm * * *.

condition and a defendant's negligent discharge of a duty related to that condition have permitted the jury to consider whether defendant's negligence increased the risk of harm and whether such increased risk was a substantial factor in producing the harm. [The opinion cites twenty-two decisions adopting this position and four adhering "to a stricter formulation of proximate cause, requiring proof that the defendant's failure properly to treat the preexisting condition was a probable cause of the resultant injury."]

* * *

* * * As the Supreme Court of Oklahoma observed:

We think in those situations where a health care provider deprives a patient of a significant chance for recovery by negligently failing to provide medical treatment, the health care professional should not be allowed to come in after the fact and allege that the result was inevitable inasmuch as that person put the patient's chance beyond the possibility of realization. Health care providers should not be given the benefit of the uncertainty created by their own negligent conduct. To hold otherwise would in effect allow care providers to evade liability for their negligent actions or inactions in situations in which patients would not necessarily have survived or recovered, but still would have a significant chance of survival or recovery. [McKellips v. Saint Francis Hosp., Inc., 741 P.2d at 474.]

We adhere to our holding in Evers. Evidence demonstrating within a reasonable degree of medical probability that negligent treatment increased the risk of harm posed by a preexistent condition raises a jury question whether the increased risk was a substantial factor in producing the ultimate result. * * *

* * *

III.

The trial court's rejection of plaintiffs' requested jury instruction on damages, affirmed by the Appellate Division, implicates the measure of damages on remand. * * * We consider and decide the issue because of its significance both on retrial and in similar litigation.

We noted in Ostrowski v. Azzara, 111 N.J. 429, 439, 545 A.2d 148 (1988), the general principle that "a defendant whose acts aggravate a plaintiff's preexisting condition is liable only for the amount of harm actually caused by the negligence." (citing 2 F. Harper & F. James, Law of Torts s 20.3 at 1128 (1956)); Prosser and Keeton on Torts, supra, s 52 at 349. In Fosgate v. Corona, 66 N.J. 268, 330 A.2d 355, we recognized that principle in the context of a claim of medical malpractice involving treatment of a preexistent disease. We held in Fosgate that where the malpractice or other tortious act aggravates a preexisting disease or condition, the innocent plaintiff should not be required to establish what expenses, pain, suffering, disability or impairment are attributable solely to the malpractice or tortious act, but that the burden of proof should be shifted to the culpable defendant who should be held responsible for all damages unless he can demonstrate that the damages for which he is responsible are capable of some reasonable apportionment and what those damages are.

* * *

The critical issue that should have determined the applicability of the Fosgate charge is whether defendant's liability for damages is capable of any apportionment. Stated differently, the question is whether plaintiffs' damage claim should be limited to the value of the lost chance for recovery, in recognition of the evidence that the infant's premature birth and death might have occurred even if defendant's treatment was non-negligent.

In Evers we acknowledged the analysis offered by Professor King, the pre-eminent commentator on the question, proposing that in Evers-type cases a plaintiff's recovery be limited to the value of the lost chance of avoiding harm. Professor King's thesis is that in such cases "[t]he defendant should be subject to liability only to the extent that he tortiously contributed to the harm by allowing a preexisting condition to progress or by aggravating or accelerating its harmful effects, or to the extent that he otherwise caused harm in excess of that attributable solely to preexisting conditions. The effect of preexisting conditions should depend on the extent to which such conditions affect the present and future value of the interest lost." [King, Causation Valuation, and Chance in Personal Injury Torts Involving Preexisting Conditions and Future Consequences, 90 Yale L.J. 1353, 1360 (1981) (hereafter King, Causation and Valuation) (footnote omitted).]

The following example is offered to illustrate application of "lost chance" damages:

> [C]onsider a patient who suffers a heart attack and dies as a result. Assume that the defendant-physician negligently misdiagnosed the patient's condition, but that the patient would have had only a 40% chance of survival even with a timely diagnosis and proper care. Regardless of whether it could be said that the defendant caused the decedent's death, he caused the loss of a chance, and that chance-interest should be completely redressed in its own right. Under the proposed rule, the plaintiff's compensation for the loss of the victim's chance of surviving the heart attack would be 40% of the compensable value of the victim's life had he survived (including what his earning capacity would otherwise have been in the years following death). The value placed on the patient's life would reflect such factors as his age, health, and earning potential, including the fact that he had suffered the heart attack and the assumption that he had survived it. The 40% computation would be applied to that base figure. [Id. at 1382 (footnote omitted).]

In a number of cases courts have adopted or acknowledged the soundness of the concept that a plaintiff's recovery in Evers-type cases should ordinarily be limited to lost-chance damages. * * *

In our view, a rule that limits a plaintiff's damages in Evers-type cases to the value of the lost chance of recovery is an essential complement to Evers' modification of the proof required to establish proximate causation. It should be a self-evident principle of tort law that valuation of allowable damages "is animated by a premise similar to that underlying causation: that a tortfeasor should be charged only with the value of the interest he destroyed." King, Causation and Valuation, supra, 90 Yale L.J. at 1356. To the extent that a plaintiff's ultimate harm may have occurred solely by virtue of a preexistent condition, without regard to a tortfeasor's intervening negligence, the defendant's liability for damages should be adjusted to reflect the likelihood of that outcome. That principle is basic in our decisional law. It also serves an important societal interest in the context of medical-malpractice litigation. A rule of law that more precisely confines physicians' liability for negligence to the value of the interest damaged should have a salutary effect on the cost and availability of medical care.

Our holding is also consistent with the principles underlying the comparative-negligence statute, N.J.S.A. 2A:15–5.1 (damages sustained shall be diminished by percentage of negligence attributable to person recovering), and the joint-tortfeasor-contribution statute, N.J.S.A. 2A:53A–3 (permitting tortfeasor paying judgment in excess of prorata share to recover contribution from other tortfeasors). * * *

* * *

[Judgment of the Appellate Division, modified and affirmed.]

RESTATEMENT OF TORTS, THIRD: LIABILITY FOR PHYSICAL HARM (BASIC PRINCIPLES)
Tent. Draft No. 2 (March 25, 2002).

§ 26. Factual Cause

Comment:

f. Framework for causal analysis. Before the causal inquiry required by this section can be conducted, it must be framed. Framing requires two steps: The initial step is to identify the relevant, legally cognizable harm for which recovery is sought. Often this step will be straightforward, but there are times when courts recognize new, unusual, or reconceptualized harms, which change the causal inquiry. See Comment *n* ("Lost opportunity or lost chance as harm"). * * *

* * *

n. Lost opportunity or lost chance as harm. A number of courts have recognized a lost opportunity (or lost chance) for cure of a medical condition as a legally cognizable harm. This new characterization of harm permits recovery when adherence to traditional categories of legally cognizable harm and rules of proof of causation would not. * * *

Concomitant with this reconceptualization of the harm for a plaintiff unable to show a probability in excess of 50 percent is an adjustment of the damages to which the plaintiff is entitled. Rather than full damages for the adverse outcome, the plaintiff is only compensated for the lost opportunity.

The lost opportunity may be thought of as the adverse outcome discounted by the probability it would have occurred due to negligence. * * *

The lost-opportunity development has been halting, as courts have sought to find appropriate limits for this reconceptualization of legally cognizable harm. Without limits, this reform is of potentially enormous scope, implicating a large swath of tortious conduct in which there is uncertainty about factual cause, including failures to warn, provide rescue or safety equipment, and otherwise take precautions to protect a person from a risk of harm that exists. To date, the courts that have accepted lost opportunity as cognizable harm have almost universally limited its recognition to medical-malpractice cases. Three features of that context are significant: 1) a contractual relationship exists between patient and physician (or physician's employer), in which the raison d'être of the contract is that the physician will take every reasonable measure to obtain an optimal outcome for the patient; 2) reasonably good empirical evidence is available about the general statistical probability of the lost opportunity; and 3) frequently the consequences of the physician's negligence will deprive the patient of a less–than–50–percent chance for recovery. * * *

Recognizing a lost opportunity for cure is not strictly a matter of factual causation; rather, it reconceptualizes the harm. * * *

———

KRAMER v. LEWISVILLE MEMORIAL HOSPITAL, 858 S.W.2d 397 (Tex. 1993). The court distinguished the *Scafidi* approach to "loss of chance" from another version of the doctrine, which the court labeled "relaxed causation."

The "relaxed causation" version of "loss of chance" doctrine, the court explained, "permit[s] the case to go to the jury based on evidence that the defendant negligently deprived the patient of a *'substantial'* or *'appreciable'* possibility of survival or recovery."(emphasis added). Under this "relaxed causation approach, the patient's ultimate death or injury, and not the lost chance itself, continues to be treated as the relevant harm when determining proximate cause. Hence, even while the lost chance may be less than even, full damages are awarded in the same manner as if the plaintiff had established causation under traditional principles." In essence, this approach allows full recovery for the ultimate harm suffered if the plaintiff can establish that the defendant's negligence was a "substantial factor" in the production of that harm.

ALBERTS v. SCHULTZ, 126 N.M. 807, 975 P.2d 1279 (1999). "The basic test for establishing loss of chance is no different from the elements required in other medical malpractice actions, or in negligence suits in general: duty, breach, loss or damage, and causation. *Loss of chance differs from other medical malpractice actions only in the nature of the harm for which relief is sought.* [emphasis in original]

* * *

"The plaintiff bears the burden of proving each of these elements. Because the issues raised in lost-chance actions are, in virtually every case, 'beyond the province of lay persons,' the plaintiff will almost always establish these elements through expert testimony.

* * *

"We see no reason at this time to limit lost-chance claims to those cases in which the chance of a better result has been utterly lost. Denying compensation for the diminution—as opposed to the loss—of a chance may lead to unreasonable hairsplitting. 'Evidence of the physical progression of the patient's disease during a negligent delay in diagnosis or treatment may be sufficient to establish that the plaintiff was "injured" by the delay.' It is possible that trial courts may conclude in some cases that the diminished chance of a better result is of negligible significance. The cost of litigating such actions will no doubt discourage claims that are insignificant."

4. Cause

"If the Alberts had brought a claim under an ordinary medical malpractice negligence theory, the injury alleged would be the loss of Dee's leg below the knee. They cannot sustain such a claim, however, because his preexisting condition—peripheral vascular disease—precludes proof to a reasonable degree of medical probability that the doctors' negligence proximately caused the loss of the leg below the knee. In contrast, Dee can submit evidence that he had a chance—even if it was a small chance—of being cured of the presenting problem of rest pain and possible impending gangrene. He can be compensated if he can demonstrate, to a reasonable degree of medical probability, a causal link between the doctor's negligence and the loss of that chance."

DILLON v. EVANSTON HOSPITAL, 199 Ill.2d 483, 264 Ill.Dec. 653, 771 N.E.2d 357 (2002). A nine centimeter fragment of a catheter used to administer chemotherapy was negligently left in plaintiff's upper chest. The fragment migrated to her heart, where its tip became lodged in the wall of the right ventricle. It was discovered during the course of a routine X ray a year later. Although it was too dangerous to attempt to remove the fragment, leaving it in place put plaintiff at risk of "infection, perforation of the heart, arrhythmia, embolization, and further migration of the fragment."

At the time plaintiff's medical malpractice claim was tried, none of the risks of leaving the catheter in place had materialized. "The evidence was that it was not reasonably certain that plaintiff would in the future suffer the injuries for which she was at risk due to the fragment's presence in her heart. Several physicians testified about the risk of infection, with the lowest estimated risk being close to zero and the highest being 20%. The risk of arrhythmia was less than 5%. The risks of perforation and migration were also small. The risk of embolization was low to nonexistent." The jury awarded plaintiff $500,000 for increased risk of future injuries, in addition to damages for past and future pain and suffering. The intermediate appellate court upheld the award, ruling "that the trial court did not err in instructing the jury that plaintiff could be compensated for the increased risk of future harm."

The Illinois Supreme Court *affirmed* recovery for increased risk of future injury and *reversed and remanded* for a new trial on damages on increased risk. "[T]he instruction which the jury received on this element of damages did not adequately state the law." The jury instruction which the court approved for use in increased risk of future injury cases reads in part:

> The plaintiff claims that he/she has suffered an increased risk of [alleged future complication] as a result of the defendant's negligence. * * * In order to award this element of damages, you must find a breach of duty that was a substantial factor in causing a present injury which has resulted in an increased risk of future harm. The increased risk must have a basis in the evidence. Your verdict must not be based on speculation. *The plaintiff is entitled to compensation to the extent that the future harm is likely to occur as measured by multiplying the total compensation to which the plaintiff would be entitled if the harm in question were certain to occur by the proven probability that the harm in question will in fact occur.* [Emphasis supplied by the Illinois Supreme Court]

In support of its decision to recognize recovery for increased risk of future injury, the court cited its own prior decisions recognizing recovery for "loss of chance." "The theories of lost chance of recovery and increased risk of future injury have similar theoretical underpinnings."

PROBABILISTIC HARM

The problem addressed by "loss of chance" doctrine is closely related to the problem presented by exposure to harmful substances—radiation, pollution, toxins—which increase the risk that those exposed to them may suffer some kind of harm. In "loss of chance" cases, the problem is that some probability of a better outcome has been lost through defendant's negligence. In "probabilistic harm" cases, the problem is that defendant's wrongful exposure of plaintiffs to some harmful substance has increased the chance that those exposed will develop an injury—typically a disease or some other injury to their health—at a later point in time. That disease is, however, a naturally occurring phenomenon as well as something whose incidence has been increased by this particular defendant's wrongful conduct. The occurrence of the disease in a person exposed to the harmful substance is therefore not sufficient to vouch for the causal connection between defendant's wrongdoing and plaintiff's injury.

Our predicament is this: We know that some members of the population exposed to the harmful substance would have developed the disease even if they hadn't been exposed, and that other members of the population would not have—they have only developed the disease because of their exposure. But we are in a poor position to determine which members of the group would have developed the harm, and which would not have. When someone exposed to a harmful substance develops the very injury threatened by that exposure, how can we tell if their exposure was the "actual cause" of the harm they have suffered? *Allen v. United States* wrestles with this problem.

ALLEN v. UNITED STATES

United States District Court, Central District of Utah, 1984.
588 F.Supp. 247.

Reversed on other grounds, 816 F.2d 1417 (10th Cir.1987).

[In this action under the Federal Tort Claims Act, the complaint alleged that plaintiffs (or their predecessors) suffered injury or death as a result of exposure to radioactive fallout that drifted from the Nevada test site for atom bomb testing to communities in parts of Utah, Arizona and Nevada. The serious injuries and deaths resulted from radiation-caused cancer or leukemia. Plaintiffs asserted that these injuries were the consequence of the negligence of the United States in conducting open-air nuclear testing up to 1963.

The action was a consolidation of claims of 1,192 plaintiffs. This trial to the court included 24 of the claims in their entirety, selected by the parties' counsel as "bellwether" cases. The court received into evidence the testimony of 98 witnesses and over 1,692 documentary exhibits. It found that defendant (1) negligently failed to warn plaintiffs adequately of known or foreseeable long-range consequences from exposure to fallout radiation, (2) negligently failed to measure adequately and concurrently with the testing the fallout in nearby communities on a "person-specific basis," and (3) negligently failed to inform nearby individuals and communities of well-known and inexpensive methods to prevent or mitigate the biological consequences of exposure. Since defendant had unreasonably placed plaintiffs at risk of injury, certain of the plaintiffs were entitled to recover damages from the United States in stated amounts. The complaints of the remaining plaintiffs of the bellwether group were dismissed for failure "to demonstrate with the requisite weight that the defendant's negligence proximately caused the condition of which each complains."

These excerpts from the opinion of Judge Jenkins treat only the issue of causation.]

In this case, the factual connection singling out the defendant as the source of the plaintiffs' injuries and deaths is very much in genuine dispute. Determination of the cause-in-fact, or factual connection, issue is complicated by the nature of the injuries suffered (various forms of cancer and leukemia), the nature of the causation mechanism alleged (ionizing radiation from nuclear fallout, as opposed to ionizing radiation from other sources, or other carcinogenic mechanisms), the extraordinary time factors and other variables involved in tracing any causal relationship between the two.

At this point, there appears to be no question whether or not ionizing radiation causes cancer and leukemia. It does. Once more, however, it seems important to clarify what is meant by "cause" in relation to radiation and cancer:

> When we refer to radiation as a cause, we do not mean that it causes every case of cancer or leukemia. Indeed, the evidence we have indicating radiation in the causation of cancer and leukemia shows that not all cases of cancer are caused by radiation. Second, when we refer to radiation as a cause of cancer, we do not mean that every individual exposed to a certain amount of radiation will develop cancer. We simply mean that a population exposed to a certain dose of radiation will show a greater incidence of cancer than that same population would have shown in the absence of the added radiation.

J. Gofman, M.D., *Radiation and Human Health* 54–55 (1981), PX–1046.

The question of cause-in-fact is additionally complicated by the long delay, known often as the *latency period*, between the exposure to radiation and the observed cancer or leukemia. Assuming that cancer originates in a single cell, or a few cells, in a particular organ or tissue, it may take years before those cells multiply into the millions or billions that comprise a detectable tumor. * * *

The problem of the latency period is one factor distinguishing radiation/cancer causation questions from the cause-in-fact relationships found in most tort cases; normally "cause" is far more direct, immediate and observable, *e.g.,* A fires a gun at B, seriously wounding him. The great length of time involved (*e.g.,* A irradiates B, who develops a tumor 22 years later) allows the possible involvement of "intervening causes," sources of injury wholly apart from the defendant's activities, which obscure the factual connection between the plaintiff's injury and the defendant's purportedly wrongful conduct. The mere passage of time is sufficient to raise doubts about "cause" in the minds of a legal system accustomed to far more immediate chains of events.

The non-specific nature of the alleged injury further obscures the causal relationship between the defendant's conduct and the biological effects which are identified as consequences. Wounds and injuries from firearms, knives, heavy machinery, or other dangerous implements, for example, have particular qualities which are readily traced to source. Acute poisoning by specific toxic chemicals may be identified by specific symptoms or effects coinciding with the detected presence of the substance itself. Even acute radiation syndrome resulting from short-term exposure to 25 or more rads is fairly easily traced to source by blood counts and more externalized symptoms now identified to such exposure.

When the injury alleged, the biological consequence, is some form of cancer or leukemia, such specific clues as to cause, or source, are usually lacking:

> First, it must be emphasized and reemphasized that when a cancer is induced by ionizing radiation, the structural and functional features

of the cancer cells, and the gross cancer itself, show *nothing specific to ionizing radiation.* Once established, a radiation-induced cancer cannot be distinguished from a cancer of the same organ arising from the unknown causes we so commonly lump together as "spontaneous." *Spontaneous* is an elegant term for describing our ignorance of the cause. The fact that radiation-induced cancers cannot be distinguished from other cancers itself indicates that there are profound common features among cancers, likely far more important than the differences.

J. Gofman, M.D., *Radiation and Human Health, supra,* at 59 (1981), PX–1046 (emphasis in original). Ionizing radiation—or other carcinogens—seem to add to the number of cancers already occurring in people, rather than producing new, distinct varieties of cancer. See *id.* PX–1046. * * *

* * *

In other cases * * * where plaintiff has produced evidence of factual connection sufficient to permit the drawing of a rational inference of causation—of some contribution by defendant's conduct to plaintiff's injury—it has been left to the defendant to prove otherwise. In *Basko v. Sterling Drug, Inc.* [416 F.2d 417 (1969)], the U.S. Court of Appeals for the Second Circuit relied upon § 432(2) of the Restatement (Second) of Torts in holding that such an inference of causation may support a finding of liability. That section states:

> If two forces are actively operating, one because of the actor's negligence, the other not because of any misconduct on his part, and each of itself sufficient to bring about harm to another, the actor's negligence may be found to be a substantial factor in bringing it about.

If defendant's negligent conduct is found to be a "substantial factor," it may in Restatement parlance be judged to be the "legal cause" of plaintiff's injury, *i.e.,* defendant could be held liable based upon determination of the *legal* issues relating to liability (scope of duty, negligence, etc.). "The reason for imposing liability in such a situation," the court explains,

> is that the "defendant has committed a wrong and this has been *a* cause of the injury; further, such negligent conduct will be more effectively deterred by imposing liability than by giving the wrongdoer a windfall in cases where an all-sufficient innocent cause happens to concur with his wrong in producing the harm." 2 Harper and James, [*The Law of Torts*] *supra* at 1123. * * *

Id. 416 F.2d at 429. Implicitly the *Basko* opinion shifts the burden to defendant to produce evidence refuting causation if he is to escape liability once plaintiff has established a "substantial" factual connection between defendant's conduct and her own injuries. The principle expressed in Restatement (Second) of Torts § 432(2) "applies not only when the second force which is operating . . . is generated by the negligent conduct of a third person, but also when it is generated by an innocent act of a third person or when its origin is unknown." Restatement (Second) of Torts § 432 comment b (1965). Thus a defendant may be held liable for negligent conduct with factual connections to plaintiff's injuries even where other concurrent forces of human, "natural" or unknown origin have similar connections. Whether he *is* held liable, of course, is a question governed by distinct ethical, legal and public policy considerations.

* * *

* * * [T]he Government's negligent failure to adequately monitor and record the actual external and internal radiation exposures of off-site residents on a person-specific basis has yielded many glaring deficiencies in the evidentiary record as it relates directly to the question of causation. The current multi-million dollar effort to reconstruct the radiation dosages received by plaintiffs or their decedents is constantly hampered by the failure of the off-site radiation safety personnel to gather whole categories of exposure data at the time that the exposures actually took place. Furthermore, had Government personnel provided adequate warnings of risk and information as to precautions minimizing the amount of exposure, a materially different picture as to appropriate inferences about factual connection and cause-in-fact might now be presented. Accurate monitoring of persons largely was not undertaken; adequate warnings and information were almost entirely omitted from the operational radiation safety activities. A strong additional reason for shifting the burden of proof on the cause-in-fact question is thus readily apparent from the record.

* * *

A useful analogy may perhaps be drawn from some of the currently proposed schemes for compensating long-term injuries to health allegedly caused by exposure to toxic chemicals and chemical wastes. The causation problems facing many toxic waste plaintiffs are strikingly similar to those facing plaintiffs alleging nuclear fallout injuries in this and other cases. Consider, for example, the problem of the "indeterminate plaintiff":

> We may know, for example, that a *group* of people has a specific type of cancer and that some of them contracted that cancer from exposure to the defendant's waste, but we do not know which *individuals* of that group were affected by the waste. The character of toxic waste injuries causes this uncertainty. We know what causes a broken leg or a black eye and can decide liability based on whether or not those causes were controlled by the defendant, but we do not know the mechanics of causation of cancers and nervous disorders. We are still at the elementary stage of knowing simply that they *can* be caused entirely or in part by exposures to certain substances; we cannot tie the exposures more precisely to the injuries.

Note, "The Inapplicability of Traditional Tort Analysis to Environmental Risks: The Example of Toxic Waste Pollution Victim Compensation," 35 *Stan.L.Rev.* 575, 582 (1983) [hereinafter cited Note, "Inapplicability of Traditional Tort Analysis"] (emphasis in original).

* * *

Several recent legislative proposals make an effort to accommodate these practical complexities. * * * A bill introduced in the United States

Senate in 1980 provided that once a claimant made a prima facie showing of causal connection, the burden of producing evidence shifted to defendant to demonstrate that exposure to its toxic chemicals was an insignificant contribution to claimant's injuries. Establishing a prima facie case required a showing that

> (1) the claimant had been exposed to a hazardous substance released by the defendant; (2) the exposure was in sufficient concentration and of sufficient duration to create a "reasonable likelihood" that it caused or contributed to the claimant's injury; and (3) there is a "reasonable likelihood" that exposure to that substance causes or contributes to the type of injury sustained by the claimant.... The defendant could rebut this showing only by demonstrating by a preponderance of the evidence that the contributing causes to the disease were apportionable and that its contribution was insignificant....

35 *Stan.L.Rev.* at 590 n. 57 (citations omitted). * * *

Each of these proposals relies upon proof by the claimant of a series of factual connections which establish a rational, reasonably exclusive relationship between defendant's conduct in releasing lethally hazardous chemicals into the environment and each claimant's asserted injury. At least as to the cause-in-fact issue, such approaches are wholly consistent with the tort law analysis expressed in this Part. * * *

A remedial framework can certainly be fashioned to meet the circumstances and requirements of the parties and issues now before this court in this action. To that end, this court now holds as follows:

Where a defendant who negligently creates a radiological hazard which puts an identifiable population group at increased risk, and a member of that group at risk develops a biological condition which is consistent with having been caused by the hazard to which he has been negligently subjected, such consistency having been demonstrated by substantial, appropriate, persuasive and connecting factors, a fact finder *may* reasonably conclude that the hazard caused the condition absent persuasive proof to the contrary offered by the defendant.

In this case, such factors shall include, among others: (1) the probability that plaintiff was exposed to ionizing radiation due to nuclear fallout from atmospheric testing at the Nevada Test Site at rates in excess of natural background radiation; (2) that plaintiff's injury is of a type consistent with those known to be caused by exposure to radiation; and (3) that plaintiff resided in geographical proximity to the Nevada Test Site for some time between 1951 and 1962. Other factual connections may include but are not limited to such things as time and extent of exposure to fallout, radiation sensitivity factors such as age or special sensitivities of the afflicted organ or tissue, retroactive internal or external dose estimation by current researchers, a latency period consistent with a radiation etiology, or an observed statistical incidence of the alleged injury greater than the expected incidence in the same population.

* * *

B.　The Problem of Mathematical Proof

In a case where a plaintiff tries to establish a factual connection between a particular "cause" and a delayed, non-specific effect such as cancer or leukemia, the strongest evidence of the relationship is likely to be statistical in form. Where the injuries are causally indistinguishable, and where experts cannot determine whether an individual injury arises from culpable human cause or non-culpable natural causes, evidence that there is an increased incidence of the injury in a population following exposure to defendant's risk-creating conduct may justify an inference of "causal linkage" between defendant's conduct and plaintiff's injuries. The search for increased incidence of injury among groups receiving more or less radiation exposure is the classic approach to researching induction of cancer and leukemia by ionizing radiation. * * * Where there is an increase of observed cases of a particular cancer or leukemia over the number statistically "expected" to normally appear, the question arises whether it may be rationally inferred that the increase is causally connected to specific human activity. The scientific papers and reports will often speak of whether a deviation from the expected numbers of cases is "statistically significant," supporting a hypothesis of causation, or whether the perceived increase is attributable to random variation in the studied population, i.e., to chance. The mathematical tests of significance commonly used in research tend to be stringent; for an increase to be considered "statistically significant," the probability that it can be attributed to random chance usually must be five percent or less (p = 0.05). In other words, if the level of significance chosen by the researcher is p = 0.05, then an observed correlation is "significant" if there is 1 chance in 20—or less—that the increase resulted from chance. H. Young, *Statistical Treatment of Experimental Data* 131–32 (pap. ed. 1962). * * * The cold statement that a given relationship is not "statistically significant" cannot be read to mean "there is no probability of a relationship." Whether a correlation between a cause and a group of effects is more likely than not—particularly in a legal sense—is a different question from that answered by tests of statistical significance, which often distinguish narrow differences in degree of probability.

The inherent limitations in the concept of statistical significance are particularly important to the evaluation of statistical studies of relatively small populations, or groups of subjects.

* * *

* * * "The fluctuations of pure chance cancel each other out when large numbers are dealt with, but these fluctuations can remain when only small numbers are involved. This is commonly referred to in science as 'the small numbers problem.' " J. Gofman, *Radiation and Human Health* 147 (1981), PX–1046. Small communities or groups of people are deemed "statistically unstable." * * *

That data from small populations must be handled with care does not mean that it cannot provide substantial evidence in aid of our effort to describe and understand events. Mathematical or statistical evidence, when properly combined with other varieties of evidence in the same case can "supply a useful link in the process of proof." Tribe, "Trial by Mathematics: Precision and Ritual in the Legal Process," 84 *Harv.L.Rev.* 1329, 1350 (1971). If relied upon as a guide rather than as an answer, the statistical evidence offered in this case provides material assistance in evaluating the factual connection between nuclear fallout and plaintiffs' injuries.

The value of the available statistical data concerning radiation and cancer in off-site communities is not confined by arbitrary tests of "statistical significance." Nor is the court constrained by simplistic models of causal probability impressed upon the judicial "preponderance of the evidence" standard.

It is suggested, for example, that in the following scenario plaintiff's proof would fail to satisfy the standard:

> Before the defendant's arrival, the region experienced a stable ("background") rate of 100 cases of the injury per year. After the defendant's arrival, the number of cases increases to 190 and remains constant. Expert testimony establishes that the increased incidence of the injury can only be attributed to the conduct of the defendant. . . .

Delgado, "Beyond *Sindell:* Relaxation of Cause-in-Fact Rules for Indeterminate Plaintiffs," 70 *Cal.L.Rev.* 881, 885 (1982) (footnotes omitted). In such a case, it is argued, "no victim can make it appear more probably than not that his or her injury stemmed from defendant's conduct." *Id.* at 887. "[S]uch evidence says little about the cause of the plaintiff's particular injury: Unless that statistical increase is greater than 100%, his injury probably was *not* caused by the exposure, and he will recover nothing." Note, "Inapplicability of Traditional Tort Analysis," *supra*, 35 *Stan.L.Rev.* at 584 (footnote omitted).

First, such argument assumes the absence of other factual connections tying the increased risk to plaintiff's particular injury. Yet even standing alone, the statistical evidence in the hypothetical cases plainly establishes the defendant's probable contribution of approximately 90 additional injuries to the community—a substantial factual connection. Whether causal inferences should be drawn which will carry the case to the additional issues of risks, scope of duty and culpable breach of duty, *e.g.,* negligence, is a question of judgment resting in part upon policy. The court must determine those risks for which the defendant should be held responsible. Whether the defendant is ultimately held responsible for an injury which may likely have occurred anyway is inherently a question of policy, not of factual connection or causation. The mechanical application of a "greater–than–100%–increase" test in this context represents merely the refabrication of the "but-for" test of causation in mathematical form: but for defendant's 50 plus percent share of the statistically identified injuries, plaintiff would probably not have been hurt.

In cases where, as here, defendant's duty extends to protection of plaintiff from even the *possibility* of harm, or where, as here, defendant's wrongful conduct arguably has denied to plaintiff a potential *opportunity* to avoid serious or lethal injury, analysis using "but-for" tests in any form falls far short of the mark.

* * *

C. THE PROBLEM OF DOSE–RESPONSE RELATIONSHIP

Evaluation of the factual connections and causal linkages between conduct and injury in this case necessarily involves some treatment of the question of the relationship between radiation exposure and human cancer and leukemia. If, for example, the evidence persuasively demonstrated that no long-term biological injury is identified in persons receiving doses of ionizing radiation smaller than 100 rads, statistical incidence or other factual connections would simply be irrelevant, unless each plaintiff could establish the likelihood of a higher radiation exposure.

* * *

Although some scientists and commentators have at times suggested the presence of a "threshold" dose, the predominant philosophical approaches to radiation protection have carefully eschewed such a view, and the overwhelming weight of currently available scientific evidence supports the view that at *any* exposure level, ionizing radiation causes *some* degree of biological damage and creates *some* long-term risk of cancer and leukemia in those persons who are exposed. * * *

The exact relationship between radiation exposure and additional risk of cancer or leukemia appears to be dependent upon a number of variable factors, some known and some unknown. * * * From the empirical evidence, we know that "age at exposure to ionizing radiation is a major factor in the carcinogenic response." *BIER–III Report,* at 167 (1980), DX–1025. For many cancers, "[t]he cancer risk from radiation is much greater for those irradiated at 0–9 years of age than for those irradiated at 10–19 years of age, and the risk declines even further for those irradiated at higher ages." J. Gofman, M.D., *Radiation and Human Health,* at xv (rev. ed. 1983). The evidence establishes that cancer may be induced by radiation in nearly all the tissues of the human body, *BIER–III Report* at 137 (1980), DX–1025, but that tissues and organs vary considerably in their sensitivity to the induction of cancer by radiation. *Id.* * * *

> With respect to excess risk of cancer from whole-body exposure to radiation, solid tumors are now known to be of greater numerical significance than leukemia. Solid cancers characteristically have long latent periods; they seldom appear before 10 yrs. after radiation exposure and may continue to appear for 30 yrs. or more after radiation exposure.

BIER–III Report, at 137 (1980), DX–1025. * * *

* * *

The empirical evidence also indicates that the incidence of radiation-induced breast and thyroid cancer is such that the total cancer risk is greater for women than for men. Age again is important: women exposed at 10–19 years of age have the highest risk of radiation-induced breast cancer. With respect to other cancers, the radiation risks for both sexes are approximately equal. *BIER–III Report* at 137–38 (1980), DX–1025.

Additional factors have been identified, yet remain shrouded in mystery. It is postulated that various internal or environmental factors may interact with radiation in a manner that affects cancer incidence in different tissues. * * *

When these variables are considered together, it is readily apparent that the dose-response relationship between ionizing radiation and cancer may vary according to (1) type of radiation; (2) type of cancer; (3) personal variables of the exposed individual (age, sex, physical characteristics); and (4) interactions with other stimuli or environmental factors. Yet when analyzed in light of these variables, the empirical evidence appears to offer a sufficient basis for at least a qualified generalization about the proportionality of dose and response. Several mathematical models have been suggested.

* * *

D. THE PROBLEM OF DOSIMETRY

Even under controlled laboratory conditions, accurate determination of absorbed dosages of radiation in human tissue is problematical. Usually where the question of radiation-induced cancer or leukemia is raised, dose must be estimated long after the fact of actual exposure. Accurate reconstruction of dose proves difficult even when a good deal is known from measurements about the source, the times and extent of exposure, effect of shielding, and other factors. * * *

* * *

This court has carefully reviewed the testimony and documentary evidence offered as relating to dosimetry. Even as much recent work as has been done still leaves the question of radiation exposure of individual plaintiffs very much in doubt. * * *

As with statistical evidence, however, the court is not confined solely to contemporaneous or reconstructed dosimetry estimates in determining whether to draw the inference that the defendant's negligent conduct has been a "substantial factor" contributing to the plaintiffs' injuries. * * * The record in this action [offers] *some* evidence pertaining to dose accompanied by *some* evidence pertaining to increased statistical incidences of various consistent injuries.

* * *

Recognizing that cancer and leukemia may be caused by radiation from other sources (natural, medical, occupational, etc.) or by other carcinogenic agents, exposure to nuclear fallout proves to be a likely "substantial factor" where the dosage materially exceeds that which is received from other sources, such as natural "background" radiation and medical x-rays or other radiological treatments. Increased incidence of injuries consistent with such exposure, particularly in radiosensitive tissues and persons, adds additional weight to the argument that the observed injuries are a real effect of radiation exposure from the additional source. Radiation exposure higher than "background" dose is the first of the factual connections set forth above that a plaintiff must establish.

All of the relevant factual connections, including dosimetry, should be considered in the evaluation of the likelihood of a relationship between fallout and cancer as to each plaintiff. Where it appears from a preponderance of the evidence that the conduct of the defendant significantly increased or augmented the risk of somatic injury to a plaintiff and that the risk has taken effect in the form of a biologically and statistically consistent somatic injury, i.e., cancer or leukemia, the inference may rationally be drawn that defendant's conduct was a substantial factor contributing to plaintiff's injury. Unless the facts are proven otherwise by sufficient evidence, the inference provides a rational basis for imposing liability, depending upon the determination of other issues (scope of duty, negligence, etc.).

E.　"Substantial Factor" Determinations

In each of the 24 cases now before this court, the plaintiffs must establish by a preponderance of the evidence that (1) the decedent or living plaintiff having cancer was probably exposed to fallout radiation significantly in excess of "background" radiation rates; (2) the injury is of a type consistent with those known to be caused by ionizing radiation; and (3) that the person injured had resided in geographical proximity to the Nevada Test Site for some if not all of the years of atmospheric testing between 1951 and 1962. If these factual connections are established, other relevant factors will also be evaluated in determining the "substantial factor" issue.

* * *

X.　Damages

After careful examination of the factors discussed in detail above in all of the preceding sections, it appears that ten of the twenty-four bellwether cases merit compensation. * * *

* * *

[The court of appeals reversed the judgment of liability to ten of the plaintiffs. It held that the challenged governmental action was immune from suit because it was within the discretionary function exception to the Federal Tort Claims Act, 28 U.S.C.A. § 2680(a). See p. 488, supra.]

———

COOK v. UNITED STATES, 545 F.Supp. 306 (N.D.Cal.1982). Plaintiffs sued under the federal Swine Flu Act and the Federal Tort Claims Act to recover damages for injuries due to Guillain–Barre Syndrome (GBS), a rare neurological disorder which plaintiffs contended was caused by their swine flu vaccinations under a federally sponsored immunization program. The three plaintiffs contracted GBS from 12 ½ to 13 weeks after vaccination. On the basis of a strong statistical correlation between the vaccinations and an increase in GBS cases that was discovered by the federal Center for Disease Control (CDC), the government had stipulated to liability in GBS cases with an onset of not more than ten weeks after vaccination. Since the etiology of GBS is not well understood, plaintiffs sought to prove their claim by relying on statistical correlations to establish causation. Those correlations were derived through their experts' interpretation of the CDC data that was different from the interpretation of CDC's experts. The district court held an evidentiary hearing on this issue of causation.

All experts agreed that the data showed that the "attack rate" of GBS rose sharply in the first few weeks after vaccination. The dispute between the parties concerned how soon the attack rate in the vaccinated population dropped below the point where the relative risk was not sufficiently large to assure the court that a given GBS case was more likely than not caused by the vaccination rather than by some other event. The government stipulated for liability up to a ten-week latency period because—according to the CDC experts—the attack rate among vaccinees dropped below twice that of non-vaccinees shortly before the tenth week. As the court explained, "[w]henever the relative risk to vaccinated persons is greater than two times the risk to unvaccinated persons, there is a greater than 50% chance that a given GBS case among vaccinees of that latency period is attributable to vaccination, thus sustaining plaintiff's burden of proof on causation." If the relative risk for vaccinated persons after nine weeks were two—that is, they were twice as likely to experience onset of GBS as persons in the unvaccinated population—the likelihood that any given vaccinated case of GBS was attributable to the vaccination would only be 50%.

After reviewing the testimony of the different experts and their related methodologies, the court concluded that "plaintiffs' data are insufficient to prove causation, inasmuch as they fail to establish a late onset attack rate in excess of twice the upper limit of the reasonable range." Judgment was entered for defendant.

TOWARDS MULTIPLE CAUSATION

The cases in this section have all involved a single negligent injurer. In single negligent injurer cases the traditional test of causation asks: Was the defendant's negligence a "but for" cause of the plaintiff's injury? The answer to that question tells us if the defendant's wrongdoing was both a necessary and a sufficient cause of the plaintiff's injury. In *Kingston*, we appear to have more than one negligent injurer, and we certainly have more than one negligent party. In the circumstances of the case, the "but for" test leads to an outcome that the court regards as unjust: neither defendants' negligence is a necessary cause of the plaintiff's injury, even though the negligence of one of the defendants is. The "but for" test therefore exculpates both defendants. The unacceptability of that exculpation drives the court's opinion.

KINGSTON v. CHICAGO & NORTHWESTERN RAILWAY

Supreme Court of Wisconsin, 1927.
191 Wis. 610, 211 N.W. 913.

[Action to recover damages caused by a fire. At the trial the jury found that on the day in question a forest fire was burning about a mile northwest of the plaintiff's property; that another fire was burning about four miles to the northeast; that these two fires were both set by locomotives belonging to the defendant; that the fires united about 1,000 feet north of the plaintiff's property; and thereafter travelled south, burning the plaintiff's logs and timber. Judgment was rendered for the plaintiff and the defendant brings this appeal.]

OWEN, J. [after finding (1) that the jury was not justified in concluding that the first fire was set by sparks emitted from the defendant's locomotives and (2) that either one of the fires, in the absence of the other, would have burned the plaintiff's property]:

It is settled in the law of negligence that any one of two or more joint tortfeasors, or one of two or more wrongdoers whose concurring acts of negligence result in injury, are each individually responsible for the entire damage resulting from their joint or concurrent acts of negligence. This rule obtains "where two causes, each attributable to the negligence of a responsible person, concur in producing an injury to another, either of which causes would produce it regardless of the other, * * * because, whether the concurrence be intentional, actual or constructive, each wrongdoer, in effect, adopts the conduct of his co-actor, and for the further reason that it is impossible to apportion the damage or to say that either perpetrated any distinct injury that can be separated from the whole. The whole loss must necessarily be considered and treated as an entirety." Cook v. Minneapolis, St. Paul & Sault Ste. Marie R. Co., 98 Wis. 624, at page 642, 74 N.W. 561, 566, 40 L.R.A. 457, 67 Am.St.Rep. 830.

That case presented a situation very similar to this. One fire, originating by sparks emitted from a locomotive, united with another fire of unknown origin and consumed plaintiff's property. There was nothing to indicate that the fire of unknown origin was not set by some human agency. The evidence in the case merely failed to identify the agency. In that case it was held that the railroad company which set one fire was not responsible for the damage committed by the united fires because the origin of the other fire was not identified. In that case a rule of law was announced, which is stated in the syllabus prepared by the writer of the opinion as follows:

> A fire started by defendant's negligence, after spreading one mile and a quarter to the northeast, near plaintiffs' property, met a fire having no responsible origin, coming from the northwest. After the union, fire swept on from the northwest to and into plaintiffs' property, causing its destruction. Either fire, if the other had not existed, would have reached the property and caused its destruction at the same time. *Held:*
>
> (1) That the rule of liability in case of joint wrongdoers does not apply.

(2) That the independent fire from the northwest became a superseding cause so that the destruction of the property could not, with reasonable certainty, be attributed in whole or in part to the fire having a responsible origin; that the chain of responsible causation was so broken by the fire from the northwest that the negligent fire, if it reached the property at all, was a remote and not the proximate cause of the loss.

Emphasis is placed upon the fact, especially in the opinion, that one fire had "no responsible origin." At other times in the opinion the fact is emphasized that it had no "known responsible origin." The plain inference from the entire opinion is that, if both fires had been of responsible origin, or of known responsible origin, each wrongdoer would have been liable for the entire damage. The conclusion of the court exempting the railroad company from liability seems to be based upon the single fact that one fire had no responsible origin, or no known responsible origin. It is difficult to determine just what weight was accorded to the fact that the origin of the fire was unknown. If the conclusion of the court was founded upon the assumption that the fire of unknown origin had no responsible origin, the conclusion announced may be sound and in harmony with well-settled principles of negligence.

From our present consideration of the subject, we are not disposed to criticize the doctrine which exempts from liability a wrongdoer who sets a fire which unites with a fire originating from natural causes, such as lightning, not attributable to any human agency, resulting in damage. It is also conceivable that a fire so set might unite with a fire of so much greater proportions, such as a raging forest fire, so as to be enveloped or swallowed up by the greater holocaust, and its identity destroyed, so that the greater fire could be said to be an intervening or superseding cause. But we have no such situation here. These fires were of comparatively equal rank. If there was any difference in their magnitude or threatening aspect the record indicates that the northeast fire was the larger fire and was really regarded as the menacing agency. At any rate, there is no intimation or suggestion that the northeast fire was enveloped and swallowed up by the northwest fire. We will err on the side of the defendant if we regard the two fires as of equal rank.

According to well-settled principles of negligence, it is undoubted that, if the proof disclosed the origin of the northwest fire, even though its origin be attributed to a third person, the railroad company, as the originator of the northeast fire, would be liable for the entire damage. There is no reason to believe that the northwest fire originated from any other than human agency. It was a small fire. It had travelled over a limited area. It had been in existence but for a day. For a time it was thought to have been extinguished. It was not in the nature of a raging forest fire. The record discloses nothing of natural phenomena which could have given rise to the fire. It is morally certain that it was set by some human agency.

Now the question is whether the railroad company, which is found to have been responsible for the origin of the northeast fire, escapes liability, because the origin of the northwest fire is not identified, although there is no reason to believe that it had any other than human origin. An affirmative answer to that question would certainly make a wrongdoer a favorite of the law at the expense of an innocent sufferer. The injustice of such a doctrine sufficiently impeaches the logic upon which it is founded. Where one who has suffered damage by fire proves the origin of a fire and the course of that fire up to the point of the destruction of his property, one has certainly established liability on the part of the originator of the fire. Granting that the union of that fire with another of natural origin, or with another of much greater proportions, is available as a defense the burden is on the defendant to show that, by reason of such union with a fire of such character, the fire set by him was not the proximate cause of the damage. No principle of justice requires that the plaintiff be placed under the burden of specifically identifying the origin of both fires in order to recover the damages for which either or both fires are responsible. * * *

Judgment affirmed.

SAUNDERS SYSTEM BIRMINGHAM CO. v. ADAMS, 217 Ala. 621, 117 So. 72, 61 A.L.R. 1333 (1928). Action for personal injuries suffered by plaintiff when she was run down by defendant's automobile rented by it to Mrs. Green. Plaintiff alleged that the defendant was negligent in renting the car to Mrs. Green with the brakes in a defective and dangerous condition. *Held,* reversing judgment for plaintiff, that the court erred in refusing to instruct the jury that if Mrs. Green "at the time and place did not use the brake until she was so close to Mrs. Adams [the plaintiff] that at the rate of speed she was traveling at said time it would have been impossible to avoid striking her with the brakes in good condition, then you cannot award Mrs. Adams any damages."

SECTION C. MULTIPLE CAUSATION

All harms have more than one cause, but not all harms are caused by more than one breach of a duty of care. The problem of multiple cause in its core form arises when two or more breaches of a duty of care combine to inflict a single, indivisible injury on a victim. (When two or more breaches of a duty of care inflict multiple injuries on a victim we simply have two or more distinct torts and tortfeasors.) In the classic multiple cause circumstance which occasions the next case, the wrongful actions of two defendants combine to inflict a single indivisible injury. Neither defendant's wrongdoing alone would have been sufficient to inflict the injury; both are necessary for the injury to be inflicted; and, taken together, the separate wrongdoings of each defendant are sufficient to inflict the injury. Once again, the "but for" test exculpates both defendants, and a new test must be formulated.

JOHNSON v. CHAPMAN

Supreme Court of Appeals of West Virginia, 1897.
43 W.Va. 639, 28 S.E. 744.

[Each of the two defendants owned a warehouse adjacent to and north of plaintiff's. The party wall between defendants' warehouses, plaintiff alleged, was defective and inadequate to support them, and defendants failed in their duty to repair the wall. As a consequence, the warehouses fell and injured plaintiff's. Demurrer sustained on ground that the declaration did not show a joint cause of action against the defendants. In reversing the judgment, the appellate court said:]

DENT, J. * * * A strong pillar and a weak one may support a wall, but, if they are both weak, the wall will fall. Two separate persons are obligated to make each pillar strong. If either does his duty, the wall may stand; but if each neglects his duty, and the wall falls, they are jointly and severally liable for the injury that follows to any one. As each contributed to the injury, they are each liable for the whole injury, and therefore can be sued jointly without in any wise increasing their separate liabilities; and of such suit neither has any right to complain. Nor is it necessary for either, to escape liability himself, to show the other at fault; but he is only called upon to defend himself, in case there is evidence tending to show his guilt, by establishing his freedom from blame. It is not a question of comparative negligence, but of contributory; for, if the negligence of one of two defendants contributed towards the injury, he cannot escape liability by showing greater negligence on the part of his codefendant. Such a question might affect the matter as between themselves, but not the right of the plaintiff to compel either or both of them to pay his whole damage.

The illustration given by defendants' counsel of two persons shooting a third, if carried far enough, would have rendered this matter plain. If two persons at the same time shoot a third, with separate pistols, in different, and not vital, parts of his body, they are separately liable for the injury produced; but if they both strike a vital part of the body, and death ensue, then they would be jointly and severally liable. And the same would follow if both should strike the same eye and destroy it, or strike separate eyes and destroy sight. In each case each would be equally to blame for the resulting injury. In the case under discussion, according to the allegations, each of the defendants was guilty of negligence, in not having a sufficient wall to sustain his building, by reason whereof both buildings fell upon and destroyed plaintiff's building. They did not fall at different times, nor on different parts of plaintiff's building as appears from the declaration, but fell together, in one mass, undistinguishable, upon and crushed the same, so that it is impossible to say which produced the greater ruin, or to separate the extent of damage by each; but, both contributing thereto, both are liable for the whole damage done, and cannot complain because they are both brought before the court in the same suit. If, on the evidence, it should turn out that either was not guilty of the negligence charged, such defendant would go free, while the other, being guilty, would have no reason to complain of the misjoinder. * * *

[Judgment reversed.]

———

KNELL v. FELTMAN, 174 F.2d 662 (D.C.Cir.1949). Passengers injured in a collision between the automobile in which they were riding, driven by Knell, and a taxicab driven by Feltman's servant, brought suit against Feltman. The jury found that both drivers, Knell and Feltman's servant, were negligent and that the conduct of each contributed to the accident. Plaintiffs obtained a judgment for the full amount of their damages against Feltman. Feltman, in turn, was held to have a right of "contribution" from Knell.

SLATER v. PACIFIC AMERICAN OIL CO., 212 Cal. 648, 300 P. 31 (1931). The plaintiff's land was damaged by a deposit of oil, salt and various hydrocarbon substances caused by the overflow upon his land, during a heavy rainfall, of oil from thirty different oil wells, of which the defendant owned two. *Held,* in reversing the judgment of the trial court, that the plaintiff could not recover damages in the absence of evidence as to the proportionate contribution of the defendant to the whole of the injury suffered by the plaintiff, but that injunction would issue.

MADDUX v. DONALDSON, 362 Mich. 425, 108 N.W.2d 33, 100 A.L.R.2d 1 (1961). Plaintiffs—Maddux, his wife and infant daughter—were driving on wet pavement at an hour near dark at a speed between 35 and 40 miles per hour. Defendant Bryie was following them at the same speed. As the cars approached a bend in the road a car coming in the opposite direction skidded in a wide arc at a speed of between 80 to 100 miles per hour. Maddux tried to get past before the skidding car reached his path, but the skidding car and plaintiffs' car collided. While plaintiffs' car was stopped with its occupants injured, it was struck in the rear by Bryie's car. The case against the skidding driver was discontinued by plaintiffs. The trial court dismissed the actions of Mrs. Maddux and her daughter against Bryie on the ground that "there is no evidence of damage before this jury from which any inference can be drawn in relation to the responsibility of Paul Bryie." Mr. Maddux' case was dismissed on the ground that he was contributorily negligent as a matter of law. *Held,* reversed and remanded for new trial. BLACK, Justice (concurring in reversal):

"Having signed Mr. Justice SMITH's opinion in this case, I would openly avow what was, and what is to be. Until now the Michigan rule has been settled. Where two or more wrongdoers separately cause the plaintiff to suffer an unknown or uncertain part or portion of the damages he has shown, each—hitherto—stood responsible to the plaintiff only for the harm caused by his tort, however difficult it may have been to establish the same. [Citations omitted.]

"In the past we have differed not upon the rule but upon its admittedly difficult application. Now we affirm that, where the trier or triers of fact find they cannot ascertain the amount of damages each wrongdoer has inflicted, then such trier or triers are authorized to assess the plaintiff's damages against any one or all of such wrongdoers on ground that the latter have—in law—participated in the infliction of a single, indivisible injury. This, it seems to me, is the only way to avoid the difficulties of our present rule."

O'BRIEN v. NATIONAL GYPSUM CO., 944 F.2d 69 (2d Cir.1991). Under a 1986 New York statute reviving certain toxic tort claims for one year, plaintiff brought this wrongful death action, "individually, and as administratrix of her late husband's estate," against a "host of entities that manufactured asbestos-containing products used at the Brooklyn Navy Yard." Her husband had worked at the Yard "from May 1944 through May 1945 as an apprentice electrician." In 1971, he developed "mesothelioma, a rare and incurable variant of lung cancer." Two years later, he died of it.

Each of the defendants except for Celotex and Raymark Industries settled with O'Brien. (Celotex was a successor entity to Philip Manufacturing Company, which manufactured some of the asbestos products to which O'Brien was exposed.) Celotex and Raymark went to trial. At trial, "the jury returned a verdict awarding plaintiff $667,000 in compensatory damages for wrongful death. Celotex's share of the liability was set at 14.28%, the same share assigned to Raymark and each of the settling defendants except for Owens–Illinois, Inc., which was assigned 0% liability." Celotex appealed the verdict, claiming in part that plaintiff's failure to produce "admissible evidence placing . . . O'Brien on a specific ship or in an asbestos-contaminated environment should be deemed a failure to establish substantial contact with asbestos and thus a fatal defect in plaintiff's proof of causation." *Held*, affirmed.

"[V]iewing the testimony below in the light most favorable to the plaintiff, plaintiff established that O'Brien contracted an exceedingly rare disease, mesothelioma, whose only known cause is exposure to asbestos. O'Brien's only known exposure to asbestos was during his tenure as an apprentice at the Brooklyn Navy Yard. These facts create a very high probability that O'Brien's illness was caused by exposure to asbestos-containing products at the Brooklyn Navy Yard. Given testimony that asbestos products were used interchangeably on virtually all of the warships under construction in the Navy Yard, O'Brien's disease might reasonably be attributed in part to exposure to Philip Carey products."

THOMPSON v. JOHNSON, 180 F.2d 431 (5th Cir.1950). Defendants Roy, Robert and Garner Johnson sought to drive plaintiff from their land, plaintiff contending that he was lawfully on it. Roy tripped and beat plaintiff, while Robert and Garner held plaintiff's mother and wife to prevent their coming to plaintiff's aid. The district court gave judgment for plaintiff against Roy for compensatory and punitive damages but denied plaintiff judgment against Robert and Garner on grounds of insufficient evidence to prove a "conspiracy." The court of appeals reversed, holding (under Mississippi Law) that the other defendants acting "in concert" with Roy were jointly liable for compensatory and punitive damages. They were "engaged in a common enterprise," especially since they acted to insure that the beating be inflicted. It was not decisive that Garner and Robert (as the District Judge found) did not know the extent of the serious injuries inflicted by Roy on plaintiff.

SUMMERS v. TICE ET AL.

Supreme Court of California, 1948.

33 Cal.2d 80, 199 P.2d 1, 5 A.L.R.2d 91.

CARTER, Justice.

* * *

Plaintiff's action was against [two] defendants, [both of whom have appealed from judgments in plaintiff's favor,] for an injury to his right eye and face as the result of bring struck by bird shot discharged from a shotgun. The case was tried by the court without a jury and the court found that on November 20, 1945, plaintiff and the two defendants were hunting quail on the open range. Each of the defendants was armed with a 12 gauge shotgun loaded with shells containing 7 1/2 size shot. Prior to going hunting plaintiff discussed the hunting procedure with defendants, indicating that they were to exercise care when shooting and to "keep in line." In the course of hunting plaintiff proceeded up a hill, thus placing the hunters at the points of a triangle. The view of defendants with reference to plaintiff was unobstructed and they knew his location. Defendant Tice flushed a quail which rose in flight to a ten foot elevation and flew between plaintiff and defendants. Both defendants shot at the quail, shooting in plaintiff's direction. At that time defendants were 75 yards from plaintiff. One shot struck plaintiff in his eye and another in his upper lip. Finally it was found by the court * * * that defendants were negligent in so shooting and plaintiff was not contributorily negligent.

* * *

The problem presented in this case is whether the judgment against both defendants may stand. It is argued by defendants that they are not joint tort feasors, and thus jointly and severally liable, as they were not acting in concert, and that there is not sufficient evidence to show which defendant was guilty of the negligence which caused the injuries[,] the shooting by Tice or that by Simonson. * * *

* * *

It has been held that where a group of persons are on a hunting party, or otherwise engaged in the use of firearms, and two of them are negligent in firing in the direction of a third person who is injured thereby, both of those so firing are liable for the injury suffered by the third person, although the negligence of only one of them could have caused the injury. * * * These cases speak of the action of defendants as being in concert as the ground of decision, yet it would seem they are straining that concept and the more reasonable basis appears in Oliver v. Miles * * *. There two persons were hunting together. Both shot at some partridges and in so doing shot across the highway injuring plaintiff who was travelling on it. The court stated they were acting in concert and thus both were liable. The court then stated: "We think that * * * each is liable for the resulting injury to the boy, although no one can say definitely who actually shot him. To hold otherwise would be to exonerate both from liability, although each was negligent, and the injury resulted from such negligence." * * *

When we consider the relative position of the parties and the results that would flow if plaintiff was required to pin the injury on one of the defendants only, a requirement that the burden of proof on that subject be shifted to defendants becomes manifest. They are both wrongdoers both negligent toward plaintiff. They brought about a situation where the negligence of one of them injured the plaintiff, hence it should rest with them each to absolve himself if he can. The injured party has been placed by defendants in the unfair position of pointing to which defendant caused the harm. If one can escape the other may also and plaintiff is remediless. Ordinarily defendants are in a far better position to offer evidence to determine which one caused the injury. * * *

* * *

[I]t should be pointed out that the same reasons of policy and justice [that support] shift[ing] the burden to each of defendants to absolve himself if he can[,] relieving the wronged person of the duty of apportioning the injury to a particular defendant, apply here where we are concerned with whether plaintiff is required to supply evidence for the apportionment of damages. * * * [W]here the matter of apportionment is incapable of proof, the innocent wronged party should not be deprived of his right to redress. * * *

* * *

The judgment is affirmed.

SECTION D.   JOINT AND PROPORTIONATE LIABILITY

The doctrines of joint and several liability, contribution and indemnity concern the financial responsibilities of joint tortfeasors, both towards the victim and towards each other. These doctrines are linked to causation by *common liability for an indivisible injury*. The rights and duties of two or more tortfeasors—especially towards each other but also towards a single victim—become an issue when two or more tortfeasors share a *common basis of responsibility in tort for the infliction of a single, indivisible injury*. If the injury is not judged indivisible—or if there is no common liability in tort for an indivisible injury—the doctrines of joint and several liability, contribution and indemnity do not apply. Compare the three cases following this note, with *Knell v. Feltman*, and *Maddux v. Donaldson*, *supra* p. 593.

————

ASSOCIATION FOR RETARDED CITIZENS–VOLUSIA, INC. v. FLETCHER, 741 So.2d 520 (Fla.App.1999). *Held*, Florida's abrogation of "the concept of joint and several liability for purposes of determining noneconomic damages caused by joint tortfeasors" did not change the common law rule that an original tortfeasor is liable for the aggravation of the victim's injuries by the subsequent negligence of a health-care provider. "Under the common law, a medical provider who aggravates an injury inflicted by the original tortfeasor is not considered to be a joint tortfeasor, but [is considered] instead, a distinct and independent tortfeasor. [citation omitted]. As Judge Cowart clearly stated in *Rucks v. Pushman*, 541 So.2d 673, 675 (Fla. 5th DCA), *rev. denied*, 549 So.2d 1014 (Fla.1989):"

> [T]he original (initial or primary) tortfeasor is liable to the victim not only for the original injuries received as a result of the initial tort, but also for the additional (or aggravated) injuries resulting from the subsequent negligence of the health care providers. This is true although the original tortfeasor and the subsequently negligent health care providers are independent tortfeasors and not joint tortfeasors jointly and severally liable for one common injury.

"In our view, this is still good law * **."

HAFF v. HETTICH, 593 N.W.2d 383 (N.D.1999). *Held*, North Dakota's statutory abolition of joint and several liability for non-economic damages "requires apportionment of damages based on the percentages of fault attributable to the original tortfeasor and medical care providers who negligently treat the original injury." The abolition of joint and several liability also abolished the "common law rule that an original tortfeasor was liable for aggravation of original injuries caused by the malpractice of a physician reasonably selected by the injured person."

CROTTA v. HOME DEPOT, INC., 249 Conn. 634, 732 A.2d 767 (1999). While under the supervision of his father, minor plaintiff fell from a shopping cart onto the concrete floor of a Home Depot store. Through his mother, he brought a negligence claim against the store, and a product liability claim against the manufacturer of the cart. *Held*, responding to a question certified by the U.S. District Court, "the doctrine of parental immunity operates to preclude the parent of a minor plaintiff from being joined as a third party defendant for purposes of: (1) apportionment of liability; (2) contribution; or (3) indemnification based on the parent's allegedly negligent supervision of the minor plaintiff."

" '[A] tortfeasor compelled to discharge a liability for a tort cannot recover contribution from a joint tortfeasor whose participation therein gave the injured person no cause of action against him, since the element of *common liability of both tortfeasors to the injured person, essential to the right of contribution, is lacking in such cases.* ... ' (Emphasis added.) 25 A.L.R.4th 1123, Joint Tortfeasor Contribution—Family §§ 2[a] (1983); 18 Am.Jur.2d, supra, § 65. 'The contribution defendant must be a tortfeasor, and *originally liable to the plaintiff.* If there was never any such liability, as where the contribution defendant has the defense of family immunity ... then there is no liability for contribution.' (Emphasis added.) W. Prosser & W. Keeton, Torts (5th Ed.1984) § 50, pp. 339–40 [further citations omitted]." Similarly, "the common-law doctrine of indemnification permits a tortfeasor to assert a claim *only* against another *liable* tortfeasor. 'As in the case of contribution, indemnity is not allowed against one who has a defense, such as family immunity against the original plaintiff.' W. Prosser & W. Keeton, supra, § 51, pp. 343–44 n. 26."

TERMINOLOGY

"Joint-and-several liability under the common law means that each defendant contributing to the same harm is liable to [the victim] for the whole amount of the recoverable damages." Uniform Comparative Fault Act, infra, p. 603. "Proportionate liability" means that each defendant contributing to the same harm is liable to the victim only in proportion to his or her tortious responsibility for the victim's injury.

"Contribution" works together with joint-and-several liability. Contribution is a right that "exists between or among two or more persons who are jointly and severally liable upon the same indivisible claim for the same injury, death, or harm, whether or not judgment has been recovered against all or any of them." Uniform Comparative Fault Act, infra, p. 603. Traditionally, contribution was *pro rata*.

In a few situations, a right of "indemnity" also exists between or among parties liable to the same victim. Traditionally, indemnity shifted the entire loss from one party to another, and was "appropriate where one party has a primary or greater liability or duty which justly requires him to bear the whole of the burden as between the parties." Hendrickson v. Minnesota Power & Light Co., 258 Minn. 368, 371, 104 N.W.2d 843, 847 (1960), quoted infra p. 604.

———

Uniform Contribution Among Tortfeasors Act

Adopted in 1955 by the Commissioners on Uniform State Laws.

Section 1. [*Right to Contribution.*]

(a) Except as otherwise provided in this Act, where two or more persons become jointly or severally liable in tort for the same injury to person or property or for the same wrongful death, there is a right of contribution among them even though judgment has not been recovered against all or any of them.

(b) The right of contribution exists only in favor of a tortfeasor who has paid more than his pro rata share of the common liability,* and his total recovery is limited to the amount paid by him in excess of his pro rata share. No tortfeasor is compelled to make contribution beyond his own pro rata share of the entire liability.

* Pro rata means divisible by a precise calculable amount. In this instance, a pro rata share would be determined by multiplying the common liability by a fraction, the numerator being 1 and the denominator being the number of tortfeasors.—Eds.

(c) There is no right of contribution in favor of any tortfeasor who has intentionally [wilfully or wantonly] caused or contributed to the injury or wrongful death.

* * *

(f) This Act does not impair any right of indemnity under existing law. Where one tortfeasor is entitled to indemnity from another, the right of the indemnity obligee is for indemnity and not contribution, and the indemnity obligor is not entitled to contribution from the obligee for any portion of his indemnity obligation.

(g) This Act shall not apply to breaches of trust or of other fiduciary obligation.

Section 2. [*Pro Rata Shares.*] In determining the pro rata shares of tortfeasors in the entire liability (a) their relative degrees of fault shall not be considered; (b) if equity requires the collective liability of some as a group shall constitute a single share; and (c) principles of equity applicable to contribution generally shall apply.

Section 3. [*Enforcement.*]

(a) Whether or not judgment has been entered in an action against two or more tortfeasors for the same injury or wrongful death, contribution may be enforced by separate action.

(b) Where a judgment has been entered in an action against two or more tortfeasors for the same injury or wrongful death, contribution may be enforced in that action by judgment in favor of one against other judgment defendants by motion upon notice to all parties to the action.

* * *

———

RULE 14(a), FEDERAL RULES OF CIVIL PROCEDURE. "At any time after commencement of the action a defending party, as a third-party plaintiff, may cause a summons and complaint to be served upon a person not a party to the action who is or may be liable to the third-party plaintiff for all or part of the plaintiff's claim against the third-party plaintiff. * * *"

THE RISE OF COMPARATIVE FAULT

The doctrines of joint and several liability, contribution and indemnity are presently being reshaped by the rise of comparative fault. The materials which follow explore the impact of comparative fault on these doctrines.

———

UNIFORM COMPARATIVE FAULT ACT

12 Unif. Laws Ann.

HISTORICAL NOTE

The Uniform Comparative Fault Act was approved by the National Conference of Commissioners on Uniform State Laws [NCCUSL] in 1977. * * *

COMMISSIONERS' PREFATORY NOTE

Plaintiff's Fault. * * * [A]t the present time (1977), the Federal Government and two-thirds of the States (33) have adopted some form of comparative fault. This is usually by statute but also by judicial decision.

* * *

[The Prefatory Note indicates that the Act will follow the "pure type" of comparative fault.]

Contribution. The original common law rule was that there is no contribution among joint tortfeasors, no matter what the nature of the tort. Some states, however, have judicially modified this rule, especially in the case of negligence. Many more states have passed statutes of various kinds providing for contribution, with the result that a substantial majority of the states now have contribution in some form * * *

The NCCUSL has promulgated two uniform contribution Acts—the first in 1939, superseded by a revised act in 1955. Both of these Acts provide for pro rata contribution, which may be suitable in a state not applying the principle of comparative fault, but is inappropriate in a comparative-fault state apportioning ultimate responsibility on the basis of the proportionate fault of the parties involved.

It has therefore been decided not to amend the separate Uniform Contribution Among Tortfeasors Act, 1955, but to leave that Act for possible use by states not adopting the principle of comparative fault. Instead, the present Act contains appropriate sections covering the rights existing between the parties who are jointly and severally liable in tort. The 1955 Act should be replaced by this Act in any state that adopts the comparative fault principle, and would be eventually replaced.

Section 1. [Effect of Contributory Fault]

(a) In an action based on fault seeking to recover damages for injury or death to person or harm to property, any contributory fault chargeable to the claimant diminishes proportionately the amount awarded as compensatory damages for an injury attributable to the claimant's contributory fault, but does not bar recovery. This rule applies whether or not under prior law the claimant's contributory fault constituted a defense or was disregarded under applicable legal doctrines, such as last clear chance.

(b) "Fault" includes acts or omissions that are in any measure negligent or reckless toward the person or property of the actor or others, or that subject a person to strict tort liability. The term also includes breach of warranty, unreasonable assumption of risk not constituting an enforceable express consent, misuse of a product for which the defendant otherwise would be liable, and unreasonable failure to avoid an injury or to mitigate damages. * * *

COMMISSIONERS' COMMENT

*

Although strict liability is sometimes called absolute liability or liability without fault, it is still included. Strict liability for both abnormally dangerous activities and for products bears a strong similarity to negligence as a matter of law (negligence per se), and the factfinder should have no real difficulty in setting percentages of fault. Putting out a product that is dangerous to the user or the public or engaging in an activity that is dangerous to those in the vicinity involves a measure of fault that can be weighed and compared, even though it is not characterized as negligence.

* * *

The Act does not include intentional torts. Statutes and decisions have not applied the comparative fault principle to them. * * *

Section 2. [Apportionment of Damages]

(a) In all actions involving fault of more than one party to the action, including third-party defendants, * * * the court, unless otherwise agreed by all parties, shall instruct the jury to answer special interrogatories or, if there is no jury, shall make findings, indicating:

(1) the amount of damages each claimant would be entitled to recover if contributory fault is disregarded; and

(2) the percentage of the total fault of all of the parties to each claim that is allocated to each claimant, defendant [and] third-party defendant * * *

(b) In determining the percentages of fault, the trier of fact shall consider both the nature of the conduct of each party at fault and the extent of the causal relation between the conduct and the damages claimed.

(c) The court shall determine the award of damages to each claimant in accordance with the findings, * * * and enter judgment against each party liable on the basis of rules of joint-and-several liability. For purposes of contribution under Sections 4 and 5, the court also shall determine and state in the judgment each party's equitable share of the obligation to each claimant in accordance with the respective percentages of fault.

* * *

COMMISSIONERS' COMMENT

* * *

Percentages of Fault. In comparing the fault of the several parties for the purpose of obtaining percentages there are a number of implications arising from the concept of fault. The conduct of the claimant or of any defendant may be more or less at fault, depending upon all the circumstances including such matters as (1) whether the conduct was mere inadvertence or engaged in with an awareness of the danger involved, (2) the magnitude of the risk created by the conduct, including the number of persons endangered and the potential seriousness of the injury, (3) the significance of what the actor was seeking to attain by his conduct, (4) the actor's superior or inferior capacities, and (5) the particular circumstances, such as the existence of an emergency requiring a hasty decision.

* * * An error in driving on the part of a bus driver with a load of passengers may properly produce an evaluation of greater fault than the same error on the part of a housewife gratuitously giving her neighbor a ride to the shopping center; and an automobile manufacturer putting out a car with a cracked brake cylinder may, even in the absence of proof of negligence in failing to discover the crack, properly be held to a greater measure of fault than another manufacturer producing a mechanical pencil with a defective clasp that due care would have discovered.

In determining the relative fault of the parties, the fact-finder will also give consideration to the relative closeness of the causal relationship of the negligent conduct of the defendants and the harm to the plaintiff. Degrees of fault and proximity of causation are inextricably mixed, as a study of last clear chance indicates, and that common law doctrine has been absorbed in this Act. * * *

Joint and Several Liability and Equitable Shares of the Obligation. The common law rule of joint-and-several liability of joint tortfeasors continues to apply under this Act. This is true whether the claimant was contributorily negligent or not. The plaintiff can recover the total amount of his judgment against any defendant who is liable.

The judgment for each claimant also sets forth, however, the equitable share of the total obligation to the claimant for each party, based on his established percentage of fault. This indicates the amount that each party should eventually be responsible for as a result of the rules of contribution. Stated in the judgment itself, it makes the information available to the parties and will normally be a basis for contribution without the need for a court order arising from motion or separate action.

* * *

Illustration No. 2. (Multiple-party situation).

A sues B, C and D. A's damages are $10,000.

A is found 40% at fault.

B is found 30% at fault.

C is found 30% at fault.

D is found 0% at fault.

A is awarded judgment jointly and severally against B & C for $6,000. The court also states in the judgment the equitable share of the obligation of each party:

A's equitable share is $4,000 (40% of $10,000).

B's equitable share is $3,000 (30% of $10,000).

C's equitable share is $3,000 (30% of $10,000).

* * *

Section 4. [Right of Contribution]

(a) A right of contribution exists between or among two or more persons who are jointly and severally liable upon the same indivisible claim for the same injury, death, or harm, whether or not judgment has been recovered against all or any of them. It may be enforced either in the original action or by a separate action brought for that purpose. The basis for contribution is each person's equitable share of the obligation, including the equitable share of a claimant at fault, as determined in accordance with the provisions of Section 2.

* * *

COMMISSIONERS' COMMENT

Sections 4, 5 and 6 are expected to replace the Uniform Contribution Among Tortfeasors Act (1955) in a state following the principle of comparative fault. The three sections, however, apply whether the plaintiff was contributorily at fault or not.

Section 4 is in general accord with the provisions of the 1955 Uniform Act, but the test for determining the measure of contribution and thus establishing the ultimate responsibility is no longer on a pro rata basis. Instead, it is on a basis of proportionate fault determined in accordance with the provisions of Section 2. A plaintiff who is contributorily at fault also shares in the proportionate responsibility.

Joint-and-several liability under the common law means that each defendant contributing to the same harm is liable to him for the whole amount of the recoverable damages. This is not changed by the Act. Between the defendants themselves, however, the apportionment is in accordance with the equitable shares of the obligation, as established under Section 2.

If the defendants cause separate harms or if the harm is found to be divisible on a reasonable basis, however, the liability may become several for a particular harm, and contribution is not appropriate. * * *

Section 5. [Enforcement of Contribution]

(a) If the proportionate fault of the parties to a claim for contribution has been established previously by the court, as provided by Section 2, a party paying more than his equitable share of the obligation, upon motion, may recover judgment for contribution.

(b) If the proportionate fault of the parties to the claim for contribution has not been established by the court, contribution may be enforced in a separate action, whether or not a judgment has been rendered against either

the person seeking contribution or the person from whom contribution is
being sought.

* * *

___

HILLMAN v. WALLIN, 298 Minn. 346, 215 N.W.2d 810 (1974). "Contribution and indemnity are both equitable remedies to provide restitution to a
tortfeasor based on the degree of his culpability for a negligent act. The
remedies differ in the character and amount of restitution allowed a joint
tortfeasor." The Court elaborated: " 'Contribution is appropriate where
there is a common liability among the parties, whereas indemnity is appropriate where one party has a primary or greater liability or duty which justly
requires him to bear the whole of the burden as between the parties.'
Hendrickson v. Minnesota Power & Light Co., 258 Minn. 368, 371, 104
N.W.2d 843, 847 (1960); Haney v. International Harvester Co., 294 Minn.
375, 378, 201 N.W.2d 140, 142 (1972)." The opinion drew one of its
illustrations of indemnity from Prosser, Torts (3d ed.) § 48, "Thus it is
generally agreed that there may be indemnity in favor of one who is held
responsible solely by imputation of law because of his relation to the actual
wrongdoer, as where an employer is vicariously liable for the tort of a
servant or an independent contractor; * * * "

___

AMERICAN MOTORCYCLE ASSOCIATION v. SUPERIOR COURT, 20
Cal.3d 578, 146 Cal.Rptr. 182, 578 P.2d 899 (1978). A minor, injured while
participating in a motorcycle race, sued defendant motorcycle clubs sponsoring the race, alleging negligent planning and supervision. AMA, one defendant, sought leave of court to file a cross-complaint against the minor's
parents, alleging their negligence in supervising the minor, and seeking
indemnity or a statement of the "allocable" negligence of the parents if AMA
were held liable. The trial court denied the motion for leave to file. *Held*,
writ of mandate issues directing trial court to permit filing of cross complaint for partial indemnity. After reviewing the decision in Li v. Yellow Cab
Co., 13 Cal.3d 804, 119 Cal.Rptr. 858, 532 P.2d 1226 (1975), p. 355, supra,
the court summarized its conclusion:

" * * * First, we conclude that our adoption of comparative negligence
to ameliorate the inequitable consequences of the contributory negligence
rule does not warrant the abolition or contraction of the established 'joint
and several liability' doctrine; each tortfeasor whose negligence is a proximate cause of an indivisible injury remains individually liable for all compensable damages attributable to that injury. Contrary to petitioner's contention, we conclude that joint and several liability does not logically conflict
with a comparative negligence regime. Indeed, as we point out, the great
majority of jurisdictions which have adopted comparative negligence have
retained the joint and several liability rule; we are aware of no judicial
decision which intimates that the adoption of comparative negligence com-

pels the abandonment of this long-standing common law rule. The joint and several liability doctrine continues, after *Li*, to play an important and legitimate role in protecting the ability of a negligently injured person to obtain adequate compensation for his injuries from those tortfeasors who have negligently inflicted the harm.

"Second, although we have determined that *Li* does not mandate a diminution of the rights of injured persons through the elimination of the joint and several liability rule, we conclude that the general principles embodied in *Li* do warrant a reevaluation of the common law equitable indemnity doctrine, which relates to the allocation of loss *among* multiple tortfeasors. As we explain, California decisions have long invoked the equitable indemnity doctrine in numerous situations to permit a 'passively' or 'secondarily' negligent tortfeasor to shift his liability completely to a more directly culpable party. While the doctrine has frequently prevented a more culpable tortfeasor from completely escaping liability, the rule has fallen short of its equitable heritage because, like the discarded contributory negligence doctrine, it has worked in an 'all-or-nothing' fashion, imposing liability on the more culpable tortfeasor only at the price of removing liability altogether from another responsible, albeit less culpable, party.

"Prior to *Li*, of course, the notion of apportioning liability on the basis of comparative fault was completely alien to California common law. In light of *Li*, however, we think that the long-recognized common law equitable indemnity doctrine should be modified to permit, in appropriate cases, a right of partial indemnity, under which liability among multiple tortfeasors may be apportioned on a comparative negligence basis. As we explain, many jurisdictions which have adopted comparative negligence have embraced similar comparative contribution or comparative indemnity systems by judicial decision. Such a doctrine conforms to *Li's* objective of establishing 'a system under which liability for damage will be borne by those whose negligence caused it in direct proportion to their respective fault.' (13 Cal.3d at p. 813, 119 Cal.Rptr. at p. 864, 532 P.2d at p. 1232.)

"Third, we conclude that California's current contribution statutes [which provide for pro rata contribution among joint tortfeasors] do not preclude our court from evolving this common law right of comparative indemnity. * * * "

BARTLETT v. NEW MEXICO WELDING SUPPLY, INC., 98 N.M. 152, 646 P.2d 579 (App.1982). Plaintiff braked suddenly to avoid hitting a negligently driven car ahead of her. Her car was then struck by defendant's truck from behind. Plaintiff sued defendant in negligence. The jury fixed damages at $100,000. It found that plaintiff was faultless, that the negligence of the unknown driver ahead of her contributed 70% to the accident and that defendant's negligence contributed 30%. The question on appeal was whether plaintiff was entitled to judgment against defendant for $100,000 or $30,000. The appellate court ordered judgment entered for $30,000. Rejecting the reasoning of the California court in American Motorcycle Association v. Superior Court, supra, it concluded that joint and several liability would not be "retained in our pure comparative negligence system. * * * " Pure comparative negligence rests on the concept "that fairness is achieved by basing liability on a person's fault." It is to be applied not simply between a plaintiff and a single defendant but also between a plaintiff and multiple defendants. Else, "a concurrent tortfeasor, 1% at fault, is liable for 100% of the damage caused by concurrent tortfeasors. * * * " It is not a defensible ground for joint and several liability "that a plaintiff must be favored." Plaintiff should bear the risk that one or several tortfeasors will be insolvent or (as in the instant case) unknown. All parties under a regime of pure comparative negligence are responsible for their own faulty acts to the extent that those acts have caused harm.

REICHERT v. ATLER

Supreme Court of New Mexico, 1994.
117 N.M. 623, 875 P.2d 379.

RANSOM, Justice.

As personal representative of the estate of Alfredo Castillo, Joseph Reichert brought this wrongful-death action against Tony and Josie Atler, doing business as the A–Mi–Gusto Lounge. Castillo was killed when assaulted by [Pablo Ochoa] another patron at the Atlers' bar. Following a bench trial, the court adjudged the Atlers liable for the entire damages. The Atlers appealed and the Court of Appeals reversed, holding that the Atlers' negligence must be compared to the assailant's conduct and that the Atlers' liability should be limited to their percentage of the fault. We issued a writ of certiorari to determine whether the negligent failure of the owner or operator of a business to protect patrons from foreseeable harm should be compared to the actions of the perpetrator of that harm and, if so, whether the owner or operator should be held liable only for proportionate fault and not jointly and severally liable with the perpetrator. We hold that the conduct should be compared and that the owner or operator is liable only for its proportionate fault, and we affirm the Court of Appeals.

* * *

In New Mexico, comparative-fault principles apply unless such application would be inconsistent with public policy. See Saiz v. Belen Sch. Dist., 113 N.M. 387, 400, 827 P.2d 102, 115 (1992); see also NMSA 1978, s 41–3A–1(C) (Repl.Pamp.1989) (stating that joint and several liability should apply only in three specific situations or in situations "having a sound basis in public policy"). We cannot find a sound basis in public policy to abrogate the legislature's determination that comparative-fault principles should apply; rather, we believe that public policy would support a holding that the bar owner may reduce his liability by the percentage of fault attributable to a third party. This analysis is most consistent with this Court's adoption of comparative-fault principles in Scott and with the rejection of joint and several liability in comparative-fault cases in Bartlett. As stated in Bartlett, the basis for comparative fault is that each individual tortfeasor should be held responsible only for his or her percentage of the harm. 98 N.M. at 159, 646 P.2d at 586. We will not stray from that reasoning in this case.

Other jurisdictions have been unwilling to apply comparative-fault principles in cases involving similar issues. See, e.g., Loeb v. Rasmussen, 822 P.2d 914, 918–19 (Alaska 1991) (holding that restaurant owner's negligent failure to protect patron could not be compared to assailant's intentional conduct); Kansas State Bank & Trust Co. v. Specialized Transp. Servs., Inc., 249 Kan. 348, 819 P.2d 587, 606 (1991) (holding that liquor store owner who negligently sells alcohol to minor is not entitled to compare his fault with the minor's intentional buying of the alcohol); Gould v. Taco Bell, 239 Kan. 564, 722 P.2d 511, 517 (1986) (holding that company's negligent failure to prevent bus driver from molesting a child could not be compared to intentional conduct of bus driver). Reichert cites the Kansas cases and argues that if we apply comparative-fault principles to this situation, the duty of the bar owner to protect patrons would be diluted or diminished because the owner could shift all blame to the third party who was the direct cause of the injury, and thus would not be held liable for any breach.

We recognize the importance of the duty of the owner or operator of a place of business to prevent the harmful conduct of a third party. Rather than hold the owner fully liable for the damages, however, we believe the jury should be given an instruction regarding the owner's duty to protect patrons and how that duty relates to the conduct of third persons. Although this Court does not normally engage in the practice of drafting jury instructions, we suggest an instruction similar to this:

> If you find that the [owner] [operator] of the [place of business] breached [his] [her] [its] duty to use ordinary care to keep the premises safe for use by the visitor, you may compare this breach of duty with the conduct of the third person(s) who actually caused the injury to the plaintiff(s) and apportion fault accordingly. In apportioning this fault, you should consider that the [owner's] [operator's] duty to protect visitors arises from the likelihood that a third party will injure a visitor and, as the risk of danger increases, the amount of care to be exercised by the [owner] [operator] also increases. Therefore, the proportionate fault of the [owner] [operator] is not necessarily reduced by the increasingly wrongful conduct of the third party.

This instruction could be given as part of SCRA 1986, 13–1309 (Repl. Pamp.1991) (providing uniform jury instruction for premises owner's duty to visitor), or as a separate instruction. In either event, it allows the jury to consider the importance of the owner's duty to protect patrons and to weigh the failure to perform that duty with the tortious conduct of the third party.

We stress that our holding is not dependent on the fact that Ochoa's conduct was intentional in this case. Here, we are not concerned with the liability of the person who acted with the intention of inflicting injury. The joint and several liability of such a person has been addressed by our legislature in Section 41–3A–1(C)(1). As stated in Restatement (Second) of Torts Section 449 (1964), when a person has a duty to protect and the third party's act is foreseeable, "such an act whether innocent, negligent, intentionally tortious, or criminal does not prevent the [person who has a duty to protect] from being liable for harm caused thereby." The owner's duty to protect patrons extends to all foreseeable harm regardless of whether that harm results from intentional or negligent conduct. Therefore, we hold that the owner's negligent failure to protect patrons from foreseeable harm may be compared to the conduct of the third party and that the owner is responsible only for its percentage of fault.

Conclusion. We affirm the Court of Appeals and the trial court with respect to the duty of the Atlers to protect Castillo from foreseeable harm, their direct liability for failure to provide adequate security, and their vicarious liability because Espinosa did nothing to stop the altercation or summon the police. We also affirm the determination of the Court of Appeals that the Atlers cannot be held jointly and severally liable for the damages, and we remand this case to the trial court for proceedings consistent with this opinion. The trial court may wish to reconsider its alternative findings of fact and conclusions of law in light of our disposition and proposed instruction.

IT IS SO ORDERED.

———

S.H., A MINOR BY AND THROUGH ROBINSON v. BISTRYSKI, 923 P.2d 1376 (Utah 1996). The three-year-old plaintiff was bitten by defendant's dog. Under Utah's dog bite statute, Bistryski was strictly liable for the injury inflicted by his dog. Under Utah's Liability Reform Act, however, defendants are liable for damages only in proportion to their fault. *Held*, the comparative fault provisions of the Liability Reform Act, which included strict liability in their definition of "fault," applied to strict liability claims. "Thus, although dog owners are strictly liable for damages arising out of injuries committed by their dogs, the percentage of those damages which the owner must pay is determined by the comparative fault provisions of the Liability Reform Act. The fault of another party may have contributed to the injury and may preclude finding a dog owner responsible for 100% of the damages arising out of such injuries."

When liability is strict, the trial must be bifurcated between liability and damages phases. "To establish liability, a plaintiff need only show that the defendant is the owner or keeper of the dog and that the plaintiff's injuries were committed by that dog." To apportion fault between the parties for purposes of awarding damages, however, the fault of the parties must be assessed. In this case, the relative culpability of plaintiff's mother and defendant must be determined. "A mother's concern may differ in the case of a seemingly friendly springer spaniel as opposed to a Doberman pinscher. These and other factors could be considered by a jury in deciding whether the mother was negligent. However, to determine her percentage of fault relative to the dog owner's fault, the jury must have something to compare it against. For instance, evidence of the dog's disposition, prior biting history, the frequency of children playing nearby, and the owner's knowledge thereof may be relevant to determine whether the dog owner was negligent in leaving the dog chained to a car in the driveway. * * * "

STATUTORY DEVELOPMENTS

During the past twenty years, more than two thirds of the states have passed legislation restricting joint-and-several liability. Roughly one third of the states now do not have joint-and-several liability as a general doctrine, although they often retain it for certain kinds of cases (e.g., for ones involving intent, concert, hazardous waste, toxic torts, vicarious liability relationships, or, more rarely, cases where a tortfeasor is insolvent or cannot be joined). Another third of the states have abolished it for certain kinds of damages (e.g., for noneconomic damages), or for certain kinds of defendants (e.g., for those whose share of liability is less than 50%) or, less frequently, for certain kinds of plaintiffs (e.g., those who are not free of fault, or whose negligence exceeds that of the defendant against whom they are claiming). The thread of common law principle woven into all of this statutory variation is the spread of the principle of proportionate responsibility from negligence (duty and breach) to liability (financial responsibility).

Following are two examples of recent statutory change. The California provisions below abolish joint-and-several liability for noneconomic damages; the Texas statute abolishes joint-and-several liability for all defendants except those (a) more than 50% responsible or (b) involved in hazardous substance cases.

1.　California Civil Code §§ 1431 et seq.:

Section 1431 was amended, and the following sections were added, by an Initiative Measure, approved by the People, June 3, 1986.

§ 1431.　Joint liability

An obligation imposed upon several persons * * * is presumed to be joint, and not [separate], except as provided in Section 1431.2 * * *.

§ 1431.1.　Findings and declaration of purpose

The People of the State of California find and declare as follows:

(a) The legal doctrine of joint and several liability, also known as "the deep pocket rule", has resulted in a system of inequity and injustice that has threatened financial bankruptcy of local governments, other public agencies, private individuals and businesses and has resulted in higher prices for goods and services to the public and in higher taxes to the taxpayers.

(b) Some governmental and private defendants are perceived to have substantial financial resources or insurance coverage and have thus been included in lawsuits even though there was little or no basis for finding them at fault. Under joint and several liability, if they are found to share even a fraction of the fault, they often are held financially liable for all the damage. The People—taxpayers and consumers alike—ultimately pay for these lawsuits in the form of higher taxes, higher prices and higher insurance premiums.

* * *

Therefore, the People of the State of California declare that to remedy these inequities, defendants in tort actions shall be held financially liable in closer proportion to their degree of fault. To treat them differently is unfair and inequitable.

* * *

§ 1431.2. *Separate liability for non-economic damages*

(a) In any action for personal injury, property damage, or wrongful death, based upon principles of comparative fault, the liability of each defendant for non-economic damages shall be [separate] and shall not be joint. Each defendant shall be liable only for the amount of non-economic damages allocated to that defendant in direct proportion to that defendant's percentage of fault, and a separate judgment shall be rendered against that defendant for that amount.

(b)(1) For purposes of this section, the term "economic damages" means objectively verifiable monetary losses including medical expenses, loss of earnings, burial costs, loss of use of property, costs of repair or replacement, costs of obtaining substitute domestic services, loss of employment and loss of business or employment opportunities.

(2) For the purposes of this section, the term "non-economic damages" means subjective, non-monetary losses including, but not limited to, pain, suffering, inconvenience, mental suffering, emotional distress, loss of society and companionship, loss of consortium, injury to reputation and humiliation.

2. Texas Civil Practice & Rem. Code § 33.013:

(a) Except as provided in subsections (b) and (c), a liable defendant is liable to a claimant only for the percentage of the damages found by the trier of fact equal to that defendant's percentage of responsibility with respect to the personal injury, property damage, death, or other harm for which the damages are allowed.

(b) Notwithstanding Subsection (a), each liable defendant is, in addition to his liability under Subsection (a), jointly and severally liable for the damages recoverable by the claimant * * * if the percentage of responsibility attributed to the defendant is greater than 50 percent.

(c) Notwithstanding Subsections (a) and (b), each liable defendant is, in addition to his liability under Subsection (a), jointly and severally liable for the damages recoverable by the claimant * * * if the percentage of responsibility attributed to the defendant is equal to or greater than 15 percent and: (1) the claimant's personal injury, property damage, death, or other harm is caused by the depositing, discharge, or release into the environment of any hazardous or harmful substance * * *; or (2) the claimant's personal injury, property damage, death, or other harm resulted from a toxic tort. * * *

———

SILER ET AL. v. 146 MONTAGUE ASSOCIATES, 228 A.D.2d 33, 652 N.Y.S.2d 315 (1997). Here the court addressed a New York statute, CPLR article 16, which abolishes joint-and-several liability for "non-economic loss" with respect to those defendants whose liability is "fifty percent or less of the total liability assigned to all persons liable." The court commented as follows on the respective policies of the common law and the statutory provisions:

" 'The policy behind the common-law rule which imposes joint and several liability upon tortfeasors who contribute, in whatever degree, to the same injury is based upon the sense that compensation of the relatively innocent victim serves a more important purpose than striking a nuanced balance between and among the relatively guilty' (Robinson v. June, 167 Misc.2d 483, 488, 637 N.Y.S.2d 1018). However, CPLR article 16 changes the common law and was intended to address the inequity which occurs when 'the disparity between minor fault and major financial punishment becomes extreme.' "

VEAZEY v. ELMWOOD PLANTATION ASSOCIATES, 650 So.2d 712 (La. 1995). Plaintiff brought suit against her landlord for negligently failing to protect her against being raped. The man who raped her was never captured. The issue before the court in the original hearing was how to apply a 1987 Louisiana statute LSA–C.C. Art. 2324, "which limited the liability of a negligent tortfeasor solidarily liable with another tortfeasor to his percentage of fault or 50% of total recoverable damages, whichever was greater."

Chief Justice Calogero, concurring in the denial of rehearing, had this to say:

"In this case, there is an intentional tortfeasor, the rapist, and a negligent tortfeasor, Southmark, the liability of both being a proper subject for the consideration of the trier-of-fact. The nature of the obligation owed by each, as previously discussed, is different. Therefore, upon a finding of liability based upon different degrees of delictual 'fault,' by operation of the third paragraph of LSA–C.C. Art. 1804 the treatment of Southmark's liability should no longer fall under the delictual articles, e.g. the 50% cap on solidarity in LSA–C.C. Art. 2324, but rather under the suretyship articles. In other words, the basis for the plaintiff's recovery against Southmark is no longer founded solely in tort; rather, Southmark is transformed by operation of law into a surety of the rapist's obligation towards the plaintiff, and the suretyship articles provide the mechanism for the plaintiff's recovery from Southmark and Southmark's recourse against the intentional tortfeasor.

* * *

"Thus, under the facts of this case LSA–C.C. Art. 2324 never comes into play because under our analysis only the intentional tortfeasor ever becomes amenable to the application of LSA–C.C. Art. 2324, the negligent tortfeasor having been removed from its operation and relegated to treatment under the suretyship articles by the third paragraph of LSA–C.C. Art. 1804. * * *

* * *

"[Consequently,] although the rapist bears complete blame for his act, a conclusion which is at least as deeply ensconced in common sense as it is in legal principle, nevertheless the injured party is entitled to collect 100% of her damages from the negligent tortfeasor. Furthermore, this system also ties the hazy notion of 'tort indemnity' to a solid codal basis, reserving to the negligent tortfeasor who is cast in judgment extensive recovery rights under the suretyship articles against the intentional tortfeasor."

MERRILL CROSSINGS ASSOCIATES v. McDONALD et al., 705 So.2d 560 (Fla.1997). Plaintiff, shot in the parking lot of a Wal–Mart store, brought suit against both Wal–Mart and Merill Crossings, the owner and developer of the shopping center. After the trial court denied Wal–Mart's request to include the assailant who shot the plaintiff on the jury verdict form, the jury found Wal–Mart seventy-five percent negligently responsible for plaintiff's injury, and Merrill Crossings twenty five percent negligently responsible. Wal–Mart appealed, arguing that its liability should be reduced by the percentage of fault attributable to the assailant.

Held, affirmed. Florida's comparative fault statute applied only to "negligence cases" and excluded "any action based upon an intentional tort." The statute expressed sound public policy: "[I]t would be irrational to allow a party who negligently fails to provide reasonable security measures to reduce its liability because there is an intervening intentional tort, where the intervening intentional tort is exactly what the security measures are supposed to protect against."

Chapter 13

EXTENT OF LIABILITY: RISK AND RESULT

To establish a *prima facie* case of negligence, a plaintiff must prove injury, duty, breach, actual cause and "proximate" cause. At first glance, this last requirement—the requirement that the defendant's breach of a duty of care be not only the actual but also the "proximate" cause of the plaintiff's injury—appears unnecessary. If the defendant has negligently breached a duty of care, thereby causing harm to the plaintiff, defenses aside, what more is there to prove? The beginning of an answer to this question is suggested by an old Mother Goose Nursery Rhyme:

> For want of a nail, the shoe was lost;
> For want of a shoe, the horse was lost;
> For want of a horse, the rider was lost;
> For want of a rider, the battle was lost;
> For want of the battle, the kingdom was lost.
> And all for the want of a horseshoe nail.

Even though the "want of a horseshoe nail" is a "but for" cause of the loss of the kingdom, and even though each step in the chain of causation is unobjectionable, we balk at the conclusion that the kingdom was lost "for the want of a horseshoe nail." The missing nail is both too remote and too trivial to count as the cause of the loss of a kingdom. That loss has more "proximate"—more immediate and more substantial—causes. At some point, apparent consequence is actually mere coincidence and the "actual" cause of an injury cannot be said to be its "proximate" cause.

Other reasons why we recoil at the thought that the kingdom was lost "for the want of a horseshoe nail" also come readily to mind. Even if we were prepared to accept the claim that the absence of the nail was the original "but for" cause of the kingdom's loss—and thus the actual cause of the loss of the kingdom—the harm is so great and so far removed from its "original cause" that we may believe it makes no sense to blame the loss of the kingdom on the missing nail. Reasons of morality and policy sometimes require us to cut responsibility for harm off long before we reach the end of some chain of actual causation.

Both of these thoughts appear in "proximate cause" cases, and both of these thoughts show how "proximate cause" might be distinct from actual cause, and make sense as an additional element of liability. It is wrong on causal grounds to hold a tortfeasor liable for a harm caused by her breach of a duty of care when the connection between that harm and her tortious conduct is no more than coincidence. Coincidence is not causation. And it is wrong on moral and policy grounds to hold a tortfeasor responsible for harms which are grossly disproportionate to her wrongdoing. Extending liability to the point where it is grossly disproportionate to the underlying wrongdoing is unfair, and probably counter-productive as well. Too little liability can lead to too much risk, but too much liability can lead to too little risk.

According to some judges and some cases—Judge Andrews' dissent in *Palsgraf v. Long Island Railroad*, (*infra* at pages 620–624) may be the most famous example—the concerns that we have identified so far are *the* keys to the doctrine. As the more expansive title we have chosen for this chapter indicates, however, other judges and other cases have brought other concerns under the rubric of "proximate cause." Benjamin Cardozo, writing for the majority in *Palsgraf*, insists that "[t]he law of causation, remote or proximate, is ... foreign to the case ... " (*infra* at page 619). For Cardozo, what counts is the conceptual—not the causal—relation between the defendant's breach of its duty of care and the plaintiff's injury. If the risk of injury to the plaintiff was not one of the risks which made the defendant's conduct wrongful, then the plaintiff should not be allowed to recover even if the defendant's breach of duty directly and immediately injures the plaintiff. Liability cannot expand beyond the boundaries of duty. So conceived, the element of plaintiff's *prima facie* case which goes by the name of "proximate cause" is concerned with conceptual connections, not causal ones. The attenuation of conceptual connections—not the attenuation of causal chains—defeats recovery.

These competing conceptions may well be attempts to realize the same end, namely, identifying the "scope of the risk" created by the tortious conduct at issue. But these conceptions approach this end along different paths, and generate competing tests for the scope of liability. The "causal" understanding finds expression in the "directness" test whereas the "conceptual" understanding finds expression in the foreseeability test. We begin our study of the doctrine with these two tests, and the broader views which inform them.

SECTION A. FORESIGHT AND HINDSIGHT

LARRIMORE v. AMERICAN NATIONAL INSURANCE CO.
Supreme Court of Oklahoma, 1939.
184 Okl. 614, 89 P.2d 340.

[The defendant, a hotel keeper, furnished rat poison to a tenant for use in exterminating rats in a coffee shop operated by the tenant. The tenant placed some of the rat poison near a coffee burner. The plaintiff, an employee in the coffee shop, was hurt when the poison, which contained phosphorous, exploded as she was lighting the burner. The defendant had no reason to know of the explosive qualities of the poison. Plaintiff contended, however, that in supplying the poison to the tenant defendant violated a statute which provided that "whoever shall, except in a safe place on his own premises, lay out strychnine or other poison, is guilty of a misdemeanor." Both sides waived a jury and the case was tried to the court, which found for the defendant; and the plaintiff appeals.]

DANNER, J. [after stating the facts]. It is clear enough that the substance laid out was poison. It may further be said that if the owner had not furnished the lessee with the rat poison the plaintiff would not have been injured; and still it does not follow that the statute makes defendant liable for plaintiff's injury. It is clear that the purpose of the above statute is to protect persons and animals from injury by being poisoned. The injury here was not the class of injury intended to be prevented by the statute. There was no connection between the poisonous nature of the substance and plaintiff's injury.

It is not enough for a plaintiff to show that the defendant neglected a duty imposed by statute. He must go further and show that his injury was caused by his exposure to a hazard from which it was the purpose of the statute to protect him [citations omitted]. Negligence is a breach of duty. Those only to whom that duty is due and who have sustained injuries of the character its discharge was designed to prevent can maintain actions for its breach.

The rule in this jurisdiction is that one who does an unlawful act is not thereby placed outside of the protection of the law, but that to have this effect the unlawful act must have some causal connection with the injury complained of [citations omitted]. Plaintiff having in no way become poisoned by the "rat doom" furnished by defendant, the above section of our statute does not, of itself, render the defendant negligent as to plaintiff's injury.

It may be observed that there is still another reason why our conclusion in this respect is correct. The statute forbids the laying out of strychnine or other poison "except in a safe place." The "safe place" contemplated by the statute obviously means that place which would be safe in regard to the substance's character as poison. What would be a safe place for poison might not be a safe place for gasoline, and vice versa. * * *

[Judgment affirmed.]

———

GORRIS v. SCOTT, L.R. 9 Ex. 125 (1874). Action to recover damages for the loss of sheep which the defendant, a shipowner, had contracted to carry, and which were washed overboard and lost by reason of his neglect to comply with an administrative order made under the Contagious Diseases Act, requiring that cattle shipped on vessels should be confined by pens. *Held,* for defendant.

DI PONZO v. RIORDAN, 89 N.Y.2d 578, 657 N.Y.S.2d 377, 679 N.E.2d 616 (1997). Plaintiff and defendant were customers at a self-service gas station. Plaintiff's leg was broken when defendant's car rolled backward, pinning the plaintiff against his own car. In violation of its own regulations, the station had allowed the defendant to pump gas without turning off his engine. *Held*, summary judgment in favor of defendant affirmed. The accident was "outside" the "limited class of hazards" which define the scope of any duty that the gas station might have to ensure that customers turned off the engines of their cars while pumping gas. "When a vehicle's engine is left running in an area where gasoline is being pumped, there is a natural and foreseeable risk of fire or explosion because of the highly flammable properties of the fuel. * * * It is this class of foreseeable hazards that defines the scope of the [gas station's] purported duty."

CIRSOSKY v. SMATHERS, 128 S.C. 358, 122 S.E. 864 (1924). Defendant permitted his son, 15 years of age and unlicensed, to drive an automobile. He ran over plaintiff's five-year-old child. There was no evidence of careless driving. *Held,* judgment for defendant affirmed. The boy's operation of the car was "unlawful and negligence per se." But mere failure of a driver to have a license does not render him liable to a person injured by the car he is driving; causal relation to the injury is required for liability.

BERRY v. SUGAR NOTCH BOROUGH, 191 Pa. 345, 43 A. 240 (1899). Defendant's negligently maintained chestnut tree was blown down in a windstorm. It fell onto a streetcar being driven by plaintiff. Plaintiff was running the car at an excessive rate of speed, in violation of a borough ordinance. "[I]t was urged on behalf of the [defendant] that the speed was the immediate cause of the plaintiff's injury, inasmuch as it was the particular speed at which he was running which brought the car to the place of the accident at the moment when the tree blew down. This argument, while we cannot deny its ingenuity, strikes us, to say the least, as being somewhat sophistical. That his speed brought him to the place of the accident at the moment of the accident was the merest chance, and a thing which no foresight could have predicted."

ZUCHOWICZ v. UNITED STATES, 140 F.3d 381 (2d Cir.1998) (Calabresi, J.) In the course of his opinion, Judge Calabresi draws a distinction between "but for" causation and the showing of a "causal linkage," noting that both must be present for a plaintiff to prevail. "The effect of the requirement that a defendant's act or omission be causally linked to, or have a causal tendency toward, the harm that occurs is demonstrated most dramatically in cases in which (a) *but for* the defendant's actions the accident would clearly not have occurred, and (b) the defendant's actions are extremely close in time and space to the harm that came about, yet no one can reasonably believe that what the defendant did, though wrong, enhanced (at the time the defendant acted) the chances of the harm occurring or that it would increase the chances of a similar accident in the future if the defendant should repeat the same wrong. In such a situation, the requirement of causal link is not met and the defendant is not held liable."

"The leading case involving this requirement is *Berry v. Sugar Notch Borough*, 191 Pa. 345, 43 A. 240 (1899). In *Berry,* a tree fell on a trolley car whose excess speed had caused the tram to be at that specific place when the tree fell. The court held that the requirement of causation was not met. This result was correct since, although the accident would not have occurred but for the trolley's speeding, speeding does not increase the probability of trees falling on trolleys. Other similar cases (termed 'darting out' cases) involve speeders who *but for* their velocity would not have been at the particular spot when children darted out from behind trees, etc., and were hit. In such cases—assuming that, had the speeders been at the same spot at the same time, they would have been unable to avoid the collision even if they were driving within the speed limit—no liability results. *See* 4 Fowler V. Harper, Fleming James, Jr., & Oscar S. Gray, The Law of Torts § 20.5, at 165 (2d ed.1986).

"In a sense, the *causal link* requirement and the *but for* requirement are two different but related ways of asking whether a defendant's actions were a substantial factor in causing the injury. Causal link says that, even if defendant's wrong was a *but for* cause of the injury in a given case, no liability ensues unless defendant's wrong increases the chances of such harm occurring in general. *But for* says even if what the defendant did greatly increased the risk of certain injuries occurring, unless it was a *sine qua non* of the specific harm that actually came about, no liability will be assessed."

PALSGRAF v. LONG ISLAND RAILROAD

Court of Appeals of New York, 1928.
248 N.Y. 339, 162 N.E. 99, 59 A.L.R. 1253.

[Appeal by defendant railroad from a judgment of the Appellate Division, affirming (3–2) a verdict for plaintiff. Opinions given in the Appellate Division, 222 App.Div. 166 (1927), characterize the negligence of the railroad's employees as follows: "The facts may have warranted the jury in finding the defendant's agents were negligent in assisting a passenger in boarding a moving train in view of the fact that a door of the train should have been closed before the train started, which would have prevented the passenger making the attempt." "Instead of aiding or assisting the passenger engaged in such an act, they might better have discouraged and warned him not to board the moving train. It is quite probable that * * * without the assistance of these employees the passenger might have desisted in his efforts to board the train." "It must be remembered that the plaintiff was * * * entitled to have the defendant exercise the highest degree of care required of common carriers."]

CARDOZO, C. J. Plaintiff was standing on a platform of defendant's railroad after buying a ticket to go to Rockaway Beach. A train stopped at the station, bound for another place. Two men ran forward to catch it. One of the men reached the platform of the car without mishap, though the train was already moving. The other man, carrying a package, jumped aboard the car, but seemed unsteady as if about to fall. A guard on the car, who had held the door open, reached forward to help him in, and another guard on the platform pushed him from behind. In this act the package was dislodged, and fell upon the rails. It was a package of small size, about fifteen inches long, and was covered by a newspaper. In fact it contained fireworks, but there was nothing in its appearance to give notice of its contents. The fireworks when they fell exploded. The shock of the explosion threw down some scales at the other end of the platform, many feet away. The scales struck the plaintiff, causing injuries for which she sues.

The conduct of the defendant's guard, if a wrong in its relation to the holder of the package, was not a wrong in its relation to the plaintiff, standing far away. Relatively to her it was not negligence at all. Nothing in the situation gave notice that the falling package had in it the potency of peril to persons thus removed. Negligence is not actionable unless it involves the invasion of a legally protected interest, the violation of a right. "Proof of negligence in the air, so to speak, will not do." Pollock, Torts, 11th Ed., p. 455. * * * If no hazard was apparent to the eye of ordinary vigilance, an act innocent and harmless, at least to outward seeming, with reference to [the plaintiff], did not take to itself the quality of a tort because it happened to be a wrong, though apparently not one involving the risk of bodily insecurity, with reference to some one else. "In every instance, before negligence can be predicated of a given act, back of the act must be sought and found a duty to the individual complaining, the observance of which would have averted or avoided the injury", McSherry, C. J., in W. Va. Central R. Co. v. State, 96 Md. 652, 666, 54 A. 669, 671, 61 L.R.A. 574; [other citations omitted.] "The ideas of negligence and duty are strictly correlative". Bowen, L. J., in Thomas v. Quartermaine, 18 Q.B.D. 685, 694. The plaintiff sues in her own right for a wrong personal to her, and not as the vicarious beneficiary of a breach of duty to another.

A different conclusion will involve us, and swiftly too, in a maze of contradictions. A guard stumbles over a package which has been left upon a platform. It seems to be a bundle of newspapers. It turns out to be a can of dynamite. To the eye of ordinary vigilance, the bundle is abandoned waste, which may be kicked or trod on with impunity. Is a passenger at the other end of the platform protected by the law against the unsuspected hazard concealed beneath the waste? If not, is the result to be any different, so far as the distant passenger is concerned, when the guard stumbles over a valise which a truckman or a porter has left upon the walk? The passenger far away, if the victim of a wrong at all, has a cause of action, not derivative, but original and primary. His claim to be protected against invasion of his bodily security is neither greater nor less because the act resulting in the invasion is a wrong to another far removed. In this case, the rights that are said to have been violated, the interests said to have been invaded, are not even of the same order. The man was not injured in his person nor even put in danger. The purpose of the act, as well as its effect, was to make his person safe. If there was a wrong to him at all, which may very well be doubted, it was a wrong to a property interest only, the safety of his package. Out of this wrong to property, which threatened injury to nothing else, there has passed, we are told, to the plaintiff by derivation or succession a right of action for the invasion of an interest of another order, the right to bodily security. The diversity of interests emphasizes the futility of the effort to build the plaintiff's right upon the basis of a wrong to some one else. The gain is one of emphasis, for a like result would follow if the interests were the same. Even then, the orbit of the danger as disclosed to the eye of reasonable vigilance would be the orbit of the duty. One who jostles one's neighbor in a crowd does not invade the rights of others standing at the outer fringe when the unintended contact casts a bomb upon the ground. The wrongdoer as to them is the man who carries the bomb, not the one who explodes it without suspicion of the danger. Life will have to be made over, and human nature transformed, before prevision so extravagant can be accepted as the norm of conduct, the customary standard to which behavior must conform.

The argument for the plaintiff is built upon the shifting meanings of such words as "wrong" and "wrongful," and shares their instability. What the plaintiff must show is "a wrong" to herself, i.e., a violation of her own right, and not merely a wrong to some one else, nor conduct "wrongful" because unsocial, but not "a wrong" to any one. We are told that one who drives at reckless speed through a crowded city street is guilty of a negligent act and, therefore, of a wrongful one irrespective of the consequences. Negligent the act is, and wrongful in the sense that it is unsocial, but wrongful and unsocial in relation to other travelers, only because the eye of vigilance perceives the risk of damage. * * * The risk reasonably to be perceived defines the duty to be obeyed, and risk imports relation; it is risk to another or to others within the range of apprehension. Seavey, Negligence, Subjective or Objective, 41 H.L.Rev. 6; Boronkay v. Robinson & Carpenter, 247 N.Y. 365, 160 N.E. 400. This does not mean, of course, that one who launches a destructive force is always relieved of liability if the force, though known to be destructive, pursues an unexpected path. "It was not necessary that the defendant should have had notice of the particular method in which an accident would occur, if the possibility of an accident was clear to the ordinarily prudent eye". Some acts, such as shooting, are so imminently dangerous to any one who may come within reach of the missile, however unexpectedly, as to impose a duty of prevision not far from that of an insurer. * * * Here, by concession, there was nothing in the situation to suggest to the most cautious mind that the parcel wrapped in newspaper would spread wreckage through the station. If the guard had thrown it down knowingly and willfully, he would not have threatened the plaintiff's safety, so far as appearances could warn him. His conduct would not have involved, even then, an unreasonable probability of invasion of her bodily security. Liability can be no greater where the act is inadvertent.

Negligence, like risk, is thus a term of relation. Negligence in the abstract, apart from things related, is surely not a tort, if indeed it is understandable at all. * * * Affront to personality is still the keynote of the wrong. * * * [One who seeks redress] sues for breach of a duty owing to himself.

The law of causation, remote or proximate, is thus foreign to the case before us. The question of liability is always anterior to the question of the measure of the consequences that go with liability. If there is no tort to be redressed, there is no occasion to consider what damage might be recovered if there were a finding of a tort. We may assume, without deciding, that negligence, not at large or in the abstract, but in relation to the plaintiff, would entail liability for any and all consequences, however novel or extraordinary. There is room for argument that a distinction is to be drawn according to the diversity of interests invaded by the act, as where conduct negligent in that it threatens an insignificant invasion of an interest in property results in an unforeseeable invasion of an interest of another order, as, e.g., one of bodily security. Perhaps other distinctions may be necessary. We do not go into the question now. The consequences to be followed must first be rooted in a wrong. * * *

[POUND, LEHMAN and KELLOGG, JJ., concur.]

ANDREWS, J. [with whom CRANE and O'BRIEN, JJ., concur] dissenting. Assisting a passenger to board a train, the defendant's servant negligently knocked a package from his arms. It fell between the platform and the cars. Of its contents the servant knew and could know nothing. A violent explosion followed. The concussion broke some scales standing a considerable distance away. In falling they injured the plaintiff, an intending passenger.

Upon these facts may she recover the damages she has suffered in an action brought against the master? The result we shall reach depends upon our theory as to the nature of negligence. Is it a relative concept—the breach of some duty owing to a particular person or to particular persons? Or where there is an act which unreasonably threatens the safety of others, is the doer liable for all its proximate consequences, even where they result in injury to one who would generally be thought to be outside the radius of danger? * * * [Given] the second hypothesis we have to inquire only as to the relation between cause and effect. We deal in terms of proximate cause, not of negligence.

* * *

But we are told that "there is no negligence unless there is in the particular case a legal duty to take care, and this duty must be one which is owed to the plaintiff himself and not merely to others." Salmond, Torts, 6th Ed., 24. This, I think too narrow a conception. Where there is the unreasonable act, and some right that may be affected there is negligence whether damage does or does not result. That is immaterial. Should we drive down Broadway at a reckless speed, we are negligent whether we strike an approaching car or miss it by an inch. The act itself is wrongful. It is a wrong not only to those who happen to be within the radius of danger but to all who might have been there—a wrong to the public at large. * * * As was said by Mr. Justice Holmes many years ago, "the measure of the defendant's duty in determining whether a wrong has been committed is one thing, the measure of liability when a wrong has been committed is another." Spade v. Lynn & Boston R. Co., 172 Mass. 488, 52 N.E. 747, 43 L.R.A. 832, 70 Am.St.Rep. 298. * * *

* * * We now permit children to recover for the negligent killing of the father. It was never prevented on the theory that no duty was owing to them. A husband may be compensated for the loss of his wife's services. To

say that the wrongdoer was negligent as to the husband as well as to the wife is merely an attempt to fit facts to theory. An insurance company paying a fire loss recovers its payment of the negligent incendiary. We speak of subrogation—of suing in the right of the insured. Behind the cloud of words is the fact they hide, that the act, wrongful as to the insured, has also injured the company. * * *

In the well-known Polemis Case, [1921] 3 K.B. 560, Scrutton, L. J., said that the dropping of a plank was negligent for it might injure "workman or cargo or ship." Because of either possibility the owner of the vessel was to be made good for his loss. The act being wrongful the doer was liable for its proximate results. Criticized and explained as this statement may have been, I think it states the law as it should be and as it is.

The proposition is this. Every one owes to the world at large the duty of refraining from those acts that may unreasonably threaten the safety of other[s]. Such an act occurs. Not only is he wronged to whom harm might reasonably be expected to result, but he also who is in fact injured, even if he be outside what would generally be thought the danger zone. There needs be duty due the one complaining but this is not a duty to a particular individual because as to him harm might be expected. Harm to some one being the natural result of the act, not only that one alone, but all those in fact injured may complain. We have never, I think, held otherwise. * * * Unreasonable risk being taken, its consequences are not confined to those who might probably be hurt.

* * *

The right to recover damages rests on additional considerations. The plaintiff's rights must be injured, and this injury must be caused by the negligence. We build a dam, but are negligent as to its foundations. Breaking, it injures property down stream. We are not liable if all this happened because of some reason other than the insecure foundation. But when injuries do result from our unlawful act we are liable for the consequences. It does not matter that they are unusual, unexpected, unforeseen, and unforeseeable. But there is one limitation. The damages must be so connected with the negligence that the latter may be said to be the proximate cause of the former.

These two words have never been given an inclusive definition. What is a cause in a legal sense, still more what is a proximate cause, depend in each case upon many considerations, as does the existence of negligence itself. Any philosophical doctrine of causation does not help us. A boy throws a stone into a pond. The ripples spread. The water level rises. The history of that pond is altered to all eternity. * * * Each cause brings about future events. Without each the future would not be the same. Each is proximate in the sense it is essential. But that is not what we mean by the word. Nor on the other hand do we mean sole cause. There is no such thing.

Should analogy be thought helpful, * * * I prefer that of a stream. The spring, starting on its journey, is joined by tributary after tributary. The river reaching the ocean, comes from a hundred sources. No man may say whence any drop of water is derived. Yet for a time distinction may be possible. Into the clear creek, brown swamp water flows from the left. Later, from the right comes water stained by its clay bed. The three remain for a space, sharply divided. But at last, inevitably no trace of separation remains. They are so commingled that all distinction is lost.

* * *

* * * What we do mean by the word "proximate" is, that because of convenience, of public policy, of a rough sense of justice, the law arbitrarily declines to trace a series of events beyond a certain point. This is not logic. It is practical politics. Take our rule as to fires. Sparks from my burning haystack set on fire my house and my neighbor's. I may recover from a negligent railroad. He may not. Yet the wrongful act as directly harmed the one as the other. We may regret that the line was drawn just where it was, but drawn somewhere it had to be. We said the act of the railroad was not the proximate cause of our neighbor's fire. Cause it surely was. The words we used were simply indicative of our notions of public policy. Other courts think differently. But somewhere they reach the point where they cannot say the stream comes from any one source.

Take the illustration given in an unpublished manuscript by a distinguished and helpful writer on the law of torts. A chauffeur negligently collides with another car which is filled with dynamite, although he could not know it. An explosion follows. A, walking on the sidewalk nearby, is killed. B, sitting in a window of a building opposite, is cut by flying glass. C, likewise sitting in a window a block away, is similarly injured, and a further illustration. A nursemaid, ten blocks away, startled by the noise, involuntarily drops a baby from her arms to the walk. We are told that C may not recover while A may. As to B it is a question for court or jury. We will all agree that the baby might not. Because, we are again told, the chauffeur had no reason to believe his conduct involved any risk of injuring either C or the baby. As to them he was not negligent.

But the chauffeur, being negligent in risking the collision, his belief that the scope of the harm he might do would be limited is immaterial. His act unreasonably jeopardized the safety of any one who might be affected by it. C's injury and that of the baby were directly traceable to the collision. Without that, the injury would not have happened. C had the right to sit in his office, secure from such dangers. The baby was entitled to use the sidewalk with reasonable safety.

The true theory is, it seems to me, that the injury to C, if in truth he is to be denied recovery, and the injury to the baby is that their several injuries were not the proximate result of the negligence. And here not what the chauffeur had reason to believe would be the result of his conduct, but what the prudent would foresee, may have a bearing. May have some bearing, for the problem of proximate cause is not to be solved by any one consideration.

It is all a question of expediency. There are no fixed rules to govern our judgment. There are simply matters of which we may take account. We have in a somewhat different connection spoken of "the stream of events." We have asked whether that stream was deflected—whether it was forced into new and unexpected channels. Donnelly v. H. C. & A. I. Piercy Contracting Co., 222 N.Y. 210, 118 N.E. 605. This is rather rhetoric than law. There is in truth little to guide us other than common sense.

There are some hints that may help us. The proximate cause, involved as it may be with many other causes, must be, at the least, something without which the event would not happen. The court must ask itself whether there was a natural and continuous sequence between cause and effect. Was the one a substantial factor in producing the other? Was there a direct connection between them, without too many intervening causes? Is the effect of cause on result not too attenuated? Is the cause likely, in the usual judgment of mankind, to produce the result? Or by the exercise of prudent foresight could the result be foreseen? Is the result too remote from the cause, and here we consider remoteness in time and space. * * * [T]he greater the distance either in time or space, the more surely do other causes intervene to affect the result. When a lantern is overturned the firing of a shed is a fairly direct consequence. Many things contribute to the spread of the conflagration—the force of the wind, the direction and width of streets, the character of intervening structures, other factors. We draw an uncertain and wavering line, but draw it we must as best we can.

* * *

* * * In the case supposed it is said, and said correctly, that the chauffeur is liable for the direct effect of the explosion although he had no reason to suppose it would follow a collision. "The fact that the injury occurred in a different manner than that which might have been expected does not prevent the chauffeur's negligence from being in law the cause of the injury." * * *

It may be said this is unjust. Why? In fairness he should make good every injury flowing from his negligence. Not because of tenderness toward him we say he need not answer for all that follows his wrong. We look back to the catastrophe, the fire kindled by the spark, or the explosion. We trace the consequences—not indefinitely, but to a certain point. And to aid us in fixing that point we ask what might ordinarily be expected to follow the fire or the explosion.

* * * The act upon which defendant's liability rests is knocking an apparently harmless package onto the platform. The act was negligent. For its proximate consequences the defendant is liable. If its contents were broken, to the owner; if it fell upon and crushed a passenger's foot, then to him. If it exploded and injured one in the immediate vicinity to him also as to A in the illustration. Mrs. Palsgraf was standing some distance away. How far cannot be told from the record—apparently twenty-five or thirty feet. Perhaps less. Except for the explosion, she would not have been injured. We are told by the appellant in his brief "it can not be denied that the explosion was the direct cause of the plaintiff's injuries." So it was a substantial factor in producing the result—there was here a natural and continuous sequence—direct connection. The only intervening cause was that instead of

blowing her to the ground the concussion smashed the weighing machine which in turn fell upon her. There was no remoteness in time, little in space. And surely, given such an explosion as here it needed no great foresight to predict that the natural result would be to injure one on the platform at no greater distance from its scene than was the plaintiff. Just how no one might be able to predict. Whether by flying fragments, by broken glass, by wreckage of machines or structures no one could say. But injury in some form was most probable.

Under these circumstances I cannot say as a matter of law that the plaintiff's injuries were not the proximate result of the negligence. * * *

———

SINRAM v. PENNSYLVANIA RAILROAD, 61 F.2d 767 (2d Cir. 1932). L. Hand, J.: "* * * [T]he usual test [for extent of liability] is said to be whether the damage could be foreseen by the actor when he acted; not indeed the precise train of events, but similar damage to the same class of persons. Yet this generally accepted canon is more equivocal than appears on the surface. * * * It must be confessed * * * that the standard so fixed scarcely advances the solution in a concrete case; it only eliminates the egregious, leaving the tribunal a free hand to do as it thinks best. But that is inevitable unless liability is to be determined by a manual, mythically prolix, and fantastically impractical. * * *"

TERRY v. NEW ORLEANS GREAT NORTHERN RAILROAD, 103 Miss. 679, 60 So. 729, 44 L.R.A.,N.S., 1069 (1912). A physician, while on his way to attend the plaintiff, who was suffering intense pain and anguish incident to a difficult childbirth, was delayed for 30 minutes at a railroad crossing by a train which blocked the highway in violation of a "five minute statute," whereby plaintiff's suffering was prolonged and greater exhaustion was caused which probably necessitated the use of different treatment and resulted in greater laceration of her body. *Held,* for plaintiff, reversing a directed judgment and remanding the cause. While the company's employees could not have anticipated that a physician on his way to plaintiff's bedside would arrive at the crossing at that particular time, they should have anticipated that some traveller might be detained, with resultant injury to him or to some third person.

WIDLOWSKI v. DURKEE FOODS, 138 Ill.2d 369, 150 Ill.Dec. 164, 562 N.E.2d 967 (1990). Plaintiff alleged that Larry Wells, an employee of Durkee Foods, entered an industrial tank in order to clean it. "The tank contained nitrogen gas, among other substances, and lacked a sufficient amount of oxygen to breathe. Wells failed to wear protective gear and failed to purge the tank of the nitrogen gas. Upon entering the tank, Wells was overcome by nitrogen gas and became restless, incoherent and delirious. He was transported to St. Joseph's Medical Center for treatment. Plaintiff, a nurse at the medical center, attended to Wells. While in a state of delirium, Wells bit off a portion of plaintiff's right middle finger." *Held,* defendant owed no duty to plaintiff. "While there can be no doubt that Wells' failure to wear protective gear upon entering the tank caused him to become ill, we do not believe that the risk of harm to plaintiff, who was removed in time and place, was reasonably foreseeable." *Palsgraf* followed: "[p]roof of negligence in the air, so to speak, will not do."

KLEINKNECHT v. GETTYSBURG COLLEGE, 989 F.2d 1360 (3d Cir. 1993). Parents of college lacrosse player who died of a heart attack during lacrosse practice brought suit alleging that the college had a duty to be reasonably prepared to handle medical emergencies arising in the course of intercollegiate athletics. *Held*, injury to plaintiff was reasonably foreseeable. "Only when even the general likelihood of some broadly definable class of events, of which the particular event that caused the plaintiff's injury is a subclass, is unforeseeable can a court hold as a matter of law that the defendant did not have a duty to the plaintiff to guard against that broad general class of risks within which the particular harm the plaintiff suffered befell." *Palsgraf* cited.

"Although the district court correctly determined that the Kleinknechts had presented evidence establishing that the occurrence of severe and life-threatening injuries is not out of the ordinary during contact sports, it held that the College had no duty because the cardiac arrest suffered by Drew, a twenty-year old athlete with no history of any severe medical problems, was not reasonably foreseeable. Its definition of foreseeability is too narrow. Although it is true that a defendant is not required to guard against every possible risk, he must take reasonable steps to guard against hazards which are generally foreseeable. * * * Though the specific risk that a person like Drew would suffer a cardiac arrest may be unforeseeable, the Kleinknechts produced ample evidence that a life-threatening injury during participation in an athletic event like lacrosse was reasonably foreseeable."

FAZZOLARI v. PORTLAND SCHOOL DISTRICT, 303 Or. 1, 734 P.2d 1326 (1987). Linde, J.: "The scope of liability for negligently-caused harm might extend to all harm that in fact resulted from the negligence, or it could be confined to those risks that made the conduct negligent: 'The risk reasonably to be perceived defines the duty to be obeyed,' as Cardozo put it in *Palsgraf.* By confining liability to those risks that the defendant was obliged to minimize, the *Palsgraf* rule demanded a closer link of negligence to its premise of fault, if only the attenuated fault of impersonal corporate defendants and objective standards of foresight and due care. But the *Palsgraf* dissenters' contrary choice between a blameless plaintiff and a defendant whose conduct has been socially substandard, faulty, toward anyone, has been defended on grounds that any resulting loss should fall on the defendant. * * *

"[Oregon's 'foreseeable risk' approach was clarified in *Stewart v. Jefferson Plywood Co.*, 255 Or. 603, 469 P.2d 783 (1970).] Stewart was a volunteer helping to fight a fire that originated at defendant's sawmill. He was sent to control sparks on the roof of a neighboring warehouse belonging to another company and was injured when he fell through a skylight opening that had been covered by a piece of plastic and was obscured by dust. The court affirmed his recovery of damages, holding that the risk of falling through a hidden skylight while protecting a neighbor's roof was not so untypical of risks created by a negligently caused fire as to withdraw the case from the jury. * * *

" * * * [F]oresight does not demand the precise mechanical imagination of a Rube Goldberg nor a paranoid view of the universe. As already noted, *Stewart v. Jefferson Plywood Co.* made clear that the concept of foreseeability refers to generalized risks of the type of incidents and injuries that occurred rather than predictability of the actual sequence of events. In that case, for instance, a factfinder could conclude that the foreseeable risks [of a negligent fire] included physical injury from falling through a roof in protecting a nearby building from fire rather than from being burned by the fire."

DELLWO v. PEARSON
Supreme Court of Minnesota, 1961.
259 Minn. 452, 107 N.W.2d 859, 97 A.L.R.2d 866.

[The 12–year-old defendant, operating a motorboat, passed too closely behind plaintiff's boat thereby crossing over plaintiff's fishing line, entangling the line in the propeller of defendant's boat and causing a pull on plaintiff's reel that jerked it against the side of her boat, forcing the reel to come apart. Part of it struck her glasses and injured her eye. The trial court instructed the jury that a negligent person "is liable for all consequences which might reasonably have been foreseen as likely to result from one's negligent act or omission under the circumstances" and "is not responsible for a consequence which is merely possible according to occasional experience, but [is responsible] only for a consequence which is probable according to ordinary and usual experience." The jury returned a verdict for defendant. From judgment on the verdict, plaintiff appeals. The part of the opinion reprinted here is only that part concerned with the issue of proximate cause. With respect to the standard for judging the child's conduct, see the abstract of this case on p. 361, supra.]

LOEVINGER, Justice * * * The instruction of the trial court limiting liability for negligence to foreseeable consequences was a part of the instruction on proximate cause and, in effect, made foreseeability a test of proximate cause.

There is no subject in the field of law upon which more has been written with less elucidation than that of proximate cause. Cases discussing it are legion. It has challenged many of the most able commentators at one time or another. It is generally agreed that there is no simple formula for defining proximate cause, but this is assumed to be a difficulty peculiar to the law, which distinguishes between "proximate cause" and "cause in fact." However, examination of the literature suggests that neither scientists nor philosophers have been more successful than judges in providing a verbal definition for this concept.[3] We can contrast the concept of cause with

3. See, Karl Pearson, The Grammar of Science, (1892) c. 4, §§ 1, 8; c. 5; P. W. Bridgman, The Logic of Modern Physics (1927) p. 91; Hans Reichenbach (1933) Atom and Cosmos, p. 268, et seq.; Cohen and Nagel, An Introduction to Logic and Scientific Method (1934) p. 246, et seq.; John Dewey, Logic: The Theory of Inquiry (1938) p. 442, et seq.; James Jeans, Physics and

that of destiny and of chance, we can use it operationally and pragmatically, but we cannot formulate a precise, rigorous, or very satisfactory verbal definition. Cause seems to be one of those elemental concepts that defies refined analysis but is known intuitively to commonsense.

Although a rigorous definition of proximate cause continues to elude us, nevertheless it is clear, in this state at least, that it is not a matter of foreseeability. We are unable now to make any better statement on this issue than that of Mr. Justice Mitchell many years ago. Speaking for this court, he said:

> It is laid down in many cases and by some text writers that, in order to warrant a finding that negligence (not wanton) is the proximate cause of an injury, it must appear that the injury was the natural and probable consequence of the negligent act, and that it (the injury) was such as might or ought, in the light of attending circumstances, to have been anticipated. Such or similar statements of law have been inadvertently borrowed and repeated in some of the decisions of this court, but never, we think, where the precise point now under consideration was involved. Hence such statements are mere obiter. The doctrine contended for by counsel would establish practically the same rule of damages resulting from tort as is applied to damages resulting from breach of contract, under the familiar doctrine of Hadley v. Baxendale, 9 Exch. 341. This mode of stating the law is misleading, if not positively inaccurate. It confounds and mixes the definition of "negligence" with that of "proximate cause."

> What a man may reasonably anticipate is important, and may be decisive, in determining whether an act is negligent, but is not at all decisive in determining whether that act is the proximate cause of an injury which ensues. If a person had no reasonable ground to anticipate that a particular act would or might result in any injury to anybody, then, of course, the act would not be negligent at all; but, if the act itself is negligent, then the person guilty of it is equally liable for all its natural and proximate consequences, whether he could have foreseen them or not. Otherwise expressed, the law is that if the act is one which the party ought, in the exercise of ordinary care, to have anticipated was liable to result in injury to others, then he is liable for any injury proximately resulting from it, although he could not have anticipated the particular injury which did happen. Consequences which follow in unbroken sequence, without an intervening efficient cause, from the original negligent act, are natural and proximate; and for such consequences the original wrongdoer is responsible, even though he could not have foreseen the particular results which did follow.[5]

Philosophy (1943) pp. 98, 102–103, 145, 173, 190, 194; C. W. Churchman, Theory of Experimental Inference (1948) pp. 198, 199; Phillipp Frank, Modern Science and Its Philosophy (1949) p. 53, et seq.; Richard von Mises, Positivism (1956) p. 152, et seq.; Mario Bunge, Causality: The Place of the Causal Principle in Modern Science (1960); Sidney Morgenbesser, Review of Bunge, supra, Scientific American, February 1961, p. 175.

5. Christianson v. Chicago, St. P., M. & O. Ry. Co., 67 Minn. 94, 96, 69 N.W. 640, 641.

Although language may be found in some opinions dealing with the specific facts of particular cases that seems to be at variance with the statement of Mr. Justice Mitchell, this court has consistently through the years followed the doctrine thus enunciated. We now reaffirm that the doctrine of the Christianson case is still the law of Minnesota and, in the words of Mr. Justice Stone, decline the invitation of this case to add further to the already excessive literature of the law dealing, or attempting to deal, with the problem of proximate cause.[7] It is enough to say that negligence is tested by foresight but proximate cause is determined by hindsight.

It follows that the trial court erred in making foreseeability a test of proximate cause. There can be no question that this was misleading to the jury and therefore prejudicial to the plaintiff, requiring reversal of the judgment. * * *

Reversed and remanded for a new trial.

———

ORWICK v. BELSHAN, 304 Minn. 338, 231 N.W.2d 90 (1975). In a negligence case the trial judge instructed the jury on the issue of causation in the following vein:

[B]y proximate cause is meant the direct or immediate cause, or the natural sequence of events without the intervention of another independent and efficient cause. Proximate cause is that which in a natural and continuous sequence, unbroken by any efficient intervening cause produces the injuries and without which the result would not have occurred.

After deliberating for a time the jury asked for further instruction on causation, and the trial judge gave another definition couched in similar terminology. On review of the jury's verdict the Supreme Court said that these formulations, put "in terms of negativing superseding causes," were technically correct, but "may be unnecessarily abstruse." It suggested that "an accurate and much simpler definition" was an instruction in terms of "direct cause" found in 4 Hetland & Adamson, Minnesota Practice, Jury Instruction Guides (2d ed.):

A direct cause is a cause which had a substantial part in bringing about the (harm) (accident) (injury) (collision) (occurrence) [either immediately or through happenings which follow one after another].

This instruction should be supplemented, in appropriate cases, with instruction on concurring cause and superseding cause.

BUNTING v. HOGSETT, 139 Pa. 363, 21 A. 31, 33 (1891). The defendant operated a dinkey engine over a track which cut the line of a railroad at two points, the defendant's track being the arc of a circle and the railroad track subtending the arc as a chord. The defendant's engineer, negligently approaching the railroad crossing, was unable to stop in time to prevent a collision with a passenger train on the railroad. Just before the collision,

———

7. Brown v. Murphy Transfer & Storage Co.,
190 Minn. 81, 86, 251 N.W. 5, 7.

however, he jumped, after reversing the engine and shutting off steam. The jar of the collision caused the throttle to be reopened and the defendant's dinkey engine, running backwards over the arc, struck the passenger train at the other intersection. In this collision the plaintiff, who was a passenger on the train, was hurt. *Held,* affirming judgment for the plaintiff, that the negligence of the defendant's engineer was a proximate cause of the result.

THE MARINER, 17 F.2d 253 (5th Cir.1927). Suit in admiralty. The tug Mariner with barges in tow left one Texas port bound for another at about 5:30 p.m. on November 19, 1924. It went aground in the evening and remained there till the next morning before being pulled off and continuing the journey. There was no sign of bad weather until a norther began to blow at about 11 a.m., increasing to 25 or 30 miles an hour, which was not unusual off the Texas coast at that time of year. Some damage was done during the norther. If the tug had not gone aground, the voyage would have been completed in 10 or 12 hours. The trial court "ruled that the grounding was due to negligence chargeable against the tug, that the tug was liable for the slight damage sustained at the time of the grounding, but was not liable for the damage of which the norther was the direct cause, the court being of opinion that the delay could not be considered the proximate cause of the injury to the pontoons, and that the sudden blow of wind or squall was an independent intervening, and the sole proximate, cause of that injury." *Held,* reversed. "The prolongation of the towage beyond the time reasonably required to complete it being an act which, according to the usual experience of mankind, would expose the tow to the hazard of such an event happening after the expiration of the time reasonably required to complete the towage, the prolongation of the towage was not kept from being a proximate cause of the injury sustained by the fact that the happening of such an ordinary and not improbable event concurred in producing that injury."

OVERSEAS TANKSHIP (U.K.), LTD. v. MORTS DOCK AND ENGINEERING CO. [THE "WAGON MOUND CASE"]
Privy Council, 1961.
[1961] 1 All E.R. 404.

VISCOUNT SIMONDS: This appeal is brought from an order of the Full Court of the Supreme Court of New South Wales dismissing an appeal by the appellants, Overseas Tankship (U.K.), Ltd., from a judgment of KINSEL-LA, J., exercising the Admiralty jurisdiction of that court in an action in which the appellants were defendants and the respondents, Morts Dock & Engineering Co., Ltd., were plaintiffs. In the action, the respondents sought to recover from the appellants compensation for the damage which its property, known as the Sheerlegs Wharf in Sydney Harbour and the equipment thereon, had suffered by reason of fire which broke out on Nov. 1, 1951. For this damage they claimed that the appellants were, in law, responsible.

The relevant facts can be comparatively shortly stated, inasmuch as not one of the findings of fact in the exhaustive judgment of the learned trial judge has been challenged. The respondents at the relevant time carried on the business of ship-building, ship-repairing and general engineering at Morts Bay, Balmain, in the Port of Sydney. They owned and used for their business the Sheerlegs Wharf, a timber wharf about four hundred feet in length and forty feet wide, where there was a quantity of tools and equipment. In October and November, 1951, a vessel known as the Corrimal was moored alongside the wharf and was being refitted by the respondents. Her mast was lying on the wharf and a number of the respondents' employees were working both on it and on the vessel itself, using for this purpose electric and oxy-acetylene welding equipment. At the same time, the appellants were charterers by demise of the S.S. Wagon Mound, an oil-burning vessel which was moored at the Caltex Wharf on the northern shore of the harbour at a distance of about six hundred feet from the Sheerlegs Wharf. She was there from about 9 a.m. on Oct. 29, until 11 a.m. on Oct. 30, 1951, for the purpose of discharging gasolene products and taking in bunkering oil. During the early hours of Oct. 30, 1951, a large quantity of bunkering oil was, through the carelessness of the appellants' servants, allowed to spill into the bay, and, by 10:30 on the morning of that day, it had spread over a considerable part of the bay, being thickly concentrated in some places and particularly along the foreshore near the respondents' property. The appellants made no attempt to disperse the oil. The Wagon Mound unberthed and set sail very shortly after. When the respondents' works manager became aware of the condition of things in the vicinity of the wharf, he instructed their workmen that no welding or burning was to be carried on until further orders. He inquired of the manager of the Caltex Oil Co., at whose wharf the Wagon Mound was then still berthed, whether they could safely continue their operations on the wharf or on the Corrimal. The results of this inquiry, coupled with his own belief as to the inflammability of furnace oil in the open, led him to think that the respondents could safely carry on their operations. He gave instructions accordingly, but directed that all safety precautions should be taken to prevent inflammable material falling off the wharf into the oil. For the remainder of Oct. 30 and until about 2 p.m. on Nov. 1, work was carried on as usual, the condition and congestion of the oil remaining substantially unaltered. But at about that time the oil under or near the wharf was ignited and a fire, fed initially by the oil, spread rapidly and burned with great intensity. The wharf and the Corrimal caught fire and considerable damage was done to the wharf and the equipment on it.

The outbreak of fire was due, as the learned judge found, to the fact that there was floating in the oil underneath the wharf a piece of débris on which lay some smouldering cotton waste or rag which had been set on fire by molten metal falling from the wharf; that the cotton waste or rag burst into flames; that the flames from the cotton waste set the floating oil afire either directly or by first setting fire to a wooden pile coated with oil and that, after the floating oil became ignited, the flames spread rapidly over the surface of the oil and quickly developed into a conflagration which severely damaged the wharf. He also made the all-important finding, which must be set out in his own words:

The raison d'être of furnace oil is, of course, that it shall burn, but I find the [appellants] did not know and could not reasonably be expected to have known that it was capable of being set afire when spread on water.

This finding was reached after a wealth of evidence which included that of a distinguished scientist, Professor Hunter. It receives strong confirmation from the fact that, at the trial, the respondents strenuously maintained that the appellants had discharged petrol into the bay on no other ground than that, as the spillage was set alight, it could not be furnace oil. An attempt was made before their Lordships' Board to limit in some way the finding of fact, but it is clear that it was intended to cover precisely the event that happened. One other finding must be mentioned. The learned judge held that, apart from damage by fire, the respondents had suffered some damage[8] from the spillage of oil in that it had got on their slipways and congealed on them and interfered with their use of the slips. He said:

> The evidence of this damage is slight and no claim for compensation is made in respect of it. Nevertheless it does establish some damage, which may be insignificant in comparison with the magnitude of the damage by fire, but which nevertheless is damage which beyond question was a direct result of the escape of the oil.

It is on this footing that their Lordships will consider the question whether the appellants are liable for the fire damage. * * *

It is inevitable that first consideration should be given to Re Polemis and Furness, Withy & Co., Ltd.,[4] which will henceforward be referred to as Polemis. * * *

What, then, did Polemis decide? * * * The case arose out of a charter party and went to arbitration under a term of it * * * [T]he case proceeded as one in which, independently of contractual obligations, the claim was for damages for negligence. It was on this footing that the Court of Appeal held that the charterers were responsible for all the consequences of their negligent act, even though those consequences could not reasonably have been anticipated. The negligent act was nothing more than the carelessness of stevedores (for whom the charterers were assumed to be responsible) in allowing a sling or rope by which it was hoisted to come into contact with certain boards, causing one of them to fall into the hold. The falling board hit some substances in the hold and caused a spark; the spark ignited petrol vapour in the hold; there was a rush of flames and the ship was destroyed. The Special Case submitted by the arbitrators found that the causing of the spark could not reasonably have been anticipated from the falling of the

---

8. Kinsella, J., dealt with the relevance of his finding as follows: "I have already stated my finding that the oil fouled the [respondents'] slipways and caused interruption to their operations and that *those consequences were foreseeable to any reasonable person.* Counsel for [the appellants] has urged that [the respondents] are not entitled to rely on this damage, inasmuch as no claim is pressed in respect of it. I do not agree * * * The [respondents'] failure to press a claim for this damage is not an admission that it was not actionable damage * * * It follows, since foreseeable damage was caused to the [respondents], that the [appellants'] careless act became impressed with the legal quality of negligence and the case therefore is covered by the principles of Re Polemis and not those laid down in Hay (or Bourhill) v. Young."

4. [1921] All E.R.Rep. 40; [1921] 3 K.B. 560.

board, though some damage to the ship might reasonably have been anticipated. They did not indicate what damage might have been so anticipated.

There can be no doubt that the decision of the Court of Appeal in Polemis plainly asserts that, if the defendant is guilty of negligence, he is responsible for all the consequences, whether reasonably foreseeable or not. The generality of the proposition is, perhaps, qualified by the fact that each of the lords justices refers to the outbreak of fire as the direct result of the negligent act. There is thus introduced the conception that the negligent actor is not responsible for consequences which are not "direct", whatever that may mean. It has to be asked, then, why this conclusion should have been reached. The answer appears to be that it was reached on a consideration of certain authorities, comparatively few in number, that were cited to the court. * * * The earliest in point of date was Smith v. London & South Western Ry. Co.[5] In that case, it was said that:

> * * * when it has been once determined that there is evidence of negligence, the person guilty of it is equally liable for its consequences, whether he could have foreseen them or not

see per CHANNELL, B. Similar observations were made by other members of the court. [It] may be noted * * * that the point to which the court directed its mind was not unforeseeable damage of a different kind from that which was foreseen, but more extensive damage of the same kind * * *.

Enough has been said to show that the authority of Polemis has been severely shaken, though lip-service has from time to time been paid to it. In their Lordships' opinion, it should no longer be regarded as good law. It is not probable that many cases will for that reason have a different result, though it is hoped that the law will be thereby simplified, and that, in some cases at least, palpable injustice will be avoided. For it does not seem consonant with current ideas of justice or morality that, for an act of negligence, however slight or venial, which results in some trivial foreseeable damage, the actor should be liable for all consequences, however unforeseeable and however grave, so long as they can be said to be "direct". It is a principle of civil liability, subject only to qualifications which have no present relevance, that a man must be considered to be responsible for the probable consequences of his act. To demand more of him is too harsh a rule, to demand less is to ignore that civilised order requires the observance of a minimum standard of behaviour. This concept, applied to the slowly developing law of negligence has led to a great variety of expressions which can, as it appears to their Lordships, be harmonised with little difficulty with the single exception of the so-called rule in Polemis. For, if it is asked why a man should be responsible for the natural or necessary or probable consequences of his act (or any other similar description of them), the answer is that it is not because they are natural or necessary or probable, but because, since they have this quality, it is judged, by the standard of the reasonable man, that he ought to have foreseen them. Thus it is that, over and over again, it has happened that, in different judgments in the same case and

5. (1870), L.R. 6 C.P. 14.

sometimes in a single judgment, liability for a consequence has been imposed on the ground that it was reasonably foreseeable, or alternatively on the ground that it was natural or necessary or probable. The two grounds have been treated as coterminous, and so they largely are. But, where they are not, the question arises to which the wrong answer was given in Polemis. For, if some limitation must be imposed on the consequences for which the negligent actor is to be held responsible—and all are agreed that some limitation there must be—why should that test (reasonable foreseeability) be rejected which, since he is judged by what the reasonable man ought to foresee, corresponds with the common conscience of mankind, and a test (the "direct" consequence) be substituted which leads to nowhere but the never-ending and insoluble problems of causation. * * *

    * * * Applying the rule in Polemis and holding, therefore, that the unforeseeability of the damage by fire afforded no defence, [the full court below] went on to consider the remaining question. Was it a "direct" consequence? On this, Manning, J., said:

        * * * I cannot escape from the conclusion that if the ordinary man in the street had been asked, as a matter of common sense, without any detailed analysis of the circumstances, to state the cause of the fire at Morts Dock, he would unhesitatingly have assigned such cause to spillage of oil by the appellants' employees.

* * * But, with great respect to the full court, this is surely irrelevant, or, if it is relevant, only serves to show that the Polemis rule works in a very strange way. After the event even a fool is wise. Yet it is not the hindsight of a fool, but it is the foresight of the reasonable man which alone can determine responsibility. The Polemis rule, by substituting "direct" for "reasonably foreseeable" consequence, leads to a conclusion equally illogical and unjust.

* * *

    * * * Just as (as it has been said) there is no such thing as negligence in the air, so there is no such thing as liability in the air. Suppose an action brought by A for damage caused by the carelessness (a neutral word) of B, for example a fire caused by the careless spillage of oil. It may, of course, become relevant to know what duty B owed to A, but the only liability that is in question is the liability for damage by fire. It is vain to isolate the liability from its context and to say that B is or is not liable, and then to ask for what damage he is liable. For his liability is in respect of that damage and no other. If, as admittedly it is, B's liability (culpability) depends on the reasonable foreseeability of the consequent damage, how is that to be determined except by the foreseeability of the damage which in fact happened—the damage in suit? And, if that damage is unforeseeable so as to displace liability at large, how can the liability be restored so as to make compensation payable? But, it is said, a different position arises if B's careless act has been shown to be negligent and has caused some foreseeable damage to A. Their Lordships have already observed that to hold B liable for consequences, however unforeseeable, of a careless act, if, but only if, he is at the same time liable for some other damage, however trivial,

appears to be neither logical nor just. * * * It is irrelevant to the question whether B is liable for unforeseeable damage that he is liable for foreseeable damage, as irrelevant as would the fact that he had trespassed on Whiteacre be to the question whether he had trespassed on Blackacre. Again, suppose a claim by A for damage by fire by the careless act of B. Of what relevance is it to that claim that he has another claim arising out of the same careless act? It would surely not prejudice his claim if that other claim failed; it cannot assist it if it succeeds. Each of them rests on its own bottom and will fail if it can be established that the damage could not reasonably be foreseen. * * *

Their Lordships conclude this part of the case with some general observations. They have been concerned primarily to displace the proposition that unforeseeability is irrelevant if damage is "direct." In doing so, they have inevitably insisted that the essential factor in determining liability is whether the damage is of such a kind as the reasonable man should have foreseen. This accords with the general view thus stated by Lord Atkin in M'Alister (or Donoghue) v. Stevenson[50]:

> The liability for negligence, whether you style it such or treat it as in other systems as a species of 'culpa,' is no doubt based upon a general public sentiment of moral wrongdoing for which the offender must pay.

It is a departure from this sovereign principle if liability is made to depend solely on the damage being the "direct" or "natural" consequence of the precedent act. Who knows or can be assumed to know all the processes of nature? But if it would be wrong that a man should be held liable for damage unpredictable by a reasonable man because it was "direct" or "natural," equally it would be wrong that he should escape liability, however "indirect" the damage, if he foresaw or could reasonably foresee the intervening events which led to its being done. Thus foreseeability becomes the effective test. In reasserting this principle, their Lordships conceive that they do not depart from, but follow and develop, the law of negligence as laid down by Alderson, B., in Blyth v. Birmingham Waterworks Co.[52]

It is proper to add that their Lordships have not found it necessary to consider the so-called rule of "strict liability" exemplified in Rylands v. Fletcher[53] and the cases that have followed or distinguished it. Nothing that they have said is intended to reflect on that rule.

One aspect of this case remains to be dealt with. The respondents claim, in the alternative, that the appellants are liable in nuisance if not in negligence. On this issue, their Lordships are of opinion that it would not be proper for them to come to any conclusion on the material before them and without the benefit of the considered view of the Supreme Court. On the other hand, having regard to the course which the case has taken, they do not think that the respondents should be finally shut out from the opportunity of advancing this plea, if they think fit. They therefore propose that, on

50. [1932] All E.R.Rep. at p. 11; [1932] A.C.   **53.** (1868), L.R. 3 H.L. 330.
at p. 580.
52. (1856), 11 Exch. 781.

the issue of nuisance alone, the case should be remitted to the full court to be dealt with as may be thought proper.

Their Lordships will humbly advise Her Majesty that this appeal should be allowed and the respondents' action so far as it related to damage caused by the negligence of the appellants be dismissed with costs but that the action so far as it related to damage caused by nuisance should be remitted to the full court to be dealt with as that court may think fit. The respondents must pay the costs of the appellants of this appeal and in the courts below.

Appeal allowed.

———

OVERSEAS TANKSHIP (U.K.) LTD. v. MILLER STEAMSHIP CO., [1967] 1 A.C. 617, [1967] 2 All E.R. 709 (P.C.) [also referred to as Wagon Mound No. 2]. Damage to two vessels from the fire of November 1, 1951, in Sydney Harbour. Walsh, J., in the S.Ct. of New South Wales, found (a) that damage to respondents' vessels was "not reasonably foreseeable by those for whose acts the defendant would be responsible"; (b) that "reasonable people in the position of the officers of the Wagon Mound would regard the furnace oil as very difficult to ignite upon water," and that "if they had given attention to the risk of fire from the spillage, they would have regarded it as a possibility, but one which could become an actuality only in very exceptional circumstances." Walsh held defendant liable in nuisance, not dependent on foreseeability; not liable in negligence.

On appeal and cross-appeal, *held:* (1) foreseeability is essential to liability for nuisance in cases of injury on highways and navigable waters; (2) both appeal and cross appeal allowed, and judgment against defendant affirmed. A reasonable man having the knowledge and experience to be expected of the appellants' chief engineer "would have known that there was a real risk of the oil on the water catching fire in some way" and that the risk, though small, did not justify defendant's taking no steps to eliminate it.

Lord Reid, delivering the judgment, says, at [1967] 1 A.C. 640, that proving foreseeability in Wagon Mound No. 1 would have proved contributory negligence as well as negligence, whereas this charge of contributory negligence would not lie against the shipowners who are plaintiffs in Wagon Mound No. 2. Lord Reid adds, at 642–644, that there was no justification whatever for not stopping the oil from discharging into the harbor.

PETITION OF KINSMAN TRANSIT CO., 338 F.2d 708 (2d Cir.1964). Friendly, J., in a case where two ships crashed into a lowered drawbridge and blocked the channel, causing flooding:

We see no reason why an actor engaging in conduct which entails a large risk of small damage and a small risk of other and greater damage, of the same general sort, from the same forces, and to the same class of persons, should be relieved of responsibility for the latter simply because the chance of its occurrence, if viewed alone, may not have been large enough to require the exercise of care. By hypothesis, the risk of the lesser harm was sufficient to render his disregard of it actionable; the existence of a less likely additional risk * * * should inculpate him further rather than limit his liability. This does not mean that the careless actor will always be held for all damages for which the forces that he risked were a cause in fact. Somewhere a point will be reached when courts will agree that the link has become too tenuous— that what is claimed to be consequence is only fortuity. * * * Where the line will be drawn will vary from age to age; as society has come to rely increasingly on insurance and other methods of loss-sharing, the point may lie further off than a century ago. Here it is surely more equitable that the losses from the operators' negligent failure to raise the Michigan Avenue Bridge should be ratably borne by Buffalo's taxpayers than left with the innocent victims of the flooding * * *.

Moore, J., dissenting, "cannot agree" with Judge Friendly's comments on loss-sharing. Since "no bridge builder or bridge operator would envision a bridge as a dam," the flood claimants ought not to recover "even if the taxpayers of Buffalo are better able to bear the loss."

SECTION B.   SPECIAL PROBLEMS AND SUPERSEDING CAUSES

The first of the "special problems" that we take up is the problem of the "hypersensitive plaintiff," also known as the "eggshell" or "thin skull" plaintiff. Such plaintiffs are "abnormal" in a particular way: Injuries which inflict only modest harm on "normal" people inflict exceptionally great harm on the hypersensitive. Hemophiliacs, for example, can bleed to death from cuts which would merely annoy an ordinary person. Hypersensitive plaintiffs thus present special problems for "proximate cause" doctrine because they suffer exceptionally extensive injuries. "Proximate cause" cases involving such plaintiffs are striking in other ways as well. First, harms to the hypersensitive involve misfortune much more than malfeasance. Neither the plaintiff nor the defendant is usually culpably responsible for the plaintiff's extraordinary susceptibility to harm, but one of them must bear the financial cost of that susceptibility. Second, harms to the hypersensitive highlight the differences between the "foreseeability" and "directness" tests of liability. The extent of the hypersensitive plaintiff's injury is generally both unforeseeable and directly caused by the defendant. The basic tests for extent of liability point towards opposite conclusions.

The negligence law of duty and breach is not, as we have seen, particularly favorable to people who are "abnormal." The conduct that it expects of actual people is largely determined by what may fairly be expected of the "average reasonable person." In this, negligence law on duty and breach is of a piece with the intentional tort law that we have studied, which is equally inclined to prefer "objective" standards of conduct. Conduct cannot constitute a battery unless it is offensive to a "reasonable person's" sense of dignity, nor an assault unless it frightens a reasonable person. Proximate cause doctrine on hypersensitive plaintiffs is an exception to this theme. Abnormally sensitive plaintiffs generally fare well when the extent of liability—not the existence of duty or the occurrence of breach—is at issue.

WATSON v. RHEINDERKNECHT
Supreme Court of Minnesota, 1901.
82 Minn. 235, 84 N.W. 798.

COLLINS, J. Civil action to recover damages alleged to have been sustained by plaintiff by reason of an assault and battery committed by the defendant. The verdict was for the latter, and from an order denying plaintiff a new trial this appeal was taken. * * *

The court also erred in some of its rulings when receiving testimony. The defendant, young and vigorous, received no injuries, while the plaintiff, a feeble man in the neighborhood of sixty years of age, was so injured that he was unable to leave his house for two weeks, and during that time was daily attended by a physician. In 1863, while serving in the army, he had been injured by the explosion of a shell, for which injury he was receiving a pension at the time of the assault and battery. His counsel attempted to show as part of his case the physical condition he was in just prior to the assault arising from this injury, and how and to what extent his condition had been affected by the acts of the defendant. The court held this evidence inadmissible * * *, and refused to permit plaintiff to show whether his condition at the time of the trial was due to injuries for which defendant was responsible.

The burden was upon the plaintiff to prove such of his injuries as were the direct and proximate result of defendant's act, and in doing this it was proper to show in what respect, and to what extent, his present condition could be attributed to the assault and battery, and what could be more properly established as the result of his army experience. The injury for which plaintiff was receiving a pension affected his health and enfeebled him unquestionably, but that fact would not deprive him of the right to recover the direct consequences of the defendant's tort—to recover such damages as could be shown to be the direct result of that wrong. That the plaintiff was in ill health, no matter what the cause, was no excuse for defendant's acts, and would not relieve him from resulting consequences. The defendant could not be held to respond for injuries arising out of other causes, but as to those for which he was the efficient cause an action would lie.

The rule is that the perpetrator of a tort is responsible for the direct and immediate consequences thereof, whether they may be regarded as natural or probable, or whether they might have been contemplated, foreseen, or expected, or not. It is not necessary, to the liability of a wrongdoer, that the result which actually follows should have been anticipated by him. It is the general character of the act, and not the general result, that the law primarily regards in this connection. 8 Am. & Eng.Enc., 2d Ed., 598, 602, and cases cited. This rule has been adopted in this state in an action for personal injuries arising out of the negligence of a common carrier, Purcell v. St. Paul City Ry. Co., 48 Minn. 134, 139, 50 N.W. 1034, where it was said:

> But when the act or omission is negligence as to any and all passengers, well or ill, any one injured by the negligence must be entitled to recover to the full extent of the injury so caused, without regard to whether, owing to his previous condition of health, he is more or less liable to injury.

It was error to exclude testimony tending to show that the injuries received by the plaintiff in the army had been aggravated, intensified, and increased by reason of the defendant's unlawful act, and to just what extent. * * *

Order reversed, and a new trial granted.

————

SMITH v. LEECH BRAIN & CO., [1962] 2 Q.B. 405. Owing to his employer's negligence Smith was exposed to a splash of molten metal that burned him on the lip. The minor lip wound developed into cancer; the cancer metastasized and caused Smith's death. At the time of the burn Smith had a pre-malignant condition, evidently traceable to previous employment in gasworks, creating a strong likelihood that at some stage of his life he would develop cancer. On the other hand, but for the trauma of the burn, cancer might never have developed. In a wrongful death action brought by Smith's widow, *held*, for plaintiff. Lord Parker, C. J., said:

> * * * I am quite satisfied that * * * the *Wagon Mound* case did not have what I may call, loosely, the thin skull cases in mind. It has always been the law of this country that a tortfeasor takes his victim as he finds him. It is unnecessary to do more than refer to the short passage in the decision of Kennedy J. in Dulieu v. White & Sons, [[1901] 2 K.B. 669], where he said: "If a man is negligently run over or otherwise negligently injured in his body, it is no answer to the sufferer's claim for damages that he would have suffered less injury, or no injury at all, if he had not had an unusually thin skull or an unusually weak heart."

> * * * [T]he work of the courts for years and years has gone on on that basis. There is not a day that goes by where some trial judge does not adopt that principle, that the tortfeasor takes his victim as he finds him. * * *

> * * * The [judges in *Wagon Mound*] were not, I think, saying that a man is only liable for the extent of damage which he could anticipate, always assuming the type of injury could have been anticipated. * * *

> In those circumstances, it seems to me that this is plainly a case which comes within the old principle. The test is not whether these employers could reasonably have foreseen that a burn would cause cancer and that he would die. The question is whether these employers could reasonably foresee the type of injury he suffered, namely, the burn. What, in the particular case, is the amount of damage which he

suffers as a result of that burn, depends upon the characteristics and constitution of the victim.

At the foot of the opinion the reporter notes that, in awarding damages, "His Lordship * * * observed that he must make a substantial reduction from the figure taken for the dependency because of the fact that the plaintiff's husband might have developed cancer even if he had not suffered the burn."

DEROSIER v. NEW ENGLAND TELEPHONE & TELEGRAPH CO., 81 N.H. 451, 463, 130 A. 145, 152 (1925). SNOW, J. "In determining how far the law will trace causation and afford a remedy, the facts as to the defendant's intent, his imputable knowledge, or his justifiable ignorance are often taken into account. The moral element is here the factor that has turned close cases one way or the other. For an intended injury the law is astute to discover even very remote causation. For one which the defendant merely ought to have anticipated it has often stopped at an earlier stage of the investigation of causal connection."

POOLE v. COPLAND, INC., 348 N.C. 260, 498 S.E.2d 602 (1998). At trial, plaintiff recovered damages for intentional infliction of emotional distress on the basis of a coworker's sexual harassment of her. Plaintiff alleged that, because she had been sexually abused as a child, her coworker's harassment triggered painful flashbacks and caused her to suffer especially severe emotional distress. *Held*, affirmed. Under the "thin skull rule," plaintiff was entitled to "recover the full extent of her damages," even though those damages were greater than normal because of plaintiff's "peculiar susceptibility to matters that cause severe emotional distress." "We presume" that the jury followed the trial court's instructions and found that the coworker's "wrongful actions under the same or similar circumstances could reasonably have been expected to injure a person of ordinary mental condition."

SCOTT v. SHEPHERD, 2 Wm.Bl. 892, 96 Eng.Rep. 525 (1773). Action of trespass. Plea not guilty. The defendant threw a lighted squib into the market house in which was a crowd. It fell near Willis, who, to prevent harm to himself, threw it across the house, where it fell near Ryal, who instantly threw it to another part, where it struck the plaintiff and exploded, injuring him. *Held*, for plaintiff.

CAUSATION AND AGENCY

The facts of *Scott v. Shepherd* raise a question: Might the actions of Willis and Ryal in passing on the "lighted squib" have intervened in the chain of causation connecting Shepherd's action to Scott's injury, thereby cutting of Shepherd's liability to Scott? This is the problem of "superseding cause," which we shall confront directly in short order. The *Scott* court, however, answers the question of superseding cause without explicitly addressing it: The court simply holds Shepherd liable. The cases which follow press the questions raised by the agency of persons other than the defendant closer to the surface. In these cases the intentional agency of either plaintiffs or third persons is arguably, causally and culpably responsible for plaintiffs' injuries. Note that in these cases, too, we can see the continuing contrast between the foreseeability and directness tests of liability.

WAGNER v. INTERNATIONAL RAILWAY

Court of Appeals of New York, 1921.
232 N.Y. 176, 133 N.E. 437, 19 A.L.R. 1.

CARDOZO, J. The action is for personal injuries.

The defendant operates an electric railway between Buffalo and Niagara Falls. There is a point on its line where an overhead crossing carries its tracks above those of the New York Central and the Erie. A gradual incline upwards over a trestle raises the tracks to a height of twenty-five feet. A turn is then made to the left at an angle of from sixty-four to eighty-four degrees. After making this turn, the line passes over a bridge which is about one hundred and fifty-eight feet long from one abutment to the other. Then comes a turn to the right at about the same angle down the same kind of an incline to grade. Above the trestles, the tracks are laid on ties, unguarded at the ends. There is thus an overhang of the cars, which is accentuated at curves. On the bridge, a narrow footpath runs between the tracks, and beyond the line of overhang there are tie rods and a protecting rail.

Plaintiff and his cousin Herbert boarded a car at a station near the bottom of one of the trestles. Other passengers, entering at the same time, filled the platform, and blocked admission to the aisle. The platform was provided with doors, but the conductor did not close them. Moving at from six to eight miles an hour, the car, without slackening, turned the curve. There was a violent lurch, and Herbert Wagner was thrown out, near the point where the trestle changes to a bridge. The cry was raised, "Man overboard." The car went on across the bridge, and stopped near the foot of the incline. Night and darkness had come on. Plaintiff walked along the trestle, a distance of four hundred and forty-five feet, until he arrived at the bridge, where he thought to find his cousin's body. He says that he was asked to go there by the conductor. He says, too, that the conductor followed with a lantern. Both of these statements the conductor denies. Several other persons, instead of ascending the trestle, went beneath it, and discovered under the bridge the body they were seeking. As they stood there, the plaintiff's body struck the ground beside them. Reaching the bridge, he had found upon a beam his cousin's hat, but nothing else. About him, there was darkness. He missed his footing, and fell.

The trial judge held that negligence toward Herbert Wagner would not charge the defendant with liability for the injuries suffered by the plaintiff unless two other facts were found: First, that the plaintiff had been invited by the conductor to go upon the bridge; and second, that the conductor had followed with a light. Thus limited, the jury found in favor of the defendant [and the Appellate Division affirmed the judgment entered thereon]. Whether the limitation may be upheld, is the question to be answered.

Danger invites rescue. The cry of distress is the summons to relief. The law does not ignore the reactions of the mind in tracing conduct to its consequences. It recognizes them as normal. It places their effects within the range of the natural and probable. The wrong that imperils life is a wrong to the imperiled victim; it is a wrong also to his rescuer. The state that leaves an opening in a bridge is liable to the child that falls into the stream, but liable also to the parent who plunges to its aid. The railroad company whose train approaches without signal is a wrongdoer toward the traveler surprised between the rails, but a wrongdoer also to the bystander who drags him from the path. [Citations omitted.] Cf. 1 Beven on Negligence, 157, 158. The risk of rescue, if only it be not wanton, is born of the occasion. The emergency begets the man. The wrongdoer may not have foreseen the coming of a deliverer. He is as accountable as if he had. Ehrgott v. Mayor, etc., of N.Y., 96 N.Y. 264, 48 Am.Rep. 622.

The defendant says that we must stop, in following the chain of causes, when action ceases to be "instinctive." By this is meant, it seems, that rescue is at the peril of the rescuer, unless spontaneous and immediate. If there has been time to deliberate, if impulse has given way to judgment, one cause, it is said, has spent its force, and another has intervened. In this case, the plaintiff walked more than four hundred feet in going to Herbert's aid. He had time to reflect and weigh; impulse has been followed by choice; and choice, in the defendant's view, intercepts and breaks the sequence. We find no warrant for thus shortening the chain of jural causes. We may assume, though we are not required to decide, that peril and rescue must be in substance one transaction; that the sight of the one must have aroused the impulse to the other; in short, that there must be unbroken continuity between the commission of the wrong and the effort to avert its consequences. If all this be assumed, the defendant is not aided. Continuity in such circumstances is not broken by the exercise of volition. So sweeping an exception, if recognized, would leave little of the rule. "The human mind", as we have said, People v. Majone, 91 N.Y. 211, 212, "acts with celerity which it is impossible sometimes to measure." The law does not discriminate between the rescuer oblivious of peril and the one who counts the cost. It is enough that the act, whether impulsive or deliberate, is the child of the occasion.

The defendant finds another obstacle, however, in the futility of the plaintiff's sacrifice. He should have gone, it is said, below the trestle with the others; he should have known, in view of the overhang of the cars, that the body would not be found above; his conduct was not responsive to the call of the emergency; it was a wanton exposure to a danger that was useless. We think the quality of his acts in the situation that confronted him was to be determined by the jury. Certainly he believed that good would come of his search upon the bridge. He was not going there to view the landscape. The law cannot say of his belief that a reasonable man would have been unable to share it. He could not know the precise point at which his cousin had fallen from the car. If the fall was from the bridge, there was no reason why the body, caught by some projection, might not be hanging on high, athwart the tie rods or the beams. Certainly no such reason was then apparent to the plaintiff, or so a jury might have found. Indeed, his judgment was confirmed by the finding of the hat. There was little time for delay, if the facts were as he states them. Another car was due, and the body, if not removed, might be ground beneath the wheels. The plaintiff had to choose at once, in agitation and with imperfect knowledge. He had seen his kinsman and companion thrown out into the darkness. Rescue could not charge the company with liability if rescue was condemned by reason. "Errors of judgment", however, would not count against him, if they resulted "from the excitement and confusion of the moment." Corbin v. City of Philadelphia, 195 Pa. 461, 472, 45 A. 1070, 49 L.R.A. 715, 78 Am.St.Rep. 825. The reason that was exacted of him was not the reason of the morrow. It was reason fitted and proportioned to the time and the event.

Whether Herbert Wagner's fall was due to the defendant's negligence, and whether plaintiff in going to the rescue, as he did, was foolhardy or reasonable in the light of the emergency confronting him, were questions for the jury.

The judgment of the Appellate Division and that of the Trial Term should be reversed, and a new trial granted, with costs to abide the event.

CARNEY v. BUYEA, 271 App.Div. 338, 65 N.Y.S.2d 902 (1946); noted in 16 Fordham L.Rev. 139; 32 Corn.L.Q. 605; 45 Mich.L.Rev. 918; 25 Tex.L.Rev. 688. Defendant started her car and left it on a slight incline with the engine running, to pick up a bottle lying in the path of the car. Apparently the car was not sufficiently braked and it started. The plaintiff, a bystander, finding that the defendant was oblivious to her peril, pushed her out of the path of the approaching car to safety and was himself hurt. At the trial term the plaintiff obtained judgment. *Held,* judgment affirmed. One who carelessly exposes himself to danger in a place where others may be expected to be commits a wrongful act towards them, as it exposes them to a recognizable risk of injury.

LYNCH v. FISHER, 34 So.2d 513 (La.App.1947). Plaintiff alleges that defendant Fisher negligently parked his truck on the road without lights; that defendant Gunter ran into it; that plaintiff, seeing the collision, went to help the Gunters from their burning car; that, finding a pistol on the floor of the car, he handed it to Gunter, who being delirious and temporarily mentally deranged by the shock of the accident, fired the pistol at the plaintiff, wounding him. The trial court sustained exceptions of no cause of action filed by all defendants. *Held,* judgment reversed and remanded. There was no break in the continuity of incidents. Because of the peculiar circumstances the general doctrine of foreseeability is not applicable. Under the allegations, Fisher's conduct was a substantial factor and Gunter's insanity no excuse, being induced by his own negligence. [In a second appeal, 41 So.2d 692 (La.App.1949), judgment against Fisher was affirmed;

that against Gunter was reversed on the ground that under the evidence he was not negligent.]

PURCHASE v. SEELYE, 231 Mass. 434, 121 N.E. 413, 8 A.L.R. 503 (1918). The plaintiff was injured by the negligence of a railroad company and was treated by the defendant, a surgeon, who, mistaking him for another patient, performed an operation on the wrong side. The plaintiff released his claim against the railroad. *Held,* sustaining exceptions to a verdict directed for defendant, that the release to the railroad did not bar the present action, since the railroad was not liable for the harm resulting from the defendant's mistake. "In an action for personal injuries arising out of the alleged negligence of the defendant, the plaintiff is entitled to recover for the injuries resulting from the defendant's negligence, although such injuries are aggravated by the negligence of an attending physician if, in his selection and employment, the plaintiff was in the exercise of reasonable care. * * * Such unskillful treatment is a result which reasonably ought to have been anticipated." In the instant case, however, "the railroad company could not be held liable because of the defendant's mistaken belief that he was operating upon some person other than the plaintiff. Such a mistake was not an act of negligence which could be found to flow legitimately as a natural and probable consequence of the original injury."

———

EXXON CORP. v. BRECHEEN, 526 S.W.2d 519 (Tex.1975). Action by widow of driver of tanker truck who had been sprayed with gasoline at refinery and, after filing suit, committed suicide with a rifle. The trial court entered judgment on a verdict in favor of the widow, and the refinery appealed. *Held,* though reversing and remanding on other points, the trial court correctly denied the refinery's contention that the evidence failed to establish that Brecheen acted without conscious volition and under an uncontrollable impulse. A review of authorities discloses a noticeable trend from the strict view that a suicide is not a result naturally and reasonably to be expected or foreseen from a negligently inflicted injury to the broader view that there may be liability if the negligent wrong causes mental illness which results in an uncontrollable impulse to commit suicide or—citing Restatement (Second) of Torts § 455 (1965)—"prevents him from realizing the nature of his act and the certainty or risk of harm involved therein."

BRUZGA v. PMR ARCHITECTS, 141 N.H. 756, 693 A.2d 401 (1997). " 'As a general rule, negligence actions seeking damages for the suicide of another will not lie because the act of suicide is considered a deliberate, intentional and intervening act which precludes a finding that a given defendant, in fact, is responsible for the harm.' *McLaughlin v. Sullivan,* 123 N.H. 335, 337, 461 A.2d 123, 124 (1983). This is because the act of suicide 'breaks the causal connection between the wrongful or negligent act and the death.' *Mayer v. Town of Hampton,* 127 N.H. 81, 84, 497 A.2d 1206, 1209 (1985). A number of jurisdictions, however, have delineated two exceptions to the general rule. *Id.*

" 'The first exception recognizes a cause of action where the defendant actually causes the suicide.' *Murdock v. City of Keene,* 137 N.H. 70, 72, 623 A.2d 755, 756 (1993). We adopted the first exception in *Mayer,* 127 N.H. at 87, 497 A.2d at 1210–11. A defendant may be found liable 'where the conduct of the defendant was an intentional tort and extreme and outrageous, and where this conduct caused severe emotional distress on the part of the victim which was a substantial factor in bringing about the victim's ensuing suicide.' *Id.* at 88, 497 A.2d at 1211. * * *

"The second exception recognizes a cause of action where the defendant has 'a specific duty of care to prevent suicide,' arising from the defendant's 'special relationship with the suicidal individual.' *McLaughlin,* 123 N.H. at 338, 461 A.2d at 125; *see Murdock,* 137 N.H. at 73, 623 A.2d at 756. In *McLaughlin,* we stated:

> [T]his duty has been imposed on: (1) institutions such as jails, hospitals and reform schools, having actual physical custody of and control over persons; and (2) persons or institutions such as mental hospitals, psychiatrists and other mental-health trained professionals, deemed to have a special training and expertise enabling them to detect mental illness and/or the potential for suicide, and which have the power or control necessary to prevent that suicide."

SUPERSEDING CAUSE

Problems of superseding cause arise when the act of a third person (or some other force) intervenes in the chain of causation connecting the defendant's wrongdoing to the plaintiff's injury. This circumstance raises the question: Does the intervening act of the third person "supersede" the defendant's wrongdoing, abrogating the defendant's responsibility for the harm suffered by the plaintiff? This question, which has been with us since *Scott v. Shepherd,* is taken up directly in *McLaughlin v. Mine Safety Appliances.* The defendant in *McLaughlin* argues not that it is free of negligence in its own right, but that the subsequent negligence of a third person cuts off its responsibility for plaintiff's injury.

McLAUGHLIN v. MINE SAFETY APPLIANCES CO.

Court of Appeals of New York, 1962.
11 N.Y.2d 62, 226 N.Y.S.2d 407, 181 N.E.2d 430.

[Plaintiff, a 6–year-old girl, nearly drowned, and a fire department rescue truck came to the scene. A woman identifying herself as a nurse volunteered her help. After the child was wrapped in blankets more heat was needed. A fireman went to the fire truck, returned with boxes containing "M–S–A Redi–Heat Blocks" (of which defendant was the exclusive distributor), removed them from their containers, activated them, and turned them over to the nurse. She applied several of them directly to the child's body under the blankets. The child later began to heave and moan.

She was taken to a car and placed on the back seat, still wrapped in the blankets, the heat blocks having fallen out. That evening, blisters were observed about her body, which were found to be third degree burns caused by the heat blocks. The instructions on the container included the following sentence: "Wrap in insulating medium, such as pouch, towel, blanket or folded cloth." Defendant's representative, at the time of sale of the blocks to the fire department, demonstrated the proper mode of use and warned that the heat block was to be covered with a towel or other material to avoid contact with the skin. The fireman who activated the blocks on the occasion in suit was present at that demonstration, four or five years earlier. Verdict and judgment for plaintiffs. The Appellate Division reversed and ordered a new trial unless plaintiffs would stipulate for reduced damages, in which case the judgment was to be affirmed. Plaintiffs so stipulated, and defendant appealed.]

FOSTER, Judge. [After discussing the evidence of negligence.] But the true problem presented in this case is one of proximate causation, and not one concerning the general duty to warn or negligence of the distributor. In this regard the trial court instructed the jury that the defendant would not be liable if "an actual warning was conveyed to the person or persons applying the blocks that they should be wrapped in insulation of some kind before being placed against the body" for in that event the "failure to heed that warning would be a new cause which intervened." Subsequently, and after the jury retired, they returned and asked this question: "Your Honor, if we, the jury, find that the M.S.A. Company was negligent in not making any warning of danger on the heat block itself, but has given proper instructions in its use up to the point of an intervening circumstance (the nurse who was not properly instructed), is the M.S.A. Company liable?"

The trial court answered as follows: "Ladies and gentlemen of the jury, if you find from the evidence that the defendant, as a reasonably prudent person under all of the circumstances should have expected use of the block by some person other than those to whom instruction as to its use had been given, either by the wording on the container or otherwise, and that under those circumstances a reasonably prudent person would have placed warning words on the heat block itself, and if you find in addition to that that the nurse was not warned at the scene and that a reasonably prudent person in the position of the nurse, absent any warning on the block itself, would have proceeded to use it without inquiry as to the proper method of use, then the defendant would be liable." Counsel for the defendant excepted to that statement. The jury then returned its verdict for the plaintiffs.

From the jury's question, it is obvious that they were concerned with the effect of the fireman's knowledge that the blocks should have been wrapped, and his apparent failure to so advise the nurse who applied the blocks in his presence. The court in answering the jury's question instructed, in essence, that the defendant could still be liable, even though the fireman had knowledge of the need for further insulation, if it was reasonably foreseeable that the blocks absent the containers, would find their way from the firemen to unwarned third persons.

We think that the instruction, as applied to the facts of this case, was erroneous. In the cases discussed above, the manufacturer or distributor failed to warn the original vendee of the latent danger, and there were no additional acts of negligence intervening between the failure to warn and the resulting injury or damage. This was not such a case, or at least the jury could find that it was not. Nor was this simply a case involving the negligent failure of the vendee to inspect and discover the danger; in such a case the intervening negligence of the immediate vendee does not necessarily insulate the manufacturer from liability to third persons, nor supersede the negligence of the manufacturer in failing to warn of the danger.

In the case before us, the jury obviously believed that the fireman, Traxler, had actual knowledge of the need for further insulation, and the jury was preoccupied with the effect of his failure to warn the nurse as she applied the blocks to the plaintiff's person. The jury also could have believed that Traxler removed the blocks from the containers, thereby depriving the nurse of *any* opportunity she might have had to read the instructions printed on the containers, and that Traxler actually activated the blocks, turned them over, uninsulated, to the nurse for her use, and stood idly by as they were placed directly on the plaintiff's wet skin.

Under the circumstances, we think the court should have charged that if the fireman did so conduct himself, without warning the nurse, his negligence was so gross as to supersede the negligence of the defendant and to insulate it from liability. This is the rule that prevails when knowledge of the latent danger or defect is *actually* possessed by the original vendee, who then deliberately passes on the product to a third person without warning.

In short, whether or not the distributor furnished ample warning on his product to third persons in general was not important here, if the jury believed that Traxler had actual notice of the danger by virtue of his presence at demonstration classes or otherwise, and that he deprived the nurse of her opportunity to read the instructions prior to applying the blocks. While the distributor might have been liable if the blocks had found their way into the hands of the nurse in a more innocent fashion, the distributor could not be expected to foresee that its demonstrations to the firemen would callously be disregarded by a member of the department. We have indicated that knowledge of the danger possessed by the original purchaser, knowledge actually brought home to him, might protect the manufacturer or distributor from liability to third persons harmed by the failure of the purchaser to warn, where the purchaser had the means and opportunity to do so. * * *

Here, the jury might have found that the fireman not only had the means to warn the nurse, but further that, by his actions, he prevented any warning from reaching her, and, indeed, that he actually had some part in the improper application of the blocks. Such conduct could not have been foreseen by the defendant.

The judgment should be reversed and a new trial granted, with costs to abide the event.

VAN VOORHIS, Judge (dissenting). The recovery by plaintiff should not, as it seems to us, be reversed on account of lack of foreseeability or a break in the chain of causation due to any intervening act of negligence on the part of a volunteer fireman. These heat blocks were dangerous instrumentalities unless wrapped in "insulating" media, "such as pouch, towel, blanket or folded cloth" as the instructions on the container directed. What happened here was that the container, with the instructions on it, was thrown away, and the nurse who applied the heat block was unaware of this safety requirement. In our minds the circumstance that the fireman who knew of the danger failed to warn the nurse, even if negligent, did not affect the fact, as the jury found it, that this was a risk which the manufacturer of the heat block ought to have anticipated in the exercise of reasonable care, nor intercept the chain of causation. The jury found by their verdict that a duty was imposed on the manufacturer to inscribe the warning on the heat block for the reason that in the exercise of reasonable care it should have anticipated that the warning written on the container might be lost or discarded under circumstances similar to those surrounding this injury.

The rule is not absolute that it is not necessary to anticipate the negligence or even the crime of another. It has been said in the Restatement of Torts (§ 449): "If the realizable likelihood that a third person may act in a particular manner is the hazard or one of the hazards which makes the actor negligent, such an act whether innocent, negligent, intentionally tortious or criminal does not prevent the actor from being liable for harm caused thereby." It is further provided by section 447: "The fact that an intervening act of a third person is negligent in itself or is done in a negligent manner does not make it a superseding cause of harm to another which the actor's negligent conduct is a substantial factor in bringing about, if (a) the actor at the time of his negligent conduct should have realized that a third person might so act."

The judgment appealed from should be affirmed.

SUBSEQUENT INTENTIONAL WRONGDOING

McLaughlin involves prior and subsequent acts of negligence. The cases that follow involve initial negligence and subsequent intentional—indeed criminal—wrongdoing.

———

STATE v. DIERKER, 961 S.W.2d 58 (Mo.1998). "Olga Maxiaeva was driving home in the early hours of February 20, 1995, in St. Louis. As she drove under the Clayton Avenue overpass, fifteen-year-old Shawn Twine dropped a twenty-pound chunk of concrete onto Maxiaeva's car, killing her. Shawn Twine later pleaded guilty to the charge of involuntary manslaughter." Maxiaeva's estate subsequently brought suit against the Missouri Highway Commission, alleging that they had created a "dangerous condition" by "leaving loose pieces of concrete" on the overpass and failing to fence it adequately.

Held, reversing the Circuit Court, summary judgment should have been granted in favor of the Highway Commission. "Although the conditions of the overpass 'had some connection' to [Maxiaeva's] death, Twine intervened to break the chain of causation." His criminal act was the "direct" cause of her death. The condition of the overpass " 'presaged' " the commission of the crime "only 'in some remote way.' " "It would be unreasonable to subject the Commission to suit for the damages caused by this manslaughter." White, J, dissented. Whether "the Commission's alleged negligence set into motion the chain of events that caused the injury" was a matter of "genuine dispute" on the pleadings and hence a question for the jury to decide, "after both sides had an opportunity to present evidence on causation."

KOZICKI v. DRAGON, 583 N.W.2d 336 (Neb.1998). Plaintiff was injured when a stolen car owned by defendant ran a stop sign and collided with her. Fifteeen-year-old Jamie L. Jacobsen, who ran into Kozicki, had stolen the car earlier that morning, when "Dragon left his car unlocked and running while he went back inside his home to get ready for work." Dragon's actions violated Neb.Rev.Stat. § 60–6, 168 (Reissue 1993), which prohibits "leaving an unattended vehicle on the roadway, unlocked and with the keys in the ignition." In her complaint, Kozicki alleged that Dragon was negligent not only in violating the statute, but also in "leaving his automobile running, unlocked, unattended, and out of his view on the street in front of his house in a high-crime area;" and in "failing to take any measure to prevent theft of his automobile when he knew or should have known that there was an unreasonable risk that the automobile would be stolen and driven in such manner as to cause injury or damage to the person and/or property of innocent parties such as Kozicki." The trial court granted Dragon's motion for summary judgment, "concluding that Dragon's acts or omissions did not proximately cause injury to Kozicki as a matter of law." *Held*, reversed and remanded. "[W]hether Dragon did or reasonably should have foreseen that thieves are more negligent at the wheel than are ordinary citizens" was "a question of fact for the jury. * * * [S]ummary judgment was inappropriate."

In light of the statute forbidding leaving a key in the ignition of an unlocked and unattended motor vehicle, there was "no question that Dragon owed Kozicki a duty." The only question was whether Jacobsen's actions constituted "an efficient intervening cause." "An efficient intervening cause is a new, independent force intervening between the defendant's negligent act and the plaintiff's injury by the negligence of a third person who had full control of the situation, whose negligence the defendant could not anticipate or contemplate, and whose negligence resulted directly in the plaintiff's injury. [citation omitted] Thus, an intervening act that is reasonably foreseeable by the defendant does not preclude the defendant's liability. [citation omitted] The question whether the negligence of a third person constitutes an intervening cause is a question of fact [citation omitted]."

"In the instant case, the plaintiff alleged in her petition that the '[d]efendant knew, or reasonably should have foreseen, that if his automobile was stolen ... it would be operated in a negligent, careless, or reckless manner.' Polikov's affidavit clearly states, '[E]xperience has shown that car thieves are not 'responsible drivers.' The affidavit also described public education efforts and stated that 'widespread media attention and public education efforts of law enforcement agencies and others have increased public awareness of . . . the stolen vehicle being wrecked' and that 'a stolen car operated on the public streets in Omaha, Nebraska, is at an increased risk of motor vehicle collision especially when it is being operated by a juvenile driver or if it should become involved in a police chase.' Moreover, data attached to the affidavit indicated that juveniles account for 53 percent of all arrests for motor vehicle theft, and Jacobsen described how she had wrecked several of the cars that she had previously stolen."

HINES, DIRECTOR GENERAL OF RAILROADS v. GARRETT, 131 Va. 125, 108 S.E. 690 (1921). Noted, 35 Harv.L.Rev. 467. The plaintiff, a girl of 18, was carried four-fifths of a mile past her station shortly before dark. She got off the train and on the way back she was twice raped at a place described as "Hobo Hollow." *Held,* although reversing judgment for plaintiff for error in instructions, that if the plaintiff was wrongfully ejected, "the very negligence alleged consists of exposing [her] to the act causing the injury."

LIBERTY NATIONAL LIFE INSURANCE CO. v. WELDON, 267 Ala. 171, 100 So.2d 696, 61 A.L.R.2d 1346 (1957). An infant, less than two years old, was murdered by her aunt-in-law (the widow of a brother of the infant's mother). Prior to the murder the aunt-in-law had applied for and obtained, from the three defendant insurance companies, insurance policies of $500, $1,000 and $5,000 on the infant's life in which the aunt-in-law was named as beneficiary. The infant's father brought a wrongful death action on the theory that negligence of the insurance companies in issuing these policies to the aunt-in-law, who was without insurable interest, supplied her with a motive for murder and was a legal cause of the infant's death. A judgment of $75,000 for the plaintiff was entered by the trial court. *Held,* affirmed. An insurance company is under a duty to use reasonable care not to issue a policy of life insurance to one without insurable interest. The relationship, standing alone, did not establish an insurable interest, and the evidence was sufficient to sustain findings of negligence and want of insurable interest. We cannot say as a matter of law that the intervening criminal act of murder was not reasonably foreseeable to defendants, who "created a situation of a kind which this court and others have consistently said affords temptation to a recognizable percentage of humanity to commit murder." "The question of proximate cause was properly left for the jury's determination."

SHERIDAN v. UNITED STATES, 487 U.S. 392, 108 S.Ct. 2449, 101 L.Ed.2d 352 (1988). Justice Kennedy, concurring in the judgment, stated the "basic rule" applicable to an injury arising from more than one wrongful act. " 'If the likelihood of the intervening act was one of the hazards that made defendant's conduct negligent—that is, if it was sufficiently foreseeable to have this effect—then defendant will generally be liable for the consequences . . . So far as scope of duty . . . is concerned, it should make no difference whether the intervening actor is negligent or intentional or criminal.' 2 F. Harper & F. James, Law of Torts, § 20.5, pp. 1143–1145 (1956) (footnotes omitted).''

SUPERSEDING CAUSE AND COMPARATIVE NEGLIGENCE

McLaughlin arose in the era of contributory negligence, with its "all or nothing" approach to liability. The rise of comparative negligence invites the blurring of the bright lines of traditional superseding cause doctrine.

GODESKY v. PROVO CITY

Supreme Court of Utah, 1984.
690 P.2d 541.

J. DENNIS FREDERICK, District Judge [sitting to fill a vacancy on the court]:

Plaintiff suffered personal injuries while working as part of a roofing crew in Provo, Utah. He brought suit against three defendants, one of whom was dismissed prior to trial. The jury returned a verdict against the remaining two defendants, Provo City and Monticello Investors, for approximately $1.6 million. Only Provo pursues this appeal, contending that the trial court erred (1) in applying the legal standard of superseding causation, (2) by improperly instructing the jury in several respects * * *. We find no error prejudicial to defendant, and we therefore affirm.

I. Facts

In August of 1978, plaintiff was traveling through Provo on his way to the West Coast in search of employment as a stained-glass artist. With his money running low, plaintiff sought temporary employment. He was hired by Pride Roofing Company to work on a two- or three-day roof repair at defendant Monticello's apartment building. Plaintiff had no experience in the roofing business.

The building has a flat asphalt roof. The job consisted of removing the old asphalt and replacing it with fresh asphalt. There were two wires that cut diagonally across the corner of the building; one was three feet above the roof, and the other was nine and one-half feet above the roof and parallel to the lower wire. The first day on the job, plaintiff contacted the lower wire numerous times without incident since the wire was not charged with electricity. He did not notice the second wire. Plaintiff had no experience with electrical wires.

On the second day, the lower wire interfered with the progress of the job. One of plaintiff's supervisors told plaintiff to "tie off" the lower wire to the upper wire. A rope was thrown over the top wire, and the wire was pulled down within plaintiff's reach so that it could be lashed to the lower wire. When he grasped the top wire with both hands, he received a shock of 2,400 volts. During the course of medical care, plaintiff underwent four amputation operations, one skin graft operation, and brain surgery to relieve an abscess. At the conclusion of the operations, both of plaintiff's arms were amputated below the elbows. At the time of trial, plaintiff still suffered from loss of use and control of his left side and from pain. At trial, contrary to defendants' theory of the case, the jury determined that plaintiff was not negligent.

Defendant Provo City owned and operated the electrical system that included the wire grasped by plaintiff. The wire was uninsulated and "hot"—it carried 2,400 volts and led directly to a transformer on a pole approximately six feet from the roof. The transformer was obscured by a tree, and plaintiff testified that he never noticed it. The wire and the lower unelectrified ground wire were installed in the 1960s by Provo over the then-one-story apartment building. A second story was later added to the building, which brought the wires in close proximity to the roof. Provo admitted that it had no inspection and maintenance program, that it had not recently trimmed the tree, and that there were no warning signs anywhere in the immediate vicinity (although Provo did use such signs within blocks of this location). Provo further admitted that stringing an uninsulated high-voltage wire over a residential property was contrary to its policy. Plaintiff's expert witness testified that Provo had violated four provisions of the National Electric Safety Code; defendants' expert testified that Provo complied with the minimum height provision of that Code. The jury found that Provo was negligent and 70 percent responsible for causing the accident.

Defendant Monticello owned the building. Two of Monticello's representatives, Sanchez and Gough, hired Pride to replace the roof and inspected the roof with Pride's representative. Both Sanchez and Gough knew about the transformer. Sanchez knew that the top wire was a hot power line, and Gough watched from the ground as the top wire was pulled down within plaintiff's reach. Neither warned Pride or plaintiff about the wire. No one from Monticello requested Provo to turn off the power or to otherwise abate the dangerous condition. The jury found that Monticello was negligent and 20 percent responsible for causing the accident.

Pride was not a party in this action. According to testimony, Pride's owner, Bill Ray, noticed the wires and traced them to the nearby electrical pole. He also observed the transformer. There was no testimony that Ray knew the upper wire was electrified, but he assumed that because of its height it would pose no problem. Neither of Pride's employees supervising the job knew that the wire was electrified, but both guessed it was either a lead-in wire or a telephone wire. Both assumed it was insulated. One of the two threw the rope to plaintiff and instructed him to tie the wires together. The jury found that Pride was negligent and 10 percent responsible for causing the accident.

II. Superseding Causation

Provo first cites as error the trial court's failure to rule as a matter of law that Pride's negligence was the sole proximate cause of plaintiff's injury. Provo argues that Pride, as an experienced roofer, "knew or should have known" of the danger from the wire and that Pride had a duty not to expose its employee to a dangerous condition. Provo relies on the jury's finding that Pride was negligent and was *a* proximate cause of plaintiff's injury to support its position that Pride was the sole proximate cause.

Provo is correct that an employer has a duty not to expose his employees to unreasonable dangers. Provo is also correct that a more recent negligent act may break the chain of causation and relieve the liability of a prior negligent actor under the proper circumstances. *See Watters v. Querry,* Utah, 626 P.2d 455 (1981) (*Watters II*); Restatement (Second) of Torts §§ 440–53 (1965). However, contrary to Provo's argument, proximate causation is generally a matter of fact to be determined by the jury. The case upon which Provo most relies, *Hillyard v. Utah By–Products Co.,* 1 Utah 2d 143, 263 P.2d 287 (1953), held that later negligence supersedes earlier negligence as a matter of law if the intervening negligent actor had actual knowledge of the danger but failed to avoid it. However, in the recent case of *Harris v. Utah Transit Authority,* Utah, 671 P.2d 217 (1983), we expressly overruled the portion of *Hillyard* that made such conduct the superseding cause as a matter of law and left the determination of relative fault (including causation) to the jury.

> [T]he unsound distinction made in *Hillyard* serves to frustrate the purpose of the Comparative Negligence Statute [U.C.A., 1953, § 78–27–37] by precluding the kind of comparison of fault that a jury ought to make. The allocation of liability should be made on the basis of the relative culpability of both parties. To do that the jury must assess the reasonableness or unreasonableness of the second [party's] actions in light of all the circumstances....

This is precisely what the jury did in this case. It compared the negligence of Provo, Monticello, and Pride and determined that each actor's negligence concurred to cause plaintiff's injury and that Pride's 10 percent negligence did not supersede Provo's 70 percent negligence as a matter of fact. The trial court acted properly when it refused to rule as a matter of law that Pride's negligence was the sole proximate cause of plaintiff's injury.

III.   JURY INSTRUCTION ON PROXIMATE CAUSE

Provo next claims that the trial court erred by refusing to give its proffered jury instruction on proximate cause. As a result, Provo was allegedly denied its opportunity to have the jury instructed on its theory of the case. Provo requested the following instructions:

> You are further instructed that Provo City Corporation's duty to the plaintiff was fulfilled and Provo City Corporation was not negligent if the plaintiff's employer knew, or, in the exercise of reasonable care as a roofer, should have known that the primary or top wire could be charged with electricity.

and:

> By 'proximate cause' is meant that cause which in a natural continuous sequence, *unbroken by any new cause,* produced the injury and without which the injury would not have occurred.

(Emphasis added.)

The proffered instructions are not correct statements of the law. An intervening negligent act does not automatically become a superseding cause that relieves the original actor of liability. The earlier actor is charged with the foreseeable negligent acts of others. Therefore, if the intervening negligence is foreseeable, the earlier negligent act is a concurring cause. "[T]his includes situations where negligent or other wrongful conduct of others should reasonably be anticipated." *Watters v. Querry*, Utah, 588 P.2d 702, 704 (1978) (*Watters I*). *See also Harris v. Utah Transit Authority*, 671 P.2d at 219 ("[a] person's negligence is not superseded by the negligence of another if the subsequent negligence of another is foreseeable"); Prosser, *Law of Torts* 275 (4th ed. 1971).

In *Watters II*, we concluded that the jury verdict was correct because the intervening actor therein "should have observed and avoided" the danger. However, the quoted language did not create a new standard for superseding causation; it merely analyzed the evidence in a light favorable to the jury verdict. The proper test is whether the subsequent negligence was foreseeable by the earlier actor.

* * *

[The court went on to approve the following instruction on Provo's duty of care given to the jury by the trial judge: "Provo City, as the operator of an electrical distribution system has under its control thereby, an instrumentality exceptionally dangerous in character and is bound to take exceptional precautions to prevent an injury being done by the instrumentality. The degree of care must be equal to the danger involved."]

* * *

The judgment of the trial court is affirmed.

———

BARRY v. QUALITY STEEL PRODUCTS, INC., 263 Conn. 424, 820 A.2d 258 (2003). *Held*, "it is no longer appropriate to give an instruction o[n] the doctrine of superseding cause in cases involving multiple acts of negligence." Shifting a defendant's liability for negligence entirely to the superseding conduct of a third person "has no place in our modern system of comparative fault and apportionment." "[I]t is inconsistent to conclude simultaneously that all negligent parties should pay in proportion to their fault * * * but that one negligent party does not have to pay its share because its negligence was somehow 'superseded' by a subsequent negligent act. [citation omitted]" Therefore, we now adopt an approach according to which "the fact finder need only determine whether the allegedly negligent conduct of any actor was a proximate cause, specifically, whether the conduct was a substantial factor in contributing to the plaintiff's injuries. If such conduct is found to be a proximate cause of the plaintiff's foreseeable injury, each actor will pay his or her proportionate share pursuant to our apportionment statute, regardless of whether another's conduct also contributed to the plaintiff's injury."

"DRAMSHOP" LIABILITY

The circumstance where one party provides liquor to another, who then becomes intoxicated and commits a tort, presents a classic question of superseding cause. On the one hand, the agency of the person who consumes the alcohol stands in a more immediate causal relation with the injury than the agency of the party who supplies the alcohol, and the wrongdoing of a person who permits himself to become intoxicated and then endanger others appears more egregious than the wrongdoing of the party who merely supplies the alcohol. On the other hand, the circumstances under which alcohol is provided have a powerful long-run effect on the incidence of intoxication and—unlike excessive consumption—the provision of alcohol does not lead to the loss of self-control.

———

LARGO CORP. v. CRESPIN, 727 P.2d 1098 (Colo.1986). James Hauenstein was served ten to thirteen beers at defendant's bar. While at the bar he suffered blackouts and stumbled over chairs, tables, and stairs. Shortly after leaving in his car he drove into oncoming traffic, colliding with the car driven by plaintiff's husband and killing him. Plaintiff brought a negligence suit against the tavern owner. On appeal from a verdict for plaintiff, *held,* affirmed. The Colorado Supreme Court discussed the evolution of "common-law dramshop liability," announcing that "we join the majority of jurisdictions" that have recognized such liability:

"Until the late 1950's, it was universally held that a common-law negligence action could not be brought by a third party against a tavern owner who sold alcoholic beverages to an intoxicated person. The rationale underlying the rule was that the consumption, and not the furnishing of alcohol, was the proximate cause of the injury to the third party. * * *

"The modern era of dramshop liability began in 1959, when two courts—the Seventh Circuit in *Waynick v. Chicago's Last Department Store,* 269 F.2d 322 (7th Cir.1959), and the New Jersey Supreme Court in *Rappaport v. Nichols,* 31 N.J. 188, 156 A.2d 1 (1959)—held that a third party injured by an intoxicated person may bring a negligence action against the commercial vendor who sold liquor to the intoxicated person. Both decisions rejected the defendants' contention that the sale or service of an alcoholic beverage could not, as a matter of law, be the proximate cause of injury to a third party. * * *

"Since *Waynick* and *Rappaport,* the overwhelming majority of courts have abandoned the old common-law rule and allowed negligence actions against commercial vendors of alcoholic beverages. * * *

"Any reasonable person would foresee that an intoxicated person will act with a lack of prudence, control, and self-restraint. With travel by automobile both commonplace and necessary in today's society, no one may justifiably claim ignorance of the danger posed by one whose abilities and judgment are impaired by alcohol. The harm is both likely and foreseeable, and the societal cost of alcohol-related injuries is enormous. Balancing the foreseeability, likelihood and extent of the probable injury against any conceivable 'utility' of serving an intoxicated person more alcohol than he or she can safely consume, we must conclude that a commercial vendor of alcohol owes a duty to third parties to act with reasonable care in the service of alcoholic beverages to its patrons. * * * "

SCHOOLEY v. PINCH'S DELI MARKET, 134 Wash.2d 468, 951 P.2d 749 (1998). Eighteen-year-old Lori Schooley fractured her spinal cord and became quadraplegic when, after consuming an "unknown quantity" of liquor, she dove into the shallow end of a swimming pool. The liquor had been purchased by her friend Russell Bowser, 19, who had purchased four cases of beer from Pinch's Deli and invited five of his friends over for a party while his parents were out of town. "He was not asked for identification." Schooley brought suit and the trial court granted Pinch's motion for summary judgment. The Court of Appeals reversed and remanded the case for trial. Pinch's petitioned the Supreme Court, arguing that "once a vendor has sold the alcohol it has no control over ensuing events." The Court of Appeals' decision would expose vendors of alcohol to "unlimited liability." *Held*, affirmed. The precaution required of vendors "is not onerous, all the vendor has to do is to ask the purchaser for valid identification in order to verify that he or she is of legal age to purchase alcohol."

" * * * [L]egal cause is satisfied in this case. The injury suffered is not so remote as to preclude liability and the policy considerations behind the legislation are best served by holding vendors liable for the foreseeable consequences of the illegal sale of alcohol to minors. The policy behind the prohibition was not intended to protect only the one minor who purchases the alcohol. Minors often share alcohol with others and this prohibition was intended to also protect those minors which share in the fruits of the illegal sale. * * * "

PHAN SON VAN v. PENA, 990 S.W.2d 751 (Tex.1999). Families of two teenage girls who were raped and murdered by intoxicated gang members, when the girls happened upon a gang initiation ceremony, brought suit against a convenience store which had sold alcohol to the underage gang members prior to the initiation. *Held*, reversing Court of Appeals and reinstating summary judgment in favor of defendant, "the gang members' intentional, violent criminal acts were a superseding cause of the girls' deaths." The "intentional sexual assault and brutal murder of two teenage girls who happen upon a gang initiation some distance in time and location from the illegal sale of alcohol is not the type of harm that would ordinarily result" from a commercial seller's breach of its duty not to sell alcohol to minors.

REYNOLDS v. HICKS, 134 Wash.2d 491, 951 P.2d 761 (1998). Plaintiff was injured in an automobile accident with a minor who allegedly became intoxicated at a wedding reception, and brought suit against the bride and groom. *Held*, summary judgment for defendants affirmed. "[W]e decline to extend social host liability to third persons injured by intoxicated minors. We have long recognized that social hosts are ill-equipped to handle the responsibilities of their guests' alcohol consumption, unlike commercial vendors who are in the business of serving and selling alcohol. Thus, we have not allowed a cause of action against social hosts to the extent that we have recognized commercial vendor liability."

Johnson, J., dissented. "[I]t is a criminal act for any person, including a social host, to furnish liquor to a minor."

STRAUSS v. BELLE REALTY CO., 65 N.Y.2d 399, 492 N.Y.S.2d 555, 482 N.E.2d 34 (1985). In other litigation, defendant Con Edison had been found grossly negligent in connection with a system-wide power outage which deprived most of New York City, including the building in which the plaintiff lived, of power for 25 hours. The power failure disabled the electric pump that supplied running water to Strauss's apartment and, on the second day of the blackout, he went to the basement of his building (part of its common areas) to obtain water. He fell on the darkened stairs. Strauss brought this action against Con Ed (as well as against Belle Realty, his landlord). *Held*, affirming the Appellate Division, Con Ed owed no duty to plaintiff "in any compensable legal sense."

" * * * The court's definition of an orbit of duty based on public policy may at times result in the exclusion of some who might otherwise have recovered for losses or injuries if the traditional tort principles had been applied.

" * * * [I]n determining the liability of utilities for consequential damages for failure to provide service—a liability which could obviously be 'enormous' and has been described as 'sui generis,' rather than strictly governed by tort or contract principles—courts have declined to extend the duty of care to noncustomers. * * *

"In the view of the Appellate Division dissenter, [these cases declining to extend the duty of care to noncustomers do] not control because the injuries here were foreseeable and plaintiff was a member of a specific, limited class with a close relationship with Con Edison. * * *

"Central to [the decisions that the dissenter relied on] was an ability to extend defendant's duty to cover specifically foreseeable parties but at the same time to contain liability to manageable levels. * * * Con Edison's duty to provide electricity to Belle Realty should not be treated separately from its broader statutory obligation to furnish power to all other applicants for such service in New York City and Westchester County. When plaintiff's relationship with Con Edison is viewed from this perspective, it is no answer to say that a duty is owed because, as a tenant in an apartment building, plaintiff belongs to a narrowly defined class.

" * * * If liability could be found here, then in logic and fairness the same result must follow in many similar situations. * * * [P]ermitting recovery to those in plaintiff's circumstances would, in our view, violate the court's responsibility to define an orbit of duty that places controllable limits on liability."

SECTION C.   BEYOND PHYSICAL HARM

The *Strauss* court's concern with placing "controllable limits on liability" reflects a recurring concern of "proximate cause" doctrine. This worry animates proximate cause limits on liability "beyond physical harm." Without some limits on liability for pure economic loss and pure emotional injury the liability arising out of mundane accidents might rapidly become crushing. "The typical downtown auto accident," the first opinion in this section remarks, "that harms a few persons physically and physically damages the property of several others, may well cause financial harm (e.g., through delay) to a vast number of potential plaintiffs." (*Barber Lines, infra* at 658.) Liability this extensive would be crushing.

Pure economic loss and pure emotional harm are subjects of "duty" cases as well as "proximate cause" ones. *Casa Clara Condominium Association v. Toppino*, studied in § C of Chapter 19, is a duty case considering liability for pure economic loss. The tort of intentional infliction of emotional distress, studied in § B of Chapter Two, imposes a duty not to intentionally inflict severe emotional harm by outrageous conduct. (Economic loss and emotional harm are also a subject of damages cases, since damages for economic loss and emotional harm are routinely recoverable when the plaintiff also suffers physical injury. Note, though, that the economic and emotional injuries here are not "pure;" they are accompanied by physical injury.)

The contrast between "duty" cases involving pure economic or emotional harm and "proximate cause" ones is both important and instructive. In "duty" cases, the basic question is: Will there be liability *in tort to anyone* for the losses at issue? This follows from the fact that duty cases fix the applicable legal standards. For example, the economic loss rule in product liability law (the rule at issue in *Casa Clara*) holds that there is no liability in tort when a product defect causes purely financial injury— product repair or replacement costs, or lost profits—but not physical injury. The harm in such cases is to economic expectations and the cases hold that contract law is better suited than tort to govern harms involving economic expectancies. In "proximate cause" cases, the assumption is that there generally *will be liability in tort* to someone. The "typical auto accident" as the opinion in *Barber Lines* puts it, "harms a few persons physically and physically damages the property of several others * **." In "proximate cause" pure emotional or economic harm cases, the question is the extent of the defendant's liability for breach of a tort duty.

Pure economic loss and pure emotional harm "proximate cause" cases come in two basic types. In the first type of case, the conduct negligently risks physical injury but—fortuitously—results only in emotional or economic harm to the plaintiff. The question in these cases is whether the negligent defendant should reap the benefits of its good luck and escape financial responsibility to the plaintiff, whose ill luck it is to be physically intact but economically or emotionally shattered. In the second type of case, there is a preexisting duty of care whose breach will not generally result in physical injury. Accountants and lawyers, for example, generally owe their clients duties of reasonable care, but breach of these duties generally leads to financial harm, not to physical injury. In these cases, unless liability beyond physical harm is recognized, defendants will generally be able to breach their duties of due care with impunity.

BARBER LINES v. DONAU MARU
United States Court of Appeals, First Circuit, 1985.
764 F.2d 50.

BREYER, Circuit Judge.

In December 1979 the ship Donau Maru spilled fuel oil into Boston Harbor. The spill prevented a different ship, the Tamara, from docking at a nearby berth. The Tamara had to discharge her cargo at another pier. In doing so, she incurred significant extra labor, fuel, transport and docking costs. The Tamara, her owners, and her charterers sued the Donau Maru and her owners in admiralty. Insofar as is here relevant, they claimed negligence and sought recovery of the extra expenses as damages. The district court denied recovery on the basis of the pleadings, * * *. The plaintiffs have appealed. We believe the district court was correct, and we affirm its judgment * * *

Plaintiffs-appellants seek recovery for a financial injury caused by defendants' negligence. We assume that the injury was foreseeable. Nonetheless controlling case law denies that a plaintiff can recover damages for negligently caused financial harm, even when foreseeable, except in special circumstances. There is present here neither the most common such special circumstance—physical injury to the plaintiffs or to their property—nor any other special feature that would permit recovery.

The leading "pure financial injury" case is Robins Dry Dock & Repair Co. v. Flint, 275 U.S. 303, 48 S.Ct. 134, 72 L.Ed. 290 (1927) (Holmes, J.). Flint had chartered a ship, agreeing with its owners to have the ship docked for repairs every few months. During that time Flint would neither use the ship nor pay rent. The dry dock negligently damaged the ship's propeller, delaying repairs, and causing Flint to lose the use of the ship for two weeks. The Court held that the ship's owners might sue for negligent damage to the ship, but the charterer, suffering no physical injury to himself or to his property, could not do so. Justice Holmes wrote,

> as a general rule, at least, a tort to the person or property of one man does not make the tortfeasor liable to another merely because the injured person was under a contract with that other unknown to the doer of the wrong. See Savings Bank v. Ward, 100 U.S. [(10 Otto)] 195 [25 L.Ed. 621]. The law does not spread its protection so far. * * *

* * * Before affirming the district court on the basis of existing precedent, we have asked ourselves whether that precedent remains good law. After all, courts have sometimes departed from past legal precedent where changing circumstances viewed in light of underlying legal policy deprived that precedent of sound support. See, e.g., Glanzer v. Shepard, 233 N.Y.

236, 135 N.E. 275 (1922) (Cardozo, J.); MacPherson v. Buick Motor Co., 217 N.Y. 382, 111 N.E. 1050 (1916) (Cardozo, J.). Here, however, precedent seems, at least in general, to rest on a firm policy foundation. The same judges who removed other recovery limitations left this one firmly in place, compare Glanzer v. Shepard, supra, and MacPherson v. Buick Motor Co., supra, with Ultramares Corp. v. Touche, supra (Cardozo, J.). * * *

The cases and commentaries, in making a plausible argument that existing precedent rests on sound considerations of policy, also reveal that these considerations are highly general and abstract. Judges lack the empirical information that would allow measurement of their force or magnitude; and, in particular, judges cannot apply these considerations on a case by case basis.

* * *

First, cases and commentators point to pragmatic or practical administrative considerations which, when taken together, offer support for a rule limiting recovery for negligently caused pure financial harm. The number of persons suffering foreseeable financial harm in a typical accident is likely to be far greater than those who suffer traditional (recoverable) physical harm. The typical downtown auto accident, that harms a few persons physically and physically damages the property of several others, may well cause financial harm (e.g., through delay) to a vast number of potential plaintiffs. The less usual, negligently caused, oil spill foreseeably harms not only ships, docks, piers, beaches, wildlife, and the like, that are covered with oil, but also harms blockaded ships, marina merchants, suppliers of those firms, the employees of marina businesses and suppliers, the suppliers' suppliers, and so forth. To use the notion of "foreseeability" that courts use in physical injury cases to separate the financially injured allowed to sue from the financially injured not allowed to sue would draw vast numbers of injured persons within the class of potential plaintiffs in even the most simple accident cases (unless it leads courts, unwarrantedly, to narrow the scope of "foreseeability" as applied to persons suffering physical harm). That possibility—a large number of different plaintiffs each with somewhat different claims—in turn threatens to raise significantly the cost of even relatively simple tort actions. * * *

At the same time many of the "financially injured" will find it easier than the "physically injured" to arrange for cheaper, alternative compensation. The typical "financial" plaintiff is likely to be a business firm that, in any event, buys insurance, and which may well be able to arrange for "first party" loss compensation for foreseeable financial harm. Other such victims will be able to sue under tort principles, for they will suffer at least some physical harm to their property. Still others may have contracts with, or be able to contract with, persons who can themselves recover from the negligent defendant. A shipowner, for example, might contract with a dock owner for "inaccessibility" compensation; and the dock owner (whose pier is physically covered with oil) might recover this compensation as part of its tort damages. * * *

A second set of considerations focuses on the "disproportionality" between liability and fault. Those who argue "disproportionality" are not reiterating the discredited nineteenth century view that tort liability would destroy industry, investment, or capitalism. See F. Wharton, A Suggestion as to Causation 11 (1874); Horwitz, The Doctrine of Objective Causation, in The Politics of Law: A Progressive Critique 201 (D. Kairys, ed. 1982). Rather, they recognize that tort liability provides a powerful set of economic incentives and disincentives to engage in economic activity or to make it safer, see generally G. Calabresi, The Costs of Accidents (1970). And, liability for pure financial harm, insofar as it proved vast, cumulative and inherently unknowable in amount, could create incentives that are perverse.

Might not unbounded liability for foreseeable financial damage, for example, make auto insurance premiums too expensive for the average driver? Is such a result desirable? After all, the high premiums would reflect not only the costs of the harm inflicted; they would also reflect administrative costs of law suits, jury verdicts in uncertain amounts, some percentage of unbounded or inflated economic claims, and lessened incentive for financial victims to avoid harm or to mitigate damage. Given the existing liability for physical injury (and for accompanying financial injury), can one say that still higher premiums are needed to make the public realize that driving is socially expensive or to provide greater incentive to drive safely (an incentive that risk spreading through insurance dilutes in any event, see Shavell, On Liability and Insurance, 13 Bell J. of Econ. 120 [1982])?

These considerations, of administrability and disproportionality, offer plausible, though highly abstract, "policy" support for the reluctance of the courts to impose tort liability for purely financial harm. While they seem unlikely to apply with equal strength to every sort of "financial harm" claim, their abstraction and generality, along with the comparative inaccessibility of the empirical information needed to confirm or to invalidate them, mean that courts cannot weigh or apply them case by case. * * *

It does not surprise us then that, under these circumstances, courts have neither enforced one clear rule nor considered the matter case by case. Cf. Michelman, Property, Utility, and Fairness: Comments on the Ethical Foundations of "Just Compensation" Law, 80 Harv.L.Rev. 1165, 1249–53 (1967). Rather, they have spoken of a general principle against liability for negligently caused financial harm, while creating many exceptions. [The court cites nine: 1) accompanying physical harm; 2) intentionally caused harm; 3) defamation; 4) injurious falsehood; 5) medical costs paid by a different family member; 6) negligent misstatements about financial matters; 7) master and servant; 8) telegraph-addressee; and 9) commercial fishermen as special "favorites of admiralty", citing Union Oil Co. v. Oppen, *infra*, pp. 662–663.] These exceptions seem designed to pick out broad categories of cases where the "administrative" and "disproportionality" problems intuitively seem insignificant or where some strong countervailing consideration militates in favor of liability. Thus an award of financial damages to one [who] also caused physical harm does not threaten proliferation of law suits, for the plaintiff could sue anyway (for physical damages). Financial harm awards to family members carry with them an obvious self-limiting principle (as perhaps does awarding such damages to fishermen, as "favorites" of admiralty). Awarding damages for financial harm caused by negligent misrepresentation is special in that, without such liability, tort law would not exert significant financial pressure to avoid negligence; a negligent accountant lacks physically harmed victims as potential plaintiffs. * * *

* * *

For these reasons, the judgment of the district court is

Affirmed.

CONNECTICUT MUTUAL LIFE INSURANCE CO. v. NEW YORK & NEW HAVEN RAILROAD CO., 25 Conn. 265 (1856). The plaintiff had issued a policy of insurance on the life of one Beach, who was killed by the negligence of the defendant while a passenger on its train. The defendant had paid Beach's administratrix damages for causing his death. The plaintiff then sued for the amount it was required to pay under the terms of its policy. *Held,* on demurrer, for defendant. "The single question is, whether a plaintiff can successfully claim a legal injury to himself from another, because the latter has injured a third person in such a manner that the plaintiffs' contract liabilities are thereby affected. * * * To open the door of legal redress to wrongs received through the mere voluntary and factitious relation of a contractor with the immediate subject of the injury, would be to encourage collusion and extravagant contracts between men, by which the death of either through the involuntary default of others, might be made a source of splendid profits to the other, and would also invite a system of litigation more portentous than our jurisprudence has yet known. * * * Had the life of Dr. Beach been taken with intent to injure the plaintiffs through their contract liability, a different question would arise, inasmuch as every man owes a duty to every other not intentionally to injure him."

CUE v. BRELAND, 78 Miss. 864, 29 So. 850 (1901). The plaintiff built a bridge for a county and agreed to maintain it for five years. The defendant's servant, in floating logs down the stream, let them loose, making no effort to guide them, as could readily have been done. They crashed into the bridge, destroying it. Plaintiff, having rebuilt it, brought trespass. *Held,* for plaintiff, since the jury could have found a willful wrong.

IN RE ONE MERIDIAN PLAZA FIRE LITIGATION, 820 F.Supp. 1460 (E.D.Pa.1993). A fire shut down two large skyscrapers in downtown Philadelphia—One Meridian Plaza and Two Mellon Bank Center. The City of Philadelphia barred access to an area surrounding One Meridian Plaza "for some time after the fire due to the threat of falling granite or other debris." Plaintiffs, individuals and businesses affected by the bar on access to the area affected by the fire, brought suit for damages, claiming "public nuisance." Section 821B of the Restatement, cited by the court, defines a "public nuisance" as "an unreasonable interference with a right common to the general public." The plaintiffs' damages consisted principally of "economic losses, including lost wages of employees and lost profits of businesses and individuals." Defendants objected that plaintiffs were not entitled to recover such damages, citing the economic loss doctrine.

"It is clear that the economic loss doctrine is not applicable to public nuisance claims, but defendants contend that plaintiffs' public nuisance claims must be dismissed entirely because plaintiffs did not sustain any special or peculiar harm as a result of the nuisance. Section 821C of the Restatement states, in pertinent part:

> In order to recover for damages in an individual action for public nuisance, one must have suffered a harm of a kind different from that suffered by other members of the public exercising the right common to the general public that was the subject of interference."

"The complaint alleges that 'the right to use and safely traverse the public streets surrounding (One Meridian Plaza) is a right common to the general public,' and that this right was interfered with by defendants. The special or peculiar harm suffered by plaintiffs is described as 'being deprived, and having their customers deprived, of safe, convenient and reasonable access to their business premises, and suffering pecuniary harm as a result of this deprivation.' * * * This is allegedly different from the harm suffered by other members of the public because '[w]hile other members of the public were inconvenienced . . . they were not denied reasonable and safe access to their business premises, nor did they lose significant business because customers, upon whom their businesses depend, were deprived of convenient access to their business premises.' * * *

* * *

"As a matter of law I find that the only parties who may have suffered peculiar harm as a result of the closure of the streets due to the fire were those businesses who can show with reasonable certainty that they lost profits due to the closure of the streets and who suffered a substantial loss of access. * * * All other plaintiffs were not uniquely affected by the closure of the streets, and inclusion of these parties would increase the number of plaintiffs so as to generalize the harm. Therefore all other parties claims for public nuisance are dismissed."

CABINED EXCEPTIONS OR COUNTER–PRINCIPLE?

The *Donau Maru* opinion treats the exceptions to the "no liability for pure economic loss" as discrete and bounded. The two cases that follow cast some doubt on that treatment

------

UNION OIL CO. v. OPPEN, 501 F.2d 558 (9th Cir.1974). Plaintiffs, commercial fisherman injured by a massive oil spill from defendant's offshore drilling operations, brought suit against defendant oil companies for "profits lost as a result of the reduction in the commercial fishing potential of the Santa Barbara Channel." *Held*, notwithstanding "the widely recognized principle that no cause of action lies against a defendant whose negligence prevents the plaintiff from obtaining a prospective pecuniary advantage" commercial fishermen, but not anyone else "whose economic or personal affairs were discommoded by the oil spill," may recover for lost profits, proved with certainty.

The court noted that "the defendants could reasonably have foreseen that negligently conducted drilling operations might diminish aquatic life and thus injure the business of commercial fishermen. * * * The dangers of pollution were and are known even by school children." The principle of reasonable foreseeability, "the public's deep disapproval of injuries to the environment and the strong policy of preventing such injuries," all require defendants "to conduct their drilling and production in a reasonably prudent manner so as to avoid the negligent diminution of aquatic life." The imposition of this duty was "not foreclosed by the fact that the defendant's negligence could constitute a public nuisance under California law. * * * The injury here asserted by the plaintiff is a pecuniary loss of a particular and special nature, limited to the class of commercial fishermen which they represent."

PEOPLE EXPRESS AIRLINES, INC. v. CONSOLIDATED RAIL CORP., 100 N.J. 246, 495 A.2d 107 (1985). Plaintiff airline brought an action for economic losses it suffered due to evacuation of its offices following a tank car accident at a nearby railroad yard. Municipal authorities, fearing a burning tank car loaded with a volatile chemical might explode, evacuated the area within a one-mile radius, which included plaintiff's facilities. No explosion occurred, but the twelve-hour interruption of plaintiff's business resulted in lost reservations and cancelled flights. The trial court ruled that plaintiff's economic loss was not compensable in tort, absent accompanying physical injury. On review by the New Jersey Supreme Court, *held*, that economic losses might be recovered here, in light of "the close proximity of [plaintiff's facility] to the Conrail freight yard; the obvious nature of the plaintiff's operations and particular foreseeability of economic losses resulting from an accident and evacuation." The court (per Handler, J.) took note of a "general rule" against recovery of purely economic loss, but emphasized that "numerous exceptions" had developed which pointed to "a distinction between those economic losses that are only generally foreseeable, and thus noncompensable, and those losses the defendant is in a position particularly to foresee." The latter sort—"particularly foreseeable" economic loss—should be compensated, as indicated by "the evolution of various exceptions." The court explained:

> A very solid exception allowing recovery for economic losses has
> * * * been created in cases akin to private actions for public nuisance.
> * * * *See, e.g., Union Oil Co. v. Oppen*, 501 F.2d 558 (9th Cir.1974)
> (fishermen making known commercial use of public waters may recover
> economic losses due to defendant's oil spill) * * *. The theory running
> throughout these cases, in which the plaintiffs depend on the exercise
> of the public or riparian right to clean water as a natural resource, is

that the pecuniary losses suffered by those who make direct use of the resource are particularly foreseeable because they are so closely linked, through the resource, to the defendants' behavior. * * *

These exceptions expose the hopeless artificiality of the *per se* rule against recovery for purely economic losses. When the plaintiffs are reasonably foreseeable, the injury is directly and proximately caused by defendant's negligence, and liability can be limited fairly, courts have endeavored to create exceptions to allow recovery. The scope and number of exceptions, while independently justified on various grounds, have nonetheless created lasting doubt as to the wisdom of the *per se* rule of nonrecovery for purely economic losses. * * *

We hold therefore that a defendant owes a duty of care to take reasonable measures to avoid the risk of causing economic damages, aside from physical injury, to particular plaintiffs or plaintiffs comprising an identifiable class with respect to whom defendant knows or has reason to know [that they] are likely to suffer such damages from its conduct. * * *

We stress that an identifiable class of plaintiffs is not simply a foreseeable class of plaintiffs. For example, members of the general public, or invitees such as sales and service persons at a particular plaintiff's business premises, or persons traveling on a highway near the scene of a negligently-caused accident, such as the one at bar, who are delayed in the conduct of their affairs and suffer varied economic losses, are certainly a foreseeable class of plaintiffs. Yet their presence within the area would be fortuitous, and the particular type of economic injury that could be suffered by such persons would be hopelessly unpredictable and not realistically foreseeable. Thus, the class itself would not be sufficiently ascertainable. An identifiable class of plaintiffs must be particularly foreseeable in terms of the type of persons or entities comprising the class, the certainty or predictability of their presence, the approximate numbers of those in the class, as well as the type of economic expectations disrupted. * * *

We appreciate that there will arise many similar cases that cannot be resolved by our decision today. The cause of action we recognize, however, is one that most appropriately should be allowed to evolve on a case-by-case basis in the context of actual adjudications. We perceive no reason, however, why our decision today should be applied only prospectively. Our holdings are well grounded in traditional tort principles and flow from well-established exceptional cases that are philosophically compatible with this decision.

PURE EMOTIONAL HARM

We began our study of liability for negligent infliction of pure economic loss with a case stating and defending the "no recovery" principle and conceptualizing the exceptions to it as specific rules. We ended with a case arguing that a broader principle of liability for "particularly foreseeable" injury informed those exceptions. Our study of liability for negligent inflic-tion of emotional distress travels in the other direction. We begin with a case—the most famous of modern negligent infliction cases—casting its lot with forseeability of injury, and move to cases which adopt or comment upon more rule like approaches to liability for pure emotional harm.

DILLON v. LEGG

Supreme Court of California, In Bank, 1968.
68 Cal.2d 728, 69 Cal.Rptr. 72, 441 P.2d 912, 29 A.L.R.3d 1316.

TOBRINER, Justice. That the courts should allow recovery to a mother who suffers emotional trauma and physical injury from witnessing the infliction of death or injury to her child for which the tort-feasor is liable in negligence would appear to be a compelling proposition. As Prosser points out, "All ordinary human feelings are in favor of her [the mother's] action against the negligent defendant. If a duty to her requires that she herself be in some recognizable danger, then it has properly been said that when a child is endangered, it is not beyond contemplation that its mother will be somewhere in the vicinity, and will suffer serious shock." (Prosser, Law of Torts (3d ed. 1964) p. 353.)

Nevertheless, past American decisions have barred the mother's recov-ery. Refusing the mother the right to take her case to the jury, these courts ground their position on an alleged absence of a required "duty" of due care of the tort-feasor to the mother. Duty, in turn, they state, must express public policy; the imposition of duty here would work disaster because it would invite fraudulent claims and it would involve the courts in the hopeless task of defining the extent of the tort-feasor's liability. * * *

We have concluded that neither of the feared dangers excuses the frustration of the natural justice upon which the mother's claim rests. * * *

[Defendant's negligent driving caused the death of young Erin Lee Dillon. Her mother and her sister Cheryl were nearby. Each witnessed the collision and, it is alleged, suffered "great emotional disturbance and shock" and "injury to her nervous system." The mother's claim based on her own emotional harm was dismissed because she had not herself been within the "zone of danger." The sister's claim was not dismissed because she had been closer to the accident and might have "feared for her own safety."]

* * *

* * * Thus we have before us a case that dramatically illustrates the difference in result flowing from the alleged requirement that a plaintiff cannot recover for emotional trauma in witnessing the death of a child or sister unless she also feared for her own safety because she was actually within the zone of physical impact.

* * * The case * * * illustrates the fallacy of the rule that would deny recovery in the one situation and grant it in the other. In the first place, we can hardly justify relief to the sister for trauma which she suffered upon

apprehension of the child's death and yet deny it to the mother merely because of a happenstance that the sister was some few yards closer to the accident. The instant case exposes the hopeless artificiality of the zone-of-danger rule. In the second place, to rest upon the zone-of-danger rule when we have rejected the impact rule becomes even less defensible. We have, indeed, held that impact is not necessary for recovery. The zone-of-danger concept must, then, inevitably collapse because the only reason for the requirement of presence in that zone lies in the fact that one within it will fear the danger of *impact*. At the threshold, then, we point to the incongruity of the rules upon which any rejection of plaintiff's recovery must rest.

* * *

The assertion that liability must nevertheless be denied because defendant bears no "duty" to plaintiff "begs the essential question—whether the plaintiff's interests are entitled to legal protection against the defendant's conduct. * * * "(Prosser, Law of Torts, supra, at pp. 332–333.)

The history of the concept of duty in itself discloses that it is not an old and deep-rooted doctrine but a legal device of the latter half of the nineteenth century designed to curtail the feared propensities of juries toward liberal awards. * * *

* * *

The Industrial Revolution, which cracked the solidity of the feudal society and opened up wide and new areas of expansion, changed the legal concepts. Just as the new competitiveness in the economic sphere figuratively broke out of the walls of the feudal community, so it broke through the rule of strict liability. In the place of strict liability it introduced the theory that an action for negligence would lie only if the defendant breached a duty which he owed to plaintiff. As Lord Esher said in Le Lievre v. Gould (1893) 1 Q.B. 491, 497: "A man is entitled to be as negligent as he pleases towards the whole world if he owes no duty to them."

We have pointed out that this late 19th century concept of duty, as applied to the instant situation, has led the courts to deny liability. We have noted that this negation of duty emanates from the twin fears that courts will be flooded with an onslaught of (1) fraudulent and (2) indefinable claims. We shall point out why we think neither fear justified.

1. *This court in the past has rejected the argument that we must deny recovery upon a legitimate claim because other fraudulent ones may be urged.*

The denial of "duty" in the instant situation rests upon the prime hypothesis that allowance of such an action would lead to successful assertion of fraudulent claims. The rationale apparently assumes that juries, confronted by irreconcilable expert medical testimony, will be unable to distinguish the deceitful from the bona fide. The argument concludes that only a per se rule denying the entire class of claims that potentially raises this administrative problem[3] can avoid this danger.

3. To the extent that this argument shades into the contention that such claims should be denied because otherwise courts would experience a "flood of litigation," we point out that

mother who observes an accident affecting her child will suffer harm than to foretell that a stranger witness will do so. Similarly, the degree of foreseeability of the third person's injury is far greater in the case of his contemporaneous observance of the accident than that in which he subsequently learns of it. * * * All these elements, of course, shade into each other; the fixing of obligation, intimately tied into the facts, depends upon each case.

In light of these factors the court will determine whether the accident and harm was *reasonably* foreseeable. Such reasonable foreseeability does not turn on whether the particular defendant as an individual would have in actuality foreseen the exact accident and loss; it contemplates that courts, on a case-to-case basis, analyzing all the circumstances, will decide what the ordinary man under such circumstances should reasonably have foreseen. The courts thus mark out the areas of liability, excluding the remote and unexpected.

In the instant case, the presence of all the above factors indicates that plaintiff has alleged a sufficient prima facie case. Surely the negligent driver who causes the death of a young child may reasonably expect that the mother will not be far distant and will upon witnessing the accident suffer emotional trauma. * * *

* * *

The fear of an inability to fix boundaries has not impelled the courts of England to deny recovery for emotional trauma caused by witnessing the death or injury of another due to defendant's negligence. * * *

* * *

In a recent [decision] an English court permitted recovery by a widow of a man who developed severe psychoneurotic symptoms as a result of harrowing experiences, not involving his personal safety, while serving as a rescuer at a gruesome train wreck. The court stated that the " 'test of liability for shock is foreseeability of injury by shock.' " (Chadwick v. British Railways Board [1967] 1 W.L.R. 912, 920, quoting from King v. Phillips [1953] 1 Q.B. 429, 441, opinion by Denning, L.J.)

* * *

Thus we see no good reason why the general rules of tort law, including the concepts of negligence, proximate cause, and foreseeability, long applied to all other types of injury, should not govern the case now before us. Any questions that the cause raises "will be solved most justly by applying general principles of duty and negligence, and * * * mechanical rules of thumb which are at variance with these principles do more harm than good." (2 Harper & James, The Law of Torts, supra, p. 1039; fn. omitted.) "The refusal to apply these general rules to actions for this particular kind of physical injury is nothing short of a denial of justice." (Throckmorton, Damages for Fright (1921) 34 Harv.L.Rev. 260, 277; fn. omitted.)

In short, the history of the cases does not show the development of a logical rule but rather a series of changes and abandonments. Upon the argument in each situation that the courts draw a Maginot Line to withstand an onslaught of false claims, the cases have assumed a variety of postures. At first they insisted that there be no recovery for emotional trauma at all. Retreating from this position, they gave relief for such trauma only if physical impact occurred. They then abandoned the requirement for physical impact but insisted that the victim fear for her own safety, holding that a mother could recover for fear for her children's safety if she simultaneously entertained a personal fear for herself. They stated that the mother need only be in the "zone of danger". The final anomaly would be the instant case in which the sister, who observed the accident, would be granted recovery because she was in the "zone of danger," but the *mother*, not far distant, would be barred from recovery.

The successive abandonment of these positions exposes the weakness of artificial abstractions which bar recovery contrary to the general rules. As the commentators have suggested, the problem should be solved by the application of the principles of tort, not by the creation of exceptions to them. Legal history shows that artificial islands of exceptions, created from the fear that the legal process will not work, usually do not withstand the waves of reality and, in time, descend into oblivion.

* * *

To deny recovery would be to chain this state to an outmoded rule of the 19th century which can claim no current credence. No good reason compels our captivity to an indefensible orthodoxy.

The judgment is reversed.

———

THING v. LA CHUSA, 48 Cal.3d 644, 257 Cal.Rptr. 865, 771 P.2d 814 (1989). "The narrow issue presented by the parties in this case is whether the Court of Appeal correctly held that a mother who did not witness an accident in which an automobile struck and injured her child may recover damages from the negligent driver for the emotional distress she suffered when she arrived at the accident scene. The more important question this issue poses for the court, however, is whether the 'guidelines' enunciated by this court in Dillon v. Legg * * * are adequate, of if they should be refined to create greater certainty in this area of the law.

* * *

" * * * The Dillon experience confirms, as one commentator observed, that '[foreseeability] proves too much.... Although it may set tolerable limits for most types of physical harm, it provides virtually no limit for nonphysical harm.' * * * It is apparent that reliance on foreseeability of injury alone in finding a duty and thus a right to recover, is not adequate when damages sought are for an intangible injury. In order to avoid limitless liability out of all proportion to the degree of defendant's negligence, and against which it is impossible to insure without imposing unacceptable costs on those among whom the risk is spread, the right to recover for negligently caused emotional distress must be limited.

* * *

"Unlike an award of damages for intentionally caused emotional distress which is punitive, the award for NIED [Negligent Infliction of Emotional Distress] simply reflects society's belief that a negligent actor bears some responsibility for the effect of his conduct on persons other than those who suffer physical injury. In identifying those persons and the circumstances in which the defendant will be held to redress the injury, it is appropriate to restrict recovery to those persons who will suffer an emotional impact beyond the impact that can be anticipated whenever one learns that a relative is injured, or dies, or the emotion felt by a 'disinterested' witness. The class of potential plaintiffs should be limited to those who because of their relationship suffer the greatest emotional distress. When the right to recover is limited in this manner, the liability bears a reasonable relationship to the culpability of the negligent defendant.

"The elements which justify and simultaneously limit an award of damages for emotional distress caused by awareness of the negligent infliction of injury to a close relative are * * * the traumatic emotional effect on the plaintiff who contemporaneously observes both the event or the conduct that causes serious injury to a close relative and the injury itself. Even if it is 'foreseeable' that persons other than closely related percipient witnesses may suffer emotional distress, this fact does not justify the imposition of what threatens to become unlimited liability for emotional distress on [a] defendant whose conduct is simply negligent. Nor does such abstract 'foreseeability' warrant continued reliance on the assumption that the limits of liability will become any clearer if lower courts are permitted to continue approaching the issue on a 'case to case' basis some 20 years after Dillon.

"We conclude, therefore, that a plaintiff may recover damages for emotional distress caused by observing the negligently inflicted injury of a third person if, but only if, said plaintiff: (1) is closely related to the injury victim; (2) is present at the scene of the injury-producing event at the time it occurs and is then aware that it is causing injury to the victim; and (3) as a result suffers serious emotional distress—a reaction beyond that which would be anticipated in a disinterested witness and which is not an abnormal reaction to the circumstances."

FENG v. METROPOLITAN TRANSPORTATION AUTHORITY, 285 A.D.2d 447, 727 N.Y.S.2d 470 (App.Div.2001). Plaintiff He Ming Zou's son, Gia Yi Feng, standing adjacent to the train tracks at a Long Island Rail Road station, was "struck by an arriving train and pushed onto" his mother. Ming Zou had no claim for physical injury because she was "not physically injured." She had no claim for emotional distress because "there is no evidence that she was within the zone of danger."

SCHULTZ v. BARBERTON GLASS CO., 4 Ohio St.3d 131, 447 N.E.2d 109 (1983). Celebrezze, C.J., for the Ohio Supreme Court: "[W]e hold that a cause of action may be stated for the negligent infliction of serious emotional distress without contemporaneous physical injury."

" * * * [W]e conclude that appellant has * ** a cause of action [for negligent infliction of emotional distress]. Due to appellee's negligence, a large sheet of glass fell off [appellee's] truck onto the highway and crashed into the windshield of appellant's vehicle. The validity of appellant's claim of serious emotional distress as a result of the accident is supported by the expert testimony of three medical doctors and a psychologist. Although the trial court awarded damages for emotional distress, the court of appeals remanded for a determination of a contemporaneous physical injury. Because of our holding, such a determination is unnecessary."

NELSON v. METRO–NORTH COMMUTER RAILROAD, 235 F.3d 101 (2d Cir.2000) (Calabresi. J.) "The traditional common-law standard for dealing with negligent infliction of emotional distress claims, and the rule still followed in some jurisdictions, required that a plaintiff have sustained a physical impact due to the defendant's negligence before she could recover emotional damages. The rule was intended to curtail what courts feared might otherwise be a flood of trivial or fraudulent claims, or claims for emotional injury causally remote from the defendant's conduct." *See, e.g., Shuamber v. Henderson,* 579 N.E.2d 452, 455 (Ind.1991).

"As originally formulated, the physical impact rule required a physical *injury.* [citations omitted] Mere physical *contact* was neither necessary nor sufficient to satisfy the impact rule. Rather, under that rule, emotional damages could be recovered only if they were caused by some physical hurt that was itself caused by the defendant's negligence. And, absent such an injury, emotional distress was not compensable even if it ultimately manifested itself in physical harm to the plaintiff. Moreover, in the latter circumstances, even the physical harm that derived from the emotional injury was not compensable. *See, e.g., Spade v. Lynn & Boston R.R. Co.,* 168 Mass. 285, 47 N.E. 88, 89 (1897) ('[T]here can be no recovery for fright, terror, alarm, anxiety, or distress of mind, if these are unaccompanied by some physical injury; and, if this rule is to stand, we think it should also be held that there can be no recovery for such physical injuries as may be caused solely by such mental disturbance, where there is no injury to the person from without.'), *overruled by Dziokonski v. Babineau,* 375 Mass. 555, 380 N.E.2d 1295 (1978).

"Thus, in *Spade,* the leading case for the traditional impact doctrine, a woman who was brushed against by a drunk who was being ejected from a train, and as a result suffered emotional damages that led to physical injury, was barred from recovery because the contact with the drunk man did not itself physically injure her. *See Spade,* 47 N.E. at 89. Conversely, under the impact rule, plaintiffs could recover emotional damages caused by a physical injury although there was no actual contact caused by the defendant; for example, a plaintiff who injured himself leaping out of the way of a train could recover for that physical injury and for any associated emotional harm. *See, e.g., Bullard v. Central Vermont Ry., Inc.,* 565 F.2d 193, 197 (1st Cir.1977) (holding, in an FELA case, that a railway employee who injured his foot when he jumped out of the way of a train collision could 'recover for his fright at the time of the accident'); *see also* 3 Fowler V. Harper, Fleming James, Jr. & Oscar S. Gray, *The Law of Torts* § 18.4, at 686 (2d ed.1986).

"Such a brittle rule, turning as it does solely on the existence *vel non* of physical impact, leaves a great deal to be desired. On the one hand, under the traditional rule, the most minimal of physical injuries suffices to allow a plaintiff to recover essentially unlimited damages for emotional distress flowing from that injury[4], even if the distress is a fear of future illness that is very unlikely to occur. *See, e.g., Marchica v. Long Island R.R. Co.,* 31 F.3d 1197, 1202–03 (2d Cir.1994). In *Marchica,* an FELA case, the plaintiff suffered a puncture wound from a hypodermic needle while cleaning up a pile of trash in the train station where he worked. Although no evidence was introduced that he had been exposed to HIV, and though medical tests eventually showed that he had not been, the plaintiff was allowed to recover damages under the FELA for negligent infliction of emotional distress due to his fear of developing AIDS (including damages for his continuing distress after he knew to a virtual certainty that he would not develop AIDS). *See id.; see also id.* at 1207–08.[5]"

"On the other hand, the physical impact rule makes no allowance for reasonable fear of physical injury stemming from defendant's negligent conduct in cases in which no impact on the plaintiff occurred. And *Gottshall* wisely ruled that such an approach was dissonant with the remedial goals of the F[ederal Employer's Liability Act]. *See Gottshall,* 512 U.S. at 556, 114 S.Ct. 2396 (commenting that '[w]e see no reason ... to allow an employer to escape liability for emotional injury caused by the apprehension of physical impact simply because of the fortuity that the impact did not occur').

"Moreover, although the impact rule sought to narrow the scope of liability by reducing the number of fraudulent and speculative claims brought, even courts in jurisdictions following that rule have recognized that the mere existence of a physical injury does little to decrease the chance of fraud or the difficulty of the task faced by a jury in deciding whether emotional distress is present. *See, e.g., Shuamber,* 579 N.E.2d at 455 ('The mere fact of a physical injury, however minor, does not make mental distress

---

4. Numerous examples of such trivial bodily impacts could be given. *See, e.g., Homans v. Boston Elevated Ry. Co.,* 180 Mass. 456, 62 N.E. 737, 737 (1902) (Holmes, *C.J.*) (a slight blow from being thrown against a seat); *Porter v. Delaware, L & W. R.R. Co.,* 73 N.J.L. 405, 63 A. 860, 860 (1906) (dust in the eyes); *Morton v. Stack,* 122 Ohio St. 115, 170 N.E. 869, 869–70 (1930) (per curiam) (smoke inhalation); *see also Christy Bros. Circus v. Turnage,* 38 Ga.App. 581, 144 S.E. 680, 680 (1928) (in case in which a circus horse evacuated its bowels in plaintiff's lap, holding that an "unlawful touching of a person's body, although no actual physical hurt may ensue therefrom, yet, since it violates a personal right, constitutes a physical injury to that person"), *overruled by OB–GYN Assocs.,* 386 S.E.2d at 149.

5. Moreover, the brittleness of the impact rule, together with the infelicity of the term "physical impact," has often led to the rule's being misunderstood. Thus, some courts have confused "impact" with "contact" and allowed unlimited emotional damages even in the absence of physical injury, as long as some physical *contact* existed. *See, e.g., Deutsch v. Shein,* 597 S.W.2d 141, 146 (Ky.1980) (while purporting to apply the impact rule, commenting that "[c]ontact, however slight, trifling, or trivial, will support a cause of action," and concluding that x-rays of the plaintiff's person were sufficient contact to support a claim for emotional damages stemming from fear that the x-rays would injure the plaintiff's fetus).

damages any less speculative, subject to exaggeration, or likely to lead to fictitious claims ... [T]he presence or absence of some physical injury does nothing to alleviate the jury's burden in deciding whether the elements of mental suffering are present.' (quoting *Cullison v. Medley,* 570 N.E.2d 27, 30 (Ind.1991)) (internal quotation marks omitted))."

"These failings have led courts to turn away from the traditional impact rule. An early exception to the doctrine developed in cases of *intentional* infliction of emotional distress. *See, e.g., Price v. Yellow Pine Paper Mill Co.,* 240 S.W. 588, 594 (Tex.Civ.App.1922) (allowing plaintiff to recover for physical and emotional damages sustained as a result of fright experienced when her husband was brought home bloody and unconscious after an on-the-job accident). And, even in cases of negligent infliction of emotional distress, the common law has, over the course of the last century, moved increasingly toward a less demanding standard for recovery.

"Thus, as the *Gottshall* Court noted, many jurisdictions have adopted the 'zone of danger' test, under which plaintiffs placed at risk of physical injury by defendant's negligent conduct can recover for resultant emotional distress. *See Gottshall,* 512 U.S. at 547–48 & n. 9, 114 S.Ct. 2396 (citing cases). And a large number of states now apply some variant of a 'bystander' test that allows recovery for emotional distress caused by witnessing the injury or death of a third party (who usually must be a close relative) even if the plaintiff was not herself at risk of injury. *See id.* at 548–49 & n. 10, 114 S.Ct. 2396 (citing cases). [footnote discussion of the "seminal case of" *Dillon v. Legg* and its subsequent limitation by *Thing v. LaChusa* omitted]"

"Finally, at least two states (Hawaii and Montana) employ a yet broader test under which liability for negligent infliction of emotional distress exists when 'a reasonable man, normally constituted, would be unable to adequately cope with the mental stress engendered by the circumstances of the case.' *Rodrigues v. State,* 472 P.2d 509, 520 (1970); *see Sacco v. High Country Indep. Press, Inc.,* 271 Mont. 209, 896 P.2d 411, 424–26 (1995). The *Rodrigues* court stated that the tests adopted by other jurisdictions were intended to 'guarantee the genuineness and seriousness of the claim' of emotional distress, and that, accordingly, 'the preferable approach is to adopt general standards to test the genuineness and seriousness of mental distress in any particular case,' rather than to limit the right to recovery through a requirement that the plaintiff experience a physical impact or be within the zone of danger of a physical impact. *Id.* at 519."

PERRY–ROGERS ET AL. v. OBASAJU
Supreme Court, Appellate Division, New York, 2001.
282 A.D.2d 231, 723 N.Y.S.2d 28.

[Plaintiffs underwent in vitro fertilization at defendants' fertility clinic. Defendants mistakenly implanted plaintiffs' embryo into the uterus of another woman, who bore the child and raised it for four months until plaintiffs gained custody. Plaintiffs brought suit against the clinic, alleging malpractice resulting in emotional harm. The trial court denied defendants' motions to disimiss plaintiffs' claim. Defendants appealed.]

We reject defendants' argument that plaintiffs' malpractice claim must be dismissed since it seeks to recover only for emotional harm caused by the creation of human life. Plaintiffs do not seek damages for the emotional harm caused by the birth of a sick or unplanned healthy child, and would not otherwise have the court calculate the difference between existence and nonexistence. Rather, plaintiffs seek damages for the emotional harm caused by their having been deprived of the opportunity of experiencing pregnancy, prenatal bonding and the birth of their child, and by their separation from the child for more than four months after his birth. Damages for emotional harm can be recovered even in the absence of physical injury "when there is a duty owed by defendant to plaintiff, [and a] breach of that duty result[s] directly in emotional harm". There is no requirement that the plaintiff must be in fear of his or her own physical safety (*see, Johnson v. State of New York,* 37 N.Y.2d 378 [App.Div.1978]; Topor v. State of New York, 176 Misc.2d 177, 180 [1997]). However, "a plaintiff must produce evidence sufficient to guarantee the genuineness of the claim" [citation omitted], such as "[c]ontemporaneous or consequential physical harm," which is "thought to provide an index of reliability otherwise absent in a claim for psychological trauma with only psychological consequences" (*Johnson v State of New York, supra,* at 381). Here, it was foreseeable that the information that defendants had mistakenly implanted plaintiffs' embryos in a person whom they would not identify, which information was not conveyed until after such person had become pregnant, would cause plaintiffs emotional distress over the possibility that the child that they wanted so desperately, as evidenced by their undertaking the rigors of in vitro fertilization, might be born to someone else and that they might never know his or her fate. These circumstances, together with plaintiffs' medical affidavits attesting to objective manifestations of their emotional trauma, create a "guarantee of genuineness" that makes plaintiffs' claim for emotional distress viable. *Johnson v. Jamaica Hosp.* (62 N.Y.2d 523 [1984]) is distinguishable in that it turned on the absence of a direct duty owing to the parents of a newborn who was abducted from the hospital. * * *

[The trial court's denial of defendant's motion to dismiss is affirmed.]

GUTH v. FREELAND, 96 Hawai'i 147, 28 P.3d 982 (2001). Defendant morgue failed to refrigerate the body of plaintiffs' mother, causing it to decompose prior to a planned open-casket funeral and making such a funeral impossible. *Held*, statute which bars recovery for negligent infliction of emotional distress arising solely out of damage to property or material objects, unless that distress results in physical injury or mental illness, does not apply to emotional distress arising from the negligent mishandling of a corpse. A duty of reasonable care in the preparation of a body for funeral, burial or cremation runs to decedent's immediate family members. "Many courts have recognized that the nearest relatives of the deceased have a quasi-property right in the deceased's body that arises from their duty to bury the deceased."

"[If decedent's immediate family members cannot recover] there will often be no one to hold defendants accountable for their negligent handling of dead bodies. A defendant does not owe a duty of care to the decedent, who is not himself actually harmed by the defendant's actions. The court in *Quesada* [*v. Oak Hill Improvement Co.*, 213 Cal.App.3d 596, 261 Cal.Rptr. 769, 774 (1989)] stated:

> As a society we want those who are entrusted with the bodies of our dead to exercise the greatest of care. Imposing liability within the limits described will promote that goal. Further, those who come in contact with the bereaved should show the greatest solicitude; it is beyond a simple business relationship—they have assumed a position of special trust toward the family. Few among us who have felt the sting of death cannot appreciate the grief of those bereaved by the loss. It is neither unreasonable nor unfair to expect the same appreciation by those who prepare our dead.

261 Cal.Rptr. at 778 (citation omitted). We agree that those who are entrusted with the care and preparation for burial of a decedent's body have a duty to exercise reasonable care. Further, we believe that the minority view, that does not require the plaintiff's emotional distress to manifest itself in a physical injury, is the better reasoned approach."

Chapter 14

COMPENSATION FOR HARM

Money damages, conceived as compensation for harm done and paid by the injurer to the victim, are both the normal remedy in the law of torts, and central to an understanding of tort as a legal institution. The common observation that tort is about reparation and aims to vindicate the "private" interest that the victims of harm wrongfully inflicted have in seeing to it that those who have wronged them repair the harm they have done, whereas criminal law is about punishment and aims to vindicate the public interest in penalizing and deterring harmful behavior, points to the prevalence of compensatory awards of money damages to support its claim. Legal economists, who emphasize the role of tort law in deterring dangerous behavior, point to the way in which money damages discourage such behavior by placing a "price" on the violation of someone's physical integrity or the damaging of their property

The truth that tort law is about money damages conceived as compensation is, however, only the beginning of an understanding of tort damages. Widespread agreement on this point masks a range of deep questions and disagreements. How is compensation to be conceived? As an effort to place the plaintiff in as good a position as he or she would have been but for the harm he or she has suffered? As the ineffable expression of the "sense of the community" about the amount of money necessary to compensate the victim for whatever loss of well-being he or she has experienced? As the amount necessary to make the injurer "internalize" the cost of its risky activity? And what are we to make of harms which do not readily lend themselves to measurement in monetary terms—to "pain and suffering" or "loss of enjoyment of life," for instance?

Practical questions of conceptualization and computation loom equally large. Conceptually, choices about what kinds of losses to recognize loom large: Emotional losses as well as economic ones? Losses which have already occurred? Losses which have yet to occur? Computationally, some harms are more easily quantified than others. This is true not only at a single moment in time, where economic losses may be easier to estimate than emotional ones. It is also true across time: Present losses tend to be easier to estimate than future ones. Damages must generally be awarded in total and in the present, but the harm inflicted by tortious conduct may continue to unfold in the future. The course of harm which has not yet come but which might yet come may, moreover, be uncertain. How shall we handle that uncertainty?

The materials with which we begin lay out the basic categories of damages and address the basic conceptual and practical difficulties of awarding money damages as redress for harm done.

SECTION A.   DAMAGES GENERALLY

CHRISTOPHER v. UNITED STATES
United States District Court, Eastern District of Pennsylvania, 1965.
237 F.Supp. 787.

WOOD, District Judge.

This non-jury action is a suit brought under the Federal Tort Claims Act 28 U.S.C.A. § 1346(b). The plaintiff seeks to recover damages for injuries which he sustained while undergoing treatment in a Veterans' Administration Hospital in Baltimore, Maryland in 1959.

After a full and complete trial from December 14, 1964, until December 22, 1964, we find the following:

FINDINGS OF FACT

1. The plaintiff, a 29 year-old Army veteran, was found to have tuberculosis of both lungs in December, 1958, after an examination conducted at a Veterans' Administration Clinic in Philadelphia, Pennsylvania.

* * *

[In the omitted paragraphs the court found that the plaintiff suffered paraplegia resulting from negligence in the performance of an operation in a Veterans' Administration hospital.]

41. The plaintiff was born and raised in Philadelphia, Pennsylvania, and he attended local elementary and secondary schools prior to his enlistment in the United States Army in 1948.

42. The plaintiff was honorably discharged with the rank of sergeant in July, 1952, and he secured local employment as a draftsman.

43. In February, 1954, he enrolled in a course of aeronautical engineering at the University of Alabama and was graduated with the degree of Bachelor of Science in Engineering in June, 1958.

44. In September, 1958, the plaintiff became employed as an associate engineer at Vertol Aircraft Corporation, Morton, Pennsylvania, with a salary of $110.00 per week.

45. The plaintiff then enrolled as a graduate student at the Drexel Institute of Technology for the purpose of obtaining a Master's Degree in Aeronautical Engineering while he was employed at Vertol. He attended evening classes two nights a week.

46. During his employment at Vertol the plaintiff was regarded by his supervisor as being very capable, conscientious and above average for a recently graduated engineer.

47. Before 1959, the plaintiff enjoyed a normal social life, attended dances and was active in Boy Scout activities. He also participated in athletics and organized a social group which was part of a larger organization known as the Order of Brotherly Love.

48. The plaintiff has never been married and now resides with his mother and sister in his own specially built home in Somerdale, New Jersey.

49. At the time of his entrance into the VA hospital in Baltimore, Maryland, the plaintiff was of a slender, muscular build, but was classified by the VA as 100 percent disabled because of his tuberculosis.

50. It was stipulated by the parties that the plaintiff is completely cured of his tuberculosis.

51. The plaintiff's lost wages from the date of the injury on May 4, 1959, until the date of trial amount to $42,314.00.

52. The plaintiff has not worked since May 4, 1959. He is unable to sit for long periods of time and must take a nap after four or five hours. He experiences muscle spasms in his legs with swelling and burning sensations in his feet and legs. In addition to these difficulties, he has involuntary bowel movements and occasional urinary accidents due to blockage of his catheter.

53. The plaintiff is embarrassed by these accidents and he has never applied for any type of work.

54. While at the Veterans' Administration Hospital, Bronx, New York, the plaintiff taught high school mathematics to some of the other patients.

55. The plaintiff, who is presently 34 years of age, has a future life expectancy of 40 years provided he gets intensive medical care. Without such intensive care he might not live one year.

56. The uncontradicted evidence in this case compels us to conclude that the plaintiff would have worked for 30 years, but for the injuries he sustained on May 4, 1959.

57. We further find that with the excellent rehabilitative treatment available to the plaintiff he could secure future employment utilizing his scientific training in some related engineering field.

58. Had the plaintiff not been disabled, his salary as an aeronautical engineer would have ranged from a minimum of $10,000.00 in 1964, to a maximum of $18,000.00 during the 1980's, and would have regressed to $14,000.00 by 1995, when he attains the age of 65.

59. The plaintiff is receiving *monthly* disability payments from the VA in the sum of $725.00. Of this amount $200.00 is allotted for special aid and care at home which the plaintiff would lose were he to enter a VA hospital. This means that he receives $525.00 unrelated to any medical expenses. The plaintiff will receive the VA disability benefits for the remainder of his life.

60. Assuming that the plaintiff would work for 30 more years and giving proper consideration to the future disability payments which he will receive from the Government; and assuming further, that the plaintiff will be able to secure some gainful employment in the future, we find that his lost future earning capacity is $6,000.00 annually.

61. This sum reduced to present value at the rate of 3.5 percent is $110,352.00.

62. There is no claim by the plaintiff for past medical expenses since such care was provided by the Government.

63. His future medical treatment will require intensive rehabilitation, evaluations by urologists, neurosurgeons, plastic surgeons, psychiatrists, reconstructive procedures if necessary on contractured feet if they arise, various neurosurgical procedures on his back or in his spinal canal if the reflex spasms in his legs become uncontrollable. He also runs the risk of infection of the bladder and the kidneys and decubitus ulcers.

64. Assuming that the plaintiff will live his projected life span of 40 years, and giving due consideration to the $200.00 monthly allowance which the plaintiff will receive during his entire life outside of a VA hospital we find that his future medical expense will be $5,000.00 annually making a total sum of $200,000.00.

65. On the issue of pain and suffering, we find that the plaintiff has suffered, is suffering, and will continue to suffer in the future grievous physical and mental distress. He has no hope for any future recovery and he will never regain the use of his lower extremities.

66. In addition to the above problems the plaintiff has become depressed and has suffered the permanent loss of his sex powers.

67. The plaintiff's sleeping hours are interrupted daily two or three times a night so that he may change his position to prevent bed sores. He must swing his legs from one side of the bed to the other taking care not to tangle the hose of his indwelling catheter.

68. One incident illustrative of the plaintiff's suffering occurred when some friends visited him in the Bronx Hospital. They took him out in the car and he had an unexpected bowel movement. He was taken back to the hospital, suspended by his arms and washed down with a hose.

69. His legs are subject to uncontrollable spasms which can only be corrected by an operation. He has undergone various collateral operations at the VA Hospital, Bronx, New York directly emanating from his present paraplegia.

70. We find that the plaintiff is entitled to a monetary award of $350,000.00 for past and future pain and suffering.

71. The plaintiff has received disability payments from the Government dating from May 4, 1959, until December 15, 1964, totalling $52,455.00. This sum includes a $10,000.00 payment for construction of his home, and a $1,600.00 payment for the purchase of an automobile.

72. We find that the Government is entitled to a deduction of $52,455.00 from the amount of the verdict.

* * *

On the question of damages we have specifically set forth in our findings each category of damages. We made our decision with the primary intention of awarding the plaintiff just *compensation*. While this is a tragic case we have not been influenced by sympathy in this regard.

We have followed the instructions of the United States Supreme Court in Brooks v. United States, 337 U.S. 49, 53, 69 S.Ct. 918, 921, 93 L.Ed. 1200 (1949) which stated that the amount payable under servicemen's benefit laws should be deducted " * * * *or taken into consideration*, when the serviceman obtains judgment under the Tort Claims Act." (emphasis supplied) It is only fair that this result should follow since the United States, as any other defendant, should not have to pay twice for the same injury. We have deducted the past disability payments because these sums have already been paid. With regard to the plaintiff's loss of future earning capacity, we have considered his present physical condition and prospects for future improvement through rehabilitation. We believe that with proper management and rehabilitation the plaintiff's scientific training will make it possible for him to secure employment in the future. This Court has personal knowledge of the improvements that can be effected through the diligent use of rehabilitative techniques available to paraplegics. In the unreported case of Hutton, Guardian of the Estate of Eddie Graybeal, *a minor* v. Fisher, C.A. No. 28261 (E.D.Pa.1963) a sixteen year-old boy who is a paraplegic, was trained to the degree that he can take care of all his needs. He has managed through operations and training to control his bowel and bladder movements. Also, he has learned the trades of a watchmaker and optician. In addition to these occupational improvements, he participates in wheelchair races and basketball games in New York City. He has also appeared on television and promoted National Hire the Handicapped Week. The law does not expect that such heroic determination will be exhibited by *all* plaintiffs and the defendant must accept the present plaintiff as it finds him.

While some hope for future rehabilitation does exist we do find that the plaintiff has established a diminution of earning capacity. He has shown by his past employment record and his pursuit of an advanced engineering degree that he is an industrious, capable person. The record shows that aeronautical engineers entering the field today could command an entrance salary of $7,600.00. The future prospects, assuming no serious national economic recessions or depressions, are very favorable with a high salary of $18,000.00 during the 1980's. This salary range gives no consideration to the possible management promotions which a superior engineer could attain.

In making our award, we balanced such factors as the plaintiff's proven earning ability, his prospects for some future employment, against his VA monthly disability benefits of $525.00 (unrelated to any medical expenses) and reached the conclusion that his future earning capacity has been reduced by $6,000.00 annually. We also found as a fact, that, but for his disability the plaintiff would have worked for thirty additional years. Thus, his loss of future earning capacity at $6,000.00 per year reduced to present value at the rate of 3.5 percent is $110,352.00.

* * *

In determining the plaintiff's future medical expenses, it is impossible to award a figure with any absolute certainty.

Where the tort itself is of such a nature as to preclude the ascertainment of the amount of damages with certainty, it would be a perversion of fundamental principles of justice to deny all relief to the injured person, and thereby relieve the wrongdoer from making any amend for his acts. In such case, while the damages may not be determined by mere speculation or guess, *it will be enough if the evidence show the extent of the damages as a matter of just and reasonable inference, although the result be only approximate.* The wrongdoer is not entitled to complain that they cannot be measured with the exactness and precision that would be possible if the case, which he alone is responsible for making, were otherwise. As the Supreme Court of Michigan has forcefully declared, *the risk of the uncertainty should be thrown upon the wrongdoer instead of upon the injured party.* [case cited] Story Parchment Co. v. Paterson Parchment Paper Co., 282 U.S. 555, 563, 51 S.Ct. 248, 250, 75 L.Ed. 544 (1931) (emphasis supplied)

The plaintiff has proved his present and future need for constant, unremitting and highly intensive care from almost every medical specialty known to man. There is sufficient evidence in the record to warrant an annual expense of $5,000.00 for his projected life expectancy of 40 years.

In reaching this figure we have considered the fact that he will receive, for the rest of his life, $200.00 monthly from the VA for aid and attendance at home. It matters not that the plaintiff has looked to the VA hospitals for all of his medical needs in the past. He has a right to select a private hospital or physician of his own choosing should he so desire in the future.

The last and most distressing element of damages concerns the plaintiff's pain and suffering. We have no desire to engage in the macabre by detailing every gruesome aspect of the plaintiff's considerable suffering. However, we find it difficult, if not impossible, to assess the loss of such fundamental ordinary human functions as the ability to stand, walk, run and eliminate. He has lost the ability to procreate and he will never know the pleasures and satisfactions of marriage and parenthood. He has a life that offers little in the way of optimism for the future. The disfigurement, humiliation and anxiety he has undergone is considerable. He is paralyzed from his chest down to his legs which are subject to uncontrollable spasms. This man's condition will only become increasingly more distressing with advancing years. We believe that $350,000.00 is just and reasonable compensation under the circumstances of this case.

* * *

CONCLUSIONS OF LAW

1. Jurisdiction and Venue are properly in this Court.

2. The operation of May 4, 1959, was performed in a negligent manner by a physician who was an agent or employee of the United States acting within the scope of his employment.

3. Such negligence was the proximate cause of the plaintiff's permanent injuries.

4. The plaintiff is entitled to damages in the following amounts:

Past Income	$ 42,314.00
Loss of Future Earning Capacity	110,352.00
Future Medical Expense	200,000.00
Pain and Suffering	350,000.00
Gross Damages	$702,666.00

5. The United States is entitled to a deduction of past disability payments totaling: $52,455.00

6. The plaintiff is entitled to a verdict in the sum of $650,211.00.

7. The plaintiff failed to prove that the Government's failure to warn was negligence.

8. Judgment will be entered on the verdict.

[Ed. Note: $1,000.00 in 1965 is about $3243 in 1995; $1,000.00 becomes $2,000.00 in a little more than 17.5 years at 4% inflation.]

SHERLOCK v. STILLWATER CLINIC, 260 N.W.2d 169 (Minn.1977). "[T]he elementary principle of compensatory damages * * * seeks to place injured plaintiffs in the position that they would have been in had no wrong occurred."

JONES v. FISHER, 42 Wis.2d 209, 166 N.W.2d 175 (1969) (at p. 46, supra). "([W]e rely primarily upon the good sense of jurors to determine the amount of money which will compensate an individual for whatever loss of well-being he has suffered as a result of injury.)"

KAWASNY v. UNITED STATES, 823 F.2d 194 (7th Cir.1987) (Posner, J.) "We disagree with those students of tort law who believe that pain and suffering are not real costs and should not be allowable items of damages in a tort suit. No one likes pain and suffering and most people would pay a good deal of money to be free from them. If they were not recoverable in damages, the cost of negligence would be less to the tortfeasors and there would be more negligence, more accidents, more pain and suffering, and hence higher social costs."

CHOI v. ANVIL, 32 P.3d 1 (Alaska 2001). Choi, a taxicab driver, rear-ended a pickup truck driven by Gloria Anvil. Choi's three passengers—and

Anvil and two of her passengers—brought suit against Choi for injuries allegedly suffered in the accident. Choi admitted negligently causing the accident, but contested damages. None of the plaintiffs sustained any visible physical injuries in the collision, or sought medical attention in its immediate aftermath. At trial, "the plaintiffs complained of various ailments like back, neck, and arm pain. None of the plaintiffs provided any expert testimony or otherwise offered any evidence beyond their own testimony to establish the causation, permanence, or extent of their alleged injuries." The jury returned substantial verdicts in plaintiffs' favor.

Choi appealed, urging the court to adopt a rule that would require expert testimony to establish causation of "subjective injuries"—injuries "where there is no observable symptom such as bleeding, swelling, or bruising, but only non-observable symptoms like pain and loss of strength." Expert testimony should be required, Choi argued, "because '[s]ubjective injuries require a lay person to speculate as to the existence and cause of [an] injury.' "

Held, *affirmed*. Expert testimony is only required "when the nature or character of a person's injuries require the special skill of an expert to help present the evidence to the trier of fact in a comprehensible format." When "alleged injuries—including purely subjective injuries—are of a common nature and arise from a readily identifiable cause, there is no need for the injured party to produce expert testimony. Requiring expert testimony in all such cases would needlessly increase the cost of litigation, discourage injured persons from bringing small but legitimate claims, and also burden defendants, who might feel compelled to hire their own experts in response."

ILLUSTRATIVE INSTRUCTIONS ON DAMAGES ADAPTED FROM ILLINOIS PATTERN JURY INSTRUCTIONS, CIVIL (2D ED. 1971)*

If you decide for the plaintiff on the question of liability, you must then fix the amount of money which will reasonably and fairly compensate him for any of the following elements of damage proved by the evidence to have resulted from the negligence of the defendant:

The nature, extent and duration of the injury.

The aggravation of any pre-existing ailment or condition.

The disability and disfigurement resulting from the injury.

The pain and suffering experienced and reasonably certain to be experienced in the future as a result of the injuries.

The reasonable expense of necessary medical care, treatment, and services received and the present cash value of the reasonable expenses of medical care, treatment, and services reasonably certain to be received in the future.

* See §§ 30.01–30.07, 34.01, 34.02.

The value of time, earnings, salaries lost; also the present cash value of the time, earnings, salaries reasonably certain to be lost in the future.

Whether any of these elements of damages has been proved by the evidence is for you to determine.

In the event that you find the plaintiff is entitled to damages arising in the future because of injuries, medical expenses, and loss of earnings you must determine the amount of these damages which will arise in the future.

If the damages are of a continuing nature, you may consider how long they will continue. If they are permanent in nature then in computing these damages you may consider how long the plaintiff is likely to live.

With respect to a loss of future earnings, you may consider that some persons work all of their lives and others do not; that a person's earnings may remain the same or may increase or decrease in the future.

In computing the damages arising in the future because of injuries, medical expenses, and loss of earnings, you must not simply multiply the damages by the length of time you have found they will continue or by the number of years you have found that the plaintiff is likely to live. Instead, you must determine their present cash value. "Present cash value" means the sum of money needed now, which, when added to what that sum may reasonably be expected to earn in the future, will equal the amount of the damages, expenses, and earnings at the time in the future when the damages from the injury will be suffered, the expenses must be paid, and the earnings would have been received.

Damages for pain and suffering, disability and disfigurement are not reduced to present cash value.

SPECIAL PROBLEMS OF NON–PECUNIARY LOSS

Non-pecuniary loss raises a number of difficult issues. Are such damages purely subjective or are they capable of objective assessment and comparison? What analytical principles, if any, should govern the award of such damages? What procedures should juries follow in awarding them and judges follow in reviewing them? How far should the idea of quantification be taken? If the loss of certain experiental capacities—the capacity to "enjoy life", for instance—is part of a plaintiff's injuries should the plaintiff recover for that injury, even though by virtue of that loss the plaintiff may be unaware of the loss itself? The cases that follow wrestle with these questions.

––––––

JUTZI–JOHNSON v. UNITED STATES, 263 F.3d 753 (7th Cir.2001) (Posner, J.). "The problem of figuring out how to value pain and suffering is acute * * *. Various solutions, none wholly satisfactory, have been suggested, such as asking the trier of fact, whether jurors or judge, to imagine how much they would pay to avoid the kind of pain and suffering that the victim of the defendant's negligence experienced or how much they would demand to experience it willingly, 2 Dan B. Dobbs, *Dobbs Law of Remedies:*

Damages Equity Restitution § 8.1(4), p. 383 (2d ed.1993); or to estimate how much it would cost the victim (if he survived) to obtain counseling or therapy to minimize the pain and suffering, Law Commission, *Damages for Personal Injury: Non Pecuniary Loss 8* (Consultation Paper No. 140, 1995); *Andrews v. Grand & Toy Alberta Ltd.*, (1978) 83 D.L.R. (3d) 452, 476–77 (Can.S.Ct.), or how much they would demand to assume the risk of the pain and suffering that the victim experienced. Mark Geistfeld, "Placing a Price on Pain and Suffering: A Method for Helping Juries Determine Tort Damages for Nonmonetary Injuries," 83 *Cal. L.Rev.* 773, 818–28 (1995). If they said they would demand $1,000 to assume a .01 risk of such a misfortune, this would imply that the victim should receive an award of $100,000, as that is the judgment that, if anticipated, would have induced the defendant to spend up to $1,000 to prevent. Talk is cheap, though; and maybe a better approach would be to present the jury with evidence of how potential victims themselves evaluate such risks, an approach that has been used to infer the value of life from people's behavior in using safety devices such as automobile seatbelts or in demanding risk premiums to work at hazardous jobs. See, e.g., Richard Thaler & Sherwin Rosen, "The Value of Saving a Life: Evidence from the Labor Market," in *Household Production and Consumption* 265 (Nestor E. Terleckyj ed.1975); W. Kip Viscusi, "The Value of Risks to Life and Health," 31 J. Econ. Lit.1912 (1992); Paul Lanoie, Carmen Pedro & Robert Latour, "The Value of a Statistical Life: A Comparison of Two Approaches," 10 J. *Risk & Uncertainty* 235 (1995).

"Most courts do not follow any of these approaches. Instead they treat the determination of how much damages for pain and suffering to award as a standardless, unguided exercise of discretion by the trier of fact, reviewable for abuse of discretion pursuant to no standard to guide the reviewing court either. To minimize the arbitrary variance in awards bound to result from such a throw-up-the-hands approach, the trier of fact should, as is done routinely in England, * * * be informed of the amounts of pain and suffering damages awarded in similar cases. And when the trier of fact is a judge, he should be required as part of his Rule 52(a) obligation to set forth in his opinion the damages awards that he considered comparable. We make such comparisons routinely in reviewing pain and suffering awards. It would be a wise practice to follow at the trial level as well."

RITTER v. STANTON, 745 N.E.2d 828 (Ind.App.2001). "We recognize that variability among awards is a problem primarily because it undermines the legal system's claim that like cases will be treated alike; the promise of equal justice under law is an important justification for our legal system. Criticisms of variability include the contention that it makes it harder to predict verdicts and, in turn, to settle cases, thereby adding unnecessary transaction costs to the tort system and delaying payment to plaintiffs. Furthermore, we acknowledge that inadequate notice of the limits of potential liability may impair planning for risk management, resulting in the overinvestment in liability avoidance, suppression of innovation, and higher insurance costs.

"A certain level of inconsistency, however, is inherent in the jury system and is unlikely to be eliminated because the discretion exercised by juries supports basic democratic values recognized in the Seventh Amendment right to a jury trial and similar provisions in most state constitutions '[M]oral diversity has been preferred to uniform outcomes imposed by rulemaking elites' and 'some inconsistent awards may result not from the role of the jury, but rather may simply reflect superior lawyering purchased in a free market, or the "luck of the draw" ' that is inherent in all social institutions.' See David Baldus et al., *Improving Judicial Oversight of Jury Damages Assessments: A Proposal for the Comparative Additur/Remittitur Review of Awards for Nonpecuniary Harms and Punitive Damages*, 80 IOWA L.REV. 1109, 1118 (1995)"

* * *

"If a comparability analysis is applied to reduce awards exceeding the range of purportedly similar cases, the effects are far-reaching. Because a comparability analysis effectively places a 'cap' on the jury's award regardless of the evidence, it can be considered to be second-guessing jury decisions in a manner not permitted by the Seventh Amendment. Without express statutory authority, no decisionmaker should have the power to alter a jury's award without regard for the evidence. If a jury's award can be subject to being set aside for exceeding an applicable range, the charge of the jury to fully compensate the plaintiff would no longer be paramount. The jury's decision on the amount of compensation would be replaced with a figure within the 'comparable range.' Although the jury would still find facts and calculate an amount that would compensate the plaintiff, it is disingenuous to claim that restricting the award after the fact by comparing it to other cases would not change the functioning of the jury by effectively rendering it less of a final decisionmaker and more of an advisory jury. The comparability analysis renders illusory the jury's discretion to compensate a victim."

* * *

"Furthermore, because all cases are unique, the search for comparable or similar cases is inherently flawed. * * * The inherently subjective basis of awards for pain and suffering confounds the measurement and quantification required for an accurate comparison. There simply are no standards by which to measure the effects of injuries or to convert them into dollar amounts. Similarly, the data currently available to many courts is inadequate to support a viable system of comparative review. [Furthermore,] the reported decisions used as comparison cases are likely unrepresentative of all damages awards approved by courts or agreed to by parties in comparable cases. The reported facts in these cases bearing on the level of nonpecuniary harm are often sparse or nonexistent. The comparison of cases can be easily manipulated, particularly when the factual bases for the awards in those cases are frequently not reported in great detail.[1] Each case is normally

---

1. This case perfectly illustrates our concern with comparing damage awards to other cases. If this case were written in a manner similar to other reported personal injury cases, it would likely merely contain a summary of Stanton's injuries, probably consisting of something to the effect that he suffered severe injuries including a crushed pelvis, underwent multiple surgeries, and had several complications. The opinion would indicate that he is permanently disabled and will continue to have pain and complications from his condition. However, without a

evaluated in terms of only a limited number of characteristics. Because of the uncertainty and variability associated with pain, suffering, and loss of enjoyment of life, comparing cases on that basis may have even less validity than comparing for other types of damages.''

FRIEDMAN v. C & S CAR SERVICE, 108 N.J. 72, 527 A.2d 871 (1987). Plaintiff sued for injuries suffered in an automobile accident traceable to a defectively designed brake cylinder installed by defendant. A wrist fracture caused extreme pain during treatment and permanent pain and suffering was predicted. New Jersey Rule of Court 1:7 permits counsel to suggest to the jury that it calculate damages on the basis of specific time periods, such as the amount of pain that a plaintiff will suffer each day of his life, but prohibits suggestions by counsel of specific sums for each period. In such circumstances, the judge is to instruct the jury that a counsel's time-unit summation is argumentative only and does not constitute evidence. This procedure was followed.

Judgment was entered for plaintiff on a jury verdict awarding $875,000 for past, present and future suffering and disability. The appellate division reversed and remanded, holding that whenever a time-unit summation is given, the jury must be instructed to discount damages for future non-economic losses. The supreme court here reinstated the trial court's judgment. It noted that most state judiciaries had concluded that damages for future non-economic losses should not be discounted to reflect their present value, and continued:

"Our decisional law in this area is compatible with the majority view. In *Botta v. Brunner*, 26 N.J. 82, 138 A.2d 713 (1958), we held that it was improper for counsel to suggest to the jury specific monetary amounts for pain and suffering per hour or day or week and ask that these figures be used as part of a mathematical or arithmetical formula for calculating the damages to be awarded. The Court based its holding on the 'universal acknowledgement' that there can be no fixed basis or mathematical rule for establishing damage awards for pain and suffering:

> [T]here is no measure by which the amount of pain and suffering endured by a particular human can be calculated. No market place exists at which such malaise is bought and sold.... It has never been suggested that a standard of value can be found and applied. The varieties and degrees of pain are almost infinite. Individuals differ greatly in susceptibility to pain and in capacity to withstand it. And the impossibility of recognizing or of isolating fixed levels or plateaus of suffering must be conceded. [*Id.* at 92–93, 138 A.2d 713.]

* * *

more thorough description of the injuries, the complications, the effects of the medical problems on his life, and the profound devastation the accident has caused him and his family, which we undertake to provide later, it would be impossible for any other case to be compared accurately to this one.

" * * * The time-unit rule [1:7] lends an aura of rationality to the determination of damages for non-economic losses. It has not, however, converted the determination of monetary damages for personal injury, pain and suffering into an objective or precise calculation. * * *

" * * * [W]e hold that the adoption of Rule 1:7–1(b) does not mandate or permit the discounting of damages for future pain and suffering.

"The rationale underlying our decision today distinguishes this case from *Tenore v. Nu Car Carriers*, 67 N.J. 466, 341 A.2d 613 (1975), where we held that the defendant in a wrongful death action is entitled to have the recovery for future pecuniary loss discounted to present value. Unlike damages for future pain, suffering, disability, and the like, the anticipated loss of future earnings can be calculated simply, accurately, and objectively. Therefore, requiring that an award for these damages be discounted to present value is neither artificial nor unrealistic. * * * "

UNCERTAIN FUTURE HARM

We have been looking at the categories of compensable harm, and at the difficulties of conceptualizing and estimating certain kinds of harm. In the case which follows this note, we encounter a circumstance where one of the basic difficulties encountered by the law of damages—the problem of estimating future harm—comes to the fore in an especially acute form. The plaintiff in *Jackson v. Johns–Manville* has contracted asbestosis from his exposure to asbestosis. Because he has done so, he will probably contract cancer (mesothelioma) as well. Doctrinally, the question is: Are these two harms and two claims, or just one? *Jackson* states the rule that "once the injury becomes actionable—once some effect appears—then the plaintiff is permitted to recover for all probable future manifestations as well." ([infra page 691]) This is a general rule of damages, although *Marinari* reports (infra p. 693) that a majority of jurisdictions have declined to follow it in the context of asbestos injuries.

The underlying predicament is this: If everyone who develops asbestosis probably will develop cancer as well, then they are all entitled to recover under the traditional rule. After recovering for future cancer, however, some of them will fail to contract it; while others will come down with it. If we discount everyone's damages by the probability that they will develop cancer, no one will be compensated correctly. Those who don't develop cancer will have been overcompensated; those who do will have been undercompensated. If we award full damages for cancer to everyone with asbestosis because they are all "more likely than not" to contract it, we will succeed in compensating the majority that does contract it adequately, but at the price of increased problems elsewhere. Plaintiffs who are fortunate enough never to develop cancer will have received an even bigger windfall, and the defendant will have paid for more harm than it has caused. If we apply the "two-disease" rule instead, the majority of plaintiffs with asbestosis will be forced to bring a second action when they do contract cancer. This is cumbersome and expensive. It is also unfair, because it subjects a class of severely injured plaintiffs to a special legal disability. This predicament is revisited in more detail in Chapter 20.

The facts of *Jackson* raise questions about another element of damages as well. Anyone who has contracted asbestosis from exposure to asbestos is likely to *fear* that he or she will develop cancer—mesothelioma—in the future. Should such a plaintiff be entitled to recover for his or her "fear of" cancer. Mississippi, like many states, subscribes to a traditional rule permitting recovery for this kind of mental distress when "the plaintiff's mental suffering is accompanied by a physical injury." (infra page 692) The plaintiff in *Jackson* is, of course, already suffering from asbestosis.

JACKSON v. JOHNS–MANVILLE SALES CORP.
United States Court of Appeals, Fifth Circuit, 1986.
781 F.2d 394.

[Jackson had been exposed to asbestos products during his employment as a shipyard worker. After developing asbestosis, he brought this diversity action against several manufacturers of asbestos products. Mississippi law governed his claims. The trial court allowed Jackson to introduce substantial evidence that he was likely to contract cancer (as well as asbestosis) because of his inhalation of asbestos fibers. After a jury trial, the court entered judgment against two defendants in the amount of $391,500 in compensatory damages and $625,000 in combined punitive damages.

On appeal, the court of appeals in an en banc decision certified to the Mississippi Supreme Court three questions. The second and third questions inquired whether a plaintiff who did not presently have cancer could recover damages in a strict liability action (a) for mental distress resulting from his knowledge that he had an increased risk of cancer in the future, and/or (b) for the reasonable medical probability of contracting cancer in the future. The Mississippi Supreme Court declined certification without discussion. In this opinion for an en banc court by Judge Randall, the court of appeals looked to Mississippi law to resolve the questions previously certified.]

A. RECOVERY FOR CANCER

* * * Jackson's position is that claim-splitting is disallowed in Mississippi and that the claim for cancer, insofar as it grows out of the same actionable tort which provides his recovery for asbestosis, must be raised now. Jackson reasons that, since the claim for cancer grows out of a single actionable tort, the statute of limitations with respect to cancer begins to run from the time the tort is actionable, that is, from the time asbestosis became manifest.

The defendants assert that claim-splitting is permitted in Mississippi when that would serve the ends of justice and fairness. In any case, the defendants insist, Mississippi would adopt the discovery rule with respect to asbestos-related injuries, with the result that the statute of limitations for cancer would not begin to run until cancer actually appears. The development of cancer would be a separate tort from the development of asbestosis. As a result, defendants conclude, recovery for cancer is neither permitted nor required at this time.

* * *

The defendants' argument must be rejected for two separate but related reasons. First, the truth of their crucial premise is not clear under Mississippi law. It is unclear whether Jackson *would* be permitted to sue to recover damages for cancer whenever cancer appears. Second, it *is* clear that under Mississippi tort law, plaintiffs may recover for probable future consequences.

* * *

* * * Jackson established that he will probably get cancer. In addition, he has already discovered, and brought suit to recover for, his asbestosis. Under these circumstances, it is clear that under Mississippi law Jackson may recover cancer damages. Further, having recovered cancer damages, he cannot later recover more if and when he develops cancer.

"The general rule is that where it is established that future consequences from an injury to a person will ensue, recovery therefor may be had, but such future consequences must be established in terms of reasonable probabilities." *Entex, Inc. v. Rasberry*, 355 So.2d 1102, 1104 (Miss. 1978). Defendants respond that cancer does not develop *from* asbestosis, that it can never be a future consequence *of* asbestosis. Cancer is presumably a separate injury, and recovery must therefore await manifestation. This assertion is medically sound, but legally awry. In a sense, the injury in this case is the inhalation of asbestos fibers. It was not an *actionable* injury, however, meaning it was not legally cognizable, until at least one evil *effect* of the inhalation became manifest. There was no cause of action at all, in other words, until the asbestosis appeared. * * * But in any event, once the injury becomes actionable—once *some* effect appears—then the plaintiff is permitted to recover for all probable future manifestations as well.

* * *

B. Fear

Jackson also maintains that the cancer evidence introduced at trial was relevant insofar as it elucidates the basis of the mental distress he has suffered due to the knowledge that he will probably get cancer. * * * [T]he crux of JM's argument, once again, is that these compensatory damages should not be awarded because so many people have been injured * * *

* * * [D]efendants are asking this court to change the rules in Mississippi in the case of a mass tort. However, without repeating our earlier views concerning the defendants' argument that the magnitude of its wrong should circumscribe the damages awarded against it, we note simply that the defendants have pointed to no Mississippi authority which supports their radical proposal. * * *

Jackson's fear is plainly a present injury. It is a fear which he experiences every day and every night. It is fear which is exacerbated each time he learns that another victim of asbestos has died of lung cancer. It is fear which, regardless of whether Jackson actually gets cancer, will haunt him for the rest of his life. Jackson's claim is not merely that he *might* get cancer, or that there is a remote possibility that he will. Jackson has established that there is a greater than fifty percent chance that he *will* get cancer. * * *

Under Mississippi law, damage awards for mental distress may be rendered when either of two conditions is satisfied: when the plaintiff's mental suffering is accompanied by a physical injury, or when the plaintiff establishes the defendant's misconduct to have been wilful, gross, or wanton. * * * We think it beyond cavil that in such a case as is before us, where the plaintiff manifests a present injury and has also succeeded in demonstrating gross misconduct, compensatory damages for mental distress are recoverable.

* * *

* * * [W]e conclude that the fact that this case involves a claim of strict liability and that it grows out of a mass tort would not incline the Mississippi Supreme Court to treat it differently from other torts, especially those where the jury has found that the defendants' conduct was wanton, reckless, or grossly indifferent to the rights of others. * * * Accordingly, the judgment of the district court is AFFIRMED.

EAGLE–PICHER INDUSTRIES, INC. v. COX, 481 So.2d 517 (Fla.App. 1985). " 'Fear of' claims have long been permitted. *See Alley v. Charlotte Pipe and Foundry Co.*, 159 N.C. 327, 74 S.E. 885 (1912) (plaintiff allowed to recover for mental suffering since wound from burn 'liable' to lead to 'early cancer' or 'sarcoma'). The justification for permitting recovery for 'fear of' is that the plaintiff suffers, since '[l]ike the sword of Damocles [plaintiff] knows not when it will fall.' *Id.* at 331, 74 S.E. at 886. But, if Damocles supplies the reason for permitting recovery, Pandora supplies the reason for at least limiting recovery."

" * * * [Several] courts have required that 'fear of' claims be available only to those who have suffered a physical injury. * * *

"The physical injury requirement is consistent with Florida law, necessary and fair. Millions of people have been exposed to asbestos. Permitting an action for fear of cancer where there has been no physical injury from the asbestos would likely devastate the court system as well as the defendant manufacturers.[19] * * * [T]he physical injury requirement for a mental distress from fear of cancer claim is linked to the merits of the claim, since plaintiffs with asbestosis may have a well-founded greater reason to fear contracting cancer than those who do not have asbestosis. * * *

---

19. As of March 1983, 24,000 claimants had filed asbestos-related suits. It has been estimated that new suits are being docketed at the rate of approximately 500 per month. While this is certainly a tremendous case load, it does not even approach the staggering 21 million figure estimated for the number of Americans significantly exposed to asbestos but who, as yet, do not claim to have asbestosis or cancer. *Jackson v. Johns–Manville Sales Corp.*, 750 F.2d at 1336.

"* * * Evidence that the plaintiff had an enhanced risk of contracting cancer was admissible as part of the proof that the plaintiff had a present mental distress caused by his fear of getting cancer in the future in a case such as this where the plaintiff already had manifested the physical disease of asbestosis. The verdict form in which the defendant acquiesced does not indicate that the jury awarded damages to the plaintiff for his enhanced risk of contracting cancer in the future, and since the other items of damages support the amount of the verdict, the defendant cannot establish that the jury considered this evidence for a purpose other than that for which it was properly admitted. Accordingly, the judgment below is

Affirmed."

MARINARI v. ASBESTOS CORP., 417 Pa.Super. 440, 612 A.2d 1021 (1992). "The general issue in this asbestos exposure action is whether Pennsylvania, in the context of asbestos actions, shall be a one disease or two-disease state." *Held*, "we today join a majority of jurisdictions which have responded to this difficult issue" by "allowing an action for nonmalignant asbestos disease and a separate action for cancer."

Although Pennsylvania "courts have generally followed the rule that all claims against a single defendant arising from a single transaction must be asserted in a single action," this "rigid rule" must be abandoned "[i]n order to accomplish just results in the resolution of claims for latent asbestos diseases." The two-disease approach serves "the integrity of the process" because "a fair and just resolution of disputes depends upon a search for truth, based on factual, non-speculative evidence." It also promotes "the fairness of the result" because "[l]itigation by an injured citizen against another citizen must result in a recovery of adequate compensation by the one and payment by the other of no more than fair and just compensation * * *.*"

SCHWEGEL v. GOLDBERG, 209 Pa.Super. 280, 228 A.2d 405 (1967). The four-year-old plaintiff, struck by an automobile driven by defendant, suffered a skull fracture and contusion of the brain. A neurosurgeon testified that the plaintiff "has one chance in twenty of developing seizures at some time in the future up to 15, 20 years from now." Defendant objected to admitting this testimony. Plaintiff had a jury verdict for $7,500. In affirming, the court said: "* * * Nor was the neurosurgeon speculating or guessing when, based on statistics in his field of expertise, he indicated the probabilities of this particular plaintiff suffering from epileptic seizures as a result of a condition caused by this accident. There is nothing evidentially improper about this testimony. If we were to rule it out we would be holding that such possible future effects are not entitled to any consideration as a matter of substantive law. See II Wigmore, Evidence § 663(1), (3rd ed. 1940). That would be unfair since the action must be brought within the time limitations fixed by our law and all damages, past, present and future, must be determined in that one action. Admittedly the probability of this child's getting epileptic seizures is low and it should be weighed by the jury accordingly. However, rather than keep this medical knowledge from the jury we are of the opinion that the defendant's remedy lies in objecting to the excessiveness of the verdict in a proper case."

———

DePASS v. UNITED STATES, 721 F.2d 203 (7th Cir.1983). Struck in Illinois by a car driven by an employee of the United States, and sustaining serious injuries including traumatic amputation of his left leg below the knee, plaintiff sued under the Federal Tort Claims Act. Admitting liability, the government contested damages only. Plaintiff's case included expert testimony by a Dr. Cohen, based on the NIH study of Hrubec and Ryder of 3,890 Americans who had suffered traumatic limb amputations, establishing a statistical connection between such amputations and future cardiovascular problems decreasing life expectancy. "Dr. Cohen testified that DePass had a 44–58 percent higher than normal risk of dying of heart disease, resulting in a 30 percent reduction in DePass's life expectancy from 37 to 26 years, a difference of 11 years." Other studies varied, some showing no statistical connection.

In explaining its award of damages, the district court stated that it found no evidence demonstrating by a preponderance that plaintiff had suffered a loss of life expectancy, and that the proffered expert testimony dealt only with "possibilities and speculation." The court of appeals affirmed, since "we cannot say that the district court was clearly erroneous * * *."

In his dissenting opinion, Judge Posner concluded that, in the light of all the evidence offered, the "district judge could have no basis for rejecting Dr. Cohen's assessment" of the relative weight of the Hrubec and Ryder study and another, inconsistent study. Rather the district judge "appears to have rejected the entire class of evidence—statistical evidence—illustrated by the medical evidence in this case * * *. Yet most knowledge, and almost all legal evidence, is probabilistic * * *. [T]he probabilities that are derived from statistical studies are no less reliable in general than the probabilities that are derived from direct observation, from intuition, or from case studies of a single person or event—all familiar sources of legal evidence." For example, in deciding how much to award a plaintiff in a personal injury case for medical attention for the rest of his life, the court must estimate how long he can be expected to live by consulting a mortality table, "which is to say by looking at a statistical summation of the experience of thousands or millions of people none of whom is a party or a witness in the case, rather than by studying the lifelines on the victim's palms."

Looking to Illinois cases, Judge Posner concluded that risk of a future consequence of an accident, even though not certain to materialize, was compensable. He found a trend toward allowing recovery for reduction in life expectancy. "As it should be. A tortfeasor should not get off scot-free because instead of killing his victim outright he inflicted an injury that is likely though not certain to shorten the victim's life." The opinion noted that "the additional loss inflicted by shortening what is now likely to be a rather miserable life may be slight in pecuniary terms, especially after being discounted to present value." Nonetheless, proving that the accident probably shortened his life would entitle DePass to some additional damages. Later, the opinion observed:

"It is of course unlikely that DePass will die exactly 11 years earlier because of the accident. He may never get heart disease. Or he may be cut down by it long before he is within 11 years of the expected end of his life. * * * That is how damages are calculated in personal-injury cases; and a judge is not free to say, in my court we do not allow statistical inference. Knowledge increasingly is statistical, and judges must not let themselves lag too far behind the progress of knowledge. * * *

"The district judge's rejection of such evidence, if widely followed, would lead to systematically undercompensating the victims of serious accidents and thus to systematically underdeterring such accidents. * * *

" * * * [T]he case should be remanded to the district court for a determination of the amount of damages necessary to compensate DePass for an 11–year reduction of his life expectancy."

PERIODIC AWARD OF DAMAGES

In *Jackson* we saw one fundamental uncertainty that afflicts the law of damages grow more acute. We knew that the plaintiff—and many others similarly situated—probably would contract cancer. We did not, however, know for certain that they would come down with cancer. One solution to this kind of uncertainty is periodic damages. These have the virtue of adjudicating liability while the evidence is still fresh, while permitting us to wait and see what kind of harm develops.

————

JANE DOE ET AL. v. STATE OF NEW YORK
Supreme Court of New York, Appellate Division, Fourth Department, 1993.
189 A.D.2d 199, 595 N.Y.S.2d 592.

[Plaintiff Jane Doe, a "registered nurse," contracted HIV after being "struck by a needle contaminated with the blood of an AIDS patient." The patient was an "inmate at Mid–State Correctional Facility" who, after becoming irrational and agitated, removed his oxygen mask and dislodged an intravenous needle inserted into his left arm. "Following a grand-mal seizure apparently induced by lack of oxygen, the patient became even more combative. While attempting to restrain the patient, the hospital staff requested assistance from two correction officers who were present, but they refused to intervene." Jane Doe's "gloved hand" was punctured by the needle when she and several other nurses attempted to restrain the patient and return him to his bed. She and her husband brought suit for their damages against the state, employer of the two officers. (Those portions of the opinion that relate only to his damages have been omitted.) At trial, "[e]xpert testimony * * * established that the average individual infected with HIV will develop full-blown AIDS within eight to 10 years following seroconversion. Jane Doe's physician testified that her condition appeared to be progressing more rapidly than most. Based upon that testimony, the court determined that Jane Doe would be likely to develop AIDS within the next four or five years and that her reasonable life expectancy would be through 1997."]

After trial, the Court of Claims determined that, based on the failure of the correction officers to intervene in the hospital employees' struggle with the inmate/patient, the State breached its duty to provide reasonable security to the hospital staff and that the state's negligence was the sole proximate cause of claimants' injuries. The Court of Claims awarded Jane Doe a total of $4,354,550 in damages allocated as follows:

Past medical expenses—$1,700

Future medical expenses—$59,000

Pain and suffering to date—$750,000

Loss of wages—$43,850

Future pain and suffering—$3,500,000.

* * *

The court denied in part Jane Doe's claim for future economic loss, without prejudice to the right of her distributees to maintain a wrongful death action for pecuniary loss subsequent to her death.

On appeal, claimants contend that the court erred in failing to make a complete award for future economic loss. In addition, they contend that CPLR article 50–B is unconstitutional.[1] * * *

* * *

1. The statute provided, in pertinent part, that:

(e) With respect to awards of future damages in excess of two hundred fifty thousand dollars in an action to recover damages for personal injury, injury to property or wrongful death, the court shall enter judgment as follows:

* * * [T]he court shall enter a judgment for the amount of the present value of an annuity contract that will provide for the payment of the remaining amounts of future damages in periodic installments. The present value of such contract shall be determined in accordance with generally accepted actuarial practices by applying the discount rate in effect at the time of the award to the full amount of the remaining future damages, as calculated pursuant to this subdivision. The period of time over which such periodic payments shall be made and the period of time used to calculate the present value of the annuity contract shall be the period of years determined by the trier of fact in arriving at the itemized verdict; provided, however, that the period of time over which such periodic payments shall be made and the period of time used to calculate the present value for damages attributable to pain and suffering shall be ten years or the period of time determined by the trier of fact, whichever is less. The court, as part of its judgment, shall direct that the defendants and their insurance carriers shall be required to offer and to guarantee the purchase and payment of such an annuity contract. Such annuity contract shall provide for the payment of the annual payments of such remaining future damages over the period of time determined pursuant to this subdivision. The annual payment for the first year shall be calculated by dividing the remaining amount of future damages by the number of years over which such payments shall be made and the payment due in each succeeding year shall be computed by adding four percent to the previous year's payment. Where payment of a portion of the future damages terminates in accordance with the provisions of this article, the four percent added payment shall be based only upon that portion of the damages that remains subject to continued payment. Unless otherwise agreed, the annual sum so arrived at shall be paid in equal monthly installments and in advance.

[FUTURE ECONOMIC LOSS]

The Court of Claims erred in limiting Jane Doe's future economic loss to her postinjury life expectancy (see Restatement [Second] of Torts § 924, comment c, at 524–26). Only an award based on one's preinjury life expectancy truly reflects the injured party's actual loss. To hold otherwise would in effect reward defendant for having successfully injured Jane Doe severely enough to shorten her life span. Thus, we conclude that, where the proof in the record permits the loss to be ascertained with reasonable certainty, damages attributable to an injured person's lost earning capacity due to injury must be awarded directly to that person during his or her lifetime utilizing a preinjury life expectancy. That rule must apply in those situations where, as here, an actual shortened life expectancy can be determined prior to death.

* * *

The economic and medical proof in the record is sufficient for us to determine the amount of damages to compensate Jane Doe adequately for her future economic loss. Based on that proof, we find that Jane Doe, who was 42 years of age at the time of trial and earning approximately $30,000 annually, will likely become completely disabled from AIDS in 1996. We further find that she has a reasonable work-life expectancy as a registered nurse through the age of 58. Utilizing the calculations offered by the economists and making allowances for lost fringe benefits as a percentage of income and without any adjustment for Jane Doe's personal consumption, we determine that the impairment of earnings and lost wage component of Jane Doe's future economic loss is $450,000. * * * Thus, the judgment should be modified to provide for such an award and the matter remitted to the Court of Claims for purposes of determining the amount of the judgment to be entered pursuant to article 50–B.

CONSTITUTIONALITY AND APPLICABILITY OF CPLR ARTICLE 50–B

Because the future damage awards made to [Jane Doe and her husband] exceed $250,000, the court was required to structure the judgment pursuant to CPLR article 50–B. After making necessary adjustments for payment of litigation expenses and attorneys' fees, the court entered judgment on the remainder of the future damages awards to Jane and Joseph Doe in excess of $250,000 "for the amount of the present value of an annuity contract that will provide for the payment of the remaining amounts of future damages in periodic installments." * * * The amended judgment in favor of Jane Doe provides for a lump-sum payment of $2,067,195.23 and total annual periodic payments of $389,794.93. * * * Claimants * * * moved after trial to have the total award paid in a lump sum and for a declaration that article 50–B was unconstitutional * * *.

Claimants contend that the periodic payment provisions of article 50–B requiring future damage awards in excess of $250,000 to be paid over a period of time instead of in one lump sum deprives them of their property without due process of law. They also maintain that the failure of the article to define 'discount rate' renders it impermissibly vague * * *. We disagree.

[The court ruled that Article 50–B did not deprive the plaintiffs of their property without due process of law because the statute pursued the "permissible" legislative objective of maintaining "the moderate cost of liability insurance premiums, while assuring adequate compensation for tort victims throughout the entire period of their loss" and did so through means "reasonably relate[d]" to this objective.]

[We also rule that Article 50–B is not "void for vagueness" because its use of] the term 'discount rate' can be determined with reasonable certainty. * * * The fact that a number of trial courts have applied different discount rates in structured judgment determinations does not, in our view, render the enactment unconstitutionally vague. In providing that present value determinations are to be made 'in accordance with generally accepted actuarial practices by applying the discount rate in effect at the time of the award' (CPLR 5041[e]), the Legislature merely provided for a flexible approach to such determinations, an approach not uncommon in previous practice. Moreover, although claimants asserted that the term 'discount rate' is confusing and impossible to implement with any consistency, their economist determined that a value of 6% was appropriate.

* * *

Accordingly, the judgment should be modified to provide Jane Doe with an award for all her future economic loss (impairment of earnings and lost wages of $450,00 * * *) and the matter remitted to the Court of Claims for purposes of determining the amount of the judgment to be entered pursuant to article 50–B.

DISCOUNTING FUTURE HARM

The dollar figure assigned to the future harm component of a personal injury award compensates the plaintiff for all of the harm caused by her injury, taking the expected course of her life had there been no injury as the baseline from which her loss is measured. In many cases, plaintiffs' injuries will extend over the course of their entire lives. The damage awards that compensate them for those injuries, however, are usually paid at the time that a final judgment in the case is entered. Because money in hand will grow over time, the payment of damages for future harm at the conclusion of the suit raises the issue of "discounting"—of whether, and how much, damage awards paid in the present to compensate for future harm should be reduced in order to avoid overcompensating the plaintiff.

Assuming that juries are naturally inclined to calculate in present dollars,[1] the conceptual answer to the question "What discount rate is appropriate?" is "A discount rate equal to the 'real interest rate.'" The

---

1. Of course, juries can be instructed, in the manner of the Illinois Jury Instructions excerpted supra p. ___, to determine the "present cash value" of the plaintiff's damages, meaning "the sum of money needed now, which, when added to what that sum may reasonably be expected to earn in the future, will equal the amount of the damages, expenses, and earnings at the time in the future when the damages from the injury will be suffered, the expenses must be paid, and the earnings would have been received." When so instructed, juries should discount their awards by the anticipated rate of inflation, as well as by the "real rate of interest."

anticipated rate of inflation, and a "risk premium" covering the chance that money owed will never be paid, should not be taken into account. Anticipated inflation should not be included in the discount rate because, if juries are naturally inclined to calculate in present dollars, their judgments can be adjusted for inflation simply by giving the plaintiff the sum that they think she is entitled to at the conclusion of the case. A jury conclusion that the plaintiff is, say, entitled to $10,000.00 ten years from now to compensate her for harm she will have suffered that year, can be effected simply by giving the plaintiff $10,000.00 today. Although inflation will cause that $10,000.00 to grow in nominal terms (e.g., to become $11,000.00), if the award grows *only at the rate of inflation* it will still be worth $10,000.00 in real dollars ten years from now. (If inflation causes $10,000.00 to become $11,000.00 in ten years, that $11,000.00 is worth $10,000.00 in today's dollars.).

Similarly, although people usually demand some "risk premium" to cover the chance that a payment promised in the future will not be made, the risk of nonpayment is properly excluded from court calculations of an appropriate discount rate. Plaintiffs are *entitled* to the damages that courts award them in tort actions. It would therefore be unjust to discount (that is, to reduce) their awards by factoring in some risk that the defendant will, in fact, successfully shirk its legal duty. Conversely, the real rate of interest is properly included in calculations of an appropriate discount rate, because money in hand today can be invested in a "riskless," readily available financial instrument (e.g., a Treasury Bill, or a Certificate of Deposit) at a rate higher than the rate of inflation. The return over and above the anticipated rate of inflation that these riskless financial instruments yield is the "real rate of interest." While plaintiffs cannot be expected to gamble with their awards, they can be expected to earn the riskless rate of return on those awards. Consequently, unless damage awards are discounted by the real rate of interest, the plaintiff will be overcompensated because her award will grow at inflation plus the real rate of interest.

In practice, courts face the same problems that everyone else faces in determining "the real rate of interest." The yields on "riskless" financial instruments such as Treasury Bills and Certificates of Deposit lump together a component covering anticipated inflation, and a component equal to the "real interest rate." Teasing these apart is a matter of guesswork. In the *Christopher* decision (supra p. 678) the court chose a discount rate of 3.5%. Other courts have chosen rates as low as 1.5%. Even in light of this indeterminacy, however, the "discount rate" of 6% suggested by plaintiff's expert in Doe is unusually high. Furthermore, using such a high rate appears to be against the plaintiff's interest, because it reduces the total dollar value of the damage award for future harm more than the use of a lower and more plausible rate of 2 to 4% would. Doe's attorney believed, however, that unless he reduced the total dollar amount of plaintiff's damages by discounting them at an abnormally high rate, the jury would be troubled by the sheer size of the award, and would reduce the total award arbitrarily and severely. Preemptively reducing the size of the award by using an unusually high discount rate would, he thought, lead to a larger award in the end.

These matters are discussed by the majority opinion, and by Judge Friendly's doubting concurrence, in Feldman v. Allegheny Airlines, Inc., 524 F.2d 384 (2d Cir.1975).

———

NORFOLK AND WESTERN RAILWAY v. LIEPELT, 444 U.S. 490, 100 S.Ct. 755, 62 L.Ed.2d 689 (1980). The Court held that, in actions for compensation (in this case, for wrongful death) brought under the Federal Employers Liability Act, the computation of future lost earnings must take account of after-tax income rather than gross income before taxes. Such a computation "provides the only realistic measure" of a wage earner's support of a family. Hence estimated future income tax liability must be deducted from estimated future gross income. The Court also held that the trial court should have given a requested instruction to the jury indicating that the federal Internal Revenue Code exempts from taxable income the amount of damages received from personal injury claims.

SECTION B.   WRONGFUL DEATH

In the early period of the common law the death of either the tortfeasor or the claimant terminated the cause of action and abated an action already begun. In the fourteenth century, however, statutes were enacted permitting the representative of a deceased person to maintain an action for a taking of property that diminished the estate, and, without statute, restitutional actions either at law or in equity could be maintained for the value of property taken before the death of either party.

At present in most states, statutes have been enacted causing tort actions to survive the death of either party. (In many statutes exceptions are made as to actions for harms peculiarly personal, such as defamation and malicious prosecution). Such statutes are commonly known as Survival Statutes; they transfer to the estate of the deceased person rights and liabilities the deceased would have had if he or she had lived.

Survival and Death Statutes Distinguished. If the defendant has injured another but has not caused death, and either the injured person or the defendant has died before trial, only the Survival Statute comes into operation. If, however, the defendant's act has caused the death of another, two distinct statutory provisions affect the recovery of damages in most jurisdictions and the rights existing under these two different provisions are usually referred to as distinct causes of action. One of these is in the estate of the deceased and includes elements of damage for which the deceased could have recovered had he not died; this is the cause of action under the Survival Statute. The other cause of action is created by the Death Statute. The first Death Statute, enacted in England in 1846, is commonly known as Lord Campbell's Act. It provided damages for near relatives who were dependents of the person killed, damages being given in accordance with pecuniary benefits they probably would have received but for the death. This statute has been widely copied in the United States with variations as to the amount of recovery and the persons who may be beneficiaries.

Damages for wrongful death are, with rare exception, an instance of recovery for "relational harm." Except when damages are awarded for the victim's loss of enjoyment of his or her life, recovery is by various person related to the victim, who have suffered through the victim's wrongful death. Because the recovery is by someone related to the victim, the question "Who may recover?" is one of the basic questions of wrongful death damages. We begin with another basic question: What kinds of damages may be recovered?

OTANI v. BROUDY

Court of Appeals of Washington, Division 1, 2002.
114 Wash.App. 545, 59 P.3d 126.

BECKER, C.J.

The issue in this appeal is whether loss of enjoyment of life is recoverable by a decedent's estate in a suvival action as an item of damage compensating for the decedent's shortened life expectancy. We conclude it is not, and reverse an award of $450,000 to the estate of a decedent who died shortly after surgery without conscious pain or awareness that she had been fatally injured. Had the decedent lived, she would have had no claim for loss of life; therefore, no such claim survived to her personal representative.

The facts are uncontested. While performing surgery upon Yaeko Otani to implant a pacemaker, appellant Dr. David Broudy punctured his patient's aorta, causing uncontrollable bleeding. Ms. Otani was unconscious when injured and died several hours later without regaining consciousness.

At the time of her death, Ms. Otani was 81 years old. She enjoyed an active life. She gardened, traveled, and cooked. She had close relationships with her two children, was active in her church, and had a wide circle of friends. If the implantation of the pacemaker had been successful, Ms. Otani would have had a normal life expectancy of an additional 7.9 years.

* * *

The only issue raised in this appeal is whether the award of $450,000 for loss of enjoyment of life was authorized under Washington's survival statutes.

A trial court's conclusions of law are reviewed *de novo. Inland Foundry Co. v. Dep't of Labor & Industries,* 106 Wash.App. 333, 340, 24 P.3d 424 (2001). Interpretation of a statute is also a question of law and is reviewed *de novo. Cockle v. Dep't of Labor & Indus.,* 142 Wash.2d 801, 807, 16 P.3d 583 (2001).

The wrongful death statutes, RCW 4.20.010 and RCW 4.20.020, create a cause of action that is not available in the common law, for the losses of specific beneficiaries caused by the wrongful death. *Gray v. Goodson,* 61 Wash.2d 319, 325, 378 P.2d 413 (1963). In contrast, Washington's survival statutes, RCW 4.20.046 and 4.20.060, do not create a new cause of action; they preserve the causes of action that the decedent could have maintained if still alive. *White v. Johns–Manville Corp.*, 103 Wash.2d 344, 358, 693 P.2d 687 (1985).

The Legislature enacted the survival statutes "to remedy an anomalous twist in the common law which allowed victims of tortious injury to sue if they survived, but barred their claims if they died." *Cavazos v. Franklin*, 73 Wash.App. 116, 118, 867 P.2d 674 (1994). The general survival statute, RCW 4.20.046, preserves all causes of action that the decedent could have brought even for injuries unrelated to the death. The special survival statute, RCW 4.20.060, is limited to claims for personal injury resulting in death. The special survival statute, also known as the death-by-personal-injury statute, has always allowed a decedent's estate to recover for all the decedent's damages, including pain and suffering. *Walton v. Absher Construction*, 101 Wash.2d 238, 245, 676 P.2d 1002 (1984). Before 1993, the proviso in the general survival statute expressly disallowed recovery of damages such as pain and suffering. [In 1993, "the Legislature amended the proviso in the general survival statute to 'close the gap' between the two statutes. *Tait v. Wahl*, 97 Wash.App. 765, 773, n. 3, 987 P.2d 127 (1999) *review denied*, 140 Wash.2d 1015, 5 P.3d 9 (2000)."]

* * *

A Supreme Court case decided under the former version of the general survival statute held that recoverable damages in a survival action do not include loss of enjoyment of life. *Wooldridge v. Woolett*, 96 Wash.2d 659, 666, 638 P.2d 566 (1981) (affirming judgment for funeral and burial expenses only, where decedent was a 22–year old high school graduate with a "spotty" job history and no spouse or dependents; trial court refused to give instruction that would have allowed recovery for the qualitative loss of life's pleasures in addition to loss of future earning capacity.). "The loss of life's amenities should be recoverable only by plaintiffs who survive compensable injuries, since such lost pleasures are personal to that individual and essentially represent pain and suffering." *Wooldridge*, 96 Wash.2d at 666, 638 P.2d 566.

The holding in *Wooldridge* did not, however, mean that loss of enjoyment of life is the same thing as pain and suffering. A plaintiff may recover for loss of enjoyment of life as a distinct item of damages in a personal injury action that is not a survival action. *Kirk v. Washington State University*, 109 Wash.2d 448, 746 P.2d 285 (1987) (personal injury action for injuries incurred during cheerleading practice; jury properly instructed to consider loss of enjoyment of life as distinct from damages for pain and suffering and disability and disfigurement). * * * Under *Kirk* it is clear that separate instructions for each item are not necessarily duplicative:

> Recovery for pain and suffering only compensates for physical and mental discomfort caused by the injury. Recovery for disability compensates for inability to lead a 'normal life' but does not imply any recovery for loss of a specific unusual activity such as ballet dancing.... Recovery for lost wages or lost earning capacity compensates for economic value,

but does not include the noneconomic rewards to the dancer. The trial court in the present case may have felt the need to alert the jury of its prerogative to include consideration of Kirk's loss of enjoyment of life based upon her inability to pursue her interests and abilities in ballet.

Kirk, 109 Wash.2d at 461, 746 P.2d 285 (citations omitted).

The trial court in this case relied on *Kirk's* distinction between loss of enjoyment of life and pain and suffering, and concluded that Ms. Otani's estate should recover for Ms. Otani's loss of the enjoyment of the remaining years of her life:

> THE COURT: With regard to Ms. Otani's claim for loss of enjoyment of life, I'm allowing the claim, and this is my brief analysis:
>
> * * *
>
> * * * the cause of action that Mrs. Otani would have had, had she not died but merely been severely injured would have been loss of enjoyment of life. Under *Kirk,* the loss of enjoyment of life is the loss of life's pleasures, the inability to enjoy the qualitative aspects of interests, avocations, vocations. The loss of enjoyment of life is conceptually different than pain and suffering for a number of reasons, but, most significantly here, pain and suffering itself ends with the death. The pain is over.
>
> But the loss of enjoyment of life begins with the death.
>
> * * *
>
> If we do not allow for recovery for this element of damage, it would perpetuate the anomaly that it is still cheaper for a defendant to [kill] the plaintiff than to [wound] the plaintiff. And there's no possibility of duplicative recovery if loss of enjoyment of life is authorized in this action because there's no other element of the damages that would cover that type of loss.

The trial court's conclusion conflicts with the *Wooldridge* court's holding that damages for loss of enjoyment of life are recoverable only by plaintiffs who survive compensable injuries. *Wooldridge,* 96 Wash.2d at 666, 638 P.2d 566. The estate argues that *Wooldridge* has been effectively overruled by *Kirk* and the 1993 amendment to RCW 4.20.046. But * * * *Kirk* did not overrule *Wooldridge;* rather, it recognized that *Wooldridge* was concerned with a survival action, not a personal injury action. The 1993 amendment did not eliminate the significance of this distinction. While both survival statutes now allow a decedent's estate to recover for the decedent's pain and suffering, there must be evidence that the decedent experienced pain and suffering even if only for a short time.[2] Loss of enjoyment of life must likewise be experienced in life before it can become the basis for an award of damages. For this reason, it is available in a personal injury action, but not in a survival action.

---

2. Conscious pain and suffering can include the awareness that "life and everything fine that it encompassed was prematurely ending." *Bin-* *gaman v. Grays Harbor Community Hosp.,* 103 Wash.2d 831, 699 P.2d 1230 (1985).

The estate argues that Ms. Otani, whether conscious or not, did experience the loss of 7.9 years of her life. * * * But the estate clearly was not seeking an award for any loss experienced by Ms. Otani in the few short hours between her injury and her death, and thus we are not asked to decide whether such damages would be available in the case of a person who was comatose for an extended period before death. Rather, the question is whether to award damages for a number of years after death. Because this was a loss which, in the trial court's words, "begins with the death," it is not a claim Ms. Otani would have been able to make if she were still alive. *See Federated Servs. v. Estate of Norberg,* 101 Wash.App. 119, 125–27, 4 P.3d 844 (2000), *review denied,* 142 Wash.2d 1025, 21 P.3d 1150 (2001) (estate cannot recover for son's loss of prospective inheritance because he could not have recovered it if he were still alive). In a survival action, shortened life expectancy is relevant "only to the extent it affects the loss of value of a decedent's future earning capacity." *Wooldridge,* 96 Wash.2d at 667, 638 P.2d 566.

The point is well explained in a case the *Wooldridge* court found persuasive, *Willinger v. Mercy Catholic Medical Center,* 482 Pa. 441, 393 A.2d 1188 (1978), cited in *Wooldridge,* 96 Wash.2d at 665, 638 P.2d 566. In *Willinger,* a five-year-old boy died while under anesthesia. The father brought wrongful death and survival actions and sought separate damages for the boy's shortened life expectancy. The trial court instructed the jury that it could consider the boy's loss of amenities or pleasures of life as part of its award of damages. The Pennsylvania Supreme Court held the instruction erroneous because such an award would be the equivalent of damages for the loss of life itself:

> Thus, to a large extent it has been the plaintiff's consciousness of his or her inability to enjoy life that we have compensated under the rubric of "loss of life's pleasures". Unlike one who is permanently injured, one who dies as a result of injuries is not condemned to watch life's amenities pass by. Unless we are to equate loss of life's pleasures with loss of life itself, we must view it as something that is compensable only for a living plaintiff who has suffered from that loss.

Willinger, 393 A.2d at 1191.

Our survival statutes preserve claims that a living person could have brought; that is, they govern only "predeath damages." *Hatch v. Tacoma Police Dept.,* 107 Wash.App. 586, 590, 27 P.3d 1223 (2001). They do not create claims on behalf of dead persons for the loss of life itself. Ms. Otani did not suffer any noneconomic "predeath damages" as a result of her fatal injury and thus no claim for such damages survived to her personal representative.

The judgment is reversed and remanded for revision consistent with this opinion.

EYOMA v. FALCO, 247 N.J.Super. 435, 589 A.2d 653 (App.Div.1991). Survival and wrongful death action brought by mother and children of patient who entered a coma following surgery and remained unconscious until his death a year later. The issue on appeal was whether "loss of enjoyment of life" damages could be awarded to a "tortiously-injured party who, before death, existed in a comatose condition, unable to perceive pain or pleasure." *Held*, "loss of enjoyment of life is a separate and distinct item of damages, recoverable in a survival action, and the fact that the victim may be in a comatose state should not preclude an award of damages for the total disability and impairment inflicted by the tortious injury."

CHOCTAW MAID FARMS, INC. v. HAILEY, 822 So.2d 911 (Miss.2002). Wrongful death action brought by wife and estate of deceased 23 year old motorist, who died when a tractor-trailer truck owned and operated by Choctaw Maid Farms collided with his pickup truck. The trial court entered judgment against the trucking company on a jury verdict which found the defendant to be 90% negligent. During closing arguments, counsel for the plaintiff-appellee asked the jury to return damages of $1,440,512 for lost wages; $2,000,000 for loss of consortium; $7,332 for miscellaneous expenses; and $1,902,318 for loss of enjoyment of life. The loss of enjoyment of life figure was calculated by multiplying Hailey's probable life expectancy by the minimum wage. The jury awarded an amount exactly equal to the sum of these figures, less 10%. *Held*, judgment of the trial court is affirmed as to all issues.

"The right to recover for loss of enjoyment of life is included in Miss.Code Ann. § 11–7–13 (Supp.2001) which states that in a wrongful death case, the person bringing suit is *entitled to recover all damages of every kind and nature which might have been awarded to the decedent had he lived,* and any damages for which the decedent's wrongful death beneficiaries sustained by reason of his death. The issue of loss of enjoyment of life was properly submitted to the jury by the trial court, and the damages awarded were not contrary to the overwhelming weight of the credible evidence.

The statute plainly states "the fact that death was instantaneous shall in no case affect the right of recovery." *Id.* Although the language employed by the Legislature in the wrongful death act is far-reaching, it is clear. In keeping with this statute, we have previously upheld an award of loss of enjoyment of life (hedonic damages) in a wrongful death suit. *See Thomas v. Hilburn,* 654 So.2d 898 (Miss.1995). The main difference between *Thomas* and the case sub judice is that the deceased in *Thomas* lived for six days before he died, whereas death was instantaneous in the present situation. *Thomas,* 654 So.2d at 900. This presents the question: How much enjoyment of life could one lose in six days? What if the deceased lived for six days (or six months or six years) in a coma? The distinction between those who may recover for loss of enjoyment of life becomes blurred when alternate scenarios are proposed. If enjoyment of life is proportional to the knowledge that one is able or unable to enjoy life, then it stands to reason that someone in a coma would not be allowed to recover hedonic damages. Following this same logic, a party who lived only a few days should only be able to recover for the loss of enjoyment he suffered in those few days. How much is one day of enjoyment of life worth? To what extent does any particular injury prevent one from enjoying life?

Loss of enjoyment of life is just that—loss of the ability to enjoy life in the manner to which one has become accustomed. Alive, dead, in a coma or with bodily injuries, the individual is unable to function in a way which allows him to enjoy life. Loss of enjoyment of life (hedonic damages) is an attempt to recompense the injured party for his loss. Nothing in Miss.Code Ann. § 11–7–13 says or should be construed otherwise. We find, as per the trial court's ruling, that Hailey was properly allowed to recover damages for loss of enjoyment of life."

MATTYASOVSZKY v. WEST TOWNS BUS CO., 61 Ill.2d 31, 330 N.E.2d 509 (1975). In an action brought by a father as administrator of his 12–year-old son's estate under the Illinois Survival Act and Wrongful Death Act considered in Murphy v. Martin Oil Co., supra, the jury found defendant guilty of wilful and wanton conduct and awarded $50,000 punitive as well as $75,000 compensatory damages. Judgment was entered on the verdict. The appellate court affirmed the award for compensatory damages but reversed the judgment for punitive damages. On appeal limited to two issues, *held*, affirmed. Punitive damages are not recoverable under the Survival Act.

The dissent noted that the majority "treats as established doctrine that punitive damages may not be recovered in an action for wrongful death." It said generally with respect to punitive damages in death actions: "I agree with the statement of the appellate court that a construction of our survival statute which did not preclude recovery of punitive damages 'would once and for all put to rest the old adage that it is cheaper to kill your victim than to leave him maimed. In addition to deterring others from wilful and wanton misconduct, it would bring death actions into complete harmony with the general body of law governing other types of tortious conduct. Logically, it would seem that punitive damages should be allowed to the estate of the decedent under the Survival Statute.' 21 Ill.App.3d 46, 54, 313 N.E.2d 496, 502."

EXCERPTS FROM ILLINOIS PATTERN JURY INSTRUCTIONS, CIVIL (2D ED. 1971)

31.04 Measure of Damages—Wrongful Death—Adult—Lineal Next of Kin Surviving

If you decide for the plaintiff on the question of liability you must then fix the amount of money which will reasonably and fairly compensate the _____ of the decedent, for the pecuniary loss
widow and lineal next of kin, e.g., daughter
proved by the evidence to have resulted to [him] [her] [them] from the death of the decedent.

Where the decedent leaves _____ the law
widow and lineal next of kin, e.g., daughter
recognizes a presumption that [he] [she] [they] has [have] sustained some substantial pecuniary loss by reason of the death.

In determining pecuniary loss and the weight to be given to the presumption of pecuniary loss you may consider what benefits of pecuniary value, including money, goods, and services the decedent might reasonably have been expected to contribute to the _____ had the

widow and lineal next of kin, e.g., daughter

decedent lived, bearing in mind the following factors concerning the decedent:

1. What he customarily contributed in the past;

2. What he earned or what he was likely to have earned in the future;

3. What he spent for customary personal expenses [and other deductions];

4. What instruction, moral training, and superintendence of education he might reasonably have been expected to give his [child] [children] had he lived;

5. His age;

6. His health;

7. His habits of industry, sobriety, and thrift;

8. His occupation.

* * *

31.07 Measure of Damages—Wrongful Death—Factors Excluded

In determining "pecuniary injuries" you may not consider the following factors:

1. The pain and suffering of the decedent;

2. The loss of decedent's society by the [widow] [and] [next of kin];

3. The grief or sorrow of the [widow] [and] [next of kin] [or;]

4. The poverty or wealth of the (widow) (and) [(next of kin)].

———

DE LONG v. COUNTY OF ERIE, 60 N.Y.2d 296, 469 N.Y.S.2d 611, 457 N.E.2d 717 (1983). This was a wrongful death action brought by the husband of a woman killed by a burglar. A jury found defendants (a county and city) liable for the negligent processing of and hence failure to respond to the victim's call to the police for emergency assistance. Defendants appealed from the adverse judgment. The Appellate Division affirmed, as did the Court of Appeals in this opinion. In the excerpts below, that court considered whether defendants were entitled to a new trial with respect to damages because the trial court permitted expert testimony concerning the monetary value of a housewife's services.

"* * * This evidence was relevant to the issue of damages on the wrongful death cause of action which is fixed by statute as follows: 'fair and just compensation for the pecuniary injuries resulting from the decedent's death to the persons for whose benefit the action is brought' (EPTL 5–4.3). When the decedent is a housewife who is not employed outside the home the financial impact on the survivors, aside from compensable losses of a personal nature, will not involve a loss of income but increased expenditures to continue the services she was providing or would have provided if she had lived.

"* * * It is now apparent, as a majority of courts have held, that qualified experts are available and may aid the jury in evaluating the housewife's services not only because jurors may not know the value of those services, but also to dispel the notion that what is provided without financial reward may be considered of little or no financial value in the marketplace. We conclude that it was not an abuse of discretion to allow the expert testimony in this case."

———

ANDERSON v. LALE, 88 S.D. 111, 216 N.W.2d 152 (1974). Action for wrongful death of seven-year-old girl who was fatally injured in an automobile-pedestrian accident. Verdict and judgment for plaintiff for $16,500. *Held,* affirmed. One issue on appeal was whether the trial court erred in giving what in substance was South Dakota Pattern Jury Instruction, Civil 31.02, the questioned portion of which follows:

> You may also consider what pecuniary loss, if any, plaintiffs have suffered and will suffer in the future with reasonable certainty, by being deprived of advice, assistance, comfort, and protection of the child.

Defendant contended that there is no right to recover for loss of companionship and association. In 1947, the legislature substituted the phrase "all advantage" for the phrase "pecuniary advantage" in the statutory statement of the measure of damages under the Wrongful Death Act. In 1967 the legislature enacted a new statute using the phrase "pecuniary injury." After reviewing a trend in decisions of other states toward a broader measure of damages in death actions, the majority opinion declares:

"We, too, feel as the courts did in the above cited cases, that the better rule is to include loss of companionship, society, advice, assistance and protection as elements of damages in wrongful death cases wherein the decedent was a minor. It is evidence that any court where more than nominal damages have been awarded must have tacitly accepted this rule in that, except in rare cases, never would a child's earnings be more than his cost of upbringing."

"We are also of the opinion that the 1967 legislature was well aware of the newer interpretations of pecuniary loss of injury, and it was their intent to only eliminate any recovery for sorrow, mental distress and grief suffered by the parents or any pain or suffering on the part of the decedent. Comment: South Dakota Pattern Jury Instruction, Civil, 31.03."

* * *

"We, therefore, hold that in a wrongful death action, wherein the decedent was a minor, it is proper for the court to instruct the jury that loss of companionship and society, which may be expressed by, but is not limited to, the words 'advice', 'assistance' and 'protection' are proper elements of damage for them to consider in reaching their verdict. We note that the word 'comfort' was used in the instruction given in this case. Comfort may connote alleviation of mental distress and we, therefore, find it objectionable since if an award for mental distress of the parents is not permitted confusion may arise. It is, however, only harmless error."

ROBERTS v. STEVENS CLINIC HOSP., INC., 176 W.Va. 492, 345 S.E.2d 791 (1986). Parents and siblings of a 2–year–old child who died as a result of medical malpractice brought a wrongful death action. They won a jury verdict, and related judgment, in the amount of $10 million. The supreme court of appeals here reversed and remanded with directions to enter a remittitur of $7 million and hence a judgment of $3 million or, at plaintiffs' option, to hold a new trial. The opinion for the court of Justice Neely explained why "we are compelled to reduce the jury's award."

"Plaintiff's counsel made a number of analogies during closing argument that could lead a juror only to believe that the juror's job was to evaluate Michael's life in terms of money. Counsel argued that if a $10,000,000 racehorse had been killed through the negligence of a veterinary hospital, the measure of damages would be exactly $10,000,000. At another point in the argument counsel asked what would have happened if someone had approached Michael's parents with an envelope containing ten, $1,000,000 winning lottery tickets and asked the parents if they would trade Michael's life for the tickets. Finally, counsel made reference to the American space program where billions of dollars are spent to avoid the loss of a single life. Representative excerpts from counsel's closing argument are as follows:

> If the race horse is worth $10,000,000, that's what the Roberts would be entitled to. It wouldn't be fair for us to come in and ask for $11,000,000 and it wouldn't be right, for the defense to say, 'We only want to pay $9,000,000' and that case would be easy. Justice would require a verdict of $10,000,000 * * *

Now if Michael were a race horse and the Stevens Clinic Hospital operated a veterinarian hospital and a race horse named Michael died as a result of the negligence of a veterinary doctor, you wouldn't have any trouble in returning a verdict for millions of dollars because you know that that's what race horses are worth. You tell me, you tell the family, are horses entitled to better care than children? And are children less valuable than horses? * * *

* * *

"Our wrongful death statute, *W.Va.Code*, 55–7–6 [1982][6] (the statute in effect at the time of Michael's death) specifically sets forth * * * the losses

---

6. *Code*, 55–7–6 [1982] provides:

The verdict of the jury shall include, but may not be limited to, damages for the following: (A)

Sorrow, mental anguish, and solace which may include society, companionship, comfort, guidance, kindly offices and advice of the decedent;

for which damages can be recovered. Obviously, if the measure of damages were the value of a human life then, arguably, no jury verdict could be excessive. The death of a family member, particularly a child, involves inconsolable grief for which no amount of money can compensate. Counsel's suggestion that the Roberts would not have traded Michael's life for $10,000,000 is entirely accurate—but they would also not have traded Michael's life for $100,000,000 or even a $1,000,000,000.

* * *

" * * * [W]e have decided to dispose of the one meritorious assignment of error, namely the excessiveness of the verdict, simply by asking ourselves: 'What is the highest jury award under the facts of this case that would not be monstrous and enormous, at first blush beyond all measure, unreasonable and outrageous, and such as manifestly shows jury passion, partiality, prejudice, or corruption?' Our answer, after substantial collegial discussion, is $3,000,000 and that is the amount that we will allow to stand. * * * "

CLYMER v. WEBSTER, 156 Vt. 614, 596 A.2d 905 (1991). "This court has recently reiterated that the 'term "pecuniary injuries" does not limit recovery to purely economic losses.' We now hold that the loss of the comfort and companionship of an adult child is real, direct and personal loss that can be measured in pecuniary terms. Children have an intrinsic value to their parents regardless of who is supporting whom at the time of death. Whether the decedent child is an adult or minor, society recognizes the destruction of the parents' investment in affection, guidance, security and love. * * * "

"In some cases, the close, familial ties that unite a minor child with his or her parents may dissipate as the child becomes an adult. Nevertheless, the WDA [Wrongful Death Act] does not preclude the parents of an adult child from showing that the death of their child did in fact injure them by depriving them of the society of that child. Every case must stand upon its own facts and circumstances. In determining whether and what amount of damages are appropriate for loss of companionship, the court or jury should consider the physical, emotional, and psychological relationship between the parents and the child. Accordingly, among other things, the factfinder should examine the living arrangements of the parties, the harmony of family relations, and the commonality of interests and activities. Prior cases contrary to our holding are overruled."

CASSANO v. DURHAM

Superior Court of New Jersey, Law Division, Passaic County, 1981.
180 N.J.Super. 620, 436 A.2d 118.

SCHWARTZ, J. S. C. The issue in this case is whether one who maintains a "live-in" relationship with another without the benefit of a marital

(B) compensation for reasonably expected loss of (i) income of the decedent, and (ii) services, protection, care and assistance provided by the decedent; (C) expenses for the care, treatment and hospitalization of the decedent incident to the injury resulting in death; and (D) reasonable funeral expenses.

ceremony may recover under the Wrongful Death Act (N.J.S.A. 2A:31–1 et seq.) for pecuniary loss sustained by reason of the partner's accidental death.

N.J.S.A. 2A:31–4 provides that the amount recovered in proceedings under this statute "shall be for the exclusive benefit of the persons entitled to take any intestate personal property of the decedent."

In this case the partner had lived with decedent for seven years and they intended to get married. The court is asked to permit her to recover for her pecuniary loss as if she qualified as a "surviving spouse" under N.J.S.A. 3A:2A–34 of the intestacy statute.

* * *

Is it arbitrary to provide a remedy for a surviving spouse and to deny a like remedy for a live-in companion who may equally suffer as the result of the tort? There is no constitutional impediment to the legislative determination to designate one, who has entered into the bonds of matrimony with decedent, as a beneficiary under the Wrongful Death Act among those who will inherit under the intestacy statute. That is solely a legislative function and the court cannot enlarge the reach of the statute.

* * *

The Legislature made provision for inheritance by other persons, such as children, parents and others within degrees of kinship. It excluded persons who failed to survive the decedent by 120 hours. If the statute was designed to accommodate unmarried companions, such legislative intent would have found expression in the law. Even illegitimate children and adopted minor children were recognized (N.J.S.A. 3A:2A–41) to accommodate a change in public policy.

* * *

The family has been the genesis of our society since the birth of civilization, and the laws of inheritance were intended to buttress the stability and continuance of the family unit. The preservation of familial law is so essential that where questions of inheritance, property, legitimacy of offspring and the like are involved, and adherence to conventional doctrine is demanded. Dawson v. Hatfield Wire & Cable Co., 59 N.J. 190, 197, 280 A.2d 173 (1971).

Since the live-in plaintiff cannot be classified as a "surviving spouse" under the legislative designation in the intestacy laws, and the Wrongful Death Act was intended to apply for the *exclusive* benefit of persons eligible to inherit under the succession provisions of the statute, the motion for summary judgment striking the claim of plaintiff shall be granted.

NO. 91. AN ACT RELATING TO CIVIL UNIONS.

[VERMONT CIVIL UNION STATUTE]

(H.847)

It is hereby enacted by the General Assembly of the State of Vermont:

Sec. 1. LEGISLATIVE FINDINGS

The General Assembly finds that:

* * *

(4) Legal recognition of civil marriage by the state is the primary and, in a number of instances, the exclusive source of numerous benefits, responsibilities and protections under the laws of the state for married persons and their children.

(5) Based on the state's tradition of equality under the law and [of] strong families, for at least 25 years, Vermont Probate Courts have qualified gay and lesbian individuals as adoptive parents.

(6) Vermont was one of the first states to adopt comprehensive legislation prohibiting discrimination on the basis of sexual orientation (Act No. 135 of 1992).

(7) The state has a strong interest in promoting stable and lasting families, including families based upon a same-sex couple.

(8) Without the legal protections, benefits and responsibilities associated with civil marriage, same-sex couples suffer numerous obstacles and hardships.

* * *

CHAPTER 23. CIVIL UNIONS

§ 1201. DEFINITIONS

As used in this chapter:

(1) "Certificate of civil union" means a document that certifies that the persons named on the certificate have established a civil union in this state in compliance with this chapter and 18 V.S.A. chapter 106.

(2) "Civil union" means that two eligible persons have established a relationship pursuant to this chapter, and may receive the benefits and protections and be subject to the responsibilities of spouses.

* * *

§ 1202. REQUISITES OF A VALID CIVIL UNION

For a civil union to be established in Vermont, it shall be necessary that the parties to a civil union satisfy all of the following criteria:

(1) Not be a party to another civil union or a marriage.

(2) Be of the same sex and therefore excluded from the marriage laws of this state.

* * *

§ 1204. BENEFITS, PROTECTIONS AND RESPONSIBILITIES OF PARTIES TO A CIVIL UNION

(a) Parties to a civil union shall have all the same benefits, protections and responsibilities under law, whether they derive from statute, administrative or court rule, policy, common law or any other source of civil law, as are granted to spouses in a marriage.

(b) A party to a civil union shall be included in any definition or use of the terms "spouse," "family," "immediate family," "dependent," "next of kin," and other terms that denote the spousal relationship, as those terms are used throughout the law.

* * *

(e) The following is a nonexclusive list of legal benefits, protections and responsibilities of spouses, which shall apply in like manner to parties to a civil union:

* * *

(2) causes of action related to or dependent upon spousal status, including an action for wrongful death, emotional distress, loss of consortium, dramshop, or other torts or actions under contracts reciting, related to, or dependent upon spousal status;

* * *

(9) workers' compensation benefits;

* * *

Approved: April 26, 2000.

SECTION C.   OTHER RELATIONAL HARM

The harm we examine here involves context where the victim has not died, either from her injuries or while trial was pending, and recovery is sought by persons related to the victim. There is an overlap between the cases here—where recovery is sought principally for "loss of consortium"— and extent of liability cases where recovery is sought for pure emotional distress. The differences are matters of emphasis. The cases in § C of Chapter 11 are primarily driven by considerations of foreseeability on the one hand, and by a concern with bringing appropriate cost-pressure to bear on harmful conduct, on the other hand. The cases that follow are also moved by these considerations, but they are shaped by concerns distinct to the law of damages as well. Is the relational harm to other people sufficiently urgent to warrant compensation? Will money damages serve as meaningful compensation for this kind of loss?

BORER v. AMERICAN AIRLINES, INC.

Supreme Court of California, 1977.

19 Cal.3d 441, 138 Cal.Rptr. 302, 563 P.2d 858.

TOBRINER, Acting Chief Justice.

In Rodriguez v. Bethlehem Steel Corp. (1974) 12 Cal.3d 382, 115 Cal.Rptr. 765, 525 P.2d 669 we held that a married person whose spouse had been injured by the negligence of a third party may maintain a cause of action for loss of "consortium." We defined loss of "consortium" as the "loss of conjugal fellowship and sexual relations" (12 Cal.3d at p. 385, 115 Cal.Rptr. at p. 766, 525 P.2d at p. 670), but ruled that the term included the loss of love, companionship, society, sexual relations, and household services. Our decision carefully avoided resolution of the question whether anyone other than the spouse of a negligently injured person, such as a child or a parent, could maintain a cause of action analogous to that upheld in *Rodriguez*. We face that issue today: the present case presents a claim by nine children for the loss of the services, companionship, affection and guidance of their mother. * * *

* * *

* * * Unpersuaded of any legal distinction between a parent's claim for loss of a child's consortium and a child's claim for loss of a parent's consortium, we granted hearings in the instant case and in [the companion case of] Baxter v. Superior Court in order to address generally the question whether to recognize a new cause of action for loss of consortium in a parent-child relationship.

Judicial recognition of a cause of action for loss of consortium, we believe, must be narrowly circumscribed. Loss of consortium is an intangible injury for which money damages do not afford an accurate measure or suitable recompense; recognition of a right to recover for such losses in the present context, moreover, may substantially increase the number of claims asserted in ordinary accident cases, the expense of settling or resolving such claims, and the ultimate liability of the defendants. Taking these considerations into account, we shall explain why we have concluded that the payment of damages to persons for the lost affection and society of a parent or child neither truly compensates for such loss nor justifies the social cost in attempting to do so. * * *

* * *

* * * Plaintiffs, the nine children of Patricia Borer, allege that on March 21, 1972, the cover on a lighting fixture at the American Airlines Terminal at Kennedy Airport fell and struck Patricia. Plaintiffs further assert that as a result of the physical injuries sustained by Patricia, each of them has been "deprived of the services, society, companionship, affection, tutelage, direction, guidance, instruction and aid in personality development, all with its accompanying psychological, educational and emotional detriment, by reason of Patricia Borer being unable to carry on her usual duties of a mother." The complaint sets forth causes of action based upon negligence, breach of warranty, and manufacture of a defective product. * * * Each plaintiff seeks damages of $100,000.

Defendant American Airlines demurred to the complaint for failure to state a cause of action. (Code Civ.Proc., § 430.10, subd. (e).) The trial court sustained the demurrer without leave to amend, and entered judgment dismissing the suit as to defendant American Airlines. Plaintiffs appealed from that judgment.

* * *

Rodriguez, * * * does not compel the conclusion that foreseeable injury to a legally recognized relationship necessarily postulates a cause of action; instead it clearly warns that social policy must at some point intervene to delimit liability. Patricia Borer, for example, foreseeably has not only a husband (who has a cause of action under *Rodriguez*) and the children who sue here, but also parents whose right of action depends upon our decision in the companion case of Baxter v. Superior Court; foreseeably, likewise, she has brothers, sisters, cousins, inlaws, friends, colleagues, and other acquaintances who will be deprived of her companionship. No one suggests that all such persons possess a right of action for loss of Patricia's consortium; all agree that somewhere a line must be drawn. As stated by Judge Breitel in Tobin v. Grossman, (1969) 24 N.Y.2d 609, 619, 301 N.Y.S.2d 554, 561, 249 N.E.2d 419, 424; "Every injury has ramifying consequences, like the ripplings of the waters, without end. The problem for the law is to limit the legal consequences of wrongs to a controllable degree."

The decision whether to limit liability for loss of consortium by denying a cause of action in the parent-child context, or to permit that action but deny any claim based upon more remote relationships, is thus a question of policy. As explained by Justice Fleming in Suter v. Leonard (1975) 45 Cal.App.3d 744, 746, 120 Cal.Rptr. 110, 111: " * * * [N]ot every loss can be made compensable in money damages, and legal causation must terminate somewhere. In delineating the extent of a tortfeasor's responsibility for damages under the general rule of tort liability (Civ.Code, § 1714), the courts must locate the line between liability and nonliability at some point, a decision which is essentially political."

In the first instance, strong policy reasons argue against extension of liability to loss of consortium of the parent-child relationship. Loss of consortium is an intangible, nonpecuniary loss; monetary compensation will not enable plaintiffs to regain the companionship and guidance of a mother; it will simply establish a fund so that upon reaching adulthood, when plaintiffs will be less in need of maternal guidance, they will be unusually wealthy men and women. To say that plaintiffs have been "compensated" for their loss is superficial; in reality they have suffered a loss for which they can never be compensated; they have obtained, instead, a future benefit essentially unrelated to that loss.

We cannot ignore the social burden of providing damages for loss of parental consortium merely because the money to pay such awards comes initially from the "negligent" defendant or his insurer. Realistically the burden of payment of awards for loss of consortium must be borne by the public generally in increased insurance premiums or, otherwise, in the enhanced danger that accrues from the greater number of people who may choose to go without any insurance. We must also take into account the cost of administration of a system to determine and pay consortium awards; since virtually every serious injury to a parent would engender a claim for loss of consortium on behalf of each of his or her children, the expense of settling or litigating such claims would be sizable.

Plaintiffs point out that courts have permitted recovery of monetary damages for intangible loss in allowing awards for pain and suffering in negligence cases and in sanctioning recovery for loss of marital consortium. The question before us in this case, however, pivots on whether we should recognize a wholly new cause of action, unsupported by statute or precedent; in this context the inadequacy of monetary damages to make whole the loss suffered, considered in light of the social cost of paying such awards, constitutes a strong reason for refusing to recognize the asserted claim. To avoid misunderstanding, we point out that our decision to refuse to recognize a cause of action for parental consortium does not remotely suggest the rejection of recovery for intangible loss; each claim must be judged on its own merits, and in many cases the involved statutes, precedents, or policy will induce acceptance of the asserted cause of action.

A second reason for rejecting a cause of action for loss of parental consortium is that, because of its intangible character, damages for such a loss are very difficult to measure. Plaintiffs here have prayed for $100,000 each; yet by what standard could we determine that an award of $10,000 was inadequate, or one of $500,000 excessive? Difficulty in defining and quantifying damages leads in turn to risk of double recovery: to ask the jury, even under carefully drafted instructions, to distinguish the loss to the mother from her inability to care for her children from the loss to the children from the mother's inability to care for them may be asking too much. Thus as observed by the New Jersey Supreme Court in Russell v. Salem Transportation Co. (1972) 61 N.J. 502, 507, 295 A.2d 862, 864: "The asserted social need for the disputed cause of action [a child's action for loss of parental consortium] may well be qualified, at least in terms of the family as an economic unit, by the practical consideration recognized by many of the cases on the point that reflection of the consequential disadvantages to children of injured parents is frequently found in jury awards to the parents on their own claims under existing law and practice."

* * *

In summary, we do not doubt the reality or the magnitude of the injury suffered by plaintiffs. We are keenly aware of the need of children for the love, affection, society and guidance of their parents; any injury which diminishes the ability of a parent to meet these needs is plainly a family tragedy, harming all members of that community. We conclude, however, that taking into account all considerations which bear on this question, including the inadequacy of monetary compensation to alleviate that tragedy, the difficulty of measuring damages, and the danger of imposing extended and disproportionate liability, we should not recognize a nonstatutory cause of action for the loss of parental consortium.

The judgment is affirmed.

[In the companion case referred to, Baxter v. Superior Court of Los Angeles County, 19 Cal.3d 461, 138 Cal.Rptr. 315, 563 P.2d 871 (1977), the court held that a parent has no cause of action in negligence to recover damages for loss of filial consortium after severe, disabling injury to the child. The court relied on the "policy considerations" developed in the

Borer opinion. Parents, under the common or statutory law of many states, can recover for loss of a child's services and earnings. But, argued the court, such recovery should be limited to services "of economic value" and not be expanded to include damages for "loss of affection and society."]

HIBPSHMAN v. PRUDHOE BAY SUPPLY, INC., 734 P.2d 991 (Alaska 1987). Hibpshman sued defendant for severe negligently inflicted injuries. In the same complaint, his wife claimed damages for loss of consortium. Their four minor children then asserted a claim against the same defendant for loss of parental consortium. The lower court entered an order dismissing the claim for loss of parental consortium. That order was reversed in this opinion by the Alaska Supreme Court, and the case remanded. The court pointed out that the state's wrongful death statute specified that loss of consortium was a part of the damages recoverable by the statutorily designated parties, including children of the decedent. The claim for loss of parental consortium in this action "is not sufficiently distinguishable from either spousal consortium claims in injury cases or children's consortium claims in death cases to warrant non-recognition." The court addressed several arguments of defendant against recognition, including the following:

" * * * [W]e think that the potential problem of double recovery can be eliminated by recognizing that pecuniary damages such as lost income which would have been used for the benefit of a child or the cost of substitute child care services are damages recoverable by the parent, not the child; the child's damages would thus be limited primarily to an emotional suffering award in most cases. * * *

* * *

" * * * Prudhoe Bay asserts that recognition of parental consortium should be withheld because the social costs, in particular increased insurance rates and a projected rise in the number of uninsured tortfeasors, outweigh the benefit to the child. We are in agreement with those courts which have concluded that any burden to society is offset by the benefit to the child. In this regard, the Oregon Supreme Court accurately observed that

[a] person's liability in our law still remains the same whether or not he has liability insurance; properly, the provision and cost of such insurance varies with potential liability under the law, not the law with the cost of the insurance. *Norwest* [v. *Presbyterian Intercommunity Hosp.*], 652 P.2d at 323.

"Lastly, Prudhoe Bay argues that recognition of loss of parental consortium will increase the potential for future complex litigation arising from multiple claims which have not been instituted contemporaneously. Other jurisdictions have required joinder of a minor's consortium claim with the injured parent's claim. * * * [W]e conclude that a practical and fair solution to the problem is to require joinder of the minors' consortium claim with the injured parent's claim whenever feasible."

FRANK v. SUPERIOR COURT, 150 Ariz. 228, 722 P.2d 955 (1986). Plaintiffs Hathaway were parents of Marilyn Hathaway, an adult, who had sued Dr. Frank in a separate action for malpractice causing her severe brain damage. That litigation was in midstream, following a jury award of $5 million and Marilyn Hathaway's refusal of a remittitur to $3.1 million. Plaintiffs alleged that because of Frank's negligence, they had been deprived of their daughter's companionship, affection, solace and moral support, and sought damages to compensate them for loss of consortium of their only child. The trial (and respondent) judge denied Frank's motion to dismiss on grounds that Arizona did not recognize an action for loss of consortium of an adult child. Frank here sought an order requiring the respondent judge to grant a motion for summary judgment.

In holding that the parents could maintain the action and thus denying Frank relief, the supreme court noted that a prior Arizona decision had allowed recovery for loss of filial consortium of a minor child severely injured by a third party's negligence. Decisions under the state wrongful death statute, which provided for parents' recovery for wrongful death of a child irrespective of the child's age, had expanded damages past pecuniary loss. "In sum we have not hesitated to assign a monetary value to the elements of consortium—society, companionship, care, support, and affection, to name a few—even in the most difficult cases. * * * Often death is separated from severe injury by mere fortuity; and it would be anomalous to distinguish between the two when the quality of consortium is negatively affected by both."

The principal argument against extending the filial consortium action from minor to adult children was that emancipation frees parents and children from reciprocal obligations of support and obedience. That argument "is premised upon an archaic and outmoded pecuniary theory of parental rights and fundamentally misapprehends the modern elements of consortium." Today's laws curbing child labor and requiring education "virtually [guarantee] that children will not be an economic asset to their parents." Parents "continue to enjoy a legitimate and protectible expectation of consortium beyond majority arising from the very bonds of the family relationship." As for the risk of heightened litigation and increased insurance costs, "[t]he rights of a new class of tort plaintiffs should be forthrightly judged without engaging in gloomy speculation as to where it will all end." In any event, "in the vast majority of cases involving injury to a child the injury will not be so severe that the parents suffer a loss of society and companionship."

BURKE ET AL. v. RIVO
Supreme Judicial Court of Massachusetts, 1990.
406 Mass. 764, 551 N.E.2d 1.

WILKINS, Justice.

A judge in the Superior Court reported to the Appeals Court * * * the question of the proper measure of damages recoverable by the parents of a normal, healthy child who was conceived and born (1) following the

defendant physician's alleged negligent performance of a sterilization procedure on the mother, and (2) following the physician's alleged guarantee that
the sterilization procedure would prevent any future pregnancy. The case,
which we transferred here on our own motion, presents an issue of first
impression.

* * *

The great weight of authority permits the parents of a normal child born
as a result of a physician's negligence to recover damages directly associated
with the birth (sometimes including damage for the parents' emotional
distress), but courts are divided on whether the parents may recover the
economic expense of rearing the child. [The court cited to approximately a
dozen decisions denying, and half a dozen permitting, recovery.] * * *

The judge below recognized that damages properly would include the
cost of the unsuccessful sterilization procedure and costs directly flowing
from the pregnancy: the wife's lost earning capacity; medical expenses of the
delivery and care following the birth; the cost of care for the other children
while the wife was incapacitated; the cost of the second sterilization procedure and any expenses flowing from that operation; and the husband's loss
of consortium. We would add the wife's pain and suffering in connection
with the pregnancy and birth and with the second sterilization procedure.
We also see no reason why the plaintiffs should not recover for emotional
distress they sustained as a result of the unwanted pregnancy. Emotional
distress could be the probable consequence of a breach of the duty the
defendant owed directly to the plaintiffs.

* * *

* * * Under normal tort and contract principles, [the cost of raising a
child] is both a reasonably foreseeable and a natural and probable consequence of the wrongs that the plaintiffs allege. The question is whether
there is any public policy consideration to which we should give effect to
limit traditional tort and contract damages. We conclude that there is none
as to parents who have elected sterilization for economic reasons.

Many justifications often relied on for declining to allow recovery of the
cost of rearing a healthy child born as a result of a physician's negligence are
outstandingly unimpressive. * * * The judicial declaration that the joy and
pride in raising a child always outweigh any economic loss the parents may
suffer, thus precluding recovery for the cost of raising the child * * * simply
lacks verisimilitude. The very fact that a person has sought medical intervention to prevent him or her from having a child demonstrates that, for that
person, the benefits of parenthood did not outweigh the burdens, economic
and otherwise, of having a child. The extensive use of contraception and
sterilization and the performance of numerous abortions each year show
that, in some instances, large numbers of people do not accept parenthood
as a net positive circumstance. We agree with those courts that have rejected
the theory that the birth of a child is for all parents at all times a net benefit.
* * *

We are also unimpressed with the reasoning that child-rearing expenses should not be allowed because some day the child could be adversely affected by learning that he or she was unwanted and that someone else had paid for the expense of rearing the child. Courts expressing concern about the effect on the child nevertheless allow the parents to recover certain direct expenses from the negligent physician without expressing concern about harm to the child when the child learns that he or she was unwanted. * * * In any event, it is for the parents, not the courts, to decide whether a lawsuit would adversely affect the child and should not be maintained.

* * *

A substantial number of jurisdictions have allowed recovery of the cost of rearing a normal child to adulthood, offset, however, by the benefits that the parents receive in having a normal, healthy child. * * * Such a balancing by the trier of fact requires a comparison of the economic loss of child-rearing with the emotional gains of having a normal, healthy child (converted into a dollar value). These courts have thought the comparison appropriate under the general principle expressed in Restatement (Second) of Torts § 920 (1979).[5] A few courts have thought that, because the benefit conferred did not affect the economic interest that was harmed, no mitigation of the cost of child-rearing should be recognized. * * *

If the parents' desire to avoid the birth of a child was founded on eugenic reasons (avoidance of a feared genetic defect) or was founded on therapeutic reasons (concern for the mother's health) and if a healthy normal baby is born, the justification for allowing recovery of the costs of rearing a normal child to maturity is far less than when, to conserve family resources, the parents sought unsuccessfully to avoid conceiving another child. * * *

We conclude that, in addition to the recoverable damages described earlier in this opinion, parents may recover the cost of rearing a normal, healthy but (at least initially) unwanted child if their reason for seeking sterilization was founded on economic or financial considerations. In such a situation, the trier of fact should offset against the cost of rearing the child the benefit, if any, the parents receive and will receive from having their child.[6] We discern no reason founded on sound public policy to immunize a

---

5. Section 920 provides: "When the defendant's tortious conduct has caused harm to the plaintiff or to his property and in so doing has conferred a special benefit to the interest of the plaintiff that was harmed, the value of the benefit conferred is considered in mitigation of damages, to the extent that this is equitable."

6. The dissent declares that a factfinder should not engage "in an inquiry concerning the probable value of a child to his or her parents." Post at 7 (O'Connor, J., dissenting). The process is not an unacceptably difficult one. Our law recognizes the propriety of measuring the loss to parents in financial terms when a child is injured (G.L. c. 231, § 85X, inserted by St. 1989, c. 259, § 1 [loss of consortium when a child is seriously injured]), or killed (G.L. c. 229,

§ 2 [1988 ed.] [loss of "society, companionship, comfort, guidance, counsel, and advice"]). To measure the benefit of having a child is simply the other side of the coin. Numerous courts have reached the same conclusion. See, e.g., Hartke v. McKelway, 707 F.2d 1544, 1552 n. 8 (D.C.Cir.1983) ("no significant distinction between the task here and the analogous task of fixing damages for wrongful death"); University of Ariz. Health Sciences Center v. Superior Court, 136 Ariz. 579, 582–583, 667 P.2d 1294 (1983) "juries in tort cases are often required to assess just such intangible factors, both emotional and pecuniary, and [we] see no reason why a new rule should be adopted for wrongful pregnancy" Ochs v. Borrelli, 187 Conn. 253, 260, 445 A.2d 883 (1982) (citations omitted) ("We

physician from having to pay for a reasonably foreseeable consequence of his negligence or from a natural and probable consequence of a breach of his guarantee, namely, the parents' expenses in rearing the child to adulthood.

O'CONNOR, Justice (dissenting, with whom NOLAN and LYNCH, Justices, join).

I agree, as do most of the relatively few courts that allow recovery of child-rearing costs, that an award of such costs without setting off the value of the child to the parents would be unfair to defendants, and therefore intolerable. However, in my view, it would be equally intolerable for a judge or jury to engage in an inquiry concerning the probable value of a child to his or her parents. The result, in my view, is that child-rearing costs should not be recoverable.

The inquiry would be intolerable because it would require a determination of whether the child represents a loss to his or her parents. Would they be better off if the child had never been born? Is the child worth less than it would cost to raise him or her and, if so, how much less? Even if such an inquiry could lead to a reasoned, and not merely speculative, conclusion, a doubtful proposition, the balancing of costs and benefits treats the child as though he or she were personal property. The very inquiry is inconsistent with the dignity that the Commonwealth, including its courts, must accord to every human life, and it should not be permitted.

see no basis for distinguishing this case from other tort cases in which the trier of fact fixes damages for wrongful death ... or for loss of consortium").

B. PASSAGES FROM FAULT TO STRICT LIABILITY

Chapter 15

THE IMPACT OF INSURANCE

The institution of insurance exerts a pervasive influence on the law of torts. Sometimes, as we have seen, this influence is explicit. *Barber Lines v. Donau Maru* (Chapter 13, p. 658), contemplating the extent of liability for pure economic loss, takes the potential effect of general liability for pure economic loss on liability insurance premiums as a reason in favor of the traditional rule of proximate cause that pure economic losses are not generally recoverable in tort. *Hibpshman v. Prudhoe Bay* (Chapter 14, p. 717) considers and rejects the argument that the recognition of claims for loss of parental consortium would have an untoward effect on insurance rates. The existence of liability insurance also figured prominently as a ground for the abolition of tort immunities in two cases in Chapter 10—*Hicks v. State* p. 486 and *Pierce v. Yakima Memorial Hospital* p. 495.

Perhaps more importantly, the institution of insurance exerts a pervasive influence on the law of torts even when it is not explicitly mentioned, because it forms part of the social and institutional background to liability. Insurance considerations first made their presence felt at the very beginning of this casebook—in *Garratt v. Dailey* (p. 7) and the squibs which followed, contrasting tort and liability insurance coverage standards of intentionality. The use of a "substantial certainty" of intentionality in *Garratt v. Dailey* and an "intend the injury" standard in *Baldinger v. Consolidated Mutual Insurance Co.* and *Connecticut Indemnity Co. v. Nestor*, (pp. 10–11) is an attempt to reconcile the partially conflicting objectives of reducing the incidence of intentional wrongdoing and compensating the victims of such wrongdoing.

Liability insurance plays a vital role in this, the most traditional domain of tort law—the domain of individual, intentional wrongdoing—because the existence of liability insurance enables victims to recover more frequently and more fully from those who have wronged them, thereby enabling the law of torts to realize one of its principal aims. The delicacy of the relation between tort and insurance is also visible in this traditional tort setting. On the one hand, the institution of liability insurance furthers the ends of tort law by enabling victims of intentional wrongdoing to recover for the harms that they have suffered. On the other hand, the provision of insurance for intentional wrongdoing can create a serious problem of "moral hazard." By insulating insureds against the costs of their own intentional wrongdoing, insurance can increase the incidence of intentional wrongdoing. This is undesirable from a tort perspective, because the law of torts seeks to discourage, not encourage, the conduct that it counts compensable. Inducing the very conduct against which insurance is provided is equally undesirable from an insurance perspective. When the provision of insurance against expected losses causes the level of losses actually experienced to spiral upward, past losses become an unreliable guide to future ones and it becomes difficult to price insurance premiums accurately. The institution of insurance malfunctions. Tort doctrine is, and must be, sensitive to this predicament.

Insurance has been equally important to tort liability for negligence, even when it has not been explicitly visible in the way that it is in *Barber Lines v. Donau Maru*, *Hibpshman v. Prudhoe Bay* and *Pierce v. Yakima Memorial Hospital*. Once again liability insurance both enables and disables the operation of tort liability. On the one hand, it expands the resources available for compensating victims of accidental injury; on the other, it complicates the task of minimizing the incidence of harmful, careless conduct. As the materials that follow this note explain, other things equal, losses are most insurable "when they are beyond the control of the insured." (p. 730) Tort liability insurance, however, insures losses that are at least partially under the control of those that it insures, because injurers are almost always in a position to affect (if not fully control) the incidence of the accidents for which they are held liable. Indeed, tort liability is most effective at minimizing the incidence of careless conduct when it is imposed on parties in an excellent position to control the incidence of such conduct, and when those parties are made to suffer financial damage sufficient to induce them to exercise appropriate care. Effecting the twin ends of compensation and accident minimization requires both the existence of insurance as an institution and the appropriate structuring of insurance mechanisms such as premiums, deductibles, and co-payments—mechanisms which counteract the tendency of insurance to make the insured indifferent to loss.

If insurance has been important all along, it is even more important to a distinctive form of modern strict liability—namely, enterprise liability. Enterprise liability seeks to disperse accident costs across the risky activities responsible for generating those accidents. Because loss dispersion is one of its principal aims, enterprise liability incorporates insurance considerations into its own internal logic. When we take up strict liability in its enterprise form (as we do in the next two chapters) the institution of insurance moves from the background of tort liability into the foreground. An introduction to the institution of insurance is therefore especially useful as a prelude to the study of modern strict liability.

SECTION A. SOME BASIC CHARACTERISTICS

MEHR, CAMMACK AND ROSE, PRINCIPLES OF INSURANCE
(8th Ed. 1985).*

[The following excerpts are taken from Chapter 2, "Risk Management and Insurance."]

* * *

Chance of loss is the long-run relative frequency of loss. Chance of loss is best expressed as a fraction or a percentage. It indicates the probable number and severity of losses out of a given number of exposures. Expressed as a fraction, the probable number of losses is the numerator, and the given number of exposures is the denominator. If a person flips a coin for a cup of coffee, the chance of loss is ½, or 50 percent. If a prize is offered for drawing a white ball out of a box that contains nine black balls and one white, the chance of loss is ⁹⁄₁₀, or 90 percent.

Thus:

$$\text{Chance of loss} = \frac{\text{Probable losses}}{\text{Total exposures to loss}}$$

In these cases chance of loss is easy to understand and measure. But what about exposure to loss by fire, windstorm, and other perils? Here one cannot rely solely on logic; instead, a mass of statistical data must be collected.

In measuring chance of loss for standard insurance loss exposures, empirical probability is computed by using statistical methods. (Statistics has been defined as using incomplete data and questionable methods to reach foregone conclusions.) Thus, if the interest is in the probability of loss or damage to a house by fire, all possible statistics must be collected concerning fires on comparable houses. One must know how many fires occurred during a given time and how many houses were exposed to fire losses during that period. If, out of 100,000 similar houses, 100 have burned, the chance of loss or damage to one of these houses by fire during any equivalent period will be 100/100,000, or 0.1 percent. This figure, however, gives the *loss frequency* only. For insurance purposes, *loss severity* figures are more important. Suppose the houses were worth $60,000 each, making a total value of $6 billion, and that the total value of the losses was $3 million (most losses were partial). The chance of loss, expressed in terms of

---

* Mehr, Cammack and Rose, Principles of Insurance (8th ed. 1985) (Homewood, Ill.: Richard D. Irwin, Inc.) © 1985 Richard D. Irwin, Inc. Reprinted with permission of The McGraw–Hill Companies.

severity, would be 3 million/6 billion, or 0.05 percent. The loss cost then would be 5 cents for each $100 of exposure, or $30 for each house.

The same principle is used in determining the chance of death at any given age. If, out of 1,000 persons alive at the age of 75, 65 die before reaching their 76th birthday, the chance of death during the 75th year can be expressed as the fraction 65/1,000, or 6.5 percent. Since death is permanent and total, loss frequency and loss severity statistics produce the same results.

Chance of loss is important in insurance, for it is a basis on which rates are established. A reasonable degree of accuracy in measuring loss probabilities is necessary if adequate, equitable, and nonexcessive insurance rates are to be developed. Furthermore, chance of loss affects the decision concerning how risk should be handled. If the chance of loss is "relatively high," risk avoidance or risk assumption coupled with a major loss prevention effort appears to be the most efficient method of dealing with risk. If the chance of loss is infinitesimal, the best approach may be simply to ignore the risk.

Definition of Risk

* * *

In this text, the focus is on an operational definition of risk for the study of insurance. The definition of risk that both facilitates communication and analysis of risk as it affects insurance is a simple one: *risk is uncertainty concerning loss.* This definition contains two concepts: uncertainty and loss. While both concepts are important to insurance, risk represents the uncertainty and not the loss, the cause of loss, or the chance of loss. The basic function of insurance is to handle risk, and this definition of risk considers effectively the question of how insurance deals with risk. * * *

Assume that the chance of loss by fire to a store is 1 in 1,000. If a person owned one store the loss cannot be predicted. Either it will or will not burn. No basis exists for predicting the outcome, so the owner is faced with complete uncertainty even though the chance of loss is low. Suppose, however, a chain of 1,000 similar stores is owned. The risk is reduced, and now at least one store can be expected to burn as the probability of loss is 1 in 1,000. But even here one has no assurance that the actual losses will equal expected losses. Because the outcome still is uncertain, risk remains. If two stores burn, the actual loss exceeds expected loss by 100 percent. However, the loss of one more store represents only 0.1 percent of the exposure.

But suppose one owns 100,000 stores. Then 100 stores can be expected to burn. If as many as 10 more burn, the actual loss exceeds the expected loss by only 10 percent or 0.01 percent of the exposure. The large number of stores improves loss predictability; that is, it reduces the probable margin of error in predicted results. Thus, with 100,000 stores, the degree of risk is reduced; yet the chance of loss still remains 1 in 1,000. The risk is not entirely eliminated, however, because actual losses will rarely, if ever, equal expected losses. * * *

* * *

DEGREE OF RISK

The accuracy with which losses can be predicted is the measure of degree of risk. The degree of risk is measured by the probable variation of actual experience from expected experience.

Thus:

$$\text{Degree of risk} = \frac{\text{Actual number of losses—Probable number of losses}}{\text{Probable number of losses}}$$

The lower the probable percentage of variation, the smaller is the risk. This percentage variation decreases as the number of exposures increases. Mathematicians express this concept by stating that as the number of exposures increases, the probable variation of actual experience from expected experience increases, but only in proportion to the square root of the increased number of exposures. This observation means that as the number of exposures increases the number of cases that vary from the expected also increases but the percentage variation decreases.

* * *

When the future course of events is perfectly predictable, no risk exists. If it is known that something will or will not occur, no uncertainty prevails and hence no risk. The inability to predict the course of future events is the essence of risk. And, as events become more predictable, risk is reduced.

Risk makes insurance both desirable and possible. If in a given case a loss were certain to occur, insurance could not be obtained. No insurer could write it at commercially feasible rates. If in a given case a loss were certain not to occur, insurance also would not be written. No one would buy it. Thus, the owners of a house located on a river bank where flood damage occurs three years out of four would be eager to buy flood insurance, if offered. The owners of houses on a nearby hill would not buy the insurance as no flood ever causes them damage. Insurance exists because people do not know what will happen to their property or to their personal earning power in the future. They prefer a small certain cost for which they can budget (the insurance premium) to an uncertain, but potentially large, loss for which they may be unable to budget (actual loss, up to the limit of the policy).

Chance of loss versus degree of risk. The distinction between chance of loss and degree of risk is clarified by a simple illustration. Assume that A and B represent two groups of exposures to loss. The chance of loss in each group is 10 out of 1,000 (1 percent). In group A, over a period of years, annual losses varied from 3 to 18, whereas in group B losses varied from 8 to 12. The annual experience is more stable for group B. Therefore, losses are more predictable because of the low degree of variability. The more predictable the loss, the less is the degree of risk. So notwithstanding an equal chance of loss (1 percent), the degree of risk is less for group B. The degree of risk is in part a function of the probability distribution of losses over time.

* * *

HAZARD

* * *

Hazard is defined as a condition that may create or increase the chance of loss arising from a given peril. Carelessness, poor housekeeping, bad highways, unguarded machines, and dangerous employments are examples of hazards, for they increase chance of loss.

Some writers distinguish three types of hazards: physical, moral, and morale. *Physical hazard* is a material condition increasing chance of loss. The production of gunpowder in a building is a physical hazard increasing chance of loss by fire or explosion. *Moral hazard* is an individual characteristic of the insured that increases the probability of loss arising from the dishonesty of the insured. For example, dishonest insureds increase arson losses. *Morale hazard,* also an individual characteristic of the insured, is indifference to loss. This condition is observed in those insureds with the general attitude expressed in the thought: "What, me worry? I've got insurance!" For example, carelessness in the safekeeping of property increases the chance of loss by theft. * * *

* * *

DEFINITION OF INSURANCE

An adequate definition of insurance must include either the accumulation of a fund or the transference of risk, but not necessarily both. In addition, it must include a combination of a large number of separate, independent exposure units having the same common risk characteristics into an interrelated group.

Insurance may be defined as a device for reducing risk by combining a sufficient number of exposure units to make their individual losses collectively predictable. The predictable loss is then shared proportionately by all units in the combination.

These exposure units include both an entity (for example, one automobile, one house, or one business) and a time unit (for example, one year). Commonly, insurance involves spreading losses over more than one entity within one unit of time. However, insurance also can involve spreading losses of one entity over a long enough time period to increase the predictability of the losses. This technique of spreading losses for a single entity over a long time span is known as self-insurance. The question of whether that technique should be called insurance has caused considerable controversy within academic circles, the accounting profession, and in Internal Revenue Service rulings. That issue is tangential to the discussion at this point. The important characteristics of the concept of insurance as used in this text is that *uncertainty is reduced* and that *losses are shared or distributed* among the exposure units.

Insurance allows the individual insured to substitute a small, definite cost (the premium) for a large but uncertain loss (not to exceed the amount of the insurance) under an arrangement whereby the fortunate many who escape loss will help compensate the unfortunate few who suffer loss. Even if no loss materializes, insurance helps to eliminate any anxiety the insured might have about a potential loss. Insurance, therefore, provides the insured not only postloss but also preloss utility.

* * *

Insurance may be distinguished from gambling. In gambling, the risk is created by the transaction; in insurance, the risk is reduced by the transaction. For example, no chance of loss exists at the racetrack until a bet has been placed; but the risk of loss of property by fire or windstorm is present until reduced or eliminated by insurance. Therefore, gambling and insurance are opposites: one creates risk, the other reduces it.

The Law of Large Numbers

At first glance, it may seem strange that a combination of individual risks would result in the reduction of total risk. The principle that explains this phenomenon is called the "law of large numbers." It is sometimes loosely termed the "law of averages," or the "law of probability." However, it is but one portion of the subject of probability. The latter is not a law but an entire branch of mathematics.

* * * This law is based on the regularity of events. What seems random occurrence in the individual happening appears so because of insufficient or incomplete knowledge of what is expected. For practical purposes, the law of large numbers may be stated as follows: The greater the number of exposures, the more nearly will the actual results obtained approach the probable result expected with an infinite number of exposures. Thus if a coin is flipped a sufficiently large number of times, the results of the trials will approach half heads and half tails—the theoretical probability if the coin is flipped an infinite number of times.

Events that seem the result of chance occur with surprising regularity as the number of observations increase. A car races around a corner one July 4th. A tire blows, and the car crashes, killing the driver. If the car had been moving slowly and its tires were in good condition, the accident might not have happened. It seems impossible to have predicted this particular accident, yet the National Safety Council predicts within a small margin of error how many motorists will die in accidents over the July 4th holiday. Even more accurate is the Safety Council's estimates of yearly accidental deaths, as the greater the number of exposures to loss, the closer are the results to the underlying probability.

Similarly, insurers with statistics on millions of lives can make a close forecast of the number of deaths in a given period; the longer the period, the greater accuracy. The prediction of the number of persons in a college class who will die during the year probably would be far from accurate. The prediction on the basis of enrollment in a large university would show a moderate degree of accuracy; and the prediction of deaths in all U.S. colleges and universities would have a high degree of accuracy.

The law of large numbers is the basis of insurance. Under this law, the impossibility of predicting a happening in an individual case is replaced by the demonstrable ability to forecast collective losses when considering a large number of cases. Applying these conclusions to insurance, one observes that every year a given number of dwellings burn or a particular number of deaths occur. If a small group of cases were isolated, a wide variation between actual loss experienced and average loss expected might be found. Insurers within their financial limits use the benefits of the law of large numbers by insuring the greatest possible number of acceptable exposure units to facilitate loss forecasting. In addition, the insurers want the units spread widely to minimize deviation from underlying probabilities occurring when the units are concentrated in one location.

Insurance does not completely eliminate risk because achieving an infinite number of exposure units is impossible. Thus some deviation of actual from expected results can be anticipated. Furthermore, statistics on which predictions are based are not perfect. Even if they were, no reason exists to believe that tomorrow's losses will conform to yesterday's because so many dynamic elements are involved. The possibility of the presence of moral hazards also may interfere with loss prediction.

Criteria of an Insurable Exposure

Considering that insurance seems such a logical method of handling risk, why not combine all uncertainties in one big pool and rid the world of most risk? The limiting factor is that several broad criteria need to be considered before attempting to operate a successful insurance plan: (1) a large group of homogeneous exposure units must be involved, (2) the loss produced by the peril must be definite, (3) the occurrence of the loss in the individual cases must be accidental or fortuitous, (4) the potential loss must be large enough to cause hardship, (5) the cost of the insurance must be economically feasible, (6) the chance of loss must be calculable, and (7) the peril must be unlikely to produce loss to a great many insured units at one time.

* * *

1. A large group of homogeneous exposure units. To predict probable loss through use of the law of large numbers, it is essential that a large number of similar, though not necessarily identical, units be exposed to the same peril. Large numbers, in this context, means numbers large enough to make losses predictable within ranges compatible to insurers. A fire insurer cannot operate with only 25 or 50 houses to insure. With so few exposures, the difference between losses experienced from those expected likely will be excessive. Insurance is impractical when the probable deviation from the predicted loss is so large that a reasonable addition to the premium to offset the risk increases insurance rates to levels unattractive to buyers. In life insurance many persons are needed in each age, health, and occupational classification. To accommodate this essential criterion, classifications in insurance frequently are broad.

* * *

3. *Accidental loss.* Although some losses are expected for the group, specific individual losses themselves must be unexpected; that is, fortuitous. Ideally, the loss should be beyond the control of the insured. Under mercantile theft insurance normal (anticipated) shoplifting losses are excluded. In credit insurance, bad debt losses which are normal for the trade are not covered. The risk of loss from death is not insurable because everyone is certain to die. Insurance, however, is written against losses arising from untimely death, as the hour of death is uncertain.

* * *

5. *Economically feasible cost.* To be insurable, the chance of loss must be small. The cost of the policy consists of the pure premium (amount needed for claims) and the expense addition. If the chance of loss is much above 40 percent, the policy cost will exceed the amount the insurer must pay under the contract. For example, a life insurer could issue a $1,000 policy on a man aged 99. The pure premium alone, however, would be about $980, to which would be added an amount for expenses increasing the total premium to more than the policy amount. For insurance to be attractive for the consumer, the coverage must exceed the premium. The amount by which the coverage must exceed the premium depends on the degree of the individual's risk aversion. The chance of loss involving small damage to autos by collision is so high that collision policies usually are written to exclude the first $100 of loss.

6. *Chance of loss must be calculable.* Some probabilities of loss can be determined by logic alone, for example, the probabilities involved in a flip of a coin. Others must be determined empirically; that is, by a tabulation of experience with a projection of that experience into the future. Most types of insurance probabilities are determined empirically. Some chances of loss, however, cannot be determined either by logic or from experience. Unemployment is an example because it occurs with such irregularity that no one, as yet, has succeeded in determining its future incidence. If no statistics on the chance of loss are available, the degree of accuracy in loss prediction is low in spite of a large number of exposures.

The essential criterion of a large number of homogeneous exposure units and the requisite of a measurable chance of loss are violated by "insurance" on loss exposures, such as the fingers of a pianist or the pitching arm of a baseball player. These types of policies are not true insurance. They are transfers of risk from "the insured" to the "insurer" but do not combine exposures to reduce risk. * * *

7. *Unlikely to produce loss to a great many at the same time.* No insurer can afford to insure a type of loss likely to happen to a large percentage of those exposed to it. A large percentage as used in this context means one so high a single occurrence could force well-managed insurers and their reinsurers into (or close to the brink of) insolvency. Life insurers write coverage against death, even though all policyowners will die eventually. Its premium rates and asset accumulations are calculated to pay claims as they mature without causing the insurer financial hardship. If all policyowners of a life insurer should die prematurely, it would be insolvent just as a fire insurer would whose policyowners all lost their houses by fire.

* * *

The foregoing criteria of insurability are not rigidly followed. Cases are on record in which coverage is written in violation of one or more of them (e.g., insurance covering the legs of an outstanding running back, or covering the obvious assets of a glamorous male or female screen personality). Insurers write policies for small amounts; they write insurance for which no adequate statistics are available for scientific ratemaking; they write contracts when the chance of loss is high or the exposure is catastrophic; they write coverage where the loss is not accidental; and they cover losses that are not definite in time, amount, and place. These criteria must be viewed as the optimum to achieve rather than characteristics to be met in every instance.

* * *

DENENBERG, EILERS, MELONE AND ZELTEN, RISK AND INSURANCE
(2d ed. 1974).*

[The following excerpts are taken from Chapter 26, "Rate–Making: Theory."]

A "rate" in insurance circles is the price an insurer charges for each unit of a risk that is transferred to it. From the standpoint of insureds, a rate may be viewed as the price paid for a unit of protection. * * *

* * *

DETERMINATION OF RISK CATEGORIES

Prior to calculating a rate, it is necessary to select the types of risks for which the rate will apply. For automobile bodily injury liability coverage the insurers must decide whether the same rate will be used for all types of automobiles (commercial and private), for all types of drivers (regardless of sex, age, health, and accident record), and for all locations (city, rural, and so forth).

The number and character of risk classes is not subject to the sole discretion of insurers. Most states impose regulatory standards that influence the development of classes for rate-making purposes. Furthermore, an insuring organization must set class limits that will facilitate a competitive, as well as profitable, rate structure.

Rate-making classifications are required both in the prediction of claims and in the allocation of expenses. In the prediction of claims they determine which expected losses will be grouped together for rate-making purposes;

* Denenberg, et al., Risk and Insurance, 2nd ed., © 1974, pp. 509–511, 516–517, 518–519, 520–521. Adapted by permission of Prentice-Hall, Inc., Englewood Cliffs, N.J.

that is, frame houses with asphalt roofs may be in a separate class from the one that includes frame houses with wooden shingle roofs. * * *

PREDICTION OF CLAIMS

* * *

* * * By observing the number and extent of losses among a sufficiently large sample, it is possible to estimate with reasonable accuracy the proportion of an insured population that will encounter a particular kind of loss, assuming there is no significant change in conditions in the future. Probabilities can be obtained even without a detailed knowledge of the underlying causes of loss; indeed, there is seldom any concern with the underlying causes in establishing the probabilities of loss.

The problem of loss prediction is complicated in all fields by the fact that most insurance rates apply to a period of time subsequent to the time they were calculated. Not only must the proportion of past losses—i.e., the ratio of losses to total exposures—be reliably estimated, but adjustments must also be made to account for any changes in conditions that are likely to modify future losses as compared with those of the past. This is particularly true for lines of insurance where there are long-term rate guarantees, for example, in life insurance. The judgment of those who make rates is of obvious importance in adjusting statistics of prior periods to anticipated future conditions, for example, inflation or changes in loss patterns. * * *

* * *

METHODS OF CALCULATING RATES

The approach taken in setting rates and premiums may use one of two fundamental and somewhat conflicting philosophies—namely, class rate-making or individual risk rating. In the latter approach the loss experience or risk characteristics and possibly the expense costs of a policyholder influence the rate to be paid much more directly than under a class rate-making procedure.

CLASS RATES

A class rate is obtained in principle by apportioning the anticipated losses and expenses (plus any profit or surplus and contingency factors) for a given class of coverage over all of the exposure units. For example, the workmen's compensation class rate for clerical employees in a given state would be determined first by ascertaining the predicted dollars of loss for all covered clerical employees in the state. Because the exposure unit in workmen's compensation is $100 of payroll, the anticipated total claims figure would be divided by the number of hundreds of dollars of payroll that would be received by the clerical workers. * * *

If, over a period of years, the clerical employees of a particular firm sustain no injuries at work and therefore receive no workmen's compensation benefits, the firm would nevertheless pay the same rate under a class rate-making system as would another employer whose clerical employees had collected a sizeable amount of workmen's compensation benefits. This procedure incorporates, of course, the pooling or averaging principle which is the foundation of insurance. The losses of particular policyholders affect the rate they pay only to the extent that such losses cause a change in the class rate.

In actuality the term "class rates" is a misnomer because all rates, even those based upon the experience of only one policyholder, may be thought of as being determined by class; that is, a rate applied to only one insured would treat that insured as a separate class. For this reason, although it does not have as obvious a connotation, the term "manual rates" is sometimes used as a synonym for class rates. Most individual buyers pay manual rates, at least initially.

The derivation of class or manual rates for specific lines and classes of insurance involves all of the problems associated with the selection of risk categories, prediction of losses and expenses, and the provision of margins, * * *. Few groupings of risks fall into distinct categories, and professional judgment is required to set the class boundary lines. Likewise, no trend in losses or expenses is so definitive as to indicate without question the future losses or expenses that will be incurred, even after risks have been classified into relatively homogeneous groups. Prediction involves an evaluation of what has occurred in the past and an estimation of how the future will vary therefrom, all of which relies heavily on the judgment of the actuaries—i.e., the rate-makers.

INDIVIDUAL RISK RATES AND PREMIUMS

Few persons or businesses are unconcerned about their financial expenditures. Cost consciousness is, for that matter, a prime requisite for successful business operations in the modern competitive environment. It is for obvious reasons, therefore, that the class rate-making system tends to be viewed with disfavor by those policyholders who consistently have a better than average loss experience. This view tends to be particularly strong among business purchasers of insurance. It is natural for such insureds to think that broad classes should be restructured into more homogeneous groups, i.e., that the "better" risks from each class should be in a separate category for rate-making purposes. It is this type of logic and pressure that has fostered individual risk rates.

Individual risk rates, with the exception of schedule rates, reflect much more directly than class rates the actual loss experience and, in some instances, expense experience of particular insureds. This is not to say that the rate paid by a policyholder under the individual risk approach to rate-making will be determined solely by the experience of the policyholder. The title merely implies that a portion of the premium paid for transferring a risk is dependent directly upon the experience of a particular insured. The nature of this approach has frequently resulted in its also being termed "experience rate-making" or "merit rate-making." * * *

The theory underlying individual risk rates is that the number of exposure units of some insureds is large enough to conclude that losses that are (or are not) incurred are not necessarily due to chance but, rather, reflect to some extent the actual character of the risks of the particular policyholders. If a firm with a large number of employees has group hospital-surgical coverage and lower than average claims are paid in aggregate to the employees, it is reasonable to assume that the firm has better than average "loss characteristics." The risk of incurring hospital and surgical expenses is probably less for employees in that firm than for "average" persons. This conclusion seems particularly well-founded if the low loss pattern continues for several years. The opposite assumption would be made if a firm with a large number of exposure units had poor loss experience. Individual risk rates seek to vary the rates charged each large insured in close accordance with the variation it presents in the chance of loss.

Under the basic form of individual risk rates, as under class rates, it is assumed that the rates reflect the anticipated average experience over the long run. Pooling is involved because those whose losses exceed expectations in a particular policy period are "subsidized" by those with fewer losses than anticipated. * * *

The application of the individual risk method of rate-making involves a basic issue and even raises a broad question concerning the function of insurance. If the individual risk rate-making technique is carried to the extreme, every insured pays his own losses and the pooling function of insurance is destroyed. Still, unless the rate-making process of an insurer is sufficiently flexible to provide what insureds consider to be an equitable procedure for sharing losses, it is likely that policyholders will either procure coverage from an insuring organization that will agree to reflect directly the individual loss experience or the risk will be retained on a self-assumption or self-insurance basis.

* * *

Experience Rates. Experience rate-making is a type of individual risk rate-making that uses the *past* loss experience of a particular insured to determine at least in part the rate to be paid in the *future*. Thus, experience rates are prospective in nature, because the future rates of a policyholder are influenced directly by his past experience. * * * [T]he rate of an insured who qualifies for experience rate-making may not be determined entirely by his past experience. Only very large policyholders have their future (pure premium) rate determined entirely by their past experience under this system. Other insureds of more moderate size have their rates determined in part by their own experience and in part by the appropriate class rate. The extent to which a particular insured's experience is used in the rate-making process is referred to as "credibility." Thus, 50 percent credibility indicates that a policyholder's future rate is calculated by giving equal weight to his own experience and to the class rate.

Retrospective Premium Plans. A retrospective rate utilizes the experience of the *past* period to determine the rate for *that period.* This differs, of course, from experience rates, because the latter use the past experience to calculate the future rate. Retrospective rating requires a deposit premium at the inception of a policy protection period, and a policyholder's experience for the period determines whether he receives a partial return of the premium or must pay an additional amount.

Retrospective rating is the closest possible approach to self-rating. If it were not for a maximum premium provision, insurance provided through retrospective rates would be merely a service contract that provided no protection against risks. The maximum premium provides assurance that an insured's payments to an insurance company will not exceed a set amount even if he has enormous losses. Policies that are rated retrospectively also have minimum premium stipulations, so that insureds with no losses must nevertheless pay the minimum premium. The minimum premium provides for the expenses of the insurer and a contingency factor, with funds obtained from the latter being used to pay insureds whose losses exceed their maximum premiums.

No small amount of consternation surrounds the use of retrospective rates, inasmuch as insurers see that the technique largely relieves them of their major function—that of risk-handling. This accounts in part for the fact that retrospective rate-making has been optional for insureds. The increased use of self-insurance has forced insurers to offer retrospective rate-making primarily in workmen's compensation coverages. In essence, the technique provides risk protection only above the maximum premium, with the insurer providing claims payment service below that level. In some instances, the policyholders (generally an employer with workmen's compensation or medical expense protection) may even physically pay the claims that occur up to the maximum premium.

Schedule Rates. Schedule rate-making was one of the earliest forms of individual risk rate-making. As is suggested by the title, the technique uses a schedule, which lists supposedly average physical characteristics for a given type of policyholder, and each insured is compared with the schedule. "Plus" points are given where an insured is better than average, and "minus" points where he is below average. The net points (plus or minus) determine the extent to which the appropriate class rate will be modified for the insured in question. Many observers therefore view the schedule approach as merely a type of class rate, although, as was noted earlier, the same generalization may be applied to any type of rate-making.

* * *

SECTION B. LIABILITY INSURANCE

Insurance comes in two basic forms—loss and liability. Liability insurance (also often called "third-party insurance") insures against specified liability to others; loss insurance compensates the insured directly for the occurrence of specified losses. Both forms affect tort liability but—in contemporary tort law—liability insurance has a more direct and immediate relation to tort liability.

The materials in this section first examine representative and nominally contractual arrangements which define terms of liability insurance coverage.

Next we consider two different approaches to covering claims. The traditional approach—called "occurrence-based"—covers claims whose underlying events occur during the policy period. A more recent innovation—called "claims-based" insurance—has been devised to wrestle with the long time lag between exposure and injury, which is characteristic of certain modern accidental injuries having their genesis in contact with toxic or harmful substances. "Claims-based" insurance covers claims made during the policy period. Finally, we examine a number of cases which show the influence of liability insurance on tort doctrine.

MASSACHUSETTS AUTOMOBILE INSURANCE POLICY

[The following excerpts from a standard form of policy used in 1988 (with some changes as of 1997 noted) treat only provisions whereby the company protects the insured against liability to third parties (so-called third-party insurance), as well as some general clauses governing the entire policy. They do not include many exceptions and conditions which qualify the undertakings of the insurer and impose duties on the insured.]

Our Agreement

This policy is a legal contract under Massachusetts law. Because this is an auto policy, it only covers accidents and losses which result from the ownership, maintenance or use of autos. The exact protection is determined by the coverages you purchased.

We agree to provide the insurance protection you purchased for accidents which happen while this policy is in force.

You agree to pay premiums and any Merit Rating surcharges when due and to cooperate with us in case of accidents or claims.

Our contract consists of this policy, the Coverage Selections page, any endorsements agreed upon, and your application for insurance. Oral promises or statements made by you or our agent are not part of this policy.

There are many laws of Massachusetts relating to automobile insurance. We and you must and do agree that, when those laws apply, they are part of this policy.

Compulsory Insurance

There are four Parts to Compulsory Insurance. They are called Compulsory Insurance because Massachusetts law requires you to buy all of them before you can register your auto. No law requires you to buy more than this Compulsory Insurance.

* * *

Part 1. Bodily Injury to Others

Under this Part, we will pay damages to people injured or killed by your auto in Massachusetts accidents. The damages we will pay are the amounts the injured person is entitled to collect for bodily injury through a court judgment or settlement. We will pay only if you or someone else using your auto with your consent is legally responsible for the accident. The most we will pay for injuries to any one person as a result of any one accident is $10,000. The most we will pay for injuries to two or more people as a result of any one accident is a total of $20,000. [These limits were increased to $20,000 and $40,000 by 1997.] This is the most we will pay as the result of a single accident no matter how many autos or premiums are shown on the Coverage Selections page.* * * *

The law provides a special protection for anyone entitled to damages under this Part. We must pay their claims even if false statements were made when applying for this policy or your auto registration. We must also pay even if you or the legally responsible person fails to cooperate with us after the accident. We will, however, be entitled to reimbursement from the person who did not cooperate or who made any false statements. * * *

Part 4. Damage to Someone Else's Property

Under this Part, we will pay damages to someone else whose auto or other property is damaged in an accident. The damages we will pay are the amounts that person is legally entitled to collect for property damage through a court judgment or settlement. We will pay only if you, or a household member, is legally responsible for the accident. We will also pay if someone else using your auto with your consent is legally responsible for the accident. Damages include any applicable sales tax and the costs resulting from the loss of use of the damaged property.

We will *not* pay for property damage which occurs:

1. While your auto is being used to carry anyone or anything for a fee. We do not consider share-the-expense car pool contributions as fees. * * *

5. To an auto or other property owned by you or the legally responsible person. * * *

6. When the property damage is caused by anyone using an auto without the consent of the owner.

The most we will pay for damage resulting from any one accident is shown on the Coverage Selections page. * * *

This Part is Compulsory. You must have limits of at least $5,000. However, you may want to buy more protection. Higher limits may be purchased if agreed upon by you and by us. * * *

OPTIONAL INSURANCE

There are seven separate Parts to Optional Insurance. They are called Optional Insurance because they are not required by law. * * *

We will not pay under any of the optional coverages:

* * *

---

* Note that we are in the "Compulsory Insurance" portion of the policy. Thus, these limits apply to policies that insurers must sell to any licensed driver, no matter how poor an insurance prospect he or she may be.—Eds.

4.   For injury or damage that is intentionally caused by you, a household member, or anyone else using your auto with your consent.

Part 5. Optional Bodily Injury to Others

Under this Part, we will pay damages to people injured or killed in accidents if you or a household member is legally responsible for the accident. We will also pay damages if someone else using your auto with your consent is legally responsible for the accident. The damages we will pay are the amounts the injured person is entitled to collect for bodily injury through a court judgment or settlement.

* * *

The most we will pay for injury to any one person as a result of any one accident is shown on the Coverage Selections page. The most we will pay for injuries to two or more people as a result of any one accident is also shown on the Coverage Selections page. This is the most we will pay as the result of a single accident no matter how many autos or premiums are shown on the Coverage Selections page.

If someone covered under this Part is using an auto he or she does not own at the time of the accident, the owner's auto insurance must pay its limits before we pay. Then, we will pay, up to the limits shown on your Coverage Selections page, for any damages not covered by that insurance.

* * *

We must sell you limits up to $25,000 per person and $60,000 per accident if you want to buy them. [By 1997, these limits had been increased to $35,000 and $80,000 respectively.] Higher limits may be purchased if agreed upon by you and by us.

GENERAL PROVISIONS AND EXCLUSIONS

2.   Our Duty to Defend You and Our Right to Settle. We have the right and duty to defend any lawsuit brought against anyone covered under this policy for damages which might be payable under this policy. We will defend the lawsuit even if it is without merit. We have the right to settle any claim or lawsuit as we see fit. Our duty to settle or defend ends when we have paid the maximum limits of coverage under this policy. If any person covered under this policy settles a claim without our consent, we will not be bound by that settlement.

MERIT RATING

This policy is subject to Merit Rating.

Under the Merit Rating system, the cost of your policy depends, in part, on your driving record and that of the other drivers insured by this policy.

If you or those drivers cause accidents or are convicted of certain traffic violations, your policy will be surcharged.

If neither you nor the other drivers insured by this policy cause accidents or have convictions, a credit will be applied to reduce your policy premium.

The amount of any credit or surcharge which applies to your policy will appear on your Coverage Selections Page. When we bill you for a surcharge, we will send you a "Statement of Surcharges Due" which itemizes each surcharge.

Failure to pay a surcharge will result in cancellation of your policy.

DEFINITIONS

3. Household Member—Means anyone living in your household who is related to you by blood, marriage or adoption. This includes wards or foster children.

5. Your Auto—means:

A. The vehicle or vehicles described on the Coverage Selections page.

It can be a private passenger auto, a trailer or a motorcycle.

It can also be a pick-up, sedan, delivery or panel truck, if it is not used in business.

B. Any auto or trailer while used as a temporary substitute for the described auto while that auto is out of normal use because of breakdown, repair, servicing, loss or destruction. But the term "your auto" does *not* include a substitute vehicle owned by you or your spouse.

C. An auto, motorcycle or non-business pick-up, sedan, delivery or panel truck to which you take title as a permanent replacement for a described auto or as an additional auto. We provide coverage for an additional auto only if you ask us to insure it within ten days after you take title. * * *

9. Accident—means an unexpected, unintended event that causes bodily injury or property damage arising out of the ownership, maintenance or use of an auto.

GENERAL BUSINESS LIABILITY INSURANCE POLICY

[This standard form of policy covers a range of liabilities that may be incurred by the insured business firm. The excerpts omit many exceptions and conditions. Basically the insurance company promises to pay on behalf of the insured "all sums which the Insured shall become legally obligated to pay as damages because of bodily injury or property damage." The exclusions, several of which appear below, limit the company's obligation. One important coverage of the policy involves products liability. Two characteristic definitions are:]

"Products hazard" includes bodily injury and property damage arising out of the Named Insured's products or reliance upon a representation or warranty made at any time with respect thereto, but only if the bodily injury or property damage occurs away from premises owned by or rented to the Named Insured and after physical possession of such products has been relinquished to others.

"Named Insured's products" means goods or products manufactured, sold, handled or distributed by the Named Insured or by others trading under his name, including any container thereof (other than a vehicle). * * *

EXCLUSIONS

This insurance does not apply: * * *

(b) to bodily injury or property damage arising out of the ownership, maintenance, operation, use, loading or unloading of

(1) any automobile or aircraft owned or operated by or rented or loaned to any Insured, or

(2) any other automobile or aircraft operated by any person in the course of his employment by any Insured; * * *

(f) to bodily injury or property damage arising out of the discharge, dispersal, release or escape of smoke, vapors, soot, fumes, acids, alkalis, toxic chemicals, liquids or gases, waste materials or other irritants, contaminants or pollutants into or upon land, the atmosphere or any water course or body of water; but this exclusion does not apply if such discharge, dispersal, release or escape is sudden and accidental; * * *

(i) to any obligation for which the Insured or any carrier as his insurer may be held liable under any workmen's compensation, unemployment compensation or disability benefits law, or under any similar law; * * *

(m) to loss of use of tangible property which has not been physically injured or destroyed resulting from

(1) a delay in or lack of performance by or on behalf of the Named Insured of any contract or agreement, or

(2) the failure of the Named Insured's products or work performed by or on behalf of the Named Insured to meet the level of performance, quality, fitness or durability warranted or represented by the Named Insured;

but this exclusion does not apply to loss of use of other tangible property resulting from the sudden and accidental physical injury to or destruction of the Named Insured's products or work performed by or on behalf of the Named Insured after such products or work have been put to use by any person or organization other than an Insured; * * *

(p) to damages claimed for the withdrawal, inspection, repair, replacement, or loss of the use of the Named Insured's products or work completed by or for the Named Insured or of any property of which such products or work form a part, if such products, work or property are withdrawn from the market or from use because of any known or suspected defect or deficiency therein; * * *

"OCCURRENCE" AND "CLAIMS–MADE"
BASES FOR LIABILITY INSURANCE

Premiums for liability insurance are established on the basis of predictions of future costs—predictions based partly on past experience but also on estimates of how future experience will differ from past experience. Some types of liability insurance confront special problems. For example, claims of plaintiffs based on medical malpractice or products liability may differ sharply from claims of traffic victims with respect to the difficulty of predicting the costs that insurance companies (or self-insurers) will incur in disposition of claims for a forthcoming year for which premiums are being established (or reserves are being set aside). A major factor in this contrast is the "long tail" of claims first made years after the occurrences on which they are based.

Many more medical malpractice claims than claims of traffic victims are initiated five to fifteen years after the alleged negligently caused injury occurred. One reason for this contrast is that, in many jurisdictions, statutes of limitations, either explicitly or as construed by the courts, do not bar a claimant until some period after the claimant knows or has a reasonable opportunity to discover facts bearing on the claim—for example, that the discomfort and disability suffered for years have been caused by a sponge left in the body during surgery.

The "long tail" of claims affects the products liability system also. For example, a product may be a factor in an injury occurring during use of the product many years after it was manufactured. If the applicable law starts counting the limitation period from the date a defective product is marketed, it may happen that a claimant injured by a defect in a product (1) has no cause of action before injury, because injury is one of the requisites, and (2) has no cause of action after injury because the limitation period had already run out before the injury occurred. If, to avoid this harsh result, the applicable law starts counting the limitation period at the time of injury, manufacturers and their insurers must plan in the year of manufacture for claims costs that include estimates of the costs of claims that will be made many years later.

The problems associated with a "long tail" of claims would be substantial even if claims costs were relatively steady from year to year. These problems increase dramatically during a period of cost growth—for example, during a period when claims costs per hundred physicians for each year run higher than for the preceding year.

As a way of responding to the "long tail" of claims, some malpractice insurers have sought to change the form of medical malpractice liability insurance from the traditional "occurrence" basis to a "claims-made" basis.

Under a traditional "occurrence" policy, the insurance company agrees, among other things, to pay on behalf of the insured all sums the insured shall become legally obligated to pay as damages because of bodily injury "caused by an occurrence" during the policy period and arising out of the defined activity (e.g., "ownership, maintenance or use" in an automobile policy, or "the rendering of or failure to render professional services" in a physician's liability policy). Thus, the premium a physician pays to an insurance company for a one-year "occurrence" policy buys coverage that continues to protect the physician against claims based on professional services the physician renders during that policy year, regardless of how many years later particular claims may be made.

In contrast, under a "claims-made" policy, the insurance company agrees as follows:

> To pay on behalf of the Insured all sums which the Insured shall become legally obligated to pay as damages because of any claim or claims made against the Insured during the policy period arising out of the performance of professional services rendered or which should have been rendered, subsequent to the retroactive date, by the Insured.
> * * *

A one-year "claims-made" policy with an "effective" date commencing the policy year on, for example, July 1 of a given year might have a "retroactive" date three years previous to the "effective" date. Such a policy would cover claims made in the policy year on the basis of services rendered any time since the "retroactive" date (a four-year period in the example given). In order to have coverage for claims made in a future year based on occurrences during past years, the physician would have to obtain and pay premiums for another claims-made policy for that future year or else obtain and pay premiums for a "reporting endorsement," as indicated in the following example of a policy provision on this subject:

> In the event of termination of insurance either by nonrenewal or cancellation of this policy, or termination of a reporting period the Insured shall have the right upon payment of an additional premium (to be computed in accordance with the Company's rules, rates, rating plans and premiums applicable on the effective date of the endorsement) to have issued an endorsement(s) providing Additional Reporting Period(s) in which claims otherwise covered by this policy may be reported. Such right hereunder must, however, be exercised by the Insured by written notice not later than thirty (30) days after such termination date.

THE IMPACT OF INSURANCE

The cases following this note illustrate the impact of liability insurance on tort doctrine. (Cases in Section C of this chapter will illustrate the impact of *loss* insurance on tort doctrine.) As the introductory note to this chapter observes, a number of the preceding opinions on intentional tort liability and negligence law have also referred to liability insurance, either as part of an institutional and social background bearing upon the issue of liability, or as part of the explicit justification for expanding or contracting the scope of liability. Those cases show a wide range of influence: on the conception of intention used in intentional tort law and insurance coverage (*Garratt v. Dailey* and the squib cases following it supra p. 7); on the extent of liability for pure economic loss (*Barber Lines v. Donau Maru* supra p. 658); on whether to expand damages to cover loss of parental consortium (*Hibpshman v. Prudhoe Bay* supra p. 717); and whether to abrogate traditional immunities from tort liability (*Hicks v. State* supra p. 486); *Pierce v. Yakima Valley Memorial Hospital Ass'n* supra p. 495; *Boone v. Boone,* supra p. 497.

In the next two chapters we will encounter and examine a distinctively modern conception of strict liability—enterprise liability—which is partially predicated on insurance considerations. In Chapters 19 and 20 we will see the emergence of modern products liability law under the influence of enterprise liability, and the subsequent contraction of that law in the wake of the liability insurance crisis of the middle and late 1980's. The latter is a specific topic of *Brown v. Superior Court*, infra, p. 1042; *Shanks v. Upjohn*, infra, p. 1046; and *Knowles v. United States*, infra, p. 1138.

BROWN v. MERLO, 8 Cal.3d 855, 106 Cal.Rptr. 388, 506 P.2d 212 (1973). The Vehicle Code deprived an automobile guest of recovery for injury from the host's careless driving unless there was willful misconduct or intoxication. The court held that this "guest statute", as applied to a negligently injured guest, violated guarantees of equal protection in the state and federal constitutions. "In considering one of the traditional explanations for guest statutes—that they protect generous and hospitable hosts against suits by ungrateful guests—the court said: * * * [I]f the characterization of an injured guest's lawsuit as an act of 'ingratitude' ever had general validity, its rationality has been completely eroded by the development of almost universal automobile liability insurance coverage in recent years. Whereas in the late 1920's and 1930's the statute's operation might realistically have been viewed as relieving most generous hosts from potentially great personal expense, today, with the widespread prevalence of insurance coverage, it is the insurance company, and not the generous host, that in the majority of instances wins protection under the guest statute. Thus, in a day in which nearly 85 percent of automobile drivers carry liability insurance, the statute can no longer sequester the defense that it is a necessary means to thwart 'ungrateful' guests. In plain language, there is simply no notion of 'ingratitude' in suing your hosts' *insurer.*"

SIMMON v. IOWA MUTUAL CASUALTY CO., 3 Ill.2d 318, 121 N.E.2d 509 (1954). In the course of an opinion holding that the injured person was entitled to give an insurer the notice of the automobile accident required by the insurance policy, the court observed: "Automobile insurance has taken an important position in the modern world. It is no longer a private contract merely between two parties. The greater part of litigation in our trial courts is concerned with claims arising out of property damage, personal injury or death caused by operation of motor vehicles. The legislatures of all our States have recognized the hazards and perils daily encountered and as a result have enacted various pieces of legislation aimed at the protection of the injured party. Financial Responsibility acts, Unsatisfied Judgment Fund acts, and other similar laws are direct results of this concern. That the general welfare is promoted by such laws can be little doubted. Government and the general public have an understandable interest in the problem. Many persons injured and disabled from automobile accidents would become public charges were it not for financial assistance received from the insurance companies."

MAYER v. HOUSING AUTHORITY OF JERSEY CITY, 44 N.J. 567, 210 A.2d 617 (1965). While playing baseball at a playground facility provided by defendant within its apartment complex, plaintiff was hit by a stone thrown by an unknown person (presumably another child). Plaintiff based his claim on defendant's negligent breach of an asserted duty to provide supervisory personnel adequate to prevent such behavior by third parties. Plaintiff had judgment below. The Superior Court, Appellate Division, affirmed. That decision was affirmed by the Supreme Court, in a per curiam decision adopting the reasoning of the Appellate Division, and over a dissent written by Justice Haneman.

The dissent criticized several aspects of the Appellate Division's opinion, including (1) the expansive concept of foreseeability of harm in that opinion, (2) the doubtful conclusion (in view of the record in the trial court) that failure of defendant to provide one or more guards "was a substantial factor" in bringing about plaintiff's injury, and (3) the vague, indeterminate character of the duty imposed on defendant (what standard to determine the reasonable number of guards and during what hours, whether the duty existed independently of notice to defendant of prior injuries). The dissent concluded:

"It seems to me that neither public policy nor fairness requires the vague type of duty here imposed, but rather dictate the opposite conclusion.

"Piercing the theoretical terms of 'foreseeability,' 'duty' and 'proximate cause' in which the Appellate Division's conclusion is couched, reveals that the real *ratio decidendi* is strict liability, which in turn is bottomed in large part upon the doctrine that among parties involved in an accident, the party best able to bear or distribute the loss should be liable. This risk-bearing, risk-distributing doctrine is predicated upon radically different concepts from the fault theory. The availability of insurance is one beam which undergirds this thesis; yet recent developments in the insurance field have demonstrated that this edifice may well be constructed on sand. It is common knowledge that in recent years public liability insurance has become more difficult to obtain. If obtainable, premiums have in many instances become so costly as to be almost prohibitive. Also, the expense incident to improvements and repairs to buildings and lands required by the prospective insurer as a condition to the issuance of a policy has placed coverage beyond the financial reach of many owners. It follows that in those circumstances where insurance is, for practical purposes, unavailable the risk is not distributed. Surely tenants in a low-cost housing project cannot be categorized as having 'deep pockets,' nor can the distribution of risk philosophy apply to them. It is no answer to say that a landowner should have the financial ability to obtain insurance. The same applies to many, if not most, landowners who will be affected by this decision.

"Furthermore, despite the availability of insurance, the ultimate expense of providing the supervisory personnel hereinafter required of all apartments and public bodies furnishing recreational facilities must rest upon the tenants of the apartment regime and the taxpayer. Only in the latter case can there be a true distribution of risk. And even in that case, might not the effect of this decision result in the deprivation of recreational facilities for children to the extent that such bodies are unable or unwilling to voluntarily assume the duty of supervision hereinafter imposed upon them by law?

"I would therefore reverse."

SHINGLETON v. BUSSEY, 223 So.2d 713 (Fla.1969). The trial court dismissed as a party defendant the insurance company in an action by plaintiff arising out of an automobile collision and brought against the company's insured. The insurance contract provided that no action would lie against the insurer until an insured's obligation had been determined by judgment and that the insurer could not be joined in any action against the insured. The intermediate appellate court reversed. Its judgment was here affirmed in an opinion concluding that "a direct cause of action now inures to a third party beneficiary against an insurer in motor vehicle liability insurance coverage cases as a product of the prevailing public policy of Florida." The contractual "no joinder" clause was judged invalid since it was found to "collide" with "the interests of the public generally" in the regulated field of automobile liability insurance. "In the modern world which is fraught with public safety hazards, it is unrealistic that mass liability insurance coverage designed to afford protective benefits for the general public" should so impede recovery by members of the protected class. The "unfettered right" of a plaintiff to sue the tortfeasor and insurer jointly "is so universal and essential to due process that it can rarely be curtailed or restricted by private contract between potential defendants." The court observed:

"In reaching the foregoing conclusion, we are cognizant that the primary reason advanced in those jurisdictions which have sustained 'no joinder clauses' in the area of liability insurance is that such a clause serves to prevent prejudice to the insurer through the prophylactic effect of isolating from the jury's consideration any knowledge that coverage for the insured exists. Such a result is deemed desirable because of the notion that a jury is prone to find negligence or to augment damages, if it thinks that an affluent institution such as an insurance company will bear the loss. See Appleman, 8 Insurance Law and Practice, § 4861. While we will not go so far as to assert that the above proposition has been all but obliterated by the more recent indications to the effect that the injection of insurance does not operate to increase the size of jury verdicts, we do think the stage has now been reached where juries are more mature. Accordingly, a candid admission at trial of the existence of insurance coverage, the policy limits of same, and an otherwise above board revelation of the interest of an insurer in the outcome of the recovery action against insured should be more beneficial to insurers in terms of diminishing their overall policy judgment payments to litigating beneficiaries than the questionable 'ostrich head in the sand' approach which may often mislead juries to think insurance coverage is greater than it is.

* * *

" * * * If joinder is allowed initially, all the cards are on the table and all interrelated claims and defenses can be heard and adjudicated reciprocally among all parties and the plaintiff will have the same initial right as insurer now avails itself against plaintiff to protect his rights against the insurer. In this manner the interests of all the parties and the concomitant right to expeditiously litigate the same in concert are preserved.

"If it should clearly appear in pretrial procedures that joinder of the insurer interposes issues between insured and insurer in particular case situations likely to unduly complicate trial of the questions pertaining to the liability of the insured to the injured third party and commensurate damages to be awarded, it would be a simple process under our liberal civil rules for the trial judge on timely motion to sever such complicating issues between insurer and insured for separate trial or adjudication. But such separation for adjudication of issues between insurer and insured would not remove from the case the identity of all parties joined nor their claims and defenses and their right to participate and protect their respective interests."

HARRELL v. TRAVELERS INDEMNITY CO.
Supreme Court of Oregon, 1977.
279 Or. 199, 567 P.2d 1013.

[In an earlier action, plaintiff had judgment against defendant's insured for $70,000 in compensatory damages and $25,000 in punitive damages, the latter award based on evidence that the insured drove recklessly after drinking. Plaintiff then brought an action against defendant insurance company to recover the punitive damages. The appellate court here held that the language of the insurance policy should be construed to cover such damages, and that such coverage would not (as the defendant contended) violate "public policy," at least where the case involved not "intentionally inflicted injury" but "reckless" conduct. The court said:]

* * * It has long been recognized that there is no empirical evidence that contracts of insurance to protect against liability for negligent conduct are invalid, as a matter of public policy, because of any "evil tendency" to make negligent conduct "more probable" or because there is any "substantial relationship" between the fact of insurance and such negligent conduct. Neither is there any such evidence that contracts of insurance to protect against liability for punitive damages have such an "evil tendency" to make reckless conduct "more probable" or that there is any "substantial relationship" between the fact of such insurance and such misconduct. * * *

* * *

* * * [I]f the rule proposed by defendant were adopted, the conduct subject to possible liability for punitive damages, and which could no longer be the subject of protection by a valid contract of insurance, would include a wide spectrum of conduct that would impose liability not only upon automobile drivers, but also upon business and professional persons, firms and corporations, as well as upon ordinary persons when engaged in a wide variety of activities. As examples:

(1) A physician whose treatment of a patient is such that a jury could properly find that it was "grossly negligent" may be held liable for punitive damages—a liability for which protection by insurance would no longer be available.

* * *

(4) One whose business involves the operation of a plant which emits smoke, fumes or "particulates" may also have an uninsurable liability for punitive damages, even in the absence of any "wanton" or "fraudulent" conduct, upon the ground that he has "intentionally" permitted fumes, smoke or particles to be released and blown by the wind upon another's property, for the reason that "[t]he intentional disregard of the interest of another is the legal equivalent of legal malice and justifies punitive damages for trespass." [Citation omitted.]

* * *

In our view, it is naive at least, if not pure fiction, to hold that an insurance contract against liability for punitive damages is invalid as contrary to public policy because such a contract would "shift the burden" to an insurance company so as to either "punish" it or have it pass that burden "on [to] the public," so as to "punish society."

On the contrary, an insurance company which deliberately enters into a contract to provide coverage against liability for punitive damages is free to charge either a separate or additional premium for that risk. Conversely, if an insurance contract excludes coverage for liability against punitive damages no such additional premium need be charged and the insurance company may charge a lower premium for such a policy.

* * *

It is significant to note, * * * that when liability for a judgment of punitive damages is imposed upon a large corporation, or even upon an individual business or professional person with a profitable and well-established business or profession, the financial "burden" of such a judgment is then usually "shifted," if not to an insurance company, then to the public in the form of its customers or consumers. Thus, there would be the same "shifting of the burden" [even without insurance, a fact which undermines defendant's argument against allowing insurance coverage for punitive damage awards.] * * *

* * *

[A dissenting opinion observed:]

A court-made public policy against otherwise lawful liability insurance can be defended, not *because* the purpose of punitive damages is always deterrence and *because* insurance will always destroy their deterrent effect, but only *when* these considerations apply. Neither premise is true in all cases. The court's frequent statements that punitive damages are meant to deter are true of any sanction in the sense that society would prefer avoidance of the harmful conduct and hopes the sanction will discourage it. * * * [C]ompensatory damages based on fault similarly rest on deterrence of harmful conduct; yet arguments against liability insurance on that ground were long since rejected. But aside from deterrence, statutory or common law measures of recovery beyond actual compensation may be designed to make a private suit worthwhile where individual damages are small or difficult to prove, or to channel plaintiff's anger from retaliation into a court when the tort is to his dignity more than to his pocketbook, or they may simply reflect social outrage apart from any remedial purpose.

* * * [I]f the basis is simply outrage at willful misconduct, liability for punitive damages will be uninsurable on the same principle as liability for a criminal fine. If statutory recovery beyond compensation aims at letting private plaintiffs with small claims hold defendants to socially responsible conduct, a derivative public policy against insurance is not so easily implied. * * *

The difficulty when we turn to the present case is that punitive damages for reckless driving while drunk are rather implausibly explained as a deterrent. A defendant who has not been deterred by the sanctions of criminal punishment, loss of license and risk of death or serious injury to himself and others, is not likely to be deterred by the probably unknown fact that his insurance policy will not cover the equally unfamiliar assessment of punitive damages, and as a lesson "not to do it again," this is too random and destructive a stroke to the average family's resources compared with, for instance, stricter enforcement of license revocation laws. If the matter were open, I would not ground punitive damages in this kind of case on a theory of deterrence.

But the matter is not open. The punitive damages involved here were awarded by a jury under express instructions to set them at the amount required as a deterrent, and this court affirmed on that premise. * * * [G]iven the premise, recovery from the liability insurer is an anomaly. * * *

HOME INSURANCE COMPANY v. AMERICAN HOME PRODUCTS CORPORATION, 75 N.Y.2d 196, 551 N.Y.S.2d 481, 550 N.E.2d 930 (1990). *Held*, "New York public policy precludes insurance indemnification for punitive damage awards, whether the punitive damages are based on intentional actions or actions which, while not intentional, amount to 'gross negligence, recklessness or wantonness,' or 'conscious disregard of the rights of others or for conduct so reckless as to amount to such disregard.'

"The main argument against coverage ... is that to allow it would defeat 'the purpose of punitive damages, which is to punish and to deter others from acting similarly, and that allowing coverage serves no useful purpose since such damages are a windfall for the plaintiff who, by hypothesis, has been made whole by the award of compensatory damages.' "

SECTION C. LOSS INSURANCE AND THE COLLATERAL SOURCE RULE

At the outset of this casebook we remarked that "the main job of the law of torts is to determine when loss shall be shifted from one to another, and when it shall be allowed to remain where it has fallen." supra, p. 1. Deciding not to shift a loss from victim to injurer is not, however, a guarantee that loss will remain concentrated "where it has fallen" on the victim. Loss insurance (also called "first-party insurance") may operate to disperse a loss which tort law leaves concentrated on the victim. The availability of loss insurance influences both "proximate cause" doctrine and damages doctrine. We have already seen the availability of loss insurance influence the extent of a defendant's liability in *Barber Lines v. Donau Maru* [supra, p. 658]. We shall see more such evidence in cases included in this. But the availability of first-party sources of compensation has been an even more explicit concern of the law of damages, where it is the subject of a traditional legal rule—the "collateral source" rule. That rule fixes the boundary between the tort system and first-party sources of compensation. It has also been one of the major sites of the "tort reform" movement of the past twenty or so years.

MASSACHUSETTS AUTOMOBILE INSURANCE POLICY

[The following excerpts from a standard form of policy used in 1988 (with one change as of 1997 noted) treat provisions covering the insured's own loss—so-called first-party insurance—and related subrogation and repayment provisions. They do not include many exceptions and conditions which qualify the undertakings of the insurer and impose duties upon the insured.]

Optional Insurance

Part 6. Medical Payments

Under this Part, we will pay reasonable expenses for necessary medical and funeral services incurred as a result of an accident.

We will pay for expenses resulting from bodily injuries to anyone occupying your auto at the time of the accident. We will also pay for expenses resulting from bodily injuries to you or any household member if struck by an auto or if occupying someone else's auto at the time of the accident. * * *

If someone covered under this Part is using an auto he or she does not own at the time of the accident, the owner's automobile Medical Payments insurance must pay its limit before we pay. Then, we will pay up to the limit shown on your Coverage Selections page for any expenses not covered by that insurance.

We will not pay benefits under this Part which duplicate payments made under the Medical Payments coverage of any other auto policy.

We must sell you limits of $5,000 per person if you want to buy them. Higher limits may be purchased if agreed upon by you and by us.

Part 7. Collision

Under this Part, we will pay for any direct and accidental damage to your auto caused by a collision. It does not matter who is at fault. We will also pay for collision damage to other private passenger autos while being used by you or a household member with the consent of the owner. However, we will not pay for damage to any auto which is owned or regularly used by you or a household member unless a premium for this Part is shown for that auto on the Coverage Selections page. * * *

We will pay for each loss up to the actual cash value of the auto at the time of the collision, but in all cases we will subtract the deductible amount you selected. Unless you selected a different amount, the law sets your deductible at $200. [By 1997, the deductible had been increased to $500.] Your deductible is shown on the Coverage Selections page.

After a collision, you must allow us to have the auto appraised. If you have your auto repaired in accordance with the appraisal, you must then send us a Completed Work Claim Form. * * *

If we fail to pay you within 7 days after receipt of the Completed Work Claim Form, you have the right to sue us. If a court decides that we were unreasonable in refusing to pay you on time, you are entitled to double the amount of damage plus costs and reasonable attorneys' fees. * * *

Part 9. Comprehensive

Under this Part, we will pay for direct and accidental damage or loss to your auto other than damage caused by collision. We will also reimburse you for substitute transportation expenses if your auto is stolen. * * *

We consider glass breakage and the following types of losses to be Comprehensive and not Collision losses: losses caused by vandalism, fire and theft, missiles, falling objects, larceny, explosion, earthquake, windstorm, hail, water, flood, malicious mischief, riot or contact with a bird or animal.

We will pay for each loss up to the actual cash value of your auto at the time of loss but in all cases we will subtract the deductible amount you selected. * * *

GENERAL PROVISIONS AND EXCLUSIONS

5. *Our Right to Be Repaid.* Sometimes we may make a payment under this policy to you or to someone else who has a separate legal right to recover damages from others. In that case, those legal rights may be exercised by us. Anyone receiving payment under those circumstances must do nothing to interfere with those rights. He or she must also do whatever is necessary to help us recover for ourselves up to the amount we have paid. If we then recover more than we paid, we will pay that person the excess, less

his or her proportionate share of the costs of recovery, including reasonable attorneys' fees.

Sometimes you or someone else may recover money from the person legally responsible for an accident and *also* receive money from us for the same accident. If so, the amount we paid must be repaid to us to the extent that you or someone else recovers. We do not have to be repaid for any money we have paid under Medical Payments (Part 6). Whenever we are entitled to repayment from anyone, the amount owed us can be reduced by our proportionate share of the costs of recovering the money, including reasonable attorneys' fees.

HOMEOWNERS POLICY

[These excerpts from a standard form of policy include only provisions insuring against loss rather than liability. Many exceptions and conditions are omitted.]

We agree to provide the insurance described in this policy. In return you must pay the premium and comply with the policy terms. * * *

Definitions Used Throughout this Policy

"You" and "your" refer to the "named insured" shown in the Declarations and the spouse if a resident of the same household. "We", "us", and "our" mean the Company providing this insurance. In addition, certain words and phrases are defined as follows:

1. **"insured"** means you and the following residents of your household:

    a.   your relatives;

    b.   any other person under the age of 21 who is in the care of any person named above. * * *

2. **"Insured Location"**—means:

    a.   the one family dwelling, other structures and grounds or that part of any other building where you reside and which is shown in the Declarations as the insured location; * * *

6. **"Property Damage"**—means physical injury to or destruction of tangible property, including loss of its use.

8. **"Occurrence"**—means:

    a.   Under Policy Section I—Your Property, a loss to covered property caused by one or more perils we insure against; * * *

Policy Section I—Your Property

Our Limit of Liability

Our limits of liability for Coverages A, B and C for each insured location are show in the Declarations. * * *

Coverage A: Dwelling

Under Coverage A, we cover:

a. the dwelling on the insured location used principally as a private residence; including structures attached to the dwelling; and

b. materials and supplies located on or adjacent to the insured location for use in construction, alteration or repair of the dwelling or other structures on the insured location.

Coverage C: Personal Property

Under Coverage C, we cover:

a. Personal property owned or used by an insured while it is anywhere in the world;

b. Personal property of a guest or a residence employee while in a residence occupied by an insured;

c. Personal property of others who are not tenants of an insured while the property is on the insured location.

Our limit of liability for personal property usually situated at any insured's residence that is not an insured location is $10,000. * * *

Coverage Limitations

We will pay no more for loss in each occurrence than:

1. $1,000 for money, bank notes, bullion, gold other than goldware, silver other than silverware, platinum, coins and medals;

7. $1,000 for theft, misplacing or losing of furs, jewelry, precious and semi-precious stones and precious metals;

8. $5,000 for theft, misplacing or losing of silverware, silver-plated ware, goldware, gold-plated ware or pewterware.

9. $1,000 for business property pertaining to a business actually conducted on the insured location;

10. $1,000 for business property in storage or held as a sample or for sale or delivery after sale.

Deductible Applying to Loss Under Section I

Loss in each occurrence to covered property is subject to the deductible shown in the Declarations. * * *

Section I—Perils Insured Against

We will pay for all direct physical loss or damage to covered property from all perils not excluded under LOSSES NOT COVERED.

["LOSSES NOT COVERED" include normal wear and tear, and specified types of damage resulting from earthquakes, floods, power interruptions, "nuclear action" and war.]

RYAN v. NEW YORK CENTRAL RAILROAD

Court of Appeals of New York, 1866.

35 N.Y. 210.

This was an action by James Ryan against the New York Central Railroad Company to recover damages for the destruction by fire of his dwelling-house, in consequence of the alleged negligence of the defendants.

On the 15th July 1854, in the city of Syracuse, the defendants, by the careless management, or through the insufficient condition, of one of their engines, set fire to their wood-shed, and a large quantity of wood therein. The plaintiff's house, situated at a distance of one hundred and thirty feet from the shed, soon took fire from the heat and sparks, and was entirely consumed, notwithstanding diligent efforts were made to save it. A number of other houses were also burned by the spreading of the fire.

These facts having been proved on the part of the plaintiff, the defendants' counsel moved for a nonsuit, which was granted, and an exception taken. And the judgment having been affirmed at general term, the plaintiff appealed to this court.

HUNT, J. [after stating the facts.]—The question may be thus stated: A house in a populous city takes fire, through the negligence of the owner or his servant; the flames extend to and destroy an adjacent building: Is the owner of the first building liable to the second owner for the damage sustained by such burning?

It is a general principle, that every person is liable for the consequences of his own acts; he is thus liable in damages for the proximate results of his own acts, but not for remote damages. It is not easy, at all times, to determine what are proximate and what are remote damages. In Thomas v. Winchester (6 N.Y. 408), Judge Ruggles defines the damages for which a party is liable, as those which are the natural or necessary consequences of his acts. Thus, the owner of a loaded gun, who puts it in the hands of a child, by whose indiscretion it is discharged, is liable for the injury sustained by a third person from such discharge. The injury is a natural and ordinary result of the folly of placing a loaded gun in the hands of one ignorant of the manner of using it, and incapable of appreciating its effects. The owner of a horse and cart, who leaves them unattended in the street is liable for an injury done to a person or his property, by the running away of the horse, for the same reason; the injury is the natural result of the negligence. If the party thus injured had, however, by the delay or confinement from his injury, been prevented from completing a valuable contract, from which he expected to make large profits, he could not recover such expected profits from the negligent party, in the cases supposed; such damages would not be the necessary or natural consequences, nor the results ordinarily to be anticipated, from the negligence committed. So, if an engineer upon a steamboat or locomotive, in passing the house of A., so carelessly manages its machinery that the coal and sparks from its fires fall upon and consume the house of A., the railroad company or the steamboat proprietors are liable to pay the value of the property thus destroyed. (Field v. New York Central Railroad Co., 32 N.Y. 339.)

Thus far the law is settled, and the principle is apparent. If, however, the fire communicates from the house of A. to that of B., and that is destroyed, is the negligent party liable for his loss? And if it spreads thence to the house of C., and thence to the house of D., and thence consecutively through the other houses, until it reaches and consumes the house of Z., is the party liable to pay the damages sustained by these twenty-four sufferers?

The counsel for the plaintiff does not distinctly claim this, and I think it would not be seriously insisted, that the sufferers could recover in such case. Where, then, is the principle upon which A. recovers and Z. fails?

* * * I prefer to place my opinion upon the ground, that, in the one case, to wit, the destruction of the building upon which the sparks were thrown by the negligent act of the party sought to be charged, the result was to have been anticipated, the moment the fire was communicated to the building; that its destruction was the ordinary and natural result of its being fired. In the second, third or twenty-fourth case, as supposed, the destruction of the building was not a natural and expected result of the first firing. That a building upon which sparks and cinders fall should be destroyed or seriously injured, must be expected, but that the fire should spread and other buildings be consumed, is not a necessary or an usual result. That it is possible, and that it is not infrequent, cannot be denied. The result, however, depends, not upon any necessity of a further communication of the fire, but upon a concurrence of accidental circumstances, such as the degree of the heat, the state of the atmosphere, the condition and materials of the adjoining structures and the direction of the wind. These are accidental and varying circumstances; the party has no control over them, and is not responsible for their effects.

My opinion, therefore, is, that this action cannot be sustained, for the reason that the damages incurred are not the immediate but the remote result of the negligence of the defendants. The immediate result was the destruction of their own wood and sheds; beyond that, it was remote.

* * *

That the defendant is not liable in this action may also be strongly argued, from the circumstance that no such action as the present has ever been sustained in any of the courts of this country, although the occasion for it has been frequent and pressing. Particular instances are familiar to all, where such claims might have been made with propriety. The instance of the Harpers, occurring a few years since, is a striking one. (23 N.Y. 441.) Their large printing establishment, in the city of New York, was destroyed by the gross carelessness of a workman, in throwing a lighted match into a vat of camphene; the fire extended, and other buildings and much other property was destroyed. The Harpers were gentlemen of wealth, and able to respond in damages to the extent of their liability; yet we have no report in the books, and no tradition, of any action brought against them to recover such damages. The novelty of the claim, as was said by Judge BEARDSLEY, in Costigan v. Mohawk and Hudson Railroad Co., where the occasion for its being made had been so common, is a strong argument against its validity. (2 Denio 609.) * * *

To sustain such a claim as the present, and to follow the same to its legitimate consequences, would subject to a liability against which no prudence could guard, and to meet which no private fortune would be adequate. Nearly all fires are caused by negligence, in its extended sense. In a country where wood, coal, gas and oils are universally used, where men are crowded into cities and villages, where servants are employed, and where children find their home in all houses, it is impossible, that the most vigilant prudence should guard against the occurrence of accidental or negligent fires. A man may insure his own house, or his own furniture, but he cannot insure his neighbor's building or furniture, for the reason that he has no interest in them. To hold that the owner must not only meet his own loss by fire, but that he must guaranty the security of his neighbors on both sides, and to an unlimited extent, would be to create a liability which would be the destruction of all civilized society. No community could long exist, under the operation of such a principle. In a commercial country, each man, to some extent, runs the hazard of his neighbor's conduct, and each, by insurance against such hazards, is enabled to obtain a reasonable security against loss. To neglect such precaution, and to call upon his neighbor, on whose premises a fire originated, to indemnify him instead would be to award a punishment quite beyond the offence committed. It is to be considered, also, that if the negligent party is liable to the owner of a remote building thus consumed, he would also be liable to the insurance companies who should pay losses to such remote owners. The principle of subrogation would entitle the companies to the benefit of every claim held by the party to whom a loss should be paid.

* * *

PETITION OF KINSMAN TRANSIT CO., 338 F.2d 708 (2d Cir.1964). Friendly, J. [The facts of the case are briefly described, and the opinions quoted at slightly greater length, at p. 635 supra]. " * * * [T]he careless actor will [not] always be held [liable] for all damages for which the forces that he risked were a cause in fact. Somewhere a point will be reached when courts will agree that the link has become too tenuous—that what is claimed to be consequence is only fortuity. * * * Where the line will be drawn will vary from age to age; as society has come to rely increasingly on insurance and other methods of loss-sharing, the point may lie further off than a century ago."

WEINBERG v. DINGER, 106 N.J. 469, 524 A.2d 366 (1987). A fire broke out in plaintiff's apartment building. Because of inadequate water pressure at nearby fire hydrants, the flames could not be extinguished and the fire gutted the entire building. Plaintiff brought suit against Penns Grove, a private water company that installed and maintained the fire hydrants and watermains pursuant to its tariffs filed with the Board of Public Utility Commissioners, and to the regulations of the Board. Plaintiff had signed a standard service contract with Penns Grove for water supply, which incorporated by reference the regulatory requirements of the Board that Penns Grove maintain sufficient pressure for fire hydrants.

The trial court granted summary judgment for Penns Grove. Controlling precedent held that, absent express contractual provision obligating the water company to provide water *for extinguishing fires*, a private water company was immune from liability for negligently failing to provide water to fire hydrants at sufficient pressure to extinguish a fire. Plaintiffs sought and obtained review from the Supreme Court. *Held,* reversed and remanded. "[W]e impose on water companies the duty to act with reasonable care in providing water for extinguishing fires, and overrule [our prior decision granting water companies immunity from liability] and cases decided in reliance on it."

The contours of the court's abrogation of the waterworks' immunity were shaped by considerations of insurance and subrogation:

"On behalf of the water company, the following arguments are made: Imposing upon private water companies a duty to act with reasonable care would not benefit the public, because homeowners would in any case need adequate fire insurance; abrogating water company immunity would only encourage redundant insurance coverage on the part of the water companies; liability insurance for water companies, if available at all, would be expensive due to the extreme risk, and this cost will be passed on to water consumers. This form of compulsory insurance through water rates, it is argued, is inefficient because water rates do not vary with fire hazard. If sufficient insurance is not obtained, large negligence judgments could force water companies into bankruptcy, thereby interrupting water service.

* * *

"We are mindful of the concern that the water company's added liability insurance cost, ultimately borne by the consumer, constitutes a less efficient method of insuring against fire loss than is afforded by property insurance. We are also acutely aware that the shrinkage of the casualty insurance market and the sharp escalation in casualty insurance premiums that has recently occurred will affect the availability and cost of liability insurance for water companies. * * *

* * *

"Ultimately, the strongest argument against liability is that it is unnecessary because most property owners are already insured against fire loss. Accordingly, since fire insurance policies are authorized by statute to include a subrogation clause assigning to the insurer the insured's claims against a responsible third party, *N.J.S.A.* 17:36–5.20, the water companies contend that the abrogation of immunity would benefit not the property-owners but the insurance carriers. Although this argument minimizes the interests of claimants who are underinsured or who sustain personal injuries, there is little question that the existence of first-party insurance and the prospect of windfall recoveries by carriers exercising subrogation rights is the most persuasive argument against the abrogation of water company immunity.

"However, elimination of the water companies' immunity does not necessarily require that we impose on them liability for the subrogation claims of fire insurance carriers. Subrogation is an equitable doctrine. * * *

* * *

"We believe that the imposition on a water company of liability for subrogation claims of carriers who pay fire losses caused by the company's negligent failure to maintain adequate water pressure would inevitably result in higher water rates paid by the class of consumers that paid for the fire insurance. The result of imposing subrogation-claim liability on water companies in such cases would be to shift the risk from the fire-insurance company to the water company, and, ultimately, to the consumer in the form of increased water rates. Thus, the consumer would pay twice—first for property insurance premiums, and then in the form of higher water rates to fund the cost of the water company's liability insurance. We find this result contrary to public policy.

"Accordingly, we abrogate the water company's immunity for losses caused by the negligent failure to maintain adequate water pressure for fire fighting only to the extent of claims that are uninsured or underinsured. To the extent that such claims are insured and thereby assigned to the insurance carrier as required by statute, *N.J.S.A.* 17:36–5.20, we hold that the carrier's subrogation claims are unenforceable against the water company. This determination is made without prejudice to the right of a subrogation claimant, either in this or other litigation, to offer proof tending to demonstrate that any increase in water rates resulting from liability for subrogation claims would be substantially offset by reductions in fire-insurance premiums. If insurance rates were set on the basis of risk and experience, one would expect a high correlation between the increase in water company liability rates and the decrease in fire-insurance rates occasioned by the abrogation of water company immunity in cases like this. If that correlation were to be proven in subsequent litigation, we would be prepared to reconsider our denial of the carrier's right to subrogation against a water company."

COMPENSATION THROUGH SOCIAL INSURANCE AND SOCIAL WELFARE PROGRAMS

The preceding materials involve arrangements between individuals and private insuring organizations that are not legally required. Such typical loss or first-party insurance includes medical insurance, disability insurance and life insurance as well as the examples above of property insurance.

For workers (and their families) protection against loss has become ever more related to employment. To some extent, as with government employment, such protection may be mandated by statute. But these employee-benefit programs grow primarily out of collective bargaining agreements. They include medical benefits, sick leave or disability benefits, guaranteed wage, and pensions.

A third category of protection against loss (of health, employment, etc.) consists of mandatory governmental programs that are generally described under the rubric of "social insurance." Unlike the prior categories, the terms of social insurance are determined by statute and administrative regulations rather than by (regulated) contracts. These programs generally cover employed persons and their families and provide benefits in cash or kind to alleviate losses stemming from such events as death, health problems or unemployment. The criteria for eligibility for benefits under these programs—criteria such as past employment or contributions by a beneficiary— tend to be stated independent of generalized need (such as a showing of need evidenced by income beneath a stated level). Hence, the programs are referred to as insurance rather than "need" or "welfare" programs. Social insurance programs, unlike welfare programs, have tended to be specially funded, financed not out of general tax revenues but out of payroll taxes paid by covered individuals and/or their employers or by direct payments by covered persons.

The three dominant social insurance programs are social security, unemployment insurance, and medicare. The federal social security system (OASDHI) has four principal components:

>   (1) retirement benefits for those retirees with minimum employment;

>   (2) survivor benefits for families of deceased workers;

>   (3) benefits for disabled workers (Social Security Disability Insurance, or SSDI); and

>   (4) medicare benefits covering hospital and medical costs for those over 65 and for some younger disabled workers.

Unemployment insurance, administered by the states, provides short-term protection for those who have lost jobs and are willing to work.

Medicare provides hospital insurance and optional supplementary medical insurance for persons eligible for social security who are either disabled or older than 65. Medicare is financed primarily through a payroll tax, and secondarily by monthly premiums paid by participants. The program is administered by the Social Security Administration with the assistance of various intermediaries, such as Blue Cross and private insurance companies. These intermediaries determine the amount of payments due, and process claims. Participation in Medicare entitles beneficiaries to inpatient hospital care, and limited post-hospital care. The optional supplementary medical insurance pays for the services of physicians, surgeons, psychologists and social workers, and other ancillary services such as physical therapy and X–Rays.

The most important social welfare programs are Supplemental Security Income (SSI), Medicaid, food stamps, and the various state programs being put in place since the dismantling of AFDC (Aid for Families with Dependent Children).

Unlike Social Security, Supplemental Security Income (SSI) is a means-tested, not an insurance, program. SSI pays benefits from general revenues to aged, blind, or disabled persons and their spouses on the basis of need; the recipient's income and resources may not exceed specified limits; in 1995 the monthly earned income cut-off was approximately $1,000 for an individual, and approximately $1,450 for a couple (with a number of excludable items).* SSI was inaugurated in 1974, replacing previous state

---

* Dollar figures in this note are taken from the Social Security Bulletin, the 1996 Annual Statistical Supplement to the Social Security Bulletin, or from information supplied directly by the Social Security Administration itself.

administered, federally reimbursed programs with a national program providing a uniform minimum cash benefit with incentives for state supplementation. In 1995 approximately 6.5 million people received assistance through SSI. The majority of these were blind or disabled, not aged.

AFDC was part of the original Social Security Act of 1935, but it became known as "welfare" rather than as "social security," a fact that had much to do with its abolition as an entitlement program some sixty years later. It provided payments to families in which there was a dependent child who had been deprived of parental support or care by reason of death, continued absence, or incapacity. In 1994, an average of slightly more than 14 million people received AFDC cash assistance each month. In 1996 AFDC was repealed and replaced with a new program called Temporary Assistance for Needy Families (TANF), which provides block grants for states to spend on time-limited cash assistance. TANF gives states complete flexibility to determine eligibility criteria and set benefit levels, thereby ending the AFDC entitlement to cash assistance.

Medicaid—like SSI and unlike Medicare—is also a means-tested program. Unlike SSI, however, Medicaid provides benefits "in kind." That is, it provides health care, not cash. Prior to 1996, Medicaid required each state to provide medical assistance to AFDC and SSI recipients, and gave each state the option of providing such assistance to the "medically needy." Only thirty-five states extended coverage to the latter group, who are defined by their income minus medical expenses. The precise criteria of eligibility vary with family status, distinguishing among single persons, single parents and families, for example. With the abolition of AFDC, states now have more freedom to define these eligibility criteria.

Prior to 1996, food stamps were available to all recipients of public assistance or general assistance and to other households falling below certain income standards. They varied in price with the size of the recipient's income. The Federal Government was committed to paying the full cost of the food stamps and half of all administrative costs. The appropriations were open-ended—the government funded the full demand for food stamps, given their criteria of eligibility. In 1995, roughly 26.5 million people received food stamps every month. The Personal Responsibility and Work Opportunity Reconciliation Act of 1996 retained the Food Stamp Program as a federal program, but required able-bodied individuals between the ages of 18 and 50 with no dependents to work at least 20 hours a week or to participate in a state work program in order to continue to receive food stamps for more than three months out of every thirty-six month period. The Act also gives states some leeway to define criteria of eligibility.

All these programs influence tort law. The *Ryan* case illustrated how the availability of private loss insurance may affect liability rules. The cases which follow treat the collateral source rule and illustrate how private and social insurance against loss as well as welfare programs such as Medicaid may influence the measure of tort damages.

HELFEND v. SOUTHERN CALIFORNIA
RAPID TRANSIT DISTRICT

Supreme Court of California, 1970.
2 Cal.3d 1, 84 Cal.Rptr. 173, 465 P.2d 61.

TOBRINER, Acting Chief Justice.

Defendants appeal from a judgment of the Los Angeles Superior Court entered on a verdict in favor of plaintiff, Julius J. Helfend, for $16,400 in general and special damages for injuries sustained in a bus-auto collision that occurred on July 19, 1965, in the City of Los Angeles.

We have concluded that the judgment for plaintiff in this tort action against the defendant governmental entity should be affirmed. The trial court properly followed the collateral source rule in excluding evidence that a portion of plaintiff's medical bills had been paid through a medical insurance plan that requires the refund of benefits from tort recoveries.

[The court described the accident, which occurred when a bus driver employed by defendant sideswiped plaintiff's vehicle while trying to pass. The impact crushed plaintiff's arm. Plaintiff required hospital care and medical therapy to regain use of the arm. The injury led to "some permanent discomfort but no permanent disability."]

Plaintiff filed a tort action against the Southern California Rapid Transit District, a public entity, and Mitchell, an employee of the transit district. At trial plaintiff claimed slightly more than $2,700 in special damages, including $921 in doctor's bills, a $336.99 hospital bill, and about $45 for medicines. Defendant requested permission to show that about 80 percent of the plaintiff's hospital bill had been paid by plaintiff's Blue Cross insurance carrier and that some of his other medical expenses may have been paid by other insurance. * * * The court ruled that defendants should not be permitted to show that plaintiff had received medical coverage from any collateral source.

After the jury verdict in favor of plaintiff in the sum of $16,300, defendants appealed, raising only two contentions: (1) The trial court committed prejudicial error in refusing to allow the introduction of evidence to the effect that a portion of the plaintiff's medical bills had been paid from a collateral source. (2) The trial court erred in denying defendant the opportunity to determine if plaintiff had been compensated from more than one collateral source for damages sustained in the accident.

* * *

2.   THE COLLATERAL SOURCE RULE

The Supreme Court of California has long adhered to the doctrine that if an injured party receives some compensation for his injuries from a source wholly independent of the tortfeasor, such payment should not be deducted from the damages which the plaintiff would otherwise collect from the tortfeasor. (See, e.g., Peri v. Los Angeles Junction Ry. Co. (1943) 22 Cal.2d 111, 131, 137 P.2d 441.)[2] As recently as August 1968 we unanimously reaffirmed our adherence to this doctrine, which is known as the "collateral source rule."

Although the collateral source rule remains generally accepted in the United States, nevertheless many other jurisdictions[4] have restricted[5] or repealed it. In this country most commentators have criticized the rule and called for its early demise. * * *

* * *

The collateral source rule as applied here embodies the venerable concept that a person who has invested years of insurance premiums to assure his medical care should receive the benefits of his thrift.[14] The tortfeasor should not garner the benefits of his victim's providence.

The collateral source rule expresses a policy judgment in favor of encouraging citizens to purchase and maintain insurance for personal injuries and for other eventualities. Courts consider insurance a form of investment, the benefits of which become payable without respect to any other possible source of funds. If we were to permit a tortfeasor to mitigate damages with payments from plaintiff's insurance, plaintiff would be in a position inferior to that of having bought no insurance, because his payment

---

2. In Peri v. Los Angeles Junction Ry. Co., supra, 22 Cal.2d 111, 131, 137 P.2d 441, 452, a case involving a negligently caused automobile accident, this court said, "While it is true that he [plaintiff] received $2 per day compensation while he was unable to work, that sum may not be deducted from his loss of earnings, because it was received from an insurance company under a policy owned and held by him. 'Damages recoverable for a wrong are not diminished by the fact that the party injured has been wholly or partly indemnified for his loss by insurance effected by him, and to the procurement of which the wrongdoer did not contribute; * * * ' [citations]."

4. After a period in which it appeared that the courts of the United Kingdom, the country of the rule's origin, would disavow it, the House of Lords in Parry v. Cleaver (1969) 2 W.L.R. 821, has recently reaffirmed the rule and applied it to a case of a tort victim who, following the automobile accident in which he was disabled, received a pension. Most other western European nations have repudiated the rule. (See Fleming, the Collateral Source Rule and Loss Allocation in Tort Law, supra, 54 Cal.L.Rev. 1478, 1480–1484, 1516–1523, 1535–1540.)

5. The New York Court of Appeals has, for example, quite reasonably held that an injured physician may not recover from a tortfeasor for the value of medical and nursing care rendered gratuitously as a matter of professional courtesy. (See Coyne v. Campbell (1962) 11 N.Y.2d 372, 230 N.Y.S.2d 1, 183 N.E.2d 891) The doctor owed at least a moral obligation to render gratuitous services in return, if ever required; but he

had neither paid premiums for the services under some form of insurance coverage nor manifested any indication that he would endeavor to repay those who had given him assistance. Thus this situation differs from that in which friends and relatives render assistance to the injured plaintiff with the expectation of repayment out of any tort recovery; in that case, the rule has been applied. On the other hand, New York has joined most states in holding that a tortfeasor may not litigate damages by showing that an injured plaintiff would receive a disability pension. In these cases the plaintiff had actually or constructively paid for the pension by having received lower wages or by having contributed directly to the pension plan.

14. See Thompson v. Mattucci (1963) 223 Cal.App.2d 208, 209–210, 35 Cal.Rptr. 741 (Blue Cross payment for hospital bills does not reduce plaintiff's recovery); Gersick v. Shilling (1950) 97 Cal.App.2d 641, 649–650, 218 P.2d 583 (error to have admitted testimony that plaintiff's medical bills had been paid by Blue Cross or that plaintiff had received United States Employment Service disability payments). In Lewis v. County of Contra Costa (1955) 130 Cal.App.2d 176, 278 P.2d 756, the court held that the collateral source rule prohibited the trial court from admitting evidence that at the time of the accident plaintiff had accumulated sufficient sick leave to cover the period of his disablement. The court reasoned that "In a very real sense of the term it is as if he had drawn upon his savings account in an amount equal to his salary during the period of his disablement." (130 Cal.App.2d at pp. 178–179, 278 P.2d at p. 758. * * *)

of premiums would have earned no benefit. Defendant should not be able to avoid payment of full compensation for the injury inflicted merely because the victim has had the foresight to provide himself with insurance.

Some commentators object that the above approach to the collateral source rule provides plaintiff with a "double recovery," rewards him for the injury, and defeats the principle that damages should compensate the victim but not punish the tortfeasor. We agree with Professor Fleming's observation, however, that "double recovery is justified only in the face of some exceptional, supervening reason, as in the case of accident or life insurance, where it is felt unjust that the tortfeasor should take advantage of the thrift and prescience of the victim in having paid the premiums." (Fleming, Introduction to the Law of Torts (1967) p. 131.) As we point out infra, recovery in a wrongful death action is not defeated by the payment of the benefit on a life insurance policy.

Furthermore, insurance policies increasingly provide for either subrogation or refund of benefits upon a tort recovery, and such refund is indeed called for in the present case. (See Fleming, The Collateral Source Rule and Loss Allocation in Tort Law, supra, 54 Cal.L.Rev. 1478, 1479.) Hence, the plaintiff receives no double recovery; the collateral source rule simply * * * permits a proper transfer of risk from the plaintiff's insurer to the tortfeasor by way of the victim's tort recovery. The double shift from the tortfeasor to the victim and then from the victim to his insurance carrier can normally occur with little cost in that the insurance carrier is often intimately involved in the initial litigation and quite automatically receives its part of the tort settlement or verdict.

Even in cases in which the contract or the law precludes subrogation or refund of benefits[17] or in situations in which the collateral source waives such subrogation or refund, the rule performs entirely necessary functions in the computation of damages. For example, the cost of medical care often provides both attorneys and juries in tort cases with an important measure for assessing the plaintiff's general damages. To permit the defendant to tell the jury that the plaintiff has been recompensed by a collateral source for his medical costs might irretrievably upset the complex, delicate, and somewhat indefinable calculations which result in the normal jury verdict.

We also note that generally the jury is not informed that plaintiff's attorney will receive a large portion of the plaintiff's recovery in contingent

---

17. "Certain insurance benefits are regarded as the proceeds of an investment rather than as an indemnity for damages. Thus it has been held that the proceeds of a life insurance contract made for a fixed sum rather than for the damages caused by the death of the insured are proceeds of an investment and can be received independently of the claim for damages against the person who caused the death of the insured. The same rule has been held applicable to accident insurance contracts. As to both kinds of insurance it has been stated: 'Such a policy is an investment contract giving the owner or beneficiary an absolute right, independent of the right against any third person responsible for the injury covered by the policy.' [Citations omitted.] * * * An insurer who fully compensates the insured, however, is subrogated to the rights of the insured * * * if the insurance was for the protection of the property of the insured, and was therefore an indemnity contract. [Citation omitted.] In such cases subrogation [or refund of benefits] is the means by which double recovery by the owner is prevented and the ultimate burden shifted to the wrongdoer where it belongs. * * *" (Anheuser–Busch, Inc. v. Starley, supra, 28 Cal.2d 347, 355, 170 P.2d 448, 453 (dissenting opn. of Traynor, J.).)

* * *

fees or that personal injury damages are not taxable to the plaintiff and are normally deductible by the defendant. Hence, the plaintiff rarely actually receives full compensation for his injuries as computed by the jury. The collateral source rule partially serves to compensate for the attorney's share and does not actually render "double recovery" for the plaintiff. Indeed, many jurisdictions that have abolished or limited the collateral source rule have also established a means for assessing the plaintiff's costs for counsel directly against the defendant rather than imposing the contingent fee system. In sum, the plaintiff's recovery for his medical expenses from both the tortfeasor and his medical insurance program will not usually give him "double recovery," but partially provides a somewhat closer approximation to full compensation for his injuries.[20]

If we consider the collateral source rule as applied here in the context of the entire American approach to the law of torts and damages, we find that the rule presently performs a number of legitimate and even indispensable functions. Without a thorough revolution in the American approach to torts and the consequent damages, the rule at least with respect to medical insurance benefits has become so integrated within our present system that its precipitous judicial nullification would work hardship. In this case the collateral source rule lies between two systems for the compensation of accident victims: the traditional tort recovery based on fault and the increasingly prevalent coverage based on non-fault insurance. Neither system possesses such universality of coverage or completeness of compensation that we can easily dispense with the collateral source rule's approach to meshing the two systems. The reforms which many academicians propose cannot easily be achieved through piecemeal common law development; the proposed changes, if desirable, would be more effectively accomplished through legislative reform. In any case, we cannot believe that the judicial repeal of the collateral source rule, as applied in the present case, would be the place to begin the needed changes.

* * * We therefore reaffirm our adherence to the collateral source rule in tort cases in which the plaintiff has been compensated by an independent collateral source—such as insurance, pension, continued wages, or disability payments—for which he had actually or constructively paid or in cases in which the collateral source would be recompensed from the tort recovery through subrogation, refund of benefits, or some other arrangement. Hence, we conclude that in a case in which a tort victim has received partial compensation from medical insurance coverage entirely independent of the tortfeasor the trial court properly followed the collateral source rule and foreclosed defendant from mitigating damages by means of the collateral payments.

---

20. Of course, only in cases in which the tort victim has received payments or services from a collateral source will he be able to mitigate attorney's fees by means of the collateral source rule. Thus the rule provides at best only an incomplete and haphazard solution to pro- viding all tort victims with full compensation. Depriving some tort victims of the salutary protections of the collateral source rule will, short of a thorough reform of our tort system, only decrease the available compensation for injuries.

3. The Collateral Source Rule, Public Entities, and Public Employees

Having concluded that the collateral source rule is not simply punitive in nature, we hold, for the reasons set out infra, that the rule as delineated here applies to governmental entities as well as to all other tortfeasors. * * *

Defendants would have this court create a special form of sovereign immunity as a novel exception to the collateral source rule for tortfeasors who are public entities or public employees. We see no justification for such special treatment. In the present case the nullification of the collateral source rule would simply frustrate the transfer of the medical costs from the medical insurance carrier, Blue Cross, to the public entity. The public entity or its insurance carrier is in at least as advantageous a position to spread the risk of loss as is the plaintiff's medical insurance carrier. To deprive Blue Cross of repayment for its expenditures on plaintiff's behalf merely because he was injured by a public entity rather than a private individual would constitute an unwarranted and arbitrary discrimination.

* * *

The judgment is affirmed.

REID v. DISTRICT OF COLUMBIA, 391 A.2d 776 (D.C.App.1978). In a suit by a mother to recover for injuries to a student allegedly caused by defendant's negligence, the jury found for defendant. Testimony was admitted that the student's mother was eligible for Medicaid but had failed to submit the bills to it for payment. *Held*, admission of the evidence was reversible error. The court said:

"To decide whether evidence of eligibility for Medicaid is admissible to mitigate damages, we must first ask the question: is Medicaid a collateral source? * * *

"When the compensation comes from someone other than the defendant, the situation is clear and courts generally deem such compensation to be collateral. The fact that it comes in part from the defendant tortfeasor does not itself preclude the possibility that it is from a collateral source. Because of the nature of the source, the defendant may not be paying twice for the same injury. * * *

* * *

"In the instant case, Medicaid is funded in very small part by the class of eligible people. * * * [T]he benefits from Medicaid are not paid in anticipation of tort liability but only on account of medical injuries and financial need. Also, Medicaid does not come from the general revenues of the District of Columbia but from a special fund created for the recipient class of Medicaid eligible people. (See, e.g., Pub.L.No. 94–333, 90 Stat. 785.)

* * *

"Medicaid is not a type of compensation for services rendered, although it may be viewed as a fringe benefit of citizenship, and it may be claimed as a matter of right without regard to liability on the part of the District of Columbia.

* * *

"Medicaid is paid for mostly by the federal government; the defendant District of Columbia pays between seventeen and fifty percent of the cost of Medicaid, depending on the per capita income of the District relative to the nation as a whole. However, as noted above, the contributions of the recipient class are very small.

"Because Medicaid was established to provide health services for the indigent and not to compensate for tort liability, because Medicaid payments may be claimed by plaintiff as a matter of right and independent of any liability on the part of the defendant, and because most of the funding for Medicaid comes from a third party, we hold that Medicaid payments come from a collateral source and are not admissible to mitigate damages."

SMITH v. UNITED STATES, 587 F.2d 1013 (3d Cir.1978). The wife and children of the decedent sued under the Federal Tort Claims Act for alleged negligence. The district court entered judgment for plaintiffs but reduced the wife's damage by social security benefits to which she was entitled as decedent's survivor. *Held,* reversed on ground that such benefits could not be deducted under the FTCA where Pennsylvania law (the applicable state law) recognized the collateral source rule. "FTCA recoveries come out of general revenues; Social Security benefits are funded almost entirely from employee and employer contributions. * * * The government here did not argue that a FTCA recovery must be reduced by that portion of Social Security benefits attributable to the government's contribution out of general revenues. * * * We believe that the government's payments are so minimal and so difficult to trace that such an approach would be impracticable."

KURTA v. PROBELSKE, 324 Mich. 179, 36 N.W.2d 889 (1949). Action for negligence, in which the damages included an amount for loss of wages. *Held,* in affirming the verdict, that it was correct not to deduct the amount received from the state for unemployment compensation.

FEIN v. PERMANENTE MEDICAL GROUP, 38 Cal.3d 137, 211 Cal.Rptr. 368, 695 P.2d 665 (1985). The judgment in a medical malpractice action awarded plaintiff substantial damages. The trial court applied provisions of the state Medical Injury Compensation Reform Act of 1975 (MICRA), including Civil Code section 3333.1 which modified the traditional collateral source rule in malpractice litigation. One of plaintiff's claims in this appeal was that section 3333.1, which allegedly lowered his damages, was unconstitutional. The California Supreme Court here concluded that the challenged provisions were constitutional, and that the judgment below should be affirmed. In his opinion for the court, Justice Kaus discussed the collateral source rule:

" * * * Section 3333.1 alters this rule in medical malpractice cases. Under section 3333.1, subdivision (a), a medical malpractice defendant is permitted to introduce evidence of such collateral source benefits received by or payable to the plaintiff; when a defendant chooses to introduce such evidence, the plaintiff may introduce evidence of the amounts he has paid— in insurance premiums, for example—to secure the benefits. Although section 333.1, subdivision (a)—as ultimately adopted—does not specify how the jury should use such evidence, the Legislature apparently assumed that in most cases the jury would set plaintiff's damages at a lower level because of its awareness of plaintiff's 'net' collateral source benefits.

"In addition, section 3333.1, subdivision (b) provides that whenever such collateral source evidence is introduced, the source of those benefits is precluded from obtaining subrogation either from the plaintiff or from the medical malpractice defendant. As far as the malpractice plaintiff is concerned, subdivision (b) assures that he will suffer no 'double deduction' from his tort recovery as a result of his receipt of collateral source benefits; because the jury that has learned of his benefits may reduce his tort award by virtue of such benefits, the Legislature eliminated any right the collateral source may have had to obtain repayment of those benefits from the plaintiff. As for the malpractice defendant, subdivision (b) assures that any reduction in malpractice awards that may result from the jury's consideration of the plaintiff's collateral source benefits will inure to its benefit rather than to the benefit of the collateral source.

* * *

"Because section 3333.1, subdivision (a) is likely to lead to lower malpractice awards, there can be no question but that [it] directly relates to MICRA's objective of reducing the costs incurred by malpractice defendants and their insurers. * * *

"Moreover, the Legislature clearly did not act irrationally in choosing to modify the collateral source rule as one means of lowering the costs of malpractice litigation. In analyzing the collateral source rule more than a decade ago in *Helfend v. Southern Cal. Rapid Transit District, supra,* 2 Cal.3d 1, 84 Cal.Rptr. 173, 465 P.2d 61, we acknowledged that most legal commentators had severely criticized the rule for affording a plaintiff a 'double recovery' for 'losses' he had not in reality sustained, and we noted that many jurisdictions had either restricted or repealed it. Although we concluded in *Helfend* that a number of policy considerations counseled against judicial abolition of the rule, we in no way suggested that it was immune from legislative revision, but, on the contrary, stated that the charges proposed by legal commentators 'if desirable, would be more effectively accomplished through legislative reform.' (*Id.* at p. 13, 84 Cal. Rptr. 173, 465 P.2d 61.) In the mid–1970's, California was only one of many states to include a modification of the collateral source rule as a part of its medical malpractice reform legislation * * * Under the circumstances, we think it is clear that the provision is rationally related to a legitimate state interest and does not violate due process."

STATUTORY DEVELOPMENTS AND THE "COLLATERAL SOURCE" RULE

The "collateral source" rule has been subject to substantial legislative modification and abolition over the past twenty-five years. Legislative action has occurred in two waves. The first wave crested in the mid–1970's. The statutes passed in this wave addressed medical malpractice claims in particular. According to a 1986 report by the United States General Accounting Office, by July of 1985, 17 states had passed legislation modifying the collateral source rule in the medical malpractice area. Some of these statutes were permissive. They *allowed* defendants to introduce evidence of collateral payments received by or payable to the plaintiff, but did not require a corresponding reduction in damages. Other states adopted mandatory offset provisions. Mandatory statutes *require* either the judge or the jury to reduce plaintiffs' damage awards upon proof of collateral payments by the amount of those payments. Statutes of either type may provide that collateral payments from certain sources (e.g., from life insurance policies) should not be used to offset damage awards. The California statute upheld in Fein v. Permanente Medical Group was permissive.

The second wave crested in the mid-to late–1980's, and continued into the 1990's. The statutes passed in this wave either abolished or modified the collateral source rule in general, not just in one particular area like medical malpractice. By 1995 more than a third, but less than half, of the fifty states had passed statutes either abolishing or modifying the "collateral source" rule generally. These modifications have taken a number of different forms. First, following the pattern of the first wave, some have been permissive, whereas others have been mandatory. The permissive statutes allow either the judge or the jury—but not both—to take collateral payments into account in calculating an appropriate damage award. Second, both kinds of statutes usually include various exclusions or qualifications. These exclusions may be broad (life insurance and other death benefits; benefits for which plaintiff has paid premiums; retirement, disability, and pension plan benefits; and federal social security benefits; may all be excluded) or narrow (only life insurance or insurance purchased by the recovering party may be excluded). Finally, just as the medical malpractice statute in *Fein* was subject to constitutional challenge, these statutes, too, have been challenged, with varying results. The materials following this note illustrate some of the characteristics of this second wave of statutory reform.

The common law "collateral source" rule was grounded upon the conviction that it would be wrong for a tortfeasor to reduce his financial responsibility for the harm he had inflicted on the plaintiff by drawing upon resources that the plaintiff had set aside to guard against such harm. To do so, would be to add a second injury (the wrongful taking of the plaintiff's financial resources) to the first (the wrongful harming of the person or property of the plaintiff). If the statutory reforms of the past twenty years can be said to express a similarly moral conviction, the conviction that they appear to express is that plaintiffs should not receive more than full compensation for their injuries.

Following are two illustrative provisions which change the common-law rule.

_____

Oregon ST § 18.580. Effect of collateral benefits.

(1) In a civil action, when a party is awarded damages for bodily injury or death of a person which are to be paid by another party to the action, and the party awarded damages or person injured or deceased received benefits for the injury or death other than from the party who is to pay the damages, the court may deduct from the amount of damages awarded, before the entry of final judgment, the total amount of those collateral benefits other than:

(a) Benefits which the party awarded damages, the person injured or that person's estate is obligated to repay;

(b) Life insurance or other death benefits;

(c) Insurance benefits for which the person injured or deceased or members of that person's family paid premiums; and

(d) Retirement, disability and pension plan benefits, and federal social security benefits.

(2) Evidence of the benefit described in subsection (1) of this section and the cost of obtaining it is not admissible at trial, but shall be received by the court by affidavit submitted after the verdict by any party to the action.

Colorado ST § 13–21–111.6. Civil actions—reduction of damages for payment from collateral source

In any action by any person or his legal representative to recover damages for a tort resulting in death or injury to person or property, the court, after the finder of fact has returned its verdict stating the amount of damages to be awarded, shall reduce the amount, of the verdict by the amount by which such person, his estate, or his personal representative has been or will be wholly or partially indemnified or compensated for his loss by any other person, corporation, insurance company, or fund in relation to the injury, damage, or death sustained; except that the verdict shall not be reduced by the amount by which such person, his estate, or his personal representative has been or will be wholly or partially indemnified or compensated by a benefit paid as a result of a contract entered into and paid for by or on behalf of such person. The court shall enter judgment on such reduced amount.

_____

THOMPSON v. KFB INSURANCE COMPANY, 252 Kan. 1010, 850 P.2d 773 (1993). "Ivan Thompson, Jr., brought this action against his automobile insurance carrier, KFB Insurance Company (KFB), claiming underinsured motorist benefits. Thompson sought to recover for personal injuries and damages suffered as a result of an automobile accident. Before trial began, the district court ruled that K.S.A.1992 Supp. 60–3801 et seq., the current Collateral Source Benefits Act, is unconstitutional. Evidence of collateral source benefits was not admitted at trial. The jury awarded $377,000 to Thompson. The district court made several reductions in the award and entered judgment for him in the amount of $226,150. KFB appeals from the jury verdict and rulings of the district court. * * *

"K.S.A.1992 Supp. 60–3802 through 60–3805 are the operative sections and provide: 'In any action for personal injury or death, in which the claimant demands judgment for damages in excess of $150,000, evidence of collateral source benefits received or evidence of collateral source benefits which are reasonably expected to be received in the future shall be admissible.' K.S.A.1992 Supp. 60–3802. 'When evidence of collateral source benefits is admitted into evidence pursuant to K.S.A.1992 Supp. 60–3802, evidence of the cost of the collateral source benefit shall be admissible.' K.S.A.1992 Supp. 60–3803. 'In determining damages in an action for personal injury or death, the trier of fact shall determine the net collateral source benefits received and the net collateral source benefits reasonably expected to be received in the future.' * * * '(a) The amount of the judgment shall be reduced by the court by the amount of net collateral source benefits received, or reasonably expected to be received in the future * * *'

"Three times in recent memory the Kansas Legislature has enacted statutes which were intended to override or limit the common-law rule. [We found the first two statutes unconstitutional. The statute now before us is the third.]

"The rational basis test is the appropriate measure of equal protection in the present case. We have consistently recognized that the equal protection clause of the Fourteenth Amendment does not preclude the legislature from treating different claims of parties in different ways. A legislative classification will be upheld if the classification itself is rationally related to a legitimate legislative purpose. The classification, however, 'must be reasonable, not arbitrary, and must rest upon some ground of difference having a fair and substantial relation to the object of the legislation, so that all persons similarly circumstanced shall be treated alike.' Royster Guano Co. v. Virginia, 253 U.S. 412, 415, 64 L.Ed. 989, 40 S.Ct. 560, 561–62 (1920).

"In the present case, * * * [o]ur first task * * * is to determine whether the classification of plaintiffs by the size of their demands is relevant to a legitimate State objective.

"The legislative purpose, as stated by KFB, is * * * 'to address concerns relating to the sky-rocketing cost and availability of insurance, and the tort system in general, by compensating all tort victims fully for their injuries while reducing or eliminating recoveries by personal injury plaintiffs in excess of total damages they have suffered.'

" * * * The question is whether discriminatory aspects of the legislation bear a rational relationship to the legislature's objective. * * *.

"Thompson contends that the classification is based on the severity of injuries suffered and that this basis is arbitrary, unreasonable, and discriminatory. He cites Roe v. Diefendorf, 236 Kan. 218, 689 P.2d 855 (1984), where a statute of limitations using the term 'substantial injury' was at issue. The court stated: 'An unsubstantial injury as contrasted to a substantial injury is only a difference in degree, i.e., the amount of damages. That is not a legal distinction. Both are injuries from which the victim is entitled to recover damages if the injury is the fault of another. A separate classification for the two, for purposes of limiting actions thereon, is in violation of the Equal Protection Clause * * * because such classification has no legitimate legislative purpose.' 236 Kan. at 222–23

"[Supporters of the statute] contend that plaintiffs seeking $150,000 or less are not similarly situated to those seeking more with respect to the legislative objective of reducing insurance costs. * * * The proponents' contention is that the line is drawn at an approximation of the dollar amount at which the potential duplicative recovery and the potential costs of discovery of collateral source converge. * * * Plaintiffs making claims below the line do not further the objective of cutting costs of insurance due to the disproportionate costs of discovery. Plaintiffs making claims above the line do further this goal. [The defendants have not supported this contention with any facts or data.]

" * * * Even assuming the objective of cutting insurance costs is a legitimate legislative goal, we do not find the classification in the present case will reasonably further that purpose. Under the rational basis test, great deference is given to the legislature in establishing classifications. However, where * * * the statutory classification is * * * without a rational basis and is arbitrary [it will not be upheld]. Here, the challenged classification unreasonably discriminates in favor of claimants demanding $150,000 or less and unduly burdens those seeking judgments in excess of $150,000. We hold that [this] provision * * * violates the equal protection clause of the Fourteenth Amendment to the United States Constitution and § 1 of the Bill of Rights of the Kansas Constitution."*

---

* Section 1 of the Kansas Bill of Rights provides: "All men are possessed of equal and inalienable natural rights, among which are life, liberty and the pursuit of happiness."—Eds.

Chapter 16

VICARIOUS LIABILITY

Tort liability for accidental injury is divided between two competing principles of responsibility—negligence, which we have been studying throughout the past eight chapters, and strict liability, which we have not engaged explicitly since Chapter Seven. With vicarious liability, we renew our study of strict forms of liability.

Vicarious liability is liability for *someone else's* tortious conduct. In its two most common incarnations, the law of vicarious liability imputes—or declines to impute—financial responsibility to a "master" for the tort of a "servant" or "independent contractor," or to a partnership for the tort of a partner. The structure of vicarious liability cases is therefore more complex than that of most of the cases that we have studied so far. Vicarious liability cases contain both "underlying torts" and the law of vicarious liability itself—the body of rules, concepts and principles that governs the attribution of these torts to the enterprises that occasion them. The law of vicarious liability presupposes underlying tortious conduct, but does not fix the basis of the underlying liability. Some other body of tort law fixes the ground of the underlying tort liability; that liability may be strict as vicarious liability is, but it may also be intentional or negligent. Vicarious liability is thus a hybrid doctrine. Its strictness lies in the criteria that it deploys for determining whether or not to charge an underlying tort to some larger enterprise which might be said to have precipitated it.

Vicarious liability comes in two forms: "vertical" and "horizontal." Vertical vicarious liability governs the attribution of torts committed by subordinates acting on behalf of their superiors; horizontal vicarious liability governs the attribution of torts among agents who are equal participants in a common venture. The vicarious liability of employers for the torts of their employees is vertical; the vicarious liability of partners for the torts of other partners is horizontal.

Vertical vicarious liability is itself split into two branches. One branch of the doctrine governs the attribution of torts committed by "servants" while laboring on behalf of their "masters." Liability under this branch of the doctrine is strict. The imputation of responsibility to the master turns not on whether the master exercised due care in controlling the servant, but on whether the servant was acting within the "scope of employment." The other branch of "vertical" vicarious liability doctrine governs the attribution of torts committed by "independent contractors" acting on behalf of their masters. The general rule here is that the acts of independent contractors are not imputed to their employers. This rule is subject to a remarkable number of exceptions, but here, too, neither the general rule, nor the exceptions to it, place primary weight on the care exercised by the master.

We start with one of the principal questions of vertical vicarious liability doctrine. When should the tort of a servant be imputed to a master under the scope of employment doctrine? The terms "master," "servant" and "scope of employment," along with the term "independent contractor," are the conceptual cornerstones of vicarious liability law.

SECTION A.   SERVANTS AND SCOPE OF EMPLOYMENT

RESTATEMENT (SECOND), AGENCY

[Sections 2, 219 and 220 are set forth at pp. 15–16, supra.]

[Sections 229 and 235 are set forth at pp. 18–19, supra.]

KOHLMAN v. HYLAND

[The opinion is set forth at p. 16, supra.]

KONRADI v. UNITED STATES

United States Court of Appeals, Seventh Circuit, 1990.
919 F.2d 1207.

POSNER, Circuit Judge: While driving to work early one morning Robert Farringer, a rural mailman, struck a car driven by the plaintiff's decedent, Glenn Konradi, killing him. * * * The district judge dismissed the suit on the government's motion for summary judgment. He ruled that the accident had not occurred within the scope of Farringer's employment by the Postal Service, which let off the Service; he then relinquished jurisdiction over the pendent party claim.

The parties agree that the question whether the accident occurred within the scope of Farringer's employment is governed by Indiana law, that under Indiana law it is a question of fact, and therefore that the judge was right to dismiss the case on summary judgment only if no reasonable jury, presented with the evidence that was before the judge when he ruled, could have answered the question in the plaintiff's favor. * * *

* * *

* * * The general rule is that an employee is not within the scope of his employment when commuting to or from his job. As the Supreme Court of Indiana put it the last time it addressed the issue, more than three decades ago, "an employee on his way to work is normally not in the employment of the corporation." Biel, Inc. v. Kirsch, 240 Ind. 69, 73, 161 N.E.2d 617, 618 (1959) (per curiam). The rub is "normally," and though omitted in the statement of the rule in Pursley v. Ford Motor Co., 462 N.E.2d 247, 249 (Ind.App.1984), this weasel word is definitely required for

the sake of accuracy. In State v. Gibbs, 166 Ind.App. 387, 336 N.E.2d 703 (1975), the employer furnished the employee with a car for use on the job but also allowed him to take it home at night. The accident occurred while he was driving home, and the employer was held liable. * * *

It is impossible to find the pattern in this carpet without a conception of what the law is trying to accomplish by making an employer liable for the torts of his employees committed within the scope of their employment and by excluding commuting from that scope—"normally." * * *

Often an employer can reduce the number of accidents caused by his employees not by being more careful—he may already be using as much care in hiring, supervising, monitoring, etc. his employees as can reasonably be demanded—but by altering the nature or extent of his operations: in a word by altering not his care but his activity. This possibility is a consideration in deciding whether to impose strict liability generally. * * * Shavell, Strict Liability versus Negligence, 9 J. Legal Stud. 1 (1980). The liability of an employer for torts committed by its employees—without any fault on his part—when they are acting within the scope of their employment, the liability that the law calls "respondeat superior," is a form of strict liability. It neither requires the plaintiff to prove fault on the part of the employer nor allows the employer to exonerate himself by proving his freedom from fault. The focus shifts from changes in care to changes in activity. For example, instead of dispatching its salesmen in cars from a central location, causing them to drive a lot and thus increasing the number of traffic accidents, a firm could open branch offices closer to its customers and have the salesmen work out of those offices. The amount of driving would be less (an activity change) and with it the number of accidents. Firms will consider these tradeoffs if they are liable for the torts of their employees committed within the scope of their employment, even if the employer was not negligent in hiring or training or monitoring or supervising or deciding not to fire the employee who committed the tort. This liability also discourages employers from hiring judgment-proof employees, which they might otherwise have an incentive to do because a judgment-proof employee, by definition, does not have to be compensated (in the form of a higher wage) for running the risk of being sued for a tort that he commits on his employer's behalf. He runs no such risk; he is not worth suing.

If it is true that one objective of the doctrine of respondeat superior is to give employers an incentive to consider changes in the nature or level of their activities, then "scope of employment" can be functionally defined by reference to the likelihood that liability would induce beneficial changes in activity. It becomes apparent for example that the employer should not be made liable for a tort committed by the employee in the employee's home, for there is no plausible alteration in the activity of the employer that would substantially reduce the likelihood of such a tort. This overstates the case a bit; one can imagine a plaintiff's arguing that if the employer had not made the employee work so hard the employee would have been more alert and therefore more careful and the accident would not have occurred. But the law has to draw some lines for ease of administration, and a rough-and-ready one is between accidents on the job and accidents off the job—

including accidents while commuting—* * *. Indiana recognizes, however, that the line is indeed a rough one, and it allows juries to cross it when particular circumstances make the line inapt to the purpose that it seeks to implement. * * *

The Postal Service, Farringer's employer, requires its rural postal carriers to furnish their own vehicle (Farringer's was a pick-up truck) in making their rounds. * * * The Postal Service's rule pretty much guarantees that its mailmen will drive to and from work, and by doing this it increases the amount of driving compared to a system in which, since the mailman does not need to have his own car at work, he can take a train or bus or join a car pool. One cost of more driving is more accidents, and this cost can be made a cost to the Postal Service, and thus influence its choice between furnishing its mailmen with vehicles and requiring them to furnish their own, if the scope of employment is defined for purposes of tort law as including commuting in all cases in which the employee is required to furnish a vehicle for use at work. * * *

All this is highly speculative. The Postal Service's rule is limited to rural deliverymen, and neither public transportation nor car pooling is common in rural America. * * * But additional evidence in this case points to employer liability. According to testimony that for purposes of this appeal (only) we must take to be true, Farringer's postmaster required the postal carriers to take the most direct route in driving to and from work, and hence not to divagate for personal business. Nor was the carrier to stop for such business, or give anyone a ride. * * *

* * *

The rules of commuting that the postmaster has imposed upon his carriers may * * * reflect a belief that the work of a rural deliveryman begins when he gets into his car in the morning and ends when he gets out of it in the evening. For during all that time he has control over an essential instrumentality of postal service—the delivery van—albeit supplied by the deliverer. * * *

* * *

[Furthermore,] the imposition of liability on the Postal Service * * * is consistent with all three of the formulas that courts in Indiana and elsewhere intone when they are trying to generalize about scope of employment. By driving to and from work Farringer conferred a benefit on his employer because he was bringing an essential instrumentality of the employer's business. (True, the employer would not have cared if Farringer had left his truck in the post office parking lot and thumbed a ride to work, but few employees would thus forgo all personal use of their vehicle.) The employer exerted substantial control over the employee's commuting, as shown by the regulations discussed earlier. And finally the employee while commuting was in the service of the employer because he was keeping and maintaining the instrumentality.

These "tests" should not be thought conclusive. Tests divorced from purposes tend not to be useful, let alone conclusive, and the linkage between the tests and what the discussion in this opinion conjectures is the underlying purpose of the scope of employment concept is obscure. The law has drawn a line between at work and at home but treats commuting as an intermediate zone that can be placed within or outside the scope of employment depending on circumstances, though the presumption is in favor of outside. The purpose of a doctrine determines what circumstances are relevant. The purpose of this doctrine may be to induce the employer to consider activity changes that might reduce the number of accidents. * * *

* * *

* * * [T]he dismissal of the United States is reversed and the case remanded for further proceedings consistent with this opinion. * * *

———

WOOD v. CENTRAL ARKANSAS MILK PRODUCERS ASSOCIATION, 233 Ark. 958, 349 S.W.2d 811 (1961). Defendant, a service station operator, allowed his employees to drive passenger cars but instructed them not to attempt to drive plaintiff's trucks. An employee damaged one of the trucks while driving it to the service station for repairs. *Held,* judgment for plaintiff affirmed. "When an employee is acting in furtherance of his employer's business the latter is liable for the employee's negligence although the particular act is unauthorized or even contrary to express instructions."

KANSALLIS FINANCE LTD. v. FERN & OTHERS, 421 Mass. 659, 659 N.E.2d 731 (1996) (Fried, J.). "* * * [A]s between two innocent parties it is not unfair that the one whom the wrongful act may have and was meant to benefit must bear the burden of the harm."

CONCEPTIONS OF STRICT LIABILITY

Judge Posner's *Konradi* opinion acknowledges that the liability of masters for the torts of their servants, committed within the scope of their employment, is strict in nature. Yet Posner goes on to present strict doctrine as the servant of negligence policy. The end of negligence liability, as Judge Posner conceives it, is to reduce the number of accidents to its appropriate level. The strictness of the scope of employment test is justified because it advances this end. Negligence induces actors to conduct their activities with appropriate care; strict liability induces actors to conduct their activities with appropriate intensity. Both care and activity levels influence the incidence of accidents. Other things equal, careful drivers precipitate fewer accidents than careless ones, and those who drive less precipitate fewer accidents than those who drive more. When accidents can only be reduced to the correct level by inducing injurers to conduct their activities with appropriate intensity, as well as with appropriate caution, the imposition of strict liability realizes the fundamental aim of negligence doctrine more faithfully than negligence liability itself does.

This conception of strict liability as the handmaiden of negligence is one among several competing conceptions. In Chapter Five, we saw examples of an older conception of strict liability, one which flowered under the various common law forms of action for trespass. *The Case of the Thorns* (1466) and *Weaver v. Ward* (1616) capture the core of this conception. Strict liability for trespass applied when an actor, by his agency, directly harmed someone else; its underlying idea was that people who act and cause harm should pay for the harm they cause. People, in short, "act at their peril." In the wake of the abandonment of the forms of action in the middle of the nineteenth century, several of the opinions in *Rylands v. Fletcher* recast strict liability for trespass as a general principle of liability. Blackburn's opinion in the Exchequer Chamber draws on strict liability cases concerning animals, straying cattle and vicious beasts, and also on cases imposing strict liability for trespass and nuisance, seepage of filth from a privy, and emission of chlorine fumes from an alkali works, to fashion a general norm of strict liability. Lord Cranworth's opinion in the House of Lords makes explicit the connection between the general doctrine of *Rylands* and the "act at your peril" conception that preceded it:

> In considering whether a defendant is liable to a plaintiff for damage which the plaintiff may have sustained, the question in general is not whether the defendant has acted with due care and caution, but whether his acts have occasioned the damage. This is all well explained in the old case of Lambert v. Bessey, reported by Sir Thomas Raymond (Sir T. Raym. 421). [Lambert v. Bessey contains, verbatim, the report of The Case of the Thorns.] And the doctrine is founded on good sense. For when one person, in managing his own affairs, causes, however innocently, damage to another, it is obviously only just that he should be the party to suffer. [supra, p. 300]

Exner v. Sherman Power Construction Co., (supra, p. 20), an American case from the early part of the twentieth century, takes the generalization of strict liability a step further. *Exner* uses the rule of *Rylands v. Fletcher*, and the ancient cases that support it, both to justify the imposition of strict liability on the "perilous activity" of blasting, and to criticize the "logical basis" for making the imposition of strict liability turn on the distinction between direct and indirect injuries, as it did under older conceptions of trespass. Strict liability in *Exner* is bottomed on a principle of responsibility as general, and as intuitively plausible, as the fault principle. Actors who, in pursuit of their own ends, deliberately impose risks on others, should not be allowed to foist the costs of their choices off on innocent victims. "[T]he owner of [a] business, rather than a third person who has no relation to [the business], other than that of injury, should bear the loss."

The principle of *Rylands* and *Exner* anticipates a third, and distinctively modern, conception of strict liability—"enterprise liability." Two prescriptive theses lie at the heart of enterprise liability. First, the costs of those accidents that are characteristic of an enterprise should be absorbed by the enterprise as an operating expense, not left on those whose bad luck it is to get in the enterprise's way. Second, the costs of such accidents should not be concentrated either on the victim who originally suffered the injury, or on the particular agent who inflicted the injury. Those costs should be distributed among those who benefit from the imposition of the enterprise's risks—among customers, employees, suppliers and shareholders, for example.

These two theses—that characteristic accident costs should be internalized and that they should be spread across the beneficiaries of the enterprise—are linked by a factual assumption. Enterprise liability assumes that, when an enterprise is made liable for its characteristic toll in life, limb and property damage, it will usually insure against that liability and will factor the cost of such insurance into the cost of its products, the prices that it pays to its suppliers, the wages of its employees, and so on. The theory of enterprise liability also assumes, as strict liability generally does, that the activity it addresses is worthwhile and ought to continue, provided it pays its way. The characteristic risks that it subjects to liability are assumed to be reasonable, not unreasonable; the burden of avoiding these risks presumably exceeds the benefits of doing so. Enterprise liability supposes, in a nutshell, that it is reasonable to impose the risks that it regulates, but unreasonable not to pay for the harms that issue from those risks.

Enterprise liability is in part a flowering of ideas internal to the law of torts and in part the expression of ideas imported into the law of torts from legislative sources of law. On the one hand, enterprise liability is the fullest flowering of common law ideas of strict liability, ideas which reach back as far as the *Case of the Thorns*. Late nineteenth and early twentieth century cases like *Rylands* and *Exner* give ever more general expression to these common law conceptions, working strict liability pure as they free it from the fetters of the old forms of action. On the other hand, enterprise liability emerges full-grown in the Workmen's Compensation Acts enacted early in the twentieth century. While these Acts are part of accident law as a whole, they displace tort law from the domain of workplace accidents, and replace it with an administrative scheme. In part, the history of enterprise liability is the history of a statutory conception reshaping the common law.

Several of the cases that follow this note—*Ira S. Bushey & Sons, Inc. v. United States*, *Fruit v. Schreiner*, and *Taber v. Maine*—evidence the influence of workers' compensation. They invoke the scope of the employer's liability under worker's compensation law as a guide to the interpretation of the scope of employment test in vicarious liability law, thereby signaling their adherence to an enterprise conception of vicarious liability. *Bushey* applies the enterprise liability idea of "characteristic risk" to a rare circumstance where the accident prevention, loss-spreading and fairness justifications for enterprise liability diverge.

IRA S. BUSHEY & SONS, INC. v. UNITED STATES
United States Court of Appeals, Second Circuit, 1968.
398 F.2d 167.

FRIENDLY, Circuit Judge: While the United States Coast Guard vessel Tamaroa was being overhauled in a floating drydock located in Brooklyn's Gowanus Canal, a seaman returning from shore leave late at night, in the condition for which seamen are famed, turned some wheels on the drydock wall. He thus opened valves that controlled the flooding of the tanks on one side of the drydock. Soon the ship listed, slid off the blocks and fell against the wall. Parts of the drydock sank, and the ship partially did—fortunately without loss of life or personal injury. The drydock owner sought and was granted compensation by the District Court for the Eastern District of New York in an amount to be determined, 276 F.Supp. 518; the United States appeals.

* * *

* * * The Tamaroa had gone into drydock on February 28, 1963; her keel rested on blocks permitting her drive shaft to be removed and repairs to be made to her hull. The contract between the Government and Bushey provided in part:

> (o) The work shall, whenever practical, be performed in such manner as not to interfere with the berthing and messing of personnel attached to the vessel undergoing repair, and provision shall be made so that personnel assigned shall have access to the vessel at all times, it being understood that such personnel will not interfere with the work or the contractor's workmen.

Access from shore to ship was provided by a route past the security guard at the gate, through the yard, up a ladder to the top of one drydock wall and along the wall to a gangway leading to the fantail deck, where men returning from leave reported at a quartermaster's shack.

Seaman Lane, whose prior record was unblemished, returned from shore leave a little after midnight on March 14. He had been drinking heavily; the quartermaster made mental note that he was "loose." For reasons not apparent to us or very likely to Lane, he took it into his head, while progressing along the gangway wall, to turn each of three large wheels some twenty times; unhappily as previously stated, these wheels controlled the water intake valves. * * *

The Government attacks imposition of liability on the ground that Lane's acts were not within the scope of his employment. It relies heavily on § 228(1) of the Restatement of Agency 2d which says that "conduct of a servant is within the scope of employment if, but only if: * * * (c) it is actuated, at least in part by a purpose to serve the master." * * * It would be going too far to find such a purpose here; while Lane's return to the Tamaroa was to serve his employer, no one has suggested how he could have thought turning the wheels to be, even if—which is by no means clear—he was unaware of the consequences.

In light of the highly artificial way in which the motive test has been applied, the district judge believed himself obliged to test the doctrine's continuing vitality by referring to the larger purposes *respondeat superior* is supposed to serve. He concluded that the old formulation failed this test. We do not find his analysis so compelling, however, as to constitute a sufficient basis in itself for discarding the old doctrine. It is not at all clear, as the court below suggested, that expansion of liability in the manner here suggested will lead to a more efficient allocation of resources. As the most astute exponent of this theory has emphasized, a more efficient allocation can only be expected if there is some reason to believe that imposing a particular cost on the enterprise will lead it to consider whether steps should be taken to prevent a recurrence of the accident. Calabresi, The Decision for Accidents: An Approach to Non-fault Allocation of Costs, 78 Harv. L. Rev. 713, 725–34 (1965). And the suggestion that imposition of liability here will lead to more intensive screening of employees rests on highly questionable premises. The unsatisfactory quality of the allocation of resource rationale is especially striking on the facts of this case. It could well be that application of the traditional rule might induce drydock owners, prodded by their insurance companies, to install locks on their valves to avoid similar incidents in the future,[6] while placing the burden on shipowners is much less likely to lead to accident prevention.[7] It is true, of course, that in many cases the plaintiff will not be in a position to insure and so expansion of liability will, at the very least, serve *respondeat superior's* loss spreading function. But the fact that the defendant is better able to afford damages is not alone sufficient to justify legal responsibility, and this overarching principle must be taken into account in deciding whether to expand the reach of *respondeat superior*.

A policy analysis thus is not sufficient to justify this proposed expansion of vicarious liability. This is not surprising since *respondeat superior*, even within its traditional limits, rests not so much on policy grounds consistent with the governing principles of tort law as in a deeply rooted sentiment that a business enterprise cannot justly disclaim responsibility for accidents which may fairly be said to be characteristic of its activities. It is in this light that the inadequacy of the motive test becomes apparent. * * * We concur in the statement of Mr. Justice Rutledge in a case involving violence injuring a fellow-worker, in this instance in the context of workmen's compensation:

> Men do not discard their personal qualities when they go to work. Into the job they carry their intelligence, skill, habits of care and rectitude. Just as inevitably they take along also their tendencies to carelessness and camaraderie, as well as emotional make-up. In bringing men together, work brings these qualities together, causes frictions between them, creates occasions for lapses into carelessness, and for fun-making and emotional flare-up. * * * These expressions of human nature are incidents inseparable from working together. They involve risks of injury and these risks are inherent in the working environment.

Hartford Accident & Indemnity Co. v. Cardillo, 72 App.D.C. 52, 112 F.2d 11, 15, * * *

Put another way, Lane's conduct was not so "unforeseeable" as to make it unfair to charge the Government with responsibility. We agree with a leading treatise that "what is reasonably foreseeable in this context [of

---

6. The record reveals that most modern drydocks have automatic locks to guard against unauthorized use of valves.

7. Although it is theoretically possible that shipowners would demand that drydock owners take appropriate action, see Coase, The Problem of Social Cost, 3 J.L. & Economics 1 (1960), this would seem unlikely to occur in real life.

respondeat superior] * * * is quite a different thing from the foreseeably unreasonable risk of harm that spells negligence * * *. The foresight that should impel the prudent man to take precautions is not the same measure as that by which he should perceive the harm likely to flow from his long-run activity in spite of all reasonable precautions on his own part. The proper test here bears far more resemblance to that which limits liability for workmen's compensation than to the test for negligence. The employer should be held to expect risks, to the public also, which arise 'out of and in the course of' his employment of labor." 2 Harper & James, The Law of Torts 1377–78 (1956). Here it was foreseeable that crew members crossing the drydock might do damage, negligently or even intentionally, such as pushing a Bushey employee or kicking property into the water. Moreover, the proclivity of seamen to find solace for solitude by copious resort to the bottle while ashore has been noted in opinions too numerous to warrant citation. Once all this is granted, it is immaterial that Lane's precise action was not to be foreseen. * * * Consequently, we can no longer accept our past decisions * * * since they do not accord with modern understanding as to when it is fair for an enterprise to disclaim the actions of its employees.

One can readily think of cases that fall on the other side of the line. If Lane had set fire to the bar where he had been imbibing or had caused an accident on the street while returning to the drydock, the Government would not be liable; the activities of the "enterprise" do not reach into areas where the servant does not create risks different from those attendant on the activities of the community in general. * * * Here Lane had come within the closed-off area where his ship lay, to occupy a berth to which the Government insisted he have access, cf. Restatement, Agency 2d, § 267, and while his act is not readily explicable, at least it was not shown to be due entirely to facets of his personal life. The risk that seamen going and coming from the Tamaroa might cause damage to the drydock is enough to make it fair that the enterprise bear the loss. It is not a fatal objection that the rule we lay down lacks sharp contours; in the end, as Judge Andrews said in a related context, "it is all a question [of expediency,] * * * of fair judgment, always keeping in mind the fact that we endeavor to make a rule in each case that will be practical and in keeping with the general understanding of mankind." Palsgraf v. Long Island R.R. Co., 248 N.Y. 339, 354–355, 162 N.E. 99, 104, 59 A.L.R. 1253 (1928) (dissenting opinion).

* * *

Affirmed.

———————

FRUIT v. SCHREINER, 502 P.2d 133 (Alaska 1972). "The basis of *respondeat superior* has been correctly stated as 'the desire to include in the costs of operation inevitable losses to third persons incident to carrying on an enterprise, and thus distribute the burden among those benefited by the enterprise.'[19]

19. Smith, Frolic and Detour, 23 Col.L.Rev. 716, 718 (1923).

" * * * Thus, if an employee is engaged in trucking merchandise for an employer and through negligence in driving injures a pedestrian, it appears more socially desirable for the employer, although faultless itself, to bear the loss than the individual harmed. Insurance is readily available for the employer so that the risk may be distributed among many like insureds paying premiums and the extra cost of doing business may be reflected in the price of the product.

"The principle has been recognized by every state in the enactment of workmen's compensation laws whereby employees may recover compensation for injuries arising out of and in the course of their employment without reference to negligence on the part of employers. The costs to the employers are distributed to the public in the price of the product.

"Indeed the concept whereby the enterprise bears the loss caused by it has been recently extended to cover any loss caused by a defect in a manufactured product even without fault of employees or employers. The rule of *respondeat superior*, however, has not been extended to that length and is limited to requiring an enterprise to bear the loss incurred as a result of the employee's negligence. The acts of the employee need be so connected to his employment as to justify requiring that the employer bear that loss."

TABER v. MAINE, 45 F.3d 598 (2d Cir.1995) (Calabresi, J.). Maine, a navy serviceman "went on liberty after having completed a grueling 24 hour duty shift. While on liberty he was free to leave the base as he pleased and travel up to 50 miles away. He could also be recalled for duty at any time." Maine spent the day drinking and partying. By 11:00 that evening he appeared drunk. At 11:30, he drove off base to get something to eat but turned around because he felt tired. While returning to base, he crashed into a car carrying Taber. The district court granted the government's motion for summary judgment, ruling that the accident was outside the scope of Maine's employment. *Held*, reversed. *Bushey* cited.

"It seems clear to us that [the law of Guam] would hold the government vicariously liable for Maine's actions [because the law of Guam has been modeled on the law of California and, as] * * * early as 1961, commentators noted that California had taken the lead in equating the scope of respondeat superior liability to the traditionally broader coverage mandated by worker's compensation statutes. Thus, California employers were subject to liability for injuries to third parties caused by the behavior of their employees whenever the employees' acts 'arose out of or in the course of' their employment relationship. See Guido Calabresi, Some Thoughts on Risk Distribution and the Law of Torts, 70 Yale L.J. 499, 545 (1961).

"The government understandably seeks to rely on an older conception of respondeat superior. This view of the doctrine required a close link between the acts of the 'agent' and 'profit' accruing to the master before vicarious liability attaches. See Restatement (Second) of Agency § 228 (1984). But today this position is in hasty retreat, if not rout. [Under California law] the employer-benefit requirement is met whenever broad potential effects on morale and customer relations exist, or where the employer has implicitly permitted or endorsed the recreational practices that led to the harm. * * *

"Of course drinking by servicemembers can be viewed as important to military morale * * * [h]ence, 'employer-benefit' can be adduced in all these cases. But in the end, 'employer-benefit' is significant only because it is one way of showing that the harm that drinking causes can properly be considered a cost of the employer's enterprise.

"Here, it is undisputed that drinking on base during off-duty hours was a commonplace, if not an officially condoned activity. * * * And in the context of the military mission, an occasional drunken servicemember who leaves government premises and causes damage is a completely foreseeable event, in the sense that it is a reasonably obvious risk of the general enterprise. As such, we do not think that it would be either 'unfair' or the slightest bit unreasonable to impose that cost on the government. To the contrary, given the pervasive control that the military exercises over its personnel while they are on a base, it is totally in keeping with the doctrine of respondeat superior to allocate the costs of base operations to the government. See William M. Landes & Richard A. Posner, The Positive Economic Theory of Tort Law, 15 Ga. L. Rev. 851, 914–15 (discussing respondeat superior as an incentive for employers to exert their control over employees to induce careful conduct). And this is so quite apart from whether the military benefits from the boost in morale achieved through fairly lenient on-base drinking policies."

MARY M. v. CITY OF LOS ANGELES, 54 Cal.3d 202, 285 Cal.Rptr. 99, 814 P.2d 1341 (1991) (Kennard, J.). Plaintiff, who had been drinking, was stopped for erratic driving by a police officer. After performing poorly on a sobriety test, she pleaded with the officer not to take her to jail. He drove her home and raped her.

Held, reversing the intermediate appellate court, when "a police officer on duty misuses his official authority by raping a woman who he has detained, the public entity that employs him can be held vicariously liable." Although "sexual assaults by police officers are fortunately uncommon," they are not so "unusual or startling" that they cannot "fairly be regarded as typical of or broadly incidental" to the "enterprise of law enforcement." "The danger that an officer will commit a sexual assault while on duty arises from the considerable authority and control inherent in the responsibilities of an officer in enforcing the law." Costs issuing from misuse of that authority "should be borne by the community, because of the substantial benefits that the community derives from the lawful exercise of police power."

LISA M. v. HENRY MAYO NEWHALL MEMORIAL HOSPITAL, 12 Cal.4th 291, 48 Cal.Rptr.2d 510, 907 P.2d 358 (1995). Nineteen year old plaintiff, who was pregnant, sought treatment in hospital emergency room for injuries suffered in a fall. An emergency room physician ordered an ultrasound examination to determine if the fetus had been injured. The ultrasound technician (Tripoli) rejected plaintiff's request that her mother and boyfriend be allowed to accompany her. After completing the prescribed examination, he asked the plaintiff if she would like to learn the gender of her baby. Under the pretense of conducting an ultrasound examination designed to determine the fetus's gender, he sexually molested her.

Held, reversing the intermediate appellate court, Tripoli's conduct fell outside the scope of his employment as a matter of law. *Mary M.* distinguished. While the technician "abused his position of trust" he "had no legal or coercive authority over plaintiff." By "employing the technician and providing the ultrasound room, [the hospital] may have set the stage for his misconduct, but the script was entirely of his own, independent invention. For this reason it would be unfair and inconsistent with the basic rationale of respondeat superior to impose liability" on the hospital.

Kennard, J., dissented. The intimate contact inherent in the job "put [the] plaintiff in a vulnerable position and permitted Tripoli to dupe plaintiff into believing that his sexual assault was actually part of a standard medical procedure." Consequently, "a reasonable trier of fact could conclude that this sexual assault * * * may fairly be attributed to risks arising from, and inherent in, the 'peculiar aspects' of Tripoli's employment."

LANE v. MODERN MUSIC, INC., 244 S.C. 299, 136 S.E.2d 713 (1964). Employee whose duty it was to place coin-operated piccolos in restaurant location, and repair, change records, etc., was engaged in horseplay outside scope of employment in frightening customer outside restaurant with "mongoose" device.

SECTION B. INDEPENDENT CONTRACTORS

The materials in this section cover the liability of "masters" for the torts committed by "independent contractors" acting on their behalf. "Independent contractors," like "servants," are a species of agent. The law governing the imputation of the torts of independent contractors to the parties who employ them is the other branch of "vertical" vicarious liability doctrine.

We start with the Restatement's formulation of the basic doctrine and its rationales, then briefly take up a central doctrinal question: When is an agent an "independent contractor" rather than a "servant"? Settled doctrine, included in Chapter One, tells us that the answer to this question turns on whether the principal has the "right to control" the conduct of the agent. Here, we look at what this doctrinal category means when the law is "in action." Is the presence of the right to control a matter of legal form—of what the contract between the parties says? Or is it a matter of social fact—of how the parties actually allocate the power of control? What is at stake in choosing between these possibilities?

Most of the cases in this section explore the principal exceptions to the general rule that masters are not liable for the torts of their independent contractors. That rule is subject to a remarkable number of exceptions—so many, in fact, that they might easily swallow the rule—though there is no present trend for them to do so. The cases is this section thus raise a number of issues: Why is the balance between rule and exception so close? What criteria, if any, distinguish those cases that are appropriately covered by the general rule, from those that are appropriately excepted from it? Is there an underlying unity of policy or principle that accounts for the diversity of formal rules?

RESTATEMENT (SECOND), TORTS

§ 409. General Principle

Except as stated in §§ 410–429, the employer of an independent contractor is not liable for physical harm caused to another by an act or omission of the contractor or his servants.

* * *

Comment:

b. The general rule stated in this Section, as to the nonliability of an employer for physical harm caused to another by the act or omission of an independent contractor, was the original common law rule. The explanation for it most commonly given is that, since the employer has no power of control over the manner in which the work is to he done by the contractor, it is to be regarded as the contractor's own enterprise, and he, rather than the employer, is the proper party to be charged with the responsibility of preventing the risk, and bearing and distributing it.

The first departure from the old common law rule was in Bower v. Peate, 1 Q.B.D. 321 (1876), in which an employer was held liable when the foundation of the plaintiff 's building was undermined by the contractor's excavation. Since that decision, the law has progressed by the recognition of a large number of "exceptions" to the "general rule." These exceptions are stated in §§ 410–429. They are so numerous, and they have so far eroded the "general rule," that it can now be said to be "general" only in the sense that it is applied where no good reason is found for departing from it. * * *

The exceptions have developed, and have tended to be stated, very largely as particular detailed rules for particular situations, which are difficult to list completely, and few courts have attempted to state any broad principles governing them, or any very satisfactory summaries. In general, the exceptions may be said to fall into three very broad categories:

    1. Negligence of the employer in selecting, instructing, or supervising the contractor.

    2. Non-delegable duties of the employer, arising out of some relation toward the public or the particular plaintiff.

    3. Work which is specially, peculiarly, or "inherently" dangerous.

———

ANDERSON v. MARATHON PETROLEUM COMPANY, 801 F.2d 936. (7th Cir.1986) (Posner, J.) "Generally a principal is not liable for an independent contractor's torts even if they are committed in the performance of the contract and even though a principal is liable under the doctrine of respondeat superior for the torts of his employees if committed in the furtherance of their employment."

"The reason for distinguishing the independent contractor from the employee is that, by definition of the relationship between a principal and an independent contractor, the principal does not supervise the details of the independent contractor's work and therefore is not in a good position to prevent negligent performance, whereas the essence of the contractual relationship known as employment is that the employee surrenders to the employer the right to direct the details of his work, in exchange for receiving a wage. The independent contractor commits himself to providing a specified output, and the principal monitors the contractor's performance not by * * * monitoring inputs—i.e., supervising the contractor—but by inspecting the contractually specified output to make sure it conforms to the specifications. * * * "

PARKER v. DOMINO'S PIZZA, 629 So.2d 1026 (Fla.Dist.Ct.App.1993). Plaintiffs were injured assisting the victims of an automobile accident negligently caused by a pizza deliveryman. An express provision of the agreement between Domino's and its franchise provided that the franchise was an independent contractor. Relying on that provision, the trial court ruled that the franchise was an independent contractor as a matter of law.

Held, grant of summary judgment for defendant reversed. "[I]t was error to determine as a matter of law that Domino's does not retain the right to control the means to be used by its franchisee to accomplish the required tasks." The terms of the agreement between Domino's and the franchise raised "a genuine and material question of fact."

"It is clear that the nature and extent of the relationship of parties said to occupy the status of principal and agent is a question of fact. * * *

"Whether one party is a mere agent rather than an independent contractor as to the other party is to be determined by measuring the right to control and not by considering only the actual control exercised by the latter over the former. If the employer's right to control the activities of an employee extends to the manner in which a task is to be performed, then the employee is not an independent contractor.

"The relationship between Domino's and J & B Enterprises is established by a franchise agreement and an operating manual. [The franchise agreement indicates that Domino's retains extensive control over the manner in which the franchise is to operate.]

" * * * The manual which Domino's provides to its franchisees is a veritable bible for overseeing a Domino's operation. It contains prescriptions for every conceivable facet of the business: from the elements of preparing the perfect pizza to maintaining accurate books; from advertising and promotional ideas to routing and delivery guidelines; from order-taking instructions to oven-tending rules; from organization to sanitation. The manual even offers a wide array of techniques for 'boxing and cutting' the pizza, as well as tips on running the franchise to achieve an optimum profit. The manual literally leaves nothing to chance. * * * "

BECKER v. INTERSTATE PROPERTIES
United States Court of Appeals, Third Circuit, 1977.
569 F.2d 1203.

ADAMS, Circuit Judge.

* * *

A.

On August 31, 1972, appellant Gary Becker, a 19–year-old construction worker, was severely injured on his job site in Windsor, New Jersey when a heavy truck drove squarely over his pelvis. Mr. Becker has sued to recover his damages, including the $35,000 in medical fees he had expended as of the time the complaint was filed.

The owner and general contractor of the $1.5 million shopping center project on which Mr. Becker was working at the time of the accident was I. P. Construction Corp. (hereinafter the developer). Mr. Becker was employed by Wood–Pine Corp., a small company hired by the developer to pave the shopping center. The developer knew, or should have known, that Wood–Pine would hire subcontractors, since Wood–Pine itself had no trucks. In fact, Wood–Pine hired Windsor Contracting Corp., whose employee, Willard Edwards, drove the truck which injured Mr. Becker.

There is evidence to indicate that I. P., at least on some occasions in the past, had required insurance coverage from its subcontractors. Also, there is evidence that the standard liability insurance coverage in the construction industry allows for recoveries of up to $250,000 per accident. In contrast, Windsor's automobile liability insurance coverage was only $10,000, and Windsor is only minimally capitalized.

To recover for his injuries in this diversity action, Mr. Becker sued Windsor and its employee for negligence, also asserting claims against the developer. Mr. Becker contends that he will be unable to recover his damages from Windsor because of Windsor's limited insurance coverage and marginal capitalization, and that the developer breached its duty in allowing such a financially-irresponsible contractor to be hired.

The district court granted summary judgment for the developer, holding that under New Jersey law the developer could not be held liable for the tort of an independent subcontractor regardless of the financial status of such subcontractor. It is this conclusion that we review here.

B.

Inasmuch as no New Jersey cases are squarely on point, it is important to make clear that our disposition of this case must be governed by a prediction of what a New Jersey court would do if confronted with the facts before us. * * *

* * *

C.

It is true, as Mr. Becker suggests, that the concept of immunity of the employer of an independent contractor is in tension with the more general tort doctrine of *respondeat superior*, and that the former represents a judicial gloss on the latter.[10] Indeed some authorities have advocated the all-out abolition of the independent contractor immunity,[11] and one noted commentator has espoused the view that the proliferation of exceptions to the immunity precept is "sufficient to cast doubt on the validity of the rule."[12]

Nonetheless, we discern no indication that the New Jersey courts are prepared to abandon on a wholesale basis the rule of an employer's immunity for the acts of his independent contractors and to adopt a pure theory of "enterprise liability." Instead, the New Jersey courts have adhered to the general doctrine of immunity, and the liability of employers has emanated from the exceptions articulated in Majestic Realty Associates, Inc. v. Toti Contracting Co.[13]

Under *Majestic*, an employer is responsible for the negligence of an independent contractor if one of three special circumstances is present:

(1) where the employer retains control over the aspect of the activity in which the negligence occurs;

(2) where the contractor employed is incompetent; or

(3) where the performance of the contract involves an inherently dangerous activity.

The sharp conflict in the case at hand centers on Mr. Becker's contention that by hiring or permitting the hiring of Windsor—a contractor financially unable to respond in damages—the developer came within the second exception to the immunity rule. Mr. Becker places his reliance primarily on a passage from *Majestic* * * *.

D.

In *Majestic*, the New Jersey Parking Authority hired Toti Contracting Co. as an independent contractor to demolish a building owned by the Authority. Toti's employees negligently allowed a part of the demolished building to collapse and to damage Majestic's adjoining property. In a unanimous opinion adjudicating Majestic's claim against the Parking Authority, the New Jersey Supreme Court * * * [stated], albeit in what was characterized as "an incidental comment,":

10. See W. Prosser, Handbook of the Law of Torts 468–69 (1971); Note, Risk Administration in the Marketplace; A Reappraisal of the Independent Contractor Rule, 40 U. Chicago L.Rev. 661–664 (1973). Indeed, the early cases, both British and American, applied the doctrine of respondeat superior to independent contractors. See Bush v. Steinman, 1 Bos. & P. 404, 121 Eng. Rep. 978 (S.P.1799); Lowell v. Boston 7 L.R.Corp., 23 Pick, Mass. 24 (1839).

11. Note, Risk Administration in the Marketplace, supra note [10] at 675–79 (suggesting joint liability of employer and contractor with indemnification agreements allowed); cf. Calabresi, Some Thoughts on Risk Distribution and the Law of Tort, 70 Yale L.J. 499, 545 (1960) (applicability of independent contractor exception should be "narrower"). * * *

12. Prosser, supra note 10 at 468. * * *

13. 30 N.J. 425, 153 A.2d 321 (1959).

Inevitably the mind turns to the fact that the injured third party is entirely innocent and that the occasion for his injury arises out of the desire of the contractee to have certain activities performed. The injured has no control over or relation with the contractor. The contractee, true, has no control over the doing of the work and in that sense is also innocent of the wrongdoing; but he does have the power of selection and in the application of concepts of distributive justice perhaps much can be said for the view that a loss arising out of the tortious conduct of a financially irresponsible contractor should fall on the contractee.

Imposition of liability under such circumstances is particularly appropriate, the Court said, in light of the ready availability of liability insurance, which is viewed as a normal cost of doing business in the construction industry. Nonetheless, the issue was expressly reserved.

* * *

* * * [S]ince its enunciation, the financial-responsibility test has not come before the New Jersey courts. We thus have no directly applicable precedent upon which to rely.

However, the New Jersey courts since *Majestic* have consistently acknowledged both the rule of immunity and its tripartite exceptions. * * * We must therefore look to the more general principles which govern New Jersey courts in their exposition of common law doctrines.

E.

* * *

* * * [W]e believe the goals of New Jersey tort law in three areas would impel a New Jersey court to hold that the failure to engage a properly solvent or adequately insured subcontractor is a violation of the duty to obtain a competent independent contractor.[27]

First, the New Jersey courts have manifested a concern in their formulation of tort law to ensure that the burden of accidental loss be shifted to those best able to bear and distribute that loss rather than having it imposed on the hapless victim. * * *

In this case, as in any case in which a financially-irresponsible contractor is hired, the choice of the party to bear the loss falls between the developer and the victim. Where, as here, the developer is a substantial entrepreneur and a member of an industry that carries large liability insurance policies as a matter of course, there is little question but that he is in the better position to bear the loss of such an accident.[31] Moreover, the developer can

27. It is true that *Majestic* involved a suit against an employer for the tort of his contractor, rather than a suit against an employer for the tort of his contractor's subcontractor, as here. As noted above, however, I. P. retained authority over the choice of subcontractors by Wood–Pine; any subcontract required specific authorization by I. P. Thus, if Wood–Pine breached a duty in choosing its subcontractor, I. P. is chargeable with Wood–Pine's negligent choice of a subcontractor under the standard tort doctrine that retention of control by the employer of an independent contractor subjects the employer to liability.

31. At the time that the doctrine of non-liability for acts of independent contractors was formulated, insurance markets were not nearly as extensive or sophisticated as they are today. * * *

spread the increased costs of insurance or liability to ultimate users of the project. It is only in rare circumstances that a victim will have a similar option. Thus in a context such as we have here the doctrine suggested in *Majestic* is indicated by the policies previously adopted by the New Jersey courts.[32]

* * *

Second, it is a well-recognized principle of tort law that, where feasible, liability for an accident should be allocated to those in the best position to control the factors leading to such accidents. Indeed, this is said to be the basis for the independent contractor exception to *respondeat superior*—the independent contractor is in a better position to control the work of his employees than is his employer.

In the situation contemplated by the financial-irresponsibility exception, however, the loss must fall either upon the developer or upon the victim, for the subcontractor is by definition incapable of bearing it. In general, the developer has more control than the victim.

More importantly, however, in the context in which the *Majestic* dictum applies, two elements have conjoined to give rise to the loss before the Court: the negligence leading to an injury and the failure to assure the financial responsibility that would allow compensation for the damages flowing from such negligence. While the developer might be in a disadvantageous position to control the negligent conduct, in a case such as this—where the developer has negotiated at length regarding the insurance coverage of his independent contractor—he is in an excellent position to assure the proper degree of financial responsibility. The doctrine suggested by *Majestic* places the costs of a failure to insure, and the consequent incentives, on the party in a superior position to evaluate and avoid such costs.

* * *

Third, the New Jersey courts have expressed the view that the costs of accidents should be borne by those who secure the benefit of the activities that engender the mishaps. Where only one party is involved, a decision declining to insure carries with it an automatic penalty: unshielded liability to tort judgments. By hiring an independent contractor, however, without the rule suggested by *Majestic*, the developer could obtain the advantage of lowered operating costs (passed on to him by his contractor in the form of reduced prices) without liability for the decision to expose third parties to the risk of uncompensated losses. This is particularly so where, as here, the

---

The New Jersey courts in other areas have been sensitive to the impact of the growth and availability of insurance upon the rationale for common law immunities. [Citations omitted to cases discussing abolition of interspousal and charitable immunities.]

32. Where the employer is likely to be impecunious, of course, different considerations come into play. Nothing but a rigid adherence to legal formalism, however, dictates that the same rule must govern the case of a private individual contracting for repairs on his house as applies to the relation between a commercial developer and his subcontractor.

subcontractor has effectively shielded himself from suit by incorporating several minimally financed business entities.

The *Majestic* doctrine would impose costs of financial irresponsibility on parties who benefit from that irresponsibility. In this respect, also, such an approach seems fully at one with the goals of New Jersey law.

* * *

No persuasive argument has been adduced by the cases that have declined to adopt the *Majestic* approach. Accordingly, it seems doubtful that a New Jersey court would give controlling weight to the decisions of tribunals of other states in the face of the considered reflections of its own Supreme Court.[50]

G.

* * *

When the objectives of spreading costs and ensuring victim compensation, the goal of encouraging action to minimize losses, and the end of placing the cost of risks upon those who profit from those risks are all served by a single doctrine, it would appear that such a precept would commend itself to the judiciary. When the effect of applying that doctrine is to assure the right of a tragically injured young person to have a day in court in which to seek recovery from a developer who failed to follow a trade practice which would have allowed compensation directly, I do not believe that application of that doctrine is at odds with intuitive notions of justice. When policy concerns and practical effect so merge to support a rule of law, and when no prior New Jersey case has rejected it, it seems reasonable to predict that such a rule would be adopted by the New Jersey courts.

[Reversed and remanded.]

———

ROBINSON v. JIFFY EXECUTIVE LIMOUSINE, 4 F.3d 237 (3d Cir.1993). "These consolidated diversity actions arise from a fatal car accident which took the lives of the appellant's father and of the driver of the limousine hired by a casino ['Showboat'] to transport one of its patrons from the Philadelphia airport. The main issue we address is whether, under New Jersey law, one (such as the casino) who hires an independent contractor who is uninsured, or financially unable to pay tort judgments, as was the limousine company and its driver, is liable in tort for that independent contractor's negligence under New Jersey's 'incompetent contractor' exception to the general rule against imputed liability. * * * The district court declined to follow Becker's majority opinion.

"Since our decision in Becker, the Superior Court of New Jersey, Appellate Division, has twice rejected the Becker majority holding. * * * "

50. The dissent suggests that the principle advanced here will significantly limit the opportunities of independent contractors without "start-up" capital. This seems unlikely because even a minimally capitalized business presumably will be able to bear insurance premiums as operating costs. Moreover, there is no evidence to indicate that New Jersey wishes to subsidize struggling construction contractors by depriving accident victims of compensation.

"At the outset we note that, although state intermediate appellate decisions are not automatically controlling where the highest court of the state has not spoken * * *, we must give serious consideration to the decisions of the intermediate appellate courts in ascertaining and applying state law. * * * "

" * * * In light of the application of New Jersey law in those [two intermediate appellate] cases, we predict now that Becker's expansion of the 'incompetent contractor' exception to impose liability on Showboat would not likely comport with the New Jersey Supreme Court's pronouncement, were it to confront the issue. * * *

"Policy considerations favor our conservative approach. As the dissent in Becker noted, the majority's standard for imposing liability would be an inexact appendage to the standard already provided by the state legislature, and would 'cause uncertainty and doubt for every financial strata and every court, as well as hinder the employment opportunities of an independent contractor trying to enter the market place but lacking much in the way of start-up capital.' Becker, 569 F.2d at 1216. Under Becker, any person or entity which contracted for transportation service, from taxis, buses and limousines, to movers and delivery services, would be obliged to make a diligent and continuing inquiry into the financial qualifications of the contractor before calling upon him to perform the transportation service, in order to guard against potential imputed negligence liability. Such a duty would not only be unprecedented, but would indeed impose prohibitive obligations on employers of independent contractors beyond what we are prepared to predict the New Jersey Supreme Court will adopt."

"PECULIAR" RISKS

SCOTT FETZER CO. v. READ, 945 S.W.2d 854 (Tex.App.1997). " * * * The general rule is that an employer or owner is not liable for the acts or omissions of its independent contractors. Texas courts, however, have recognized many exceptions to this general rule of non-liability. Both the rule and its exceptions are derived from the same underlying polices. The general rule encompasses the notion that employers should not be held responsible for activities they do not control and, in many instances, lack the knowledge and resources to direct. *See* Restatement (Second) of Torts [hereinafter 'Restatement'] § 409, cmt. b (1965). The exceptions largely reflect special situations where the employer is in the best position to identify, minimize, and administer the risks involved in the contractor's activities. *See* W. Prosser & W.P. Keeton, *Prosser and Keeton on the Law of Torts* § 71, at 509–10 (5th ed. 1983); Fowler V. Harper, *The Basis of the Immunity of an Employer of an Independent Contractor,* 10 Ind. L.J. 494, 498–500 (1935); *see also* Restatement §§ 410–429 (1965) (listing 24 exceptions to the general rule of non-liability). One of these long-recognized exceptions is encompassed by the doctrine of 'peculiar risk.'

"The peculiar-risk exception establishes liability for an employer who hires an independent contractor to do work that the employer knows is likely to create 'a peculiar risk of physical harm to others' absent special precautions. The peculiar-risk exception is premised on the putative existence of a duty to third parties that the employer, for policy reasons, may not delegate to an independent contractor. Its use is traced to the leading English case of *Bower v. Peate*, 1 Q.B.D. 321 (1876), in which an independent contractor undermined the plaintiff's building by negligently failing to shore up an excavation on his employer's adjacent land. The court held the independent contractor's employer liable, finding that:

> [A] man who orders a work to be executed, from which, in the natural course of things, injurious consequences to his neighbours must be expected to arise unless means are adopted by which such consequences may be prevented, is bound to see to the doing of that which is necessary to prevent the mischief, and cannot relieve himself of his responsibility by employing some one else....

Id. at 326. The peculiar-risk exception represents an allocation of risk and prevents unscrupulous employers of independent contractors from hiding behind the drawbridge of immunity of the independent contractor's general rule of non-liability. The peculiar-risk exception is exemplified by section 413 of the Restatement:

> One who employs an independent contractor to do work which the employer should recognize as likely to create a peculiar unreasonable risk of physical harm to others unless special precautions are taken, is subject to liability for physical harm caused by the absence of such precautions if the employer:
>
> (a) fails to provide in the contract that the contractor shall take such precautions, or
>
> (b) fails to exercise reasonable care to provide in some other manner for the taking of such precautions.

Restatement § 413 (1965). Thus, under the peculiar-risk exception, liability may be imposed on the employer of an independent contractor if the employer has reason to know that the independent contractor's work is likely to create a peculiar risk of harm to others absent special precautions and if the employer takes no steps to minimize that risk.

"A peculiar risk * * * does not mean that the risk must be one that is abnormal to the type of work done, or that it must be an abnormally great risk. It has reference only to a special, recognizable danger arising out of the work itself, of which special precautions can be taken to avert the risk. [Wilson v.] Good Humor[Corp.], 757 F.2d at 1304–05 [(D.C.Cir.1985)].

"The peculiar-risk doctrine has been applied to many situations. For example, in *Good Humor*, a child was fatally struck by a car as she responded to a Good Humor ice cream vendor who parked his truck on the street and began "ringing the distinctive Good Humor jingle bells." 757 F.2d at 1296. In holding Good Humor liable under the doctrine of peculiar risk, the court explained:

> [The evidence] was sufficient to permit a jury finding that Good Humor knew or had special reason to know of the risks to children likely to arise from the street vending of ice cream * * *

* * * The vendors do not possess any special experience or knowledge concerning the risk peculiar to their task. Good Humor, by contrast, has special and detailed knowledge of the peculiar risks to children involved in its operation and is in the best position to ensure reasonable safety awareness. * * *.

Id. at 1305–06. [fn. omitted]

"Kirby argues that peculiar risk is not a separate degree of dangerous activity, but is instead merely a part of the 'inherently dangerous work' exception to the general rule of non-liability for acts of independent contractors. * * * The inherent-danger and peculiar-risk exceptions are closely related because both focus on the independent-contractor relationship and the particular circumstances surrounding a specific job. Although the doctrines of peculiar risk and inherently dangerous activities are related, however, 'they are not identical and ought not to be confused.' *Good Humor,* 757 F.2d at 1311 n. 7 (Bork, J., concurring).

" * * * The difference between the doctrines of peculiar risk and inherently dangerous work is that peculiar risk occupies an intermediate position between the employer's absolute *immunity* for an independent contractor's negligence in ordinary circumstances and the employer's absolute *liability* for inherently dangerous activities. *El-Meswari v. Washington Gas Light Co.,* 785 F.2d 483, 492 (4th Cir.1986). Inherently dangerous work has been described as that which is dangerous no matter how skillfully done. Work is inherently dangerous if it '*must* result in probable injury to third persons or the public.' *Goolsby v. Kenney,* 545 S.W.2d 591, 594 (Tex.Civ.App.—Tyler 1976, writ ref'd n.r.e.) (emphasis added). The peculiar-risk doctrine, on the other hand, applies to work that can be done safely if the risk peculiar to that work is known and appropriate precautionary steps are taken."

The court went on to uphold the imposition of liability under the "peculiar risk" doctrine on a company which hired independent contractors to market vacuum cleaners door-to-door, but which failed to conduct background checks on prospective salespeople.

"ABNORMAL" AND "INHERENT" DANGERS

ANDERSON v. MARATHON PETROLEUM COMPANY, 801 F.2d 936 (7th Cir.1986) (Posner, J.) "The rule [that employers are not liable for the torts of their independent contractors] is not applied, however, when the activity for which the independent contractor was hired is 'abnormally dangerous,' see Restatement (Second) of Torts § 427A (1964), or in an older terminology 'ultrahazardous,' see, e.g., Cities Service Co. v. State, 312 So.2d 799, 802 (Fla.Dist.Ct.App.1975)—i.e., if the activity might very well result in injury even if conducted with all due skill and caution. When an activity is abnormally dangerous, it is important not only that the people engaged in it use the highest practicable degree of skill and caution, but also—since even if they do so, accidents may well result—that the people who have authorized the activity consider the possibility of preventing some accidents by curtailing the activity or even eliminating it altogether. On both scores there is an argument for making the principal as well as the independent contractor liable if an accident occurs that is due to the hazardous character of the performance called for by the contract. The fact that a very high degree of care is cost-justified implies that the principal should be induced to wrack his brain, as well as the independent contractor his own brain, for ways of minimizing the danger posed by the activity. And the fact that the only feasible method of accident prevention may be to reduce the amount of the activity or substitute another activity argues for placing liability on the principal, who makes the decision whether to undertake the activity in the first place. * * *

"True, the principal would in any event be liable indirectly if the price it paid the independent contractor fully reflected the dangers of the undertaking; but this condition would be fulfilled only if the contractor were fully answerable for an accident if one occurred. * * *

* * *

"[The concept of an 'abnormally dangerous' undertaking must be distinguished from both the concept of a 'peculiar risk' and from the concept of 'inherent dangerousness.'] * * * Johnson v. Central Tile & Terrazzo Co., 59 Ill.App.2d 262, 276–77, 207 N.E.2d 160, 167 (1965), * * * says that 'if one employs another to do work which he should recognize as involving some peculiar risk to others unless special precautions are taken, the one doing the employing will remain liable if harm results because these precautions are not taken,' even though the person 'employed' is actually an independent contractor. The words 'peculiar risk' bring to mind section 416 of the Restatement. And the closely related section 427 speaks of a danger that is 'inherent,' a concept apparently distinguishable in the restaters' minds from the 'abnormally dangerous' concept of 427A (an a fortiori ground for not allowing the principal to shift his duty of care to the independent contractor). This concept, too, is echoed in Illinois cases, * * *"

"The distinction between an abnormal risk on the one hand and a peculiar or inherent risk on the other hand is easiest to understand in situations where the activity, though not always or generally hazardous, is so in the particular case. Thus in Donohue v. George W. Stiles Construction Co., 214 Ill.App. 82, 89–91 (1919) * * * the prime contractor hired a subcontractor to do structural steel repair work in a post office, right over the heads of the postal employees—and sure enough, one of them was injured. * * *"

NON-DELEGABLE DUTIES

MALONEY v. RATH, 69 Cal.2d 442, 71 Cal.Rptr. 897, 445 P.2d 513 (1968). Plaintiff sued for damages for injuries from a collision with defendant's car, whose brakes failed. Defendant had the brakes overhauled three months before the accident and had no reason to know of their defective condition after the faulty overhauling. The Vehicle Code required brakes to be "maintained * * * in good working order." The trial court entered judgment for defendant. In an opinion by Chief Justice Traynor, the Supreme Court reversed. The court first held that "violation of a safety provision of the Vehicle Code does not make the violator strictly liable for damage caused by the violation." It then considered a distinct ground for liability.

"It does not follow, however, that the duty to exercise reasonable care to maintain brakes so that they comply with the provisions of the Vehicle Code can be delegated. * * *

"Unlike strict liability, a nondelegable duty operates, not as a substitute for liability based on negligence, but to assure that when a negligently caused harm occurs, the injured party will be compensated by the person whose activity caused the harm and who may therefore properly be held liable for the negligence of his agent, whether his agent was an employee or an independent contractor. To the extent that recognition of nondelegable duties tends to insure that there will be financially responsible defendant available to compensate for the negligent harms caused by that defendant's activity, it ameliorates the need for strict liability to secure compensation.

"* * * [W]e have found nondelegable duties in a wide variety of situations * * *. Such duties include those imposed by a public authority as a condition of granting a franchise; * * * the duty of a general contractor to construct a building safely; the duty to exercise due care when an '* * * independent contractor is employed to do work which the employer should recognize as necessarily creating a condition involving an unreasonable risk of bodily harm to others unless special precautions are taken,' Courtell v. McEachen (1959) 51 Cal.2d 448, 457, 334 P.2d 870, 874; the duty of landowners to maintain their property in a reasonably safe condition and to comply with applicable safety ordinances; and the duty of employers and suppliers to comply with the safety provisions of the Labor Code.

"* * * The statutory provisions regulating the maintenance and equipment of automobiles constitute express legislative recognition of the fact that improperly maintained motor vehicles threaten 'a grave risk of serious bodily harm or death.' [Section 423, Restatement Second of Torts]. The responsibility for minimizing that risk or compensating for the failure to do so properly rests with the person who owns and operates the vehicle. He is the party primarily to be benefited by its use; he selects the contractor and is free to insist upon one who is financially responsible and to demand indemnity from him; the cost of his liability insurance that distributes the risk is properly attributable to his activities; and the discharge of the duty to exercise reasonable care in the maintenance of his vehicle is of the utmost importance to the public.

"In the present case it is undisputed that the accident was caused by a failure of defendant's brakes that resulted from her independent contractor's negligence in overhauling or in thereafter inspecting the brakes. Since her duty to maintain her brakes in compliance with the provisions of the Vehicle Code is nondelegable, the fact that the brake failure was the result of her independent contractor's negligence is no defense."

MISIULIS v. MILBRAND MAINTENANCE CORP., 52 Mich.App. 494, 218 N.W.2d 68 (1974). Plaintiff, a business invitee, was injured when his motorcycle struck debris on an unlit roadway leading to an exit from a shopping center parking lot. The debris had been left by an independent contractor employed by defendants Fastenberg, owners and lessors of the shopping center, to repair the roof of a leased store in the center. The court affirmed a jury verdict of liability, holding defendants vicariously liable for the negligence of their independent contractor in making repairs on the leased premises. It said:

" * * * Generally, [the exceptional vicarious liability for the negligence of an independent contractor] is predicated upon a finding that the contractee owed a nondelegable or absolute duty to the third person which prevents the contractee from shifting the responsibility for the proper performance of the work to the contractor. * * *

"In the present case, defendants Fastenberg were responsible for setting in motion the course of events which resulted in plaintiff's injuries; it is they who benefited economically, along with their tenants, from the operation of the shopping center; and it is they who can most easily bear and distribute the loss occasioned by plaintiff's injury.

"The considerations support the conclusion that defendants Fastenberg owed plaintiff, a foreseeable business invitee, a nondelegable duty to exercise reasonable care in making repairs, whether gratuitously or otherwise, on the leased premises. * * * "

BAPTIST MEMORIAL HOSP. SYSTEM v. SAMPSON, 969 S.W.2d 945 (Tex.1998). "[W]e reject the suggestion of the court of appeals quoted above that we disregard the traditional rules and take 'the full leap' of imposing a nondelegable duty on Texas hospitals for the malpractice of emergency room physicians. Imposing such a duty is not necessary to safeguard patients in hospital emergency rooms. A patient injured by a physician's malpractice is not without a remedy. The injured patient ordinarily has a cause of action against the negligent physician, and may retain a direct cause of action against the hospital if the hospital was negligent in the performance of a duty owed directly to the patient."

WARD v. LUTHERAN HOSPITALS & HOMES SOC., 963 P.2d 1031 (Alaska 1998). "Alaska * * * imposes on hospitals a nondelegable duty to provide quality emergency medical care. Unless the patient selects the physician herself, a general acute care hospital will be liable for the physician's negligence in the emergency room." The court noted that Alaska is the only state to impose a nondelegable duty; other jurisdictions apply the doctrine of ostensible agency.

VICARIOUS LIABILITY BY OSTENSIBLE AGENCY

Vicarious liability is usually established (or negated) "objectively." It is established, in other words by the application of criteria which show that the principal does (or does not) control the conduct of the agent, can or cannot spread the risks of the activity more fairly, is or is not the best insurer, and so on. But there is one important route to the establishment of vicarious liability which is "subjective" in the sense that the (reasonable) perceptions of the victim are essential to it. This is the doctrine of vicarious liability by ostensible agency, also called apparent agency, apparent authority, and agency by estoppel.

———

MEIJA v. COMMUNITY HOSPITAL OF SAN BERNARDINO, 99 Cal. App.4th 1448, 122 Cal.Rptr.2d 233 (2002). *Held*, summary judgment in favor of defendant radiologist, reversed. "[A]bsent evidence that plaintiff should have known that the radiologist was not an agent of respondent hospital, plaintiff has alleged sufficient evidence to get to the jury merely by claiming that she sought treatment at the hospital.

"Although the cases discussing ostensible agency use various linguistic formulations to describe the elements of the doctrine, in essence, they require the same two elements: (1) conduct by the hospital that would cause a reasonable person to believe that the physician was an agent of the hospital, and (2) reliance on that apparent agency relationship by the plaintiff.

"Regarding the first element, courts generally conclude that it is satisfied when the hospital 'holds itself out' to the public as a provider of care * * * [and] a hospital is generally deemed to have held itself out as the provider of care, unless it gave the patient contrary notice. Many courts have even concluded that prior notice may not be sufficient to avoid liability in an emergency room context, where an injured patient in need of immediate medical care cannot be expected to understand or act upon that information.

"The second element, reliance, is established when the plaintiff 'looks to' the hospital for services, rather than to an individual physician. However, reliance need not be proven by direct testimony. (* * * see also *Pamperin* [v. Trinity Memorial Hospital, 423 N.W.2d 848], at p. 857 ['[I]f a person voluntarily enters a hospital without objecting to his or her admission to the hospital, then that person is seeking care from the hospital itself.'].) In fact, many courts presume reliance, absent evidence that the plaintiff knew or should have known the physician was not an agent of the hospital.

"As should be apparent to an astute observer, there is really only one relevant factual issue: whether the patient had reason to know that the physician was not an agent of the hospital. As noted above, hospitals are generally deemed to have held themselves out as the provider of services unless they gave the patient contrary notice, and the patient is generally presumed to have looked to the hospital for care unless he or she was treated by his or her personal physician. Thus, unless the patient had some reason to know of the true relationship between the hospital and the physician—i.e., because the hospital gave the patient actual notice or because the patient was treated by his or her personal physician—ostensible agency is readily inferred."

BAPTIST MEMORIAL HOSP. SYSTEM v. SAMPSON, 969 S.W.2d 945 (Tex.1998). "[T]o establish a hospital's liability for an independent contractor's medical malpractice based on ostensible agency, a plaintiff must show that (1) he or she had a reasonable belief that the physician was the agent or employee of the hospital, (2) such belief was generated by the hospital affirmatively holding out the physician as its agent or employee or knowingly permitting the physician to hold herself out as the hospital's agent or employee, and (3) he or she justifiably relied on the representation of authority."

Held, reversing Court of Appeals and reinstating summary judgment for defendant, hospital was not vicariously liable for negligence of its emergency room physicians under theory of ostensible agency. "Even if Sampson's belief that Dr. Zakula was a hospital employee were reasonable, that belief * * * must be based on or generated by some conduct on the part of the Hospital. * * * The summary judgment proof establishes that the Hospital took no affirmative act to make actual or prospective patients think the emergency room physicians were its agents or employees, and did not fail to take reasonable efforts to disabuse them of such a notion. As a matter of law, on this record, no conduct by the Hospital would lead a reasonable patient to believe that the treating emergency room physicians were hospital employees."

SECTION C.   OTHER FORMS OF VICARIOUS LIABILITY

The materials in this section cover the vicarious liability of partners; vicarious liability under the doctrine of joint enterprise; the imputation of victim negligence; and the vicarious liability of parents. The vicarious liability of partners, and vicarious liability under the doctrine of joint enterprise, are examples of "horizontal" vicarious liability. When vicarious liability is horizontal, "the person acting and the persons who might be held liable for his actions usually stand on an equal footing and may be thought of as equally implicated in a joint enterprise." (*Kansallis*, p. 799) The vicarious liability of partners—the leading example of horizontal vicarious liability—therefore differs from the vicarious liability of masters, in at least two ways. First, the vicarious liability of partners involves a "reciprocity" not found in master-servant relationships—each partner may be bound by the acts of each other partner, and each partner may bind her partners through her acts. (*Id.*) Second, the concept of "apparent authority" plays the role that "scope of employment" does in the master-servant context.

Kansallis, the main case in this section, addresses a particular doctrinal puzzle in the vicarious liability of partners: When, if ever, is there vicarious liability beyond "apparent authority"? *Kansallis* also asserts that the two branches of vicarious liability doctrine are unified by adherence to a common principle—"that as between two innocent parties—the principal-master and the third party—the principal-master who for his own purposes places another in a position to do harm to a third party should bear the loss."

KANSALLIS FINANCE LTD. v. FERN & OTHERS

Supreme Judicial Court of Massachusetts, 1996.
421 Mass. 659, 659 N.E.2d 731.

FRIED, Justice.

The United States Court of Appeals for the First Circuit has certified [the following question to this court]: " * * *. Under Massachusetts law, to find that a certain act is within the scope of a partnership for the purpose of applying the doctrine of vicarious liability, must a plaintiff show, inter alia, that the act was taken at least in part with the intent to serve or benefit the partnership?" * * *

* * *

* * * [The] defendants were law partners in Massachusetts when, in connection with a loan and lease financing transaction, the plaintiff sought and obtained an opinion letter from Jones. * * * [T]he letter, executed in Massachusetts and issued on "Fern, Anderson, Donahue, Jones & Sabatt, P.A." letterhead, "contained several intentional misrepresentations concerning the transaction and was part of a conspiracy by Jones and others (though not any of the defendants here) to defraud Kansallis." Although Jones did not personally sign the letter, he arranged for a third party to do so, and both the District Court judge and the jury found that Jones adopted or ratified the issuance of the letter. Jones was later convicted on criminal charges for his part in the fraud, but the plaintiff was unable to collect its $880,000 loss from Jones or his coconspirators.

[The plaintiff sued Jones' law partners, claiming that they were] liable for the letter because: (1) [they] gave Jones apparent authority to issue the letter; [and] (2) Jones acted within the scope of the partnership in issuing the letter * * * [The jury found that the defendants were not vicariously liable for Jones conduct.] The Court of Appeals affirmed * * * the jury's factual findings * * *.

* * * [T]he jury based their verdict on their findings that (1) Jones did not have apparent authority to issue the opinion letter and (2) that his action in issuing the opinion letter was outside the scope of the partnership. On appeal the plaintiff contended that the jury based their second finding on an erroneous instruction directing that, to find Jones's actions within the scope of the partnership, the issuance of the letter must satisfy a three-prong test. It must have: (1) been "the kind of thing a law partner would do"; (2) "occurred substantially within the authorized time and geographic limits of the partnership; and" (3) been "motivated at least in part by a purpose to serve the partnership." Although the jury did not indicate which prong the plaintiff failed to satisfy, the plaintiff objected to the addition of the third prong, and it is on the correctness of including this third prong in the test that the Court of Appeals now seeks guidance. * * *

* * *

[The vicarious liability of partners differs in important ways from the vicarious liability of masters for the torts of their servants.] In the context of a partnership, the person acting and the persons who might be held liable for his actions usually stand on an equal footing and may be thought of as equally implicated in a joint enterprise. By contrast, the law of the vicarious liability of a master for the acts of his servant grew up in circumstances where the actor was often in a subordinate position and had a limited interest in the enterprise which he assists. Yet both servants and partners are categorized as agents of their principals. In the partnership context, while each partner is the agent of the partnership, he also stands in the role of a principal—a reciprocity that is lacking in the master-servant relation. Finally, there is an important practical distinction between determining vicarious liability for harms that come about through the victim's voluntary interactions with the purported agent—as in the case of contracts, of fraud and of misrepresentation—and those that are inflicted on a victim who has made no choice to deal with the agent, as in the case of an accident, an assault or a trespass. Only in the former instance is the inquiry into apparent authority particularly apt, since where the victim transacts business with the agent, the victim's ability to assess the agent's authority will bear on whether and in what ways he chooses to deal with him. By contrast, where the victim has not chosen to deal with the agent by whose act he suffers harm—as in an automobile accident—the scope of employment seems the natural determinant of vicarious liability, and that is where the concept has had its most usual application.

Standing behind these diverse concepts of vicarious liability is a principle that helps to rationalize them. This is the principle that as between two innocent parties—the principal-master and the third party—the principal-master who for his own purposes places another in a position to do harm to a third party should bear the loss. A principal who requires an agent to transact his business, and can only get that business done if third parties deal with the agent as if with the principal, cannot complain if the innocent third party suffers loss by reason of the agent's act. Similarly, the master who must put an instrument into his servant's hands in order to get his business done, must also bear the loss if the servant causes harm to a stranger in the use of that instrument as the business is transacted.

* * *

In the case before us here, the jury instructions required the jury to consider [two] routes to vicarious liability. The jury found that Jones acted without actual or apparent authority, presumably because the form and circumstances of the letter were such that they concluded that no reasonable person in the plaintiff's position would have believed that the letter was issued with the partnership's authority. But then they were asked in the alternative whether Jones "acted in the scope of the partnership." This further question was taken to ask whether writing this opinion letter was the kind of thing that the partnership did—even if there was no apparent authority for this particular letter. This is the alternative theory, which the District Court labeled "vicarious liability," and under this alternative the defendants might yet be liable if the jury found all three of the conditions set out above in its charge on that issue. The rationale for this possibly more extended liability recognizes an authority in each partner to take the initiative to enlarge the partnership enterprise even without the authority—actual or apparent—of his partners, so long as what he does is within the generic description of the type of partnership involved. Whatever the harshness may be of such a rule extending vicarious liability past apparent authority, it is mitigated by the third factor, requiring that the unauthorized but law partner-like act be intended at least in part to serve the partnership. Since there is then some possibility that the partnership will benefit from the errant partner's act, then as between two innocent parties it is not unfair that the one whom the wrongful act may have and was meant to benefit must bear the burden of the harm.

* * *

Accordingly, if we take the * * * certified question to ask whether a partner must necessarily at least in part act for the benefit of the partnership if the partnership is to be liable for his actions, the answer is "no." But the answer is "no" only because under our law—and the law of partnership and agency generally—there are two routes by which vicarious liability may be found. If the partner has apparent authority to do the act, that will be sufficient to ground vicarious liability, whether or not he acted to benefit the partnership. It is only where there is no apparent authority, which is what the jury found on the common law counts here, that there may yet be vicarious liability on the alternative ground requiring such an intent to benefit the partnership. Since there is no evidence that Jones was acting to benefit the partnership, the District Court's judgment for the defendants on the common law counts accords with our statutes and precedents. The jury instructions on the common law claims were correct.

SHOEMAKER v. ESTATE OF WHISTLER, 513 S.W.2d 10 (Tex.1974). Action for death of plaintiff's son, in crash of private plane, against the estate and widow of one of the owner-occupants of the plane. *Held,* for defendants. Previous decisions of this court support the conclusion that negligence of the pilot is to be imputed to the joint owner under the doctrine of joint enterprise. On reconsideration, however, the doctrine is now modified so as to apply "to an enterprise having a business or pecuniary purpose." In this case, negligence will not be imputed since the purpose of the flight was to engage in a voluntary search mission in which owners of the aircraft had no pecuniary interest.

SAMSON v. RIESING, 62 Wis.2d 698, 215 N.W.2d 662 (1974). One of the plaintiffs ate turkey salad at a luncheon put on by an unincorporated association of high school band mothers and became ill from salmonella food poisoning. Plaintiff sued eleven members of the association, nine of whom had cooked one turkey each; all eleven had participated in preparation of the salad. The trial court directed a verdict for defendants.

Held, affirmed. The most that has been proved among the elements of res ipsa loquitur is that, taking all defendants together, it is more probable than not that the negligence of one of them caused plaintiff's injury. But "exclusive control in any one of the defendants or in the defendants, collectively, on a theory of vicarious liability, has not been shown * * * " As for vicarious liability, plaintiff has shown neither that any one of the defendants had control over the work of others (respondeat superior) nor that there was concerted action or a joint venture among them. "While it seems clear that the purpose of the luncheon was to secure funds to support the activities of the band, the venture does not come within the purview of 'a special business arrangement * * * partaking of some essentials of a partnership.' "

RESTATEMENT (SECOND) OF TORTS (1965)

§ 485. Imputed Negligence: General Principle

Except as stated in §§ 486, 491, and 494, a plaintiff is not barred from recovery by the negligent act or omission of a third person.

Comment:

a. The rule stated in this Section rejects, except as indicated by the reference to other Sections, the doctrine of "imputed contributory negligence," under which the plaintiff is barred from recovery against the defendant because the negligence of a third person, with whom the plaintiff stands in some relation, has contributed to his harm. During the latter part of the nineteenth century a good many courts "imputed" the negligence of the third person to the plaintiff in a number of situations, because of theories of a fictitious agency relation, which are now generally recognized as pure fiction, and no longer valid. * * *

§ 486. Master and Servant

A master is barred from recovery against a negligent defendant by the negligence of his servant acting within the scope of his employment.

Comment:

b. The rule stated in this Section applies only to the extent that the master would be barred from recovery if the negligence were his own rather than that of the servant.

WEBER v. STOKELY–VAN CAMP, INC., 274 Minn. 482, 144 N.W.2d 540 (1966). "Essentially, imputation of the [contributory] negligence of a servant to a master rests on a so-called 'both-way test'—that is, if the master is vicariously liable to a third party due to the agent's negligence, he is also barred from recovery because his agent's negligence is imputed to him. * * *

" * * * [F]rom vicarious liability has come the companion rule imputing to the master the negligence of the servant when the master seeks to recover for his own damage and injury, even though the master was not at fault. There is no necessity for creating a solvent defendant in that situation, nor can any of the reasons given for holding a master vicariously liable in a suit by third persons be defended on any rational ground when applied to imputing negligence of a servant to a faultless master who seeks recovery from a third person for his own injury or damage. * * *

"We are convinced the time has come to discard this rule which is defensible only on the grounds of its antiquity. In doing so we realize we may stand alone, but a doctrine so untenable should not be followed so as to bar recovery of one entitled to damages. We limit this decision to automobile negligence cases. There may be other situations where the same result should follow, but we leave those decisions for the future as they come before us. * * * "

———

LASH ET AL. v. CUTTS, 943 F.2d 147 (1st Cir.1991). Five-year-old Caleb Lash was visiting a neighbor's house when he rode his tricycle down the neighbor's steep driveway and into the street, where he was struck by Richard Cutts, who was speeding. "Although the jury determined that all parties were negligent, Cutts successfully established that Mrs. Lash had been negligent in failing to supervise Caleb, that her negligence should be imputed to Caleb, and that the combined negligence of Mrs. Lash and Caleb exceeded the negligence of Cutts, thereby precluding any recovery by Caleb." Plaintiffs contended that Maine had abandoned the doctrine of imputed parental negligence. *Held*, affirmed. The imputation of Mrs. Lash's negligence was proper.

"At common law, the imputation of parental contributory negligence to an injured child was based on the theory that the special parent-child relationship amounted to an agency, requiring reasonable parental control over the actions of the child." Although Maine "did adopt Restatement (Second) of Torts § 316 (1985)* in Merchant v. Mansir, 572 A.2d 493 (Me.1990), by its terms Restatement § 316 applies only to the parent's duty to prevent the child from causing harm to *others*, and not to the parental duty to protect the child from *harm*."

CALIFORNIA CIVIL CODE § 1714.1

Liability of parents and guardians for willful misconduct of minor

(a) Any act of willful misconduct of a minor which results in injury or death to another person or in any injury to the property of another shall be imputed to the parent or guardian having custody and control of the minor for all purposes of civil damages, and the parent or guardian having custody and control shall be jointly and severally liable with the minor for any damages resulting from the willful misconduct.

Subject to the provisions of subdivision (c), the joint and several liability of the parent or guardian having custody and control of a minor under this

---

* When certain conditions are met, this section imposes on parents a duty to exercise reasonable care to prevent their children from creating unreasonable risks of bodily injury to others.—Eds.

subdivision shall not exceed twenty-five thousand dollars ($25,000) for each tort of the minor, and in the case of injury to a person, imputed liability shall be further limited to medical, dental and hospital expenses incurred by the injured person, not to exceed twenty-five thousand dollars ($25,000). The liability imposed by this section is in addition to any liability now imposed by law.

(b) Any act of willful misconduct of a minor which results in the defacement of property of another with paint or a similar substance shall be imputed to the parent or guardian having custody and control of the minor for all purposes of civil damages, including court costs, and attorney's fees, to the prevailing party, and the parent or guardian having custody and control shall be jointly and severally liable with the minor for any damages resulting from the willful misconduct, not to exceed twenty-five thousand dollars ($25,000), except as provided in subdivision (c), for each tort of the minor.

(c) The amounts listed in subdivisions (a) and (b) shall be adjusted every two years by the Judicial Council to reflect any increases in the cost of living in California, as indicated by the annual average of the California Consumer Price Index. The Judicial Council shall round this adjusted amount up or down to the nearest hundred dollars. On or before January 1, 1997, and on or before January 1 of each odd-numbered year thereafter, the Judicial Council shall compute and publish the amounts listed in subdivisions (a) and (b), as adjusted according to this subdivision.

(d) The maximum liability imposed by this section is the maximum liability authorized under this section at the time that the act of willful misconduct by a minor was committed.

(e) Nothing in this section shall impose liability on an insurer for a loss caused by the willful act of the insured for purposes of Section 533 of the Insurance Code. An insurer shall not be liable for the conduct imputed to a parent or guardian by this section for any amount in excess of ten thousand dollars ($10,000).

C. LIABILITY WITHOUT FAULT

Chapter 17

STRICT LIABILITY

This chapter addresses strict liability for harm caused by dangerous activity. It encompasses a number of related liability rules, both traditional and distinctively modern. The title of the chapter is simply "Strict Liability," though in fact the doctrines examined herein make up but one—the second—of four main areas of liability without fault, presented in successive chapters. Still, the title is apt, since all the liabilities discussed in the present chapter are quite strict, whereas the other three areas of strict liability each have an admixture of fault. Vicarious liability, discussed in the prior chapter, usually depends on the fault of someone related to the strictly liable party; nuisance and products liability, up-coming, are fields which include fault-based as well as strict liabilities.

A strict liability for harm caused by accident is one which attaches even though the risk that gives rise to harm is entirely reasonable—even though, in terms of the Hand formula, $B > P \times L$. Assertion of strict liability does not involve any criticism of the primary conduct that created the risk and so caused injury. There's no necessary assertion that the conduct leading up to the harm should be discontinued or changed in any way. Assertion of strict liability does involve criticism of the actor's failure to make reparation after the fact. The persistent policy question is: what's objectionable about defendant's failure to pay for harm done? Put affirmatively, the question is: what aim or objective is served by imposition of liability without fault? These questions come up throughout the chapter, and they come to the fore in Section C, where we pause to consider the general policy commitments of modern strict liability.

SECTION A.   COMMON LAW BACKGROUND

Today's strict liability for harm caused by dangerous activity has roots in very early doctrines of the common law. The main ideas of traditional strict liability, associated with the old writ of trespass, are displayed by two pithy case reports at the start of Chapter 7, *The Case of the Thorns* (1466) and *Weaver* v. *Ward* (1616). Traditional trespassory liability attached when someone's agency, or feasance, directly harmed another; its basic prescription is that the one who acts and causes harm should pay for harm done; in short, one acts at one's peril. Such liability, founded on the doing of an "act," could be avoided by a showing, in the nature of an excuse, that defendant's movements did not amount to a voluntary act, or that the harm should be attributed to the act of another. At the outset of the modern period of American tort law, Augustus Hand invoked traditional conceptions in support of strict or "absolute" liability for injury caused by handling of explosive materials:

> Furthermore, the imposition of absolute liability is not out of accord with any general principles of law. As Professor Holdsworth has said: "The dominant idea of Anglo–Saxon law" was "that man acts at his peril." 2 History of English Law, 52. ... Accordingly the earlier forms of action such as trespass and trespass quare clausum fregit allowed recovery for a direct invasion of person or property without regard to fault. After the later action "sur case" arose, there was a growing tendency to excuse an act causing damage if the defendant was without fault. But, in trespass, fault ordinarily remained a matter of no consequence, and even in cases of damage to the person the early decisions prior to Brown v. Kendall, 6 Cush. 292, 60 Mass. 292, seemed to have imposed liability where there was no negligence. ... Although liability for injury to the person has not in most instances survived except where there has been fault, there still remains absolute liability for trespasses to real estate and for actionable wrongs committed by servants no matter how carefully they are selected by the master. The extent to which one man in the lawful conduct of his business is liable for injuries to another involves an adjustment of conflicting interests. The solution of the problem in each particular case has never been dependent upon any universal criterion of liability (such as "fault") applicable to all situations. If damage is inflicted, there ordinarily is liability, in the absence of excuse.

See *Exner* v. *Sherman Power Construc. Co.* (1931), in Section D, Chapter 1.

In the famous case of *Rylands* v. *Fletcher*, which appears in Chapter 7, Justice Blackburn fashioned a general norm of strict liability which has clear links to traditional doctrines of liability without fault. Blackburn's opinion (1866) builds on old strict liabilities concerning animals, straying cattle and vicious beasts, and also on cases imposing strict liability for trespass and nuisance, seepage of filth from a privy and emission of chlorine fumes from an alkali works. Blackburn's ruling was affirmed by the House of Lords (1868), from which two opinions issued. One of them, Lord Cranworth's, makes evident the connection between the nineteenth century "rule of *Rylands*" and the traditional idea of act-based liability:

> In considering whether a defendant is liable to a plaintiff for damage which the plaintiff may have sustained, the question in general is not whether the defendant has acted with due care and caution, but whether his acts have occasioned the damage. This is all well explained in the old case of Lambert v. Bessey, reported by Sir Thomas Raymond (Sir T. Raym. 421). [The case mentioned contains, verbatim, the report of *The Case of the Thorns* that appears in the casebook's Chapter 7.] And the doctrine is founded on good sense. For when one person, in managing his own affairs, causes, however innocently, damage to another, it is obviously only just that he should be the party to suffer. He is bound sic uti suo ut non loedat alienum.

The Latin expression recited by Cranworth is the traditional maxim of strict liability, usually put in the form "sic utere tuo ut alienum non laedas" (so use your own as not to injure that of another).

The *Rylands* decision, whose roots go back to *The Case of the Thorns*, is in turn a source of inspiration for the modern development of strict tort liability. The present section begins with materials on contemporary liability for harm done by animals, and then shows how "the rule of *Rylands*" has been received over time in American courts.

MARSHALL v. RANNE
Supreme Court of Texas, 1974.
511 S.W.2d 255.

POPE, Justice. Paul Marshall instituted this suit against John C. Ranne seeking damages for injuries he sustained when Ranne's vicious hog attacked him and severely injured his hand. The jury made findings that plaintiff Marshall was contributorily negligent and also that he voluntarily assumed the risk of the hog. The trial court rendered judgment for the defendant on the verdict. The court of civil appeals ruled that the findings of the jury concerning the plaintiff's assumption of the risk supported the judgment and affirmed. 493 S.W.2d 533. We reverse the judgments of the courts below and render judgment for the plaintiff Marshall.

The opinion of the court of civil appeals correctly states these operative facts:

The only witness to the occurrence was plaintiff. He and defendant both lived in Dallas, but they owned neighboring farms in Van Zandt County. Plaintiff's principal occupation was raising hogs. At the time of the injury he had about two hundred on his farm. The hog in question was a boar which had escaped from defendant's farm and had been seen on plaintiff's land during several weeks before the day of the injury. According to plaintiff, defendant's boar had charged him ten to twelve times before this occurrence, had held him prisoner in his outhouse several times, and had attacked his wife on four or five occasions. On the day of the injury plaintiff had hauled in several barrels of old bread in his pickup and had put it out for his hogs at the barn. At that time he saw defendant's boar about a hundred yards behind the barn, but it came no nearer. After feeding his hogs, he went into the house and changed clothes to get ready to go back to Dallas. On emerging from the house, he looked for the boar because, as he testified, he always had to look before he made a move, but he did not see it. He started toward his pickup, and when he was about thirty feet from it, near the outhouse, he heard a noise behind him, turned around and saw the boar charging toward him. He put out his hand defensively, but the boar grabbed it and bit it severely.

Plaintiff testified that the first time the hog had jeopardized his safety was about a week or ten days before he was hurt. He did not shoot the hog because he did not consider that the neighborly thing to do, although he was an expert with a gun and had two available. He made no complaint about the hog to defendant until the day of the injury, when he wrote a note and put it on defendant's gate. The note read:

"John, your boar has gone bad. He is trying to chase me off the farm. He stalks us just like a cat stalks a mouse every time he catches us out of the house. We are going to have to get him out before he hurts someone."

This note did not come to defendant's attention until he came in late that afternoon, and the evidence does not reveal whether he saw it before plaintiff was injured. Plaintiff testified that he and defendant had previously discussed the hog's viciousness on several occasions.

The answers to the special issues were: (1) defendant's boar hog bit the plaintiff's right hand on January 21, 1970, (2) immediately prior to that date, the boar hog had vicious propensities and was likely to cause injury to persons, (3) refused to find that at any time before plaintiff's injury, the defendant actually knew that the defendant's boar hog was vicious and was likely to cause injury to persons, (4) the defendant prior to plaintiff's injury in the exercise of ordinary care should have known that the boar hog was vicious and likely to cause injury to persons, (5) defendant permitted his boar hog to run at large after he knew or should have known that the hog was vicious and likely to cause injury to persons, (6) plaintiff, Paul Marshall, had knowledge of the vicious propensities of the defendant's boar hog and that it was likely to cause injury to persons at and prior to the time the hog bit him, (7) plaintiff, Paul Marshall, with knowledge of the nature of defendant's boar hog voluntarily exposed himself to the risk of attack by the animal, (8) plaintiff's failure to shoot the defendant's boar hog prior to the time the hog bit plaintiff was negligence, (9) which failure was a proximate cause of plaintiff's injuries, (10) plaintiff failed to maintain a fence about his premises sufficiently close to prevent hogs passing through, (11) which was negligence, and (12) a proximate cause of plaintiff's injuries, (13) plaintiff was damaged in the amount of $4,146.00.

The questions presented by this cause are (1) the true nature of an action for damages caused by a vicious animal, (2) whether contributory negligence is a defense to this action, and (3) whether plaintiff Marshall was, as a matter of law, deprived of a voluntary and free choice in confronting the risk.

NATURE OF VICIOUS ANIMAL CASES

A correct classification of this case is important, since that decision also controls the nature of the acceptable defenses to the action. In Texas, actions for damages caused by vicious domestic animals have sometimes been cast as common law negligence cases, at other times as strict liability cases, and sometimes as either. Comment, Personal Injuries by Animals in Texas, 4 Baylor L.Rev. 183 (1952).

* * *

Strict liability has been applied in about an equal number of vicious animal cases.

* * *

We approve the rule expressed in Moore v. McKay, [55 S.W.2d 865 (Tex.Civ.App.1933)], that suits for damages caused by vicious animals should be governed by principles of strict liability, and disapprove the cases which hold the contrary. W. Prosser, Law of Torts § 76 (4th ed. 1971); 2 F. Harper & F. James, the Law of Torts § 14.11 (1956). The correct rule is expressed in Restatement of Torts §§ 507, 509 (1938):

§ 507. Liability of Possessor of Wild Animal

Except as stated in §§ 508 and 517, a possessor of a wild animal is subject to liability to others, except trespassers on his land, for such harm done by the animal to their persons, lands or chattels as results from a dangerous propensity which is characteristic of wild animals of its class or of which the possessor has reason to know, although he has exercised the utmost care to confine the animal or otherwise prevent it from doing harm.

§ 509. Harm Done by Abnormally Dangerous Domestic Animals

Except as stated in § 517, a possessor of a domestic animal which he has reason to know has dangerous propensities abnormal to its class, is subject to liability for harm caused thereby to others, except trespassers on his land, although he has exercised the utmost care to prevent it from doing the harm.

The jury in this case refused to find that the defendant actually knew that the hog was vicious and was likely to cause injury to persons, but it did find in answer to special issue four that the defendant prior to plaintiff's injury should have known that fact. Defendant Ranne does not challenge the finding to issue four.

The Restatement, quoted above, uses the phrase "has reason to know" and the fourth special issue submitted in this case used the phrase "should have known." There is no essential distinction between the two terms * * *.

CONTRIBUTORY NEGLIGENCE IS NO DEFENSE TO STRICT LIABILITY

The trial court over plaintiff's objection, submitted contributory negligence issues and the jury found that plaintiff Marshall was negligent in several particulars. We hold that contributory negligence is not a defense to this action. The court in Copley v. Wills, 152 S.W. 830 (Tex.Civ.App.1913, no writ), confronted this question and rejected contributory negligence as an applicable defense to an action for strict liability for keeping a vicious animal which one knew or had reason to know was vicious. This is also the view expressed in Restatement (Second) of Torts § 515, Comment b (Tent.Draft No. 10, 1964):

> b. Since the strict liability of the possessor of an animal is not founded on his negligence, the ordinary contributory negligence of the plaintiff is not a defense to such an action. The reason is the policy of the law which places the full responsibility for preventing the harm upon the defendant. Thus where the plaintiff merely fails to exercise reasonable care to discover the presence of the animal, or to take precautions against the harm which may result from it, his recovery on the basis of strict liability is not barred.

We conclude that the findings of plaintiff's contributory negligence as contained in the answers to special issues eight through twelve have no place in this case and did not bar the plaintiff from recovery. 2 F. Harper & F. James, The Law of Torts § 14.12, at 843 (1956). We do not hold that negligence and contributory negligence can never be a correct theory in a case which concerns animals. All animals are not vicious and a possessor of a non-vicious animal may be subject to liability for his negligent handling of such an animal. * * *

Did Marshall Voluntarily Assume the Risk?

Plaintiff Marshall does not contend that voluntary assumption of risk is no defense to an action which asserts the defendant's strict liability. He alludes to the truth that it has been abolished as a defense in a number of states in actions grounded upon negligence. Marshall's argument is that he did not, as a matter of law voluntarily expose himself to the risk of the attack by the hog. The jury found that plaintiff Marshall had knowledge of the vicious propensities of the hog and that it was likely to cause injury to persons, and also found that plaintiff, with knowledge of the nature of defendant's boar hog, voluntarily exposed himself to the risk of attack by the animal. We hold that there was no proof that plaintiff had a free and voluntary choice, because he did not have a free choice of alternatives. He had, instead, only a choice of evils, both of which were wrongfully imposed upon him by the defendant. He could remain a prisoner inside his own house or he could take the risk of reaching his car before defendant's hog attacked him. Plaintiff could have remained inside his house, but in doing so, he would have surrendered his legal right to proceed over his own property to his car so he could return to his home in Dallas. The latter alternative was forced upon him against his will and was a choice he was not legally required to accept. W. Prosser, Law of Torts § 68, at 450–453 (4th ed. 1971). We approve and follow the rule expressed in Restatement (Second) of Torts § 496E (1965):

> (1) A plaintiff does not assume a risk of harm unless he voluntarily accepts the risk.

(2) The plaintiff's acceptance of a risk is not voluntary if the defendant's tortious conduct has left him no reasonable alternative course of conduct in order to

(a) avert harm to himself or another, or

(b) exercise or protect a right or privilege of which the defendant has no right to deprive him.

The dilemma which defendant forced upon plaintiff was that of facing the danger or surrendering his rights with respect to his own real property, and that was not, as a matter of law the voluntary choice to which the law entitled him.

We held in Harvey v. Seale, 362 S.W.2d 310, 313 (Tex.1962), that a choice afforded a nine-year-old child to cease playing on a porch that her parents held by lease or to risk stepping in a hole was not a voluntary one. We wrote in that case:

By virtue of her father's lease, she was entitled to be on the front porch of her home without regard to respondent's consent. Respondent was not privileged, therefore, to adopt a "take it or leave it" attitude, and his duty to petitioner was not fully discharged when she learned of the danger. The negligent failure to repair the hole placed her in a position where she was compelled to choose between foregoing her legal right to play on the porch and encountering the risk involved in playing there. If her choice was unreasonable under the circumstances, she was guilty of contributory negligence, but respondent will not be heard to say that she voluntarily exposed herself to the danger, and that he owed her no duty with respect thereto, when she decided to play on the porch.

* * *

Defendant Ranne argues also that the plaintiff Marshall had yet another alternative, that of shooting the hog. The proof showed that Marshall was an expert marksman and had a gun in his house with which he could have killed the hog. Plaintiff Marshall testified that he was reluctant to destroy his neighbor's animal because he did not know how Ranne would react. We do not regard the slaughter of the animal as a reasonable alternative, because plaintiff would have subjected himself arguably to charges under the provision of two criminal statutes.

We accordingly hold that contributory negligence is not a defense in a strict liability action. Voluntary assumption of risk, if established, would be a valid defense. In this case as a matter of law, the proof shows that plaintiff Marshall did not voluntarily encounter the vicious hog. We, therefore, reverse the judgments of the courts below and render judgment that plaintiff recover the sum of $4,146.00, the amount of damages found by the jury.

On Rehearing

Defendant, John C. Ranne, urges in his motion for rehearing that there was neither finding nor evidence that he permitted the hog to run at large after he should have known the animal was vicious. The jury found as a fact that he permitted his hog to run at large after he knew, or should have known that the hog was vicious and likely to cause injury to persons. Ranne himself testified concerning the nature of the animal, "I knew that he had been raised alone and wasn't, you know, a regular yard type animal." According to the plaintiff, Ranne visited him in the hospital and told him, "I knew the bugger was mean." A witness told of Ranne's visit to the hospital after the animal attacked plaintiff. She testified that Ranne then told Marshall, "I knew he was vicious, why didn't you kill him?" We overrule defendant's motion for rehearing.

ANDRADE v. SHIERS, 564 So.2d 787 (La.Ct.App.1990). Plaintiff saw a two-hour-old calf nearing a river bank, and attempted to move the calf away from that danger. The mother cow butted plaintiff, who sues the cow's owners for damages. The trial court said that the "mother cow of a two-hour-old calf would be explosively dangerous." Since plaintiff, who had been "around cattle most of his life," should have known this, and "could have easily and temporarily secured the cow," he was guilty of contributory negligence and barred from recovery. On appeal, *held*, reversed. Liability of the cow's owners is strict. "The injured person need not prove the 'negligence' of the owner." Plaintiff's conduct was unreasonable, but after the advent of comparative negligence, victim fault does not totally bar recovery. "The victim's fault or conduct that substantially causes in fact the injury" must be "compared and weighed" against the responsibility "that is legally imposed on the owner of the animal." The appellate court concluded that "responsibility for plaintiff's injury" should be allocated 80% to plaintiff and 20% to the owners. "[R]ecovery of damages by plaintiff on remand shall be reduced by his 80 percent fault."

GALLICK v. BARTO, 828 F.Supp. 1168 (M.D.Pa.1993). Plaintiff, an infant, was brought along by her parents when they made a social visit at the home of two of the defendants. There plaintiff was bitten by these defendants' pet ferret. The issue was whether a ferret is a "wild animal." *Held*, under Pennsylvania law, for plaintiff. The doctrine of strict liability has, in Pennsylvania, "long been applied to the keeping of wild animals." Granted a pet ferret is different from "a tiger or a venomous reptile," still a ferret is an animal "which has traditionally been kept for the purpose of hunting rabbits and rats." Just as a pit bull may be considered "a domestic animal with dangerous propensities," a ferret "is a wild animal with domestic propensities. However, those propensities do not change its essential character as a wild animal."

WORMALD v. COLE, [1954] 1 All E.R. 683 (C.A.). Defendant's well-behaved cattle escaped without negligence of defendant, and entered plaintiff's grounds. While plaintiff, without doing anything to frighten them, was trying in the dark to prevent their getting into her garden, one of the cattle, apparently moved by natural instincts to rejoin the others, and being clumsy in the dark, knocked plaintiff down and injured her. *Held*, for plaintiff.

Originally liability without negligence for cattle trespass was limited to crop damage and the like, when the trespassing animal was not known to be vicious. But liability has been extended to injury done by trespassing cattle to a plaintiff's own animals. Since one can recover for injury to his own animals, he should also be allowed recovery for injuries to himself naturally resulting from the trespass. Cases of injury to persons by cattle on the highway, where negligence has been required for liability, are distinguishable as not involving cattle trespass since those injured did not own the soil in the highway.

FLETCHER v. RYLANDS
Exchèquer Chamber, 1866. L.R. 1 Exch. 265.

RYLANDS v. FLETCHER
House of Lords, 1868. L.R. 3 H.L. 330.

[See p. 294, supra]

EKSTROM v. DEAGON, [1946] 1 D.L.R. 208 (S.Ct.Alberta). Action for damages. Defendant Montgomery was driving a truck that stopped. He had it towed to the front of plaintiff's garage where, apparently with plaintiff's acquiescence but without his help, he looked for the cause of the trouble, getting permission to use a "trouble light", an electric bulb on the end of a cord. He came to the conclusion that there was dirt in the fuel tank. He was draining this, without plaintiff's knowledge, when the gasoline fumes ignited. The resulting fire destroyed the garage. *Held*, judgment for plaintiff, under the principle of Rylands v. Fletcher. "Now it seems to me this: If a person brings on his own land a dangerous substance which escapes and injury results to another and for which he thus becomes liable, then much more so would a person who takes a dangerous article on another person's property and causes damage to the latter be liable."

BRENNAN CONSTRUCTION CO. v. CUMBERLAND, 29 App.D.C. 554 (1907). The defendant stored liquid asphalt in tanks on a hillside bordering on the Potomac River. Some asphalt escaped, flowed down the hillside to the river and was carried by the water to an inlet where it settled and injured the plaintiff's boats anchored there. *Held*, for plaintiff. The case falls within the rule of Fletcher v. Rylands. "[A] person who places some potentially dangerous substance upon his property—something which if permitted to escape is certain to injure others—must make good the damages occasioned by the escape of such substance, regardless of the question of negligence."

SHIPLEY v. FIFTY ASSOCIATES
Supreme Judicial Court of Massachusetts, 1870.
106 Mass. 194.

[Plaintiff was injured by a sudden fall of ice and snow from the peaked roof of defendants' building onto the sidewalk where she was walking. After a trial conducted by the chief justice plaintiff was awarded her damages, and the case was reported for determination by the full court.]

AMES, J. * * * [Defendants contend] that the damage to the plaintiff was the result of an inevitable accident; that travellers in the streets in cities, in this climate, take the risk of such accidents upon themselves, as they do the danger of injury from runaway horses, or from the slippery or crowded condition of the streets; and that the defendants cannot be said to be to blame, or to be responsible, unless it can be shown that their building was of an unusual or improper construction, or that they neglected to take proper precautions in its care and management. In other words, they claim the right to erect or maintain a building, provided it be of no unusual construction, so near to the street, and of such a shape and character that snow and ice collected upon the roof must inevitably and in the natural course of things be liable to slide down and fall upon the sidewalk, thereby exposing foot-passengers to the risk of great bodily injury. Does the law give them any such right? * * *

The plaintiff, at the time of the accident, was where she had a right to be, and was not guilty of any want of due and reasonable care. For the purpose for which she was using the sidewalk, her rights were exactly the same as if she owned the soil in fee simple. The case in our judgment depends on the same rules, and is to be decided on the same principles, as if it raised a question between adjoining proprietors * * *. In contemplation of law, the person is at least as much entitled to protection as the estate. The right to discharge snow and ice from one's own house upon the person of the next door neighbor is certainly no better or stronger than the right to subject that neighbor's building or land to the same kind of inconvenience. Shipley v. Fifty Associates, 101 Mass. 251. It is well settled that, although every landowner has a right to use his own land for any lawful purpose for which in the natural course of enjoyment it can be used, yet he cannot use his neighbor's land, except upon proof of express grant or permission, or prescription which furnishes a presumption of a grant. * * * [In] Fletcher v. Rylands, Law Rep. 1 Ex. 265, Mr. Justice Blackburn, in giving the judgment which was afterwards affirmed in the house of lords, expresses himself substantially thus: Whoever for his own purposes brings on his land, and collects and keeps there any thing likely to do mischief if it escapes, must keep it in at his peril. He illustrates this proposition by putting various cases in which a party is damnified without any fault of his own * * *.

* * * It is well settled * * * that no man has a right so to construct his roof as to discharge upon his neighbor's land water which would not naturally fall there. Washburn on Easements, 890. In such a case, the maxim *Sic utere tuo ut alienum non laedas* [use your own property in such a manner as not to injure that of another] would be applicable. It is not at all a question of reasonable care and diligence * * *. He must at his peril keep the ice or the snow that collects upon his own roof, within his own limits; and is responsible for all damages, if the shape of his roof is such as to throw them upon his neighbor's land, in the same manner as he would be if he threw them there himself. He has no right to appropriate his neighbor's land in that manner for his own convenience, as a place into which he may pour the accumulated snow from his own premises.

It appears to us, therefore, that the defendants have no right to erect or maintain a building so near to the street, and with a roof of such a construction, that, notwithstanding all the care that can be taken, passengers upon the sidewalk shall be subjected to the kind of injury complained of in this case. This would be an appropriation of the sidewalk, or an application of it to their own convenience, at the risk of the traveller and without regard to public right, which they cannot lawfully make. No man would claim for them the right to collect in one stream the rain that falls upon their roof and pour it by means of a spout upon the street below. They have no better right to collect and retain the snow till it falls by its own weight. In either case, it would be an attempt to extend their right as proprietors, beyond the limits of their own property, and to secure an advantage that does not belong to them, at the expense of their neighbor, or of the traveller, whose rights for this special purpose are as complete as those of an adjoining proprietor.

* * *

Judgment for the plaintiff upon the verdict.

———

AINSWORTH v. LAKIN, 180 Mass. 397, 62 N.E. 746 (1902). Liability for injury from collapse of walls or buildings is fault-based, not strict. " 'As it is desirable that buildings and fences should be put up, the law of this commonwealth does not throw the risk of that act, any more than of other necessary conduct, upon the actor' " (quoting Justice Holmes). The rule of Rylands v. Fletcher is reserved for "unwarrantable and extremely dangerous uses of property" that are "fraught with peril to others," as opposed to risks "which are ordinary and usual, and, in a sense, natural, as incident to the ownership of the land." "This rule is rightly applicable only to such unusual and extraordinary uses of property in reference to the benefits to be derived from the use and the dangers or losses to which others are exposed as should not be permitted except at the sole risk of the user."

TOY v. ATLANTIC GULF & PACIFIC CO., 176 Md. 197, 4 A.2d 757 (1939). "If carried to its logical consequences, the rule [of Rylands v. Fletcher] would impose grievous burdens as incident to the ownership of land, and, therefore, the courts have strictly limited the application of the rule."

STATE, DEPARTMENT OF ENVIRONMENTAL PROTECTION v. VENTRON CORP., 94 N.J. 473, 468 A.2d 150 (1983). Defendants are four corporations successively responsible for operating a mercury processing plant on a forty-acre tract. For years the plant dumped untreated waste material containing mercury on the site. The waste seeped into a creek, causing mercury pollution of a tidal estuary. The New Jersey Department of Environmental Protection sued to recover costs required by its cleanup plan. Lower courts imposed strict liability for "unleashing a dangerous substance during non-natural use of the land," relying on "the early English decision of *Rylands v. Fletcher*, L.R. 1 Ex. 265 (1866), aff'd, L.R. 3 H.L. 330 (1868)." *Held*, affirmed.

The New Jersey Supreme Court (Pollack, J.) said that it had, in 1876, become "one of the first courts to reject the doctrine of *Rylands v. Fletcher*." Its decision in Marshall v. Welwood, 38 N.J.L. 339 (Sup.Ct.1876), "refused to adopt *Rylands*." But a decision of 1962, "without referring to either" Rylands or Marshall, imposed strict liability on landowners because of considerations of "fairness and morality." Berg v. Reaction Motors Divison, 37 N.J. 396, 405, 181 A.2d 487, 492 (1962) (see p. 904 infra). "More recently, the *Restatement (Second) of Torts*" formulated a standard of strict liability which "incorporates the theory developed in *Rylands v. Fletcher*." "We believe it is time to recognize expressly that the law of liability has evolved so that a landowner is strictly liable to others for harm caused by toxic wastes that are stored on his property and flow onto the property of others. Therefore, we overrule *Marshall v. Welwood* and adopt the principle of liability originally declared in *Rylands v. Fletcher*."

"Pollution from toxic wastes that seeps onto the land of others and into streams necessarily harms the environment. * * * [D]isposal of toxic waste may cause a variety of harms, including ground water contamination via leachate, surface water contamination via runoff or overflow, and poison via the food chain. * * * [W]e conclude that mercury and other toxic wastes are 'abnormally dangerous,' and the disposal of them, past or present, is an abnormally dangerous activity. * * * Even if they did not intend to pollute or adhered to the standards of the time, all of these parties remain liable. Those who poison the land must pay for its cure."

SPLENDORIO v. BILRAY DEMOLITION CO., 682 A.2d 461 (R.I.1996). Here the Rhode Island Supreme Court approved "absolute liability for ultrahazardous or abnormally dangerous activities," and in doing so, expressly overruled its prior decision in Rose v. Socony–Vacuum Corp. (1934), which had rejected "absolute liability as espoused in Rylands v. Fletcher." "Although the theory was originally developed in *Rylands*, courts now use the same terms as the Restatements when discussing the absolute liability theory." In rejecting *Rylands*, the opinion in Rose v. Socony–Vacuum Corp. had said: "If, in the process of refining petroleum, injury is occasioned to those in the vicinity, not through negligence * * * such injury is damnum absque injuria."

"We believe that *Rose* has succumbed to 'the inaudible and noiseless foot of Time.' " (Citation to William Shakespeare, All's Well That Ends Well.) "As Justice Holmes observed * * *, 'precedents should be overruled when they become inconsistent with present conditions.' *Rose* is today inconsistent with present conditions."

SECTION B.   ABNORMALLY DANGEROUS ACTIVITY

This section explores modern strict liability for harm caused by dangerous activity. Doctrine in this area is crystallized by Sections 519 and 520 of the Second Restatement of Torts. The Restatement scheme of 1977 is hardly followed slavishly in the courts, but it serves as a point of reference for more recent case materials that follow. The Second Restatement supplies a list of factors which, when present, count in favor of strict liability. The three main cases below discuss these factors together with associated policies pro and con.

Many of the decisions in this chapter imposing strict liability have to do with two broad categories of activity: handling of explosive or flammable agencies (blasting, storing explosives, hauling gasoline), and handling of poisonous or toxic materials (fumigating, crop dusting, disposal of hazardous waste). Situations involving "explosives and poisons" are indeed core examples of abnormally dangerous activity, but they do not exhaust the category. Strict liability is imposed as well in cases involving other sorts of hazards. Moreover, even when a very hazardous substance—"explosive" or "poison"—is involved in a case, it remains a question whether defendant's activity with respect to the substance is suitable for strict liability. Strict liability attaches to activities, not substances, as the materials of the present section show.

A noteworthy point about terminology is made by the second main case below. The legal category "abnormally dangerous activity," at the center of the present section, applies in situations where no fault on the part of anyone is shown. This category is not the same as—is not coextensive with—the category "inherently dangerous activity," which figures in the doctrine of vicarious liability addressed in the prior chapter.

EXNER v. SHERMAN POWER CONSTRUCTION CO.
United States Court of Appeals, Second Circuit, 1931.
54 F.2d 510, 80 A.L.R. 686.

[See p. 20, supra]

RESTATEMENT OF TORTS, FIRST (1938)

§ 519.   Miscarriage of Ultrahazardous Activities Carefully Carried on

* * * [O]ne who carries on an ultrahazardous activity is liable to another whose person, land or chattels the actor should recognize as likely to be harmed by the unpreventable miscarriage of the activity for harm resulting thereto from that which makes the activity ultrahazardous, although the utmost care is exercised to prevent the harm.

§ 520.   Definition of Ultrahazardous Activity

An activity is ultrahazardous if it

(a) necessarily involves a risk of serious harm to the person, land or chattels of others which cannot be eliminated by the exercise of the utmost care, and

(b) is not a matter of common usage.

———

GREEN v. GENERAL PETROLEUM CORP., 205 Cal. 328, 270 P. 952 (1928). Plaintiffs' property was covered with "oil, sand, mud, and rocks" as a result of the "blowing out" of an oil well during prudently conducted drilling operations by defendant. In affirming a judgment against the oil company, the California Supreme Court said:

" * * * The present case * * * presents a situation to which the doctrine of 'sic utere tuo ut alienum non laedas' may be applied in its broad and fundamental import. That ancient maxim of jurisprudence is incorporated, in substance, in the statutory law of this state. The Civil Code provides (section 3514): 'One must so use his own rights as not to infringe upon the rights of another.'

"Where one, in the conduct and maintenance of an enterprise lawful and proper in itself, deliberately does an act under known conditions, and, with knowledge that injury may result to another, proceeds, and injury is done to the other as the direct and proximate consequence of the act, however carefully done, the one who does the act and causes the injury should, in all fairness, be required to compensate the other for the damage done. * * *

" * * * In our judgment, no other legal construction can be placed upon the operations of the appellant in this case than that, by its deliberate act of boring its well, it undertook the burden and responsibility of controlling and confining whatever force or power it uncovered. Any other construction would permit one owner, under like circumstances, to use the land of another for his own purpose and benefit, without making compensation for such use. We do not conceive that to be the law."

AIRCRAFT GROUND DAMAGE. The Uniform Aeronautics Act, approved by the Conference of Commissioners on Uniform State Laws in 1922, and adopted in substance by a number of states, provided (§ 5) for strict liability of the owner or lessee of an airplane for damages caused by its fall, but for liability of the operator only if negligent. Section 520A of the Second Restatement of Torts (1977) provides that both the aircraft owner and the operator are strictly liable for ground damage "caused by the ascent, descent or flight of aircraft, or by the dropping or falling of an object from the aircraft."

ADLER'S QUALITY BAKERY, INC. v. GASETERIA, INC., 32 N.J. 55, 159 A.2d 97 (1960). Actions arising out of collision of an airplane with a television tower, debris causing damage to properties and incidental pecuniary losses to several persons in the area. Defendant Gaseteria was the owner of the plane. A statute provided that the owner of every aircraft operating in the state "is absolutely liable for injuries to persons or property on the land or water beneath, * * * unless the injury is caused in whole or in part by the negligence of the person injured, or of the owner or bailee of the property injured." *Held*, summary judgment for plaintiff on the issue of liability sustained. But the statute does not preclude Gaseteria's claims for contribution or indemnity from RKO, which was in control of the television tower with which the plane collided.

CROSBY v. COX AIRCRAFT CO., 109 Wash.2d 581, 746 P.2d 1198 (1987). Defendants' airplane crash-landed onto plaintiff's property. *Held* (5–4), against strict liability. According to the majority opinion, "The number of states imposing strict liability [for aircraft ground damage] has diminished significantly. At present, only six states retain the rule * * *." "The defendants urge us to reject Restatement § 520A. They contend that aviation can no longer be designated an 'abnormally dangerous activity' requiring special rules of liability. We agree." A strong dissent rejected the majority's approach: "Compelling, persuasive policy reasons exist to impose such strict liability. Those reasons should be explored and evaluated rather than simply accepting the pigeonhole conclusion that aviation is not abnormally dangerous as defined by the black letter rule * * *."

RESTATEMENT OF TORTS, SECOND (1977)

§ 519. General Principle

(1) One who carries on an abnormally dangerous activity is subject to liability for harm to the person, land or chattels of another resulting from the activity, although he has exercised the utmost care to prevent the harm.

(2) This strict liability is limited to the kind of harm, the possibility of which makes the activity abnormally dangerous.

Comment:

* * *

* * * The liability * * * is founded upon a policy of the law that imposes upon anyone who for his own purposes creates an abnormal risk of harm to his neighbors, the responsibility of relieving against that harm when it does in fact occur. The defendant's enterprise, in other words, is required to pay its way by compensating for the harm it causes, because of its special, abnormal and dangerous character.

* * *

§ 520. Abnormally Dangerous Activities

In determining whether an activity is abnormally dangerous, the following factors are to be considered:

(a) existence of a high degree of risk of some harm to the person, land or chattels of others;

(b) likelihood that the harm that results from it will be great;

(c) inability to eliminate the risk by the exercise of reasonable care;

(d) extent to which the activity is not a matter of common usage;

(e) inappropriateness of the activity to the place where it is carried on; and

(f) extent to which its value to the community is outweighed by its dangerous attributes.

Comment:

* * *

f. *"Abnormally Dangerous."* * * * The essential question is whether the risk created is so unusual, either because of its magnitude or because of the circumstances surrounding it, as to justify the imposition of strict liability for the harm that results from it, even though it is carried on with all reasonable care. * * *

Comment on Clauses (a) and (b):

g. Risk of Harm. An activity that is abnormally dangerous ordinarily involves a high degree of risk of serious harm to the person, land or chattels of others. * * * If the potential harm is sufficiently great, however, as in the case of a nuclear explosion, the likelihood that it will take place may be comparatively slight and yet the activity be regarded as abnormally dangerous.

                              * * *

Comment on Clause (c):

h. Risk Not Eliminated by Reasonable Care. * * *

* * * What is referred to here is the unavoidable risk remaining in the activity, even though the actor has taken all reasonable precautions * * *. The utility of his conduct may be such that he is socially justified in proceeding with his activity, but the unavoidable risk of harm that is inherent in it requires that it be carried on at his peril, rather than at the expense of the innocent person who suffers harm as a result of it. * * *

                              * * *

Comment on Clause (d):

i. Common Usage. An activity is a matter of common usage if it is customarily carried on by the great mass of mankind or by many people in the community. It does not cease to be so because it is carried on for a purpose peculiar to the individual who engages in it. Certain activities, notwithstanding their recognizable danger, are so generally carried on as to be regarded as customary. Thus automobiles have come into such general use that their operation is a matter of common usage. This, notwithstanding the residue of unavoidable risk of serious harm that may result even from their careful operation, is sufficient to prevent their use from being regarded as an abnormally dangerous activity. * * *

Although blasting is recognized as a proper means of excavation for building purposes or of clearing woodland for cultivation, it is not carried on by any large percentage of the population, and therefore it is not a matter of common usage. Likewise the manufacture, storage, transportation and use of high explosives, although necessary to the construction of many public and private works, are carried on by only a comparatively small number of persons and therefore are not matters of common usage. * * *

The usual dangers resulting from an activity that is one of common usage are not regarded as abnormal, even though a serious risk of harm cannot be eliminated by all reasonable care. * * * Water collected in large quantity in a hillside reservoir in the midst of a city or in coal mining country is not the activity of any considerable portion of the population, and may therefore be regarded as abnormally dangerous; while water in a cistern or in household pipes or in a barnyard tank supplying cattle, although it may involve much the same danger of escape, differing only in degree if at all, still is a matter of common usage and therefore not abnormal. The same is true of gas and electricity in household pipes and wires, as contrasted with large gas storage tanks or high tension power lines. Fire in a fireplace or in an ordinary railway engine is a matter of common usage, while a traction engine shooting out sparks in its passage along the public highway is an abnormal danger.

Comment on Clause (e):

j. Locality. Another factor to be taken into account in determining whether an activity is abnormally dangerous is the place where it is carried on. If the place is one inappropriate to the particular activity, and other factors are present, the danger created may be regarded as an abnormal one.

* * *

Comment on Clause (f):

k. Value to the Community. Even though the activity involves a serious risk of harm that cannot be eliminated with reasonable care and it is not a matter of common usage, its value to the community may be such that the danger will not be regarded as an abnormal one. This is true particularly when the community is largely devoted to the dangerous enterprise and its prosperity largely depends upon it. Thus the interests of a particular town whose livelihood depends upon such an activity as manufacturing cement may be such that cement plants will be regarded as a normal activity for that community notwithstanding the risk of serious harm from the emission of cement dust. There is an analogy here to the consideration of the same elements in determining the existence of a nuisance * * *.

Thus in Texas and Oklahoma, a properly conducted oil or gas well, at least in a rural area, is not regarded as abnormally dangerous, while a different conclusion has been reached in Kansas and Indiana. California, whose oil industry is far from insignificant, has concluded that an oil well drilled in a thickly settled residential area in the city of Los Angeles is a matter of strict liability.

* * *

———

KOOS v. ROTH, 293 Or. 670, 652 P.2d 1255 (1982). Linde, J.: " * * * [T]he value of a hazardous activity does not preclude strict liability for its consequences * * *. In an action for damages, the question is not whether the activity threatens such harm that it should not be continued. The question is who shall pay for harm that has been done."

BENNETT v. MALLINCKRODT, INC., 698 S.W.2d 854 (Mo.App.1985). Plaintiffs allege harm from radioactive emissions caused by defendant's radiopharmaceutical processing plant. *Held*, that "strict liability, as defined by the Restatement (Second) of Torts, should be adopted and applied to claims based on radiation damage." The "potential danger" of the nuclear industry is "enormous."

T & E INDUSTRIES, INC. v. SAFETY LIGHT CORP., 123 N.J. 371, 587 A.2d 1249 (1991). Defendant is a corporation legally responsible for the activities, years ago, of a plant which processed radium on an industrial site. The plant extracted radium from ore and discarded solid waste, radium "tailings," on the property. This went on from 1917 to 1926, when radium processing ceased. In 1943 the property was sold, and then changed hands several times. In 1974 plaintiff, "unaware of the presence" of the tailings, bought the property. Subsequently environmental authorities established that the discarded tailings posed "significant potential threats to human health," and required remedial action at the radium-contaminated site. Plaintiff sued defendant to recover cleanup costs and related damages. *Held*, for plaintiff. The New Jersey Supreme Court said that "despite the usefulness of radium," radium processing is "an abnormally-dangerous activity."

Defendant had invoked "the principle of caveat emptor" which says that, in the absence of express agreement, a seller is not liable to a buyer for the condition of land existing at the time of transfer. The court responded: "As between an unsuspecting purchaser and a seller who has engaged in an abnormally-dangerous activity and polluted the property, the polluter should bear the cleanup expense." Strict liability will " 'internalize' the external costs" of dangerous activity. This serves "the underlying policy of the abnormally-dangerous-activity doctrine: certain enterprises should bear the costs attributable to their activities."

Defendant also had argued that it should not be held strictly liable because it did not know "at the time of performance that its activity was in fact abnormally dangerous." The court noted that the scientific community "was not aware of the problems generated by radioactive tailings until the late 1960's," but rejected defendant's argument. It said "requirements such as 'knowledge' and 'foreseeability' smack of negligence and may be inappropriate in the realm of strict liability." Moreover, while defendant may not have known "the precise dangers associated with the disposal of the tailings," it knew it was dealing with a substance "fraught with hazardous potential" and so, "[i]f knowledge be a requirement, defendant knew enough."

SIEGLER v. KUHLMAN
Supreme Court of Washington, 1972.
81 Wn.2d 448, 502 P.2d 1181.

HALE, Associate Justice. Seventeen-year-old Carol J. House died in the flames of a gasoline explosion when her car encountered a pool of thousands of gallons of spilled gasoline. She was driving home from her after-school job in the early evening of November 22, 1967, along Capitol Lake Drive in Olympia; it was dark but dry; her car's headlamps were burning. There was a slight impact with some object, a muffled explosion, and then searing flames from gasoline pouring out of an overturned trailer tank engulfed her car. The result of the explosion is clear, but the real causes of what happened will remain something of an eternal mystery.

Aaron L. Kuhlman had been a truck driver for nearly 11 years after he completed the tenth grade in high school and after he had worked at other jobs for a few years. He had been driving for Pacific Intermountain Express for about 4 months, usually the night shift out of the Texaco bulk plant in Tumwater. That evening of November 22nd, he was scheduled to drive a gasoline truck and trailer unit, fully loaded with gasoline, from Tumwater to Port Angeles. Before leaving the Texaco plant, he inspected the trailer, checking the lights, hitch, air hoses and tires. Finding nothing wrong, he then set out, driving the fully loaded truck tank and trailer tank, stopping briefly at the Trail's End Cafe for a cup of coffee. It was just a few minutes after 6 p.m., and dark, but the roads were dry when he started the drive to deliver his cargo—3,800 gallons of gasoline in the truck tank and 4,800 gallons of gasoline in the trailer tank. With all vehicle and trailer running lights on, he drove the truck and trailer onto Interstate Highway 5, proceeded north on that freeway at about 50 miles per hour, he said, and took the offramp about 1 mile later to enter Highway 101 at the Capitol Lake interchange. Running downgrade on the offramp, he felt a jerk, looked into his left-hand mirror and then his right-hand mirror to see that the trailer lights were not in place. The trailer was still moving but leaning over hard, he observed, onto its right side. The trailer then came loose. Realizing that the tank trailer had disengaged from his tank truck, he stopped the truck without skidding its tires. He got out and ran back to see that the tank trailer had crashed through a chain-link highway fence and had come to rest upside down on Capitol Lake Drive below. He heard a sound, he said, "like somebody kicking an empty fifty-gallon drum and that is when the fire started." The fire spread, he thought, about 100 feet down the road.

The trailer was owned by defendant Pacific Intermountain Express. It had traveled about 329,000 miles prior to November 22, 1967, and had been driven by Mr. Kuhlman without incident down the particular underpass above Capitol Lake Drive about 50 times. When the trailer landed upside down on Capitol Lake Drive, its lights were out, and it was unilluminated when Carol House's car in one way or another ignited the spilled gasoline.

Carol House was burned to death in the flames. There was no evidence of impact on the vehicle she had driven, Kuhlman said, except that the left front headlight was broken.

Why the tank trailer disengaged and catapulted off the freeway down through a chain-link fence to land upside down on Capitol Lake Drive below remains a mystery. What caused it to separate from the truck towing it, despite many theories offered in explanation, is still an enigma. Various theories as to the facts and cause were advanced in the trial. Plaintiff sought to prove both negligence on the part of the driver and owner of the vehicle and to bring the proven circumstances within the res ipsa loquitur doctrine. Defendants sought to obviate all inferences of negligence and the circumstances leading to the application of res ipsa loquitur by showing due care in inspection, maintenance and operation. Plaintiff argued negligence per se and requested a directed verdict on liability. On appeal, plaintiff relied in part on RCW 46.44.070 and RCW 46.61.655,[1] relating to the drawbar connecting trailer to truck, and provisions prohibiting a load from dropping, shifting, leaking or escaping from the vehicle.

The jury apparently found that defendants had met and overcome the charges of negligence. * * * From a judgment entered upon a verdict for defendants, plaintiff appealed to the Court of Appeals which affirmed. We granted review, and reverse.

In the Court of Appeals, the principal claim of error was directed to the trial court's refusal to give an instruction on res ipsa loquitur, and we think that claim of error well taken. Our reasons for ruling that an instruction on res ipsa loquitur should have been given and that an inference of negligence could have been drawn from the event are found, we believe, in our statement on the subject: ZeBarth v. Swedish Hosp. Medical Center, 81 Wash.2d 12, 499 P.2d 1 (1972); Miles v. St. Regis Paper Co., 77 Wash.2d 828, 467 P.2d 307 (1970); Douglas v. Bussabarger, 73 Wash.2d 476, 438 P.2d 829 (1968); Pederson v. Dumouchel, 72 Wash.2d 73, 431 P.2d 973 (1967). We think, therefore, that plaintiff was entitled to an instruction permitting the jury to infer negligence from the occurrence.

But there exists here an even more impelling basis for liability in this case than its derivation by allowable inference of fact under the res ipsa loquitur doctrine, and that is the proposition of strict liability arising as a matter of law from all of the circumstances of the event.

Strict liability is not a novel concept; it is at least as old as Fletcher v. Rylands, L.R. 1 Ex. 265, 278 (1866), affirmed, House of Lords, 3 H.L. 330 (1868). In that famous case, where water impounded in a reservoir on defendant's property escaped and damaged neighboring coal mines, the landowner who had impounded the water was held liable without proof of fault or negligence. Acknowledging a distinction between the natural and nonnatural use of land, and holding the maintenance of a reservoir to be a nonnatural use, the Court of Exchequer Chamber imposed a rule of strict liability on the landowner. The ratio decidendi included adoption of what is now called *strict liability,* and at page 278 announced, we think, principles which should be applied in the instant case:

> [T]he person who for his own purposes brings on his lands and collects and keeps there anything likely to do mischief if it escapes, must keep it in at his peril, and, if he does not do so, is prima facie answerable for all the damage which is the natural consequence of its escape.

---

1. RCW 46.44.070 reads in part as follows:

"The drawbar or other *connection* between vehicles in combination *shall be of sufficient strength,* to hold the weight of the towed vehicle on any grade where operated. *No trailer shall* whip, weave or oscillate or *fail to follow substantially in the course* of the towing vehicle." (Italics ours.)

RCW 46.61.655 reads in part as follows:

"*No vehicle shall be driven or moved on any public highway unless* such vehicle is so *constructed or loaded as to prevent any of its load from* dropping, sifting, leaking or otherwise *escaping therefrom,* except that sand may be dropped for the purpose of securing traction, or water or other substance may be sprinkled on a roadway in the cleaning or maintaining of such roadway by public authority having jurisdiction." (Italics ours.)

All of the Justices in Fletcher v. Rylands, supra, did not draw a distinction between the natural and nonnatural use of land, but such a distinction would, we think, be irrelevant to the transportation of gasoline. The basic principles supporting the *Fletcher* doctrine, we think, control the transportation of gasoline as freight along the public highways the same as it does the impounding of waters and for largely the same reasons. *See* Prosser, Torts, § 78 (4th ed. 1971).

In many respects, hauling gasoline as freight is no more unusual, but more dangerous, than collecting water. When gasoline is carried as cargo— as distinguished from fuel for the carrier vehicle—it takes on uniquely hazardous characteristics, as does water impounded in large quantities. Dangerous in itself, gasoline develops even greater potential for harm when carried as freight—extraordinary dangers deriving from sheer quantity, bulk and weight, which enormously multiply its hazardous properties. And the very hazards inhering from the size of the load, its bulk or quantity and its movement along the highways presents another reason for application of the Fletcher v. Rylands, supra, rule not present in the impounding of large quantities of water—the likely destruction of cogent evidence from which negligence or want of it may be proved or disproved. It is quite probable that the most important ingredients of proof will be lost in a gasoline explosion and fire. Gasoline is always dangerous whether kept in large or small quantities because of its volatility, inflammability and explosiveness. But when several thousand gallons of it are allowed to spill across a public highway—that is, if, while in transit as freight, it is not kept impounded—the hazards to third persons are so great as to be almost beyond calculation. * * *

That this is a sound case for the imposition of a rule of strict liability finds strong support in Professor Cornelius J. Peck's analysis in Negligence and Liability Without Fault in Tort Law, 46 Wash.L.Rev. 225 (1971). Pointing out that strict liability was imposed at common law prior to Fletcher v. Rylands supra, that study shows the application of a rule of strict liability in a number of instances, i.e., for harm done by trespassing animals; on a bona fide purchaser of stolen goods to their true owner; on a bailee for the misdelivery of bailed property regardless of his good faith or negligence; and on innkeepers and hotels at common law. But there are other examples of strict liability: The Supreme Court of Minnesota, for example, imposed liability without fault for damage to a dock inflicted by a ship moored there during a storm. Vincent v. Lake Erie Transp. Co., 109 Minn. 456, 124 N.W. 221 (1910).

The rule of strict liability rests not only upon the ultimate idea of rectifying a wrong and putting the burden where it should belong as a matter of abstract justice, that is, upon the one of the two innocent parties whose acts instigated or made the harm possible, but it also rests on problems of proof:

> * * * [T]he disasters caused by those who engage in abnormally dangerous or extra-hazardous activities frequently destroy all evidence of what in fact occurred, other than that the activity was being carried

on. Certainly this is true with explosions of dynamite, large quantities of gasoline, or other explosives. It frequently is the case with falling aircraft. Tracing the course followed by gases or other poisons used by exterminators may be difficult if not impossible. The explosion of an atomic reactor may leave little evidence of the circumstances which caused it. * * *

C. Peck, Negligence and Liability Without Fault in Tort Law, 46 Wash.L.Rev. 225, 240 (1971).

See, also, G. P. Fletcher, Fairness and Utility in Tort Theory, 85 Harv.L.Rev. 537 (1972), for an analysis of the judicial philosophy relating to tort liability as affecting or affected by concepts of fault and negligence; and Comment, Liability Without Fault: Logic and Potential of a Developing Concept, 1970 Wis.L.Rev. 1201.

Thus, the reasons for applying a rule of strict liability obtain in this case. We have a situation where a highly flammable, volatile and explosive substance is being carried at a comparatively high rate of speed, in great and dangerous quantities as cargo upon the public highways, subject to all of the hazards of high-speed traffic, multiplied by the great dangers inherent in the volatile and explosive nature of the substance, and multiplied again by the quantity and size of the load. Then we have the added dangers of ignition and explosion generated when a load of this size, that is, about 5,000 gallons of gasoline, breaks its container and, cascading from it, spreads over the highway so as to release an invisible but highly volatile and explosive vapor above it. * * *

Stored in commercial quantities, gasoline has been recognized to be a substance of such dangerous characteristics that it invites a rule of strict liability—even where the hazard is contamination to underground water supply and not its more dangerous properties such as its explosiveness and flammability. See, Yommer v. McKenzie, 255 Md. 220, 257 A.2d 138 (1969). It is even more appropriate, therefore, to apply this principle to the more highly hazardous act of transporting it as freight upon the freeways and public thoroughfares.

Recently this court, while declining to apply strict liability in a particular case, did acknowledge the suitability of the rule in a proper case. In Pacific Northwest Bell Tel. Co. v. Port of Seattle, 80 Wash.2d 59, 491 P.2d 1037 (1971), we observed that strict liability had its beginning in Fletcher v. Rylands, supra, but said that it ought not be applied in a situation where a bursting water main, installed and maintained by the defendant Port of Seattle, damaged plaintiff telephone company's underground wires. There the court divided—not on the basic justice of a rule of strict liability in some cases—but in its application in a particular case to what on its face was a situation of comparatively minor hazards. * * *

The rule of strict liability, when applied to an abnormally dangerous activity, as stated in the Restatement (Second) of Torts § 519 (Tent.Draft No. 10, 1964), was adopted as the rule of decision in this state in Pacific Northwest Bell Tel. Co. v. Port of Seattle, supra, at 64, 491 P.2d, at 1039, 1040 * * *.

* * * [W]e rejected the application of strict liability in Pacific Northwest Bell Tel. Co. v. Port of Seattle solely because the installation of underground water mains by a municipality was not, under the circumstances shown, an abnormally dangerous activity. Had the activity been found abnormally dangerous, this court would have applied in that case the rule of strict liability.

* * *

Transporting gasoline as freight by truck along the public highways and streets is obviously an activity involving a high degree of risk; it is a risk of great harm and injury; it creates dangers that cannot be eliminated by the exercise of reasonable care. That gasoline cannot be practicably transported except upon the public highways does not decrease the abnormally high risk arising from its transportation. Nor will the exercise of due and reasonable care assure protection to the public from the disastrous consequences of concealed or latent mechanical or metallurgical defects in the carrier's equipment, from the negligence of third parties, from latent defects in the highways and streets, and from all of the other hazards not generally disclosed or guarded against by reasonable care, prudence and foresight. Hauling gasoline in great quantities as freight, we think, is an activity that calls for the application of principles of strict liability.

The case is therefore reversed and remanded to the trial court for trial to the jury on the sole issue of damages.

ROSELLINI, Associate Justice (concurring).

I agree with the majority that the transporting of highly volatile and flammable substances upon the public highways in commercial quantities and for commercial purposes is an activity which carries with it such a great risk of harm to defenseless users of the highway, if it is not kept contained, that the common-law principles of strict liability should apply. In my opinion, a good reason to apply these principles, which is not mentioned in the majority opinion, is that the commercial transporter can spread the loss among his customers—who benefit from this extrahazardous use of the highways. Also, if the defect which caused the substance to escape was one of manufacture, the owner is in the best position to hold the manufacturer to account. * * *

———

LANGAN v. VALICOPTERS, INC., 88 Wn.2d 855, 567 P.2d 218 (1977). Organic farmers brought an action for loss of their crop caused by aerial spraying of agricultural pesticides on a neighboring farm. Tests conducted after the spraying indicated the presence of poisonous chemicals on plaintiffs' crops. Amounts detected were not excessive under standards of the federal Food and Drug Administration but were sufficient to cause plaintiffs' certification as organic food growers to be revoked by the Northwest Organic Food Producers' Association. Decertification left plaintiffs without a market for their crop. They sought damages from persons involved in the crop-dusting operation. Held, for plaintiffs. Crop-dusting is an "abnormally dangerous activity" as defined in the Second Restatement of Torts (Tent. Draft No. 10, 1964). Each of the six factors listed in Section 520 points toward strict liability here. With respect to the last three factors the court commented:

"§ 520(d): *Whether the activity is not a matter of common usage.* * * * Although we recognize the prevalence of crop dusting and acknowledge that it is ordinarily done in large portions of the Yakima Valley, it is carried on by only a comparatively small number of persons (approximately 287 aircraft were used in 1975) and is not a matter of common usage.

"§ 520(e): *Whether the activity is inappropriate to the place where it is carried on.* Given the nature of organic farming, the use of pesticides adjacent to such an area must be considered an activity conducted in an inappropriate place.

"§ 520(f): *The value of the activity to the community.* As a criterion for determining strict liability, this factor has received some criticism among legal writers. * * *

"There is no doubt that pesticides are socially valuable in the control of insects, weeds and other pests. * * * Whether strict liability or negligence principles should be applied amounts to a balancing of conflicting social interest[s] * * *.

"In the present case, the Langans were eliminated from the organic food market * * * through no fault of their own. * * * Appellants, on the other hand, will all profit from the continued application of pesticides. Under these circumstances, there can be an equitable balancing of social interests only if appellants are made to pay for the consequences of their acts."

CITIES SERVICE CO. v. STATE OF FLORIDA, 312 So.2d 799 (Fla.Dist.Ct. App.1975). Wastes from Cities Service's phosphate mine are stored in large settling ponds. A dam break permitted phosphate slimes to escape into a nearby stream, killing fish and inflicting other injury. In this action for damages the appellate court approved the approach of the Second Restatement of Torts. Hazardous activities should "pay their own way." "It is too much to ask an innocent neighbor to bear the burden thrust upon him as a consequence of an abnormal use of the land next door." Strict liability should be imposed here, considering the six factors of Section 520, even though "the last two [factors] favor Cities Service."

" * * * Cities Service filed an affidavit of the manager of the plant where the dam break occurred. The affidavit points out that the property is peculiarly suitable for the mining of phosphate and that the central Florida area of which Polk County is the hub is the largest producer of phosphate rock in Florida. It further appears that Florida produced over 80% of the nation's marketable phosphate rock and one-third of the world production thereof in 1973. The affidavit goes on to explain that the storing of phosphate slimes in diked settling ponds is an essential part of the traditional method of mining phosphate rock. * * *

" * * * All of the assertions of Cities Service relative to the need to maintain settling ponds in its mining operations, the suitability of the land for this purpose and the importance of phosphate to the community as well as to the world at large may be accepted at face value. Admitting the desirability of phosphate and the necessity of mining in this manner, the rights of adjoining landowners and the interests of the public in our environment require the imposition of a doctrine which places the burden upon the parties whose activity made it possible for the damages to occur."

CADENA v. CHICAGO FIREWORKS MFG. CO.

Illinois Appellate Court, 1998.
297 Ill.App.3d 945, 232 Ill.Dec. 60, 697 N.E.2d 802.
Appeal denied, 181 Ill.2d 568, 235 Ill.Dec. 940, 706 N.E.2d 495 (1998).

Justice BURKE delivered the opinion of the court:

Plaintiffs Manual Anthony Cadena, Larisa Cadena, Andres Cadena, and Marcella Garcia (Cadenas) and plaintiffs Dale Baikauskas and Christopher Baikauskas (Baikauskases) appeal from an order of the circuit court granting summary judgment in favor of defendant City of Chicago Heights (City) * * *. For the reasons set forth below, we affirm.

On July 3, 1991, Chicago Fireworks Manufacturing Company, who is not a party to this appeal, conducted a Fourth of July fireworks display at Bloom Township High School in the City of Chicago Heights. The City's administrator, Enrico Doggett (Doggett), was in charge of coordinating all activities surrounding the fireworks display. Chicago Fireworks was responsible for putting on the display on July 3, 1991, and had been responsible for the display from 1976 to 1992. * * * The procedures for setting up the fireworks display and the barricades had been essentially the same since Doggett began as the City's administrator in 1975, and "everyone knew where the barricades went, * * * how it was supposed to be set up." * * *

Doggett * * * stated that after an accident during the 1975 fireworks display, which was held at the Bloom Township High School football field, the display was moved in 1976 to a large field at the high school where the display in 1991 was subsequently held. A perimeter was also established in 1976 and the perimeter remained basically the same from then on * * *.

On July 3, 1991, it rained at approximately 6 p.m. and, while it was raining, workers from Chicago Fireworks placed tarps over the fireworks. During the fireworks display, one of the fireworks misfired and landed in the crowd which had gathered to view the display, injuring the Cadenas and Baikauskases. * * *

[Six members of the Cadena and Baikauskas families who were injured by the explosion of the errant projectile within the crowd of spectators brought suit against both the City and its contractor Chicago Fireworks. Initially plaintiffs alleged negligence on the part of the defendants. Negligence was said to lie in the defendants' "permitting the fireworks to be ignited when wet, placing the barricades too close to the ignition area of the fireworks, and designating a spectator viewing area too close to the ignition area." Later plaintiffs amended their complaint to include assertion of strict liability for injury caused by the miscarriage of an ultrahazardous activity. The City moved for summary judgment on the ground that suit against it was barred by the Illinois Governmental and Governmental Employees Tort Immunity Act. The trial court ruled that the City was immune from suit. That ruling gave rise to the present appeal.

[The appellate court first concluded that the negligence claims against the City were indeed barred by the Immunity Act. Then it turned to plaintiffs' claim that the City, in sponsoring the fireworks display, was engaged in an ultrahazardous activity. The court declined to decide whether strict liability for ultrahazardous activity "should be an exception" to the Immunity Act "because it is clear * * * the displaying of fireworks is not an ultrahazardous activity."]

* * * Plaintiffs argue that fireworks displays are an ultrahazardous activity because (1) the detonation of explosives has been found to be ultrahazardous and fireworks are a form of explosives; (2) the absolute liability which attaches to employers or property owners authorizing inherently dangerous activity is directly analogous to the operation of the ultrahazardous doctrine and property owners have been found vicariously liable for fireworks displays on their property * * *.

* * *

Illinois courts have either implicitly or explicitly adopted the Restatement (Second) of Torts in analyzing whether an activity should be considered ultrahazardous. See *Miller v. Civil Constructors, Inc.,* 272 Ill.App.3d 263, 269, 209 Ill.Dec. 311, 651 N.E.2d 239 (1995) * * *.

* * *

Based on the factors listed in section 520 of the Restatement, we find that the displaying of fireworks is not an ultrahazardous activity. While plaintiffs argue that because the detonation of explosives has been found to be ultrahazardous and fireworks are a form of explosives, therefore this court should find that fireworks displays constitute an ultrahazardous activity, this comparison alone is not enough to support a finding that a fireworks display is an ultrahazardous activity under an analysis of the factors listed in section 520 of the Restatement. While factors (a) and (b) of the Restatement are arguably met because there exists a high degree of risk of some harm to a person during a fireworks display, and the likelihood that the harm that results from it will be great because of the explosive nature of fireworks, the other factors listed in the Restatement are not met. Under factor (c), the exercise of reasonable care in displaying fireworks will significantly reduce the risks involved. Moreover, section (c) does not require the reduction of *all* risk, and indeed, there exists significant risk using a firearm, an activity which this court has previously determined is not an ultrahazardous activity. Under factor (d), while displaying fireworks is not a common activity undertaken by a large amount of individuals, certainly many individuals view them and many municipalities display fireworks. Thus, fireworks displays *are* a matter of common usage. Under factor (e), we assume that the location was appropriate for the fireworks display in the absence of factual allegations in plaintiffs' complaint specifically describing the area as inappropriate for fireworks displays. Lastly, we determine, based on the fact that the general public enjoys fireworks displays to celebrate every July 4, they are of some social utility to communities. Therefore, we find that the value of the fireworks display is not outweighed by its dangerous attributes. Accordingly, we find that a fireworks display is not an ultrahazardous activity as a matter of law.

We also reject plaintiffs' argument that the absolute liability which attaches to employers or property owners who authorize inherently dangerous activity is directly analogous to the operation of the ultrahazardous doctrine. Plaintiffs argue that because property owners have been found vicariously liable for fireworks displays on their property, this court should find that the display of fireworks is an ultrahazardous activity. We find that the analysis utilized under the "inherently dangerous activity" [doctrine] as it relates to property owners, however, is not substantially similar to the analysis utilized under the ultrahazardous doctrine. The "inherently dangerous activity" doctrine is analyzed under section 427 of the Restatement, which provides:

> "One who employs an independent contractor to do work involving a special danger to others which the employer knows or has reason to know to be inherent in or normal to the work, or which he contemplates or has reason to contemplate when making the contract, is subject to liability for physical harm caused to such others by the contractor's failure to take reasonable precautions against such danger."
> Restatement (Second) of Torts § 427 (1977).

This doctrine is clearly distinct from the ultrahazardous activity doctrine set forth in section 520 of the Restatement because while an activity may be considered inherently dangerous, the imposition of strict liability under an ultrahazardous activity theory may not be warranted in certain situations. See *Miller*, 272 Ill.App.3d at 270, 209 Ill.Dec. 311, 651 N.E.2d 239 (where the court stated that the use of firearms has been classified as highly dangerous but their use does not constitute an ultrahazardous activity). In addition, liability under section 427 can be avoided by taking reasonable precautions against the danger, whereas under the ultrahazardous doctrine, reasonable precautions will not preclude the imposition of liability.

[Affirmed.]

————

KLEIN v. PYRODYNE CORP., 117 Wash.2d 1, 810 P.2d 917 (1991). At a public fireworks display on the Fourth of July, an aerial shell went astray and exploded near spectators, causing serious injury. Suit was brought against the pyrotechnic company in charge of the display. The trial judge ruled that defendant was strictly liable. On appeal, *held*, affirmed. Four of the six factors listed by Section 520 of the Second Restatement of Torts support the conclusion that "conducting public fireworks displays is an abnormally dangerous activity justifying the imposition of strict liability."

"We find that the factors stated in clauses (a), (b), and (c) [of Section 520] are all present in the case of fireworks displays. Any time a person ignites aerial shells or rockets with the intention of sending them aloft to explode in the presence of large crowds of people, a high risk of serious personal injury or property damage is created. * * *

"The dangerousness of fireworks displays is evidenced by the elaborate scheme of administrative regulations with which pyrotechnicians must comply. * * *

"Pyrodyne argues that if the regulations are complied with, then the high degree of risk otherwise inherent in the displays can be eliminated. Although we recognize that the high risk can be reduced, we do not agree that it can be eliminated. Setting off powerful fireworks near large crowds remains a highly risky activity even when the safety precautions mandated by statutes and regulations are followed. The Legislature appears to agree, for it has declared that in order to obtain a license to conduct a public fireworks display, a pyrotechnician must first obtain a surety bond or a certificate of insurance, the amount of which must be at least $1,000,000 for each event.

* * *

"The factor expressed in clause (d) concerns the extent to which the activity is not a matter 'of common usage.' * * *

"Pyrodyne argues that the factor stated in clause (d) is not met because fireworks are a common way to celebrate the 4th of July. We reject this argument. Although fireworks are frequently and regularly enjoyed by the public, few persons set off special fireworks displays. Indeed, the general public is prohibited by statute from making public fireworks displays insofar as anyone wishing to do so must first obtain a license.

* * *

" * * * Most basic is the question as to who should bear the loss when an innocent person suffers injury through the nonculpable but abnormally dangerous activities of another. In the case of public fireworks displays, fairness weighs in favor of requiring the pyrotechnicians who present the displays to bear the loss rather than the unfortunate spectators who suffer the injuries."

RESTATEMENT OF TORTS, SECOND (1965). Section 427A, titled "Work Involving Abnormally Dangerous Activity," provides:

> One who employs an independent contractor to do work which the employer knows or has reason to know to involve an abnormally dangerous activity, is subject to liability to the same extent as the contractor for physical harm to others caused by the activity.

INDIANA HARBOR BELT RAILROAD
v. AMERICAN CYANAMID CO.

United States Court of Appeals, Seventh Circuit, 1990.
916 F.2d 1174.

POSNER, Circuit Judge.

American Cyanamid Company, the defendant in this diversity tort suit governed by Illinois law, is a major manufacturer of chemicals, including acrylonitrile, a chemical used in large quantities in making acrylic fibers, plastics, dyes, pharmaceutical chemicals, and other intermediate and final goods. On January 2, 1979, at its manufacturing plant in Louisiana, Cyanamid loaded 20,000 gallons of liquid acrylonitrile into a railroad tank car that it had leased from the North American Car Corporation. The next day, a train of the Missouri Pacific Railroad picked up the car at Cyanamid's siding. * * * The Missouri Pacific train carried the car north to the Blue Island railroad yard of Indiana Harbor Belt Railroad, the plaintiff in this case, a small switching line that has a contract with Conrail to switch cars from other lines to Conrail, in this case for travel east. The Blue Island yard is in the Village of Riverdale, which is just south of Chicago and part of the Chicago metropolitan area.

The car arrived in the Blue Island yard on the morning of January 9, 1979. Several hours after it arrived, employees of the switching line noticed fluid gushing from the bottom outlet of the car. The lid on the outlet was broken. After two hours, the line's supervisor of equipment was able to stop the leak by closing a shut-off valve controlled from the top of the car. * * * [S]ince acrylonitrile is flammable at a temperature of 30 degrees Fahrenheit or above, highly toxic, and possibly carcinogenic, the local authorities ordered the homes near the yard evacuated. The evacuation lasted only a few hours, until the car was moved to a remote part of the yard and it was discovered that only about a quarter of the acrylonitrile had leaked. Concerned nevertheless that there had been some contamination of soil and water, the Illinois Department of Environmental Protection ordered the switching line to take decontamination measures that cost the line $981,022.75, which it sought to recover by this suit.

One count of the two-count complaint charges Cyanamid with having maintained the leased tank car negligently. The other count asserts that the transportation of acrylonitrile in bulk through the Chicago metropolitan area is an abnormally dangerous activity, for the consequences of which the shipper (Cyanamid) is strictly liable to the switching line, which bore the financial brunt of those consequences because of the decontamination measures that it was forced to take. After the district judge denied Cyanamid's motion to dismiss the strict liability count, 517 F.Supp. 314 (N.D.Ill. 1981), the switching line moved for summary judgment on that count—and won. 662 F.Supp. 635 (N.D.Ill.1987). [The judge directed the entry of judgment for $981,022.75. Cyanamid appealed.]

The question whether the shipper of a hazardous chemical by rail should be strictly liable for the consequences of a spill or other accident to the shipment en route is a novel one in Illinois * * *.

The parties agree * * * that the Supreme Court of Illinois would treat as authoritative the provisions of the Restatement [(Second) of Torts] governing abnormally dangerous activities. * * *

* * *

* * * The baseline common law regime of tort liability is negligence. When it is a workable regime, because the hazards of an activity can be avoided by being careful (which is to say, nonnegligent), there is no need to switch to strict liability. Sometimes, however, a particular type of accident cannot be prevented by taking care but can be avoided, or its consequences minimized, by shifting the activity in which the accident occurs to another locale, where the risk or harm of an accident will be less, or by reducing the scale of the activity in order to minimize the number of accidents caused by it. Bethlehem Steel Corp. v. EPA, 782 F.2d 645, 652 (7th Cir.1986); Shavell, Strict Liability versus Negligence, 9 J. Legal Stud. 1 (1980). By making the actor strictly liable—by denying him in other words an excuse based on his inability to avoid accidents by being more careful—we give him an incentive, missing in a negligence regime, to experiment with methods of preventing accidents that involve not greater exertions of care, assumed to be futile, but instead relocating, changing, or reducing (perhaps to the vanishing point) the activity giving rise to the accident. * * *

The largest class of cases in which strict liability has been imposed under the standard codified in the Second Restatement of Torts involves the use of dynamite and other explosives for demolition in residential or urban areas. Restatement, supra, § 519, comment d; City of Joliet v. Harwood, 86 Ill. 110 (1877). Explosives are dangerous even when handled carefully, and we therefore want blasters to choose the location of the activity with care and also to explore the feasibility of using safer substitutes (such as a wrecking ball), as well as to be careful in the blasting itself. * * *

[The court discussed several cases imposing strict liability for transportation or storage of dangerous chemicals, including Siegler v. Kuhlman, 81 Wash.2d 448, 502 P.2d 1181 (1972), but found them not on point. It added:] We shall see that a further distinction of great importance between the present case and Siegler is that the defendant there was the transporter, and here it is the shipper.

* * *

So we can get little help from precedent, and might as well apply [Restatement] section 520 to the acrylonitrile problem from the ground up. To begin with, we have been given no reason * * * for believing that a negligence regime is not perfectly adequate to remedy and deter, at reasonable cost, the accidental spillage of acrylonitrile from rail cars. * * * [The accident here] was caused by carelessness—whether that of the North American Car Corporation in failing to maintain or inspect the car properly, or that of Cyanamid in failing to maintain or inspect it, or that of the Missouri Pacific when it had custody of the car, or that of the switching line itself in failing to notice the ruptured lid, or some combination of these possible failures of care. * * *

* * * For all that appears from the record of the case or any other sources of information that we have found, if a tank car is carefully maintained the danger of a spill of acrylonitrile is negligible. If this is right, there is no compelling reason to move to a regime of strict liability, especially one that might embrace all other hazardous materials shipped by rail as well. * * *

* * *

The district judge and the plaintiff's lawyer make much of the fact that the spill occurred in a densely inhabited metropolitan area. Only 4,000 gallons spilled; what if all 20,000 had done so? Isn't the risk that this might happen even if everybody were careful sufficient to warrant giving the shipper an incentive to explore alternative routes? Strict liability would supply that incentive. But this argument overlooks the fact that, like other transportation networks, the railroad network is a hub-and-spoke system. And the hubs are in metropolitan areas. Chicago is one of the nation's largest railroad hubs. In 1983, the latest date for which we have figures, Chicago's railroad yards handled the third highest volume of hazardous-material shipments in the nation. * * * With most hazardous chemicals (by volume of shipments) being at least as hazardous as acrylonitrile, it is unlikely—and certainly not demonstrated by the plaintiff—that they can be rerouted around all the metropolitan areas in the country, except at prohibitive cost. Even if it were feasible to reroute them one would hardly expect shippers, as distinct from carriers, to be the firms best situated to do the rerouting. * * *

The difference between shipper and carrier points to a deep flaw in the plaintiff's case. * * * A shipper can in the bill of lading designate the route of his shipment if he likes, but is it realistic to suppose that shippers will become students of railroading in order to lay out the safest route by which to ship their goods? Anyway, rerouting is no panacea. Often it will increase the length of the journey, or compel the use of poorer track, or both. When this happens, the probability of an accident is increased, even if the consequences of an accident if one occurs are reduced; so the expected accident cost, being the product of the probability of an accident and the harm if the accident occurs, may rise. It is easy to see how the accident in this case might have been prevented at reasonable cost by greater care on the part of those who handled the tank car of acrylonitrile. It is difficult to see how it might have been prevented at reasonable cost by a change in the activity of transporting the chemical. This is therefore not an apt case for strict liability.

We [note] that Cyanamid, because of the role it played in the transportation of the acrylonitrile—leasing, and especially loading, and also it appears undertaking by contract with North American Car Corporation to maintain, the tank car in which the railroad carried Cyanamid's acrylonitrile to Riverdale—might be viewed as a special type of shipper (call it a "transporter"), rather than as a passive shipper. But neither the district judge nor the plaintiff's counsel has attempted to distinguish Cyanamid from an ordinary manufacturer of chemicals on this ground, and we consider it waived. Which is not to say that had it not been waived it would have changed the outcome of the case. The very fact that Cyanamid participated actively in the transportation of the acrylonitrile imposed upon it a duty of due care and by doing so brought into play a threat of negligence liability that, for all we know, may provide an adequate regime of accident control in the transportation of this particular chemical.

* * *

The judgment is reversed (with no award of costs in this court) and the case remanded for further proceedings, consistent with this opinion, on the plaintiff's claim for negligence.

———

SPLENDORIO v. BILRAY DEMOLITION CO., 682 A.2d 461 (R.I.1996). A building inspection firm, Certified Engineering (Certified), found asbestos in three public housing buildings slated for demolition. After asbestos removal was undertaken, Certified declared the buildings asbestos-free, and demolition proceeded. Later Certified learned that it had overlooked a possible locus of asbestos within the buildings, and it tested demolition debris being stored in a wrecking yard. Asbestos was found in the debris, which was then removed to a special facility. This lawsuit was brought against Certified and other defendants by homeowners whose property had been exposed to asbestos dust emanating from the wrecking yard. The complaint included a claim of strict liability against Certified. The trial court granted summary judgment in favor of Certified on that claim. *Held*, affirmed. "Absolute liability attaches only to ultrahazardous or abnormally dangerous *activities* and not to ultrahazardous or abnormally dangerous *materials*." "Although asbestos is understandably an ultrahazardous or abnormally dangerous material, Certified's activities in this case were not ultrahazardous or abnormally dangerous."

"[I]n the demolition of buildings possibly containing asbestos it is necessary prior to demolition to inspect for asbestos in order to reduce potential health risks. * * * '[C]leanup operations serve the valuable and essential social function of *reducing* the danger' of potentially harmful substances such as asbestos. Therefore, public policy * * * support[s] our conclusion that Certified could not on the facts present in this case be held strictly liable for its activities."

ARLINGTON FOREST ASSOCIATES v. EXXON CORP., 774 F.Supp. 387 (E.D.Va.1991). Defendant maintained underground gasoline storage tanks at a gasoline station in Arlington, Virginia. Plaintiff purchased the property and afterward discovered that the tanks had leaked, causing gasoline contamination of the soil. Plaintiff claims defendant should be strictly liable for damage done. *Held*, under Virginia law, that storage of gasoline in underground tanks "is not an abnormally dangerous activity for which common law strict liability should be imposed." The court noted that two other jurisdictions (Colorado and Maryland) had reached "the opposite result." But past Virginia decisions "apply strict liability narrowly," declining, for example, to apply it to "disposal of pentaborane" (a toxic chemical). In the present case, liability for abnormally dangerous activity "does not apply" for two reasons.

First, when maintained with due care, "underground gasoline storage tanks present virtually no risk of injury from seepage of their contents." "If an activity can be performed safely with ordinary care, negligence serves both as an adequate remedy for injury and a sufficient deterrent to carelessness. Strict liability is reserved for selected uncommon and extraordinarily dangerous activities for which negligence is an inadequate deterrent or remedy."

Second, "filling stations with underground tanks are commonplace in most communities throughout the country." "[A]lthough gasoline service stations may not themselves be operated by 'the great mass of mankind,' they are so pervasive as reasonably to be considered 'matters of common usage.'"

DOE v. JOHNSON, 817 F.Supp. 1382 (W.D.Mich.1993). Plaintiff, Jane Doe, alleges that the male defendant transmitted the human immunodeficiency virus (HIV) to her through consensual sexual intercourse. The complaint says defendant should have known he had a "high risk of becoming infected" with HIV because of his "promiscuous lifestyle." It claims, inter alia, that defendant is strictly liable for harm suffered by Ms. Doe because his activity was "abnormally dangerous and ultrahazardous." *Held*, that "sexual activity (homosexual or heterosexual)" is not "abnormally dangerous activity under strict liability." "[T]he risk associated with sexual activity, spread of disease, can be reduced (although not completely eliminated) by use of a condom. Also, the Restatement suggests * * * that in order to be abnormally dangerous, the activity must not be a matter of common usage. Sexual activity is not an uncommon endeavor."

SECTION C. STRICT RATIONALES

This section focuses on the idea of enterprise liability. The theory of enterprise liability is a modern understanding of the aims of strict liability for accidental injury, such as liability for harm caused by dangerous activities. The theory came to prominence in legal thinking with the advent of workers' compensation early in the twentieth century; always embattled, it has figured in tort argument throughout the modern period.

The prescriptive conception of enterprise liability can be boiled down into two basic normative assertions: (1) that accident costs should be internalized; (2) that accident costs should be spread. First, an enterprise should pay for losses caused by its characteristic risks. Such losses should be absorbed by the enterprise as an operating expense, not left with the random victims of the enterprise's risk. Second, accident costs should be distributed among those who benefit from the risky enterprise, such as its customers. Costs of a given injury should be shared, not concentrated on the one who got injured.

The theory of enterprise liability includes a factual assumption which links the aims of internalization and spreading. It is assumed that the enterprise, made liable for its accident costs, will usually arrange to provide compensation through liability insurance, and will include the insurance expense in the price of its product, thereby spreading the burden of compensation among all its customers. The theory also makes the standard assumption of a strict liability, that the activity it addresses is worthwhile and ought to continue, provided it pays its way. It is assumed that risky enterprise made subject to liability does, on balance, more good than harm, in that the gains from running its risk over time are greater than expected losses from accidents, and in that the costs of avoiding the risk would outweigh the benefits of avoidance.

The materials that follow put forward two different lines of policy argument in support of internalization and spreading. The two main justificatory grounds of enterprise liability are utility and fairness. The utilitarian rationale and the fairness rationale are convergent in prescription, but they proceed from distinct substantive commitments. Utilitarian considerations are emphasized in the first main case below, which speaks of "economic resources . . . efficiently allocated"; fairness concerns are underscored in the second main case, which speaks of "natural justice"; both sorts of policy justification are invoked in the third.

CHAVEZ v. SOUTHERN PACIFIC TRANSPORTATION CO.
United States District Court, Eastern District of California, 1976.
413 F.Supp. 1203.

MacBRIDE, Chief Judge. On April 28, 1973, approximately eighteen bomb loaded boxcars exploded in Southern Pacific Transportation Company's Antelope Yard in Roseville, California. These boxcars and bombs, both the property of the United States, were being hauled by the Southern Pacific Transportation Company (hereinafter Southern Pacific), under a contract with the Department of the Navy, from Hawthorne, Nevada, to Port Chicago, California. Plaintiffs in the above entitled cases seek to recover damages for personal injuries and property destruction allegedly caused by the Roseville explosions.

Southern Pacific has moved this court * * * to dismiss the plaintiffs' claims against Southern Pacific which are premised on a theory of strict liability for the miscarriage of an ultrahazardous activity. * * *

* * *

* * * [According to California caselaw, which controls this controversy,] where one intentionally engages in an ultrahazardous enterprise and thereby exposes others to risks of harm which cannot be eliminated by the exercise of due care, fairness or abstract justice requires the precipitator of the risk to pay for resulting damages. Although the actor's conduct is not so unreasonable as to constitute negligence itself, it is sufficiently anti-social that, as between two innocents, the actor and not the injured should pay for mishaps.

This "fairness" rationale for imposing strict liability for the miscarriage of an ultrahazardous activity has been undergoing a metamorphosis. * * *

Notwithstanding Southern Pacific's protestations to the contrary, one public policy now recognized in California as justifying the imposition of strict liability for the miscarriage of an ultrahazardous activity is the social and economic desirability of distributing the losses, resulting from such activity, among the general public. Smith v. Lockheed Propulsion Co., 247 Cal.App.2d 774, 56 Cal.Rptr. 128 (1967). The defendant in *Smith*, Lockheed Propulsion Co., under a contract with the United States Air Force, had been engaged in testing a solid fuel rocket motor by firing the motor nosedown while it was affixed to a test stand. Resulting tremors damaged nearby property belonging to the plaintiffs. After finding that this test firing involved the inherent risk of damage which could not be eliminated by the exercise of due care, the *Smith* court concluded:

> "In these circumstances, public policy calls for strict liability. There is no basis, either in reason or justice, for requiring the innocent neighboring landowner to bear the loss. Defendant, who is engaged in the enterprise for profit, is in a position best able to administer the loss so that it will ultimately be borne by the public. As Professor Prosser summarizes the rationale for the imposition of strict liability: 'The problem is dealt with as one of allocating a more or less inevitable loss to be charged against a complex and dangerous civilization, and liability is placed, upon the party best able to shoulder it.' (Prosser, Law of Torts, (2d ed. 1955) page 318)." * * *

The *Smith* court's justification of strict liability on a risk distribution theory is consistent with developments in other areas of California strict liability tort law. See Escola v. Coca Cola Bottling Co., 24 Cal.2d 453, 150 P.2d 436 (1944) (concurring opinion); Greenman v. Yuba Power Products, Inc., 59 Cal.2d 57, 27 Cal.Rptr. 697, 377 P.2d 897 (1963); Price v. Shell Oil Co., 2 Cal.3d 245, 85 Cal.Rptr. 178, 466 P.2d 722 (1970).

The first articulate use of the risk distribution rationale for imposing strict liability in California came in Justice Traynor's often cited concurring opinion in Escola v. Coca Cola Bottling Co., supra, an exploding bottle case. While the majority affirmed the plaintiff's judgment on a res ipsa loquitur theory, Justice Traynor reasoned that the same result should be reached on a theory of strict liability:

> "Those who suffer injury from defective products are unprepared to meet its consequences. The cost of an injury and the loss of time or health may be an overwhelming misfortune to the person injured, and a needless one, for the risk of injury can be insured by the manufacturer and distributed among the public as a cost of doing business." 24 Cal.2d at 462, 150 P.2d at 441.

Justice Traynor firmly imprinted this reasoning into California strict liability law in the landmark case of Greenman v. Yuba Power Products, Inc., supra, in which California led other jurisdictions by finding that the products liability of a manufacturer was governed by the law of strict liability in tort, and not by the law of contract warranties. In support of this new proposition, Justice Traynor opined:

"We need not recanvass the reasons for imposing strict liability on the manufacturer. * * * The purpose of such liability is to insure that the costs of injuries resulting from defective products are borne by the manufacturers that put such products on the market rather than by the injured persons who are powerless to protect themselves." 59 Cal.2d at 63, 27 Cal.Rptr. at 701, 377 P.2d at 901.

The Supreme Court of California, in the recent case of Price v. Shell Oil Co., supra, applied the risk distribution rationale to impose strict liability on the lessor of a truck for damages caused by defects existing in the truck when leased. Finding his inspiration in the *Greenman* and *Escola* cases, Justice Sullivan stated:

"Essentially the paramount policy to be promoted by the rule is the protection of otherwise defenseless victims of manufacturing defects and the spreading throughout society of the cost of compensating them. * * * " 2 Cal.3d at 251, 85 Cal.Rptr. at 181, 466 P.2d at 725.

As was found by the court in Smith v. Lockheed Propulsion Co., supra, the risk distribution justification for imposing strict liability is well suited to claims arising out of the conduct of ultrahazardous activity. The victims of such activity are defenseless. Due to the very nature of the activity, the losses suffered as a result of such activity are likely to be substantial—an "overwhelming misfortune to the person injured." 24 Cal.2d at 462, 150 P.2d at 441. Southern Pacific, like the manufacturer in *Greenman,* like the lessor in *Price,* and like Lockheed Propulsion Co. in *Smith,* is in a position to "administer the loss so that it will ultimately be borne by the public." 247 Cal.App.2d at 785, 56 Cal.Rptr. at 137. By indirectly imposing liability on those that benefit from the dangerous activity, risk distribution benefits the social-economic body in two ways: (1) the adverse impact of any particular misfortune is lessened by spreading its cost over a greater population and over a larger time period, and (2) social and economic resources can be more efficiently allocated when the actual costs of goods and services (including the losses they entail) are reflected in their price to the consumer.[4] Both of these benefits may be achieved by subjecting Southern Pacific to strict liability.

Southern Pacific argues that the California courts would not subject it to strict liability on a risk distribution theory because they would find that common carriers may not be held absolutely liable for damages resulting from the transportation of bombs the carrier was bound to ship. In support, it cites a number of decisions in other jurisdictions which have held that a common carrier may not be held strictly liable.

Actually, the cases cited by Southern Pacific proceed on two theories. First, several decisions have found carriers to be excepted from the general rule of strict liability simply because they have the right to engage in the ultrahazardous activity. * * *

4. See Calabresi, Some Thoughts on Risk Distribution and the Law of Torts, 70 Yale L.J. 499 (1961).

A public authorization exception does have some basis in reason when strict liability is imposed * * * only as an equitable arrangement between the injured party and the risk creating actor. Insofar as strict liability is imposed on the innocent but dangerous actor because his conduct is anti-social, such liability would be inappropriate if specific public authorization is read to mean that the conduct is socially desirable.

However, California also imposes strict liability because certain activity is so dangerous that such a standard is thought necessary to distribute the loss among the general public. Smith v. Lockheed Propulsion Co., supra. There is no logical basis for a public authorization exception when this risk distribution rationale is utilized to justify the strict liability standard. The need to distribute the risk and the benefits to be derived from the distributions do not vary according to whether the dangerous activity is authorized by the state in some manner.

* * *

The second basis for not imposing strict liability on common carriers is the one upon which Southern Pacific has relied in its briefs: that where a common carrier has a duty to transport dangerous cargo, it is unjust to hold it strictly liable when damages result from the transportation. * * *

The argument that no strict liability should be imposed where the carrier is acting pursuant to a public duty was adopted by the American Law Institute (ALI) in 1937, when it set forth in its Restatement of Torts its scheme for imposing strict liability for the miscarriage of an ultrahazardous activity. * * *

The ALI carved out an exception to the general rule of § 519 in § 521, which provides:

> "The rule stated in § 519 does not apply if the activity is carried on in pursuance of a public duty imposed upon the actor as a public officer or employee or as a common carrier."*

* * *

But, there is no logical reason for creating a "public duty" exception when the rationale for subjecting the carrier to absolute liability is the carrier's ability to distribute the loss to the public. Whether the carrier is free to reject or bound to take the explosive cargo, the plaintiffs are equally defenseless. Bound or not, Southern Pacific is in a position to pass along the loss to the public. Bound or not, the social and economic benefits which are ordinarily derived from imposing strict liability are achieved. Those which benefit from the dangerous activity bear the inherent costs. The harsh impact of inevitable disasters is softened by spreading the cost among a greater population and over a larger time period. A more efficient allocation of resources results. Thus, the reasonable inference to be drawn from the adoption of the risk distribution rationale in Smith v. Lockheed Propulsion Co., supra, is that California would follow the path of the Supreme Court of

* Ed. note: Section 521 is retained in The Second Restatement of Torts (1977).

Washington in Siegler v. Kuhlman and find that carriers engaged in ultrahazardous activity are subject to strict liability.

It is therefore ordered that Southern Pacific's motions to dismiss the ultrahazardous activity strict liability claims stated against it in the above entitled cases are denied.

LUBIN v. IOWA CITY

Supreme Court of Iowa, 1964.
257 Iowa 383, 131 N.W.2d 765.

[Action against the city seeking damages for injuries sustained when a city water main broke, flooding the basement of plaintiffs' store and damaging merchandise. Various counts were based, respectively, on theories of liability without fault, res ipsa loquitur, and specific acts of negligence. The trial court submitted only the second and third theories to the jury, and the jury returned a verdict for the defendant. The trial court then granted a motion for new trial on the ground that the verdict failed to do substantial justice, explicitly inviting the Supreme Court of Iowa to reverse his refusal to submit the theory of liability without fault.]

STUART, Justice. * * *

III.   Plaintiffs argue the facts in this case are such that the doctrine of Rylands v. Fletcher imposing strict liability, or liability without fault, should be applied. This leading and controversial case was decided in England in 1866 and has been the subject of much discussion by the legal scholars ever since. Bohlen, Studies in the Law of Torts, pp. 344–440; Prosser, the Law of Torts, 2d Ed. 329–349. There a millowner was held liable for damages sustained when water broke through the bottom of a pond into some unused mine shafts and flooded plaintiff's mine through connecting passages. No negligence was found. The facts did not satisfy the technical requirements of either trespass or nuisance. Justice Blackburn in the Exchequer Chamber said: "We think that the true rule of law is that a person who for his own purposes brings on his land and collects and keeps there anything likely to do mischief if it escapes, must keep it at his peril, and if he does not do so is prima facie answerable for all the damage which is a natural consequence of its escape." Fletcher v. Rylands (1866) L.R. 1 Ex. 265, 279–280.

On appeal to the House of Lords this broad statement was limited to a "non-natural" user of the land as distinguished from "any purpose for which it might in the ordinary course of enjoyment of the land be used". Rylands v. Fletcher (1868) L.R. 3 H.L. 330, 338.

While this doctrine was readily followed in England, it is generally thought that it has not been widely accepted in the United States. However, Prosser in 1955 found 20 jurisdictions including Iowa, which have accepted it in name or principle. Law of Torts, p. 332–333. In many other jurisdictions strict liability has been imposed on other theories for damages sustained when an escaping substance or force has invaded the real estate of another.

Many recent cases have applied strict liability on the theory of trespass. [Citations omitted.]

Strict liability has frequently been imposed on the theories of absolute nuisance or private nuisance—Prosser, The Law of Torts, pp. 336–337, pp. 399–400, pp. 405–416; and cases cited.

However, most of the broken water main cases have been founded upon negligence.

* * *

We have not been asked, prior to this case, to apply strict liability to broken watermains. We have, however, applied strict liability in other instances. The doctrine of Ryland v. Fletcher, supra, was discussed and approved in the case of percolating water or water seepage in Healey v. Citizens' Gas and Electric Company, 199 Iowa 82, 201 N.W. 118, 38 A.L.R. 1226. Strict liability has also been imposed on the theory of nuisance (Ryan v. City of Emmetsburg, 232 Iowa 600, 4 N.W.2d 435) and trespass. Watson v. Mississippi River Power Co., 174 Iowa 23, 156 N.W. 188, L.R.A. 1916D,101.

The Ryan case approved of an action for damages from a continuing nuisance alleged to have been created by odors from a sewage disposal plant. There were no allegations of negligence. In that case a distinction was drawn between a private nuisance and a trespass, which we say "comprehends an actual physical invasion by tangible matter." This definition would seem to include the present situation. In the Watson case recovery was allowed for damages to a building caused by the concussion of air and vibrations of the earth brought about by blasting operations on the theory of trespass through the use of an inherently dangerous instrumentality. There was no proof of negligence and the case was tried on the theory of liability without fault. Some of the general language contained in that case is both enlightening and pertinent. We say:

"The employment of force of any kind which, when so put in operation, extends its energy into the premises of another to their material injury, and renders them uninhabitable, is as much a physical invasion as if the wrongdoer had entered thereon in person and by overpowering strength had cast the owner into the street."

In the recent case of Pumphrey v. J.A. Jones Construction Co., 250 Iowa 559, 94 N.W.2d 737, 738, which was also a blasting case, we recognize that we have accepted the doctrine of liability without fault when one "uses on his own lands something inherently dangerous and likely to damage his neighbor's property" p. 738.

In Healey v. Citizens' Gas and Electric Co., 199 Iowa 82, 201 N.W. 118, 38 A.L.R. 1226, Rylands v. Fletcher was discussed and approved and other cases which had applied strict liability were exhaustively reviewed. The defendant had obtained the required permit to raise its dam across a stream to increase its capacity to produce electricity. It had condemned the land included in the increased water reservoir. Plaintiff's land did not lie next to the river and was not condemned, however the higher water level caused water to seep through the ground and come to the surface on plaintiff's land damaging it and his crops. In holding that the question of damages from the percolating water should have been submitted to the jury, we said: "(W)e think the action is more like an action for nuisance, and that the Pixley (Pixley v. Clark, 35 N.Y. 520) and like cases relied upon by appellant (including Ryland v. Fletcher stated to be directly in point, p. 88 [201 N.W. p. 120]) are the better reasoned and more numerous * * * " p. 108, 201 N.W. p. 129. (Words in parenthesis are ours.)

Whether we say the invasion of plaintiffs' property by water escaping from defendant's broken watermain constitutes a trespass or nuisance or results from an extra-hazardous activity as defined in the Restatement of Torts, Section 520, or is an application of the doctrine of Rylands v. Fletcher, or that the practice of leaving pipes in place until they break is negligence per se, we believe the facts in this case disclose a situation in which liability should be imposed upon the city without a showing of negligent conduct.

It is neither just nor reasonable that the city engaged in a proprietary activity can deliberately and intentionally plan to leave a watermain underground beyond inspection and maintenance until a break occurs and escape liability. A city or corporation so operating knows that eventually a break will occur, water will escape and in all probability flow onto the premises of another with resulting damage. We do not ordinarily think of watermains as being extra-hazardous but when such a practice is followed they become "inherently dangerous and likely to damage the neighbor's property" within the meaning of Pumphrey v. J.A. Jones Construction Co., supra. The risks from such a method of operation should be borne by the water supplier who is in a position to spread the cost among the consumers who are in fact the true beneficiaries of this practice and of the resulting savings in inspection and maintenance costs. When the expected and inevitable occurs, they should bear the loss and not the unfortunate individual whose property is damaged without fault of his own.

The Circuit Court of Appeals, Fourth Circuit applied similar reasoning in Norfolk & Western Railway Co. v. Amicon Fruit Co. (1920) 269 F. 559, 14 A.L.R. 547 in which a private company was held liable for damages caused by recurring leaks in a 16 cast iron pipe although "the pipeline was built in the best manner and maintained at all times with due care, so that defendant was not negligent in those respects". The court said: "We are not here dealing with an accident, an unexpected and unlikely happening, but with the continuous or frequently recurring results of what may be called the normal operation of this pipeline, though properly constructed and carefully maintained. It is not a question of negligence, in the ordinary sense of that term. Defendant in effect says that it cannot keep its pipeline from leaking and therefore is not liable for the consequences. In our judgment the position is plainly untenable." While the leak occurring here was not continuous or frequent, it was certainly not accidental or unexpected and was within the normal operation of the water system.

The reasons stated by the Supreme Court of Minnesota in adhering to the doctrine of Rylands v. Fletcher in Bridgeman–Russell [v. City of Duluth, 158 Minn. 509, 197 N.W. 971 (1924)], are appropriate here.

"Congestion of population in large cities is on the increase. This calls for water systems on a vast scale either by the cities themselves or by strong corporations. Water in immense quantities must be accumulated and held where none of it existed before. If a break occurs in the reservoir itself, or in the principal mains, the flood may utterly ruin an individual financially. In such a case, even though negligence be absent, natural justice would seem to demand that the enterprise, or what really is the same thing, the whole community benefited by the enterprise, should stand the loss rather than the individual. It is too heavy a burden upon one. The trend of modern legislation is to relieve the individual from the mischance of business or industry without regard to its being caused by negligence." 197 N.W. 971, 972. We see no logical distinction between mains leading from a reservoir and other mains. Damage may utterly ruin an individual financially in either case.

If the city accepts the advantages of lower maintenance costs and other benefits which result from its practice of burying long lasting cast iron pipe six feet underground beyond any reasonable opportunity to inspect and intentionally leaves them there until breaks began to occur, it should also expect to pay for the damages resulting from such practice as a cost of its doing business in this manner.

The result reached here seems to be in line with modern trends. Legal scholars, with justification, accuse the courts of tending to fix tort liability, not by determining which party is at fault but by deciding which party can best stand the loss. 1963 Annual Survey of American Law, p. 363. While we cannot accept such a basis for determining liability in most tort cases, it seems to be appropriate here. Most jurisdictions which rejected Rylands v. Fletcher did so during that period of time when our country was still young and expanding. "Dangerous enterprises, involving a high degree of risk to others, were clearly indispensable to the industrial and commercial development of a new country and it was considered that the interests of those in the vicinity of such enterprises must give way to them, and that too great a burden must not be placed upon them. With the disappearance of the frontier, and the development of the country's resources, it was to be expected that the force of this objection would be weakened, and that it would be replaced in time by the view that the hazardous enterprise, even though it be socially valuable, must pay its way, and make good the damage inflicted. After a long period during which Rylands v. Fletcher was rejected by the large majority of the American courts which considered it, the pendulum has swung to acceptance of the case and its doctrine in the United States." Prosser, Law of Torts, p. 332, see also Bohlen, Studies in the Law of Torts, p. 367–370.

Appellant cites 3 cases in which the rule of Rylands v. Fletcher has been rejected in broken watermains. Interstate Sash and Door Co. v. City of Cleveland (1947) 148 Ohio St. 325, 74 N.E.2d 239; Midwest Oil Co. v. City of Aberdeen (1943) 69 S.D. 343, 10 N.W.2d 701; A.J. Brown & Son, Inc. v. City of Grand Rapids (1933) 265 Mich. 465, 251 N.W. 561. In none of these cases does it appear whether the city engaged in the practice of leaving the watermains in place until a break would occur. In any event, the courts gave no indication that such a practice was considered of importance in the decisions. We cannot justify a decision which would permit one party to engage in an activity upon his land that will inevitably result in an invasion of the land of another with resulting damage and escape liability for that damage.

IV. Defendant suggests that the record here does not justify the application of strict liability even if we accept it in watermain cases. It claims the injury resulted either from a "vis major" or the conduct of the plaintiffs. Evidence was introduced that breaks were sometimes caused by the shifting of the earth. No authorities are furnished by either party to aid in deciding whether this is sufficient to constitute a "vis major". There is also evidence that the ground was soft under the connections to service line of the plaintiffs and that of another party on each side of the break and that resulting beaming action could have caused the break. Neither piece of evidence is so conclusive to require us to hold the defendant not liable as a matter of law. The defendant is entitled to have all valid defences to strict liability which are supported by the evidence submitted to the jury. We believe the evidence is sufficient to require the court to submit the question of the fault of the plaintiffs to the jury. We do not pass upon the defense of "vis major".

* * *

JENNINGS BUICK, INC. v. CITY OF CINCINNATI, 56 Ohio St.2d 459, 384 N.E.2d 303 (1978). An underground water main broke and released a significant quantity of water into the showroom of plaintiff's automobile agency, causing extensive damage. The 12–inch cast iron main was of the same type used throughout Cincinnati's water system, and there was "no reasonable method of inspection * * * to predetermine whether a pipe might rupture." No negligence on the part of the city was found, and the trial court entered a judgment for defendant. The intermediate appellate court reversed, holding that the city should be strictly liable. Prior Ohio decisions had imposed strict liability in a case involving seepage from a municipal reservoir, but had rejected strict liability with respect to the bursting of a 4–inch "feeder" water main. The intermediate court concluded that the water main in the present case—"a high pressure transmission main"—was more like the reservoir than the 4–inch feeder. "[A]n eruption of this type of main with its potential to discharge large quantities of water in a very short period of time creates a substantial risk of harm to adjacent property owners."

On further review in the Ohio Supreme Court, held (5–2), for defendant. "To apply different standards of liability solely upon the basis of the size or utility of the water main would result in an artificial and arbitrary distinction." The reservoir case is distinguishable since harmful seepage from the city reservoir had continued for more than five years, was well known to the city and therefore "intentional." Strict liability turns on "whether the actor is knowingly doing an unlawful act; if not, then is the actor engaged in a process or activity which is inherently dangerous or hazardous?" It cannot be said that an underground water main is "a dangerous instrumentality" absent evidence that such mains are "likely to burst," posing "a risk of serious harm," and are "not in common usage." Here there is no such evidence. "On the contrary, the laying of mains in public streets * * * is universally recognized as proper, necessary and legal in modern cities." Accordingly a city's liability for the breaking of a water main is not strict, but depends on a finding of negligence. This is "the general rule," embraced by "the majority of states, as well as federal courts."

PACIFIC NORTHWEST BELL TELEPHONE CO. v. PORT OF SEATTLE, 80 Wn.2d 59, 491 P.2d 1037 (1971). An underground pipe which formed part of the fire protection system operated by the Port of Seattle suddenly broke. Water ran into a Telephone Company manhole, damaging exposed wires therein. The Company sued the Port on theories of negligence, nuisance, trespass, and strict liability. The jury, despite a res ipsa loquitur instruction, found no negligence on the part of the Port. Its cast iron pipe was expected to last for 75 more years before replacement and was "buried beyond practical inspection and maintenance." On appeal from a judgment against the Port based on strict liability, *held* (7–2), for defendant, since "the principle of liability without fault does not apply." Using the standards of the Second Restatement of Torts, "we do not find the activity to be abnormally dangerous." Water mains are "universally in use in cities" and "commonly used for fire protection." Their placement underground is "customary" and "of course, appropriate." Nor is water in an underground pipe "something that is inherently dangerous." To say that water mains create a high risk of harm "would be contrary to the experience of at least several generations." "Our conclusion that underground water mains do not constitute an abnormal condition warranting strict liability is supported by * * * the great weight of authority." In dissent from this conclusion Justice Finley wrote:

"I do not think it would open any Pandora's Box—certainly not to any alarming or objectionable extent—if strict liability were applied in the instant case. I believe this is particularly so in view of the unique circumstances of this case, the fact that the Port of Seattle, a municipality or public entity, is involved, and the Port of Seattle would simply be required to assume and pay as a cost of doing business the damages incurred by plaintiff Pacific Northwest Bell Telephone Company * * *. In other words, the public or social *benefits* provided by the business or functions of the Port of Seattle should simply be expected to be assessed with the special *expense* here involved; i.e., the damages to the plaintiff telephone company would be one of the costs of such benefits * * *."

BIERMAN v. CITY OF NEW YORK

Civil Court of the City of New York, 1969.
60 Misc.2d 497, 302 N.Y.S.2d 696.

IRVING YOUNGER, Judge. Jean Bierman, a lady no longer young, owns a small house at 149 Rivington Street, New York City, where, assisted by Social Security payments, she makes her home.

On February 11, 1968, at about 6:30 a.m., water poured into Mrs. Bierman's basement. It damaged the boiler, floor, and walls. The source of the flood was a ruptured water main in front of her house.

She filed a claim for property damage against the City, which responded with a letter stating, in substance, that Consolidated Edison had been working on the main, and hence that Mrs. Bierman's grievance, if any, was against Consolidated Edison. Mrs. Bierman then commenced an action in the Small Claims Part of this Court, against both the City and Consolidated Edison, seeking damages in the amount of $300.00. Because of a crowded calendar in the Small Claims Part, the case was referred to Part 20, where, on May 20, 1969, it was tried.

Neither the City nor Consolidated Edison offered any evidence. Rather, at the close of Mrs. Bierman's case, each moved to dismiss the complaint on the ground that there was no proof of negligence. There was none. Although it has been held that without such proof a plaintiff may not recover for harm caused by a broken water main, George Foltis, Inc. v. City of New York, 287 N.Y. 108, 38 N.E.2d 455 (1941), I find that simple citation of authority will not suffice as a basis for decision here.

This is a Small Claims case, and in Small Claims cases we are adjured "to do substantial justice between the parties according to the rules of substantive law." N.Y.City Civ.Ct.Act, Sec. 1804. The rule of substantive law says that Mrs. Bierman may not recover because she cannot prove negligence on the part of the City or of Consolidated Edison. Is this substantial justice? Only a very backward lawyer could think so. Why should a lady little able to bear the loss nevertheless bear it? Because the metropolis and the great utility were not at fault, we are told. Yet the concept of fault is beside the point. When called upon to decide the rights of a farmer into whose cabbages the flock wandered while the shepherd dallied, a court can preach a sermon on culpability and still appear to reason its way to a just result. But when the task is the allocation of burdens between a plaintiff who is little more than a bystander in his own society and government itself, talk of negligence leaves the highroad to justice in darkness. Accidents happen. Injuries occur. People suffer. Frequently nobody is at fault. The problem is one of mechanics, not morals. The law should therefore turn from fault as a rule of decision. Rather, judges must find a rule to decide whose the cost and whose the compensation so as to satisfy the legislature's command in a case like this "to do substantial justice."

Modern legal scholarship provides at least three signposts pointing to such a rule.

(1) Cost-spreading. See Calabresi, "Some Thoughts on Risk Distribution and the Law of Torts," 70 Yale L.J. 499 (1961). The rule should operate to alleviate the expense of accidents. Can Mrs. Bierman recover only by proving negligence here where no one was negligent? Then she will bear the whole expense and defendants none. Can Mrs. Bierman recover without proving negligence? Then defendants will in the first instance bear the whole expense and Mrs. Bierman none. That whole expense defendants will thereupon spread among all who benefit from the water main: the City in taxes, Consolidated Edison in rates. Mrs. Bierman obviously can do no such thing. So the defendants should pay. If they must, they argue, they have become insurers. Precisely. Let them charge each person something so that no person pays everything.

(2) Injury-prevention. See Seavey, "Speculations as to 'Respondeat Superior,' "in Harvard Legal Essays 433 (1934); Calabresi, "The Decision for Accidents: An Approach to Nonfault Allocation of Costs," 78 Harv.L.Rev. 713 (1965). The rule should assign liability to the party who will thereby be moved to take all possible precautions against recurrence of the accident. That party is not Mrs. Bierman. It is the defendants.

(3) Fairness. See Ira S. Bushey & Sons, Inc. v. United States, 398 F.2d 167 (2d Cir.1968). The rule should impress an onlooker as fair. Here, defendants maintained a water main in the street. It was their business to do it. They created a hazard. The hazard gave issue to the accident. I believe that fairness calls for a defendant to pay for accidents which occur because of his business activities. Thus the City and Consolidated Edison should pay Mrs. Bierman for her damages here.

I recognize that Mrs. Bierman was a beneficiary of defendants' water main. So were many others. There is nothing in Mrs. Bierman's use of her share of the water to require that she sustain the entire loss brought about by the accident. At most, she should sustain her share; and that is the result forecast under "cost-spreading," above.

I conclude that "substantial justice" in this case demands a rule of strict liability rather than a rule of fault. Accordingly, plaintiff shall have judgment against defendants, jointly and severally, in the sum of $300, together with interest from February 11, 1968.

MAHOWALD v. MINNESOTA GAS CO., 344 N.W.2d 856 (Minn.1984). Plaintiffs suffered personal injury and property damage in an explosion of natural gas caused by fracture of a corroded main pipe buried in the street on which they resided. In their suit against the gas company the jury found damages of $110,850 but no negligence. On appeal to the Minnesota Supreme Court, *held,* that plaintiffs should have had the benefit of res ipsa loquitur in proving negligence of the gas company, even though at least three other companies dug up the street at various times and could have damaged the pipe, since the gas distributor "has the non-delegable responsibility to maintain and inspect its mains in the public streets at all times." But the majority (per Kelley, J.) refused to apply strict liability. "[T]he court in New Meadows Holding Co. v. Washington Water Power Co., 34 Wash.App. 25, 659 P.2d 1113 (1983), indicated that its research revealed no jurisdiction which had imposed strict liability for accidents arising out of escaping gas from lines maintained in the public streets." The majority opinion continued:

> The insurance rationale for imposing liability on a gas distributor which we are urged to adopt, and which the minority thinks we should adopt, is not without its attractiveness. If adopted, the ratepayers pay the damage for those few who may sustain damage to person or property. On the other hand, in the typical explosion case involving a home, such as the one at bar, the insurance rationale is likewise present under the negligence standard. For example, the record here shows that the [plaintiffs] had homeowners insurance. Their property damage to both real estate and personal property was largely compensated by their homeowners insurance. Thus, should we adopt a rule making the gas distributor an insurer, what we would be doing in a great majority of cases would be allowing, in substance, subrogation insurers to shift the risk for which they have collected premiums to the gas company and its ratepayers, notwithstanding the gas company may be free of negligence. * * * [I]n most cases, as in this case, it is not the innocent victim who bears the loss, but rather an insurance company which collected premiums to insure the loss * * *.

A footnote added that the plaintiffs

> likewise claimed to have sustained personal injuries. The record does not show that they had health and accident insurance which presumably would cover any medical expenses and costs; but considering the employment of the parties and their education and experience, it is most likely that they did. Notwithstanding, we acknowledge that they could not recover for damages generally recognized as general damages, such as for pain and suffering, loss of consortium, etc.

In support of strict liability, the dissenting opinion (Todd, J.) emphasized that "this is the first case in more than 20 years" in which the gas company itself had not pinpointed the negligent cause of a gas explosion, and objected to "saddling an innocent victim with substantial property and personal injury losses which, for the most part, are not covered by insurance." It quoted as follows from the dissent in the New Meadows Holding Co. case:

> "During periods of technological or industrial advance which promise great societal benefits, theories of loss allocation which place the risk of serious loss upon the members of society for technological or industrial accidents not attributable to an identifiable person breaching an articulable standard, may be acceptable for the well-being of society and consequently, just. To hold otherwise places unreasonable restraints upon the development of society as a whole that ultimately would be adverse to the well-being of its individual members. But once the promised benefits, such as here—the wide-spread use of a relatively

clean and inexpensive energy source—have become a reality, the risk of serious loss should be spread among the beneficiaries of the advance and not thrust upon a faultless victim.

"Just how prevalent are injuries and damage from natural gas explosions? The majority correctly states there are fewer than 25 deaths each year in the United States from this kind of malfunction. Six years ago 466 failures involving transmission and gathering lines were reported to the Department of Transportation. 10 United States Dep't of Transp., *Natural Gas Pipeline Safety Act Annual Report* (1977) at note 1, p. 3. So the possible liability of any natural gas transmission company is not at a level so high as to be economically prohibitive when measured against the cost of insurance to compensate persons injured, or payment for property damaged by a gas explosion. The loss would be spread among its customers."

SECTION D.   DEFENSES AND LIMITS

Here we should assume that defendant's activity, which harmed plaintiff, is subject to a rule of strict liability. That is, we assume both that the activity carried on by defendant is the type of undertaking to which strict liability attaches, and that but for the carrying on of this activity the harm to plaintiff would not have happened. Before strict liability for damages is finally established, two sets of issues remain to be addressed.

First, does plaintiff conduct or plaintiff choice cut against liability? Unreasonable plaintiff conduct in a situation of peril is contributory negligence; knowing plaintiff choice to encounter peril is assumption of risk. Materials below investigate how these two standard defenses operate in the context of strict liability. A related question is whether someone who participates in defendant's dangerous undertaking—an insider, not a stranger to the activity—should be allowed to recover for harm caused by the perilous enterprise.

Second, is the casual nexus between defendant's activity and plaintiff's harm close enough, or is it so attenuated that liability should be withheld? In a negligence case, plaintiff must show that defendant's conduct is the "legal cause" of injury. Likewise, in the area of strict liability, "legal cause" questions may arise. Materials below show that, even if defendant is carrying on the type of activity to which strict liability attaches, such liability does not extend to every possible harm that may result from the carrying on of the activity.

RESTATEMENT OF TORTS, SECOND (1977)

§ 523.   Assumption of Risk

The plaintiff's assumption of the risk of harm from an abnormally dangerous activity bars his recovery for the harm.

§ 524. Contributory Negligence

(1) Except as stated in Subsection (2), the contributory negligence of the plaintiff is not a defense to the strict liability of one who carries on an abnormally dangerous activity.

(2) The plaintiff's contributory negligence in knowingly and unreasonably subjecting himself to the risk of harm from the activity is a defense to the strict liability.

McLANE v. NORTHWEST NATURAL GAS CO.

Supreme Court of Oregon, 1970.
255 Or. 324, 467 P.2d 635.

HOLMAN, J. This is an action for damages for wrongful death brought by the administratrix of decedent's estate for the benefit of decedent's widow and minor children. Plaintiff appealed from a judgment in favor of defendant which was entered after a demurrer to plaintiff's complaint was sustained and plaintiff elected not to plead further.

The sole question upon this appeal is whether plaintiff's complaint states a cause of action based upon strict liability. The relevant parts of plaintiff's complaint are as follows:

"III

" * * * [D]efendant was the owner of * * * property on N.W. St. Helen's Road, Portland, Oregon, whereupon it maintained * * * storage units wherein it collected and controlled large amounts of natural gas.

"IV

" * * * said commodity was capable of great harm if it escaped from control.

"V

" * * * [P]laintiff's decedent was on a portion of the property of the defendant away from the aforementioned collection of gas, to-wit, the plaintiff's decedent was preparing to assist in insulating a part of a * * * gas storage tank then under construction * * *.

"VI

"A portion of the gas so collected escaped from the defendant's control and entered the aforesaid * * * gas storage tank, and then and there exploded, causing the death * * *."

Plaintiff relies on the rule of Rylands v. Fletcher and Restatement of Torts § 519. * * *

The first question which arises in this case is whether defendant was engaged in an activity in which abnormal risks were inherent. Such an activity is spoken of as ultrahazardous or abnormally dangerous. Whether an activity is abnormally dangerous is a question for the court. It is our opinion that natural gas in vaporous form is sufficiently volatile to be capable of great harm and that the danger of explosion and/or fire from its storage in large quantities cannot be completely eliminated by the use of reasonable care. It is usually held that the storage of explosives in a settled area is abnormally dangerous. We view natural gas as of the same nature as an explosive.

* * *

The trial judge ruled that the storage of natural gas is not abnormally dangerous (ultrahazardous) because if care is used, the risk of an explosion or a fire is minimal. We agree that miscarriage is not frequent, probably because a high degree of care is usually used and, therefore, the risk of some harm cannot be said to be great. However, when miscarriage does occur, it can be lethal. We rather suspect that a blending process goes on and that the risk of some harm may be less if the gravity of the possible harm is great enough. * * *

We believe the principal factor which brings the activity within the abnormally dangerous classification is not so much the frequency of miscarriage (although this may be important) as it is the creation of an additional risk to others which cannot be alleviated and which arises from the extraordinary, exceptional, or abnormal nature of the activity. There is no reason why defendant's activity should not pay the cost of the additional risk of harm to others which arises from the activity's unusual nature. It is a risk which does not result from customary industrial activity. It is not a normal risk which is mutually created and borne by all.

* * * Undoubtedly, another factor which enters the picture is the feeling that where one of two innocent persons must suffer, the loss should fall upon the one who created the risk causing the harm.

* * *

Defendant next contends that the Rylands v. Fletcher type of absolute liability is not applicable because neither the stored gas nor the force of its explosion escaped from defendant's premises. This contention raises a problem on which there is very little law. * * *

We can see no meaningful reason, in terms of the policies behind imposing strict liability, why, in all cases, liability should be limited to damage which occurs off a defendant's premises. * * * The basis of the liability is the creation of an abnormal risk. This risk can be present both on and off defendant's premises. There may be reasons why a plaintiff should not recover which revolve around the circumstances under which plaintiff happened to be upon defendant's premises. Such reasons are usually grouped under the doctrine of assumption of risk. However, we cannot say that in all instances plaintiff's presence on defendant's premises should prevent recovery without more. It does not appear that in all instances the boundaries of a defendant's premises are relevant to any reasons for applying or not applying absolute liability.

Mere proximity to the area of danger may or may not be greater in the case of one who is on the premises as compared with one who is not. A person who is off the premises may be only across the street from the explosion while a person on defendant's premises may be a half mile away from it. No relevant distinction which is applicable in all instances is discernible between a person who is one foot within the boundary of defendant's premises as compared with one who is one foot from defendant's premises.

* * *

Defendant also contends that plaintiff's complaint is insufficient to state a cause of action because it alleges that decedent was engaged in the construction of a gas tank upon defendant's premises when the explosion occurred. Defendant argues that under Restatement (Second) Torts § 523, decedent, as a matter of law, assumed the risk of explosion because he took part in the abnormally dangerous activity. The complaint does not disclose the circumstances under which decedent was working upon defendant's premises. Two possibilities exist: he could have been an employee of defendant or an employee of an independent contractor. Our treatment of the subject of assumption of risk presupposes that he could have been either.

Assumption of risk is presently the source of much controversy among courts and legal scholars. Harper and James contend that assumption of risk is duplicated in other more widely understood concepts, such as scope of defendant's duty or plaintiff's contributory negligence, and that the defense of assumption of risk should be abolished except in those instances where there is an actual express agreement by plaintiff to incur the risk and to relieve defendant of responsibility. 2 Harper and James, The Law of Torts 1191, § 21.8 (1956). In effect, their concept distributes everything that was formerly known as assumption of risk between no-duty upon defendant and contributory negligence on the part of plaintiff, with the exception of an express agreement to assume the risk and to hold defendant harmless. Other legal scholars disagree that the concept should be limited to this extent.

Disregarding terminology, whether the reason for not allowing plaintiff to recover is described as assumption of risk, no-duty on the part of defendant, or contributory negligence by decedent, all authorities would agree that before decedent's participation in the work will bar plaintiff's recovery, such participation must have been with the full realization by decedent of the risks which resulted in his death, and he must have voluntarily incurred them. Plaintiff's complaint does not allege facts from which it must necessarily be concluded that decedent, with knowledge, voluntarily submitted himself to such risks. Such a conclusion does not have to be drawn just because decedent was working on defendant's premises in the furtherance of defendant's activity. Before knowledge and voluntariness will be inferred as a matter of law from decedent's actions in engaging in the work, the situation with which decedent was faced must have presented a more obvious and immediate danger than that which is disclosed by plaintiff's complaint. Even if we assume that this court will follow the Restatement (Second) rule which recognizes assumption of risk as a defense to strict liability, the questions of decedent's knowledge and voluntariness are still viable and outstanding in this case.

* * *

The judgment of the circuit court is reversed and the case is remanded for further proceedings.

———

IRVINE v. RARE FELINE BREEDING CENTER, INC., 685 N.E.2d 120 (Ind.App.1997). Irvine's arm was severely mauled when he tried to pet defendant Schaffer's tiger through an opening in a wire fence. He asserted strict liability. The trial court declined to render summary judgment on the question whether plaintiff's conduct barred his recovery, and certified an interlocutory appeal to clarify the law bearing on defenses to strict liability. *Held*, "we adopt the Restatement's approach in wild animal cases." Indiana recognizes strict liability for harm done by "a naturally ferocious or dangerous animal." The Indiana Comparative Fault Act governs actions "based on fault," and does not apply to a strict liability claim. The Second Restatement of Torts, which says that "voluntarily and unreasonably encountering a known danger" is a defense to strict liability, will be followed.

"[T]here was evidence that Irvine was aware of a prior incident wherein the tiger which injured him grabbed another man's thumb. However, there was other evidence tending to indicate that Schaffer and others had petted the tiger safely in the past. * * * In view of the conflicting evidence and inferences, summary judgment was properly denied on the issue of whether a defense was appropriate in this case."

RESTATEMENT OF TORTS, THIRD: LIABILITY FOR PHYSICAL HARM (BASIC PRINCIPLES)
Tent. Draft No. 1 (March 28, 2001).

§ 25. Comparative Responsibility
If the plaintiff has been contributorily negligent in failing to take precautions against an abnormally dangerous activity * * *, the plaintiff's recovery for physical harm resulting from the contributory negligence is reduced in accordance with the share of responsibility assigned to the plaintiff.

Comment:

c. Effect of contributory negligence. * * * In the years intervening since the drafting of the Second Restatement, comparative negligence has been introduced and widely accepted as a defense in negligence actions. * * * It is widely perceived that in negligence actions comparative negligence provides an appealing compromise between, on the one hand, allowing the plaintiff's contributory negligence to defeat the plaintiff's claim and, on the other hand, regarding the plaintiff's contributory negligence as irrelevant to the defendant's liability. This appeal extends to strict-liability claims as well. Especially in the context of defendant strict liability, the term "comparative negligence" does not suffice; however, the term "comparative responsibility" is satisfactory. * * *

d. Assigning proportionate shares. * * * When the defendant is held liable under a theory of strict liability, no literal comparison of the fault of the two parties may be possible. According to Restatement Third, Torts: Apportionment of Liability § 8, Comment *a*, while "comparative responsibility" is the common legal term, "assigning shares of responsibility" might be a better term, "because it suggests that the factfinder, after considering the relevant factors, *assigns* shares of responsibility rather than *compares* incommensurate quantities." * * *

e. Assumption of risk. The Restatement Second of Torts, while generally rejecting contributory negligence as an affirmative defense [to strict liability], singled out one form of contributory negligence as a complete defense. Plaintiffs who knowingly and unreasonably subjected themselves to the risk of harm were barred from any recovery. * * * The Second Restatement, in a separate but related section, declared that assumption of risk operates as a full defense against a strict-liability claim.

[Section 25 of the present Restatement provides] that all forms of contributory negligence are subject to the comparative-responsibility process. No separate defense of assumption of risk is recognized. Accordingly, under this section particular plaintiffs whose recovery would have been barred under the Second Restatement can secure a partial, although generally small, recovery. * * *

————

NEW YORK CIVIL PRACTICE LAW & RULES (McKinney 1976). Section 1411, enacted in 1975, provides for pure comparative fault as follows:

In any action to recover damages for personal injury, injury to property, or wrongful death, the culpable conduct attributable to the claimant or to the decedent, including contributory negligence or assumption of risk, shall not bar recovery, but the amount of damages otherwise recoverable shall be diminished in the proportion which the culpable conduct attributable to the claimant or decedent bears to the culpable conduct which caused the damages.

In his Practice Commentaries Joseph M. McLaughlin notes:

By its terms, section 1411 is not limited to negligence actions. Thus, in an action for breach of warranty, strict liability in tort, or strict products liability, where it has become increasingly common to hold that contributory negligence or assumption of the risk is a defense, CPLR 1411 now directs that the recovery be diminished by the proportion of the plaintiff's "culpable conduct." * * *

It is interesting (and edifying) that the new statute treats contributory negligence and assumption of the risk interchangeably. The writer has never clearly understood the difference between the two doctrines, and it is well that the statute handles both defenses identically.

FRASER–PATTERSON LUMBER CO. v. SOUTHERN RAILWAY CO., 79 F.Supp. 424 (W.D.S.C.1948). A South Carolina statute provides that a railroad "shall be responsible in damages to any person * * * injured by fire communicated by its locomotive engines * * * and shall have an insurable interest in the property upon its route for which it may be so held responsible, and may procure insurance thereon in its own behalf." Plaintiff lumber company brought suit under the statute to recover damages for property destroyed in a fire caused by defendant's locomotive. The railroad posed two defenses: (1) contributory negligence and "contributory wilfullness"; (2) a written contract whereby the railroad agreed to maintain a special "industrial track" to carry plaintiff's freight onto the main line, and plaintiff in turn agreed to "indemnify and save harmless the defendant against any and all claims * * * for loss or damage by fire." With respect to the first defense the court said:

> It appears * * * that the liability of a railroad company for the results of communicated fires is, under the statute, absolute; no question of negligence, due care, proximate cause, or remote cause can arise in an action under the statute; the only question is whether the conditions under the statute are found to exist, and not whether, under the general law, apart from the provisions of the statute, liability would exist. It seems to me to follow, therefore, that there can be no defense of contributory negligence on the part of the plaintiff in this case. For the same reasons there can be no question of contributory wilfullness.

However, the court went on to say that the written contract constituted a good defense, since it "is a valid contract, and is not against public policy."

YUKON EQUIPMENT, INC. v. FIREMAN'S FUND INSURANCE CO.
Supreme Court of Alaska, 1978.
585 P.2d 1206.

MATTHEWS, Justice. A large explosion occurred at 2:47 a.m. on December 7, 1973, in the suburbs north of the city of Anchorage. The explosion originated at a storage magazine for explosives * * * which was operated by petitioner Yukon Equipment, Inc. The storage magazine is located on a 1,870 acre tract * * *. The magazine which exploded was located 3,820 feet from the nearest building not used to store explosives and 4,330 feet from the nearest public highway. At the time of the explosion it contained approximately 80,000 pounds of explosives. The blast damaged dwellings and other buildings within a two mile radius of the magazine and, in some instances, beyond a two mile radius. The ground concussion it caused registered 1.8 on the Richter scale at the earthquake observation station in Palmer, some 30 miles away.

The explosion was caused by thieves. Four young men had driven onto the tract where the magazine was located, broken into the storage magazine, set a prepared charge, and fled. They apparently did so in an effort to conceal the fact that they had stolen explosives from the site a day or two earlier.

This consolidated lawsuit was brought to recover for property damage caused by the explosion. Cross-motions for partial summary judgment were filed, and summary judgment on the issue of liability was granted in favor of the respondents [plaintiffs below]. * * *

* * * Respondents argue that the summary judgment is sustainable under the theory of absolute liability and that the intentional nature of the explosion is not a defense. We agree with respondents and affirm.

I

* * *

[After sketching the development of strict liability the court concluded:] Thus the particular rule of *Exner,* absolute liability for damage caused by the storage of explosives, was preserved by the Restatement and a general rule, inferred from *Exner* and the authorities on which it was based, and from Rylands v. Fletcher and its antecedents, was stated * * *.

* * *

However, we do not believe that the Restatement (Second) approach should be used in cases involving the use or storage of explosives. Instead, we adhere to the rule of Exner v. Sherman Power Constr. Co. and its progeny imposing absolute liability in such cases. The Restatement (Second) approach requires an analysis of degrees of risk and harm, difficulty of eliminating risk, and appropriateness of place, before absolute liability may be imposed. Such factors suggest a negligence standard.[10] * * *

The reasons for imposing absolute liability on those who have created a grave risk of harm to others by storing or using explosives are largely independent of considerations of locational appropriateness. We see no reason for making a distinction between the right of a homesteader to recover when his property has been damaged by a blast set off in a remote corner of the state, and the right to compensation of an urban resident whose home is destroyed by an explosion originating in a settled area. In each case, the loss is properly to be regarded as a cost of the business of storing or using explosives. Every incentive remains to conduct such activities in locations which are as safe as possible, because there the damages resulting from an accident will be kept to a minimum.

II

The next question is whether the intentional detonation of the storage magazine was a superseding cause relieving petitioners from liability. In

---

10. In the analogous area of strict liability for defective products we have rejected the approach of § 402(a) of the Restatement (Second) of Torts which requires proof that a product is "unreasonably dangerous." "It represents a step backwards in the development of products liability cases. The purpose of strict liability is to overcome the difficulty of proof inherent in negligent and warranty theories, thereby insuring that the costs of physical injuries are borne by those who market defective products." Butaud v. Suburban Marine & Sporting Goods, Inc., 543 P.2d 209, 214 (Alaska 1975).

Sharp v. Fairbanks North Star Borough, 569 P.2d 178 (Alaska 1977), a negligence case, we stated that a superseding cause exists where "after the event and looking back from the harm to the actor's negligent conduct, it appears to the court highly extraordinary that it should have brought about the harm." 569 P.2d at 182, quoting from Restatement (Second) of Torts § 435 (1965). We further explained in *Sharp,*

> [w]here the defendant's conduct threatens a particular kind of result which will injure the plaintiff and an intervening cause which could not have been anticipated changes the situation but produces the same result as originally threatened, such a result is within the scope of the defendant's negligence.

Id. at 183 n. 9. The considerations which impel cutting off liability where there is a superseding cause in negligence cases also apply to cases of absolute liability.

Prior to the explosion in question the petitioners' magazines had been illegally broken into at least six times. Most of these entries involved the theft of explosives. Petitioners had knowledge of all of this.

Applying the standards set forth in *Sharp,* supra, to these facts we find there to have been no superseding cause. The incendiary destruction of premises by thieves to cover evidence of theft is not so uncommon an occurrence that it can be regarded as highly extraordinary.[12] Moreover, the particular kind of result threatened by the defendant's conduct, the storage of explosives, was an explosion at the storage site. Since the threatened result occurred it would not be consistent with the principles stated in *Sharp,* supra, to hold there to have been a superseding cause. Absolute liability is imposed on those who store or use explosives because they have created an unusual risk to others. As between those who have created the risk for the benefit of their own enterprise and those whose only connection with the enterprise is to have suffered damage because of it, the law places the risk of loss on the former. When the risk created causes damage in fact, insistence that the precise details of the intervening cause be foreseeable would subvert the purpose of that rule of law.

The partial summary judgment is Affirmed.

OLD ISLAND FUMIGATION, INC. v. BARBEE, 604 So.2d 1246 (Fla.Dist. Ct.App.1992). Defendant fumigated buildings A and B, but not building C, of a condominium complex. Several residents of building C became ill. It turned out that the fire wall between buildings B and C was defective, allowing fumigating gas to enter building C. The fumigator defended against a strict liability claim "on the ground that third parties the architect and

---

12. See Chicago, Wilmington & Vermillion Coal Co. v. Glass, 34 Ill.App. 364 (1889), where the court stated with reference to stored explosives:

It is because no human skill can tell when or where the fatal spark from the clouds or the incendiary's torch may light this dangerous mass and involve everything within its reach in instant destruction that its presence and close contact with human habitation will not be tolerated.

34 Ill.App. at 370.

contractors had actually caused plaintiffs' injuries by failing to construct properly the fire wall between buildings B and C." *Held*, for plaintiffs. "Fumigation is an ultrahazardous activity," and "[a]ny alleged negligence by a third party does not free the fumigation company from liability."

The court relied on Restatement (Second) of Torts § 522 ("One carrying on an abnormally dangerous activity is subject to strict liability for the resulting harm although it is caused by the unexpectable (a) innocent, negligent or reckless conduct of a third person, or (b) action of an animal, or (c) operation of a force of nature") and quoted as follows from the Restatement's comment on § 522:

> The reason for imposing strict liability upon those who carry on abnormally dangerous activities is that they have for their own purposes created a risk that is not a usual incident of the ordinary life of a community. If the risk ripens into injury, it is immaterial that the harm occurs through the unexpectable action of a human being.... This is true irrespective of whether the action of the human being which makes the abnormally dangerous activity harmful is innocent, negligent or even reckless.

BOSTOCK–FERARI AMUSEMENT CO. v. BROCKSMITH, 34 Ind.App. 566, 73 N.E. 281 (1905). Defendant's bear, within the control of defendant's servant, was walking along the road. Plaintiff's horse bolted at sight of the bear and plaintiff was injured. *Held* for defendant, reversing judgment. There was no evidence that the bear was an animal likely to frighten a horse of ordinary gentleness.

MADSEN v. EAST JORDAN IRRIGATION CO., 101 Utah 552, 125 P.2d 794 (1942). Action by mink farmer for loss of mink when mother mink were frightened and destroyed their young. The fright was caused by defendant's blasting, about 100 yards away, while repairing its canal. The complaint alleged that by nature all mink are highly excitable and, when disturbed, will become terrified and kill their young. A general demurrer was sustained, and the plaintiff appealed. *Held,* affirmed. Assuming the rule of absolute liability for damages from use of explosives, "[d]id the mother minks' intervention break the chain of causation and therefore require an allegation of negligence?" One "who fires explosives is not liable for every occurrence following the explosion which has a semblance of connection to it. Jake's horse might become so excited that he would run next door and kick a few ribs out of Cy's jersey cow, but is such a thing to be anticipated from an explosion? * * * In the instant case, the killing of their kittens was not an act of self-preservation on the part of the mother mink but a peculiarity of disposition which was not within the realm of matters to be anticipated."

FOSTER v. PRESTON MILL CO., 44 Wn.2d 440, 268 P.2d 645 (1954). Blasting caused frightened mother mink to kill their kittens. *Held,* for defendant, on two grounds. First, "strict liability should be confined to consequences which lie within the extraordinary risk whose existence calls for such responsibility," just as negligence liability must be restricted to consequences proximately caused. No case can be found granting recovery in strict liability for injury caused by a frightened farm animal. Second, the harm herein is attributable to "the plaintiff's extraordinary and unusual use of land," rather than "risks inherent in blasting operations." The "relatively moderate" effect of the blasting, which injured no nearby landowner except plaintiff, "was no more than a usual incident of the ordinary life of the community." Therefore plaintiff's activity—not defendant's—"must, as a matter of sound policy, bear the responsibility for the loss here sustained." The court noted that a state statute "requiring notice to be given * * * when blasting is to be undertaken within fifteen hundred feet of any fur farm or commercial hatchery" did not apply to present facts.

Chapter 18

NUISANCE

_____

The legal category "nuisance," historically and at present, covers a wide variety of situations. In Chapter 4, where nuisance is introduced, the materials consider situations of private nuisance in which defendant's use of land interferes with plaintiff's interest in use and enjoyment of neighboring land. This focus on land-to-land interference continues.

The present chapter concentrates on cases in which fallout from defendant's use of land—noise, smells, air pollution, water pollution—hurts defendant's neighbors. Detrimental "fallout" arising from productive use of land is the most important topic addressed by nuisance doctrine. Here liability for nuisance goes beyond negligence, and tort law connects with public law of environmental protection.

The "fallout" situation of greatest interest has the following features. Defendant, a landowner, engages in productive activity within the confines of a parcel of land. But defendant's activity has a negative side effect; fallout from the activity results in injury to occupants of other parcels of land nearby. Defendant's activity is on-going, and the bad side effect is continuous. This fallout is not created on purpose; defendant would be glad if no harm befell others. But defendant knows that the harmful impact is happening; in the circumstances, involving continuous perceptible fallout from on-going activity, defendant's knowledge of the harmful impact is readily inferred. Therefore it may be said that defendant "intends" the harm. (Notice that, if many are harmed, the situation may be regarded as one of public nuisance; see materials at the end of Section B.)

All of the ten main cases in Chapter 18 are fallout situations; six involve air-borne pollution, molecular or larger, which literally falls upon neighboring land; one involves airport noise; three involve water-borne pollution.

SECTION A. NUISANCE AND TRESPASS

This section looks at distinctions—and connections—between liability for nuisance and liability for trespass to land. Both torts address interferences affecting landed property. At first glance the two, trespass and nuisance, seem rather distinct. In the conventional phraseology, they protect different interests: trespass, the interest in exclusive possession of land;

862

nuisance, the interest in use and enjoyment of land. The elements of the two land-related torts, which are different, were presented in Chapter 4.

The basic nuisance situation, as described a moment ago, is a case of "fallout." By contrast, the core case of trespass is an invasion in the nature of a "takeover." A dramatic example of a hard-core continuing trespass is the *Crescent Mining Co. v. Silver King Mining Co.* case at the end of Chapter 4. There the defendant, without right and despite protest, entered plaintiff's land; dug a trench, laid a pipeline, and mounted an armed guard to maintain the invasion by force if necessary. Here is a direct and purposeful appropriation of someone else's property, an aggressive exercise of dominion—"takeover" indeed. In a case involving purposeful and continuous bodily trespass, an injunction against the defendant, protecting plaintiff's property entitlement, would today be pretty automatic.

The three main cases that follow are situations of acoustic or chemical fallout, not bodily takeover. But they show that trespass categories, which are quite general, might be thought to apply in some fallout situations. These materials explore circumstances where the same conduct by defendant might be regarded as a trespass or as a nuisance. They pose a number of questions about the overlap of trespass and nuisance. If both sets of categories apply, does it matter which tort is found? In a suit for damages? In a suit for an injunction? How far will trespass categories stretch?

ATKINSON v. BERNARD, INC.
Supreme Court of Oregon, 1960.
223 Or. 624, 355 P.2d 229.

GOODWIN, J. The defendant operator of a small airport appeals, and the plaintiff landowners cross-appeal, from a decree of the circuit court enjoining part, but not all, of the flights from the airport over the lands of the plaintiffs. The parties will be referred to in this opinion as the Airport and the plaintiffs.

In 1918 the Airport commenced operation about one mile north of the city center of Beaverton. The Airport serves mainly single-engine, non-commercial aircraft of the type commonly flown for business and pleasure by persons having private licenses as distinguished from larger aircraft found in military and airline service. The present runway is about 2,500 feet long.

Some time after 1948, a suburban residential area known as Cedar Hills was developed directly north of the airport. Building sites and homes were sold to persons desiring to purchase them. Some 68 property owners joined as plaintiffs in 1955 in the present suit, and 21 of them testified at the trial. The plaintiffs located nearest the airport are approximately 1,000 feet north of the runway. Others are located at varying distances greater than 1,000 feet from the end of the runway, but all are within an area affected in some degree by the sound of aircraft landing and taking off.

The evidence showed that during fair weather the wind commonly blows from the north, and most of the flights take off toward the north during fair weather. The evidence further showed that a substantial number of flights take place early on Sunday mornings when the air is calm but when the plaintiffs are not necessarily ready to greet the new day.

The complaint alleged that, in taking off over the plaintiffs' homes, the planes fly at altitudes varying from 50 to 300 feet above the rooftops, and in so doing create noises and vibrations which substantially interfere with the use and enjoyment of the lands of the plaintiffs. There was testimony in support of these allegations, but the matter of altitude was sharply disputed.

The complaint further alleged that such flights constitute a hazard. There was evidence that during the past thirty years at least two planes had crashed to the north of the airport premises and near the property occupied by certain of the plaintiffs. Two others had crashed to the south of the airport. The plaintiffs expressed concern that future crashes could be expected with disastrous results for nearby householders.

The plaintiffs demanded an injunction of all flights taking off to the north, as such flights necessarily pass over one or more of their homes before gaining cruising altitude. As the only runway lies north and south, such an injunction would, for all practical purposes, put an end to fair-weather flying from the airport. During the winter, the evidence showed, the prevailing winds are from the south.

The trial judge viewed the premises, and, upon stipulation of the parties, observed a demonstration of several flights over the property of the plaintiffs.

The decree enjoined flights taking off over the property of the plaintiffs by all aircraft which make "appreciably more noise than [a certain 1954 Piper Tri–Pacer 135 HP owned at that time by the State of Oregon]."

The Airport appeals from the decree, contending that it is too vague and indefinite for enforcement. The plaintiffs cross-appeal and demand an end to all take-offs over their lands.

No decibel readings or other objective acoustical data were made available to the trial court. The evidence showed that atmospheric conditions have some influence upon what those on the ground may hear as the result of flights over their property, but the nature and extent of such influence was undisclosed.

There are a number of problems raised in the briefs and argued before this court, but the principal question dealt with below was the extent to which the plaintiffs were entitled to noise abatement.

The trial court found, and the evidence supports the finding, that at least some of the plaintiffs were annoyed and inconvenienced by the noise of unspecified "larger" or "noisier" planes taking off over their rooftops. The noise on take-off bears some relation to the kind of engine, the pitch of the propeller, and the angle of climb between the time the plane leaves the runway and the point where it reaches flying or cruising altitude. The evidence left the exact relationship somewhat obscure, but mere size of aircraft alone appeared to be less significant than the other factors.

Here we are dealing with a privately operated airport and the question of enjoining certain flights, all of which, to some extent, invade the airspace below navigable heights and above the surface. This was the situation in Anderson v. Souza, 38 Cal.2d 825, 844, 243 P.2d 497, 509. There the court indicated that the landowners were entitled to limited relief and remanded the cause for further evidence.

To the facts in the instant case, the trial court applied the "privileged trespass" theory found in the Restatement, 1 Torts 460 § 194 (1934). The Restatement rule is as follows:

Travel Through Air Space.

An entry above the surface of the earth, in the air space in the possession of another, by a person who is traveling in an aircraft, is privileged if the flight is conducted

    (a) for the purpose of travel through the air space or for any other legitimate purpose,

    (b) in a reasonable manner,

    (c) at such a height as not to interfere unreasonably with the possessor's enjoyment of the surface of the earth and the air space above it, and

    (d) in conformity with such regulations of the State and federal aeronautical authorities as are in force in the particular State.
   * * *

Under the "privileged trespass" theory, two considerations determine whether the invasion of the landowner's airspace will be privileged: (1) the flight itself must be reasonable, thus eliminating stunting, whimsical changes of propeller pitch and the like, at altitudes which affect those on the ground; and (2) the flights must be at such a height as not to interfere unreasonably with the enjoyment of the surface by the person in possession. [Citations omitted.] As will be seen later, reasonableness becomes the key issue in each case.

It is the process of becoming airborne which causes the difficulty in the case now before the court, as in most of the litigation elsewhere. A partial bibliography, together with a challenging presentation of the "take-off" problem, may be found in William B. Harvey, Landowners' Rights in the Air Age: The Airport Dilemma, 56 Mich.L.Rev. 1313 (1958).

Most heavier-than-air flying machines presently used by private citizens require a horizontal space beyond the end of the runway in which to ascend or descend to or from a flying, or cruising, altitude. The so-called glide-angle or "glide plane" needed for taking off may vary from a ratio of seven feet of horizontal movement to one foot of ascent or descent for light aircraft of modest speed to a ratio of 50 to 1 for high-powered planes of greater weight and velocity. Harvey, 56 Mich.L.Rev., supra at 1314.

Many courts have considered the problems which are inherent in every airport lacking sufficient surface ownership to escort its patrons aloft to navigable airspace entirely over its own land. As noted by Professor Harvey:

"If the prime method for ascertaining the limits of the ownership-trespass zone in airspace is by determining whether the landowner's use and enjoyment of the surface have been subjected to unreasonable interference, it is apparent that the concept of nuisance is equally available with trespass as an analytical tool. In fact, some decisions range freely over both the trespass and the nuisance rationales—the airspace zone in which intrusion by aircraft would be a nuisance apparently being considered in certain opinions as coterminous with that in which it would constitute a trespass * * *, while others which rely upon nuisance as the ground of decision might easily be interpreted in trespass terms * * *." 56 Mich.L.Rev., supra at 1315.

At the point where "reasonableness" enters the judicial process we take leave of trespass and steer into the discretionary byways of nuisance. Each case then must be decided on its own peculiar facts, balancing the interest before the court. * * *

In addition to balancing the private interests of the contesting parties, at least one court has recognized that there is a coexistent element of public interest. There are really two public interests: (1) in protecting the property rights of all landowners, and (2) in protecting the freedom of air travel. The point at which the two interests come into conflict is the point where the unreasonable must give way to the reasonable. * * * See also C. Z. German, The Conflicting Interest of Airport Owners and Nearby Property Owners, 20 Kan.City L.Rev. 138. The writer of the law review article, who was at that time a regional attorney for the Civil Aeronautics Administration, suggested that the test of reasonableness may be used equally well when an airport seeks to enjoin activity on neighboring lands which may be claimed to be a hazard to navigation.

We hold that whenever the aid of equity is sought to enjoin all or part of the operations of a private airport, including flights over the land of the plaintiff, the suit is for the abatement of a nuisance, and the law of nuisance rather than that of trespass applies.

The nuisance theory is in accordance with modern thinking in the field, and with common sense. The flexibility of nuisance law enables the trial judge to take into consideration, openly with proper pleadings and evidence, all relevant factors which will assist him in balancing the interests of the parties before the court in light of relevant public interest.

The Restatement rule which attempts to pour new wine into the old bottle of trespass appears to be losing adherents, and does not commend itself to this court as a rule to be cemented into the case law of Oregon. See Herbert David Klein, Cujus Est Solum Ejus Est * * * Quousque Tandem?, 26 J Air L & Co 237, 254; Wherry and Condon, Aerial Trespass under the Restatement of the Law of Torts, 6 Air L Rev 113, 124.

We have previously said that reasonableness in such cases is primarily a question for the trial judge to determine from all the facts; " * * * whether a particular annoyance or inconvenience is sufficient to constitute a nuisance depends upon its effect upon an ordinarily reasonable man, that is, a normal person of ordinary habits and sensibilities * * * [citing cases]." Amphitheaters, Inc. v. Portland Meadows, 184 Or. at page 349, 198 P.2d at page 852.

The trial judge found that flights which make sufficient noise to constitute an unreasonable interference with the rights of the landowners consisted mainly of isolated flights of planes heavier than those ordinarily using the airport at the time of trial. We are unable to learn from the record just how such aircraft might accurately be described, but presumably the line can be drawn somewhere.

The trial judge attempted to draw the line by using a specific model of plane which he described in the decree. For the purpose of regulating its future conduct, the Airport is entitled to know with greater certainty what flights will be permitted and what flights will be enjoined. The state-owned Tri–Pacer may not always be available as a template for measuring excessive sound. * * *

Before the court can arrive at an objective standard of reasonableness, it will be necessary to perform acoustical studies under the supervision of the trial court. A decree thereafter should be drawn in terms of decibel readings set forth in relation to relevant atmospheric conditions with sufficient latitude for inconsequential deviations. An objective measurement of noise levels will then be established and such a decree can be properly enforced.

The decree appealed from is vacated and the cause remanded for further evidence in accordance with the views expressed herein. Counsel should be given a reasonable time in the trial court in which to prepare and submit additional evidence.

———

SMITH v. NEW ENGLAND AIRCRAFT CO., 270 Mass. 511, 170 N.E. 385 (1930). The question in the case was whether aircraft, in order to reach or leave an airport, may of right fly so low as 100 feet over brush and woodland not otherwise utilized. *Held,* that invasions at such a low level were trespass. The court said: "If, in the interest of aerial navigation, rights of flight at such a low altitude over lands of others are of sufficient public importance doubtless the power of eminent domain for acquisition of rights of way in airspaces might be authorized."

GRIGGS v. COUNTY OF ALLEGHENY, PENNSYLVANIA, 369 U.S. 84, 82 S.Ct. 531, 7 L.Ed.2d 585 (1962). Action by a property owner against county for an alleged taking or appropriation of his property resulting from take-off and landing of aircraft at county airport. No flights were in violation of pertinent regulations nor were any flights lower than necessary for safe landing or take-off. The planes taking off observed regular flight patterns ranging from 30 feet to 300 feet over plaintiff's residence, and on let-down they were within 53 feet to 153 feet. On take-off the noise of the planes was comparable "to the noise of a riveting machine or steam hammer." On the let-down the planes made a noise comparable "to that of a noisy factory." *Held,* that defendant county had "taken" an air easement over plaintiff's property for which it must pay just compensation as required by the Fourteenth Amendment.

WHITTAKER v. STANGVICK, 100 Minn. 386, 111 N.W. 295 (1907). Plaintiff owning a narrow strip of land, known as a "duck pass", situated between two lakes, sought to enjoin defendant from setting up a "blind" directly in front of the pass and shooting at ducks from the blind in the direction of the pass. Some of the shot, it was shown, would cross over the pass, while other shot would come to rest thereon. No damage was shown other than the interference with the facilities for shooting wild fowl afforded by the pass. *Held*, that the threatened conduct of defendant would constitute trespass, against which an injunction should be granted.

SMITH v. SMITH, 110 Mass. 302 (1872). The eaves of defendant's barn projected some 15 inches over plaintiff's land. *Held*, that "projecting his eaves over the plaintiff's land is a wrongful act on the part of the defendant which, if continued for twenty years, might give him a title to the land by adverse occupation. It is a wrongful occupation of the plaintiff's land, for which he may maintain an action of trespass."

MARTIN v. REYNOLDS METALS CO.
Supreme Court of Oregon, 1959.
221 Or. 86, 342 P.2d 790.

O'CONNELL, Justice. This is an action of trespass. The plaintiffs allege that during the period from August 22, 1951 to January 1, 1956 the defendant, in the operation of its aluminum reduction plant near Troutdale, Oregon caused certain fluoride compounds in the form of gases and particulates to become airborne and settle upon the plaintiffs' land rendering it unfit for raising livestock during that period. Plaintiffs allege that their cattle were poisoned by ingesting the fluorides which contaminate the forage and water on their land. They sought damages in the amount of $450,000 for the loss of use of their land for grazing purposes and for the deterioration of the land through the growth of brush, trees and weeds resulting from the lack of use of the premises for grazing purposes. The plaintiffs also sought punitive damages in the amount of $30,000.

The plaintiffs and the defendant each moved for a directed verdict, whereupon the trial court found that the plaintiffs had suffered damage in the amount of $71,500 in the loss of use of their land and $20,000 for the deterioration of their land and entered judgment accordingly. The trial court rejected the plaintiffs' claim for punitive damages.

In the course of the pleadings the defendant raised the issue as to whether the complaint alleged a cause of action in trespass. The defendant contended that at most a cause of action in nuisance was stated. The trial court accepted the plaintiff's theory of the case. The principal assignments of error rest upon the defendant's contention that the trial court was mistaken in identifying the defendant's invasion of the plaintiffs' land as a trespass; that there was not sufficient evidence to establish a cause of action under any theory, but that if the court should find the evidence sufficient to give rise to liability the defendant's conduct constituted a nuisance and not a trespass.

Through appropriate pleadings the defendant set up the two-year statute of limitations applicable to nontrespassory injuries to land (ORS 12.110). If the defendant's conduct created a nuisance and not a trespass the defendant would be liable only for such damage as resulted from its conduct during a period of two years immediately preceding the date upon which plaintiffs' action was instituted. On the other hand, if the defendant's conduct resulted in a trespass upon plaintiffs' land the six-year statute of limitations provided for in ORS 12.080 would be applicable and plaintiffs would be entitled to recover damages resulting from the trespasses by defendant during the period from August 22, 1951 to January 1, 1956.

The gist of the defendant's argument is as follows: a trespass arises only when there has been a "breaking and entering upon real property," constituting a direct, as distinguished from a consequential, invasion of the possessor's interest in land; and the settling upon the land of fluoride compounds consisting of gases, fumes and particulates is not sufficient to satisfy these requirements.

Before appraising the argument we shall first describe more particularly the physical and chemical nature of the substance which was deposited upon plaintiffs' land. In reducing alumina (the oxide of aluminum) to aluminum the alumina is subjected to an electrolytic process which causes the emanation of fluoridic compounds * * *. The individual particulates which form these chemical compounds are not visible to the naked eye. A part of them were captured by a fume collection system which was installed in November, 1950; the remainder became airborne and a part of the uncaptured particles eventually were deposited upon plaintiffs' land.

There is evidence to prove that during the period from August, 1951, to January, 1956 the emanation of fluorides from defendant's plant averaged approximately 800 pounds daily. Some of this discharge was deposited upon the plaintiffs' land. There is sufficient evidence to support the trial court's finding that the quantity of fluorides deposited upon plaintiffs' land was great enough to cause $91,500 damage to the plaintiffs in the use of their land for grazing purposes and in the deterioration of their land as alleged.

We must determine, however, whether all or only a part of this damage may be shown; all, if the invasion constitutes a trespass, a part only (i.e., the damage which resulted within the two-year period of the statute of limitations) if the invasion was a nuisance and not a trespass.

Trespass and private nuisance are separate fields of tort liability relating to actionable interference with the possession of land. They may be distinguished by comparing the interest invaded; an actionable invasion of a possessor's interest in the exclusive possession of land is a trespass; an actionable invasion of a possessor's interest in the use and enjoyment of his land is a nuisance. 4 Restatement, Torts 224, Intro. Note Chapter 40.

The same conduct on the part of a defendant may and often does result in the actionable invasion of both of these interests, in which case the choice between the two remedies is, in most cases, a matter of little consequence. Where the action is brought on the theory of nuisance alone the court ordinarily is not called upon to determine whether the conduct would also result in a trespassory invasion. In such cases the courts' treatment of the invasion solely in terms of the law of nuisance does not mean that the same conduct could not also be regarded as a trespass. * * *

However, there are cases which have held that the defendant's interference with plaintiff's possession resulting from the settling upon his land of effluents emanating from defendant's operations is exclusively nontrespassory. [Citations omitted.] Although in such cases the separate particles which collectively cause the invasion are minute, the deposit of each of the particles constitutes a physical intrusion and, but for the size of the particle, would clearly give rise to an action of trespass. The defendant asks us to take account of the difference in size of the physical agency through which the intrusion occurs and relegate entirely to the field of nuisance law certain invasions which do not meet the dimensional test, whatever that is. In pressing this argument upon us the defendant must admit that there are cases which have held that a trespass results from the movement or deposit of rather small objects over or upon the surface of the possessor's land.

Thus it has been held that causing shot from a gun to fall upon the possessor's land is a trespass. * * *

The dropping of particles of molten lead upon the plaintiff's land has been held to be a trespass. Van Alstyne v. Rochester Telephone Corp., 163 Misc. 258, 296 N.Y.S. 726. And the defendant was held liable in trespass where spray from a cooling tower on the roof of its theater fell upon the plaintiff's land. B & R Luncheonette, Inc. v. Fairmont Theatre Corp., 278 App.Div. 133, 103 N.Y.S.2d 747.

The deposit of soot and carbon from defendant's mill upon plaintiff's land was held to be a trespass in Young v. Fort Frances Pulp and Paper Co., Canada 1919, 17 Ont.Wkly.Notes 6.

And liability on the theory of trespass has been recognized where the harm was produced by the vibration of the soil or by the concussion of the air which, of course, is nothing more than the movement of molecules one against the other. McNeill v. Redington, 1945, 67 Cal.App.2d 315, 154 P.2d 428. Liability on this basis was clearly recognized in Bedell v. Goulter, 1953, 199 Or. 344, 361, 261 P.2d 842, 850, where Justice Lusk, after discussing the rule of Rylands v. Fletcher, LR 3 HL 330, continued with the following observation:

> * * * And there is slight difficulty in holding that one who engages in blasting operations which set in motion vibrations and concussions of the earth and air which reach to another's land—no matter how far distant—and shatter his dwelling, commits a trespass no less than one who accomplishes the same result by the propulsion of rocks or other material. "Is not a concussion of the air, and jarring, breaking, and cracking the ground with such force as to wreck the buildings thereon, as much an invasion of the rights of the owner as the hurling of a

missile thereon?" Louden v. City of Cincinnati [90 Ohio St. 144, 106 N.E. 970, 974, L.R.A.1915E, 356, Ann.Cas.1916C, 1171].

The view recognizing a trespassory invasion where there is no "thing" which can be seen with the naked eye undoubtedly runs counter to the definition of trespass expressed in some quarters. 1 Restatement, Torts § 158, Comment h (1934); Prosser, Torts § 13 (2d Ed. 1955). It is quite possible that in an earlier day when science had not yet peered into the molecular and atomic world of small particles, the courts could not fit an invasion through unseen physical instrumentalities into the requirement that a trespass can result only from a *direct* invasion. But in this atomic age even the uneducated know the great and awful force contained in the atom and what it can do to a man's property if it is released. In fact, the now famous equation E $= mc^2$ has taught us that mass and energy are equivalents and that our concept of "things" must be reframed. If these observations on science in relation to the law of trespass should appear theoretical and unreal in the abstract, they become very practical and real to the possessor of land when the unseen force cracks the foundation of his house. The force is just as real if it is chemical in nature and must be awakened by the intervention of another agency before it does harm.

If, then, we must look to the character of the instrumentality which is used in making an intrusion upon another's land we prefer to emphasize the object's energy or force rather than its size. Viewed in this way we may define trespass as any intrusion which invades the possessor's protected interest in exclusive possession, whether that intrusion is by visible or invisible pieces of matter or by energy which can be measured only by the mathematical language of the physicist.

We are of the opinion, therefore, that the intrusion of the fluoride particulates in the present case constituted a trespass.

The defendant argues that our decision in Amphitheaters, Inc. v. Portland Meadows, 1948, 184 Or. 336, 198 P.2d 847, 851, 5 A.L.R.2d 690, requires a contrary conclusion. In discussing the distinction between trespass and nuisance the court referred to a difference between "a cannon ball and a ray of light" indicating that the former but not the latter could produce a trespassory invasion. * * * In that case the plaintiff contended that he had suffered damage in the form of a less efficient cinema screen due to the defendant's lights. In denying recovery the court found that there was no damage, apparently because whatever harm the plaintiff suffered was damnum absque injuria.

In every case in which trespass is alleged the court is presented with a problem of deciding whether the defendant's intrusion has violated a legally protected interest of the plaintiff. * * *

In some cases the solution can be based upon the ground that the defendant's conduct is not substantial enough to be regarded as a trespassory intrusion. Thus, the casting of a candle beam upon the screen of a drive-in theater would not constitute an actionable invasion, simply because the intrusion is so trifling that the law will not consider it and the principle de minimis non curat lex is applicable. In some cases the solution may be arrived at by admitting that the intrusion is substantial but refusing to recognize that plaintiff has a legally protected interest in the particular possessory use as against the particular conduct of the defendant. And so the glare of flood lights upon an adjoining owner's cinema screen, as in the Amphitheaters case, may not be a trespass, not because the intrusion is trifling, but because the law does not wish to protect such a use from an invasion, whether the cause of the interference be viewed as a physical intrusion or as a nontrespassory act and covered by the law of nuisance.

The Amphitheaters case can be explained in terms of this latter point of view, i.e., that the glare of the defendant's lights could be regarded as an intrusion within the law of trespass, but that the plaintiff had no right to treat the intrusion as actionable in view of the nature of plaintiff's use and the manner in which the defendant interfered with it. Had the defendant purposely, and not as an incidence of his own legitimate use, directed the rays of light against the plaintiff's screen the court might well have taken the position that the plaintiff could have recovered in a trespass action. These illustrations demonstrate that the tort of trespass involves a weighing process, similar to that involved in the law of nuisance, although to a more limited extent than in nuisance and for a different purpose, i.e., in the one case to define the possessor's interest in exclusive possession, and in the other to define the possessor's interest in use and enjoyment. * * *

* * *

Probably the most important factor which describes the nature of the interest protected under the law of trespass is nothing more than a feeling which a possessor has with respect to land which he holds. It is a sense of ownership; a feeling that what one owns or possesses should not be interfered with, and that it is entitled to protection through law. This being the nature of the plaintiff's interest, it is understandable why actual damage is not an essential ingredient in the law of trespass. As pointed out in 1 Harper & James, Torts, § 1.8, p. 26, the rule permitting recovery in spite of the absence of actual damages "is probably justified as a vindicatory right to protect the possessor's proprietary or dignitary interest in his land." * * *

We hold that the defendant's conduct in causing chemical substances to be deposited upon the plaintiffs' land fulfilled all of the requirements under the law of trespass. * * *

The judgment of the lower court is affirmed.

McALLISTER, Chief Justice (specially concurring). I concur in the result of the above opinion but dissent from that portion thereof that attempts to reconcile the holding in this case with the holding in the case of Amphitheaters, Inc. v. Portland Meadows, 184 Or. 336, 198 P.2d 847.

———

REAM v. KEEN, 314 Ore. 370, 838 P.2d 1073 (1992). Plaintiff landowners brought suit for damages due to "the intrusion of smoke and its lingering odor" caused by defendant's open field burning of grass stubble on his adjacent land. Defendant admitted that he knew smoke would drift onto adjoining property. *Held*, citing *Martin* v. *Reynolds Metals Co.*, supra, that trespass is established. The court rejected defendant's argument that a "weighing process" should be followed, similar to that used when an injunction is sought to abate a nuisance. Here "the plaintiff seeks damages," and it is inappropriate to weigh "the hardship to the defendant against the injury sustained by the plaintiff." In a footnote the court added: "The relative hardship likely to result to the defendant if [an] injunction is granted and to the plaintiff if it is denied, is one of the factors to be considered in determining the appropriateness of an injunction against tort."

RUSSO FARMS, INC. v. VINELAND BOARD OF EDUCATION, 144 N.J. 84, 675 A.2d 1077 (1996). Plaintiffs complained that the improper siting and construction of a public school (by the School Board), plus an inadequate drainage system (maintained by the City), caused repeated flooding of their nearby farmlands, damaging the soil and the crops. The New Jersey Supreme Court said: "Plaintiffs claim that the Board and City are liable under a nuisance theory because the Board and City's use of their property has invaded plaintiffs' use and enjoyment of their land. The invasion was a physical invasion, which ordinarily sounds in trespass, but 'the flooding of the plaintiff's land, which is a trespass, is also a nuisance if it is repeated or of long duration.' " Restatement (Second) of Torts § 821D, cmt. e (1977); cf. Hennessey v. Carmony, 50 N.J.Eq. 616, 618, 25 A. 374 (Ch.1892) (throwing water on another's property once constitutes a trespass, 'to continue to do so constitutes a nuisance'). Plaintiffs could have pled either claim, but chose to plead nuisance."

STATE OF NEW YORK v. FERMENTA ASC CORP., 166 Misc.2d 524, 630 N.Y.S.2d 884 (N.Y.Sup.Ct.1995). Defendants are the manufacturers and distributors of a herbicide called Dachtal. When used in agriculture, Dachtal's active ingredient ("DCPA") degrades into an acid ("TCPA") which enters the subsoil. Excessive amounts of TCPA were found to have contaminated wells which supply drinking water for Suffolk County. The Suffolk County Water Authority undertook costly measures to reduce the level of TCPA in water from its wells, and brought suit in trespass to recover its costs. *Held*, for plaintiff, "[t]here being a direct and intentional invasion of [Water Authority] land by the chemical TCPA." The court summarized: "[Plaintiff] has established that the defendants manufactured and distributed Dachtal which * * * was sold in Suffolk County; that the defendants advised consumers that it be applied to the soil; that Dachtal contains DCPA; that DCPA ultimately breaks down to TCPA and, therefore, that the unlawful invasion of TCPA to the ground water was direct and intentional."

SAN DIEGO GAS & ELECTRIC CO. v. SUPERIOR COURT, 13 Cal.4th 893, 55 Cal.Rptr.2d 724, 920 P.2d 669 (1996). Next to the home owned by plaintiffs are electric power lines maintained by defendant power company. The lines give rise to electric and magnetic fields. Such fields are regions of space pervaded by electromagnetic force; fields from power lines are detectable by instruments but not directly perceived by the senses. Plaintiffs sued defendant for damages and injunctive relief, alleging inter alia trespass. The complaint says defendant "intended to and did emit electromagnetic radiation onto plaintiffs' property without plaintiffs' consent." Plaintiffs fear this "physical invasion" may cause cancer or other disease, but do not allege present physical injury. *Held*, for defendant. Intrusion of electromagnetic fields is "wholly intangible" and does not amount to a trespass. The court quoted with approval from an earlier decision:

" * * * Recovery allowed in prior trespass actions predicated upon noise, gas emissions, or vibration intrusions has, in each instance, been predicated upon the deposit of particulate matter upon the plaintiffs' property or on actual physical damage thereto. All intangible intrusions, such as noise, odor, or light alone, are dealt with as nuisance cases, not trespass. Succinctly stated, the rule is that actionable trespass may not be predicated upon nondamaging noise, odor, or light intrusion * * *."

MERCER v. ROCKWELL INTERNATIONAL CORP.

United States District Court, Western District of Kentucky, 1998.
24 F.Supp.2d 735.

[Defendant's manufacturing plant in Russellville, Kentucky, generated liquid waste containing PCB's (polychlorinated biphenyls). Owing to defendant's negligence, a large amount of PCB-laden waste escaped into a drainage system and then into the Mud River. Plaintiffs own properties on the Mud River some 50 miles downstream. They brought suit seeking recovery for "negligent trespass."

[Plaintiffs alleged that their properties had been contaminated by defendant's PCB waste; that PCB's are cancer-causing chemicals hazardous to health; and that fear of PCB's on the part of prospective purchasers had depressed the market value of their land. Plaintiffs' cause went to trial, but the jury was unable to agree. Defendant then moved for dismissal of the case, on the ground that plaintiffs' evidence was insufficient to establish liability. The trial court (Heyburn, J.) granted defendant's motion. The following excerpts from Judge Heyburn's opinion discuss the elements of a negligent trespass claim.]

The Restatement (Second) of Torts § 165 provides:

One who recklessly or negligently, or as a result of an abnormally dangerous activity, enters land in the possession of another or causes a thing or third person so to enter is subject to liability to the possessor if, but only if, his presence or the presence of the thing or the third person upon the land causes harm to the land, to the possessor, or to a thing or a third person in whose security the possessor has a legally protected interest.

The Restatement distinguishes intentional trespasses and negligent trespasses by requiring "harm" for negligent trespass. *See* Restatement (Second) Torts § 165 cmt. b. Liability is imposed for intentional trespasses when there is an intrusion, even when it is harmless, and liability is imposed for negligent trespasses only when there has been harm to the property. *See id.*

* * *

Plaintiffs contend that the PCB's are an entry of a thing onto their land causing harm.[1] This would be obvious if PCB's were as big as a house or as noticeable as red paint. Unfortunately, the PCB's are as invisible as the wind and as unobtrusive as a grain of sand. In circumstances such as this, courts have been reluctant to find a trespass. *See e.g., Bradley v. American Smelting & Refining Co.,* 104 Wash.2d 677, 709 P.2d 782 (Wash.1985). Indeed, even in * * * the context of intentional trespass, courts have reasoned that "entry" by an invisible object * * * cannot be proven without a showing of harm to the property. The analysis in these cases is directly applicable to a claim for negligent trespass because negligent trespass has as its express elements "entry" *and* harm.

Trespass does not protect against mere entrance; it protects against another's interference with an owner's right to exclusive possession of the property. *See* W. Page Keeton, et al., Prosser & Keeton in the Law of Torts § 13, at 71 (5th Ed.1984). Normally, entry would qualify as interference. However, not every touching of the land interferes with that right to exclusive possession of the property. Although the "right to exclusive possession" is liberally interpreted so as to not subject property owners to most uninvited intrusions, some entries may be so insubstantial or so trifling that they will not infringe upon the legally protected interest in freedom from interference with exclusive possession. *See Martin v. Reynolds Metals Co.,* 221 Or. 86, 342 P.2d 790 (Or.1959).

* * *

Many other courts have allowed trespass claims for invisible particles, but like the Oregon court [in *Martin v. Reynolds Metals*] they circumscribe the reach of this rule by requiring actual damage to the property. [Discussion of cases omitted.]

Although this Court agrees with much of these cases' reasoning, the Court rejects language requiring "real and substantial" or "actual and substantial" damage. If what is at issue in those cases is whether the intrusion is sufficient to rank as a trespass onto the land, proof of actual damage should be sufficient. * * * *Cf. Karpiak v. Russo,* 450 Pa.Super. 471, 676 A.2d 270, 275 (Pa.Super.1996) (A plaintiff claimed nuisance and negligent trespass against the defendant landscaping company because dust had settled on her property. The court easily dismissed plaintiffs' negligent trespass claim because there was no evidence that they "suffered ailments from the dust nor was there evidence that the dust caused any corrosive damage to their property.").

* * * Trespass is designed to protect against interference with exclusive possession, and not just mere entry. When an object can be seen or sensed in some manner, one may even assume that a landowner's right to exclusively possess his property is infringed. When the "thing" that has entered plaintiff's property is imperceptible to ordinary human senses, it does not so obviously infringe upon a landowner's right to exclusive possession. In such cases, only when the substance actually damages the property does it

---

1.　They say that the harm is the loss of fair　market value.

intrude upon the landowner's right to exclusive possession. Therefore, an essential element of Plaintiffs' claim is that the PCB's interfere with their right to exclusive possession by causing actual harm to the property.

[The court went on to discuss plaintiffs' proffered proof of actual harm caused by the presence of PCB's on their land. It said that "stigma" damage—reduced land value owing to fear of PCB's on the part of potential buyers—was, by itself, insufficient: "Kentucky law will not allow recovery for stigma absent some physical harm to the property." "Plaintiffs may recover if they demonstrate that the amount of PCB's on their property now [is] a health hazard. If Plaintiffs demonstrate this, then the issue of stigma will not present itself because Plaintiffs can recover any decreased fair market value resulting from the permanent injury." However, the court concluded that plaintiffs' evidence was "simply insufficient" to prove the existence of a health hazard. "The Court does not doubt for a moment that the fear and uncertainty about PCB's is so great that some persons will not want to remain on these properties," but "[t]he Court cannot find any scientific basis for such fears at these levels of PCB's."]

[Dismissed with prejudice.]

———

WALKER DRUG CO. v. LA SAL OIL CO., 972 P.2d 1238 (Utah 1998). Plaintiffs, suing in trespass and nuisance, alleged that their property had been contaminated by gasoline that leaked from defendant's nearby service stations. Plaintiffs' remediation efforts were effective and thus the physical injury to their property was temporary. *Held*, "stigma damages" to compensate lost market value due to negative public perceptions are recoverable, in addition to the cost of remediation.

" * * * [R]ecovery for stigma damages is compensation for a property's diminished market value in the absence of 'permanent "physical" ' harm. This Court has not assessed the availability of stigma damages in any prior case.

"A majority of courts from other jurisdictions, however, allows recovery when a defendant's trespass or nuisance has caused some *temporary* physical injury to the property but, despite the temporary injury's remediation, the property's market value remains depressed. Thus, stigma damages compensate for loss to the property's market value resulting from the long-term negative perception of the property in excess of any recovery obtained for the temporary injury itself. Were this residual loss due to stigma not compensated, the plaintiff's property would be permanently deprived of significant value without compensation.

"We find the majority position convincing. Stigma damages are therefore recoverable in Utah when a plaintiff demonstrates that (1) defendant caused some temporary physical injury to plaintiff's land and (2) repair of this temporary injury will not return the value of the property to its prior level because of a lingering negative public perception."

SECTION B.   ABATEMENT, CLEANUP, PUBLIC NUISANCE

When should an injunction be available in a nuisance situation? The first two main cases below conduct a sharp debate on this question. In both continuing nuisance is found (not trespass), and an injunction is sought to stop the harmful fallout complained of for the future. There are two basic approaches used in deciding whether continuing nuisance should be enjoined. They may be called the "entitlement" approach and the "balancing" approach. On the first approach, given substantial harm to plaintiff from continuing nuisance, an injunction is granted fairly automatically—that is, even if the activity to be enjoined does, on balance, more good than harm—in order to protect plaintiff's property entitlement. This is the line taken by the first case (1913). On the second approach, an injunction is not at all automatic, but depends on a balancing of interests: the harm to plaintiff caused by the nuisance is weighed against the harm to defendant that an injunction would cause. This is the method upheld by the majority in *Boomer v. Atlantic Cement Co.* (1970), over forceful dissent; it is the dominant approach today.

The section ends with materials on public nuisance. The last main case is "public" in several senses. It involves claims by public agencies to recover costs incurred in the governmental response to a massive release of hazardous waste into the environment. It links the common law of nuisance with the public law and policy of environmental protection.

WHALEN v. UNION BAG & PAPER CO.
Court of Appeals of New York, 1913.
208 N.Y. 1, 101 N.E. 805.

WERNER, J. The plaintiff is a lower riparian owner upon Kayaderosseras creek, in Saratoga county, and the defendant owns and operates on this stream a pulp mill a few miles above plaintiff's land. This mill represents an investment of more than $1,000,000, and gives employment to 400 or 500 operatives. It discharges into the waters of the creek large quantities of a liquid effluent containing sulphurous acid, lime, sulphur, and waste material consisting of pulp wood, sawdust, slivers, knots, gums, resins, and fiber. The pollution thus created, together with the discharge from other industries located along the stream and its principal tributary, has greatly diminished the purity of the water.

The plaintiff brought this action to restrain the defendant from continuing to pollute the stream. The trial court granted an injunction to take effect one year after the final affirmance of its decision upon appeal, and awarded damages at the rate of $312 a year. The Appellate Division reversed the judgment of the Special Term upon the law and facts, unless the plaintiff should consent to a reduction of damages to the sum of $100 a year, in which event the judgment as modified should be affirmed, and eliminated that part of the trial court's decree granting an injunction. The plaintiff thereupon stipulated for a reduction of damages, and then appealed to this court from the modified judgment. The facts found by the trial court, which do not appear to have been disturbed by the Appellate Division, establish a clear case of wrongful pollution of the stream, and need not be set forth in detail.

The plaintiff is the owner of a farm of 255 acres, and the trial court has found that its use and value have been injuriously affected by the pollution of the stream caused by the defendant. The defendant conducts a business in which it has invested a large sum of money, and employs great numbers of the inhabitants of the locality. * * * The setting aside of the injunction was apparently induced by a consideration of the great loss likely to be inflicted on the defendant by the granting of the injunction as compared with the small injury done to the plaintiff's land by that portion of the pollution which was regarded as attributable to the defendant. Such a balancing of injuries cannot be justified by the circumstances of this case. * * *

One of the troublesome phases of this kind of litigation is the difficulty of deciding when an injunction shall issue in a case where the evidence clearly establishes an unlawful invasion of a plaintiff's rights, but his actual injury from the continuance of the alleged wrong will be small as compared with the great loss which will be caused by the issuance of the injunction. This appeal has been presented as though that question were involved in the case at bar, but we take a different view. Even as reduced at the Appellate Division, the damages to the plaintiff's farm amount to $100 a year. It can hardly be said that this injury is unsubstantial, even if we should leave out of consideration the peculiarly noxious character of the pollution of which the plaintiff complains. The waste from the defendant's mill is very destructive, both to vegetable and animal life, and tends to deprive the waters with which it is mixed of their purifying qualities. It should be borne in mind also that there is no claim on the part of the defendant that the nuisance may become less injurious in the future. Although the damage to the plaintiff may be slight as compared with the defendant's expense of abating the condition, that is not a good reason for refusing an injunction. Neither courts of equity nor law can be guided by such a rule, for if followed to its logical conclusion it would deprive the poor litigant of his little property by giving it to those already rich. It is always to be remembered in such cases that "denying the injunction puts the hardship on the party in whose favor the legal right exists, instead of on the wrongdoer." Pomeroy's Eq. Juris. vol. 5, § 530. In speaking of the injustice which sometimes results from the balancing of injuries between parties, the learned author from whom we have just quoted sums up the discussion by saying, "The weight of authority is against allowing a balancing of injury as a means of determining the propriety of issuing an injunction." To the same effect is the decision in Weston Paper Co. v. Pope, 155 Ind. 394, 57 N.E. 719, 56 L.R.A. 899: "The fact that the appellant has expended a large sum of money in the construction of its plant, and that it conducts its business in a careful manner and without malice, can make no difference in its rights to the stream. Before locating the plant the owners were bound to know that every riparian proprietor is entitled to have the waters of the stream that washes his land come to it without obstruction, diversion, or corruption, subject only to the reasonable use of the water, by those similarly entitled, for such domestic purposes as are inseparable from and necessary for the free use of their land; they were bound also to know the character of their proposed business, and to take notice of the size, course, and capacity of the stream, and to determine for themselves at their own peril whether they should be able to conduct their business upon a stream of the size and character of Brandywine creek without injury to their neighbors; and the magnitude of their investment and their freedom from malice furnish no reason why they should escape the consequences of their own folly." This language very aptly expresses the rule which we think should be applied to the case at bar.

The judgment of the Appellate Division, in so far as it denied the injunction, should be reversed and the judgment of the Special Term in that respect reinstated, with costs to the appellant.

———

McCLEERY v. HIGHLAND BOY GOLD MINING CO., 140 Fed. 951 (C.C.Utah 1904). Plaintiffs are owners of farms located near defendant's mine and smelter. The smelter employs 450 workers and processes 500 tons of ore daily. It creates sulfur dioxide fumes and dust—emissions "incident to the smelting and not due to any negligence"—which are injurious to crops and animals, causing plaintiffs "substantial damage." In assessing plaintiffs' request for an injunction against continuation of smelting operations, the court said:

The title of the complainants to their respective farms is admitted. The substantial invasion of their rights to some extent and the purpose to continue this invasion is also admitted. * * * The substantial contention of the defendant is that it is engaged in a business of such extent and involving such a large capital that the value of the plaintiffs' rights sought to be protected is relatively small, and that therefore an injunction, destroying the defendant's business, would inflict a much greater injury on it than it would confer benefit upon the plaintiffs. Under such circumstances, it is asserted, courts of equity refuse to protect legal rights by injunction and remit the injured party to the partial relief to be obtained in actions at law. Stated in another way, the claim in effect is that one wrongfully invading the legal rights of his neighbor will be permitted by a court of equity to continue the wrong indefinitely on condition that he invests sufficient capital in the undertaking.

I am unable to accede to this statement of the law. If correct, the property of the poor is held by uncertain tenure, and the constitutional provisions forbidding the taking of property for private use would be of no avail. As a substitute it would be declared that private property is held on the condition that it may be taken by any person who can make a more profitable use of it, provided that such person shall be answerable in damage to the former owner for his injury. In a state of society the rights of the individual must to some extent be sacrificed to the rights of the social body; but this does not warrant the forcible taking of property from a man of small means to give it to the wealthy man, on the ground that the public will be indirectly advantaged by the greater activity of the capitalist. Public policy, I think, is more concerned in the protection of individual rights than in the profits to inure to individuals by the invasion of those rights. As said by Judge Sawyer in Woodruff v. North Bloomfield Gravel Mining Co. (C.C.) 18 Fed. 753, 807:

> "Of course, great interests should not be overthrown on trifling or frivolous grounds, as where the maxim 'de minimis non curat lex' is applicable; but every substantial, material right of person or property is entitled to protection against all the world. It is by protecting the most humble in his small estate against the encroachments of large capital and large interests that the poor man is ultimately enabled to become a capitalist himself. If the smaller interest must yield to the larger, all small property rights, and all smaller and less important enterprises, industries, and pursuits, would sooner or later be absorbed by the large, more powerful, few; and their development to a condition of great value and importance, both to the individual and the public, would be arrested in its incipiency."

While I recognize a conflict of authority upon this question, I think the better considered cases support the conclusion here reached. If it be said that an owner of property may refuse to sell unless he gets a fancy price, and in this way use his injunction for purposes of extortion, that is but saying that he has the rights of the ordinary owner of property to sell at what price he pleases, or to refuse to sell if he so desires. * * *

(Despite the foregoing, abatement was refused on the ground that plaintiffs had delayed seeking an injunction until two or three years after harm to them commenced, and in the meantime defendant had made substantial additional investments in its smelter. Permanent damages granted in lieu of an injunction.)

CRUSHED STONE CO. v. MOORE, 369 P.2d 811 (Okl.S.Ct.1962). Operations at defendants' limestone quarry produced large amounts of rock dust as well as noise and vibrations from blasting. Plaintiffs, owners and inhabitants of nearby rural acreages, testified that the dust made it hard to breathe, damaged their furniture, and kept them from opening windows or hanging clothes out to dry; that the concussions caused cracks in their houses and the noise interfered with sleep. Defendants showed that their operations were planned to minimize dust, noise, and vibrations; that they had recently invested some $13,000 to control the ill effects complained of; and that the value of the quarry was "well over $300,000." The trial court found that the quarry amounted to a nuisance and ordered that all quarrying operations cease. On appeal, *held*, for plaintiffs. The injunction is proper despite the contention that its issuance will cause defendants "grossly disproportionate hardship * * * in comparison with the * * * lesser injuries plaintiffs will suffer" from continued quarrying. Also "the fact that some of the plaintiffs have obtained damages" in prior lawsuits does not preclude them from obtaining injunctive relief.

"While we recognize that in proper cases, especially those involving businesses upon which the public's interest, or necessity, depends, the matter of 'comparative injury' should be given prominent consideration, this court is among those holding that where damages in an action at law will not give plaintiffs an adequate remedy against a business operated in such a way that it has become a nuisance, and such operation causes plaintiffs substantial and irremediable injury, they are entitled, as a matter of right, to have same abated, by injunction ' * * * notwithstanding the comparative benefits conferred thereby or the comparative injury resulting therefrom.' See Kenyon v. Edmundson, 80 Okl. 3, 193 P. 739."

BOOMER v. ATLANTIC CEMENT CO.

Court of Appeals of New York, 1970.
26 N.Y.2d 219, 309 N.Y.S.2d 312, 257 N.E.2d 870.

BERGAN, Judge. [FULD, C.J., and BURKE and SCILEPPI, JJ., concurring.]

Defendant operates a large cement plant near Albany. These are actions for injunction and damages by neighboring land owners alleging injury to property from dirt, smoke and vibration emanating from the plant. A nuisance has been found after trial, temporary damages have been allowed; but an injunction has been denied.**

The public concern with air pollution arising from many sources in industry and in transportation is currently accorded ever wider recognition accompanied by a growing sense of responsibility in State and Federal Governments to control it. Cement plants are obvious sources of air pollution in the neighborhoods where they operate.

But there is now before the court private litigation in which individual property owners have sought specific relief from a single plant operation. The threshold question raised by the division of view on this appeal is whether the court should resolve the litigation between the parties now before it as equitably as seems possible; or whether, seeking promotion of the general public welfare, it should channel private litigation into broad public objectives.

A court performs its essential function when it decides the rights of parties before it. Its decision of private controversies may sometimes greatly affect public issues. Large questions of law are often resolved by the manner in which private litigation is decided. But this is normally an incident to the court's main function to settle controversy. It is a rare exercise of judicial power to use a decision in private litigation as a purposeful mechanism to achieve direct public objectives greatly beyond the rights and interests before the court.

** Ed. note: The trial court found that "[t]he company installed at great expense the most efficient devices available to prevent the discharge of dust and polluted air into the atmosphere." It went on: "Although the evidence in this case establishes that Atlantic took every available and possible precaution to protect the plaintiffs from dust, nevertheless, I find * * * that Atlantic in the operation of its cement plant * * * created a nuisance insofar as the lands of the plaintiffs are concerned." Damages were granted but an injunction was denied because it would produce "great * * * hardship."

Effective control of air pollution is a problem presently far from solution even with the full public and financial powers of government. In large measure adequate technical procedures are yet to be developed and some that appear possible may be economically impracticable.

It seems apparent that the amelioration of air pollution will depend on technical research in great depth; on a carefully balanced consideration of the economic impact of close regulation; and of the actual effect on public health. It is likely to require massive public expenditure and to demand more than any local community can accomplish and to depend on regional and interstate controls.

A court should not try to do this on its own as a by-product of private litigation and it seems manifest that the judicial establishment is neither equipped in the limited nature of any judgment it can pronounce nor prepared to lay down and implement an effective policy for the elimination of air pollution. This is an area beyond the circumference of one private lawsuit. It is a direct responsibility for government and should not thus be undertaken as an incident to solving a dispute between property owners and a single cement plant—one of many—in the Hudson River valley.

The cement making operations of defendant have been found by the court at Special Term to have damaged the nearby properties of plaintiffs in these two actions. That court, as it has been noted, accordingly found defendant maintained a nuisance and this has been affirmed at the Appellate Division. The total damage to plaintiffs' properties is, however, relatively small in comparison with the value of defendant's operation and with the consequences of the injunction which plaintiffs seek.

The ground for the denial of injunction, notwithstanding the finding both that there is a nuisance and that plaintiffs have been damaged substantially, is the large disparity in economic consequences of the nuisance and of the injunction. This theory cannot, however, be sustained without overruling a doctrine which has been consistently reaffirmed in several leading cases in this court and which has never been disavowed here, namely that where a nuisance has been found and where there has been any substantial damage shown by the party complaining an injunction will be granted.

The rule in New York has been that such a nuisance will be enjoined although marked disparity be shown in economic consequence between the effect of the injunction and the effect of the nuisance.

The problem of disparity in economic consequence was sharply in focus in Whalen v. Union Bag & Paper Co., 208 N.Y. 1, 101 N.E. 805. A pulp mill entailing an investment of more than a million dollars polluted a stream in which plaintiff, who owned a farm, was "a lower riparian owner". The economic loss to plaintiff from this pollution was small. This court, reversing the Appellate Division, reinstated the injunction granted by the Special Term against the argument of the mill owner that in view of "the slight advantage to plaintiff and the great loss that will be inflicted on defendant" an injunction should not be granted (p. 2, 101 N.E. p. 805). "Such a balancing of injuries cannot be justified by the circumstances of this case", Judge Werner noted (p. 4, 101 N.E. p. 805). He continued: "Although the damage to the plaintiff may be slight as compared with the defendant's expense of abating the condition, that is not a good reason for refusing an injunction" (p. 5, 101 N.E. p. 806).

Thus the unconditional injunction granted at Special Term was reinstated. The rule laid down in that case, then, is that whenever the damage resulting from a nuisance is found not "unsubstantial", viz., $100 a year, injunction would follow. This states a rule that had been followed in this court with marked consistency (McCarty v. Natural Carbonic Gas Co., 189 N.Y. 40, 81 N.E. 549; Strobel v. Kerr Salt Co., 164 N.Y. 303, 58 N.E. 142; Campbell v. Seaman, 63 N.Y. 568).

There are cases where injunction has been denied. McCann v. Chasm Power Co., 211 N.Y. 301, 105 N.E. 416 is one of them. There, however, the damage shown by plaintiffs was not only unsubstantial, it was non-existent. Plaintiffs owned a rocky bank of the stream in which defendant had raised the level of the water. This had no economic or other adverse consequence to plaintiffs, and thus injunctive relief was denied. Similar is the basis for denial of injunction in Forstmann v. Joray Holding Co., 244 N.Y. 22, 154 N.E. 652 where no benefit to plaintiffs could be seen from the injunction sought (p. 32, 154 N.E. 655). Thus if, within Whalen v. Union Bag & Paper Co., supra which authoritatively states the rule in New York, the damage to plaintiffs in these present cases from defendant's cement plant is "not unsubstantial", an injunction should follow.

Although the court at Special Term and the Appellate Division held that injunction should be denied, it was found that plaintiffs had been damaged in various specific amounts up to the time of the trial and damages to the respective plaintiffs were awarded for those amounts. The effect of this was, injunction having been denied, plaintiffs could maintain successive actions at law for damages thereafter as further damage was incurred.

The court at Special Term also found the amount of permanent damage attributable to each plaintiff, for the guidance of the parties in the event both sides stipulated to the payment and acceptance of such permanent damage as a settlement of all the controversies among the parties. The total of permanent damages to all plaintiffs thus found was $185,000. This basis of adjustment has not resulted in any stipulation by the parties.

This result at Special Term and at the Appellate Division is a departure from a rule that has become settled; but to follow the rule literally in these cases would be to close down the plant at once. This court is fully agreed to avoid that immediately drastic remedy; the difference in view is how best to avoid it.*

One alternative is to grant the injunction but postpone its effect to a specified future date to give opportunity for technical advances to permit defendant to eliminate the nuisance; another is to grant the injunction conditioned on the payment of permanent damages to plaintiffs which would compensate them for the total economic loss to their property

* Respondent's investment in the plant is in excess of $45,000,000. There are over 300 peo- ple employed there.

present and future caused by defendant's operations. For reasons which will be developed the court chooses the latter alternative.

If the injunction were to be granted unless within a short period—e.g., 18 months—the nuisance be abated by improved methods, there would be no assurance that any significant technical improvement would occur.

The parties could settle this private litigation at any time if defendant paid enough money and the imminent threat of closing the plant would build up the pressure on defendant. If there were no improved techniques found, there would inevitably be applications to the court at Special Term for extensions of time to perform on showing of good faith efforts to find such techniques.

Moreover, techniques to eliminate dust and other annoying by-products of cement making are unlikely to be developed by any research the defendant can undertake within any short period, but will depend on the total resources of the cement industry nationwide and throughout the world. The problem is universal wherever cement is made.

For obvious reasons the rate of the research is beyond control of defendant. If at the end of 18 months the whole industry has not found a technical solution a court would be hard put to close down this one cement plant if due regard be given to equitable principles.

On the other hand, to grant the injunction unless defendant pays plaintiffs such permanent damages as may be fixed by the court seems to do justice between the contending parties. All of the attributions of economic loss to the properties on which plaintiffs' complaints are based will have been redressed.

The nuisance complained of by these plaintiffs may have other public or private consequences, but these particular parties are the only ones who have sought remedies and the judgment proposed will fully redress them. The limitation of relief granted is a limitation only within the four corners of these actions and does not foreclose public health or other public agencies from seeking proper relief in a proper court.

It seems reasonable to think that the risk of being required to pay permanent damages to injured property owners by cement plant owners would itself be a reasonable effective spur to research for improved techniques to minimize nuisance.

The power of the court to condition on equitable grounds the continuance of an injunction on the payment of permanent damages seems undoubted. * * *

* * *

Thus it seems fair to both sides to grant permanent damages to plaintiffs which will terminate this private litigation. The theory of damage is the "servitude on land" of plaintiffs imposed by defendant's nuisance. (See United States v. Causby, 328 U.S. 256, 261, 262, 267, 66 S.Ct. 1062, 90 L.Ed. 1206, where the term "servitude" addressed to the land was used by Justice Douglas relating to the effect of airplane noise on property near an airport.)

The judgment, by allowance of permanent damages imposing a servitude on land, which is the basis of the actions, would preclude future recovery by plaintiffs or their grantees.

This should be placed beyond debate by a provision of the judgment that the payment by defendant and the acceptance by plaintiffs of permanent damages found by the court shall be in compensation for a servitude on the land.

Although the Trial Term has found permanent damages as a possible basis of settlement of the litigation, on remission the court should be entirely free to reexamine this subject. It may again find the permanent damage already found; or make new findings.

The orders should be reversed, without costs, and the cases remitted to Supreme Court, Albany County to grant an injunction which shall be vacated upon payment by defendant of such amounts of permanent damage to the respective plaintiffs as shall for this purpose be determined by the court.

JASEN, Judge (dissenting).

I agree with the majority that a reversal is required here, but I do not subscribe to the newly enunciated doctrine of assessment of permanent damages, in lieu of an injunction, where substantial property rights have been impaired by the creation of a nuisance.

It has long been the rule in this State, as the majority acknowledges, that a nuisance which results in substantial continuing damage to neighbors must be enjoined. (Whalen v. Union Bag & Paper Co., 208 N.Y. 1, 101 N.E. 805; Campbell v. Seaman, 63 N.Y. 568; see, also, Kennedy v. Moog Servocontrols, 21 N.Y.2d 966, 290 N.Y.S.2d 193, 237 N.E.2d 356.) To now change the rule to permit the cement company to continue polluting the air indefinitely upon the payment of permanent damages is, in my opinion, compounding the magnitude of a very serious problem in our State and Nation today.

In recognition of this problem, the Legislature of this State has enacted the Air Pollution Control Act (Public Health Law, Consol.Laws, c. 45, §§ 1264 to 1299–m) declaring that it is the State policy to require the use of all available and reasonable methods to prevent and control air pollution (Public Health Law § 1265[1]).

The harmful nature and widespread occurrence of air pollution have been extensively documented. Congressional hearings have revealed that air pollution causes substantial property damage, as well as being a contributing factor to a rising incidence of lung cancer, emphysema, bronchitis and asthma.

The specific problem faced here is known as particulate contamination because of the fine dust particles emanating from defendant's cement plant. The particular type of nuisance is not new, having appeared in many cases for at least the past 60 years. (See Hulbert v. California Portland Cement Co., 161 Cal. 239, 118 P. 928 [1911].) It is interesting to note that cement

---

1. See, also, Air Quality Act of 1967, 81   U.S.Stat. 485 (1967).

production has recently been identified as a significant source of particulate contamination in the Hudson Valley.[3] This type of pollution, wherein very small particles escape and stay in the atmosphere, has been denominated as the type of air pollution which produces the greatest hazard to human health.[4] We have thus a nuisance which not only is damaging to the plaintiffs,[5] but also is decidedly harmful to the general public.

I see grave dangers in overruling our long-established rule of granting an injunction where a nuisance results in substantial continuing damage. In permitting the injunction to become inoperative upon the payment of permanent damages, the majority is, in effect, licensing a continuing wrong. It is the same as saying to the cement company, you may continue to do harm to your neighbors so long as you pay a fee for it. Furthermore, once such permanent damages are assessed and paid, the incentive to alleviate the wrong would be eliminated, thereby continuing air pollution of an area without abatement.

It is true that some courts have sanctioned the remedy here proposed by the majority in a number of cases,[6] but none of the authorities relied upon by the majority are analogous to the situation before us. In those cases, the courts, in denying an injunction and awarding money damages, grounded their decision on a showing that the use to which the property was intended to be put was primarily for the public benefit. Here, on the other hand, it is clearly established that the cement company is creating a continuing air pollution nuisance primarily for its own private interest with no public benefit.

This kind of inverse condemnation (Ferguson v. Village of Hamburg, 272 N.Y. 234, 5 N.E.2d 801) may not be invoked by a private person or corporation for private gain or advantage. Inverse condemnation should only be permitted when the public is primarily served in the taking or impairment of property. The promotion of the interests of the polluting cement company has, in my opinion, no public use or benefit.

Nor is it constitutionally permissible to impose servitude on land, without consent of the owner, by payment of permanent damages where the continuing impairment of the land is for a private use. (See Fifth Ave. Coach Lines v. City of New York, 11 N.Y.2d 342, 347, 229 N.Y.S.2d 400, 403, 183 N.E.2d 684, 686; Walker v. City of Hutchinson, 352 U.S. 112, 77 S.Ct. 200, 1 L.Ed.2d 178.) This is made clear by the State Constitution (art. I, § 7, subd. [a]) which provides that "[p]rivate property shall not be taken for *public*

---

3. New York State Bureau of Air Pollution Control Services, Air Pollution Capital District, 1968, at p. 8.

4. J. Ludwig, Air Pollution Control Technology: Research and Development on New and Improved Systems, 33 Law & Contemp.Prob., 217, 219 (1968).

5. There are seven plaintiffs here who have been substantially damaged by the maintenance of this nuisance. The trial court found their total permanent damages to equal $185,000.

6. See United States v. Causby, 328 U.S. 256, 66 S.Ct. 1062, 90 L.Ed. 1206; Kentucky–Ohio Gas Co. v. Bowling, 264 Ky. 470, 477, 95 S.W.2d 1; Northern Indiana Public Service Co. v. W.J. & M.S. Vesey, 210 Ind. 338, 200 N.E. 620; City of Amarillo v. Ware, 120 Tex. 456, 40 S.W.2d 57; Pappenheim v. Metropolitan El. Ry. Co., 128 N.Y. 436, 28 N.E. 518; Ferguson v. Village of Hamburg, 272 N.Y. 234, 5 N.E.2d 801.

use without just compensation" (emphasis added). It is, of course, significant that the section makes no mention of taking for a *private* use.

In sum, then, by constitutional mandate as well as by judicial pronouncement, the permanent impairment of private property for private purposes is not authorized in the absence of clearly demonstrated public benefit and use.

I would enjoin the defendant cement company from continuing the discharge of dust particles upon its neighbors' properties unless, within 18 months, the cement company abated this nuisance.[7]

It is not my intention to cause the removal of the cement plant from the Albany area, but to recognize the urgency of the problem stemming from this stationary source of air pollution, and to allow the company a specified period of time to develop a means to alleviate this nuisance.

I am aware that the trial court found that the most modern dust control devices available have been installed in defendant's plant, but, I submit, this does not mean that *better* and more effective dust control devices could not be developed within the time allowed to abate the pollution.

Moreover, I believe it is incumbent upon the defendant to develop such devices, since the cement company, at the time the plant commenced production (1962), was well aware of the plaintiffs' presence in the area, as well as the probable consequences of its contemplated operation. Yet, it still chose to build and operate the plant at this site.

In a day when there is a growing concern for clean air, highly developed industry should not expect acquiescence by the courts, but should, instead, plan its operations to eliminate contamination of our air and damage to its neighbors.

Accordingly, the orders of the Appellate Division, insofar as they denied the injunction, should be reversed, and the actions remitted to Supreme Court, Albany County to grant an injunction to take effect 18 months hence, unless the nuisance is abated by improved techniques prior to said date.

BREITEL and GIBSON, JJ., taking no part.

MADISON v. DUCKTOWN SULPHUR, COPPER & IRON CO., 113 Tenn. 331, 83 S.W. 658 (1904). Defendants are two copper mining companies whose process for reducing their ore—open-air "roasting"—produces large volumes of sulfurous smoke. Plaintiffs are nearby farmers complaining of crop and timber damage caused by the smoke, as well as household inconvenience, personal annoyance, and ill health. Plaintiffs' nuisance suit seeks an injunction to prevent continued injury. Since roasting is "the only known method" of ore reduction, and integral to defendants' operations, an

---

7. The issuance of an injunction to become effective in the future is not an entirely new concept. For instance, in Schwarzenbach v. Oneonta Light & Power Co., 207 N.Y. 671, 100 N.E. 1134, an injunction against the maintenance of a dam spilling water on plaintiff's property was issued to become effective one year hence.

abatement decree would compel defendants "to stop operations" and "withdraw from the state." The two companies together employ some 2,500 workers; their tax assessment amounts to half the tax aggregate for their county. On appeal in the Tennessee Supreme Court from the grant of injunctive relief by the Court of Chancery Appeals, *held*, for defendants. "While there can be no doubt that the facts stated make out a case of nuisance, * * * the remedy in equity is not a matter of course. * * * A judgment for damages in this class of cases is a matter of absolute right, where injury is shown. A decree for an injunction is a matter of sound legal discretion * * *." Equitable discretion must consider "all of the special circumstances of each case * * * with a view to effect the ends of justice." Two principles of equity compel denial of an injunction here.

First, undue delay in seeking an injunction—or "laches"—is a bar to equitable relief. A party who has "slept on his rights" cannot later obtain a remedy whose basis is "the real equity of the case." Quoting, the court said:

> Relief by injunction is not controlled by arbitrary or technical rules, but the application for its exercise is addressed to the conscience and sound discretion of the court. * * * [A] court of equity will not grant relief by injunction where the party seeking it, being cognizant of his rights, does not take those steps which are open to him, but lies by and suffers his adversary to incur expenses and enter into burdensome engagements which would render the granting of an injunction against the completion of the undertaking, or the use thereof when completed, a great injury to him. A suitor who by his laches has made it impossible for a court to enjoin his adversary without inflicting great injury upon him will be left to pursue his ordinary legal remedy.

In the present case, several plaintiffs are barred by laches because they waited ten years before bringing suit, and in the meantime large expenditures were made to improve the copper extraction facilities complained of. It would be "inequitable to grant the severe remedy of injunction" to these complainants, who rather "should be left to their actions for damages." However, other claims for injunctive relief were brought little more than two years after injuries began, and they are not barred.

The second ground for denying an injunction—applicable to all complainants—is developed in the following excerpts from the court's opinion:

> In Wood on Nuisances (3d Ed.) p. 1182, it is said: "* * * if the injury on the one hand is small and fairly compensable in damages, and the loss to the other party would be large and disastrous, an injunction will be refused and the party left to his legal remedy."

> In Demarest v. Hardham it is said: "* * * The defendant's business is not only lawful, but necessary. It is carried on in a part of the city of Newark devoted almost exclusively to manufacturing and business purposes. * * * It should not, therefore, be enjoined except under a stern necessity. * * * [T]he court is bound to compare consequences. If the fact of an actionable nuisance is clearly established, then the court is bound to consider whether a greater injury will not be done by granting an injunction, and thus destroying a citizen's property and taking away

from him his means of livelihood, than will result from a refusal, and leaving the injured party to his ordinary legal remedy * * *." 34 N.J.Eq. 469 (1881).

In Powell v. Bentley & Gerwig Furniture Co. (W.Va.) it is said: " * * * to abate or restrain in case of nuisance is not a matter of strict right, but of orderly and reasonable discretion, according to the right of the particular case, and hence [a court of equity] will refuse relief, and send the party to a court of law, when damages would be a fairer approximation to common justice, because to silence a useful and costly factory is often a matter of serious moment to the state and town as well as to the owner." 34 W.Va. 804, 12 S.E. 1085 (1891).

In Clifton Iron Co. v. Dye it is said: " * * * it is not every case of nuisance or continuing trespass which a court of equity will restrain by injunction. In determining this question the court should weigh the injury that may accrue to the one or the other party, and also to the public, by granting or refusing the injunction. * * * The utilization of these ores, which must be washed before using, necessitates in some measure the placing of sediment where it may flow into streams * * *, and, while this invasion of the rights of the lower riparian owner may produce injury, entitling him to redress, the great public interests and benefits to flow from the conversion of these ores into pig metal should not be lost sight of." 87 Ala. 468, 6 So. 192 (1888).

* * *

The question now to be considered is, what is the proper exercise of discretion, under the facts appearing in the present case? * * *

In order to protect by injunction several small tracts of land, aggregating in value less than $1,000, we are asked to destroy other property worth nearly $2,000,000, and wreck two great mining and manufacturing enterprises, that are engaged in work of very great importance, not only to their owners, but to the state, and to the whole country as well, to depopulate a large town, and deprive thousands of working people of their homes and livelihood, and scatter them broadcast. The result would be practically a confiscation of the property of the defendants for the benefit of the complainants—an appropriation without compensation. The defendants cannot reduce their ores in a manner different from that they are now employing, and there is no more remote place to which they can remove. The decree asked for would deprive them of all of their rights. We appreciate the argument based on the fact that the homes of the complainants who live on the small tracts of land referred to are not so comfortable and useful to their owners as they were before they were affected by the smoke complained of, and we are deeply sensible of the truth of the proposition that no man is entitled to any more rights than another on the ground that he has or owns more property than that other. But in a case of conflicting rights, where neither party can enjoy his own without in some measure restricting the liberty of the other in the use of property, the law must make the best arrangement it can between the contending parties, with a view to preserving to each one the largest measure of liberty possible under the circumstances. We see no escape from the conclusion in the present case that the only proper decree is to allow the complainants a reference for the ascertainment of damages, and that the injunction must be denied to them * * *.

LITTLE JOSEPH REALTY, INC. v. TOWN OF BABYLON, 41 N.Y.2d 738, 395 N.Y.S.2d 428, 363 N.E.2d 1163 (1977). Plaintiff sued to enjoin construction and operation of an asphalt plant in violation of local zoning law. The trial court ruled against plaintiff, but the Appellate Division held that the plant—by then in full operation—contravened the zoning ordinance. However, since "a disparity existed between plaintiff's damages and the larger economic consequences of an injunction," the intermediate court refused an order shutting down the plant, provided a specified filter were installed to reduce dust emission. Following Boomer v. Atlantic Cement Co., it held plaintiff should recover permanent damages in lieu of abatement. On certification to the New York Court of Appeals, *held*, for plaintiff. The remedy granted below "runs counter to firmly established law and sound public policy," since under it "defendants are * * * in effect buying the right to violate the law." *Boomer* is inapplicable here because "no zoning violation, or for that matter, the violation of any other statute, was involved in that case." The court explained:

"The law of nuisance and that of zoning both relate to the use of property, but they each protect a different interest. So a use which fully complies with a zoning ordinance may still be enjoined as a nuisance albeit 'the plaintiff assumes a heavy burden of proof.'

"Nuisance is based upon the maxim that 'a man shall not use his property so as to harm another.' It traditionally required that, after a balancing of risk-utility considerations, the gravity of the harm to a plaintiff be found to outweigh the social usefulness of a defendant's activity. (Prosser, Law of Torts [4th ed.], p. 581; see, also, Restatement, Torts 2d [Tent.Draft No. 18], § 826, pp. 3–4). On that basis, it was logical in *Boomer,* where the adverse economic effects of a permanent injunction far outweighed the loss plaintiffs there would suffer, to limit the relief to monetary damages as compensation for the 'servitude' which had been imposed upon them.

"Zoning is far more comprehensive. Its design is, on a planned basis, to serve as 'a vital tool for maintaining a civilized form of existence' for the benefit and welfare of an entire community (Udell v. Haas, 21 N.Y.2d 463, 469, 288 N.Y.S.2d 888, 893, 235 N.E.2d 897, 900; see, also, Comment, Zoning and the Law of Nuisance, 29 Ford.L.Rev. 749, 750–751; Comment, Zoning Ordinances and Common–Law Nuisance, 16 Syracuse L.Rev. 860). Its provisions must be enforced with these goals in mind. It follows that, when a continuing use flies in the face of a valid zoning restriction, it must, subject to the existence of any appropriate equitable defenses, be enjoined unconditionally.

"Consequently, however appropriate the remedy fashioned by the Appellate Division might be in resolving a private nuisance case, it is inappropriate here. In private nuisance, there is frequently a need to resolve a dispute between a plaintiff and a defendant over conflicting though valid uses of land. In such a case, the remedial options delineated in *Boomer* provide means by which courts can adjust such competing uses with a view towards maximizing the social value of each.

"On the other hand, when it has been established that a defendant violates a valid zoning ordinance, there is no need for judicial accommodation of the defendant's use to that of the plaintiff. For a court to do so would be for it to usurp the legislative function. Specifically, in the case now before us, if the defendants can continue the unlawful use of the property after complying with the relief granted on remand, the trial court's judgment would have worked to rezone the land with conditions notwithstanding the fact that the power to do so is reserved to the town board alone.

"This is not to say that risk-utility considerations have not entered into the adoption of a zoning law's restriction on use. It is rather that presumptively they have already been weighed and disposed of by the Legislature which enacted them."

UNITED STATES v. HOOKER CHEMICALS & PLASTICS CORP.

United States District Court, Western District of New York, 1989.

722 F.Supp. 960.

CURTIN, District Judge.

Pending for decision is plaintiff State of New York's motion, pursuant to Fed.R.Civ.P. 56, for partial summary judgment as to defendant Occidental Chemical Corporation [OCC]'s liability in this action under the New York common law of nuisance. Specifically, the State seeks this court's determination that OCC is liable as a matter of law for the creation of a public nuisance at the Love Canal landfill site, as well as for the costs incurred by the State in cleaning up the site. * * *

* * * In May of 1894, William T. Love began construction of a canal to connect the upper and lower portions of the Niagara River as part of a comprehensive project to develop and utilize the area's water power potential. The construction was subsequently abandoned when industrial financiers of Love's company (the Niagara Power and Development Corporation [NPDC]) withdrew their backing * * *. The unfinished canal, about three-quarters of a mile long, thirty feet deep, eighty feet wide at the top and forty feet wide at the base, was essentially intact when, in the early 1940s, OCC's corporate predecessor the Hooker Electrochemical Company [Hooker] sought to purchase the sixteen-acre canal site from NPDC.

In April, 1942, OCC and NPDC entered an agreement allowing OCC to use the Love Canal property for disposal of chemical wastes generated at its Niagara Falls plant while negotiations continued for purchasing the site. OCC actually purchased the property in 1947, and continued to dispose of chemical wastes there until it sold the property to the City of Niagara Falls Board of Education [the Board], for one dollar, in April, 1953. During its ownership and use of the property between April, 1942, and April, 1953,

OCC deposited some 21,800 tons—more than 40 million pounds—of liquid and solid chemical waste in the Love Canal, including several substances designated as hazardous under the Clean Water Act, 33 U.S.C. §§ 1317(a) and 1321(b)(4), and the Comprehensive Environmental Response, Compensation and Liability Act [CERCLA], 42 U.S.C. § 9601(14). * * *

* * *

During the 1970s, "[h]azardous substances were ... detected in the surface water, groundwater, soil, the basements of homes, sewers, creeks, and other locations in the area surrounding the Love Canal landfill.... " United States v. Hooker Chemicals and Plastics Corp., 680 F.Supp. 546, 549 (W.D.N.Y.1988). On June 20, 1978, New York State Commissioner of Health Robert H. Whalen, M.D., ordered the Niagara County Board of Health "to abate the public health nuisance now existing at the Love Canal Chemical Waste Landfill site," and subsequently issued an order on August 2, 1978, declaring the site a public health emergency. Five days later, on August 7, 1978, President Jimmy Carter declared the site a federal emergency. * * *

This action was filed on December 20, 1979, to recover costs incurred by the federal and state governments to prevent further migration of wastes, to relocate families, and for other actions taken in response to these emergency orders. In addition to ruling on several discovery motions throughout the already long history of this case, the court, in its order dated February 23, 1988, found OCC jointly and severally liable for these response costs under section 107(a) of CERCLA, 42 U.S.C. § 9607(a), and granted the plaintiffs' motions for partial summary judgment in that regard.

In support of its instant motion, the State contends that the record is sufficiently well-developed for the court to further enter partial summary judgment, this time as to OCC's liability for public nuisance. According to the State, in an action brought in the exercise of its police power to abate a public nuisance or to seek reimbursement for the cost of abating the nuisance, New York common law imposes joint and several liability on those responsible for the nuisance without the need to show negligence or fault. The State contends that this "strict" liability extends to OCC for its waste disposal activities at Love Canal both prior to and during its ownership of the property, and cannot be avoided by OCC's sale of the property to the Board * * *.

* * *

Under the common law as it has developed in New York, [summarized in Copart Industries, Inc. v. Consolidated Edison Co., 41 N.Y.2d 564, 394 N.Y.S.2d 169, 362 N.E.2d 968 (1977),]

> [a] public, or as sometimes termed a common, nuisance is an offense against the State and is subject to abatement or prosecution on application of the proper governmental agency. It consists of conduct or omissions which offend, interfere with or cause damage to the public in the exercise of rights common to all, in a manner such as to offend public morals, interfere with use by the public of a public place or

endanger or injure the property, health, safety or comfort of a considerable number of persons.

An action for private nuisance may be maintained by a person with a legally protected interest in respect to the particular use and enjoyment of the land against one whose conduct is a legal cause of the invasion of such interest * * *. Id.; see also State of New York v. Schenectady Chemicals, Inc., 117 Misc.2d 960, 459 N.Y.S.2d 971, 976 (Sup.Ct.1983) [Schenectady I], aff'd as modified, 103 A.D.2d 33, 479 N.Y.S.2d 1010 (3d Dept. 1984) [Schenectady II]. * * *

The court in Schenectady I denied defendant's motion to dismiss an action brought by the State of New York under the common law of public nuisance to compel the defendant chemical company to pay for the costs of cleaning up a chemical dump site owned by an independent contractor at which defendant had disposed hazardous wastes some 15 to 30 years earlier. In sustaining the cause of action, the court [proceeded] * * * on the premise that, "with respect to public nuisances and inherently dangerous activities, fault is not an issue, the ultimate inquiry being limited to whether the condition created, not the conduct creating it, is causing damage to the public."

Relying on the Schenectady Chemical cases, the Second Circuit in [State of New York v. Shore Realty Corp., 759 F.2d 1032 (2d Cir.1985),] extended public nuisance liability "irrespective of negligence or fault" to a party responsible not for creating but for maintaining the nuisance. * * *

> * * * [We are convinced] that a New York court would find as a matter of law that Shore's maintenance of the site—for example, allowing corroding tanks to hold hundreds of thousands of gallons of hazardous waste—constitutes abnormally dangerous activity and thus constitutes a public nuisance.

Shore Realty, 759 F.2d at 1051–52 (citing New Jersey State Department of Environmental Protection v. Ventron Corp., 94 N.J. 473, 492, 468 A.2d 150, 160 (1983) (holding that "simply dumping [a hazardous substance] onto land or into water" is an abnormally dangerous activity)).

* * *

* * * While the New York courts have not explicitly held that the disposal of hazardous wastes by the generator is, in itself, an abnormally dangerous activity requiring the application of strict liability standards, the language employed by the leading cases certainly indicate[s] that such a holding would not be unreasonable in a case such as the instant one, in which it is undisputed that such wastes have been released into the environment so as to "endanger or injure the property, health, safety or comfort of a considerable number of persons." Copart, 394 N.Y.S.2d at 172, 362 N.E.2d at 971. The Schenectady I court found that * * * defendant's disposal of chemical wastes several years earlier * * * [gave] rise to a cause of action for public nuisance, since "[o]ne who creates a nuisance through an inherently dangerous activity or use of an unreasonably dangerous product is absolutely liable for resulting damages, irregardless of fault, and

despite adhering to the highest standard of care." In its affirmance, the court in Schenectady II stated that it "[did] not hesitate in recognizing that the seepage of chemical wastes into a public water supply constitutes a public nuisance", (citing Amax, Inc. v. Sohio Prods. Co., 121 Misc.2d 814, 469 N.Y.S.2d 282 (1983) (sustaining nuisance cause of action on theory of strict liability for abnormally dangerous activity)), and that it "may reasonably be deemed the case [that the activity is inherently dangerous] where the disposal of hazardous wastes [is] involved. . . . " Further, the Second Circuit in Shore Realty had little difficulty in granting the State's motion for summary judgment against the current owner and maintainer of a site at which several other parties had disposed hazardous wastes, since it "[had] no doubt that the release or threat of release of hazardous waste into the environment unreasonably infringes upon a public right and thus is a public nuisance as a matter of New York law."

The instant case presents an even more compelling set of facts and circumstances for finding the existence of a public nuisance than did Shore Realty. * * * It is undisputed that, during the period of its use and ownership of the Love Canal property, OCC deposited over 21,800 tons of liquid and solid chemical waste[s] in the Canal, several of which have been identified as hazardous substances under CERCLA. It is also undisputed that water which infiltrated the Love Canal mixed with the wastes to form leachate, which eventually migrated offsite to contaminate the groundwater, soil, and other areas surrounding the Canal.

* * *

I therefore find that there is no genuine issue of material fact remaining in the case as to OCC's joint and several liability under the common law of public nuisance, and hereby enter summary judgment in favor of plaintiffs on their public nuisance claim as a matter of law. * * *

So ordered.

UNITED STATES v. ALCAN ALUMINUM CORP., 964 F.2d 252 (3d Cir. 1992). Here the Court of Appeals discussed the remedial structure and purpose of CERCLA, the federal Comprehensive Environmental Response, Compensation and Liability Act, 94 Stat. 2767. Also known as the "Superfund" law, CERCLA was enacted in 1980, two years after the federal emergency was declared at Love Canal. In the present case, brought under CERCLA in 1989, the United States sued 20 defendants, including Alcan, for the recovery of cleanup costs incurred as a result of the release of hazardous wastes from a Pennsylvania disposal site into the Susquehanna River. Over the years "liquid wastes from numerous industrial facilities," including Alcan's, were deposited at the site; in 1985 some 100,000 gallons of contaminated liquid escaped into the river. Alcan defended on the ground that the government could not prove that Alcan's own wastes caused the environmental damage that led to response costs incurred by the government. The trial court ruled against Alcan.

The appellate court said CERCLA was enacted "[i]n response to widespread concern over the improper disposal of hazardous wastes," and was designed "to force polluters to pay for costs associated with remedying their pollution" at disposal sites. Under the Act, administered by the Environmental Protection Agency (EPA), "the Government can clean the sites itself" using monies from the Hazardous Substance Superfund. "EPA can then seek reimbursement from responsible parties, as it has done in this case"; "of great significance in this case, CERCLA imposes strict liability on responsible parties." The court rejected Alcan's argument that the government must prove a specific causal connection between Alcan's own wastes and the government's response costs:

> * * * [T]he fact that a single generator's waste would not in itself justify a response is irrelevant in the multi-generator context, as this would permit a generator to escape liability where the amount of harm it engendered to the environment was minimal, though it was significant when added to other generators' waste. Accordingly, we find that the district court's construction of the statute furthers important environmental goals.

A principal goal of CERCLA, the court pointed out, is "assuring that those who caused chemical harm bear the costs of that harm."

LEFEBVRE v. CENTRAL MAIN POWER CO., 7 F.Supp.2d 64 (D.Me.1998). From 1919 to 1949 defendant operated a gas plant on a site in Waterville, Maine, and disposed of coal tar waste on the site. In 1949 defendant sold the property, which was subsequently resold twice and then sold to plaintiff in 1985. After discovering that the site had been contaminated by defendant's waste, plaintiff brought this suit to compel defendant to clean up the site. Defendant argued that plaintiff's claims under the federal Resource Conservation and Recovery Act (RCRA) and Maine common law were barred by the statute of limitations. *Held*, for plaintiff. There is "no applicable limitations period for a citizen suit under RCRA" seeking to compel cleanup of waste that poses a present danger to health or the environment. With respect to the common law claim, the court said:

> " * * * Plaintiff alleges that the manufacturing of gas and the disposal of the associated wastes is an ultrahazardous activity giving rise to strict liability under Maine law. This Court has held that Maine 'would likely recognize a cause of action for strict liability for the disposal and storage of hazardous waste.' * * * Generally under Maine law, * * * the statute of limitations is six years * * *. In the context of common law trespass and nuisance claims arising out of the disposal of hazardous waste, however, both this Court and the Maine Law Court have held that so long as a plaintiff can demonstrate that the hazardous waste remains present on the land and can be abated, a plaintiff may assert an action for continuing nuisance or trespass regardless of when the hazardous substance entered the land. When a trespass or nuisance continues, a new cause of action accrues each day, and the statute of limitations provides no bar so long as the tort is ongoing."

PUBLIC NUISANCE

In the course of his opinion for the court in *Copart Industries, Inc. v. Consolidated Edison Co.,* 41 N.Y.2d 564, 394 N.Y.S.2d 169, 362 N.E.2d 968 (1977), Justice Cooke defined the realms of "private" and "public" nuisance as follows:

"A private nuisance threatens one person or a relatively few, an essential feature being an interference with the use or enjoyment of land. It is actionable by the individual person or persons whose rights have been disturbed (Restatement, Torts, notes preceding § 822, p. 217). A public, or as sometimes termed a common, nuisance is an offense against the State and is subject to abatement or prosecution on application of the proper governmental agency. It consists of conduct or omissions which offend, interfere with or cause damage to the public in the exercise of rights common to all, in a manner such as to offend public morals, interfere with use by the public of a public place or endanger or injure the property, health, safety or comfort of a considerable number of persons.

"As observed by Professor Prosser, public and private nuisances 'have almost nothing in common, except that each causes inconvenience to someone, and it would have been fortunate if they had been called from the beginning by different names' (Prosser, Torts [4th ed.], p. 573). Not only does confusion arise from sameness in denomination and from the lack of it in applicability, but also from the fact that, although an individual cannot institute an action for public nuisance as such, he may maintain an action when he suffers special damage from a public nuisance."

DUY v. ALABAMA WESTERN RAILWAY CO., 175 Ala. 162, 57 So. 724 (1912). Plaintiff sued to recover damages for the obstruction of a highway by defendant's construction of a freight depot. Plaintiff's property was rendered less accessible. *Held,* that the pecuniary loss suffered by plaintiff was peculiar injury and different in kind from that suffered by the public generally.

BISHOP PROCESSING CO. v. DAVIS, 213 Md. 465, 132 A.2d 445 (1957). Owners of realty brought suit to enjoin the operation of a processing plant. The material processed consisted of chicken feathers, offal, viscera, blood, heads, feet, beef bones, and any other poultry by-products. The liquids are extracted and solids ground into a fine meal, which was high in protein and widely used in fertilizers and poultry feeds. It was alleged to be a nuisance because of nauseating odor emanating from plant. *Held,* that even if the operation of the plant is a public nuisance, the plaintiffs proved sufficient discomfort to themselves and injury to their properties to entitle them to injunctive relief, and damages different in character from that sustained by public generally do not have to be proved.

IN RE THE EXXON VALDEZ, 104 F.3d 1196 (9th Cir.1997). In the wake of the 1989 grounding of the Exxon Valdez oil tanker and the resulting oil spill in Prince William Sound, a class of 3,455 Alaska Natives brought suit against Exxon in public nuisance seeking recovery for (1) economic damage flowing from loss of fishing resources and (2) non-economic damage to the Natives' "subsistence way of life." The first claim (loss of fishing) was settled by the parties, and so removed from the litigation. The second claim ("cultural" damage) was rejected by the trial court. *Held*, affirmed. The appellate court explained:

"Admittedly, the oil spill affected the communal life of Alaska Natives, but whatever injury they suffered (other than the [fishing] loss), though potentially different in degree than that suffered by other Alaskans, was not different in kind. We agree with the district court that the right to lead subsistence lifestyles is not limited to Alaska Natives. While the oil spill may have affected Alaska Natives more severely than other members of the public, 'the right to obtain and share wild food, enjoy uncontaminated nature, and cultivate traditional, cultural, spiritual, and psychological benefits in pristine natural surroundings' is shared by all Alaskans. The Class therefore has failed to prove any 'special injury' to support a public nuisance action."

SECTION C. COMPENSATION

This section addresses nuisance liability for compensatory damages. The focus is upon fallout-causing activity of the sort which is actionable as private nuisance and is not regarded as abnormally dangerous. The section investigates two main topics, "strict nuisance" and "nuisance limits."

Nuisance is often said to be a "field of liability," not a "type of conduct." This means that the field of (private) nuisance is concerned with a certain sort of injury, harm from interference with use and enjoyment of land. But the conduct giving rise to a nuisance may be any of three familiar kinds: (a) intentional, (b) negligent, (c) abnormally dangerous. This raises an interesting question. What happens if we put aside—subtract—all nuisance cases where liability could be established under other tort doctrines, in particular those concerning negligence or dangerous activity? What remains? What is added by having a tort liability for damages called "nuisance"?

One answer is that the harms actionable as nuisance include annoyances and inconveniences (bad smells, noise) which, while physical in character, do not rise to the level of physical harm ordinarily handled by negligence or by liability for dangerous activity. But in many nuisance cases the harm (like the crop damage in the first main case below) is not especially distinct.

The main thing nuisance adds is another kind of strict liability, based on "intent." Nuisance recovery may be had though there is no negligence, and no abnormal danger. "Strict nuisance" provides reparation even though the fallout-causing activity survives negligence scrutiny, because all cost-justified precautions have been taken; and even though no abatement injunction would issue, because the harming activity on balance does more good than harm. The claim asserted in strict nuisance is not that the primary conduct causing harm should be changed; the claim is that the actor should make reparation for harm done. Materials below explore the doctrinal basis of, and policy rationale for, strict nuisance.

The materials below also explore the topic of "nuisance limits." A way to approach that topic is to imagine that plaintiff has made out the following case: defendant is creating harmful fallout—say, air pollution that causes physical injury—continuously, knowledgeably, and thus "intentionally," with the result that plaintiff has suffered substantial injury. What additional elements in the situation would lead us, despite the intentional harming, to withhold reparation? This inquiry will expose a number of notable factors that operate as limits of nuisance liability.

WHEAT v. FREEMAN COAL MINING CORP.
Appellate Court of Illinois, Fifth District, 1974.
23 Ill.App.3d 14, 319 N.E.2d 290.

[See p. 129, supra]

JOST v. DAIRYLAND POWER COOPERATIVE
Supreme Court of Wisconsin, 1969.
45 Wis.2d 164, 172 N.W.2d 647.

The action is one for damages for injury to crops and loss of market value of farm lands. The plaintiffs are farmers living within, or near, the city limits of Alma, Wisconsin. Their farms are located on the bluffs overlooking the Mississippi River. In 1947 the Dairyland Power Cooperative erected a coal burning electric generating plant at Alma. It is the contention of the farmers that consumption of high-sulfur-content coal at this plant has increased from 300 tons per day in 1948 to 1,670 tons per day in 1967. There was testimony that the 1967 coal consumption resulted in discharging approximately 90 tons of sulfur-dioxide gas into the atmosphere each day. There was substantial evidence to show that the sulphur-dioxide gas, under certain atmospheric conditions, settled on the fields, causing a whitening of the alfalfa leaves and a dropping off of some of the vegetation. There was also testimony to show that the sulphur compounds resulting from the industrial pollution killed pine trees, caused screens to rust through rapidly, and made flower raising difficult or impossible. There was some testimony to show that some of the sulphur came from locomotives or from river barges, but there was testimony that the power plant was the source of most of the contamination. Defendant's witness, a farmer who was "hit" less frequently by the sulphurous fumes, estimated his crop damage at 5 percent. There was also evidence of damage to apple trees, sumac, and wild grape, in addition to the alfalfa damage.

Each of the plaintiff farmers testified that his land had diminished in value as the result of the continuing crop loss. * * *

The jury found that the alfalfa crop on the three farms sustained damage. It concluded, however, that the damage was not substantial. The jury found a diminution of the market value of the Andrew Noll farm but no loss in the market value of the farms of Andrew Jost or Norbert Noll.

The trial judge changed the jury's answer in regard to "substantial" damage from "no" to "yes." Judgment was entered upon the verdict as amended. Defendant has appealed from the whole of the judgment, and plaintiffs have filed for a review of the judgment which sustained the jury's finding in regard to loss of market value.

HEFFERNAN, Justice. One of defendant's principal objections to the judgment is that plaintiffs' counsel was permitted to proceed until almost the close of his case before electing to rely on a theory of nuisance rather than negligence. * * * Our review of the 900 page record gives no support to the defendant's contention. In the entire transcript only a very few questions could be construed as bearing upon negligence. Contrary to defendant's claim, Attorney Kostner almost immediately dispelled any question in regard to the legal theory on which he was relying. After a defense objection to questions posed to the first witness, Attorney Kostner stated:

"If the Court please, our purpose in asking the question is to show that at the present time there is no control of the diffusion of sulfur dioxide gases from the Alma plant into the atmosphere. Whether or not it's possible, or whether or not there is no method of doing it, is not material because if the sulfur dioxide gases are diffused in the atmosphere and that causes damage to the property the question of whether or not it can, by proper scientific methods, be controlled is not material. The question is did it."

It seems eminently clear that, from the very outset, the case was tried on the theory of nuisance and not on the ground that the defendant had failed to exercise due care.

* * *

Negligence and nuisance, of course, are not always mutually exclusive legal concepts. Prosser points out:

"Another fertile source of confusion is the fact that nuisance is a field of tort liability, rather than a type of tortious conduct. It has reference to the interests invaded, to the damage or harm inflicted, and not to any particular kind of act or omission which has led to the invasion. The attempt frequently made to distinguish between nuisance and negligence, for example, is based upon an entirely mistaken emphasis upon what the defendant has done rather than the result which has followed, and forgets completely the well established fact that negligence is merely one type of conduct which may give rise to a nuisance." Prosser, Law of Torts (hornbook series, 3d ed.), Nuisance, p. 594, sec. 88.

In the instant cause there was no reason for confusion. Plaintiff's attorney from the outset made it clear that liability was predicated on the *fact* that sulphur dioxide gases were emitted into the atmosphere, despite complaints over a period of several years. There was no attempt to hinge plaintiffs' case on the theory that the defendant was not exercising due care. Under the plaintiffs' theory, which we deem to be a correct one, it is irrelevant that defendant was conforming to industry standards of due care if its conduct created a nuisance. We see no error in plaintiffs' pleading of the case, nor can we conclude that the trial conduct of plaintiffs in any way misled defendant or prejudiced its defense by requiring it to prepare for trial on a theory subsequently abandoned.

The jury found that Dairyland Power Cooperative produced its power in such a manner as to constitute a continuing nuisance to the plaintiffs. The following question was, however, answered "no" by the jury, "Did such nuisance cause substantial damage to their alfalfa crops and lands?" Nevertheless, the jury found the damage to the Jost alfalfa crops amount to $250 for each of the two years, the Andrew Noll damage to $145 for each year, and the Norbert Noll damage to $145 for each year. In addition, Andrew Noll's farm was found to have sustained a $500 diminution in market value.

Appellant claims that the trial judge erred in changing the answer to the substantial damage question from "no" to "yes." * * * The rule is clear. A trial court may not change the jury's answer to a question unless it appears that the answer is not supported by any "credible evidence."

The damage to the alfalfa crop was undisputed. Even Danzinger, the neighboring farmer who testified, ostensibly for the defendant, estimated the crop damage at 5 percent. * * *

* * * In the oft-quoted case, Pennoyer v. Allen (1883), 56 Wis. 502, 14 N.W. 609, the court points out that only a "substantial injury" is compensable or protected against by law. Substantial injury is defined as "tangible" injury, or as a "discomfort perceptible to the senses of ordinary people." The Restatement, 4 Torts, p. 246, sec. 827, follows the same rationale * * *.

Here the damage was to tangible property. The damage was apparent and undisputed. The trial judge summarized the nature of the damage:

"Aside from this testimony [Danzinger, discussed supra], exhibits and testimony of the plaintiffs which showed that plants and vegetation were affected by the sulphur fumes; that flowers could not be raised; that screens became rusty within a short time and totally unusable within two years. To buy the defendant's theory that the plaintiffs were not ordinary sensitive people would mean that the ordinary common housewife likes rusty screens, enjoys barn insects in her home, does not like flowers, delights in buying all her garden vegetables in a store and that her farm husband says, 'so what' if alfalfa plants turn a little yellow and the leaves drop off."

We conclude that the injury was substantial as a matter of law, since under the reasoning of *Pennoyer,* supra, and the Restatement, the injury was obvious injury to tangible property. Moreover, it was, in fact, of such a nature that the jury placed more than a nominal value upon the injury done.

Defendant strenuously argues that it was prejudiced by the court's refusal to permit certain testimony, particularly testimony that tended to show that defendant had used due care in the construction and operation of its plant, and to show that the social and economic utility of the Alma plant outweighed the gravity of damage to the plaintiffs.

Defendant's contention that the evidence should have been admitted rests on two theories; one, that due care, if shown, defeats a claim for nuisance, and, two, that, if the social utility of the offending industry substantially outweighs the gravity of the harm, the plaintiffs cannot recover damages.

We can agree with neither proposition. As this court pointed out in Bell v. Gray–Robinson Construction Co. (1954), 265 Wis. 652, 657, 62 N.W.2d 390, 392:

"A nuisance does not rest on the degree of care used * * * but on the degree of danger existing even with the best of care. To constitute a nuisance, the wrongfulness must have been in the acts themselves [*i.e.,* the consequence of the acts] rather than in the failure to use the requisite degree of care in doing them * * *."

* * *

In any event it is apparent that a continued invasion of a plaintiff's interests by non-negligent conduct, when the actor knows of the nature of the injury inflicted, is an intentional tort, and the fact the hurt is administered non-negligently is not a defense to liability. See Prosser supra, pp. 594 ff., sec. 88; Restatement, supra, p. 226, sec. 822.

It is thus apparent that the facts tending to show freedom from negligence would not have constituted a defense to plaintiffs' nuisance action. It was therefore proper that such evidence was excluded (the nominal character of plaintiffs' proof as to negligence has been commented on above).

While there are some jurisdictions that permit the balancing of the utility of the offending conduct against the gravity of the injury inflicted, it is clear that the rule, permitting such balancing, is not approved in Wisconsin where the action is for damages. We said in Pennoyer v. Allen, supra, 56 Wis. at p. 512, 14 N.W. at p. 613:

"When such comfort and enjoyment are so impaired, and compensation is demanded, it is no defense to show that such business was conducted in a reasonable and proper manner, and with more than ordinary cleanliness, and that the odors so sent over and upon such adjacent premises were only such as were incident to the business when properly conducted. It is the interruption of such enjoyment and the destruction of such comfort that furnishes the ground of action, and it is no satisfaction to the injured party to be informed that it might have been done with more aggravation. The business is lawful; but such interruption and destruction is an invasion of private rights, and to that extent unlawful. It is not so much the manner of doing as the proximity of such a business to the adjacent occupant which causes the annoyance. A business necessarily contaminating the atmosphere to the extent indicated should be located where it will not necessarily deprive others of the enjoyment of their property, or lessen their comfort while enjoying the same."

In Dolata v. Berthelet Fuel & Supply Co. (1949), 254 Wis. 194, 198, 36 N.W.2d 97, 8 A.L.R.2d 413, relying on *Pennoyer,* this court concluded that even though a coalyard was operated properly, nevertheless, it, a socially and economically useful business, would be abated if it caused substantial damage to the adjoining plaintiff.

It appears clear that the doctrine of comparative injury is not entertained in Wisconsin in damage suits for nuisance. * * * [The] problem was discussed in the earlier case of Holman v. Mineral Point Zinc Co. (1908), 135 Wis. 132, 115 N.W. 327, where, in an action for *damages* occasioned by *sulphurous* fumes, defendant sought to rely on the theory that injury to a socially and economically useful factory by the granting of relief would outweigh the possible or actual injury to the plaintiff. This court stated, in discussing a case cited by the parties therein:

"That was a suit to enjoin the operation of a copper smelter as a nuisance, and for damages occasioned by the destruction of timber on nearby lands. It is there held that * * * the court will consider the comparative injury which will result from the granting or refusing of an injunction, and that it will not be granted when it would cause a large loss to the defendant, while the injury to the plaintiff, if refused, will be comparatively slight and can be compensated by damages. That decision could only be applicable on the question of the abatement of the nuisance, as the right of the plaintiff to recover damages is distinctly recognized. * * * "

As in *Holman,* the question of comparative injury is not before us, since this is a suit for damages, not abatement of a nuisance. Defendant nevertheless urges us to adopt the rule of the Restatement, which he contends applies the rule to damage suits for nuisance. It should be pointed out, however, that the Restatement recognizes that:

"For the purpose of determining liability for damages for private nuisance, conduct may be regarded as unreasonable even though its utility is great and the amount of harm is relatively small * * *. It may be reasonable to continue an important activity if payment is made for the harm it is causing, but unreasonable to continue it without paying." Restatement, 4 Torts, p. 224, ch. 40. * * *

We therefore conclude that the court properly excluded all evidence that tended to show the utility of the Dairyland Cooperative's enterprise. Whether its economic or social importance dwarfed the claim of a small farmer is of no consequence in this lawsuit. It will not be said that, because a great and socially useful enterprise will be liable in damages, an injury small by comparison should go unredressed. We know of no acceptable rule of jurisprudence that permits those who are engaged in important and desirable enterprises to injure with impunity those who are engaged in enterprises of lesser economic significance. Even the government or other entities, including public utilities, endowed with the power of eminent domain—the power to take private property in order to devote it to a purpose beneficial to the public good—are obliged to pay a fair market value for what is taken or damaged. To contend that a public utility, in the pursuit of its praiseworthy and legitimate enterprise, can, in effect, deprive others of the full use of their property without compensation, poses a theory unknown to the law of Wisconsin, and in our opinion would constitute the taking of property without due process of law.

We adhere to the rule of Pennoyer v. Allen. Although written in 1883, we believe it remains completely applicable under modern conditions. We conclude that injuries caused by air pollution or other nuisance must be compensated irrespective of the utility of the offending conduct as compared to the injury. Nor do we imply that a different rule should apply where the remedy sought is abatement rather than damages. That point is not considered herein. We consider that the rule of *Dolata* continues to be the law in Wisconsin where the action is for abatement.

We conclude, however, that the court erred in concluding that the evidence failed to show a diminution in the market value. The evidence was uncontradicted that the value of crops raised had diminished in value and that certain types of vegetation were dying out or had died out completely. It is clear that the nuisance has continued for several years and will continue for an indefinite period into the future.

The jury found there was a continuing nuisance. Under these circumstances, we conclude that the injury was permanent and that, as a matter of law, the market value of the land was diminished. *See* McCormick, Damages (hornbook series), p. 500, sec. 127. How much it was diminished we need not determine, since we are satisfied that there should be a new trial on the issue of diminution of market value only in regard to the real property of all plaintiffs.

* * *

We conclude that the plaintiffs are entitled to recover for the crops and damage to vegetation for the years complained of—1965 and 1966—as found by the jury, but after those years recovery cannot again be for specific items of damage on a year-by-year basis. Their avenue for compensation is for permanent and continuing nuisance as may be reflected in a diminution of market value. Of course, permitting recovery now for a permanent loss of market value presupposes that the degree of nuisance will not increase. If such be the case, an award of damages for loss of market value is final. If, however, the level of nuisance and air pollution should be increased above the level that may now be determined by a jury, with a consequent additional injury the plaintiffs would have the right to seek additional permanent damage to compensate them for the additional diminished market value.

Judgment affirmed in part and reversed in part consistent with this opinion.

————

WASHINGTON SUBURBAN SANITARY COMMN. v. CAE–LINK CORP., 330 Md. 115, 622 A.2d 745 (1993). In compliance with a court order enforcing the federal Clean Water Act, the Washington Suburban Sanitary Commission (WSSC) built a facility to treat sewage sludge. The facility was located on a tract called "Site II" in Montgomery County, Maryland, adjacent to the Montgomery Industrial Park. Neighboring landowners who maintained business operations on their properties (including The Washington Post Company) claimed that noxious odors emitted by WSSC's facility constituted a nuisance under Maryland common law. Defendant conceded that, in general, "nuisance is a matter of strict liability" in Maryland, but argued that in this case strict liability should be held "inapplicable" because its action in building the sewage facility was compelled by court order and "not voluntarily undertaken." The trial court agreed with defendant's argument, ruling that plaintiffs must "prove that WSSC negligently created the nuisance" in order to recover damages. The intermediate appellate court reversed this ruling. On defendant's petition for review by Maryland's highest court, *held*, that "[a] strict liability standard should apply." WSSC was ordered to build a facility that treats sewage sludge, not a facility "that emits obnoxious odors that invade the property of others."

"Moreover, in order to build the [sewage] facility, the petitioner had to condemn 115 acres of land [and pay for the property taken]. That was a cost of the facility. The elimination of odors, or compensating those affected, is likewise a cost of the facility if the plant emits the odors. The Court of Special Appeals put it thusly [:] 'If the users [of water] within the entire area serviced by * * * the operation of Site II, are going to inflict the odors generated by the treatment of their sludge on a limited number of Site II neighbors, we see no reason why they should not be required to alleviate that damage or compensate those they damage.' "

BERG v. REACTION MOTORS DIVISION, 37 N.J. 396, 181 A.2d 487 (1962). For over a year defendant regularly test-fired a rocket engine that it was under contract with the Air Force to produce "for the X–15 supersonic airplane." Property owners and residents near the test site repeatedly complained about resultant noise, vibrations, and air blasts. Plaintiffs, homeowners, sued in nuisance to recover the cost of repairing structural damage to their homes caused by the testing. *Held*, for plaintiffs, though no negligence was found. Said the court:

" * * * [T]he defendant first stresses the utility of its activities * * *. It then urges that there was legal error in the trial court's charge which, after referring to a landowner's obligation to avoid unreasonable interference with his neighbor's land, set forth the textbook classifications of nuisances grounded on interference which may be negligent, intentional, or the result of abnormally dangerous activities. * * * We are here primarily concerned with the underlying considerations of reasonableness, fairness and morality rather than with the formulary labels to be attached to the plaintiffs' causes of action or the legalistic classifications in which they are to be placed. * * *

" * * * It may be assumed, for present purposes, that the defendant's activities were conducted with great care and had great public utility and that a court would hesitate to enjoin them notwithstanding the resulting structural damage to the neighboring property. But the issue before us is not whether there should be an injunction but whether the defendant may reasonably be expected to make monetary payment. On that issue there would appear to be little room for difference of opinion—every consideration of fairness and justness dictates that the defendant at least make its neighbors whole for the structural damage it caused. Professor Keeton in his article on Trespass, Nuisance, and Strict Liability, 59 Colum.L.Rev. 457, 470 (1959), points out that when a defendant is put on notice that his conduct, such as blasting or other dangerous activity, is causing damage to neighbors' homes, the question is whether he may destroy another's property 'to serve his own and the public interest.' The Professor notes that 'the answer would seem clearly to be that the enterprise that must do such physical damage is liable therefor, however socially desirable the actor's conduct might be, even though the operations might not be enjoinable.' * * *

* * *

"The cited blasting cases embody current notions as to what is right and just. * * * A business enterprise which engages in blasting operations knows that despite the precautions it takes, neighboring properties may be damaged. If damage does occur, it should in all fairness be absorbed as an operating business expense, for the enterprise may not reasonably expect its wholly innocent neighbors to shoulder the loss. It seems to us that the foregoing considerations apply with even greater force to the case at hand. The extraordinary activities of the defendant may readily be classed as ultrahazardous and, unlike the situation in many of the blasting cases, the significant structural damage resulted from their continuation after receipt of repeated complaints from the neighboring landowners."

SAN DIEGO GAS & ELECTRIC CO. v. CITY OF SAN DIEGO, 450 U.S. 621, 101 S.Ct. 1287, 67 L.Ed.2d 551 (1981). Comments of Brennan, J., on the constitutional Just Compensation Clause, which provides: "[N]or shall private property be taken for public use, without just compensation."

* * * The typical "taking" occurs when a government entity formally condemns a landowner's property and obtains the fee simple pursuant to its sovereign power of eminent domain. However, * * * the Court frequently has found "takings" outside the context of formal condemnation proceedings or transfer of fee simple, in cases where government action benefiting the public resulted in destruction of the use and enjoyment of private property. E.g., Kaiser Aetna v. United States, 444 U.S. 164, 178–180, 100 S.Ct. 383, 392 (1979) (navigational servitude allowing public right of access); United States v. Dickinson, 331 U.S. 745, 750–751, 67 S.Ct. 1382, 1385 (1947) (property flooded because of government dam project); United States v. Causby, 328 U.S. 256, 261–262, 66 S.Ct. 1062, 1065 (1946) (frequent low altitude flights of Army and Navy aircraft over property); Pennsylvania Coal Co. v. Mahon, 260 U.S. 393, 414–416, 43 S.Ct. 158, 159 (1922) (state regulation forbidding mining of coal).

* * * In Jacobs v. United States, 290 U.S. 13, 54 S.Ct. 26 (1933), for example, a government dam project creating intermittent overflows onto petitioners' property resulted in the "taking" of a servitude. Petitioners brought suit against the government to recover just compensation for the partial "taking." Commenting on the nature of the landowners' action, the Court observed: "The suits were based on the right to recover just compensation for property taken by the United States for public use in the exercise of its power of eminent domain. That right was guaranteed by the Constitution. The fact that condemnation proceedings were not instituted and that the right was asserted in suits by the owners did not change the essential nature of the claim. * * * "

[Payment of damages for de facto "takings" is necessary to fulfill] the fundamental purpose of the Just Compensation Clause. That guarantee was designed to bar the government from forcing some individuals to bear burdens which, in all fairness, should be borne by the public as a whole. Armstrong v. United States, 364 U.S. 40, 49, 80 S.Ct. 1563, 1569 (1960). When one person is asked to assume more than a fair share of the public burden, the payment of just compensation operates to redistribute that economic cost from the individual to the public at large. See United States v. Willow River Power Co., 324 U.S. 499, 502, 65 S.Ct. 761, 763 (1945); Monongahela Navigation Co. v. United States, 148 U.S. 312, 325, 13 S.Ct. 622, 625 (1893). * * * If [government action] denies the private property owner the use and enjoyment of his land and is found to effect a "taking," it is only fair that the public bear the cost of benefits received * * *.

COPART INDUSTRIES, INC. v. CONSOLIDATED EDISON COMPANY OF NEW YORK, INC.

Court of Appeals of New York, 1977.
41 N.Y.2d 564, 394 N.Y.S.2d 169, 362 N.E.2d 968.

COOKE, Justice.

"There is perhaps no more impenetrable jungle in the entire law than that which surrounds the word 'nuisance'. It has meant all things to all men" (Prosser, Torts [4th ed.], p. 571). From a point someplace within this oft-noted thicket envisioned by Professor Prosser, this appeal emerges.

Plaintiff leased a portion of the former Brooklyn Navy Yard for a period of five years commencing September 1, 1970. On the demised premises during the ensuing eight or nine months it conducted a storage and new car preparation business, the latter entailing over 50 steps ranging from services such as checking brakes to vehicle cleaning, catering to automobile dealers in the metropolitan area of New York City. Adjacent to the navy yard was defendant's Hudson Avenue plant, engaged in the production of steam and electricity since about 1926. This generating system had five smokestacks and during the time in question its burners were fired with oil having a sulphur content of 1% or less. Prior to 1968, coal had been the fuel employed and the main boiler was equipped with an electrostatic precipitator to remove or control the discharged fly ash. Upon conversion to oil, the precipitator had been deactivated.

Based on allegations that noxious emissions from defendant's nearby stacks caused damage to the exterior of autos stored for its customers such as to require many to be repainted, that reports were received in early 1971 from patrons of paint discoloration and pitting, and that dealers served by plaintiff terminated their business by early May, plaintiff contends that because of said emissions it was caused to cease doing business on May 28, 1971. This action was instituted seeking $1,300,000 for loss of investment and loss of profit, under three causes of action respectively asserting "a deliberate and willful violation of the rights of plaintiff, constituting a nuisance", a "wrongful and unlawful trespass" and violations of "New York City, New York State and federal laws, regulations and guidelines with respect to air pollution." A fourth cause demanded exemplary and punitive damages of $1,000,000 because of defendant's "wrongful and illegal acts."

The case came on for jury trial in 1974. As a result of rulings made at junctures prior to submission for verdict, the third and fourth causes of action were dismissed and the second was merged with the first. After pointing out that plaintiff "framed his case on a branch of the law of wrongdoing called nuisance", the trial court charged nuisance based on negligence and nuisance grounded on an intentional invasion of plaintiff's rights. Negligence was defined and it was pointed out that, although contributory negligence may be a defense where the basis of the nuisance is merely negligent conduct, it would not be where the wrongdoing is founded on the intentional, deliberate misconduct of defendant. Contending that "nuisance is entirely separate and apart from negligence" and that "defendant's intent or negligence is not * * * an essential element of the cause of action of nuisance", plaintiff excepted to the portions of the charge relating to said subjects.

The jury found in defendant's favor and judgment was entered dismissing the complaint. The Appellate Division, by a divided court, affirmed * * * On appeal to this court, plaintiff maintains that the trial court erred in charging (1) that plaintiff was required to prove an intent of the defendant to cause damages, and (2) that plaintiff had a burden of proof as to defendant's negligence and plaintiff's freedom from contributory negligence.

* * *

* * * [N]uisance, as a general term, describes the consequences of conduct, the inconvenience to others, rather than the type of conduct involved (2 N.Y.P.J.I. 653). It is a field of tort liability rather than a single type of tortious conduct (Prosser, Torts [4th ed.], p. 573).

Despite early private nuisance cases, which apparently assumed that the defendant was strictly liable, today it is recognized that one is subject to liability for a private nuisance if his conduct is a legal cause of the invasion of the interest in the private use and enjoyment of land and such invasion is (1) intentional and unreasonable, (2) negligent or reckless, or (3) actionable under the rules governing liability for abnormally dangerous conditions or activities (Restatement, Torts 2d [Tent.Draft No. 16], § 822).

In urging that the charge in respect to negligence constituted error, plaintiff's brief opens its discussion with the assertion that "[t]he complaint contained no allegations of negligence and its theory was that of nuisance." This statement is significant in that not only does it miss the fundamental difference between types of conduct which may result in nuisance and the invasion of interests in land, which is the nuisance, but it also overlooks the firmly established principle that negligence is merely one type of conduct which may give rise to a nuisance. A nuisance, either public or private, based on negligence and whether characterized as either negligence or nuisance, is but a single wrong, and "whenever a nuisance has its origin in negligence", negligence must be proven and a plaintiff "may not avert the consequences of his [or her] own contributory negligence by affixing to the negligence of the wrongdoer the label of a nuisance" (McFarlane v. City of Niagara Falls, 247 N.Y. 340, 344–345, 160 N.E. 391, 392, supra). Although during trial an issue as to causation developed, whether the deleterious substances reaching the customers' vehicles in plaintiff's custody had their origin at defendant's Hudson Avenue property or elsewhere, plaintiff introduced the testimony of different witnesses in support of its contention that defendant operated its plant in a negligent manner. While plaintiff offered expert proof to the effect that it was the general custom or usage in the power plant industry, during the period in question, to use collectors or precipitators, or both, on oil-fired boilers and also to use magnesium as a fuel oil additive to reduce the formation of acid bearing particulates, defendant submitted testimony from similar sources that mechanical and electrostatic precipitators are not commonly utilized on oil-fired burners and that defendant actually was using manganese as an additive.

Besides liability for nuisance arising out of negligence and apart from consideration of a nuisance resulting from abnormally dangerous or ultrahazardous conduct or conditions, the latter of which obviously is not applicable here (see Restatement, Torts 2d, § 822 [Tent.Draft No. 16]), one may be liable for a private nuisance where the wrongful invasion of the use and enjoyment of another's land is intentional and unreasonable. It is distinguished from trespass which involves the invasion of a person's interest in the exclusive possession of land. The elements of such a private nuisance, as charged in effect by the Trial Justice, are: (1) an interference substantial in nature, (2) intentional in origin, (3) unreasonable in character, (4) with a person's property right to use and enjoy land, (5) caused by another's conduct in acting or failure to act. Thus, plaintiff's exception that "defendant's intent * * * is not * * * an essential element of the cause of action of nuisance" and its criticism of the charge, which was to the effect that as to the private nuisance plaintiff was required to prove that defendant's conduct was intentional, are not well taken. "An invasion of another's interest in the use and enjoyment of land is intentional when the actor (a) acts for the purpose of causing it; or (b) knows that it is resulting or is substantially certain to result from his conduct" (Restatement, Torts, § 825).

Negligence and nuisance were explained to the jury at considerable length and its attention was explicitly directed to the two categories of nuisance, that based on negligence and that dependent upon intentional conduct. The causes accrued, if at all, prior to the applicable date of the new CPLR article 14–A (CPLR 1411–1413)*, and the trial court properly charged that contributory negligence may be a defense where the nuisance is based on negligent conduct. As to nuisance involving a willful or intentional invasion of plaintiff's rights, the jury was instructed that contributory negligence was not a defense and, in this respect, plaintiff was not prejudiced and has no right to complain.

* Ed. note: CPLR Section 1411, establishing pure comparative fault, is noted supra at p. 520.

Boomer v. Atlantic Cement Co., 26 N.Y.2d 219, 309 N.Y.S.2d 312, 257 N.E.2d 870, revg. 30 A.D.2d 480, 294 N.Y.S.2d 452 and 55 Misc.2d 1023, 287 N.Y.S.2d 112, relied on by plaintiff, does not dictate a contrary result. There, Supreme Court found that defendant maintained a nuisance, same was affirmed by the Appellate Division, and the Court of Appeals concerned itself with the relief to be granted. Although Trial Term did [not] specifically mention the type of nuisance it found, it is obvious that it was not a nuisance in which the substance of the wrong was negligence since it was held that "the evidence in this case establishes that Atlantic took every available and possible precaution to protect the plaintiffs from dust" (55 Misc.2d, at p. 1024, 287 N.Y.S.2d at p. 113). Rather, it would appear that the nuisance found was based on an intentional and unreasonable invasion, as it was stated that "[t]he discharge of large quantities of dust upon each of the properties and excessive vibration from blasting deprived each party of the reasonable use of his property and thereby prevented his enjoyment of life and liberty therein" (55 Misc.2d, at pp. 1024–1025, 287 N.Y.S.2d at p. 114). Contrary to plaintiff's assertion, *Boomer* does not negate the necessity of proving negligence in some nuisance actions involving harmful emissions since negligence is one of the types of conduct on which a nuisance may depend.

Although there are some Judges in the majority who are of the opinion that the charge did not furnish a model of discussion on some subjects, all of that group agree that reversal on the basis of the charge would not be warranted.

The order of the Appellate Division should be affirmed, with costs.

FUCHSBERG, Judge (dissenting).

I believe, as did Justices Markewich and Kupferman, who dissented at the Appellate Division, that the charge in this case, by repeatedly presenting an admixture of nuisance and negligence in a manner and to an extent that could have misled the jury, should bring a reversal. All the more is that so because of the Trial Judge's insistent refrain that the injury to the plaintiff's property was required to be intentionally inflicted. Accordingly, I must dissent.

In doing so, I should note that, while in the main I am in agreement with the majority of our court in its discussion of the substantive law of nuisance, I believe the readiness with which it uses the term "negligence" in the context of this action for nuisance is counterproductive to the eradication of the confusion which has so long plagued that subject. Words such as "intent", "negligence" and "absolute liability" refer *not* to the result of the conduct of a defendant who intrudes unreasonably on the use and enjoyment of another's property, but rather to the method of bringing it about. Too often, as here, it serves to divert from focusing on the basic legal issue.

* * *

Interestingly, sections 826 and 829A of the Restatement of Torts 2d (Tent.Draft Nos. 17, 18) have now given recognition to developments in the law of torts by moving past the traditional rule to favor recovery for nuisance even when a defendant's conduct is not unreasonable. To be exact, section 826 (Tent.Draft No. 18, pp. 3–4) reads: "An intentional invasion of another's interest in the use and enjoyment of land is unreasonable under the rule stated in section 822, if (a) the gravity of the harm outweighs the utility of the actor's conduct, or (b) the harm caused by the conduct is substantial and the financial burden of compensating for this and other harms does not render infeasible the continuation of the conduct".

Indeed, a fair reading of Boomer v. Atlantic Cement Co., 26 N.Y.2d 219, 309 N.Y.S.2d 312, 257 N.E.2d 870, would indicate that the position articulated by the Restatement's Tentative Draft is consistent with the decision of our court in that case. The plaintiffs in *Boomer* were landowners who were substantially damaged by air pollution caused by the defendant's cement plant. However, since the court found that the adverse economic effects of a permanent injunction which would close the plant would far outweigh the loss plaintiffs would suffer if the nuisance continued, it limited the relief it granted to an award of monetary damages as compensation to the defendants for the "servitude" which had been imposed on their lands. Taken into account was the fact that an injunction would have put 300 employees out of work and caused forfeiture of a $45,000,000 investment, while plaintiffs' permanent damages were only $185,000 and that the burden of compensating for the harm did "not render infeasible the continuation of the conduct" (Restatement, Torts 2d, § 826 [Tent.Draft No. 18], pp. 3–4).

On the basis of these principles, it follows that, on reversal the plaintiff in this case should be permitted to sustain its action for damages on proof that the harm is substantial and that the financial burden of compensating for the harm does not render "infeasible" the continuation of the defendant's business activity.

RESTATEMENT OF TORTS, SECOND (1979)

[1. *Compensation Despite Cost–Justification*]

[The following provisions and comments address nuisance situations in which (a) defendant continuously imposes harm on plaintiff, not by desire but knowingly and so "intentionally"; (b) defendant's conduct is cost-justified, meaning the costs of avoiding the harm would be greater than benefits to be derived; and (c) plaintiff seeks compensation but not abatement.]

§ 826. Unreasonableness of Intentional Invasion

An intentional invasion of another's interest in the use and enjoyment of land is unreasonable if

(a) the gravity of the harm outweighs the utility of the actor's conduct, or

(b) the harm caused by the conduct is serious and the financial burden of compensating for this and similar harm to others would not make the continuation of the conduct not feasible.

* * *

Comment on Clause (b):

f. It may sometimes be reasonable to operate an important activity if payment is made for the harm it is causing, but unreasonable to continue it without paying. * * * The process of comparing the general utility of the activity with the harm suffered as a result is adequate if the suit is for an injunction prohibiting the activity. But it may sometimes be incomplete and therefore inappropriate when the suit is for compensation for the harm imposed. The action for damages does not seek to stop the activity; it seeks instead to place on the activity the cost of compensating for the harm it causes. The financial burden of this cost is therefore a significant factor in determining whether the conduct of causing the harm without paying for it is unreasonable. In estimating this burden, consideration is given not only to the cost of compensating for the harm in the suit before the court but also to the potential liability for compensating the other persons who may also have been injured by the activity.

In a damage action for an intentional invasion of another's interest in the use and enjoyment of land, therefore, the invasion is unreasonable not only when the gravity of the harm outweighs the utility of the conduct, but also when the utility outweighs the gravity—provided the financial burden of compensating for the harms caused by the activity would not render it unfeasible to continue conducting the activity. If imposition of this financial burden would make continuation of the activity not feasible, the weighing process for determining unreasonableness is similar to that in a suit for injunction. * * *

The extent of the burden of compensating may also affect the determination of what persons can recover. Thus in the case of a factory emitting smoke and odors, the granting of compensation for annoyance and inconvenience to all persons located in the general vicinity may create a burden so heavy as to make it not feasible to continue to operate the factory. Compensation may therefore be granted only to those in closer vicinity to the plant whose annoyance is more severe, and not to those farther away whose annoyance is less. The failure to award damages to those farther away from the factory may sometimes be placed on the ground that the harm to them is not significant (see § 821F), but even when the injury is found to be significant, the extent of the financial burden on the actor may mean that not all plaintiffs can recover. Cases involving airport noise illustrate this principle.

§ 829A. Gravity vs. Utility—Severe Harm

An intentional invasion of another's interest in the use and enjoyment of land is unreasonable if the harm resulting from the invasion is severe and greater than the other should be required to bear without compensation.

Comment:

* * *

b. The rule stated in this Section is a specific application of the general rule stated in § 826. * * * [C]ertain types of harm may be so severe as to require a holding of unreasonableness as a matter of law, regardless of the utility of the conduct. This is particularly true if the harm resulting from the invasion is physical in character. * * *

Illustrations:

1.   A's factory produces severe vibrations that reach B's house 100 feet away. The vibrations shake window panes loose, cause ceilings to fall and produce cracks in the plaster. A's invasion is unreasonable.

2.   A's smelter produces sulphurous fumes that waft over B's adjoining farm, killing some of his crops and severely damaging others. A's invasion is unreasonable.

3.   A's chemical factory occasionally emits for short times unpleasant odors that are disturbing to B, a next-door neighbor, and his family. Whether the invasion is unreasonable is a question to be determined by the trier of fact under the principles of § 826, depending upon all of the circumstances involved.

[2. *Some Complexities*]

[Despite the foregoing, not all clear and continuing harms from conflicting uses of land are compensable in nuisance, much less abatable. The following comments indicate distinctions and limits that operate in plenary nuisance analysis.]

Particular Community. The location, character and habits of the particular community are to be taken into account in determining what is offensive or annoying to a normal individual living in it. Thus the odors of a hen house, which would be highly objectionable in a residential area in a city, may be acceptable and normally regarded as harmless and inoffensive in a rural district. [Comment on § 821F]

Intentional Invasions—Unreasonableness. * * * Not every intentional and significant invasion of a person's interest in the use and enjoyment of land is actionable, even when he is the owner of the land in fee simple absolute and the conduct of the defendant is the sole and direct cause of the invasion. Life in organized society and especially in populous communities involves an unavoidable clash of individual interests. Practically all human activities unless carried on in a wilderness interfere to some extent with others or involve some risk of interference, and these interferences range from mere trifling annoyances to serious harms. It is an obvious truth that each individual in a community must put up with a certain amount of annoyance, inconvenience and interference and must take a certain amount of risk in order that all may get on together. The very existence of organized society depends upon the principle of "give and take, live and let live," and therefore the law of torts does not attempt to impose liability or shift the loss in every case in which one person's conduct has some detrimental effect on another. Liability for damages is imposed in those cases in which the harm or risk to one is greater than he ought to be required to bear under the circumstances, at least without compensation. (See § 829A). In respect to unintentional invasions of another's interests, certain broad general principles of liability have been developed. These principles are embodied in the rules governing liability for negligent, reckless and abnormally dangerous conduct and apply to unintentional invasions of interest in the use and enjoyment of land as well as to other interests. In respect to intentional invasions of interests, however, there are no broad general principles of liability applicable to different types of interests. In respect to certain types of interests, such as those in bodily security and in the exclusive possession of land, the law has developed strict rules of liability for intentional invasions, qualified by specific privileges. In respect to interests in the use and enjoyment of land, however, the law has developed a broader, more indefinite and more comprehensive, rule of liability for intentional invasions. This rule is expressed in terms of unreasonableness and * * * requires that an intentional invasion be unreasonable before one is liable for causing it. [Comment on § 822(a)]

Character of the Harm Involved. The gravity of the harm involved in an intentional invasion of another's interest in the use and enjoyment of land depends to some extent upon what kind of harm is involved. The harm that one suffers from an interference with his use or enjoyment of land may arise out of physical damage to the land or to the vegetation, buildings and other things on it; or it may arise out of personal discomfort or annoyance. The loss or detriment to a person from personal discomfort or annoyance may be, and often is, just as serious to him as the loss or detriment from the destruction or impairment of the physical things he is using. It is, however, more difficult to show the existence of substantial harm in respect to personal discomfort than in respect to physical damage to things. * * * Furthermore, if the invasion involves physical damage to tangible property, the gravity of the harm is ordinarily regarded as great even though the extent of the harm is relatively small. But if the invasion involves only minor and temporary personal discomfort and annoyance, the gravity of the harm may be regarded as slight. [Comment on § 827(b)]

Character of the Locality. The gravity of the harm from an invasion of a particular use or enjoyment of land depends not only upon the extent and character of the harm and the general social value of the type of use or enjoyment invaded, but also upon the suitability of the particular use or enjoyment to the character of the locality. Even between socially desirable and valuable uses of land there is a degree of incompatibility that, in some cases, is so great that they cannot be carried on in the same locality. A slaughterhouse, for example, may be indispensable to the community, but it usually renders other land in its immediate vicinity unfit for residential use and enjoyment. This incompatibility between the various beneficial uses to which land may be put has, in nearly all communities, resulted in a segregation of certain uses in certain localities in order to avoid unnecessary conflict between those that are highly incompatible. Thus some localities come to be devoted primarily to residential purposes, others to industrial purposes, others to agricultural purposes and so on. Sound public policy demands that the land in each locality be used for purposes suited to the character of that locality and that persons desiring to make a particular use of land should make it in a suitable locality. If a particular use or enjoyment of land is well suited to the character of the locality, an interference with it is more serious and the gravity of the harm involved is greater than it is if the particular use or enjoyment is not suited to the locality. The harm, for example, that results from an invasion of the comfortable enjoyment of a residence is more serious when the residence is located in a strictly residential district than it is when the residence is located in a business or industrial district even though the harm is the same in kind and extent in both places. The character of a particular locality is, of course, subject to change over a period of time and therefore the suitability of a particular use of land to the locality will also vary with the passage of time. A use of land ideally suited to the character of a particular locality at a particular time may be wholly unsuited to that locality twenty years later. Hence the suitability of the particular use or enjoyment invaded must be determined as of the time of the invasion rather than the time when the use or enjoyment began. [Comment on § 827(d)]

[*Burden on Person Harmed of Avoiding the Harm.*] The harm involved in an intentional invasion of another's interest in the use and enjoyment of land can sometimes be partially or wholly avoided by the other. In most cases, however, the avoidance of one harm involves another in the form of expense and inconvenience, and the burden involved in avoiding is often as great as that sought to be avoided. Nevertheless, there are some situations in which one can avoid most of the harm from an interference with his use or enjoyment of land with very little trouble or expense. For example, one may be able by closing the windows in his building to shut out much of the noise or smoke from his neighbor's activities. In these cases the gravity of the harm is less than it would be if the harm were unavoidable or could only be avoided with difficulty. This does not mean that the person whose conduct causes an invasion is automatically relieved of liability whenever the person harmed can avoid the harm without much trouble. The one whose conduct causes the invasion may be able to reduce or eliminate the harm without undue hardship, and if so, he is the one to do the avoiding. * * * This factor of the burden to the person harmed of avoiding the harm is not often decisive as to gravity. It merely embodies the common sense idea that persons living in society must make a reasonable effort to adjust their uses of land to those of their fellowmen before complaining that they are being unreasonably interfered with in what they are doing. [Comment on § 827(e)]

BAMFORD v. TURNLEY
Court of Exchequer Chamber, 1862.
3 B. & S. 66.

[A large estate was divided into lots which were sold as building sites for houses. Lots were advertised as containing abundant brick clay suitable for building. Plaintiff's house was finished in 1858. In 1860 defendant put up a brick kiln on one of four lots he had bought, and began burning bricks for use in building. Plaintiff brought a nuisance action for damages, complaining of smoke and fumes emitted from the brick kiln some 180 yards from his house. A judgment for defendant was reversed (5–1) on appeal in Exchequer Chamber.]

BRAMWELL, B.—I am of opinion that this judgment should be reversed. The defendant has done that which, if done wantonly or maliciously, would be actionable as being a nuisance to the plaintiff's habitation by causing a sensible diminution of the comfortable enjoyment of it. This, therefore, calls on the defendant to justify or excuse what he has done. And his justification is this: He says that the nuisance is not to the health of the inhabitants of the plaintiff's house, that it is of a temporary character, and is necessary for the beneficial use of his, the defendant's, land, and that the public good requires he should be entitled to do what he claims to do.

The question seems to me to be, Is this a justification in law,—and, in order not to make a verbal mistake, I will say,—a justification for what is done, or a matter which makes what is done no nuisance? It is to be borne in mind, however, that, in fact, the act of the defendant is a nuisance such that it would be actionable if done wantonly or maliciously. The plaintiff, then, has a prima facie case. The defendant has infringed the maxim Sic utere tuo ut alienum non laedas. Then, what principle or rule of law can he rely on to defend himself? It is clear to my mind that there is some exception to the general application of the maxim mentioned. The instances put during the argument, of burning weeds, emptying cesspools, making noises during repairs, and other instances which would be nuisances if done wantonly or maliciously, nevertheless may be lawfully done. It cannot be said that such acts are not nuisances, because, by the hypothesis, they are; and it cannot be doubted that, if a person maliciously and without cause made close to a dwelling-house the same offensive smells as may be made in emptying a cesspool, an action would lie. Nor can these cases be got rid of as extreme cases, because such cases properly test a principle. Nor can it be said that the jury settle such questions by finding there is no nuisance, though there is. For that is to suppose they violate their duty, and that, if they discharged their duty, such matters would be actionable, which I think they could not and ought not to be. There must be, then, some principle on which such cases must be excepted. It seems to me that that principle may be deduced from the character of these cases, and is this, viz., that those acts necessary for the common and ordinary use and occupation of land and houses may be done, if conveniently done, without subjecting those who do them to an action. This principle would comprehend all the cases I have mentioned, but would not comprehend the present, where what has been done was not the using of land in a common and ordinary way, but in an exceptional manner—not unnatural nor unusual, but not the common and ordinary use of land. There is an obvious necessity for such a principle as I have mentioned. It is as much for the advantage of one owner as of another; for the very nuisance the one complains of, as the result of the ordinary use of his neighbour's land, he himself will create in the ordinary use of his own, and the reciprocal nuisances are of a comparatively trifling character. The convenience of such a rule may be indicated by calling it a rule of give and take, live and let live.

Then can this principle be extended to, or is there any other principle which will comprehend, the present case? I know of none: it is for the defendant to show it. None of the above reasoning is applicable to such a cause of nuisance as the present. It had occurred to me, that any not unnatural use of the land, if of a temporary character, might be justified; but I cannot see why its being of a temporary nature should warrant it. What is temporary,—one, five, or twenty years? If twenty, it would be difficult to say that a brick kiln in the direction of the prevalent wind for twenty years would not be as objectionable as a permanent one in the opposite direction. If temporary in order to build a house on the land, why not temporary in order to exhaust the brick earth? I cannot think then that the nuisance being temporary makes a difference.

But it is said that, temporary or permanent, it is lawful because it is for the public benefit. Now, in the first place, that law to my mind is a bad one which, for the public benefit, inflicts loss on an individual without compensation. But further, with great respect, I think this consideration misapplied in this and in many other cases. The public consists of all the individuals of it, and a thing is only for the public benefit when it is productive of good to those individuals on the balance of loss and gain to all. So that if all the loss and all the gain were borne and received by one individual, he on the whole would be a gainer. But whenever this is the case,—whenever a thing is for the public benefit, properly understood,—the loss to the individuals of the public who lose will bear compensation out of the gains of those who gain. It is for the public benefit there should be railways, but it would not be unless the gain of having the railway was sufficient to compensate the loss occasioned by the use of the land required for its site; and accordingly no one thinks it would be right to take an individual's land without compensation to make a railway. It is for the public benefit that trains should run, but not unless they pay their expenses. If one of those expenses is the burning down of a wood of such value that the railway owners would not run the train and burn down the wood if it were their own, neither is it for the public benefit they should if the wood is not their own. If, though the wood were their own, they still would find it compensated them to run trains at the cost of burning the wood, then they obviously ought to compensate the owner of such wood, not being themselves, if they burn it down in making their gains. So in like way in this case a money value indeed cannot easily be put on the plaintiff's loss, but it is equal to some number of pounds or pence, 10*l.*, 50*l.*, or what not: unless the defendant's profits are enough to compensate this, I deny that it is for the public benefit he should do what he has done; if they are, he ought to compensate.

The only objection I can see to this reasoning is, that by injunction or by abatement of the nuisance a man who would not accept a pecuniary compensation might put a stop to works of great value, and much more than enough to compensate him. This objection, however, is comparatively of small practical importance; it may be that the law ought to be amended, and some means be provided to legalize such cases, as I believe is the case in some foreign countries on giving compensation; but I am clearly of opinion that, though the present law may be defective, it would be much worse, and be unjust and inexpedient, if it permitted such power of inflicting loss and damage to individuals, without compensation, as is claimed by the argument for the defendant. * * *

If we look to analogous cases I find nothing to countenance the defendant's contention. A riparian owner cannot take water for the public benefit; he cannot foul it for the public benefit, if to the prejudice of another owner. A common cannot be enclosed on such principle. A window, the fee simple of which is 5*s.*, cannot be stopped up by a building worth 1,000,000*l.*, of the greatest public benefit, nor a way. * * *

As to the somewhat remote illustration of taking a man's land in case of foreign invasion, it is said that is a case of "necessity;" but it can hardly be a "necessity" to burn bricks on the defendant's land, to the nuisance of the plaintiff, without compensation.

I confess then I can see no reason or principle in the defendant's contention.

* * *

Judgment reversed, and entered for the plaintiff for 40*s.*

ALEVIZOS v. METROPOLITAN AIRPORTS COMMISSION, 298 Minn. 471, 216 N.W.2d 651 (1974). The Minnesota Constitution provides that "private property shall not be taken, destroyed or damaged for public use without just compensation therefor." Plaintiffs are property owners who reside under or near the take-off and landing flight paths for the Minneapolis–St. Paul airport. They allege that "noise, vibrations, dust, and oily grime" from airport operations so interfere with use and enjoyment of their property "as to amount to a taking, requiring compensation." Their suit seeks to compel the airport authority "to institute condemnation proceedings" and pay permanent damages for the "easements" already taken. On appeal, *held* for plaintiffs. An action for "inverse condemnation" is proper whether or not plaintiffs were injured by direct overflights. Moreover, balancing "the utility of the airport" against the harm to plaintiffs "is irrelevant." The test for compensation is "whether the interference is sufficiently direct, sufficiently peculiar, and of sufficient magnitude to cause us to conclude that fairness and justice, as between the State and the citizen, requires the burden imposed to be borne by the public and not by the individual alone." The court went on:

" * * * Not every economic, social, or other interest or advantage is a property right, the taking of which must be compensated. * * *

" * * * [Not] every noise or interference with a property owner's use and enjoyment thereof constitutes a taking. Every landowner must continue to endure that level of inconvenience, discomfort, and loss of peace and quiet which can be reasonably anticipated by any average member of a vibrant and progressive society. But when those interferences reach the point where they cause a measurable decrease in property market value, it is reasonable to assume that, considering the permanency of the air flights, a property right has been, if not 'taken or destroyed,' at the very least 'damaged,' for which our constitution requires that compensation be paid. This will not give relief to the unusually sensitive person because the measure of recovery is decrease in market value of the property due to its decreased desirability in the general market place rather than the amount of discomfort to the individual.

"We recognize that most property in a metropolitan area would have a higher value if it were completely free of any noise, smog, or other undesirable features, provided the same conveniences were available. We are sure that if the metropolitan area had no airports, freeways, buses, trucks, trains, ambulances, and many other conveniences that are sources of noise, fumes, and whatnot, that property values would be substantially reduced. Property owners cannot—and we are sure they do not expect to—have the advantages created by conveniences and yet be paid for the undesirable effects created by the same conveniences unless those effects adversely affect their property so directly and so substantially that it is manifestly unfair to require them to sustain a measurable loss in market value which the property-owning public in general does not suffer. Thus, not every inconvenience, annoyance, or loss of peace and quiet caused by air flights will give rise to a cause of action in inverse condemnation against an airport operator.

"The test, then, that we prescribe will give relief to any property owner who can show a direct and substantial invasion of his property rights of such a magnitude he is deprived of the practical enjoyment of the property and that such invasion results in a definite and measurable diminution of the market value of the property.

* * *

"Another issued raised and argued in the briefs is: Should property owners who purchased their homes at a reduced price because of the overflight be required to set off this saving against the award of damages in this case? This question was not reached in the lower court and should be passed upon in the lower court, with respect to the damages sustained by such property owner."

ADKINS v. THOMAS SOLVENT CO., 440 Mich. 293, 487 N.W.2d 715 (1992). Plaintiffs are a group of 22 property owners whose parcels lie south and east of defendants' facilities. Suing in nuisance, plaintiffs allege that "toxic chemicals and industrial wastes" escaped from the facilities, contaminating the groundwater. However, in discovery it became clear that owing to a subsurface "ground water divide," the contaminated water flowed north and west; it never actually reached these plaintiffs' properties, and never would. Plaintiffs seek recovery for "loss in property values due to public concern about the contaminants in the general area." *Held*, for defendants, since the facts do not show "a significant interference with the use and enjoyment of land." "Diminution in property values caused by negative publicity is, on these facts, damnum absque injuria—a loss without an injury in the legal sense."

The court noted that, according to prior cases, "property depreciation alone is insufficient to constitute a nuisance," and "a cause of action for nuisance may not be based on unfounded fears." "[W]e would think it

* * * anachronistic that a claim of nuisance in fact could be based on unfounded fears regarding persons with AIDS moving into a neighborhood, the establishment of otherwise lawful group homes for the disabled, or unrelated persons living together, merely because the fears experienced by third parties would cause a decline in property values.''

SPUR INDUSTRIES, INC. v. DEL E. WEBB DEVELOPMENT CO.
Supreme Court of Arizona, 1972.
108 Ariz. 178, 494 P.2d 700.

CAMERON, Vice Chief Justice. From a judgment permanently enjoining the defendant, Spur Industries, Inc., from operating a cattle feedlot near the plaintiff Del E. Webb Development Company's Sun City, Spur appeals. Webb cross-appeals. Although numerous issues are raised, we feel that it is necessary to answer only two questions. They are:

1. Where the operation of a business, such as a cattle feedlot is lawful in the first instance, but becomes a nuisance by reason of a nearby residential area, may the feedlot operation be enjoined in an action brought by the developer of the residential area?

2. Assuming that the nuisance may be enjoined, may the developer of a completely new town or urban area in a previously agricultural area be required to indemnify the operator of the feedlot who must move or cease operation because of the presence of the residential area created by the developer?

[Spur operates a large cattle feeding facility, or feed lot, about 15 miles from Phoenix. When begun in 1956 the feed lot was located in a predominantly rural area. About 2 miles to the north was Youngtown, "a retirement community appealing primarily to senior citizens." In 1959 Del Webb, a development company, bought some 20,000 acres of farmland around Youngtown as the site of a much larger residential development called Sun City. The purchase price "was considerably less than the price of land located near the urban area of Phoenix."]

By September 1959, Del Webb had started construction of a golf course * * * and Spur's predecessors had started to level ground for more feedlot area. * * * By 1962 Spur's expansion program was completed and [the feedlot] had expanded from approximately 35 acres to 114 acres.

Accompanied by an extensive advertising campaign, homes were first offered by Del Webb in January 1960 and the first unit to be completed was * * * approximately 2 ½ miles north of Spur. By 2 May 1960, there were 450 to 500 houses completed or under construction. At this time, Del Webb did not consider odors from the Spur feed pens a problem and Del Webb continued to develop in a southerly direction, until sales resistance became so great that the parcels were difficult if not impossible to sell.

* * *

By December 1967, Del Webb's property had extended south to [within a half mile of Spur]. Del Webb filed its original complaint alleging that in excess of 1,300 lots in the southwest portion were unfit for development for sale as residential lots because of the operation of the Spur feedlot.

Del Webb's suit complained that the Spur feeding operation was a public nuisance because of the flies and the odor which were drifting or being blown by the prevailing south to north wind over the southern portion of Sun City. At the time of the suit, Spur was feeding between 20,000 and 30,000 head of cattle, and the facts amply support the finding of the trial court that the feed pens had become a nuisance to the people who resided in the southern part of Del Webb's development. The testimony indicated that cattle in a commercial feedlot will produce 35 to 40 pounds of wet manure per day, per head, or over a million pounds of wet manure per day for 30,000 head of cattle, and that despite the admittedly good feedlot management and good housekeeping practices by Spur, the resulting odor and flies produced an annoying if not unhealthy situation as far as the senior citizens of southern Sun City were concerned. There is no doubt that some of the citizens of Sun City were unable to enjoy the outdoor living which Del Webb had advertised and that Del Webb was faced with sales resistance from prospective purchasers as well as strong and persistent complaints from the people who had purchased homes in that area.

Trial was commenced before the court with an advisory jury. The advisory jury was later discharged and the trial was continued before the court alone. Findings of fact and conclusions of law were requested and given. The case was vigorously contested, including special actions in this court on some of the matters. In one of the special actions before this court, Spur agreed to, and did, shut down its operation without prejudice to a determination of the matter on appeal. On appeal the many questions raised were extensively briefed.

It is noted, however, that neither the citizens of Sun City nor Youngtown are represented in this lawsuit and the suit is solely between Del E. Webb Development Company and Spur Industries, Inc.

MAY SPUR BE ENJOINED?

The difference between a private nuisance and a public nuisance is generally one of degree. A private nuisance is one affecting a single individual or a definite small number of persons in the enjoyment of private rights not common to the public, while a public nuisance is one affecting the rights enjoyed by citizens as a part of the public. To constitute a public nuisance, the nuisance must affect a considerable number of people or an entire community or neighborhood. City of Phoenix v. Johnson, 51 Ariz. 115, 75 P.2d 30 (1938).

Where the injury is slight, the remedy for minor inconveniences lies in an action for damages rather than in one for an injunction. Kubby v. Hammond, 68 Ariz. 17, 198 P.2d 134 (1948). Moreover, some courts have held, in the "balancing of conveniences" cases, that damages may be the sole remedy. See Boomer v. Atlantic Cement Co., 26 N.Y.2d 219, 309 N.Y.S.2d 312, 257 N.E.2d 870, 40 A.L.R.3d 590 (1970), and annotation comments, 40 A.L.R.3d 601.

Thus, it would appear from the admittedly incomplete record as developed in the trial court, that, at most, residents of Youngtown would be entitled to damages rather than injunctive relief.

We have no difficulty, however, in agreeing with the conclusion of the trial court that Spur's operation was an enjoinable public nuisance as far as the people in the southern portion of Del Webb's Sun City were concerned.

* * *

It is clear that as to the citizens of Sun City, the operation of Spur's feedlot was both a public and a private nuisance. They could have successfully maintained an action to abate the nuisance. Del Webb, having shown a special injury in the loss of sales, had a standing to bring suit to enjoin the nuisance. Engle v. Clark, 53 Ariz. 472, 90 P.2d 994 (1939); City of Phoenix v. Johnson, supra. The judgment of the trial court permanently enjoining the operation of the feedlot is affirmed.

Must Del Webb Indemnify Spur?

A suit to enjoin a nuisance sounds in equity and the courts have long recognized a special responsibility to the public when acting as a court of equity: * * * "Courts of equity may, and frequently do, go much further both to give and withhold relief in furtherance of the public interest than they are accustomed to go when only private interests are involved. Accordingly, the granting or withholding of relief may properly be dependent upon considerations of public interest. * * *." 27 Am.Jur.2d, Equity, page 626.

In addition to protecting the public interest, however, courts of equity are concerned with protecting the operator of a lawful, albeit noxious, business from the result of a knowing and willful encroachment by others near his business.

In the so-called "coming to the nuisance" cases, the courts have held that the residential landowner may not have relief if he knowingly came into a neighborhood reserved for industrial or agricultural endeavors and has been damaged thereby:

"Plaintiffs chose to live in an area uncontrolled by zoning laws or restrictive covenants and remote from urban development. In such an area plaintiffs cannot complain that legitimate agricultural pursuits are being carried on in the vicinity, nor can plaintiffs, having chosen to build in an agricultural area, complain that the agricultural pursuits carried on in the area depreciate the value of their homes. The area being *primarily agricultural,* any opinion reflecting the value of such property must take this factor into account. The standards affecting the value of residence property in an urban setting, subject to zoning controls and controlled planning techniques, cannot be the standards by which agricultural properties are judged.

"People employed in a city who build their homes in suburban areas of the county beyond the limits of a city and zoning regulations do so for a reason. Some do so to avoid the high taxation rate imposed by cities, or to avoid special assessments for street, sewer and water projects. They usually build on improved or hard surface highways, which have been built either at state or county expense and thereby avoid special assessments for these improvements. It may be that they desire to get away from the congestion of traffic, smoke, noise, foul air and the many other annoyances of city life. But with all these advantages in going beyond the area which is zoned and restricted to protect them in their homes, they must be prepared to take the disadvantages." Dill v. Excel Packing Company, 183 Kan. 513, 525, 526, 331 P.2d 539, 548, 549 (1958).

And:

"* * * a party cannot justly call upon the law to make that place suitable for his residence which was not so when he selected it. * * *." Gilbert v. Showerman, 23 Mich. 448, 455, 2 Brown 158 (1871).

Were Webb the only party injured, we would feel justified in holding that the doctrine of "coming to the nuisance" would have been a bar to the relief asked by Webb, and, on the other hand, had Spur located the feedlot near the outskirts of a city and had the city grown toward the feedlot, Spur would have to suffer the cost of abating the nuisance as to those people locating within the growth pattern of the expanding city:

"The case affords, perhaps, an example where a business established at a place remote from population is gradually surrounded and becomes part of a populous center, so that a business which formerly was not an interference with the rights of others has become so by the encroachment of the population * * *." City of Ft. Smith v. Western Hide & Fur Co., 153 Ark. 99, 103, 239 S.W. 724, 726 (1922).

We agree, however, with the Massachusetts court that:

"The law of nuisance affords no rigid rule to be applied in all instances. It is elastic. It undertakes to require only that which is fair and reasonable under all the circumstances. In a commonwealth like this, which depends for its material prosperity so largely on the continued growth and enlargement of manufacturing of diverse varieties, 'extreme rights' cannot be enforced. * * *." Stevens v. Rockport Granite Co., 216 Mass. 486, 488, 104 N.E. 371, 373 (1914).

There was no indication in the instant case at the time Spur and its predecessors located in western Maricopa County that a new city would spring up, full-blown, alongside the feeding operation and that the developer of that city would ask the court to order Spur to move because of the new city. Spur is required to move not because of any wrongdoing on the part of Spur, but because of a proper and legitimate regard of the courts for the rights and interests of the public.

Del Webb, on the other hand, is entitled to the relief prayed for (a permanent injunction), not because Webb is blameless, but because of the damage to the people who have been encouraged to purchase homes in Sun City. It does not equitably or legally follow, however, that Webb, being entitled to the injunction, is then free of any liability to Spur if Webb has in fact been the cause of the damage Spur has sustained. It does not seem harsh to require a developer, who has taken advantage of the lesser land values in a rural area as well as the availability of large tracts of land on which to build and develop a new town or city in the area, to indemnify those who are forced to leave as a result.

Having brought people to the nuisance to the foreseeable detriment of Spur, Webb must indemnify Spur for a reasonable amount of the cost of moving or shutting down. It should be noted that this relief to Spur is limited to a case wherein a developer has, with foreseeability, brought into a previously agricultural or industrial area the population which makes necessary the granting of an injunction against a lawful business and for which the business has no adequate relief.

It is therefore the decision of this court that the matter be remanded to the trial court for a hearing upon the damages sustained by the defendant Spur as a reasonable and direct result of the granting of the permanent injunction. Since the result of the appeal may appear novel and both sides have obtained a measure of relief, it is ordered that each side will bear its own costs.

Affirmed in part, reversed in part, and remanded for further proceedings consistent with this opinion.

HAYS, C. J., STRUCKMEYER and LOCKWOOD, JJ., and UDALL, Retired Justice.

————

HOFFMAN v. UNITED IRON & METAL CO., 108 Md.App. 117, 671 A.2d 55 (1996). In 1971 defendants began operating an automobile shredder at their scrap metal yard. In 1993 plaintiffs—37 neighborhood residents plus a church—commenced a nuisance suit for damages. They complain that the shredder causes four kinds of interferences: periodic explosions, constant noise, air pollutants, and lead contamination. Because defendants' operation had continued for more than 20 years, the trial court granted summary judgment against plaintiffs. On appeal, *held*, reversed in part.

The appellate court noted that "Maryland does not recognize the defense of 'coming to the nuisance.'" Maryland law does provide that "[a] prescriptive right to maintain a nuisance may be acquired by continuance of the nuisance, uninterrupted, for twenty years." Such a right, in the nature of an easement, covers types of interferences by defendants' shredder which had been going on since 1971 (explosions, noise, pollutants). However, suit could proceed as to the fourth type, since "it was not until July 1994 that tests of soil revealed high lead levels in the backyards of plaintiffs' houses."

The court also noted that "[a]n existing easement may be extinguished by the subsequent purchase of the servient estate by a bona fide purchaser without notice of the easement." "It is logical to conclude that, because prescriptive rights are designed to disadvantage those who sleep on their rights, the prescriptive period did not begin to run against the adult plaintiffs until they had notice * * * of the nuisance." Therefore summary judgment should not have been granted, as to any type of interference, against those plaintiffs who moved into the neighborhood less than 20 years ago.

RESTATEMENT OF TORTS, SECOND (1979). Contributory negligence is a defense "[w]hen a nuisance results from negligent conduct," but not "[w]hen the harm is intentional" (§ 840B). Intent is shown if a defendant knew harm was occurring but "nevertheless continued to act" (Comment f). Assumption of risk is an available defense (§ 840C), but "plaintiff is not required to forego a valuable right or privilege, such as the use of his own land or dwelling, in order to avoid assuming the risk" (Comment d). Section 840D, titled "Coming to the Nuisance," provides:

> The fact that the plaintiff has acquired or improved his land after a nuisance interfering with it has come into existence is not in itself sufficient to bar his action, but it is a factor to be considered in determining whether the nuisance is actionable.

Chapter 19

PRODUCTS LIABILITY: RISE
AND BASIC DOCTRINE

The basic situation addressed by products liability is this: a manufacturer sells a product containing a defect to a distributor, who sells it to a consumer, who puts the product to use and is injured because of the defect. There is a chain of contracts linking the parties, from manufacturer to distributor to consumer. The injured consumer brings suit against the manufacturer seeking compensation for injuries caused by the defective product. The basic question is whether the manufacturer is liable to the consumer and if so, on what basis.

In the development of products liability, four different answers have been given to the question of a manufacturer's liability for product defect. Four main ideas, doctrinal conceptions, underlie the divergent answers. In sequence the ideas, and the answers, are as follows:

    1. privity: the manufacturer is not liable to a person who is not "in privity of contract" with the manufacturer;

    2. negligence: the manufacturer is liable in tort if the defect is attributable to its negligent conduct;

    3. warranty: the manufacturer is liable for breach of an implied warranty of safety running to the consumer;

    4. strictness: the manufacturer is strictly liable in tort for injuries caused by its defective products.

These answers come alternatively from contract doctrine (privity), then from tort doctrine (negligence), then again from contract (warranty), and again from tort (strictness).

The materials that follow present the four answers as four successive stages in the historical evolution of products liability. The sequence ends with strict liability in tort, which is the object of detailed study both below and, especially, in the following chapter. The first stage, with its negative answer (manufacturer not liable in tort), is largely superseded—but not entirely, as we shall see. Though products liability is today ensconced in the field of tort, contract-related ideas remain vital. Though strict liability is well established in certain respects, the battle between tort ideas of negligence and strictness continues—particularly in the area of "design defect," discussed in the following chapter.

SECTION A.   FROM PRIVITY TO NEGLIGENCE

Parties are in privity of contract when they have contractual relations with one another. The doctrine of privity of contract says that legal liability is bounded by the contractual relation; there's no liability to persons—strangers—outside the contractual relationship. On this view, the manufacturer of a product has obligations to the immediate buyer of the product, who is privy to the contract of sale; but the manufacturer has no obligation—in particular, no tort liability for negligence—to other persons, with whom the manufacturer never dealt, who happen to be affected by the product. This approach is in line with a deep predilection of classical private law, which is to let contract govern, and let tort recede, when contract ideas are able to take hold of a legal problem.

The first stage in the evolution of products liability doctrine, dominated by the idea of privity just recounted, is distinctively pre-modern. The second stage, wherein the idea of negligence displaces the idea of privity, is recognizably modern. Two main cases below, both decided in 1916, reject privity in favor of negligence, and thus take the conceptual leap that establishes contemporary legal understanding. Today it seems quite unexceptionable that the general principles of negligence should apply to the activity of product manufacture, as to all sorts of other risky activities. But today's commonplace understanding is the hard-won result of a dramatic intellectual struggle between tort and contract.

THOMAS v. WINCHESTER
Court of Appeals of New York, 1852.
6 N.Y. 397, 57 Am.Dec. 455.

[In the course of debating the liability of a seller who falsely labeled a poison to a plaintiff who purchased the poison from an intermediate druggist, the court said:]

If A. build a wagon and sell it to B., who sells it to C., and C. hires it to D., who in consequence of the gross negligence of A., in building the wagon, is overturned and injured, D. cannot recover damages against A., the builder. A.'s obligation to build the wagon faithfully, arises solely out of his contract with B.; the public have nothing to do with it. Misfortune to third persons, not parties to the contract, would not be a natural and necessary consequence of the builder's negligence; and such negligence is not an act imminently dangerous to human life. So, for the same reason, if a horse be defectively shod by a smith, and a person hiring the horse from the owner, is thrown and injured, in consequence of the smith's negligence in shoeing; the smith is not liable for the injury. The smith's duty in such case grows exclusively out of his contract with the owner of the horse; it was a duty which the smith owed to him alone, and to no one else. And although the injury to the rider may have happened, in consequence of the negligence of the smith, the latter was not bound, either by his contract, or by any considerations of public policy or safety, to respond for his breach of duty to any one except the person he contracted with.

———

LOSEE v. CLUTE, 51 N.Y. 494, 10 Am.Rep. 638 (1873). In this case, related to Losee v. Buchanan, p. 300, supra, plaintiff sued the manufacturer of a boiler which exploded when used by a paper company at its mill and thereby damaged plaintiff's nearby property. Testimony showed the boiler to be improperly constructed. The court, affirming dismissal of the complaint, said:

"* * * [Defendants] contracted with the company, and did what was done by them for it and to its satisfaction, and when the boiler was accepted they ceased to have any further control over it or its management, and all responsibility for what was subsequently done with it devolved upon the company and those having charge of it, and the case falls within the principle decided by the Court of Appeals in The Mayor, etc., of Albany v. Cunliff (2 Comst., 165), which is, that the * * * architect or builder of a work is answerable only to his employees for any want of care or skill in the execution thereof, and he is not liable for accidents or injuries which may occur after the execution of the work; and the opinions published in that case clearly show that there is no ground of liability by the defendants to the plaintiff in this action. They owed *him* no *duty* whatever at the time of the explosion either growing out of contract or imposed by law."

WARD v. MOREHEAD CITY SEA FOOD CO.
Supreme Court of North Carolina, 1916.
171 N.C. 33, 87 S.E. 958.

[Action for causing the death of the plaintiff's intestate. The defendant had sold fish to a grocery dealer from whom the intestate had purchased it. The fish was bad and caused the death of the intestate. Under various issues which were framed, the jury found for the plaintiff. The defendant appealed.]

CLARK, C. J. * * * The fourth issue is, "Was the death of the plaintiff's intestate brought about by the negligence of defendant, as alleged?" This issue was comprehensive of the idea of negligence, alleged in the complaint in the preparation, care, and packing of the fish, and also as to the duty and care of giving notice if the defendant could thereby have avoided the injury, and it was sufficient, for the defendant presented its evidence upon both points.

Both the State and Federal Governments have enacted statutes to protect the public against impure articles of food. Our statutes, Revisal, sec. 3969, et seq., and Revisal, secs. 3442 and 3444, make it an indictable offense, under certain circumstances, to sell adulterated food. When the defendant had put this food on the market for sale, if it was in a dangerous condition it was the defendant's duty to protect the public from the consequences thereof. There was evidence that there was a delay by the defendant in cleaning and packing this fish for some thirty-six hours after they were placed on the wharf in the month of September. They knew the effect upon fish of that delay in one of the most heated months of the year.

The defendant learned, on the very day that this particular lot was shipped to the retail dealer who sold the plaintiff's intestate, that fish from this lot were making people sick. A second notice was received on the following day that this had happened in several localities. A little later the defendant learned that a man had been actually killed by eating fish from the same lot. The defendant recognized its duty to notify those to whom it had sold to stop the sale, by writing letters, but it failed to do what an ordinarily prudent man would have done under the circumstances, in that it did not wire immediately to the parties to whom this lot had been sold and did not even mail a letter till twenty-four hours after receiving notice. There was evidence that if a telegram had been promptly sent the life of the intestate might have been saved. * * *

There was evidence to justify the finding of the jury that there was negligence on the part of the defendant which was the proximate cause of the death of plaintiff's intestate.

[Judgment was affirmed.]

MacPHERSON v. BUICK MOTOR CO.

Court of Appeals of New York, 1916.
217 N.Y. 382, 111 N.E. 1050.

CARDOZO, J. The defendant is a manufacturer of automobiles. It sold an automobile to a retail dealer. The retail dealer resold to the plaintiff. While the plaintiff was in the car it suddenly collapsed. He was thrown out and injured. One of the wheels was made of defective wood, and its spokes crumbled into fragments. The wheel was not made by the defendant; it was bought from another manufacturer. There is evidence, however, that its defects could have been discovered by reasonable inspection, and that inspection was omitted. There is no claim that the defendant knew of the defect and wilfully concealed it. * * * The charge is one, not of fraud, but of negligence. The question to be determined is whether the defendant owed a duty of care and vigilance to any one but the immediate purchaser.

The foundations of this branch of the law, at least in this state, were laid in Thomas v. Winchester, 6 N.Y. 397, 57 Am.Dec. 455. A poison was falsely labeled. The sale was made to a druggist, who in turn sold to a customer. The customer recovered damages from the seller who affixed the label. "The defendant's negligence," it was said, "put human life in imminent danger." A poison, falsely labeled, is likely to injure any one who gets it. Because the danger is to be foreseen, there is a duty to avoid the injury. Cases were cited by way of illustration in which manufacturers were not subject to any duty irrespective of contract. The distinction was said to be that their conduct, though negligent, was not likely to result in injury to any one except the purchaser. We are not required to say whether the chance of injury was always as remote as the distinction assumes. Some of the illustrations might be rejected to-day. The principle of the distinction is, for present purposes, the important thing. Thomas v. Winchester became quickly a landmark of the law. In the application of its principle there may, at times, have been uncertainty or even error. There has never in this state been doubt or disavowal of the principle itself. The chief cases are well known, yet to recall some of them will be helpful. Loop v. Litchfield, 42 N.Y. 351, 1 Am.Rep. 543, is the earliest. It was the case of a defect in a small balance wheel used on a circular saw. The manufacturer pointed out the defect to the buyer, who wished a cheap article and was ready to assume the risk. The risk can hardly have been an imminent one, for the wheel lasted five years before it broke. In the meanwhile the buyer had made a lease of the machinery. It was held that the manufacturer was not answerable to the lessee. Loop v. Litchfield was followed in Losee v. Clute, 51 N.Y. 494, 10 Am.Rep. 638, the case of the explosion of a steam boiler. That decision has been criticized, Thompson on Negligence, 233; Shearman & Redfield on Negligence, 6th Ed., § 117; but it must be confined to its special facts. It was put upon the ground that the risk of injury was too remote. The buyer in that case had not only accepted the boiler, but had tested it. The manufacturer knew that his own test was not the final one. The finality of the test has a bearing on the measure of diligence owing to persons other than the purchaser.

These early cases suggest a narrow construction of the rule. Later cases, however, evince a more liberal spirit. First in importance is Devlin v. Smith, 89 N.Y. 470, 42 Am.Rep. 311. The defendant, a contractor, built a scaffold for a painter. The painter's servants were injured. The contractor was held liable. He knew that the scaffold, if improperly constructed, was a most dangerous trap. He knew that it was to be used by the workmen. He was building it for that very purpose. Building it for their use, he owed them a duty, irrespective of his contract with their master, to build it with care.

From Devlin v. Smith we pass over intermediate cases and turn to the latest case in this court in which Thomas v. Winchester was followed. That case is Statler v. Ray Mfg. Co., 195 N.Y. 478, 480, 88 N.E. 1063. The defendant manufactured a large coffee urn. It was installed in a restaurant. When heated, the urn exploded and injured the plaintiff. We held that the manufacturer was liable. We said that the urn "was of such a character inherently that, when applied to the purposes for which it was designed, it was liable to become a source of great danger to many people if not carefully and properly constructed."

It may be that Devlin v. Smith and Statler v. Ray Mfg. Co. have extended the rule of Thomas v. Winchester. If so, this court is committed to the extension. The defendant argues that things imminently dangerous to life are poisons, explosives, deadly weapons—things whose normal function it is to injure or destroy. But whatever the rule in Thomas v. Winchester may once have been, it has no longer that restricted meaning. A scaffold is not inherently a destructive instrument. It becomes destructive only if imperfectly constructed. A large coffee urn may have within itself, if negligently made, the potency of danger, yet no one thinks of it as an implement whose normal function is destruction. What is true of the coffee urn is equally true of bottles of aerated water. * * *

Devlin v. Smith was decided in 1882. A year later a very similar case came before the Court of Appeal in England, Heaven v. Pender, 11 Q.B.D. 503. We find in the opinion of Brett, M.R., afterwards Lord Esher, the same conception of a duty, irrespective of contract, imposed upon the manufacturer by the law itself:

"Whenever one person supplies goods or machinery, or the like, for the purpose of their being used by another person under such circumstances that every one of ordinary sense would, if he thought, recognize at once that unless he used ordinary care and skill with regard to the condition of the thing supplied, or the mode of supplying it, there will be danger of injury to the person or property of him for whose use the thing is supplied, and who is to use it, a duty arises to use ordinary care and skill as to the condition or manner of supplying such thing."

He then points out that for a neglect of such ordinary care or skill whereby injury happens, the appropriate remedy is an action for negligence. The right to enforce this liability is not to be confined to the immediate buyer. The right, he says, extends to the persons or class of persons for whose use the thing is supplied. * * * What was said by Lord Esher in that case did not command the full assent of his associates. His opinion has been criticised "as requiring every man to take affirmative precautions to protect his neighbors as well as to refrain from injuring them." Bohlen, Affirmative Obligations in the Law of Torts, 44 Am.Law Reg.,N.S., 341. It may not be an accurate exposition of the law of England. * * * But its tests and standards, at least in their underlying principles with whatever qualification may be called for as they are applied to varying conditions, are the tests and standards of our law.

We hold, then, that the principle of Thomas v. Winchester is not limited to poisons, explosives, and things of like nature, to things which in their normal operation are implements of destruction. If the nature of a thing is such that it is reasonably certain to place life and limb in peril when negligently made, it is then a thing of danger. Its nature gives warning of the consequences to be expected. If to the element of danger there is added knowledge that the thing will be used by persons other than the purchaser, and used without new tests, then, irrespective of contract, the manufacturer of this thing of danger is under a duty to make it carefully. That is as far as we are required to go for the decision of this case. There must be knowledge of a danger, not merely possible, but probable. It is possible to use almost anything in a way that will make it dangerous if defective. That is not enough to charge the manufacturer with a duty independent of his contract. Whether a given thing is dangerous may be sometimes a question for the court and sometimes a question for the jury. There must also be knowledge that in the usual course of events the danger will be shared by others than the buyer. Such knowledge may often be inferred from the nature of the transaction. But it is possible that even knowledge of the danger and of the use will not always be enough. The proximity or remoteness of the relation is a factor to be considered. We are dealing now with the liability of the manufacturer of the finished product, who puts it on the market to be used without inspection by his customer. If he is negligent, where danger is to be foreseen, a liability will follow.

We are not required at this time to say that it is legitimate to go back of the manufacturer of the finished product and hold the manufacturers of the component parts. To make their negligence a cause of imminent danger, an independent cause must often intervene; the manufacturer of the finished product must also fail in his duty of inspection. It may be that in those circumstances the negligence of the earlier members of the series is too remote to constitute, as to the ultimate user, an actionable wrong. We leave that question open. We shall have to deal with it when it arises. The difficulty which it suggests is not present in this case. There is here no break in the chain of cause and effect. In such circumstances, the presence of a known danger, attendant upon a known use, makes vigilance a duty. We have put aside the notion that the duty to safeguard life and limb, when the consequences of negligence may be foreseen, grows out of contract and nothing else. We have put the source of the obligation where it ought to be. We have put its source in the law.

From this survey of the decisions, there thus emerges a definition of the duty of a manufacturer which enables us to measure this defendant's liability. Beyond all question, the nature of an automobile gives warning of probable danger if its construction is defective. This automobile was de-signed to go 50 miles an hour. Unless its wheels were sound and strong, injury was almost certain. It was as much a thing of danger as a defective engine for a railroad. The defendant knew the danger. It knew also that the car would be used by persons other than the buyer. This was apparent from its size; there were seats for three persons. It was apparent also from the fact that the buyer was a dealer in cars, who bought to resell. The maker of this car supplied it for the use of purchasers from the dealer just as plainly as the contractor in Devlin v. Smith supplied the scaffold for use by the servants of the owner. The dealer was indeed the one person of whom it might be said with some approach to certainty that by him the car would not be used. Yet the defendant would have us say that he was the one person whom it was under a legal duty to protect. The law does not lead us to so inconsequent a conclusion. Precedents drawn from the days of travel by stage-coach do not fit the conditions of travel to-day. The principle that the danger must be imminent does not change, but the things subject to the principle do change. They are whatever the needs of life in a developing civilization requires them to be.

In reaching this conclusion, we do not ignore the decisions to the contrary in other jurisdictions. * * * The earlier cases are summarized by Judge Sanborn in Huset v. J. I. Case Threshing Machine Co., 120 F. 865. Some of them, at first sight inconsistent with our conclusion, may be reconciled upon the ground that the negligence was too remote, and that another cause had intervened. But even when they cannot be reconciled the difference is rather in the application of the principle than in the principle itself. Judge Sanborn says, for example, that the contractor who builds a bridge, or the manufacturer who builds a car, cannot ordinarily foresee injury to other persons than the owner as the probable result. We take a different view. * * *

In England the limits of the rule are still unsettled. Winterbottom v. Wright, 10 M. & W. 109, is often cited. The defendant undertook to provide a mail coach to carry the mail bags. The coach broke down from latent defects in its construction. The defendant, however, was not the manufacturer. The court held that he was not liable for injuries to a passenger. The case was decided on a demurrer to the declaration. Lord Esher points out in Heaven v. Pender, supra, at page 513, that the form of the declaration was subject to criticism. It did not fairly suggest the existence of a duty aside from the special contract which was the plaintiff's main reliance. See the criticism of Winterbottom v. Wright, in Bohlen, supra, at pages 281, 283. At all events, in Heaven v. Pender, supra, the defendant, a dock owner, who put up a staging outside a ship, was held liable to the servants of the shipowner. * * * There seems to have been a return to the doctrine of Winterbottom v. Wright in Earl v. Lubbock [1905] 1 K.B. 253. In that case, however, as in the earlier one, the defendant was not the manufacturer. He had merely made a contract to keep the van in repair. * * * From these cases a consistent principle is with difficulty extracted. * * *

There is nothing anomalous in a rule which imposes upon A, who has contracted with B, a duty to C and D and others according as he knows or does not know that the subject-matter of the contract is intended for their use. We may find an analogy in the law which measures the liability of landlords. If A leases to B a tumble-down house, he is not liable, in the absence of fraud, to B's guests who enter it and are injured. This is because B is then under the duty to repair it; the lessor has the right to suppose that he will fulfill that duty, and, if he omits to do so, his guests must look to him. Bohlen, supra, at page 276. But if A leases a building to be used by the lessee at once as a place of public entertainment, the rule is different. There injury to persons other than the lessee is to be foreseen, and foresight of the consequences involves the creation of a duty.

* * * Subtle distinctions are drawn by the defendant between things inherently dangerous and things imminently dangerous, but the case does not turn upon these verbal niceties. If danger was to be expected as reasonably certain, there was a duty of vigilance, and this whether you call the danger inherent or imminent. In varying forms that thought was put before the jury. We do not say that the court would not have been justified in ruling as a matter of law that the car was a dangerous thing. If there was any error, it was none of which the defendant can complain.

We think the defendant was not absolved from a duty of inspection because it bought the wheels from a reputable manufacturer. It was not merely a dealer in automobiles. It was a manufacturer of automobiles. It was responsible for the finished product. It was not at liberty to put the finished product on the market without subjecting the component parts to ordinary and simple tests. Under the charge of the trial judge nothing more was required of it. The obligation to inspect must vary with the nature of the thing to be inspected. The more probable the danger the greater the need of caution. * * *

The judgment should be affirmed, with costs.

WILLARD BARTLETT, C.J. (dissenting). The plaintiff was injured in consequence of the collapse of a wheel of an automobile manufactured by the defendant corporation which sold it to a firm of automobile dealers in Schenectady, who in turn sold the car to the plaintiff. The wheel was purchased by the Buick Motor Company, ready made, from the Imperial Wheel Company of Flint, Mich., a reputable manufacturer of automobile wheels which had furnished the defendant with 80,000 wheels, none of which had proved to be made of defective wood prior to the accident in the present case. The defendant relied upon the wheel manufacturer to make all necessary tests as to the strength of the material therein, and made no such test itself. * * *

The late Chief Justice Cooley of Michigan, one of the most learned and accurate of American law writers, states the general rule thus:

"The general rule is that a contractor, manufacturer, vendor or furnisher of an article is not liable to third parties who have no contractual relations with him, for negligence in the construction, manufacture, or sale of such article." 2 Cooley on Torts (3d Ed.), 1486.

The leading English authority in support of this rule, to which all the later cases on the same subject refer, is Winterbottom v. Wright, 10 Meeson & Welsby, 109, which was an action by the driver of a stagecoach against a contractor who had agreed with the postmaster general to provide and keep the vehicle in repair for the purpose of conveying the royal mail over a prescribed route. The coach broke down and upset, injuring the driver, who sought to recover against the contractor on account of its defective construction. The Court of Exchequer denied him any right of recovery on the ground that there was no privity of contract between the parties, the agreement having been made with the postmaster general alone.

"If the plaintiff can sue," said Lord Abinger, the Chief Baron, "every passenger or even any person passing along the road who was injured by the upsetting of the coach might bring a similar action. Unless we confine the operation of such contracts as this to the parties who enter into them the most absurd and outrageous consequences, to which I can see no limit, would ensue."

The doctrine of that decision was recognized as the law of this state by the leading New York case of Thomas v. Winchester, 6 N.Y. 397, 408, 57 Am.Dec. 455, which, however, involved an exception to the general rule. There the defendant, who was a dealer in medicines, sold to a druggist a quantity of belladonna, which is a deadly poison, negligently labeled as extract of dandelion. The druggist in good faith used the poison in filling a prescription calling for the harmless dandelion extract, and the plaintiff for whom the prescription was put up was poisoned by the belladonna. This court held that the original vendor was liable for the injuries suffered by the patient. Chief Judge Ruggles, who delivered the opinion of the court, distinguished between an act of negligence imminently dangerous to the lives of others and one that is not so, saying:

"If A. build a wagon and sell it to B., who sells it to C., and C. hires it to D., who in consequence of the gross negligence of A. in building the wagon is overturned and injured, D. cannot recover damages against A., the builder. A.'s obligation to build the wagon faithfully arises solely out of his contract with B. The public have nothing to do with it. * * * So, for the same reason, if a horse be defectively shod by a smith, and a person hiring the horse from the owner is thrown and injured in consequence of the smith's negligence in shoeing, the smith is not liable for the injury."

* * *

The character of the exception to the general rule limiting liability for negligence to the original parties to the contract of sale, was still more clearly stated by Judge Hiscock, writing for the court in Statler v. Ray Manufacturing Co., 195 N.Y. 478, 482, 88 N.E. 1063, where he said that:

"In the case of an article of an inherently dangerous nature, a manufacturer may become liable for a negligent construction which, when added to the inherent character of the appliance, makes it imminently dangerous, and causes or contributes to a resulting injury not necessarily incident to the use of such an article if properly constructed, but naturally following from a defective construction."

In that case the injuries were inflicted by the explosion of a battery of steamdriven coffee urns, constituting an appliance liable to become dangerous in the course of ordinary usage.

The case of Devlin v. Smith, 89 N.Y. 470, 42 Am.Rep. 311, is cited as an authority in conflict with the view that the liability of manufacturer and vendor extends to third parties only when the article manufactured and sold is inherently dangerous. In that case the builder of a scaffold 90 feet high, which was erected for the purpose of enabling painters to stand upon it, was held to be liable to the administratrix of a painter who fell therefrom and was killed, being at the time in the employ of the person for whom the scaffold was built. It is said that the scaffold, if properly constructed, was not inherently dangerous, and hence that this decision affirms the existence of liability in the case of an article not dangerous in itself, but made so only in consequence of negligent construction. Whatever logical force there may be in this view it seems to me clear from the language of Judge Rapallo, who wrote the opinion of the court that the scaffold was deemed to be an inherently dangerous structure, and that the case was decided as it was because the court entertained that view. Otherwise he would hardly have said, as he did, that the circumstances seemed to bring the case fairly within the principle of Thomas v. Winchester.

I do not see how we can uphold the judgment in the present case without overruling what has been so often said by this court and other courts of like authority in reference to the absence of any liability for negligence on the part of the original vendor of an ordinary carriage to any one except his immediate vendee. The absence of such liability was the very point actually decided in the English case of Winterbottom v. Wright, supra, and the illustration quoted from the opinion of Chief Judge Ruggles in Thomas v. Winchester, supra, assumes that the law on the subject was so plain that the statement would be accepted almost as a matter of course. In the case at bar the defective wheel on an automobile, moving only eight miles an hour, was not any more dangerous to the occupants of the car than a similarly defective wheel would be to the occupants of a carriage drawn by a horse at the same speed, and yet, unless the courts have been all wrong on this question up to the present time, there would be no liability to strangers to the original sale in the case of the horsedrawn carriage.

The rule upon which, in my judgment, the determination of this case depends, and the recognized exceptions thereto, were discussed by Circuit Judge Sanborn, of the United States Circuit Court of Appeals in the Eighth Circuit, in Huset v. J. I. Case Threshing Machine Co., 120 F. 865, in an opinion which reviews all the leading American and English decisions on the subject up to the time when it was rendered (1903). * * *

* * * That the federal courts still adhere to the general rule, as I have stated it, appears by the decision of the Circuit Court of Appeal in the Second Circuit, in March, 1915, in the case of Cadillac Motor Car Co. v. Johnson, 221 F. 801. That case, like this, was an action by a subvendee against a manufacturer of automobiles for negligence in failing to discover that one of its wheels was defective, the court holding that such an action could not be maintained. It is true there was a dissenting opinion in that case, but it was based chiefly upon the proposition that rules applicable to stagecoaches are archaic when applied to automobiles, and that if the law did not afford a remedy to strangers to the contract, the law should be changed. If this be true, the change should be effected by the Legislature and not by the courts. A perusal of the opinion in that case and in the Huset Case will disclose how uniformly the courts throughout this country have adhered to the rule and how consistently they have refused to broaden the scope of the exceptions. I think we should adhere to it in the case at bar, and therefore I vote for a reversal of this judgment.

CARTER v. YARDLEY & CO., 319 Mass. 92, 64 N.E.2d 693, 164 A.L.R. 559 (1946). Plaintiff bought and used a bottle of perfume manufactured by defendant. The manufacturer had sold the perfume to a retailer from whom plaintiff purchased it. Plaintiff offered evidence that she suffered a second degree burn from applying it to her skin. Jury verdict for plaintiff. *Held*, judgment on the verdict. Prior decisions led to "an asserted 'general rule' that a manufacturer or supplier is never liable for negligence to a remote vendee or other person with whom he has had no contractual relation." But exceptions to that rule have become so extensive that it is time "to recognize that the asserted general rule no longer exists."

FORD MOTOR CO. v. MATHIS, 322 F.2d 267 (5th Cir. 1963). Action by car owner against car manufacturer for personal injuries and property damage sustained in collision with a tree after his lights went out completely because of a defective dimmer switch manufactured by an independent supplier and incorporated into the car by the defendant. In response to special questions, the jury found that the independent supplier of the switch was negligent, but that the defendant could not have discovered the defect by reasonable inspection. The trial court entered judgment for the plaintiff. *Held* (2–1), affirmed. The defendant, as assembler, is liable for the negligence of its component-part manufacturer.

SECTION B.   WARRANTY AND BEYOND

The third stage in the development of products liability is dominated by the contract-based notion of implied warranty. Warranty doctrine is part of the modern law of sales contracts. Liability for breach of contract, including warranty, is strict. When applicable, the implied warranty of a product's safety results in strict liability for injury caused by product failure. When freed from privity limitations and held to be non-disclaimable (as in the well-known case, *Henningsen v. Bloomfield Motors, Inc.,* infra), the warranty obligation of contract law has precisely the same effect as strict liability in tort.

In the overall evolution of products liability, the warranty theory played the historical role of a ladder of the fourth stage, that of strict tort liability: once climbed, the ladder could be set aside. Today the warranty theory is largely superfluous in establishing a producer's liability for harm caused by the basic sort of product defect, a defect that develops in the manufacturing process. But still, implied warranty remains an available tool, and it may come in handy in establishing "design defect," a more esoteric type of defect which is discussed in the following chapter.

UNIFORM COMMERCIAL CODE

2–313.   Express Warranties by Affirmation, Promise, Description, Sample

(1) Express warranties by the seller are created as follows:

(a) Any affirmation of fact or promise made by the seller to the buyer which relates to the goods and becomes part of the basis of the bargain creates an express warranty that the goods shall conform to the affirmation or promise.

(b) Any description of the goods which is made part of the basis of the bargain creates an express warranty that the goods shall conform to the description.

(c) Any sample or model which is made part of the basis of the bargain creates an express warranty that the whole of the goods shall conform to the sample or model.

(2) It is not necessary to the creation of an express warranty that the seller use formal words such as "warrant" or "guarantee" or that he have a specific intention to make a warranty, but an affirmation merely of the value

of the goods or a statement purporting to be merely the seller's opinion or commendation of the goods does not create a warranty.

2–314. Implied Warranty: Merchantability; Usage of Trade

(1) Unless excluded or modified (Section 2–316), a warranty that the goods shall be merchantable is implied in a contract for their sale if the seller is a merchant with respect to goods of that kind. Under this section the serving for value of food or drink to be consumed either on the premises or elsewhere is a sale.

(2) Goods to be merchantable must be at least such as

(a) pass without objection in the trade under the contract description; and

(b) in the case of fungible goods, are of fair average quality within the description; and

(c) are fit for the ordinary purposes for which such goods are used; and

(d) run, within the variations permitted by the agreement, of even kind, quality and quantity within each unit and among all units involved; and

(e) are adequately contained, packaged, and labeled as the agreement may require; and

(f) conform to the promises or affirmations of fact made on the container or label if any.

(3) Unless excluded or modified (Section 2–316) other implied warranties may arise from course of dealing or usage of trade.

2–315. Implied Warranty; Fitness for Particular Purpose

Where the seller at the time of contracting has reason to know any particular purpose for which the goods are required and that the buyer is relying on the seller's skill or judgment to select or furnish suitable goods, there is unless excluded or modified under the next section an implied warranty that the goods shall be fit for such purpose.

2–316. Exclusion or Modification of Warranties

(1) Words or conduct relevant to the creation of an express warranty and words or conduct tending to negate or limit warranty shall be construed whenever reasonable as consistent with each other; but subject to the provisions of this Article on parol or extrinsic evidence (Section 2–202) negation or limitation is inoperative to the extent that such construction is unreasonable.

(2) Subject to subsection (3), to exclude or modify the implied warranty of merchantability or any part of it the language must mention merchantability and in case of a writing must be conspicuous, and to exclude or modify any implied warranty of fitness the exclusion must be by a writing and conspicuous. Language to exclude all implied warranties of fitness is

sufficient if it states, for example, that "There are no warranties which extend beyond the description on the face hereof."

(3) Notwithstanding subsection (2)

(a) unless the circumstances indicate otherwise, all implied warranties are excluded by expressions like "as is", "with all faults" or other language which in common understanding calls the buyer's attention to the exclusion of warranties and makes plain that there is no implied warranty; and

(b) when the buyer before entering into the contract has examined the goods or the sample or model as fully as he desired or has refused to examine the goods there is no implied warranty with regard to defects which an examination ought in the circumstances to have revealed to him; and

(c) an implied warranty can also be excluded or modified by course of dealing or course of performance or usage of trade.

(4) Remedies for breach of warranty can be limited in accordance with the provisions of this Article on liquidation or limitation of damages and on contractual modification of remedy (Sections 2–718 and 2–719).

2–318.   Third Party Beneficiaries of Warranties Express or Implied

Alternative A

A seller's warranty whether express or implied extends to any natural person who is in the family or household of his buyer or who is a guest in his home if it is reasonable to expect that such person may use, consume or be affected by the goods and who is injured in person by breach of the warranty. A seller may not exclude or limit the operation of this section.

Alternative B

A seller's warranty whether express or implied extends to any natural person who may reasonably be expected to use, consume or be affected by the goods and who is injured in person by breach of the warranty. A seller may not exclude or limit the operation of this section.

Alternative C

A seller's warranty whether express or implied extends to any person who may reasonably be expected to use, consume or be affected by the goods and who is injured by breach of the warranty. A seller may not exclude or limit the operation of this section with respect to injury to the person of an individual to whom the warranty extends. As amended 1966.

2–714.   Buyer's Damages for Breach in Regard to Accepted Goods

(1) Where the buyer has accepted goods and given notification (subsection (3) of Section 2–607) he may recover as damages for any nonconformity of tender the loss resulting in the ordinary course of events from the seller's breach as determined in any manner which is reasonable.

(2) The measure of damages for breach of warranty is the difference at the time and place of acceptance between the value of the goods accepted and the value they would have had if they had been as warranted, unless special circumstances show proximate damages of a different amount.

(3) In a proper case any incidental and consequential damages under the next section may also be recovered.

2–715. Buyer's Incidental and Consequential Damages

(1) * * *

(2) Consequential damages resulting from the seller's breach include

(a) * * *

(b) injury to person or property proximately resulting from any breach of warranty.

2–719. Contractual Modification or Limitation of Remedy

(1) * * *

(2) * * *

(3) Consequential damages may be limited or excluded unless the limitation or exclusion is unconscionable. Limitation of consequential damages for injury to the person in the case of consumer goods is prima facie unconscionable but limitation of damages where the loss is commercial is not.

———

FORD MOTOR CO. v. MOULTON, 511 S.W.2d 690 (Tenn.1974). Suit against Ford Motor Co. and dealer by purchaser and wife. Purchaser was seriously injured when his car suddenly veered to right, jumped the guard rail and fell twenty-six feet to a street below. Held: (a) implied warranties can be disclaimed pursuant to Sec. 2–316(2) of the U.C.C.; (b) Section 2–719(3) does not prevent a total disclaimer of a warranty, rather it states that a limitation of damages for personal injuries is prima facie unconscionable when a warranty has not been specifically disclaimed; (c) a warranty disclaimer which meets the provisions of 2–316(2) cannot be considered unconscionable within the meaning of that term as used in 2–302 of the U.C.C.

UNCONSCIONABILITY. Section 2–302 of the Uniform Commercial Code provides:

§ 2–302. **Unconscionable Contract or Clause.** (1) If the court as a matter of law finds the contract or any clause of the contract to have been unconscionable at the time it was made the court may refuse to enforce the contract, or it may enforce the remainder of the contract without the unconscionable clause, or it may so limit the application of any unconscionable clause as to avoid any unconscionable result.

(2) When it is claimed or appears to the court that the contract or any clause thereof may be unconscionable the parties shall be afforded a

reasonable opportunity to present evidence as to its commercial setting, purpose and effect to aid the court in making the determination.

The drafters' Comment on this provision explains:

> This section is intended to make it possible for the courts to police explicitly against the contracts or clauses which they find to be unconscionable. In the past such policing has been accomplished by adverse construction of language, by manipulation of the rules of offer and acceptance or by determinations that the clause is contrary to public policy or to the dominant purpose of the contract. This section is intended to allow the court to pass directly on the unconscionability of the contract or particular clause therein and to make a conclusion of law as to its unconscionability. The basic test is whether, in the light of the general commercial background and the commercial needs of the particular trade or case, the clauses involved are so one-sided as to be unconscionable under the circumstances existing at the time of the making of the contract. * * * The principle is one of the prevention of oppression and unfair surprise and not of disturbance of allocation of risks because of superior bargaining power. * * *

HENNINGSEN v. BLOOMFIELD MOTORS, INC.

Supreme Court of New Jersey, 1960.
32 N.J. 358, 161 A.2d 69.

FRANCIS, J. Plaintiff Claus H. Henningsen purchased a Plymouth automobile, manufactured by defendant Chrysler Corporation, from defendant Bloomfield Motors, Inc. His wife, plaintiff Helen Henningsen, was injured while driving it and instituted suit against both defendants to recover damages on account of her injuries. Her husband joined in the action seeking compensation for his consequential losses. The complaint was predicated upon breach of express and implied warranties and upon negligence. At the trial the negligence counts were dismissed by the court and the cause was submitted to the jury for determination solely on the issues of implied warranty of merchantability. Verdicts were returned against both defendants and in favor of the plaintiffs. Defendants appealed * * *.

The facts are not complicated, but a general outline of them is necessary to an understanding of the case.

On May 7, 1955 Mr. and Mrs. Henningsen visited the place of business of Bloomfield Motors, Inc., an authorized De Soto and Plymouth dealer, to look at a Plymouth. * * * They were shown a Plymouth which appealed to them and the purchase followed. The record indicates that Mr. Henningsen intended the car as a Mother's Day gift to his wife. He said the intention was communicated to the dealer. When the purchase order or contract was prepared and presented, the husband executed it alone. His wife did not join as a party.

The purchase order was a printed form of one page. On the front it contained blanks to be filled in with a description of the automobile to be sold, the various accessories to be included, and the details of the financing.

The particular car selected was described as a 1955 Plymouth, Plaza "6", Club Sedan. The type used in the printed parts of the form became smaller in size, different in style, and less readable toward the bottom where the line for the purchaser's signature was placed. The smallest type on the page appears in the two paragraphs, one of two and one-quarter lines and the second of one and one-half lines, on which great stress is laid by the defense in the case. These two paragraphs are the least legible and the most difficult to read in the instrument, but they are most important in the evaluation of the rights of the contesting parties. * * *

The two paragraphs are:

"The front and back of this Order comprise the entire agreement affecting this purchase and no other agreement or understanding of any nature concerning same has been made or entered into, or will be recognized. I hereby certify that no credit has been extended to me for the purchase of this motor vehicle except as appears in writing on the face of this agreement.

"I have read the matter printed on the back hereof and agree to it as a part of this order the same as if it were printed above my signature. I certify that I am 21 years of age, or older, and hereby acknowledge receipt of a copy of this order."

* * *

The testimony of Claus Henningsen justifies the conclusion that he did not read the two fine print paragraphs referring to the back of the purchase contract. And it is uncontradicted that no one made any reference to them, or called them to his attention. With respect to the matter appearing on the back, it is likewise uncontradicted that he did not read it and that no one called it to his attention.

The reverse side of the contract contains 8 ½ inches of fine print. * * * The page is headed "Conditions" and contains ten separate paragraphs consisting of 65 lines in all. The paragraphs do not have headnotes or margin notes denoting their particular subject * * *. In the seventh paragraph, about two-thirds of the way down the page, the warranty, which is the focal point of the case, is set forth. It is as follows:

"7. It is expressly agreed that there are no warranties, express or implied, *made* by either the dealer or the manufacturer on the motor vehicle, chassis, or parts furnished hereunder except as follows.

" 'The manufacturer warrants each new motor vehicle (including original equipment placed thereon by the manufacturer except tires), chassis or parts manufactured by it to be free from defects in material or workmanship under normal use and service. Its obligation under this warranty being limited to making good at its factory any part or parts thereof which shall, within ninety (90) days after delivery of such vehicle *to the original purchaser* or before such vehicle has been driven 4,000 miles, whichever event shall first occur, be returned to it with transportation charges prepaid and which its examination shall disclose to its satisfaction to have been thus defective; *this warranty being expressly in lieu of all other warranties* *expressed or implied, and all other obligations or liabilities on its part,* and it neither assumes nor authorizes any other person to assume for it any other liability in connection with the sale of its vehicles. * * * ' "(Emphasis ours.)

* * *

The new Plymouth was turned over to the Henningsens on May 9, 1955. * * * It had no servicing and no mishaps of any kind before the event of May 19. That day, Mrs. Henningsen drove to Asbury Park. On the way down and in returning the car performed in normal fashion until the accident occurred. She was proceeding north on Route 36 in Highlands, New Jersey, at 20–22 miles per hour. The highway was paved and smooth, and contained two lanes for northbound travel. She was riding in the righthand lane. Suddenly she heard a loud noise "from the bottom, by the hood." It "felt as if something cracked." The steering wheel spun in her hands; the car veered sharply to the right and crashed into a highway sign and a brick wall. No other vehicle was in any way involved. A bus operator driving in the left-hand lane testified that he observed plaintiffs' car approaching in normal fashion in the opposite direction; "all of a sudden [it] veered at 90 degrees * * * and right into this wall." * * *

The insurance carrier's inspector and appraiser of damaged cars, with 11 years of experience, advanced the opinion, based on the history and his examination, that something definitely went "wrong from the steering wheel down to the front wheels" and that the untoward happening must have been due to mechanical defect or failure; "something down there had to drop off or break loose to cause the car" to act in the manner described.

As has been indicated, the trial court felt that the proof was not sufficient to make out a *prima facie* case as to the negligence of either the manufacturer or the dealer. The case was given to the jury, therefore, solely on the warranty theory, with results favorable to the plaintiffs against both defendants.

I.

The Claim of Implied Warranty against the Manufacturer

In the ordinary case of sale of goods by description an implied warranty of merchantability is an integral part of the transaction. R.S. 46:30–20, N.J.S.A. * * * [This] type of warranty simply means that the thing sold is reasonably fit for the general purpose for which it is manufactured and sold. * * *

* * *

Of course such sales, whether oral or written, may be accompanied by an express warranty. Under the broad terms of the Uniform Sale of Goods Law any affirmation of fact relating to the goods is an express warranty if the natural tendency of the statement is to induce the buyer to make the purchase. R.S. 46:30–18, N.J.S.A. And over the years since the almost universal adoption of the act, a growing awareness of the tremendous development of modern business methods has prompted the courts to administer that provision with a liberal hand. Vold, Law of Sales, § 86, p. 429 (2d ed. 1959). Solicitude toward the buyer plainly harmonizes with the intention of the Legislature. * * *

The uniform act codified, extended and liberalized the common law of sales. The motivation in part was to ameliorate the harsh doctrine of *caveat emptor,* and in some measure to impose a reciprocal obligation on the seller to beware. The transcendent value of the legislation, particularly with respect to implied warranties, rests in the fact that obligations on the part of the seller were imposed by operation of law, and did not depend for their existence upon express agreement of the parties. And of tremendous significance in a rapidly expanding commercial society was the recognition of the right to recover damages on account of personal injuries arising from a breach of warranty. The particular importance of this advance resides in the fact that under such circumstances strict liability is imposed upon the maker or seller of the product. Recovery of damages does not depend upon proof of negligence or knowledge of the defect.

* * *

* * * It must be noted, however, that the sections of the Sales Act, to which reference has been made, do not impose warranties in terms of unalterable absolutes. R.S. 46:30–3, N.J.S.A., provides in general terms that an applicable warranty may be negatived or varied by express agreement. As to disclaimers or limitations of the obligations that normally attend a sale, it seems sufficient at this juncture to say they are not favored, and that they are strictly construed against the seller.

With these considerations in mind, we come to a study of the express warranty on the reverse side of the purchase order signed by Claus Henningsen. At the outset we take notice that it was made only by the manufacturer and that by its terms it runs directly to Claus Henningsen. On the facts detailed above, it was to be extended to him by the dealer as the agent of Chrysler Corporation. * * *

* * * [T]he language of this warranty is that of the uniform warranty of the Automobile Manufacturers Association, of which Chrysler is a member. * * * The evidence is overwhelming that the dealer acted for Chrysler in including the warranty in the purchase contract.

The terms of the warranty are a sad commentary upon the automobile manufacturers' marketing practices. Warranties developed in the law in the interest of and to protect the ordinary consumer who cannot be expected to have the knowledge or capacity or even the opportunity to make adequate inspection of mechanical instrumentalities, like automobiles, and to decide for himself whether they are reasonably fit for the designed purpose. But the ingenuity of the Automobile Manufacturers Association, by means of its standardized form, has metamorphosed the warranty into a device to limit the maker's liability. * * *

The manufacturer agrees to replace defective parts for 90 days after the sale or until the car has been driven 4,000 miles, whichever is first to occur, *if the part is sent to the factory, transportation charges prepaid, and if* *examination discloses to its satisfaction that the part is defective.* It is difficult to imagine a greater burden on the consumer, or less satisfactory remedy. Aside from imposing on the buyer the trouble of removing and shipping the part, the maker has sought to retain the uncontrolled discretion to decide the issue of defectiveness. * * *

* * *

* * * [A]fter reciting that defective parts will be replaced at the factory, the alleged agreement relied upon by Chrysler provides that the manufacturer's "obligation under this warranty" is limited to that undertaking; further, that such remedy is "in lieu of all other warranties, express or implied, and all other obligations or liabilities on its part." * * *

Putting aside for the time being the problem of the efficacy of the disclaimer provisions contained in the express warranty a question of first importance to be decided is whether an implied warranty of merchantability by Chrysler Corporation accompanied the sale of the automobile to Claus Henningsen.

* * *

Chrysler points out that an implied warranty of merchantability is an incident of a contract of sale. It concedes, of course, the making of the original sale to Bloomfield Motors, Inc., but maintains that this transaction marked the terminal point of its contractual connection with the car. Then Chrysler urges that since it was not a party to the sale by the dealer to Henningsen, there is no privity of contract between it and the plaintiffs, and the absence of this privity eliminates any such implied warranty.

There is no doubt that under early common-law concepts of contractual liability only those persons who were parties to the bargain could sue for a breach of it. In more recent times a noticeable disposition has appeared in a number of jurisdictions to break through the narrow barrier of privity when dealing with sales of goods in order to give realistic recognition to a universally accepted fact. The fact is that the dealer and the ordinary buyer do not, and are not expected to, buy goods, whether they be foodstuffs or automobiles, exclusively for their own consumption or use. Makers and manufacturers know this and advertise and market their products on that assumption; witness, the "family" car, the baby foods, etc. The limitations of privity in contracts for the sale of goods developed their place in the law when marketing conditions were simple, when maker and buyer frequently met face to face on an equal bargaining plane and when many of the products were relatively uncomplicated and conducive to inspection by a buyer competent to evaluate their quality. See, Freezer, "Manufacturer's Liability for Injuries Caused by His Products," 37 Mich.L.Rev. 1 (1938). With the advent of mass marketing, the manufacturer became remote from the purchaser, sales were accomplished through intermediaries, and the demand for the product was created by advertising media. In such an economy it became obvious that the consumer was the person being cultivated. Manifestly, the connotation of "consumer" was broader than that of "buyer." He signified such a person who, in the reasonable contemplation of the parties to the sale, might be expected to use the product. Thus, where the commodities sold are such that if defectively manufactured they will be dangerous to life or limb, then society's interests can only be protected by eliminating the requirement of privity between the maker and his dealers and the reasonably expected ultimate consumer. In that way the burden of losses consequent upon use of defective articles is borne by those who are in a position to either control the danger or make an equitable distribution of the losses when they do occur. As Harper & James put it, "The interest in consumer protection calls for warranties by the maker that *do* run with the goods, to reach all who are likely to be hurt by the use of the unfit commodity for a purpose ordinarily to be expected." 2 Harper & James, [The Law of Torts], 1571, 1572 [(1956).] * * *

* * *

Although only a minority of jurisdictions have thus far departed from the requirement of privity, the movement in that direction is most certainly gathering momentum. Liability to the ultimate consumer in the absence of direct contractual connection has been predicated upon a variety of theories. Some courts hold that the warranty runs with the article like a covenant running with land; others recognize a third-party beneficiary thesis; still others rest their decision on the ground that public policy requires recognition of a warranty made directly to the consumer.

* * *

Under modern conditions the ordinary layman, on responding to the importuning of colorful advertising, has neither the opportunity nor the capacity to inspect or to determine the fitness of an automobile for use; he must rely on the manufacturer who has control of its construction, and to some degree on the dealer who, to the limited extent called for by the manufacturer's instructions, inspects and services it before delivery. In such a marketing milieu his remedies and those of persons who properly claim through him should not depend "upon the intricacies of the law of sales. The obligation of the manufacturer should not be based alone on privity of contract. It should rest, as was once said, upon 'the demands of social justice.'" Mazetti v. Armour & Co., 75 Wash. 622, 135 P. 633, 635, 48 L.R.A.,N.S., 213 (Sup.Ct.1913). * * *

Accordingly, we hold that under modern marketing conditions, when a manufacturer puts a new automobile in the stream of trade and promotes its purchase by the public, an implied warranty that it is reasonably suitable for use as such accompanies it into the hands of the ultimate purchaser. Absence of agency between the manufacturer and the dealer who makes the ultimate sale is immaterial.

II.

THE EFFECT OF THE DISCLAIMER AND LIMITATION OF LIABILITY
CLAUSES ON THE IMPLIED WARRANTY OF MERCHANTABILITY

* * *

* * * [W]hat effect should be given to the express warranty in question which seeks to limit the manufacturer's liability to replacement of defective parts, and which disclaims all other warranties, express or implied? In assessing its significance we must keep in mind the general principle that, in the absence of fraud, one who does not choose to read a contract before signing it, cannot later relieve himself of its burdens. Fivey v. Pennsylvania R. R. Co., 67 N.J.L. 627, 52 A. 472, (E. & A.1902). And in applying that principle, the basic tenet of freedom of competent parties to contract is a factor of importance. But in the framework of modern commercial life and business practices, such rules cannot be applied on a strict, doctrinal basis. The conflicting interests of the buyer and seller must be evaluated realistically and justly, giving due weight to the social policy evinced by the Uniform Sales Act, the progressive decisions of the courts engaged in administering it, the mass production methods of manufacture and distribution to the public, and the bargaining position occupied by the ordinary consumer in such an economy. * * *

* * *

In the modern consideration of problems such as this, Corbin suggests that practically all judges are "chancellors" and cannot fail to be influenced by any equitable doctrines that are available. And he opines that "there is sufficient flexibility in the concepts of fraud, duress, misrepresentation and undue influence, not to mention differences in economic bargaining power" to enable the courts to avoid enforcement of unconscionable provisions in long printed standardized contracts. 1 Corbin on Contracts (1950) § 128, p. 188. Freedom of contract is not such an immutable doctrine as to admit of no qualification in the area in which we are concerned.

* * *

The traditional contract is the result of free bargaining of parties who are brought together by the play of the market, and who meet each other on a footing of approximate economic equality. In such a society there is no danger that freedom of contract will be a threat to the social order as a whole. But in present-day commercial life the standardized mass contract has appeared. It is used primarily by enterprises with strong bargaining power and position. "The weaker party, in need of the goods or services, is frequently not in a position to shop around for better terms, either because the author of the standard contract has a monopoly (natural or artificial) or because all competitors use the same clauses. His contractual intention is but a subjection more or less voluntary to terms dictated by the stronger party, terms whose consequences are often understood in a vague way, if at all." Kessler, "Contracts of Adhesion—Some Thoughts About Freedom of Contract," 43 Colum.L.Rev. 629, 632 (1943); Ehrenzweig, "Adhesion Contracts in the Conflict of Laws," 53 Colum.L.Rev. 1072, 1075, 1089 (1953). Such standardized contracts have been described as those in which one predominant party will dictate its law to an undetermined multiple rather than to an individual. They are said to resemble a law rather than a meeting of the minds. Siegelman v. Cunard White Star, 221 F.2d 189, 206 (2 Cir.1955).

* * *

The warranty before us is a standardized form designed for mass use. It is imposed upon the automobile consumer. He takes it or leaves it, and he must take it to buy an automobile. No bargaining is engaged in with respect to it. In fact, the dealer through whom it comes to the buyer is without authority to alter it; his function is ministerial—simply to deliver it. The form warranty is not only standard with Chrysler but, as mentioned above, it is the uniform warranty of the Automobile Manufacturers Association. * * *

The gross inequality of bargaining position occupied by the consumer in the automobile industry is thus apparent. There is no competition among the car makers in the area of the express warranty. Where can the buyer go to negotiate for better protection? Such control and limitation of his remedies are inimical to the public welfare and, at the very least, call for great care by the courts to avoid injustice through application of strict common-law principles of freedom of contract. Because there is no competition among the motor vehicle manufacturers with respect to the scope of protection guaranteed to the buyer, there is no incentive on their part to stimulate good will in that field of public relations. Thus, there is lacking a factor existing in more competitive fields, one which tends to guarantee the safe construction of the article sold. Since all competitors operate in the same way, the urge to be careful is not so pressing. See "Warranties of Kind and Quality," 57 Yale L.J. 1389, 1400 (1948).

Although the courts, with few exceptions, have been most sensitive to problems presented by contracts resulting from gross disparity in buyer-seller bargaining positions, they have not articulated a general principle condemning, as opposed to public policy, the imposition on the buyer of a skeleton warranty as a means of limiting the responsibility of the manufacturer. They have endeavored thus far to avoid a drastic departure from age-old tenets of freedom of contract by adopting doctrines of strict construction, and notice and knowledgeable assent by the buyer to the attempted exculpation of the seller.

* * *

It is undisputed that the president of the dealer with whom Henningsen dealt did not specifically call attention to the warranty on the back of the purchase order. The form and the arrangement of its face, as described above, certainly would cause the minds of reasonable men to differ as to whether notice of a yielding of basic rights stemming from the relationship with the manufacturer was adequately given. * * *

But there is more than this. Assuming that a jury might find that the fine print referred to reasonably served the objective of directing a buyer's attention to the warranty on the reverse side, and, therefore, that he should be charged with awareness of its language, can it be said that an ordinary layman would realize what he was relinquishing in return for what he was being granted? Under the law, breach of warranty against defective parts or workmanship which caused personal injuries would entitle a buyer to damages even if due care were used in the manufacturing process. Because of the great potential for harm if the vehicle was defective, that right is the most important and fundamental one arising from the relationship. Difficulties so frequently encountered in establishing negligence in manufacture in the ordinary case make this manifest. Any ordinary layman of reasonable intelligence, looking at the phraseology, might well conclude that Chrysler was agreeing to replace defective parts and perhaps replace anything that went wrong because of defective workmanship during the first 90 days or 4,000 miles of operation, but that he would not be entitled to a new car. It is not unreasonable to believe that the entire scheme being conveyed was a proposed remedy for physical deficiencies in the car. *In the context* of this warranty, only the abandonment of all sense of justice would permit us to hold that, as a matter of law, the phrase "its obligation under this warranty being limited to making good at its factory any part or parts thereof" signifies to an ordinary reasonable person that he is relinquishing any personal injury claim that might flow from the use of a defective automobile. Such claims are nowhere mentioned. The draftsmanship is reflective of the care and skill of the Automobile Manufacturers Association in undertaking to avoid warranty obligations without drawing too much attention to its effort in that regard. * * *

* * *

The task of the judiciary is to administer the spirit as well as the letter of the law. * * *

Public policy is a term not easily defined. It significance varies as the habits and needs of a people may vary. It is not static and the field of application is an ever increasing one. A contract, or a particular provision therein, valid in one era may be wholly opposed to the public policy of another. See Collopy v. Newark Eye & Ear Infirmary, 27 N.J. 29, 39, 141 A.2d 276 (1958). Courts keep in mind the principle that the best interests of society demand that persons should not be unnecessarily restricted in their freedom to contract. But they do not hesitate to declare void as against public policy contractual provisions which clearly tend to the injury of the public in some way. Hodnick v. Fidelity Trust Co., 96 Ind.App. 342, 183 N.E. 488 (App.Ct.1932).

Public policy at a given time finds expression in the Constitution, the statutory law and in judicial decisions. In the area of sale of goods, the legislative will has imposed an implied warranty of merchantability as a general incident of sale of an automobile by description. The warranty does not depend upon the affirmative intention of the parties. It is a child of the law * * *. True, the Sales Act authorizes agreements between buyer and seller qualifying the warranty obligations. But quite obviously the Legislature contemplated lawful stipulations (which are determined by the circumstances of a particular case) arrived at freely by parties of relatively equal bargaining strength. The lawmakers did not authorize the automobile manufacturer to use its grossly disproportionate bargaining power to relieve itself from liability and to impose on the ordinary buyer, who in effect has no real freedom of choice, the grave danger of injury to himself and others that attends the sale of such a dangerous instrumentality as a defectively made automobile. In the framework of this case, illuminated as it is by the facts and the many decisions noted, we are of the opinion that Chrysler's attempted disclaimer of an implied warranty of merchantability and of the obligations arising therefrom is so inimical to the public good as to compel an adjudication of its invalidity.

* * *

V.

THE DEFENSE OF LACK OF PRIVITY AGAINST MRS. HENNINGSEN

Both defendants contend that since there was no privity of contract between them and Mrs. Henningsen, she cannot recover for breach of any warranty made by either of them. On the facts, as they were developed, we agree that she was not a party to the purchase agreement. Faber v. Creswick, 31 N.J. 234, 156 A.2d 252 (1959). Her right to maintain the action, therefore, depends upon whether she occupies such legal status thereunder as to permit her to take advantage of a breach of defendants' implied warranties.

* * * In the present matter, the basic contractual relationship is between Claus Henningsen, Chrysler, and Bloomfield Motors, Inc. The precise issue presented is whether Mrs. Henningsen, who is not a party to their respective warranties, may claim under them. In our judgment, the principles [discussed earlier] are just as proximately applicable to her situation. We are convinced that the cause of justice in this area of the law can be served only by recognizing that she is such a person who, in the reasonable contemplation of the parties to the warranty, might be expected to become a user of the automobile. Accordingly, her lack of privity does not stand in the way of prosecution of the injury suit against the defendant Chrysler.

* * *

The situation before us in its legal aspects is very similar to that which we dealt with recently in Faber v. Creswick, supra. There, in a landlord and tenant relationship the lease contained a covenant to have the premises in good repair at the inception of the occupancy. The wife of the tenant was injured by reason of a breach of that agreement. We held that she was entitled to recover damages even though she was not a party to the lease. * * * True, the suit in Faber was in tort while this one is in contract. But it cannot be overlooked that historically actions on warranties were in tort also, sounding in deceit. The contract theory gradually emerged, although the tort idea has continued to lurk in the background, making the warranty "a curious hybrid of tort and contract." * * * An awareness of this evolution makes for ready acceptance of the relaxation of rigid concepts of privity when third persons, who in the reasonable contemplation of the parties to a warranty might be expected to use or consume the product sold, are injured by its unwholesome or defective state.

It is important to express the right of Mrs. Henningsen to maintain her action in terms of a general principle. To what extent may lack of privity be disregarded in suits on such warranties? In that regard, the Faber case points the way. By a parity of reasoning, it is our opinion that an implied warranty of merchantability chargeable to either an automobile manufacturer or a dealer extends to the purchaser of the car, members of his family, and to other persons occupying or using it with his consent. It would be wholly opposed to reality to say that use by such persons is not within the anticipation of parties to such a warranty of reasonable suitability of an automobile for ordinary highway operation. Those persons must be considered within the distributive chain.

Harper and James suggest that this remedy ought to run to members of the public, bystanders, for example, who are in the path of harm from a defective automobile. [Supra at p. 1572.] * * *

It is not necessary in this case to establish the outside limits of the warranty protection. For present purposes, with respect to automobiles, it suffices to promulgate the principle set forth above.

* * *

Under all of the circumstances outlined above, the judgments in favor of the plaintiffs and against the defendants are affirmed.

———

STERNER AERO A. B. v. PAGE AIRMOTIVE INC., 499 F.2d 709 (10th Cir.1974). Defendant was seller of a rebuilt aeroplane engine. Plaintiff was an enterpriser-purchaser. The engine failed on take off about one year after it was sold. Plaintiff's aeroplane was destroyed. There was a disclaimer clause. The Court seems to hold that party to contract can when in a relatively equal bargaining position waive rights to recover on theories of warranty and negligence, but a waiver of strict liability in tort would not appear to be possible. The Court was applying Oklahoma law.

DIPPEL v. SCIANO, 37 Wis.2d 443, 155 N.W.2d 55 (1967). Here the court decided that the rule requiring privity of contract should not defeat a claim based upon a defective product unreasonably dangerous to a nonprivity user. It said:

"The rule that there could be no liability upon warranty, express or implied, without privity of contract came into being in England in Winterbottom v. Wright (1842), 10 M & W 109, 152 Eng.Rep. 402. It was an outgrowth of the beginning of the industrial revolution when it was thought it was necessary to protect struggling and unstable industry against an onslaught of disastrous claims. Typical of the disregard of the claims of persons injured by products is a quotation from *Winterbottom*, 'it is, no doubt, a hardship upon the plaintiff to be without a remedy, but by that consideration we ought not to be influenced.' We have long since passed from the unsure days of industrial revolution to a settled and affluent society where we must be concerned about the just claims of the injured and hapless user or consumer of industrial products. The doctrines of laissez nous faire and caveat emptor have given way to more humane considerations."

SECTION C.   BASIC STRICT LIABILITY

In his famous concurrence in *Escola v. Coca Cola Bottling Co.* (which follows immediately below), Justice Traynor does three things. First, he argues that a manufacturer's tort liability to an injured product user should be strict (he says "absolute"), not negligence-based. Second, he proposes that the warranty theory of a manufacturer's liability for product defect be abandoned in favor of strict liability in tort. Third, he invokes the modern conception of enterprise liability as the justification of strictness: "the risk of injury can be insured by the manufacturer and distributed among the public as a cost of doing business." This prescient opinion (1944) calls for the approach to product-caused injury which is adopted by Section 402A of the Second Restatement of Torts (1965).

The materials below show the consolidation of strict liability in tort for harm caused by manufacturing defects. Liability for manufacturing defect is the basic form of strict products liability. A product containing a manufacturing defect, which causes an accident, is "defective" in a straightforward sense: the particular item that causes injury is flawed, not up to par; it is unsafe because it deviates in some way from the manufacturer's own specifications for design, construction, and marketable quality. It is a particularly sour lemon.

The liability we investigate is both tortious and strict. It runs beyond privity, exists without negligence, is independent of warranty. Materials of the section invite reflection on the policy aims that direct strict tort liability for harm caused by defective products. A recurring question is how liability should be targeted: when a number of enterprises are involved in the making and distribution of an injurious product, which should be the bearer (or bearers) of strict responsibility?

ESCOLA v. COCA COLA BOTTLING CO. OF FRESNO
Supreme Court of California, 1944.
24 Cal.2d 453, 150 P.2d 436.

[Plaintiff, a waitress, was injured when a bottle of Coca Cola, bottled and delivered to her employer by the defendant, "exploded" in her hand. Her claim for damages was based on defendant's negligence, but "being unable to show any specific acts of negligence she relied completely on the doctrine of res ipsa loquitur." Plaintiff had judgment upon a jury verdict, and defendant appealed.

The majority of the Supreme Court affirmed, finding the evidence sufficient to support a reasonable inference that the bottle "was not damaged by any extraneous force after delivery to the restaurant by defendant," and that under the evidence plaintiff properly relied upon the doctrine of res ipsa loquitur "to supply an inference that defendant's negligence was responsible for the defective condition of the bottle at the time it was delivered to the restaurant." The majority opinion concluded as follows:]

It is true that defendant presented evidence tending to show that it exercised considerable precaution by carefully regulating and checking the pressure in the bottles and by making visual inspections for defects in the glass at several stages during the bottling process. It is well settled, however, that when a defendant produces evidence to rebut the inference of negligence which arises upon application of the doctrine of res ipsa loquitur, it is ordinarily a question of fact for the jury to determine whether the inference has been dispelled.

The judgment is affirmed.

TRAYNOR, Justice.

I concur in the judgment, but I believe the manufacturer's negligence should no longer be singled out as the basis of a plaintiff's right to recover in cases like the present one. In my opinion it should now be recognized that a manufacturer incurs an absolute liability when an article that he has placed on the market, knowing that it is to be used without inspection, proves to have a defect that causes injury to human beings. MacPherson v. Buick Motor Co., 217 N.Y. 382, 111 N.E. 1050, L.R.A.1916F, 696, Ann.Cas. 1916C, 440 established the principle, recognized by this court, that irrespective of privity of contract, the manufacturer is responsible for an injury caused by such an article to any person who comes in lawful contact with it. Sheward v. Virtue, 20 Cal.2d 410, 126 P.2d 345; Kalash v. Los Angeles Ladder Co., 1 Cal.2d 229, 34 P.2d 481. In these cases the source of the manufacturer's liability was his negligence in the manufacturing process or in the inspection of component parts supplied by others. Even if there is no negligence, however, public policy demands that responsibility be fixed wherever it will most effectively reduce the hazards to life and health inherent in defective products that reach the market. It is evident that the manufacturer can anticipate some hazards and guard against the recurrence of others, as the public cannot. Those who suffer injury from defective products are unprepared to meet its consequences. The cost of an injury and the loss of time or health may be an overwhelming misfortune to the person injured, and a needless one, for the risk of injury can be insured by the manufacturer and distributed among the public as a cost of doing business. It is to the public interest to discourage the marketing of products having defects that are a menace to the public. If such products nevertheless find their way into the market it is to the public interest to place the responsibility for whatever injury they may cause upon the manufacturer, who, even if he is not negligent in the manufacture of the product, is responsible for its reaching the market. However intermittently such injuries may occur and however haphazardly they may strike, the risk of their occurrence is a constant risk and a general one. Against such a risk there should be general and constant protection and the manufacturer is best situated to afford such protection.

The injury from a defective product does not become a matter of indifference because the defect arises from causes other than the negligence of the manufacturer, such as negligence of a submanufacturer of a component part whose defects could not be revealed by inspection, or unknown causes that even by the device of res ipsa loquitur cannot be classified as negligence of the manufacturer. The inference of negligence may be dispelled by an affirmative showing of proper care. If the evidence against the fact inferred is "clear, positive, uncontradicted, and of such a nature that it cannot rationally be disbelieved, the court must instruct the jury that the nonexistence of the fact has been established as a matter of law." Blank v. Coffin, 20 Cal.2d 457, 461, 126 P.2d 868, 870. An injured person, however, is not ordinarily in a position to refute such evidence or identify the cause of the defect, for he can hardly be familiar with the manufacturing process as the manufacturer himself is. In leaving it to the jury to decide whether the inference has been dispelled, regardless of the evidence against it, the negligence rule approaches the rule of strict liability. It is needlessly circuitous to make negligence the basis of recovery and impose what is in reality liability without negligence. If public policy demands that a manufacturer of goods be responsible for their quality regardless of negligence there is no reason not to fix that responsibility openly.

In the case of foodstuffs, the public policy of the state is formulated in a criminal statute. Section 26510 of the Health and Safety Code, St.1939, p. 989, prohibits the manufacturing, preparing, compounding, packing, selling, offering for sale, or keeping for sale, or advertising within the state, of any adulterated food. * * * The criminal liability under the statute attaches without proof of fault, so that the manufacturer is under the duty of ascertaining whether an article manufactured by him is safe. Statutes of this kind result in a strict liability of the manufacturer in tort to the member of the public injured.

The statute may well be applicable to a bottle whose defects cause it to explode. In any event it is significant that the statute imposes criminal liability without fault, reflecting the public policy of protecting the public from dangerous products placed on the market, irrespective of negligence in their manufacture. While the Legislature imposes criminal liability only with regard to food products and their containers, there are many other sources of danger. It is to the public interest to prevent injury to the public from any defective goods by the imposition of civil liability generally.

The retailer, even though not equipped to test a product, is under an absolute liability to his customer, for the implied warranties of fitness for proposed use and merchantable quality include a warranty of safety of the product. This warranty is not necessarily a contractual one, for public policy requires that the buyer be insured at the seller's expense against injury. The courts recognize, however, that the retailer cannot bear the burden of this warranty, and allow him to recoup any losses by means of the warranty of safety attending the wholesaler's or manufacturer's sale to him. Such a procedure, however, is needlessly circuitous and engenders wasteful litigation. Much would be gained if the injured person could base his action directly on the manufacturer's warranty.

The liability of the manufacturer to an immediate buyer injured by a defective product follows without proof of negligence from the implied warranty of safety attending the sale. Ordinarily, however, the immediate buyer is a dealer who does not intend to use the product himself, and if the warranty of safety is to serve the purpose of protecting health and safety it must give rights to others than the dealer. * * *

* * *

In the food products cases the courts have resorted to various fictions to rationalize the extension of the manufacturer's warranty to the consumer: that a warranty runs with the chattel; that the cause of action of the dealer is assigned to the consumer; that the consumer is a third party beneficiary of the manufacturer's contract with the dealer. They have also held the manufacturer liable on a mere fiction of negligence: "Practically he must know it [the product] is fit, or take the consequences, if it proves destructive." Parks v. G. C. Yost Pie Co., 93 Kan. 334, 144 P. 202, 203. Such fictions are not necessary to fix the manufacturer's liability under a warranty if the warranty is severed from the contract of sale between the dealer and the consumer and based on the law of torts as a strict liability. Warranties are not necessarily rights arising under a contract. An action on a warranty "was, in its origin, a pure action of tort" * * *.

As handicrafts have been replaced by mass production with its great markets and transportation facilities, the close relationship between the producer and consumer of a product has been altered. Manufacturing processes, frequently valuable secrets, are ordinarily either inaccessible to or beyond the ken of the general public. The consumer no longer has means or skill enough to investigate for himself the soundness of a product, even when it is not contained in a sealed package, and his erstwhile vigilance has been lulled by the steady efforts of manufacturers to build up confidence by advertising and marketing devices such as trade-marks. Consumers no longer approach products warily but accept them on faith, relying on the reputation of the manufacturer or the trade mark. Manufacturers have sought to justify that faith by increasingly high standards of inspection and a readiness to make good on defective products by way of replacements and refunds. The manufacturer's obligation to the consumer must keep pace with the changing relationship between them; it cannot be escaped because the marketing of a product has become so complicated as to require one or more intermediaries. Certainly there is greater reason to impose liability on the manufacturer than on the retailer who is but a conduit of a product that he is not himself able to test.

The manufacturer's liability should, of course, be defined in terms of the safety of the product in normal and proper use, and should not extend to injuries that cannot be traced to the product as it reached the market.

RESTATEMENT OF TORTS, SECOND (1965)

§ 402A. Special Liability of Seller of Product for Physical Harm to User or Consumer

(1) One who sells any product in a defective condition unreasonably dangerous to the user or consumer or to his property is subject to liability for physical harm thereby caused to the ultimate user or consumer, or to his property, if

　　(a) the seller is engaged in the business of selling such a product, and

　　(b) it is expected to and does reach the user or consumer without substantial change in the condition in which it is sold.

(2) The rule stated in Subsection (1) applies although

　　(a) the seller has exercised all possible care in the preparation and sale of his product, and

　　(b) the user or consumer has not bought the product from or entered into any contractual relation with the seller.

Caveat:

The Institute expresses no opinion as to whether the rules stated in this Section may not apply

(1) to harm to persons other than users or consumers;

(2) to the seller of a product expected to be processed or otherwise substantially changed before it reaches the user or consumer; or

(3) to the seller of a component part of a product to be assembled.

Comment:

* * *

c. * * * [T]he justification for the strict liability has been said to be that the seller, by marketing his product for use and consumption, has undertaken and assumed a special responsibility toward any member of the consuming public who may be injured by it; that the public has the right to and does expect, in the case of products which it needs and for which it is forced to rely upon the seller, that reputable sellers will stand behind their goods; that public policy demands that the burden of accidental injuries caused by products intended for consumption be placed upon those who market them, and be treated as a cost of production against which liability insurance can be obtained; and that the consumer of such products is entitled to the maximum of protection at the hands of someone, and the proper persons to afford it are those who market the products.

* * *

§ 402B. Misrepresentation by Seller of Chattels to Consumer

One engaged in the business of selling chattels who, by advertising, labels, or otherwise, makes to the public a misrepresentation of a material fact concerning the character or quality of a chattel sold by him is subject to liability for physical harm to a consumer of the chattel caused by justifiable reliance upon the misrepresentation, even though

(a) it is not made fraudulently or negligently, and

(b) the consumer has not bought the chattel from or entered into any contractual relation with the seller.

Caveat:

The Institute expresses no opinion as to whether the rule stated in this Section may apply

(1) where the representation is not made to the public, but to an individual, or

(2) where physical harm is caused to one who is not a consumer of the chattel.

CODLING v. PAGLIA, 32 N.Y.2d 330, 345 N.Y.S.2d 461, 298 N.E.2d 622 (1973). In explaining its approval of strict products liability, the New York Court of Appeals (per Jones, J.) said:

"The dynamic growth of the law in this area has been a testimonial to the adaptability of our judicial system and its resilient capacity to respond to new developments both of economics and of manufacturing and marketing techniques. A developing and more analytical sense of justice, as regards both the economics and the operational aspects of production and distribution has imposed a heavier and heavier burden of responsibility on the manufacturer. * * *

* * *

"Today as never before the product in the hands of the consumer is often a most sophisticated and even mysterious article. Not only does it usually emerge as a sealed unit with an alluring exterior rather than as a visible assembly of component parts, but its functional validity and usefulness often depend on the application of electronic, chemical or hydraulic principles far beyond the ken of the average consumer. Advances in the technologies of materials, of processes, of operational means have put it almost entirely out of the reach of the consumer to comprehend why or how the article operates, and thus even farther out of his reach to detect when there may be a defect or a danger present in its design or manufacture. In today's world it is often only the manufacturer who can fairly be said to know and to understand when an article is suitably designed and safely made for its intended purpose. * * * Further, as has been noted, in all this the bystander, the nonuser, is even worse off than the user—to the point of total exclusion from any opportunity either to choose manufacturers or retailers or to detect defects. We are accordingly persuaded that from the standpoint of justice as regards the operating aspect of today's products, responsibility should be laid on the manufacturer [for injuries caused by product defects]."

"Consideration of the economics of production and distribution point in the same direction. We take as a highly desirable objective the widest feasible availability of useful, nondefective products. We know that in many, if not most instances, today this calls for mass production, mass advertising, mass distribution. It is this mass system which makes possible the development and availability of the benefits which may flow from new inventions and new discoveries. Justice and equity would dictate the apportionment across the system of all related costs—of production, of distribution, of postdistribution liability. Obviously, if manufacturers are to be held for financial losses of nonusers, the economic burden will ultimately be passed on in part, if not in whole, to the purchasing users. But considerations of competitive disadvantage will delay or dilute automatic transferral of such added costs. Whatever the total cost it will then be borne by those in the system, the producer, the distributor and the consumer. Pressures will converge on the manufacturer, however, who alone has the practical opportunity, as well as a considerable incentive, to turn out useful, attractive, but safe products. To impose this economic burden on the manufacturer should encourage safety in design and production; and the diffusion of this cost in the purchase price of individual units should be acceptable to the user if thereby he is given added assurance of his own protection."

DOE v. MILES LABORATORIES, INC., 675 F.Supp. 1466 (D.Md.1987). Here the court argues that "strict liability promotes a rational market place." It promotes "a more efficient allocation of social resources" by making the price of a product reflect the product's "true costs." The court (Ramsey, D.J.) explained:

"Society has chosen to allow market forces to set the price for goods and thus to determine their availability and distribution. In some respects the market is very efficient. The price purchasers pay invariably reflects direct costs such as raw products, capital investment, labor, plus a reasonable rate of return. However, in other respects the market is not efficient. Prices often do not reflect indirect costs. These hidden costs can include the effects of pollution or the expenses of accidents, and are what economists refer to as 'externalities.'

"When the price of an item does not reflect both its direct costs and its externalities, the price will be lower than its actual cost. This lower price will stimulate an inefficient allocation of resources, for persons will be encouraged to buy more of the product than they might if they were paying its true price. Society thus may increase the consumption of the very goods that create pollution, and thus have indirect cleanup costs, or that are defective, and thus have indirect accident costs. Strict products liability shifts the cost back to manufacturers, who will then reprice the goods to reflect their actual costs. Strict products liability therefore affords society a mechanism for a rational allocation of resources. Absent it, the costs of externalities are thrust upon victims or upon society through its governmental welfare programs. In essence, without it there is a subsidy given to the polluting or defective products."

ELMORE v. AMERICAN MOTORS CORP.

Supreme Court of California, 1969.

70 Cal.2d 578, 75 Cal.Rptr. 652, 451 P.2d 84.

PETERS, Justice. In these consolidated personal injury and wrongful death actions growing out of an automobile collision, the trial court at the conclusion of the plaintiffs' cases in chief granted motions for nonsuit by defendants American Motors Corporation and Mission Rambler Company and dismissed the jury. Plaintiffs have appealed from the ensuing judgments.

On March 16, 1962, plaintiff Mrs. Sandra Elmore and her husband purchased a 1962 Rambler American station wagon from Mission. The car had a standard transmission. It was not equipped with power steering or power brakes. Mrs. Elmore used the car to commute to work. The car was serviced by Mission after it had been driven about 1,500 miles. The car was lubricated and the oil and oil filter changed. Subsequently, Mrs. Elmore noticed that the car was shimmying when she drove it between 60 and 65 miles per hour.

She told her husband about the shimmying and asked him to drive the car. He could barely detect the shimmying and did not think it was sufficiently serious to warrant Mrs. Elmore taking time from her work to return the car for servicing. The Rambler had been driven 2,751 miles before the accident.

The accident occurred shortly after noon on April 29, 1962, a bright clear day. Mrs. Elmore was driving in a southerly direction on a three-lane road near Northridge. She suffered head injuries and was unable to remember anything about the day of the accident.

Mr. Hendley testified that he was following the Rambler for about a mile and a half before the collision, that Mrs. Elmore was travelling about 45 miles per hour, that she had caught up with the traffic in front of her and had started to pull out as if to overtake the vehicle in front of her, that a car honked to pass her, and that as she returned to the right hand lane, there was a series of "sparks underneath the car like something fell * * * like something in front was dragging. * * * like a big hunk of metal suddenly hitting the ground." Hendley stated that the sparks were "strong" ones, not like the little spark from a dragging chain. He also said that Mrs. Elmore started "fishtailing," and that as the "fishtailing" got worse the automobile went over to the wrong side of the road and struck the vehicle of plaintiff Waters, that the "fishtailing" continued until the collision, and that the impact hurled Mrs. Elmore from her vehicle onto the embankment.

A highway patrol officer investigating the accident shortly after the collision found skid and gouge marks on the pavement on the northbound lane. * * *

Mr. Ausburn, a licensed engineer, examined the Waters and Elmore vehicles at a wrecking yard apparently eight days after the accident. * * *

When Ausburn examined the Rambler, the drive shaft, a metal tube about three inches in diameter, was not attached in its proper place but was in the rear of the Rambler station wagon. The drive shaft was buckled. * * *

Ausburn also testified that the drive shaft is attached at the forward and rear portions of the car to universal joints; that if a drive shaft fell down while the car was moving, it would dig into the roadway, make sparks, and cause the rear of the car to lift and to swerve or be thrown around; that normal wear and tear or "anything the driver did" would not cause a drive shaft to fall down in a space of 2,700 miles; that the cause of a drive shaft falling would be either loose fastenings or a metal failure; and that a drive shaft would not ordinarily be expected to become separated from the car in the accident which occurred.

* * *

"A manufacturer is strictly liable in tort when an article he places on the market, knowing that it is to be used without inspection for defects, proves to have a defect that causes injury to a human being." (Greenman v. Yuba Power Products, Inc., 59 Cal.2d 57, 62, 27 Cal.Rptr. 697, 700, 377 P.2d 897, 900, 13 A.L.R.3d 1049; Vandermark v. Ford Motor Co., 61 Cal.2d 256, 260–261, 37 Cal.Rptr. 896, 391 P.2d 168.) Similarly, a retailer engaged in the business of distributing automobiles to the public is strictly liable in tort for personal injuries caused by defects in cars sold by it. In the last-cited case, it was recognized that a plaintiff is entitled to establish the existence of the defect and the defendants' responsibility for it by circumstantial evidence. No reason appears why the same rule should not apply where the plaintiff is seeking to prove that the defect caused his injuries.

When the evidence is viewed, as it must be, most strongly in favor of plaintiffs, it furnishes an inference that their injuries were proximately caused by a defect in the Rambler which existed at the time of sale. Ausburn testified that in his opinion the car was defective prior to the accident in that the drive shaft was disconnected, and in the light of his further testimony as to what occurs when the drive shaft becomes disconnected, the presence of the gouge mark, and Mr. Hendley's testimony as to the sparks and the motions of the car prior to the accident, it could properly be inferred that the disconnected drive shaft gouged the roadway and caused the rear of the car to lift and to swerve or be thrown around which in turn caused the Rambler to go to the wrong side of the road. Thus, it could properly be found that the disconnected drive shaft was a proximate cause of the accident.

* * *

The authors of the restatement have refrained from expressing a view as to whether the doctrine of strict liability of the manufacturer and retailer for defects is applicable to third parties who are bystanders and who are not purchasers or users of the defective chattel. (Rest.2d Torts, § 402A, com. *o.*) The authors pointed out that as yet (1965) no case had applied strict liability to a person who was not a user or consumer. Two recent cases, however, have held manufacturers of defective goods strictly liable in tort for injuries caused to persons who were mere bystanders and were not users or consumers. (Piercefield v. Remington Arms Company, 375 Mich. 85, 133

N.W.2d 129, 134–136; Mitchell v. Miller, 26 Conn.Sup. 142, 214 A.2d 694, 697–699.) * * *

In Greenman v. Yuba Power Products, Inc., supra, 59 Cal.2d 57, 63, 27 Cal.Rptr. 697, 701, 377 P.2d 897, 901, we pointed out that the purpose of strict liability upon the manufacturer in tort is to insure that "the costs of injuries resulting from defective products are borne by the manufacturers that put such products on the market rather than by the injured persons who are powerless to protect themselves." We further pointed out that the rejection of the view that such liability was governed by contract warranties rather than tort rules was shown by cases which had recognized that the liability is not assumed by agreement but imposed by law and which had refused to permit the manufacturer to define its own responsibility for defective products. Similarly, in Vandermark v. Ford Motor Co., supra, 61 Cal.2d 256, 263, 37 Cal.Rptr. 896, 391 P.2d 168, we held that, since the retailer is strictly liable in tort, the fact that it restricted its contractual liability was immaterial.

These cases make it clear that the doctrine of strict liability may not be restricted on a theory of privity of contract. Since the doctrine applies even where the manufacturer has attempted to limit liability, they further make it clear that the doctrine may not be limited on the theory that no representation of safety is made to the bystander.

The liability has been based upon the existence of a defective product which caused injury to a human being, and in both *Greenman* and *Vandermark* we did not limit the rules stated to consumers and users but instead used language applicable to human beings generally.

It has been pointed out that an injury to a bystander "is often a perfectly foreseeable risk of the maker's enterprise, and the considerations for imposing such risks on the maker without regard to his fault do not stop with those who undertake to use the chattel. [A restriction on the recovery by bystanders] is only the distorted shadow of a vanishing privity which is itself a reflection of the habit of viewing the problem as a commercial one between traders, rather than as part of the accident problem." (2 Harper and James, The Law of Torts, (1956) p. 1572, fn. 6.)

If anything, bystanders should be entitled to greater protection than the consumer or user where injury to bystanders from the defect is reasonably foreseeable. Consumers and users, at least, have the opportunity to inspect for defects and to limit their purchases to articles manufactured by reputable manufacturers and sold by reputable retailers, whereas the bystander ordinarily has no such opportunities. In short, the bystander is in greater need of protection from defective products which are dangerous, and if any distinction should be made between bystanders and users, it should be made, contrary to the position of defendants, to extend greater liability in favor of the bystanders.

* * *

It is urged that even assuming that the doctrine of strict liability in tort is available to an injured bystander in an action against the manufacturer, the doctrine should not be available against the retailer. In *Vandermark,* we considered the related question of the liability of the retailer to the purchaser and user, and we stated: "Retailers like manufacturers are engaged in the business of distributing goods to the public. They are an integral part of the overall producing and marketing enterprise that should bear the cost of injuries resulting from defective products. In some cases the retailer may be the only member of that enterprise reasonably available to the injured plaintiff. In other cases the retailer himself may play a substantial part in insuring that the product is safe or may be in a position to exert pressure on the manufacturer to that end; the retailer's strict liability thus serves as an added incentive to safety. Strict liability on the manufacturer and retailer alike affords maximum protection to the injured plaintiff and works no injustice to the defendants, for they can adjust the costs of such protection between them in the course of their continuing business relationship. Accordingly, as a retailer engaged in the business of distributing goods to the public, Maywood Bell is strictly liable in tort for personal injuries caused by defects in cars sold by it." (61 Cal.2d at pp. 262–263, 37 Cal.Rptr. 896, 899–890, 391 P.2d 168, 171–172.)

All of the foregoing considerations are as applicable to the bystander's action as that of the purchaser or user, and we are satisfied that the doctrine of strict liability in tort is available in an action for personal injuries by a bystander against the manufacturer and the retailer.

The judgments are reversed.

BROOKS v. BEECH AIRCRAFT CORP., 120 N.M. 372, 902 P.2d 54 (1995). According to the New Mexico Supreme Court, "the law of New Mexico and the law of other jurisdictions" makes retailers and other suppliers, as well as manufacturers, liable for harm caused by defective products, in order to promote the policy of "full chain of supply protection." The court explained:

" * * * Because suppliers are in a better economic bargaining position, they may be more likely than individual consumers to get a manufacturer to bear financial responsibility for product-related injuries. See 1 Timothy E. Travers et al. American Law of Products Liability 3d § 5:7, at 21–22 (1994). At any rate, the injured consumer is thus provided with an alternative remedy in the event that the manufacturer is insolvent, out of business, or so remote that it is either impossible to obtain jurisdiction or unduly burdensome to bring suit.

" * * * [T]his Court has noted that 'the extension of strict liability to non-negligent retailers provides two pockets from which the injured consumer can obtain relief, one being the usually local and more accessible retailer.' [Aalco Mfg. Co. v. City of Espanola, 95 N.M. 66, 67, 618 P.2d 1230, 1231 (1980).] * * *

" * * * Suppliers should be encouraged to exercise great care in selecting the manufacturers whose products they choose to distribute and to pressure manufacturers to accept financial responsibility for injuries caused by their products. Such a result cannot be achieved through negligence law. * * * Thus the goal of providing greater consumer protection is served by imposing strict products liability."

KANSAS STATUTES ANNOTATED SECTION 60–3306. A number of states have enacted legislation shielding passive, nonnegligent retailers and other distributors from strict products liability. Some of these statutes (like Kansas') create immunity from warranty claims as well as tort claims arising out of product injury. The Kansas provision is as follows.

"60–3306. A product seller shall not be subject to liability in a product liability claim arising from an alleged defect in a product, if the product seller establishes that:

"(a) Such seller had no knowledge of the defect;

"(b) such seller * * * could not have discovered the defect while exercising reasonable care;

"(c) the seller was not a manufacturer of the defective product or product component;

"(d) the manufacturer of the defective product or product component is subject to service of process either under the laws of the state of Kansas or the domicile of the person making the product liability claim; and

"(e) any judgment against the manufacturer obtained by the person making the product liability claim would be reasonably certain of being satisfied."

ROYER v. CATHOLIC MEDICAL CENTER, 144 N.H. 330, 741 A.2d 74 (1999). Plaintiff underwent knee replacement surgery at Catholic Medical Center (CMC). His surgically implanted prosthetic knee proved defective. The prosthesis was manufactured by Dow Corning Corp., sold to CMC (defendant), and sold by the hospital to plaintiff in connection with the surgical procedure. After Dow Corning went bankrupt, plaintiff sued the hospital, claiming CMC was strictly liable for harm caused by the defective product. *Held*, for defendant. According to Section 402A of the Second Restatement of Torts, strict products liability applies to "[o]ne who sells any product in a defective condition" provided "the seller is engaged in the business of selling such a product." It does not apply to someone, like an architect, who "merely provides a service." Here "the health care provider primarily renders a service"; "the provision of a prosthetic device is merely incidental to that service."

MOODY v. CITY OF GALVESTON, 524 S.W.2d 583 (Tex.Civ.App.1975). Gas was in water supplied by the city. Gas being emitted from water faucet caught fire when plaintiff approached near the faucet with a lighted cigarette. *Held*, (1) the furnishing of water constitutes a sale of goods; (2) the doctrine of strict liability is applicable to city when engaged in the sale of water; and (3) the fact that the injury occurred not as a result of drinking or washing with the water but from an ignition of the gas which had accumulated in plaintiff's lines should not insulate the city.

GOLDBERG v. KOLLSMAN INSTRUMENT CORP.

Court of Appeals of New York, 1963.

12 N.Y.2d 432, 240 N.Y.S.2d 592, 191 N.E.2d 81.

DESMOND, Chief Judge. * * *

The suit is by an administratrix for damages for the death of her daughter-intestate as the result of injuries suffered in the crash near La Guardia Airport, New York City, of an airplane in which the daughter was a fare-paying passenger on a flight from Chicago to New York. American Airlines, Inc., owner and operator of the plane, is sued here for negligence (with present respondents Lockheed and Kollsman) but that cause of action is not the subject of this appeal. The two causes of action [at issue in the present appeal] run against Kollsman Instrument Corporation, manufacturer or supplier of the plane's altimeter, and Lockheed Aircraft Corporation, maker of the plane itself. Kollsman and Lockheed are charged with breaching their respective implied warranties of merchantability and fitness. [A defect in the altimeter], it is alleged, caused the fatal crash. [An altimeter measures the altitude at which a plane is flying.]

* * *

* * * A breach of warranty, it is now clear, is not only a violation of the sales contract out of which the warranty arises but is a tortious wrong suable by a noncontracting party whose use of the warranted article is within the reasonable contemplation of the vendor or manufacturer. * * *

The concept that as to "things of danger" the manufacturer must answer to intended users for faulty design or manufacture is an old one in this State. The most famous decision is MacPherson v. Buick Motor Co., 217 N.Y. 382, 111 N.E. 1050, L.R.A.1916F, 696, holding the manufacturer liable in negligence to one who purchased a faulty Buick automobile from a dealer * * *. MacPherson and its successors dispelled the idea that a manufacturer was immune from liability in tort for violation of his duty to make his [products] fit and safe. In MacPherson's day enforcement required a suit in negligence. Today, we know * * * that, at least where an article is of such a character that when used for the purpose for which it is made it is likely to be a source of danger to several or many people if not properly designed and fashioned, the manufacturer as well as the vendor is liable, for breach of law-implied warranties, to the persons whose use is contemplated. * * * [I]t is no extension at all to include airplanes and the passengers for whose use they are built—and, indeed, decisions are at hand which have upheld complaints, sounding in breach of warranty, against manufacturers of aircraft where passengers lost their lives when the planes crashed * * *.

As we all know, a number of courts outside New York State have for the best of reasons dispensed with the privity requirement (see Jaeger, Privity of Warranty: Has the Tocsin Sounded?, 1 Duquesne U.L.Rev. 1). Very recently the Supreme Court of California (Greenman v. Yuba Power Prods., Inc., 59 Cal.2d 57, 27 Cal.Rptr. 697, 377 P.2d 897 [1963]) in a unanimous opinion imposed "strict tort liability" (surely a more accurate phrase) regardless of privity on a manufacturer in a case where a power tool threw a piece of wood at a user who was not the purchaser. The California court said that the purpose of such a holding is to see to it that the costs of injuries resulting from defective products are borne by the manufacturers who put the products on the market rather than by injured persons who are powerless to protect themselves and that implicit in putting such articles on the market are representations that they will safely do the job for which they were built. However, for the present at least we do not think it necessary so to extend this rule as to hold liable the manufacturer (defendant Kollsman) of a component part. Adequate protection is provided for the passengers by casting in liability the airplane manufacturer which put into the market the completed aircraft.

* * *

BURKE, Judge (dissenting). We dissent. * * * The conditions present in [prior cases establishing products liability] are entirely different. There the manufacturer knew that the article he made was not to be inspected thereafter. Here Federal regulations provide for rigorous inspection and certification from the Federal Aviation Agency. There the risk of loss was a trap for the unwary. Here all are aware of the hazards attending air travel and accident and special insurance is readily available at moderate rates. Plaintiff[1] is a purchaser of a service from an airline seeking to assert a warranty cause of action against Lockheed, the assembler of an airplane, and Kollsman, the manufacturer of an allegedly defective component part thereof. In such a situation we see no satisfactory basis on which to uphold against Lockheed a cause of action not grounded in negligence, while disallowing it against the manufacturer of an alleged defective part.

First, we do not find a cause of action stated under the implied warranty provisions of section 96 of the Personal Property Law, Consol.Laws, c. 41. Plaintiff purchased no goods; she entered into a contract of carriage with American Airlines. By a long line of cases in this court, the most recent being Kilberg v. Northeast Airlines, Inc., 9 N.Y.2d 34, 211 N.Y.S.2d 133, 172 N.E.2d 526, it is settled that the measure of American Airlines' duty towards plaintiff was an undertaking of reasonably safe carriage. This duty is, of course, discharged by the use of due care. Crucial is the fact that this duty would be unaffected if American assembled its own planes, even if they contained a latent defect. Why, then, should plaintiff's rights be any greater simply because American chose to contract this work out instead of doing it itself? * * *

* * * We note that the argument made in some cases based on the avoidance of a multiplicity of actions is inapplicable here. In such cases, the plaintiff himself is the recipient of a warranty incident to the sale of goods and if the defect is in the manufacture it is at least reasonable to suggest a procedure by which liability may be imposed * * * directly against the one who, through a chain of warranties, is ultimately liable. Here, however, plaintiff (or her family, etc.) was not sold the chattel which caused her injury and hence there is no warranty.

---

1. Edith Feis, for whose death this action is brought, will be referred to herein as plaintiff.

It is true we have extended the benefit of an implied warranty beyond the immediate purchaser to those who could be fairly called indirect vendees of the product. Without stressing the weakness of the analogy that plaintiff here is the indirect vendee of the airplane and its parts, or the effect of the interposition between plaintiff and defendants of a federally regulated service industry of dominant economic and legal significance, it must be recognized that the true grounds of decision in a case of this sort lie outside the purpose and policy of the Sales Act and must be evaluated accordingly. Most scholars who have considered this question acknowledge that the warranty rationale is at best a useful fiction. (See, e.g., Prosser, The Assault upon the Citadel [Strict Liability to the Consumer], 69 Yale L.J. 1099; James, Products Liability, 34 Tex.L.Rev. 192.) If a strict products or enterprise liability is to be imposed here, this court cannot escape the responsibility of justifying it. * * *

Inherent in the question of strict products or enterprise liability is the question of the proper enterprise on which to fasten it. Here the majority have imposed this burden on the assembler of the finished product, Lockheed. The principle of selection stated is that the injured passenger needs no more protection. We suggest that this approach to the identification of an appropriate defendant does not answer the question: Which enterprise should be selected if the selection is to be in accord with the rationale upon which the doctrine of strict products liability rests?

The purpose of such liability is not to regulate conduct with a view to eliminating accidents,[2] but rather to remove the economic consequences of accidents from the victim who is unprepared to bear them and place the risk on the enterprise in the course of whose business they arise. The risk, it is said, becomes part of the cost of doing business and can be effectively distributed among the public through insurance or by a direct reflection in the price of the goods or service. As applied to this case we think the enterprise to which accidents such as the present are incident is the carriage of passengers by air—American Airlines. The fact that this accident was due to a defective altimeter should be of no legal significance to plaintiff absent some fault (negligence) on the part of Kollsman or Lockheed. Here, the dominant enterprise and the one with which plaintiff did business and relied upon was the airline.

If the carrier which immediately profited from plaintiff's custom is the proper party on which to fasten whatever enterprise liability the social conscience demands, enterprises which supply the devices with which the carrier conducts its business should not be subject to an action based on this theory. This seems most persuasive where the business that deals directly with the public is not merely a conduit for the distribution of the manufacturer's consumer goods but assumes the responsibility of selecting and using those goods itself as a capital asset in the conduct of a service

---

2. In view of the ease with which lack of care can be brought to light through devices such as *res ipsa loquitur,* any marginal increase in the stimulus to care would be clearly outweighed by the harshness of the means used to achieve it— the removal of due care as a defense. Apparently the majority agree since Kollsman, the actual manufacturer of the chattel that allegedly caused the accident, is not held liable.

enterprise such as common carriage. * * * In a theory of liability based, not on the regulation of conduct, but on economic considerations of distributing the risk of accidents that occur through no one's neglect, the enterprise most strategically placed to perform this function—the carrier, rather than the enterprise that supplies an assembled chattel thereto, is the logical subject of the liability, if liability there is to be.

* * * To extend warranty law to allow plaintiff to select a defendant from a multiplicity of enterprises in a case such as this would not comport with the rationale of enterprise liability * * *. If, on the other hand, plaintiff's maximum rights lie against the carrier, the rules of warranty can perform their real function of adjusting the rights of the parties to the agreements through which the airline acquired the chattel that caused the accident. * * *

We are therefore of the opinion that any claim in respect of an airplane accident that is grounded in strict enterprise liability should be fixed on the airline or none at all. Only in this way do we meet and resolve, one way or another, the anomaly presented by the reasoning of the majority, which, through reliance on warranty incident to sales, grants a recovery to a passenger injured through a nonnegligent failure of equipment but denies it to one injured through a nonnegligent failure of maintenance or operation.

* * * [A]s we stated earlier, it is clear that our cases limit the airline's duty to that of due care. It is this rule, avowedly formed to deal with the problem of accidents, that must be re-evaluated by those who would support the theory of strict enterprise liability. * * * [A]s long as our law holds a carrier chargeable only with negligence, what part of reason is it to hold to a greater duty an enterprise which supplied an assembled aircraft which was certified for commercial service by the Federal Aviation Agency?

Our reluctance to hold an air carrier to strict liability for the inevitable toll of injury incident to its enterprise is only the counsel of prudence. Aside from the responsibility imposed on us to be slow to cast aside a well-established law in deference to a theory of social planning that is still much in dispute (Prosser, Torts, [2d ed.] § 84; Patterson, The Apportionment of Business Risks through Legal Devices, 24 Colum.L.Rev. 335, 358; Pound, Introduction to the Philosophy of Law 100–104 [1954]), there remains the inquiry whether the facts fit the theory. It is easy, in a completely free economy, to envision the unimpeded distribution of risk by an enterprise on which it is imposed; but how well will such a scheme work in an industry which is closely regulated by Federal agencies? In consideration of international competition and other factors weighed by those responsible for rate regulation, how likely is it that rate scales will rise in reflection of increased liability? In turn, how likely is it that the additional risk will be effectively distributed as a cost of doing business? Such questions can be intelligently resolved only by analysis of facts and figures compiled after hearings in which all interested groups have an opportunity to present economic arguments. These matters, which are the factual cornerstones supporting the theory adopted by the majority, aside from our view that they apply it to the wrong enterprise, are classically within the special competence of the

Legislature to ascertain. For a court to assume them in order to support a theory that displaces much of the law of negligence from its ancestral environment involves an omniscience not shared by us. For a court to apply them, not to the enterprise with which plaintiff dealt and relied upon, or to the enterprise which manufactured the alleged defective part, but to the assembler of the aircraft used by the carrier, involves a principle of selection which is purely arbitrary.

DYE, FULD and FOSTER, JJ., concur with DESMOND, C.J.

BURKE, J., dissents in an opinion in which VAN VOORHIS and SCILEP-PI, JJ., concur.

————

CITY OF FRANKLIN v. BADGER FORD TRUCK SALES, INC., 58 Wis.2d 641, 207 N.W.2d 866 (1973). "Some states hold component manufacturers and suppliers subject to strict liability; some do not. Where there is no change in the component part itself, but it is merely incorporated into something larger, and where the cause of harm or injury is found, as here, to be a defect in the component part, we hold that, as to the ultimate user or consumer, the strict liability standard applies to the maker and supplier of the defective component part. Where the component part is subject to further processing or substantial change, or where the causing of injury is not directly attributable to defective construction of the component part, the result might be different."

ROURKE v. GARZA, 530 S.W.2d 794 (Tex.1975). The defendant was engaged in the business of leasing scaffolding materials, and supplied as a bailor the necessary component parts for the erection of a scaffold. The materials, including the steel pipe frames, boards, and connecting pins, were delivered at the job site, and the scaffold was erected by plaintiff's employer, a contractor. The scaffold was "unreasonably dangerous" in that the boards failed to have cleat-type devices to prevent slippage, and plaintiff was seriously injured when boards slipped. *Held*, that since the supplier of component parts knew that boards would be used without cleats, the bailor was strictly liable in tort.

PROMAULAYKO v. JOHNS MANVILLE SALES CORP., 116 N.J. 505, 562 A.2d 202 (1989). Here the defective product (asbestos fiber) was sold by the foreign producer to Amtorg; Amtorg sold it to Buck; Buck sold it to plaintiff's employer. Buck was held strictly liable to plaintiff, and sought complete indemnification from Amtorg. *Held*, indemnification allowed under common law indemnity doctrine, in light of the aims of strict products liability.

"Two basic principles underlie the development of strict liability in tort. The first principle is the allocation of the risk of loss to the party best able to control it. The second is the allocation of the risk to the party best able to distribute it. [Citations omitted.] * * *

"In the absence of an express agreement between them, allocation of the risk of loss between the parties in the chain of distribution is achieved through common-law indemnity, an equitable doctrine that allows a court to shift the cost from one tortfeasor to another. The right to common-law indemnity arises 'without agreement, and by operation of law to prevent a result which is regarded as unjust or unsatisfactory.' W.Keeton, D.Dobbs, R.Keeton, & D.Owens, Prosser & Keeton on The Law of Torts § 51 at 341 (5th ed. 1984). One branch of common-law indemnity shifts the cost of liability from one who is constructively or vicariously liable to the tortfeasor who is primarily liable. * * * Consistent with this principle, [indemnity] actions by retailers against manufacturers have been recognized in this State for twenty years. * * *

"In allowing claims for common-law indemnification by one party in the chain of distribution against a party higher up the chain, * * * courts have proceeded in a manner consistent with the principle of allocating the risk of loss to the party better able to control the risk and to distribute its costs. * * * In general, the effect of requiring the party closest to the original producer to indemnify parties farther down the chain is to shift the risk of loss to the most efficient accident avoider. See R. Posner, Economic Analysis of the Law 173–74 (1986). Passing the cost of the risk up the distributive chain also fulfills, as a general rule, the goal of distributing the risk to the party best able to bear it. The manufacturer to whom the cost is shifted can distribute that cost among all purchasers of its product. Similarly, a wholesale distributor can generally pass the risk among a greater number of potential users than a distributor farther down the chain. When viewed in terms of these economic consequences, the principle of unjust enrichment * * * similarly supports the allocation of the risk to the distributor closest to the manufacturer. * * *

"Conceivably, a set of facts might arise in which the party at the end of the distributive chain will be a better risk-bearer than a party higher in the chain. As a general rule, however, we expect indemnification to follow the chain of distribution. Finally, we recognize that parties in a distributive chain may contract for a different allocation of the risk of loss."

SECTION D. ECONOMIC LOSS

The basic idea behind the classical doctrine of privity of contract is this: when an area of interaction is marked by contractual relations, contract should govern, not tort; and so a contracting party should have no tort liability to a person with whom the party has not contracted. In the development of products liability, as we have seen, this classical notion is defeated with respect to the core concern of tort law, which is physical harm to person or property. As to physical injury caused by products, tort, not contract, is regnant.

Still, the classical conception lives on, in two ways. First, contractarian admonitions—you get what you bargain for, you must live with your choices—continue to operate *within* tort law of products liability, especially in doctrine concerning product warnings, addressed later on. Second, the classical conception retains formal preeminence outside the core area of tort concern, by virtue of the economic loss rule discussed in the materials that follow. According to the economic loss rule, when the harm complained of is a matter of disappointed economic expectation—rather than physical injury—contract should govern, not tort.

VICTORSON v. BOCK LAUNDRY MACHINE CO.

New York Court of Appeals, 1975.
37 N.Y.2d 395, 373 N.Y.S.2d 39, 335 N.E.2d 275.

[Previous New York cases had established that manufacturers are liable to persons injured by defective products regardless of fault. Here the question was "whether this form of liability sounds in tort or in contract" for purposes of the Statute of Limitations. For tort claims the period of limitations would begin to run on the date of injury; for contract claims, on the date of sale of the defective product. In the present case the allegedly defective laundry equipment was sold in 1948 and the injury occurred in 1969. The court concluded that "strict products liability" is a matter of tort, not contract. It reasoned:]

Initially we recognize the general distinction between these two areas of the law. "The fundamental difference between tort and contract lies in the nature of the interests protected. Tort actions are created to protect the interest in freedom from various kinds of harm. The duties of conduct which give rise to them are imposed by the law, and are based primarily upon social policy, and not necessarily upon the will or intention of the parties." (Prosser, Torts [4th ed.], § 92, p. 613.)

* * *

* * * Rather than arising out of the "will or intention of the parties", the liability imposed on the manufacturer under strict products liability, whether it be to purchaser, user, or innocent bystander, is predicated largely on considerations of sound social policy.

That in the emerging growth and development of the law of liability in these matters, in the best traditions of the common law, it has from time to time been found useful in justification or exposition to use terminology familiar to the law of contracts rather than of torts should be neither surprising nor diverting. As we have recognized, depending on the factual context in which the issue arises or the alternative theory pursued by the litigant, the liability of the product-manufacturer could indeed have been grounded in contract rather than tort theory, or indeed sometimes in both. Historically it even appears that these two fields have not been so categorically discrete as we are sometimes inclined to suppose. * * *

Whatever may have been earlier doubt and confusion, the authorities are now in general agreement that strict products liability sounds in tort rather than in contract. "It has been said over and over again that this warranty—if that is the name for it—is not the old sales warranty, it is not the warranty covered by the Uniform Sales Act or the Uniform Commercial Code. It is not a warranty of the seller to the buyer at all, but it is something separate and distinct which sounds in tort exclusively, and not at all in contract; which exists apart from any contract between the parties; and which makes for strict liability in tort." (Prosser, Spectacular Change: Products Liability in General, 36 Cleveland Bar Assn.J. 167–168.)

CASA CLARA CONDOMINIUM ASSOCIATION
v. CHARLEY TOPPINO AND SONS, INC.
Supreme Court of Florida, 1993.
620 So.2d 1244.

McDONALD, J.

* * *

Charley Toppino & Sons, Inc., a dissolved corporation, supplied concrete for numerous construction projects in Monroe County. Apparently, some of the concrete supplied by Toppino contained a high content of salt that caused the reinforcing steel inserted in the concrete to rust, which, in turn, caused the concrete to crack and break off. The petitioners own condominium units and single-family homes built with, and now allegedly damaged by, Toppino's concrete. In separate actions the homeowners sued numerous defendants and included claims against Toppino for breach of common law implied warranty, products liability, negligence, and violation of the building code. The circuit court dismissed all counts against Toppino in each case. On appeal the district court applied the economic loss rule and held that, because no person was injured and no other property damaged, the homeowners had no cause of action against Toppino in tort. * * *

Plaintiffs find a tort remedy attractive because it often permits the recovery of greater damages than an action on a contract and may avoid the conditions of a contract. [There is an important] distinction between "tort recovery for physical injuries and warranty recovery for economic loss" * * *. Seely v. White Motor Co., 63 Cal.2d 9, 403 P.2d 145, 151, 45 Cal.Rptr. 17, (Cal.1965). An individual consumer * * * "should not be charged at the will of the manufacturer with bearing the risk of physical injury when he buys a product on the market. He can, however, be fairly charged with the risk that the product will not match his economic expectations unless the manufacturer agrees that it will." Id. Seely sets out the economic loss rule, which prohibits tort recovery when a product damages itself, causing economic loss, but does not cause personal injury or damage to any property other than itself.[3] E.g., East River Steamship Corp. v. Transamerica Delaval, Inc., 476 U.S. 858, 106 S.Ct. 2295, 90 L.Ed.2d 865 (1986); Florida Power & Light Co. v. Westinghouse Elec. Corp., 510 So.2d 899 (Fla.1987) * * *.

Economic loss has been defined as "damages for inadequate value, costs of repair and replacement of the defective product, or consequent loss of profits—without any claim of personal injury or damage to other property." Note, Economic Loss in Products Liability Jurisprudence, 66 Colum.L.Rev.

---

3. The economic loss rule has been adopted in a majority of jurisdictions. See the cases collected in the appendix to William K. Jones, Product Defects Causing Commercial Loss: The Ascendency of Contract over Tort, 44 U.Miami L.Rev. 731, 799 (1990). The rule applies in Florida.* * *

917, 918 (1966). * * * In other words, economic losses are "disappointed economic expectations," which are protected by contract law, rather than tort law. Sensenbrenner v. Rust, Orling & Neale, Architects, Inc., 236 Va. 419, 374 S.E.2d 55, 58 (Va.1988) * * *. This is the basic difference between contract law, which protects expectations, and tort law, which is determined by the duty owed to an injured party. For recovery in tort "there must be a showing of harm above and beyond disappointed expectations. A buyer's desire to enjoy the benefit of his bargain is not an interest that tort law traditionally protects." Redarowicz v. Ohlendorf, 92 Ill.2d 171, 441 N.E.2d 324, 327, 65 Ill.Dec. 411 (Ill.1982).

* * *

In tort a manufacturer or producer of goods "is liable whether or not it is negligent because 'public policy demands that responsibility be fixed wherever it will most effectively reduce the hazards to life and health inherent in defective products that reach the market.' " East River, 476 U.S. at 866 (quoting Escola v. Coca Cola Bottling Co., 24 Cal.2d 453, 150 P.2d 436, 441 (Cal.1944) (Traynor, J., concurring)). Thus, the "basic function of tort law is to shift the burden of loss from the injured plaintiff to one who is at fault ... or to one who is better able to bear the loss and prevent its occurrence." Barrett, [Recovery of Economic Loss In Tort For Construction Defects, 40 S.C.L.Rev. 891, 935 (1989)]. * * * Contractual duties, on the other hand, come from society's interest in the performance of promises. When only economic harm is involved, the question becomes "whether the consuming public as a whole should bear the cost of economic losses sustained by those who failed to bargain for adequate contract remedies." Barrett, supra at 933.

We are urged to make an exception to the economic loss doctrine for homeowners. Buying a house is the largest investment many consumers ever make, and homeowners are an appealing, sympathetic class. [But if] a house causes economic disappointment by not meeting a purchaser's expectations, the resulting failure to receive the benefit of the bargain is a core concern of contract, not tort, law. East River, 476 U.S. at 870. * * * Therefore, we again "hold contract principles more appropriate than tort principles for recovering economic loss without an accompanying physical injury or property damage." Florida Power & Light, 510 So.2d at 902. If we held otherwise, "contract law would drown in a sea of tort." East River, 476 U.S. at 866. We refuse to hold that homeowners are not subject to the economic loss rule.

* * *

OVERTON, GRIMES and HARDING, JJ., concur.

SHAW, J., concurring and dissenting.

* * *

While I agree with the majority opinion that parties who have freely bargained and entered a contract relative to a particular subject matter should be bound by the terms of that contract including the distribution of loss, I feel that the theory is stretched when it is used to deny a cause of action to an innocent third party who the defendant knew or should have known would be injured by the tortious conduct. Toppino knew that the concrete that was the subject matter of the bargain between Toppino and the general contractor would be incorporated into homes that would be bought and occupied by innocent third parties.

When the concrete proved to be contaminated, damages were not limited to simply the loss of concrete; innocent third parties suffered various degrees of damage to structures using the concrete. In my mind, the economic loss theory was never intended to defeat a tort cause of action that would otherwise lie for damages caused to a third party by a defective product. * * *

BARKETT, C.J., and KOGAN, J., concur.

———

MOORMAN MANUFACTURING CO. v. NATIONAL TANK CO., 91 Ill.2d 69, 61 Ill.Dec. 746, 435 N.E.2d 443 (1982). Defendant sold plaintiff a grain storage tank. The tank developed a crack. Plaintiff sued defendant for the cost of repairing the tank and also profits lost when the tank was out of use. Plaintiff's action was based on tort doctrine of strict products liability, as well as warranty provisions of the Uniform Commercial Code (UCC). *Held*, that the law of sales contracts should govern in a case of "solely economic loss." The court explained:

" * * * [T]he law of sales has been carefully articulated to govern the economic relations between suppliers and consumers of goods. * * * Although warranty rules frustrate just compensation for physical injury, they function well in a commercial setting. These rules determine the quality of the product the manufacturer promises and thereby determine the quality he must deliver.

"We note, for example, section 2–316 of the UCC, which permits parties to a sales contract to limit warranties in any reasonable manner, or to agree that the buyer possesses no warranty protection at all. * * *

" * * * [A] large purchaser, such as plaintiff in the instant case, can protect itself against the risk of unsatisfactory performance by bargaining for a warranty. Or, it may choose to accept a lower purchase price for the product in lieu of warranty protection. Subsequent purchasers may do likewise in bargaining over the price of the product. We believe it is preferable to relegate the consumer to the comprehensive scheme of remedies fashioned by the UCC, rather than requiring the consuming public to pay more for their products so that a manufacturer can insure against the possibility that some of his products will not meet the business needs of some of his customers."

2–J CORPORATION v. TICE, 126 F.3d 539 (3d Cir.1997). Defendant sold a pre-fabricated warehouse to plaintiff. Plaintiff used the warehouse as a site for storing commercial inventory. One year after the five-year warranty expired, the warehouse collapsed, destroying the goods stored in the warehouse. Plaintiff brought suit to recover for loss of the contents of the warehouse, asserting "negligence and strict products liability tort claims." *Held*, applying Pennsylvania law, for plaintiff. "An essential aspect of the * * * economic loss doctrine is that while tort recovery is barred for damage a product causes to itself, such recovery is available for damage the failing product causes to 'other property.' " "[T]he proper line to be drawn between the spheres of tort and warranty law is the line between damage to 'the product' and damage to 'other property.' "

" * * * [F]or purposes of applying the economic loss doctrine, 'the product' is no more and no less than whatever the manufacturer placed in the stream of commerce by selling it to the initial user * * *. '[O]ther property' [comprises] both property added to a defective product by the initial user/owner as well as property used by the initial user/owner in connection with the defective product."

AMERICAN FIRE AND CASUALTY CO. v. FORD MOTOR COMPANY, 588 N.W.2d 437 (Iowa 1999). A pickup truck manufactured by defendant was damaged when the truck suddenly caught fire. Plaintiff brought suit in products liability to recover for damage to the truck, claiming that a defect in the truck caused the fire. The trial court dismissed the suit "because it involved a claim only for loss of the product itself." *Held*, reversing the trial court, that Iowa's economic loss doctrine does not bar plaintiff's claim.

Acknowledging that "courts widely disagree" in the "interpretation of the economic loss theory," the Iowa Supreme Court affirmed that "the line to be drawn is one between tort and contract." Contract covers cases in which a product "failed to work at all," while tort applies in situations involving "danger created by the defective product." "[I]f a fire alarm fails to work and a building burns down, that is considered an 'economic loss' even though the building was physically harmed. It was a foreseeable consequence from the failure of the product to work properly. But if the fire was caused by a short circuit in the fire alarm itself, it is not economic loss."

"[Prior Iowa cases] emphasized that hazard and danger distinguished tort liability from contract law. They distinguished the disappointed consumers from the endangered ones. * * * A truck starting itself on fire would certainly qualify more as a danger than as a disappointment."

Chapter 20

PRODUCTS LIABILITY: DEVELOPMENT
AND DEBATE

The present chapter continues to explore the doctrines and policies that constitute tort law of products liability. The first two sections present, respectively, the main ideas of doctrine concerning design defects, and the contemporary debate about the limits of design liability. The last three sections address, chiefly, doctrine and policy concerning product warnings, user conduct, and availability of punitive damages.

The chapter is host to a jamboree of legal conceptions. In the field of products liability, contract vies with tort, negligence liability with strict liability, and their associated policies tilt with one another in multi-sided competition.

SECTION A.   DESIGN DEFECT: TWO TESTS

A "manufacturing defect" is a flaw that affects a particular sold item— say, one of many units of a mass-produced device—and makes it fail to work according to the product's intended design. A "design defect" is a flaw that inheres in the design itself and therefore afflicts all the units produced. It may be said that the standard for identifying a manufacturing flaw in a product is the product's own design. But what then is the standard for identifying a defective design?

A claim of design defect impugns a whole run of products, so the intuitive notion of a defective product—the idea of a lemon—won't suffice. Articulable criteria of defectiveness are needed, in order to decide whether an injury arising from a product's use should be attributed to the product (and be paid for by the producer or other purveyor).

Plainly a simple test of but-for causation is not enough: on account of their designs, skis may cause you to fall, and a knife may cut you. Product injuries arise at the intersection of two purposeful activities, which are mutually dependent and aware of one another, the activity of making and marketing the product and the activity of putting the product to use. Rules of products liability aim to single out those injuries which are attributable to making and marketing because something untoward about the product is responsible for causing injury.

In the evolution of products doctrine, two basic tests for assessment of design defect have emerged. They may be called the "expectation test" and the "balancing test." The two tests are distinct. They look at a challenged design from different viewpoints; they provide separate criteria for identifying defectiveness of design; and they arise from independent legal roots.

The expectation test looks at a challenged design from the standpoint of a product user. It asks these questions: do the risks of the design meet the expectations of an average consumer?—or, to the contrary, does the product's performance offend expectations about safety? This test is rooted in contract law, specifically, in warranty doctrine.

The balancing test takes the perspective of a product engineer, or a manufacturer. It asks these questions: is the design of the product, on balance, reasonably safe?—or, to the contrary, do the risks of the design outweigh the design's utility? This test has roots in tort, particularly, in risk-utility analysis of negligence law.

The duality of design defect doctrine—its use of two tests—is displayed by materials of the present section, in particular by the last main case (*Barker v. Lull Engineering Co.*), which provides a systematic summation.

GREEN v. SMITH & NEPHEW AHP, INC.

Supreme Court of Wisconsin, 2001.
245 Wis.2d 772, 629 N.W.2d 727.

JON P. WILCOX, J.

This case arises from a products liability claim brought by Linda M. Green (Green) against Smith & Nephew AHP, Inc. (S & N). Green alleged that S & N manufactured defective and unreasonably dangerous latex medical gloves, which caused her to suffer injuries arising from allergic reactions to the proteins in those gloves. Accordingly, Green claimed, S & N should be held strictly liable for these injuries.

At the close of the trial on Green's claim, the jury returned a verdict in favor of Green and against S & N. The Milwaukee County Circuit Court, Judge Charles F. Kahn, Jr., entered judgment on the verdict. S & N subsequently appealed, but the court of appeals affirmed the circuit court judgment in its entirety.

* * *

* * * [W]e hold that the jury verdict in this case was not the result of reversible error. Thus, we hold that the court of appeals correctly affirmed the circuit court's entry of judgment on the verdict.

* * *

[Green worked as a medical technologist at a hospital in Milwaukee starting in 1978. Her job required her to wear protective gloves while attending patients, up to 40 pairs of gloves per shift. She wore powdered latex gloves manufactured by S & N. During 1989 Green experienced increasingly severe health problems—cold-like symptoms, wide-spread rash, acute shortness of breath. She was hospitalized four times. In 1991 Green was diagnosed with latex allergy. Given her allergy, Green must avoid contact with latex. So she had to change jobs and must limit the items she buys, things she eats, and activities she pursues. On account of the allergy, Green developed asthma.

[Latex allergy is caused by exposure to latex proteins. In some people's bodies such exposure triggers a certain immune system response, and these persons become "sensitized" to latex. Subsequent exposure of a sensitized person to latex may produce progressively worse allergic reactions including irreversible asthma and life-threatening anaphylactic shock (which Green suffered). Since latex allergy is caused mainly by use of latex gloves, it disproportionately afflicts health care workers. The frequency of the allergy among health care workers in the United States is 5 to 17 percent, according to Green's trial evidence.

[Green's evidence at trial showed that S & N's gloves were dangerous in two respects: they contained high levels of allergy-causing latex proteins, and they were powdered with cornstarch, which allowed the latex proteins to become aerosolized and thus easily inhaled. Studies at the Mayo Clinic found S & N's gloves to have considerably higher protein levels than almost all other tested brands of latex medical gloves. Green's medical experts testified that high-protein gloves are much more likely than low-protein gloves to cause latex sensitization and allergic reactions, and that the likelihood of Green's developing a latex allergy would have been "very remote" had she been exposed only to low-protein, powderless gloves. Green's evidence included a statement of the American College of Allergy, Asthma, and Immunology (ACAAI), issued in 1997, that said: "Only low-allergen latex gloves should be purchased and used. This will reduce the occurrence of reactions among sensitized personnel and should reduce the rate of sensitization." The ACAAI statement of 1997 also said: "Only powder-free latex gloves should be purchased and used."

[Both parties agreed that in 1989, when Green became sensitized to latex, the medical community was unaware of the possibility of latex allergy. Thus in 1989, S & N neither knew, nor could have known, that its glove design posed an allergenic risk. Likewise Linda Green neither knew, nor could have known, that using the gloves was dangerous to her health.]

* * *

At the close of the case, the circuit court instructed the jury on the law surrounding Green's claim for strict liability. The court explained:

> * * * A product is said to be defective when it is * * * dangerous to an extent beyond that which would be contemplated by the ordinary user or consumer possessing the knowledge of the product's characteristics which [was] common to the community. * * *

The court then put this law into the context of Green's case:

> * * * Lack of knowledge on the part of [S & N] that proteins in natural rubber latex may sensitize and cause allergic reactions to some individuals is not a defense to the claims made by the plaintiff [Green] in this

action. A manufacturer is responsible for harm caused by a defective and unreasonably dangerous product even if the manufacturer had no knowledge or could [not] have known of the risk of harm presented by the condition of the product.

After receiving these instructions, the jury returned a verdict in favor of Green. The jury * * * awarded Green $1,000,000 in damages.

* * *

A

We first review whether the circuit court erred in instructing the jury that a product can be deemed defective and unreasonably dangerous based solely on consumer expectations about that product. * * *

S & N maintains that the consumer-contemplation standard enunciated in the jury instructions is at odds with current Wisconsin law. * * *

* * *

We disagree. In *Vincer v. Esther Williams All–Aluminum Swimming Pool Co.,* 69 Wis.2d 326, 230 N.W.2d 794 (1975), this court adopted Comment g to 402A, which provides that a product is defective where the product is, at the time it leaves the seller's hands, *in a condition not contemplated by the ultimate consumer,* which will be unreasonably dangerous to him [or her]. *Id.* at 330, 230 N.W.2d 794 (quoting *Restatement (Second) of Torts* 402A (1965)) (emphasis added).* * * [W]e concluded in *Vincer:*

> [T]he test in Wisconsin of whether a product contains an unreasonably dangerous defect depends upon the reasonable expectations of the ordinary consumer concerning the characteristics of this type of product. If the average consumer would reasonably anticipate the dangerous condition of the product and fully appreciate the attendant risk of injury, it would not be unreasonably dangerous and defective. This is an objective test and is not dependent upon the knowledge of the particular injured consumer.

Vincer, 69 Wis.2d at 332, 230 N.W.2d 794 (emphasis added). Indeed, since *Vincer,* we frequently have reiterated that Wisconsin applies a consumer-contemplation test in strict products liability cases. * * *

[In *Sumnicht v. Toyota Motor Sales,* 121 Wis.2d. 338, 360 N.W.2d 2 (1984),] we explained:

> Two separate approaches have emerged to evaluate design defect— a consumer-contemplation test and a danger-utility [*i.e.,* risk-benefit] test. . . .

> Under the consumer-contemplation test, . . . a product is defectively dangerous if it is dangerous to an extent beyond that which would be contemplated by the ordinary consumer who purchased it with the ordinary knowledge common to the community as to the product's characteristics.

Under [the danger-utility test] approach, a product is defective as designed if, but only if, the magnitude of the danger outweighs the utility of the product. The theory underlying this approach is that virtually all products have both risks and benefits and that there is no way to go about evaluating design hazards intelligently without weighing danger against utility. * * *

Id. at 367–68, 360 N.W.2d 2. We then unequivocally held that "Wisconsin is committed to the consumer-contemplation test for determining whether a product is defective." *Id.* at 368, 360 N.W.2d 2.

* * *

[The *Sumnicht* decision expressly rejected] a risk-benefit analysis. *Id.* at 368, 360 N.W.2d 2; *see also id.* at 371, 360 N.W.2d 2 ("A product may be defective and unreasonably dangerous even though there are no alternative, safer designs available."). * * *

* * *

According to S & N, consumers do not always have expectations regarding the relevant design aspects of a product. S & N suggests that while most consumers likely have expectations about how safely a product will perform its basic functions or serve its intended use, they generally do not have expectations about—or, oftentimes, even know of—technical or mechanical design aspects of the product. Thus, in cases involving technical or mechanical matters, consumer contemplation may be an inappropriate measure for liability.

* * *

* * * First, we do not agree with S & N that the consumer-contemplation test is inappropriate in cases involving complex products. The consumer-contemplation test imposes liability where a product is: (1) "in a condition not contemplated by the ultimate consumer"; and (2) "dangerous to an extent beyond that which would be contemplated by the ordinary consumer." *Vincer,* 69 Wis.2d at 330–31, 230 N.W.2d 794 (quoting *Restatement (Second) of Torts* 402A cmts. g and i).* * *

We agree with S & N that in many instances, ordinary consumers may not know of or fully understand the technical or mechanical design aspects of the product at issue. In such instances, the technical or mechanical product design features of the product will comprise "condition[s] not contemplated by the ultimate consumer."[10] *Id.* at 330, 230 N.W.2d 794. Thus, the inquiry in those cases must focus on whether the design features present an unreasonable danger to the ordinary consumer.

A determination of "unreasonable danger," like a determination that a product is in a condition not contemplated by the ordinary consumer, does not inevitably require any degree of scientific understanding about the

---

10. Indeed, if an injured consumer knows of and understands—*i.e* ., contemplates—at the time of his or her injury the condition of the design feature that caused that injury, the consumer likely would be unable to prove that the injury-causing product was defective and/or unreasonably dangerous.

product itself. Rather, it requires understanding of how safely the ordinary consumer would expect the product to serve its intended purpose. If the product falls below such minimum consumer expectations, the product is unreasonably dangerous.

* * *

And * * * this court does not agree with S & N that the consumer-contemplation test unnecessarily eliminates products from the marketplace. An otherwise defective and unreasonably dangerous product may in many cases be made safe for consumer use by means of adequate warnings or instructions. If, even in light of warnings or instructions, a product remains defective and unreasonably dangerous to the ordinary consumer, we see no reason that the product should remain on the market.

For these reasons, we decline S & N's invitation to abandon or qualify this state's exclusive reliance on the consumer-contemplation test. We reaffirm that Wisconsin is committed to the consumer-contemplation test in all strict products liability cases.

B

We next review whether the circuit court erred in instructing the jury that a product can be deemed defective and unreasonably dangerous regardless of whether the manufacturer of that product knew or could have known of the risk of harm the product presented to consumers. * * *

* * *

* * * S & N argues that where, as in the present case, a manufacturer does not and cannot foresee the risk of harm presented by its product, strict products liability does not apply.

We reject this argument. Foreseeability of harm is an element of negligence. * * *

By contrast, unlike negligence liability, strict products liability focuses not on the defendant's conduct, but on the nature of the defendant's product. * * * In other words, strict products liability imposes liability without regard to negligence and its attendant factors of duty of care and foreseeability. Thus, regardless of whether a manufacturer could foresee potential risks of harm inherent in its defective and unreasonably dangerous product, strict products liability holds that manufacturer responsible for injuries caused by that product.

* * *

* * * [W]hen this court recognized the cause of action for strict liability in tort, we identified several policy considerations supporting our decision to make manufacturers and other sellers of products responsible for placing defective and unreasonably dangerous products into the stream of commerce: (1) the seller of a product is " 'in the paramount position to distribute the costs of the risks' " presented by the products by passing along costs to consumers or by purchasing insurance; (2) consumers have " 'the right to rely on the apparent safety of the product and . . . it is the seller in the first instance who creates the risk by placing the defective product on the market' "; and (3) " 'the manufacturer has the greatest ability to control the risk created by [its] product since [it] may initiate or adopt inspection and quality control measures thereby preventing defective products from reaching the consumer.' " [*Glassey v. Continental Ins. Co.*, 176 Wis.2d 587, 602–03, 500 N.W.2d 295 (1993), quoting *Dippel v. Sciano*, 37 Wis.2d 443, 450–51, 155 N.W.2d 55 (1967).]

* * *

* * * Although products liability law is intended in part to make products safer for consumers, the primary "rationale underlying the imposition of strict liability on manufacturers and sellers is that the risk of the loss associated with the use of defective products should be borne by those who have created the risk and who have reaped the profit by placing a defective product in the stream of commerce." [*Kemp v. Miller*, 154 Wis.2d 538, 556, 453 N.W.2d 872 (1990).] * * * In a case where a manufacturer places an unforeseeably defective and unreasonably dangerous product on the market, the manufacturer both creates the risk of harm and reaps the profit from the defective and unreasonably dangerous product * * *. To be certain, imposing liability on the manufacturer [for injuries caused by a risk that was not foreseeable] may not materially affect a reduction of future risk. However, holding the manufacturer accountable * * * will serve the equitable purpose of imposing the cost of the risk on the party that created the risk. * * *

* * *

* * * [T]he circuit court correctly instructed the jury that a product can be deemed defective and unreasonably dangerous regardless of whether the manufacturer of that product knew or could have known of the risk of harm the product presented. As this court repeatedly has emphasized, foreseeability is not an element of this state's strict products liability law.

* * * In the present case, because the evidence introduced at trial indicated that the ordinary consumer was not aware at the time of Green's injuries that the protein levels and cornstarch powder in S & N's gloves could cause an allergic reaction in 5 to 17 percent of the gloves' consumers, we conclude that the jury reasonably found S & N's gloves to be defective and unreasonably dangerous.

* * *

For the foregoing reasons, we conclude that [the] jury verdict in the case at hand is legally sound. Accordingly, we affirm the decision of the court of appeals, which upheld the circuit court's entry of judgment on the verdict.

[A dissenting opinion for two of the seven Justices is omitted. Paragraph numbers in the majority opinion have been left out.]

COUCH v. MINE SAFETY APPLIANCES CO., 107 Wash.2d 232, 728 P.2d 585 (1986). Plaintiff's husband was a logger killed when struck on the head by a falling tree. At the time of the accident decedent was wearing an aluminum helmet manufactured by defendant. The helmet was found beside him with a dent in the crown and without two of four rivets needed to hold the internal suspension in place. Plaintiff claimed that the helmet's defective design caused her husband's death, since he would have suffered only "minor damage" had the helmet been safe. The jury was instructed that a product "is not reasonably safe as designed, if * * * it is unsafe as designed to an extent beyond that which would be contemplated by the ordinary user." Defendant asked for an instruction that plaintiff must prove "that an alternative, reasonably safe design was available" to the helmet manufacturer, but this charge was refused. The jury found for plaintiff. On appeal the Washington Supreme Court approved the "consumer expectations test" of defectiveness and ruled: "We affirm the judgment for the plaintiff, and hold that the availability of an alternative, reasonably safe design is not a necessary element of a plaintiff's burden of proof in a product liability action based on defective design."

LINEGAR v. ARMOUR OF AMERICA, INC., 909 F.2d 1150 (8th Cir.1990). Highway Patrol officer Linegar was shot and killed in the line of duty. He was wearing a standard-issue "bulletproof" vest which left his sides uncovered. The fatal bullet struck him in the side, under his armpit. His widow claimed the vest, manufactured by Armour of America, was defectively designed. *Held*, for defendant. "The Missouri Highway Patrol could have chosen to buy, and Armour could have sold the Patrol, a vest with more coverage; no one contests that. But it is not the place of courts or juries to set specifications as to the parts of the body a bullet-resistant garment must cover. A manufacturer is not obliged to market only one version of a product, that being the very safest design possible. If that were so, automobile manufacturers could not offer consumers sports cars, convertibles, jeeps, or compact cars. All boaters would have to buy full life vests instead of choosing a ski belt or even a flotation cushion. Personal safety devices, in particular, require personal choices * * *."

TABIEROS v. CLARK EQUIPMENT CO., 85 Haw. 336, 944 P.2d 1279 (1997). Plaintiff, a dock worker, had his legs crushed when a vehicle used to move shipping containers, called a "straddle carrier," ran into him. Plaintiff sued the manufacturer alleging design defect. Plaintiff's theory was that the carrier had a "blind zone" preventing the operator from fully seeing the surroundings. Defendant argued that this blind zone was an "open and obvious" condition. The jury, instructed that it might find defective design under either a "consumer expectation" test or a "risk-utility" test, found for plaintiff. On review by the Hawaii Supreme Court, *held*, that the consumer expectation test should not have been used, given the obviousness of the carrier's danger. The case was remanded for a new trial subject to the risk-utility test for design defect. The court (Levinson, J.) explained:

"The logic of the proposition that an open and obvious danger inherent in the use of a given product precludes the imposition of liability pursuant to the consumer expectation test is self-evident. If the danger involved in using a product is 'obvious and apparent, discernible by casual inspection,' and 'generally known and recognized,' then the danger must necessarily be within the ordinary user's expectation.''

"The consumer expectation test for determining the defectiveness of products the use of which involves open and obvious dangers 'can result in finding products to be not defective that could easily have been designed safer without great expense or effect on the benefits or functions to be served by the product.' W. Page Keeton et al., *Prosser and Keeton on the Law of Torts* § 99, at 698 (5th ed. 1984). It is for this reason that Hawai'i and most other jurisdictions have forsaken consumer expectations as the *sole* basis for denominating a product as defective, opting at the very least to extend the analysis to include the risk-utility test. Thus, a manufacturer may still be strictly liable under a product liability theory for injuries caused by a product, the use of which involves an open and obvious danger, in accordance with the risk-utility test.''

HENDERSON v. FORD MOTOR CO.

Supreme Court of Texas, 1974.
519 S.W.2d 87.

REAVLEY, Justice. This is a products liability case which raises questions of proof of a defective design * * *. Irene S. Henderson was badly hurt when, because she could not reduce the speed of her automobile, she intentionally drove it into a metal pole. She brought this suit against the manufacturer (Ford Motor Company) and her dealer (Snelling Motor Company). Mrs. Henderson obtained judgment against the defendants in the trial court; the Court of Civil Appeals reversed that judgment and remanded the case for retrial. * * *

On April 15, 1969 Mrs. Henderson was driving her 1968 Lincoln Continental in Houston city traffic. After accelerating to enter a freeway, she found that the speed of the car was not responsive to her control. Her first impression was that the problem was with the brakes. She drove the car from the freeway at the first exit and onto South Post Oak Road, continuing her efforts to stop. She determined that the accelerator pedal was not depressed. She pumped the brake and pushed with both feet against the brake pedal, but the speed continued. Seeing a busy intersection ahead and recognizing the peril to other persons, she drove onto the esplanade in the center of the street and finally crashed into the large signal light pole.

The Continental automobile had been purchased from Snelling Motor Company seven months earlier; it had been driven approximately 9,000 miles. * * * [After the accident a mechanic] examined the wreckage. He found nothing wrong with the carburetor linkage but when he looked into the carburetor itself, he found a piece of rubber between the throttle blades and the bore of the chamber of the carburetor. The piece of rubber turned out to be part of the gasket which was originally installed around the bottom of the air filter housing where that housing was seated on top of the carburetor.

The purpose of the air filter is to prevent dirt and foreign objects from entering the carburetor * * *. The lightweight filter housing requires some type of rubber or fibre gasket along the area where it fits upon the carburetor housing. In the engine installed in Mrs. Henderson's automobile, which Ford designated as model number 462, the gasket was glued into a trough or groove around the underside of the air filter housing. An alternative design, the one used on the successor model 460 Lincoln engine, substitutes a separate fibre gasket (on and around the carburetor housing at the place where the filter housing is seated) for the gasket previously fixed in the filter housing.

The chief contention of the plaintiff at the trial was that the gasket was not properly placed in its groove during manufacture, that it protruded from the groove when first sold to plaintiff and was finally cut free, that the piece then lodged in the carburetor and held open the gas feed during Mrs. Henderson's frightful ride. The jury, however, answered in the negative the issues of whether the gasket was defectively installed by Ford or defectively installed when sold by Snelling. The judgment for plaintiff was based upon jury findings that the design of the air filter housing was defective and that this design defect was the producing cause of Mrs. Henderson's damages.

* * *

* * * The question is whether this filter housing [with its attached gasket], and *all housings of the same design,* were unreasonably dangerous from the time of installation. Did some feature of the form or material or operation of the housing threaten harm to persons using the automobile to the extent that any automobile so designed would not be placed in the channels of commerce by a prudent manufacturer aware of the risks involved in its use or to the extent that the automobile would not meet the reasonable expectations of the ordinary consumer as to its safety?

* * * Dr. Douglas Muster, Professor of Engineering at the University of Houston, also a witness for the plaintiff, testified at some length to his reasons for believing that the gasket had not been properly installed during production of the car. As for the design itself, he would only say that it was his opinion that positioning of the gasket on top of the carburetor "would be better" than this installation on the bottom of the filter housing. He objected to the straight side edge of the housing adjacent to the rubber gasket, which he thought would have a tendency to be cut if dislocated, but he would not term the latter design as unsafe or dangerous. He also stated that he saw no reason why the rubber gasket would not be expected to remain in place throughout the life of the car if the gasket were properly installed.

* * *

After studying this record carefully and viewing the evidence in favor of the jury finding and trial court judgment, we conclude that there is no evidence of danger or lack of reasonable safety in the design itself. One witness says that the design could be better and that an edge or ridge has a tendency to cut a softer object bound across it. Liability is not predicated upon such bare criticism. The same statements could be made about reasonably safe products, for few machines within our ability to purchase, could not be designed "better" in some respect. This determination will not suffice as a predicate for a finding of improper or defective design and a basis for liability of the manufacturer. Garst v. General Motors Corp., 207 Kan. 2, 484 P.2d 47 (1971).

Ford engineers testified that the 462 model air filter housing design was changed at the time of an overall engine change in 1968. They described the 462 design as superior and more expensive to produce than the successor scheme which used a loose gasket rather than one fixed on the underside of the air filter housing. Over 300,000 Lincolns have been produced with the older design and it has been used on over 1,500,000 vehicles. These witnesses testified that they had no notice of any prior claim that the earlier design caused a malfunction or any problem caused by torn pieces of the gasket.

The purchaser of an automobile is entitled to expect that its manufacturer has designed the vehicle to meet the demands of its usage without deficiencies that will make it unreasonably dangerous during the course of that usage, but the manufacturer is not charged by the law nor expected by the purchasing public to design every part to be the best that science can produce or to guarantee that no harm will befall the user. This particular Lincoln Continental had been driven across the United States; no attempt was made to prove all the instances when this filter housing had been removed or all of the hands that had touched the gasket. * * *

The judgments are reversed; judgment is here rendered that plaintiffs take nothing from defendants.

SAM D. JOHNSON, Justice (dissenting).

* * * The holding to which this writer is diametrically opposed is the majority's determination that there is no evidence of design defect.

* * *

The clear import of Dr. Muster's testimony was that using sharp edges on the air filter housing in conjunction with a rubber gasket was dangerous because there is an inherent tendency for the sharp edge to cut the rubber. A design which uses sharp metal edges with rubber in a location where pieces of rubber could be cut and fall into an automobile carburetor, threatening human life, is unreasonably dangerous and thus defective. * * *

The above testimony is, however, not the only evidence supporting plaintiffs' theory and the jury's verdict. The air filter housing of course is a unit created to be removed and replaced frequently for routine maintenance operations. There was evidence that an individual placing or replacing an air filter housing of this particular design on a carburetor would have difficulty in ascertaining whether he had done so correctly.

* * *

Still further, several experts testified that the air filter housing and the gasket could have been designed so that the parts of the gasket did not have a propensity to fall into the barrel of the carburetor. They indicated that using a gasket which would fit on top of the carburetor would be a safer design. * * *

The record, furthermore, explicitly shows that Ford, in fact, later changed the design which the jury found to be defective; the new design conformed to that which [experts] testified would be a safer design. It placed the gasket on top of the carburetor rather than gluing it onto the underside of the air filter housing. In addition, the improved design incorporated "rolled" edges on the air filter housing rather than sharp edges and used a gasket of a different and more durable material than the gasket in the instant case, which became brittle after extended use. * * *

Judgment should be entered for plaintiffs on the jury verdict.

POPE, McGEE and DANIEL, JJ., join in this dissent.

On Motion for Rehearing

SAM D. JOHNSON, Justice (dissenting).

* * *

* * * In determining whether the air filter housing in the instant case is unreasonably dangerous, the majority asks the following question:

"Did some feature of the form or material or operation of the housing threaten harm to persons using the automobile to the extent that any automobile so designed would not be placed in the channels of commerce by a prudent manufacturer aware of the risks involved in its use *or* to the extent that the automobile would not meet the reasonable expectations of the ordinary consumer as to its safety?" [Emphasis added.]

* * * In other words, in the same case, the question of whether a product is defective will apparently be viewed both from the perspective of the manufacturer and from the perspective of the consumer. It is entirely possible that the proof of the consumer will fully establish that the product would not meet the reasonable expectations of the ordinary user, while the proof of the manufacturer will equally establish that a prudent manufacturer might market the product notwithstanding the risks involved in its use. In such a case, will there be recovery since one element of the majority's bifurcated test has been met, or will recovery be defeated since the other element of the majority's bifurcated test has been negated? Is the trial court, on being confronted with jury answers equally establishing the theory of the consumer and the manufacturer, free to give judgment to the party it feels developed the stronger case? If so, the practical effect is that it is incumbent upon the consumer to show *both* that the product would disappoint the reasonable expectations of the ordinary consumer *and* that a prudent manufacturer would not market the product. The onerous and unwarranted burden thus put upon the consumer to prove a product is defective is obvious.

* * * Though the test established by the majority would ostensibly view the question of the defectiveness of a product from *either* the perspective of the manufacturer or the consumer, the majority's application of the test in

the instant case stresses *only* the view of the manufacturer. The analysis of the majority is wholly directed toward whether a prudent manufacturer aware of the risks involved in the use of the product would market the air filter housing involved. There is not the slightest discussion directed toward whether an automobile equipped with the type of air filter housing involved would meet the reasonable expectations of the ordinary consumer as to its safety.

Certainly an automobile equipped with an air filter gasket which has a propensity to come loose and fall in the carburetor barrel, threatening human life, "would not meet the reasonable expectations of the ordinary consumer as to its safety." On the contrary, the ordinary consumer would undoubtedly reasonably expect an automobile which had traveled only 9,000 miles to carry the occupant safely to his destination. When that automobile malfunctions due to a cause not in control of the occupant, the reasonable expectations of that occupant as to the automobile's safety are, of course, disappointed.

If the majority * * * means to suggest that the decisive portion of its test for finding a design defect is whether a prudent manufacturer would market the product, additional problems are created. Not only does this approach violate the majority's own test by ignoring the perspective of the consumer, but it also misperceives the basis of the strict liability concept that a seller will be liable even though he has "exercised all possible care in the preparation and sale of his product." Restatement (Second) of Torts § 402A. If strict liability is, as indicated by the Restatement, to be predicated upon the condition of the product regardless of the exercise of "all possible care in the preparation and sale" of it by the seller, then questions of whether a "prudent manufacturer" would market a product have no place in the strict liability field. To inquire whether a prudent manufacturer would have marketed the product had he known of the risks involved injects an inappropriate element of negligence into the strict liability question. A "prudent manufacturer" is, after all, simply a manufacturer which exercises ordinary care. * * *

If the majority, in purporting to consider the question of design defect from both the viewpoint of the manufacturer and the expectations of the consumer, is attempting to articulate a risk versus utility balancing approach to design defect questions, it has failed in its application of such an approach to the facts of the instant case. Any risk versus utility approach for determining the acceptability of a product should consider, among others, the following factors:

"(1) the usefulness and desirability of the product, (2) the availability of other, safer products to meet the same need, (3) the likelihood and probable seriousness of injury, (4) the obviousness of the danger, (5) common knowledge and normal public expectation of the danger (particularly for established products), (6) the avoidability of injury by care in use of the product (including the effect of instructions or warnings), and (7) the ability to eliminate the danger without seriously impairing the product's usefulness or making it unduly expensive." W. Donaher, et al., The Technological Expert in Products Liability Litigation, 52 Texas L.Rev. 1303, at 1307–08 (1974).

An analysis of the majority opinion reveals no indication that an objective balancing of the foregoing considerations is attempted.

* * *

POPE, McGEE and DANIEL, JJ., join in this dissent.

———

BOATLAND OF HOUSTON, INC. v. BAILEY, 609 S.W.2d 743 (Tex.Sup. Ct.1980). "[W]hen the plaintiff alleges that a product was defectively designed because it lacked a specific feature, attention may become focused on the feasibility of that feature—the capacity to provide the feature without greatly increasing the product's cost or impairing usefulness. This feasibility is a relative, not an absolute, concept; the more scientifically and economically feasible the alternative was, the more likely that a jury may find that the product was defectively designed. A plaintiff may advance the argument that a safer alternative was feasible with evidence that it was in actual use or was available at the time of manufacture. Feasibility may also be shown with evidence of the scientific and economic capacity to develop the safer alternative. Thus, evidence of the actual use of, or capacity to use, safer alternatives is relevant insofar as it depicts the available scientific knowledge and the practicalities of applying that knowledge to a product's design."

PHILLIPS v. KIMWOOD MACHINE CO., 269 Or. 485, 525 P.2d 1033 (1974). The product was a sanding machine alleged to be defective because it was sold without safeguards (including a sufficient warning) to protect the operator. Plaintiff appealed from a directed verdict and the case was remanded. On the matter of design defect the court said:

"The problem with strict liability of products has been one of limitation. No one wants absolute liability where all the article has to do is to cause injury. To impose liability there has to be something about the article which makes it dangerously defective without regard to whether the manufacturer was or was not at fault for such condition. A test for unreasonable danger is therefore vital. A dangerously defective article would be one which a reasonable person would not put into the stream of commerce *if he had knowledge of its harmful character.* The test, therefore, is whether the seller would be negligent if he sold the article *knowing of the risk involved.*[11] Strict liability imposes what amounts to constructive knowledge of the condition of the product.

"On the surface such a test would seem to be different than the test of 2 Restatement (Second) of Torts § 402A, Comment *i*, of 'dangerous to an extent beyond that which would be contemplated by the ordinary consumer who purchases it.' This court has used this test in the past. These are not

---

11. See generally, Wade, [On the Nature of Strict Tort Liability for Products, 44 Miss.L.J. 825 (1973)], at 834–835; P. Keeton, Products Liability—Some Observations About Allocation of Risks, 64 Mich.L.Rev. 1329, 1335 (1966). * * * Keeton would impute the knowledge of dangers at time of trial to the manufacturer * * *.

necessarily different standards, however. As stated in Welch v. Outboard Marine Corp.,[8] where the court affirmed an instruction containing both standards: 'We see no necessary inconsistency between a seller-oriented standard and a user-oriented standard when, as here, each turns on foreseeable risks. They are two sides of the same standard. A product is defective and unreasonably dangerous when a reasonable seller would not sell the product if he knew of the risks involved or if the risks are greater than a reasonable buyer would expect.' To elucidate this point further, we feel that the two standards are the same because a seller acting reasonably would be selling the same product which a reasonable consumer believes he is purchasing. * * *

* * *

" * * * The issue has been raised in some courts concerning whether, in this context, there is any distinction between strict liability and negligence. * * * We discussed this matter recently in the case of Roach v. Kononen, 99 Or.Adv.Sch. 1092, 525 P.2d 125 (1974), and pointed out that there is a difference between strict liability for misdesign and negligence. We said:

" ' * * * [I]t is generally recognized that the basic difference between negligence on the one hand and strict liability for a design defect on the other is that in strict liability we are talking about the condition (dangerousness) of an article which is designed in a particular way, while in negligence we are talking about the reasonableness of the manufacturer's actions in designing and selling the article as he did. The article can have a degree of dangerousness which the law of strict liability will not tolerate even though the actions of the designer were entirely reasonable in view of what he knew at the time he planned and sold the manufactured article. As Professor Wade points out, a way of determining whether the condition of the article is of the requisite degree of dangerousness to be defective (unreasonably dangerous; greater degree of danger than a consumer has a right to expect; not duly safe) is to assume that the manufacturer knew of the product's propensity to injure as it did, and then to ask whether, with such knowledge, something should have been done about the danger before it was sold.'

* * *

"[Thus, for example, an] article can have a degree of dangerousness because of a lack of warning which the law of strict liability will not tolerate even though the actions of the seller were entirely reasonable in selling the article without a warning considering what he knew or should have known at the time he sold it. A way to determine the dangerousness of the article, as distinguished from the seller's culpability, is to assume the seller knew of the product's propensity to injure as it did, and then to ask whether, with such knowledge, he would have been negligent in selling it without a warning."

8.   481 F.2d 252, 254 (5th Cir.1973).

BARKER v. LULL ENGINEERING CO.

Supreme Court of California, 1978.
20 Cal.3d 413, 143 Cal.Rptr. 225, 573 P.2d 443.

TOBRINER, Acting Chief Justice. In August 1970, plaintiff Ray Barker was injured at a construction site at the University of California at Santa Cruz while operating a high-lift loader manufactured by defendant Lull Engineering Co. and leased to plaintiff's employer by defendant George M. Philpott Co., Inc. Claiming that his injuries were proximately caused, inter alia, by the alleged defective design of the loader, Barker instituted the present tort action seeking to recover damages for his injuries. The jury returned a verdict in favor of defendants, and plaintiff appeals from the judgment entered upon that verdict, contending primarily that in view of this court's decision in Cronin v. J. B. E. Olson Corp. (1972) 8 Cal.3d 121, 104 Cal.Rptr. 433, 501 P.2d 1153, the trial court erred in instructing the jury "that strict liability for a defect in design of a product is based on a finding that the product was unreasonably dangerous for its intended use * * *."

As we explain, we agree with plaintiff's objection to the challenged instruction and conclude that the judgment must be reversed. In *Cronin*, we reviewed the development of the strict product liability doctrine in California at some length, and concluded that, for a variety of reasons, the "unreasonably dangerous" element which section 402A of the Restatement Second of Torts had introduced into the definition of a defective product should not be incorporated into a plaintiff's burden of proof in a product liability action in this state. Although defendants maintain that our *Cronin* decision should properly be interpreted as applying only to "manufacturing defects" and not to the alleged "design defects" at issue here, we shall point out that the *Cronin* decision itself refutes any such distinction. Consequently, we conclude that the instruction was erroneous and that the judgment in favor of defendants must be reversed.

* * *

As we noted in *Cronin*, the Restatement draftsmen adopted the "unreasonably dangerous" language primarily as a means of confining the application of strict tort liability to an article which is "dangerous to an extent beyond that which would be contemplated by the ordinary consumer who purchases it, with the ordinary knowledge common to the community as to its characteristics." (Rest.2d Torts, § 402A, com. i.) In *Cronin*, however, we flatly rejected the suggestion that recovery in a products liability action should be permitted *only* if a product is more dangerous than contemplated by the average consumer, refusing to permit the low esteem in which the public might hold a dangerous product to diminish the manufacturer's responsibility for injuries caused by that product. * * * Indeed, our decision in Luque v. McLean (1972) 8 Cal.3d 136, 104 Cal.Rptr. 443, 501 P.2d 1163— decided the same day as *Cronin*—aptly reflects our disagreement with the restrictive implications of the Restatement formulation, for in *Luque* we held that a power rotary lawn mower with an unguarded hole could properly be found defective, in spite of the fact that the defect in the product was patent and hence in all probability within the reasonable contemplation of the ordinary consumer.

Thus, our rejection of the use of the "unreasonably dangerous" terminology in *Cronin* rested in part on a concern that a jury might interpret such an instruction, as the Restatement draftsman had indeed intended, as shielding a defendant from liability so long as the product did not fall below the ordinary consumer's expectations as to the product's safety.[7] As *Luque* demonstrates, the dangers posed by such a misconception by the jury extend to cases involving design defects as well as to actions involving manufacturing defects: indeed, the danger of confusion is perhaps more pronounced in design cases in which the manufacturer could frequently argue that its product satisfied ordinary consumer expectations since it was identical to other items of the same product line with which the consumer may well have been familiar.

Accordingly, contrary to defendants' contention, the reasoning of *Cronin* does not dictate that that decision be confined to the manufacturing defect context. * * * Consequently, we conclude that the design defect instruction given in the instant case was erroneous.[9]

* * *

* * * We held in *Cronin* that a plaintiff satisfies his burden of proof * * *, in both a "manufacturing defect" and "design defect" context, when he proves the existence of a "defect" and that such defect was a proximate cause of his injuries. * * *

As this court has recognized on numerous occasions, the term defect as utilized in the strict liability context is neither self-defining nor susceptible to a single definition applicable in all contexts. * * *

Resort to the numerous product liability precedents in California demonstrates that the defect or defectiveness concept has embraced a great variety of injury-producing deficiencies, ranging from products that cause injury because they deviate from the manufacturer's intended result (e.g., the one soda bottle in ten thousand that explodes without explanation (Escola v. Coca Cola Bottling Co. (1944) 24 Cal.2d 453, 150 P.2d 436)), to products which, though "perfectly" manufactured, are unsafe because of the

---

7. This is not to say that the expectations of the ordinary consumer are irrelevant to the determination of whether a product is defective, for as we point out below we believe that ordinary consumer expectations are frequently of direct significance to the defectiveness issue. The flaw in the Restatement's analysis, in our view, is that it treats such consumer expectations as a "ceiling" on a manufacturer's responsibility under strict liability principles, rather than as a "floor." As we shall explain, past California decisions establish that *at a minimum* a product must meet ordinary consumer expectations as to safety to avoid being found defective.

9. Indeed, the challenged instruction * * * was additionally erroneous because it suggested that in evaluating defectiveness, only the "in-

tended use" of the product is relevant, rather than the product's "reasonably foreseeable use." In *Cronin*, we specifically held that the adequacy of a product must be determined in light of its reasonably foreseeable use, declaring that "[t]he design and manufacture of products should not be carried out in an industrial vacuum but with recognition of the realities of their everyday use." (8 Cal.3d at p. 126, 104 Cal.Rptr. at p. 437, 501 P.2d at p. 1157.)

Because, in the instant case, the jury may have concluded that the use of the loader by a relatively inexperienced worker was not an "intended use" of the loader, but was a "reasonably foreseeable use," this aspect of the instruction may well have prejudiced the plaintiff.

absence of a safety device (e.g., a paydozer without rear view mirrors (Pike v. Frank G. Hough Co., supra, 2 Cal.3d 465, 85 Cal.Rptr. 629, 467 P.2d 229), and including products that are dangerous because they lack adequate warnings or instructions (e.g., a telescope that contains inadequate instructions for assembling a "sun filter" attachment (Midgley v. S. S. Kresge Co. (1976) 55 Cal.App.3d 67, 127 Cal.Rptr. 217)).

* * *

In general, a manufacturing or production defect is readily identifiable because a defective product is one that differs from the manufacturer's intended result or from other ostensibly identical units of the same product line. For example, when a product comes off the assembly line in a substandard condition it has incurred a manufacturing defect. A design defect, by contrast, cannot be identified simply by comparing the injury-producing product with the manufacturer's plans or with other units of the same product line, since by definition the plans and all such units will reflect the same design. Rather than applying any sort of deviation-from-the-norm test in determining whether a product is defective in design for strict liability purposes, our cases have employed two alternative criteria in ascertaining, in Justice Traynor's words, whether there is something "wrong, if not in the manufacturer's manner of production, at least in his product." (Traynor, The Ways and Meanings of Defective Products and Strict Liability, supra, 32 Tenn.L.Rev. 363, 366.)

First, our cases establish that a product may be found defective in design if the plaintiff demonstrates that the product failed to perform as safely as an ordinary consumer would expect when used in an intended or reasonably foreseeable manner. This initial standard, somewhat analogous to the Uniform Commercial Code's warranty of fitness and merchantability (Cal.U.Com.Code, § 2314), reflects the warranty heritage upon which California product liability doctrine in part rests. As we noted in Greenman [v. Yuba Power Products, Inc. (1963)], "implicit in [a product's] presence on the market * * * [is] a representation that it [will] safely do the jobs for which it was built." (59 Cal.2d at p. 64, 27 Cal.Rptr. at p. 701, 377 P.2d at p. 901.) When a product fails to satisfy such ordinary consumer expectations as to safety in its intended or reasonably foreseeable operation, a manufacturer is strictly liable for resulting injuries. * * *

As Professor Wade has pointed out, however, the expectations of the ordinary consumer cannot be viewed as the exclusive yardstick for evaluating design defectiveness because "[i]n many situations * * * the consumer would not know what to expect, because he would have no idea how safe the product could be made." (Wade, On the Nature of Strict Tort Liability for Products, supra, 44 Miss.L.J. 825, 829.) Numerous California decisions have implicitly recognized this fact and have made clear, through varying linguistic formulations, that a product may be found defective in design, even if it satisfies ordinary consumer expectations, if through hindsight the jury determines that the product's design embodies "excessive preventable danger," or, in other words, if the jury finds that the risk of danger inherent in the challenged design outweighs the benefits of such design.

A review of past cases indicates that in evaluating the adequacy of a product's design pursuant to this latter standard, a jury may consider, among other relevant factors, the gravity of the danger posed by the challenged design, the likelihood that such danger would occur, the mechanical feasibility of a safer alternative design, the financial cost of an improved design, and the adverse consequences to the product and to the consumer that would result from an alternative design.

Although our cases have thus recognized a variety of considerations that may be relevant to the determination of the adequacy of a product's design, past authorities have generally not devoted much attention to the appropriate allocation of the burden of proof with respect to these matters. The allocation of such burden is particularly significant in this context inasmuch as this court's product liability decisions, from *Greenman* to *Cronin,* have repeatedly emphasized that one of the principal purposes behind the strict product liability doctrine is to relieve an injured plaintiff of many of the onerous evidentiary burdens inherent in a negligence cause of action. Because most of the evidentiary matters which may be relevant to the determination of the adequacy of a product's design under the "risk-benefit" standard—e.g., the feasibility and cost of alternative designs—are similar to issues typically presented in a negligent design case and involve technical matters peculiarly within the knowledge of the manufacturer, we conclude that once the plaintiff makes a prima facie showing that the injury was proximately caused by the product's design, the burden should appropriately shift to the defendant to prove, in light of the relevant factors, that the product is not defective. Moreover, inasmuch as this conclusion flows from our determination that the fundamental public policies embraced in *Greenman* dictate that a manufacturer who seeks to escape liability for an injury proximately caused by its product's design on a risk-benefit theory should bear the burden of persuading the trier of fact that its product should not be judged defective, the defendant's burden is one affecting the burden of proof, rather than simply the burden of producing evidence.

Thus, to reiterate, a product may be found defective in design, so as to subject a manufacturer to strict liability for resulting injuries, under either of two alternative tests. First, a product may be found defective in design if the plaintiff establishes that the product failed to perform as safely as an ordinary consumer would expect when used in an intended or reasonably foreseeable manner. Second, a product may alternatively be found defective in design if the plaintiff demonstrates that the product's design proximately caused his injury and the defendant fails to establish, in light of the relevant factors, that, on balance, the benefits of the challenged design outweigh the risk of danger inherent in such design.

* * * As we have indicated, we believe that the test for defective design set out above is appropriate in light of the rationale and limits of the strict liability doctrine, for it subjects a manufacturer to liability whenever there is something "wrong" with its product's design—either because the product fails to meet ordinary consumer expectations as to safety or because, on balance, the design is not as safe as it should be—while stopping short of making the manufacturer an insurer for all injuries which may result from

the use of its product. This test, moreover, explicitly focuses the trier of fact's attention on the adequacy of the product itself, rather than on the manufacturer's conduct, and places the burden on the manufacturer, rather than the plaintiff, to establish that because of the complexity of, and trade-offs implicit in, the design process, an injury-producing product should nevertheless not be found defective.

Amicus CTLA [California Trial Lawyer Association] on behalf of the plaintiff, anticipating to some extent the latter half of the design defect standard articulated above, contends that any instruction which directs the jury to "weigh" or "balance" a number of factors, or which sets forth a list of completing considerations for the jury to evaluate in determining the existence of a design defect, introduces an element which "rings of negligence" into the determination of defect, and consequently is inconsistent with our decision in *Cronin*. As amicus interprets the decision, *Cronin* broadly precludes any consideration of "reasonableness" or "balancing" in a product liability action.

* * *

[However,] design defect decisions demonstrate that, as a practical matter, in many instances it is simply impossible to eliminate the balancing or weighing of competing considerations in determining whether a product is defectively designed or not. In Self v. General Motors Corp., 42 Cal. App.3d 1, 116 Cal.Rptr. 575 [(1974)], for example, an automobile passenger, injured when the car in which she was riding exploded during an accident, brought suit against the manufacturer claiming that the car was defective in that the fuel tank had been placed in a particularly vulnerable position in the left rear bumper. One issue in the case, of course, was whether it was technically feasible to locate the fuel tank in a different position which would have averted the explosion in question. But, as the *Self* court recognized, feasibility was not the sole issue, for another relevant consideration was whether an alternative design of the car, while averting the particular accident, would have created a greater risk of injury in other, more common situations.

In similar fashion, weighing the extent of the risks and the advantages posed by alternative designs is inevitable in many design defect cases. As the *Self* court stated: "[W]e appreciate the need to balance one consideration against another in designing a complicated product so as to achieve reasonable and practical safety under a multitude of varying conditions." * * *

Finally, contrary to the suggestion of amicus CTLA, an instruction which advises the jury that it may evaluate the adequacy of a product's design by weighing the benefits of the challenged design against the risk of danger inherent in such design is not simply the equivalent of an instruction which requires the jury to determine whether the manufacturer was negligent in designing the product. It is true, of course, that in many cases proof that a product is defective in design may also demonstrate that the manufacturer was negligent in choosing such a design. As we have indicated, however, in a strict liability case, as contrasted with a negligent design action, the jury's focus is properly directed to the condition of the product itself, and not to the reasonableness of the manufacturer's conduct.

Thus, the fact that the manufacturer took reasonable precautions in an attempt to design a safe product or otherwise acted as a reasonably prudent manufacturer would have under the circumstances, while perhaps absolving the manufacturer of liability under a negligence theory, will not preclude the imposition of liability under strict liability principles if, upon hindsight, the trier of fact concludes that the product's design is unsafe to consumers, users, or bystanders.

The technological revolution has created a society that contains dangers to the individual never before contemplated. The individual must face the threat to life and limb not only from the car on the street or highway but from a massive array of hazardous mechanisms and products. The radical change from a comparatively safe, largely agricultural, society to this industrial unsafe one has been reflected in the decisions that formerly tied liability to the fault of a tortfeasor but now are more concerned with the safety of the individual who suffers the loss. As Dean Keeton has written, "The change in the substantive law as regards the liability of makers of products and other sellers in the marketing chain has been from fault to defect. The plaintiff is no longer required to impugn the maker, but he is required to impugn the product." (Keeton, Product Liability and the Meaning of Defect (1973) 5 St. Mary's L.J. 30, 33.)

* * *

DART v. WIEBE MANUFACTURING, INC., 147 Ariz. 242, 709 P.2d 876 (1985). Plaintiff's arm was torn off by the conveyor belt of a paper shredding machine manufactured by defendant and owned by plaintiff's employer. Plaintiff claimed the machine, lacking safety guards that would have prevented the accident, was defectively designed. On appeal from a verdict against plaintiff, *held* (4–1), that the trial court erred in instructing the jury to judge defendant's design under "negligence principles" alone. The Arizona Supreme Court approved the approach taken by the California court in *Barker v. Lull Engineering Co.* Design defect "should, if possible, be decided upon the consumer expectation test," and if that test "fails to provide a complete answer," then the question should be "whether a reasonable manufacturer would continue to market his product in the same condition * * * *with knowledge of the potential dangerous consequences the trial just revealed*" (emphasis in original). A "hindsight test" is necessary to preserve the "fundamental difference" between negligence and strict liability. The court explained:

"It is important to bear in mind that both the consumer expectation test and the risk/benefit analysis test 'can embody strict liability because the manufacturer-designer may be held liable in situations where due or even utmost care would not have prevented the design hazard.' Henderson, Strict Products Liability and Design Defects in Arizona, 26 Ariz.L.Rev. 261, 264

(1984). The true distinction, we believe, between negligent design cases applying the risk/benefit analysis and strict liability cases applying the same word formulation is the time frame in which this determination is made. For a plaintiff to prove negligence he must prove that the designer or manufacturer acted unreasonably at the time of manufacture or design of the product. * * *

"In a strict liability risk/benefit analysis, however, it is not the conduct of the manufacturer or designer which is primarily in question, but rather the quality of the end result; the product is the focus of the inquiry. The quality of the product may be measured not only by the information available to the manufacturer at the time of design, but also by the information available to the trier of fact at the time of trial. * * * This 'hindsight' test is generally recommended by the commentators, and by precedent, if the case is to be pursued in strict liability. See, e.g., Keeton, Product Liability and the Meaning of Defect, 5 St. Mary's L.J. 30, 38 (1973); * * * Barker v. Lull, supra; Phillips v. Kimwood Machine Co., 269 Or. 485, 525 P.2d 1033 (1974)."

ELMORE v. OWENS–ILLINOIS, INC., 673 S.W.2d 434 (Mo.1984). During 1948 to 1958 Arthur Elmore's job involved working with Kaylo, an insulation material containing 15% asbestos manufactured by defendant. In 1976 Elmore was diagnosed as having asbestosis, a long-latency lung disease concededly caused by exposure to asbestos dust. Elmore and his wife sued claiming Kaylo, containing asbestos, was defectively designed. Defendant sought to present a "state of the art" defense: that given available scientific knowledge "before 1958, the date it ceased to manufacture Kaylo," defendant "could not have known" that a health hazard would arise from use of insulation products containing asbestos. According to defendant, there is no product defect unless "defendant knew or could have known that Kaylo could have been designed in a way that rendered it safer than it was." But the trial judge ruled "state of the art" at the time of manufacture irrelevant in a design defect case, and the jury found for plaintiffs. On review by the Missouri Supreme Court, *held* (5–2), for plaintiffs.

"Although jurisdictions differ on admission of state of the art evidence in design defect cases, Robb, A Practical Approach to Use of State of the Art Evidence in Strict Products Liability Cases, 77 Nw.U.L.Rev. 1, 3–19 (1982), the law in Missouri holds that state of the art evidence has no bearing on the outcome of a strict liability claim; the sole subject of inquiry is the defective condition of the product and not the manufacturer's knowledge, negligence or fault. The manufacturer's standard of care is irrelevant because it relates to the reasonableness of the manufacturer's design choice; fault is an irrelevant consideration on the issue of liability in the strict liability context. Thus, plaintiffs established that Kaylo was 'defective' when they proved that it was unreasonably dangerous as designed; they were not required to show additionally that the manufacturer or designer was 'at fault,' as that concept is employed in the negligence context. The trial court properly denied the proffered state of the art argument * * *."

EVIDENCE OF SUBSEQUENT DESIGN CHANGE

Suppose that, after an accident, safety measures are instituted to prevent its recurrence. A common-law rule says that evidence of post-accident safety measures is not admissible to prove prior negligence. The traditional rationale for the bar on evidence of subsequent remedial measures focusses on two dangers. First, given evidence of precautions undertaken by the clear light of hindsight, juries may wrongly conclude that culpable foresight—negligence—existed at the time of the accident. Second, if their remedial efforts may be used against them in court, defendants may be deterred from taking steps to repair dangerous conditions.

Should the traditional exclusionary rule for negligence cases be applied in the modern context of strict liability for defective design of a product? Rule 407 of the Federal Rules of Evidence, as amended in 1997, says that evidence of remedial measures taken "after an injury" is not admissible to prove "a defect in a product, a defect in a product's design, or a need for a warning or instruction." However, Rule 407 goes on to say that such evidence may be admitted to prove the "feasibility of precautionary measures."

The federal rule applies only to cases in federal courts. Many states take a more permissive view.

————

AULT v. INTERNATIONAL HARVESTER CO., 13 Cal.3d 113, 117 Cal.Rptr. 812, 528 P.2d 1148 (1974). Plaintiff was injured in an accident involving a motor vehicle called a "Scout," manufactured by defendant. He claimed the Scout's gear box, made of aluminum 380, was defectively designed. At trial plaintiff introduced evidence, over defendant's objection, of other accidents in which aluminum gear boxes allegedly failed; and also evidence that after plaintiff's accident defendant changed from aluminum 380 to malleable iron in the manufacture of the gear box. *Held*, plaintiff's evidence was properly admitted. "Evidence of other accidents is admissible to prove a defective condition * * * or the cause of an accident, provided that the circumstances of the other accidents are similar and not too remote." Further, evidence of a subsequent design change may be introduced in a strict liability action where the defectiveness of a product's previous design is at issue. According to section 1151 of the California Evidence Code, proof of repairs or precautions undertaken after an accident "is inadmissible to prove negligence," but the court held that this exclusionary rule does not apply to "evidentiary use of subsequent design changes in strict liability cases."

FORMA SCIENTIFIC, INC. v. BIOSERA, INC., 960 P.2d 108 (Colo.1998). Plaintiff's medical products were stored in a freezer manufactured by defendant. The products were destroyed when the freezer was accidentally switched off. Plaintiff asserted that the on/off switch should have been protected against accidental switching, and sought to introduce evidence that the manufacturer had changed the switch design for subsequent models. *Held*, that evidence of subsequent design change is admissible to establish strict liability for design defect. "We decline to follow the newly amended Rule 407 [of the Federal Rules of Evidence]."

" * * * [W]e agree with *Ault* [*v. International Harvester*, supra] and its progeny that the public policy rationale underlying [the traditional rule barring evidence of remedial measures]—not to discourage entities from taking safety precautions—is largely inapplicable in the context of today's mass manufacturers. It is unreasonable to presume that a mass manufacturer of goods takes its cue from evidentiary rules rather than considerations of consumer safety and/or the safety of consumer property. Even taking a less rosy view, recognizing that not all manufacturers necessarily place the best interests of their consumers at the forefront, market forces generally operate to compel manufacturers to improve their products."

COMPLIANCE WITH REGULATORY STANDARDS

Some states have enacted legislation providing that a manufacturer's compliance with pertinent regulatory standards is a defense in product defect litigation. Following are two examples of such provisions, from Colorado and Kansas. Both set up a presumption in defendant's favor, not a conclusive defense. In addition, the Kansas statute establishes an irrebuttable "government contractor defense."

Colorado Revised Statutes Section 13–21–403:

(1) In any product liability action, it shall be rebuttably presumed that the product which caused the injury, death, or property damage was not defective and that the manufacturer or seller thereof was not negligent if the product: * * * (b) Complied with, at the time of sale by the manufacturer, any applicable code, standard, or regulation adopted or promulgated by the United States or by this state, or by any agency of the United States or of this state.

(2) In like manner, noncompliance with a government code, standard, or regulation existing and in effect at the time of sale of the product by the manufacturer which contributed to the claim or injury shall create a rebuttable presumption that the product was defective or negligently manufactured.

Kansas Statutes Annotated Section 60–3304:

(a) When the injury-causing aspect of the product was, at the time of manufacture, in compliance with legislative regulatory standards or administrative regulatory safety standards relating to design or performance, the product shall be deemed not defective by reason of design or performance, * * * unless the claimant proves by a preponderance of the evidence that a reasonably prudent product seller could and would have taken additional precautions. * * *

(c) When the injury-causing aspect of the product was, at the time of manufacture, in compliance with a mandatory government contract specification relating to design, this shall be an absolute defense and the product shall be deemed not defective for that reason * * *.

DAWSON v. CHRYSLER CORP., 630 F.2d 950 (3d Cir.1980). At issue was the design of Chrysler's 1974 Dodge Monaco. Plaintiff claimed his injuries in a side collision were much greater because the car lacked a "full, continuous steel frame." The appellate court (per Adams, J.) upheld a jury verdict in plaintiff's favor, but recorded the following misgivings:

" * * * Congress, in enacting the National Traffic and Motor Vehicle Safety Act, provided that compliance with [design safety regulations issued pursuant to] the Act does not exempt any person from liability under the common law of the state of injury. The effect of this provision is that the states are free, not only to create various standards of liability for automobile manufacturers with respect to design and structure, but also to delegate to the triers of fact in civil cases arising out of automobile accidents the power to determine whether a particular product conforms to such standards. * * *

"The result of such arrangement is that while the jury found Chrysler liable for not producing a rigid enough vehicular frame, a factfinder in another case might well hold the manufacturer liable for producing a frame that is too rigid. Yet, as pointed out at trial, in certain types of accidents—head-on collisions—it is desirable to have a car designed to collapse upon impact because the deformation would absorb much of the shock of the collision, and divert the force of deceleration away from the vehicle's passengers. In effect, this permits individual juries applying varying laws in different jurisdictions to set nationwide automobile safety standards and to impose on automobile manufacturers conflicting requirements. It would be difficult for members of the industry to alter their design and production behavior in response to jury verdicts in such cases, because their response might well be at variance with what some other jury decides is a defective design. Under these circumstances, the law imposes on the industry the responsibility of insuring vast numbers of persons involved in automobile accidents.

"Equally serious is the impact on other national social and economic goals of the existing case-by-case system of establishing automobile safety requirements. As we have become more dependent on foreign sources of energy, and as the price of that energy has increased, the attention of the federal government has been drawn to a search to find alternative supplies and the means of conserving energy. More recently, the domestic automobile industry has been struggling to compete with foreign manufacturers which have stressed smaller, more fuel-efficient cars. Yet, during this same period, Congress has permitted a system of regulation by ad hoc adjudications under which a jury can hold an automobile manufacturer culpable for not producing a car that is considerably heavier, and likely to have less fuel efficiency.

"In sum, this appeal has brought to our attention an important conflict that implicates broad national concerns. Although it is important that society devise a proper system for compensating those injured in automobile collisions, it is not at all clear that the present arrangement of permitting individual juries, under varying standards of liability, to impose this obligation on manufacturers is fair or efficient. * * * "

BROOKS v. BEECH AIRCRAFT CORP., 120 N.M. 372, 902 P.2d 54 (1995). "We adhere to the principle that evidence of industry custom or usage, and evidence of compliance with applicable regulations, is relevant to whether the manufacturer was negligent or whether the product poses an unreasonable risk of injury, but that such evidence should not conclusively demonstrate whether the manufacturer was negligent or the product was defective. * * *

" * * * Beech cautions that allowing juries to determine on a case-by-case basis whether a manufacturer is liable for adopting a particular design ' "permits individual juries applying varying laws in different jurisdictions to set nationwide ... safety standards and to impose on ... manufacturers conflicting requirements" ' [quoting Dawson v. Chrysler Corp., supra]. It is speculated that * * * one jury may decide that a windshield should have been designed to 'pop out' on impact, while another may determine that the windshield should have been designed to stay in place.

"We are persuaded to the contrary, that * * * the courts should continue to apply to products the general and traditional rules of relevance and materiality for all evidence upon which negligence and unreasonable risk of harm is to be decided. * * *

" * * * The general [jury] instruction on ordinary care in products liability actions, UJI 13–1405, provides in relevant part: 'Industry customs [standards] [codes] [rules] are evidence of ordinary care, but they are not conclusive.' Similarly, the general instruction on unreasonable risk provides: 'Industry customs [standards] [codes] [rules] are evidence of the acceptability of the risk, but they are not conclusive.' UJI 13–1408. These instructions should be given in cases involving a claimed defect in design.

" * * * Further, we hold that design-defect claims may be proved without showing that the manufacturer's design violated any applicable regulations, codes, or standards."

ALLISON v. MERCK & CO., INC., 110 Nev. 762, 878 P.2d 948 (1994). The product at issue was a vaccine used in a government-sponsored inoculation program. The vaccine manufacturer asserted the "government contractor defense." The Nevada Supreme Court said:

" * * * This defense is very ill-defined, and we see no justification for applying it to this case. Generally speaking, the defense has been made available to a manufacturer who contracts to produce a military product for the federal government. The idea is that sovereign immunity should be extended to private contractors acting pursuant to and in conformance with a government contract for military equipment. If such contractors can show that the government approved reasonably precise specifications for the product, that the specifications were followed, and that the manufacturer warned the government of dangers known to the manufacturer but not to the government, then, the government contractor defense may be success-fully interposed. Boyle v. United Technologies, 487 U.S. 500, 108 S.Ct. 2510 (1988). * * *

"Almost all of the cases relating to the government contractor defense are military cases in which the government has told the manufacturer how to make the product. * * *

"In Nielsen v. George Diamond Vogel Paint Co., 892 F.2d 1450 (9th Cir.1990), a civilian employee of the Army Corps of Engineers painted a dam in Idaho over a period of several years, using a certain type of paint. The employee was diagnosed as suffering from brain damage as a result of inhaling the toxic paint fumes. Nielsen brought suit against two paint manufacturers * * *. In denying the government contractor defense, the Ninth Circuit Court stated: 'We do not read Boyle to establish the broad immunity for all government procurement contractors urged by the defen-dants. . . . ' * * * Noting Justice Scalia's reasoning in Boyle, the court stated that the defense is most applicable where there is a need to '[avoid] scrutiny of sensitive military decisions, as, for example, the design of a fighter plane.' Of course, no such concerns apply here."

MEDTRONIC, INC. v. LOHR, 518 U.S. 470, 116 S.Ct. 2240, 135 L.Ed.2d 700 (1996). The recipient of a malfunctioning pacemaker (designed to control the heart's contractions) sued the manufacturer under Florida's law of products liability. The complaint asserted defective design, improper manufacture, and inadequate warning claims. The manufacturer argued that a federal statute which regulates medical devices such as pacemakers has the effect of precluding—by "pre-emption"—the operation of state tort law. The statute, called the Medical Device Amendments of 1976 (the Act), provides that "no State" may establish "any requirement * * * which is different from, or in addition to, any requirement applicable under [the Act]."

In the United States Supreme Court, *held* (5–4), that the Act, adminis-tered by the Food and Drug Administration (FDA), should not be read to pre-empt any of the common law claims asserted here. The majority opinion (Stevens, J.) said that interpretation of the Act's "pre-emptive language" should be guided by a "presumption against pre-emption," and emphasized that "[t]he purpose of Congress is the ultimate touchstone" in every pre-emption case.

In a concurring opinion Justice Breyer said that "basic pre-emption principles" support the conclusion that there is no pre-emption here:

" * * * Those principles make clear that a federal requirement pre-empts a state requirement if (1) the state requirement actually conflicts with the federal requirement—either because compliance with both is impossible, or because the state requirement 'stands as an obstacle to the accomplish-ment and execution of the full purposes and objectives of Congress'—or (2) the scheme of federal regulation is 'so pervasive as to make reasonable the inference that Congress left no room for the States to supplement it' [citations omitted]."

SECTION B. THE ROLE OF NEGLIGENCE

The materials of the prior section show the development of two notable aspects of the body of law dealing with design defect liability: "duality" and "strictness." Both duality and strictness are affirmed by the synoptic decision in Barker v. Lull Engineering Co., supra at p. 989.

"Duality" refers to the use of two separate tests for design defect, an expectation test and a balancing test. The expectation test asks whether a product's performance offends consumers' expectations about safety. The balancing test asks whether the risks of a challenged design outweigh its utility. "Strictness" refers to the fact that both tests may be the basis of strict liability, as opposed to liability for negligence. The expectation test, rooted in warranty law, does not inquire into a manufacturer's negligence. The balancing test also goes beyond negligence when it is administered by hindsight—that is, when knowledge of design risks available at the time of trial is imputed to the manufacturer.

Duality and strictness are rejected in the first main item of the present section, the *Restatement of Torts, Third: Products Liability*. The American Law Institute, author of the several restatements of American common law, has decided to restate the law of torts a third time, but not all at once. The initial project of the Third Restatement was to craft a new, self-contained exposition of products liability law. As excerpts below show, the Third Restatement rejects the consumer expectation test for design defect liability, leaving the balancing test as the sole general basis for such liability; and it disapproves application of the balancing test by hindsight, leaving design risks to be assessed by the same sort of analysis that is used to establish negligence.

The object of the present section is to canvass the views that collide in the contemporary debate, going on in courts and outside, about design defect law. This conflict of ideas centers on the question whether design defect assessment should be equivalent to negligence analysis. The Third Restatement sums up one side in the debate. The next main items are some statutes and a case which likewise push design liability toward negligence. The two main cases that complete the section consider, but decline to follow, the Third Restatement's lead; they embrace strictness, and also duality, and reaffirm the policies underlying these commitments.

RESTATEMENT OF TORTS, THIRD: PRODUCTS LIABILITY (1998)

§ 1.   Liability of Commercial Seller or Distributor for Harm Caused by Defective Products

One engaged in the business of selling or otherwise distributing products who sells or distributes a defective product is subject to liability for harm to persons or property caused by the defect.

§ 2.   Categories of Product Defect

A product is defective when, at the time of sale or distribution, it contains a manufacturing defect, is defective in design, or is defective because of inadequate instructions or warnings. A product:

(a) contains a manufacturing defect when the product departs from its intended design even though all possible care was exercised in the preparation and marketing of the product;

(b) is defective in design when the foreseeable risks of harm posed by the product could have been reduced or avoided by the adoption of a reasonable alternative design by the seller or other distributor, or a predecessor in the commercial chain of distribution, and the omission of the alternative design renders the product not reasonably safe;

(c) is defective because of inadequate instructions or warnings when the foreseeable risks of harm posed by the product could have been reduced or avoided by the provision of reasonable instructions or warnings by the seller or other distributor, or a predecessor in the commercial chain of distribution, and the omission of the instructions or warnings renders the product not reasonably safe.

Comment:

a. Rationale. The rules set forth in this Section [§ 2 above] establish separate standards of liability for manufacturing defects, design defects, and defects based on inadequate instructions or warnings. * * *

[The comment characterizes liability for a manufacturing defect, under section 2(a), as "strict liability" or "liability without fault." Product sellers are made "strictly liable for harm caused by manufacturing defects." Section 2(a), "by eliminating the issue of manufacturer fault from plaintiff's case," imposes liability "even if the plaintiff is unable to show that the manufacturer's quality control fails to meet risk-utility norms." Legal responsibility is independent of "standards of reasonableness."]

In contrast to manufacturing defects, design defects and defects based on inadequate instructions or warnings are predicated on a different concept of responsibility. In the first place, such defects cannot be determined by reference to the manufacturer's own design or marketing standards because those standards are the very ones that plaintiffs attack as unreasonable. Some sort of independent assessment of advantages and disadvantages, to which some attach the label "risk-utility balancing," is necessary. Products are not generically defective merely because they are dangerous. Many product-related accident costs can be eliminated only by excessively sacrificing product features that make the products useful and desirable. Thus, * * * trade-offs need to be considered * * *.

Subsections (b) and (c) [of § 2], which impose liability for products that are defectively designed or sold without adequate warnings or instructions and are thus not reasonably safe, achieve the same general objectives as does liability predicated on negligence. The emphasis is on creating incentives for manufacturers to achieve optimal levels of safety in designing and marketing products. Society does not benefit from products that are excessively safe—for example, automobiles designed with maximum speeds of 20 miles per hour—any more than it benefits from products that are too risky. Society benefits most when the right, or optimal, amount of product safety is achieved. * * *

In general, the rationale for imposing strict liability on manufacturers for harm caused by manufacturing defects does not apply in the context of imposing liability for defective design and defects based on inadequate instruction or warning. * * * A reasonably designed product still carries with it elements of risk that must be protected against by the user or consumer since some risks cannot be designed out of the product at reasonable cost.

Most courts agree that, for the liability system to be fair and efficient, the balancing of risks and benefits in judging product design and marketing must be done in light of the knowledge of risks and risk-avoidance techniques reasonably attainable at the time of distribution. To hold a manufacturer liable for a risk that was not foreseeable when the product was marketed might foster increased manufacturer investment in safety. But such investment by definition would be a matter of guesswork. Furthermore, manufacturers may persuasively ask to be judged by a normative behavior standard to which it is reasonably possible for manufacturers to conform. For these reasons, Subsections (b) and (c) speak of products being defective only when risks were reasonably foreseeable.

d. Design defects: general considerations. * * * Subsection (b) adopts a reasonableness ("risk-utility balancing") test as the standard for judging the defectiveness of product designs. More specifically, the test is whether a reasonable alternative design would, at reasonable cost, have reduced the foreseeable risks of harm posed by the product and, if so, whether the omission of the alternative design * * * rendered the product not reasonably safe. * * * Under prevailing rules concerning allocation of burden of proof, the plaintiff must prove that such a reasonable alternative was, or reasonably could have been, available at time of sale or distribution. * * *

Assessment of a product design in most instances requires a comparison between an alternative design and the product design that caused the injury, undertaken from the viewpoint of a reasonable person. That standard is also used in administering the traditional reasonableness standard in negligence. See Restatement, Second, Torts § 283, Comment c. The policy reasons that support use of a reasonable person perspective in connection with the general negligence standard also support its use in the products liability context.

* * * [Section 2(b)] states that a design is defective if the product could have been made safer by the adoption of a reasonable alternative design. If such a design could have been practically adopted at the time of sale * * *, the plaintiff establishes defect under Subsection (b). When a defendant demonstrates that its product design was the safest in use at the time of sale, it may be difficult for the plaintiff to prove that an alternative design could have been practically adopted. The defendant is thus allowed to introduce evidence with regard to industry practice that bears on whether an alternative design was practicable. * * * While such evidence is admissible, it is not necessarily dispositive. If the plaintiff introduces expert testimony to establish that a reasonable alternative design could practically have been adopted, a trier of fact may conclude that the product was defective notwithstanding

that such a design was not adopted by any manufacturer, or even considered for commercial use, at the time of sale.

f. Design defects: factors relevant in determining whether the omission of a reasonable alternative design renders a product not reasonably safe. Subsection (b) states that a product is defective in design if the omission of a reasonable alternative design renders the product not reasonably safe. A broad range of factors may be considered in determining whether an alternative design is reasonable and whether its omission renders a product not reasonably safe. The factors include, among others, the magnitude and probability of the foreseeable risks of harm, the instructions and warnings accompanying the product, and the nature and strength of consumer expectations regarding the product, including expectations arising from product portrayal and marketing. See Comment *g.* The relative advantages and disadvantages of the product as designed and as it alternatively could have been designed may also be considered. Thus, the likely effects of the alternative design on production costs; the effects of the alternative design on product longevity, maintenance, repair, and esthetics; and the range of consumer choice among products are factors that may be taken into account. A plaintiff is not necessarily required to introduce proof on all of these factors; their relevance, and the relevance of other factors, will vary from case to case. * * *

In sum, the requirement of Subsection (b) that a product is defective in design if the foreseeable risks of harm could have been reduced by a reasonable alternative design is based on the commonsense notion that liability for harm caused by product designs should attach only when harm is reasonably preventable. * * *

g. Consumer expectations: general considerations. Under Subsection (b), consumer expectations do not constitute an independent standard for judging the defectiveness of product designs. Courts frequently rely, in part, on consumer expectations when discussing liability based on other theories of liability. * * * However, consumer expectations do not play a determinative role in determining defectiveness. See Comment *h.* Consumer expectations, standing alone, do not take into account whether the proposed alternative design could be implemented at reasonable cost, or whether an alternative design would provide greater overall safety. Nevertheless, consumer expectations about product performance and the dangers attendant to product use affect how risks are perceived and relate to foreseeability and frequency of the risks of harm, both of which are relevant under Subsection (b). * * *

h. Consumer expectations: food products and used products. With regard to two special product categories consumer expectations play a special role in determining product defect. * * * On occasion it is difficult to determine whether a given food component is an inherent aspect of a product or constitutes an adulteration of the product. Whether, for example, a fish bone in commercially distributed fish chowder constitutes a manufacturing defect within the meaning of § 2(a) is best determined by focusing on reasonable consumer expectations.

* * * On occasion the seller of a used product may market the product in a manner that would cause a reasonable person in the position of the buyer to expect the used product to present no greater risk of defect than if it were new * * *. [Then] it is appropriate to treat the sale under rules similar to those applicable to new products. * * *

MISSTATEMENT OF THE LAW? It is a perplexing question how one can "restate" the law developed by courts in an unequivocal way if the courts are in fact sharply divided on matters to be "restated." One approach is to count cases in order to find the "majority view," but this is difficult when caselaw is complex, contains multiple strands, and is readable by skillful lawyers different ways. Certainly design defect caselaw is complex, containing strands of negligence and strict liability, of contract and tort. Undeniably, a debate about the right rendering of this law is going on.

One critique of the Third Restatement counts the design cases very differently from the restaters. See Vandall, The Restatement (Third) of Torts, Products Liability, Section 2(b): Design Defect, 68 Temple L.Rev. 167 (1995). According to this critique, the following propositions (italicized in the original) are true: "a majority of jurisdictions do not support the [exclusive] use of risk-utility balancing in design defect cases"; "a majority of the jurisdictions do not support the reasonable-alternative-design requirement"; "the jurisdictions are split evenly on whether a seller should be charged with knowledge at the time of sale or the time of trial." On the last point the author says:

> The issue whether the manufacturer should be held to know of a risk at the date of trial or the date of sale is a subject that is presently being debated in the courts. By selecting the date-of-sale approach the reporters [of the Third Restatement] essentially rewrote strict liability law into negligence * * *.

POTTER v. CHICAGO PNEUMATIC TOOL CO., 241 Conn. 199, 694 A.2d 1319 (1997). In rejecting the Third Restatement's requirement that plaintiff must show a reasonable alternative design in order to establish design defect, the court said:

"Our research reveals that, of the jurisdictions that have considered the role of feasible alternative designs in design defect cases: (1) six jurisdictions affirmatively state that a plaintiff need not show a feasible alternative design in order to establish a manufacturer's liability for design defect; (2) sixteen jurisdictions hold that a feasible alternative design is merely one of several factors that the jury may consider in determining whether a product design is defective; (3) three jurisdictions require the defendant, not the plaintiff, to prove that the product was not defective; and (4) eight jurisdictions require that the plaintiff prove a feasible alternative design in order to establish a prima facie case of design defect [citations omitted]."

GREEN v. SMITH & NEPHEW AHP, 245 Wis.2d 772, 629 N.W.2d 727 (2001). The court rejected the approach of Section 2(b) of the Third

Restatement requiring that "foreseeability of risk of harm" be shown and "a risk-benefit test" be used to establish design defect liability. "Where a manufacturer places a defective and unreasonably dangerous product into the stream of commerce, the manufacturer, not the injured consumer, should bear the costs of the risks posed by the product. Because 2(b) unduly obstructs this equitable principle, we refuse to adopt 2(b) into Wisconsin law."

"We note that there has been considerable controversy over the *Restatement (Third) of Torts* § 2(b). *See, e.g.*, Marshall S. Shapo, *A New Legislation: Remarks on the Draft Restatement of Products Liability*, 30 U.Mich. J.L. Reform 215, 218 (1997) (stating that the *Restatement (Third) of Torts* is not a description of the existing law, but rather is the creation of drafters who acted as 'a sounding board for essentially political discussion'); Frank J. Vandall, *Constructing a Roof Before the Foundation is Prepared: The Restatement (Third) of Torts: Products Liability Section 2(b) Design Defect*, 30 U.Mich. J.L. Reform 261, 261–65 (1997) (characterizing § 2(b) as 'a wish list from manufacturing America' in which '[m]essy and awkward concepts such as precedent, policy, and case accuracy have been brushed aside for the purpose of tort reform'); Symposium, *A Critical Analysis of the Proposed Restatement (Third) of Torts: Products Liability*, 21 Wm. Mitchell L.Rev. 411, 412–13, 419–20 (1995) (criticizing § 2(b) as being 'a vehicle for social reform' rather than a restatement of the existing law, and citing numerous articles with similar observations)."

RESTRICTIVE PRODUCTS STATUTES

Some states have enacted statutory provisions which restrict design defect liability by controlling the time frame of design assessment. The time frame of assessment may determine the outcome when courts and juries apply the balancing test for design defect. Balancing asks whether the risks of a design feature are prudent in light of the design's utility, and in light of any alternative, safer designs.

A balancer might consider only those risks of a challenged design, and those design alternatives, which were actually known—or reasonably knowable—at the time of the product's manufacture or marketing. Such balancing is equivalent to negligence analysis. Or a balancer might consider all product risks and alternative techniques that are known at the time of trial, even if they were not reasonably knowable at an earlier date. The latter sort of balancing is done by hindsight, and "hindsight balancing" may go beyond negligence.

Two kinds of restrictive statutes operate to block hindsight balancing. Each type has been adopted in several states. "State of the art" provisions shield a manufacturer from design liability, presumptively or completely, if its product conformed to the state of the art at the time of manufacture or marketing. "Alternative design" provisions require a design defect claimant to show that an alternative, safer design was available at the time the challenged product was manufactured or sold.

Following are examples of such enactments. Notice that these statutes affect, not just balancing by hindsight, but also conventional negligence analysis as well.

State of the art provisions:

Colorado Revised Statutes Section 13–21–403(1):

In any product liability action, it shall be rebuttably presumed that the product which caused the injury, death, or property damage was not defective and that the manufacturer or seller thereof was not negligent if the product: (a) Prior to sale by the manufacturer, conformed to the state of the art, as distinguished from industry standards, applicable to such product in existence at the time of sale * * *.

Kentucky Revised Statutes Section 411.310(2):

In any product liability action, it shall be presumed, until rebutted by a preponderance of the evidence to the contrary, that the product was not defective if the design, methods of manufacture, and testing conformed to the generally recognized and prevailing standards or the state of the art in existence at the time the design was prepared, and the product was manufactured.

Nebraska Revised Statutes Section 25–21,182:

In any product liability action based upon negligent or defective design, testing, or labeling, proof establishing that such design, testing, or labeling was in conformity with the generally recognized and prevailing state of the art in the industry at the time the specific product involved in the action was first sold to any person not engaged in the business of selling such product shall be a defense. State of the art as used in this section shall be defined as the best technology reasonably available at the time.

Alternative design provisions:

New Jersey Statutes Annotated Section 2A:58c–3:

a. In any product liability action against a manufacturer or seller for harm allegedly caused by a product that was designed in a defective manner, the manufacturer or seller shall not be liable if: (1) At the time the product left the control of the manufacturer, there was not a practical and technically feasible alternative design that would have prevented the harm without substantially impairing the reasonably anticipated or intended function of the product * * *.

b. The provisions of paragraph (1) of subsection a. of this section shall not apply if the court, on the basis of clear and convincing evidence, makes all of the following determinations: (1) The product is egregiously unsafe or ultra-hazardous; (2) The ordinary user or consumer of the product cannot reasonably be expected to have knowledge of the product's risks, or the product poses a risk of serious injury to persons other than the user or consumer; and (3) The product has little or no usefulness.

Texas Civil Practice and Remedies Code Ann. Section 82.005:

(a) In a products liability action in which a claimant alleges a design defect, the burden is on the claimant to prove by a preponderance of the evidence that: (1) there was a safer alternative design * * *.

(b) In this section, "safer alternative design" means a product design other than the one actually used that in reasonable probability: (1) would have prevented or significantly reduced the risk of [injury] without substantially impairing the product's utility; and (2) was economically and technologically feasible at the time the product left the control of the manufacturer or seller by the application of existing or reasonably achievable scientific knowledge. * * *

(d) This section does not apply to: (1) a cause of action based on a toxic or environmental tort * * *; or (2) a drug or device, as those terms are defined in the federal Food, Drug, and Cosmetic Act * * *.

———

STATUTES OF LIMITATION AND REPOSE. One way of limiting manufacturers' liability for defective products—and the cost of liability insurance—is the blunt method of limiting the time during which a claim may be brought. A statute of limitation does this by saying that claims for product injury must be brought to court within some number of years after the date of injury, or the date the cause of action arises. A different but related approach has been adopted in a number of states: the statute of repose. A statute of repose says a product claim must be brought within so many years after the injuring product was manufactured or sold. For example, an Indiana statute provides that "a product liability action must be commenced * * * within ten (10) years after the delivery of the product to the initial user or consumer." Ind. Code Ann. § 33–1–1.5–5(b).

The effect of a statute of repose, as noted in Hazine v. Montgomery Elevator Co., 176 Ariz. 340, 861 P.2d 625 (1993), is that a claim may be "abolished before any injury occurs." In *Hazine* the plaintiff was injured while working on an escalator manufactured by defendant. Plaintiff sued, alleging negligence and strict products liability, "well within" the 2–year statute of limitation. But the escalator had been made and sold more than 12 years prior to the accident, so plaintiff's strict liability action was blocked by Arizona's statute of repose, which provided:

> * * * no product liability action may be commenced and prosecuted if the cause of action accrues more than twelve years after the product was first sold for use or consumption, unless the cause of action is based upon the negligence of the manufacturer or seller or a breach of an express warranty * * *.

Plaintiff argued that the statute of repose violated a clause of the Arizona Constitution of 1912 which says, "The right of action to recover damages for injuries shall never be abrogated * * *." The Arizona Supreme Court (4–1) agreed, and held the statute to be constitutionally invalid. The court wrote:

Strict products liability developed because other theories of recovery proved inadequate to protect injured users and consumers. Thus, a right to sue in negligence or express warranty is not a reasonable alternative to a products liability action.

Defendant had contended that the anti-abrogation clause of 1912 should not apply to strict products liability, developed by Arizona courts in the 1960's. The court rejoined (quoting with approval): "All that has happened since 1912 is the logical application of Rylands v. Fletcher's strict liability theory to the right to bring a product liability action."

BANKS v. ICI AMERICAS, INC.
Supreme Court of Georgia, 1994.
264 Ga. 732, 450 S.E.2d 671.

[A nine-year-old boy died after consuming a quantity of rat poison, thinking it was candy. The rat poison product, called Talon–G, was manufactured by ICI Americas, Inc. The child found the poison pellets in an unmarked container in a cabinet at a Boy's Club, where the container had been put by a pest control company. The poison, an anticoagulant, was designed to be slow-acting; the boy suffered no symptoms for several days; by the time doctors traced his ensuing condition (unstoppable bleeding) to rat poison, it was too late for the antidote to work.

[The boy's parents brought a products liability suit against ICI, the rodenticide manufacturer, alleging defective design. (Claims against the boy's club and the pest control company were settled.) At trial ICI sought to prove that, at the time the poison at issue was manufactured, no safer alternative design was feasible. Plaintiffs' trial evidence is summarized in the following paragraph from a Court of Appeals opinion, 440 S.E.2d 38, 43:

["Although it was foreseeable that the rat poison would be consumed by children who mistook it for candy, ICI failed to add an emetic or an aversive agent to the product. Plaintiffs produced expert testimony that an emetic will cause any human who ingests the poison to immediately vomit, thereby expelling the poison, but will not have the same effect on rats because they do not have a vomit reflex. They also submitted expert evidence that the aversive agent Bitrex would make the poison taste bad to children but would not keep rats from eating it; that Bitrex was in use in a variety of products as early as the late 1970's; and that there was no reason ICI could not have begun testing its use in rat poison at that time."

[The jury found for plaintiffs and awarded compensatory damages plus $1 million punitive damages. The Court of Appeals reversed, holding that there was no liability for inherent design risks of useful products if an adequate warning (here to the pest control company) were given: "[t]here is no requirement" imposing design liability "solely because ICI did not make the product safer." This ruling was in turn reversed by the Georgia Supreme Court. Excerpts from the Supreme Court's opinion which follow explain the general approach to be used in a Georgia design defect case.]

HUNSTEIN, Justice.

* * *

* * * Unlike a manufacturing defect case, wherein it is assumed that the design of the product is safe and had the product been manufactured in accordance with the design it would have been safe for consumer use, in a design defect case the entire product line may be called into question and there is typically no readily ascertainable external measure of defectiveness. It is only in design defect cases that the court is called upon to supply the standard for defectiveness: the term "defect" in design defect cases is an expression of the legal conclusion to be reached, rather than a test for reaching that conclusion. Wade, On Product Design Defects and Their Actionability, 33 Vand.L.Rev. 551, 552 (1980); 2 American Law of Products Liability 3d (1987), § 28:1.

* * *

To arrive at the appropriate test for reaching the legal conclusion that a product's design specifications were partly or totally defective, this Court has conducted an exhaustive review of foreign jurisdictions and learned treatises. That review has revealed a general consensus regarding the utilization in design defect cases of a balancing test whereby the risks inherent in a product design are weighed against the utility or benefit derived from the product. See, e.g., 1 Am. L. Prod. Liab., § 1:49; Preliminary Draft No. 1 (April 20, 1993), Restatement (Third) of Torts: Products Liability, § 101, Reporters' Notes to Comment G * * *. This risk-utility analysis incorporates the concept of "reasonableness," i.e., whether the manufacturer acted reasonably in choosing a particular product design, given the probability and seriousness of the risk posed by the design, the usefulness of the product in that condition, and the burden on the manufacturer to take the necessary steps to eliminate the risk. * * *

The balancing test that forms the risk-utility analysis is * * * consistent with Georgia law, which has long applied negligence principles in making the determination whether a product was defectively designed.[3] Accord Hunt v. Harley–Davidson Motor Co., 147 Ga.App. 44(4), 248 S.E.2d 15 (1978), in which it was noted that "[a]lthough the benefits of safer products are certainly desirable, there is a point at which they are outweighed by the cost of attaining them." Therefore, because the risk-utility analysis is consistent with Georgia law and represents the overwhelming consensus among courts deciding design defect cases, 1 Am. L. Prod. Liab., supra at § 1:50, we conclude that the better approach is to evaluate design defectiveness under

---

3. * * * While we recognize that the determination of whether a product was defective (involving the reasonableness of a manufacturer's design decisions), which is a basic inquiry for strict liability purposes, generally will overlap the determination of whether the manufacturer's conduct was reasonable, which is a basic inquiry for negligence purposes, we cannot agree that the use of negligence principles to determine whether the design of a product was

"defective" necessarily obliterates under every conceivable factual scenario the distinction Georgia law has long recognized between negligence and strict liability theories of liability. See * * * OCGA § 51–1–11(b)(2) and (c) (creating exceptions to statute of repose in negligence claims not applicable to strict liability claims). Hence, we see no reason to conclude definitively that the two theories merge in design defect cases.

a test balancing the risks inherent in a product design against the utility of the product so designed. Hence, we hereby adopt the risk-utility analysis.

* * * One factor consistently recognized as integral to the assessment of the utility of a design is the availability of alternative designs, in that the existence and feasibility of a safer and equally efficacious design diminishes the justification for using a challenged design. O'Brien v. Muskin Corp., 463 A.2d 298, 305 (N.J.1983). * * * Indeed, the reasonableness of choosing from among various alternative product designs and adopting the safest one if it is feasible is considered the "heart" of design defect cases, 78 ALR 4th 154, § 2, since it is only at their most extreme that design defect cases reflect the position that a product is simply so dangerous that it should not have been made available at all. See O'Brien, supra, 463 A.2d at 306; Prosser and Keeton, The Law of Torts (5th ed.) § 96, pp. 688–689.

We agree with the importance placed on the alternative safer design factor and now hold that in determining whether a product was defectively designed, the trier of fact may consider evidence establishing that at the time the product was manufactured, an alternative design would have made the product safer than the original design and was a marketable reality and technologically feasible. * * *

* * *

[Reversed and remanded for consideration of other issues.]

FLETCHER, Justice, concurring in part and dissenting in part.

* * *

I write to emphasize that an essential element of a plaintiff's cause of action is proof that the "seller . . . failed to adopt a reasonable, safer design that would have reduced the foreseeable risks of harm presented by the product." See Preliminary Draft No. 1 (April 20, 1993), Restatement (Third) of Torts: Products Liability, § 101 * * *. [B]y suggesting that a safer feasible alternative is a mere factor to be considered, rather than an essential element, the majority endorses a standard that is inconsistent with the reality that although "[m]any products can not be made completely safe for use and some can not be made safe at all . . . such products may be useful and desirable." Center Chemical Co. v. Parzini, 234 Ga. 868, 870, 218 S.E.2d 580 (1975).

* * * In order to demonstrate proximate cause, proof that the alternative design provides a "materially significant increase in safety" that would have prevented or reduced the plaintiff's injury is required, rather than evidence that the alternative design merely "could have" prevented the injury, as the majority suggests. See Restatement [Third], supra, * * *.

———

OGLETREE v. NAVISTAR INT'L TRANSP. CORP., 269 Ga. 443, 500 S.E.2d 570 (1998). The Georgia Supreme Court characterized its decision in *Banks v. ICI Americas*, supra: "[T]his court's mandate in *Banks* [is] that the product's risk must be weighed against its utility. Furthermore, that mandate incorporates the concept of 'reasonableness' and applies negligence principles to the determination of whether a product [design] is defective for strict liability purposes. Thus, the distinction between negligence and strict liability is not significant * * *."

GAWENDA v. WERNER CO., 127 F.3d 1102 (6th Cir.1997) (per curiam), *aff'g* 932 F.Supp. 183 (E.D.Mich.1996). "Plaintiffs, Daniel and Audrey Gawenda, appeal the district court's grant of summary judgment for defendant, Werner Company. * * * The Gawendas sued for product liability under a design defect theory, but the district court granted summary judgment because they failed to show the utility of alternative designs. * * *

"Werner manufactures an eight-foot aluminum stepladder. * * * Daniel Gawenda injured himself when he fell from one of these ladders. The Gawendas sued Werner and claimed that Werner designed the stepladder defectively. The Gawendas alleged that Werner should have built more rigid rear rails into the ladder. The Gawendas, however, offered no stepladder that used more rigid rear rails than Werner's. Moreover, the Gawendas' expert presented no evidence describing the feasibility of alternative designs.

* * *

"Michigan law governs this diversity action. Michigan employs a pure negligence, risk-utility test in design defect cases. *Prentis v. Yale Mfg. Co.*, 365 N.W.2d 176, 185–86 (Mich.1984). To establish a *prima facie* case, a plaintiff must include evidence concerning 'the utility or relative safety of the proposed alternatives, or evidence otherwise concerning the "unreasonableness" of risks arising from [the alleged defect].' *Owens v. Allis–Chalmers Corp.*, 326 N.W.2d 372, 379 (Mich.1982).

" * * * Because the Gawendas failed to present evidence concerning the reasonableness of their proposed alternative designs, this court AFFIRMS."

BROOKS v. BEECH AIRCRAFT CORP.
Supreme Court of New Mexico, 1995.
120 N.M. 372, 902 P.2d 54.

RANSOM, Justice.

As personal representative of her deceased husband, Virginia Brooks brought a wrongful death action against Beech Aircraft Corporation in connection with a 1988 plane crash. In relevant part Brooks sued in negligence and strict liability for an alleged design defect, claiming that the absence of shoulder harnesses caused the death of Thomas Brooks. The trial court granted Beech Aircraft's motion for summary judgment and Brooks appeals * * *. We hold that a design-defect claim may be brought in both negligence and strict liability, and we further hold that such claim may be proved without showing that the manufacturer has violated regulations, codes, or standards applicable to the 1968 plane that crashed. Finding disputed issues of material fact precluding summary judgment on the questions of negligence and unreasonable risk, we reverse and remand.

Thomas Brooks died on August 2, 1988, when the 1968 Beech Musketeer he was piloting crashed near Cimarron, New Mexico. Mr. Brooks bought his Musketeer used in 1984. Although his plane was equipped with lap belts, it was neither designed nor equipped with shoulder harnesses. When the Musketeer was designed, manufactured, and sold in 1968, Federal Aviation Administration (FAA) regulations did not require the installation of shoulder harnesses in "general aviation" aircraft such as the Musketeer. Further, no aircraft industry standard or guideline applicable at that time required the installation of such harnesses. The FAA did not adopt a regulation requiring the installation of shoulder harnesses in the front seats of general aviation aircraft until 1977, and this regulation applied only to planes manufactured after July 18, 1978. * * *

Brooks filed suit in 1990 * * *. [She] claimed that the absence of shoulder harnesses rendered the plane not crashworthy and that, while not causing her husband's plane to crash, the absence of shoulder harnesses proximately caused enhanced injury resulting in her husband's death. At the close of discovery Beech moved for summary judgment * * *.

In response to the motion for summary judgment, Brooks presented the deposition of Dr. Richard G. Snyder, a forensic anthropologist who testified that Beech Aircraft had developed a workable shoulder harness as early as 1951. Dr. Snyder also testified that Beech had included shoulder restraints as standard equipment on some of its aircraft before 1968. Finally, stating that he had considered the "state of the art" in 1968 and that he had determined shoulder harnesses were available when Mr. Brooks' plane was designed and manufactured, Dr. Snyder expressed the opinion that the Musketeer was not crashworthy without shoulder harnesses * * *.

* * * The trial court * * * concluded that enhanced-injury claims sound only in negligence and that negligence in design must be proved by showing the product violated the government regulations or industry standards applicable at the time of design * * *.

[New Mexico, like "the majority of jurisdictions," has adopted the "crashworthiness" theory of liability developed by] the landmark decision of Larsen v. General Motors Corp., 391 F.2d 495, 502 (8th Cir.1968). Reasoning that it is readily foreseeable that an automobile will be involved in an accident and that a user will be injured—often as a result of a "second collision" with the interior of the automobile—the court held that a user may recover damages for enhanced injury if, even though an alleged design defect did not cause the injury-producing accident, the victim can show that the defect proximately caused an injury more severe in degree than would have resulted had the defect not been present. Id.

* * *

* * * [T]he issue before us has been briefed and argued not so much as whether all crashworthiness liability should be limited to negligence, but whether all design-defect liability should be so limited. * * *

* * *

Beech and supporting amici point out that in determining whether a product is defectively designed there is an inherent difficulty that does not arise when determining whether that same product contains a manufacturing flaw. In the case of a manufacturing flaw the product leaves the manufacturer's hands in a condition unintended by the manufacturer. * * * By contrast, in the case of a design defect, the product leaves the manufacturer's hands in the exact condition intended by the manufacturer. Thus, "while manufacturing flaws can be evaluated against the intended design of the product, no such objective standard exists in the design defect context." Caterpillar Tractor Co. v. Beck, 593 P.2d 871, 880 (Alaska 1979).

Beech contends that precisely because there is no objective standard of defectiveness in the design context, the concept of defect may be understood only by reference to the manufacturer's conduct; whether a design is "safe enough" depends on the reasonableness of the manufacturer's choice between safety and other imperatives such as price and product utility. Thus Beech contends that negligence is the appropriate standard by which to measure a supplier's liability for defective design.

Beech also contends that negligence must be adopted as the sole standard of liability to avoid depriving the public of useful and beneficial products. * * *

* * *

Since Greenman v. Yuba Power Products, Inc., 59 Cal.2d 57, 27 Cal. Rptr. 697, 377 P.2d 897 (1963) (in bank), nearly every American jurisdiction has adopted some form of strict liability in tort as a measure of manufacturer responsibility for injuries caused by defective products. See, e.g., Stang v. Hertz Corp., 83 N.M. 730, 735, 497 P.2d 732, 737 (1972) (adopting strict liability in tort). * * *

The policy of risk-or cost-distribution continues to serve as a primary basis for imposing strict products liability. Thus, in adhering to strict liability as an appropriate standard of liability for a manufacturer's failure to include a safety device in the design of a sheet metal rolling machine, the New Jersey Supreme Court observed that "[s]trict liability in a sense is but an attempt to minimize the costs of accidents and to consider who should bear those costs." Suter v. San Angelo Foundry & Mach. Co., 81 N.J. 150, 406 A.2d 140, 151 (1979); see also Azzarello v. Black Bros. Co., 480 Pa. 547, 391 A.2d 1020, 1023 (1978) (concluding that "the realities of our economic society as it exists today force the conclusion that the risk of loss for injury resulting from defective products should be borne by the suppliers, principally because they are in a position to absorb the loss by distributing it as a cost of doing business").

* * *

* * * [I]mposing strict products liability serves the interests of fairness. As articulated by the New Jersey Supreme Court in Beshada v. Johns–Manville Products Corp., 90 N.J. 191, 447 A.2d 539, 549 (1982):

The burden of illness from dangerous products such as asbestos should be placed upon those who profit from its production and, more generally, upon society at large, which reaps the benefits of the various products our economy manufactures. That burden should not be imposed exclusively on the innocent victim.

The fairness rationale embodies a normative judgment that plaintiffs injured by an unreasonably dangerous product should be compensated for their injuries. At the heart of this judgment lies the conclusion that although the manufacturer has provided a valuable service by supplying the public with a product that it wants or needs, it is more fair that the cost of an unreasonable risk of harm lie with the product and its possibly innocent manufacturer than it is to visit the entire loss upon the often unsuspecting consumer who has relied upon the expertise of the manufacturer when selecting the injury-producing product.

* * *

Beech contends that in the case of injuries caused by defectively designed products, manufacturers are neither able to pass on to consumers the cost of such injuries nor able to insure themselves against losses occasioned by such injuries. Beech speculates that injuries caused by a design defect are more likely to occur several years after the injury-producing product has hit the market than are injuries caused by a manufacturing flaw. In the interim the manufacturer may have replaced the injury-producing design with an alternative design that does not pose the same risk of injury. Beech thus argues that it is impossible for the manufacturer to pass on the cost of injury from a replaced product. * * *

* * * As noted by West Virginia's highest court, however, actual behavior demonstrates that manufacturers collect a "product liability premium" at the time of sale. Blankenship v. General Motors Corp., 185 W.Va. 350, 406 S.E.2d 781, 784 (1991) (noting that General Motors collects a "product liability premium" each time it sells a vehicle). Because "product liability is concerned with spreading the cost of inevitable accidents" and because such cost spreading actually occurs, id. 406 S.E.2d at 784–85, West Virginia has adopted strict products liability as the standard in design-defect cases. Id. at 786 * * *. As long as the price of a defective product line or successive product lines reflect some element of injury costs, the policy goal of cost distribution has been served.

* * *

* * * [S]trict liability against manufacturers for injuries caused by defective product design also furthers the goal of achieving a fair allocation of the risk of loss. * * * Whether the product user's injury is caused by a manufacturing flaw or a design defect, this Court must still answer a fundamental policy question: To whom as between two innocent parties should the risk of loss from product-related injuries be allocated? When answering this policy question in cases involving manufacturing flaws, courts have concluded almost unanimously that although the manufacturer may have exercised reasonable care in its manufacturing and quality control operations, because the manufacturer is in a better position than the consumer to control product risks and because the manufacturer has profited from the sale of the injury-producing product, the manufacturer should bear the risk of loss.

* * * In the case of design defects, as in the case of manufacturing flaws, the manufacturer controls the design decision and is in a better position than the consumer to control the amount of risk that the product contains. Similarly, as in the case of a defectively manufactured product, the manufacturer of a defectively designed product has profited from its sale. Under these circumstances, it is only fair that the manufacturer bear the loss from product related injuries that are proved to result from an unreasonable risk of injury attributable to product design.

* * *

* * * In New Mexico * * * [w]e have for fifteen years rejected the definitions of "defect"—"defect is defect," "consumer expectations," "risk-utility," "reasonable alternative"—that have fueled much of the controversy as product-supply interests strike back at liability for defective products. Our "unreasonable-risk-of-injury" test seems to have allowed for proof and argument under any rational theory of defect.

Under the current product liability jury instructions, SCRA 1986, 13–1401 to 13–1433 (Repl.Pamp.1991), the jury is instructed that a supplier's liability is measured by "an unreasonable risk of injury resulting from a condition of the product or from a manner of its use." UJI 13–1406. As to either flaw or design, the jury is informed that "an unreasonable risk of injury is a risk which a reasonably prudent person having full knowledge of the risk would find unacceptable." UJI 13–1407. * * *

* * *

* * * The proposed Restatement (Third) of Torts: Products Liability § 2(b), at 9, 13 cmt. a (Tentative Draft No. 1, 1994) adopts [the position] that " * * * the balancing of risk in judging product design and marketing must be done in light of the knowledge of risks and risk-avoidance techniques reasonably attainable at the time of distribution. * * * " Hence, * * * the proposed Restatement advocate[s] a negligence approach to design defects.

* * * The distinction between the negligence approach proposed by the Restatement and strict liability is the time frame in which the risk-benefit calculation is made. * * *

In most instances a manufacturer is aware of the risks posed by any given design and of the availability of an alternative design. This case is a perfect example; Dr. Snyder testified that Beech had developed and used a workable shoulder harness prior to the design and manufacture of Mr. Brooks' plane. * * *

Further, in those hypothetical instances in which technology known at the time of trial and technology knowable at the time of distribution differ * * * it is more fair that the manufacturers and suppliers who have profited from the sale of the product bear the risk of loss. Given the risk-benefit calculation on which the jury is instructed in New Mexico, and the policy considerations that favor strict products liability, we believe that it is logical and consistent to take the same approach to design defects as to manufacturing flaws. * * *

* * *

SOULE v. GENERAL MOTORS CORP., 8 Cal.4th 548, 882 P.2d 298, 34 Cal.Rptr.2d 607 (1994). On a rainy day, another car skidded into the path of plaintiff's car. The resulting collision caused plaintiff's left front wheel to break free, collapse rearward, and smash the floorboard into her feet. Plaintiff suffered severe ankle fractures; one ankle joint had eventually to be fused, so plaintiff can walk only with considerable difficulty. Plaintiff brought suit against the manufacturer of her automobile to recover damages for "enhanced collision injuries caused by an uncrashworthy vehicle." She alleged that the design of the bracket that attached the car's wheel assembly to its frame, and the design of the frame, were defective because they permitted the wheel to tear loose and to thrust rearward into the floorboard. The jury found for plaintiff. The intermediate appellate court affirmed.

On review in the California Supreme Court, the manufacturer urged reconsideration of the holding of Barker v. Lull Engineering Co. (p. 989 supra) that "the manufacturer has the burden of proving that the utility of the challenged design outweighs its dangers." This holding was embodied in the "standard instruction" given to the jury at trial. *Held*, affirmed. The Supreme Court noted two reasons in favor of "placement of the risk-benefit burden on the manufacturer." First, the considerations which influence product design are "peculiarly within" the knowledge of the manufacturer. Second, as emphasized in *Barker*, the "fundamental policies" of products liability prescribe that a manufacturer who seeks to escape design defect liability on risk-benefit grounds "should bear the burden of persuading the trier of fact that its product should not be judged defective."

IN RE HAWAII FEDERAL ASBESTOS CASES, 960 F.2d 806 (9th Cir.1992), aff'g 699 F.Supp. 233 (D.Hawai'i 1988). Products liability claims were brought by or on behalf of persons who were exposed to asbestos dust while serving in the United States Navy, at the Pearl Harbor Naval Shipyard and elsewhere, and who suffered asbestosis or cancer as a result. Defendants supplied insulation products containing asbestos to the Navy during World War II and after. In these suits arising under Hawaii law, plaintiffs alleged defective design, because product dangers were greater than users would expect, and also failure to warn of product risks.

Defendants sought to introduce evidence showing that they were not aware of health risks posed by asbestos until the 1960's, and that they could not have become aware at an earlier time given the state of the art. "State of the art" here refers to facts discoverable in light of the scientific and technological knowledge available at the time the products were produced.

The District Court ruled that state-of-the-art evidence is inadmissible since, under strict liability, "culpability is irrelevant." It said that liability for risk unknowable at the time of manufacture would not make the manufacturer "an absolute insurer of its product," because plaintiffs "are never relieved of their primary burden of proof, that of establishing the product's dangerousness" by a preponderance of the evidence. "That the product was unsafe because of the state of the technology does not change the fact that it was unsafe."

> Spreading the costs of injuries among all those who produce, distribute and purchase manufactured products is far preferable to imposing it on the innocent victims who suffer disability or even death from defective products. This premise is at the very heart of our strict liability rules. Moreover, this important public policy consideration is unaffected by the state of scientific knowledge available at the time of manufacture.

On appeal from jury verdicts in favor of plaintiffs, the Ninth Circuit Court of Appeals affirmed the trial court's ruling. It agreed that "evidence regarding a defendant's actual or constructive knowledge of the perils of its products is irrelevant." The appellate court explained:

> "In [a prior case also involving asbestos exposure] we certified to the Hawaii Supreme Court the following question: ' * * * is the manufacturer conclusively presumed to know the dangers inherent in his product, or is state of the art evidence admissible * * *?' The Hawaii Supreme Court responded that, in strict liability actions, ' * * * the issue of whether the seller knew or reasonably should have known of the dangers inherent in his or her product is irrelevant to the issue of liability. Although highly relevant to a negligence action, it has absolutely no bearing on the elements of a strict products liability claim. * * * ' Johnson v. Raybestos–Manhattan, Inc., 69 Haw. 287, 740 P.2d 548, 549 (1987). * * *

> "Under Hawaii law * * *, therefore, evidence as to the possible extent of a defendant's knowledge concerning the dangerousness of its own products is not admissible in either consumer expectations or failure-to-warn cases. The district court did not err in rejecting the state-of-the-art evidence."

STERNHAGEN v. DOW COMPANY, 282 Mont. 168, 935 P.2d 1139 (1997). Marlene Sternhagen brought a wrongful death action against manufacturers of the herbicide 2,4–D. She alleged that the decedent Charles Sternhagen was exposed to 2,4–D when employed by a crop spraying business during the period 1948–1950, and that this exposure caused the cancer that developed in 1981 and led to his death. Defendants rejoined that during 1948–1950 "neither they, nor medical science, knew or had reason to know" that 2,4–D was a cancer-causing substance. The trial court certified this question to the Montana Supreme Court: is a manufacturer "conclusively presumed to know the dangers inherent in his product, or is state-of-the-art evidence admissible"? The supreme court (Nelson, J.) said "we address the certified question by addressing strict products liability law in Montana generally and without differentiating as among manufacturing defect, design defect, or failure to warn cases." *Held*, Montana law affirms "the imputation of knowledge doctrine" and rejects "the state-of-the-art defense."

"[F]or the past two-plus decades, we have consistently adhered to the core public policy principles underlying strict products liability * * *. [T]he state-of-the-art defense raises issues of reasonableness and foreseeability—concepts fundamental to negligence law—to determine a manufacturer's liability. To recognize the state-of-the-art defense now would inject negligence principles into strict liability law and thereby sever Montana's strict products liability law from the core principles for which it was adopted—maximum protection for consumers against dangerous defects in manufactured products with the focus on the condition of the product, and not on the manufacturer's conduct or knowledge. * * *

"Despite the adoption of the state-of-the-art defense in other jurisdictions, recognition of the defense in the Restatement (Third) of the Law of Torts: Products Liability (Proposed Final Draft, Preliminary Version) (Oct. 18, 1996) and the Chemical Companies' assertion that public policy supports adoption of the defense, we choose to continue to adhere to the clear precedent we have heretofore established which focuses on the core principles and remedial purposes underlying strict products liability. Strict liability without regard to fault is the only doctrine that fulfills the public interest goals of protecting consumers, compensating the injured and making those who profit from the market bear the risks and costs associated with the defective or dangerous products which they place in the stream of commerce. * * *

"Accordingly, in answer to the question certified, we conclude that, in a strict products liability case, knowledge of any undiscovered or undiscoverable dangers should be imputed to the manufacturer. Furthermore, we conclude that, in a strict products liability case, state-of-the-art evidence is not admissible to establish whether the manufacturer knew or through the exercise of reasonable human foresight should have known of the danger."

DENNY v. FORD MOTOR CO.
Court of Appeals of New York, 1995.
87 N.Y.2d 248, 639 N.Y.S.2d 250, 662 N.E.2d 730.

TITONE, J.:

Are the elements of New York's causes of action for strict products liability and breach of implied warranty always coextensive? If not, can the latter be broader than the former? These are the core issues presented by the questions that the United States Court of Appeals for the Second Circuit has certified to us in this diversity action involving an allegedly defective vehicle. On the facts set forth by the Second Circuit, we hold that the causes of action are not identical and that, under the circumstances presented here, it is possible to be liable for breach of implied warranty even though a claim of strict products liability has not been satisfactorily established.

As stated by the Second Circuit, this action arises out of a June 9, 1986 accident in which plaintiff Nancy Denny was severely injured when the Ford

Bronco II that she was driving rolled over. The rollover accident occurred when Denny slammed on her brakes in an effort to avoid a deer that had walked directly into her motor vehicle's path. Denny and her spouse sued Ford Motor Co., the vehicle's manufacturer, asserting claims for negligence, strict products liability and breach of implied warranty of merchantability (see, UCC §§ 2–314[c], –318). * * *

The trial evidence centered on the particular characteristics of utility vehicles, which are generally made for off-road use on unpaved and often rugged terrain. Such use sometimes necessitates climbing over obstacles such as fallen logs and rocks. While utility vehicles are traditionally considerably larger than passenger cars, some manufacturers have created a category of down-sized "small" utility vehicles, which are designed to be lighter, to achieve better fuel economy and, presumably, to appeal to a wider consumer market. The Bronco II in which Denny was injured falls into this category.

Plaintiffs introduced evidence at trial to show that small utility vehicles in general, and the Bronco II in particular, present a significantly higher risk of rollover accidents than do ordinary passenger automobiles. Plaintiffs' evidence also showed that the Bronco II had a low stability index attributable to its high center of gravity and relatively narrow track width. The vehicle's shorter wheel base and suspension system were additional factors contributing to its instability. * * *

Ford argued at trial that the design features of which plaintiffs complained were necessary to the vehicle's off-road capabilities. According to Ford, the vehicle had been intended to be used as an off-road vehicle and had not been designed to be sold as a conventional passenger automobile. Ford's own engineer stated that he would not recommend the Bronco II to someone whose primary interest was to use it as a passenger car, since the features of a four-wheel-drive utility vehicle were not helpful for that purpose and the vehicle's design made it inherently less stable.

Despite the engineer's testimony, plaintiffs introduced a Ford marketing manual which predicted that many buyers would be attracted to the Bronco II because utility vehicles were "suitable to contemporary life styles" and were "considered fashionable" in some suburban areas. According to this manual, the sales presentation of the Bronco II should take into account the vehicle's "suitability for commuting and for suburban and city driving." Additionally, the vehicle's ability to switch between two-wheel and four-wheel drive would "be particularly appealing to women who may be concerned about driving in snow and ice with their children." Plaintiffs both testified that the perceived safety benefits of its four-wheel-drive capacity were what attracted them to the Bronco II. They were not at all interested in its off-road use.

At the close of the evidence, the District Court Judge submitted both the strict-products-liability claim and the breach-of-implied-warranty claim, despite Ford's objection that the two causes of action were identical. With respect to the strict-products-liability claim the court told the jury that * * *:

A product is defective if it is not reasonably safe. * * * [T]he plaintiffs must prove by a preponderance of the evidence that a reasonable person * * * who knew of the product's potential for causing injury and the existence of available alternative designs * * * would have concluded that such a product should not have been marketed in that condition. * * *

With respect to the breach-of-implied-warranty claim, the court told the jury:

The law implies a warranty by a manufacturer who places its product on the market that the product is reasonably fit for the ordinary purpose for which it was intended. If it is, in fact, * * * not reasonably fit to be used for its intended purpose, the warranty is breached.

[Ed. note: This implied warranty of safety is not limited by a privity requirement.]

In response to interrogatories, the jury found that the Bronco II was not "defective" and that defendant was therefore not liable under plaintiffs' strict-products-liability cause of action. However, the jury also found that defendant had breached its implied warranty of merchantability and that the breach was the proximate cause of Nancy Denny's injuries. Following apportionment of damages, plaintiff was awarded judgment in the amount of $1.2 million.

* * *

In this proceeding, Ford's sole argument is that plaintiffs' strict-products-liability and breach-of-implied-warranty causes of action were identical and that, accordingly, a defendant's verdict on the former cannot be reconciled with a plaintiff's verdict on the latter. This argument is, in turn, premised on both the intertwined history of the two doctrines and the close similarity in their elements and legal functions. * * * However, in the final analysis, the argument is flawed because it overlooks the continued existence of a separate statutory predicate for the breach-of-warranty theory and the subtle but important distinction between the two theories that arises from their different historical and doctrinal root[s].

* * *

Although the products-liability theory sounding in tort and the breach-of-implied-warranty theory authorized by the UCC coexist and are often invoked in tandem, the core element of "defect" is subtly different in the two causes of action. * * * Since this Court's decision in Voss v. Black & Decker Mfg. Co. (59 N.Y.2d 102, 108, 463 N.Y.S.2d 398, 450 N.E.2d 204), the New York standard for determining the existence of a design defect has required an assessment of whether "if the design defect were known at the time of manufacture, a reasonable person would conclude that the utility of the product did not outweigh the risk inherent in marketing a product designed in that manner" * * *.

* * *

It is this negligence-like risk/benefit component of the defect element that differentiates strict-products-liability claims from UCC-based breach-of-implied-warranty claims in cases involving design defects. While the strict products concept of a product that is "not reasonably safe" requires a weighing of the product's dangers against its overall advantages, the UCC's concept of a "defective" product requires an inquiry only into whether the product in question was "fit for the ordinary purposes for which such goods are used" (UCC § 2–314[2][c]). The latter inquiry focuses on the expectations for the performance of the product when used in the customary, usual and reasonably foreseeable manners. The cause of action is one involving true "strict" liability, since recovery may be had upon a showing that the product was not minimally safe for its expected purpose—without regard to the feasibility of alternative designs or the manufacturer's "reasonableness" in marketing it in that unsafe condition.

This distinction between the "defect" analysis in breach-of-implied-warranty actions and the "defect" analysis in strict-products-liability actions is explained by the differing etiology and doctrinal underpinnings of the two distinct theories. The former class of actions originates in contract law, which directs its attention to the purchaser's disappointed expectations; the latter originates in tort law, which traditionally has concerned itself with social policy and risk allocation by means other than those dictated by the marketplace.

* * *

[T]he dissent's novel proposal that the contract-based consumer-expectation test should be abandoned for the tort-based risk/utility approach even for contract-based warranty claims has not been embraced or even suggested by any of the risk/utility advocates that the dissent cites. For example, although the drafters of the Third Restatement have endorsed risk/utility analysis for design defect cases sounding in tort, they also have made clear that claims based on warranty theories are "not within the scope" of the newly drafted section and are, in fact, "unaffected by it" (ALI, Restatement of Torts: Products Liability, Tentative Draft No. 2 [March 13, 1995], § 2, comment m, p 42). Further, the drafters have noted that "warranty law as a body of legal doctrine separate from tort may impose legal obligations that go beyond those set forth" in the Restatement of Torts (id., comment q, p 46).

* * *

Significantly, the consumer-expectation test has its advocates as well as its critics. * * * [There is] "considerable support for a threshold test which does not require that the complexities of risk-utility analysis be undertaken in every design defect case" (Twerski & Weinstein, [A Critique of the Uniform Products Liability Law, 28 Drake L.Rev.221], pp. 230–233). In view of the "rigors of the risk-utility test," it has been suggested that it is "worthwhile" to retain the consumer-expectation test and "explore solutions to [its] subjectivity problem" rather than simply abandoning it (id.).[6]

* * *

6. The authors note that "the fear that almost any defective product claim will pass under the rubric of consumer expectations can be dealt with by requiring that such expectations must be clearly and widely perceived to be attendant to the normal use of the product."

As a practical matter, the distinction between the defect concepts in tort law and in implied-warranty theory may have little or no effect in most cases. In this case, however, the nature of the proof and the way in which the fact issues were litigated demonstrates how the two causes of action can diverge. In the trial court, Ford took the position that the design features of which plaintiffs complain, i.e., the Bronco II's high center of gravity, narrow track width, short wheel base and specially tailored suspension system, were important to preserving the vehicle's ability to drive over the highly irregular terrain that typifies off-road travel. Ford's proof in this regard was relevant to the strict-products-liability risk/utility equation, which required the factfinder to determine whether the Bronco II's value as an off-road vehicle outweighed the risk of the rollover accidents that could occur when the vehicle was used for other driving tasks.

On the other hand, plaintiffs' proof focused, in part, on the sale of the Bronco II for suburban driving and everyday road travel. Plaintiffs also adduced proof that the Bronco II's design characteristics made it unusually susceptible to rollover accidents when used on paved roads. All of this evidence was useful in showing that routine highway and street driving was the "ordinary purpose" for which the Bronco II was sold and that it was not "fit"—or safe—for that purpose.

Thus, under the evidence in this case, a rational factfinder could have simultaneously concluded that the Bronco II's utility as an off-road vehicle outweighed the risk of injury resulting from rollover accidents and that the vehicle was not safe for the "ordinary purpose" of daily driving for which it was marketed and sold. * * *

* * *

[Chief Judge Kaye and Judges Bellacosa, Smith, Levine and Ciparick concur. Judge Simons dissents in an opinion.]

SIMONS, J. (dissenting):

* * *

The majority concludes that the implied warranty and strict products liability causes of action are different because the existence of an actionable defect is determined by two different analyses. Viewing implied warranty from a contract perspective, it would define defectiveness by whether the product lived up to the consumer's expectations whereas defectiveness, for strict products liability purposes, is determined by application of the risk/utility standard. In my judgment, the consumer expectation standard, appropriate to commercial sales transactions, has no place in personal injury litigation alleging a design defect and may result in imposing absolute liability on marketers of consumers' products. Whether a product has been defectively designed should be determined in a personal injury action by a risk/utility analysis.

* * *

* * * The correct standard in strict liability claims, according to the Third Restatement, should include a balancing of the risk of danger against the utility of the product as designed. In its words, "consumer expectations do not constitute an independent standard for judging the defectiveness of product designs" (Restatement [Third] Torts [Tent. Draft No. 2], § 2, comment f.). They are "not determinative of defectiveness" because they do not take into account "whether the proposed alternative design could be implemented at reasonable cost, or whether an alternative design would provide greater overall safety", i.e., the test does not take into consideration risk/utility factors (id.). * * *

––––––––––

SOULE v. GENERAL MOTORS CORP., 8 Cal.4th 548, 34 Cal.Rptr.2d 607, 882 P.2d 298 (1994). In this crashworthiness case, the California Supreme Court reaffirmed the two tests for design defect articulated in Barker v. Lull Engineering Co., supra, p. 989. (Facts of the present case are summarized at p. 1017 supra.)

At trial the judge gave the jury "the standard design defect instruction" which says that a product is defective "if it fails to perform as safely as an ordinary consumer would expect * * * or if there is a risk of danger inherent in the design which outweighs the benefit of the design." In the Supreme Court the manufacturer argued that design expectations of consumers are subjective, unstable, often ignorant and unreasonable, and that the consumer expectation test "should be entirely abolished as a basis for design defect," leaving all design claims to be resolved by "risk-benefit analysis."

The Supreme Court said: "We * * * find no compelling reason to overrule the consumer expectations prong of Barker at this late date, and we decline to do so." "In Barker, we offered two alternative ways to prove a design defect, each appropriate to its own circumstances." The test based on expectations of consumers is related to "the common law doctrine of warranty," which holds that "a product's presence on the market includes an implied representation" that the product is fit for safe performance. The court said that "a substantial number of jurisdictions expressly recognize, consistent with Barker," the test of conformance with safety expectations (citing cases from Arizona, Hawaii, Illinois, Ohio). "Consumers govern their own conduct by these expectations, and products on the market should conform to them." Within proper limits, the consumer expectation test "remains a workable means of determining the existence of design defect."

The court emphasized that the expectation test is not appropriate in all design cases. In many situations involving complex design characteristics and complex circumstances of injury, the consumer "would not know what to expect." The expectation test "is reserved for cases in which the everyday experience of the product's users permits a conclusion" of defectiveness. "The crucial question in each individual case is whether the circumstances of the product's failure permit an inference that the product's design performed below the legitimate, commonly accepted minimum safety assumptions of its ordinary consumers." A design claim based on the expectation test appeals to "the common knowledge of lay jurors"; therefore expert testimony "may not be used to demonstrate what an ordinary consumer would or should expect."

The court added that reliance on the expectation test is not foreclosed "simply because the product at issue is only in specialized use, so that the general public may not be familiar with its safety characteristics." "[I]f the expectations of the product's limited group of ordinary consumers are beyond the lay experience common to all jurors, expert testimony on * * * what the product's actual consumers do expect may be proper."

POTTER v. CHICAGO PNEUMATIC TOOL CO., 241 Conn. 199, 694 A.2d 1319 (1997). Plaintiffs alleged that they had suffered permanent impairment of their hands because of their long-term use, as shipyard workers, of pneumatic hand tools manufactured by defendants. According to plaintiffs' expert, defendants' tools exceeded the maximum limits for vibration exposure consistent with avoiding harm to long-term users set by the American Conference of Governmental and Industrial Hygienists. The trial judge instructed the jury "that, in determining whether the tools were unreasonably dangerous, it may draw its conclusions based on the reasonable expectations of an ordinary user of the defendants' tools," and the jury found for plaintiffs. On appeal to the Connecticut Supreme Court, *held*, that the quoted instruction—called the "ordinary consumer expectation test"—was proper. In the present case "there was sufficient evidence as a matter of law to support the determination that the tools were unreasonably dangerous based on the ordinary consumer expectation test." The court (Katz, J.) elaborated:

"Although today we continue to adhere to our long-standing rule that a product's defectiveness is to be determined by the expectations of an ordinary consumer, we nevertheless recognize that there may be instances involving complex product designs in which an ordinary consumer may not be able to form expectations of safety. In such cases, a consumer's expectations may be viewed in light of various factors that balance the utility of the product's design with the magnitude of its risks. We find persuasive the reasoning of those jurisdictions that have modified their formulation of the consumer expectation test by incorporating risk-utility factors into the ordinary consumer expectation analysis. Thus, the modified consumer expectation test provides the jury with the product's risks and utility and then inquires whether a reasonable consumer would consider the product unreasonably dangerous. * * * "

"Under this formulation, a sample jury instruction could provide: ' * * * In determining what an ordinary consumer would reasonably expect, you should consider the usefulness of the product, the likelihood and severity of the danger posed by the design, the feasibility of an alternative design, the financial cost of an improved design, the ability to reduce the product's danger without impairing its usefulness or making it too expensive, and the feasibility of spreading the loss by increasing the product's price or by purchasing insurance * * *.' "

"Although today we adopt a modified formulation of the consumer expectation test, we emphasize that we do not require a plaintiff to present evidence relating to the product's risks and utility in every case. As the California Court of Appeals has stated: 'There are certain kinds of accidents—even where fairly complex machinery is involved—[that] are so bizarre that the average juror, upon hearing the particulars, might reasonably think: "Whatever the user may have expected from that contraption, it certainly wasn't that." ' *Akers v. Kelley Co.*, 173 Cal.App.3d 633, 651, 219 Cal.Rptr. 513 (1985). Accordingly, the ordinary consumer expectation test is appropriate when the everyday experience of the particular product's users permits the inference that the product did not meet minimum safety expectations."

SECTION C. WARNINGS

Modern product warning law was originally organized by the conceptual framework set out in *Comments i, j,* and *k* to § 402A of the *Second Restatement of Torts*. These comments, which begin our study of product warning law, distinguish between "unreasonably dangerous" products and "unavoidably unsafe" ones, and between "warnings" and "directions" (or instructions). The framework they establish permits sellers to discharge their duty to market a non-defective product by warning of the product's otherwise unacceptable risks when the product is: (1) "unavoidably unsafe", but worth consuming nonetheless; or (2) "unreasonably dangerous" without a warning, but reasonably safe with one.

An "unavoidably unsafe" product is one that cannot be made less risky, given the state of knowledge at the time that the product was placed on the market. The prototype examples of "unavoidably unsafe" products are prescription drugs. For example, at the time that § *402A* of the *Second Restatement* was drafted, the Pasteur vaccine for rabies was "unavoidably unsafe"; it "not uncommonly [led] to very serious and damaging consequences when it [was] injected." (infra, p. 1028, *Comment k*) The vaccine was worth consuming despite its grim side effects because "the disease itself invariably leads to a dreadful death * * *." (id.) "Unreasonably dangerous" products are also "dangerous to an extent beyond that which would be contemplated by the ordinary consumer who purchases it, with the ordinary knowledge common to the community as to its characteristics" (infra, p. 1028 *Comment i*) The excessive risks of "unreasonably dangerous" products, however, are present not by default but *by design*.

Why would a product be "unreasonably dangerous" by design? In some circumstances, risky design features further the legitimate interests of at least some users. Jeeps are a case in point. Their high and narrow wheelbase renders Jeeps less safe than passenger cars on paved roads—especially in slick road conditions—because that wheelbase makes them more prone to tip over. (The sport utility vehicle that is the subject of *Denny* supra, p. 1019, an overgrown cousin of the Jeep, suffered from just this flaw.) Yet that wheelbase also enables the off road driving for which Jeeps were originally designed, and to which they are especially suited. Lowering and widening a Jeep's wheelbase diminishes its suitability for off-road excursions.

"Unreasonably dangerous" products bring the second part of the § 402A framework—the duty to provide appropriate directions or instructions for the safe use of a product—into play, because it is generally possible to minimize the risks of "unreasonably dangerous" products by using them more carefully. Jeep owners—or, more exactly, Jeep drivers—can minimize the risks of rollover accidents by driving more cautiously, especially in slick conditions. "Unavoidably unsafe" products, by contrast, generally cannot be used more or less carefully. The only choice a rabies victim has with respect to the Pasteur vaccine for the disease is to take the vaccine or not. The usual point of issuing warnings in connection with "unavoidably unsafe" products, then, is to enable *informed consumer choice, not* to enable *effective user precaution*. By contrast, when a product is "unreasonably dangerous"—and when user precaution is essential but not evident—"[a] duty to warn actually consists of two duties: One is to give adequate instructions for safe use, and the other is to give a warning as to dangers." *Ontai v. Straub Clinic & Hosp. Inc.*, 66 Haw. 237, 659 P.2d 734, 743 (1983).

The warnings required in connection with "unreasonably dangerous" products serve two purposes. First, they too enable informed consumer choice. Some people may decline to buy Jeeps once they realize that their off-road capabilities have an on-road cost. Second, warnings alert users to the need for special precautions. When the appropriate precautions are not evident to the average reasonable consumer, the duty to instruct comes into play. The seller must tell users how to avoid or reduce the product's risk through careful use.

RESTATEMENT OF TORTS, SECOND (1977)

§ 402A, Comments i, j, k

i. Unreasonably Dangerous. The rule stated in this Section applies only where the defective condition of the product makes it unreasonably dangerous to the user or consumer. Many products cannot possibly be made entirely safe for all consumption, and any food or drug necessarily involves some risk of harm, if only from over-consumption. Ordinary sugar is a deadly poison to diabetics, and castor oil found use under Mussolini as an instrument of torture. That is not what is meant by "unreasonably dangerous" in this Section. The article sold must be dangerous to an extent beyond that which would be contemplated by the ordinary consumer who purchases it, with the ordinary knowledge common to the community as to its characteristics. Good whiskey is not unreasonably dangerous merely because it will make some people drunk, and is especially dangerous to alcoholics; but bad whiskey, containing a dangerous amount of fusel oil, is unreasonably dangerous. Good tobacco is not unreasonably dangerous merely because the effects of smoking may be harmful; but tobacco containing something like marijuana may be unreasonably dangerous. * * *

j. Directions or Warning. In order to prevent the product from being unreasonably dangerous, the seller may be required to give directions or warning, on the container, as to its use. The seller may reasonably assume that those with common allergies, as for example to eggs or strawberries, will be aware of them, and he is not required to warn against them. Where, however, the product contains an ingredient to which a substantial number of the population are allergic, and the ingredient is one whose danger is not generally known, or if known is one which the consumer would reasonably not expect to find in the product, the seller is required to give warning against it, if he has knowledge, or by the application of reasonable, developed human skill and foresight should have knowledge, of the presence of the ingredient and the danger. Likewise in the case of poisonous drugs, or those unduly dangerous for other reasons, warning as to use may be required.

But a seller is not required to warn with respect to products, or ingredients in them, which are only dangerous, or potentially so, when consumed in excessive quantity, or over a long period of time, when the danger, or potentiality of danger, is generally known and recognized. * * *

Where warning is given, the seller may reasonably assume that it will be read and heeded; and a product bearing such a warning, which is safe for use if it is followed, is not in defective condition, nor is it unreasonably dangerous.

k.   Unavoidably Unsafe Products. There are some products which, in the present state of human knowledge, are quite incapable of being made safe for their intended and ordinary use. These are especially common in the field of drugs. An outstanding example is the vaccine for the Pasteur treatment of rabies, which not uncommonly leads to very serious and damaging consequences when it is injected. Since the disease itself invariably leads to a dreadful death, both the marketing and the use of the vaccine are fully justified, notwithstanding the unavoidable high degree of risk which they involve. Such a product, properly prepared, and accompanied by proper directions and warning, is not defective, nor is it *unreasonably* dangerous. The same is true of many other drugs, vaccines, and the like, many of which for this very reason cannot legally be sold except to physicians, or under the prescription of a physician. It is also true in particular of many new or experimental drugs as to which, because of lack of time and opportunity for sufficient medical experience, there can be no assurance of safety, or perhaps even of purity of ingredients, but such experience as there is justifies the marketing and use of the drug notwithstanding a medically recognizable risk. The seller of such products, again with the qualification that they are properly prepared and marketed, and proper warning is given, where the situation calls for it, is not to be held to strict liability for unfortunate consequences attending their use, merely because he has undertaken to supply the public with an apparently useful and desirable product, attended with a known but apparently reasonable risk.

WHEN DOES THE DUTY TO WARN ARISE?

Comment i states that the duty to warn attaches when a product is "dangerous to an extent beyond that which would be contemplated by the ordinary consumer who purchases it, with the ordinary knowledge common to the community as to its characteristics." When a risk is evident, the product itself informs the consumer of its dangers. Whether a risk is obvious even in the absence of a warning is thus the first question of warning law.

JOSUE v. ISUZU MOTORS AMERICA, INC., 87 Hawai'i 413, 958 P.2d 535 (1998). "[I]t should be readily apparent and patently obvious to a passenger who chooses to ride in the bed of a pickup truck that he or she is completely unrestrained and unprotected from being ejected from the bed in an accident. We therefore hold, as a matter of law, that the dangers of traveling in the bed of a pickup truck are 'open and obvious, discernible by casual inspection.' Accordingly, Isuzu had no duty to warn potential passengers of such dangers." Summary judgment in favor of Isuzu affirmed.

BELLING v. HAUGH'S POOLS, LTD., 126 A.D.2d 958, 511 N.Y.S.2d 732 (1987). Plaintiff was seriously injured diving into an above-ground pool. *Held*, reversing the trial court, summary judgment in favor of defendants granted. The plaintiff's "vertical dive" into "four feet of water involved an open and obvious risk."

The dissent observed: "This record reveals that defendants knew, or should have known, that similar dives into similar pools had resulted in over 100 quadriplegic injuries per year during the past ten years." Defendants had not warned of this fact, and had confined their warnings about the risks of diving into the pool to the owner's manual. There was, then, "a question of fact whether the warnings given were adequate, giving due consideration to the fact that plaintiff was a non-owner of the pool who could not be expected to read the owner's manual before using the pool."

LIRIANO v. HOBART CORPORATION, 170 F.3d 264 (2d Cir.1999) (Calabresi, J.). Seventeen-year-old Luis Liriano "was severely injured on the job in 1993 when his hand was caught in a meat grinder manufactured by Hobart Corporation ('Hobart') and owned by his employer, Super Associated ('Super'). The meat grinder had been sold to Super with a safety guard, but the safety guard was removed while the machine was in Super's possession and was not affixed to the meat grinder at the time of the accident. The machine bore no warning indicating that the grinder should be operated only with a safety guard attached." After a trial and partial retrial on a failure to warn theory, the jury attributed five per cent of the liability to Hobart, thirty-three percent to the plaintiff himself, and the remainder to Super. Hobart appealed, arguing in part that the obviousness of the danger relieved the company of its duty to warn. *Held*, affirmed. The jury was entitled to decide the issue, even though "meat grinders are widely known to be dangerous." The claim that Hobart was relieved of its duty to warn because the danger was open and obvious as a matter of law ignored "the complex functions of warnings."

" * * * [A] warning can do more than exhort its audience to be careful. It can also affect what activities the people warned choose to engage in. * * * And where the function of a warning is to assist the reader in making choices, the value of the warning can lie as much in making known the existence of alternatives as in communicating the fact that a particular choice is dangerous. It follows that the duty to warn is not necessarily obviated merely because a danger is clear.

"To be more concrete, a warning can convey at least two types of messages. One states that a particular place, object, or activity is dangerous. Another explains that people need not risk the danger posed by such a place, object, or activity in order to achieve the purpose for which they might have taken that risk. Thus, a highway sign that says 'Danger—Steep Grade' says less than a sign that says 'Steep Grade Ahead—Follow Suggested Detour to Avoid Dangerous Areas.'

"If the hills or mountains responsible for the steep grade are plainly visible, the first sign merely states what a reasonable person would know without having to be warned. The second sign tells drivers what they might not have otherwise known: that there is another road that is flatter and less hazardous. A driver who believes the road through the mountainous area to be the only way to reach her destination might well choose to drive on that road despite the steep grades, but a driver who knows herself to have an alternative might not, even though her understanding of the risks posed by the steep grade is exactly the same as those of the first driver. Accordingly, a certain level of obviousness as to the grade of a road might, in principle, eliminate the reason for posting a sign of the first variety. But no matter how patently steep the road, the second kind of sign might still have a beneficial effect. As a result, the duty to post a sign of the second variety may persist even when the danger of the road is obvious and a sign of the first type would not be warranted.

"One who grinds meat, like one who drives on a steep road, can benefit not only from being told that his activity is dangerous but from being told of a safer way. As we have said, one can argue about whether the risk involved in grinding meat is sufficiently obvious that a responsible person would fail to warn of that risk, believing reasonably that it would convey no helpful information. But if it is also the case—as it is—that the risk posed by meat grinders can feasibly be reduced by attaching a safety guard, we have a different question. Given that attaching guards is feasible, does reasonable care require that meat workers be informed that they need not accept the risks of using unguarded grinders? Even if most ordinary users may—as a matter of law—know of the risk of using a guardless meat grinder, it does not follow that a sufficient number of them will—as a matter of law—also know that protective guards are available, that using them is a realistic possibility, and that they may ask that such guards be used. It is precisely these last pieces of information that a reasonable manufacturer may have a duty to convey even if the danger of using a grinder were itself deemed obvious."

STRICT CONCEPTIONS OF THE DUTY TO WARN

Risks that are known by the manufacturer, but are not obvious to the user or consumer, raise an important doctrinal question: Should the manufacturer's duty to warn be governed by negligence concepts, or by strict liability ones? If so, what does "strict liability" demand in this context? Products liability as formulated by § 402A of the *Second Restatement* is self-consciously strict, and cases arising under its influence seek to articulate a "strict" duty to warn. The *Third Restatement*, and other cases, take the contrary position that a negligence standard is appropriate.

MacDONALD v. ORTHO PHARMACEUTICAL CORP.

Supreme Judicial Court of Massachusetts, 1985.
394 Mass. 131, 475 N.E.2d 65.

ABRAMS, Justice.

* * *

* * * In September, 1973, the plaintiff Carole D. MacDonald (MacDonald), who was twenty-six years old at the time, obtained from her gynecologist a prescription for Ortho–Novum contraceptive pills, manufactured by Ortho [Pharmaceutical Corp. (Ortho)]. As required by the then effective regulations promulgated by the United States Food and Drug Administration (FDA), the pill dispenser she received was labeled with a warning that "oral contraceptives are powerful and effective drugs which can cause side effects in some users and should not be used at all by some women," and that "[t]he most serious known side effect is abnormal blood clotting which can be fatal." The warning also referred MacDonald to a booklet which she obtained from her gynecologist, and which was distributed by Ortho pursuant to FDA requirements. The booklet contained detailed information about the contraceptive pill, including the increased risk to pill users that vital organs such as the brain may be damaged by abnormal blood clotting.[4] The word "stroke" did not appear on the dispenser warning or in the booklet.

MacDonald's prescription for Ortho–Novum pills was renewed at subsequent annual visits to her gynecologist. The prescription was filled annually. On July 24, 1976, after approximately three years of using the pills, MacDonald suffered an occlusion of a cerebral artery by a blood clot, an injury commonly referred to as a stroke. The injury caused the death of approxi-

----

4. * * * Ortho's booklet contained the following information:

"About blood clots

"Blood clots occasionally form in the blood vessels of the legs and the pelvis of apparently healthy people and may threaten life if the clots break loose and then lodge in the lung or if they form in other vital organs, such as the brain. It

has been estimated that about one woman in 2,000 on the pill each year suffers a blood clotting disorder severe enough to require hospitalization. The estimated death rate from abnormal blood clotting in healthy women under 35 not taking the pill is 1 in 500,000; whereas for the same group taking the pill it is 1 in 66,000. * * * "

mately twenty per cent of MacDonald's brain tissue, and left her permanently disabled. She and her husband initiated an action in the Superior Court against Ortho, seeking recovery for her personal injuries and his consequential damages and loss of consortium.

MacDonald testified that, during the time she used the pills, she was unaware that the risk of abnormal blood clotting encompassed the risk of stroke, and that she would not have used the pills had she been warned that stroke is an associated risk.[6] The case was submitted to a jury on the plaintiffs' theories that Ortho was negligent in failing to warn adequately of the dangers associated with the pills and that Ortho breached its warranty of merchantability. These two theories were treated, in effect, as a single claim of failure to warn. The jury returned a special verdict, finding no negligence or breach of warranty in the manufacture of the pills. The jury also found that Ortho adequately advised the gynecologist of the risks inherent in the pills;[7] the jury found, however, that Ortho was negligent and in breach of warranty because it failed to give MacDonald sufficient warning of such dangers. The jury further found that MacDonald's injury was caused by Ortho's pills, that the inadequacy of the warnings to MacDonald was the proximate cause of her injury, and that Ortho was liable to MacDonald and her husband.

After the jury verdict, the judge granted Ortho's motion for judgment notwithstanding the verdict, concluding that, because oral contraceptives are prescription drugs, a manufacturer's duty to warn the consumer is satisfied if the manufacturer gives adequate warnings to the prescribing physician, and that the manufacturer has no duty to warn the consumer directly.

* * *

1. *Extent of duty to warn.* Ordinarily, "a manufacturer of a product, which the manufacturer knows or should know is dangerous by nature or is in a dangerous condition," is under a duty to give warning of those dangers to "persons who it is foreseeable will come in contact with, and consequently be endangered by, that product." *H.P. Hood & Sons v. Ford Motor Co.,* 370 Mass. 69, 75, 345 N.E.2d 683 (1976). The element of privity being long discarded, a manufacturer's warning to the immediate purchaser will not, as a general matter, discharge this duty. However, "there are limits to that principle." *Carter v. Yardley & Co.,* 319 Mass. 92, 98, 64 N.E.2d 693 (1946). Thus, "a manufacturer may be absolved from blame because of a justified reliance upon ... a middleman." *Id.* at 99, 64 N.E.2d 693. * * *

---

6. Subsequent to the events in this case, the FDA regulation was amended by 43 Fed.Reg. 4221 (1978), which replaced the regulation requirement of a specified warning on the pill dispenser with a requirement that the dispenser contain a warning "of the serious side effects of oral contraceptives, such as thrombophlebitis, pulmonary embolism, myocardial infarction, retinal artery thrombosis, *stroke,* benign hepatic adenomas, induction of fetal abnormalities, and gallbladder disease" (emphasis added). See 21 C.F.R. § 310.501(a)(2)(iv) (1984).

7. MacDonald stated at trial that her gynecologist had informed her only that oral contraceptives might cause bloating, and had not advised her of the increased risk of stroke associated with consumption of birth control pills. The physician was not joined as a defendant in this action, and no questions relating to any potential liability on his part are before us.

MacDonald further testified at trial that she had read both the warning on the Dialpak tablet dispenser as well as the booklet which she received from her gynecologist.

The rule in jurisdictions that have addressed the question of the extent of a manufacturer's duty to warn in cases involving prescription drugs is that the prescribing physician acts as a "learned intermediary" between the manufacturer and the patient, and "the duty of the ethical drug manufacturer is to warn the doctor, rather than the patient, [although] the manufacturer is directly liable to the patient for a breach of such duty." *McEwen v. Ortho Pharmaceutical Corp.,* 270 Or. 375, 386–387, 528 P.2d 522 (1974). Oral contraceptives, however, bear peculiar characteristics which warrant the imposition of a common law duty on the manufacturer to warn users directly of associated risks. Whereas a patient's involvement in decision-making concerning use of a prescription drug necessary to treat a malady is typically minimal or nonexistent, the healthy, young consumer of oral contraceptives is usually actively involved in the decision to use "the pill," as opposed to other available birth control products, and the prescribing physician is relegated to a relatively passive role.

Furthermore, the physician prescribing "the pill," as a matter of course, examines the patient once before prescribing an oral contraceptive and only annually thereafter. * * * Even if the physician, on those occasions, were scrupulously to remind the patient of the risks attendant on continuation of the oral contraceptive, "the patient cannot be expected to remember all of the details for a protracted period of time." 35 Fed.Reg. 9002 (1970).

Last, the birth control pill is specifically subject to extensive Federal regulation. The FDA has promulgated regulations designed to ensure that the choice of "the pill" as a contraceptive method is informed by comprehensible warnings of potential side effects. * * *

The oral contraceptive thus stands apart from other prescription drugs in light of the heightened participation of patients in decisions relating to use of "the pill"; the substantial risks affiliated with the product's use; the feasibility of direct warnings by the manufacturer to the user; the limited participation of the physician (annual prescriptions); and the possibility that oral communications between physicians and consumers may be insufficient or too scanty standing alone fully to apprise consumers of the product's dangers at the time the initial selection of a contraceptive method is made as well as at subsequent points when alternative methods may be considered. We conclude that the manufacturer of oral contraceptives is not justified in relying on warnings to the medical profession to satisfy its common law duty to warn, and that the manufacturer's obligation encompasses a duty to warn the ultimate user. Thus, the manufacturer's duty is to provide to the consumer written warnings conveying reasonable notice of the nature, gravity, and likelihood of known or knowable side effects, and advising the consumer to seek fuller explanation from the prescribing physician or other doctor of any such information of concern to the consumer.

2. *Adequacy of the warning.* Because we reject the judge's conclusion that Ortho had no duty to warn MacDonald, we turn to Ortho's separate argument, not reached by the judge, that the evidence was insufficient to warrant the jury's finding that Ortho's warnings to MacDonald were inadequate. Ortho contends initially that its warnings complied with FDA labeling

requirements, and that those requirements preempt or define the bounds of the common law duty to warn. We disagree. The regulatory history of the FDA requirements belies any objective to cloak them with preemptive effect. * * * Although the common law duty we today recognize is to a large degree coextensive with the regulatory duties imposed by the FDA, we are persuaded that, in instances where a trier of fact could reasonably conclude that a manufacturer's compliance with FDA labeling requirements or guidelines did not adequately apprise oral contraceptive users of inherent risks, the manufacturer should not be shielded from liability by such compliance. Thus, compliance with FDA requirements, though admissible to demonstrate lack of negligence, is not conclusive on this issue, just as violation of FDA requirements is evidence, but not conclusive evidence, of negligence. * * *

* * *

Ortho argues that reasonable minds could not differ as to whether MacDonald was adequately informed of the risk of the injury she sustained by Ortho's warning that the oral contraceptives could cause "abnormal blood clotting which can be fatal" and further warning of the incremental likelihood of hospitalization or death due to blood clotting in "vital organs, such as the brain." We disagree. "The fact finder may find a warning to be unreasonable, hence inadequate, in its factual content, its expression of the facts, or the method or form in which it is conveyed.... The adequacy of such warnings is measured not only by what is stated, but also by the manner in which it is stated. A reasonable warning not only conveys a fair indication of the nature of the dangers involved, but also warns with the degree of intensity demanded by the nature of the risk. A warning may be found to be unreasonable in that it was unduly delayed, reluctant in tone or lacking in a sense of urgency." *Seley v. G.D. Searle & Co.,* 67 Ohio St.2d 192, 198, 423 N.E.2d 831 (1981). We cannot say that this jury's decision that the warning was inadequate is so unreasonable as to require the opposite conclusion as a matter of law. The jury may well have concluded, in light of their common experience and MacDonald's testimony, that the absence of a reference to "stroke" in the warning unduly minimized the warning's impact or failed to make the nature of the risk reasonably comprehensible to the average consumer. Similarly, the jury may have concluded that there are fates worse than death, such as the permanent disablement suffered by MacDonald, and that the mention of the risk of death did not, therefore, suffice to apprise an average consumer of the material risks of oral contraceptive use.

Ortho's argument that, as a matter of law, there was insufficient evidence that MacDonald's injury was proximately caused by a deficiency in the warnings is substantially similar to its argument on the issue of the adequacy of the warnings, and is likewise unavailing. * * * The jury were free, however, to credit MacDonald's testimony that she would not have used the pills had she been advised of the danger of "stroke," and to infer that an explicit reference to the risk of stroke might tip the balance in a reasonable person's choice of a contraceptive method. * * *

We reverse the judgment, which the judge ordered notwithstanding the verdict, and remand the case to the Superior Court for the entry of judgment for the plaintiffs.

CARLIN v. SUPERIOR COURT, 13 Cal.4th 1104, 56 Cal.Rptr.2d 162, 920 P.2d 1347 (1996) (Mosk, Acting C. J.). "In this case we address the question whether a plaintiff alleging injury from ingesting a prescription drug can state a claim against the manufacturer for strict liability * * * for failure to warn about the known or reasonably scientifically knowable dangerous propensities of its product. We conclude that she can.

" '[F]ailure to warn in strict liability differs markedly from failure to warn in the negligence context. Negligence law in a failure-to-warn case requires a plaintiff to prove that a manufacturer or distributor did not warn of a particular risk for reasons which fell below the acceptable standard of care, i.e., what a reasonably prudent manufacturer would have known and warned about. Strict liability is not concerned with the standard of due care or the reasonableness of a manufacturer's conduct. The rules of strict liability require a plaintiff to prove only that the defendant did not adequately warn of a particular risk that was known or knowable in light of the generally recognized and prevailing best scientific and medical knowledge available at the time of manufacture and distribution. Thus, in strict liability, as opposed to negligence, the reasonableness of the defendant's failure to warn is immaterial. * * * [U]nder strict liability principles the manufacturer * * * is liable if it failed to give warning of dangers that were known to the scientific community at the time it manufactured or distributed the product.' (Anderson [v. Owens–Corning Fiberglas], 53 Cal.3d at pp. 1002–1003, 281 Cal.Rptr. 528, 810 P.2d 549, fn. omitted.) * * *

"We explained the policy behind our strict liability standard for failure to warn as follows: ' "When, in a particular case, the risk qualitatively (e.g., of death or major disability) as well as quantitatively, on balance with the end sought to be achieved, is such as to call for a true choice judgment, *medical* or *personal*, the warning must be given. . . ." ' Thus, the fact that a manufacturer acted as a reasonably prudent manufacturer in deciding not to warn, while perhaps absolving the manufacturer of liability under the negligence theory, will not preclude liability under strict liability principles if the trier of fact concludes that, based on the information scientifically available to the manufacturer, the manufacturer's failure to warn rendered the product unsafe to its users.' (Anderson, supra, 53 Cal.3d at p. 1003, 281 Cal.Rptr. 528, 810 P.2d 549, italics added, quoting Davis v. Wyeth Laboratories, Inc. (9th Cir.1968) 399 F.2d 121, 129–130 [applying strict liability to a manufacturer of prescription drugs].)"

PEREZ v. WYETH LABORATORIES, 161 N.J. 1, 734 A.2d 1245 (1999). *Held*, in litigation involving Norplant—a long-term birth control method whereby the recipient has six thin capsules of the hormone progestin inserted just below the skin of her upper arm—"the learned intermediary doctrine does not apply to the direct marketing of drugs to consumers."

"Our medical-legal jurisprudence is based on images of health care that no longer exist. At an earlier time, medical advice was received in the doctor's office from a physician who most likely made house calls if needed. The patient usually paid a small sum of money to the doctor. Neighborhood pharmacists compounded prescribed medicines. Without being pejorative, it is safe to say that the prevailing attitude of law and medicine was that the 'doctor knows best.' .

"Pharmaceutical manufacturers never advertised their products to patients, but rather directed all sales efforts at physicians. In this comforting setting, the law created an exception to the traditional duty of manufacturers to warn consumers directly of risks associated with the product as long as they warned health-care providers of those risks.

"For good or ill, that has all changed. Medical services are in large measure provided by managed care organizations. Medicines are purchased in the pharmacy department of supermarkets and often paid for by third-party providers. Drug manufacturers now directly advertise products to consumers on the radio, television, the Internet, billboards on public transportation, and in magazines. For example, a recent magazine advertisement for a seasonal allergy medicine in which a person is standing in a pastoral field filled with grass and goldenrod, attests that to 'TAKE [THE PRODUCT]' is to 'TAKE CLEAR CONTROL.' Another recent ad features a former presidential candidate, encouraging the consumer to 'take a little courage' to speak with 'your physician.' " The first ad features major side effects, encourages the reader to 'talk to your doctor,' and lists a brief summary of risks and contraindications on the opposite page. The second ad provides a phone number and the name of the pharmaceutical company, but does not provide the name of the drug.

"The question in this case, broadly stated, is whether our law should follow these changes in the marketplace or reflect the images of the past. We believe that when mass marketing of prescription drugs seeks to influence a patient's choice of a drug, a pharmaceutical manufacturer that makes direct claims to consumers for the efficacy of its product should not be unqualifiedly relieved of a duty to provide proper warnings of the dangers or side effects of the product."

In defining the manufacturer's duty to warn when it directly advertises its products to consumers, the court adopted a "rebuttable presumption" that compliance with "FDA advertising, labeling and warning requirements" applicable to such warning discharges the manufacturer's duty to warn the patient directly.

IN RE NORPLANT CONTRACEPTIVE PRODUCTS LIABILITY LITIGATION, 165 F.3d 374 (5th Cir.1999). Applying Texas law, the District Court held that the learned intermediary doctrine barred the claims of five patients who received Norplant from their personal physicians. *Held*, affirmed. There was "no evidence that the Texas Supreme Court would be inclined to" recognize an exception to learned intermediary doctrine in this case.

"[Plaintiffs argue] that, for reasons of public policy, Norplant should have had a duty to warn the end user of Norplant's side effects because of the reduced role physicians play in selecting contraceptives for their patients. [They contend] that the physician's reduced role invalidates the rationale of the learned intermediary doctrine because the patient cannot rely on the physician to provide an adequate warning. Although it may be true that physicians may seek to provide greater freedom to their patients in selecting an appropriate form of contraception, Norplant is nevertheless a prescription drug. The record makes it clear that physicians play a significant role in prescribing Norplant and in educating their patients about the benefits and disadvantages to using it. [Plaintiffs'] argument therefore is unavailing."

THE APPROACH OF THE FDA. Under FDA regulations, written warnings for prescription drugs must be provided directly to patients when "one or more of the following circumstances exist: (1) The drug product is one for which patient labeling could help prevent serious adverse effects. (2) The drug product is one that has serious risk(s) (relative to benefits) of which patients should be made aware because information concerning the risk(s) could affect patients' decision to use, or to continue to use, the product. (3) The drug product is important to health and patient adherence to directions for use is crucial to the drug's effectiveness." 21 C.F.R. 208.1. There are currently about 45 drugs that include FDA-approved information written specifically for patients.

NEGLIGENCE CONCEPTIONS OF THE DUTY TO WARN

RESTATEMENT OF TORTS, THIRD: PRODUCTS LIABILITY (1998)

§ 2. Categories of Product Defect

* * * A product:

(c) is defective because of inadequate instructions or warnings when the foreseeable risks of harm posed by the product could have been reduced or avoided by the provision of reasonable instructions or warnings by the seller or other distributor, or a predecessor in the commercial chain of distribution, and the omission of the instructions or warnings renders the product not reasonably safe.

COTTON v. BUCKEYE GAS PRODUCTS CO., 840 F.2d 935, 937–39 (D.C.Cir.1988). The plaintiff worked as a "night heater watcher" at a construction company. His job was to monitor portable heaters used to cure concrete in cold weather and to change the propane cylinders supplied by the defendant as they ran low on gas. The plaintiff neglected to close the valves on the used cylinders and stored them in the vicinity of the active heaters within the polyethylene enclosed areas. Gas escaped from the "spent" cylinders, ignited, and burned the plaintiff severely. The trial court entered judgment notwithstanding the verdict for defendant. *Held,* affirmed.

"The cylinders supplied to plaintiff's employer by Buckeye bore labels clearly and conspicuously warning that the cylinders contained 'flammable' gas and should not be used or stored in 'living areas.' According to plaintiff, this warning was inadequate because it failed (1) to warn about the explosive properties of propane; (2) to instruct users to shut the valves on used cylinders; (3) to advise users not to use or store the cylinders in enclosed, unventilated areas; and (4) to warn that gas might escape from used cylinders believed to be empty.

"Failure-to-warn cases have the curious property that, when the episode is examined in hindsight, it appears as though addition of warnings keyed to a particular accident would be virtually cost free. What could be simpler than for the manufacturer to add the few simple items noted above? The primary cost is, in fact, the increase in time and effort required for the user to grasp the message. The inclusion of each extra item dilutes the punch of every other item. Given short attention spans, items crowd each other out; they get lost in fine print. Here, in fact, Buckeye responded to the information-cost problem with a dual approach: a brief message on the canisters themselves and a more detailed one in [a] pamphlet delivered to [the construction company] (and posted on the bulletin board at the Leesburg Pike construction site where Cotton was employed.)

"Plaintiff's analysis completely disregards the problem of information costs. He asserts that 'it would have been neither difficult nor costly for Buckeye to have purchased or created for attachment to its propane cylinders a clearer more explicit label, such as the alternatives introduced at trial, warning of propane's dangers and instructing how to avoid them.' But he offers no reason to suppose that any alternative package of warnings was preferable. He discounts altogether the warnings in the pamphlet, without even considering what the canister warning would have looked like if Buckeye had supplemented it not only with the special items he is personally interested in—in hindsight—but also with all other equally valuable items (i.e., 'equally' in terms of the scope and probability of the danger likely to be averted and the incremental impact of the information on user conduct.) If every foreseeable possibility must be covered, 'The list of foolish practices warned against would be so long, it would fill a volume.' Kerr v. Koemm, 557 F.Supp. 283, 288 n. 2 (S.D.N.Y.1983). Unlike plaintiff, we must review the record in light of these obvious information costs.

"Cotton's first complaint is that in neglecting to mention that propane is explosive, as well as flammable, the label failed to 'convey a fair indication of the nature and extent of the danger to the mind of a reasonably prudent person.' True, warnings must identify the nature of a product's risks to ensure that the user is apprised of their seriousness. But the record here gives no suggestion of any relevant differences between 'flammable' and 'explosive.' Cotton admitted that he knew propane was flammable and could ignite and burn him. That is precisely what happened. * * * Although the gas 'exploded,' he suffered no injury from that fact insofar as it may be different from simply igniting. Cotton was thus fully aware of the relevant essential consequences of allowing gas to escape from the cylinders.

"Although the other warnings that plaintiff contends should have been given were not contained in the cylinder labels, they were embodied in the * * * pamphlet. It warned that the cylinders should be used only in ventilated areas and that the cylinder valves should be closed. (While the pamphlets did not explicitly warn that the valves should be closed on cylinders withdrawn from use because they might still have propane left in them, this was inferable as a matter of common sense from the pamphlet's insistence on keeping valves shut, on specific safety criteria for valves, and on proper use of valves. Again, a warning need not dot every i.)"

USER PRECAUTION AND SELLER DUTY

The duties of product sellers may be affected by the extent to which product users can and should be expected to exercise care to avoid accidents. Where appropriate, for example, manufacturers have duties both to warn and to instruct. Instructions are *not* appropriate in *MacDonald v. Ortho Pharmaceutical* because, wilful misuse aside, there are no safer or riskier ways of consuming oral contraceptives. Warnings *are* appropriate, because consumers must be alerted to the risks of oral contraceptives so that they may make informed choices about whether or not to use them. In *Cotton v. Buckeye, both* warnings—of the risk that "spent" cylinders will explode—and instructions—on how to minimize that risk through careful handling and storage—are appropriate.

Pure warning cases, where users cannot reduce product risks though safe use and can only choose either to use the product or not, are cases of "unilateral precaution." Only the manufacturer can make the product safer. In "unilateral precaution" cases, does it make sense to place more of the burden of accident minimization on the seller through a "strict" conception of the duty to warn? Cases where both warning and instructions are appropriate, by contrast, are cases of "bilateral precaution." Both manufacturers and users can reduce product risks. In "bilateral precaution" cases, does it make sense to demand less of sellers and more of users through a "negligence" conception of the duty to warn?

THE DUTY TO WARN OF "UNKNOWN" RISKS

Some product risks have only become known after they have caused injuries—often mass injuries—to users of a product. Arguably, this was true of some of the most famous mass disasters with which modern tort law has struggled—asbestos and DES, for example. How should responsibility for these kinds of risks be apportioned? Should these losses be left on victims who were utterly unaware of the dangers to which they were exposed? Or on the manufacturers who unknowingly exposed them? Should the answer to this question turn on the urgency of the need for the product involved? In answering these questions courts must once again choose between negligence and strict liability, and give content to these competing conceptions.

We begin with a special case—the case of affirmative misrepresentation where defendant's liability is predicated on the representations that it has made—and move on to the general case, where defendant's liability is predicated on its failure to speak. In this general case, the debate between strict liability conceptions and negligence ones revolves primarily around two issues: (1) whether *Comment k* to § 402A of the Second Restatement is recognized and, if it is recognized, how broadly it is construed and (2) whether the "state of the art" defense is recognized and, if it is recognized, how strictly it is construed.

CROCKER v. WINTHROP LABORATORIES, DIVISION OF STERLING DRUG, INC.

Supreme Court of Texas, 1974.
514 S.W.2d 429.

REAVLEY, Justice. Glenn E. Crocker became addicted to a new drug produced by Winthrop Laboratories and known as "talwin" which had been previously thought to be non-addictive. [Because of his addiction, he was hospitalized "for a process of detoxification (to remove the toxic agents in his body) and treatment of his drug dependency. After six days in the hospital being withdrawn from talwin as well as all narcotics, and at a time when his tolerance for potent drugs was very low, Crocker walked out of the hospital and went to his home. Because of his agitated condition and the threats he made against his wife, he was finally successful in having her call Dr. Eugene Engel who, on June 10, 1968, came to the Crocker home and gave Mr. Crocker an injection of demerol. Crocker went to his bed for the last time."] His widow and representative, Clarissa Crocker, brought this action for damages due to his suffering while alive as well as for his wrongful death. She recovered judgment against Winthrop Laboratories in the trial court. The Court of Civil Appeals reversed and rendered judgment for the drug company, holding that while some of the facts found by the jury (including the positive misrepresentation by the drug company that talwin was non-addictive) would warrant the recovery, the additional finding that the drug company could not reasonably have foreseen Crocker's addiction (because of his unusual susceptibility and the state of medical knowledge when the drug was marketed), constituted a complete defense.

[The jury below found that "at the time Cracker was taking talwin under doctors' prescriptions, the state of medical knowledge was such that Winthrop Laboratories could not have reasonably foreseen, in the exercise of ordinary care, that talwin would cause an addiction in an appreciable number of persons."]

* * *

Winthrop Laboratories first put talwin on the market in July of 1967 after extensive testing and approval by the Federal Drug Administration. The descriptive material on the new drug circulated by Winthrop Laboratories in 1967 gives no warning of the possibilities of addiction. There is a heading of a paragraph in the product information of the 1967 edition of Physicians' Desk Reference Book which reads: "Absence of addiction liability." This might be considered misleading, but in view of the evidence of verbal assurances as to the properties of talwin by the drug company's representative, there is no need to deal further with the printed materials. Dr. Palafox, a prominent orthopedic surgeon in El Paso, allowed Crocker to have liberal use of talwin and assured him that it was non-addictive because of the assurance by a representative of the drug company who had detailed the doctor on the nature of the drug. There had been an extended and specific conversation between the drug company representative and Dr. Palafox about talwin, and Dr. Palafox was told that talwin was as harmless as aspirin and could be given as long as desired. Dr. Palafox testified that the representative of the defendant insisted that talwin could have no addicting effect.

Subsequent experience has proved that talwin is an extremely useful drug for the relief of pain but that it cannot be regarded as non-addictive.
* * *

* * *

Section 402B applies to those cases of misrepresentation by seller of chattels to the consumer; it reads:

> One engaged in the business of selling chattels who, by advertising, labels, or otherwise, makes to the public a misrepresentation of a material fact concerning the character or quality of a chattel sold by him is subject to liability for physical harm to a consumer of the chattel caused by justifiable reliance upon the misrepresentation, even though
>
> > (a) it is not made fraudulently or negligently, and
> >
> > (b) the consumer has not bought the chattel from or entered into any contractual relation with the seller.

* * *

[Winthrop is subject to liability under § 402B because it misrepresented] that the drug would not cause physical dependence, a fact conceded by the attorney for the company in his jury argument, [and because the trial court reasonably found] reliance and causation. Whatever the danger and state of medical knowledge, and however rare the susceptibility of the user, when the drug company positively and specifically represents its product to be free and safe from all dangers of addiction, and when the treating physician relies upon that representation, the drug company is liable when the representation proves to be false and harm results. * * *

[The judgment of the Court of Civil Appeals is reversed, and the judgment of the trial court is affirmed.]

BROWN v. SUPERIOR COURT
Supreme Court of California, 1988.
44 Cal.3d 1049, 245 Cal.Rptr. 412, 751 P.2d 470.

MOSK, Justice.

In current litigation several significant issues have arisen relating to the liability of manufacturers of prescription drugs for injuries caused by their products. Our first and broadest inquiry is whether such a manufacturer may be held strictly liable for a product that is defective in design. * * *

A number of plaintiffs filed actions in the San Francisco Superior Court against numerous drug manufacturers which allegedly produced DES, a substance plaintiffs claimed was used by their mothers to prevent miscarriage. They alleged that the drug was defective and they were injured in utero when their mothers ingested it. The cases raised several common issues and, in order to facilitate their resolution and conserve judicial resources, the presiding judge, pursuant to a procedure recommended by the Judicial Council, designated the actions as "complex litigation." (Cal.Standards Jud.Admin., § 19 [Deering's Cal.Ann.Codes, Rules (Appen.) (1987 pocket supp.) p. 199].)

Each case was assigned its own number and had an independent existence, but the court's pretrial rulings on the law were made in a separate case with a separate number, and were to be binding on the other actions. At least 69 cases are involved. * * *

* * *

The trial court * * * determined that defendants could not be held strictly liable for the alleged defect in DES but only for their failure to warn of known or knowable side effects of the drug. * * *

Plaintiff sought a writ of mandate or prohibition in the Court of Appeal to review the foregoing rulings. That court issued an alternative writ and, after considering the issues, upheld the trial court's determination * * *. We granted review to examine the conclusions of the Court of Appeal * * * on the issue of strict liability of a drug manufacturer for a defect in the design of a prescription drug.

* * *

[In Barker v. Lull we identified three types of product defects. The first two types were manufacturing and design defects.] The third type of defect identified in Barker is a product that is dangerous because it lacks adequate warnings or instructions. According to plaintiff, defendants here failed to warn of the dangers inherent in the use of DES. We are concerned, therefore, with the second and third types of defects described in Barker.

[When drafting Section 402A of the Restatement 2d of Torts] the members of the American Law Institute * * * pondered whether the manufacturer of a prescription drug should be subject to the doctrine [of strict liability]. (38 ALI Proc. 19, 90–92, 98 (1961).) During [their deliberations] a member of the institute proposed that drugs should be exempted from strict liability on the ground that it would be "against the public interest" to apply the doctrine to such products because of "the very serious tendency to stifle medical research and testing." * * * At the next meeting of the institute in 1962, section 402A was approved together with comment k thereto. (41 ALI Proc. 227, 244 (1962).)

The comment provides that the producer of a properly manufactured prescription drug may be held liable for injuries caused by the product only if it was not accompanied by a warning of dangers that the manufacturer knew or should have known about. * * *

Comment k has been analyzed and criticized by numerous commentators. While there is some disagreement as to its scope and meaning, there is a general consensus that, although it purports to explain the strict liability doctrine, in fact the principle it states is based on negligence. * * * That is, comment k would impose liability on a drug manufacturer only if it failed to warn of a defect of which it either knew or should have known. This concept focuses not on a deficiency in the product—the hallmark of strict liability—but on the fault of the producer in failing to warn of dangers inherent in the use of its product that were either known or knowable—an idea which "rings of negligence," * * *

Comment k has been adopted in the overwhelming majority of jurisdictions that have considered the matter. [citations omitted] In California, several decisions of the Courts of Appeal have embraced the comment k exemption [citations omitted], but this court has never spoken to the issue.

* * *

We appear * * * to have three distinct choices: (1) to hold that the manufacturer of a prescription drug is strictly liable for a defect in its product because it was defectively designed, as that term is defined in Barker, or because of a failure to warn of its dangerous propensities even though such dangers were neither known nor scientifically knowable at the time of distribution; (2) to determine that liability attaches only if a manufacturer fails to warn of dangerous propensities of which it was or should have been aware, in conformity with comment k; or (3) to decide * * * that strict liability for design defects should apply to prescription drugs unless the particular drug which caused the injury is found to be "unavoidably dangerous."

We shall conclude that (1) a drug manufacturer's liability for a defectively designed drug should not be measured by the standards of strict liability; (2) because of the public interest in the development, availability, and reasonable price of drugs, the appropriate test for determining responsibility is the test stated in comment k; and (3) for these same reasons of policy, we disapprove the holding of [an intermediate California appellate court in

Kearl v. Lederle Laboratories] that only those prescription drugs found to be "unavoidably dangerous" should be measured by the comment k standard and that strict liability should apply to drugs that do not meet that description.

1. DESIGN DEFECT

Barker, * * * set forth two alternative tests to measure a design defect: first, whether the product performed as safely as the ordinary consumer would expect when used in an intended and reasonably foreseeable manner, and second, whether, on balance, the benefits of the challenged design outweighed the risk of danger inherent in the design. In making the latter determination, the jury may consider these factors: "the gravity of the danger posed by the challenged design, the likelihood that such danger would occur, the mechanical feasibility of a safer alternative design, the financial cost of an improved design, and the adverse consequences to the product and to the consumer that would result from an alternative design." (20 Cal.3d at p. 431, 143 Cal.Rptr. 225, 573 P.2d 443.)

Defendants assert that neither of these tests is applicable to a prescription drug like DES. * * * We agree that the "consumer expectation" aspect of the Barker test is inappropriate to prescription drugs. While the "ordinary consumer" may have a reasonable expectation that a product such as a machine he purchases will operate safely when used as intended, a patient's expectations regarding the effects of such a drug are those related to him by his physician, to whom the manufacturer directs the warnings regarding the drug's properties. The manufacturer cannot be held liable if it has provided appropriate warnings and the doctor fails in his duty to transmit these warnings to the patient or if the patient relies on inaccurate information from others regarding side effects of the drug.

The second test * * * calls for the balancing of risks and benefits * * * [and asks if] a safer alternative design is feasible. * * *

[This test might be applied to prescription drugs.] For example, plaintiff might be able to demonstrate at trial that a particular component of DES rendered it unsafe as a miscarriage preventative and that removal of that component would not have affected the efficacy of the drug. * * *

Or plaintiff might be able to prove that other, less harmful drugs were available to prevent miscarriage; the benefit of such alternate drugs could be weighed against the advantages of DES in making the risk/benefit analysis of Barker. * * *

Of course, the fact that a drug with dangerous side effects may be characterized as containing a defect in design does not necessarily mean that its producer is to be held strictly liable for the defect. The determination of that issue depends on whether the public interest would be served by the imposition of such liability. As we have seen, the fundamental reasons underlying the imposition of strict liability are to deter manufacturers from marketing products that are unsafe, and to spread the cost of injury from the plaintiff to the consuming public, which will pay a higher price for the product to reflect the increased expense of insurance to the manufacturer resulting from its greater exposure to liability.

These reasons could justify application of the doctrine to the manufacturers of prescription drugs. It is indisputable, as plaintiff contends, that the risk of injury from such drugs is unavoidable, that a consumer may be helpless to protect himself from serious harm caused by them, and that, like other products, the cost of insuring against strict liability can be passed on by the producer to the consumer who buys the item. Moreover, * * * in some cases additional testing of drugs before they are marketed might reveal dangerous side effects, resulting in a safer product.

But there is an important distinction between prescription drugs and other products such as construction machinery, a lawnmower, or perfume, the producers of which were held strictly liable. [citations omitted] In the latter cases, the product is used to make work easier or to provide pleasure, while in the former it may be necessary to alleviate pain and suffering or to sustain life. Moreover, unlike other important medical products (wheelchairs, for example), harm to some users from prescription drugs is unavoidable. Because of these distinctions, the broader public interest in the availability of drugs at an affordable price must be considered in deciding the appropriate standard of liability for injuries resulting from their use.

Perhaps a drug might be made safer if it was withheld from the market until scientific skill and knowledge advanced to the point at which additional dangerous side effects would be revealed. But in most cases such a delay in marketing new drugs—added to the delay required to obtain approval for release of the product from the Food and Drug Administration—would not serve the public welfare. Public policy favors the development and marketing of beneficial new drugs, even though some risks, perhaps serious ones, might accompany their introduction, because drugs can save lives and reduce pain and suffering.

If drug manufacturers were subject to strict liability, they might be reluctant to undertake research programs to develop some pharmaceuticals that would prove beneficial or to distribute others that are available to be marketed, because of the fear of large adverse monetary judgments. Further, the additional expense of insuring against such liability—assuming insurance would be available—and of research programs to reveal possible dangers not detectable by available scientific methods could place the cost of medication beyond the reach of those who need it most.

* * *

The possibility that the cost of insurance and of defending against lawsuits will diminish the availability and increase the price of pharmaceuticals is far from theoretical. Defendants cite a host of examples of products which have greatly increased in price or have been withdrawn or withheld from the market because of the fear that their producers would be held liable for large judgments.

For example, according to defendant E.R. Squibb & Sons, Inc., Benedictin, the only antinauseant drug available for pregnant women, was withdrawn from sale in 1983 because the cost of insurance almost equalled the entire income from sale of the drug. Before it was withdrawn, the price of Benedictin increased by over 300 percent. (132 Chemical Week (June 12, 1983) p. 14.)

Drug manufacturers refused to supply a newly discovered vaccine for influenza on the ground that mass inoculation would subject them to enormous liability. The government therefore assumed the risk of lawsuits resulting from injuries caused by the vaccine. (Franklin & Mais, Tort Law and Mass Immunization Programs (1977) 65 Cal.L.Rev. 754, 769 et seq.; * * *.) One producer of diphtheria-tetanus-pertussis vaccine withdrew from the market, giving as its reason "extreme liability exposure, cost of litigation and the difficulty of continuing to obtain adequate insurance." (Hearing Before Subcom. on Health and the Environment of House Com. on Energy and Commerce on Vaccine Injury Compensation, 98th Cong., 2d Sess. (Sept. 10, 1984) p. 295.) There are only two manufacturers of the vaccine remaining in the market, and the cost of each dose rose a hundredfold from 11 cents in 1982 to $11.40 in 1986, $8 of which was for an insurance reserve. The price increase roughly paralleled an increase in the number of lawsuits from one in 1978 to 219 in 1985. (232 Science (June 13, 1986) p. 1339.) Finally, a manufacturer was unable to market a new drug for the treatment of vision problems because it could not obtain adequate liability insurance at a reasonable cost. (N.Y.Times (Oct. 14, 1986) p. 10.)

There is no doubt that, from the public's standpoint, these are unfortunate consequences. And they occurred even though almost all jurisdictions follow the negligence standard of comment k. It is not unreasonable to conclude in these circumstances that the imposition of a harsher test for liability would not further the public interest in the development and availability of these important products.

We decline to hold, therefore, that a drug manufacturer's liability for injuries caused by the defective design of a prescription drug should be measured by the standard set forth in Barker.

2. Failure to Warn

For these same reasons of policy, we reject plaintiff's assertion that a drug manufacturer should be held strictly liable for failure to warn of risks inherent in a drug even though it neither knew nor could have known by the application of scientific knowledge available at the time of distribution that the drug could produce the undesirable side effects suffered by the plaintiff.

The judgment of the Court of Appeal is affirmed.

SHANKS v. UPJOHN
Supreme Court of Alaska, 1992.
835 P.2d 1189.

MOORE, Justice.

Shanks represents the estate of a decedent who committed suicide shortly after he began taking a prescription drug manufactured by The

Upjohn Company. Shanks sued Upjohn under negligence, negligence per se, strict liability design defect, strict liability failure to warn, and breach of warranty theories. On Upjohn's motions for partial summary judgment, the superior court dismissed all but Shanks' strict liability failure to warn claim. At trial, the superior court instructed the jury on negligence principles alone. After a jury verdict for Upjohn and an award of costs and attorney's fees against the estate, Shanks' personal representative appeals. We vacate the award of attorney's fees and reverse and remand for a new trial on the issues of strict liability design defect and failure to warn.

On August 29, 1984, Harvey Rice, complaining of back pain, made a visit to his physician, Dr. Richard K. Dobyns. Dr. Dobyns prescribed two drugs, Xanax[1] and Tylenol #3[2], and advised Mr. Rice to return in two days for a follow-up examination. The doctor warned Mr. Rice, a pilot, that the drugs would cause sedation and that he should not fly, drive or operate machinery.[3] The following evening, after taking the medication, Mr. Rice shot himself in the head following an argument with his wife. He died in the hospital a few hours later. Tests performed on Mr. Rice at the hospital indicated the presence in his system of Xanax, Tylenol, and codeine as well as another CNS depressant, meprobromate.

Sharon L. Shanks, as personal representative of Mr. Rice's estate, sued the Upjohn Company, the manufacturer of Xanax. * * * Shanks asserted claims against Upjohn under several theories, including strict products liability, breach of warranty, and negligence. In her strict liability claim, Shanks alleged that Xanax was defective both in its design and in its failure to include adequate warnings. * * *

Upjohn filed separate motions for partial summary judgment as to all of Shanks' claims. The superior court granted Upjohn's motions dismissing the design defect, warranty, negligent failure to warn and the negligence per se claims. Thus the strict liability failure to warn claim was the only claim remaining at the time of trial.

* * *

The jury returned a verdict for Upjohn. By special verdict, the jury found that Upjohn was not negligent in failing to adequately warn and direct Mr. Rice's physician regarding the effects of Xanax. Based on the verdict, the superior court entered judgment for Upjohn. In its final judgment, the

---

1. Xanax is the manufacturer's trade name for the drug Alprazolam, a member of the benzodiazepine class of drugs. It is a central nervous system (CNS) depressant used for the treatment of anxiety disorders and anxiety associated with depression.

2. Tylenol #3 is the trade name for acetaminophen with codeine. Codeine is a CNS depressant.

3. Prescription drugs such as Xanax are accompanied by a "package insert" containing warnings and directions for use approved by the United States Food and Drug Administration (FDA). The information contained in the insert, also published in the Physicians' Desk Refer-

ence, is intended for the use of the physician, not the patient. The Xanax package insert warns that because of its CNS effect, patients using Xanax "should be cautioned against engaging in hazardous occupations" and "about the simultaneous ingestion of ... other CNS depressant drugs during treatment with XANAX." In the section of the insert labeled "Precautions" is the following: As with other psychotropic medications, the usual precautions with respect to administration of the drug and size of the prescription are indicated for severely depressed patients or those in whom there is reason to expect concealed suicidal ideation or plans.

superior court assessed costs and attorney's fees against the estate, refusing to assess them against Mr. Rice's widow and three minor children, as requested by Upjohn. The superior court ordered the estate to pay Upjohn $225,000.00 in attorney's fees. Shanks' motion for J.N.O.V. or in the alternative for new trial, in which she alleged misconduct by Upjohn's counsel, was denied.

Shanks appeals, challenging the grant of summary judgment and the denial of her motion for new trial. * * *

A.   Design Defect

Shanks' first assignment of error is that the superior court improperly dismissed her strict liability design defect claim on Upjohn's motion for partial summary judgment. Upjohn urges us to adopt a rule of law which would exempt manufacturers of prescription drugs from such claims. Specifically, Upjohn argues that we should adopt the approach of the California Supreme Court in Brown v. Superior Court, 44 Cal.3d 1049, 245 Cal.Rptr. 412, 751 P.2d 470 (1988). We decline to do so.

* * *

[We have previously] adopted the two-prong defective design test set forth by the California Supreme Court in Barker v. Lull Eng'g Co., 20 Cal.3d 413, 143 Cal.Rptr. 225, 573 P.2d 443, 457–58 (1978). [We have held] that a product is defectively designed if: (1) the plaintiff proves that the product failed to perform as safely as an ordinary consumer would expect when used in an intended or reasonably foreseeable manner, or (2) the plaintiff proves that the product's design proximately caused injury and the defendant fails to prove, in light of the relevant factors, that on balance the benefits of the challenged design outweigh the risk of danger inherent in such design.

The issue of the applicability of the Barker test in the context of prescription drugs is before this court for the first time. With respect to the first prong, Shanks argues that the "consumer expectation" prong of the Barker test should be consistently applied in all cases, regardless of the nature of the product involved. We disagree.

* * *

However, rather than completely discard an expectation prong, we believe one can be tailored to reflect the unique nature of prescription drugs and the role of the doctor in the decision to use a particular drug. In a sense, prescribing doctors are the consumers of prescription drugs. It is the doctor's evaluation of the patient's condition and consideration of the available treatment alternatives which leads to the choice of a specific prescription drug product. Also, the doctor has ready access to the FDA-approved warning information contained in the package insert and the Physicians' Desk Reference. Thus it is the doctor's expectation, and not that of the patient, regarding the performance and safety of prescription drugs which is the relevant inquiry in the imposition of strict liability. In light of this, we conclude that a prescription drug is defectively designed and strict liability should be imposed on its manufacturer if the prescription drug failed to perform as safely as an ordinary doctor would expect, when used by the patient in an intended and reasonably foreseeable manner.[4]

As to the second prong of the Barker test, we find the reasoning of the Brown court in declining to apply the "risk/benefit" analysis in the prescription drug context to be unpersuasive, and we decline to follow it. While the social utility and value of prescription drugs as a class of products may exceed that of most other classes of products, we do not believe that this generalization warrants granting "the same protection from liability to those who gave us thalidomide as to the producers of penicillin."* 245 Cal.Rptr. at 423, 751 P.2d at 481. Furthermore, we find it speculative at best that restricting strict liability design defect claims against prescription drug manufacturers will serve the public interest by enhancing the availability and affordability of prescription drugs.[5] While we recognize that the threat of products liability litigation in general may impair the ability of drug manufacturers to obtain liability insurance and may cause beneficial drugs to be withdrawn from the market, it is far from obvious that strict liability doctrines, rather than the awards of compensatory and punitive damages in negligence actions, are responsible. Products liability suits against drug manufacturers are almost invariably brought under both negligence and strict liability theories. There is nothing in the record of this case to indicate, nor does the Brown court explain, the impact of design defect claims alone on the cost of products liability litigation, on the cost to drug manufacturers of liability insurance or on the availability and affordability of prescription drugs. Finally, we find it consistent with the purposes underlying strict products liability that manufacturers should be deterred from marketing certain products and that the cost of the defense of strict products liability litigation and any resulting judgments should be borne by the manufacturer

---

4. With certain types of prescription drugs, the role of the doctor in the decision to use a specific product is significantly reduced. Examples of such atypical prescription products include contraceptives, where the patient initiates and directs the usage, drugs typically administered in a clinical setting with little or no physician involvement, or drugs marketed under a strategy designed to appeal directly to the consuming public. These are areas where courts have held that manufacturers have a duty to warn patients directly. In strict liability design defect cases involving such products, it may be appropriate to apply the "ordinary consumer expectation" test rather than the "ordinary doctor expectation" test.

* Thalidomide was a sedative, prescribed to pregnant women (among others) in 48 countries, but not the United States, in the 1950's and early 1960's. It was banned world-wide in the early 1960's, after it caused horrible birth defects in thousands of children whose mothers took it while pregnant. Many of the more than 12,000 children affected were born with short "flippers" for limbs, or no limbs at all. In September of 1997, the FDA announced its intention to license the drug for use on leprosy patients. Under U.S. law, once a drug is approved for any use, physicians can legally pre-

scribe it for "off-label," or officially untested, uses. Because studies have suggested that the thalidomide might be very useful in treating certain cancers and advanced AIDS, some "off-label" prescription of thalidomide is expected. To avoid a repeat of the earlier disaster, the FDA has proposed requiring women of childbearing age to show proof that they are using contraceptives before they can be considered for treatment.—Eds.

5. The Brown court states that "[w]e are aware of only one decision that has applied the doctrine of strict liability to prescription drugs." Id. 245 Cal.Rptr. at 418, 751 P.2d at 476 (citing Brochu v. Ortho Pharmaceutical Corp., 642 F.2d 652, 654–57 (1st Cir.1981)). Yet the court goes on to discuss the adverse effect of products liability litigation on the availability and cost of prescription drugs. Id. 245 Cal.Rptr. at 421, 751 P.2d at 479–80. If, as the Brown court claims, theories other than strict liability have been the basis of recovery under these claims in the past, it is unclear how limiting strict liability causes of action will serve the policy interest in enhancing the availability and affordability of prescription drugs in the future.

who is able to spread the cost through insurance and by charging more for its products. See 245 Cal.Rptr. at 420, 751 P.2d at 478.

We find the language of the Eighth Circuit Court of Appeals, explicitly rejecting the policy basis of the Brown decision in Hill v. Searle Laboratories, 884 F.2d 1064, 1069 (8th Cir.1989), to be particularly apt. There the court stated that "the premise generally relied on by those courts [exempting all prescription drugs from strict liability design defect claims]—that the public interest in the development of prescription drug products requires the user to bear all the costs of injury unless the drug product was negligently manufactured or designed or unaccompanied by proper warnings—is unconvincing. In our view, this policy has no greater relevance to prescription drug products than to other products having life-saving or life-bettering characteristics." Id. The public policy concerns underlying the doctrine of strict products liability must be balanced with, rather than yield to, the public interest in the availability and affordability of safe prescription drugs. We believe that these interests are best balanced and served by applying the risk/benefit prong of the Barker test in determining the liability of prescription drug manufacturers. We hold that the superior court erred in not doing so.

In deciding whether a defendant has met the burden of proving that the benefits of the design outweigh the risk, * * * the fact finder should consider the seriousness of the side effects or reactions posed by the drug, the likelihood that such side effects or reactions would occur, the feasibility of an alternative design which would eliminate or reduce the side effects or reactions without affecting the efficacy of the drug, and the harm to the consumer in terms of reduced efficacy and any new side effects or reactions that would result from an alternative design. In evaluating the benefits, the fact finder should be permitted to consider the seriousness of the condition for which the drug is indicated. In summary, what the trier of fact should determine in balancing these factors is whether the drug confers an important benefit and whether the interest in its availability outweighs the interest in promoting the enhanced accountability which strict products liability design defect review provides. See Kearl v. Lederle Laboratories, 172 Cal. App.3d 812, 218 Cal.Rptr. 453, 464 (1985).[6]

On appeal, the parties extensively briefed the issue of the applicability and scope of comment k to § 402A of the Restatement (Second) of Torts. Most courts that have considered the issue have adopted comment k to § 402A. See Brown, 245 Cal.Rptr. at 417, 751 P.2d at 476. Upjohn now urges us to adopt comment k and follow the Brown court in interpreting it to grant immunity from strict liability design defect claims to manufacturers of all prescription drugs.

6. We reject Upjohn's argument that courts should defer to the determination of the Food and Drug Administration as to the safety and efficacy of a prescription drug. While a deferential standard of review is appropriate when directly reviewing an agency decision, we feel that such deference in the face of allegations of serious injuries caused by FDA-approved drugs would amount to an abdication of judicial responsibility. See Grundberg v. Upjohn Co., 813 P.2d 89, 100–04 (Utah 1991) (Stewart, J., dissenting).

While we accept the soundness of the policy underlying comment k that manufacturers of certain highly beneficial products which have inherent unavoidable risks of which the user is adequately warned should not be held strictly liable for injuries resulting from their products, we decline to formally adopt comment k for three reasons. First, we believe that comment k has contributed to the confusion which permeates this area of law and blurs the distinctions between negligence and strict liability principles, a distinction we believe warrants preservation.

Secondly, courts are unable to agree as to the comment's scope. Some courts have interpreted comment k to exempt all prescription drugs from strict liability design defect claims. See, e.g., Brown, 245 Cal.Rptr. at 415–24, 751 P.2d at 473–83. In Grundberg v. Upjohn Co., 813 P.2d 89 (Utah 1991), the most recent case addressing this issue, the Utah Supreme Court arrived at the same conclusion but refused to rely on a strained interpretation of the plain language of comment k to reach this result. Id. at 95. Other courts, without confronting the issue squarely, discuss comment k as if it applies to all prescription drugs. [citations to three opinions omitted] Still other courts interpret comment k to provide the exemption only to those prescription drugs determined on a case-by-case basis to be "unavoidably dangerous." [citations to six opinions omitted] By declining to adopt comment k, we hope to avoid contributing to this confusion.

Finally, we believe that the risk/benefit prong of the Barker test offers the manufacturers of those products intended to be protected by comment k an opportunity to avoid liability for strict liability claims based on a design defect theory. For these reasons, we find it undesirable and unnecessary to impose the additional layer of comment k on an area of law which is already strained under its own doctrinal weight. We recognize that by holding that the liability of drug manufacturers should be measured by the second prong of the Barker test, we are taking a position similar to those jurisdictions which apply comment k to prescription drugs on a case-by-case basis. However, we arrive at this result without specifically relying on comment k.

In summary, the superior court erred in its conclusion that prescription drugs are exempt from strict liability design defect claims. Alaska recognizes such claims and makes no exception for prescription drugs. Neither policy nor reason supports the approach taken by some courts in barring such claims. * * *

B. FAILURE TO WARN

While it dismissed all but Shanks' strict liability failure to warn claim before trial, the superior court's jury instructions presented only a negligence theory to the jury. Shanks argues that the superior court erred when it introduced negligence principles while instructing the jury on the strict liability failure to warn claim. * * *

We recognize the conceptual problems that exist in determining the boundary between negligent and strict liability failure to warn and the practical difficulties facing courts and juries in applying these principles. See W. Page Keeton et al., Prosser and Keeton on the Law of Torts § 99, at 697–

98 (5th ed. 1984). * * * Negligence-like language inevitably creeps into strict liability failure to warn analysis, both in the context of determining which risks require a warning and in determining whether a warning is adequate. However, we believe that the policy underlying strict liability warrants preserving the distinction between the doctrines.

* * *

* * * Under a strict liability failure to warn theory, if the plaintiff proves that the product as marketed posed a risk of injury to one who uses the product in a reasonably foreseeable manner and the product is marketed without adequate warnings of the risk, the product is defective. If such a defect is the proximate cause of the plaintiff's injuries, the manufacturer is strictly liable unless the defendant manufacturer can prove that the risk was scientifically unknowable at the time the product was distributed to the plaintiff. The superior court committed reversible error in only presenting a negligent failure to warn theory to the jury and in depriving Shanks of her strict liability failure to warn claim.

* * *

The judgment of the superior court is REVERSED and REMANDED for further proceedings consistent with this opinion. The award of attorney's fees is VACATED.

THE "STATE OF THE ART" DEFENSE

BESHADA v. JOHNS–MANVILLE PRODUCTS CORP., 90 N.J. 191, 447 A.2d 539 (1982). "The sole question here is whether defendants in a product liability case based on strict liability for failure to warn may raise a 'state of the art' defense. Defendants assert that the danger of which they failed to warn was undiscovered at the time the product was marketed and that it was undiscoverable given the state of scientific knowledge at that time. The case comes to us on appeal from the trial court's denial of plaintiffs' motion to strike the state-of-the-art defense. For the reasons stated below, we reverse the trial court judgment and strike the defense.

* * *

"These cases involve asbestos exposure dating back perhaps as far as the 1930's. The suits are first arising now because of the long latent period between exposure and the discernible symptoms of asbestosis and mesothelioma. Plaintiffs have raised a variety of legal theories to support their claims for damages. The important claim, for purposes of this appeal, is strict liability for failure to warn. Prior to the 1960's, defendants' products allegedly contained no warning of their hazardous nature. Defendants respond by asserting the state-of-the-art defense. They allege that no one knew or could have known that asbestos was dangerous when it was marketed.

"There is substantial factual dispute about what defendants knew and when they knew it. A trial judge in the Eastern District of Texas, the forum for numerous asbestos-related cases, has concluded that '[k]nowledge of the

danger can be attributed to the industry as early as the mid–1930's * * *.'
Hardy v. Johns–Manville Sales Corp., 509 F.Supp. 1353, 1355 (E.D.Tex.1981)
(footnote omitted). Defendants respond, however, that [before] the 1960's
* * * the danger from asbestos was believed limited to workers in asbestos
textile mills, who were exposed to much higher concentrations of asbestos
dust than were the workers at other sites, such as shipyards. Defendants
claim that it was not discovered until recently that the much smaller
concentration these workers faced were also hazardous.

"We need not resolve the factual issues raised. * * * The issue is
whether the medical community's presumed unawareness of the dangers of
asbestos is a defense to plaintiffs' claims.

* * *

" * * * For purposes of analysis, we can distinguish two tests for
determining whether a product is safe: (1) does its utility outweigh its risk?
and (2) if so, has that risk been reduced to the greatest extent possible
consistent with the product's utility? * * * The second aspect of strict
liability * * * requires that the risk from the product be reduced to the
greatest extent possible without hindering its utility. Whether or not the
product passes the initial risk-utility test, it is not reasonably safe if the same
product could have been made or marketed more safely.

"Warning cases are of this second type. * * *

" * * * [The issue in some earlier decisions] was whether there is any
difference between negligence and strict liability in warning cases. We stated
unequivocally that there is. That difference is * * *:

> when a plaintiff sues under strict liability, there is no need to prove
> that the manufacturer knew or should have known of any dangerous
> propensities of its product—such knowledge is imputed to the manufac-
> turer. [Freund v. Cellofilm Properties, Inc., 87 N.J. at 239, 432 A.2d 925]

Thus, we held in *Freund* that it was reversible error for the trial judge to
instruct the jury only with a negligence charge.

" * * * Essentially, state-of-the-art is a negligence defense. It seeks to
explain why defendants are not culpable for failing to provide a warning.
They assert, in effect, that because they could not have known the product
was dangerous, they acted reasonably in marketing it without a warning. But
in strict liability cases, culpability is irrelevant. The product was unsafe. That
it was unsafe because of the state of technology does not change the fact
that it was unsafe. Strict liability focuses on the product, not the fault of the
manufacturer. * * *

"When the defendants argue that it is unreasonable to impose a duty on
them to warn of the unknowable, they misconstrue both the purpose and
effect of strict liability. By imposing strict liability, we are not requiring
defendants to have done something that is impossible. In this sense, the
phrase 'duty to warn' is misleading. It implies negligence concepts with their
attendant focus on the reasonableness of defendant's behavior. However, a
major concern of strict liability—ignored by defendants—is the conclusion

that if a product was in fact defective, the distributor of the product should compensate its victims for the misfortune that it inflicted on them.

"The most important inquiry * * * is whether imposition of liability for failure to warn of dangers which were undiscoverable at the time of manufacture will advance the goals and policies sought to be achieved by our strict liability rules. We believe that it will [further the goal of risk-spreading by dispersing the costs of product accidents across 'the manufacturers and distributors who profit from its sale and the buyers who profit from its use." Eliminating the "state of the art" defense will also further the policy of allocative efficiency because it will "force the price of any particular product to reflect the cost of insuring against the possibility that the product will turn out to be defective."]

" * * * The analysis thus far has assumed that it is possible to define what constitutes 'undiscoverable' knowledge and that it will be reasonably possible to determine what knowledge was technologically discoverable at a given time. In fact, both assumptions are highly questionable. * * *

"Scientific knowability, as we understand it, refers not to what in fact was known at the time, but to what *could have been* known at the time. In other words, even if no scientist had actually formed the belief that asbestos was dangerous, the hazards would be deemed 'knowable' if a scientist could have formed that belief by applying research or performing tests that were available at the time. Proof of what could have been known will inevitably be complicated, costly, confusing and time-consuming. * * *

"The concept of knowability is complicated further by the fact * * * that the level of investment in safety research by manufacturers is one determinant of the state-of-the-art at any given time. Fairness suggests that manufacturers not be excused from liability because their prior inadequate investment in safety rendered the hazards of their product unknowable. Thus, a judgment will have to be made as to whether defendants' investment in safety research in the years preceding distribution of the product was adequate. If not, the experts in the history of technology will have to testify as to what would have been knowable at the time of distribution if manufacturers had spent the proper amount on safety in prior years. To state the issue is to fully understand the great difficulties it would engender in a courtroom.

"For the reasons expressed above, we conclude that plaintiffs' position is consistent with our holding in *Freund* and prior cases and will achieve the various policies underlying strict liability. The burden of illness from dangerous products such as asbestos should be placed upon those who profit from its production and, more generally, upon society at large, which reaps the benefits of the various products our economy manufactures. That burden should not be imposed exclusively on the innocent victim. Although victims must in any case suffer the pain involved, they should be spared the burdensome financial consequences of unfit products. At the same time, we believe this position will serve the salutary goals of increasing product safety research and simplifying tort trials.

"* * * We impose strict liability because * * * [a]s between * * * innocent victims and [product] distributors, it is the distributors—and the public which consumes their products—which should bear the unforeseen costs of the product.

"The judgment of the trial court is reversed; the plaintiff's motion to strike the state-of-the-art defense is granted."

FELDMAN v. LEDERLE LABORATORIES, 97 N.J. 429, 479 A.2d 374 (1984). Plaintiff's teeth were permanently discolored as a result of her use of a prescription antibiotic. She brought suit on the ground that the manufacturer had failed to warn physicians of this side effect. Lederle, the manufacturer of the drug, asserted the "state of the art" defense, arguing that the possibility of tooth discoloration was unknown at the time that the product was marketed. The trial court entered judgment on a jury verdict for the defendant and the intermediate appellate court affirmed. *Held,* reversed in part, and remanded. "We do not overrule *Beshada* but restrict *Beshada* to the circumstances giving rise to its holding." *Beshada* should not "hold generally or in all cases, particularly with respect to a situation like the present one involving drugs vital to health."

"* * * [Generally, the adequacy of a warning] should be measured by knowledge at the time the manufacturer distributed the product. Did the defendant know, or should he have known, of the danger, given the scientific, technological, and other information available when the product was distributed; or, in other words, did he have actual or constructive knowledge of the danger? The *Restatement* has adopted this test in comment j to section 402A, * * *. Under this standard negligence and strict liability in warning cases may be deemed to be functional equivalents. Constructive knowledge embraces knowledge that should have been known based on information that was reasonably available or obtainable and should have alerted a reasonably prudent person to act. Put another way, would a person of reasonable intelligence or of the superior expertise of the defendant charged with such knowledge conclude that defendant should have alerted the consuming public?"

STERNHAGEN v. DOW CO., 282 Mont. 168, 935 P.2d 1139 (1997). "Strict liability without regard to fault is the only doctrine that fulfills the public interest goals of protecting consumers, compensating the injured and making those who profit from the market bear the risks and costs associated with the defective or dangerous products which they place in the stream of commerce. * * *

"* * * [B]oth our case law and statutory law make it clear that even careful manufacturers may be strictly liable for unreasonably dangerous products whose dangers could not be foreseen. [citations omitted] Moreover, given strict liability's focus on the product and not on the manufacturer's conduct, knowledge of any undiscovered or undiscoverable dangers should be imputed to the manufacturer. That is, while a plaintiff must still prove [a traceable defect, causation, and damage or injury], evidence that a manufacturer knew or through the exercise of reasonable human foresight should have known of the dangers inherent in his product is irrelevant. [citation omitted]

Accordingly, in answer to the question certified, we conclude that, in a strict products liability case, knowledge of any undiscovered or undiscoverable dangers should be imputed to the manufacturer. Furthermore, we conclude that, in a strict products liability case, state-of-the-art evidence is not admissible to establish whether the manufacturer knew or through the exercise of reasonable human foresight should have known of the danger."

POTTER v. CHICAGO PNEUMATIC TOOL CO., 241 Conn. 199, 694 A.2d 1319 (1997). "In Tomer v. American Home Products Corp., 170 Conn. 681, 687, 368 A.2d 35 (1976), this court recognized the applicability of state-of-the-art evidence to failure to warn claims, stating that '[s]ince the defendants could not be held to standards which exceeded the limits of scientific advances existing at the time of their allegedly tortious conduct, expert testimony tending to show the scope of duties owed could have been properly limited to scientific knowledge existing at that time.' "

SECTION D.   USER CONDUCT

Product liability differs from the standard accident to which tort law applies in that the victims of product accidents are not usually "strangers," legally speaking, to the enterprises which injure them. The prototypical victim of a product accident is both the user and the purchaser of the product. The participation of product accident victims in the activities which result in their own injury affects the law of products liability in a number of ways. One aspect of that participation is the chain of contracts liking manufacturer, distributor and consumer, noted at the outset of Chapter 19. That chain makes contract a live alternative to tort as the legal regime for regulating product accidents.

A second aspect of the victim's participation in the activity which injures him, is brought out by product warning and instruction law. Because victims purchase products, the risks of those products might be transferred to them at the time of purchase, through an adequate and appropriate warning. Because victims use products, they may be enlisted in the pursuit of product safety, by being instructed in the safe operation of otherwise risky objects. Not surprisingly, victim use of products—and resultant participation in the genesis of product accidents—has at least as important an influence on the articulation and application of product defenses.

Contemporary product liability doctrine on defenses shows the influence of two distinct movements and regimes. The first is the original product liability regime of § 402A, with which we start. This is a strict liability regime—an enterprise liability regime—formulated at a time when contributory negligence was a bar to all recovery. The second is the comparative negligence regime, which arose after the promulgation of § 402A, and which has spread from negligence law into products liability law. These two regimes have different conceptual structures, although much of the conceptual structure of the § 402A regime can be incorporated into a comparative regime, as *Hernandez v. Barbo Machinery Co.*, the first main case in this section, shows.

In thinking about product defenses, it helps to recognize that the victim's participation in the genesis of product accidents—the victim's encounter with a product defect—makes it difficult to disentangle "duty" from "defense". In considering cases where victim negligence is at issue, for instance, you may wish to ask yourself if the victim's conduct would be negligent, absent the defect in the defendant's product. In considering assumption of risk, you may wish to ask how we disentangle defendant's duty to make a reasonably safe product from plaintiff's assumption of the risk.

RESTATEMENT OF TORTS, SECOND (1977)

§ 402A, Comments h, n

h. [Defective Condition.] A product is not in a defective condition when it is safe for normal handling and consumption. If the injury results from abnormal handling, as where a bottled beverage is knocked against a radiator to remove the cap, or from abnormal preparation for use, as where too much salt is added to food, or from abnormal consumption, as where a child eats too much candy and is made ill, the seller is not liable. Where, however, he has reason to anticipate that danger may result from a particular use, as where a drug is sold which is safe only in limited doses, he may be required to give adequate warning of the danger (see Comment *j*), and a product sold without such warning is in a defective condition.

* * *

n. Contributory Negligence. Since the liability with which this Section deals is not based upon negligence of the seller, but is strict liability, the rule applied to strict liability cases applies. Contributory negligence of the plaintiff is not a defense when such negligence consists merely in a failure to discover the defect in the product, or to guard against the possibility of its existence. On the other hand the form of contributory negligence which consists in voluntarily and unreasonably proceeding to encounter a known danger, and commonly passes under the name of assumption of risk, is a defense under this Section as in other cases of strict liability. If the user or consumer discovers the defect and is aware of the danger, and nevertheless proceeds unreasonably to make use of the product and is injured by it, he is barred from recovery.

HERNANDEZ v. BARBO MACHINERY CO.

Supreme Court of Oregon, 1998.
327 Or. 99, 957 P.2d 147.

KULONGOSKI, Justice.

The issue in this products liability case is whether the trial court committed reversible error in refusing to give plaintiff's requested jury instruction [that "contributory negligence of the plaintiff is not a defense when such negligence consists merely in a failure to discover the defect in the product, or to guard against the possibility of its existence."]. * * *

We take the following facts from the opinion of the Court of Appeals: [footnote omitted]

Plaintiff is a maintenance mechanic who serviced Westwood Manufacturing Company's (Westwood) machinery. On June 25, 1993, plaintiff discovered a new saw at the Westwood work site, which he had never seen before, and with which he was unfamiliar. The saw, called a Belsaw, is sold by defendants. It consists of a cabinet, in which the saw blade is encased, with a work area on top where the wood is cut. The blade is not visible when the cabinet door is closed.

Plaintiff decided to investigate the saw more closely to see if it needed maintenance. He looked for the on/off switch to determine whether the saw was turned off, but because the area was dark and because the switch was not located in any of the customary positions, plaintiff could not find the switch. He also placed his hand on the top of the cabinet, but could not feel a vibration from the saw, nor could he hear any sound emanating from the cabinet. However, unbeknownst to plaintiff, the saw was operating.

Plaintiff then opened the cabinet door and squatted on the floor to get a closer look at the inside of the cabinet. Using a flashlight, he looked inside the cabinet. While he was looking, he slipped on sawdust, causing his right hand to go inside the cabinet and into the moving saw blade. The accident resulted in the partial amputation of plaintiff's right hand." 141 Or.App. at 36, 917 P.2d 30.

* * *

Plaintiff sued defendants under the theory of strict products liability. He alleged that defendants' machine was dangerously defective in four respects:

A. It was not equipped with a readily observable on/off switch which clearly showed what mode the saw was in at all times;

B. It was not equipped with a limit switch on, or in conjunction with, its access door which would terminate the power to the blade in the event the door was opened;

C. It was not equipped with a decal or similar device warning its users of the risk of opening the access door without first making certain that the saw was in the 'off' mode; and

D. It was not equipped with a guard sufficient to prevent a user from coming into contact with the saw's revolving blade.

Defendants raised the affirmative defense of comparative fault, setting forth the following ten allegations of plaintiff's negligence:

1. Plaintiff, as an experienced maintenance person, knew that machines contain on-off switches and further knew that with respect to this specific machine he had not yet located the on-off switch when he

opened the door to the interior of the machine, thereby knowingly encountering the risk that the saw blade might be turning.

2. Plaintiff knowingly encountered the risk that the machine might be running by opening the door to the interior of the Belsaw when he heard or should have been able to hear the sound of the saw blade running.

3. Plaintiff knowingly encountered the risk that the machine might be running by ignoring the fact that when the door to the Belsaw was opened the noise from the blade was louder than when the door was closed, thereby indicating that the machine was running and the blade was turning.

4. Plaintiff negligently set his feet in sawdust in an area in which the floor was obviously covered with sawdust which he could slip on.

5. Plaintiff knowingly encountered a risk of injury when he, having possession of a flashlight, failed to use it first on the exterior of the machine to locate the on-off switch and turn the machine off, before attempting to use the flashlight to see the interior of the machine.

6. Plaintiff knowingly encountered a risk of injury when he failed to follow standard and generally recognized safety rules of first unplugging the Belsaw before he attempted to inspect its interior.

7. Plaintiff knowingly encountered the risk of injury when he failed to ask any Westwood employee for a manual or for instructions as to how to turn the Belsaw off before he began his inspection.

8. Plaintiff knowingly encountered the risk of injuring himself on a machine whose blade was still moving by failing to follow a safe shutdown procedure prior to performing inspection or maintenance on the machine.

9. Plaintiff knowingly encountered the risk of injury to himself by placing his hand into the cabinet of the saw when the presence of the blade was open, obvious and constituted an observable danger.

10. Plaintiff knowingly encountered the risk of injuring himself on a machine when he saw the on-off switch on the Belsaw and failed to push the off button to shut the machine down.

Defendants' fourth allegation of plaintiff's comparative fault is the only one that does not allege that plaintiff knowingly encountered the risk of injury created by the alleged defects in the saw.

At trial, plaintiff requested the following jury instruction:

Defendants have charged plaintiff with comparative fault; that is, they have alleged that the subject accident and any injuries that plaintiff may have sustained as a result thereof, were caused, at least in part, by plaintiff's own fault in certain particulars. In that connection, I instruct you that an injured person's conduct which in fact was a cause of his or her injury, and which constitutes 'fault,' including negligence, may be considered in a products liability action, unless that person's alleged negligence consists in the kind of unobservant, inattentive, ignorant, or awkward failure to discover or to guard against the defect that goes toward making the product dangerously defective in the first place. In other words, contributory negligence of the plaintiff is not a defense when such negligence consists merely in a failure to discover the defect in the product, or to guard against the possibility of its existence.

Plaintiff's requested jury instruction relied on this court's treatment of comparative fault in a products liability action in *Sandford v. Chev. Div. Gen. Motors*, 292 Or. 590, 610, 642 P.2d 624 (1982).

The trial court refused to give plaintiff's requested jury instruction * * *

The jury returned a verdict, finding that defendants were at fault in one or more of the ways alleged in the complaint and that plaintiff was at fault in one or more of the ways alleged in defendants' answer. The jury further found plaintiff's fault to be 50.5 percent and defendants' fault to be 49.5 percent. Because plaintiff's fault exceeded that of defendants, the trial court entered a judgment in favor of defendants. ORS 18.470. On appeal, the Court of Appeals concluded that the trial court's refusal to give plaintiff's requested jury instruction constituted reversible error. For the reasons discussed below, we agree.

* * *

* * * [A]n error in refusing to give a requested jury instruction requires reversal only if the jury instructions given by the trial court, considered as a whole, cause prejudice to the party requesting the instruction. [citations omitted] The party requesting an instruction is prejudiced if the trial court's failure to give the requested instruction probably created an erroneous impression of the law in the minds of the members of the jury, and if that erroneous impression may have affected the outcome of the case. [citations omitted]

* * *

In *Sandford*, this court held that a plaintiff's comparative fault could defeat a products liability claim if the plaintiff's fault is greater than the defendant's fault. In describing what conduct by a plaintiff properly could be attributed to the plaintiff as fault, this court stated:

> 'Fault' includes contributory negligence except for such unobservant, inattentive, ignorant, or awkward failure of the injured party to discover the defect or to guard against it as is taken into account in finding the particular product dangerously defective.

292 Or. at 610, 642 P.2d 624.

* * *

Th[is] passage from *Sandford* on which plaintiff relies for his requested jury instruction represented the court's conclusion that the legislature carried forward, into the comparative fault regime adopted by the legislature in the 1975 version of ORS 18.470, the long-established principle that a plaintiff's incidental carelessness or negligent failure to discover or guard against a product defect is not an appropriate defense to that plaintiff's products liability action for injuries suffered because of the product defect.[7] * * * Other forms of negligent conduct by a plaintiff, such as unreasonable misuse of the product, or unreasonable use despite knowledge of a dangerous defect in the product and awareness of the risk posed by that defect, are defenses to a strict products liability action. The jury instruction that plaintiff requested is a correct statement of the law regarding the kinds of negligent behavior that the jury can and cannot attribute to a plaintiff in considering that party's proportional fault in a strict products liability action.

* * *

* * * [W]here a plaintiff requests a *Sandford* instruction such as the one requested by plaintiff here, the court must determine whether the pleadings and evidence are such that a jury reasonably could conclude that the plaintiff has established that the plaintiff's injury resulted, in whole or in part, from an "unobservant, inattentive, ignorant, or awkward" failure to discover or guard against alleged defects in the product. If so, the giving of a *Sandford* instruction is appropriate. The plaintiff is entitled to have the jury instructed correctly and adequately as to the kinds of negligent conduct that the jury may and may not attribute to him as a defense to a strict products liability action.

The instructions that the trial court gave in this case informed the jury that it could attribute fault to plaintiff if he engaged in the type of behavior specified by defendants' affirmative answer, *i.e.*, either by "knowingly" encountering a risk of injury or by engaging in negligent conduct in the face of an "obvious" danger. However, defendants' allegations of plaintiff's fault also encompass negligence that this court has ruled cannot be attributed to a plaintiff as fault.

Defendants alleged that plaintiff "negligently set his feet in sawdust * * * which he could slip on" (affirmative defense, * * * allegation no. 4). * * * If the court had instructed the jury properly, as requested by plaintiff, the jury reasonably could have found that, even if plaintiff was negligent in setting his feet in the sawdust while he worked on the saw, thereby creating a risk of injury from the alleged defects in the saw, such negligence consisted of an "unobservant, inattentive, ignorant or awkward failure" to discover or guard against the alleged defects in the saw. Instructed properly, the jury would have understood that it could not attribute that negligence to plaintiff as comparative fault. We conclude that the trial court failed to instruct the jury on an issue material to the outcome of the case.

In this case, plaintiff was harmed, because the jury may have based its comparative fault assessment on a misperception of the evidence resulting directly from the court's failure to give plaintiff's requested jury instruction. * * *

---

7. In an omitted portion of the opinion, the court comments that *Sanford's* holding that "fault" in a product liability action does not include "unobservant, inattentive, ignorant, or awkward failure of the injured party to discover the defect or to guard against it" was carrying forward a doctrine which originated in *Findlay* *v. Copeland Lumber Co.*, 265 Or. 300, 509 P.2d 28 (1973). The omitted portion of the opinion goes on to explain that *Findlay* was applying *Comment n* to § 402A of the **Second Restatement,** and the strict liability policies of § 402A more generally.—Eds.

The decision of the Court of Appeals is affirmed. The judgment of the circuit court is reversed, and the case is remanded to the circuit court for further proceedings.

———

MESSICK v. GENERAL MOTORS CORP., 460 F.2d 485 (5th Cir.1972). Plaintiff knew the defect in the front suspension system of his automobile and had been told by a mechanic that if he continued to drive the car it would kill him. He did continue to drive it and, though he was not killed, he was injured. He argued that his use of the automobile after knowledge of the danger was reasonable because of economic duress since he depended on his car in his work as a salesman and he was unable to obtain any substitute transportation. The Fifth Circuit upheld an instruction that "a person is not at fault in voluntarily exposing himself to a known and appreciated danger, if, under the same or similar circumstances, an ordinarily prudent person would have incurred the risk which such conduct involved."

"MISUSE", "FORESEEABLE MISUSE" AND ASSUMPTION OF THE RISK

MICALLEF v. MIEHLE CO., DIVISION OF MIEHLE–GOSS DEXTER, INC.

Court of Appeals of New York, 1976.
39 N.Y.2d 376, 384 N.Y.S.2d 115, 348 N.E.2d 571.

COOKE, Judge. The time has come to depart from the patent danger rule enunciated in Campo v. Scofield, 301 N.Y. 468, 95 N.E.2d 802.

This action was initiated to recover damages for personal injuries, allegedly resulting from negligent design and breach of an implied warranty. Paul Micallef, plaintiff, was employed by Lincoln Graphic Arts at its Farmingdale plant as a printing-press operator. For eight months he had been assigned to operate a photo-offset press, model RU 1, manufactured and sold by defendant Miehle–Goss Dexter, Inc., to his employer. The machine was 150 feet long, 15 feet high and 5 feet wide and was capable of printing at least 20,000 sheets an hour. Then, while working on January 22, 1969, plaintiff discovered that a foreign object had made its way onto the plate of the unit. Such a substance, known to the trade as a "hickie," causes a blemish or imperfection on the printed pages. Plaintiff informed his superior of the problem and told him he was going to "chase the hickie," whereupon the foreman warned him to be careful. "Chasing a hickie" consisted of applying, very lightly, a piece of plastic about eight inches wide to the printing plate, which is wrapped around a circular plate cylinder which spins at high speed. The revolving action of the plate against the plastic removes the "hickie." Unsuccessful in his first removal attempt, plaintiff started anew but this time the plastic was drawn into the nip point between the plate cylinder and an ink-form roller along with his hand. The machine had no safety guards to prevent such occurrence. Plaintiff testified that while his hand was trapped he reached for a shut-off button but couldn't contact it because of its location.

Plaintiff was aware of the danger of getting caught in the press in "chasing hickies." However, it was the custom and usage in the industry to "chase hickies on the run", because once the machine was stopped, it required at least three hours to resume printing and, in such event, the financial advantage of the high speed machine would be lessened. Although it was possible to have "chased the hickie" from another side of the machine, such approach would have caused plaintiff to be in a leaning position and would have increased the chances of scratching the plate. Through its representatives and engineers, defendant had observed the machine in operation and was cognizant of the manner in which "hickies were chased" by Lincoln's employees.

Samuel Aidlin, a professional engineer, had inspected the machine subsequent to the mishap. In his opinion, based upon the custom in the printing industry, it would have been good custom and practice to have placed guards near the rollers where plaintiff's hand entered the machine, the danger of human contact being well known. Moreover, he testified that at least three different types of guards were available, two for over 30 years, that they would not have impeded the practice of "chasing hickies," and that these guards would have protected an employee from exposure to the risk. * * *

[Judgment for plaintiff in the trial court.]

Defendant appealed and the Appellate Division, * * * [reversed, relying on the "patent danger" rule.] It found that the danger of being caught in the machine was well known in the trade and, more importantly, the plaintiff had actual knowledge of the possible consequences in "chasing a hickie."

* * *

We are confronted here with the question as to the continued validity of the patent-danger doctrine * * *.

* * *

[We conclude that the "patent danger" rule should be relaxed.] A casting of increased responsibility upon the manufacturer, who stands in a superior position to recognize and cure defects, for improper conduct in the placement of finished products into the channels of commerce furthers the public interest. To this end, we hold that a manufacturer is obligated to exercise that degree of care in his plan or design so as to avoid any unreasonable risk of harm to anyone who is likely to be exposed to the danger when the product is used in the manner for which the product was intended, as well as an unintended yet reasonably foreseeable use.

What constitutes "reasonable care" will, of course, vary with the surrounding circumstances and will involve "a balancing of the likelihood of harm, and the gravity of harm if it happens, against the burden of the precaution which would be effective to avoid the harm" (2 Harper & James, Torts, § 28.4; see Pike v. Hough Co., 2 Cal.3d 465, 85 Cal.Rptr. 629, 467

P.2d 229, supra). Under this approach, "the plaintiff endeavors to show the jury such facts as that competitors used the safety device which was missing here, or that a 'cotter pin costing a penny' could have prevented the accident. The defendant points to such matters as cost, function, and competition as narrowing the design choices. He stresses 'trade-offs'. If the product would be unworkable when the alleged missing feature was added, or would be so expensive as to be priced out of the market, that would be relevant defensive matter" (Rheingold, Expanding Liability of the Product Supplier: A Primer, 2 Hofstra L.Rev., 521, 537). In this case, there was no evidence submitted at trial to show the cost of guards that could have been attached in relation to the entire cost of the machine.

* * *

We next examine the duty owing from a plaintiff or, in other words, the conduct on a plaintiff's part which will bar recovery from a manufacturer. As now enunciated, the patent-danger doctrine should not, in and of itself, prevent a plaintiff from establishing his case. That does not mean, however, that the obviousness of the danger as a factor in the ultimate injury is thereby eliminated, for it must be remembered that in actions for negligent design, the ordinary rules of negligence apply. Rather, the openness and obviousness of the danger should be available to the defendant on the issue of whether plaintiff exercised that degree of reasonable care as was required under the circumstances. [In a footnote, the court observed that New York's pure comparative fault statute would apply.]

The order of the Appellate Division should be reversed and a new trial granted, with costs to abide the event.

OGLETREE v. NAVISTAR INTERNATIONAL TRANSP. CORP., 269 Ga. 443, 500 S.E.2d 570 (1998). Plaintiff brought a wrongful death action against the manufacturer of the cab and chassis of a fertilizer spreader truck that had backed over and killed her husband. She alleged that the truck was defective because the defendant had not installed an audible back-up alarm. The trial court entered JNOV after the jury returned a verdict for plaintiff's funeral and medical expenses. Plaintiff appealed and the Court of Appeals affirmed, applying the "open and obvious" danger rule. *Held*, reversed. "[T]he 'open and obvious danger' rule is not controlling in a case where, as here, it is alleged that a product has a design defect." Cases applying the rule to design defects "are hereby overruled."

"The open and obvious nature of the danger in a product is logically only one of many factors which affect the product's risk and, therefore, making that single factor dispositive is not consistent with this court's mandate in *Banks [v. ICI America*, supra 1009] that the product's risk must be weighed against its utility. * * * Accordingly, we find no justification for the "open and obvious danger" rule as to design defect cases whether brought in strict liability or in negligence."

SCHEMEL v. GENERAL MOTORS CORP., 384 F.2d 802 (7th Cir.1967). Plaintiff alleged negligence and improper design in making the Chevrolet Impala capable of being driven at a rate of speed in excess of 115 miles per hour. In denying recovery, the court asserted two propositions: (1) an automobile is not dangerous for use for which it was made by its unlawful use in the manner and for the purpose for which it was supplied; (2) the dangers attendant on excessive and unlawful speed are neither latent nor concealed.

LeBOUEF v. GOODYEAR, 623 F.2d 985 (5th Cir.1980). Plaintiff's decedent was killed, and his passenger seriously injured, when their Mercury Cougar "veered off the Louisiana back road on which it had been travelling at over 100 miles per hour and crashed into a cement culvert. The accident occurred when the tread separated from the body of the Cougar's left rear tire." Ford appealed from the judgment entered against it, "arguing that: (1) it had no duty to warn of or otherwise to guard against the danger of tread separation in situations like that involved here: * * * and (3) the court should have held Leleux and Dugas to be barred from recovery on the basis of their own conduct in connection with the accident." *Held,* affirmed.

"Certainly the operation of the Cougar in excess of 100 miles per hour was not 'normal' in the sense of being a routine or intended use. 'Normal use,' however, is a term of art in the parlance of Louisiana products liability law, delineating the scope of a manufacturer's duty and consequent liability; it encompasses all reasonably foreseeable uses of a product. [citations omitted] The sports car involved here was marketed with an intended and recognized appeal to youthful drivers. The 425 horsepower engine with which Ford had equipped it provided a capability of speeds over 100 miles per hour, and the car's allure, no doubt exploited in its marketing, lay in no small measure in this power and potential speed. It was not simply foreseeable, but was to be readily expected, that the Cougar would, on occasion, be driven in excess of the 85 mile per hour proven maximum safe operating speed of its Goodyear tires. Consequently, Ford cannot, on the basis of abnormal use, escape its duty either to provide an adequate warning of the specific danger of tread separation at such high speeds or to ameliorate the danger in some other way."

VENEZIA v. MILLER BREWING COMPANY, 626 F.2d 188 (1st Cir.1980). The plaintiff, who was eight years old at the time, severely injured his eye when he threw a discarded beer bottle against a telephone pole, shattering it. He brought suit alleging that "Miller and the bottle manufacturers should have been aware of the dangers inherent in their 'thin walled' 'non-returnable' bottles and should have accordingly designed and marketed a product better able to withstand such foreseeable misuse as breakage in the course of improper handling by children." The district court dismissed plaintiff's complaint for failure to state a claim. *Held,* affirmed.

"Under Massachusetts law the question of fitness for ordinary purposes is largely one centering around reasonable consumer expectations. * * * No reasonable consumer would expect anything but that a glass beer bottle, apparently well suited for its immediate intended use, would fail to safely withstand the type of purposeful abuse involved here. What, if not the possibility of shattering the bottle, would lead him to throw it against the pole in the first place? * * *

" * * * [We are convinced] that the Massachusetts courts would not be prepared to hold a manufacturer liable for injuries sustained by * * * his own intentional misuse of an otherwise 'fit' product in a manner in no reasonable way related to the * * * intended uses for which the product was designed, manufactured and marketed. * * * [T]he impact of endorsing a contrary conclusion would be overwhelming, with every discarded glass object holding the potential for generating a future lawsuit."

PERSONAL AND WORKPLACE USE OF PRODUCTS

Both the extent of the manufacturer's duty and the availability of defenses pertaining to victim conduct can be affected by the context in which a product is to be used. The primary distinction here is between "personal" and "workplace" use.

HILLRICHS v. AVCO CORP., 514 N.W.2d 94 (Iowa 1994). Plaintiff was operating a cornpicking machine, which he had purchased, when "the husking bed became plugged with corn 'trash.' Hillrichs left the machine running and attempted to unplug it. While doing so, he caught his right (dominant) hand between two rollers * * *." As a result he had to have four fingers on the hand amputated. At trial, a "jury found Hillrichs to be 100% at fault for his injuries" and judgment was entered against him.

On appeal, the Supreme Court affirmed in part, but reversed and remanded for a new trial "with respect to Avco's liability, if any, for plaintiff's 'enhanced injuries.' Hillrichs claimed that Avco negligently failed to include an emergency stop device on the rear of the husking bed near the point where he caught his hand and that this failure resulted in an unnecessary enhancement of his injuries." At the second trial, the "jury returned a verdict finding Avco eighty percent at fault and Hillrichs twenty percent at fault." Avco appealed. *Held*, affirmed.

" * * * Avco had a duty to design the husking be reasonably safe when used in a reasonably foreseeable manner. This duty required Avco to anticipate the possibility that the machine would be used in a dangerous but foreseeable manner. See Tafoya v. Sears Roebuck & Co., 884 F.2d 1330, 1338 (10th Cir.1989) ('Collisions and accidents are natural, foreseeable consequences of automobile use.')."

CARREL v. ALLIED PRODUCTS CORPORATION, 78 Ohio St.3d 284, 677 N.E.2d 795 (1997). Plaintiff, an experienced and skilled press operator, lost parts of his index and ring fingers and all of his middle finger when a newly trained co-worker, Steven Price, reactivitated a six-hundred-ton transfer press "approximately twenty feet in length and five feet in width." The press was misfeeding. Plaintiff and Price were trying to determine why. To do so, they had to take the press out of automatic mode and "place it in the inch mode." The electrically interlocked guards which protected users when the press was operating in the automatic mode did not operated when the press was operating in the inch mode. Plaintiff brought suit on a defective design claim, among other claims, and Allied moved for summary judgment, arguing in part that the plaintiff had assumed the risk. The trial court granted Allied's motion and the Court of Appeals affirmed. *Held*, reversed and remanded.

The defense of assumption of risk is a "viable defense against an employee injured by a defective product in the workplace," but "is unavailable in those situations where the job duties require the employee to encounter the risk, and the employee is injured while engaging in normal job-related tasks." "An employee will be deemed to have voluntarily exposed himself or herself to a risk when he or she has elected to use a defective product. However, the defense of assumption of the risk is not available when the employee is required to encounter the risk while performing normal job duties.

Here, there is some question as to whether appellant voluntarily assumed the risk. Appellant's supervisor testified that although appellant had been trained in the procedures for adjusting the dies, and was aware that he needed first to pull the safety cord, or to use one of the other safety devices when adjusting a misaligned part, he failed to follow these procedures. However, there is also evidence that the press was dangerous because of the inability of the operator to see someone in the die area. Appellant's experts averred that barrier guards which would have electrically interlocked in the inch mode would have eliminated the risk. This feature was available at the time the press was designed, and had been incorporated into other Verson Transmat presses. Additionally, appellant testified that his co-worker observed him working in the die space. Further, he did not anticipate that his co-worker would activate the press without being told to do so. Thus, there is a question as to whether appellant appreciated the full danger of the press. In light of this evidence, a reasonable jury could determine that appellant did not appreciate or voluntarily encounter the risk associated with the press."

NICHOLAS v. HOMELITE CORP., A DIVISION OF TEXTRON, INC., 780 F.2d 1150 (5th Cir.1986). Decedent was killed when a bow blade chain saw manufactured by defendant kicked back into his neck. In a wrongful death action alleging a product defect, the jury found that the defendant and decedent were each 50% negligent. The widow had judgment for $300,000. Defendant appealed, arguing among other points that Louisiana law required the judge to reduce the damage award by one-half. The court of appeals turned for guidance on this issue to the recent Louisiana decision in *Bell v. Jet Wheel Blast*, 462 So.2d 166 (La.1985). Under that decision, "we must determine whether the application of comparative fault on the facts of this case will provide an incentive to careful use by consumers. If it will not, comparative fault will not apply. * * * [The decedent] purchased and used the Homelite saw for personal rather than commercial or business use. No employer required his use of the saw. Furthermore, he had experienced a previous kickback from the saw he was using when he was killed. Under these circumstances the threat of a reduction in recovery will provide future consumers with the very incentive for more careful use which the doctrine of comparative fault was intended to engender." Hence comparative fault applied to reduce damages in proportion to decedent's negligence.

COMPARATIVE NEGLIGENCE

The product liability regime of § 402A of the *Second Restatement* rejects ordinary contributory negligence, but recognizes it in the form of assumption of the risk (on one conception of that doctrine). It also recognizes misuse as a defense, and this gives rise to foreseeable misuse as an exception to the defense of misuse. The alternative to this regime of defenses is a relatively undifferentiated comparative negligence regime. The cases which follow elaborate this regime.

HUFFMAN v. CATERPILLAR TRACTOR CO.

United States Court of Appeals, Tenth Circuit, 1990.
908 F.2d 1470.

HOLLOWAY, Chief Judge.

Plaintiff Susan Huffman prevailed in the district court in a product liability action against defendant Caterpillar Tractor Co. (Caterpillar) for damages arising from the death of her husband, Garry Huffman. The jury assessed $950,000 in damages. However, pursuant to Colorado's Comparative Fault statute, this figure was reduced to $475,000 to reflect the jury's determination that the decedent had been 50 percent responsible for his own injuries.

In her appeal, Huffman challenges the district court's interpretation of the term "fault" as it is employed in Colorado's Comparative Fault statute. She argues, inter alia, that the court erred when it instructed the jury that under the Colorado statute, ordinary negligence constitutes "fault." She contends that under the correct interpretation of the term "fault," her damages should be $950,000 instead of the $475,000 awarded. * * *

In its cross-appeal defendant Caterpillar raises [the additional question]: Did the district court err when it denied Caterpillar's motion for a directed verdict, JNOV, or a new trial on the ground that plaintiff failed to establish a prima facie case of strict product liability? * * *

* * * We affirm [the judgment of the district court on both of these issues].

I. FACTS

There is evidence tending to show these facts when the record is considered favorably to plaintiff. Decedent Garry Huffman was fatally injured at the Steamboat Springs, Colorado, Ski Area on July 29, 1981. At that time Mr. Huffman was employed by The Industrial Corporation (TIC), a contractor retained by the operators of the Steamboat Springs ski slopes to install snowmaking facilities.

Huffman was operating a Caterpillar Model 561D pipelayer, a model manufactured in 1977, on a ski slope the day of the accident. The parties stipulated that the particular pipelayer Huffman was then using was manufactured in February 1981. The pipelayer—a large, tracked, construction vehicle which combines elements of a bulldozer and a crane—is used in the installation of snowmaking equipment to haul large sections of pipe for placement in trenches running up the side of the ski slope. An important feature of the 561D is its braking system, which combines mechanical brakes with an hydraulic boost. The hydraulic assist substantially enhances braking capacity, but only when the vehicle's engine is running. When the engine is not running, the operator must rely exclusively on the mechanical brakes.[8] Beginning in 1981 Caterpillar altered the braking system on successor models of the 561D in order to add a spring-applied emergency braking system to the hydraulically-assisted brakes with which the TIC 561D was equipped (TR 309). Spring-applied brakes automatically and immediately stop the pipelayer whenever the engine is shut off.

To perform the task assigned to the decedent, the operator of a pipelayer must pick up a section of pipe at the bottom of the ski slope, drag it up the incline, and then use the crane-like apparatus of the pipelayer to place the section in the trench running up the side of the slope so that the pipe section can be connected to the rest of the underground piping by weld. Since the sections of pipe are heavy and cumbersome, and the slope quite steep (in this case the slope of the "See Me" trail was 53%), it requires some effort and skill to maintain the balance of the load and keep the pipelayer stable on the hill. Although the decedent had worked at Steamboat for several months and had previously operated a bulldozer for the Forest Service, at the time of the accident he had only two weeks' experience on the 561D.

The accident occurred as Huffman was operating the pipelayer to adjust the position of a large length of pipe that had already been placed in the trench on the "See Me" slope by another operator. Huffman had been instructed to close the gap between the pipe just placed in the ditch and the pipe to which it would be welded. As Huffman tried to move the pipe into place, his co-worker, assistant welder Mike Gardner, shouted words to the effect that he should adjust the counterweight mechanism on the pipelayer in order to improve the machine's stability during this operation. Huffman, apparently unable to hear over the noise of the vehicle, shut off the engine, and the machine began rolling down the hill.

As the pipelayer accelerated, Huffman was observed "stomping" on the brake pedals, but to no avail. Approximately 100 feet down the hill, with the pipelayer gaining speed, Huffman rose from his seat and tried to climb off of

---

8. One of the central arguments of the plaintiff at trial was that Caterpillar should have equipped the 561D with "spring-applied" brakes. The technology * * * was said to have been technically feasible at the time the 561D leased by TIC was manufactured * * *. Plaintiff contends that this technology would have saved the decedent's life * * *.

the vehicle. He became tangled in the machine's cable works and then fell on to the tracks of the vehicle. In an instant, he was crushed to death.

* * *

III. DISCUSSION

* * *

1. *Comparative Fault: Doctrinal Development*

Plaintiff's central argument on appeal is that the district court's jury instructions regarding the issue of comparative fault erroneously stated the law under Colorado's comparative fault statute, § 13–21–406 C.R.S. (1980 & 1988 Supp.). Jury instruction 31, it is contended, incorrectly defined "fault," as used in the comparative fault statute, to subsume ordinary negligence. In place of the district court's interpretation, plaintiff urges a construction of the statute that would allow a jury to consider only a plaintiff's assumption of risk and/or product misuse in deciding the extent to which a judgment should be reduced after a finding of manufacturer liability. Thus plaintiff should be entitled to the full $950,000 in assessed damages; because the decedent's measure of "fault" for his fatal accident did not rise to the level of assumption of risk or misuse, there was no basis for any reduction in the damage award.

Plaintiff's argument is not without some foundation, especially when we consider the doctrinal origin of comparative fault. * * *

In some jurisdictions it has been held either through the construction of or inference from a state comparative negligence statute, or by means of judicially-adopted rules, that comparative negligence or comparative fault principles are applicable to strict products liability actions. Other courts by contrast, have held that such principles could not be applied to the analysis of strict products liability claims. Before the adoption in 1981 of its comparative fault statute, § 13–21–406 C.R.S. (1980 & 1988 Supp.), Colorado's common law clearly placed it in the latter category.

The rationale for separating comparative fault or comparative negligence from products liability derives from the understanding that strict products liability analysis is not fundamentally based on a culpability or "blameworthiness" inquiry. Rather, the doctrine imposes liability where a product was defective when it left the defendant manufacturer's hands, even though the manufacturer is not proven negligent in the production of the item.

Viewed in this light, the doctrinal tension between strict products liability and comparative fault or comparative negligence becomes clear: Strict liability reflects the effort to remove the issue of negligence or fault from product liability analysis, and to place the emphasis on causation. Comparative negligence or comparative fault rules, as applied to product liability actions, inject a culpability inquiry into the process of apportioning damages. Nevertheless, it is quite conceivable that in enacting its comparative fault statute, § 13–21–406 C.R.S. (1980 & 1988 Supp.), the Colorado legislature intended to change the state's product liability law in order to establish a hybrid system, combining elements of strict liability with elements of a fault or negligence regime. Indeed, the evolution of such hybrid systems appears to have become something of a national trend: "[i]n recent years there has been widespread adoption of comparative negligence, either judicially or by statutes, either expressly adopting comparative fault in products liability cases or in statutes construed to include products liability actions." 2 L. FRUMER 7 M. FRIEDMAN, PRODUCTS LIABILITY § 3.01[5][f] (1988).

2. Colorado's Comparative Fault Statute

We cannot agree that the trial court's construction of Colorado's comparative fault statute constitutes reversible error. From our examination of the Colorado statute, its legislative history, the relevant decisional law, and canons of statutory construction, we conclude that the trial court's instructions on the issue of comparative fault were correct.

* * *

The key passage of C.R.S. 13–21–406 reads as follows: Comparative fault as measure of damages. (1) In any product liability action, the fault of the person suffering the harm, as well as the fault of all others who are parties to the action for causing the harm, shall be compared by the trier of fact in accordance with this section. The fault of the person suffering the harm shall not bar such person, or a party bringing an action on behalf of such a person ... from recovering damages, but the award of damages to such person or the party bringing the action shall be diminished in proportion to the amount of causal fault attributed to the person suffering the harm. * * * § 13–21–406 C.R.S. (1980 & 1988 Supp.) (emphasis added).

* * *

B.   CATERPILLAR'S CROSS-APPEAL

1.   Failure to Establish Prima Facie Case

In its cross-appeal, Caterpillar challenges the trial court's denial of its motions for judgment notwithstanding the verdict. It claims that it was entitled to judgment on plaintiff's defective design claim because plaintiff failed to establish a prima facie case that (1) the 561D's braking system was defective and unreasonably dangerous, (2) that the defect caused the fatal accident, * * *.

* * *

Evidence marshalled by the plaintiff was more than adequate to support a jury determination that the Caterpillar 561D was unreasonably dangerous under the consumer expectation test. Plaintiff presented testimony on which the jury could have reasonably based the conclusions that (a) the placement of the brake pedals made it excessively difficult for a man of average height to brake the 561D in an emergency, (b) that the near impossibility of stopping the machine on an incline once it began to roll for more than 20 feet with its engine off presented an unreasonable and unexpected hazard, and/or (c) that the absence of the feasible spring-applied braking system created an unreasonable danger beyond the expectation of the ordinary user of the 561D.

Caterpillar's claim that plaintiff failed to establish a prima facie case that the defect[s] of the 561D caused the accident is similarly unpersuasive. Caterpillar argues that the 561D was "risk-neutral," that Huffman's operation of the machine amounted to misuse, and that Huffman's inexperience was the sole cause of the accident. However, plaintiff presented testimony that it is not uncommon for an operator to shut off his pipelayer on a slope. Construction machines also stall and break down on occasion, on the mountainous work-sites where they are frequently used. Viewing the record in its entirety, the jury had before it an adequate evidentiary basis for concluding that Huffman did not misuse the 561D and that the machine's defect or defects caused, or partially caused, the decedent's death.

AFFIRMED.

———————

DALY v. GENERAL MOTORS CORP., 20 Cal.3d 725, 144 Cal.Rptr. 380, 575 P.2d 1162 (1978). In this decision, the California Supreme Court decided to apply "the principles of comparative negligence * * * to actions founded on strict products liability." The court explained the operation of, and justification for, comparative negligence principles in the following paragraphs:

> * * * [Where a consumer sues a manufacturer] technically, neither fault nor conduct is really compared functionally. The conduct of one party in combination with the product of another * * * produce[s] the ultimate injury. In such a case * * * we think 'equitable apportionment or allocation of loss' may be more descriptive than 'comparative fault.'

> * * * Defendant's liability for injuries caused by a defective product remains strict. The principle of protecting the defenseless is likewise preserved, for plaintiff's recovery will be reduced only to the extent that his own lack of reasonable care contributed to his injury. The cost of compensating the victim of a defective product, albeit proportionately reduced, remains on defendant manufacturer, and will, through him, be 'spread among society.' However, * * * as to that share of plaintiff's damages which flows from his own fault we discern no reason of policy why it should * * * be borne by others. Such a result would directly contravene the principle * * * that loss should be assessed equitably in proportion to fault.

Dissenting from the decision, Justice Mosk protested:

> This will be remembered as the dark day when this court, which heroically took the lead in originating the doctrine of products liability and steadfastly resisted efforts to inject concepts of negligence * * * into the newly designed tort inexplicably turned 180 degrees and beat an hasty retreat almost back to square one. * * *

> The majority injects a foreign object—the tort of negligence—into the tort of products liability by the simple expedient of calling negli-

gence something else: on some pages the opinion speaks of "comparative fault," on others reference is to "comparative principles," and elsewhere the term "equitable apportionment" is employed, although this is clearly not a proceeding in equity. But a rose is a rose and negligence is negligence; * * *.

The defective product is comparable to a time bomb ready to explode; it maims its victims indiscriminately, the righteous and the evil, the careful and the careless. Thus when a faulty design or otherwise defective product is involved, the litigation should not be diverted to consideration of the negligence of the plaintiff. * * *

The majority deny their opinion diminishes the therapeutic effect of products liability upon producers of defective products. It seems self-evident that procedures which evaluate the injured consumer's conduct in each instance, and thus eliminate or reduce the award against the producer of a defective product, are not designed as an effective incentive to maximize responsibility to consumers. The converse is more accurate: the motivation to avoid polluting the stream of commerce with defective products increases in direct relation to the size of potential damage awards.

LEWIS v. TIMCO, INC., 716 F.2d 1425 (5th Cir.1983). The court of appeals held that the doctrine of comparative fault applied in a products liability suit maintained under the maritime jurisdiction of the federal courts. Before concluding that "general considerations of fairness and efficiency support a comparative fault defense in product liability actions," Judge Higginbotham observed:

"It is relevant to an analysis[3] of how a rule allocates liability for accident losses resulting from use of a product to consider: (1) short-term and long-term cost; (2) amount of use of the product in the economy or 'activity'; and (3) cost of administering the rules of liability. It is relevant because fault has both an ethical and an efficiency dimension. The latter is expressed by asking which party can prevent the injury at the least costs.

"The short-term costs are the immediate expenditures to avoid accidents as well as the immediate costs of accidents themselves. Of course the two primary actors influenced by the rule choice are the manufacturer and the user. The manufacturer will alter its product to avoid an accident if the manufacturer's share of the expected cost of the accident (coverage cost times the probability it will occur) exceeds the cost of altering the product. A system of strict liability with comparative fault includes in the manufacturer's share of the accident costs only those costs caused by product defects. In that case the manufacturer will have the correct economic incentive to adjust the design of the product to minimize accident costs caused by the design. A system of strict liability with no comparative fault would add to the manufacturer's share those accident costs caused by negligent use and not by any

---

3. The "analysis" * * * presents nothing novel. It describes what maritime jurists intuitively sensed long ago. We do no more than talk in an analytical way about judgments intuitively made. * * * While ultimately choices among potential tort rules may turn on notions of "fairness" as viewed through the eyes of each judge's ethical regimen, those choices will only be guesses if the judges are inadequately informed of their impact.

product defect. This increase in the manufacturer's share would result in an increased, and therefore inefficient, level of expenditures on preventive measures.

"The situation with respect to the user's expenditures is precisely complementary. The user will intentionally alter his use of the product only if his perceived cost of altering his use to avoid an accident is less than his expected cost from an accident resulting from his failure to alter his behavior. The inclusion of comparative fault will affect user behavior in a manner that results in a more efficient utilization of resources. Under simple strict liability, as proposed by the plaintiff, the user has no economic incentive to avoid an accident that he could avoid more cheaply than the manufacturer.

"Besides affecting long-term research for safe products and the immediate decisions on how much to invest in preventive measures, rules of liability affect the level of product use. When the liability for blameless accidents is placed on the manufacturer, the price of products whose use results in high accident costs will go up relative to those whose use results in small accident costs. The use of the comparative fault standard reduces the risks of non-negligent users indirectly paying for negligent users. The comparative fault standard allows the price of the product to reflect the cost of its non-negligent use. Hence a comparative fault standard allows the economically efficient amount of the product to be used. * * *

"The final economic consideration in choosing a rule of liability is the cost of administering the system. It might appear that strict liability without comparative fault would be less expensive to administer both because it simplifies the issues at litigation and because it removes uncertainty thereby facilitating settlements, which are cheaper than trials. The matter, however, is more complex: by increasing the certainty of victory, if it does, strict liability may increase the plaintiff's willingness to spend money on litigation and decrease his willingness to settle. There is no indication that strict liability with comparative fault would increase cost."

RESTATEMENT OF TORTS, THIRD: PRODUCTS LIABILITY (1998)

§ 17. Apportionment of Responsibility Between of Among Plaintiff, Sellers and Distributors of Defective Products, and Others

(a) A plaintiff's recovery of damages for harm caused by a product defect may be reduced if the conduct of the plaintiff combines with the product defect to cause the harm and the plaintiff's conduct fails to conform to generally applicable rules establishing appropriate standards of care.

Comment:

d. Particular forms or categories of plaintiff's conduct. Some courts accord different treatment to special categories of plaintiff conduct. For example, some decisions hold that when the plaintiffs negligence is the failure to discover a product defect, reduction of damages on the basis of apportionment of responsibility is improper, reasoning that a consumer has a right to expect a defect-free product and should not be burdened with a duty to inspect for defects. Other decisions hold that apportionment of responsibility is improper when the product lacked a safety feature that would protect against the risk that resulted in the injury in question, reasoning that the defendant's responsibility should not be diminished when the plaintiff engages in the very conduct that the product design should have prevented. On the other hand, some decisions hold that a plaintiffs assumption of the risk is a complete defense to a products liability action, not merely a basis for apportionment of responsibility. Product misuse * * * [has] been treated by some courts as an absolute bar to recovery * * *. The majority position is that all forms of plaintiffs failure to conform to applicable standards of care are to be considered for the purpose of apportioning responsibility between the plaintiff and the product seller or distributor.

SECTION E.   SPECIAL PROBLEMS AND DAMAGES

WARNINGS AND CAUSATION

Warnings are often taken to present special problems of causation. *GMC v. Saenz*, 873 S.W.2d 353 (Tex.1993) excerpted in this section, formulates the problem in the following terms:

> Proving causation in a failure-to-warn case has peculiar difficulties. Proof that a collision between two cars would not have happened had defendant swerved or braked or driven within the speed limit is mostly a matter of physics. Proof that an accident would not have occurred if defendant had provided adequate warnings concerning the use of a product is more psychology and does not admit of the same degree of certainty. A plaintiff must show that adequate warnings would have made a difference in the outcome, that is, that they would have been followed. In the best case a plaintiff can offer evidence of his habitual, careful adherence to all warnings and instructions. In many cases, however, plaintiff's evidence may be little more than the self-serving assertion that whatever his usual practice may have been, in the circumstances critical to his claim for damages he would have been mindful of an adequate warning had it been given. In the worst case, where the user of the product is deceased, proof of what the decedent would or would not have done may be virtually impossible.

The *Magro* court, as we shall see, takes the view that the best solution to this predicament is to adopt a presumption that an *adequate* warning would have been heeded. Other courts have done so as well, often citing *Comment j* to § 402A of the *Second Restatement*, quoted supra, pp. 1027–28 as authority for their position. The *Third Restatement*, quoted infra p. 1077 conspicuously declines to adopt such a presumption. Courts have gone in several different directions.

In thinking about the special problems of causation posed by warnings, and the role that a "heeding presumption" might play in addressing those problems, it helps to distinguish between the warnings and instructions. The primary point of warnings—in the case of "unavoidably unsafe" products the only point—is to enable informed consumer choice. We require warnings in the case of "unavoidably unsafe" products even though well informed users of those products cannot reduce their risks by careful use, because we wish to enable consumers to make an informed decision as to whether the "game is worth candle." In *MacDonald v. Ortho Pharmeceutical*, supra p. 1031, for example, the court insists on a vivid warning in order to enable consumers to make an informed decision whether an increased risk of stroke is worth the advantages of oral contraception.

In cases where a product is not "unavoidably unsafe" but might be made safer by redesign, we usually tolerate the otherwise unreasonable risks of the product because we believe that consumers have heterogeneous interests and that some consumers will choose to buy unusually risky products even if they fully appreciate their risks. We believe, for example, that reasonable consumers may be unaware of the increased risks of rollover presented by many sport-utility vehicles, and we therefore require warnings to alert consumers to those risks. But we also believe that some well-informed consumers will nevertheless wish to buy sport-utility vehicles, perhaps because they value the off-road capability that a high, narrow wheelbase enables. Here, too, warnings enable informed consumer choice.

Instructions serve a different purpose. They promote the safe use of an otherwise unreasonably unsafe product. All reasonable consumers have an interest in using products safely, even if they are prepared to purchase products which are, by design, more risky than normal. No reasonable consumer wants to roll his or her sport-utility vehicle over. As product purchasers consumers have *heterogeneous* interests, but as product users they have *homogeneous* ones. This difference bears on the desirability of adopting a heeding presumption. A presumption that an adequate instruction would be heeded is more plausible than a presumption that an adequate warning would have been heeded.

A presumption that no well-informed buyer would purchase a sport-utility vehicle, for example, is untenable. We require warnings in large part because we believe that some well informed consumers will choose to buy sport-utility vehicles whose risks of rolling over are substantially greater than average, and others will not. It is contradictory to then presume that no well-informed consumer would, in fact, purchase such a vehicle. A presumption that all would heed adequate instructions is, on the other hand, entirely reasonable. All reasonable product users have the same interest in minimizing product risks through careful use. All reasonable users of propane cylinders, for example[4], share an interest in minimizing the risk that "spent" canisters will ignite. From this it follows that all users should heed instructions on safe use, and that all users have an interest in being well-instructed in how to use products safely. Penalizing manufacturers for providing inadequate instructions by presuming that adequate instructions would be heeded creates a powerful incentive to provide adequate instructions.

Note, too, that inadequate warnings present more acute causal difficulties than inadequate instructions do. After an accident has occurred how can we distinguish those victims who really would not have purchased the

---

4. Propane cylinders were the subject of *Cotton v. Buckeye*, supra p. 1037.

product had they been adequately informed of its risks, from those who have undergone a change of heart since being injured? This difference in the relative causal tractability of warnings and instructions may have a powerful effect on the course of product liability litigation. One commentator has suggested that the relatively greater tractability of instruction problems leads plaintiffs' lawyers to present cases where the "real" issue is the adequacy of the product warning, as cases where inadequate instructions were given. Does *Ayers v. Johnson & Johnson*, the last case in this section, support this claim?

RESTATEMENT OF TORTS, THIRD: PRODUCTS LIABILITY (1998)

§ 2.　Categories of Product Defect

i.　Inadequate instructions or warnings. * * * Whether or not many persons would, when warned, nonetheless decide to use or consume the product, warnings are required to protect the interests of those reasonably foreseeable users or consumers who would, based on their own reasonable assessments of the risks and benefits, decline product use or consumption. When such warnings are necessary, their omission renders the product not reasonably safe at time of sale. Notwithstanding the defective condition of the product in the absence of adequate warnings, if a particular user or consumer would have decided to use or consume even if warned, the lack of warnings is not a legal cause of that plaintiff's harm.

§ 15.　General Rule Governing Causal Connection Between Product Defect and Harm

Whether a product defect caused harm to persons or property is determined by the prevailing rules and principles governing causation in tort.

GMC v. SAENZ, 873 S.W.2d 353 (Tex.1993). "We recognized [the special problems] of proving causation [in warning cases] in Technical Chemical Co. v. Jacobs, 480 S.W.2d 602, 606 (Tex.1972). As one solution, we observed: 'It has been suggested that the law should supply the presumption that an adequate warning would have been read.' * * *"

"This Court did not actually adopt the presumption suggested in Technical Chemical until our opinion in Magro v. Ragsdale Brothers, Inc., 721 S.W.2d 832, 834 (Tex.1986) * * *

"The arguments against a presumption that adequate warnings will be heeded were not examined in Technical Chemical or Magro. One such argument is that the authority usually cited for the presumption, and referred to in both cases, comment j to section 402A of the Restatement (Second) of Torts, is not supportive. Comment j states in relevant part: 'Where a warning is given, the seller may reasonably assume that it will be read and heeded; and a product bearing such a warning, which is safe for use if followed, is not in defective condition, nor is it unreasonably dangerous.' This sentence, the argument runs, is nothing more than a recognition of the obvious, that if the seller provides adequate instructions for use of his product, he cannot be liable for the buyer's failure to follow them. After all, you can lead a horse to water but you can't make him drink. * * *

"This argument against reliance on comment j is persuasive, but it is not conclusive. * * * The real reason for the presumption, the problem of proving causation in failure-to-warn cases, remains. This basis for the presumption is attacked by the argument that while the proof problem is real, a presumption does not solve it and may even make it worse. James A. Henderson Jr. & Aaron D. Twerski, Doctrinal Collapse in Products Liability: The Empty Shell of Failure to Warn, 65 N.Y.U. L. REV. 265, 325–326 (1990).* While the proof problem affects parties differently in different cases, a presumption solution always operates to benefit the favored party and thus ignores the reality of many situations. The presumption here always helps the plaintiff even, according to the argument, when he does not need it, and never helps the defendant, even when he does. The only real solution to the problem, the argument concludes, is a case-by-case analysis of the causation evidence. Id.

"This argument is far more logical than practical. It ends where it begins, calling for a better solution to the problem of proving causation in failure-to-warn cases, but suggesting no rules or procedures to accomplish this goal. We continue to believe the Magro presumption remains the best solution to the problem. It excuses plaintiff from the necessity of making self-serving assertions that he would have followed adequate instructions, simply to put the issue of causation in sufficient dispute to avoid summary judgment or directed verdict, and it assists plaintiffs in cases where the person injured has died and evidence of what he would have done is unavailable for that reason. The presumption is not conclusive but subject to rebuttal by the defendant.

"The presumption is subject to the same rules governing presumptions generally. Its effect is to shift the burden of producing evidence to the party against whom it operates. * * *

"Thus, the presumption that adequate warning on products will be heeded places upon the defendant in a failure-to-warn case the burden of going forward with the evidence on causation. If * * * defendant offers evidence contrary to the presumption, then plaintiff must prove causation by a preponderance of the evidence, and the presumption has no further legal consequence."

LIRIANO v. HOBART CORPORATION, 170 F.3d 264 (2d Cir.1999) (Calabresi, J.) The facts of this case are summarized supra, p. 1029, where the adequacy of the defendant's warning is discussed. The following excerpts address the causation question.

---

* Professors Henderson and Twerski were the Reporters for the Third Restatement.—Eds.

"On rebriefing following the Court of Appeals decision, Hobart has made another argument as to why the jury should not have been allowed to find for the plaintiff. In this argument, Hobart raises the issue of causation. It maintains that Liriano 'failed to present any evidence that Hobart's failure to place a warning [on the machine] was causally related to his injury.' Whether or not there had been a warning, Hobart says, Liriano might well have operated the machine as he did and suffered the injuries that he suffered. Liriano introduced no evidence, Hobart notes, suggesting either that he would have refused to grind meat had the machine borne a warning or that a warning would have persuaded Super not to direct its employees to use the grinder without the safety attachment.

Hobart's argument about causation follows logically from the notion that its duty to warn in this case merely required Hobart to inform Liriano that a guard was available and that he should not use an unguarded grinder. The contention is tightly reasoned, but it rests on a false premise. It assumes that the burden was on Liriano to introduce additional evidence showing that the failure to warn was a but-for cause of his injury, even after he had shown that Hobart's wrong greatly increased the likelihood of the harm that occurred. But Liriano does not bear that burden. When a defendant's negligent act is deemed wrongful precisely because it has a strong propensity to cause the type of injury that ensued, that very causal tendency is evidence enough to establish a *prima facie* case of cause-in-fact. The burden then shifts to the *defendant* to come forward with evidence that its negligence was *not* such a but-for cause.

* * *

This shifting of the *onus procedendi* has long been established in New York. Its classic statement was made more than seventy years ago, when the Court of Appeals decided a case in which a car collided with a buggy driving after sundown without lights. *See Martin v. Herzog*, 228 N.Y. 164, 170, 126 N.E. 814, 816 (1920). The driver of the buggy argued that his negligence in driving without lights had not been shown to be the cause-in-fact of the accident. Writing for the Court, Judge Cardozo reasoned that the legislature deemed driving without lights after sundown to be negligent precisely because not using lights tended to cause accidents of the sort that had occurred in the case. *See id.* at 168, 126 N.E. at 815. The simple fact of an accident under those conditions, he said, was enough to support the inference of but-for causal connection between the negligence and the particular accident. *See id.* at 170, 126 N.E. at 816. The inference, he noted, could be rebutted. But it was up to the negligent party to produce the evidence supporting such a rebuttal. *See id.*

The words that Judge Cardozo applied to the buggy's failure to use lights are equally applicable to Hobart's failure to warn: 'If nothing else is shown to break the connection, we have a case, prima facie sufficient, of negligence contributing to the result.' *Id.* Under that approach, the fact that Liriano did not introduce detailed evidence of but-for causal connection between Hobart's failure to warn and his injury cannot bar his claim. His *prima facie* case arose from the strong causal linkage between Hobart's negligence and the harm that occurred. *See* Guido Calabresi, *Concerning Cause and the Law of Torts: An Essay for Harry Kalven, Jr.,* 43 U. Chi. L.Rev. 69 (1975) (describing the concept of 'causal link'). And, since the *prima facie* case was not rebutted, it suffices."

AYERS v. JOHNSON & JOHNSON BABY PRODUCTS CO., 117 Wash.2d 747, 818 P.2d 1337 (1991). David Ayers, then 15 months old, aspirated baby oil which he found in an unmarked bottle in his older sister's purse. As a result, he suffered permanent brain damage. "Today David cannot move his arms or legs, which are stiff and spastic. He has limited control of his head movements. He cannot speak, is mentally retarded, and is subject to seizures." The Ayerses brought suit against Johnson and Johnson for failing to warn of the dangers of aspirating baby oil. At trial, they presented testimony by Dr. Marvin Scotvold, chief of dermatology at Children's Hospital & Medical Center in Seattle. He "testified that he teaches resident physicians training under him not to use baby oil on children under the age of 3 years because of the danger of aspiration. Dr. Scotvold further testified that he felt strongly that there should be a warning about aspiration on bottles of baby oil. Among the reasons he gave for this view is that the product is sold for use on and around babies, who have a well-known tendency to put things in their mouths, and for use in and around water, where the chances of the baby aspirating some liquid containing the oil are increased."

The trial court entered judgment notwithstanding the verdict in favor of Johnson & Johnson, partly on the ground that the plaintiffs had failed to prove causation. The Court of Appeals reversed, and reinstated the verdict. *Held,* affirmed. The jury's finding that absence of a warning caused the child's injury "was not so unsupported or unreasonable that a judgment notwithstanding the verdict was appropriate."

"Expert testimony established that once David inhaled the oil there was no way to get it out, and medical attention would not have prevented injury to his lungs. Therefore, the issue as regards cause in fact does not concern whether had there been an adequate warning, Mrs. Ayers would have been alerted to the danger when she inspected the label on the bottle and so sought immediate medical help. Rather, the issue concerns whether had there been an adequate warning, David never would have inhaled the oil because the Ayerses would have kept it out of his reach. This was what the parties contested at trial and is the issue we examine here.

"As the Court of Appeals noted, members of the Ayers family testified that they kept items they knew to be dangerous out of the reach of the twin baby boys. Mrs. Ayers testified that she made a practice of reading labels on products, and that she shelved them at home according to what she read on the labels. Items she knew to be particularly dangerous, such as cleaning waxes or bathroom cleansers, were shelved up high in a cupboard above the kitchen stove or in a box on the top shelf of the bathroom closet. Items she perceived as less dangerous were treated with less care. Before David's accident, she regarded baby oil as one of these less dangerous items, thinking that the only danger it presents is diarrhea if ingested. Accordingly, she usually kept it on the dresser in the babies' room, where she could reach it easily. This location was not, she testified, out of the babies' reach. She testified that if she had been aware of the dangers of aspiration, the baby oil would have been kept up high in the medicine box. She also said that if she had been aware of the dangers, she would have alerted other members of the family. She had specifically told her teenage daughters that if they were carrying in their purses anything that could be dangerous to the twins, such as personal toiletries like perfume, they were to keep the purses out of the twins' reach. David's sister, Laurie, in whose purse David found the baby oil, testified that she thought baby oil might cause an upset stomach if digested, but that she too had no idea of the dangers of aspiration.

"On the basis of this evidence, the jury was entitled to infer that if the Ayerses had known of the dangers of aspiration, they would have treated baby oil with greater care; that they would have treated it with the caution they used in relation to items they recognized as highly dangerous, like cleaning products; and that had they done so, the accident never would have occurred. We conclude that the evidence of causation presented to the jury was sufficient to sustain the jury's verdict.

"Johnson & Johnson argues that the absence of any warning on the baby oil container was not a cause in fact of David's injury. First, Johnson & Johnson asserts that the Ayerses knew before the accident occurred that baby oil is for external use only and should be kept out of the reach of children. Johnson & Johnson reasons that since the Ayerses already knew this, it is wholly speculative that a further warning on the container would have caused them to modify their behavior in a way that would have prevented the accident. Johnson & Johnson also emphasizes that to reach the conclusion that the absence of a warning caused David's injury, one must assume that had there been a warning, it would have been heeded by Mrs. Ayers, that she would have communicated the need for caution to the other members of her family, and that Laurie would not have left her purse on the bedroom floor. Johnson & Johnson asserts that under these circumstances it is 'rank speculation' to suppose a warning would have prevented the injury.

"We reject this argument. All the Ayerses apparently knew was that baby oil could cause diarrhea if swallowed. They did not know of the risks of aspiration, and the evidence they presented, as described above, is sufficient to support the jury's conclusion that if they had been alert to those risks, they would have treated the product more carefully. At most, Johnson & Johnson's argument suggests that reasonable persons might disagree as to whether a warning would have made any difference. For this court to uphold the trial court's judgment notwithstanding the verdict, however, more is required. This court must be prepared to conclude that no reasonable person could infer, as did the jury, that a warning would have altered the Ayerses' behavior. The evidence presented at trial was not so weak as to permit such a conclusion."

SPECIAL KINDS OF GOODS

The materials that follow comment briefly on special kinds of products: leased and used ones, products sold in bulk and to be integrated as components in other products, services, and products which exert their influence on and through people's minds. Each of these presents special questions about whether and how to apply products liability law.

———

Leased and Used Goods

PRICE v. SHELL OIL CO., 2 Cal.3d 245, 85 Cal.Rptr. 178, 466 P.2d 722 (1970). "We hold in this case that the doctrine of strict liability in tort which we have heretofore made applicable to sellers of personal property is also applicable to bailors and lessors of such property."

"[The expansion of categories of persons benefiting from strict liability] evolves naturally from the purpose of imposing strict liability which 'is to insure that the costs of injuries resulting from defective products are borne by the manufacturers that put such products on the market rather than by the injured persons who are powerless to protect themselves.' (Greenman v. Yuba Power Products, Inc., supra, 59 Cal.2d 57, 63, 27 Cal.Rptr. 697, 701, 377 P.2d 897, 901.) Essentially the paramount policy to be promoted by the rule is the protection of otherwise defenseless victims of manufacturing defects and the spreading throughout society of the cost of compensating them. * * *

"Similarly we can perceive no substantial difference between *sellers* of personal property and *non-sellers*, such as bailors and lessors. In each instance, the seller or non-seller 'places [an article] on the market, knowing that it is to be used without inspection for defects, * * *.' (*Greenman [v. Yuba Power Products, Inc.]*, 59 Cal.2d at p. 62, 27 Cal.Rptr. at p. 700, 377 P.2d at p. 900) In the light of the policy to be subserved, it should make no difference that the party distributing the article has retained title to it. Nor can we see how the risk of harm associated with the use of the chattel can vary with the legal form under which it is held. Having in mind the market realities and the widespread use of the lease of personalty in today's business world, we think it makes good sense to impose on the lessors of chattels the same liability for physical harm which has been imposed on the manufacturers and retailers. The former, like the latter, are able to bear the cost of compensating for injuries resulting from defects by spreading the loss through an adjustment of the rental.

" * * * [F]or the doctrine of strict liability in tort to apply to a lessor of personalty, the lessor should be found to be in the business of leasing, in the same general sense as the seller of personalty is found to be in the business of manufacturing or retailing."

TILLMAN v. VANCE EQUIPMENT CO., 286 Or. 747, 596 P.2d 1299 (1979). Durametal asked defendant to locate a used crane. Defendant did so, purchased it and immediately resold it to Durametal under an "as is" contract. Plaintiff, Durametal's employee, had his hand drawn into the gears while greasing them and sued defendant in strict liability on grounds of a design defect. The Supreme Court, affirming judgment for defendant, concluded that "the trial court was correct in holding that a seller of used goods is not strictly liable in tort for a defect in a used crane when that defect was created by the manufacturer." It said:

"This court has never been willing to rely on enterprise liability alone as a justification for strict liability for defective products. Instead, we have identified three justifications for the doctrine:

> * * * [C]ompensation (ability to spread the risk), satisfaction of the reasonable expectations of the purchaser or user (implied representational aspect), and over-all risk reduction (the impetus to manufacture a better product) * * *. Fulbright v. Klamath Gas Co., 271 Or. 449, 460, 533 P.2d 316, 321 (1975).

"While dealers in used goods are, as a class, capable like other businesses of providing for the compensation of injured parties and the allocation of the cost of injuries caused by the products they sell, we are not convinced that the other two considerations identified in *Fulbright* weigh sufficiently in this class of cases to justify imposing strict liability on sellers of used goods generally.

" * * * [H]olding every dealer in used goods responsible regardless of fault for injuries caused by defects in his goods would not only affect the prices of used goods; it would work a significant change in the very nature of used goods markets. Those markets, generally speaking, operate on the apparent understanding that the seller, even though he is in the business of selling such goods, makes no particular representation about their quality simply by offering them for sale. If a buyer wants some assurance of quality, he typically either bargains for it in the specific transaction or seeks out a dealer who routinely offers it, * * *. The flexibility of this kind of market appears to serve legitimate interests of buyers as well as sellers.

" * * * [A]ny risk reduction which would be accomplished by imposing strict liability on the dealer in used goods would not be significant enough to justify our taking that step. The dealer in used goods generally has no direct relationship with either manufacturers or distributors. Thus, there is no ready channel of communication by which the dealer and the manufacturer can exchange information about possible dangerous defects in particular product lines or about actual and potential liability claims."

BELL v. PRECISION AIRMOTIVE CORPORATION, 42 P.3d 1071 (Alaska 2002). "[S]trict liability applies to sellers of used items when 'the product has undergone extensive repair, inspection and testing at the hands of the seller prior to resale.' "

Generic Goods and Component Parts

HOFFMAN v. HOUGHTON CHEMICAL CORPORATION et al., 434 Mass. 624, 751 N.E.2d 848 (2001). Plaintiffs brought personal injury and wrongful death actions against three suppliers of chemicals which were involved in an explosion at an ink manufacturer. The explosion killed two workers and severely injured several others. The three chemicals—acetone, methanol and toluene—were "highly volatile, flammable solvents." At trial, the jury was instructed "to determine whether the products were delivered in bulk; to assess whether the defendants gave 'adequate and sufficient' warning about the products to the 'immediate purchaser' (that is, to Gotham); and to determine whether the defendants' reliance on Gotham to warn the ultimate users of the products was reasonable in light of the latter's sophistication and ability to pass on its knowledge of product hazards." The jury returned verdicts in favor of all defendants. *Held*, affirmed. "We adopt the 'bulk supplier doctrine' as an affirmative defense in products liabilities actions." The doctrine "allows a manufacturer-supplier (supplier) of bulk products, in certain circumstances, to discharge its duty to warn end users of a product's hazards by reasonable reliance on an intermediary."

"In MacDonald v. Ortho Pharmaceutical Corp., [supra, p. 1031], we held that a supplier of a potentially dangerous product has a duty to warn all foreseeable users of known or reasonably foreseeable hazards of the product's use, but that, in certain limited circumstances, 'a manufacturer may be absolved from blame [for failure to warn] because of a justified reliance upon ... a middleman,' so long as such reliance is reasonable. * * *

"We can imagine few more appropriate circumstances in which to apply these principles than in the context of bulk sales. First, as a practical matter, the nature and function of bulk products are different from those of many other consumer and industrial goods and thus require separate consideration. Bulk products often are delivered in tank trucks, box cars, or large industrial drums, and stored in bulk by the intermediary, who generally repackages or reformulates the bulk product. Even if the product *could* be labeled by the supplier, any label warnings provided to the intermediary would be unlikely to reach the end user. Often, too, the bulk product has multitudinous commercial uses. Toluene, for instance, is used in gasoline, as well as printing ink; acetone is an ingredient of both nail polish remover and press wash; methanol, another press wash component, commonly known as 'wood alcohol,' is used in antifreeze. To impose on bulk suppliers a duty to warn all foreseeable end users *directly* where the product cannot readily be labeled for such users (if it can be labeled at all); where the intermediary is often in a different industry from that of the supplier, with different means of production; and where the end users themselves are a remote and varied lot would be unduly, indeed crushingly, burdensome.

"Second, the intermediary vendee, particularly the large industrial company, has its own independent obligation to provide adequate safety measures for its end users, an obligation on which bulk suppliers should be entitled to rely. The bulk supplier rarely has any control over the intermediary's personnel policies or day-to-day safety operations. Thus, the bulk supplier simply is 'not in a position to constantly monitor the turnover of an employer's workforce' or 'to provide the good housekeeping measures, training and warnings to [the intermediary's] workers on a continuous and systemic basis.' Fisher v. Monsanto Co., [863 F.Supp. 285 (W.D.Va.1994)]at 289, quoting Goodbar v. Whitehead Bros., [591 F.Supp. 552 (W.D.Va.1984)] at 566. In the oft-quoted words of the authors of comment n [to § 388 of the Restatement (Second of Torts)]: 'Modern life would be intolerable unless one were permitted to rely to a certain extent on others' doing what they normally do, particularly if it is their duty to do so.' "

BUONANNO v. COLMAR BELTING CO., 733 A.2d 712 (R.I.1999). Plaintiff's right, dominant arm was severely crushed and had to be amputated when it was pulled into the "nip point" of a conveyor belt system, used to transport debris at a recycling transfer station where he worked as a supervisor. The "nip point" was unguarded, "notwithstanding the fact that an unguarded nip point was generally known to be a hazardous aspect of the system." He brought suit against, inter alia, Colmar Belting Systems, the distributor who had supplied most of the component parts for the system. Colmar did not dispute the defectiveness of the conveyor belt design, but argued that it had " 'no duty' as a as a component part seller" with respect to the design of the final product into which its parts were integrated.

Held, summary judgment in favor of Colmar reversed. "We adopt the Restatement's conclusion that the manufacturer or seller of a component part may be liable to the ultimate user, particularly when it has substantially participated in the integration of the component into the design of the final product. *Restatement (Third) Torts* § 5." There were facts in the record which might "create a reasonable inference that Colmar 'substantially participated' in the design of the conveyor belt system."

Services and Expressions

In re BREAST IMPLANT PRODUCT LIABILITY LITIGATION, 331 S.C. 540, 503 S.E.2d 445 (1998). "We hold that health care providers who perform breast implant procedures are, in essence, providing a service. Although the breast implant procedure requires the use of a product, the implant, the health care provider is fundamentally and predominantly offering a service. The provider must have medical knowledge and skill to conduct the procedure. He must advise the patient of the medical consequences and must recommend to the patient the preferable type of procedure. The product may not be purchased independently of the service. One does not "buy" a breast implant procedure in the same way as one would buy a product, such as a lawn-mower. At its heart, the breast implant procedure is a service and not a product." Health care providers are not strictly liable under products liability law.

WILSON v. MIDWAY GAMES, INCORPORATED, 198 F.Supp.2d 167 (D.Conn.2002). Plaintiff's thirteen-year-old son was grabbed around the neck in a "headlock" and knifed to death by one of his friends. Plaintiff filed suit against Midway Games, Inc., alleging that at the time the friend stabbed and killed her son, the friend was "addicted to a video game manufactured by Midway called Mortal Kombat," and was "so obsessed with the game that he actually believed he was the character Cyrax." Cyrax kills his opponents "by grabbing them around the neck in a 'headlock' and stabbing them in the chest." She also alleged that Midway designed Mortal Kombat to "addict players to the exhilaration of violence" and "specifically targeted a young audience, intending to addict them to the game."

Plaintiff's product liability claim was dismissed for failure to state a claim. The properties of the video game that plaintiff claimed were responsible for the harm were insufficiently "tangible." The game involved "ideas and expression," and the harm was alleged to have been caused by "exhortation, inspiration or 'brainwashing.' " Product liability claims apply only to harms caused by the "tangible" properties of a product. The distinction is "reflected in the Restatement, which defines a product as 'tangible personal property distributed commercially for use or consumption.' Restatement (Third) Torts: Products Liability § 19 (1998)."

In its opinion, the court distinguished the case before it from "commercial intellect or faulty instruction" cases, which also involve "ideas or expression." *Winter v. G.P. Putnam's Sons,* 938 F.2d 1033 (9th Cir.1991), which held that "mushroom enthusiasts who relied on erroneous information in encyclopedia of mushrooms had no strict products liability claim against publisher when they became ill," illustrated the "faulty instruction" class of case. Cases in this class "involve harm resulting from reliance on instruction manuals, cookbooks, navigational charts and similar materials," and "are about misinformation." Most courts, the opinion observed, have declined to impose strict liability in such cases " 'expressing concern that imposing strict liability for the dissemination of false and defective information would significantly impinge on free speech * * * ' Restatement (Third) Torts: Products Liability § 19 cmt. d (1998)." The court thought, however, that "persuasive arguments can be raised both in support of and in opposition to the imposition of products liability for misinformation in various circumstances," citing to an academic commentator who calls for the creation of a " 'commercial intellectual products liability' doctrine that would provide a remedy for the harm that befalls a cook, for example, when preparing a recipe from a cookbook that calls for the use of a poisonous root."

DAMAGES

Because design defects and inadequate warnings or instructions pervade an entire product line, so that a single product defect may give rise to hundreds and even thousands of accidents, damages in products liability law present a special problems. These problems become even more acute in the case of mass accidents, studied in the next chapter, and help to shape and justify the restrictions on damages characteristic of administrative plans, studied in Chapter 22.

ACOSTA v. HONDA MOTOR CO., LTD.
United States Court of Appeals, Third Circuit, 1983.
717 F.2d 828.

[Plaintiff bought a used Honda motorcycle in the Virgin Islands, for which the restatements of law approved by the American Law Institute provided the rules of decision in this case. Plaintiff suffered injuries from an accident caused by the collapse of the motorcycle's rear wheel when it hit the back edge of a ditch through which the motorcycle had been driven. He sued the two manufacturers and distributor in strict product liability and negligence, alleging defective design and manufacture and failure to warn. The jury found for plaintiffs on the strict-liability count, and also awarded punitive damages of $210,000 against each defendant. The court, on motions of defendants for judgment n.o.v., concluded that the evidence disclosed sufficiently "outrageous or reckless conduct" to sustain punitive damages against two defendants, but granted the motion of a third (American Honda).

One issue on appeal was the appropriateness of punitive damages in a strict-liability action. In his opinion for the court, Judge Becker considered three arguments suggesting that the policies animating punitive damages were incompatible with those animating strict products liability:]

1. WOULD THE AVAILABILITY OF PUNITIVE DAMAGES DISRUPT THE REGIME OF STRICT PRODUCTS LIABILITY?

* * *

* * * [T]he drafters of the Restatement explicitly noted that 402A "does not preclude liability based upon the alternative ground of negligence of the seller, where such negligence can be proved." Comment a. Rather, the rule is intended to expand recovery by circumventing the restrictions imposed by fault-based standards. The fact that some sellers therefore will be found liable in the absence of fault does not mean that those who are at fault—and outrageously so—should not be punished. * * *

* * *

2. DOES THE STRICT LIABILITY CONTEXT LIMIT THE EFFECTIVENESS OF PUNITIVE DAMAGES?

* * *

Proponents of this argument point out that the magnitude of recent jury verdicts, coupled with the potential for a single design defect to serve as the template for hundreds or thousands of defective, injury-causing products, means that a manufacturer may be liable for many millions of dollars merely as compensation to injured victims. Thus, the argument runs, compensatory damages have reached such a level in products-liability litigation that, despite their more limited purpose, they have begun to perform the functions heretofore performed by punitive damages. Manufacturers, the argument concludes, therefore already have every incentive to insure that their products are as safe as possible. Indeed the Court of Appeals for the Second Circuit observed as early as 1967:

> Many awards of compensatory damages doubtless contain something of a punitive element, and more would do so if a separate award for exemplary damages were eliminated. Even though products liability insurance blunts the deterrent effect of compensatory awards to a considerable extent, the total coverage under such policies is often limited, bad experience is usually reflected in future rates, and insur-

ance affords no protection to the damage to reputation among [users, consumers, and distributors] which an instance like the present must inevitably produce.

Roginsky v. Richardson–Merrell, Inc., 378 F.2d 832, 841 (2d Cir.1967). Thus the *Roginsky* court concluded that punitive damages were unnecessary to punish and deter the reckless marketing of defective products.

We are not persuaded that limiting recovery to compensatory damages will, in all cases, provide an effective deterrent against the type of wrongful conduct for which punitive damages are usually available. For example, the cost of litigation relative to the likely recovery may deter victims of product defects from suing the manufacturer, even under a regime of strict liability, where products causing numerous minor injuries are involved. The availability of punitive damages to those who do sue may offset the decreased deterrence attributable to those who thus could but do not. Similarly, consumers will not always be aware of the source of an injury caused by a product defect, * * * or they may wrongfully attribute the accident to their own clumsiness; the manufacturer's reprieve in such cases will be offset by the availability of punitive damages in other cases. Finally, under existing doctrine, compensatory damages may prove an inadequate deterrent even when victims do bring suit. Current doctrine does not, for example, allow the estate of a decedent killed by a defective product to recover the value of life to the decedent himself; recovery is instead limited to the pecuniary loss to those immediately surrounding the decedent. In many instances, this doctrine may lead to inadequate compensation. In addition, those peripherally injured by accidents to another generally are not allowed to bring suit, yet their loss may be, in moral or practical terms, extremely substantial. While punitive damages may not be a logically perfect method of remedying these perhaps unavoidable flaws in our system of justice, they are a useful surrogate not necessarily precluded by a strict products liability regime.

3. WILL PUNITIVE DAMAGES HAVE UNDESIRABLE ECONOMIC AND SOCIAL CONSEQUENCES?

Perhaps recognizing that mere redundancy would not be sufficient to supersede considerations in favor of allowing punitive damages, the *Roginsky* court predicted that the availability of such damages would have unfortunate results. The court noted that there are frequently numerous potential plaintiffs with claims arising from the same defect in design or manufacture; if each such plaintiff can recover punitive damages, the court warned, the aggregate recovery could be "catastrophic."

If liability policies can protect against this risk as several courts have held, the cost of providing this probably needless deterrence, not only to the few manufacturers from whom punitive damages for highly negligent conduct are sought but to the thousands from whom it never will be, is passed on to the consuming public; if they cannot, as is held by other courts and recommended by most commentators, a sufficiently egregious error to one product can end the business life of a concern that has wrought much good in the past and might otherwise have continued to do so in the future, with many innocent stockholders suffering extinction of their investments for a single management sin.

Id. at 841.

Although we recognize that the effect of punitive damages may be harsh, we find somewhat excessive the *Roginsky* court's dire predictions about the consequences of allowing punitive damages. First, even assuming that policy considerations would permit manufacturers to insure against punitive damages,[14] it is not clear that such insurance would necessarily emasculate the effectiveness of the remedy or result in "needless deterrence." Rather, a 1976 study by the Department of Commerce noted that recent increases in the number of products liability claims, policy cancellations, insurance premiums, and average loss per claim have contributed to a situation in which manufacturers are finding it more and more difficult to obtain adequate coverage. * * *

More importantly, we do not share *Roginsky's* in terrorem vision of the consequences of punitive damages for which insurance is unavailable. It is, of course, possible that "a sufficiently egregious error as to one product" could result in the demise of its manufacturer, but such a result is not inevitable.[15] Comment e to section 908 of the Restatement makes clear that one factor to be taken into account in calculating punitive damages is the existence of multiple claims by numerous persons affected by the wrongdoer's conduct. It seems appropriate to take into consideration both the punitive damages that have been awarded in prior suits and those that may be granted in the future, with greater weight being given to the prior awards. In a class action involving all claims, full assessment of the punitive damages can be made.

* * *

B. Standard of Proof

Although we reject each of the various arguments against awarding punitive damages in the strict liability context, we agree with Judge Friendly's observation in *Roginsky, supra,* that "the consequences of imposing punitive damages in a case like the present are so serious" that "particularly careful scrutiny" is warranted. * * * We therefore hold under Virgin Islands law that a plaintiff seeking punitive damages, at least in an action in which

---

14. It would seem obvious that the availability of insurance to cover awards of punitive damages would undercut their punitive and deterrent effect. Indeed the Court of Appeals for the Fifth Circuit has so recognized in refusing to enforce such provisions of automobile insurance policies:

Where a person is able to insure himself against punishment he gains a freedom of misconduct inconsistent with the establishment of sanctions against such misconduct. It is not disputed that insurance against criminal fines or penalties would be void as violative of public policy. The same public policy should invalidate any contract of insurance against the civil punishment that punitive damages represent.

Northwestern National Casualty Co. v. McNulty, 307 F.2d 432, 440 (5th Cir.1962).

15. Nor is such a result necessarily untenable. We note, however, that no empirical evidence has been offered that Roginsky's forebodings have been realized in the sixteen years since it was written. * * *

liability is predicated on section 402A, must prove the requisite "outrageous" conduct by clear and convincing proof.

* * *

We have examined the evidence; viewed in the light most favorable to plaintiff, it does not show that the conduct of any defendant was outrageous or reckless. Indeed we discern no basis upon which the jury could have concluded that defendants knew or had reason to know that the rear wheel of Acosta's motorcycle was defective in design or manufacture and that they decided not to remedy the defect in conscious disregard of or indifference to the risk thereby created. Although the wheel had been used in over 275,000 motorcycles, and the model first offered in 1970 (six years before plaintiff's accident), there was no evidence of previous consumer complaints or lawsuits that might have called to defendants' attention that there might be a problem. Moreover, plaintiff offered no proof that defendants developed or failed to modify the engineering designs for the rear wheel of the CB750 with any knowledge or reason to know of its alleged lack of safety. Such matters would have been admissible on the punitive damages issues.

In short, a jury could not have reasonably concluded that the evidence by the clear and convincing standard showed defendants to have acted with reckless disregard for the safety of users of the CB750. Accordingly, we hold that the district court should have granted defendants' motions for directed verdicts on the punitive damage claim * * *.

DUNN v. HOVIC, 1 F.3d 1371 (3d Cir.1993). The plaintiff recovered both compensatory and punitive damages for injuries resulting from his exposure to asbestos. On appeal, defendant challenged the punitive damage award on the ground that it constituted repetitive punishment for the same course of conduct. In affirming the award, the court asserted that unilateral action by a single court or state legislature to limit the number of punitive damage awards against a single defendant for a single course of action, or a particular product defect, would be "illogical and unfair." The opinion quoted from the 1991 American Law Institute Reporter's Study, Enterprise Responsibility for Personal Injury.

" * * * '[T]he state that acts alone may simply provide some relief to out-of-state manufacturers at the expense of its own citizen-victims, a situation that hardly [serves the interests of its citizens.] Moreover, * * * formulas which give the lion's share of the punitive award to the first victim able to win a judgment against a particular defendant, are unfair to the subsequent plaintiffs and concomitantly risk providing too little deterrence to behavior of this type.' As an alternative to state action, the Study supported a federal legislative solution 'to authorize mandatory class actions for multiple punitive damages arising out of large-scale mass torts.'

"These concerns are equally applicable to our role in reviewing punitive damage awards emanating from the Virgin Islands. * * * "

GRIMSHAW v. FORD MOTOR CO.
Court of Appeals, Fourth District, California, 1981.
119 Cal.App.3d 757, 174 Cal.Rptr. 348.

TAMURA, Acting Presiding Justice. A 1972 Ford Pinto hatchback automobile unexpectedly stalled on a freeway, erupting into flames when it was rear ended by a car proceeding in the same direction. Mrs. Lilly Gray, the driver of the Pinto, suffered fatal burns and 13–year-old Richard Grimshaw, a passenger in the Pinto, suffered severe and permanently disfiguring burns on his face and entire body. Grimshaw and the heirs of Mrs. Gray (Grays) sued Ford Motor Company and others. Following a six-month jury trial, verdicts were returned in favor of plaintiffs against Ford Motor Company. Grimshaw was awarded $2,516,000 compensatory damages and $125 million punitive damages; the Grays were awarded $559,680 in compensatory damages. On Ford's motion for a new trial, Grimshaw was required to remit all but $3 ½ million of the punitive award as a condition of denial of the motion.

* * *

Ford assails the judgment as a whole, assigning a multitude of errors and irregularities, including misconduct of counsel, but the primary thrust of its appeal is directed against the punitive damage award. * * * Grimshaw's cross-appeal challenges the validity of the new trial order and the conditional reduction of the punitive damage award. * * *

[Grimshaw's case was submitted to the jury on theories of negligence and strict liability, while the Grays' case was submitted only on the latter theory. Ford did not contest on appeal the amount of compensatory damages.

The court reviewed the evidence in the light most favorable to plaintiffs. The accident occurred in 1972, when the Pinto stalled (a problem since its purchase which the dealer had sought to repair) on the middle lane of a freeway and coasted to a halt. The Ford Galaxie behind that collided with the Pinto had braked from 37 to 28 m.p.h. The impact drove the gas tank forward and caused it to be punctured by the flange or a bolt on the differential housing. Fuel sprayed from the punctured tank and entered the car through a gap caused by the collision.

The court summarized the history of the design of the Pinto fuel system. Some excerpts from that history follow.]

* * * Ford's objective was to build a car at or below 2,000 pounds to sell for no more than $2,000.

Ordinarily marketing surveys and preliminary engineering studies precede the styling of a new automobile line. Pinto, however, was a rush project, so that styling preceded engineering and dictated engineering design to a greater degree than usual. Among the engineering decisions dictated by styling was the placement of the fuel tank. It was then the preferred practice in Europe and Japan to locate the gas tank over the rear axle in subcompacts because a small vehicle has less "crush space" between the rear axle and the bumper than larger cars. The Pinto's styling, however, required the tank to be placed behind the rear axle leaving only 9 or 10 inches of "crush space"—far less than in any other American automobile or Ford overseas subcompact. In addition, the Pinto was designed so that its bumper was little more than a chrome strip, less substantial than the bumper of any other American car produced then or later. The Pinto's rear structure also lacked reinforcing members known as "hat sections" (2 longitudinal side members) and horizontal cross-members running between them such as were found in cars of larger unitized construction and in all automobiles produced by Ford's overseas operations. The absence of the reinforcing members rendered the Pinto less crush resistant than other vehicles. Finally, the differential housing selected for the Pinto had an exposed flange and a line of exposed bolt heads. These protrusions were sufficient to puncture a gas tank driven forward against the differential upon rear impact.

During the development of the Pinto, prototypes were built and tested. * * * Ford also conducted the tests to see if the Pinto as designed would meet a proposed federal regulation requiring all automobiles manufactured in 1972 to be able to withstand a 20–mile-per-hour fixed barrier impact without significant fuel spillage and all automobiles manufactured after January 1, 1973, to withstand a 30–mile-per-hour fixed barrier impact without significant fuel spillage.

The crash tests revealed that the Pinto's fuel system as designed could not meet the 20–mile-per-hour proposed standard. * * * In at least one test, spilled fuel entered the driver's compartment through gaps resulting from the separation of the seams joining the rear wheel wells to the floor pan. The seam separation was occasioned by the lack of reinforcement in the rear structure and insufficient welds of the wheel wells to the floor pan.

Tests conducted by Ford on other vehicles, including modified or reinforced mechanical Pinto prototypes, proved safe at speeds at which the Pinto failed. * * *

When a prototype failed the fuel system integrity test, the standard of care for engineers in the industry was to redesign and retest it. The vulnerability of the production Pinto's fuel tank at speeds of 20 and 30–miles-per-hour fixed barrier tests could have been remedied by inexpensive "fixes," but Ford produced and sold the Pinto to the public without doing anything to remedy the defects. Design changes that would have enhanced the integrity of the fuel tank system at relatively little cost per car included the following: Longitudinal side members and cross members at $2.40 and $1.80, respectively; a single shock absorbent "flak suit" to protect the tank at $4; a tank within a tank and placement of the tank over the axle at $5.08 to $5.79; a nylon bladder within the tank at $5.25 to $8; placement of the tank over the axle surrounded with a protective barrier at a cost of $9.95 per car; substitution of a rear axle with a smooth differential housing at a cost of $2.10; imposition of a protective shield between the differential housing and the tank at $2.35; improvement and reenforcement of the bumper at $2.60;

addition of eight inches of crush space [at] a cost of $6.40. Equipping the car with a reinforced rear structure, smooth axle, improved bumper and additional crush space at a total cost of $15.30 would have made the fuel tank safe in a 34 to 38–mile-per-hour rear end collision by a vehicle the size of the Ford Galaxie. If, in addition to the foregoing, a bladder or tank within a tank were used or if the tank were protected with a shield, it would have been safe in a 40 to 45–mile-per-hour rear impact. If the tank had been located over the rear axle, it would have been safe in a rear impact at 50 miles per hour or more.

The idea for the Pinto, as has been noted, was conceived by Mr. Iacocco, then Executive Vice President of Ford. * * * As the project approached actual production, the engineers responsible for the components of the project "signed off" to their immediate supervisors who in turn "signed off" to their superiors and so on up the chain of command until the entire project was approved for public release by Vice Presidents Alexander and MacDonald and ultimately by Mr. Iacocco. The Pinto crash tests results had been forwarded up the chain of command to the ultimate decision-makers and were known to the Ford officials who decided to go forward with production.

Harley Copp, a former Ford engineer and executive in charge of the crash testing program, testified that the highest level of Ford's management made the decision to go forward with the production of the Pinto, knowing that the gas tank was vulnerable to puncture and rupture at low rear impact speeds creating a significant risk of death or injury from fire and knowing that "fixes" were feasible at nominal cost. He testified that management's decision was based on the cost savings which would inure from omitting or delaying the "fixes."

* * * At an April 1971 product review meeting chaired by Mr. Mac-Donald, those present received and discussed a report (Exhibit 125) prepared by Ford engineers pertaining to the financial impact of a proposed federal standard on fuel system integrity and the cost savings which would accrue from deferring even minimal "fixes." The report refers to crash tests of the integrity of the fuel system of Ford vehicles and design changes needed to meet anticipated federal standards. Also in evidence was a September 23, 1970, report (Exhibit 124) by Ford's "Chassis Design Office" concerning a program "to establish a corporate [Ford] position and reply to the government" on the proposed federal fuel system integrity standard which included zero fuel spillage at 20 miles per hour fixed barrier crash by January 1, 1972, and 30 miles per hour by January 1, 1973. * * *

The fact that two of the crash tests were run at the request of the Ford Chassis and Vehicle Engineering Department for the specific purpose of demonstrating the advisability of moving the fuel tank over the axle as a possible "fix" further corroborated Mr. Copp's testimony that management knew the results of the crash tests. * * *

* * *

In the ensuing analysis (ad nauseam) of Ford's wideranging assault on the judgment, we have concluded that Ford has failed to demonstrate that any errors or irregularities occurred during the trial which resulted in a miscarriage of justice requiring reversal. * * *

* * *

PUNITIVE DAMAGES

Ford contends that it was entitled to a judgment notwithstanding the verdict on the issue of punitive damages on two grounds: First, punitive damages are statutorily and constitutionally impermissible in a design defect case; second, there was no evidentiary support for a finding of malice or of corporate responsibility for malice. In any event, Ford maintains that the punitive damage award must be reversed because of erroneous instructions and excessiveness of the award.

(1) *"Malice" Under Civil Code Section 3294:*

* * * When our laws were codified in 1872, the doctrine [of punitive damages] was incorporated in Civil Code section 3294, which at the time of trial read: "In an action for the breach of an obligation not arising from contract, where the defendant has been guilty of oppression, fraud, or malice, express or implied, the plaintiff, in addition to the actual damages, may recover damages for the sake of example and by way of punishing the defendant."

Ford argues that "malice" as used in section 3294 and as interpreted by our Supreme Court in Davis v. Hearst, 160 Cal. 143, 116 P. 530, requires *animus malus* or evil motive—an intention to injure the person harmed— and that the term is therefore conceptually incompatible with an unintentional tort such as the manufacture and marketing of a defectively designed product. This contention runs counter to our decisional law. As this court recently noted, numerous California cases after Davis v. Hearst, supra have interpreted the term "malice" as used in section 3294 to include, not only a malicious intention to injure the specific person harmed, but conduct evincing "a conscious disregard of the probability that the actor's conduct will result in injury to others." (Dawes v. Superior Court, 111 Cal.App.3d 82, 88, 168 Cal.Rptr. 319, hg. den. (Dec. 17, 1980). [String citations omitted. The court notes that three of the cases cited "were strict products liability cases."]

* * *

The interpretation of the word "malice" as used in section 3294 to encompass conduct evincing callous and conscious disregard of public safety by those who manufacture and market mass produced articles is consonant with and furthers the objectives of punitive damages. The primary purposes of punitive damages are punishment and deterrence of like conduct by the wrongdoer and others. In the traditional noncommercial intentional tort, compensatory damages alone may serve as an effective deterrent against future wrongful conduct but in commerce related torts, the manufacturer may find it more profitable to treat compensatory damages as a part of the cost of doing business rather than to remedy the defect. Deterrence of such "objectionable corporate policies" serves one of the principal purposes of Civil Code section 3294. (Egan v. Mutual of Omaha Ins. Co., 24 Cal.3d 809, 820, 157 Cal.Rptr. 482, 598 P.2d 452.) Governmental safety standards and the criminal law have failed to provide adequate consumer protection against the manufacture and distribution of defective products. Punitive damages thus remain as the most effective remedy for consumer protection against defectively designed mass produced articles. They provide a motive for private individuals to enforce rules of law and enable them to recoup the expenses of doing so which can be considerable and not otherwise recoverable.

We find no statutory impediments to the application of Civil Code section 3294 to a strict products liability case based on design defect.

(2) *Constitutional Attacks On Civil Code Section 3294:*

* * *

The argument that application of Civil Code section 3294 violates the constitutional prohibition against double jeopardy is equally fallacious. This prohibition like the ex post facto concept is applicable only to criminal proceedings.

The related contention that the potential liability for punitive damages in other cases for the same design defect renders the imposition of such damages violative of Ford's due process rights also lacks merit. Followed to its logical conclusion, it would mean that punitive damages could never be assessed against a manufacturer of a mass produced article. No authorities are cited for such a proposition; indeed, as we have seen, the cases are to the contrary. We recognize the fact that multiplicity of awards may present a problem, but the mere possibility of a future award in a different case is not a ground for setting aside the award in this case, particularly as reduced by the trial judge. If Ford should be confronted with the possibility of an award in another case for the same conduct, it may raise the issue in that case. We add, moreover, that there is no necessary unfairness should the plaintiff in this case be rewarded to a greater extent than later plaintiffs. * * *

(3) *Sufficiency Of The Evidence To Support The Finding Of Malice And Corporate Responsibility:*

Ford contends that its motion for judgment notwithstanding the verdict should have been granted because the evidence was insufficient to support a finding of malice or corporate responsibility for such malice. The record fails to support the contention.

* * *

Through the results of the crash tests Ford knew that the Pinto's fuel tank and rear structure would expose consumers to serious injury or death in a 20 to 30 mile-per-hour collision. There was evidence that Ford could have corrected the hazardous design defects at minimal cost but decided to defer correction of the shortcomings by engaging in a cost-benefit analysis balancing human lives and limbs against corporate profits. Ford's institutional mentality was shown to be one of callous indifference to public safety. There was substantial evidence that Ford's conduct constituted "conscious disregard" of the probability of injury to members of the consuming public.

* * *

(4) *Instructions On Malice:*

In its instructions to the jury, the trial court defined malice as follows: " 'Malice' means a motive and willingness to vex, harass, annoy or injure another person. Malice may be inferred from acts and conduct, such as by showing that the defendant's conduct was wilful, intentional, and done in conscious disregard of its possible results." * * *

On appeal, Ford contends that the phrase "conscious disregard of its possible results" * * * would permit a plaintiff to impugn almost every design decision as made in conscious disregard of some perceivable risk because safer alternative designs are almost always a possibility. Ford * * * maintains that an instruction on "malice" in products liability must contain the phrase "conscious disregard of [the probability/a high probability] of injury to others," in order to preclude prejudicial error. * * *

* * *

* * * When the instructions are read as a whole, the jury could not possibly have interpreted the words "conscious disregard of its possible results" to extend to the innocent conduct depicted by Ford. The term "motive and willingness . . . to injure" and the words "wilful," "intentional," and "conscious disregard" signify *animus malus* or evil motive. * * *

The jury was instructed that Ford was not required under the law to produce either the safest possible vehicle or one which was incapable of producing injury. The instructions on malice manifestly referred to conduct constituting conscious and callous disregard of a substantial likelihood of injury to others and not to innocent conduct by the manufacturer. Further, plaintiffs made no attempt in their arguments to the jury to give the instructions on malice the interpretation to which Ford says they are susceptible. Plaintiffs did not argue possibility of injury; they argued that injury was a virtual certainty and that Ford's management knew it from the results of the crash tests. Thus, the instructions on malice, even assuming them to have been erroneous because the word "possible" was used instead of "probable," did not constitute prejudicial error.

* * *

(6) *Amount of Punitive Damage Award:*

Ford's final contention is that the amount of punitive damages awarded, even as reduced by the trial court, was so excessive that a new trial on that issue must be granted. Ford argues that its conduct was less reprehensible than those for which punitive damages have been awarded in California in the past; that the 3 ½ million dollar award is many times over the highest award for such damages ever upheld in California; and that the award exceeds maximum civil penalties that may be enforced under federal or state statutes against a manufacturer for marketing a defective automobile. We are unpersuaded.

* * * In deciding whether an award is excessive as a matter of law or was so grossly disproportionate as to raise the presumption that it was the product of passion or prejudice, the following factors should be weighed: The degree of reprehensibility of defendant's conduct, the wealth of the defendant, the amount of compensatory damages, and an amount which would serve as a deterrent effect on like conduct by defendant and others who may be so inclined. Applying the foregoing criteria to the instant case, the punitive damage award as reduced by the trial court was well within reason.

In assessing the propriety of a punitive damage award, as in assessing the propriety of any other judicial ruling based upon factual determinations, the evidence must be viewed in the light most favorable to the judgment. Viewing the record thusly in the instant case, the conduct of Ford's management was reprehensible in the extreme. It exhibited a conscious and callous disregard of public safety in order to maximize corporate profits. Ford's self-evaluation of its conduct is based on a review of the evidence most favorable to it instead of on the basis of the evidence most favorable to the judgment. Unlike malicious conduct directed toward a single specific individual, Ford's tortious conduct endangered the lives of thousands of Pinto purchasers. Weighed against the factor of reprehensibility, the punitive damage award as reduced by the trial judge was not excessive.

Nor was the reduced award excessive taking into account defendant's wealth and the size of the compensatory award. Ford's net worth was 7.7 billion dollars and its income after taxes for 1976 was over 983 million dollars. The punitive award was approximately .005% of Ford's net worth and approximately .03% of its 1976 net income. The ratio of the punitive damages to compensatory damages was approximately 1.4 to one. Significantly, Ford does not quarrel with the amount of the compensatory award to Grimshaw.

Nor was the size of the award excessive in light of its deterrent purpose. An award which is so small that it can be simply written off as a part of the cost of doing business would have no deterrent effect. An award which affects the company's pricing of its product and thereby affects its competitive advantage would serve as a deterrent. The award in question was far from excessive as a deterrent against future wrongful conduct by Ford and others.

Ford complains that the punitive award is far greater than the maximum penalty that may be imposed under California or federal law prohibiting the sale of defective automobiles or other products. * * * It is precisely because monetary penalties under government regulations prescribing business standards or the criminal law are so inadequate and ineffective as deterrents against a manufacturer and distributor of mass produced defective products that punitive damages must be of sufficient amount to discourage such practices. Instead of showing that the punitive damage award was excessive, the comparison between the award and the maximum penalties under state and federal statutes and regulations governing automotive safety demonstrates the propriety of the amount of punitive damages awarded.

GRIMSHAW'S APPEAL

Grimshaw has appealed from the order conditionally granting Ford a new trial on the issue of punitive damages and from the amended judgment entered pursuant to that order.

Grimshaw contends that the new trial order is erroneous because (1) the punitive damages awarded by the jury were not excessive as a matter of law, (2) the specification of reasons was inadequate; and (3) the court abused its discretion in cutting the award so drastically. For reasons to be stated, we have concluded that the contentions lack merit.

The court prefaced its specification of reasons with a recitation of the judicially established guidelines[16] for determining whether a punitive award is excessive. * * * The court then noted, based on the fact that Ford's net worth was 7.7 billion and its profits during the last quarter of the year referred to in the financial statement introduced into evidence were more than twice the punitive award, that the award was not disproportionate to Ford's net assets or to its profit generating capacity. The court noted, however, that the amount of the punitive award was 44 times the compensatory award, the court stated that while it did not consider that ratio alone to be controlling because aggravating circumstances may justify a ratio as high as the one represented by the jury verdict, it reasoned that the ratio coupled with the amount by which the punitive exceeded the compensatory damages (over 122 million dollars) rendered the jury's punitive award excessive as a matter of law.

Grimshaw contends that the court erred in determining that the ratio of punitive to compensatory damages rendered the punitive excessive as a matter of law. The trial court, however, did not base its decision solely on the ratio of punitive to compensatory. It took into account the ratio, the "aggravating circumstances" (the degree of reprehensibility), the wealth of the defendant and its profit generating capacity, the magnitude of the punitive award, including the amount by which it exceeded the compensatory. Those were proper considerations for determining whether the award was excessive as a matter of law. * * * In the case at bench, we find no abuse of discretion.

* * *

* * * Finally, while the trial judge may not have taken into account Ford's potential liability for punitive damages in other cases involving the same tortious conduct in reducing the award, it is a factor we may consider in passing on the request to increase the award. Considering such potential liability, we find the amount as reduced by the trial judge to be reasonable

---

16. The court stated that "the principles by which the propriety of the amount of punitive damages awarded will be judged are threefold: (1) Is the sum so large as to raise a presumption that the award was the result of passion and prejudice and therefore excessive as a matter of law; (2) Does the award bear a reasonable relationship to the net assets of the defendant; and (3) Does the award bear a reasonable relationship to the compensatory damages awarded."

and just. We therefore decline the invitation to modify the judgment by reducing the amount of the remittitur.

DISPOSITION

In Richard Grimshaw v. Ford Motor Company, the judgment, the conditional new trial order, and the order denying Ford's motion for judgment notwithstanding the verdict on the issue of punitive damages are affirmed.

THE GRAYS' CASE

[Discussion omitted. The court affirmed the judgment, finding against the arguments in both Ford's appeal and in the Grays' cross-appeal.]

HILLRICHS v. AVCO CORP., 514 N.W.2d 94 (Iowa 1994). In this case, the facts of which are summarized supra, p. 1066, the jury in the second trial awarded plaintiff $1 million in punitive damages, in addition to compensatory damages. The trial court set aside the punitive award on the ground that the plaintiff failed to prove that the defendant acted with "willful and wanton disregard for the rights of another." *Held*, affirmed.

"Plaintiff does not dispute defendant's evidence that when Avco engineers decided not to install emergency stop devices on the Unisystem's husker apparatus, they based their decision on the so-called 'dependency hypothesis,' the theory that the product as designed would discourage farmers from making contact with the roller bed and that the plaintiff's proposed device would invite farmers to unreasonably depend on it despite the dangerousness of the husking roller bed.

" * * * [W]e agree that plaintiff generated a jury question on the negligence issue as to the reasonableness of this decision based on the foreseeability that farmers might nevertheless attempt by hand to unplug a running machine. Plaintiff contends that this generalized knowledge of possible danger, coupled with defendant's failure to test an emergency stop device, generated a jury question on punitive damages. We believe this evidence supports precisely the opposite conclusion—namely, that an award of punitive damages is inappropriate where room exists for reasonable disagreement over the relative risks and utilities of the conduct and device at issue."

D. BEYOND TORT

Chapter 21

BEYOND TRADITIONAL TORT PROCESSES

SECTION A. MASS TORTS

The materials of the present section deal with mass tort situations. These are situations in which many people are put at risk, and many ultimately hurt, by the same tortious conduct. The multiple injuries of a mass tort may be produced all at once, caused by the same explosion, fire, air crash, oil spill. Or the common source of injury may be a set of circumstances persisting over time, as in the gradual leaching of a hazardous substance from a dump site. Or the common risk may arise again and again across time and space, as in the case of a nationally marketed product containing a defect that imperils all users. Mass tort situations include great bursts of risk which, like risks of asbestos or the drug DES, produce public health disaster on a national level. These are the supernovas of tort law's firmament.

Materials that follow focus on two problems which develop in mass tort litigation. Both problems have to do with difficulty in proving causation of a particular plaintiff's injury. The first problem raises issues of collective responsibility; the second has to do with collective harm. Each is most acute when the physical harm at issue is long-latency disease. The two matters addressed are "the problem of generic injury" and "the problem of toxic exposure."

The problem of generic injury involves the following situation. Many firms within an industry produce an identical product or substance. The product turns out to create characteristic harm. A plaintiff is harmed by the product, but is unable to prove which firm within the industry marketed the specific item that caused the harm in plaintiff's case. The claimant can show that harm was caused by the generic output of the industry as a whole. Should courts grant recovery on some theory of collective responsibility?

The problem of toxic exposure is a kind of dilemma. The dilemma happens when a population is exposed to a toxic substance that can be shown to create an increased risk of disease for the group as a whole. Increased risk means additional risk over and above an underlying or background chance that the disease will be contracted from other sources. On the one hand, an exposed person might bring suit right away and seek to recover damages for the increased risk itself. The difficulty is that such recovery is a matter of probabilities; there's a chance the particular claimant will never get sick. On the other hand, an exposed person may wait and bring suit only after disease actually develops. The difficulty is that recovery is still a matter of probabilities, since there's a chance the particular claimant's illness arose from other sources. How should courts proceed in the face of these difficulties?

SINDELL v. ABBOTT LABORATORIES

Supreme Court of California, 1980.
26 Cal.3d 588, 163 Cal.Rptr. 132, 607 P.2d 924.

MOSK, Justice. This case involves a complex problem both timely and significant: may a plaintiff, injured as the result of a drug administered to her mother during pregnancy, who knows the type of drug involved but cannot identify the manufacturer of the precise product, hold liable for her injuries a maker of a drug produced from an identical formula?

Plaintiff Judith Sindell brought an action against eleven drug companies and Does 1 through 100, on behalf of herself and other women similarly situated. The complaint alleges as follows:

Between 1941 and 1971, defendants were engaged in the business of manufacturing, promoting, and marketing diethylstilbesterol (DES), a drug which is a synthetic compound of the female hormone estrogen. The drug was administered to plaintiff's mother and the mothers of the class she represents,[1] for the purpose of preventing miscarriage. In 1947, the Food and Drug Administration authorized the marketing of DES as a miscarriage preventative * * *.

DES may cause cancerous vaginal and cervical growths in the daughters exposed to it before birth, because their mothers took the drug during pregnancy. The form of cancer from which these daughters suffer is known as adenocarcinoma, and it manifests itself after a minimum latent period of 10 or 12 years. It is a fast-spreading and deadly disease, and radical surgery is required to prevent it from spreading. DES also causes adenosis, precancerous vaginal and cervical growths which may spread to other areas of the body. The treatment for adenosis is cauterization, surgery, or cryosurgery. Women who suffer from this condition must be monitored by biopsy or

---

1. The plaintiff class alleged consists of "girls and women who are residents of California and who have been exposed to DES before birth and who may or may not know that fact or the dangers" to which they were exposed. Defendants are also sued as representatives of a class of drug manufacturers which sold DES after 1941.

colposcopic examination twice a year, a painful and expensive procedure. Thousands of women whose mothers received DES during pregnancy are unaware of the effects of the drug.

In 1971, the Food and Drug Administration ordered defendants to cease marketing and promoting DES for the purpose of preventing miscarriages, and to warn physicians and the public that the drug should not be used by pregnant women because of the danger to their unborn children.

During the period defendants marketed DES, they knew or should have known that it was a carcinogenic substance, that there was a grave danger after varying periods of latency it would cause cancerous and precancerous growths in the daughters of the mothers who took it, and that it was ineffective to prevent miscarriage. Nevertheless, defendants continued to advertise and market the drug as a miscarriage preventative. They failed to test DES for efficacy and safety; the tests performed by others, upon which they relied, indicated that it was not safe or effective. In violation of the authorization of the Food and Drug Administration, defendants marketed DES on an unlimited basis rather than as an experimental drug, and they failed to warn of its potential danger.

Because of defendants' advertised assurances that DES was safe and effective to prevent miscarriage, plaintiff was exposed to the drug prior to her birth. She became aware of the danger from such exposure within one year of the time she filed her complaint. As a result of the DES ingested by her mother, plaintiff developed a malignant bladder tumor which was removed by surgery. She suffers from adenosis and must constantly be monitored by biopsy or colposcopy to insure early warning of further malignancy.

The first cause of action alleges that defendants were jointly and individually negligent in that they manufactured, marketed and promoted DES as a safe and efficacious drug to prevent miscarriage, without adequate testing or warning, and without monitoring or reporting its effects.

[The complaint] alleges that defendants are jointly liable regardless of which particular brand of DES was ingested by plaintiff's mother because defendants collaborated in marketing, promoting and testing the drug, relied upon each other's tests, and adhered to an industry-wide safety standard. DES was produced from a common and mutually agreed upon formula as a fungible drug interchangeable with other brands of the same product; defendants knew or should have known that it was customary for doctors to prescribe the drug by its generic rather than its brand name and that pharmacists filled prescriptions from whatever brand of the drug happened to be in stock.

Other causes of action are based upon theories of strict liability, violation of express and implied warranties, [and] false and fraudulent representations * * *.

* * *

Plaintiff seeks compensatory damages of $1 million and punitive damages of $10 million for herself. For the members of her class, she prays for equitable relief in the form of an order that defendants warn physicians and others of the danger of DES and the necessity of performing certain tests to determine the presence of disease caused by the drug, and that they establish free clinics in California to perform such tests.

Defendants demurred to the complaint. While the complaint did not expressly allege that plaintiff could not identify the manufacturer of the precise drug ingested by her mother, she stated in her points and authorities in opposition to the demurrers filed by some of the defendants that she was unable to make the identification, and the trial court sustained the demurrers of these defendants without leave to amend on the ground that plaintiff did not and stated she could not identify which defendant had manufactured the drug responsible for her injuries. Thereupon, the court dismissed the action. This appeal involves only five of ten defendants named in the complaint.

* * *

This case is but one of a number filed throughout the country seeking to hold drug manufacturers liable for injuries allegedly resulting from DES prescribed to the plaintiffs' mothers since 1947. According to a note in the Fordham Law Review, estimates of the number of women who took the drug during pregnancy range from 1½ million to 3 million. Hundreds, perhaps thousands, of the daughters of these women suffer from adenocarcinoma, and the incidence of vaginal adenosis among them is 30 to 90 percent. (Comment, DES and a Proposed Theory of Enterprise Liability (1978) 46 Fordham L.Rev. 963, 964–967 [hereafter Fordham Comment].) Most of the cases are still pending. With two exceptions, those that have been decided resulted in judgments in favor of the drug company defendants because of the failure of the plaintiffs to identify the manufacturer of the DES prescribed to their mothers. * * *

We begin with the proposition that, as a general rule, the imposition of liability depends upon a showing by the plaintiff that his or her injuries were caused by the act of the defendant or by an instrumentality under the defendant's control. * * *

There are, however, exceptions to this rule. * * *

I

Plaintiff places primary reliance upon cases which hold that if a party cannot identify which of two or more defendants caused an injury, the burden of proof may shift to the defendants to show that they were not responsible for the harm. This principle is sometimes referred to as the "alternative liability" theory.

The celebrated case of Summers v. Tice, 33 Cal.2d 80, 199 P.2d 1 [1948], a unanimous opinion of this court, best exemplifies the rule. In *Summers*, the plaintiff was injured when two hunters negligently shot in his direction. It could not be determined which of them had fired the shot which actually caused the injury to the plaintiff's eye, but both defendants were nevertheless held jointly and severally liable for the whole of the damages. We reasoned that both were wrongdoers, both were negligent toward the plaintiff, and that it would be unfair to require plaintiff to isolate the defendant responsible, because if the one pointed out were to escape liability, the other might also, and the plaintiff-victim would be shorn of any remedy. In these circumstances, we held, the burden of proof shifted to the defendants, "each to absolve himself if he can." * * *

In *Summers*, we relied upon Ybarra v. Spangard (1944) 25 Cal.2d 486, 154 P.2d 687. * * *

* * *

Here, as in *Summers*, the circumstances of the injury appear to render identification of the manufacturer of the drug ingested by plaintiff's mother impossible by either plaintiff or defendants, and it cannot reasonably be said that one is in a better position than the other to make the identification. Because many years elapsed between the time the drug was taken and the manifestation of plaintiff's injuries she, and many other daughters of mothers who took DES, are unable to make such identification. * * *

On the other hand, it cannot be said with assurance that defendants have the means to make the identification. In this connection, they point out that drug manufacturers ordinarily have no direct contact with the patients who take a drug prescribed by their doctors. Defendants sell to wholesalers, who in turn supply the product to physicians and pharmacies. * * *

* * *

* * * There is an important difference between the situation involved in *Summers* and the present case. There, all the parties who were or could have been responsible for the harm to the plaintiff were joined as defendants. Here, by contrast, there are approximately 200 drug companies which made DES, any of which might have manufactured the injury-producing drug.

Defendants maintain that, while in *Summers* there was a 50 percent chance that one of the two defendants was responsible for the plaintiff's injuries, here * * * any one of 200 companies which manufactured DES might have made the product which harmed plaintiff * * *.

These arguments are persuasive if we measure the chance that any one of the defendants supplied the injury-causing drug by the number of possible tortfeasors. In such a context, the possibility that any of the five defendants supplied the DES to plaintiff's mother is so remote that it would be unfair to require each defendant to exonerate itself. * * * While we propose, infra, an adaptation of the rule in *Summers* which will substantially overcome these difficulties, defendants appear to be correct that the rule, as previously applied, cannot relieve plaintiff of the burden of proving the identity of the manufacturer which made the drug causing her injuries.

II

The second principle upon which plaintiff relies is the so-called "concert of action" theory. * * *

* * * The elements of this doctrine are prescribed in section 876 of the Restatement of Torts. The section provides, "For harm resulting to a third person from the tortious conduct of another, one is subject to liability if he (a) does a tortious act in concert with the other or pursuant to a common design with him, or (b) knows that the other's conduct constitutes a breach of duty and gives substantial assistance or encouragement to the other so to conduct himself * * *."

* * *

In our view, [plaintiff's] litany of charges is insufficient to allege a cause of action under the rules stated above. The gravamen of the charge of concert is that defendants failed to adequately test the drug or to give sufficient warning of its dangers and that they relied upon the tests performed by one another and took advantage of each others' promotional and marketing techniques. These allegations do not amount to a charge that there was a tacit understanding or a common plan among defendants to fail to conduct adequate tests or give sufficient warnings, and that they substantially aided and encouraged one another in these omissions.

* * *

What the complaint appears to charge is defendants' parallel or imitative conduct in that they relied upon each others' testing and promotion methods. But such conduct describes a common practice in industry: a producer avails himself of the experience and methods of others making the same or similar products. Application of the concept of concert of action to this situation would expand the doctrine far beyond its intended scope and would render virtually any manufacturer liable for the defective products of an entire industry, even if it could be demonstrated that the product which caused the injury was not made by the defendant.

* * *

IV

If we were confined to the theories [discussed], we would be constrained to hold that the judgment must be sustained. Should we require that plaintiff identify the manufacturer which supplied the DES used by her mother or that all DES manufacturers be joined in the action, she would effectively be precluded from any recovery. As defendants candidly admit, there is little likelihood that all the manufacturers who made DES at the time in question are still in business or that they are subject to the jurisdiction of the California courts. There are, however, forceful arguments in favor of holding that plaintiff has a cause of action.

In our contemporary complex industrialized society, advances in science and technology create fungible goods which may harm consumers and which cannot be traced to any specific producer. The response of the courts can be either to adhere rigidly to prior doctrine, denying recovery to those injured by such products, or to fashion remedies to meet these changing needs. * * *

The most persuasive reason for finding plaintiff states a cause of action is that advanced in *Summers*: as between an innocent plaintiff and negligent defendants, the latter should bear the cost of the injury. Here, as in *Summers*, plaintiff is not at fault in failing to provide evidence of causation, and although the absence of such evidence is not attributable to the defendants either, their conduct in marketing a drug the effects of which are delayed for many years played a significant role in creating the unavailability of proof.

From a broader policy standpoint, defendants are better able to bear the cost of injury resulting from the manufacture of a defective product. * * * The manufacturer is in the best position to discover and guard against defects in its products and to warn of harmful effects; thus, holding it liable for defects and failure to warn of harmful effects will provide an incentive to product safety. These considerations are particularly significant where medication is involved, for the consumer is virtually helpless to protect himself from serious, sometimes permanent, sometimes fatal, injuries caused by deleterious drugs.

Where, as here, all defendants produced a drug from an identical formula and the manufacturer of the DES which caused plaintiff's injuries cannot be identified through no fault of plaintiff, a modification of the rule of *Summers* is warranted. * * *

* * * [W]e hold it to be reasonable in the present context to measure the likelihood that any of the defendants supplied the product which allegedly injured plaintiff by the percentage which the DES sold by each of them for the purpose of preventing miscarriage bears to the entire production of the drug sold by all for that purpose. Plaintiff asserts in her briefs that Eli Lilly and Company and 5 or 6 other companies produced 90 percent of the DES marketed. If at trial this is established to be the fact, then there is a corresponding likelihood that this comparative handful of producers manufactured the DES which caused plaintiff's injuries, and only a 10 percent likelihood that the offending producer would escape liability.

If plaintiff joins in the action the manufacturers of a substantial share of the DES which her mother might have taken, the injustice of shifting the burden of proof to defendants to demonstrate that they could not have made the substance which injured plaintiff is significantly diminished. While 75 to 80 percent of the market is suggested as the requirement by the Fordham Comment (at p. 996), we hold only that a substantial percentage is required.

The presence in the action of a substantial share of the appropriate market also provides a ready means to apportion damages among the defendants. Each defendant will be held liable for the proportion of the judgment represented by its share of that market unless it demonstrates that it could not have made the product which caused plaintiff's injuries. In the present case, * * * one DES manufacturer was dismissed from the action upon filing a declaration that it had not manufactured DES until after plaintiff was born. Once plaintiff has met her burden of joining the required defendants, they in turn may cross-complaint against other DES manufacturers, not joined in the action, which they can allege might have supplied the injury-causing product.

* * * It is probably impossible, with the passage of time, to determine market share with mathematical exactitude. But just as a jury cannot be expected to determine the precise relationship between fault and liability in applying the doctrine of comparative fault * * *, the difficulty of apportioning damages among the defendant producers in exact relation to their market share does not seriously militate against the rule we adopt. * * *

* * * [U]nder the rule we adopt, each manufacturer's liability for an injury would be approximately equivalent to the damages caused by the DES it manufactured.

The judgments are reversed.

RICHARDSON, Justice, dissenting.

* * *

The majority attempts to justify its new liability on the ground that defendants herein are "better able to bear the cost of injury resulting from the manufacture of a defective product." * * * In the absence of proof that a particular defendant caused or at least probably caused plaintiff's injuries, a defendant's ability to bear the cost thereof is no more pertinent to the underlying issue of liability than its "substantial" share of the relevant market. * * * Moreover, considerable doubts have been expressed regarding the ability of the drug industry, and especially its smaller members, to bear the substantial economic costs (from both damage awards and high insurance premiums) inherent in imposing an industry-wide liability.

* * * [Section 402A, Rest.2d Torts, including its comment k,] *implicitly recognizes the social policy behind the development of new pharmaceutical preparations.* As one commentator states, " '[t]he social and economic benefits from mobilizing the industry's resources in the war against disease and in reducing the costs of medical care are potentially enormous. The development of new drugs in the last three decades has already resulted in great social benefits. The potential gains from further advances remain large. To risk such gains is unwise. Our major objective should be to encourage a continued high level of industry investment in pharmaceutical R & D [research and development].' " (Schwartzman, The Expected Return from Pharmaceutical Research: Sources of New Drugs and the Profitability of R & D Investment (1975) p. 54.)

In the present case the majority imposes liability more than 20 years after ingestion of drugs which at the time they were used, after careful testing, had the full approval of the United States Food and Drug Administration. It seems to me that liability in the manner created by the majority must inevitably inhibit, if not the research or development, at least the dissemination of new pharmaceutical drugs. Such a result, as explained by the Restatement, is wholly inconsistent with traditional tort theory.

* * *

* * * In my opinion, common sense and reality combine to warn that a "market share" theory goes too far. Legally, it expects too much.

———

MARKET SHARE LIABILITY REFINED. Suppose a plaintiff, proceeding under *Sindell*, joins several defendants who together represent 80% of the relevant market. Plaintiff establishes liability, and proves damages of $100,000. Granting each defendant is liable for the proportion of the judgment corresponding to its market share, what is the amount of the judgment? Does the plaintiff recover the entire $100,000 from the group of joined defendants, or only $80,000 (80%)? Courts interpreting *Sindell* have divided on this matter. Compare Collins v. Eli Lilly Co., 116 Wis.2d 166, 190 n. 9, 342 N.W.2d 37, 47 n. 9 (1984) (entire damages recovered) with Brown v. Superior Court, 44 Cal.3d 1049, 245 Cal.Rptr. 412, 751 P.2d 470 (1988) (diminished recovery).

In Brown v. Superior Court, supra, the California Supreme Court (per Mosk, J.) refined its market share theory in two ways. First, as indicated above, it rejected joint and several liability of defendants in market share suits, saying each manufacturer should be liable only for the percent of the plaintiff's damages that corresponds to its own market share. And second, it said that the *Sindell* approach is not available with respect to claims asserting breach of warranty or fraud.

VARIATIONS AND REJECTIONS. *Sindell* has proved more provocative than persuasive. Courts have continued to struggle with cases in which plaintiff was harmed by an industry's product but is unable to identify the firm whose product caused injury. Some courts have embraced the underlying justification for *Sindell*'s market share approach, but have declined to embrace the approach itself, instead developing alternatives. Two main variations are briefly described below: the "single defendant" approach and the "national market" approach. Other courts have firmly rejected *Sindell*'s invitation to innovate; reasons for rejections are also noted.

1. The single defendant approach was adopted in Collins v. Eli Lilly Co., 116 Wis.2d 166, 342 N.W.2d 37 (1984). The Wisconsin Supreme Court decided not to adopt market share liability because of "the practical difficulty of defining and proving market share" in fluid markets. The court concluded that a DES plaintiff should be allowed to assert strict liability as well as negligence, and to proceed against any one manufacturer whose product "could have caused the plaintiff's injuries"; "the plaintiff may recover all damages from the one defendant." The court reasoned that "as between the injured plaintiff and the possibly responsible drug company, the drug company is in a better position to absorb the cost of the injury." The single defendant might "implead as third-party defendants other drug companies," in which case total liability–100% of plaintiff's damages—would be allocated by the jury among all liable companies on the basis of a judgment of "relative fault." The court said that "the interests of justice and fundamental fairness" require a workable method of recovery for injured

persons, and added: "We note that this method of recovery could apply in situations which are factually similar to the DES cases."

Collins was followed, up to a point, in Martin v. Abbott Laboratories, 102 Wash.2d 581, 689 P.2d 368 (1984). The Washington Supreme Court said a DES plaintiff may maintain suit against a single manufacturer whose product was marketed in the relevant time and place; other manufacturers might be impleaded. "[D]efendants are initially presumed to have equal shares of the market." But any defendant which succeeds in proving its own actual percentage of the market would be liable only for that percentage of damages. So if all joined defendants prove their shares, and their shares total less than 100% of the market, plaintiff would recover less than 100% of damages. On the other hand, if one or more defendants "fail to establish their actual market share, their presumed market share is adjusted so that 100 percent of the market is accounted for"—then plaintiff recovers 100%.

2.   The national market approach was adopted in Hymowitz v. Eli Lilly & Co., 73 N.Y.2d 487, 539 N.E.2d 1069, 541 N.Y.S.2d 941 (1989). According to *Sindell*, a manufacturer is liable if its product could have caused the plaintiff's injury—that is, if its product was sold in the relevant place. But what is the relevant place: a given state, or a particular city, or a specific pharmacy? In *Hymowitz* the New York Court of Appeals abandoned as unworkable the idea of defining a geographical market less extensive than the whole United States. "[F]or essentially practical reasons, we adopt a market share theory using a national market." Each defendant who marketed DES for pregnancy use anywhere in the United States would be liable for its share of the national market; no defendant would escape liability because its product, for geographical reasons, could not have harmed the plaintiff. "[W]e choose to apportion liability so as to correspond to the overall culpability of each defendant, measured by the amount of risk of injury each defendant created to the public-at-large."

Hymowitz was followed, but with a difference, in Smith v. Cutter Biological, Inc., 72 Haw. 416, 823 P.2d 717 (1991). In *Smith* the plaintiff, a hemophiliac, was infected by an AIDS-contaminated blood product called "Factor VIII," but was unable to prove which of four manufacturers made the specific batch of Factor VIII that infected him. The Hawaii Supreme Court approved market share liability and said that the relevant market was "the national one." It held that any manufacturer who sold Factor VIII at the time plaintiff was infected would be "liable for its market share." But borrowing from *Martin*, supra, it added: "Defendants failing to establish their proportionate share of the market will be liable for the difference in the judgment to 100 percent of the market."

3.   The theme of *Sindell*, and foregoing variations, have been rejected by a number of courts. The majority opinion in Smith v. Eli Lilly & Co., 137 Ill.2d 222, 148 Ill.Dec. 22, 560 N.E.2d 324 (1990), provides a compendium of reasons for rejection. There the Illinois Supreme Court pointed to decisions from other states (Iowa, Missouri, New Jersey, Ohio, Oklahoma) refusing to embrace *Sindell* in general or in particular applications. According to the Illinois court, "market share liability is not a sound theory" for

reasons of practicality, principle, and policy. First, the market share approach is impractical, indeed "markedly flawed." It attempts "to establish percentages based on unreliable or insufficient data"; it leads to "arbitrary" determinations and "wide variances between judgments"; it "will imprudently bog down the judiciary in an almost futile endeavor." Second, market share liability "is too great a deviation from a tort principle which * * * serve[s] a vital function in the law, causation in fact." It imposes liability on "defendants wholly innocent of wrongdoing toward the particular plaintiff"; thus it violates the "fundamental principle" that "creation of risk or breach of a duty alone is not sufficient in imposing liability"; it also violates "the principle that manufacturers are not insurers of their industry." Third, the market share innovation jeopardizes the policy behind law's requirement of causation. This requirement "limits the scope of potential liability and thereby encourages useful activity that would otherwise be deterred." The market share approach, applied to drug manufacturers, "will likely contribute to diminishing participants in the market as well as research and availability of drugs." Such innovation "is most appropriate for the legislature to develop, with its added ability to hold hearings and determine public policy."

ISSUES IN TOXIC TORTS

Tort liability to compensate people who have been exposed to risk of disease from toxic substances might come "after the fact" or "before the fact" of actual serious illness. The tort system might wait until the harm feared has actually occurred, and some among an exposed population have developed serious health injury. Or it might act on the basis of toxic risk rather than manifest harm, at the point that all within the population have been put in jeopardy.

Tort reparation after the fact—after harm has matured from risk—is the conventional approach. In the area of toxic torts this poses the difficulty of proving that a given toxic exposure actually caused a particular illness, such as a case of cancer. When we say a substance causes cancer usually we mean that exposure of a group to the substance will over time bring about "excess" cancers within the group, though some cancers would have occurred anyway and not everyone will become ill. How can a particular cancer be connected causally to the group's exposure when our basic knowledge of causation remains statistical or probabilistic in nature? For a discussion of these matters, see the note on "collective health injury" later in this section.

Tort liability before the fact of serious health injury might aim at four types of reparation: (a) recovery just for the fact of having been exposed to an enhanced risk of future illness imposed by the defendant, perhaps on a showing that anyone so exposed would already have suffered adverse bodily changes at a subclinical level; (b) compensation for present fear, stress, and other emotional harm—and stress-induced physical conditions—arising from knowledge of the risk of latent disease; (c) reparation for losses and inconveniences involved in efforts to avoid further peril (such as evacuation, relocation, or arranging alternative water supplies); (d) reparation for the expense of special medical tests and periodic monitoring for signs of the feared disease, perhaps through a program for group-wide health surveillance funded by the defendant. The case that follows addresses all four types of recovery.

AYERS v. TOWNSHIP OF JACKSON

Supreme Court of New Jersey, 1987.
106 N.J. 557, 525 A.2d 287.

STEIN, Justice.

In this case we consider the application of the New Jersey Tort Claims Act (the Act), *N.J.S.A.* 59:1–1 to 12–3, to the claims asserted by 339 residents of Jackson Township against that municipality.

The litigation involves claims for damages sustained because plaintiffs' well water was contaminated by toxic pollutants leaching into the Cohansey Aquifer from a landfill established and operated by Jackson Township. After an extensive trial, the jury found that the township had created a "nuisance" and a "dangerous condition" by virtue of its operation of the landfill, that its conduct was "palpably unreasonable,"—a prerequisite to recovery under *N.J.S.A.* 59:4–2—and that it was the proximate cause of the contamination of plaintiffs' water supply. The jury verdict resulted in an aggregate judgment of $15,854,392.78, to be divided among the plaintiffs in varying amounts. The jury returned individual awards for each of the plaintiffs that varied in accordance with such factors as proximity to the landfill, duration and extent of the exposure to contaminants, and the age of the claimant.

The verdict provided compensation for three distinct claims of injury: $2,056,480 was awarded for emotional distress caused by the knowledge that they had ingested water contaminated by toxic chemicals for up to six years; $5,396,940 was awarded for the deterioration of their quality of life during the twenty months when they were deprived of running water; and $8,204,500 was awarded to cover the future cost of annual medical surveillance that plaintiffs' expert testified would be necessary because of plaintiffs' increased susceptibility to cancer and other diseases. * * *

The Appellate Division upheld that portion of the judgment awarding plaintiffs damages for impairment of their quality of life. It reversed the award for emotional distress, concluding that such damages constituted "pain and suffering" for which recovery is barred by *N.J.S.A.* 59:9–2(d). The Appellate Division also set aside the $8,204,500 award for medical surveillance expenses, concluding that it is "impossible to say that defendant has so significantly increased the 'reasonable probability' that any of the plaintiffs will develop cancer so as to justify imposing upon defendant the financial burden of lifetime medical surveillance for early clinical signs of cancer."

In addition, the Appellate Division affirmed the trial court's dismissal of plaintiffs' claim for damages for their enhanced risk of disease * * *.

We granted plaintiffs' petition for certification to review the adverse portions of the Appellate Division decision, and granted defendant's cross-petition to review the affirmance of the damage award for impairment of plaintiffs' quality of life. We now affirm in part and reverse in part the judgment of the Appellate Division.

* * *

QUALITY OF LIFE

In November 1978, the residents of the Legler area of Jackson Township were advised by the local Board of Health not to drink their well water, and to limit washing and bathing to avoid prolonged exposure to the water. This warning was issued by the Board after tests disclosed that a number of wells in the Legler area of the township were contaminated by toxic chemicals. Initially, the township provided water to the affected residents in water tanks that were transported by tank trucks to various locations in the neighborhood. Plaintiffs brought their own containers, filled them with water from the tanks, and transported the water to their homes.

* * *

In the Appellate Division and before this Court, defendant argues that [quality of life recovery] is barred by the New Jersey Tort Claims Act, which provides:

> No damages shall be awarded against a public entity or public employee for pain and suffering resulting from any injury; provided, however, that this limitation on the recovery of damages for pain and suffering shall not apply in cases of permanent loss of a bodily function, permanent disfigurement or dismemberment where the medical treatment expenses are in excess of $1,000.00. [*N.J.S.A.* 59:9–2(d).]

* * *

As the Appellate Division acknowledged, plaintiffs' claim for quality of life damages is derived from the law of nuisance. It has long been recognized that damages for inconvenience, annoyance, and discomfort are recoverable in a nuisance action. The *Restatement (Second) of Torts* § 929 (1977) sets out three distinct categories of compensation with respect to invasions of an interest in land:

> (a) the difference between the value of the land before the harm and the value after the harm, or at [plaintiff's] election in an appropriate case, the cost of restoration that has been or may be reasonably incurred;
>
> (b) the loss of use of the land, and
>
> (c) discomfort and annoyance to him as occupant.

While the first two of these components constitute damages for the interference with plaintiff's use and enjoyment of his land, the third category compensates the plaintiff for his personal losses flowing directly from such an invasion. As such, damages for inconvenience, discomfort, and annoyance constitute "distinct grounds of compensation for which in ordinary cases the person in possession is entitled to recover *in addition to* the harm to his proprietary interests." *Restatement Second of Torts* § 929 Comment e (1977).

Accordingly, we conclude that the quality of life damages represent compensation for losses associated with damage to property, and agree with the Appellate Division that they do not constitute pain and suffering under the Tort Claims Act. We therefore sustain the judgment for quality of life damages.

EMOTIONAL DISTRESS

The jury verdict awarded plaintiffs damages for emotional distress in the aggregate amount of $2,056,480. The individual verdicts ranged from $40 to $14,000.

Many of the plaintiffs testified about their emotional reactions to the knowledge that their well-water was contaminated. Most of the plaintiffs' testimony on the issue of emotional distress was relatively brief and general. Typically, their testimony did not indicate that the emotional distress resulted in physical symptoms or required medical treatment. * * * Nevertheless, the consistent thrust of the testimony offered by numerous witnesses was that they suffered anxiety, stress, fear, and depression, and that these feelings were directly and causally related to the knowledge that they and members of their family had ingested and been exposed to contaminated water for a substantial time period.

* * * [T]he township contended that the jury verdict for emotional distress constituted damages for "pain and suffering resulting from any injury," recovery for which is expressly barred by the Tort Claims Act, *N.J.S.A.* 59:9–2(d). The Appellate Division, without deciding the issue of the sufficiency of plaintiffs' proofs, agreed that the verdict for emotional distress was barred by the Act:

> * * * [W]e conclude that although damages for these intangible harms might be recoverable from a non-governmental entity, as consequential to a nuisance, the language of *N.J.S.A.* 59:9–2(d), barring damages from a public entity "for pain and suffering resulting from any injury," clearly precludes recovery herein.

* * *

We acknowledge that our cases no longer require proof of causally-related physical impact to sustain a recovery for emotional distress. Nevertheless, we reject plaintiffs' assertion that the Tort Claims Act's limitation against recovery for "pain and suffering resulting from any injury" does not apply to claims based on emotional distress. * * *

* * * The New Jersey Tort Claims Act bars the recovery of such damages. Accordingly, we affirm the Appellate Division's reversal of that portion of the jury verdict awarding damages for emotional distress.

CLAIMS FOR ENHANCED RISK AND MEDICAL SURVEILLANCE

No claims were asserted by plaintiffs seeking recovery for specific illnesses caused by their exposure to chemicals. Rather, they claim damages for the enhanced risk of future illness attributable to such exposure. They also seek to recover the expenses of annual medical examinations to monitor their physical health and detect symptoms of disease at the earliest possible opportunity. [The enhanced risk and medical surveillance claims were rejected by lower courts.]

As a result of the trial court's and Appellate Division's rulings, plaintiffs are left to await actual manifestation of physical injury attributable to their exposure to toxic chemicals before they can institute and sustain a damage claim for personal injuries against the defendant. * * *

* * *

1.

Our evaluation of the enhanced risk and medical surveillance claims requires that we focus on a critical issue in the management of toxic tort litigation: at what stage in the evolution of a toxic injury should tort law intercede by requiring the responsible party to pay damages?

* * *

By far the most difficult problem for plaintiffs to overcome in toxic tort litigation is the burden of proving causation. In the typical tort case, the plaintiff must prove tortious conduct, injury and proximate cause. Ordinarily, proof of causation requires the establishment of a sufficient nexus between the defendant's conduct and the plaintiff's injury. In toxic tort cases, the task of proving causation is invariably made more complex because of the long latency period of illnesses caused by carcinogens or other toxic chemicals. The fact that ten or twenty years or more may intervene between the exposure and the manifestation of disease highlights the practical difficulties encountered in the effort to prove causation. Moreover, the fact that segments of the entire population are afflicted by cancer and other toxically-induced diseases requires plaintiffs, years after their exposure, to counter the argument that other intervening exposures or forces were the "cause" of their injury. The thoughtful analysis by District Judge Jenkins in *Allen v. United States,* 588 *F.Supp.* 247 (D.Utah 1984), rev'd on other grounds, 816 *F.*2d 1417 (10th Cir.1987), a case involving the causal relationship between nuclear fallout and cancer, graphically explains the causation problem in mass exposure litigation:

* * *

At this point, there appears to be no question whether or not ionizing radiation causes cancer and leukemia. It does. Once more, however, it seems important to clarify what is meant by "cause" in relation to radiation and cancer.

When we refer to radiation as a cause, we do not mean that it causes *every* case of cancer or leukemia. Indeed, the evidence we have indicating radiation in the causation of cancer and leukemia shows that not all cases of cancer are caused by radiation. Second, when we refer to radiation as a cause of cancer, we do not mean that every individual exposed to a certain amount of radiation will develop cancer. We simply mean that a population exposed to a certain dose of radiation will show a greater incidence of cancer than that same population would have shown in the absence of the added radiation.

J. Gofman, M.D., *Radiation and Human Health* 54–55 (1981), PX–1046.

* * *

Although we acknowledge, as we must, the array of complex practical and doctrinal problems that confound litigants and courts in toxic-tort mass-exposure litigation, we are confronted in this case with fairly narrow and manageable issues. * * * The legal issue we must resolve, in the context of the jury's determination of defendant's liability under the Act, is whether the proof of an unquantified enhanced risk of illness or a need for medical surveillance is sufficient to justify compensation under the Tort Claims Act. In view of the acknowledged difficulties of proving causation once evidence of disease is manifest, a determination of the compensability of post-exposure, pre-symptom injuries is particularly important in assessing the ability of tort law to redress the claims of plaintiffs in toxic-tort litigation.

2.

Much of the same evidence was material to both the enhanced risk and medical surveillance claims. * * *

Dr. Highland testified that the Legler area residents, because of their exposure to toxic chemicals, had an increased risk of cancer * * *. Dr. Highland testified that *he could not quantify the extent of the enhanced risk of cancer* because of the lack of scientific information concerning the effect of the interaction of the various chemicals to which plaintiffs were exposed. However, the jury could reasonably have inferred from his testimony that the risk, although unquantified, was medically significant.

* * * Dr. Highland also testified that the exposure to chemicals had already caused actual physical injury to plaintiffs through its adverse effects on the genetic material within their cells. * * *

* * * [P]laintiffs contend that the unquantified injury to their health and life expectancy should be presently compensable, even though no evidence of disease is manifest. Defendant does not dispute the causal relationship between the plaintiffs' exposure to toxic chemicals and the plaintiffs' increased risk of diseases, but contends that the probability that plaintiffs will actually become ill from their exposure to chemicals is too remote to warrant compensation under principles of tort law.

* * *

3.

The trial court declined to submit to the jury the issue of defendant's liability for the plaintiffs' increased risk of contracting cancer, kidney or liver damage, or other diseases associated with the chemicals that had migrated from the landfill to their wells. * * *

* * *

Except for a handful of cases involving traumatic torts causing presently discernible injuries in addition to an enhanced risk of future injuries,[9] courts have generally been reluctant to recognize claims for potential but unrealized injury unless the proof that the injury will occur is substantial. * * *

Among the recent toxic tort cases rejecting liability for damages based on enhanced risk is *Anderson v. W.R. Grace & Co.*, 628 *F.Supp.* 1219 (D.Mass.1986). * * *

The court in *Anderson* explained that its reluctance to recognize the enhanced risk claims was based on two policy considerations. Its first concern was that recognition of the cause of action would create a flood of speculative lawsuits. In addition, the court stated:

> A further reason for denying plaintiffs' damages for the increased risk of future harm in this action is the inevitable inequity which would result if recovery were allowed. "To award damages based on a mere mathematical probability would significantly undercompensate those who actually do develop cancer and would be a windfall to those who do not."

The majority of courts that have considered the enhanced risk issue have agreed with the disposition of the District Court in *Anderson. See Schweitzer v. Consolidated Rail Corp.*, 758 F.2d 936, 942 (3d Cir.1985) ("[S]ubclinical injury resulting from exposure to asbestos is insufficient to constitute the actual loss or damage to a plaintiff's interest required to sustain a cause of action * * *.") * * *.

Other courts have acknowledged the propriety of the enhanced risk cause of action, but have emphasized the requirement that proof of future injury be reasonably certain. * * *

Additionally, several courts have permitted recovery for increased risk of disease, but only where the plaintiff exhibited some present manifestation of disease. *See Jackson v. Johns–Manville Sales Corp.*, 781 F.2d 394, 412–13 (5th Cir.) (allowing recovery for increased risk of cancer where evidence indicated that due to asbestos exposure, plaintiff had greater than fifty percent chance of contracting cancer; "[o]nce the injury becomes actionable—once *some* effect appears—then the plaintiff is permitted to recover for all probable future manifestations as well"); *Brafford v. Susquehanna Corp.*, 586 F.Supp. 14, 17–18 (D.Colo.1984) (acknowledging that cause of action for increased risk of cancer requires proof of present physical injury, but denying defendant's motion for summary judgment to permit plaintiff to offer proof of present genetic and chromosomal damage due to exposure to radiation) * * *.

---

9. *See, e.g., Martin v. City of New Orleans,* 678 *F.*2d 1321, 1327 (5th Cir.1982) (bullet lodged in neck; despite plaintiff's favorable prognosis, the fact that there would always be a risk of life threatening future complications supported large damage award) * * *.

We observe that the overwhelming weight of the scholarship on this issue favors a right of recovery for tortious conduct that causes a significantly enhanced risk of injury. Gale & Goyer, "Recovery for Cancerphobia and Increased Risk of Cancer," 15 *Cum.L.Rev.* 723 (1985) * * *. For the most part, the commentators concede the inadequacy of common-law remedies for toxic-tort victims. Instead, they recommend statutory or administrative mechanisms that would permit compensation to be awarded on the basis of exposure and significant risk of disease, without the necessity of proving the existence of present injury.

Our disposition of this difficult and important issue requires that we choose between two alternatives, each having a potential for imposing unfair and undesirable consequences on the affected interests. A holding that recognizes a cause of action for unquantified enhanced risk claims exposes the tort system, and the public it serves, to the task of litigating vast numbers of claims for compensation based on threats of injuries that may never occur. It imposes on judges and juries the burden of assessing damages for the risk of potential disease, without clear guidelines to determine what level of compensation may be appropriate. * * *

On the other hand, denial of the enhanced-risk cause of action may mean that some of these plaintiffs will be unable to obtain compensation for their injury. Despite the collateral estoppel effect of the jury's finding that defendant's wrongful conduct caused the contamination of plaintiffs' wells, those who contract diseases in the future because of their exposure to chemicals in their well water may be unable to prove a causal relationship between such exposure and their disease. * * *

* * *

In deciding between recognition or non-recognition of plaintiffs' enhanced-risk claim, we feel constrained to choose the alternative that most closely reflects the legislative purpose in enacting the Tort Claims Act. We are conscious of the admonition that in construing the Act courts should "exercise restraint in the acceptance of novel causes of action against public entities." Comment, *N.J.S.A.* 59:2–1. In our view, the speculative nature of an unquantified enhanced risk claim, the difficulties inherent in adjudicating such claims, and the policies underlying the Tort Claims Act argue persuasively against the recognition of this cause of action. Accordingly, we decline to recognize plaintiffs' cause of action for the *unquantified* enhanced risk of disease, and affirm the judgment of the Appellate Division dismissing such claims. * * *

4.

The claim for medical surveillance expenses stands on a different footing from the claim based on enhanced risk. It seeks to recover the cost of periodic medical examinations intended to monitor plaintiffs' health and facilitate early diagnosis and treatment of disease caused by plaintiffs' exposure to toxic chemicals. At trial, competent medical testimony was offered to prove that a program of regular medical testing and evaluation was reasonably necessary and consistent with contemporary scientific principles applied by physicians experienced in the diagnosis and treatment of chemically-induced injuries.[12]

* * *

Compensation for reasonable and necessary medical expenses is consistent with well-accepted legal principles. It is also consistent with the important public health interest in fostering access to medical testing for individuals whose exposure to toxic chemicals creates an enhanced risk of disease. * * *

Recognition of pre-symptom claims for medical surveillance serves other important public interests. The difficulty of proving causation, where the disease is manifested years after exposure, has caused many commentators to suggest that tort law has no capacity to deter polluters, because the costs of proper disposal are often viewed by polluters as exceeding the risk of tort liability. However, permitting recovery for reasonable pre-symptom, medical-surveillance expenses subjects polluters to significant liability when proof of the causal connection between the tortious conduct and the plaintiffs' exposure to chemicals is likely to be most readily available. * * *

* * *

Accordingly, we hold that the cost of medical surveillance is a compensable item of damages where the proofs demonstrate, through reliable expert testimony predicated upon the significance and extent of exposure to chemicals, the toxicity of the chemicals, the seriousness of the diseases for which individuals are at risk, the relative increase in the chance of onset of disease in those exposed, and the value of early diagnosis, that such surveillance to monitor the effect of exposure to toxic chemicals is reasonable and necessary. In our view, this holding is thoroughly consistent with our rejection of plaintiffs' claim for damages based on their enhanced risk of injury. That claim seeks damages for the impairment of plaintiffs' health, without proof of its likelihood, extent, or monetary value. In contrast, the medical surveillance claim seeks reimbursement for the specific dollar costs of periodic examinations that are medically necessary notwithstanding the fact that the extent of plaintiffs' impaired health is unquantified. * * *

5.

The medical surveillance issue was tried as if it were a conventional claim for compensatory damages susceptible to a jury verdict in a lump sum. The jury was so instructed by the trial court, and neither plaintiffs' nor defendant's request to charge on this issue sought a different instruction.

In the Appellate Division, defendant argued for the first time that a lump-sum damage award for medical surveillance was inappropriate. Defendant contended that if the court were to uphold all or any part of the medical surveillance award, it should "create an actuar[i]ally-sound fund, to

---

12. Plaintiff's expert, Dr. Daum, testified that it would be appropriate to initiate the medical surveillance testing for a period ranging from one to three years after the exposure, for the purpose of establishing baseline data. She testi- fied that regular medical surveillance examinations should then be commenced at the onset of the risk of disease, which she estimated to be ten years after exposure, and that the surveillance should be continued annually thereafter.

which the plaintiffs may apply in the future for the cost of medical surveillance upon proof [of costs incurred]." * * *

The indeterminate nature of damage claims in toxic-tort litigation suggests that the use of court-supervised funds to pay medical-surveillance claims as they accrue, rather than lump-sum verdicts, may provide a more efficient mechanism for compensating plaintiffs. A funded settlement was used in the Agent Orange litigation. *In re "Agent Orange" Prod. Liab. Litig.*, 611 F.Supp. 1396, 1399 (E.D.N.Y.1985), aff'd, 818 *F.*2d 194 (2d Cir.1987). The use of insurance to fund future medical claims is frequently recommended by commentators. * * *

In our view, the use of a court-supervised fund to administer medical-surveillance payments in mass exposure cases, particularly for claims under the Tort Claims Act, is a highly appropriate exercise of the Court's equitable powers. * * *

* * *

However, we decline to upset the jury verdict awarding medical-surveillance damages in this case. Such a result would be unfair to these plaintiffs, since the medical-surveillance issue was tried conventionally, and neither party requested the trial court to withhold from the jury the power to return a lump-sum verdict for each plaintiff in order that relief by way of a fund could be provided. * * * Accordingly, the verdict for medical-surveillance damages was in a specific amount for each of the plaintiffs, thereby limiting in this case the applicability of the fund concept, which contemplates an aggregate lump-sum award available to reimburse the medical-surveillance expenses of any plaintiff, without the constraint of individually-allocated limitations. * * * Under the circumstances, we think it would be inappropriate to impose this effective but novel procedure on these litigants at this late stage in litigation that has already been protracted and extensive. Accordingly, the judgment of the Appellate Division setting aside the jury verdict for medical surveillance damages is reversed and the jury verdict is reinstated.

* * *

For the reasons stated in this opinion, the judgment of the Appellate Division is affirmed in part and reversed in part.

HANDLER, J., concurring in part and dissenting in part.

This case involves a municipality that operated a landfill over a long period of time in a palpably unreasonable way, directly subjecting its own residents to carcinogenic and otherwise toxic chemicals. These chemicals caused medical injury in the residents, creating a significant risk that they would develop cancer and other diseases equally grave. The risk of disease to these residents is indisputably greater than the risk of disease experienced by the general population. Because of limitations in current scientific knowledge and because of the number and variety of toxic chemicals involved, the victims of this toxic exposure were unable to measure or quantify the enhancement of their risk of disease. The Court focuses on this inability to measure the risk, rather than on the fact of contamination, and rules that these residents cannot therefore recover any damages referable to that enhanced risk. Further, while the majority does recognize a claim for medical monitoring that is clearly referable to the enhanced risk of disease, it rules that in the future the award of this limited item of special damages is not to be treated as compensation paid directly to aggrieved plaintiffs, but will be used only to reimburse actual expenses through a court-supervised fund. In effect, the Court's holding leaves these grievously wronged persons uncompensated for the injuries caused by the defendant's palpably unreasonable conduct. The Court thus affords the victims of tortious toxic exposure significantly less protection than it would plaintiffs in other tort actions. While in some respects the Court is influenced by the provisions of the New Jersey Tort Claims Act, *N.J.S.A.* 59:1–1 to 59:12–3, and the status of defendant as a governmental entity covered by the Act, these considerations do not require or justify the unfairness to plaintiffs. Accordingly, I dissent in part from the majority's reasoning and holding.

* * *

MAURO v. RAYMARK INDUSTRIES, INC., 116 N.J. 126, 561 A.2d 257 (1989). Plaintiff was a plumber-steamfitter. From 1964 to well into the 1970's he was exposed to materials containing asbestos manufactured by defendants, including pipe covering and asbestos cement. In 1981 X-ray tests showed an abnormal condition of plaintiff's lungs, diagnosed as "pleural asbestosis," though plaintiff's lung function remained "normal." Plaintiff was told that because of his asbestos exposure "the risk of cancer" in the future was "a major concern." Lower courts upheld plaintiff's claims for damages based on his fear of developing cancer, and the costs of ongoing medical surveillance, but rejected his claim based on "enhanced risk of developing cancer" because plaintiff could not prove "that cancer was more probable than not." On certification to the New Jersey Supreme Court, *held*, affirmed (Handler, J., dissenting).

The court noted that its decision in Ayers v. Township of Jackson, supra, which involved a governmental defendant subject to the New Jersey Tort Claims Act, left open the question "whether a claim for enhanced risk of disease is cognizable in a case involving personal injury claims against private-entity defendants." The court concluded that damages for increased risk of disease, caused by toxic exposure, may not be recovered unless the claimant can show a "reasonable medical probability that disease will occur." Unlike claims for present fear of cancer and ongoing costs of medical monitoring, an enhanced risk claim concerning a prospective illness that is "less than likely to occur" is a matter of "speculation." The court added:

"Equally persuasive to this Court, however, is the availability of a future opportunity to assert [toxic tort] claims if and when the disease occurs, combined with the present availability of medical surveillance and emotional distress damages in appropriate cases. * * * Recognition of present claims for medical surveillance and emotional distress realistically addresses significant aspects of the present injuries sustained by toxic-tort plaintiffs, and serves as an added deterrent to polluters and others responsible for the wrongful use of toxic chemicals."

STITES v. SUNDSTRAND HEAT TRANSFER, INC., 660 F.Supp. 1516 (W.D.Mich.1987). Plaintiffs allege toxic chemicals from defendant's manufacturing plant contaminated their drinking water, subjecting them to an enhanced risk of contracting cancer and causing present "fear of cancer, as well as humiliation, anxiety, mortification, anguish, emotional distress, [and] outrage," plus "physical symptoms of anguish due to fear of drastic consequences." On motion for summary judgment, *held,* under applicable Michigan law, that plaintiffs cannot recover for "risk of cancer" but several plaintiffs' claims for "fear of cancer" should be resolved by the jury. "To recover on their fear of cancer claim, plaintiffs must establish [that their] emotional distress has manifested itself in definite and objective physical injury," but "a plaintiff's burden in this regard is minimal" and might be satisfied by "claims of nervousness." Michigan law expresses "a strong presumption that the jury should decide whether a plaintiff's claim of negligent infliction of emotional distress is valid."

HAGERTY v. L & L MARINE SERVICES, 788 F.2d 315 (5th Cir.1986). Working as a tankerman on a barge being loaded with chemicals, Hagerty was accidentally drenched with a fluid known to be carcinogenic. That day and the next he experienced some dizziness, leg cramps, and a stinging sensation, but "has suffered no manifestations of any symptoms or ailments attributed to cancer." He sues to recover damages for "cancerphobia," that is, "present fear or anxiety due to the possibility of contracting cancer." The lower court ruled no cause of action had accrued. On appeal, *held,* for plaintiff. The appellate court commented:

> Defendants contend that a plaintiff's cancerphobia should not be considered a present injury unless accompanied by "physical manifestations." Only a physical injury requirement, they argue, will ensure against the proliferation of "unworthy claims." It would also deny worthy claims, perhaps that of Hagerty. We believe the courts have better devices with which to choose between the worthy and the unworthy.

> Cancerphobia is merely a specific type of mental anguish or emotional distress. * * *

> The physical injury requirement, like its counterpart, the physical impact requirement, was developed to provide courts with an objective means of ensuring that the alleged mental injury is not feigned. We believe that notion to be unrealistic. * * * With or without physical injury or impact, a plaintiff is entitled to recover damages for serious mental distress arising from fear of developing cancer where his fear is reasonable and causally related to the defendant's negligence. * * * It is for the jury to decide questions such as the existence, severity and reasonableness of the fear.

MARLIN v. BILL RICH CONSTRUCTION, INC., 198 W.Va. 635, 482 S.E.2d 620 (1996). In a case involving construction workers negligently exposed to asbestos, the West Virginia Supreme Court of Appeals approved recovery for mental distress without physical injury. "[W]e hold that in order to recover for negligent infliction of emotional distress based upon the fear of contracting a disease, a plaintiff must prove that he or she was actually exposed to the disease by the negligent conduct of the defendant [and] that his or her serious emotional distress was reasonably foreseeable * * *." "[T]he evidence must show first, that the exposure upon which the claim is based raises a medically established possibility of contracting a disease, and second, that the disease will produce death or substantial disability requiring prolonged treatment to mitigate and manage or promising imminent death."

TEMPLE–INLAND FOREST PRODUCTS CORP. v. CARTER, 993 S.W.2d 88 (Tex.1999). Electrical workers exposed to asbestos on defendant's business premises brought an action to recover "mental anguish damages" for their fear of developing asbestos-related diseases "that they do not currently have." Evidence showed that their risk of developing such disease is "no higher than one chance in a hundred over twenty to thirty years." *Held*, by the Texas Supreme Court, that "no such action should be recognized." "The difficulty in predicting whether exposure will cause any disease and if so, what disease, and the long latency period characteristic of asbestos-related diseases, make it very difficult for judges and juries to evaluate which exposure claims are serious and which are not. This difficulty in turn makes liability unpredictable, with some claims resulting in significant recovery while virtually indistinguishable claims are denied altogether."

"We add this cautionary note. The principles we have used to deny recovery of mental anguish damages for fear of the possibility of developing a disease as a result of an exposure to asbestos may not yield the same result when the exposure is to some other dangerous or toxic element. * * * The consequences of exposure to other toxic materials vary, and * * * the outcomes may be different."

HANSEN v. MOUNTAIN FUEL SUPPLY CO., 858 P.2d 970 (Utah Sup.Ct. 1993). Plaintiffs were exposed to asbestos when renovating an office building. They sought, inter alia, to recover the cost of medical monitoring. *Held*, that medical monitoring costs are recoverable in Utah. The court noted that "many other jurisdictions have recognized the legitimacy of medical surveillance damages for toxic-tort plaintiffs." It said that "the physical injury resulting from exposure to toxic substances usually manifests itself years after exposure," and that for toxic tort victims "other sorts of recovery may prove difficult." Recovery of monitoring costs "furthers the deterrent function of the tort system by compelling those who expose others to toxic substances to minimize risks and costs of exposure."

COLLECTIVE HEALTH INJURY

Consider the following simplified situation. Actor A exposes each of 1000 people equally to a cancer-causing condition—say, through use of a carcinogenic substance in the workplace or through release of radiation or hazardous waste into a local environment—such that over time 5 of the 1000 contract cancer. However, another 5 persons in the group contract the same sort of cancer anyway, from causes not attributable to A. We know that A's activity doubles the probability of cancer for a definable population, and that one of every two cancers suffered will have been "caused" by A—but which one? Here it is plain that A is causing harm to the group, but it is not patent that A has caused harm to any given individual within the group.

We may "know" that A is harming the group—will cause so many cancers over time—on the basis of two different types of evidence. First, laboratory analysis, animal tests, or other medical evidence about a substance for which A is responsible may indicate its carcinogenic propensity. Second, epidemiological studies may show "excess cancer incidence" among various human populations subjected to the condition or substance in question. Either kind of evidence may ground a probabilistic theory of cancer causation, one positing that a certain sort of exposure gives rise to an increased probability of disease. Given such a theory, plus facts about exposure over time, calculation of harm to a particular exposed group— such as the group subjected to A's activity—becomes possible. But so long as the underlying theory remains statistical in character, and does not account for all of the cancers of a given type, it will not entail the conclusion that a particular cancer suffered after average exposure is attributable to A's activity rather than other causes.

The foregoing pattern might occur with respect to any disease that arises from a variety of causes or conditions, and does in fact appear in a host of areas, albeit in contexts vastly more complex than the one sketched. The key is that harm to a group taken as a whole is evident, but harm to the individual is uncertain. Collective injury is clear, since increased probability of disease created by a social activity yields calculable damage to a group continuously exposed. Individual injury is unclear—quite apart from difficulty in ascertaining particular facts or inevitable uncertainties in medical assessment—because the available account of disease causation has a probabilistic structure.

Now suppose a particular victim of disease seeks reparation from A and proves that A's risk was negligently imposed. If so, relevant law says A should pay for harms the risk "caused."

Alternatively, there may be a basis for nonfault recovery. The unhealthy condition created by A might be judged an abnormal danger or a nuisance or a product defect suitable for strict liability in tort, or A may be covered by a no-fault plan such as workers compensation or the federal scheme for nuclear accidents. If so, relevant law embodies the proposition that actors engaged in A's activity should pay for characteristic physical harm they "cause."

The problem, in either case, is that proof of membership in a group subjected to an increased probability of harm does not equal proof of actual causation in the particular. Even if the victim can show that A's activity trebled or quadrupled the chances of disease—so that A is responsible for any given illness "more likely than not"—such proof is available to every stricken member of the group and, if taken as sufficient, would produce overcompensation. The probabilistic evidence by itself is gross, diffuse, impersonal. Statistical harm is not the same as personal injury, conventionally understood.

How might a reparation system be engineered so that probabilistic harm is offset in proper amount? The challenge is to devise a scheme that authorizes individual reparation on the basis of gross statistical evidence, and also ensures that the sum of individuated recoveries equals the total injury calculable at a collective level. There are four main possibilities.

First, statistical proofs of all varieties might be received as valid evidence that the victim's illness was caused by A's activity, and be assigned whatever probative weight the finder of fact deems proper under the circumstances. Second, presumptions might be developed such that the burden of explaining causation would shift to A given sufficient gross likelihood that a particular disease is accountable to A's activity—or given specified facts associated with a gross likelihood. Third, when members of a group are exposed in varying degrees to A's unhealthy condition, those disease victims subject to high exposure—above some threshold level—might be granted full recovery, and the others no recovery. The threshold should be set so that the sum of allowable recoveries equals the total harm done to the group taken as a whole. Fourth, every stricken group member might be granted partial or scaled-down recovery—thus, when A's activity doubles the incidence of a disease, all victims would recover 50% of their loss from A, assuming all were equally exposed.

For discussion of the first two of the foregoing alternatives, see Allen v. United States (statistical proofs), p. 578, supra, and Usery v. Turner Elkhorn Mining Co. (presumptions), p. 1172, infra.

The four alternatives—statistical proof, presumptions, thresholds, pro rata recovery—aim to offset collective injury with individuated reparation. A different sort of response is "collective reparation." Instead of trying to determine which particular illnesses should be compensated by A, legal institutions might calculate the collective injury caused by A's activity, exact a sum of money equal to the total injury, and apply the money to projects meant to benefit whole classes of people. For example, funds gotten from A might be used to finance medical screening and diagnosis of an entire exposed population, or to support relevant programs of scientific research, or to reduce the cost of health insurance or medical treatment for groups put in jeopardy. Collective reparation might be engineered on an ad hoc basis through class actions in the courts, or through systematic extraction of revenue—in the form of premiums or taxes—from disease-causing activities.

AMERICAN LAW INSTITUTE, REPORTERS' STUDY ON ENTERPRISE RESPONSIBILITY FOR PERSONAL INJURY, vol. II (1991). This ALI-sponsored report on accident law, jointly authored by a study team of fourteen scholars, makes four recommendations about how the law should handle "tort claims for diseases caused by toxic environmental exposures."

The first recommendation is that statutes of limitation should accommodate claims having to do with long-latency diseases. The second is that strict liability should be accepted "as the principal basis for legal responsibility of enterprises that create substantial environmental risks which cause personal injury." The third and fourth recommendations follow:

"3. In situations in which the causal connection between toxic exposure and eventual disease must be established on the basis of epidemiological studies of large classes of victims, the amount of damages awarded to any one claimant should be prorated in accordance with the probability (as revealed by the epidemiological studies relied on * * *) that the disease was caused by the exposure.

"4. In cases in which the toxic exposure has already occurred and been identified but the disease has not yet manifested itself, courts should entertain tort actions for the creation of a fund to pay the financial costs of appropriate medical surveillance of the population at risk, with full damages to be awarded (on the proportionate basis described above) to victims of the disease when the condition manifests itself."

In addition, the Study proposes expanded use of the class action device and other procedural changes—amounting to a "collective regime"—in order to address "large-scale, long-latency mass-exposure disasters, exemplified by asbestos, Agent Orange, the Dalkon Shield, and DES." The procedure for mass disasters "would authorize insurance fund judgments to cover future losses predicted to ensue from * * * past exposures, and for this purpose would calculate damages using schedules of average losses developed for different subclasses of victims."

SECTION B. TORT DEVELOPMENTS
APPROACHING PLANS

TORT STATUTES AND NONTORT PLANS

Legislative intervention into matters once handled predominantly by the common law of tort has become an ever more frequent phenomenon. During the last quarter of the twentieth century, starting roughly in the mid—1970's, state legislatures have produced a large volume of statutory provisions changing the law of tort.

The recent legislative activity in the states has not only been intense in frequency. Its products have also been different in spirit and thrust from the traditional types of legislation which have addressed one or another aspect of tort law—for example, comparative fault statutes moderating the effect of contributory negligence, or statutes providing for contribution suits or wrongful death actions, filling gaps in common law.

It is instructive to compare the approach of the recent tort legislation and the approach of nontort plans like workers' compensation. Such plans, presented in Chapter 22, are administrative compensation schemes that displace the common law of tort in whole or part. In the present context, three features of plans are notable: their simplified process, their compensation limits, and their undertaking to see that insurance is available to satisfy valid claims.

First, plans like workers' compensation provide a simplified process for resolving claims. Plans aim to avoid the costly and time-consuming procedures of full-scale civil adjudication. Second, plans embody compensation limits. An award of compensation for injury under a plan is, characteristically, less than the full reparation that would be available for the same sort of injury in tort. Third, plans are insurance schemes. They do not simply declare liabilities and calculate awards. They seek to provide or foster properly functioning insurance mechanisms for the regular financing of awards.

The recent tort legislation addressed in the present section stops shy of actually embracing the planning model of workers' compensation. The usual approach of the tort legislation is to retain the common law's liability rule as the basis of recovery, not to displace the common law. Nonetheless, the recent tort statutes may be seen to possess plan-like attributes.

The Indiana statute on medical malpractice, which follows immediately after this note, is a good illustration of the plan-like character of much recent tort legislation. Indiana's malpractice statute, enacted in 1975, adopts each of the three features of plans noted above: simplified process, compensation limits, and insurance planning. At the same time it retains the familiar tort liability rule for medical malpractice. It grafts the three plan-like features onto the ordinary common law suit for professional negligence, yielding an interesting hybrid.

In the mid–1970's, in response to a perceived crisis concerning the availability of malpractice insurance, there was a flurry of legislative activity in the states. Most states adopted some sort of legislation affecting medical malpractice lawsuits. Many adopted one or more of the provisions combined in the Indiana statute. The cases in this section discuss various legislative approaches, in the area of medical malpractice, including periodic payment of damages, which is also plan-like in nature. The cases comment on the insurance crisis, and assess the constitutionality of legislative responses, comparing them to plans.

The section concludes with materials on tort statutes of broader reach. These are general statutes, passed in several states over the last twenty-five years or so, whose effect is not confined to a particular field of tort liability. Rather they apply to all tort claims, of whatever sort, brought in their respective states. The provisions presented restrict the availability of tort damages that go beyond compensation for pecuniary loss: they restrict award of damages for pain and suffering, and award of punitive or exemplary damages. Damages limits of these sorts are plan-like. Accident plans like workers' compensation do not provide individuated pain and suffering awards, and do not make available punitive damages. Thus the general damages limits discussed below may be viewed as pushing tort closer to the approach of the nontort plans.

INDIANA MEDICAL MALPRACTICE PROVISIONS

Ind.Code Ann. (West 1995), Title 27, Article 12.
Acts 1975, P.L. 146, as amended.

1. REVIEW PANEL PROVISIONS

27–12–8–1. Filing of complaints.

Subject to [provisions below], a patient or the representative of a patient who has a claim under this article for bodily injury or death on account of malpractice may do the following:

> (1) File a complaint in any court of law having requisite jurisdiction.

> (2) By demand, exercise the right to a trial by jury.

27–12–8–3. Damages claimed.

* * * [A] dollar amount or figure may not be included in the demand in a malpractice complaint, but the prayer must be for such damages as are reasonable in the premises.

27–12–8–4. Presentation of claims to medical review panels.

* * * [A]n action against a health care provider may not be commenced in a court in Indiana before:

> (1) the claimant's proposed complaint has been presented to a medical review panel * * *; and

> (2) an opinion is given by the panel.

27–12–10–1. Establishment of panels.

This chapter provides for the establishment of medical review panels to review proposed malpractice complaints against health care providers covered by this article.

27–12–10–3. Members.

(a) A medical review panel consists of one (1) attorney and three (3) health care providers.

(b) The attorney member of the medical review panel shall act as chairman of the panel and in an advisory capacity but may not vote.

* * *

27–12–10–13. Time limit for opinions.

(a) The panel shall give its expert opinion within one hundred eighty (180) days after the selection of the last member * * *.

* * *

27–12–10–17. Evidence.

(a) The evidence in written form to be considered by the medical review panel shall be promptly submitted by the respective parties.

(b) The evidence may consist of medical charts, x-rays, lab tests, excerpts of treatises, depositions of witnesses including parties, and any other form of evidence allowable by the medical review panel.

(c) Depositions of parties and witnesses may be taken before the convening of the panel.

* * *

27–12–10–19. Legal advice.

The chairman of the panel shall advise the panel relative to any legal question involved in the review proceeding and shall prepare the opinion of the panel * * *.

27–12–10–20. Convening and questioning of panel.

(a) Either party, after submission of all evidence and upon ten (10) days notice to the other side, has the right to convene the panel at a time and place agreeable to the members of the panel. Either party may question the panel concerning any matters relevant to issues to be decided by the panel before the issuance of the panel's report.

(b) The chairman of the panel shall preside at all meetings. Meetings shall be informal.

27–12–10–21. Access to information.

(a) The panel has the right and duty to request all necessary information.

(b) The panel may consult with medical authorities.

(c) The panel may examine reports of other health care providers necessary to fully inform the panel regarding the issue to be decided.

(d) Both parties shall have full access to any material submitted to the panel.

27–12–10–22. Expert opinions.

(a) The panel has the sole duty to express the panel's expert opinion as to whether or not the evidence supports the conclusion that the defendant or defendants acted or failed to act within the appropriate standards of care as charged in the complaint.

(b) After reviewing all evidence and after any examination of the panel by counsel representing either party, the panel shall, within thirty (30) days, give one (1) or more of the following expert opinions, which must be in writing and signed by the panelists:

(1) The evidence supports the conclusion that the defendant or defendants failed to comply with the appropriate standard of care as charged in the complaint.

(2) The evidence does not support the conclusion that the defendant or defendants failed to meet the applicable standard of care as charged in the complaint.

(3) There is a material issue of fact, not requiring expert opinion, bearing on liability for consideration by the court or jury.

(4) The conduct complained of was or was not a factor of the resultant damages. If so, whether the plaintiff suffered: (A) any disability and the extent and duration of the disability; and (B) any permanent impairment and the percentage of the impairment.

27–12–10–23. Evidentiary value of expert opinions.

A report of the expert opinion reached by the medical review panel is admissible as evidence in any action subsequently brought by the claimant in a court of law. However, the expert opinion is not conclusive, and either party, at the party's cost, has the right to call any member of the medical review panel as a witness. If called, a witness shall appear and testify.

2. COMPENSATION FUND PROVISIONS

27–12–2–14. Health care provider.

"Health care provider" means any of the following:

(1) An individual, a partnership, a limited liability company, a corporation, a professional corporation, a facility, or an institution licensed or legally authorized by this state to provide health care or professional services as a physician, psychiatric hospital, hospital, health facility, emergency ambulance service * * *, dentist, registered or licensed practical nurse, physician assistant, midwife, optometrist, podiatrist, chiropractor, physical therapist, respiratory care practitioner, occupational therapist, psychologist, paramedic, [or] emergency medical technician * * *.

(2) A college, university, or junior college that provides health care to a student, faculty member, or employee, and the governing board or a person who is an officer, employee, or agent of the college, university, or junior college acting in the course and scope of the person's employment.

(3) A blood bank, community mental health center, community mental retardation center, community health center, or migrant health center.

(4) A home health agency * * *.

(5) A health maintenance organization * * *.

* * *

27–12–3–1. Application of article.

A health care provider who fails to qualify under this article is not covered by this article and is subject to liability under the law without regard to this article. If a health care provider does not qualify, the patient's remedy is not affected by this article.

27–12–3–2. Qualification of health care providers.

For a health care provider to be qualified under this article, the health care provider or the health care provider's insurance carrier shall:

(1) cause to be filed with the commissioner proof of financial responsibility established [below]; and

(2) pay the surcharge assessed on all health care providers * * *.

27–12–14–3. Recovery limitations.

(a) The total amount recoverable for an injury or death of a patient may not exceed five hundred thousand dollars ($500,000) except that, as to an act of malpractice that occurs on or after January 1, 1990, the total amount recovered for an injury or death may not exceed seven hundred fifty thousand dollars ($750,000).

(b) A health care provider qualified under this article is not liable for an amount in excess of one hundred thousand dollars ($100,000) for an occurrence of malpractice.

(c) Any amount due from a judgment or settlement that is in excess of the total liability of all liable health care providers * * * shall be paid from the patient's compensation fund * * *.

* * *

27–12–4–1. Establishment of financial responsibility.

Financial responsibility of a health care provider and the provider's officers, agents, and employees while acting in the course and scope of their employment with the health care provider may be established * * *:

(1) By the health care provider's insurance carrier filing with the commissioner proof that the health care provider is insured by a policy of malpractice liability insurance in the amount of at least one hundred thousand dollars ($100,000) per occurrence and three hundred thousand dollars ($300,000) in the annual aggregate, except for the following: (A) If the health care provider is a hospital, as defined in this article, the minimum annual aggregate insurance amount is as follows: (i) For hospitals of not more than one hundred (100) beds, two million dollars ($2,000,000) [;] (ii) For hospitals of more than one hundred (100) beds, three million dollars ($3,000,000).

* * *

27–12–6–6. Payments from fund.

(a) If an annual aggregate for a health care provider qualified under this article has been paid by or on behalf of the health care provider, all amounts that may subsequently become due and payable to a claimant arising out of an act of malpractice of the health care provider occurring during the year in which the annual aggregate was exhausted shall be paid from the patient's compensation fund * * *.

* * *

27–12–6–1. Collection and deposit of fund.

(a) The patient's compensation fund is created to be collected and received by the commissioner for exclusive use for the purposes stated in this article.

(b) The fund and any income from the fund shall be held in trust, deposited in a segregated account, invested, and reinvested by the commissioner * * * and does not become a part of the state general fund.

* * *

27–12–5–1. Annual levy.

To create a source of money for the patient's compensation fund, an annual surcharge shall be levied on all health care providers in Indiana.

27–12–5–2. Amount of surcharge.

* * *

(b) The amount of the surcharge shall be determined based upon actuarial principles and actuarial studies and must be adequate for the payment of claims and expenses from the patient's compensation fund.

(c) The surcharge may not exceed two hundred percent (200%) of the cost to each health care provider for maintenance of financial responsibility.

* * *

JONES v. STATE BOARD OF MEDICINE, 97 Idaho 859, 555 P.2d 399 (1976). In this declaratory judgment action, the lower court held Idaho's 1975 Hospital–Medical Liability Act unconstitutional. On appeal, the Supreme Court concluded that the resolution of challenges to provisions of the Act required the development of certain facts, and it remanded for further proceedings. In the course of its opinion, it described some aspects of the "malpractice crisis":

" * * * [W]e have examined some of the growing body of literature on medical malpractice insurance. Therein we find general agreement that there is a growing problem in medical malpractice insurance which is manifested by increasing rates and a threat of curtailment of health care. Four dominant factors appear of prominent concern although the overall causes of the problem appear intricate, highly interrelated and difficult of ascertainment. The HEW Report [U.S. Dep't of Health, Education and Welfare Report to the Secretary's Commission on Medical Malpractice (1972)] at 24, attributes the root cause of medical malpractice problems to an increase in patient injuries. While those iatrogenic injuries (those induced during treatment) may or may not be caused by negligence, their numerical increase is a reality. The second causal factor is the increase in number of malpractice claims. * * * The Insurance Services Organization estimates nationally an increase in claims of 12%. In contrast, an estimate of 225% annual increase between 1970 and 1975 was made by St. Paul Fire & Marine Insurance Co. That same data, however, indicates a 130% increase between 1969 and 1974. * * *

"A third factor exerting an effect upon medical malpractice insurance is the dollar amount of damages awarded in verdicts and the rise in that dollar amount in recent years. * * *

"A final factor indicated by the literature has been the difficulty in providing medical malpractice insurance at reasonable rates. Rate-setting in medical malpractice insurance has been described as an 'actuarial nightmare.' Therein it is stated:

'The basic objective of any insurance company is to sell insurance at a rate which is competitive and which will result in a profit for the company. In order to do this companies employ actuaries to predict future losses that must be paid from present premiums. * * * Rates must produce a sufficient premium volume to (1) cover the losses that will occur during the period, (2) cover the administrative expenses of running the business, and (3) provide a small margin for the unknown contingencies, which may become a profit if not used.' HEW Report, supra, at 41–42.

* * *

"Perhaps the most vexing problem in malpractice rate setting nationally has been the protracted period of time that passes prior to the reporting and settlement of malpractice claims. * * * What has been described as the 'long tail' on malpractice losses is the period during which doctors and hospitals may be exposed to liability for iatrogenic injuries following actual patient contact. In part, this results from some statutes of limitations which may not begin to run until several years after the incident which caused the injury. As a result a claim may be far removed in time from the point at which the patient received the actual treatment. * * * "

AMERICAN LAW INSTITUTE, REPORTERS' STUDY ON ENTERPRISE RESPONSIBILITY FOR PERSONAL INJURY, vol. II (1991). The ALI-sponsored Study notes concerns about medical malpractice insurance which have motivated adoption of legislation like the Indiana malpractice statute, presented at p. 1127, supra. It acknowledges the "burden imposed on doctors by the spiraling rates of malpractice litigation and insurance," and in particular, "the difficulty of pricing insurance for individual physicians, especially in high-risk specialties and areas." But it does not endorse the package of provisions contained in the Indiana statute: screening of claims, limits on provider liability and patient recovery, a patient's compensation fund to hold insurance costs down through state-wide pooling of risk.

The Study recommends a different approach. It proposes that liability for medical malpractice should not be limited, but rather should be redirected: "The primary bearer of liability (and provider of insurance) for negligently caused injuries to hospitalized patients should be the hospital * * *." The Study's authors explain:

"Our proposal is to relieve doctors of the direct financial burden of malpractice insurance by shifting the locus of legal liability from the physician to the hospital or other health care institution connected with the incident. * * * [A hospital would be liable] for physician malpractice that injures patients who are treated within that hospital. This enterprise liability rule would cover roughly 90 percent of the incidents now giving rise to malpractice claims and payments.

" * * * [W]e would exculpate doctors from personal liability for negligence (and thus eliminate their need to purchase insurance against such liability), on the condition that the hospital assume such liability and provide the insurance, a change that would leave untouched the patient's present entitlement to recover for injuries caused by the doctor's negligence."

JOHNSON v. ST. VINCENT HOSPITAL, INC.
Supreme Court of Indiana, 1980.
273 Ind. 374, 404 N.E.2d 585.

[The Supreme Court here upheld as constitutional the Indiana Medical Malpractice Act, p. 1127, supra. It held, under the state and federal constitutions, that the requirement of submitting malpractice claims to panels did not violate rights to trial by jury and access to the courts; that the procedural requirements burdening patient claimants and benefiting health care providers were consistent with guarantees of equal protection; and that the limitations on recovery were consistent with due process and equal protection.

In considering the challenges to the panel requirements under the equal protection clause, the court said:]

The legislative purpose to be served by this statute as a whole is clear. Its goal is to protect the health of the citizens of this State by preventing a reduction of health care services. The question for our determination is whether there is some "ground of difference" that makes clear the reason for the different and more burdensome treatment accorded medical malpractice tort claimants and explains the corresponding special consideration given the health care provider. We conclude that a ground does exist and was not negatived by appellants in the courts below. Each citizen is dependent upon practicing health care providers for the treatment of his illnesses and injuries. Medical malpractice cases against health care providers, by reason of their potential number and size, pose a special economic threat to the rewards which health care providers may enjoy in return for their services. They also routinely require the ascertainment of technical and scientific facts, procedures, and expert opinions for the purposes of determining whether a breach of legal duty has occurred. The panel submission requirement serves this requirement and tends to insure that a resolution of a dispute will be based upon the ascertainment of the true facts and circumstances and will be fair; and also tends to insure that the cost to the health care providers participating in a risk spreading combine will be no more than is reasonable and necessary.

[In finding the limitations on recovery consistent with due process and equal protection, the court said:]

Of particular salience here is the recent case of Duke Power Co. v. Carolina Environmental Study Group, Inc., (1978) 438 U.S. 59, 98 S.Ct. 2620, 57 L.Ed.2d 595 [p. 1198, infra] * * *. The court considered the constitutionality of the Price–Anderson Act wherein it placed a dollar limit upon the aggregate liability of licensed private companies and the government due to a single nuclear incident. The limitation was upheld as against a due process and equal protection attack. The court held that the statutory limitation on liability bears a rational relationship to the intent of Congress to encourage private industry to become involved in the production of electricity by use of atomic power. It was recognized that the liability figure would not be sufficient to guarantee full compensation to those injured as the result of a nuclear disaster. There are parallels between the situation dealt with by Congress and the one dealt with by our Legislature. Both involved the lack of an effective risk spreading device for a private industry and a public need to have the industry provide its services. Both involved a private industry which was reluctant to provide its services because of the shortage of effective insurances for the risks attendant to production. In both the Price–Anderson Act and the Indiana Malpractice Act the governments established a form of government sponsored insurance, set limitations upon liability, and placed the burden of the limitation upon persons injured by the industry.

It would appear that the limitation upon recovery is the natural consequent of the establishment of an insurance type program. It provides a factor for calculating premiums and charges to those covered. An insurance operation cannot be sound if the funds collected are insufficient to meet the obligations incurred. It must, however, be accepted that the badly injured plaintiff who may require constant care will not recover full damages, yet at the same time we are impressed with the large amount which is recoverable and its probable ability to fully compensate a large proportion of injured patients. * * *

* * *

In the record before us evidence was presented for constitutional purposes that part of the private insurance industry did cease making malpractice insurance available to some health care providers in the State. * * * The Legislature responded by creating the patient compensation fund and the residual malpractice insurance authority, thereby providing a government sponsored risk spreading mechanism as an alternative to insurance strictly from private sources. In so doing it set the limitations upon recovery. The mechanism cannot operate without the voluntary participation of health care providers. The limitation may well provide health care providers with the incentive to participate. It also facilitates the determination of an annual surcharge to be paid by participating health care providers * * *. In effect it would serve the same purpose for the patient compensation fund that such limitations serve in private insurance contracts. The Legislature could have reasonably considered a set limitation upon recoveries to be an essential part of any operable plan to spread the risk of loss to participating health care providers and to regulate the cost to them, and thereby meet the danger it perceived to the public welfare. The classifications of health care providers and injured patients challenged here are but composite parts of the limitation itself and are likewise justified. Duke Power Co. v. Carolina Environmental Study Group, Inc., supra. We are aware that the Supreme Court of Illinois was unable to find a justification for a limitation of recovery in malpractice actions against health care providers erected by their own act at this same level. Wright v. Central Du Page Hospital Ass'n, [excerpted below]. Unlike that court, we find a rational justification for the difference in treatment accorded the various groups identified within the rationality of the program launched by the Legislature to protect vital societal interests.

———

STATE EX REL. STRYKOWSKI v. WILKIE, 81 Wis.2d 491, 261 N.W.2d 434 (1978). This original action was brought to determine the constitutionality of W.S.A. 655.001 et seq., a 1975 statute relating to health care liability and patient compensation. The statute established an exclusive procedure for prosecuting malpractice claims against a "health care provider." The court summarized the statute as follows:

"Under Chapter 655, Stats., no court action may be maintained for injuries arising from medical malpractice until the matter has been reviewed by a patients' compensation panel. * * *

"Once convened, a panel determines the issues of negligence, causation and damages, applying comparative negligence principles. Sec. 655.065(1), (2) Stats. These determinations are made by a majority vote. Sec. 655.16(2).

"A court action may be commenced within 120 days after the panel's decision. The findings of a * * * panel with regard to causation and negligence are admissible at trial; the damage award may be admitted in the judge's discretion. Sec. 655.19(1), Stats. No panel member may appear at the trial as counsel or as a witness. Sec. 655.19. If no action is commenced within 120 days, judgment may be rendered in accordance with the panel's order. Sec. 655.20.

"The Patients Compensation Fund, created by sec. 655.27, Stats., pays that portion of medical malpractice awards above certain limits. Sec. 655.27(1). It is financed by assessments against health care providers. * * * Malpractice claimants seeking damages in excess of $200,000 must name the fund as a defendant, and the fund may appear and defend against the action. Sec. 655.27(5).

"Chapter 655, Stats., also imposes certain limitations upon the payment of malpractice awards. Awards for future medical payments in excess of $25,000 are paid to a medical expenses fund and are disbursed as future medical expenses are incurred. These payments continue until the amount is exhausted or the patient dies. Sec. 655.015. * * * After July 1, 1979, awards will be automatically limited to $500,000 per incident if the fund falls below certain levels. Sec. 655.27(6)."

(The court concluded that these provisions, as interpreted by the court, did not violate constitutional guarantees of equal protection and due process, did not amount to an unlawful delegation of judicial authority and did not impair the right to trial by jury. Hence Chapter 655 was constitutionally valid.)

WRIGHT v. CENTRAL DU PAGE HOSPITAL ASSOCIATION
Supreme Court of Illinois, 1976.
63 Ill.2d 313, 347 N.E.2d 736.

[Plaintiffs sought a declaratory judgment that basic provisions of the 1975 "Act to revise the law in relation to medical practice" were invalid. The lower court held parts of the Act unconstitutional. Excerpts from the opinion upon appeal in the Supreme Court follow.]

We consider next the provision * * * that the maximum recovery "on account of injuries by reason of medical, hospital or other healing art malpractice" shall be $500,000. * * *

Plaintiff argues that by denying recovery for loss and damage in excess of $500,000 the General Assembly has arbitrarily classified, and unreasonably discriminated against, the most seriously injured victims of medical malpractice, but has not limited the recovery of those victims who suffer moderate or minor injuries. She points out that the burden of this legislative effort to reduce or maintain the level of malpractice insurance premiums falls exclusively on those extremely unfortunate victims who most need financial protection.

Defendants argue that such unequal treatment is necessary to deal with what they describe as the "medical malpractice crisis." * * *

Defendants cite the Workmen's Compensation Act (Ill.Rev.Stat. 1975, ch. 48, par. 138.1 et seq.) as precedent for the limitation of monetary recovery for injuries. The Workmen's Compensation Act provided a *quid pro quo* in that the employer assumed a new liability without fault but was relieved of the prospect of large damage judgments, while the employee, whose monetary recovery was limited, was awarded compensation without regard to the employer's negligence. * * *

* * * [The 1975 Act] abolished no common law defenses, nor did it purport either to alter the essential elements of a cause of action for medical malpractice or lessen the plaintiff's burden of proof. Furthermore, the very seriously injured malpractice victim, because of the recovery limitation, might be unable to recover even all the medical expenses he might incur, in which event he would recover nothing for any other loss suffered.

Defendants argue that there is a societal *quid pro quo* in that the loss of recovery potential to some malpractice victims is offset by "lower insurance premiums and lower medical care costs for all recipients of medical care." This *quid pro quo* does not extend to the seriously injured medical malpractice victim and does not serve to bring the limited recovery provision within the rationale of the cases upholding the constitutionality of the Workmen's Compensation Act.

* * *

* * * We are of the opinion that limiting recovery only in medical malpractice actions to $500,000 is arbitrary and constitutes a special law in

violation of section 13 of article IV of the 1970 [Illinois] Constitution, and we so hold.

[The court held that a further provision of the Act limiting rate increases in malpractice insurance policies violated the Illinois Constitution. It affirmed in part and vacated in part.]

UNDERWOOD, Justice (concurring in part and dissenting in part):

* * *

Much has been written and said in recent times about the current "crisis" in the area of medical malpractice resulting from substantial increases in the numbers of cases filed and amounts of jury verdicts, enormous increases in malpractice insurance premiums, threatened walkouts and strikes by doctors, etc. * * * [I]t is clear that serious problems do exist to which a majority of the States have responded with legislative action in various forms, including new means of providing malpractice insurance, limitations upon contingency fees of lawyers, screening panels to hear claims, maximum liability limits, etc. * * *

Given the fact that serious problems do exist; that, while not all of them are unique to the medical malpractice area, it is that area in which they appear most acute; that health care costs affect virtually all persons; * * * and that the $500,000 limitation still affords entirely adequate protection to the vast majority of victims of medical malpractice, I am not prepared to hold it an impermissible exercise of legislative discretion.

———

CARSON v. MAURER, 120 N.H. 925, 424 A.2d 825 (1980). In considering the constitutionality of the portion of a 1979 statute on medical malpractice actions that treated the periodic rather than lump-sum payment of medical malpractice awards, the court said:

"The plaintiffs next attack RSA 507–C:7 IV (Supp.1979) on equal protection grounds. The provision allowing the court to order periodic payments in certain circumstances is apparently designed to ensure that the claimant with substantial injuries requiring long-term treatment would have money available to pay for future medical care. The purpose of the provision relating to payments following the death of the injured person is to reduce medical reparations system costs by eliminating a 'bonus element,' namely, the payment of portions of the award no longer required to compensate the malpractice victim.

"Regardless whether the provision substantially furthers its stated purpose, we conclude that it unreasonably discriminates in favor of health care defendants and unduly burdens seriously injured malpractice plaintiffs. * * * [A]lthough there may be a windfall to the claimant's family if the periodic payments are not terminated at the claimant's death, there is also a windfall benefit to the defendant's insurer under RSA 507–C:7 IV (Supp. 1979) if the claimant dies. Furthermore, the money represented by the judgment becomes the plaintiff's property when he obtains a judgment. Yet he is denied the right to dispose of that property, as and when he pleases. In return he obtains only the questionable benefit of having money available to meet future expenses, which money, it may turn out, he does not even need. Finally, a statute which singles out seriously injured malpractice victims whose future damages exceed $50,000 and requires one class to shoulder the burden inherent in a periodic payments scheme from which the general public benefits offends basic notions of fairness and justice. Accordingly, we hold that RSA 507–C:7 IV (Supp.1979) is an unreasonable exercise of the legislature's police power and violates the State's equal protection guarantees."

KNOWLES v. UNITED STATES

Supreme Court of South Dakota, 1996.
1996 SD 10, 544 N.W.2d 183.

[In 1976 South Dakota's legislature imposed a $500,000 cap on non-economic damages (pain and suffering) in medical malpractice cases. In 1986 a new cap on malpractice awards was substituted: all damages, economic and non-economic, were limited to a total of $1 million. In this case the South Dakota Supreme Court addressed the question (certified to it) whether the 1986 cap was valid under the state's constitution. Following are excerpts from the two "majority" opinions issued by the five member court.]

SABERS, Justice, writing the majority opinion on the result of unconstitutionality of the damages cap of SDCL 21–3–11 based on due process * * *.

* * *

Kris Knowles was twelve days old when he was admitted for treatment of a fever at the Ellsworth Air Force Base Hospital, near Rapid City, South Dakota. * * * On the night before his discharge, the [nurses' aides on duty] failed to report to nurses or physicians that Kris' temperature had been dropping throughout that night. Kris developed hypoglycemia and suffered respiratory arrest resulting in severe, permanent brain damage.

* * * The United States admitted liability for medical malpractice and filed a motion for entry of judgment of $1 million based on SDCL 21–3–11, which limits damages in medical malpractice actions to $1 million. * * *

* * *

Under South Dakota Constitution article VI, § 2, "[n]o person shall be deprived of life, liberty or property without due process of law." * * * We apply a more stringent test than the federal courts' rational basis test [in judging whether a statute satisfies due process]. Katz v. Bd. of Med. & Osteopathic Examiners, 432 N.W.2d 274, 278 n. 6 (S.D.1988). The statute must "bear a real and substantial relation to the objects sought to be attained." Id.

Ohio uses the same test. In Morris [v. Savoy, 61 Ohio St.3d 684, 576 N.E.2d 765 (1991)], the Supreme Court of Ohio held that a medical malpractice damages cap was a violation of due process. A 1987 study by the Insurance Service Organization, which sets the rates of the insurance industry, found that the savings from various tort reforms including a damages cap were "marginal to nonexistent." Id. 576 N.E.2d at 771. The court concluded that the cap was irrational and arbitrary and that it did "not bear a real and substantial relation to public health or welfare[.]" Id.

* * *

The arbitrary classification of malpractice claimants based on the amount of damages is not rationally related to the stated purpose of curbing medical malpractice claims. See Lyons [v. Lederle Laboratories, 440 N.W.2d 769 (S.D.1989)] at 773 (Sabers, J. concurring specially). The legislation was adopted as a result of "some perceived malpractice crisis." Id. at 771. Many courts and commentators have argued that there was no "crisis" at all.[6] Gail Eiesland, note, Miller v. Gilmore: The Constitutionality of South Dakota's Medical Malpractice Statute of Limitations, 38 S.D.L.Rev. 672, 703 (1993) * * *.

In Moore [v. Mobile Infirmary Assn., 592 So.2d 156 (Ala.1991)], the court examined several studies to conclude that the connection between recovery caps and decreased malpractice insurance rates was "at best, indirect and remote." Id. at 168. The court balanced this remote connection against the "direct and concrete" burden on severely injured claimants. * * * "[T]he statute operates to the advantage not only of negligent health care providers over other tortfeasors, but of those health care providers who are *most irresponsible*." Moore, 592 So.2d at 169 (emphasis in original).

* * *

Despite a claimed medical malpractice crisis in the rural areas of this state, this legislation wholly failed to differentiate between rural and urban problems and solutions. It purported to cover all practitioners of the healing arts, including chiropractors and dentists. There is no showing of a shortage of chiropractors or dentists. The statutes purported to cover the entire state even though there was no medical malpractice crisis in the urban areas such as Minnehaha and Pennington Counties, as opposed to the rural areas.

Even in this case, we are dealing with a United States Air Force hospital situated in Pennington County. There is no showing that any United States

---

6. SDCL 21–3–11 was adopted as a result of recommendations by the 1975 South Dakota Legislature's Special Committee on Medical Malpractice. As noted by one commentator:

Statements made by insurance representatives before the [Committee], referring to the low number of medical malpractice claims brought in the state, can only create significant doubt that South Dakota was experiencing a genuine insurance crisis at that time. Startling data on medical malpractice claims in South Dakota, North Dakota, and Minnesota, collected by the Minnesota Department of Commerce from 1982–1987 [the Hatch Study], also tend to call into question the

basis for cries of *any* insurance crisis; if claim frequency and severity did not change significantly in those years, and if in those same six years only one-half of one percent of all medical malpractice plaintiffs were awarded any damages, why then did physicians' insurance premiums *triple* in that same time period?

Eiesland, infra, at 703 (emphasis in original). * * *

In addition, a 1986 report by the National Association of Attorneys General concluded that "insurance premium increases were not related to any purported liability crisis, but 'result[ed] largely from the insurance industry's own mismanagement.' "[Id.] at 685 n. 121 * * *.

Air Force hospital had any difficulty obtaining and keeping practitioners of the healing arts. This legislation does not bear a *real* and *substantial* relation to the objects sought to be attained and it violates many rights in the process. The fact that certain fringe benefits may result to the public in general is insufficient to save this statute. * * *

* * *

AMUNDSON, J., concurs specially.

MILLER, C.J., and KONENKAMP and GILBERTSON, JJ., concur in part, concur in result in part and dissent in part.

* * *

GILBERTSON, Justice, writing the majority opinion on the rationale for unconstitutionality and on the revival of the [1976 provision].

I agree with the writing of Justice Sabers only insofar as it holds our [1986] cap violates substantive due process. This cap requires the most seriously injured malpractice victims to bear the burden of alleviating a perceived medical malpractice insurance crisis by limiting recovery for actual economic losses.

* * *

It is vitally important to an analysis of this issue to understand and respect the circumstances under which South Dakota enacted [the original 1976 version of] SDCL 21–3–11. In the mid–1970s, our Legislature, along with many legislatures throughout the country, became gravely concerned about the availability and cost of health care, especially in rural areas and small communities. Seeing a direct correlation between the availability of health services and skyrocketing medical malpractice insurance premiums, these state legislatures attempted to alleviate the increasing cost of such insurance by enacting statutes limiting the damages recoverable in medical malpractice suits.

South Dakota's Legislature prudently responded to this perceived crisis by first setting up a special fact-finding committee to study the problem. After considering public testimony taken over a period of months, the Legislature responded with a $500,000 cap on general (noneconomic) damages for medical malpractice awards * * *.

* * *

An unsettled argument persists over whether a malpractice crisis ever actually existed. Yet there can be no doubt, for whatever reason, malpractice premiums were increasing at an alarming rate. Umbrella coverage for a general or family practitioner in South Dakota rose from a rate of $640 a year in 1970 to approximately $8,400 a year in 1976. The problem was especially acute in rural areas. * * *

Unfortunately we are not reviewing the 1976 enactment. In 1986 the Legislature amended SDCL 21–3–11 * * *. While most other jurisdictions where malpractice caps had been upheld adhered to capping only noneconomic damages, the South Dakota Legislature for reasons unknown adopted a flat cap on "total damages." This caps not only noneconomic damages as in 1976, but also caps actual out-of-pocket expenses and future losses. Therefore, in 1986, the distinction between economic and noneconomic damages disappeared from the statute.

* * *

Certainly the 1976 version sought only to cut the fat out of malpractice awards. Medical bills, lost wages, and prescription costs are tangible damages, whereas pain and suffering and like damages are largely intangible. Unbridled noneconomic damage awards present a real threat to maintaining reasonable malpractice insurance premiums, because such awards are unpredictable and based on highly subjective perceptions.[22] In truth, however, the 1986 flat cap on total damages potentially cuts not only fat, but muscle, bone and marrow. If a malpractice patient's hospital bill, for example, exceeds the cap, then the patient can recover nothing for the remaining medical bills, future bills, past and future income lost, prescriptions, etc. The 1976 enactment did not have this problem.

When the Legislature imposed the $1 million cap, it acted without any showing of need. Out of the hundreds of pages of the record concerning a medical crisis of the mid–1970's in this state, there is not any evidence in the record which shows that in 1986 the "crisis" had worsened to require a cap on economic damages. In fact the only post–1976 evidence in the record points to the contrary. * * * Under appropriate circumstances such a cap may have been warranted, but without adequate justification, its adoption was plainly an unreasonable and arbitrary imposition of an economic burden upon the most severely injured malpractice victims.

* * *

Based on the analysis as set forth above, I would find the cap on economic damages of SDCL 21–3–11 to be in violation of the substantive due process clause of the South Dakota Constitution. I would find the cap on non-economic damages to be constitutional for the reasons previously set forth.

* * *

If the 1986 amended form of SDCL 21–3–11 is declared unconstitutional in toto, does the prior version of that statute survive? The effect of an invalid amendment on the prior statute was clearly answered in State v. Reed, 75 S.D. 300, 303, 63 N.W.2d 803, 804 (1954) wherein this Court stated, "[i]f such amendatory act is unconstitutional in its entirety, the law prior to its enactment is still in effect." * * *

---

22. No exactness of calculation can be established for non-economic damages which we call upon a jury to quantify into a dollar award. Trial and appellate courts can review jury awards for economic damages in light of the evidence * * * and determine whether an award is justified or in excess of the plaintiff's loss. No such similar assurance can be provided for intangible non-economic losses which, from the standpoint of the insurer and the insured medical provider, pose the real threat of risk of run-away verdicts. * * *

* * * Thus, I conclude that as the 1986 amended version of SDCL 21–3–11 is wholly unconstitutional, the pre-amendment [1976] version remains in full force and effect.

* * *

MILLER, C.J., and KONENKAMP, J., concur.

SABERS and AMUNDSON, JJ., dissent.

RESTRICTIONS ON NONECONOMIC DAMAGES

The legislative approach that ultimately survives constitutional scrutiny in Knowles v. United States, supra—limitation of noneconomic damages in medical malpractice—has been generalized by a minority of states. Some states have adopted general statutes setting upper limits or caps on noneconomic damages for all tort suits. The general provisions differ as to the dollar amount of the ceiling imposed, and also in their handling of different types of noneconomic loss, but they have a common thrust.

These restrictions are responsive to doubt and concern about award of damages for pain and suffering. The doubt has to do with the fact that pain and suffering, unlike medical expense and wage loss, cannot be undone by money, but only offset. The concerns have to do with the lack of objective standards to measure detriment that is subjective and personal, the high costs and enhanced controversy involved in adjudicating the issue of pain and suffering, and the danger that jury discretion will produce irregular judgments and outsized awards. Truncation of recovery for noneconomic injury is a sharp departure from the traditional commitment of common law to recompense all loss of well-being caused by tortious impact. Truncated recovery is akin to the approach of the plans beyond tort, which characteristically do not attempt to award individualized compensation for noneconomic losses.

Nonpecuniary harm is redressed at common law in a wide variety of settings. The most familiar case is physical pain and suffering attending substantial personal injury. Also there are situations in which the main harm done by the tort is emotional or experiential in character. Then there is the class of cases in which noneconomic injury is suffered by persons other than the primary victim of tortious impact. Physical harm to the primary victim may cause nonphysical harm to others, as valuable relationships with the victim, particularly family relations, are interrupted or cut off. Relational harms include the anguish felt because of a loved one's plight, and the associational disruptions called loss of consortium.

Following below are illustrative provisions from statutes enacted in Colorado and Maryland to restrict noneconomic recovery in all tort suits. The Colorado and Maryland statutes have been parsed, so that provisions applying to noneconomic recovery for primary injury are separated from provisions that speak to recovery for relational harm of a nonpecuniary nature.

Recovery for primary injury:

Colorado Revised Statutes Section 13–21–102.5:

(2)(b) "Noneconomic loss or injury" means nonpecuniary harm for which damages are recoverable by the person suffering the direct or primary loss or injury, including pain and suffering, inconvenience, emotional stress, and impairment of the quality of life. * * *

(3)(a) In any civil action in which damages for noneconomic loss or injury may be awarded, the total of such damages shall not exceed the sum of two hundred fifty thousand dollars, unless the court finds justification by clear and convincing evidence therefor. In no case shall the amount of such damages exceed five hundred thousand dollars.

(4) The limitations specified * * * shall not be disclosed to a jury * * *, but shall be imposed by the court before judgment.

(5) Nothing in this section shall be construed to limit the recovery of compensatory damages for physical impairment or disfigurement.

Maryland Courts and Judicial Proceedings Code Ann. Section 11–108:

(a)(1) "Noneconomic damages": (i) In an action for personal injury, means pain, suffering, inconvenience, physical impairment, disfigurement, * * * or other nonpecuniary injury * * *.

(b)(2)(i) * * * [I]n any action for damages for personal injury * * * in which the cause of action arises on or after October 1, 1994, an award for noneconomic damages may not exceed $500,000. (ii) The limitation on noneconomic damages * * * shall increase by $15,000 on October 1 of each year beginning on October 1, 1995. * * *

Recovery for relational harm:

Colorado Revised Statutes Section 13–21–102.5:

(2)(a) "Derivative noneconomic loss or injury" means nonpecuniary harm or emotional stress to persons other than the person suffering the direct or primary loss or injury [in cases not involving wrongful death].

(3)(b) In any civil action, no damages for derivative noneconomic loss or injury may be awarded unless the court finds justification by clear and convincing evidence therefor. In no case shall the amount of such damages exceed two hundred fifty thousand dollars.

Maryland Courts and Judicial Proceedings Code Ann. Section 11–108:

(a)(1) "Noneconomic damages": * * * (ii) In an action for wrongful death, means mental anguish, emotional pain and suffering, loss of society, companionship, comfort, protection, care, marital care, parental care, filial care, attention, advice, counsel, training, guidance, or education * * *.

(b)(3)(ii) In a wrongful death action in which there are two or more claimants or beneficiaries, an award for noneconomic damages may not exceed 150% of the limitation established [for recovery for primary injury, supra], regardless of the number of claimants or beneficiaries who share in the award.

RESTRICTIONS ON PUNITIVE DAMAGES

Over the last twenty-five years, most states have adopted statutory provisions that, in one way or another, affect the awarding of punitive damages in tort suits. These are general provisions applicable to all sorts of tort actions in which punitive recovery is sought. Their main thrust is restrictive: they tend to restrict the number of occasions in which punitive recovery is available, to confine jury discretion in deciding punitive claims, and to control the amount of damages recoverable.

One state, New Hampshire, has chosen to abolish the common law of punitive damages: "No punitive damages shall be awarded in any action, unless otherwise provided by statute." N.H. Rev. Stat. Ann. § 507:16. Other legislative interventions preserve, but revise, the doctrine of punitive damages. Revisionary statutes address three aspects of the law of punitive recovery: (1) standard, (2) process, (3) amount.

First, many states have adopted statutory standards defining the sort of bad conduct that must be proved in order for punitive damages to be awarded. Often these statutes say that proof of the defined bad conduct must be "clear and convincing." Various standards of heightened culpability have been enacted. This is the area of greatest legislative intervention.

Second, a number of state statutes address one or another aspect of the process for adjudicating punitive claims. Three notable types of process-oriented enactments are provisions for preliminary screening of punitive claims by the court, for bifurcated trial whereby the jury determines the amount of a punitive award in a separate proceeding, and for judicial review of jury decisions about punitive damages.

Third, recent state statutes have limited the amount of punitive damages recoverable by a claimant, by use of two techniques. Some states require that a stated percentage of the punitive award assessed against a defendant be given to a designated state fund, not to the winning plaintiff. A number of states have imposed statutory "caps" or upper limits on the total amount of punitive damages that may be exacted from a defendant.

Following are some illustrative provisions grouped under the three categories just discussed.

Standard and proof:

Kentucky Revised Statutes Section 411.184:

(1) As used in this section * * *: (a) "Oppression" means conduct which is specifically intended by the defendant to subject the plaintiff to cruel and unjust hardship. (b) "Fraud" means an intentional misrepresentation, deceit, or concealment of material fact * * * made with the intention of causing injury to the plaintiff. (c) "Malice" means either conduct which is specifically intended by the defendant to cause * * * injury to the plaintiff or conduct that is carried out by the defendant both with a flagrant

indifference to the rights of the plaintiff and with a subjective awareness that such conduct will result in human death or bodily harm. * * *

(2) A plaintiff shall recover punitive damages only upon proving, by clear and convincing evidence, that the defendant from whom such damages are sought acted toward the plaintiff with oppression, fraud or malice.

Oregon Revised Statutes Section 18.537(1):

Punitive damages are not recoverable in a civil action unless it is proven by clear and convincing evidence that the party against whom punitive damages are sought has acted with malice or has shown a reckless and outrageous indifference to a highly unreasonable risk of harm and has acted with a conscious indifference to the health, safety and welfare of others.

Montana Code Annotated Section 27–1–221(5):

* * * Clear and convincing evidence means evidence in which there is no serious or substantial doubt about the correctness of the conclusions drawn from the evidence. It is more than a preponderance of evidence but less than beyond a reasonable doubt.

Process of adjudication:

Minnesota Statutes Annotated Section 549.191:

Upon commencement of a civil action, the complaint must not seek punitive damages. After filing the suit a party may make a motion to amend the pleadings to claim punitive damages. The motion must allege the applicable legal basis * * * and must be accompanied by one or more affidavits showing the factual basis for the claim. At the hearing on the motion, if the court finds prima facie evidence in support of the motion, the court shall grant the moving party permission to amend the pleadings to claim punitive damages. * * *

Montana Code Annotated Section 27–1–221(7):

(a) Evidence regarding a defendant's financial affairs, financial condition, and net worth is not admissible in a trial to determine whether a defendant is liable for punitive damages. When the jury returns a verdict finding a defendant liable for punitive damages, the amount of punitive damages must then be determined by the jury in an immediate, separate proceeding * * *. In the separate proceeding to determine the amount of punitive damages to be awarded, the defendant's financial affairs, financial condition, and net worth must be considered.

* * *

(c) The judge shall review a jury award of punitive damages * * *. If after review the judge determines that the jury award of punitive damages should be increased or decreased, he may do so. The judge shall clearly state his reasons for increasing, decreasing, or not increasing or decreasing the punitive damages award of the jury in findings of fact and conclusions of law * * *.

Amount recoverable:

Utah Code Annotated Section 78–18–1(3):

In any judgment where punitive damages are awarded and paid, 50% of the amount of the punitive damages in excess of $20,000 shall, after payment of attorneys' fees and costs, be remitted to the state treasurer for deposit into the General Fund.

Nevada Revised Statutes Section 42.005:

1. * * * Except as otherwise provided in this section or by specific statute, an award of exemplary or punitive damages * * * may not exceed: (a) Three times the amount of compensatory damages awarded to the plaintiff if the amount of compensatory damages is $100,000 or more; or (b) Three hundred thousand dollars if the amount of compensatory damages awarded to the plaintiff is less than $100,000.

2. The limitations on the amount of an award of exemplary or punitive damages prescribed in subsection 1 do not apply to [actions involving products liability, an insurer acting in bad faith, discriminatory housing practices, toxic materials, defamation].

FORD v. UNIROYAL GOODRICH TIRE CO., 267 Ga. 226, 476 S.E.2d 565 (1996). In a Georgia products liability suit against a tire manufacturer, plaintiff sought punitive damages. The trial court instructed the jury that, as required by a Georgia statute, 75 percent of any punitive damages award would be paid into the state treasury. The jury awarded plaintiff $17 million in compensatory damages and $25 million in punitive damages. *Held*, that instructing the jury about the distribution of the punitive damages award was error. "[T]he purpose of * * * the 75–percent allocation rule [is] not to generate additional state revenue." "[T]he sole issue for a jury is the amount of money necessary to punish the defendant and deter future misconduct. Therefore, it is irrelevant who will be compensated by the award or how much the plaintiff will ultimately receive. By instructing the jury on the statutory scheme for allocating a punitive damages award, the trial court improperly shifted the jury's focus from the critical question of the defendant's conduct to the inappropriate question of the plaintiff's compensation."

WILLIAMS v. WILSON
Supreme Court of Kentucky, 1998.
972 S.W.2d 260.

LAMBERT, Justice.

This Court granted discretionary review to consider whether KRS 411.184 violates one or more provisions of the Constitution of Kentucky, thereby rendering the statute invalid and unenforceable. To resolve this question of constitutional law, it is necessary to first determine whether, in material respects, the statute impairs the common law of this Commonwealth as it existed prior to adoption of our present Constitution [in 1891] * * *.

[The statutory provision at issue—Kentucky Revised Statutes Section 411.184, enacted in 1988—is quoted within the foregoing note on "Restrictions on Punitive Damages."]

* * * [T]he intent of the Legislature was to redefine the circumstances in which punitive damages were recoverable, and toward that end a new legal standard was established. Departing from the traditional common law standard which permitted a jury to impose punitive damages upon a finding of gross negligence as measured by an objective standard, the new statutory standard, here under review, requires a determination that the defendant acted with "flagrant indifference to the rights of the plaintiff and with a subjective awareness that such conduct will result in human death or bodily harm." * * *

The facts which give rise to this litigation are unremarkable but not unimportant. On May 18, 1990, at 7:00 a.m., [plaintiff], Patricia Lynn Herald Wilson, was en route to the place of her employment as a school teacher. As she approached the intersection of Man–O–War and Palumbo in Lexington, she was struck by the vehicle being driven by [defendant, Teri Williams], a person who was intoxicated. At the scene, [defendant] was arrested and charged with DUI. She subsequently pled guilty to DUI in the Fayette District Court.

[Plaintiff sought punitive as well as compensatory damages, but the trial court ruled that the statutory conditions for a punitive award were not met.]

* * * While the trial court believed the fact of [defendant's] intoxication would authorize a finding that she acted with flagrant indifference, the court found no evidence of [defendant's] subjective awareness that her conduct would result in death or bodily harm. On the other hand, the court found the evidence sufficient to satisfy the gross negligence standard of "wanton or reckless indifference to the rights of others." * * *

* * *

* * * [F]rom our review of the cases, there is little doubt that prior to 1891, Kentucky law was well established that punitive damages could be recovered for negligent conduct which exceeded ordinary negligence whether such conduct was expressed as gross negligence, recklessness, wantonness, or some other such term.

* * *

* * * Recent case law reaffirms the continued viability of these venerable decisions.

Older cases, a number of which pre-date our constitution, recognize and approve the award of punitive damages in addition to compensatory damages against corporations and other employers based on gross negligence of their employees.

Horton v. Union Light, Heat & Power Co., Ky., 690 S.W.2d 382, 388 (1985). *Horton* * * * re-states the prevailing rule in this jurisdiction:

> In order to justify punitive damages there must be first a finding of failure to exercise reasonable care, and then an additional finding that this negligence was accompanied by a "wanton or reckless disregard for the lives, safety or property of others." * * *

Id. at 389–90.

* * * As shown by the decisions discussed hereinabove, the well established common law standard for awarding punitive damages was gross negligence. While the concept was not expressed in the same language in every opinion rendered prior to adoption of our Constitution, and while the language has not remained perfectly constant in this century, there is no doubt that unintentional conduct amounting to gross negligence, as that concept is well defined in *Horton,* was sufficient to authorize recovery of punitive damages. As the new statute requires proof of a subjective awareness that harm will result, it amounts to a vastly elevated standard for the recovery of punitive damages and a clear departure from the common law. The facts of this case well illustrate the fundamental change brought about by the statute.

* * *

* * * Gross negligence, however it may be qualified, is conduct lacking intent or actual knowledge of the result. Moreover, and while recognizing that at some point along the continuum between negligent conduct and intentional conduct there may be a convergence of the concepts, this Court must remain mindful that where statutes are applicable, trial courts must instruct in statutory language. * * *

* * * [W]hatever theoretical merger of gross negligence and subjective awareness of harm might be perceived by the court and counsel, the jury would be informed only of the legal standard contained in the statute and by any reasonable reckoning, the statutory standard far exceeds gross negligence. * * *

[The court went on to hold unconstitutional the statute's standard for award of punitive damages, since it would deny a right of recovery that was well established at the time of the adoption of Kentucky's constitution (1891). The court relied on Section 14 of the constitution, which provides that "every person for an injury done him in his lands, goods, person or reputation, shall have remedy by due course of law."]

[Case remanded. One of the seven Justices dissented.]

COOPER, Justice, dissenting.

* * *

The only possible argument for the proposition that KRS 411.184 "abolished" the right to punitive damages is * * * that the element of "subjective awareness" set forth in the definition of malice, KRS 411.184(1)(c), can be proven only by the direct testimony of the person against whom punitive damages are sought. Since the defendant/Appellant was unavailable to testify, the trial court reasoned that Appellee could not prove Appellant's "subjective awareness," thus was not entitled to an instruction on punitive damages. However, * * * "a plaintiff is entitled to prove a defendant's state of mind through circumstantial evidence." *Ball v. E.W. Scripps Co.*, Ky., 801 S.W.2d 684, 689 (1990). Even in a criminal case, where the elements of the offense must be proven beyond a reasonable doubt, *mens rea* may be inferred from the act itself and/or the circumstances surrounding it.

It is no longer arguable in this day and age that proof of the act of driving while intoxicated creates an inference of "subjective awareness" on the part of the actor of the potential consequences of the act. If that inference would satisfy the "beyond a reasonable doubt" standard of proof in a criminal case, it is sufficient to satisfy the "clear and convincing evidence" standard set forth in KRS 411.184(2).

PUNITIVE DAMAGES IN THE SUPREME COURT. Starting in 1989, the United States Supreme Court has rendered a series of decisions addressing the constitutionality of punitive damages in civil lawsuits. In two cases the Court rejected broad challenges to the basic common-law doctrine and practice of punitive imposition. It said the award of punitive damages in cases between private parties does not violate the constitutional ban on "excessive fines," Browning–Ferris Industries v. Kelco Disposal, Inc., 492 U.S. 257, 109 S.Ct. 2909, 106 L.Ed.2d 219 (1989); and that "the common-law method for assessing punitive awards," which relies primarily on jury discretion, does not violate the constitutional requirement of "due process." Pacific Mutual Life Ins. Co. v. Haslip, 499 U.S. 1, 111 S.Ct. 1032, 113 L.Ed.2d 1 (1991). In a third case the Court held that a $10 million punitive award was, in the circumstances, not so "grossly excessive" as to violate due process. TXO Production Corp. v. Alliance Resources Corp., 509 U.S. 443, 113 S.Ct. 2711, 125 L.Ed.2d 366 (1993). Then came cases that raised constitutional hackles.

In Honda Motor Co. v. Oberg, 512 U.S. 415, 114 S.Ct. 2331, 129 L.Ed.2d 336 (1994), the Court vacated an Oregon punitive damages award because, in that state, the amount of a jury's award was not subject to postverdict or appellate review. The Court said that judicial review of the amount of a punitive award was a safeguard against arbitrariness required by due process. It noted that some such review has been undertaken by common law courts "for as long as punitive damages have been awarded"; "[i]n the federal courts and in every State, except Oregon, judges review the size of damage awards." (An Oregon statute enacted in 1995 requires review by the trial court. See Ore. Rev. Stat. § 18.537(2).)

In BMW of North America, Inc. v. Gore, 517 U.S. 559, 116 S.Ct. 1589, 134 L.Ed.2d 809 (1996), the Court for the first time found a punitive award to be constitutionally excessive, and struck it down. Plaintiff Gore, a new car buyer, brought a fraud suit alleging that he was not told his new BMW had, before delivery, suffered minor damage and been repainted. BMW said its nationwide policy was not to advise dealers about predelivery damage when the cost of repair was minor, and that this policy complied with all the state statutes (in 25 other states) on the subject. The Alabama jury found common law fraud; an award of $4,000 compensatory damages plus $2 million punitive damages was upheld in Alabama courts. The U.S. Supreme Court ruled (5–4) that the punitive award was "grossly excessive" and so violated due process. The Court (per Justice Stevens) said three "guideposts" should be used in assessing the propriety of a punitive amount: (1) degree of reprehensibility of a defendant's misconduct (here there was no disregard of "the health and safety of others"); (2) the ratio between compensatory and punitive amounts (here the punitive award was 500 times greater than the "purely economic" actual harm); (3) the level of any statutory penalties for comparable misconduct (here much lower). With respect to the second guidepost, the punitive-compensatory ratio, the Court said that "the constitutional line" cannot be defined "by a simple mathematical formula":

> [T]he proper inquiry is " 'whether there is a reasonable relationship between the punitive damages award and *the harm likely to result* from the defendant's conduct as well as the harm that actually has occurred' " [quoting *TXO*, supra, quoting *Haslip*, supra]. * * *

> * * * [L]ow awards of compensatory damages may properly support [high ratios] if, for example, a particularly egregious act has resulted in only a small amount of economic damages. A higher ratio may also be justified in cases in which the injury is hard to detect or the monetary value of noneconomic harm might have been difficult to determine. It is appropriate, therefore, to reiterate our rejection of a categorical approach.

(On remand, the Alabama Supreme Court reduced Gore's punitive award to $50,000. 701 So.2d 507 (Ala.1997).)

The three "guideposts" of *Gore* were reaffirmed in Cooper Industries, Inc. v. Leatherman Tool Group, Inc., 532 U.S. 424, 121 S.Ct. 1678, 149 L.Ed.2d 674 (2001), where the Court said that, in the federal system, "courts of appeals should apply a *de novo* standard of review when passing on district courts' determinations of the constitutionality of punitive damages awards."

The *Gore* guideposts were tightened in State Farm Mutual Ins. Co. v. Campbell, 538 U.S. 408, 123 S.Ct. 1513, 155 L.Ed.2d 585 (2003), and applied to upset a state court punitive award. The case from Utah involved improper refusal by an insurance company (State Farm) to make timely payment under a liability insurance policy, causing emotional distress to the insureds (plaintiffs) in the interval before payment was finally made. Plaintiffs' evidence showed a nationwide practice by State Farm of delaying timely payment under policies it had issued. The Utah courts upheld recovery of $1 million in compensation for emotional distress, and $145 million in punitive damages. The U.S. Supreme Court (per Kennedy, J.) found the punitive award to be "excessive and in violation of the Due Process Clause." First, it held that the "reprehensibility" of a defendant's conduct should be measured by focussing on the misconduct at issue in the particular case, not on "dissimilar" activity by the defendant performed "out-of-state" which, while unsavory, "may have been lawful where it occurred." Second, the Court said the following about the appropriate ratio between punitive and compensatory awards:

> We decline again to impose a bright-line ratio which a punitive damages award cannot exceed. * * * [H]owever, * * * in practice, few awards exceeding a single-digit ratio between punitive and compensatory damages, to a significant degree, will satisfy due process.

The Court said "there is a presumption against" the very high punitive-to-compensatory ratio (145–to–1) in the present case, where "[t]he harm arose from a transaction in the economic realm" and "there were no physical injuries."

Chapter 22

NO–FAULT PLANS FOR ACCIDENT VICTIMS

SECTION A. WORKERS' COMPENSATION PLANS

Workers' compensation has long had an ambiguous relation to tort law. On the one hand, it is a rejection of tort, a different way of providing reparation to accident victims. On the other hand, its prescription of enterprise liability is an impetus to the expansion of strict tort doctrines. The materials of the present section explore workers' compensation by addressing in sequence three topics: historical development, general features, contemporary operation.

The section starts with historical materials, some notable cases from the second decade of the twentieth century, the founding period of American workers' compensation. The first case (*Ives v. South Buffalo Railway*) shows the shocked reaction of classical legal thinking to the idea of nonfault liability for workplace accidents.

Next is a note which describes basic features of workers' compensation plans, especially their distinctive limits on compensation for wage loss and bodily impairment. The note also identifies main areas of legal debate about the operation of the plans.

The section ends with a selection of contemporary cases which come to grips with the questions identified in the preceding note. Here the aim is not detailed doctrinal explication, but rather exposure of general ideas used to direct an evolving institution of accident law.

IVES v. SOUTH BUFFALO RAILWAY CO.

Court of Appeals of New York, 1911.
201 N.Y. 271, 94 N.E. 431.

[Plaintiff, a railroad employee, was injured on the job "solely by reason of a necessary risk or danger of his employment." He brought an action to recover compensation under New York's 1910 workmen's compensation law, modeled upon the English act of 1897. The law was enacted upon the recommendation of a legislatively appointed commission on industrial accidents. Defendant, pleading the law's unconstitutionality, lost below and appealed.]

* * *

The statute, judged by our common-law standards, is plainly revolutionary. Its central and controlling feature is that every employer who is engaged in any of the classified industries shall be liable for any injury to a workman arising out of and in the course of the employment by "a necessary risk or danger of the employment or one inherent in the nature thereof; * * * provided that the employer shall not be liable in respect of any injury to the workman which is caused in whole or in part by the serious and willful misconduct of the workman." * * * Just now our purpose is to present in sharp juxtaposition the fundamentals of these two opposing rules, namely, that under the common law an employer is liable to his injured employé only when the employer is at fault and the employé is free from fault; while under the new statute the employer is liable, although not at fault, even when the employé is at fault, unless this latter fault amounts to serious and willful misconduct. The reasons for this departure from our long-established law and usage are summarized in the language of the commission as follows:

"First, that the present system in New York rests on a basis that is economically unwise and unfair, and that in operation it is wasteful, uncertain, and productive of antagonism between workmen and employers.

"Second, that it is satisfactory to none, and tolerable only to those employers and workmen who practically disregard their legal rights and obligations, and fairly share the burden of accidents in industries.

* * *

" * * * [We propose] an elective plan of compensation which, if generally adopted, will do away with many of the evils of the present system. Its adoption will, we believe, be profitable to both employer and employé, and prove to be the simplest way for the state to change its system of liability without disturbance of industrial conditions. Not the least of the motives moving us is the hope that by these means a source of antagonism between employer and employed, pregnant with danger for the state, may be eliminated."

* * *

This legislation is challenged as void under the fourteenth amendment to the federal Constitution and under section 6, art. 1 of our state Constitution, which guarantee all persons against deprivation of life, liberty, or property without due process of law. * * * One of the inalienable rights of every citizen is to hold and enjoy his property until it is taken from him by due process of law. When our Constitutions were adopted, it was the law of the land that no man who was without fault or negligence could be held liable in damages for injuries sustained by another. That is still the law, except as to the employers enumerated in the new statute * * *.

It is conceded that this is a liability unknown to the common law, and we think it plainly constitutes a deprivation of liberty and property under the federal and state Constitutions, unless its imposition can be justified under the police power which will be discussed under a separate head. In arriving at this conclusion we do not overlook the cogent economic and sociological arguments which are urged in support of the statute. There can be no doubt as to the theory of this law. It is based upon the proposition that the inherent risks of an employment should in justice be placed upon the shoulders of the employer, who can protect himself against loss by insurance and by such an addition to the price of his wares as to cast the burden ultimately upon the consumer; that indemnity to an injured employé should be as much a charge upon the business as the cost of replacing or repairing disabled or defective machinery, appliances, or tools; that, under our present system, the loss falls immediately upon the employé who is almost invariably unable to bear it, and ultimately upon the community which is taxed for the support of the indigent; and that our present system is uncertain, unscientific, and wasteful, and fosters a spirit of antagonism between employer and employé which it is to the interests of the state to remove. We have already admitted the strength of this appeal to a recognized and widely prevalent sentiment; but we think it is an appeal which must be made to the people, and not to the courts. The right of property rests, not upon philosophical or scientific speculations, nor upon the commendable impulses of benevolence or charity, nor yet upon the dictates of natural justice. The right has its foundation in the fundamental law. That can be changed by the people, but not by Legislatures. * * *

* * * If such economic and sociologic arguments as are here advanced in support of this statute can be allowed to subvert the fundamental idea of property, then there is no private right entirely safe, because there is no limitation upon the absolute discretion of Legislatures, and the guarantees of the Constitution are a mere waste of words. * * * If the argument in support of this statute is sound, we do not see why it cannot logically be carried much further. Poverty and misfortune from every cause are detrimental to the state. It would probably conduce to the welfare of all concerned if there could be a more equal distribution of wealth. Many persons have much more property than they can use to advantage and many more find it impossible to get the means for a comfortable existence. If the Legislature can say to an employer, "You must compensate your employé for an injury not caused by you or by your fault," why can it not go further and say to the man of wealth, "You have more property than you need, and your neighbor is so poor that he can barely subsist; in the interest of natural justice you must divide with your neighbor, so that he and his dependents shall not become a charge upon the state"?

* * * In its final and simple analysis that is taking the property of A. and giving it to B., and that cannot be done under our Constitutions. * * *

* * *

We conclude, therefore, that in its basic and vital features the right given to the employé by this statute does not preserve to the employer the "due process" of law guaranteed by the Constitutions, for it authorizes the taking of the employer's property without his consent and without his fault. * * *

* * *

[The court then concluded that the legislation could not be justified under the police power. Judgment reversed.]

NEW YORK CENTRAL RAILROAD CO. v. WHITE
Supreme Court of the United States, 1917.
243 U.S. 188, 37 S.Ct. 247, 61 L.Ed. 667.

[Following the decision in Ives v. South Buffalo Railway Co., a constitutional amendment authorizing workmen's compensation legislation was adopted in New York and a new statute was enacted. The New York Court of Appeals sustained that act "as not inconsistent with the Fourteenth Amendment", and the Supreme Court here affirmed in an opinion by Justice Pitney. With respect to the arguments that the act took an employer's property without due process of law, interfered with an employee's rights to compensation "commensurate with the damages actually sustained", and deprived employers and employees of their "liberty" in "making such agreement as they choose" about terms of employment, the court said:]

The close relation of the rules governing responsibility as between employer and employee to the fundamental rights of liberty and property, is of course recognized. But those rules, as guides of conduct, are not beyond alteration by legislation in the public interest. No person has a vested interest in any rule of law entitling him to insist that it shall remain unchanged for his benefit. [The Court referred to the fellow servant rule, contributory fault and assumption of risk, aspects of a negligence action against employers which were all "plainly" subject to legislative modification or abolition. Such state legislation had long been sustained.]

It is true that in the case of the statutes thus sustained there were reasons rendering the particular departures appropriate. Nor is it necessary, for the purposes of the present case, to say that a State might, without violence to the constitutional guaranty of "due process of law," suddenly set aside all common-law rules respecting liability as between employer and employee, without providing a reasonably just substitute. Considering the vast industrial organization of the State of New York, for instance, with hundreds of thousands of plants and millions of wage-earners, each employer on the one hand having embarked his capital, and each employee on the other having taken up his particular mode of earning a livelihood, in reliance upon the probable permanence of an established body of law governing the relation, it perhaps may be doubted whether the State could abolish all rights of action on the one hand, or all defenses on the other, without setting up something adequate in their stead. No such question is here presented, and we intimate no opinion upon it. The statute under consideration sets aside one body of rules only to establish another system in its place. If the employee is no longer able to recover as much as before in case of being injured through the employer's negligence, he is entitled to moderate compensation in all cases of injury, and has a certain and speedy remedy without the difficulty and expense of establishing negligence or proving the amount of the damages. Instead of assuming the entire consequences of all ordinary risks of the occupation, he assumes the consequences, in excess of the scheduled compensation, of risks ordinary and extraordinary. On the other hand, if the employer is left without defense respecting the question of fault, he at the same time is assured that the recovery is limited, and that it goes directly to the relief of the designated beneficiary. And just as the employee's assumption of ordinary risks at common law presumably was taken into account in fixing the rate of wages, so the fixed responsibility of the employer, and the modified assumption of risk by the employee under the new system, presumably will be reflected in the wage scale. The act evidently is intended as a just settlement of a difficult problem, affecting one of the most important of social relations, and it is to be judged in its entirety. * * *

* * *

Much emphasis is laid upon the criticism that the act creates liability without fault. This is sufficiently answered by what has been said, but we may add that liability without fault is not a novelty in the law. The common-law liability of the carrier, of the inn-keeper, of him who employed fire or other dangerous agency or harbored a mischievous animal, was not dependent altogether upon questions of fault or negligence. Statutes imposing liability without fault have been sustained.

We have referred to the maxim *respondeat superior*. In a well-known English case, Hall v. Smith, 2 Bing. 156, 160, this maxim was said by Best, C.J., to be "bottomed on this principle, that he who expects to derive advantage from an act which is done by another for him, must answer for any injury which a third person may sustain from it." And this view has been adopted in New York. Cardot v. Barney, 63 N.Y. 281, 287. The provision for compulsory compensation, in the act under consideration, cannot be deemed to be an arbitrary and unreasonable application of the principle, so as to amount to a deprivation of the employer's property without due process of law. The pecuniary loss resulting from the employee's death or disablement must fall somewhere. It results from something done in the course of an operation from which the employer expects to derive a profit. In excluding the question of fault as a cause of the injury, the act in effect disregards the proximate cause and looks to one more remote—the primary cause, as it may be deemed—and that is, the employment itself. For this, both parties are responsible, since they voluntarily engage in it as co-adventurers, with personal injury to the employee as a probable and foreseen result. * * * And it is evident that the consequences of a disabling or fatal injury are precisely the same to the parties immediately affected, and to the community, whether the proximate cause be culpable or innocent. * * *

This, of course, is not to say that any scale of compensation, however insignificant on the one hand or onerous on the other, would be supportable. In this case, no criticism is made on the ground that the compensation prescribed by the statute in question is unreasonable in amount, either in general or in the particular case. Any question of that kind may be met when it arises.

* * *

We have not overlooked the criticism that the act imposes no rule of conduct upon the employer with respect to the conditions of labor in the various industries embraced within its terms, prescribes no duty with regard to where the workmen shall work, the character of the machinery, tools, or appliances, the rules or regulations to be established, or the safety devices to be maintained. This statute does not concern itself with measures of prevention, which presumably are embraced in other laws. But the interest of the public is not confined to these. One of the grounds of its concern with the continued life and earning power of the individual is its interest in the prevention of pauperism, with its concomitants of vice and crime. And, in our opinion, laws regulating the responsibility of employers for the injury or death of employees arising out of the employment bears so close a relation to the protection of the lives and safety of those concerned that they properly may be regarded as coming within the category of police regulations.

———

BORGNIS v. FALK CO., 147 Wis. 327, 133 N.W. 209 (1911). The Wisconsin Workmen's Compensation Law of 1911 provided for elections by employers and employees to come within its terms. The court here upheld the Law over a constitutional challenge. In discussing the occasion for such legislation, it said:

"It is matter of common knowledge that this law forms the legislative response to an emphatic, if not a peremptory, public demand. It was admitted by lawyers as well as laymen that the personal injury action brought by the employee against his employer to recover damages for injuries sustained by reason of the negligence of the employer had wholly failed to meet or remedy a great economic and social problem which modern industrialism has forced upon us, namely, the problem of who shall make pecuniary recompense for the toll of suffering and death which that industrialism levies and must continue to levy upon the civilized world. This problem is distinctly a modern problem. In the days of manual labor, the small shop with few employees, and the stage-coach, there was no such problem, or if there was it was almost negligible. Accidents there were in those days and distressing ones, but they were relatively few, and the employee who exercised any reasonable degree of care was comparatively secure from injury. There was no army of injured and dying with constantly swelling ranks marching with halting step and dimming eyes to the great hereafter. This is what we have with us now, thanks to the wonderful material progress of our age, and this is what we shall have with us for many a day to come. Legislate as we may in the line of stringent requirements for safety devices or the abolition of employers' common-law defenses, the army of the injured will still increase, the price of our manufacturing greatness will still have to be paid in human blood and tears. To speak of the common-law personal injury action as a remedy for this problem is to jest with serious subjects, to give a stone to one who asks for bread. The terrible economic waste, the overwhelming temptation to the commission of perjury, and the relatively small proportion of the sums recovered which comes to the injured parties in such actions, condemn them as wholly inadequate to meet the difficulty.

* * *

"When an eighteenth century constitution forms the charter of liberty of a twentieth century government must its general provisions be construed and interpreted by an eighteenth century mind in the light of eighteenth century conditions and ideals? Clearly not. This were to command the race to halt in its progress, to stretch the state upon a veritable bed of Procrustes.

"Where there is no express command or prohibition, but only general language or policy to be considered, the conditions prevailing at the time of its adoption must have their due weight; but the changed social, economic, and governmental conditions and ideals of the time, as well as the problems which the changes have produced, must also logically enter into the consideration, and become influential factors in the settlement of problems of construction and interpretation.

"These general propositions are here laid down not because they are considered either new or in serious controversy, but because they are believed to be peculiarly applicable to a case like the present, where a law which is framed to meet new economic conditions and difficulties resulting therefrom is attacked principally because it is believed to offend against constitutional guaranties or prohibitions couched in general terms, or supposed general policies drawn from the whole body of the instrument."

* * *

MARSHALL, J., concurring.

" * * * The difficulty here has been, want of appreciation of the great economic truth, that personal injury losses incident to industrial pursuits, as certainly as wages, are a part of the cost of production of those things essential to or proper for human consumption, and the more directly they are incorporated therein the less the enhancement of cost and the better for all.

* * *

" * * * It is needless to add that I heartily indorse all said in the court's opinion regarding the importance of the legislation which has received approval. May it be the beginning of a well rounded out constitutional system making every one who consumes any product of labor for hire pay his proportionate amount of the cost of the creation representing the personal injury misfortunes of those whose hands have enabled him to secure the objects of human desire, thus minimizing the sufferings which are the natural incidents of industry and should be borne, so far as they represent pecuniary sacrifice, by the mass of mankind whose desires are administered to by such industry."

STERTZ v. INDUSTRIAL INSURANCE COMMISSION, 91 Wash. 588, 158 P. 256 (1916). In the course of an opinion interpreting the state workmen's compensation law, the court said:

"Our act came of a great compromise between employers and employed. Both had suffered under the old system, the employers by heavy judgments of which half was opposing lawyers' booty, the workmen through the old defenses or exhaustion in wasteful litigation. Both wanted peace. The master in exchange for limited liability was willing to pay on some claims in future where in the past there had been no liability at all. The servant was willing not only to give up trial by jury but to accept far less than he had often won in court, provided he was sure to get the small sum without having to fight for it. All agreed that the blood of the workman was a cost of production, that the industry should bear the charge.

"By the working class the new legislation was craved from a horror of lawyers and judicial trials. * * *

"They knew, and both economists and progressive jurists were pointing out, what is now generally conceded, that two generations ought never to have suffered from the baleful judgments of Abinger and Shaw."

[Ed. note: Judge Shaw wrote the 1842 opinion on the fellow-servant rule in Farwell v. The Boston and Worcester Rail Road Corp., p. 530, supra. That opinion drew upon the 1837 opinion of Lord Abinger in Priestly v. Fowler, 3 Mees. & Welsb. 1.]

LARSON'S WORKER'S COMPENSATION LAW

[See p. 25, supra.]

WORKERS' COMPENSATION SCHEMES

As the foregoing historical materials show, statutory schemes for workers' compensation have been around for a long time. Today every state has a workers' compensation program. Workers' compensation stands alongside the common law of tort as a major institution of accident law. It represents an alternative approach to the problem of providing reparation to victims of physical harm. The following comments emphasize distinctive aspects of the workers' compensation model of accident reparation, plus some characteristic issues involved in the model's application.

1. *Basic Features*—Workers' compensation is a legislative approach to employment-related accidents which, within its area of operation, displaces tort law. It abolishes the tort liability of an employer to an employee for accidental injuries "arising out of" employment. It requires the employer to provide, through a process it specifies, compensation for work-related injury and death on a nonfault basis.

A workers' compensation plan can be viewed as a sort of statutory strict liability of employer to employee, comparable to strict liability in tort. But the approach of a typical plan differs significantly, in important respects, from the approach of tort law. Four main features of workers' compensation, taken together, constitute a distinctive kind of reparation system. The four features are: (a) broad coverage, (b) simplified process, (c) compensation limits, (d) insurance planning.

First, workers' compensation draws a broad circle around a large class of accidental injuries, employment-related accidents, and says that employers should provide reparation for such accidents without regard to anyone's fault. The requirement is that the employer must pay for any accidental injury to a worker "arising out of and in the course of" employment. This "arising out of" requirement is the fundamental legal norm of workers' compensation. It is meant to be a much simpler basis for awarding reparation than the liability-determining rules of tort law.

Second, workers' compensation aims to simplify process as well as substance. Costs of claiming are reduced by simplified substantive law, intended to minimize disputes, and also by relaxed procedures in case of contest. Disputed claims are resolved by examining officials who are part of the agency of state government that administers the workers' compensation program. Administrative fact-finding is relatively informal, designed to be less cumbersome and expensive than the procedures of lawyer-driven civil adjudication in common law courts.

Third, benefits paid on account of employee injury or death are limited, compared to damages for personal injury or wrongful death available in tort. In cases of nonfatal injury, tort aims to provide full reparation for the victim's medical expense, wage loss, and pain and suffering. In general, workers' compensation aims to provide full recovery of medical and rehabilitation expense, but only limited recovery of wage loss, and no recovery for pain and suffering as such. Also there is a death benefit, for surviving spouse and dependent children, covering pecuniary loss on account of an employee's death—again, in limited amount.

Fourth, workers' compensation was planned, from the beginning, as an insurance program. Employers responsible for compensation are required to maintain sufficient insurance by arrangement with qualified private liability insurers, or—in some states—by insuring with a state fund, or—in the case of larger employers—by instituting an appropriate regimen of self-insurance. Workers' compensation is a "plan" for accident reparation because the insurance mechanism for financing awards is made an integral part of the whole approach. A plan not only draws a circle around a class of accidents and says who ought to pay for them, but also makes affirmative provision to ensure that needed funds for payment of awards are regularly collected in sufficient amount.

The picture of workers' compensation just given is very sketchy. Other materials of the casebook flesh it out. But the third point—about compensation limits—needs more sustained exposition here. The model of workers' compensation is perhaps most distinctive, compared to tort, in its approach to compensation of wage loss, and to redress of so-called scheduled injuries.

2. *Wage Loss*—Consider the situation of a worker who suffers a serious nonfatal accident on the job. The worker is out of work, in the hospital and at home recuperating, for an extended period of time. Eventually the worker recovers completely, suffering no permanent impairment, and returns to the old job. This is a case of "temporary total" disability. How much of the wage loss is compensated?

The basic approach of workers' compensation schemes is to grant (after a waiting period) an award for lost earnings, paid periodically, which is limited by use of two techniques. First, a percentage of lost earnings—not 100%—is compensated. Second, the award for lost earnings is subject to an upper limit, or maximum amount. These two techniques—scale-down and maximum—produce lower awards than would be available for wage loss in tort.

There are two main methods of scaling down awards. In New York, for example, a disabled employee receives 66⅔% of his or her weekly wage. This percentage—66⅔%, applied to the basic weekly wage—is the traditional scale-down used in most states. Michigan follows the alternative approach, which is to compensate 80% of spendable earnings. In Michigan an employee's weekly wage (including overtime that would have been earned) is reduced by the amount of tax owed on the wage, and 80% of the after-tax wage loss is compensated.

New York and Michigan also use different methods to establish the maximum amount of a wage-loss award—in this respect most states are like Michigan. In New York compensation for wage loss may not exceed a weekly rate fixed (and periodically revised) by law: for 2001 the maximum benefit for disability was $400 per week. In Michigan the maximum award is set at 90% of the statewide average weekly wage: for 2001 the average wage for all employments in Michigan was calculated to be $714 per week, so the maximum weekly award (90%) was $643.

The same two techniques—scale-down and maximum—are used in compensating the most gravely injured workers, who suffer "permanent total" (as opposed to "temporary total") disability. Also workers' compensation schemes characteristically set a minimum as well as a maximum award. In Michigan, for example, the minimum award for wage loss owing to total disability is one quarter of the statewide average weekly wage. For 2001 the Michigan minimum comes out to $179: this means a low earner will receive at least $179 per week even if the usual calculation would have set an award below that figure.

(Dollar amounts given in the last two paragraphs are drawn from Commerce Clearing House (CCH), Workers' Compensation: Business Management Guide (2001).)

3. *Scheduled Injuries*—The approach of workers' compensation to a case of "permanent partial" disability is like the approach sketched above. In such a case the worker is able eventually to go back to work, but remains permanently disabled in some respect, and as a result earns less than before. Here the wage loss is the drop in pay: the difference between pre-accident

and post-accident earnings. This wage loss is characteristically compensated (a) after a scale-down, (b) subject to a maximum.

Now consider the case of a worker who is seriously injured, recovers, goes back to work and earns the same as before, but now has a permanent physical impairment. A useful distinction defines "impairment" as loss of bodily function, and "disability" as the consequent loss of earning capacity. The hypothetical worker is impaired, but not disabled: back on the job, the worker suffers no diminution of earning power. In tort, of course, the "permanent partial impairment" itself is compensable—but what about workers' compensation?

A notable feature of workers' compensation is its provision of set amounts of money for the loss of specified limbs and organs. Most states have schedules covering a number of recurrent injuries involving loss, or loss of use, of body members. The schedules say that a worker suffering a listed injury shall receive so many weeks of wage-loss benefits (calculated by application of scale-down and maximum to pre-injury earnings). In these cases wage loss is "presumed," even if the worker is in fact able to reenter the job market after recuperation. Thus a worker may receive compensation for permanent impairment going beyond economic loss. Though workers' compensation characteristically does not award reparation for pain and suffering as such, scheduled benefits in effect compensate some workers for their loss of enjoyment of life owing to a listed injury. Unlike pain and suffering awards in tort, scheduled benefits do not vary depending on personal circumstances of an injured worker. The only individuation involved is the process of fitting a particular injury into the schedule, whereupon—if the injury happens to be listed—a fixed amount of compensation ensues.

Scheduled benefits may be received as periodic payments for the number of weeks specified or, in many states, may be converted to a single lump-sum award. Most states allow payment for scheduled injuries in addition to compensation for temporary total disability; some states deduct payments for temporary disability from the scheduled award. States' schedules vary widely in generosity. Below are the maximum dollar amounts provided by a selection of states for six scheduled injuries:

	Arm at Shoulder	Hand	Thumb	Leg at Hip	One Eye	Hearing Both Ears
Calif.	108,445	58,863	5,335	65,663	21,420	58,863
Ill.	269,943	170,964	62,987	247,448	143,970	97,130
Mass.	25,183	19,912	—	22,841	22,841	45,096
Mich.	156,020	124,700	37,700	124,700	93,960	—
N.Y.	124,800	97,600	30,000	115,200	64,000	60,000

(Figures are drawn from U.S. Chamber of Commerce, 2000 Analysis of Workers' Compensation Laws, Chart VII.)

There is a conceptually ambitious alternative to the approach of the schedules, which is to relate all particular bodily impairments to a common denominator. The American Medical Association (AMA) has devised guide-lines whereby a particular sort of physical impairment can be translated into a percentage "impairment of the whole person." See American Medical Association, Guides to the Evaluation of Permanent Impairment (4th ed. 1993). According to the AMA Guides (at pp. 19–20), loss of an arm is a 60% impairment of the whole person; loss of a hand is a 54% impairment of the whole person; loss of a thumb works out to 22%. A few states have rejected detailed schedules listing a number of specific injuries and instead adopted the concept of degree of whole-person impairment. For example, Alaska's "permanent partial" provision says that a given dollar amount should be scaled downward to fit any particular loss of bodily function. The provision, Alaska Stat. § 23.30.190 (2001), reads:

> (a) In case of impairment partial in character but permanent in quality, and not resulting in permanent total disability, the compensa-tion is $177,000 multiplied by the employee's percentage of permanent impairment of the whole person. The percentage of permanent impair-ment of the whole person is the percentage of impairment to the particular body part, system, or function converted to the percentage of impairment to the whole person as provided under (b) of this section. The compensation is payable in a single lump sum * * *.

> (b) All determinations of the existence and degree of permanent impairment shall be made strictly and solely under the whole person determination as set out in the American Medical Association Guides to the Evaluation of Permanent Impairment * * *.

4. *Major Issues*—The law of workers' compensation, framed by legisla-tion and developed by courts, encounters a number of persistent problems as it tries to define the proper reach of the statutory program and its relation to tort adjudication. Five basic problems—issues, questions—are discussed in the cases of the present section following this note, and also elsewhere in the casebook.

First is the fundamental issue of coverage: what sorts of accidents are sufficiently work-connected to come within the scope of workers' compensa-tion? In the conventional phraseology, workers' compensation covers acci-dents "arising out of and in the course of employment"—but which accidents are these, and how are they known? The issue of work-connected-ness is addressed in Chapter 1, and also, briefly, below.

Second is the issue of the employer's immunity from suit in tort. Workers' compensation schemes abolish tort liability of employers to acci-dentally injured employees. But what about an employee's tort suit against the employer alleging "intentional" misconduct? And what happens to the tort claims of family members of an injured worker? The question of employer immunity is addressed in Chapter 2, and briefly below.

Third is the matter of tort suits by workers, injured on the job, against third parties, such as product manufacturers. There is no general obstacle to an employee's suit against a third party (as opposed to the employer) involved in a workplace accident. Such suits appear at various points in the casebook, particularly in Chapter 20. But what if the "third party" sued by the employee in tort is the liability insurance company which provides workers' compensation insurance for the employer? Tort liability of a workers' compensation insurer is discussed in the first main case below.

The fourth question develops when an injured employee is entitled to workers' compensation benefits from the employer, and also succeeds in establishing liability of a responsible third party for full tort damages. Should the third party end up paying the amount that otherwise would be covered by workers' compensation? Or can the third party force the employer to make contribution, despite the employer's immunity from liability in tort? The problem of coordinating tort liability and workers' compensation for the same accident is examined in the second main case below.

Fifth is the problem of health injury. In principle a worker who is exposed to a disease on the job, and so later gets sick, is just as much entitled to workers' compensation as someone who suffers a time-definite accident on the job. In practice it is much harder to get compensation for occupational disease than for a traumatic accident. The big difficulty is establishing causation of the disease by the employment, when the same illness might have been contracted from other sources. One technique for easing the burden on disease claimants is to set up a presumption that a type of disease arose out of employment, not other causes, given proof of exposure to the disease on the job. The last main case within the present section discusses the use of presumptions in the context of the federal black lung program, a special workers' compensation scheme which provides benefits for total disability or death caused by respiratory illness attributable to coal mining.

WHETRO v. AWKERMAN

[See p. 27, supra.]

CIRCLE K STORE v. INDUSTRIAL COMMISSION OF ARIZONA, 165 Ariz. 91, 796 P.2d 893 (1990). Claimant, an employee of Circle K Store, left work at the end of her shift. She deposited trash from her shift in the dumpster in Circle K's parking lot, turned to pick up her personal belongings, and fell, suffering injury. Claimant couldn't say just why she fell other than "my ankle turned." She received an award of workers' compensation benefits, pursuant to Arizona's statute which covers accidents "arising out of and in the course of" employment, but her award was overturned on review in the court of appeals. The appellate court reasoned that the phrase "in the course of" refers to the time and place of the accident in relation to the employment, while the phrase "arising out of" refers to the origin or cause of injury; that here the accident did occur "in the course of" employment, as the claimant was using a customary route from her workplace; but that since the fall was unexplained, claimant failed to prove her injuries "arose out of" employment.

The Arizona Supreme Court reinstated the award, saying: "We hold that in the case of a neutral injury, the positional-risk doctrine applies." A neutral injury is one "neither distinctly associated with the employment nor personal to claimant." According to the positional-risk doctrine,

An injury arises out of the employment if it would not have occurred but for the fact that the conditions and obligations of the employment placed claimant in the position where he was injured. * * * This theory supports compensation, for example, in cases of stray bullets, roving lunatics, and other situations in which the only connection of the employment with the injury is that its obligations placed the employee in the particular place at the particular time when he was injured * * *.

The court noted that a number of states "recognize the doctrine in Act of God cases," citing decisions involving injury by lightning and tornado, including Whetro v. Awkerman (supra at p. 27).

Under the positional-risk doctrine, "if the 'in course of' employment test is met, the injury will be presumed to 'arise out of the employment." The supreme court (Cameron, J.) explained:

" * * * In this case, claimant would not have been at the place of injury but for the duties of her employment. She was required to throw out the trash from her shift, and was performing this duty on her way home. Consequently, a presumption arises that her injuries 'arose out of' her employment. We reach our holding keeping in mind the policy of construing the Worker's Compensation Act liberally with a view of effectuating the principle of placing the burden of death and injury on the industry. In addition, because fault concepts have no bearing on whether or not worker's compensation should be awarded, an employee should not have to explain how an injury occurs, as long as it occurs in connection with her employment."

DOROSZ v. GREEN & SEIFTER, 92 N.Y.2d 672, 708 N.E.2d 162, 685 N.Y.S.2d 406 (1999). The decedent, an accountant employed by an accounting firm, suffered a fatal heart attack while bowling with a client of his employer. The decedent had regularly bowled with the client, and the two discussed business while bowling. Decedent's widow sought workers' compensation death benefits. *Held*, compensation denied. New York's workers' compensation law does not cover injury "caused by voluntary participation in an off-duty athletic activity" unless the employer "compensates" or "sponsors" the activity. "That the employer may have known of the activity, and even acquiesced in it, does not constitute overt encouragement, let alone formal sponsorship of the activity. An employee's activity * * * may confer a benefit on the employer, but that alone is not enough to justify an award * * *."

BEAUCHAMP v. DOW CHEMICAL CO.

[See p. 36, supra.]

FERRITER v. DANIEL O'CONNELL'S SONS, INC., 381 Mass. 507, 413 N.E.2d 690 (1980). A wife (and minor children) brought an action for loss of consortium and society of the husband (and father), alleging that he was seriously injured as a result of the negligence of his employer (the defendant). Defendant's principal argument was that the Workmen's Compensation Act, G.L. c. 152, barred the claims. In addressing this defense, the court said:

"In the present case, the employee not only failed to give notice that he wished to preserve his rights at common law, G.L. c. 152, § 24,[15] but he also accepted compensation payments, G.L. c. 152, § 23.[16] His waiver of rights is undisputed. However, we must decide whether his waiver bars his family from recovering against the employer at common law for damage suffered by them. We first addressed this question in King v. Viscoloid Co., [219 Mass. 420, 106 N.E. 988 (1914)], only three years after St.1911, c. 751, inserted the Workmen's Compensation Act.

"In *King*, a mother sued her son's employer for loss of the son's services and for expenses incurred in nursing and caring for him. The workmen's compensation insurer had made various payments to the son. This court upheld the mother's claim. Her right of action 'was not in any just sense consequential upon that of the son.' Id. at 422, 106 N.E. at 989. She sought redress for her own injury, not his. Furthermore, her action was distinct from the action that the son had waived under St.1911, c. 751, Part I, § 5, the progenitor of G.L. c. 152, § 24.

'[H]e had waived his right of action; but he had not waived, by his own mere act he could not waive, his parent's independent right.' *King*, supra at 422, 106 N.E. at 988.

* * *

"Rejecting the defendant's arguments, we conclude that the rule of King v. Viscoloid Co., supra, governs the present case. The Workmen's Compensation Act does not bar the plaintiffs' claims for loss of consortium and society."

[A dissenting opinion declined to recognize a spouse's or child's right to recover for loss of consortium and society "where the injury sustained by the parent-spouse was covered by the Workmen's Compensation Act."]

WEISS v. CITY OF MILWAUKEE, 208 Wis.2d 95, 559 N.W.2d 588 (1997). Holly Weiss's employer, against her wishes, gave her new address and phone number to her abusive former spouse, who then telephoned her regularly to say "he now knew her home address and * * * he would kill her and their two children." Plaintiff brought a tort suit against her employer, the City of Milwaukee, alleging negligent infliction of emotional distress (NIED). *Held*, that plaintiff's tort suit is barred because the "accident" that gave rise to injury was employment-related, and so the Worker's Compensation Act (WCA) provides the "exclusive remedy." "Weiss was required to provide her

---

15. General Laws c. 152, § 24, as amended through St.1955, c. 174, § 5, provides in pertinent part: "An employee shall be held to have waived his right of action at common law * * * to recover damages for personal injuries if he shall not have given his employer, at the time of his contract of hire, written notice that he claimed such right, or, if the contract of hire was made before the employer became an insured person or self-insurer, if the employee shall not have given the said notice within thirty days of the time said employer became an insured person or a self-insurer."

16. General Laws c. 152, § 23, as amended through St.1953, c. 314, § 6, provides: "If an employee files any claim for, or accepts payment of compensation on account of personal injury under this chapter, or makes any agreement, or submits to a hearing before a member of the division under section eight, such action shall constitute a release to the insured or self-insurer of all claims or demands at law, if any, arising from the injury."

residential information to the City as a condition of employment. That condition of employment facilitated the City's subsequent accidental release of the information * * *. We therefore conclude that the accident causing Weiss's injury arose out of her employment * * *."

The court added in a footnote: "The legal positions of the employer and employee in this instance are the reverse of those found in many worker's compensation cases. Often it is the employer who resists coverage under the WCA * * *. [T]he City invokes the WCA in this instance in order to limit Weiss's potential recovery for its allegedly wrongful disclosure of her residential information."

PRATT v. LIBERTY MUTUAL INSURANCE CO.

United States Court of Appeals, Second Circuit, 1992.
952 F.2d 667.

McLAUGHLIN, Circuit Judge:

Plaintiff injured her back while working for the Cersosimo Lumber Company. She sued Cersosimo's workers' compensation carrier, Liberty Mutual Insurance Company, in the District Court for the District of Vermont (Billings, C.J.). She alleged that Liberty Mutual undertook to conduct an active loss-prevention program at Cersosimo's facilities, but that it discharged that duty negligently, thereby causing her injuries.

After plaintiff presented her case-in-chief, Liberty Mutual moved under Fed.R.Civ.P. 50(a) for a directed verdict. The district court granted the motion and entered judgment for Liberty Mutual dismissing the complaint. Upon plaintiff's appeal, we vacated the judgment and remanded the case for reconsideration in light of the Vermont Supreme Court's intervening decision in Derosia v. Liberty Mut. Ins. Co., 155 Vt. 178, 583 A.2d 881 (1990) ["Derosia III"]. The district court reconsidered, but saw nothing in Derosia III requiring a different result. Accordingly, the district court reinstated its decision dismissing plaintiff's case. Pratt now appeals the district court's reinstatement of its decision. * * *

Cersosimo supplies wood products. Plaintiff Pratt worked at Cersosimo's Brattleboro, Vermont facility as a "manual materials handler," i.e., she lifted lumber repeatedly from a pallet and loaded it on a conveyer belt. On November 5, 1986, she injured her back while lifting and she alleges that her injuries resulted from the cumulative effect of performing this repetitive, strenuous task. Pratt maintains that her injuries could have been avoided if Cersosimo had simply installed lift tables to facilitate this arduous exercise.

Liberty Mutual issued Cersosimo's workers' compensation insurance policy and is one of the largest underwriters of such insurance in the country. Liberty Mutual advertises its services in various media, including print, radio and television. One of the major themes of Liberty's campaign is its expertise in loss prevention. It boasts that it maintains a network of safety consultants and loss prevention representatives ("LPRs") who will assist its insureds in creating a safe workplace. This program inures to the benefit of both insured and insurer in the form of lower premiums and fewer claims.

Pratt alleged that Liberty Mutual's LPRs inspected Cersosimo's facilities several times in the five years preceding November 5, 1986, when she injured her back. During this period, Liberty Mutual's LPRs concluded that manual materials handling was a major source of injuries at Cersosimo's. Pratt alleges that Liberty Mutual should therefore have gone one step further by recommending to Cersosimo that it install lift tables to assist its manual materials handlers in the strenuous and repetitive lifting their jobs required. Had Liberty Mutual so recommended, and had Cersosimo complied with this advice, Pratt maintains that she would not have been injured.

Vermont's workers' compensation statute, of course, bars Pratt from bringing a tort action against Cersosimo for maintaining an unsafe workplace. See Vt.Stat.Ann. tit. 21, § 622 (1987). The statute, however, does not bar an employee from bringing a tort action against her employer's workers' compensation insurer. See Derosia v. Duro Metal Prods. Co., 147 Vt. 410, 519 A.2d 601 (1986) ["Derosia I"]. Pratt brought such an action for negligent inspection against Liberty Mutual * * *.

* * *

We apply the law of Vermont in this diversity action and we begin with the Vermont Supreme Court's exposition in Derosia III.

Lyman Derosia cut his hand while operating a table saw on the job. He sued Liberty Mutual, his employer's workers' compensation carrier, alleging that it negligently conducted safety inspections of his employer's facilities by not insisting that the employer follow Liberty's recommendation that it use a safety blade guard on its table saws. * * *

* * *

[In Derosia III] the Vermont Supreme Court explicitly adopted Section 324A of the Restatement (Second) of Torts, which provides:

> One who undertakes, gratuitously or for consideration, to render services to another which he should recognize as necessary for the protection of a third person or his things, is subject to liability to the third person for physical harm resulting from his failure to exercise reasonable care to protect his undertaking, if
>
> (a) his failure to exercise reasonable care increases the risk of such harm, or
>
> (b) he has undertaken to perform a duty owed by the other to the third person, or
>
> (c) the harm is suffered because of reliance of the other or the third person upon the undertaking.

Restatement (Second) of Torts § 324A (1965) ["Restatement"].

Liberty Mutual argued that Derosia had not proven an undertaking by Liberty Mutual to provide safety inspection services for Derosia or his employer. The Vermont Supreme Court rejected this argument, "disagree[ing] with defendant that there was no evidence from which the jury could reasonably have concluded that defendant undertook an obligation to provide a safe workplace, notwithstanding the statements in its written contract to the contrary."

Evidence of Liberty Mutual's undertaking included testimony that it regularly inspected the company's facilities; that it proffered and pursued specific safety recommendations; that the company relied on Liberty Mutual for safety and loss prevention advice; and that Liberty Mutual held itself out as providing comprehensive loss prevention expertise for its insureds. Proof of the latter was provided by Liberty Mutual's advertisements, introduction of which was proper to "address[ ] the substantive question of whether defendant's entire course of conduct represented an undertaking to conduct an active loss-prevention program [for Derosia's employer], so that negligent performance of such undertaking might give rise to liability."

With Derosia III as our blueprint, we turn to the issues raised on this appeal.

* * *

* * * Viewing the evidence in the light most favorable to Pratt, and giving her the benefit of all reasonable inferences that may be drawn from the evidence, see 9 C. Wright & A. Miller, Federal Practice and Procedure § 2524, at 543–45 (1971), a reasonable jury could conclude that Liberty Mutual undertook to conduct an active loss prevention program at Cersosimo. Thus, the directed verdict was improper.

[In the present case] Liberty Mutual's loss-prevention activities were substantial: it maintained a sophisticated loss-prevention department; its LPRs regularly inspected the insured's facilities; and it provided recommendations for improved safety in the workplace. Indeed, Pratt introduced into evidence internal training memoranda in which Liberty Mutual acknowledged an "obligation to offer real, tangible assistance by [its] Loss Prevention Department to every policyholder." Moreover, * * * there was evidence that the insured relied on Liberty Mutual for loss-prevention expertise. At trial, individuals who had been employed by Cersosimo and Liberty Mutual testified that Cersosimo relied to some degree on Liberty Mutual for its loss prevention expertise. Finally, * * * there was evidence that Liberty Mutual identified the very risk which ultimately manifested itself, resulting in [Pratt's] injuries.

Liberty Mutual also argues that the directed verdict was required because Pratt's evidence was not sufficient to establish that Liberty Mutual's conduct was a proximate cause of her injuries. We disagree. The Vermont Supreme Court summarily rejected the same claim in Derosia III: "[o]nce the jury decided that defendant had undertaken that duty, it was free to conclude that defendant had not performed the duty with reasonable care, resulting in physical harm to plaintiff." The issue is manifestly one for the jury.

LAMBERTSON v. CINCINNATI CORP.

Supreme Court of Minnesota, 1977.
312 Minn. 114, 257 N.W.2d 679.

[Cincinnati Corp. manufactures press brakes. Hutchinson Manufacturing and Sales, Inc. bought one, and its employee (plaintiff) was injured while operating it. Plaintiff recovered workers' compensation benefits from Hutchinson, and sued Cincinnati on grounds that safety devices which could have been included in the press brake would have prevented the accident. Prior to the accident, Cincinnati had called problems in the machine to Hutchinson's attention and suggested the addition of two devices to the press brake. Hutchinson ordered neither. There was testimony that the absence of these devices "constituted defects in the machine that were causally related to this accident." Cincinnati sought contribution or indemnity from Hutchinson.]

The case was submitted to the jury on special verdict on a theory of negligence. The jury found all parties causally negligent and apportioned their comparative negligence as follows: Plaintiff—15 percent; Cincinnati—25 percent; Hutchinson—60 percent. The jury found damages of $40,000. The trial court ordered judgment against Cincinnati for $34,000, the full amount of the verdict less 15 percent for plaintiff's negligence, and denied Cincinnati's claim for contribution or indemnity from Hutchinson.

* * *

Did the trial court err in refusing to grant contribution or indemnity to Cincinnati?

* * *

* * * The essence of the controversy is this: If contribution or indemnity is allowed, the employer may be forced to pay his employee—through the conduit of the third-party tortfeasor—an amount in excess of his statutory workers' compensation liability. This arguably thwarts the central concept behind workers' compensation, i.e., that the employer and employee receive the benefits of a guaranteed, fixed-schedule, nonfault recovery system, which then constitutes the exclusive liability of the employer to his employee. See, Minn.St. 176.031. If contribution or indemnity is not allowed, a third-party stranger to the workers' compensation system is made to bear the burden of a full common-law judgment despite possibly greater fault on the part of the employer. This obvious inequity is further exacerbated by the right of the employer to recover directly or indirectly from the third party the amount he has paid in compensation regardless of the employer's own negligence. Minn.St. 176.061, subds. 5, 6(d). Thus, the third party is forced to subsidize a workers' compensation system in a proportion greater than his own fault and at a financial level far in excess of the workers' compensation schedule.

The even balance in this controversy results from conflicts among the policies underlying workers' compensation, contribution/indemnity, and comparative negligence and the fault concept of tort recovery. * * *

Despite its essential nonfault character, the workers' compensation system retains an important common-law aspect—the third-party action. See,

Minn.St. 176.061. The employee, and in some instances the employer, is allowed to bring an action against a third party who is legally responsible for the employee's injury. Such an action accomplishes two beneficial results for the workers' compensation system: (1) The at-fault third party is made to reimburse the employer who has been forced to bear the cost of the third party's activity; and (2) the employee obtains a full common-law recovery against the third party, who is not subject to the benefits and burdens of the workers' compensation system. While some states have placed the former result first in importance and have decreed that the employer must be reimbursed for all compensation benefits before the employee receives anything from a third-party judgment, Minnesota has given paramount importance to the latter object in mandating that the employee receive a third of the judgment after litigation expenses are paid and before the employer can collect compensation paid. Minn.St. 176.061, subd. 6 * * *

In summary, the interests of the respective parties in the workers' compensation system are therefore as follows: The employer has a primary interest in limiting his payment for employee injury to the workers' compensation schedule and a secondary interest in receiving reimbursement when a third party has caused him to incur obligations to his employee. The employee has a primary interest in receiving full workers' compensation benefits and, to the extent a third party has caused him injury, a common-law recovery from that third party.

In contrast, the third party's interest is that of any other cotortfeasor— to limit its liability to no more than its established fault. This interest is vindicated through contribution or indemnity. * * *

* * *

Comparative negligence, which is embodied in Minn.St. 604.01 and was substantially borrowed from our sister state of Wisconsin in 1969, introduces yet another dimension to the third-party tortfeasor's predicament. By abolishing the defense of contributory negligence in cases where plaintiff's percentage of total causal negligence is less than defendant's, it permits an injured workman to recover against the third party more frequently. In addition, Minn.St. 604.01, subd. 1, specifies a rule for contribution:

> " * * * When there are two or more persons who are jointly liable, contributions to awards shall be in proportion to the percentage of negligence attributable to each, provided, however, that each shall remain jointly and severally liable for the whole award."

Thus, a jointly liable tortfeasor has an interest, at least where the other tortfeasors are solvent and otherwise available for contribution, in contributing no more to the plaintiff's recovery than the percentage of negligence attributable to him.

* * *

Cincinnati initially seeks indemnity from Hutchinson chiefly on the ground that it offered safety devices to Hutchinson which, if installed on the press brake, could have prevented the accident. The difficulty with this argument lies in the jury's unchallenged finding that Cincinnati was 25–percent negligent in the first instance, when it placed its press brake in the stream of commerce without certain kinds of safety devices. Since the independent acts of negligent manufacture and sale by Cincinnati and refusal of safety devices by Hutchinson combined to produce plaintiff's injury, liability should be apportioned between them, not shifted entirely to one or the other. Therefore, if Cincinnati is entitled to any remedy, that remedy is contribution.

* * *

* * * The problem is discussed in Larson, Workmen's Compensation: Third Party's Action Over Against Employer, 65 Nw.U.L.Rev. 351, 419:

"* * * The question here becomes very precise: did the compensation acts, in conferring immunity on the employer from common-law suits, mean to do so only at the expense of the injured employee, or also at the expense of outsiders? One answer is that whereas the injured employee got *quid pro quo* in receiving assured compensation payments as a substitute for tort recoveries, the third party has received absolutely nothing and, hence, should not be impliedly held to have given up rights which he had before. It is unfair, so the argument runs, to pull the third party within the principle of mutual sacrifice when his part is to be all sacrifice and no corresponding gain.

"A situation like this ought to be dealt with legislatively. * * *"

* * * [W]e have found direction in the approach taken by the Pennsylvania Supreme Court. That court has allowed contribution from the employer up to the amount of the workers' compensation benefits. Maio v. Fahs, 339 Pa. 180, 14 A.2d 105 (1940); Brown v. Dickey, 397 Pa. 454, 155 A.2d 836 (1959). This approach allows the third party to obtain limited contribution, but substantially preserves the employer's interest in not paying more than workers' compensation liability. While this approach may not allow full contribution recovery to the third party in all cases, it is the solution we consider most consistent with fairness and the various statutory schemes before us. If further reform is to be accomplished, it must be effected by legislative changes in workers'-compensation-third-party law.

For the reasons expressed above, the judgment is reversed and the case is remanded with instructions to grant contribution against Hutchinson in an amount proportional to its percentage of negligence, but not to exceed its total workers' compensation liability to plaintiff.

USERY v. TURNER ELKHORN MINING CO.

Supreme Court of the United States, 1976.
428 U.S. 1, 96 S.Ct. 2882, 49 L.Ed.2d 752.

Mr. Justice MARSHALL delivered the opinion of the Court.

Twenty-two coal mine operators (Operators) brought this suit to test the constitutionality of certain aspects of Title IV of the Federal Coal Mine Health and Safety Act of 1969, as amended by the Black Lung Benefits Act of

1972. The Operators, potentially liable under the amended Act to compensate certain miners, former miners, and their survivors for death or total disability due to pneumoconiosis arising out of employment in coal mines, sought declaratory and injunctive relief against the Secretary of Labor and the Secretary of Health, Education, and Welfare, who are responsible for the administration of the Act and the promulgation of regulations under the Act.

* * *

Coal workers' pneumoconiosis—black lung disease—affects a high percentage of American coal miners with severe, and frequently crippling, chronic respiratory impairment. The disease is caused by long-term inhalation of coal dust. * * *

* * *

In order to curb the incidence of pneumoconiosis, Congress provided in Title II of the Federal Coal Mine Health and Safety Act of 1969 for limits on the amount of dust to be permitted in the ambient air of coal mines. Additionally, in view of the then-established prevalence of irreversible pneumoconiosis among miners, and the insufficiency of state compensation programs, Congress passed Title IV of the 1969 Act to provide benefits to afflicted miners and their survivors. These benefit provisions were subsequently broadened by the Black Lung Benefits Act of 1972.

* * * Under Part B of Title IV, claims filed between [1969 and 1973] are adjudicated by the Secretary of Health, Education, and Welfare and paid by the United States.

Under Part C of Title IV, claims filed after December 31, 1973, are to be processed under an applicable state workmen's compensation law approved by the Secretary of Labor * * *. In the absence of such an approved state program, and to date no state program has been approved, claims are to be filed with and adjudicated by the Secretary of Labor, and paid by the mine operators. * * *

* * *

* * * The Act * * * prescribes several "presumptions" for use in determining compensable disability. * * * [A] miner shown by X-ray or other clinical evidence to be afflicted with complicated pneumoconiosis is "irrebuttably presumed" to be totally disabled due to pneumoconiosis; if he has died, it is irrebuttably presumed that he was totally disabled by pneumoconiosis at the time of his death, and that his death was due to pneumoconiosis. * * *

The other presumptions are each explicitly rebuttable by an operator seeking to avoid liability. There are three such presumptions. First, if a miner with 10 or more years' employment in the mines contracts pneumoconiosis, it is rebuttably presumed that the disease arose out of such employment. Second, if a miner with 10 or more years' employment in the mines died from a "respirable disease", it is rebuttably presumed that his death was due to pneumoconiosis. Finally, if a miner * * * with 15 or more years' employment in underground coal mines is able, despite the absence of clinical evidence of complicated pneumoconiosis, to demonstrate a totally disabling respiratory or pulmonary impairment, the Act rebuttably presumes that the total disability is due to pneumoconiosis * * *. [N]one of these three rebuttable presumptions may be defeated solely on the basis of a chest X-ray.

In initiating this suit against the defendant Secretaries (hereafter Federal Parties), the Operators contended that the amended Act is unconstitutional insofar as it requires the payment of benefits with respect to miners who left employment in the industry before the effective date of the Act; [and] that the Act's definitions, presumptions, and limitations on rebuttal evidence unconstitutionally impair the operators' ability to defend against benefit claims * * *.

* * *

The Operators contend that the amended Act violates the Fifth Amendment Due Process Clause by requiring them to compensate former employees who terminated their work in the industry before the Act was passed, and the survivors of such employees. The Operators accept the liability imposed upon them to compensate employees working in coal mines now and in the future who are disabled by pneumoconiosis * * *. But the Operators complain that to impose liability upon them for former employees' disabilities is impermissibly to charge them with an unexpected liability for past, completed acts that were legally proper and, at least in part, unknown to be dangerous at the time.

It is by now well established that legislative Acts adjusting the burdens and benefits of economic life come to the Court with a presumption of constitutionality * * *.

* * * [O]ur cases are clear that legislation readjusting rights and burdens is not unlawful solely because it upsets otherwise settled expectations. * * *

It does not follow, however, that what Congress can legislate prospectively it can legislate retrospectively. The retrospective aspects of legislation, as well as the prospective aspects, must meet the test of due process, and the justifications for the latter may not suffice for the former. Thus * * * we would * * * hesitate to approve the retrospective imposition of liability on any theory of deterrence, or blameworthiness.

We find, however, that the imposition of liability for the effects of disabilities bred in the past is justified as a rational measure to spread the costs of the employees' disabilities to those who have profited from the fruits of their labor—the operators and the coal consumers. The Operators do not challenge Congress' power to impose the burden of past mine working conditions on the industry. They do claim, however, that the Act spreads costs in an arbitrary and irrational manner by basing liability upon past employment relationships, rather than taxing all coal mine operators presently in business. * * *

* * * [I]t is for Congress to choose between imposing the burden of inactive miners' disabilities on all operators, including new entrants and

farsighted early operators who might have taken steps to minimize black lung dangers, or to impose that liability solely on those early operators whose profits may have been increased at the expense of their employees' health. We are unwilling to assess the wisdom of Congress' chosen scheme by examining the degree to which the "cost-savings" enjoyed by operators in the pre-enactment period produced "excess" profits, or the degree to which the retrospective liability imposed on the early operators can now be passed on to the consumer. It is enough to say that the Act approaches the problem of cost spreading rationally; whether a broader cost-spreading scheme would have been wiser or more practical under the circumstances is not a question of constitutional dimension.

* * *

We turn next to a consideration of the Operators' challenge to the "presumptions" and evidentiary rules governing adjudications of compensable disability under the Act.

* * *

[The Court upheld all the statutory presumptions. Under the three rebuttable presumptions, conclusions are based on duration of employment—two presumptions arise given 10 years employment as a coal miner, and another arises given 15 years. As to the durational presumptions the Court said:]

* * * The Operators focus their attack on the rationality of the presumptions' bases in duration of employment. But it is agreed here that pneumoconiosis is caused by breathing coal dust, and that the likelihood of a miner's developing the disease rests upon both the concentration of dust to which he was exposed and the duration of his exposure. Against this scientific background, it was not beyond Congress' authority to refer to exposure factors in establishing a presumption that throws the burden of going forward on the operators. And in view of the medical evidence before Congress indicating the noticeable incidence of pneumoconiosis in cases of miners with 10 years' employment in the mines, we cannot say that it was "purely arbitrary" for Congress to select the 10–year figure as a point of reference for these presumptions. No greater mathematical precision is required.

The Operators insist, however, that the 10–year presumptions are arbitrary, because they fail to account for varying degrees of exposure, some of which would pose lesser dangers than others. We reject this contention. In providing for a shifting of the burden of going forward to the operators, Congress was no more constrained to require a preliminary showing of the degree of dust concentration to which a miner was exposed, a historical fact difficult for the miner to prove, than it was to require a preliminary showing with respect to all other factors that might bear on the danger of infection. * * *

The Operators press the same due process attack upon the durational basis of the rebuttable presumption * * * which provides * * * that a miner employed for 15 years in underground mines, who is able to marshal evidence demonstrating a totally disabling respiratory or pulmonary impairment, shall be rebuttably presumed to be totally disabled by pneumoconiosis. Particularly in light of the Surgeon General's testimony at the Senate hearings on the 1969 Act to the effect that the 15–year point marks the beginning of linear increase in the prevalence of the disease * * *, we think it clear that the durational basis of this presumption is equally unassailable.

The Operators also challenge [the provision] that "no claim for benefits * * * shall be denied solely on the basis of the results of a chest roentgenogram [X-ray]." * * * The Operators contend * * * that * * * X-ray evidence is frequently the sole evidence they can marshal to rebut a claim of pneumoconiosis. We conclude that, given Congress' reasoned reservations regarding the reliability of negative X-ray evidence, it was entitled to preclude exclusive reliance on such evidence.

Congress was presented with significant evidence demonstrating that X-ray testing that fails to disclose pneumoconiosis cannot be depended upon as a trustworthy indicator of the absence of the disease. In particular, the findings of the Surgeon General and others indicated that * * * autopsy frequently disclosed pneumoconiosis where X-ray evidence had disclosed none; and that pneumoconiosis may be masked from X-ray detection by other disease.

Taking these indications of the unreliability of negative X-ray diagnosis at face value, Congress was faced with the problem of determining which side should bear the burden of the unreliability. * * * [R]eliance on uncorroborated negative X-ray evidence would risk the denial of benefits in a significant number of meritorious cases. * * *

* * * That Congress ultimately determined "to resolve doubts in favor of the disabled miner" does not render the enactment arbitrary under the standard of rationality appropriate to this legislation.

SECTION B. AUTO NO–FAULT PLANS

This section proceeds in three stages. The materials investigate, in sequence, three topics having to do with motoring accidents: (1) shortcomings of tort adjudication, (2) architecture of auto plans, (3) policy objectives and practical effects of no-fault plans.

Shortcomings of the tort system, as seen by advocates of auto no-fault, are summed up in the initial items of the section. Here "the tort system" refers both to negligence doctrines used by courts to decide cases involving motoring accidents, and to liability insurance which pays reparation on behalf of motorists deemed negligent. Central to the critique of tort is the finding that, out of a dollar spent on auto liability insurance, the amount paid out as compensation for injury is in the neighborhood of 44 cents.

The architecture of a compulsory auto no-fault plan is distinctively different from that of workers' compensation. The typical plan abolishes tort for claims below a specified "threshold" (some dollar amount of loss or described level of injury), but preserves tort for claims above the stated cut-off point. Below the threshold, economic loss is compensated without regard to fault by the no-fault plan; above it, tort suits based on negligence proceed, and tort damages for pain and suffering may be obtained. The crucial question of legal engineering, then, is how to formulate the threshold: how high should it be?

FINANCIAL RESPONSIBILITY FOR NEGLIGENT DRIVING

In the period before 1970, the year in which Massachusetts enacted the first auto no-fault statute, liability for unintended injuries from the operation of motor vehicles was based generally on negligence. Within the framework of negligence doctrine, statutory changes of rules determining liability in motor vehicles cases were common. Guest statutes are an example. Comparative negligence statutes are another example. They have much broader application than merely to motor vehicle cases, but most of the impetus for their enactment came from dissatisfaction with the results reached in the large body of cases based on motor vehicle injuries.

Another type of statutory development was aimed at making certain that in a maximum number of cases there would be available a solvent defendant against whom the victim might press a claim for damages, at least up to a moderate figure. This type of statute—generally referred to as "financial responsibility legislation"—did not attack the doctrine of negligence as the basis for liability, but it substantially improved the victim's chances of obtaining compensation.

The most stringent form of financial responsibility legislation is "compulsory" in the sense that no vehicle can be registered without a showing of minimum financial responsibility (usually made by filing a certificate of automobile liability insurance).

Statutes requiring liability insurance for the operation of particular vehicles, such as those of public carriers, were common, but, in the 1970's only a few states had compulsory insurance provisions of general application. All other states and the District of Columbia had some other form of motor vehicle financial responsibility legislation. The most favored type was a Safety–Responsibility Act. Such legislation required in specified circumstances that a driver, in order to avoid revocation of driving privileges, (1) give "proof" (usually a certificate of insurance) of financial responsibility to cover future accidents and (2) deposit "security" for payment of damages arising from a past accident.

Another type of legislation was aimed at closing the gap in financial responsibility that remained because Safety–Responsibility Acts and even compulsory insurance acts did not assure that the victims of negligent driving would have financially responsible persons in sight as potential defendants. The first legislation of this type was called an Unsatisfied Judgment Fund Act. This type of act provided for accumulation of a state fund from sources including automobile registration fees and levies against insurers of a percentage of their premiums on automobile insurance. A person who had an unsatisfied judgment in excess of a minimum figure (e.g., $200) for damages arising from a motor vehicle accident could apply to the court for an order directing payment out of the fund, subject to limits and terms comparable to those of an insurance policy issued in compliance with a Safety–Responsibility Act. These acts had provisions for benefits to victims of hit-and-run accidents also.

Beyond statutes such as these, voluntary developments within the insurance industry aided in closing the gap in assurance to victims that legal responsibility would be backed up by financial responsibility. One such development produced an insurance coverage now called uninsured motorist coverage. Within its limits and conditions, it protects the named insured (and usually other members of the household as well) against loss from inability to collect a valid claim against an uninsured motorist. This coverage is now available in most states on a voluntary basis, at an annual charge of only a few dollars, and in many states there are statutes requiring its inclusion in each policy issued, with few exceptions.

Since 1939, Medical Payments coverage, providing for payments regardless of fault, has been offered by automobile liability insurers, and revisions of standard policy forms in intervening years have gradually improved this coverage. It applies only to medical and hospital expenses, however, and it is customarily written in rather small amounts.

DATA ON THE "NEGLIGENCE–WITH–LIABILITY– INSURANCE" COMPENSATION SYSTEM

The first major empirical inquiry into the practical performance of the negligence system was the Columbia Study. Perhaps the most striking findings were these: (1) when there was liability insurance, some payment was made in 87 per cent of the cases involving fairly serious personal injury; (2) victims with relatively slight injuries were paid quickly and in amounts many times greater than their losses; (3) those with more serious injuries were severely underpaid and ordinarily only after long delay.[1] Later studies have repeatedly confirmed this general pattern.[2]

In 1964 Professor Conard and his colleagues published their report of the Michigan Study[3]—a more thorough and extensive empirical inquiry than any of those that had preceded it. To a much greater extent than before, the Michigan Study developed a picture of the increasing importance of nontort sources of compensation. They found that compensation from nontort sources had risen to the point of being about half of the total compensation received by traffic victims.[4]

1. Columbia University Council for Research in the Social Sciences, Report by the Committee to Study Compensation for Automobile Accidents (1932). See Report and Appendix, particularly data at 261, 264, 269, from which the figure of 87 per cent was computed, as explained in R. Keeton & J. O'Connell, Basic Protection for the Traffic Victim 35, n. 88 (1965).

2. James & Law, Compensation for Auto Accident Victims: A Story of Too Little and Too Late, 26 Conn.B.J. 70 (1952); Morris & Paul, The Financial Impact of Automobile Accidents, 110 U.Pa.L.Rev. 913 (1962).

3. Conard, Morgan, Pratt, Voltz & Bombaugh, Automobile Accident Costs and Payments—Studies in the Economics of Injury Reparation (1964) [Hereinafter cited as Conard et al.]

4. Id. at 147, 174.

The data developed in this study also showed a greater gap in tort compensation than might have been expected on the basis of the earlier studies.[5] Of 86,120 who suffered economic loss in automobile accidents involving personal injury, only 77 per cent received compensation from any source.[6] Only 37 per cent received something from a tort claim.[7]

A Department of Transportation study released in 1970 disclosed the continued existence of a very substantial gap between economic losses from automobile accidents and total compensation from all sources.[8] According to this study compensation from all sources amounted to only $2.5 billion of $5.1 billion in out-of-pocket losses resulting from 1967 accidents involving deaths or serious bodily injuries, and of the $2.5 billion compensation, only $1.1 billion came from automobile insurance.[9]

The data developed through these and other studies—including data published in 1968 from a study executed within a segment of the insurance industry, the American Insurance Association (AIA)[10]—made it possible to calculate where the premium dollar was going. The combined data revealed the stunning fact that, of the premium dollar collected for automobile bodily injury liability insurance, the part paid net to victims in compensation for out-of-pocket losses not already compensated from other sources amounted to only 14½ cents.[11] The distribution of the entire premium dollar is shown in the pie chart below.

5. For a comparison of the findings of the different studies in some detail, see Basic Protection for the Traffic Victim 49–64.

6. Conard et al. at 138, 139.

7. Id. at 139, 149.

8. Economic Consequences of Automobile Accident Injuries, Report of the Westat Research Corp., vols. I, II (1970).

9. Id., vol. I, at 40, 118, 145–147.

10. AIA, Report of Special Committee to Study and Evaluate the Keeton–O'Connell Basic Protection Plan and Automobile Accident Reparations 13–16 (1968).

11. The principal sources of data relied upon in making this computation were the following: the American Insurance Association Cost Study, reported in this Section supra; the Michigan Study of Conard and his colleagues, discussed in this Section supra; Harwayne, Automobile Basic Protection Costs Evaluated (1968); and Harwayne, Insurance Costs of Basic Protection Plan in Michigan, 1967 U.Ill.L.Forum 479 (1967), also published in Crisis in Car Insurance 119. See also N.Y. Ins. Dept. Report 34–37 (1970).

Where the Automobile Bodily Injury Liability
Insurance Premium Dollar Goes

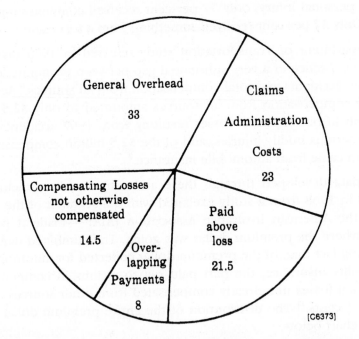

The Report of the Columbia Study presented a proposal for a system of compulsory accident insurance, closely analogous to employee compensation insurance. It would have completely eliminated the application of negligence law and negligence liability insurance to automobile accident cases. This proposal remained the center of controversy over reform of the negligence system for about two decades. As hopes for enactment of the Columbia proposal waned, however, the search for a viable alternative to negligence law continued. Public controversy over proposals for reforming the automobile accident reparations system intensified in the late 1960's and led to the publication of many additional plans and proposals.

STANDARDS FOR NO–FAULT MOTOR VEHICLE
ACCIDENT BENEFITS ACT

Senate Committee on Commerce, Science, and Transportation,
S. Rep. No. 95–975, 95th Cong., 2d Sess. (1978).

[This Report accompanied S. 1381, a bill to provide basic standards to be met by state no-fault motor vehicle acts. The Committee reported favorably thereon, but S. 1381 was not enacted.]

THE NEED FOR AUTO ACCIDENT REFORM

The tort liability system on which automobile accident insurance is based in the majority of States is an unfair and ineffective means for compensating automobile accident victims. In order to recover benefits, a victim must first identify and show that another driver was at fault. (There will be no compensation if the accident involves only one vehicle.) Second, a victim must show that he or she was without fault or less at fault than the other driver. Third, the victim must obtain a settlement or prevail in a lawsuit. Fourth, the party at fault must have sufficient insurance or other financial resources to pay for the victim's loss.

Not surprisingly, fewer than 50 percent of motor vehicle accident victims meet all these prerequisites and recover benefits under the fault system. The others are left to their own financial resources, or other insurance, *even though they have purchased automobile insurance.* Some victims even become dependent on Federal or State assistance.

The committee believes that such a system is inadequate, and should be replaced by a no-fault insurance system. A no-fault insurance system for the compensation of automobile accident victims will assure victims substantial benefits in a more timely manner, will provide a more efficient accident compensation system, and will reduce court burdens. These advantages are possible without increasing the costs of automobile insurance premiums and without disturbing the actual provisions of or philosophy behind the McCarran–Ferguson Act, which makes the regulation of insurance a state responsibility.

Sixteen States have enacted some form of no-fault insurance;* however, most of the plans provide for inadequate benefits or do not sufficiently restrict tort lawsuits, causing increases in insurance costs. * * *

1. *The Fault–Liability System Is an Unfair and Ineffective Means for Compensating Auto Accident Victims*

The deficiencies of the fault system are well documented. Seven years ago, the Department of Transportation completed a comprehensive $2 million study[3] of the present tort liability system of compensation for automobile accident victims. Highlights of that study illustrate graphically the shortcomings of the existing system:

(a) Inefficiency.—Consumers, who buy automobile accident insurance receive back an average of only 44 cents for each dollar paid into the system in the form of benefits to compensate for injuries. This ratio of return for auto insurance compares to a benefit return of 70 to 90 percent for other insurance systems such as private health insurance, workmen's compensation, and social security—all of which are no-fault systems. Twenty-seven percent of all claims dollars paid to auto accident victims go to lawyers.

(b) Inadequacy of compensation.—Hundreds of thousands of accident victims suffer uncompensated loss, either because they are found to be partially negligent or because the other party either had no insurance or had inadequate insurance. Only 45 percent of the seriously injured victims recovered *anything* from the tort system. Of that 45 percent who did recover, more than 25 percent recovered less than one-half of their economic loss. In all, 53 percent of the innocent victims entitled to recover under

---

* [Eds.] Since publication of the Committee Report, there have been both repeals and enactments of no-fault laws. The chart on p. 1187, infra, summarizes the enacted laws as of 1996.

3. Motor Vehicle Crash Losses and Their Compensation in the United States (DOT 1971).

the fault system recovered less than their total economic loss and absolutely nothing for intangible loss, such as pain and suffering.

(c) Unfair and unreasonable distribution of benefits.—The tort system unfairly overcompensates victims with less serious injuries and compensates the more seriously injured victims inadequately or not at all. Where out-of-pocket victim losses are under $500, a victim recovers an average of 4.5 times his economic losses. These distorted settlements result from the dynamics of the tort-liability insurance system. Small claims are overcompensated because settlement is cheaper than the cost of litigating these claims. In contrast, where losses are $25,000 or more, even successful tort claimants average a net recovery of only about one-third of their out-of-pocket loss, because in cases of large losses, insurers can attempt to induce lower settlements and can delay the case until the insured is so financially strapped that he will accept a less than adequate amount.

(d) Unreasonable delay.—Seriously injured victims are required to wait an average of 16 months to settle their claims. This lengthy settlement time imposes an economic hardship upon the accident victim.

More importantly, the delay frequently poses a medical hardship because lack of settlement may mean necessary rehabilitation cannot be started. Failure to begin rehabilitation promptly frequently means there will not be a chance for complete physical recovery.

In addition, the internal dynamics of the tort negligence system encourage victims to remain disabled for possible jury appearance until the most favorable possible settlement or verdict can be achieved. By that time, it is generally too late for rehabilitation to help the person involved.

(e) Excessive court use.—Auto accident litigation consumes 17% of the U.S. court system's resources. This burden results in excessive delay not only for auto accident claims but other civil claims and serious criminal cases as well.

* * *

2. The Requirements of an Effective Auto Accident Compensation System

There are two basic requirements for an adequate bodily injury automobile accident compensation system:

* It should compensate all insured accident victims for their basic economic loss, including expenses for medical and rehabilitation care and lost wages, in order to prevent victims and their families from experiencing the financial hardship, delay and uncertainty that are inherent in the fault system.

* It should maximize the return of premium dollars to injured victims in order to provide adequate compensation for their losses in the most efficient, effective, and inexpensive manner.

* * *

ROGER C. HENDERSON, NO–FAULT INSURANCE
FOR AUTOMOBILE ACCIDENTS
56 Oregon Law Review 287 (1977).*

* * *

Massachusetts was the first state to enact no-fault automobile insurance. Since this landmark legislation, effective January 1, 1971, there have been twenty-three more no-fault automobile insurance statutes passed in the United States. In addition to the variety of plans passed by the state legislatures, other plans are being considered, including some by Congress and by states which have already passed no-fault legislation.

Although the enacted and proposed plans vary considerably in detail as well as basic structure, patterns have emerged. At least with regard to compensation schemes for bodily injury, the no-fault plans that have been enacted and that are being proposed can be grouped into three basic categories. The first category has been denominated "add-on" plans, the second "modified" plans, and the third "pure" no-fault plans.

A.　ADD–ON PLANS

The first category includes those plans that merely require that additional coverages be provided in standard automobile liability insurance policies. These plans are generally referred to as add-on plans because they merely add to the present tort-liability insurance system and do not abolish tort liability. Automobile insurance, in states without no-fault, typically includes tort liability, collision, comprehensive, medical payments, and uninsured motorist coverage. Add-on no-fault insurance provides increased benefits for medical and related expenses, and offers new benefits for lost wages and for loss of essential services that do not produce income. A few of the add-on plans include a life insurance benefit in the event of death. These additional coverages are no-fault coverages like the present collision, comprehensive, and medical payments coverages, but are limited to damages arising from bodily injury. Of the twenty-four states which have enacted no-fault automobile insurance plans, eight have add-on type schemes.**

Add-on plans can be subcategorized into three groups. The first group includes those plans that require any insurance company writing automobile liability insurance in the state to offer these additional coverages to anyone purchasing a standard automobile liability insurance policy. The automobile owner has the option either to buy or reject the additional coverages, just as he or she may do today with collision, comprehensive, medical payments, and, in some states, uninsured motorist coverage. * * *

A second group of add-on plans consists of those plans that require the additional coverages to be included in any automobile liability insurance policy sold or issued for delivery in the enacting state; when one buys the

---

* Reprinted by permission. Copyright ©1977 by University of Oregon.

** [Eds.] Since the publication of this article, there have been several changes in no-fault laws.

See the chart on p. 1187, infra, for the enacted laws as of 2001.

policy the additional no-fault coverages are automatically included as part of the package. * * * [T]his kind of plan * * * is referred to as mandatory add-on no-fault insurance. One is not required to buy an automobile liability insurance policy under the laws of these states, but if a policy is purchased one has no choice and receives the additional no-fault coverages.

The third group includes those plans that require that the additional coverages must not only be included in every automobile liability insurance policy sold or issued for delivery in the enacting state, but also that one must purchase the policy before he or she can legally operate an automobile on the highways of that state. This type of law is referred to as compulsory add-on no-fault insurance * * *.

No-fault coverage in the add-on plans ranges from $1,000 to about $15,000. The add-on coverages also are sometimes conditioned on the loss being incurred within a certain time from the date of the accident, for example, within one year.

Under add-on plans there is no change in the existing legal system which determines when one may or may not successfully sue or be sued in tort for personal injury or property damage resulting from the operation or use of a motor vehicle. Before or after collecting the additional no-fault benefits, a person is free to pursue his or her claim under the fault-based tort system, subject to any rights of setoff, reimbursement, or subrogation on behalf of the no-fault insurer.

B. Modified Plans

The second basic category of plans is referred to as the modified no-fault plan, and differs from the add-on plans in its elimination of some of the present tort-liability insurance system for bodily injury. When injured in an automobile accident the victim receives, from the additional no-fault coverages under the modified plans, benefits which are similar in type but in some instances much larger in dollar amounts than those provided in the add-on plans. The victim, however, is limited to some extent in his or her right to sue the tortfeasor under the rules of law pertaining to negligence. He or she is also free, usually to the same extent, from being sued.

Modified no-fault plans can be broken down into two groups, depending upon the extent to which different kinds of damages under the tort-liability insurance system are abolished. The plans in the first group limit one's right to sue in tort for general damages. One is still able to sue for any economic loss suffered as a result of an automobile accident, but the right to sue for pain and suffering and similar damages is limited. Typically, the limitation placed on the recovery for noneconomic losses applies only in cases of less than serious injury. This is accomplished through the use of techniques called "thresholds."

The modified plans generally use one or both of two types of thresholds. The first type of threshold relates to the amount of medical expense that one incurs as a result of the accident. The second type describes certain injuries for which a cause of action for pain and suffering is retained. Thus, the right to sue for general damages is eliminated in cases in which the medical expenses do not exceed a certain figure, for example, $500, or do not meet narrative thresholds which attempt to delineate certain serious injuries, for example, death, permanent serious disfigurement, fracture, or loss of body function. Conversely, where the medical expense threshold or a narrative threshold is met there is no limitation and one can still sue in tort for the full amount of general damages suffered.

As mentioned, these plans do not involve any limitations or restriction on the tort cause of action for economic loss such as loss of earnings or medical expenses. A right of subrogation or reimbursement is usually provided for the no-fault insurer so as to adhere to the principle of indemnity by preventing the insured from collecting twice for the same economic loss. * * *

The second group of modified no-fault insurance plans includes those plans that not only limit one's right to recover general damages in the minor or less than serious personal injury cases, but also eliminate the right to sue or be sued in tort for economic loss to the extent that one is entitled to collect no-fault benefits. Each insured injured party collects for economic loss from his or her own insurance carrier up to the limits provided, and to that extent the cause of action for negligence against the other motorist is abolished. A cause of action is retained for any economic loss above the amount compensated by no-fault benefits. * * * All of the plans falling in both types make the additional no-fault insurance coverages compulsory, save Kentucky.

C. Plans Approaching Pure No–Fault

The third basic category includes plans which more nearly approach what has been termed pure no-fault insurance. A pure no-fault insurance plan would eliminate entirely the negligence system as the basis for compensating traffic victims for bodily injury and substitute a comprehensive insurance scheme in its stead. None of the plans that have been included in the third category goes this far, but they do provide for much more extensive compulsory no-fault benefits and abolition of tort liability than the modified no-fault plans described above. For this reason they deserve to be distinguished; they constitute a more definite decision to favor the compensation of traffic accident victims without regard to negligence. Like most modified no-fault plans, they make the additional no-fault coverages compulsory. New York and Michigan have moved furthest towards abolishing the negligence system and substituting no-fault insurance. Neither, however, has gone as far as the Uniform Motor Vehicle Accident Reparations Act (UMVARA), although much of the language and basic structure of the New York and Michigan laws are taken from the Uniform Act.

The New York law provides up to $50,000 of no-fault benefits for most personal injury losses suffered as a result of a motor vehicle accident, and abolishes to the same extent causes of action for pecuniary losses arising from the negligent operation of a motor vehicle. Death cases are not covered by the New York plan.

The Michigan law provides for unlimited reimbursement of medical losses and up to $1,000 per month for three years for other specific categories of economic loss.[33] It too abolishes negligence actions for economic loss to the extent no-fault benefits are payable. The Michigan plan is designed to eliminate all causes of action for general damages except those involving especially serious injury. Thus, the plan abolishes the great majority of causes of action arising out of the ownership, maintenance, or use of motor vehicles which previously have been based on negligence concepts. It represents a shift to a different system of compensating traffic accident victims.

D. FEDERAL LEGISLATION

In addition to the activity in state legislatures, Congress has become increasingly interested in the problem of automobile accident reparations. In 1974 the United States Senate passed the National No–Fault Motor Vehicle Insurance Act (S. 354), which is patterned after UMVARA. This legislation would have required the states to meet minimum federal standards by a certain date. The House of Representatives, however, failed to act on no-fault insurance during 1974 and the Senate bill died with the adjournment of the 93d Congress.

* * *

E. NO–FAULT FOR PROPERTY DAMAGE

While most legislation has been directed primarily at the problem of compensating victims of bodily injury, there also has been movement in the area of tort liability for property damage. * * *

* * *

Although there are cogent arguments for adopting no-fault for damage to motor vehicles, the concept has never been embraced by the insurance industry. * * * [T]he concept has not fared well in court challenges and, moreover, after five years of turmoil, Massachusetts recently repealed its statute, returning damage to motor vehicles to the tort-liability insurance system. What all this portends is not clear. * * *

* * *

---

33. The income loss benefits, one of the specified categories of economic loss, have increased under the statutory cost-of-living provision from the original $1,000 per month to a current level of $1,285. Mich.Comp.Laws Ann. § 500.3107(b) (Supp.1976–1977). Potential aggregate income loss benefits per person have therefore risen from $36,000 to $46,260, an increase of 29 percent, since the act went into effect on October 1, 1973. * * *

ENACTED NO–FAULT LAWS AND UMVARA (2001)

Plan	Tort Threshold For Bodily Injury*	Approximate Bodily Injury No–Fault Benefits "Cap"		
		Medical	Wage	Combined
Arkansas	_____	5,000	7,280	
Colorado	medium	50,000	20,800	
Delaware	_____			15,000
District of Columbia[1]	high	50,000	12,000	
Florida	high			10,000
Hawaii	medium	10,000	10,000	
Kansas	medium	4,500	10,800	
Maryland	_____			2,500
Massachusetts	medium		2,000	8,000
Michigan	high	no cap	36,000	
Minnesota	medium	20,000	20,000	
New Jersey[2]	high (option a)	15,000	5,200	
	_____ (option b)	15,000	5,200	
New York	high			50,000
North Dakota	medium			30,000
Oregon	_____	10,000	15,000	
Pennsylvania[3]	_____	5,000	5,000	
Puerto Rico	low	no cap	7,800	
Utah	medium	3,000	13,000	
Virginia	_____	2,000	5,200	
UMVARA	very high	no cap	no cap	no cap

Source: Based on descriptions of state statutes in 4 I. Schermer & W. Schermer, *Automobile Liability Insurance* (3d ed. Supp. 2001).

* This column classifies no-fault statutes according to the threshold which must be reached before an accident victim can sue in tort to recover damages for pain and suffering. Statutes without a threshold—that is, add-on statutes—are designated by a dash. "Low" statutes include a dollar threshold of $1,000 or less. "Medium" statutes include a dollar threshold of more than $1,000 (and less than $10,000). "High" statutes have a verbal threshold of serious injuries and/or a dollar threshold over $10,000. The "very high" UMVARA has no dollar threshold but rather a verbal threshold of severe injury.

The add-on plans listed on the table are all (in the terms of Henderson's article, supra) "mandatory" or "compulsory," rather than "optional." In addition, Kentucky, Texas, and Washington have optional add-on laws, which require insurers to offer no-fault coverage but give insured drivers the option of declining such coverage. Some states (Hawaii, New Jersey, Pennsylvania) with non-optional no-fault coverage likewise require insurers to offer higher coverage but give drivers the option of declining.

1. The District of Columbia accident victim must elect within 60 days whether or not to accept no-fault benefits. The "high" threshold assumes acceptance.

2. New Jersey drivers can elect to buy less expensive (option a) or more expensive (option b) no-fault insurance. Those who buy less expensive insurance are subject to a high threshold; buyers of the more expensive insurance are not subject to a threshold.

3. Pennsylvania drivers can elect no-fault coverage that comes with a "medium" threshold.

A PRAGMATIC JUSTIFICATION OF AUTO NO–FAULT

[Ed. note: What follows is an attempt to state in summary form major arguments and assessments advanced in public debate in support of the no-fault approach to auto accidents, as compared to the system of fault plus liability insurance. The line of advocacy sketched below aims to make out a case for reform that is pragmatic, eclectic, and empirical in character. Readers should consider whether the case succeeds in light of its own aims and in light of pertinent principles of legal and moral justification.]

1. *Fault Adjudication*—Imposing liability on the basis of negligence inflicts a penalty for fault fortuitously on those who happen to be unlucky enough that their negligence causes loss, while others whose conduct is similar are lucky enough to escape having an accident. Similarly, denying benefits because of contributory fault or on the theory of unavoidable accident inflicts the penalty for fault fortuitously on those who happen to be unlucky—but worse still, most severely on those who happen to be unlucky enough to be severely injured though slightly at fault. Making rights to compensation depend on fault in these ways forces an arbitrary gamble on drivers rather than sensibly and fairly fixing legal consequences commensurate with fault. If real equity according to fault is the objective, would it not be better to seek it through insurance rating than through rules basing rights to compensation on negligence and contributory negligence?

Arguments about whether the fault criterion of modern negligence law can be realistically applied to automobile accidents have produced two sets of very different illustrations.

One set is concerned with accidents in which plainly innocent victims (such as the pedestrian who is on the sidewalk when struck by a car) are injured by plainly blameworthy driving (such as driving while intoxicated). One who gives attention only to this set of cases is likely to conclude that negligence law can be realistically applied and that justice requires that negligence be taken into account either as a basis for awards or as a basis for higher premium charges to negligent drivers.

The second set of illustrations concerns accidents of a very different nature. One example is an intersection collision occurring under circumstances such that determining who had the right of way depends on unreliable reconstruction of relative speeds, distances and movements of vehicles during a time interval of only seconds. Another example is an expressway pile-up injuring a dozen people and damaging two dozen cars. One who gives attention only to cases such as these is likely to conclude that negligence law is out of touch with reality.

Probably the automobile accidents to which negligence law can be faithfully and realistically applied are fewer than those for which it is an unrealistic criterion. Moreover, the settlement process tends to dispose of cases in which fault can be readily determined, leaving for trial a disproportionately high percentage of those cases in which the negligence criterion is at its worst.

This tendency of the system to select for trial the cases to which it is least well adapted would not be remedied by shifting from jury trial to some other form of adjudication. The answer, instead, is to change the criterion of liability.

Is it reasonable to make such a change of criterion for cases of less than severe injury only, as no-fault laws with strong tort exemptions do? It is commonly reported that in a high percentage of death cases one or more persons (drivers or pedestrians) were under the influence of alcohol. In cases of less than severe injury, the percentage involving intoxication is much lower. Thus, it may be argued that the cases involving severe injury tend, more than those of lesser injury, to be cases in which the fault criterion can be realistically applied. But perhaps considerations of equity and cost are the principal justifications for a dual system of the no-fault type. If the criterion for compensation were simplified for the overwhelming number of cases involving less than severe injury, the cost of maintaining jury trial—at least for claims based on severe injury and perhaps even for the small claims as well—would be tolerable.

If cost is to be considered, it becomes relevant that a substantial percentage of the automobile accident cases tried result in plaintiff's verdicts for amounts less than the tax money expended to provide the jury trial. Should legislatures be persuaded to spend enough more in tax money to assure prompt jury trial of every negligence claim, regardless of how limited the injury may be?

Individualizing compensation for pain and suffering, under either a fault system or a no-fault system, inherently gives cases of minor injury a substantial nuisance value. In large part this grows out of the defense costs involved in disputing the valuation of pain and suffering. The nuisance value is even higher under a fault than under a no-fault system, because of the added defense costs of disputing the issues of fault. Thus, not all but nevertheless a substantial part of the administrative savings envisioned under no-fault systems would be sacrificed by extending individualized compensation to all pain and suffering claims. For this reason, those who regard compensation for pain and suffering as much less important than compensation for out-of-pocket loss tend not to favor individualizing compensation for pain and suffering. It seems objectionable for a system to impose the high administrative cost of individualized pain and suffering awards on everybody who pays any share of the burden. This is what the negligence system does.

2. *Deterrence and Equity*—The theory that negligence law deters dangerous driving is founded on the assumption that it penalizes dangerous drivers. Under the liability insurance system, this is no longer true to any substantial extent.

Under the present system, compensation is ordinarily paid by liability insurance companies rather than individuals. To some extent, it is true, the negligence liability insurance system imposes higher costs on wrongdoers by charging them higher insurance premiums, but it does so only in very rough terms, and to whatever extent this serves as a deterrent to dangerous driving the same could be accomplished through insurance rating even if compensation were paid without regard to fault.

The present system does not in fact make wrongdoers pay for their own wrongs. It does not even make all wrongdoers together pay for all the damages they have caused. Rather, even when merit rating is used, the present system spreads the burden of paying damages widely among all insured drivers, using the premiums collected from innocent as well as blameworthy drivers so those who are in the category of having been both highly blameworthy and a cause of the most harm end up paying only a tiny fraction of the losses they have caused. This is true whether their cases are viewed one by one or instead as a group. Any system that actually collected back enough in lifetime premiums from persons in this group of drivers to pay for the damages they have caused over a lifetime would cease to be an insurance system and would be, instead, simply a financing or borrowing system. It would give up all the advantages of risk-spreading that a true insurance system offers.

Even the deterrent effect of denying compensation because of contributory fault is more fanciful than real. The public, knowing that in fact compensation is to be paid ordinarily through insurance rather than by individuals, will not tolerate faithful enforcement of the rule that contributory fault bars recovery. Decisions on negligence are increasingly divorced from standards genuinely concerned with fault.

The supposed deterrent effect of the compensation system appears weaker still in view of other influences on driver behavior—including fear of injury to oneself and members of one's family, fear of criminal sanctions, and fear of suspension or revocation of the license to drive. If all these factors will not deter dangerous driving, what possible hope can there be that the design of the compensation system will do so?

Perhaps the international favorite among horrible hypotheticals advanced by opponents of no-fault insurance is that of the drunken drivers who grievously injure others and still receive full compensation for their own losses.

Insofar as the charge of inequity concerns the responsibility of drunken drivers for providing benefits *for others,* arguments against rewarding drunken drivers are, as noted above, more cogently addressed to liability insurance than to no-fault insurance.

Insofar as the charge of inequity concerns the payment of benefits to drunken drivers, or their dependents, *for their own injuries,* it is very easy under a no-fault system to meet the problem by exclusion of benefits to persons whose injuries result from their own activities such as driving under the influence of alcohol or drugs. Then no one is forced to pay premiums to create assets from which drunk drivers will receive benefits.

Of course it would not be feasible to meet the argument of inequity among good and bad drivers generally (as distinguished from drunken drivers particularly) by such an exclusion. But there is a full answer to the argument of inequity on more fundamental grounds: A well designed no-fault system will give both innocent victims and good drivers better protection at lower cost than the fault system.

Cost comparisons show that a no-fault system for small claims, preserving the fault system for larger claims, as no-fault partial-exemption statutes do, would cost less than the present system. Thus the good drivers' costs of buying liability insurance to protect against the possibility that they will negligently injure other persons is greater than the cost to them of buying no-fault and liability insurance combined, which would give them protection against liability to other persons as well as a right to recover no-fault benefits from their own insurance companies. Looking at the matter purely as a matter of economics, they would prefer the no-fault system as the better deal.

To say under these circumstances that no-fault would be unfair to good drivers is to say that we must make them pay more because it would be unjust to them to create a system under which they pay less even though receiving greater assurance of reimbursement of their losses. It is misguided paternalism of the worst kind to keep the fault system, thereby making good drivers continue to pay unnecessarily high premiums, all the while telling them the reason for doing this is that it would be an injustice to them to make the change.

This misguided view results from the fundamental error of viewing the system fictionally as if individuals paid compensation rather than seeing it realistically as an insurance system. The fact that under most no-fault systems the policyholders' own insurance companies pay benefits to them when other persons negligently injure them does not mean that the injured policyholders bear the burden of paying for injuries caused by the other persons. The injured policyholders pay premiums into an insurance system, and so do the other persons. Whether the injured policyholders and the others are fairly treated depends not on which companies pay benefits but on what each group pays and what protection persons in that group receive—that is, on the comparison between their respective deals under the system.

3. *Insurance Rating*—The real assessment of burdens under an insurance system is determined not by the theoretical basis of liability for compensation (that is, whether compensation is based on fault or instead is payable without regard to fault) but by the way liability for insurance premiums is allocated. If making determinations of who are good and bad drivers is thought to be worth the cost, this can be done, and burdens of cost can be assigned accordingly, even though compensation is paid without regard to fault. For example, merit rating or any other system that in some degree considers driver records in fixing premium charges can be used as well under a system that pays compensation regardless of fault as under a negligence system.

Further, it is true that the loss-causing potential of various classes of vehicles is one of the factors that ought to be taken into account in setting rates, regardless of whether compensation is based on fault. It is quite possible and practical to do this under a no-fault system. A sound and fair rating system must also make provision for reallocating burdens among insurance companies if it happens that different classes of coverage are unevenly distributed. This would require some innovation in the insurance industry, but it is well within the capabilities of actuaries, especially since they now have the aid of computers.

Note that the rating system used with liability insurance focuses on only the probability of the policyholder's involvement in an accident, totally disregarding all factors bearing on the probable size of the loss in the event of injury—including matters such as whether the policyholder's annual earnings are $5,000 or $50,000. There have been numerous variations in methods of rating used with liability insurance, but all have had in common the characteristic that they have dealt with potential size of loss as a random factor. That is, they have used average claim cost in calculating rates rather than trying to tailor a policyholder's rates to factors bearing on the probable size of the policyholder's loss from a given severity of injury. It is quite natural to proceed in this way since under a liability insurance system an injured person claims against somebody else's insurance company, not the injured person's own company. Thus it does not reduce costs for the injured policyholder's own company if the injured policyholder happens to be a person of such low earning power that the claim for loss of earnings would be lower than average. But when one looks at the system as a whole one can see that this is grossly unfair to low wage earners. Their injuries cost the system less but they have to pay just as much into the system as policyholders whose wage losses will run much higher on the average. It is basically as unfair to charge the same rate to $5,000–a-year and $50,000–a-year earners as it is to charge the same total fire insurance premium for full coverage on a $5,000 house and a $50,000 house. Yet that is just what the liability insurance system does.

A fair system of rating for automobile insurance ought to take into account not only the probability of accident involvement (predicted accident frequency), as liability insurance rating has done, but also the probable size of loss (predicted claim cost). This could be done either with a negligence liability insurance system or with a no-fault system. Perhaps it is more likely to be done with a no-fault system, however, since it is difficult to make such a change in the well established tradition of liability insurance rating.

Finally, under a net-loss form of automobile insurance (where benefits are limited to net loss remaining after taking into account other sources of reimbursement), lower-than-average rates can and should be charged to policyholders with higher-than-average coverages of other types.

Opponents of net-loss insurance have advanced numerous hypotheticals like that of a person who has a loss of $4,750, receives reimbursement of $4,250 from other sources, and in view of the income tax saving and a deductible, receives no benefits under net-loss automobile insurance. Equity in rating is a complete answer to the charge of inequity under such a hypothetical. A policyholder with such remarkably generous coverages of other types—a person probably less frequently encountered in real life than in the debates over automobile insurance reform—would represent a lower risk to the company, and this could and should be reflected in the rating system. Another way equity can be achieved in this setting is to permit the person with excellent coverages of other types to elect a deductible as to no-fault automobile insurance benefits, at an appropriate premium saving. This method was adopted in the Massachusetts Personal Injury Protection Act of 1970.

The present system forces people to pay premiums for overlapping coverage they do not need. That is, if one wants to have both adequate liability insurance and adequate medical and disability insurance, as a practical matter there is no choice but to buy coverages at premiums that are higher just because payments under liability insurance overlap with payments from other sources.

4. *Coercion to Insure*—An argument of principle against legislative coercion to insure is contrary to the spirit of legislation in all 50 states. Many states have "compulsory" automobile liability insurance, requiring insurance or other proof of financial responsibility as a prerequisite to registering an automobile. All other states have financial responsibility laws imposing such a compulsory requirement in more limited circumstances—generally after one has negligently caused injuries and failed to pay or has been convicted of a serious driving offense such as drunken driving or greatly excessive speeding. Moreover, the primary purpose of these laws is to coerce all others to buy liability insurance under threat of the sanctions that can be invoked if, for example, one happens to cause injuries negligently—sanctions that extend beyond the insurance requirement and may involve suspension of the license to drive.

The impact of legal coercion to insure is to cause the individual motorist to pay an insurance premium in order to be able to operate a car. By changing the form of the insurance to loss insurance that pays benefits regardless of fault, one can eliminate inequities of the present insurance system and increase its efficiency so motorists get more in benefits for their premium dollars. To argue that this change is objectionable in principle because it compels people to insure themselves is to argue that form prevails over substance. Moreover, even in relation to form there are precedents for compulsory self-insurance, the most dramatic of which (social security) goes far beyond proposals for loss insurance since it also uses a government rather than a private financing system.

The history of changing attitudes toward coercion to insure, reflected in legislation and court decisions on constitutionality, is striking.

The first workmen's compensation legislation enacted in New York was successfully attacked on constitutional grounds, and similar challenges occurred in many other states. The hurdles were cleared in due course—in some instances by state constitutional amendment and in others by court decisions expressing a point of view on constitutional issues quite in contrast with the early New York court decision.

Compulsory automobile liability insurance was opposed on constitutional grounds also, but unsuccessfully. Attacks on constitutional grounds have been leveled at other forms of financial responsibility legislation too, but have achieved only the very limited success of striking down some detail rather than an entire statute.

In the 1960s, another form of coercive legislation was developed to supplement financial responsibility legislation, moving even closer to assuring that every victim has a financially responsible target for a claim. This legislation requires that every policy of automobile liability insurance issued in the state include uninsured motorist coverage (or that it do so unless the policyholder has declined such coverage in writing). This form of legislation has also been enacted in combination with compulsory liability insurance.

The major battle over the principle of legal coercion on motorists to insure had already been fought and won, it would seem, before compulsory no-fault laws were enacted in the 1970s. Also, the increasing use of uninsured motorist coverage as part of the statutory system of coercive legislation could be seen as an indication of a clear trend toward including self-insurance within the types of coverage a legislature may coerce motorists to buy.

Once the legislative judgment has been reached to use legal sanctions to coerce motorists to buy self-insurance, it is a small step indeed to change the form of that self-insurance from uninsured motorist coverage (paying benefits to policyholders only when they can prove tort claims against uninsured motorists) to no-fault insurance. And no different principle is presented though further steps of degree are involved, in pushing as far as the compulsory no-fault partial-tort-exemption statutes go, combining compulsory automobile liability insurance with compulsory no-fault coverage up to the specified limits. Though attacks on the constitutionality of no-fault acts have been common and have succeeded in some measure, a clearly stronger current of authority sustains the constitutionality of compulsory no-fault partial-tort-exemption statutes.

U.S. DEPARTMENT OF TRANSPORTATION, COMPENSATING AUTO ACCIDENT VICTIMS (1985)

[This report describes experience under no-fault auto insurance plans.]

The report distinguishes "no-lawsuit" plans (restricting lawsuits in exchange for assured no-fault benefits) from add-on plans (making no-fault benefits a supplement to, rather than a substitute for, traditional tort actions). It compares no-fault (personal injury protection), (or PIP) insurance plans with traditional bodily injury (BI) liability insurance.

The excerpts below use the term "balance" to refer to the trade-off between (a) savings from restrictions on lawsuits and (b) the added costs of no-fault benefits. The report stresses that, in order to keep insurance rates down, there must be effective restrictions on lawsuits so that the savings generated by constraining tort recoveries will cover the cost of no-fault benefits. In this connection it assesses types of thresholds: the magnitude of injury that the victim must sustain (verbal threshold), or the amount of medical expense that the victim must incur (dollar threshold), to be able to bring a tort action in a no-lawsuit, no-fault state.

The report finds that "highway fatality and injury rates in no-fault States exhibit no significant difference from those in traditional States." In addition, it offers the following general conclusions about no-fault auto insurance based on experience in twenty-four jurisdictions.]

1. *Significantly more motor vehicle accident victims receive auto insurance compensation in no-fault States than in other States.* No-fault auto insurance, whether of the no-lawsuit or add-on type, compensates many more personal injury victims of motor vehicle accidents than does traditional or liability auto insurance. Almost twice as many victims per hundred insured cars receive PIP benefits in no-fault States as receive BI liability payments in traditional States. * * *

2. *In general, accident victims in no-fault States have access to a greater amount of money from auto insurance than victims in traditional States.* * * *

3. *Although no-fault States, on average, have higher total insurance premiums than traditional States, this seems to be due to the inclusion in the average of no-fault States with laws that are out of balance.* From 1976 to 1983, the average auto insurance premium in the average traditional State rose 50%. During the same period, the average auto insurance premium rose (a) 54% in the average no-fault State with a law that is in balance, and (b) 126% in the average no-fault State with a law that is not in balance.

4. *"Balance" in no-fault systems seems to be closely linked to the presence of an exclusively verbal or a high medical-expense dollar threshold.* Some systems which provide no-fault benefits to all motor vehicle accident victims do so at a cost which is more or less equal to (or less than) the savings which are produced in those systems by having a threshold. In fact, the appropriateness of the threshold is likely to be the principal factor in determining whether a system is in balance.

All of the States which permit recovery of [full tort damages] only upon satisfaction of a verbal threshold are in balance. Three out of four of the States which permit recovery of [tort damages] upon satisfaction of a high-dollar threshold ($1,000 or more in medical expenses) are in balance. Three out of eight of the States which permit recovery of [tort damages] upon satisfaction of a low-dollar threshold (less than $1,000 in medical expenses) are in balance. Only one out of the three States that have no threshold at all is in balance. * * *

5. *Compensation payments under no-fault insurance are made far more swiftly than under traditional auto insurance.* * * * One year after notification, the PIP claimants had received 95.5% of the money they would ever receive; by contrast, the BI liability claimants had received only 51.7% of the money they would ever receive.

6. *No-fault insurance systems pay a greater percentage of premium income to injured claimants than do traditional liability systems.* * * * An analysis found that out of each personal injury premium dollar the average no-fault State returned 50.2 cents in personal benefits to claimants whereas the average traditional State returned 43.2 cents. One of the highest rates,

55.1 cents, was reached by the State of Michigan, the State which provides the greatest amount of no-fault benefits to accident victims and which puts the strongest restrictions on lawsuits * * * .

7. *State auto insurance laws which provide high no-fault benefits would appear to better facilitate the rehabilitation of seriously injured motor vehicle accident victims than traditional laws * * * .*

No-fault laws which provide high PIP benefit levels are particularly helpful in facilitating rehabilitation because rehabilitation treatment is expensive. While larger awards may be intermittently made under traditional insurance, the average amount generally available under traditional insurance is less than the average amount generally available in a no-fault State.

8. *No-fault has led to reductions in the number of lawsuits and, thus, to significant savings in court and other public legal costs paid by the taxpayer.* The evidence is clear that each no-fault auto insurance statute has led to some reduction in the number of motor vehicle accident lawsuits. According to Chief Justice Warren Burger, each jury trial tort case costs the taxpayer approximately $8,300 in court and other public costs. While the precise level of savings in each State is not known, nevertheless, the amount of savings for public entities is substantial.

9. *Typical auto insurance benefits in both no-fault and traditional States fall short of the needs of catastrophically injured victims.* The amount of auto insurance compensation available, in most no-fault and all traditional States, is not sufficient to meet all the economic-loss needs of the average catastrophically injured victim of a motor vehicle accident. A 1982 study, based upon review of 410 motor vehicle accident victims with economic losses expected to exceed $100,000, found that the average projected total medical and rehabilitation costs for each would be $408,700.

Each year, approximately 20,000 people receive severe to critical injuries in motor vehicle accidents. Only the no-fault laws * * * which provide for unlimited medical benefits, meet the medical needs of all of these victims. * * *

THE INSTITUTE FOR CIVIL JUSTICE, ANNUAL REPORT (Rand Corp. 1993–1994). The Institute's report describes the results of recent studies, conducted by its researchers, which assess the performance of auto no-fault plans in comparison with that of the traditional tort-plus-liability insurance system. Following is a summary of findings:

"Growing dissatisfaction with the liability-based system and rising insurance costs have prompted many states to switch to some form of auto no-fault compensation system. In many states that still use the traditional tort-based system, no-fault proposals have been hotly debated. * * *

"Our work has looked at both the effects of existing no-fault plans and the likely effects of switching from tort-based compensation to a variety of no-fault plans.

"We first looked at how claimants fare under the various state insurance programs. * * * We concluded that injured claimants in no-fault states are more likely to receive some form of compensation, which frequently comes in the form of first-party insurance (i.e., from their own insurer). Compensation in tort states was less predictable and slower.

"What would happen to costs and compensation if a state adopted no-fault? This question was the focus of recent work on no-fault * * *. The study found that

- No-fault can reduce costs substantially compared to the traditional liability system; some no-fault plans, however, may increase costs. Most of the savings from no-fault plans result from reduced compensation for noneconomic losses to those who fall below the plan's threshold.

- No-fault plans reduce transaction costs by approximately 20 to 40 percent.

- No-fault aligns compensation more closely with economic loss.

- No-fault generally speeds up compensation.

"The study illustrates its analysis by comparing outcomes for the average case in the liability system with those for the average case under an illustrative no-fault plan whose provisions include a verbal threshold and $15,000 [no-fault] benefit level. The no-fault plan reduces the costs of injury compensation by 22 percent, including a one-third reduction in legal fees and processing costs. * * *

"The critical trade-off in designing an auto-accident injury compensation plan involves deciding how much to emphasize lower premiums versus preserving or increasing compensation. No-fault plans that reduce costs also reduce compensation to claimants with less-serious injuries and have little effect on compensation for those with severe injuries. Plans that increase compensation to severely injured people also tend to increase costs. Therefore, policymakers choosing among the traditional liability system and no-fault alternatives confront difficult trade-offs in deciding whether to maintain the status quo, to cut costs, or to increase injury compensation."

SECTION C.   OTHER PLANS DISPLACING TORT

The present section introduces three more accident compensation plans which share the basic features of workers' compensation and auto no-fault. Each of the three, to one extent or another, displaces tort: each restricts recourse to tort and substitutes an administrative no-fault scheme. Each plan uses a statutory basis of recovery simpler than pertinent tort doctrine; all three provide less than the full measure of tort reparation. At the same time, the three approaches are quite different from one another.

First is the Price–Anderson Act, the federal program for compensating victims of catastrophe at a nuclear power plant. All nuclear operators are required to contribute to a fund; in the event of a nuclear disaster, total liability would be limited by the size of the fund. The Supreme Court decision upholding the Act, excerpted below, is a basic text on the constitutionality of tort displacement.

Second is the federal plan to compensate victims of childhood vaccines. These are persons who contract disease from a vaccine meant to prevent disease. This nation-wide plan is financed by a flat tax on sales by vaccine manufacturers. It greatly eases a claimant's burden in proving a causal connection between the event of inoculation and the illness suffered.

The third scheme is far and away the most ambitious. New Zealand, since 1972, has embraced a comprehensive legislative alternative to tort. The New Zealand enactment abolishes tort recovery for personal injuries caused by accident, and substitutes an administrative compensation program. It covers accidental injuries in the workplace, on the highway, and anywhere else.

DUKE POWER CO. v. CAROLINA ENVIRONMENTAL STUDY GROUP

Supreme Court of the United States, 1978.
438 U.S. 59, 98 S.Ct. 2620, 57 L.Ed.2d 595.

[According to the Court, this case presents "the question of whether Congress may, consistent with the Constitution, impose a limitation on liability for nuclear accidents resulting from the operations of private nuclear power plants licensed by the Federal Government." At issue was the Price–Anderson Act's limitation of total liability for a single nuclear disaster to roughly $560 million.* The Act establishes strict liability for nuclear tort damage, by requiring waiver of common law defenses. Compensation would come from a $560 million fund made up of contributions by the power companies, their private insurers, and the federal government. Once settlements growing out of a disaster exceed $84,000,000, payments stop, the problem is referred to a district judge, and claims must then be settled in terms of a proportion of the available funds. Plaintiffs (now appellees) attacked the tort liability limitation on constitutional grounds.]

Mr. Chief Justice BURGER delivered the opinion of the Court.

* * *

The District Court held the Price–Anderson Act contravened the Due Process Clause because "[t]he amount of recovery is not rationally related to the potential losses"; because "[the Act] tends to encourage irresponsibility in matters of safety and environmental protection * * * "; and finally because "there is no *quid pro quo*" for the liability limitations. 431 F.Supp. 222–223. An equal protection violation was also found because the Act "places the cost of [nuclear power] on an arbitrarily chosen segment of society, those injured by nuclear catastrophe." Application of the relevant

---

* [Eds.] The Price–Anderson amendments of 1988 increased the liability limit for a nuclear disaster, as follows. In the event of a catastrophe at any one plant, each nuclear operator is required to make a contribution ($63 million, subject to adjustment for inflation) to a compensation fund for victims of the disaster. The limit of liability is set by the size of the industry-financed fund. With over 100 nuclear power plants operating, the aggregate amount of the fund (subject to inflation adjustment) becomes approximately $7 billion. See 42 U.S.C.A. § 2210, subsections (b), (e), & (t).

constitutional principles forces the conclusion that these holdings of the District Court cannot be sustained.

* * *

* * * [T]he Price–Anderson Act, in our view, passes constitutional muster. The record before us fully supports the need for the imposition of a statutory limit on liability to encourage private industry participation and hence bears a rational relationship to Congress' concern for stimulating the involvement of private enterprise in the production of electric energy through the use of atomic power; nor do we understand appellees or the District Court to be of a different view. Rather their challenge is to the alleged arbitrariness of the *particular figure* of $560 million, which is the statutory ceiling on liability. The District Court aptly summarized its position:

> "[t]he amount of recovery is not rationally related to the potential losses. Abundant evidence in the record shows that although major catastrophe in any particular place is not certain and may not be extremely likely, nevertheless, in the territory where these plants are located, damage to life and property for this and future generations could well be many, many times the limit which the law places on liability." 431 F.Supp. 222.

Assuming, *arguendo,* that the $560 million fund would not insure full recovery in all conceivable circumstances,[28]—and the hard truth is that no one can ever know—it does not by any means follow that the liability limitation is therefore irrational and violative of due process. The legislative history clearly indicates that the $560 million figure was not arrived at on the supposition that it alone would necessarily be sufficient to guarantee full compensation in the event of a nuclear incident. Instead, it was conceived of as a "starting point" or a working hypothesis. The reasonableness of the statute's assumed ceiling on liability was predicated on two corollary considerations—expert appraisals of the exceedingly small risk of a nuclear incident involving claims in excess of $560 million, and the recognition that in the event of such an incident, Congress would likely enact extraordinary relief provisions to provide additional relief, in accord with prior practice.

* * *

Given our conclusion that in general limiting liability is an acceptable method for Congress to utilize in encouraging the private development of electric energy by atomic power, candor requires acknowledgment that whatever ceiling figure is selected will, of necessity, be arbitrary in the sense that any choice of a figure based on imponderables like those at issue here can always be so characterized. This is not, however, the kind of arbitrari-

28. As the various studies considered by the District Court indicate, there is considerable uncertainty as to the amount of damages which would result from a catastrophic nuclear accident. See 431 F.Supp., at 210–214. The Reactor Safety Study published by the NRC in 1975 suggested that there was a one in 20,000 chance (per reactor year) of an accident causing property damage approaching $100 million and having only minor health effects. By contrast, when the odds were reduced to the range of one in one billion (per reactor year), the level of damages approached $14 billion, and 3,300 early fatalities and 45,000 early illnesses were predicted. * * *

ness which flaws otherwise constitutional action. When appraised in terms of both the extremely remote possibility of an accident where liability would exceed the limitation and Congress' now statutory commitment to "take whatever action is deemed necessary and appropriate to protect the public from the consequences of" any such disaster, 42 U.S.C.A. (Supp. V) § 2210(e),[31] we hold the congressional decision to fix a $560 million ceiling at this stage in the private development and production of electric energy by nuclear power, to be within permissible limits and not violative of due process.

This District Court's further conclusion that the Price–Anderson Act "tends to encourage irresponsibility * * * on the part of builders and owners" of the nuclear power plants, 431 F.Supp. 222, simply cannot withstand careful scrutiny. We recently outlined the multitude of detailed steps involved in the review of any application for a license to construct or to operate a nuclear power plant, Vermont Yankee Nuclear Power Corp. v. NRDC, 435 U.S. 519, at 526–529, 98 S.Ct. 1197, at 1203–1204, 55 L.Ed.2d 460 (1978); nothing in the liability limitation provision undermines or alters in any respect the rigor and integrity of that process. Moreover, in the event of a nuclear accident the utility itself would suffer perhaps the largest damages. While obviously not to be compared with the loss of human life and injury to health, the risk of financial loss and possible bankruptcy to the utility is in itself no small incentive to avoid the kind of irresponsible and cavalier conduct implicitly attributed to licensees by the District Court.

The remaining due process objection to the liability limitation provision is that it fails to provide those injured by a nuclear accident with a satisfactory *quid pro quo* for the common-law rights of recovery which the Act abrogates. Initially, it is not at all clear that the Due Process Clause in fact requires that a legislatively enacted compensation scheme either duplicate the recovery at common law or provide a reasonable substitute remedy.[32] However, we need not resolve this question here since the Price–

---

31. In the past Congress has provided emergency assistance for victims of catastrophic accidents even in the absence of a prior statutory commitment to do so. For example in 1955, Congress passed the Texas City Disaster Relief Act, 69 Stat. 707, to provide relief for victims of the explosion of ammonium nitrate fertilizer in 1947. Congress took this action despite the decision in Dalehite v. United States, 346 U.S. 15, 73 S.Ct. 956, 97 L.Ed. 1427 (1953), holding the United States free from any liability under the Federal Tort Claims Act for the damages incurred and injuries suffered. More recently Congress enacted legislation to provide relief for victims of the flood resulting from the collapse of the Teton Dam in Idaho. Pub.L. 94–400, 90 Stat. 1211. Under the Act, the Secretary of the Interior was authorized to provide full compensation for any deaths, personal injuries or property damage caused by the failure of the dam. Ibid.

The Price–Anderson Act is, of course, a significant improvement on these prior relief efforts because it provides an advance guarantee of recovery up to $560 million plus an express commitment by Congress to take whatever further steps are necessary to aid the victims of a nuclear incident.

32. Our cases have clearly established that "[a] person has no property, no vested interest, in any rule of the common law." Second Employers' Liability Cases, 223 U.S. 1, 50, 32 S.Ct. 169, 175, 56 L.Ed. 327 (1912), quoting Munn v. Illinois, 94 U.S. 113, 134, 24 L.Ed. 77 (1876). The "Constitution does not forbid the creation of new rights, or the abolition of old ones recognized by the common law to attain a permissible legislative objective," Silver v. Silver, 280 U.S. 117, 122, 50 S.Ct. 57, 58, 74 L.Ed. 221 (1929), despite the fact that "otherwise settled expectations" may be upset thereby. Usery v. Turner Elkhorn Mining Co., 428 U.S., at 16, 96 S.Ct., at 2892. See also Arizona Employers' Liability Cases, 250 U.S. 400, 419–422, 39 S.Ct. 553, 555–556, 63 L.Ed. 1058 (1919). Indeed, statutes limiting liability are relatively commonplace and have consistently been enforced by the courts.

Anderson Act does, in our view, provide a reasonably just substitute for the common or state tort law remedies it replaces. Cf. New York Central R. Co. v. White, 243 U.S. 188, 37 S.Ct. 247, 61 L.Ed. 667 (1917); Crowell v. Benson, 285 U.S. 22, 52 S.Ct. 285, 76 L.Ed. 598 (1932).

The legislative history of the liability limitation provisions and the accompanying compensation mechanism reflects Congress' determination that reliance on state tort law remedies and state court procedures was an unsatisfactory approach to assuring public compensation for nuclear accidents, while at the same time providing the necessary incentives for private development of nuclear produced energy. The marks of Chairman Anders of the Joint Committee on Atomic Energy during the 1975 hearings on the need for renewal of Price–Anderson are illustrative of this concern and of the expectation that the Act would provide a more efficient and certain vehicle for assuring compensation in the unlikely event of a nuclear incident.

* * *

Appellees, like the District Court, differ with this appraisal on several grounds. They argue, *inter alia,* that recovery under the Act would not be greater than without it, that the waiver of defenses required by the Act, 42 U.S.C.A. § 2210(n), is an idle gesture since those involved in the development of nuclear energy would likely be held strictly liable under common-law principles;[34] that the claim-administration procedure under the Act delays rather than expedites individual recovery, and finally that recovery of even limited compensation is uncertain since the liability ceiling does not vary with the number of persons injured or amount of property damaged. * * *

We disagree. We view the congressional *assurance* of a $560 million fund for recovery, accompanied by an express statutory commitment, to "take whatever action is deemed necessary and appropriate to protect the public from the consequences of" a nuclear accident, 42 U.S.C.A. § 2210(e), to be a fair and reasonable substitute for the uncertain recovery of damages of this magnitude from a utility or component manufacturer, whose resources might well be exhausted at an early stage. The record in this case raises serious questions about the ability of a utility or component manufacturer to satisfy a judgment approaching $560 million—the amount guaranteed under the Price–Anderson Act. Nor are we persuaded that the mandatory waiver of defenses required by the Act is of no benefit to potential claimants. Since there has never been, to our knowledge, a case arising out of a nuclear incident like those covered by the Price–Anderson Act, any discussion of the standard of liability that state courts will apply is necessari-

See, e.g., Silver v. Silver, 280 U.S. 117, 50 S.Ct. 57, 74 L.Ed. 221 (automobile guest statute); Providence & NYSS Co. v. Hill Mfg. Co., 109 U.S. 578, 3 S.Ct. 379, 27 L.Ed. 1038 (limitation of vessel owner's liability); Indemnity Ins. Co. of North America v. Pan Amer. Airways, 58 F.Supp. 338 (S.D.N.Y.1944) (Warsaw Convention limitation on recovery for injuries suffered during international air travel). Cf. Thomason v. San-chez, 539 F.2d 955 (C.A.3 1976) (Federal Driver's Act).

34. See Rylands v. Fletcher, LR 3 H. L. 330 (1868). See generally Prosser, The Law of Torts 516 (1971); Cavers, Improving Financial Protection of the Public Against the Hazards of Nuclear Power, 77 Harv.L.Rev. 644, 649 (1964).

ly speculative. At the minimum, the statutorily mandated waiver of defenses establishes at the threshold the right of injured parties to compensation without proof of fault and eliminates the burden of delay and uncertainty which would follow from the need to litigate the question of liability after an accident. Further, even if strict liability were routinely applied, the common-law doctrine is subject to exceptions for acts of God or of third parties—two of the very factors which appellees emphasized in the District Court in the course of arguing that the risks of a nuclear accident are greater than generally admitted. All of these considerations belie the suggestion that the Act leaves the potential victims of a nuclear disaster in a more disadvantageous position than they would be in if left to their common-law remedies—not known in modern times for either their speed or economy.

* * *

In the course of adjudicating a similar challenge to the Workmen's Compensation Act in New York Central R. Co. v. White, 243 U.S. 188, 201, 37 S.Ct. 247, 252, 61 L.Ed. 667 (1917), the Court observed that the Due Process Clause of the Fourteenth Amendment was not violated simply because an injured party would not be able to recover as much under the Act as before its enactment. "[H]e is entitled to moderate compensation in all cases of injury, and has a certain and speedy remedy without the difficulty and expense of establishing negligence or proving the amount of damages." The logic of *New York Central* would seem to apply with renewed force in the context of this challenge to the Price–Anderson Act.
* * *

Although the District Court also found the Price–Anderson Act to contravene the "equal protection provision that is included within the Due Process Clause of the Fifth Amendment," 431 F.Supp., at 224–225, appellees have not relied on this ground since the equal protection arguments largely track and duplicate those made in support of the due process claim. In any event, we conclude that there is no equal protection violation. The general rationality of the Price–Anderson Act liability limitations—particularly with reference to the important congressional purpose of encouraging private participation in the exploitation of nuclear energy—is ample justification for the difference in treatment between those injured in nuclear accidents and those whose injuries are derived from other causes. Speculation regarding other arrangements that might be used to spread the risk of liability in ways different from Price–Anderson is, of course, not pertinent to the equal protection analysis. See Mourning v. Family Publications Service, Inc., 411 U.S. 356, 378, 93 S.Ct. 1652, 1665, 36 L.Ed.2d 318 (1973).

Accordingly, the decision of the District Court is reversed and the case is remanded for proceedings consistent with this opinion.

Reversed.

———

ADDENDUM ON BENEFITS AND BURDENS. In developing its argument that the Act violated equal protection, the District Court had said (431 F.Supp. at 223–225):

"The philosophy behind the imposition of strict liability is that '[t]he law casts the risk of the venture on the person who introduces peril into the community. Blasting operations are dangerous and should pay their own way.' Trull v. Carolina–Virginia Well Co., 264 N.C. at 691, 142 S.E.2d at 624. This allocation of risk is applicable to the generation of nuclear energy as it is to blasting.

* * *

"The Act violates the equal protection provision that is included within the Due Process Clause of the Fifth Amendment because it provides for what Congress deemed to be a benefit to the whole society (the encouragement of the generation of nuclear power), but places the cost of that benefit on an arbitrarily chosen segment of society, those injured by nuclear catastrophe. * * *

"The statute irrationally places the risk of major nuclear accident upon people who happen to live in the areas which may be touched by radioactive debris. No necessity is suggested for using such geographical happenstance as the basis for allocating the burden of loss.

* * *

"The Act unreasonably and irrationally relieves the owners of power plants of financial responsibility for nuclear accidents and places that loss upon the people injured by such accidents who are by definition least able to stand such losses.

"The limitation is unnecessary to serve any legitimate public purpose. Other arrangements rationally related to the interests asserted could easily be devised. For example, a liability pool could be established, requiring either contributions in advance, or liability for assessment on a unit basis or otherwise, of all power companies building or operating nuclear generators. This would effectively place the responsibility upon the group most directly profiting from any improvement in the costs or usefulness of electric power—the power company stockholders and the customers themselves. Another rational alternative would be to make such accidents a national loss and to pay those damaged out of the federal treasury. This would spread the loss among those who benefitted indirectly by having the nation's power supply increased as well as among those who presumably benefitted directly."

NATIONAL CHILDHOOD VACCINE INJURY ACT OF 1986
P.L. 99–660, codified principally at 42 U.S.C.A. §§ 300aa–10 to–34.

This Act creates a no-fault system for compensating individuals who have been injured by vaccines routinely administered to children. Report No. 99–908, Sept. 26, 1986, of the House Energy and Commerce Committee accompanying H.R. 5546, the bill giving rise to the Act, explained the need for legislation:

Vaccination of children against deadly, disabling, but preventable infectious diseases has been one of the most spectacularly effective public health initiatives this country has ever undertaken. Use of vaccines has prevented thousands of children's deaths each year and has substantially reduced the effects resulting from disease. Billions of medical and health-related dollars have been saved by immunizations. * * *

In recent years, however, the Nation's ability to maintain this level of success has come into question. Previously unrecognized injuries associated with vaccines have become more widely known. While most of the Nation's children enjoy great benefit from immunization programs, a small but significant number have been gravely injured. These children are often without a source of payment or compensation for their medical and rehabilitative needs, and they and their families have resorted in greater numbers to the tort system for some form of financial relief.

At least in part as a result of this increase in litigation, the prices of vaccines have jumped enormously. The number of childhood vaccine manufacturers has declined significantly. In certain areas, the level of immunization against some preventable diseases has decreased while the incidence of those diseases has increased. * * *

* * *

* * * Through Federal support, State and local health agencies are able to plan, develop, and conduct programs to immunize children against polio, measles, mumps, rubella (German measles), diphtheria, pertussis (whooping cough), and tetanus.

* * *

* * * There is today no "perfect" or reaction-free childhood vaccine on the market. A relatively small number of children who receive immunizations each year have serious reactions to them. But it is not always possible to predict who they will be or what reactions they will have. And since State law requires that all children be immunized before entering school, most parents have no choice but to risk the chance—small as that may be—that their child may be injured from a vaccine.

Despite these possibilities, public health officials, private physician groups, and parent organizations have repeatedly stated that it is safer to take the required shots than to risk the health consequences of contracting the diseases immunizations are designed to prevent. * * *

But for the relatively few who are injured by vaccines—through no fault of their own—the opportunities for redress and restitution are limited, time-consuming, expensive, and often unanswered. Currently, vaccine-injured persons can seek recovery for their damages only through the civil tort system or through a settlement arrangement with the vaccine manufacturer. Over time, neither approach has proven satisfactory. Lawsuits and settlement negotiations can take months and even years to complete. Transaction costs—including attorneys' fees and court payments—are high. And in the end, no recovery may be available. Yet futures have been destroyed and mounting expenses must be met.

This approach has also been ineffective for the manufacturers of childhood vaccines. This has become especially true in more recent years as the number of lawsuits—particularly those concerning the DPT [diphtheria, pertussis, tetanus] vaccine—has increased. * * * Manufacturers have become concerned not only with the problems of time and expense, but with the issue of the availability of affordable product liability insurance that is used to cover losses related to vaccine injury cases. * * * This lack of insurance was the stated reason for one manufacturer to withdraw temporarily from the vaccine market in 1984. Others have suggested that they may follow a similar course of action. This factor, coupled with the possibility that vaccine-injured persons may recover substantial awards in tort claims, has prompted manufacturers to question their continued participation in the vaccine market.

The loss of any of the existing manufacturers of childhood vaccines at this time could create a genuine public health hazard in this country. Currently, there is only one manufacturer of the polio vaccine, one manufacturer of the measles, mumps, rubella (MMR) vaccine, and two manufacturers of the DPT vaccine. Two States, Michigan and Massachusetts, produce their own DPT vaccine. * * *

Before bringing a tort action against the manufacturer of a vaccine that is listed in the Act's Vaccine Injury Table, persons alleging injuries derived from that vaccine must seek relief within the Act's no-fault compensation program. The process begins with the filing of a petition in federal court which is referred to a court-appointed master. Petitioner can recover damages by proving the vaccination, and the onset of an injury listed in the Table within a designated time period after the vaccination. In effect, causation is then deemed to exist, provided that respondent does not demonstrate by a preponderance of the evidence that the injury was caused by factors unrelated to the vaccine. Petitioner can also seek recovery for nonlisted injuries, but then must show causation from a listed vaccine. After conducting such hearings and requiring such evidence as appears appropriate, the master makes fact findings and conclusions of law. Those are submitted to the judge, who may adopt them or make de novo determinations and issue judgment accordingly or remand.

Compensation is paid from a Trust Fund created by the Act. It includes both the direct injury from the vaccine and further complications from that injury. Compensation consists of unreimbursable medical and rehabilitative expenses, death benefits, lost earnings, and pain and suffering. Death benefits are fixed at $250,000, and compensation for pain and suffering cannot exceed $250,000. There are no punitive damages. Awards for compensation include reasonable attorney fees (which may be awarded for petitions made in good faith on reasonable grounds even when compensation is denied), and attorneys for petitioners cannot charge fees other than those authorized by the Act.

Payments for projected medical and rehabilitative expenses are made on a periodic basis. Persons receiving such payments are required to disclose to the compensation program any changes significantly affecting the compensation to be paid. If an audit determines that a need has been terminated, the program may petition the court for appropriate revision of compensation. On the other hand, a petitioner finding an award inadequate to meet expenses may request a court to increase the award and modify the payment schedule.

The ongoing revenues of the Trust Fund created by the Act are derived from a tax imposed on the sale of childhood vaccines, plus amounts recovered from manufacturers of vaccines pursuant to subrogation rights given the Trust Fund with respect to compensation paid from the Fund to petitioners.

The Act seeks to divert injured persons from litigation by persuading them to accept awards because of their speed, low transaction costs and fairness. But a petitioner may reject an award and bring a tort action for damages. Except as provided by the Act, state law governs such an action. Those exceptions include: (1) No manufacturer is liable if the injury/death resulted from side effects that were unavoidable even though the vaccine was properly prepared and accompanied by proper directions and warnings. Compare comment *K* to Section 402a of the Restatement (Second) of Torts, p. 1208, supra. (2) Warnings are proper if the manufacturer complied with requirements of the Federal Food, Drug and Cosmetic Act, unless the plaintiff shows fraudulent or intentional withholding of information or failure to exercise due care. (3) No manufacturer is liable solely because of failure to give warnings of danger directly to the injured party, provided that required warnings were given to designated intermediaries such as prescribing physicians. (4) Punitive damages may be awarded against a manufacturer meeting all requirements of the Federal Food, Drug and Cosmetic Act only by proving fraud or wrongful withholding of information under that Act in seeking approval of the vaccine, or wrongful withholding of information relating to safety of the vaccine after approval.

––––––––––

SHACKIL v. LEDERLE LABORATORIES, 116 N.J. 155, 561 A.2d 511 (1989). In 1972 plaintiff, then an infant, was inoculated with a combined diphtheria-pertussis-tetanus (DPT) vaccine. Within 24 hours she became sick. Her illness led to severe brain damage. In 1984 her mother "became aware of the linkage between brain damage and the pertussis portion of the DPT vaccine," and plaintiff, by her parents, brought this product liability suit against 5 drug companies that manufactured DPT vaccine in 1972. Plaintiff became eligible to receive compensation under the subsequently enacted National Childhood Vaccine Injury Act of 1986, but elected to continue her tort action. Despite "extensive discovery," plaintiff was unable to show which DPT manufacturer's product was administered to her, and sought to rely on the theory of "market share liability" developed in Sindell v. Abbott Laboratories (p. 1101, supra).

The New Jersey Supreme Court held (4–2) that the Sindell theory of "collective liability" should not be applied. It argued that society's goal of "encouraging the use and development of needed drugs" would be "thwarted" if the Sindell approach were followed. It said that exposure to tort liability led to "the exorbitant increase in price of the DPT vaccine from eleven cents a dose [in 1982] to $11.40 a dose in 1986 (eight dollars of which [went] to insurance costs)." And it emphasized that the "alternative compensation scheme established by Congress * * * will fulfill in large measure the goal of providing compensatory relief to vaccine-injured plaintiffs."

> * * * [B]y eliminating traditional elements of proof that often prove fatal to a tort-law claim, the compensation scheme contained in the [Vaccine] Act went "beyond even the most [expansive] ruling issued by a court in a vaccine case." * * * It could even be argued that in one sense the Act embodies a theory of collective liability, inasmuch as it does not require identification of a manufacturer; moreover, it allocates the cost of vaccine-related accidents among all manufacturers by imposing a tax on each dose of vaccine produced.

The dissenting opinion (O'Hern, J.) questioned "the extent to which liability expenses are the cause of the price increases." "[E]ven if one accepts the Court's 'findings' " that price per DPT dose increased from around 11 cents to $11.40, of which $8.00 represented insurance costs, that would leave $3.40 of the higher price unaccounted for—"a twenty-seven-fold increase in non-insurance-related costs" in "a market with only two suppliers." The dissent quoted from Schwartz & Mahshigian, National Childhood Vaccine Injury Act of 1986: An Ad Hoc Remedy or a Window for the Future?, 48 Ohio St.L.J. 387, 393 (1987): "unlike some other products, the incidence of serious injury with children's vaccines is very low. Thus, a vaccine compensation system can be self-funding by adding a very small excise tax to the price of vaccines." The dissent's author added:

> From my perspective, the most critical and significant provision of the Act is that it creates the Vaccine Injury Compensation Trust Fund with money collected from an excise tax on vaccines. 26 U.S.C.A. § 9510. In other words, the industry as a whole shares the risk of financial compensation for injuries * * * attributable to individual manufacturers. I think that we would do well to mold our tort law to this model.

SCHAFER v. AMERICAN CYANAMID CO., 20 F.3d 1 (1st Cir.1994). A child received an oral polio vaccine and subsequently her mother, Lenita Schafer, contracted polio. The mother sought recovery under the National Childhood Vaccine Injury Act and received a $750,000 award from the Vaccine Court for her injuries, "thereby giving up her right to bring a tort action." The polio victim's husband and child brought suit on their own behalf against the vaccine manufacturer, seeking damages under Massachusetts tort law "for loss of Lenita's companionship and consortium." *Held* (per Breyer, C.J.), that the Act does not bar tort suits under state law by family members. Since the Act only provides compensation for "the person who suffered the vaccine-related injury" (except for death benefits), it does not affect the tort rights of the sufferer's family members. "Given the difficulties of prevailing in a traditional tort suit, it is, at least, unclear that plaintiff families—particularly families of victims who have already received Vaccine Act compensation—will prevail so often, and obtain verdicts so large, that the jury awards, or the threat of those awards, would significantly raise vaccine prices or retard their distribution."

TERENCE ISON, ACCIDENT COMPENSATION: A COMMENTARY ON THE NEW ZEALAND SCHEME (1980)*

[The excerpts below drawn from several chapters first summarize the New Zealand Accident Compensation Act of 1972 and the compensation scheme which it introduced. They then address a few aspects of the scheme.]

[Introduction]

Stated over-simply, the main features of the system are as follows. A statutory body, the ACC [Accident Compensation Commission], is the administering agency and adjudicating tribunal. The main revenues of the system are derived in three ways and recorded in three funds.

1. Levies on employers and the self-employed are collected by the Inland Revenue (a collecting agent for the ACC), and paid into an "earners' fund". The rate of levy payable in respect of employees ranges from 50 cents to $5.00 per $100.00 of payroll (as of 1 April 1979) depending on the risk classification of the employment. For the self-employed there is a standard rate of $1.00 per $100.00 of earnings.

2. Levies on motor vehicles are collected by the Post Office (a collecting agent for the ACC) as part of the motor vehicle license fee. These levies are paid into a "motor vehicle fund". The rate of levy for an ordinary motor car is $14.20 per annum, with other rates applying to other types of motor vehicles.

3. A "supplementary fund" is created from general government revenues to provide benefits in respect of injuries not covered by either of the other two funds, for example, housewives injured at home.

The distribution of the benefit cost among the three funds is determined by the following general principles.

1. Benefits paid in respect of earners are charged to the earners' fund regardless of the cause of injury, unless the injury was caused by a motor vehicle accident while the earner was not at work, [nor] commuting to or from work.

2. Benefits paid in respect of injuries caused by motor vehicle accidents are charged to the motor vehicle fund, except for an injury to an earner who was at work, or commuting to or from work.

* The following excerpts from Terence Ison, Accident Compensation: A Commentary on the　New Zealand Scheme (1980), are reprinted by permission of Croom Helm Ltd. Publishers.

3. Where an injury is compensable under the Act and the benefits are not chargeable to either of the other two funds, they are paid out of the supplementary fund.

There are special provisions relating to members of the Armed Forces.

All three funds are administered by the ACC.

All cases of "personal injury by accident" are covered by the plan, and that phrase is defined to include occupational diseases. Most other disabilities from disease are excluded.

The benefits depend on the nature and duration of the injury, its economic significance, and the losses suffered by the claimant. The full cost of medical care is usually covered. Apart from that, the main benefits are:

1. Earnings related compensation (ERC). Periodic payments are made to those who, by reason of injury, are wholly or partly disabled from work. After the first week, the rate of payment for temporary or permanent total disability is 80 percent of pre-accident earnings with a maximum compensation payment for this benefit of $288.00 per week (as of 1 April 1979). These payments may continue up to the age of 65, or a later age if the claimant was injured after the age of 60 years. These benefits are taxable income and PAYE tax is deducted at source.

2. Lump sums for permanent disability.

3. Rehabilitation aids and services.

4. Expenses and losses resulting from the injury, for example, the costs of attending for medical treatment, damage to clothing, and housekeeping services.

In fatal cases the main benefits are:

1. Earnings related compensation, i.e., periodic payments for a surviving dependent spouse, and dependent children.

2. Lump sums for a surviving dependent spouse, and dependent children.

3. Funeral and other expenses.

Most claims are decided and administered in the local offices of the State Insurance Office (SIO), which are located in towns throughout the country. The SIO is a state-owned company running a general insurance business in competition with other insurance companies. With regard to claims under the Accident Compensation Act, however, the SIO acts as agent for the ACC.

* * *

Apart from dealing with compensation claims and rehabilitation, the ACC also has a statutory role in relation to safety.

* * *

The Act abolishes tort liability in respect of injuries covered by the scheme. Injuries sustained in industry, on military service, or as a result of crime are now included in the comprehensive plan rather than being covered by separate systems. There are, however, other systems of compensation for disablement that still survive independently of the Accident Compensation Act. In particular, those disabled by disease or congenital abnormality may be eligible for benefits under the general welfare system. Also company sick pay plans still survive. Similarly private policies of sickness and accident insurance are not prohibited, nor have they disappeared. But of course the need for private coverage is diminished in respect of injuries covered by the scheme.

* * *

The reasons for the reform are clear. The humanity, efficiency, justice and economy that can be achieved by compensating all victims of injury under a comprehensive plan, rather than in separate categories by reference to the cause of disablement, have been well documented.

Exactly why New Zealand was the first country to adopt a reform of this type is less clear. An imaginative attempt to find an explanation in the values implicit in New Zealand culture did not produce any easy or definite answers. It is clear, however, that New Zealand has a tradition of communal as well as individual responsibility, and a tradition of organising communal responsibility in a systematic way. In particular, the country already had an organised system of public medical care. Thus the *Woodhouse Report* [Report of the Royal Commission on Compensation for Personal Injury in New Zealand, 1967] was not embracing any alien view when it began its statement of objectives with a principle of community responsibility.

> Just as a modern society benefits from the productive work of its citizens, so should society accept responsibility for those willing to work but prevented from doing so by physical incapacity. And, since we all persist in following community activities, which year by year exact a predictable and inevitable price in bodily injury, so should we all share in sustaining those who become the random but statistically necessary victims. The inherent cost of these community purposes should be borne on a basis of equity by the community. (Para. 56)

* * *

[*Coverage*]

The system generally covers all cases of "personal injury by accident" without inquiry into fault, without inquiry into cause, and for the most part, without other qualifying requirements that would delay or complicate the payment of benefits. Thus apart from being desirable in itself, the universality of coverage helps to facilitate the quick and efficient administration of claims, and it helps to avoid anxieties by allowing each injured person to know from the start that he is covered by the Act.

Unfortunately, however, the principle of universal coverage has been applied to injuries, not to all disabilities.

* * *

* * * [T]he following categories of disease are covered:

(a) Any disease that is a consequence of a compensable injury or a consequence of the accident. For example, where a wound is compensable, a disease resulting from the infection of the wound would be compensable.

(b) Occupational diseases.

(c) A disease resulting from "medical misadventure".

(d) Any disease wilfully inflicted by one person upon another in violation of section 201 of the Crimes Act, 1961.

Subject to those exceptions, the general rule is that disabilities and deaths resulting from disease are not covered.

* * *

It is difficult to see why, in the allocation of resources to compensation for human disablement, the victims of disease should be assigned a lower priority than the victims of injury. The needs of the disabled reflect the consequences of disablement, which depend on the nature, the extent, the duration, and the social and environmental significance of the disability. The needs of the disabled do not vary according to the cause of disablement.

* * *

[*Benefits: Lump Sums*]

Two sections of the Act result in lump sums being paid in cases of permanent disability (total or partial). These sums differ from the lump sums normally discussed in compensation literature in that they are not paid for loss of earnings or earning capacity. They are separate from ERC [Earnings related compensation] and are payable regardless of any entitlement to ERC.

Under section 119, a lump sum is payable for "permanent loss or impairment of any bodily function". The maximum is $7,000 and this is the amount paid in cases of total permanent disability. Partial disabilities are classified as a percentage of total disability. For guidance in assessing the percentage, Schedule 2 of the Act lists a variety of physical impairments to each of which is ascribed a percentage figure.

The second lump sum under section 120 is payable in respect of—

(a) The loss suffered by the person of amenities or capacity for enjoying life, including loss from disfigurement; and

(b) Pain and mental suffering, including nervous shock and neurosis:

Provided that no such compensation shall be payable in respect of that loss, pain, or suffering unless, in the opinion of the Commission, the loss, pain, or suffering (having regard to its nature, intensity, duration, and any other relevant circumstances) has been or is or may become of a sufficient degree to justify payment of compensation under this subsection.

The maximum under this section is $10,000. The amount payable in each case under section 120 is decided by a judgment, inevitably subjective, about the effect of the injury on the claimant. The proportion of the maximum that is awarded under section 120 may be higher or lower than the proportion of the maximum awarded under section 119.

* * *

Perhaps the greatest concern about the lump sums relates to section 120. Compensation for pain and suffering and for loss of the amenities of life, assessed on an intuitive basis, is a concept inherited from the tort system, and one that has no rational place in a system of social insurance. There are no objective criteria for assessing the amount and the administrative cost can be high in relation to the compensation awarded. Some guidelines can be established, but the decisions inevitably rest on intuitive judgments, and whatever the award, a good advocate can always find arguments for an appeal. It is hard to explain section 120 except as a political concession to overcome the opposition of those interest groups that would have benefited from the retention of tort liability.

* * *

[*Financing the Compensation Scheme*]

No one knows, or ever will know comprehensively, how the cost of the system is distributed. The earners' fund is drawn from levies imposed on employers and the self-employed. But the cost of the levy imposed on an employer, for example a freezing company, might be:

(1) absorbed by the company in the form of lower profits;

(2) passed on to consumers in the form of higher prices;

(3) passed back to labour in the form of lower wage rates; or

(4) passed back to suppliers (e.g., farmers) in the form of lower net prices.

The actual distribution will depend upon the relevant markets and the bargaining position of the parties concerned. It may change from time to time, and as a practical matter, it will be obscured by inflation and other events that have a more profound and noticeable impact on wages and prices.

* * *

The distribution of the cost is, however, rarely recognised in political and public discussion. * * * The notion that the cost is borne where it is first imposed is one that doggedly persists and that remains impervious to any contrary evidence or argument. For example, the Employers' Federation has been arguing that the cost of non-work accidents ought not to be paid out of the earners' fund because these costs ought not to be borne by employers. There is no recognition of the hidden contributions that employees and consumers make to the employment levy, and which could exceed the contributions of employers.

The self-employed pay a flat rate levy of $1.00 per $100.00 of earnings. For levies paid by employers there is a classification system. Each employment is assigned to an industrial class, and the employer pays the rate of levy applicable to that class. There is a statutory minimum of 25 per $100.00 of payroll, though as of 1 April 1979, the lowest actual rate is 50 per $100.00. There is a maximum of $5.00 per $100.00 of payroll and several classes of employment are at that rate. One industrial operation, however, may be split into several classifications. For example, at a manufacturing plant, the production workers may be assigned to one class and the managerial and clerical workers to another class.

* * *

The primary argument for classification is good social cost accounting. The contribution of each industry to the fund should be roughly proportionate to the costs imposed by that industry on the fund, so that each product will bear in the market the cost of its own production. Another argument is that the employers in an industry often collaborate in trade associations and a classification system can encourage these associations to promote safety programs among their members.

* * *

A classification system is also used for the motor vehicle fund, but it is more rudimentary. The classification is by type of vehicle. There is no classification by make. There is, however, surely an opportunity here for making the safety features of a vehicle more relevant in the market by classifying motor vehicles by type, with sub-classes by make. It could well be that the dollar differences in the levy per make among the sub-classes would not be very great. But those differences would at least provide the public with some indicator of the claims experience relating to different makes of motor vehicles, and if those differences are used by consumers as a buying guide, that could help to make manufacturers more sensitive to safety features.

An alternative system might be to raise the motor vehicle levy in the form of a petrol tax rather than an insurance premium. The levy would then be more risk-related on a mileage basis; but it would be less risk-related in other ways. For example, in relation to the risk of claims resulting from their use, trucks would be over-paying compared with motor cycles.

* * *

———

NEW ZEALAND AMENDMENTS. In 1992 the New Zealand accident compensation scheme was amended in a number of respects. Following is a summary of notable changes. For a more detailed examination, see Miller, An Analysis and Critique of the 1992 Changes to New Zealand's Accident Compensation Scheme, 52 Md.L.Rev. 1070 (1993).

The basic commitment of the New Zealand scheme—its grand displacement of tort—remains. The scheme continues to abolish tort for all covered injuries. It continues to provide compensation of medical expense, and earnings-related compensation, for workplace injuries, auto accidents, and all other personal injuries caused by accident. One general change of the 1992 amendments was the elimination of the "lump sum" recoveries for permanent impairment and for pain and suffering which had been awarded, on an individuated basis, in limited amount. A very modest "independence allowance" for the disabled, paid weekly, was added.

The three main sources of revenue for the system, established in 1972, remain. The three sources cover, respectively, workplace injuries, auto accidents, and injuries to non-earners. (1) Workplace injuries are paid for by employer contributions. The New Zealand scheme continues to operate as a comprehensive workers' compensation plan, barring tort suits for on-the-job accidents against employers and anyone else (e.g., product suppliers). Employer contributions vary according to the classification of employment involved. In addition to rating by industrial category, the 1992 amendments require experience-rating of employers. (2) Injuries from auto accidents are paid for by contributions from operators of motor vehicles. In this respect the New Zealand scheme remains a pure auto no-fault plan, involving complete—not partial—tort abolition. The 1972 financing mechanism, a fee collected annually from each vehicle owner, remains. The 1992 amendments impose a per-liter gasoline tax as another source of revenue for auto-related injuries. (3) The funding source for accidents involving non-workers— children, students, homemakers, the elderly—remains the same. Except for auto-related accidents, injuries to non-earners—for example, a homemaker injured at home—are paid for out of general government revenues.

One quite interesting change involves the handling of injuries to earners that occur off the job. Under the 1972 statute, non-work accidents of workers were paid for by employer contributions, the same as on-the-job injuries. The 1992 amendments set up a new funding mechanism in the nature of a payroll tax on employees. Workers are obligated to contribute a flat percent of earnings; employers withhold the assessment from employees' wages. The result is a compulsory "first party" insurance program for employees' off-the-job accidents.

The biggest change involves injuries arising out of medical treatment. The 1972 legislation included compensation for "medical misadventure," but that term was left undefined by statute. The 1992 amendments break down medical misadventure into two categories: "medical mishap" and "medical error." A "medical mishap" is an adverse consequence of treatment that is both "rare" (likely to occur in no more than 1% of cases) and "severe." A finding of medical mishap does not require a finding of malpractice, but the same is not true with respect to the more encompassing category, "medical error." "Medical error" is defined as the failure to exercise proper care and skill—in other words, as medical malpractice. Thus the 1992 amendments introduce the idea of negligence or fault, on the part of a medical provider, into what had previously been a staunchly nonfault compensation scheme. The 1992 amendments also set up a new financing mechanism for medical misadventure awards: health professionals, divided into classes, are required to make contributions to pay for the injuries caused by their activities.

Chapter 23

PHYSICAL HARM IN THE MODERN STATE

The present chapter takes a look at direct regulation of physical risk by modern administrative agencies. It does so through materials that are, of necessity, rather general and introductory in nature. A question immediately presents itself: why should the study of tort lead to an examination of regulation? Regulatory rule-making is very different from tort adjudication. It is based on statutory interpretation, not common law. It does not provide reparation, unlike tort and also unlike no-fault plans.

One reason for such examination is that direct regulation of risk—health, safety, and environmental regulation—is an important part of the background of the tort law of accidents. Direct regulation is a major mechanism of accident law. Like tort, it aims to control the harmful fallout of productive activity in our society. To some extent, regulation is an alternative to tort. Indeed, regulation enters tort, as in the doctrine of negligence per se. Pertinent regulation gets noted in tort discussion of dangerous activity, nuisance, and products liability. We have, in a way, been looking at regulation right along—at least, we have seen how regulation appears within tort cases, refracted by tort law's lens.

The main idea behind the present chapter is this: some further study of how regulation is conducted by administrative bodies may throw a powerful light on tort law proper. That is, the main reason for going more deeply into the topic of regulation is to gain a deeper understanding of the regulatory aspects of tort, particularly tort law of negligence. The materials on administrative regulation that follow are rather basic. They raise fundamental issues that relate to the most famous expression of tort law's regulatory purpose, the Hand Formula for determining negligence.

In the notation of the Hand Formula, introduced at p. 14 supra, negligence is the situation in which "B < P x L." Negligence analysis assesses the probability of loss ("P x L") that might be avoided by a safety precaution; estimates the burden ("B") that would have to be borne in order to avoid that risk; then weighs "B" against "PL," in order to strike a balance. Due care is achieved when any further B would be greater than the PL it would reduce.

The following materials raise two fundamental questions that challenge use of the BPL framework. These broad questions lurk in the background of every negligence case involving serious physical risk. But common law judges and juries proceed case by case, always attentive to particularities of the concrete situation at hand, and the broad questions tend to remain in the background. By contrast, regulators who make rules designed to control whole industries over large stretches of time are more exposed to basic critique. The two fundamental questions are at the heart of the contemporary debate about regulation of physical risk.

The first question is very basic: what is the justifiable level of risk for social life? According to the Hand Formula, the proper level of risk is, of course, the BPL level. In the jargon of regulation, this is the cost-benefit level, the level at which marginal costs of regulation are just offset by marginal benefits. But is this level indeed right? Is it fair? The following materials show that regulators sometimes go beyond the cost-benefit level, seeking to reduce risk to the lowest level "feasible," or seeking to ensure "safety" regardless of cost. A fierce debate is going on between champions of cost-benefit balancing, and those who insist that health, safety, and environmental regulation must be more protective. In this debate claims of utility clash with claims of fairness.

The second question is, if anything, more basic: what is the value of life? Loss of life, the thing we most fear from undue risk, is the most important "L" for BPL analysis. Avoiding premature death is the most important "benefit" to be weighed in cost-benefit balancing. How can regulators determine the value of a life saved, in order to decide whether costs of life-saving regulation are justified? Materials that follow present alternative approaches, used in regulatory contexts, for determining the value of a life. Included is a curious line of tort cases in which the question surfaces, only to be brushed aside as unanswerable. But if the value of life is unknowable, how can cost-benefit regulation—or BPL analysis—proceed?

The two vital questions canvassed above are addressed, respectively, in the second and third sections of this chapter. The first section, just below, briefly reviews the recent history and defining characteristics of direct regulation, thus setting the stage.

SECTION A. REGULATION OF RISK

REPARATION AND REGULATION

Tort liability and no-fault plans are "reparation systems." That is, they seek to offset the harm caused by an accident by providing full or partial compensation to the accident victim, and they impose the duty of making reparation on an actor or activity deemed responsible for causing the harm. Thus reparation systems at the same time compensate victims and regulate risk. Their regulatory impact lies in the fact that they impose costs of accidents on accident-causing activities, and so create cost pressures toward greater safety.

Now given that reparation systems all pursue dual aims—compensation and regulation alike—it is possible to set them off as a distinct type in contrast to other mechanisms of accident law, here called "background institutions." Background institutions are defined as legal mechanisms that *either* compensate accident victims, *or* regulate risky activity, but do not do both.

Compensation apart from regulation is undertaken by private loss insurance and government benefit programs (discussed in Chapter 15). These mechanisms handle an enormous volume of accident costs, but they are not "reparation systems." They do not operate on the principle that an actor who has done harm to another should repair all or part of the harm caused.

Loss insurance operates on the principle of contract, paying benefits up to policy limits to those potential victims who have arranged in advance for such protection. Government programs of social insurance or welfare, reflecting ideals of social justice, transfer funds in restricted amount to all eligible persons suffering certain defined needs or economic misfortunes, whether arising from physical accident or otherwise. Such mechanisms lack a "regulatory impact" because they do not undertake to fasten particular accident costs on the specific risky activity that gave rise to them. Thus an accident caused, say, by blasting or a product defect may end up being compensated by all premium-payers who contribute to Blue Cross, or all taxpayers who contribute to Social Security.

Regulation apart from compensation is undertaken in a host of substantive and procedural modes at all levels of government in order to induce safety and avoid accidents. Among notable forms of such regulation are statutory norms backed by injunctions or criminal process, criteria for permits or licenses administered in screening systems, municipal codes or industry standards enforced by inspections plus fines, recalls, shut-down orders, and the like.

Direct regulation of risk, conducted independently of any attempt to compensate victims, is a perennial legal endeavor that has burgeoned in recent years. It rivals reparation as society's chief means for controlling the harmful physical fallout of productive activity. The regulatory form of greatest contemporary importance involves the fashioning of safety, health, and environmental standards by administrative agencies. The present chapter is devoted to an examination of this phenomenon—modern complex regulation. It provides an occasion for reexamining rationales commonly said to underlie the tort law of reparation.

DAVID VOGEL, THE "NEW" SOCIAL REGULATION IN HISTORICAL AND COMPARATIVE PERSPECTIVE

McCraw, ed., Regulation in Perspective (1981).*

Between 1900 and 1980, the United States experienced three sustained political efforts to transform the structure and dynamics of business-govern-

* Reprinted by permission of Harvard Business School Press, from McCraw, ed., Regulation in Perspective, Boston, MA, 1981, pp. 155–165.

Copyright © 1981 by the President and Fellows of Harvard College; all rights reserved.

ment relations. The first two of these periods are familiar to historians as the Progressive Era and the New Deal; the third—which still lacks a convenient label—is rooted in the consumer, civil rights, and antiwar movements that emerged during the sixties. * * *

* * *

The boundaries of the most recent wave of governmental intervention in the economy are * * * difficult to determine. Unlike the two previous periods, this one does not correspond to sudden shifts in focus of any particular presidential administration, but spans four administrations of widely disparate character. Although lack of an adequate historical perspective makes any assessment hazardous, the years 1964 through 1977 appear to be reasonable boundary dates.

* * *

* * * In the public debate over business-government relations during the 1960s and 1970s, the importance of corporate social performance has been unprecedented, not only in the United States, but in any industrial democracy. The exposés of the muckrakers [in the Progressive period], like the accusations of corporate malfeasance that surfaced during the thirties, focused heavily on corporate abuses that affected the economic welfare of consumers, workers, investors, and taxpayers. The prime corporate villains for the Progressives were the trusts that victimized both consumers and small businessmen, while supporters of the New Deal aimed most of their antibusiness rhetoric at manipulations by the financial community.

In sharp contrast, the accusations of corporate misconduct that so preoccupied public opinion during the 1960s and 1970s concentrated on dangers to the health and safety of the citizenry. The following is a partial list of those corporate products that, during the sixties and seventies, were alleged to cause irreparable harm to the public: DDT, cigarettes, the Corvair, flammable children's pajamas, phosphates, poisonous household cleaners, Firestone radial tires, Kepone, DCP, DES, Tris, leaded gasoline, vinyl chloride, the Pinto, aerosol spray cans, asbestos, tampons, cyclamates, saccharin, Dalkon Shields, and the DC–10. And to this list, which could be expanded almost indefinitely, should be added the environmental hazards associated with the nuclear power plant at Three Mile Island and the toxic chemical wastes dumped at Love Canal, as well as the more generalized threats to public health reportedly caused by the presence of various chemicals and particles in the nation's air and water. In short, we are dealing with a level of public consciousness about environmental, consumer, and occupational hazards that appears to be of a different order of magnitude from public outrage over such issues during both the Progressive Era and the New Deal.

During the New Deal, consumer and environmental protection were on the periphery of the political agenda, while during the Progressive Era, they shared the spotlight with such issues as industrial concentration, tariff policy, banking reform, and the rights of workers. But during the last two decades, while other issues directly involving the relationship between business and government, such as the urban crisis, Watergate, overseas payments, and unemployment, have come and gone, battles over consumer and environmental protection have persisted with extraordinary regularity. Legislation in the areas of environmental and consumer protection was debated and acted upon by every session of Congress from the beginning of the sixties through the end of the seventies. Moreover, growing public concern with the economy's poor performance throughout the seventies did not succeed in pushing social regulatory issues off the political agenda; on the contrary, their relative costs and benefits underlay a significant portion of the public debate over energy shortages, inflation, declining productivity, and reindustrialization. * * *

In addition to their relative political saliency, the controls over corporate social conduct enacted during the 1960s and 1970s differ in number and impact from those initiated during both the Progressive Era and the New Deal. Prior to the 1960s, social regulatory programs were administered almost exclusively by state and local governments. From 1900 through 1965, only one regulatory agency was established at the federal level whose primary responsibility was to protect either consumers, employees, or the public from physical harm due to corporate activities: the Food and Drug Administration, established in 1931. Between [1966] and 1977, [nine] federal regulatory agencies were created with this as their mandate: * * * the National Transportation Safety Board (1966), the Council on Environmental Quality (1969), the Environmental Protection Agency (1970), the National Highway Traffic Safety Administration (1970), the Occupational Safety and Health Administration (1970), the Consumer Product Safety Commission (1972), the Mining Enforcement and Safety Administration (1973), the Materials Transportation Bureau (1975), and the Office of Strip Mining Regulation and Enforcement (1977).

Equally striking is the comparative increase in each period in the number of laws restricting corporate social conduct. In the broad area of consumer safety and health, five new laws were enacted by the federal government during the Progressive Era, eleven during the New Deal, and a total of sixty-two between 1964 and 1979. Job safety and other working conditions were the focus of a total of five pieces of national legislation during both the Progressive Era and the New Deal; from 1960 through 1978, twenty-one laws were approved in this area. Two statutes regulating energy and the environment were enacted by the federal government during the Progressive Era, five during the New Deal, and thirty-two during the most recent period of increased government intervention.

Even more significant is the relative impact of the newer regulatory statutes. Government regulations enacted prior to the sixties generally tended to affect either one or a handful of related industries. Additional such laws were enacted during the sixties and seventies, including the Traffic Safety Act, the Child Protection and Toy Safety Act, the Coal Mine Safety Amendments, the Lead Based Paint Elimination Act, the Wholesale Poultry Products Act, and the Toxic Substances Control Act. What is novel about the social regulatory laws of the sixties and seventies is that a significant portion of them cut across industry lines: this is true of all the air and water pollution control statutes, * * * as well as both the Occupational Safety and

Health Act and the Consumer Product Safety Act. By vastly expanding the scope of federal social regulation, these laws have succeeded in undermining much of the historic distinction between regulated and unregulated industries.

The result of the increased number of new regulatory laws and agencies, with their expanded scope, was an increase in the intrusion of the federal government into an array of what formerly were private corporate decisions. Regulatory officials began routinely to shape and influence virtually every important decision made by virtually every firm. * * *

* * *

The direct and indirect costs of compliance by business are * * * difficult to determine. Some regulations may force companies to make expenditures they would have made anyway, while in other cases the costs may be passed on to consumers. Nor do regulations affect all companies or industries equally: the costs of compliance, in the area of environmental protection, the single most expensive category of regulations, disproportionately affect four industries—utilities, paper, chemicals, and steel—while other companies have managed to carve out a profitable market selling pollution control equipment to companies in those industries. Moreover the debate over the costs of regulation has become highly polarized with supporters of regulation prone to minimize them and critics of regulation likely to exaggerate them. Nevertheless, the overall costs of corporate compliance with the regulations affecting health, safety, and environmental protection that were enacted during the sixties and seventies totaled in the tens of billions of dollars by 1980. According to one reliable study, environmental and worker health and safety programs cut conventionally measured productivity by 1.4 percent between 1970 and 1975.

In sum, we are dealing with an increase in government intervention in the economy at least proportionately as great as that which occurred during the Progressive Era and the New Deal; the difference is that in the sixties and seventies, this expansion primarily took the form of increased regulation of corporate social conduct.

* * *

* * * [W]hat is novel about the politics of business-government relations during the last fifteen years is that conflicts over the scope of social regulation have affected directly the power and wealth of the private sector vis-à-vis nonbusiness interest groups. In essence, during the seventies, the controversy over the social regulation of business became the focus of class conflict: it pitted the interests of business as a whole against the public interest movement as well as much of organized labor. The nature of the conflict over regulation became analogous to the struggle over the adoption of the welfare state and the recognition of unions that defined class conflict during the 1930s.

This perspective makes sense out of an episode that at first appears puzzling: the extraordinary mobilization of business political resources during the mid-seventies to defeat the proposal to create a Consumer

Protection Agency. A coalition of more than 450 separate organizations and institutions was organized to defeat the CPA—even though the agency itself would have no enforcement powers against business and was certainly among the more innocuous of the newer social regulatory agencies that had been proposed since the early sixties. Only the labor reform bill—a traditional focus of class conflict—stimulated as much corporate coalition building. The explanation is that by 1977 business had come to see regulation as a class issue: executives became concerned not simply with the impact of particular regulatory policies on their companies' balance sheets, but with the broader principle of government regulation itself. * * *

REGULATORY STANDARDS

Modern regulation of physical risk uses the technique of administrative standard-setting to control the physical fallout of social activity—accidents, health injury, environmental harm. In fact regulatory bodies in this area have multiple functions and enforcement tools, and engage in individualized screening or licensing as well as standard-setting. But their key function is to translate broad statutory norms into detailed regulatory standards.

The regulatory process begins with legislative enactment of a scheme of restraints meant to govern a type of harm. A statutory scheme may be complex and ramified, but normally its provisions include highly general language authorizing control of undue risk. Characteristically the job of implementing the open-ended statutory precepts is delegated to executive officials. The recipient of delegated powers is the modern administrative agency, a bureaucratically organized body having specialized functions and personnel that serves as a center for enforcement of related statutes. The typical agency focusses its attention and accumulated expertise on risks that arise as the side-effect of many sorts of activities or industries. It aspires to develop systematic policy and coordinated strategy within its area of regulatory concern. In reducing broad precepts to specific standards, the agency employs conventional administrative methods such as notice-and-comment rule-making. The upshot is detailed regulation specifying kinds of risk and degrees of exposure allowable in various activities, and prescribing safeguards and control technologies that must be undertaken, all in order to discipline and restructure harmful behavior. Thus the regulatory norm, in the hands of the agency, is an implement for deep and precise criticism of risky social practice.

Direct regulation of physical risk is a major institution of modern accident law. In order to understand how the law affects any given category of risky activity and its characteristic physical fallout, it is important to remember the operation and impact of regulatory schemes as well as reparation systems. Regulation and reparation each aim to bring about proper levels of precaution. Reparation systems—that is, tort and no-fault plans—require actors to compensate victims of risk, and so induce safety by fastening cost pressures on risky activity. Regulatory schemes impose non-compensatory sanctions—fines and imprisonment—on actors who deviate from prescribed safety norms.

Three notable phenomena of modern reparation law are products liability, workers compensation, and auto no-fault. Their counterparts in regulation are three of the most active and controversial administrative agencies of federal government—the Consumer Product Safety Commission (CPSC), the Occupational Safety and Health Administration (OSHA), and the National Highway Traffic Safety Administration (NHTSA), all created during the period 1966–1972. A fourth federal agency set up at the same time—the Environmental Protection Agency (EPA)—has regulatory jurisdiction over types of fallout also addressed by the tort law of abnormally dangerous activity and nuisance. These four regulatory bodies—CPSC, OSHA, NHTSA, EPA—by themselves have sufficient institutional weight and prominence to render regulation a central, not a peripheral, mechanism of accident law.

Direct regulation—the sort addressed in the present chapter—sets the permitted level of risk that actors must, through various means, maintain. An alternative approach is indirect regulation, which relies on incentives constructed by government plus market pressures. An example would be a tax on pollution. A tax scheme would induce actors to adopt pollution control devices, but allow them to pollute—and pay the tax—when prevention would be unduly expensive. The virtues of indirect regulation are debated in excerpts that follow from a report on regulation commissioned by the American Bar Association and approved by the ABA House of Delegates.

AMERICAN BAR ASSOCIATION COMMISSION ON LAW AND THE ECONOMY, FEDERAL REGULATION: ROADS TO REFORM (1979)*

[1. The Commission's Preference for Market-Based Alternatives]

The Commission's review of the characteristics of classical regulation leads it to make the following recommendations:

RECOMMENDATION 1: In lieu of governmental intervention in the economy, reliance should be placed when feasible upon the competitive market as regulator supported by antitrust laws. Where governmental intervention is required, consideration should be given to disclosure or to incentive-based modes of regulation before turning to the classical command and control modes.

RECOMMENDATION 2: Careful consideration and utilization by Congress and the Executive Branch of analytical principles, such as the following four "rules of thumb," are urged to avoid mismatches between a particular need for governmental intervention and the regulatory method used to meet that need:

* * *

* Reprinted with permission from the American Bar Association, Federal Regulation: Roads to Reform, Copyright ©1979 American Bar Association.

(d) Classical standard-setting is needed to protect the public by controlling dangerous conditions and substances, but where possible in dealing with problems of "spillovers" (such as environmental pollution or safety) less restrictive tools (such as taxes, disclosure, or bargaining) should be considered as supplements to, or as partial substitutes for, classical standard-setting.

* * *

[The Commission canvassed various types of "market defects" that provide "reasons typically given to justify regulation." Apart from "unequal bargaining power," "inadequate information," and "paternalism," the justification of greatest relevance to regulation of physical risk is "the asserted need to correct for 'spillovers' ":]

Regulation is frequently justified by the need to compensate for the fact that the price of a product does not reflect major costs that its production and use impose upon society.

Thus, the price of steel in the past did not reflect the "spillover" costs (sometimes referred to as "externalities") that its manufacture imposes in the form of air pollution. Neither the manufacturer nor the consumer bears these costs. As a result, the demand for steel will be greater than it would be if buyers had to pay for the cost of its manufacture's adverse side effects.

Of course, the harmful effects of pollution result both from the steel company's production process and the fact that people live near the plant. In theory, steel users and pollution sufferers might agree to share the cost of pollution reduction through the installation of antipollution equipment if they could readily bargain between themselves. However, it is likely that such bargaining is impracticable, and regulation in the presence of spillover costs is a way of correcting for that fact.

* * *

* * * [C]lassical standard-setting is difficult to administer and can cause significant anticompetitive and "technology freezing" harm. The more complex the problem, the more points that must be monitored, the more modifications and exceptions needed, the more technologically related the problems, the more likely it is that these harms will occur. Thus, one should search for less restrictive alternatives, where feasible.

To many economists, some type of tax system offers a promising approach to spillover problems, such as environmental pollution. Since the problem is that the price of product A does not reflect an important social cost it imposes (i.e., pollution), the economist proposes raising the price by means of a tax, to reflect the harm. * * *

* * * [T]he virtue of a tax lies * * * in its power to act as an incentive to develop more cost-effective antipollution methods. A tax also avoids freezing current technology while preserving a degree of individual choice. * * *

* * * [I]n many respects, the problem involves achievement of a better balance between two competing goods—clean environment and industrial production—which are in part mutually exclusive, but both of which are desired. The solution requires both a balancing among goods and strong incentives (1) to consumers to shift away from pollution-causing products, and (2) to producers to shift to, or to develop, pollution-free processes. Relative prices perform just such functions throughout the economy. Except where especially serious health hazards exist, thus justifying an outright prohibition on polluting substances, a price tag on pollution allows buyers to balance the competing "environmental" and "industrial" goods and provides incentives in the right direction. A tax allows those with a special need or desire for the polluting item to obtain it (thus permitting continuous individual balancing) while providing a continuing incentive to manufacturers to find cleaner production methods.

* * *

It is important to remember that a pollution tax is only one possible market-related approach to the problem. Under this approach, an agency would set a tax per unit of pollutant emitted. A firm would be free to pollute provided it paid the tax. Another market-related approach is for an agency to set an absolute limit on the amount of pollutant that can be emitted in a given region and to issue "marketable rights" to pollute up to this level. Those "rights" could be sold by the government to firms which would either use them or sell them to others. To pollute without a permit would be unlawful.

* * *

When compared with classical standard-setting * * * either system seems more efficient. A tax, for example, would encourage firms to buy nonpolluting equipment up to the point where the equipment's cost exceeded the amount of the tax. Thus, units of pollution would be eliminated in rank order of least cost. Under such a system the only pollution remaining would be that which was the most expensive to eliminate. Similarly, "marketable rights" would be sold and exchanged until they fell into the hands of those to whom they were most valuable—namely, the creators of those units of pollution that were the most expensive to prevent. * * *

In sum, the needs for balancing the extent to which resources are put to conflicting use, for providing incentives, for producing a broad variety of different end results, and for dealing with a large number of enterprises all point toward the use of a tax or similar incentive-based system. These advantages, weighed against the problems of standard-setting, make the effort to devise a practical * * * regulatory taxation mechanism important to substantive regulatory reform.

A stronger case for standard-setting can be made with regard to workplace health and safety. * * * [B]ut the total elimination of all [occupational] risks is not feasible. * * * A proper balance would include creation of incentives to avoid the more dangerous activities, products, and production processes, and to invent safer technology.

Inadequate information is often part of the problem, and disclosure requirements would provide a useful supplement to standard-setting. Where union contracts are in place, the bargaining system may help to resolve some safety problems in particular plants. An improved system of workers compensation would be a useful adjunct to safety standards by providing employers with enhanced incentives to improve safety conditions. These and other mechanisms used as supplements to safety standards, would allow those standards to be used only for the most severe problems, where standards are both essential and practical.

[2. Dissenting Statement of Commissioner Elliot Bredhoff]

The Commission's critique of classical standard-setting as a regulatory tool strikes me as unduly harsh. * * *

Nor do I believe that the problems which the Commission considers to be inherent in classical standard-setting justify the conclusion that a tax system would be a desirable alternative in many contexts. * * * The difficulties in arriving at proper tax rates are as great as those entailed in setting proper standards. I disagree also with the Commission's apparent belief that standards necessarily freeze technology. In my judgment a tax system provides no greater incentive for innovation than a standard which allows for flexibility in the mode of compliance or which permits variances for new technology.

* * *

I am particularly troubled by the Commission's remarks regarding the regulation of workplace health and safety. * * * [There] the Commission's ultimate conclusion is that with better utilization of various mechanisms such as collective bargaining, disclosure of information, and an improved system of workers compensation, standards would not be needed except for "the most severe problems." That assessment is entirely unrealistic.

* * * [T]here will be few instances in which a regulatory agency could prudently decide to leave significant aspects of worker safety and health to bargaining rather than regulation. By the same token, while it is certainly important for employees to be given better knowledge of the hazards of their jobs, only rarely would disclosure of information obviate the need for a protective standard. * * *

Finally, an "improved system of workers compensation" would be desirable for several reasons, including the fact that it would provide employers with a somewhat greater incentive to provide a safe and healthy workplace. But the possibility of this enhanced incentive would not justify any lessened reliance on standards. * * * [T]he incentive created by workers compensation would not be very large in most situations. The likelihood of many types of industrial accidents and illnesses is perceived to be so small in absolute terms, that many employers would be willing to run the risk of incurring even a large potential penalty in the belief that "it can't happen here." In addition, for many hazards, particularly occupational diseases, proof of causality is so difficult as to greatly weaken the incentive effect of any potential penalty. * * *

* * *

* * * I cannot agree that the regulatory agencies have proved themselves to be incapable of making balancing choices which involve national goals other than the particular goals primarily entrusted to each agency. The fact is that in large part the agencies simply have not been called upon by their enabling statutes to undertake that task.

* * *

Indeed, the philosophy of many regulatory statutes, particularly those concerned with health and safety, is fundamentally at odds with the concept of "balancing" espoused by the Commission. * * *

SECTION B. REGULATORY PRINCIPLES

RISK–ASSESSMENT

Underlying regulation of physical risk are two types of inquiry. "Risk-assessment" predicts the positive effect of regulation, or the amount of physical harm that might be avoided by a specified control on risky activity. "Cost-assessment" considers negative consequences, or what must be given up in order to achieve the postulated level of safety. These two aspects of regulatory analysis correspond to the two elements of the Hand Formula for determining negligence in tort. According to Judge Hand, negligence analysis should calculate the probability of loss ("PL") generated by a risky condition, and also estimate the burden ("B") that would have to be borne in order to eliminate that risk. United States v. Carroll Towing Co., 159 F.2d 169 (2d Cir.1947); see p. 14, supra.

Risk-assessment by modern administrative agencies is an affair of considerable complexity and often, considerable uncertainty. In major standard-setting proceedings, regulatory bodies use statistical technique and probabilistic theory in order to calculate general classes of risks across situations and over time. Regulatory risk-assessment determines "PL"—the magnitude of avoidable detriment arising from risky activity—on rather a grand scale.

The case that follows this introductory note—The Benzene Case, decided by the Supreme Court in 1980—discusses a notable risk-assessment conducted by OSHA, the federal Occupational Safety and Health Administration. OSHA's task was to determine the permissible level of occupational exposure to benzene, a petroleum-derived substance used in making a variety of chemical products. Benzene was known to be a toxic substance: it was known to cause cancer at high exposure levels. The problem was to determine the magnitude of health injury likely to occur at varying levels of occupational exposure. At issue in the Benzene Case was OSHA's reliance on the broad assumption that there is no safe level of exposure to a human carcinogen—that is, that there exists no threshold level below which a cancer-causing substance like benzene has no effect at all.

This no-threshold principle had been invoked in prior risk-assessments by OSHA, and had been upheld in reviewing courts. For example, in American Iron & Steel Institute v. OSHA, 577 F.2d 825 (3d Cir.1978), OSHA's exposure limit for coke oven emissions was upheld given "substantial evidence that coke oven emissions are carcinogenic":

> Evidence of carcinogenicity has been derived from chemical analysis and various epidemiological studies. Such studies indicate a significantly higher rate of mortality among coke oven workers than the general population. For example, the rate of mortality for lung cancer among employees working on top of the coke oven batteries for five or more years is ten times greater than normal. Furthermore, the incidence of contracting various nonmalignant respiratory diseases—bronchitis, emphysema, pneumoconiosis—is also substantially increased, particularly for long term workers.

> Having established the existence of a health hazard created by coke oven emissions, [OSHA] endeavored to ascertain a safe level of exposure. Edward Baier, Deputy Director of NIOSH [National Institute for Occupational Safety and Health], testified in hearings that it is impossible to set a safe threshold exposure limit above zero for a carcinogen. In a 1970 report to the Surgeon General entitled "Evaluation of Environmental Carcinogens" the Ad Hoc Committee on the Evaluation of Low Levels of Environmental Chemical Carcinogens stated, "no level of exposure to a chemical carcinogen should be considered toxicologically insignificant for man. For carcinogenic agents a safe level for man cannot be established by application of our present knowledge. The concept of 'socially acceptable risk' represents a more realistic notion." * * * Finally, the majority report of the Secretary's Advisory Committee based its recommendations to the Secretary [of Labor] on the finding that "coke oven emissions are carcinogenic and there [are] no scientific data to demonstrate that there is a safe level of exposure to carcinogens * * *."

In 1980 OSHA sought to crystallize and generalize the approach to carcinogenic risk it had used in particular regulatory proceedings, including benzene regulation. It promulgated a generic "cancer policy" designed to be used in any regulatory proceeding involving a carcinogen. 45 Fed.Reg. 5001 (1980). In devising its general policy, OSHA conducted extensive hearings and received numerous submissions from interested parties. The resulting OSHA Cancer Policy, adopted in 1980, and amended in part in response to the Supreme Court's decision in The Benzene Case, 46 Fed.Reg. 5878 (1981), became a final standard governing all carcinogenic risk-assessment by the agency. See 29 C.F.R. §§ 1990.101 et seq. (1995).

In the lengthy preamble of its cancer policy, OSHA summarized the many presentations made to it, and its own approach to contested matters. The OSHA Cancer Policy, at 45 Fed.Reg. 5001 (1980), is a remarkable document. It provides a concentrated discussion of issues that dominate contemporary debate about regulation of risk. Within it may be found, succinctly argued, the basic positions whose continuing clash defines the modern debate about acceptable risk, about cost-benefit balancing, about the value of life. In it an uncommonly self-conscious regulatory body tries to articulate its own coherent position on the fundamental issues. Excerpts from the OSHA Cancer Policy will appear from time to time in pages that follow.

The preamble to the Cancer Policy emphasizes a "regulatory dilemma" that is particularly acute with respect to carcinogenic risk, but apparent also in other areas of regulation. 45 Fed.Reg. 5001, at 5008. Given significant but uncertain evidence about physical risk, regulators must either act or await certainty. Action may turn out to have created erroneous overregulation; inaction may turn out to have permitted avoidable injury and death. This dilemma is at the heart of The Benzene Case.

THE BENZENE CASE

INDUSTRIAL UNION DEPARTMENT v. AMERICAN PETROLEUM INSTITUTE

Supreme Court of the United States, 1980.
448 U.S. 607, 100 S.Ct. 2844, 65 L.Ed.2d 1010.

Mr. Justice STEVENS announced the judgment of the Court and delivered an opinion in which THE CHIEF JUSTICE and Mr. Justice STEWART join and in [parts] of which Mr. Justice POWELL joins.

The Occupational Safety and Health Act of 1970, 29 U.S.C.A. § 651 et seq. (the Act), was enacted for the purpose of ensuring safe and healthful working conditions for every working man and woman in the Nation. This case concerns a standard promulgated by the Secretary of Labor to regulate occupational exposure to benzene, a substance which has been shown to cause cancer at high exposure levels. The principal question is whether such a showing is a sufficient basis for a standard that places the most stringent limitation on exposure to benzene that is technologically and economically possible.

The Act delegates broad authority to the Secretary to promulgate different kinds of standards. The basic definition of an "occupational safety and health standard" is found in § 3(8), which provides:

> "The term 'occupational safety and health standard' means a standard which requires conditions, or the adoption or use of one or more practices, means, methods, operations, or processes, reasonably necessary or appropriate to provide safe or healthful employment and places of employment." 29 U.S.C.A. § 652(8).

Where toxic materials or harmful physical agents are concerned, a standard must also comply with § 6(b)(5), which provides:

> "The Secretary, in promulgating standards dealing with toxic materials or harmful physical agents under this subsection, shall set the standard which most adequately assures, to the extent feasible, on the basis of the best available evidence, that no employee will suffer material impairment of health or functional capacity even if such

employee has regular exposure to the hazard dealt with by such standard for the period of his working life. * * * "29 U.S.C.A. § 655(b)(5).

Wherever the toxic material to be regulated is a carcinogen, the Secretary has taken the position that no safe exposure level can be determined and that § 6(b)(5) requires him to set an exposure limit at the lowest technologically feasible level that will not impair the viability of the industries regulated. In this case, after having determined that there is a causal connection between benzene and leukemia (a cancer of the white blood cells), the Secretary set an exposure limit on airborne concentrations of benzene of one part benzene per million parts of air (1 ppm), regulated dermal and eye contact with solutions containing benzene, and imposed complex monitoring and medical testing requirements on employers whose workplaces contain 0.5 ppm or more of benzene. 29 CFR § 1910.1028, 43 Fed.Reg. 5918 (Feb. 10, 1978), as amended, 43 Fed.Reg. 27962 (June 27, 1978).

On pre-enforcement review * * * the United States Court of Appeals for the Fifth Circuit held the regulation invalid. 581 F.2d 493 (1978). * * *

We agree with the Fifth Circuit's holding that § 3(8) requires the Secretary to find, as a threshold matter, that the toxic substance in question poses a significant health risk in the workplace and that a new, lower standard is therefore "reasonably necessary or appropriate to provide safe or healthful employment and places of employment." Unless and until such a finding is made it is not necessary to address the further question whether the Court of Appeals correctly held that there must be a reasonable correlation between costs and benefits, or whether, as the Government argues, the Secretary is then required by § 6(b)(5) to promulgate a standard that goes as far as technologically and economically possible to eliminate the risk.

* * *

As presently formulated, the benzene standard is an expensive way of providing some additional protection for a relatively small number of employees. According to OSHA's figures, the standard will require capital investments in engineering controls of approximately $266 million, first-year operating costs (for monitoring, medical testing, employee training, and respirators) of $187 million to $205 million and recurring annual costs of approximately $34 million. * * *

* * *

Any discussion of the 1 ppm exposure limit must, of course, begin with the Agency's rationale for imposing that limit. The written explanation of the standard fills 184 pages * * *. Much of it is devoted to a discussion of the voluminous evidence of the adverse effects of exposure to benzene at levels of concentration well above 10 ppm. This discussion demonstrates that there is ample justification for regulating occupational exposure to benzene and that the prior limit of 10 ppm * * * was reasonable. It does not, however, provide direct support for the Agency's conclusion that the limit should be reduced from 10 ppm to 1 ppm.

* * *

In the end OSHA's rationale for lowering the permissible exposure limit to 1 ppm was based * * * on a series of assumptions * * *. [T]he Agency first unequivocally concluded that benzene is a human carcinogen. Second, it concluded that industry had failed to prove that there is a safe threshold level of exposure to benzene below which no excess leukemia cases would occur. In reaching this conclusion OSHA rejected industry contentions that certain epidemiological studies * * * were sufficient to establish that the threshold level of safe exposure was at or above 10 ppm. It also rejected an industry witness' testimony that a dose-response curve could be constructed on the basis of the reported epidemiological studies and that this curve indicated that reducing the permissible exposure limit from 10 to 1 ppm would prevent at most one leukemia and one other cancer death every six years.

Third, the Agency applied its standard policy with respect to carcinogens, concluding that, in the absence of definitive proof of a safe level, it must be assumed that *any* level above zero presents *some* increased risk of cancer. As the Government points out in its brief, there are a number of scientists and public health specialists who subscribe to this view, theorizing that a susceptible person may contract cancer from the absorption of even one molecule of a carcinogen like benzene.

Fourth, the Agency reiterated its view of the Act, stating that it was required by § 6(b)(5) to set the standard either at the level that has been demonstrated to be safe or at the lowest level feasible, whichever is higher. If no safe level is established, as in this case, the Secretary's interpretation of the statute automatically leads to the selection of an exposure limit that is the lowest feasible. Because of benzene's importance to the economy, no one has ever suggested that it would be feasible to eliminate its use entirely, or to try to limit exposures to the small amounts that are omnipresent. Rather, the Agency selected 1 ppm as a workable exposure level, and then determined that compliance with that level was technologically feasible and that "the economic impact of * * * [compliance] will not be such as to threaten the financial welfare of the affected firms or the general economy." 43 Fed.Reg., at 5939. * * *

* * *

If the purpose of the statute were to eliminate completely and with absolute certainty any risk of serious harm, we would agree that [OSHA's approach] would be proper * * *. But we think it is clear that the statute was not designed to require employers to provide absolutely risk-free workplaces whenever it is technologically feasible to do so, so long as the cost is not great enough to destroy an entire industry. Rather, both the language and structure of the Act, as well as its legislative history, indicate that it was intended to require the elimination, as far as feasible, of significant risks of harm.

By empowering the Secretary to promulgate standards that are "reasonably necessary or appropriate to provide safe or healthful employment and places of employment," the Act implies that, before promulgating any standard, the Secretary must make a finding that the workplaces in question are not safe. But "safe" is not the equivalent of "risk-free." There are many activities that we engage in every day—such as driving a car or even breathing city air—that entail some risk of accident or material health impairment; nevertheless, few people would consider these activities "unsafe." Similarly, a workplace can hardly be considered "unsafe" unless it threatens the workers with a significant risk of harm.

Therefore, before he can promulgate *any* permanent health or safety standard, the Secretary is required to make a threshold finding that a place of employment is unsafe—in the sense that significant risks are present and can be eliminated or lessened by a change in practices. * * *

* * *

In the absence of a clear mandate in the Act, it is unreasonable to assume that Congress intended to give the Secretary the unprecedented power over American industry that would result from the Government's view of §§ 3(8) and 6(b)(5), coupled with OSHA's cancer policy. Expert testimony that a substance is probably a human carcinogen—either because it has caused cancer in animals or because individuals have contracted cancer following extremely high exposures—would justify the conclusion that the substance poses some risk of serious harm no matter how minute the exposure and no matter how many experts testified that they regarded the risk as insignificant. That conclusion would in turn justify pervasive regulation limited only by the constraint of feasibility. In light of the fact that there are literally thousands of substances used in the workplace that have been identified as carcinogens or suspect carcinogens, the Government's theory would give OSHA power to impose enormous costs that might produce little, if any, discernible benefit.

* * *

Contrary to the Government's contentions, imposing a burden on the Agency of demonstrating a significant risk of harm will not strip it of its ability to regulate carcinogens, nor will it require the Agency to wait for deaths to occur before taking any action. First, the requirement that a "significant" risk be identified is not a mathematical straitjacket. It is the Agency's responsibility to determine, in the first instance, what it considers to be a "significant" risk. Some risks are plainly acceptable and others are plainly unacceptable. If, for example, the odds are one in a billion that a person will die from cancer by taking a drink of chlorinated water, the risk clearly could not be considered significant. On the other hand, if the odds are one in a thousand that regular inhalation of gasoline vapors that are two percent benzene will be fatal, a reasonable person might well consider the risk significant and take appropriate steps to decrease or eliminate it. Although the Agency has no duty to calculate the exact probability of harm, it does have an obligation to find that a significant risk is present before it can characterize a place of employment as "unsafe."

Second, OSHA is not required to support its finding that a significant risk exists with anything approaching scientific certainty. * * *

* * *

Mr. Justice POWELL, concurring in part and in the judgment.

* * *

Although I regard the question as close, I do not disagree with the plurality's view that OSHA has failed, on this record, to carry its burden of proof on the threshold issues summarized above. But even if one assumes that OSHA properly met this burden, I conclude that the statute also requires the agency to determine that the economic effects of its standard bear a reasonable relationship to the expected benefits. An occupational health standard is neither "reasonably necessary" nor "feasible," as required by statute, if it calls for expenditures wholly disproportionate to the expected health and safety benefits.

OSHA contends that § 6(b)(5) not only permits but actually requires it to promulgate standards that reduce health risks without regard to economic effects, unless those effects would cause widespread dislocation throughout an entire industry. Under the threshold test adopted by the plurality today, this authority will exist only with respect to "significant" risks. But the plurality does not reject OSHA's claim that it must reduce such risks without considering economic consequences less serious than massive dislocation. In my view, that claim is untenable.

* * * It is simply unreasonable to believe that Congress intended OSHA to pursue the desirable goal of risk-free workplaces to the extent that the economic viability of particular industries—or significant segments thereof—is threatened. As the plurality observes, OSHA itself has not chosen to carry out such a self-defeating policy in all instances. If it did, OSHA regulations would impair the ability of American industries to compete effectively with foreign businesses and to provide employment for American workers.

I therefore would not lightly assume that Congress intended OSHA to require reduction of health risks found to be significant *whenever* it also finds that the affected industry can bear the costs. * * * [A] standard-setting process that ignored economic considerations would result in a serious misallocation of resources and a lower effective level of safety than could be achieved under standards set with reference to the comparative benefits available at a lower cost. I would not attribute such an irrational intention to Congress.

* * *

Mr. Justice MARSHALL, with whom Mr. Justice BRENNAN, Mr. Justice WHITE, and Mr. Justice BLACKMUN join, dissenting.

* * *

Unlike the plurality, I do not purport to know whether the actions taken by Congress and its delegates to ensure occupational safety represent sound or unsound regulatory policy. The critical problem in cases like the one at bar is scientific uncertainty. While science has determined that exposure to benzene at levels above 1 ppm creates a definite risk of health impairment, the magnitude of the risk cannot be quantified at the present time. The risk at issue has hardly been shown to be insignificant; indeed, future research may reveal that the risk is in fact considerable. But the existing evidence may frequently be inadequate to enable the Secretary to make the threshold finding of "significance" that the Court requires today. If so, the consequence of the plurality's approach would be to subject American workers to a continuing risk of cancer and other fatal diseases, and to render the Federal Government powerless to take protective action on their behalf. Such an approach would place the burden of medical uncertainty squarely on the shoulders of the American worker, the intended beneficiary of the Occupational Safety and Health Act. * * *

* * *

The Secretary rejected the hypothesis that the [benzene] standard would save only two lives in six years. This estimate, he concluded, was impossible to reconcile with the evidence in the record. He determined that, because of numerous uncertainties in the existing data, it was impossible to construct a dose-response curve by extrapolating from those data to lower exposure levels. More generally, the Secretary observed that it had not been established that there was a safe level of exposure for benzene. Since there was considerable testimony that the risk would decline with the exposure level, the new standard would save lives. The number of lives saved "may be appreciable," but there was no way to make a more precise determination. The question was "on the frontiers of scientific knowledge."

* * *

Under these circumstances, the plurality's requirement of identification of a "significant" risk will have one of two consequences. If the plurality means to require the Secretary realistically to "quantify" the risk in order to satisfy a court that it is "significant," the record shows that the plurality means to require him to do the impossible. But the regulatory inaction has very significant costs of its own. The adoption of such a test would subject American workers to a continuing risk of cancer and other serious diseases; it would disable the Secretary from regulating a wide variety of carcinogens for which quantification simply cannot be undertaken at the present time.

There are encouraging signs that today's decision does not extend that far. My Brother Powell concludes that the Secretary is not prevented from taking regulatory action "when reasonable quantification cannot be accomplished by any known methods." The plurality also indicates that it would not prohibit the Secretary from promulgating safety standards when quantification of the benefits is impossible. The Court might thus allow the Secretary to attempt to make a very rough quantification of the risk imposed by a carcinogenic substance, and give considerable deference to his finding that the risk was significant. If so, the Court would permit the Secretary to promulgate precisely the same regulation involved in this case if he had not relied on a carcinogen "policy," but undertaken a review of the evidence and the expert testimony and concluded, on the basis of conservative assumptions, that the risk addressed is a significant one. Any other interpretation of the plurality's approach would allow a court to displace the agency's judgment with its own subjective conception of "significance," a duty to be performed without statutory guidance.

* * *

In recent years there has been increasing recognition that the products of technological development may have harmful effects whose incidence and severity cannot be predicted with certainty. The responsibility to regulate such products has fallen to administrative agencies. * * *

Those delegations, in turn, have been made on the understanding that judicial review would be available to ensure that the agency's determinations are supported by substantial evidence and that its actions do not exceed the limits set by Congress. * * * But in this case the plurality has far exceeded its authority. The plurality's "threshold finding" requirement is nowhere to be found in the Act and is antithetical to its basic purposes. * * *

Because the approach taken by the plurality is so plainly irreconcilable with the Court's proper institutional role, I am certain that it will not stand the test of time. In all likelihood, today's decision will come to be regarded as extreme reaction to a regulatory scheme that, as the Members of the plurality perceived it, imposed an unduly harsh burden on regulated industries. * * *

BENZENE REVISITED. In September 1987, seven years after the Supreme Court's decision, OSHA completed another rulemaking proceeding on benzene, again determined that the exposure limit should be reduced from 10 ppm to 1 ppm, and amended its benzene standard accordingly. 52 Fed.Reg. 34460 (1987). Based on laboratory and epidemiological studies, OSHA concluded that the relationship between occupational exposure to benzene, even at low doses, and resulting health injury, primarily leukemia and aplastic anemia, should be regarded as linear. With respect to leukemia alone, OSHA estimated "an excess risk per 1000 exposed workers of 95 leukemia deaths at 10 ppm and 10 [deaths] at 1 ppm"—in other words, lowering benzene exposure from 10 ppm to 1 ppm "would result in 85 fewer leukemia deaths per 1000 workers exposed at the current 10 ppm level for a working lifetime." This risk is "clearly greater" than all the risks of the riskiest occupations:

> For example, in the high risk occupations of fire fighting and mining and quarrying the average risk of death from all causes of occupational injury or an acute occupationally related illness from a lifetime of employment (45 years) is 27.45 and 20.16 per 1,000 employees respectively. Typical occupational risk of death in occupations of average risk

are 2.7 per 1,000 for all manufacturing and 1.62 per 1,000 for all service employment. Typical lifetime occupational risks of death in occupations of relatively low risk are 0.48 per 1,000 in electric equipment and 0.07 per 1,000 in retail clothing. * * * OSHA believes Congress intended to reduce risks of average magnitude * * *.

Using conservative assumptions about the number of workers being exposed to benzene at levels between 1 ppm and 10 ppm, the agency calculated that "the new standard will prevent a minimum of 326 deaths from leukemia and diseases of the blood and blood-forming organs over a working lifetime of 45 years."

BLY v. TRI–CONTINENTAL INDUSTRIES, INC., 663 A.2d 1232 (D.C.App. 1995). Plaintiffs alleged that their decedents, Leo Bly and Edward Seals, died from leukemia caused by exposure to benzene in the course of their work as automotive mechanics for the District of Columbia Department of Public Works (DPW). Defendants are 15 refiners and distributors of petroleum products containing benzene. Plaintiffs alleged that each defendant knew the benzene in its product "caused leukemia and other diseases of the blood," but provided no warnings regarding the risk of exposure to the product. But plaintiffs conceded they were unable to develop definite information showing which of the defendants supplied gasoline to DPW, in what amounts, at particular times during the period of Bly's and Seals' occupational exposure (1949 to 1979). The lawsuit was dismissed by the trial court. *Held*, affirmed. The appellate court said that the "market share theory of liability" developed in Sindell v. Abbott Laboratories (p. 1101, supra) should not be applied in the present case, since the gasoline market "may have fluctuated greatly" over the 30–year exposure period. "The task of identifying the market and apportioning damages among manufacturers would present a substantial burden." The court added:

> Nor have [plaintiffs] claimed that exposure to benzene is the only cause of the illnesses that the decedents suffered. Leukemia, which the decedents contracted, has not been shown * * * to be a so-called signature illness which results from only benzene.

ACCEPTABLE RISK. Supposing risk-assessment to have done its job to perfection, and yielded a precise calculation of the degree of avoidable risk associated with a particular substance or condition, what then? Presumably regulation will not try to eliminate any physical risk whatever its magnitude, since social life appears to be irreducibly risky. As Justice Stevens wrote in The Benzene Case, "Some risks are plainly acceptable"—but which ones? Testimony at agency hearings on the OSHA Cancer Policy addressed the question whether there is a definable threshold level of "acceptable risk" beneath which regulatory concern should cease:

> The AIHC [American Industrial Health Council] presented Dr. Richard Wilson, a physicist from Harvard University, who recommended a specific procedure * * * for defining health protection in terms of acceptable risk levels. * * *
>
> * * * Wilson's recommendation attempted to define an overall objective function for determining acceptable levels of risk. Using

comparative risk analysis, Dr. Wilson calculated single-point estimates of risks which individuals voluntarily (engaging in certain sports activities) or involuntarily live with (pedestrian in a motor age). For example, he calculated that some individuals voluntarily accept a risk of death of 1/1000 per year of activity to engage in risky sports such as auto racing and rock climbing. Smokers "voluntarily" accept a level of risk three times higher. People "involuntarily" accept a risk of 1/5000 per year from motor vehicles—his highest estimate of involuntarily accepted life-style risk. The highest fatality rates that Wilson reports among occupational groups in the workforce presently are approximately 1/1000 per year for coal miners, railroad workers and firefighters. However, the risk of death for coal miners from work-related causes approaches 1 death per 100 annually when fatalities from black lung disease are included.

He argued as an appropriate benchmark for risk reduction that OSHA not attempt to lower occupational risks below other voluntarily accepted risk levels. He used his estimates of non-occupational risks voluntarily accepted or involuntarily lived with to develop risk categories for structuring occupational regulatory actions.

Dr. Wilson recommended different regulatory responses for risks in excess of one death per 100 employees per year (regulation irrespective of cost) and for risks below one death per 100,000 annually (no regulation). For occupational risks of death between these boundaries, cost-benefit analysis would determine the reduction in risks. [For risks of death between 1/100 and 1/100,000 per year Wilson recommended controls "only to the extent that they save one life for every $1 million in expenditures, his implicit estimate of the value of human life."]

* * *

Other [participants] discussed the concepts behind Dr. Wilson's methodology for determining "acceptable" risk based on historically observed levels of voluntary or involuntary risks. Dr. [Lester] Lave [of Carnegie–Mellon University] discussed at length various research attempts to analyze the risks that humans are willing to accept. He discussed the conceptual and practical difficulties inherent in evaluations of risk, including the large variations in the risks that humans view as acceptable, the difficulties that individuals face in assessing risks, and the characteristics of risk that influence individual preferences for risk. These dimensions include whether the risk is voluntary or imposed, familiar or unknown, controllable or uncontrollable, of immediate occurrence or indeterminate in the future, and whether the risk affects large numbers of humans with low probability or small numbers of individuals with high probability. He also stated,

"Another major complication evolves from intertemporal changes in preferences due to higher standards of living and improved knowledge. The higher our standard of living, the more protection and greater safety we desire (are willing to pay for); also, the greater our knowledge about the adverse effects of exposures, the more we desire to lower exposures."

45 Fed.Reg. 5001, 5235–36 & 5246–47 (1980).

Compare Dr. Wilson's recommended lower limit (no regulation below 1 in 100,000 annual risk of death) with the performance of the Environmental Protection Agency (EPA), summarized as follows: "[T]here seems to be a tendency for EPA * * * to insist on reducing lifetime cancer risk below the broad range of 10^{-4} to 10^{-6}. * * * [I]ndividual risks greater than 10^{-4} [1 in 10,000] are highly likely to be regulated, while risks less than 10^{-6} [1 in one million] are rarely regulated." Rosenthal, Gray, & Graham, Legislating Acceptable Cancer Risk from Exposure to Toxic Chemicals, 19 Ecology L.Q. 269, 320 (1992).

COST–ASSESSMENT

Risk-assessment defines the direct benefit of regulation: reduction of the physical harm caused by a risky condition or substance. The "other side of the equation" is regulatory cost. Costs may be calculated by figuring the amount of money it would take to achieve compliance with prescribed standards by installing new technology, rearranging work practices, or otherwise restructuring the regulated activity. But calculation of direct compliance costs is only the beginning of plenary cost-assessment. On a broad view costs include any negative consequences of compliance with respect to economic viability of firms and industries, employment and sales, energy requirements, inflation and trade balances, availability of resources for other safety purposes, stimulation of other activities having their own detrimental fallout.

What role should cost-assessment play in fashioning of regulatory standards by administrative agencies? There are many possibilities, ranging from no consideration of costs to plenary balancing of costs against benefits. Following are some major alternatives, assembled in a sort of continuum, reflecting disparate approaches actually taken by federal legislation authorizing regulation of physical risk.

1. *Safe Levels*—Regulation may aim to eliminate significant risks regardless of the cost. Then risk-assessment is the sole governor of regulatory standards. This approach is taken in some aspects of legislation having to do with toxic substances that may endanger public health.

An example of safety-based regulation is the Food Quality Protection Act of 1996. 110 Stat. 1489. This legislation controls the amount of pesticide residue that may be present on foods, both fresh food ("a raw agricultural commodity") and processed food. Tolerances set pursuant to the Act must be "safe," meaning "there is a reasonable certainty that no harm will result from aggregate exposure to the pesticide chemical residue, including all anticipated dietary exposures and all other exposures." 21 U.S.C.A. § 346a(b)(2). Regulators are directed to set limits that provide "an additional margin of safety" in light of the special susceptibility to harm of infants and children. Id.

Safety-based regulation says that toxic exposures should be kept to such and such a level regardless of cost. In Union Electric Co. v. Environmental

Protection Agency, 427 U.S. 246, 96 S.Ct. 2518, 49 L.Ed.2d 474 (1976), the Supreme Court upheld EPA's approval of a state air quality plan despite the objection that emission controls required by the plan were "prohibitively expensive." The plan was formulated, pursuant to the 1970 Amendments to the Clean Air Act, to implement "primary" or health-related ambient air standards. According to the Court, the legislative scheme "leaves no room for claims of technological or economic infeasibility" to avoid compliance with primary air standards. The scheme is based on Congress' determination "that existing sources of pollutants either should meet the standard of the law or be closed down," and is "designed to force regulated sources to develop pollution control devices."

> Technology forcing is a concept somewhat new to our national experience and it necessarily entails certain risks. But Congress considered those risks in passing the 1970 Amendments and decided that the dangers posed by uncontrolled air pollution made them worth taking.

An interesting provision of the Clean Air Act Amendments of 1990 focusses on carcinogenic risks remaining after technology-based regulations for hazardous pollutants have been in effect for eight years. 42 U.S.C.A. § 7412(f). If by that time a numerically defined level of cancer risk has not been achieved, EPA is directed to promulgate additional regulations that will "provide an ample margin of safety to protect public health." The numerical objective is to "reduce lifetime excess cancer risks to the individual most exposed to emissions * * * to less than one in one million."

2. *Feasibility*—Regulation may seek to reduce risk to the lowest level that is technologically and economically "feasible." Here there is no requirement that marginal costs of regulation be offset by marginal benefits. Rather costs are assessed in order to determine whether an on-going activity is in fact able to bear the burden of regulatory controls and remain viable. The limit of regulation is practical possibility, or achievability, not maximum utility. The main practitioner of regulation subject to feasibility has been OSHA—see The Cotton Dust Case, immediately below. Feasibility also governs aspects of clean air and clean water regulation.

The Clean Air Act, as amended in 1990, provides that regulatory standards for hazardous air pollutants "shall require the maximum degree of reduction in emissions" that EPA, "taking into consideration the cost of achieving such emission reduction," determines to be "achievable." 42 U.S.C.A. § 7412(d)(2). Standards for new sources "shall not be less stringent than the emission control that is achieved in practice by the best controlled similar source." 42 U.S.C.A. § 7412(d)(3).

In Portland Cement Association v. Ruckelshaus, 486 F.2d 375 (D.C.Cir. 1973), the court addressed similar language of the Clean Air Amendments of 1970, requiring "the degree of emission limitation achievable * * * taking into account the cost of achieving such reduction." The court said that EPA was not obliged to conduct "a quantified cost-benefit analysis" in order to justify its air pollution standard for new or modified cement plants, since the operative statutory test is "achievability." EPA had determined that the cement industry could absorb the cost of control devices without detriment to competition between cement and substitute products, though some plants might have to close. The court held that such cost-assessment was sufficient to answer the "essential question" under the Act: "whether the mandated standards can be met by a particular industry for which they are set."

Feasibility-based regulation is also prescribed by the so-called "BAT" provisions of the Clean Water Act, which mandate pollution control to the extent "technologically and economically achievable." 33 U.S.C.A. §§ 1311(b)(2)(A), 1314(b)(2)(B), 1317(a)(2) (as amended through 1995). Under the legislative scheme, water pollution sources are subject to two different sorts of effluent limitations: ones based on "the best practicable control technology currently available" (BPT), and limits based on "the best available technology economically achievable" (BAT).

As characterized by the Supreme Court in EPA v. National Crushed Stone Assn., 449 U.S. 64, 101 S.Ct. 295, 66 L.Ed.2d 268 (1980), the less-stringent BPT standards should generalize "the best existing performance" in an industry—"control practices in exemplary plants"—despite an expectation of "economic hardship, including the closing of some plants." The more-stringent BAT standards should go further and require "a commitment of the maximum resources economically possible to the ultimate goal of eliminating all polluting discharges." In Rybachek v. EPA, 904 F.2d 1276 (9th Cir.1990), the court said that while "cost-benefit analysis" is involved in the setting of BPT standards, it is not a part of BAT determinations: "In determining the economic achievability of a technology, the EPA must consider the 'cost' of meeting BAT limitations, but need not compare such cost with the benefits of effluent reduction."

3. *Unreasonable Risk*—Regulators may be authorized to eliminate only risk that is "unreasonable." Such provisions are notable in the area of product safety. For example, a finding of "unreasonable risk" is a necessary predicate for the setting of safety standards under the Consumer Product Safety Act, 15 U.S.C.A. § 2056(a); for determination of mechanical or thermal hazard under the Federal Hazardous Substances Act, 15 U.S.C.A. § 1261(s) & (t); and for issuance of a flammability standard pursuant to the Flammable Fabrics Act, 15 U.S.C.A. § 1193(a). See also the Toxic Substances Control Act, which authorizes EPA to regulate chemicals that present "an unreasonable risk of injury to health or the environment." 15 U.S.C.A. § 2605(a).

Determination of reasonableness requires some sort of balancing. According to Aqua Slide 'N' Dive Corp. v. Consumer Product Safety Commission, 569 F.2d 831 (5th Cir.1978), CPSC product safety standards are governed by "a balancing test like that familiar in tort law":

> The regulation may issue if the severity of the injury that may result from the product, factored by the likelihood of the injury, offsets the harm the regulation itself imposes upon manufacturers and consumers.

The court added that while the Commission "does not have to conduct an elaborate cost-benefit analysis," it does have to bear "the burden of examining the relevant factors and producing substantial evidence to support its conclusion that they weigh in favor of the standard."

The National Traffic and Motor Vehicle Safety Act, administered by the National Highway Traffic Safety Administration (NHTSA), authorizes motor vehicle safety standards to protect against "unreasonable risk" of accidental injury. 49 U.S.C.A. § 30102(a)(8). It also provides that when a type of automobile "contains a defect," the manufacturer must provide "notification" and "remedy the defect." 49 U.S.C.A. §§ 30118(c) & 30120(a). The relationship between statutory terminology and common law definitions was discussed in United States v. General Motors, 518 F.2d 420 (D.C.Cir.1975). According to the court, the general requirement that NHTSA's regulations address "unreasonable risk" was meant "to signify a 'commonsense' balancing of safety benefits and economic cost." However, the term "defect" has a broader meaning in the Act than in "the common law of negligence and product liability":

> The Act was designed as a preventive measure * * *. Determinations * * * relevant to the award of damages at common law are not controlling on the interpretation of the scope of this prophylactic defect notification legislation.

A statutory defect is established by showing "a significant number of failures in performance," including failures resulting from foreseeable "owner abuse" and "inadequate maintenance."

4. *Costs and Benefits*—Regulatory statutes may say in so many words that costs must be balanced against benefits. Two pertinent examples are the Clean Air Act, which authorizes EPA to regulate auto fuel additives that impair operation of emission control devices only after "consideration of available scientific and economic data, including a cost benefit analysis," 42 U.S.C.A. § 7545(c)(2)(B); and the Federal Insecticide, Fungicide, and Rodenticide Act, which requires that "unreasonable adverse effects on the environment" be determined "taking into account the economic, social, and environmental costs and benefits of the use of any pesticide." 7 U.S.C.A. § 136(bb).

Cost-benefit analysis may be restricted in its focus, or quite comprehensive—it may be "focussed" or "plenary." The distinction has to do with how many factors are placed in the cost-benefit scales and weighed against one another.

"Focussed" analysis balances the direct monetary costs of achieving compliance with a regulatory standard against the direct benefits of reduced risk. Focussed balancing by EPA was approved in Weyerhaeuser Co. v. Costle, 590 F.2d 1011 (D.C.Cir.1978). There the court addressed a provision of the Clean Water Act, 33 U.S.C.A. § 1314(b)(1)(B), which specifies factors to be taken into account in determining "best practicable control technology currently available" (BPT):

> [F]actors * * * shall include * * * the total cost of application of technology in relation to the effluent reduction benefits to be achieved

* * * and * * * non-water quality environmental impact (including energy requirements) * * *.

The court read this language to mean that two factors (technology costs and effluent benefits) were subject to "comparison" by EPA, while other regulatory impacts were simply matters for "consideration." As to "consideration factors," EPA had "discretion to decide * * * how much weight to give each factor." As to "comparison factors," EPA had to undertake what the court called "limited balancing." Balancing was constrained in three ways. First, only technology costs—not other consequences—need be balanced against effluent reduction benefits. "[T]he comparison factors are a closed set of two, making it possible to have a definite structure and weight in considering them and preventing extraneous factors from intruding on the balance." Second, "cost need not be balanced against benefits with pinpoint precision." In particular, "calculation of the overall cost-benefit balance" is sufficient, and there is no requirement of "marginal or incremental analysis." Third, balancing is a "relatively subsidiary task" in the regulatory process, and regulation is to be foregone "only where" technology costs and effluent benefits are "wholly out of proportion."

"Plenary" cost-benefit balancing surveys and weighs all the positive and negative consequences of regulation. On the cost side, plenary analysis not only calculates financial costs of compliance, but also forecasts the multifarious effects of requiring these monetary costs to be borne, their concrete impact in given social and economic circumstances. The breadth of plenary analysis is suggested by a provision of the Clean Air Act requiring (for a limited purpose) "economic impact assessment" which "shall contain an analysis of":

    (1) the costs of compliance * * *;

    (2) the potential inflationary or recessionary effects of the standard * * *;

    (3) the effects on competition * * * with respect to small business;

    (4) the effects * * * on consumer costs; and

    (5) the effects * * * on energy use.

42 U.S.C.A. § 7617(c).

WHITMAN v. AMERICAN TRUCKING ASSOCIATIONS, 531 U.S. 457, 121 S.Ct. 903, 149 L.Ed.2d 1 (2001). Here a unanimous Supreme Court held that the Environmental Protection Agency (EPA) "may not consider implementation costs" in setting ambient air quality standards under the Clean Air Act (CAA). Writing for the Court, Justice Scalia said:

"In *Lead Industries Assn., Inc. v. EPA,* [647 F.2d 1130 (1980),] at 1148, the District of Columbia Circuit held that 'economic considerations [may] play no part in the promulgation of ambient air quality standards under Section 109' of the CAA. In the present cases, the court adhered to that holding, as it had done on many other occasions. [Citations omitted.] Respondents argue that these decisions are incorrect. We disagree * * *.

"Section 109(b)(1) instructs the EPA to set primary ambient air quality standards 'the attainment and maintenance of which . . . are requisite to protect the public health' with 'an adequate margin of safety.' 42 U.S.C. § 7409(b)(1). Were it not for the hundreds of pages of briefing respondents have submitted on the issue, one would have thought it fairly clear that this text does not permit the EPA to consider costs in setting the standards. The language, as one scholar has noted, 'is absolute.' D. Currie, Air Pollution: Federal Law and Analysis 4–15 (1981). The EPA, 'based on' the information about health effects [it has compiled], is to identify the maximum airborne concentration of a pollutant that the public health can tolerate, decrease the concentration to provide an 'adequate' margin of safety, and set the standard at that level."

In a concurring opinion, Justice Breyer wrote:

" * * * [T]he legislative history shows that Congress intended the statute to be 'technology forcing.' Senator Edmund Muskie, the primary sponsor of the 1970 amendments to the Act, introduced them by saying that Congress' primary responsibility in drafting the Act was not 'to be limited by what is or appears to be technologically or economically feasible,' but 'to establish what the public interest requires to protect the health of persons,' even if that means that *industries will be asked to do what seems to be impossible at the present time.*' 116 Cong. Rec. 32901–32902 (1970) (emphasis added).

" * * * Subsequent legislative history confirms that the technology-forcing goals of the 1970 amendments are still paramount in today's Act. See * * * S.Rep. No. 101–228, p. 5 (1989) (stating that the 1990 amendments to the Act require ambient air quality standards to be set at 'the level that "protects the public health" with an "adequate margin of safety," *without regard to the economic or technical feasibility of attainment*' (emphasis added)).

"To read this legislative history as meaning what it says does not impute to Congress an irrational intent. Technology-forcing hopes can prove realistic. Those persons, for example, who opposed the 1970 Act's insistence on a 90% reduction in auto emission pollutants, on the ground of excessive cost, saw the development of catalytic converter technology that helped achieve substantial reductions without the economic catastrophe that some had feared."

THE COTTON DUST CASE

AMERICAN TEXTILE MANUFACTURERS INSTITUTE v. DONOVAN

Supreme Court of the United States, 1981.
452 U.S. 490, 101 S.Ct. 2478, 69 L.Ed.2d 185.

Justice BRENNAN delivered the opinion of the Court.

Congress enacted the Occupational Safety and Health Act of 1970 (the Act) "to assure so far as possible every working man and woman in the

Nation safe and healthful working conditions * * *." 29 U.S.C. § 651(b). The Act authorizes the Secretary of Labor to establish, after notice and opportunity to comment, mandatory nationwide standards governing health and safety in the workplace. In 1978, the Secretary, acting through the Occupational Safety and Health Administration (OSHA),[1] promulgated a standard limiting occupational exposure to cotton dust, an airborne particle byproduct of the preparation and manufacture of cotton products, exposure to which induces a "constellation of respiratory effects" known as "byssinosis." 43 Fed.Reg. 27352, col. 3 (1978). * * *

Petitioners in these consolidated cases, representing the interests of the cotton industry, challenged the validity of the "Cotton Dust Standard" in the Court of Appeals for the District of Columbia Circuit * * *. They contend in this Court, as they did below, that the Act requires OSHA to demonstrate that its Standard reflects a reasonable relationship between the costs and benefits associated with the Standard. Respondents, the Secretary of Labor and two labor organizations, counter that Congress balanced the costs and benefits in the Act itself, and that the Act should therefore be construed not to require OSHA to do so. They interpret the Act as mandating that OSHA enact the most protective standard possible to eliminate a significant risk of material health impairment, subject to the constraints of economic and technological feasibility. The Court of Appeals held that the Act did not require OSHA to compare costs and benefits. 617 F.2d 636 (1979). We granted certiorari to resolve this important question, which was presented but not decided in last Term's Industrial Union Department v. American Petroleum Institute, 448 U.S. 607, 100 S.Ct. 2844, 65 L.Ed.2d 1010 (1980) * * *.

I

Byssinosis, known in its more severe manifestations as "brown lung" disease, is a serious and potentially disabling respiratory disease primarily caused by the inhalation of cotton dust. Byssinosis is a "continuum * * * disease" that has been categorized into four grades. * * *

* * *

Estimates indicate that at least 35,000 employed and retired cotton mill workers, or 1 in 12 such workers, suffers from the most disabling form of byssinosis. The Senate Report accompanying the Act cited estimates that 100,000 active and retired workers suffer from some grade of the disease. * * *

Not until the early 1960's was byssinosis recognized in the United States as a distinct occupational hazard associated with cotton mills. In 1966, the American Conference of Governmental Industrial Hygienists (ACGIH), a private organization, recommended that exposure to total cotton dust be limited to a "threshold limit value" of 1,000 micrograms per cubic meter of air (1000 $\mu g/m^3$) averaged over an 8–hour workday. The United States Government first regulated exposure to cotton dust in 1968 * * *.

---

1. This opinion will use the terms OSHA and the Secretary interchangeably * * *.

In 1974, ACGIH, adopting a new measurement unit of respirable rather than total dust, lowered its previous exposure limit recommendation to 200 $\mu g/m^3$ measured by a vertical elutriator, a device that measures cotton dust particles 15 microns or less in diameter. That same year, the Director of the National Institute for Occupational Safety and Health (NIOSH) * * * submitted to the Secretary of Labor a recommendation for a cotton dust standard with a permissible exposure limit (PEL) that "should be set at the lowest level feasible, but in no case at an environmental concentration as high as 0.2 mg lint-free cotton dust/cu. m.," or 200 $\mu g/m^3$ of lint-free respirable dust. * * *

On December 28, 1976, OSHA published a proposal to replace the existing Federal standard on cotton dust with a new permanent standard * * *. The proposed standard contained a PEL of 200 $\mu g/m^3$ of vertical elutriated lint-free respirable cotton dust for all segments of the cotton industry. * * * OSHA invited interested parties to submit written comments within a 90–day period.

Following the comment period, OSHA conducted three hearings in Washington, D.C., Greenville, Miss., and Lubbock, Tex. that lasted over 14 days. Public participation was widespread, involving representatives from industry and the workforce, scientists, economists, industrial hygienists, and many others. By the time the informal rule-making procedure had terminated, OSHA had received 263 comments and 109 notices of intent to appear at the hearings. The voluminous record, composed of a transcript of written and oral testimony, exhibits, and post-hearing comments and briefs, totaled some 105,000 pages. OSHA issued its final Cotton Dust Standard—the one challenged in the instant case—on June 23, 1978. * * *

The Cotton Dust Standard promulgated by OSHA establishes mandatory PELs over an 8–hour period of 200 $\mu g/m^3$ for yarn manufacturing, 750 $\mu g/m^3$ for slashing and weaving operations, and 500 $\mu g/m^3$ for all other processes in the cotton industry. These levels represent a relaxation of the proposed PEL of 200 $\mu g/m^3$ for all segments of the cotton industry.

OSHA chose an implementation strategy for the Standard that depended primarily on a mix of engineering controls, such as installation of ventilation systems, and work practice controls, such as special floor sweeping procedures. Full compliance with the PELs is required within 4 years, except to the extent that employers can establish that the engineering and work practice controls are infeasible. During this compliance period, and at certain other times, the Standard requires employers to provide respirators to employees. Other requirements include monitoring of cotton dust exposure, medical surveillance of all employees, annual medical examinations, employee education and training programs, and the posting of warning signs. A specific provision also under challenge in the instant case requires employers to transfer employees unable to wear respirators to another position, if available, having a dust level at or below the Standard's PELs, with "no loss of earnings or other employment rights or benefits as a result of the transfer."

* * * In assessing the health risks from cotton dust and the risk reduction obtained from lowered exposure, OSHA relied particularly on data showing a strong linear relationship between the prevalence of byssinosis and the concentration of lint-free respirable cotton dust. * * *

* * * OSHA interpreted the Act to require adoption of the most stringent standard to protect against material health impairment, bounded only by technological and economic feasibility. OSHA therefore rejected the industry's alternative proposal for a PEL of 500 $\mu g/m^3$ in yarn manufacturing, a proposal which would produce a 25% prevalence of at least Grade ½ byssinosis. The agency expressly found the Standard to be both technologically and economically feasible based on the evidence in the record as a whole. Although recognizing that permitted levels of exposure to cotton dust would still cause some byssinosis, OSHA nevertheless rejected the union proposal for a 100 $\mu g/m^3$ PEL because it was not within the "technological capabilities of the industry." Similarly, OSHA set PELs for some segments of the cotton industry at 500 $\mu g/m^3$ in part because of limitations of technological feasibility. Finally, the Secretary found that "engineering dust controls in weaving may not be feasible even with massive expenditures by the industry," and for that and other reasons adopted a less stringent PEL of 750 $\mu g/m^3$ for weaving and slashing.

The Court of Appeals upheld the Standard in all major respects. * * * The court held that "Congress itself struck the balance between costs and benefits in the mandate to the agency" * * * and that OSHA is powerless to circumvent that judgment by adopting less than the most protective feasible standard. Finally, the court held that the agency's determination of technological and economic feasibility was supported by substantial evidence in the record as a whole.

We affirm in part, and vacate in part.[25]

25. * * * At oral argument, and in a letter addressed to the Court after oral argument, petitioners contended that the Secretary's recent amendment of OSHA's so-called "Cancer Policy" in light of this Court's decision in Industrial Union Department v. American Petroleum Institute, 448 U.S. 607, 100 S.Ct. 2844, 65 L.Ed.2d 1010 (1980), was relevant to the issues in the present case. We disagree.

OSHA amended its Cancer Policy to "carry out the Court's interpretation of the Occupational Safety and Health Act of 1970 that consideration must be given to the significance of the risk in the issuance of a carcinogen standard and that OSHA must consider all relevant evidence in making these determinations." 46 Fed.Reg. 4889, col. 3 (1981). Previously, although lacking such evidence as dose response data, the Secretary presumed that no safe exposure level existed for carcinogenic substances. Following this Court's decision, OSHA deleted those provisions of the Cancer Policy which required the "auto-

matic setting of the lowest feasible level" without regard to determinations of risk significance.

In distinct contrast with its Cancer Policy, OSHA expressly found that "exposure to cotton dust presents a significant health hazard to employees," 43 Fed.Reg. 27350, col. 1, and that "cotton dust produced significant health effects at low levels of exposure." In addition, the agency noted that "grade ½ byssinosis and associated pulmonary function decrements are significant health effects in themselves and should be prevented in so far as possible." In making its assessment of significant risk, OSHA relied on dose response curve data (the Merchant Study) showing that 25% of employees suffered at least Grade ½ byssinosis at a 500 $\mu g/m^3$ PEL, and that 12.7% of all employees would suffer byssinosis at the 200 $\mu g/m^3$ PEL standard. * * * OSHA concluded that the "prevalence of byssinosis should be significantly reduced" by the 200 $\mu g/m^3$ PEL. * * * It is difficult to imagine what else the agency could do to comply with this

II

The principal question presented in this case is whether the Occupational Safety and Health Act requires the Secretary, in promulgating a standard pursuant to § 6(b)(5) of the Act, to determine that the costs of the standard bear a reasonable relationship to its benefits. Relying on §§ 6(b)(5) and 3(8) of the Act, petitioners urge not only that OSHA must show that a standard addresses a significant risk of material health impairment, see Industrial Union Department v. American Petroleum Institute, supra, but also that OSHA must demonstrate that the reduction in risk of material health impairment is significant in light of the costs of attaining that reduction.[26] Respondents on the other hand contend that the Act requires OSHA to promulgate standards that eliminate or reduce such risks "to the extent such protection is technologically and economically feasible."[27] To resolve this debate, we must turn to the language, structure, and legislative history of the Occupational Safety and Health Act.

A

The starting point of our analysis is the language of the statute itself. Section 6(b)(5) of the Act, 29 U.S.C. § 655(b)(5) (emphasis added), provides:

> "The Secretary, in promulgating standards dealing with toxic materials or harmful physical agents under this subsection, shall set the standard which most adequately assures, *to the extent feasible,* on the basis of the best available evidence, that no employee will suffer material impairment of health or functional capacity even if such employee has regular exposure to the hazard dealt with by such standard for the period of his working life."

Court's decision in *Industrial Union Department v. American Petroleum Institute.*

26. Petitioners ATMI et al. express their position in several ways. They maintain that OSHA "is required to show that a reasonable relationship exists between the risk reduction benefits and the costs of its standards." * * * Allowing that "[t]his does not mean that OSHA must engage in a rigidly formal cost-benefit calculation that places a dollar value on employee lives or health," petitioners describe the required exercise as follows:

"First, OSHA must make a responsible determination of the costs and risk reduction benefits of its standard. * * * The subsequent determination whether the reduction in health risk is 'significant' (based upon the factual assessment of costs and benefits) is a judgment to be made by the agency in the first instance."

Respondent disputes petitioners' description of the exercise, claiming that any meaningful balancing must involve "placing a [dollar] value on human life and freedom from suffering," and that there is no other way but through formal cost-benefit analysis to accomplish petitioners' desired balancing. Cost-benefit analysis contemplates "systematic enumeration of all benefits and all costs, tangible and intangible, whether readily quantifiable or difficult to measure, that will accrue to all members of society if a particular project is adopted." E. Stokey and R. Zeckhauser, A Primer for Policy Analysis 134 (1978); see National Academy of Sciences, Decision Making for Regulating Chemicals in the Environment 38 (1975). See generally E. Mishan, Cost–Benefit Analysis (1976); Prest and Turvey, Cost–Benefit Analysis, in 300 Economic Journal 683 (1965). Whether petitioners' or respondent's characterization is correct, we will sometimes refer to petitioners' proposed exercise as "cost-benefit analysis."

27. As described by the union respondents, the test for determining whether a standard promulgated to regulate a "toxic material or harmful physical agent" satisfies the Act has three parts:

"First, whether the 'place of employment is unsafe—in the sense that significant risks are present and can be eliminated or lessened by a change in practices.' Second, whether of the possible available correctives the Secretary had selected 'the standard * * * that is most protective'. Third, whether that standard is 'feasible.' "

We will sometimes refer to this test as "feasibility analysis."

Although their interpretations differ, all parties agree that the phrase "to the extent feasible" contains the critical language in § 6(b)(5) for purposes of this case.

The plain meaning of the word "feasible" supports respondents' interpretation of the statute. According to Webster's Third New International Dictionary of the English Language, "feasible" means "capable of being done, executed, or effected." * * * Thus, § 6(b)(5) directs the Secretary to issue the standard that "most adequately assures * * * that no employee will suffer material impairment of health," limited only by the extent to which this is "capable of being done." In effect then, as the Court of Appeals held, Congress itself defined the basic relationship between costs and benefits, by placing the "benefit" of worker health above all other considerations save those making attainment of this "benefit" unachievable. Any standard based on a balancing of costs and benefits by the Secretary that strikes a different balance than that struck by Congress would be inconsistent with the command set forth in § 6(b)(5). Thus, cost-benefit analysis by OSHA is not required by the statute because feasibility analysis is.[29]

When Congress has intended that an agency engage in cost-benefit analysis, it has clearly indicated such intent on the face of the statute. One early example is the Flood Control Act of 1936, 33 U.S.C. § 701a.

> "[T]he Federal Government should improve or participate in the improvement of navigable waters or their tributaries, including watersheds thereof, for flood-control purposes if the *benefits to whomsoever they may accrue are in excess of the estimated costs,* and if the lives and social security of people are otherwise adversely affected."

A more recent example is the Outer Continental Shelf Lands Act Amendments of 1978, 43 U.S.C. § 1347(b), providing that offshore drilling operations shall use

> "the best available and safest technologies which the Secretary determines to be economically *feasible,* wherever failure of equipment would have significant effect on safety, health, or the environment, except where the Secretary determines that the *incremental benefits are clearly insufficient to justify the incremental costs of using such technologies."*

These and other statutes[30] demonstrate that Congress uses specific language when intending that an agency engage in cost-benefit analysis. Certainly in

---

29. In this case we are faced with the issue whether the Act requires OSHA to balance costs and benefits in promulgating a *single* toxic material and harmful physical agent standard under § 6(b)(5). Petitioners argue that without cost-benefit balancing, the issuance of a single standard might result in a "serious misallocation of the finite resources that are available for the protection of worker safety and health," given the other health hazards in the workplace. This argument is more properly addressed to other provisions of the Act which may authorize OSHA to explore costs and benefits for deciding between issuance of several standards regulating

different varieties of health and safety hazards, e.g., § 6(g) of the Act, or for promulgating other types of standards not issued under § 6(b)(5). We express no view on these questions.

30. See, e.g., Energy Policy and Conservation Act of 1975, 42 U.S.C. § 6295(c), (d); Federal Water Pollution Control Act Amendments of 1972, 33 U.S.C. § 1312(b)(1), (2); § 1314(b)(1)(B); Clean Water Act Amendments of 1977, 33 U.S.C. § 1314(b)(4)(B); Clean Air Act Amendments of 1970, 42 U.S.C. § 7545(c)(2)(B). * * *

In other statutes, Congress has used the phrase "unreasonable risk," accompanied by ex-light of its ordinary meaning, the word "feasible" cannot be construed to articulate such congressional intent. We therefore reject the argument that Congress required cost-benefit analysis in § 6(b)(5).

B

Even though the plain language of § 6(b)(5) supports this construction, we must still decide whether § 3(8), the general definition of an occupational safety and health standard, either alone or in tandem with § 6(b)(5), incorporates a cost-benefit requirement for standards dealing with toxic materials or harmful physical agents. Section 3(8) of the Act, 29 U.S.C. § 652(8) (emphasis added), provides:

> "The term 'occupational safety and health standard' means a standard which requires conditions, or the adoption or use of one or more practices, means, methods, operations, or processes, *reasonably necessary or appropriate* to provide safe or healthful employment and places of employment."

Taken alone, the phrase "reasonably necessary or appropriate" might be construed to contemplate some balancing of the costs and benefits of a standard. Petitioners urge that, so construed, § 3(8) engrafts a cost-benefit analysis requirement on the issuance of § 6(b)(5) standards, even if § 6(b)(5) itself does not authorize such analysis. We need not decide whether § 3(8), standing alone, would contemplate some form of cost-benefit analysis. For even if it does, Congress specifically chose in § 6(b)(5) to impose separate and additional requirements for issuance of a subcategory of occupational safety and health standards dealing with toxic materials and harmful physical agents: it required that those standards be issued to prevent material impairment of health *to the extent feasible.* Congress could reasonably have concluded that *health* standards should be subject to different criteria than *safety* standards because of the special problems presented in regulating them.

Agreement with petitioners' argument * * * would eviscerate the "to the extent feasible" requirement. Standards would inevitably be set at the level indicated by cost-benefit analysis, and not at the level specified by § 6(b)(5). For example, if cost-benefit analysis indicated a protective standard of 1000 $\mu g/m^3$ PEL, while feasibility analysis indicated a 500 $\mu g/m^3$ PEL, the agency would be forced by the cost-benefit requirement to chose the less stringent point.[31] We cannot believe that Congress intended the general

planation in legislative history, to signify a generalized balancing of costs and benefits. See, e.g., the Consumer Product Safety Act of 1972, 15 U.S.C. § 2056(a) ("unreasonable risk of injury"); H.R.Rep. No. 92–1153, 92d Cong., 2d Sess., 33 (1972) (where the House stated * * * "the determination of unreasonable hazard will involve the Commission in balancing the probability that risk will result in harm and the gravity of such harm against the effect on the product's utility, costs, and availability to the consumer."). The error of several cases finding a cost-benefit

analysis mandate in the Occupational Safety and Health Act is their reliance on the different language and clear legislative history of the Consumer Product Safety Act to reach their conclusions. * * *

31. In addition, as the legislative history makes plain, any standard that was not economically or technologically feasible would *a fortiori* not be "reasonably necessary or appropriate" under the Act. See Industrial Union Department v. Hodgson, 162 U.S.App.D.C. 331, 499 F.2d 467, 478 (1974) ("Congress does not appear to

terms of § 3(8) to countermand the specific feasibility requirement of § 6(b)(5). Adoption of petitioners' interpretation would effectively write § 6(b)(5) out of the Act. We decline to render Congress' decision to include a feasibility requirement nugatory, thereby offending the well-settled rule that all parts of a statute, if possible, are to be given effect. Congress did not contemplate any further balancing by the agency for toxic material and harmful physical agents standards * * *.[32]

C

The legislative history of the Act, while concededly not crystal clear, provides general support for respondents' interpretation of the Act. The congressional reports and debates certainly confirm that Congress meant "feasible" and nothing else in using that term. Congress was concerned that the Act might be thought to require achievement of absolute safety, an impossible standard, and therefore insisted that health and safety goals be capable of economic and technological accomplishment. Perhaps most telling is the absence of any indication whatsoever that Congress intended OSHA to conduct its own cost-benefit analysis before promulgating a toxic material or harmful physical agent standard. The legislative history demonstrates conclusively that Congress was fully aware that the Act would impose real and substantial costs of compliance on industry, and believed that such costs were part of the cost of doing business. * * *

* * *

Not only does the legislative history confirm that Congress meant "feasible" rather than "cost-benefit" when it used the former term, but it also shows that Congress understood that the Act would create substantial costs for employers, yet intended to impose such costs when necessary to create a safe and healthful working environment.[37] Congress viewed the costs of health and safety as a cost of doing business. Senator Yarborough * * * stated: "We know the costs would be put into consumer goods but that is the price we should pay for the 80 million workers in America." He asked:

> "One may well ask too expensive for whom? * * * Is it too expensive for the employee who loses his hand or leg or eyesight? Is it too expensive for the widow trying to raise her children on meager

have intended to protect employees by putting their employers out of business").

32. This is not to say that § 3(8) might not require the balancing of costs and benefits for standards promulgated under provisions other than § 6(b)(5) of the Act. * * * Furthermore, the mere fact that a § 6(b)(5) standard is "feasible" does not mean that § 3(8)'s "reasonably necessary or appropriate" language might not impose additional restraints on OSHA. For example, all § 6(b)(5) standards must be addressed to "significant risks" of material health impairment. In addition, if the use of one respirator would achieve the same reduction in health risk as the use of five, the use of five respirators was "technologically and economically feasible," and OSHA thus insisted on the use of five, then the "reasonably necessary or appropriate" limitation might come into play as an additional restriction on OSHA to choose the one-respirator standard. In this case we need not decide all the applications that § 3(8) might have either alone or together with § 6(b)(5).

37. Because the costs of compliance would weigh particularly heavily on small businesses, Congress provided in § 28 of the Act an amendment to the Small Business Act, 15 U.S.C. § 636, making small businesses eligible for economic assistance through the Small Business Administration to comply with standards promulgated by the Secretary. * * *

allowance under workmen's compensation and social security? And what about the man—a good hardworking man—tied to a wheel chair or hospital bed for the rest of his life? That is what we are dealing with when we talk about industrial safety. * * * We are talking about people's lives, not the indifference of some cost accountants."

Senator Eagleton commented that "[t]he costs that will be incurred by employers in meeting the standards of health and safety to be established under this bill are, in my view, *reasonable and necessary costs of doing business*" (emphasis added).[38]

Other Members of Congress voiced similar views.[39] Nowhere is there any indication that Congress contemplated a different balancing by OSHA of the benefits of worker health and safety against the costs of achieving them. Indeed Congress thought that the *financial costs* of health and safety problems in the workplace were as large or larger than the *financial costs* of eliminating these problems. * * *

"[T]he economic impact of industrial deaths and disability is staggering. Over $1.5 billion is wasted in lost wages, and the annual loss to the Gross National Product is estimated to be over $8 billion. Vast resources that could be available for productive use are siphoned off to pay workmen's compensation benefits and medical expenses." S.Rep. No. 91–1282 at 2 U.S.Code & Admin.News 1970, p. 5178.

Senator Eagleton summarized, "Whether we, as individuals, are motivated by simple humanity or by simple economics, we can no longer permit profits to be dependent upon an unsafe or unhealthy worksite."

* * *

[The Court then went on to uphold OSHA's determination that the cotton dust standard is economically feasible—see Feasibility Analysis, infra—and to disapprove one minor element of the standard. The Court concluded:]

When Congress passed the Occupational Safety and Health Act in 1970, it chose to place pre-eminent value on assuring employees a safe and healthful working environment, limited only by the feasibility of achieving such an environment. We must measure the validity of the Secretary's actions against the requirements of that Act. For "[t]he judicial function does not extend to substantive revision of regulatory policy. That function lies elsewhere—in Congressional and Executive oversight or amendatory

38. Congress was concerned that some employers not obtain a competitive advantage over others by declining to invest in worker health and safety: " * * * [T]he fact is that many employers—particularly smaller ones—simply cannot make the necessary investment in health and safety, and survive competitively, unless all are compelled to do so." S.Rep. 91–1282, 91st Cong., 2d Sess. 4.

39. See, e.g., Legis.Hist. 1030–1031 (remarks of Congressman Dent):

"Although I am very much disturbed over adding new costs to the operation of our production facilities because of the threats from abroad, I would say there is a greater concern and that must be for the production men who do the producing—the men who work in the service industries and the men and women in this country who daily go out and keep the economy moving and make it safe for all of us to live and to work and to be able to prosper in it."

legislation." Industrial Union Department v. American Petroleum Institute, supra, 448 U.S., at 663, 100 S.Ct., at 2875 (BURGER, C. J., concurring).

Accordingly, the judgment of the Court of Appeals is affirmed in all respects except to the extent of its approval of the * * * wage guarantee provision of the Cotton Dust Standard * * *.

[Justice Powell did not participate in the decision. A dissent by Justice Stewart is omitted.]

Justice REHNQUIST, with whom THE CHIEF JUSTICE joins, dissenting.

A year ago I stated my belief that Congress in enacting § 6(b)(5) of the Occupational Safety and Health Act of 1970 unconstitutionally delegated to the Executive Branch the authority to make the "hard policy choices" properly the task of the legislature. Industrial Union Department v. American Petroleum Institute, 448 U.S. 607, 100 S.Ct. 2844, 65 L.Ed.2d 1010 (1980) (concurring opinion). Because I continue to believe that the Act exceeds Congress' power to delegate legislative authority to nonelected officials, I dissent.

WHITMAN v. AMERICAN TRUCKING ASSOCIATIONS, 531 U.S. 457, 121 S.Ct. 903, 149 L.Ed.2d 1 (2001). A unanimous Supreme Court (per Scalia, J.) held that the federal Clean Air Act "does not delegate legislative power to the EPA [Environmental Protection Agency] in contravention of Art. I, § 1, of the [United States] Constitution." "The scope of discretion [the Act] allows is in fact well within the outer limits of our nondelegation precedents." Concurring, Justice Breyer wrote:

"Section 109(b)(1) directs the Administrator [of EPA] to set standards that are 'requisite to protect the public health' with 'an adequate margin of safety.' * * * [T]hese words do not describe a world that is free of all risk– an impossible and undesirable objective. See *Industrial Union Dept., AFL–CIO v. American Petroleum Institute*, 448 U.S. 607, 642, 100 S.Ct. 2844, 65 L.Ed.2d 1010 (1980) (plurality opinion) (the word 'safe' does not mean 'risk-free'). Nor are the words 'requisite' and 'public health' to be understood independent of context. We consider football equipment 'safe' even if its use entails a level of risk that would make drinking water 'unsafe' for consumption. And what counts as 'requisite' to protecting the public health will similarly vary with background circumstances, such as the public's ordinary tolerance of the particular health risk in the particular context at issue. The Administrator can consider such background circumstances when 'decid[ing] what risks are acceptable in the world in which we live.' *Natural Resources Defense Council, Inc. v. EPA*, 824 F.2d 1146, 1165 (C.A.D.C.1987). * * *

"This discretion would seem sufficient to avoid the extreme results that some of the industry parties fear. After all, the EPA, in setting standards that 'protect the public health' with 'an adequate margin of safety,' retains discretionary authority to avoid regulating risks that it reasonably concludes are trivial in context. Nor need regulation lead to deindustrialization.

Preindustrial society was not a very healthy society; hence a standard demanding the return of the Stone Age would not prove 'requisite to protect the public health.' "

FEASIBILITY ANALYSIS

Regulators aiming to reduce physical risk "to the extent feasible" must first analyze the capacity of an activity to control its harmful side-effects, while continuing to meet its primary objectives, and then prescribe the lowest level of risk that appears to be practically attainable. Analysis of an industry's capacity for risk-control has two aspects: "technological" and "economic" feasibility.

1. *Technological Feasibility*—Technological inquiry asks what is the lowest level of risk achievable by an on-going activity simply as a matter of physical technique. Agencies and reviewing courts must be confident that any limit on risk set by regulation—such as the "permissible exposure level" (PEL) for a toxic substance—can in fact be engineered. On the other hand, an entire industry may have failed to exploit technological potential for control of its risks, so that even the best control equipment and devices in operation are less than what is "feasible." An agency may specify a risk limit or PEL only partly attainable through control measures already developed, if it is able to predict that further technical developments can be accomplished within the time frame of regulation. Such predictions are complex, turning on assessment of specific technological possibilities and also the general capacities of an industry, its record in innovation, financial and technical resources available to it, experience of technological change in related areas. Regulatory judgments about these matters are based on expert opinion and studies conducted by agency staff, consultants, or industry sources. The ultimate question is what might be achieved given full determination to succeed—something not entirely knowable until the attempt has been made.

In American Iron & Steel Institute v. Occupational Safety and Health Administration, 577 F.2d 825 (3d Cir.1978), OSHA's standard for coke oven emissions was upheld as technologically feasible though "the most modern and clean coke oven battery operating" met the standard only one-third of the time. Evidence of one-third compliance using less than all suitable technology—plus dramatic progress toward compliance at another plant after new engineering controls were implemented—shows sufficiently that the standard is not "impossible of attainment." As in prior cases involving OSHA standards for asbestos and vinyl chloride, the question is "what the industry could achieve in an effort to best protect its * * * employees," given resolve to develop "technological potentialities." The court approved OSHA's reliance on "innovative technology currently in the experimental stage," and its faith in new techniques "looming over the horizon."

In United Steelworkers v. Marshall, 647 F.2d 1189 (D.C.Cir.1980), which upholds OSHA's airborne lead standard for ten industries, Judge Wright offered the following summary:

The oft-stated view of technological feasibility under the OSH Act is that Congress meant the statute to be "technology-forcing." AFL–CIO v. Brennan, 530 F.2d 109, 121 (3d Cir.1975). This view means, at the very least, that OSHA can impose a standard which only the most technologically advanced plants in an industry have been able to achieve—even if only in some of their operations some of the time. But under this view OSHA can also force industry to develop and diffuse new technology. At least where the agency gives industry a reasonable time to develop new technology, OSHA is not bound to the technological status quo. So long as it presents substantial evidence that companies acting vigorously and in good faith can develop the technology, OSHA can require industry to meet PEL's never attained anywhere.

* * *

As for [proof of] technological feasibility, we know that we cannot require of OSHA anything like certainty. Since "technology-forcing" assumes the agency will make highly speculative projections about future technology, a standard is obviously not infeasible solely because OSHA has no hard evidence to show that the standard has been met. More to the point here, we cannot require OSHA to prove with any certainty that industry will be able to develop the necessary technology, or even to identify the single technological means by which it expects industry to meet the PEL. OSHA can force employers to invest all reasonable faith in their own capacity for technological innovation, and can thereby shift to industry some of the burden of choosing the best strategy for compliance. OSHA's duty is to show that modern technology has at least conceived some industrial strategies or devices which are likely to be capable of meeting the PEL and which the industries are generally capable of adopting.

Our view finds support in the statutory requirement that OSHA act according to the "best *available* evidence." 29 U.S.C. § 655(b)(5) (1976) (emphasis added). OSHA cannot let workers suffer while it awaits the Godot of scientific certainty. * * *

2. *Economic Feasibility*—Economic assessment undertakes to estimate the costs of complying with a regulatory standard, and to analyze the economic impact of such costs upon a regulated industry, in order to determine whether the prescribed level of risk is "economically feasible." Cost estimates focus on financial outlays necessary to achieve and maintain compliance—both capital and operating costs. Impact analysis considers the effects of compliance costs on prices, production, employment, capital financing, competition, and profit, given the underlying economics of the regulated industry. Feasibility determination asks the ultimate question: not whether costs are outweighed by benefits, but whether the industry is able to bear the cost. Regulation by OSHA subject to economic feasibility, according to Judge Wright in United Steelworkers v. Marshall, supra, means "protecting worker health and safety within the limits of economic possibility":

The most useful general judicial criteria for economic feasibility come from Judge McGowan's opinion in Industrial Union Dep't, AFL–CIO v. Hodgson, [499 F.2d 467 (D.C.Cir.1974) (OSHA asbestos standard)]. A standard is not infeasible simply because it is financially burdensome, or even because it threatens the survival of some companies within an industry:

> Nor does the concept of economic feasibility necessarily guarantee the continued existence of individual employers. It would appear to be consistent with the purposes of the Act to envisage the economic demise of an employer who has lagged behind the rest of the industry in protecting the health and safety of employees and is consequently financially unable to comply with new standards as quickly as other employers. * * *

[Id. at 478.] A standard is feasible if it does not threaten "massive dislocation" to, or imperil the existence of, the industry. No matter how initially frightening the projected total or annual costs of compliance appear, a court must examine those costs in relation to the financial health and profitability of the industry and the likely effect of such costs on unit consumer prices. * * * [T]he practical question is whether the standard threatens the competitive stability of an industry, or whether any intra-industry or inter-industry discrimination in the standard might wreck such stability or lead to undue concentration.

* * *

* * * [A]s for [proof of] economic feasibility, OSHA must construct a reasonable estimate of compliance costs and demonstrate a reasonable likelihood that these costs will not threaten the existence or competitive structure of an industry, even if it does portend disaster for some marginal firms. * * *

In the Cotton Dust Case, both the Court of Appeals and the Supreme Court upheld OSHA's assessment of economic feasibility. AFL–CIO v. Marshall, 617 F.2d 636, 659–662 (D.C.Cir.1979), affirmed sub nom. American Textile Manufacturers Institute v. Donovan, 452 U.S. 490, 522–536, 101 S.Ct. 2478, 2497–2504, 69 L.Ed.2d 185 (1981). Following is a summary under three headings: (a) cost estimation; (b) impact analysis; (c) feasibility determination.

(a) OSHA had available two calculations of the capital cost of engineering controls made necessary by its cotton dust standard: a consultant figured such costs at $1.1 billion, while the textile industry submitted an estimate of $543 million. OSHA subjected the industry estimate, which it regarded as the more realistic, to critical analysis and concluded that even the lesser sum overstated probable costs. As the Court of Appeals said, OSHA's analysis took into account "cost advantages available when compliance is achieved through modernizing rather than retrofitting the machinery," and also "improvements in technology that can reasonably be expected during the four-year compliance period." Both courts approved OSHA's technique of appraising and revising cost calculations done by others, especially since the industry would not make underlying data available to the agency. The Supreme Court noted "the inherent crudeness of estimation tools," which have to "rely on assumptions the truth or falsity of which could wreak havoc on * * * numerical cost estimates." It said OSHA is "obligated to subject such assumptions to careful scrutiny."

(b) OSHA's impact analysis considered likely economic consequences of the cotton dust standard with respect to particular sectors of the cotton industry, the industry as a whole, and the economy generally. The analysis calculated increases in production costs and consequent price increases needed to maintain prior rates of return on investment, and forecast the effect of higher prices on consumption given pertinent price elasticities of demand, concluding that the industry would be able to pass compliance costs on to consumers. It investigated capital requirements and capital financing problems, particularly for smaller firms; effects on profitability and market structure of the cotton industry; on competition between cotton and synthetics, and between domestic and foreign producers; on employment, energy consumption, and inflation. The Supreme Court approved OSHA's "comprehensive economic evaluation" as a "responsible prediction" of the impact of cotton dust regulation.

(c) Finally, OSHA concluded that "compliance with the standard is well within the financial capability" of the cotton industry. The agency noted that "although some marginal employers may shut down rather than comply, the industry as a whole will not be threatened." Both courts agreed that OSHA had amply demonstrated the industry's ability to absorb projected costs. For the Court of Appeals, regulatory requirements remain economically feasible even though they "impose substantial costs on an industry * * * or even force some employers out of business," provided controls are not "prohibitively expensive" and do not make "financial viability generally impossible." For the Supreme Court, the cotton dust controls fit "the plain meaning of the word 'feasible,'" given OSHA's determination "that the industry will maintain long-term profitability and competitiveness."

3. *Feasibility and Fairness*—What is the moral basis for pressing regulation of risk beyond the point at which costs are offset by benefits, and requiring the lowest level of risk that is technologically and economically feasible? OSHA has argued that regulation must be guided by feasibility in order to bring about fair distribution of benefits and burdens in social life. The OSHA Cancer Policy declares that "equity considerations" are "paramount to occupational health regulation." 45 Fed.Reg. 5001, 5250 (1980). OSHA's emphasis on the link between fairness and feasibility follows the approach of testimony given at agency hearings on the cancer policy:

> Dr. Nicholas A. Ashford (MIT) testified that cost-benefit criteria, while useful as analytical tools, were not appropriate as decision rules for occupational health regulation. He argued that occupational health differed from some environmental problems. The public, by and large, equally benefited from and paid the costs for cleaner water. If a cost-benefit analysis determined that the costs necessary to achieve cleaner water exceeded the benefits, the same public would forego both the

reductions in risk and water quality and the regulatory costs. However, in the case of occupational safety and health, different groups enjoy the economic savings of not regulating and take the risks. Consumers save through lower prices and employers benefit through higher profits from not regulating, while risks are borne by workers, often in the lower economic groups. Therefore, occupational safety and health posed an "equity" question. Dr. Ashford believed it was inappropriate to ignore equity considerations and pay attention to efficiency criteria alone. He believed that cost-benefit analyses are not neutral when the costs and benefits accrue to different parties. Therefore, Dr. Ashford stated that efficiency criteria cannot form the major basis for decision-making on occupational health questions and that inequalities in the distribution of costs and benefits must be given heavy consideration.

* * *

* * * OSHA believes that as a matter of policy, efficiency criteria alone are not appropriate because they ignore equity considerations. The economic savings from less protective regulation accrue to industry in the form of higher profits and to consumers in the form of lower prices. But the costs are borne by workers through increased industrial illness and death rates.

Efficiency analysis cannot accommodate the distributional implications involved when the costs and benefits accrue to different subgroups. * * *

Dr. Ashford (MIT), discussed the implications of equity for cost-benefit analysis. He stated:

"The most serious limitation (of cost-benefit analysis), however, lies in the failure to successfully deal with the fact that the cost and benefit streams accrue to different parties. One person's benefit cannot be neatly traded off from another's cost. * * * Equity and economic efficiency are sometimes conflicting goals. As a decision tool, cost-benefit analysis can be useful in identifying the nature of the trade-offs; as a decision rule it is useless. Regulation of toxic substances is an expression of social policy, not economic policy, and the social decision does not end with internalizing the social costs of producing and using chemicals and * * * equating costs and benefits at the margin."

OSHA believes that it would be inappropriate for an agency statutorily required "to assure so far as possible every working man and woman in the nation safe and healthful working conditions" to ignore such equity considerations.

Id. at 5237 & 5249.

Fairness was also advanced as a rationale for feasibility in argument to the Supreme Court in the Cotton Dust Case. The Solicitor General's brief for OSHA argues that cost-benefit balancing may be appropriate in the area of product safety, since "the risks and benefits of a consumer product accrue to the same party, the consumer, who can choose to avoid the risk. Employees, on the other hand, rarely have such a choice—they must bear the risk of occupational health hazards, while benefits accrue largely to employers and consumers." Brief for Federal Respondent at 55. The brief concludes:

* * * [T]raditional cost-benefit analysis * * * cannot account for those considerations of equity that underlay the very concept of occupational health regulation. While the cost-benefit technique has gained some adherents as an allegedly value-free method for dealing with all manner of difficult questions, this technique originated in the context of investment capital decisions, where costs and benefits not only were already expressed in dollars, but also accrued to the same party. In occupational health regulation, however, * * * [t]he unequal distribution of costs and benefits * * * necessarily raises the question of this statute's purpose and its determination of what is equitable; the mere calculation of costs and benefits cannot supply that answer.

Id. at 61. See also E. J. Mishan, Economics for Social Decisions: Elements of Cost–Benefit Analysis 13 (1973):

* * * A project that is adjudged feasible by reference to a cost-benefit analysis is * * * quite consistent with an economic arrangement that makes the rich richer and the poor poorer. It is also consistent with manifest inequity, for an enterprise that is an attractive proposition by the lights of a cost-benefit calculation may be one that offers opportunities for greater profits and pleasure to one group, in the pursuit of which substantial damages and suffering may be endured by other groups.

In order, then, for a mooted enterprise to be socially approved, it is not enough that the outcome of an ideal cost-benefit analysis is positive. It must also be shown that the resulting distributional changes are not regressive, and no gross inequities are perpetrated.

––––––––

COTTON DUST REVISITED. In December 1985, four years after the Supreme Court upheld the cotton dust standard, OSHA adopted several technical amendments and commented generally on the regulation's effects and costs:

No changes are being made in the permissible exposure limit (PEL) and compliance strategy for the textile industry. The PELs remain 200 Sg/m^3 for yarn production, 750 $\mu g/m^3$ for slashing and weaving and 500 Sg/m^3 for wastehouses in textile mills. The studies by Imbus and ELB indicate that the standard has substantially reduced the incidence of byssinosis and declines in lung function from the levels of the early 1970's, a greater reduction than had been previously predicted. The Beck study confirms and expands on the prior studies by Merchant that the higher exposures of the early seventies and earlier lead not only to significant risk of acute byssinotic symptoms but also to chronic lung disease. OSHA expects that the much lower levels now in effect will substantially reduce and could possibly eliminate this chronic disease for newer employees. Both the American Textile Manufacturers Institute (ATMI) and the Amalgamated Clothing and Textile Workers Union (ACTWU) agree to the retention of the exposure limits. OSHA commends both the industry and the union whose efforts along with OSHA's have led to this substantial improvement in the health of workers currently employed in the cotton textile industry.

Current studies by Centaur and others show that it has been technically and economically feasible to comply with the standard in the textile industry. Virtually the entire industry has come into compliance utilizing modern production equipment in conjunction with increased ventilation * * *. Such new equipment (chute fed cards, projectile looms, open end spinning, etc.) has substantially increased industry productivity while lowering both cotton dust and noise levels. The cost of the standard has proven to be half of the cost predicted by OSHA in 1978 and has proven to be economically feasible for the industry. Therefore, OSHA finds no basis for changing the compliance strategy. Again, both ATMI and ACTWU agree with this conclusion.

50 Fed.Reg. 51120, 51121 (1985).

COST–BENEFIT BALANCING

Advocates of cost-benefit balancing oppose single-minded pursuit of any regulatory goal beyond the point at which marginal costs are offset by marginal benefits. They prescribe that each regulatory intervention be subjected to exacting cost-benefit analysis, in order to promote economic efficiency and maximize social utility. The key thought is that pursuit of the regulatory goal—reduction of risk—should not involve too much sacrifice of other values. So regulators must strike a balance between costs and benefits of regulation.

1. *Single–Minded Agencies*—According to Murray L. Weidenbaum, chair of the Council of Economic Advisers in the Reagan administration, regulatory programs should be managed by people "who are sympathetic with the important social objectives to be achieved—and who are equally concerned with minimizing the costs and intrusions." Otherwise, "the costs of the 'government failure' that poor regulation represents [will] far exceed the costs of the 'market failure' with which regulation attempts to deal." Cost-benefit analysis, "a neutral policy concept," is a needed corrective to single-minded regulation by "uncritical enthusiasts":

> * * * We need open-minded regulators who understand that good policy making means a careful balancing of important and bona fide considerations—clean air *and* lower unemployment, safer products *and* less inflation, healthier working conditions *and* rising productivity. * * *

> * * *

Government regulation * * * should be carried to the point where the incremental costs equal the incremental benefits, and no further.

Overregulation, that is to say, is the economist's shorthand for regulation where costs exceed benefits.

Weidenbaum, Reforming Government Regulation, Regulation (Nov./Dec. 1980) 15.

A similar diagnosis is offered by Christopher C. DeMuth, administrator for regulatory affairs in the Office of Management and Budget during 1981–1984:

> Market failures—such as natural monopoly, externality, and consumer uncertainty over product quality—are a consequence of the costs of voluntary market transactions, such as the costs buyers and sellers incur in finding each other and negotiating and enforcing agreements. In the usual formulation, a market failure is said to exist when these kinds of costs prevent mutually beneficial transactions from taking place. * * * [Then] the government might use its coercive powers to effect certain transactions more cheaply than the private market. For example, a regulation might obtain the reduction in pollution that would have resulted, in the absence of transaction costs, from voluntary agreements between polluting firms and their neighbors. * * * The correction of market failure is the only non-paternalistic rationale for government regulation, and largely for this reason it permeates the official rhetoric of most regulatory programs as well as the logic of most regulatory decisions.

> If regulation in fact operated purely to correct for market failure, [it would promote] the efficiency of the economic system. But in the real world regulation departs from the economic ideal in two related ways—which may be called "regulatory failures." First, regulation frequently operates not to improve the efficiency of markets, but rather to redistribute income and wealth in the direction of politically effective groups, typically at the *expense* of economic efficiency. Second, regulators have skewed incentives resulting from their institutional responsibility to pursue a single policy single-mindedly, which frequently lead them to go far beyond the point of zero marginal returns in correcting market failures. Fearing above all a conspicuous disaster within their jurisdiction—deformed babies or a major accident—they issue regulations requiring (say) the elimination of 95 percent of some risk where a 90 percent reduction would cost only half as much and would be the equilibrium point in a perfectly functioning market. The first "regulatory failure" is most often associated with economic regulation and the second with health, safety, and environmental regulation, but the two overlap insensibly.

DeMuth, The Regulatory Budget, Regulation (Mar./Apr.1980) 29.

2. *Agency Balancing*—At hearings conducted by OSHA on the agency's Cancer Policy, industry representatives objected to feasibility-based regulation, proposing that regulation should find the point of balance between costs and benefits, and go no further. The approach recommended by advocates of cost-benefit balancing is summarized by the agency as follows:

Several of the major industrial participants advocated that an "efficiency-based" approach be used to determine permissible exposure limits. Their approach would estimate risks to workers and compliance costs at alternative levels of exposure for each substance regulated. * * * Efficiency criteria would determine the stringency of control technology mandated.

* * *

Industry representatives recommended that numerical estimates balancing social costs and benefits form the primary basis for the setting of standards for individual carcinogenic agents. These parties argued that the OSHA Cancer Policy as proposed was designed to achieve a risk-free society, and that this is an undesirable goal because it is impossible to achieve and wasteful of economic resources. * * *

* * *

* * * Under this cost-benefit framework, if benefits exceed costs, there is a net social benefit and the project should be undertaken. Regarding occupational health investments, estimates of the costs of compliance at a particular control level would be compared to the permanent or long-term benefits of improved occupational health defined as the costs of nonregulation. Exposure levels would be lowered only [to] the extent that the benefits of improved health (including extended longevity) exceed hazard abatement costs; otherwise, resources would be more efficiently spent elsewhere.

Cost-benefit balancing "at the margin" was recommended. This means that each increment of regulatory control—especially the last, and costliest—must itself yield a sufficiently large increment of benefit.

A * * * cost-benefit approach to setting permissible exposure levels would balance control costs and predicted benefits at the margin. Dr. [Richard] Zeckhauser [of Harvard University] explained marginal analysis and its use in setting exposure levels as follows:

"[I]t is important to determine not only how much is achieved on average for a particular level of expenditure but how much is achieved at the margin. * * * We might look at a standard that reduces exposure by an amount X at an expenditure of $100 million. The gain may seem worth it. But the gain at the margin may be rather minimal. What if we would achieve a reduction of 99% of X for an expenditure of merely $50 million? Well, that last small reduction in exposure would be costing a very great deal."

Another sort of analysis—cost-effectiveness—was also recommended. Such analysis aims to discover how to spend limited resources and achieve the greatest amount of risk-reduction possible, but does not itself say how to determine the total "budget" to be expended.

Both Drs. Zeckhauser and [Lester] Lave argued that placing a monetary value on human life is not necessary to achieve optimal allocation of available health resources. They recommended a cost-effective approach both to structure priorities for regulatory actions and to set standards.

It should be noted that the term "cost-effective" [denotes] the least-costly method of achieving a particular level of health benefits.

The cost-effectiveness analysis advocated by Drs. Lave and Zeckhauser would involve estimating risks to workers and compliance costs at alternative levels of exposure for each substance. * * * Industrial substances would be ordered and regulated to levels according to the number of lives saved per dollar expended. They stated that OSHA should first regulate the substance to the level which would save the most lives per dollar of control costs, then the next substance to the level which would save the second greatest number of lives per dollar, etc. They argued that OSHA should continue to regulate until the cost to save one life was greater than the risk that the Nation was willing to accept (however determined).

45 Fed.Reg. 5001, 5236–37 & 5245–46 (1980).

SECTION C.   THE VALUE OF LIFE

The materials in this section all deal, one way or another, with this question: what is the value of life? Put in monetary terms, the question is: what dollar amount should be assigned to the loss that occurs when life is lost? Or, more elaborately, for purposes of cost-benefit analysis: what is the quantity of benefit that is realized when loss of life is avoided by the reduction of life-threatening physical risk through costly regulation? And how can we determine that quantity?

The following materials show two different ways of arriving at a monetary sum that may represent the value of a life for purposes of regulatory policy. One method is to calculate the "societal cost" incurred when economically productive life-activity is cut off. This approach is used in the initial readings below. The other way is to calculate the "implicit valuation" of life reflected in peoples' choices to pay money in order to avoid risks of death, or to accept money in exchange for running mortal risks. This approach is discussed in the subsequent readings.

E.S. GRUSH & C. S. SAUNBY, FATALITIES ASSOCIATED WITH CRASH INDUCED FUEL LEAKAGE AND FIRES

[In August 1973 the National Highway Traffic Safety Administration (NHTSA) gave notice of a new standard concerning "fuel system integrity." 38 Fed.Reg. 22397 & 22417. Under the announced Federal Motor Vehicle Safety Standard (FMVSS) No. 301, vehicles must be engineered so that only a limited amount of fuel spillage would occur in collisions. Tests are specified—including a "static rollover requirement"—in which fuel leakage is measured in typical crash situations. The present document, which has come to be known as the "Grush–Saunby Report," offers an evaluation of NHTSA's standard. An internal Ford Motor Company memorandum authored by employees in "impact factors," the Grush–Saunby Report undertakes (a) risk-assessment and (b) cost-benefit balancing. It concludes that FMVSS No. 301 is not cost-justified.

[The Grush–Saunby Report deals with a general standard for fuel system safety. The specific design of the Ford Pinto gas tank was at issue in Grimshaw v. Ford Motor Company (see p. 1091 supra). In that celebrated case the jury found the Pinto gas tank defective and awarded punitive damages of $125 million against Ford, later reduced to $3.5 million. Plaintiffs in *Grimshaw* sought unsuccessfully to have the Grush–Saunby Report admitted in evidence, but were able to elicit testimony from a former Ford employee "that Ford did in fact engage in cost-benefit analyses which balanced life and limb against corporate savings and profits." 174 Cal.Rptr. at 376. In affirming the reduced award of punitive damages, the California Court of Appeal noted that "Ford could have corrected the hazardous design defects at minimal cost but decided to defer correction of the shortcomings by engaging in a cost-benefit analysis * * *. Ford's institutional mentality was shown to be one of callous indifference to public safety." Id. at 384.]

* * *

The NHTSA estimate of 2000 to 3500 fatalities yearly in fire-involved motor vehicle crashes appears to overstate the seriousness of the fire problem. Examination of in-depth accident data sources indicates that most fatalities in fire-accompanied crashes die from injuries not associated with the fire itself. Thus the National Safety Council estimate of 600 to 700 fire deaths each year is probably more appropriate than the higher NHTSA figure.

The actual number of fuel leakage incidents is relatively evenly distributed into four basic crash types: frontal, side, rear, and rollover. However, the likelihood of a given crash resulting in fuel spillage is much higher for rear impacts (26 percent with spillage in the sample studied) than for other crash types, such as frontals (3.5 percent spillage).

The cost of implementing the rollover portion of the amended Standard has been calculated to be almost three times the expected benefit, even using very favorable benefit assumptions. The yearly benefits of compliance were estimated at just under $50 million, with an associated customer cost of $137 million. Analyses of other portions of the proposed regulation would also be expected to yield poor benefit-to-cost ratios.

METHOD AND RESULTS

Number of Fire Fatalities

The NHTSA states that "motor vehicle collisions accompanied by fire account for between 2000 and 3500 fatalities annually." This range is about the same as that proposed by Sliepcevich and others from the University of Oklahoma Research Institute in an NHTSA-sponsored report. The National Safety Council (NSC), on the other hand, has suggested a somewhat lesser number (600–700) of persons dying annually in motor-vehicle fires resulting from accidents.

One explanation for the large difference in these estimates may relate to what is actually being counted: *total* deaths in fire-involved motor vehicle crashes or deaths *from fire* in fire-involved crashes. It has been reported that, as crash severity increases, the chance of a resultant fire increases in turn. Thus the set of crashes which do involve fire tends to include severe accidents which are believed to be more likely to result in fatality regardless of the occurrence of fire. It may be, therefore, that many fatalities in fire-involved crashes result from the crash forces themselves, with fire being simply a concomitant and not causal variable.

The data source available to check this proposition was the CPIR III File of in-depth accident investigations maintained by the University of Michigan Highway Safety Research Institute. * * *

From this data source were selected those occupants who were fatally injured in vehicles which sustained crash-induced fires. The 24 such occupants who were found comprise about seven percent of the total of 358 fatalities in the data sample. Extending this percentage to the nationwide total of some 40,000 occupant fatalities yields an estimate of 2800 deaths in motor vehicle accidents in which a fire took place, a number in agreement with the NHTSA and Oklahoma estimate.

The complete crash history on file for each of the 24 supposed fire fatalities was examined in detail to ascertain the actual circumstances surrounding the death * * *. In over half of the instances the deceased was not burned at all, and death can be attributed only to the impact injuries. In these instances the occupant was typically ejected or extracted prior to spread of the fire. In one-fourth of the fatalities, fatal injuries were attributed to both impact and burns. These occupants most likely would have died even had there been no fire—in fact, the fire may well have burned an already-dead body. For only five of the 24 fatalities examined was fire reasonably classifiable as the clear cause of the death. * * *

* * *

Results from this rather small sample of fatalities taken from a specialized data source perhaps cannot be considered definitive, in terms of predicting exact numbers. The analysis does indicate, however, that the NSC estimate of 600 to 700 yearly motor vehicle fire fatalities is certainly within reason. In addition, the detailed evaluation shows that, while the higher NHTSA estimate of deaths in cars with fire may be correct, most of these occupants in fact sustain fatal injuries not at all related to the associated fire.

The results discussed here refer to the types of vehicles in service at the present time. In future cars, with improved ejection-prevention and injury-mitigation properties, fewer occupants may sustain impact-induced fatal injuries. This would brighten the overall fatality and injury picture, of course, but might increase occupant exposure to situations in which fire would be the only hazard. On the other hand, occupants sustaining lesser injuries might be better able to cope with and escape from fire impacts which do occur, thereby reducing the risk of serious burns. Thus the influence vehicle improvements will have on the relative risk associated with fire is not clear, and cannot be practicably quantified with the limited data available.

Fuel Spillage

An NHTSA-sponsored study conducted by Brayman at Calspan, Inc. contains data concerning fuel leakage for different impact directions. The source for these data was the Automotive Crash Injury Research (ACIR) accident file maintained by Calspan. The ACIR data concern rural, injury-producing accidents. Accident cases analyzed by Calspan between June 1968 and May 1969 were used by Brayman as the data sample for his study.

* * * [I]nformation developed from the Brayman study * * * indicates that fuel leaks themselves are relatively evenly split among four basic crash types: frontal, side (mostly to rear half of car), rear and rollover. Thus no particular crash type is especially outstanding with regard to its contribution to any fuel spillage problem.

Certain crash types have a much greater likelihood of producing fuel spillage, however. Among 933 frontal impacts in the sample, 33, or 3.5 percent, resulted in fuel spillage. In contrast, over one-fourth of all rear impacts produced fuel leakage. Other crash types had intermediate likelihoods of leaking fuel. Thus it is clear that different crash types have widely varying propensities for resulting in fuel leaks.

It is noteworthy that, while seven percent of the cars in the Brayman sample developed fuel leaks, fires (both fuel-fed and otherwise) were reported for .5 percent of the cars in this ACIR data file. Thus it appears as though less than seven percent of cars which develop fuel leaks subsequently burn.

COST/BENEFIT ANALYSIS OF STATIC ROLLOVER REQUIREMENT

The analysis discussed below concerns the static rollover requirement proposed for FMVSS 301. This discussion represents an attempt to outline an approach which can be used to address this and similar problems. While the benefit analysis is not meant to be definitive and beyond criticism, it is based on assumptions and derivations believed to be quite representative of an *upper bound* on the possible benefits accruing from compliance with the requirement.

Table 3 outlines the pertinent benefit and cost. The relevant benefits are those associated with the consequences of reduction in the frequency of fires in rollovers, while the presented costs relate to the incremental cost associated with meeting the specific static rollover aspects of the Standard.

Table 3

BENEFITS AND COSTS RELATING TO FUEL LEAKAGE ASSOCIATED WITH
THE STATIC ROLLOVER TEST PORTION OF FMVSS [301]

BENEFITS:

Savings—180 burn deaths, 180 serious burn injuries, 2100 burned vehicles.

Unit Cost—$200,000 per death, $67,000 per injury, $700 per vehicle.

Total Benefit—180 × ($200,000) + 180 × ($67,000) + 2100 × ($700) =
$49.5 million.

COSTS:

Sales—11 million cars, 1.5 million light trucks.

Unit Cost—$11 per car, $11 per truck.

Total Cost—11,000,000 × ($11) + 1,500,000 × ($11) = $137 million.

Benefits

The appropriateness of the estimate of 700 burn deaths each year
resulting from motor vehicle crashes has been discussed in the main text of
this study. Data from both the Calspan fire study and the Oklahoma analysis
of a New York State fire study suggest that when occupants are burned, the
injuries tend to be quite serious, and about half of the casualties sustain fatal
injuries. Thus the 700 fatalities should be complemented by another 700
non-fatally (though seriously) injured occupants. Given the NSC estimate of
10,000 yearly crash induced vehicle fires, about 8,500 of these fire crashes
occur with no resultant occupant burns each year. * * *

The proportion of fuel leaks which occur in rollovers is * * * slightly
less than one-fourth. If this proportion is applied to the fire numbers
themselves, the consequences of fire in rollovers can be estimated as 180
deaths, 180 non-fatal injuries, and 2100 other fire crashes. These values are
predicated upon two postulations: rollover fuel leaks result in fire just as
often as other fuel leaks, and rollover fires are just as likely to result in burns
as other fires.

This analysis assumes that *all* these fires and the resultant casualties can
be eliminated entirely through compliance with the rollover requirement. In
addition, it is assumed that vehicle modifications designed to ensure compliance with non-rollover portions of the Standard will not reduce at all the
number of rollover fires. The extent to which either of these assumptions is
not completely accurate represents a measure of the extent to which
benefits derived here are overestimates of the true values.

To compare the benefits of eliminating the consequences of these
rollover fires with the requisite costs, the benefits and costs must be
expressed in terms of some common measure. The measure typically chosen
is dollars; this requires, then, converting the casualty losses to this metric.
The casualty to dollars conversion factors used in this study were the
societal cost values prepared by the NHTSA. These values are generally
higher than similarly-defined costs from other sources, and their use does
not signify that Ford accepts or concurs in the values. Rather, the NHTSA

figures are used only to be consistent with the attempt not to understate the relevant benefits.

The NHTSA has calculated a value of $200,000 for each fatality. While the major portion of this amount relates to lost future wages, the total also includes some consideration for property damage. The NHTSA average loss for all injuries was about $7000. Burn injuries which do occur tend to be quite serious, however, as discussed above. Thus a higher value of $67,000, which is the NHTSA estimate of partial disability injuries, was used for each of the 180 non-fatal burn injuries. The $700 property damage per vehicle is the NHTSA estimate of vehicle property damage costs in non-disabling injury crashes.

Costs

The Retail Price Equivalent (the customer sticker price with no provision for Ford profit) of vehicle modifications necessary to assure compliance with the static rollover portion of the proposed Standard has been determined by Ford to be an average of $11 per passenger car and $11 per light truck. While these are Ford costs, they have been applied across the industry in this analysis. Total yearly sales estimates of 11 million passenger cars and 1.5 million light trucks (under 6,000 lbs. GVW) were used in conjunction with the unit cost determinations.

Benefit and Cost Comparison

The total benefit is shown in Table 3 to be just under $50 million, while the associated cost is $137 million. Thus the cost is almost three times the benefits, even using a number of highly favorable benefit assumptions. As better estimates of the parameters used in the benefit analysis become available, they could be inserted into the general analysis framework. It does not appear likely, however, that such alternate estimates could lead to the substantial benefit estimate increase which would be required to make compliance with the rollover requirement cost effective.

Benefits and Costs for Other Impact Modes

The analysis discussed above concerns only rollover consequences and costs. Similar analysis for other impact modes would be expected to yield comparable results, with the implementation costs far outweighing the expected benefits.

* * *

NOTE ON $200,000 PER LIFE. The Grush–Saunby Report uses the cost-of-fatality calculation found in NHTSA's Preliminary Report on Societal Costs of Motor Vehicle Accidents (April 1972). There NHTSA arrives at a figure of $200,700 per fatality, but admonishes (at p. A–1): "*We have not quantified all losses associated with the tragedy of a highway accident. We have not placed a value on a human life * * **" (emphasis in original). NHTSA's calculation focusses on the value of production lost by reason of a fatal accident—this approach is refined in its 1975 report on societal costs, excerpted below.

Notice that the Grush–Saunby Report's cost-benefit analysis would come out in favor of regulation, not against it, if lives are assumed to be worth $750,000 each rather than $200,000.

NATIONAL HIGHWAY TRAFFIC SAFETY ADMINISTRATION, SOCIETAL COSTS OF MOTOR VEHICLE ACCIDENTS (1975)

Motor vehicle accidents result in significant costs to individuals and to society at large. This report, which is an update and revision of a societal cost study published in 1972, presents estimates of societal costs through quantification of societal loss components.

The purpose of this study is to assess some basic losses to society from motor vehicle accidents. Measurable cost components are identified to provide some indication of the scope of the human problem. However, the total of individual cost estimates of accidents should not be interpreted as the value placed on a life or as the total cost of a fatality or injury to society. Neither is it the total amount that society is willing to spend to save a life or to prevent an injury. Rather, the cost components and the total of these components are indicators of the significance of the motor vehicle accident problem.

The basic concept of societal loss is a decrease in individual and group welfare. Societal welfare is, in general terms, the sum total of individual well-being; and, in specific terms, it includes levels of health, production of goods and services (both qualitative and quantitative), personal satisfaction and happiness, and physical comfort. The concept goes beyond economic welfare. Precise specification of societal welfare would require determination of a consistent ordering of individual values and probably will never be specified in totality. In addition, quantification is not possible on all factors. The broad concept of societal welfare just described is embraced in this study with the recognition that all factors cannot be identified or measured.

SUMMARY OF COSTS

Application of the societal cost components and totals should be considered with this conceptual basis in mind. The primary usefulness of the cost estimates is to serve as an indication of the magnitude of the problem. Though the societal cost estimates can be useful in a benefit-cost context, it should be recognized that a benefit-cost ratio or net benefit figure is only one component of a relatively substantial array of social and technological factors that must be considered in evaluating the worth of a program.

The general approach of this study is to derive cost estimates that adequately reflect certain losses to society. Some losses are to individuals as a part of society and others are to society external to the individual. The two basic criteria for identifying loss components are (1) resources consumed in the repair of damage to people and vehicles that could be shifted in the long run to welfare-producing activities and (2) the consumption losses of individuals and society at large caused by losses in production and the ability to produce.

Costs of medical care, repair costs of vehicle damage, legal and court costs, accident investigation costs and insurance administration costs relate to the first concept of loss. The resources consumed in these activities could be shifted to raise the existing level of economic and social welfare of society were they not devoted to "cleaning up" the damage from accidents. On the other hand, losses in production relate to the accident victim's inability to produce in the market context, in home and family activities, and in community service. Losses in production are also related to the time spent by others in response to accident ramifications and in the delay caused by the accident to others on the road.

The current measurement does not identify the redistributions that occur between individuals as a result of an accident; nor does the quantification determine how much of a loss is compensated and by whom the compensation is provided, whether by the individual, by private insurance, or by government. Redistributions in the Gross National Product (GNP) occur as the result of accidents; in fact, the overall level of GNP may be increased by the occurrence of accidents. Therefore, in the context of losses in societal welfare, a GNP approach to measurement is neither valid nor relevant. Losses may be largely to the individual for some cost components, but these are losses to society as a whole because the individual is an integral part of society.

* * *

SOCIETAL COST COMPONENTS

The conceptual basis and the measurement of societal cost components are presented in the following sections. The basic concepts are explained in the context of the two criteria for component identification: resources devoted to accidents and production losses. * * *

[Given all the study's "cost components," the average cost of a fatal accident in 1975 is calculated to be $287,175. Of this amount, production losses make up $275,365 or fully 96%—$211,820 in loss of workweek production, and $63,545 in home, family and community production. All other costs—medical, funeral, legal and court, insurance administration, accident investigation, losses to others, vehicle damage, traffic delay—amount to $11,810 or 4%. At the rate of 46,800 traffic fatalities per year, the total "societal cost" for fatal accidents alone is 13.44 billion dollars annually.]

PRODUCTION LOSSES

Losses in present and future production resulting from the casualties of highway accidents are significant societal costs. The basic concept of production loss relates to decreases in individual and group welfare. The following scenario describes the concept better than a general discussion. When a person dies accidentally, future potential production by that individual ceases; the deceased individual no longer produces the units of production that would have been consumed by the individual and his family and by others in society. Individual and societal welfare would have been derived from that person's production. Whether the loss is largely to the individual and his immediate family or to the rest of society is inconsequential, since the well-being of each individual in society is part of total societal welfare. This is the case for persons temporarily or permanently injured as well. Measurement of the value of lost production is, in effect, only a proxy measure of these losses in societal welfare. Assigned compensation to the individual is one means to determine societal valuation of production. In this context, the quantity to be measured is average compensation in the marketplace. That an individual might be replaced by an unemployed individual is not relevant, since the quantity to be measured is the value of life activity of that individual. When a person dies prematurely or is permanently disabled, the value of life activity of that individual is lost to society.

There are two components to lost production. The first is the market or market-proxy portion, which is the measurement of the 8–hour day or 40–hour week. The second component of total production loss is those production losses in the home and community context outside the 8–hour day. * * *

[The study then proceeds to calculate production losses as follows. It uses "average income" to represent the value of production "within the 40–hour workweek." The weighted average includes a "market proxy" estimate of the value of unpaid labor (e.g., by housewives) done within workweek hours. Then workweek production loss is calculated by multiplying average income times the average duration of lost production at various levels of injury. Finally, production losses beyond the 40–hour workweek are calculated in the manner described below.]

The production losses outside the 40–hour workweek related to home, family, and community services are significant and are amenable to measurement on application of the opportunity cost principle. * * *

The average home, family, and community production losses for fatalities and injuries were determined on the basis of time devoted to the identified functions. The production time devoted to home and community was estimated, and the resulting percent of the 40–hour week was applied to the average dollar loss for [workweek] losses for each severity level. * * * The average production was determined to be 10 hours per week for home and family sector production and 2 hours per week for volunteer activity. The combined total is 30% of the 40–hour week. * * *

[Home and family sector] loss components include the following service production functions: home maintenance; household tasks; training, teaching, and counseling children; and many other functions. These productive services are lost if a fatality occurs and are diminished in proportion to disability and activity restrictions for injuries. The method of calculation is to estimate a percent of market production for these tasks and to apply the percentage to the previously determined opportunity-cost measurement of the workweek loss for fatalities and injuries.

* * *

LOSSES TO OTHERS

Costs associated with losses to others include employer losses (temporary or permanent replacement costs), time spent visiting patients, transportation for medical attention, home care, and time spent in vehicle repair and replacement. The basic concept for loss measurement is the opportunity cost of time spent by others in these activities.

* * *

———

SUBSEQUENT NHTSA REPORTS. NHTSA has continued to calculate the cost associated with a traffic fatality, using essentially the same approach as that just described. In *The Economic Cost of Motor Vehicle Crashes: 1990* (1992), the agency reckoned the cost of fatal injury to be $702,000. In its similarly titled study covering 1994, when traffic accidents caused 40,676 fatalities, NHTSA said that "[e]ach fatality resulted in an average discounted lifetime cost of $830,000"; "[o]ver 85 percent of this cost is due to lost workplace and household productivity."

Following are excerpts from *The Economic Cost of Motor Vehicle Crashes: 1994* (1996), which comment on the methodology NHTSA uses:

"The costs documented in this report are the economic or 'human capital' cost components for motor vehicle injuries and crashes. The conceptual framework of human capital costs encompasses direct and indirect costs to individuals and to society as a whole from decreases in the general health status of those injured in motor vehicle crashes. Individuals are seen as producers and consumers of a stream of output throughout their lifetime. Injured individuals are considered part of total societal impact, hence, the value of their decreased production and their decreased consumption is included in total cost." Id. at 13.

"The costs examined * * * are the economic costs that result from goods and services that must be purchased or productivity that is lost as a result of motor vehicle crashes. They do not represent the more intangible consequences of these events to individuals and families such as pain, suffering and loss of life. Measurement of the dollar value of those consequences has been undertaken through numerous studies. These studies have estimated values based on wages for risky occupations and purchases of products for improvements in safety among other measurement techniques. These 'willingness-to-pay' costs can be an order of magnitude higher than the economic costs of injuries. Currently, most authors seem to agree that the value of fatal risk reduction lies in the range of $2–5 million per life saved." Id. at 59.

MONTALVO v. LAPEZ
Supreme Court of Hawaii, 1994.
77 Hawai'i 282, 884 P.2d 345.

MOON, Chief Justice.

* * * John Lapez and the City and County of Honolulu [the defendants in the case] appeal from a jury verdict in the First Circuit Court awarding $770,000.00 in damages against the City in favor of [the plaintiff] Obidio Montalvo resulting from a multi-vehicle rearend accident caused by the negligent operation of a City refuse truck.

On appeal, the City asserts that the trial court erred [in a number of particulars]. * * * On his cross-appeal, Montalvo asserts that the trial court erred by excluding expert testimony on hedonic damages,[2] and therefore, if the case is remanded for further proceedings, he should be allowed to present such expert testimony.

We vacate the trial court's judgment and remand for a new trial. With respect to Montalvo's cross-appeal, we affirm the trial court's decision to exclude expert testimony on hedonic damages.

[Discussion of issues that led to remand is omitted.]

* * *

Because we are remanding this case to the trial court, we address the merits of Montalvo's cross-appeal. [Montalvo, who suffered a back injury in the accident at issue here,] contends that the trial court erred in excluding expert testimony on hedonic (or loss of enjoyment of life) damages. * * *

We note first that, indisputably, hedonic damages are recoverable [as compensation for permanent nonfatal injury, such as Montalvo's]. HRS § 663–8.5(a) (Supp. 1992) provides that "[n]oneconomic damages which are recoverable in tort actions include damages for pain and suffering, mental anguish, disfigurement, *loss of enjoyment of life,* loss of consortium, and all other nonpecuniary losses or claims" (emphasis added). Thus, the important issue-of-first-impression we face is strictly whether the trial court abused its discretion in excluding expert testimony on such damages. "The question of admissibility of expert testimony on how the value of [hedonic] damages is calculated is the focus of controversy and debate. Decisions continue to go both ways." T. Branch, Seeking Recovery for Loss of Enjoyment of Life, Trial, April 1994, at 40, 43 [hereinafter, Branch, Seeking Recovery].

* * *

At trial, Montalvo offered the testimony of Dr. Louis Rose, a professor of economics at the University of Hawaii, who testified as an expert on lost wages. * * * Montalvo made a lengthy offer of proof on Rose's proposed testimony regarding hedonic damages. Montalvo argued, in part:

> Doctor Rose would be testifying * * * based upon more than 40 studies [which calculate] the value of life [by looking at] people taking riskier jobs [for] greater amounts of pay, safety factors such as what people are willing to pay for airbags and things of that nature.

* * *

[Dr. Rose's proffered testimony was to do three things: (1) establish a monetary value for an average human life, based on "willingness to pay" studies; (2) show how much of that value remained for Montalvo at the time of his accident, given his age and life expectancy; (3) permit the jury to

---

2. Hedonic damages are damages "for the loss of enjoyment of life, or for the value of life itself, as measured separately from the economic productive value that an injured or deceased person would have had." Black's Law Dictionary 391 (6th ed. 1990).

consider the value of Montalvo's life when deciding what dollar amount of "hedonic damages" to award him on account of his permanent injury.]

Montalvo also noted that Rose's theory of estimating hedonic damages was based on "(1) [w]orker's wages for risk of death, (2) [c]onsumer expenditures on safety, and (3) [s]urvey questionnaires."

"Perhaps surprising to some, the development of methodologies to place a value on human life is not a new science.... [Economists] have come up with two basic approaches for valuing human life: the human capital approach and the willingness-to-pay approach." A. McClurg, It's a Wonderful Life: The Case for Hedonic Damages in Wrongful Death Cases, 66 Notre Dame L.Rev. 57, 100 (1990) [hereinafter, McClurg, It's a Wonderful Life]. "[T]he willingness-to-pay approach studies people's consumption behavior to determine how much they are willing to pay to reduce the possibility of dying. The theory is that the amount people are willing to pay for lifesaving products like smoke alarms or automobile safety devices shows what dollar value people place on life." Branch, Seeking Recovery, supra, at 42 * * * . Rose's proffered expert testimony clearly was based on the willingness-to-pay approach discussed in the McClurg and Branch articles.

Recent decisions, however, have specifically rejected expert testimony on hedonic damages based upon willingness-to-pay studies.[23] Some courts have allowed such testimony. However, we reject the minority view and agree with the majority trend towards inadmissibility of expert testimony on hedonic damages based on willingness-to-pay studies.

We stress that the narrow issue is whether an expert can assist a jury in valuing loss of *enjoyment* of life due to an injury; the value of life itself is, at most, tangentially related. * * *

Moreover, we agree with other courts that *assumptions* made in willingness-to-pay studies are questionable. "[T]he calculations are based on assumptions that appear to controvert logic and good sense." [Wilt v. Buracker, 443 S.E.2d 196, 205 (W.Va.1993).] As did the *Wilt* court, we find the following analysis of the United States Court of Appeals for the Seventh Circuit persuasive:

We have serious doubts about [the] assertion that the studies [relied] upon actually measure how much Americans value life.... [S]pending on safety items reflects a consumer's willingness to pay to reduce *risk*, perhaps more a measure of how cautious a person is than how much he or she

---

23. See Wilt v. Buracker, 443 S.E.2d 196, 205 (W.Va.1993) ("[t]he majority of jurisdictions that have addressed whether expert testimony based upon willingness-to-pay studies is relevant to one's loss of enjoyment of life have concluded that such testimony is inadmissible"); Mercado v. Ahmed, 974 F.2d 863, 871 (7th Cir.1992) ("we have serious doubts about [the expert's] assertion that [willingness-to-pay] studies ... actually measure how much Americans value life"); * * * see also McClurg, It's a Wonderful Life, supra, at 105–06 ("[t]he most basic flaw in the willingness-to-pay theory ... is that it simply does not comport with the reality of how people behave.... Given the flaws of the willingness-to-pay theory and the wide-ranging values it generates, the extent to which willingness-to-pay evidence meaningfully assists a jury in calculating damages for the intrinsic value of life is suspect at best"); cf. Foster v. Trafalgar House Oil & Gas, 603 So.2d 284, 286 (La.App.1992) ("economic theories which attempt to extrapolate the 'value' of human life from various studies of wages, costs, etc., have no place in the calculation of general damages").

values life. Few of us, when confronted with the threat, "Your money or your life!" would, like Jack Benny, pause and respond, "I'm thinking, I'm thinking." Most of us would empty our wallets. Why that decision reflects less the value we place on life than whether we buy an airbag is not immediately obvious.

[Mercado v. Ahmed, 974 F.2d 863, 871 (7th Cir.1992)] (emphasis in original).

The measurement of the joy of life is intangible. A jury may draw upon its own life experiences in attempting to put a monetary figure on the pleasure of living. It is "a uniquely human endeavor ... requiring the trier of fact to draw upon the virtually unlimited factors unique to us as human beings." Foster, 603 So.2d at 286. Testimony of an economist would not aid the jury in making such measurements because an economist is no more expert at valuing the pleasure of life than the average juror. * * *

Thus, because the proffered expert testimony on hedonic damages * * * would not have assisted the jury, and would not have added to the common understanding of the jury, we hold that the trial court did not abuse its discretion by excluding it.

————

WILT v. BURACKER, 191 W.Va. 39, 443 S.E.2d 196 (1993). In this case the trial judge permitted expert testimony of an economist about the value of life, in order to assist the jury in calculating hedonic damages. According to the reviewing court, the expert, Dr. Brookshire, testified that "every human life has the same whole-life value," which he "set at $2.5 million." Dr. Brookshire derived this dollar amount "by combining and averaging the economic values arrived at in over 50 'willingness-to-pay' studies." He gave simplified numerical examples to explain the studies' methodology:

> * * * [O]ne example was based on wage-versus-risk studies and involved a hypothetical illustration of 10,000 window washers working on skyscrapers and the risk of death between those working on the first-floor windows and those working on the top floors. From federal statistics, [Dr. Brookshire] found a 1 in 10,000 greater chance of death for top-floor window washers than other window washers. He then assumed a wage differential of $300 per year for top-floor washers. Thus, the bottom-floor washers were willing to accept $300 less a year to avoid the top-floor work. He concluded that if the 10,000 workers were willing to accept $300 less, then the value of one life in that context is $3,000,000. * * *

Another illustration was given to disclose the methodology [involved in calculating the value of life] by using studies on consumers' willingness to pay for safety devices to protect their lives. Dr. Brookshire set the cost of an automobile airbag at $300 and indicated that highway death statistics showed that with an airbag the risk of death went down by 1 in 10,000, that is, one life will be saved if 10,000 people have air bags. He then concluded: " * * * What does that mean? 10,000 people spend $300.00 each, that is three million in total, to save one life."

The West Virginia Supreme Court of Appeals held that Dr. Brookshire's testimony ought not to have been allowed, because the loss of enjoyment of life "is not subject to an economic calculation." It said that "[a]nyone who is familiar with the wages of coal miners, policemen, and firefighters would scoff at the assertion that these high risk jobs have any meaningful extra wage component for the risks undertaken by workers in those professions." The court quoted with approval the following passages from the opinion in Mercado v. Ahmed, 974 F.2d 863, 871 (7th Cir.1992):

> * * * [S]pending on items like air bags and smoke detectors is probably influenced as much by advertising and marketing decisions made by profit-seeking manufacturers and by government-mandated safety requirements as it is by any consideration by consumers of how much life is worth. Also, many people may be interested in a whole range of safety devices and believe they are worthwhile, but are unable to afford them. * * *

> * * * To say that the salary paid to those who hold risky jobs tells us something significant about how much we value life ignores the fact that humans are moved by more than monetary incentives. For example, someone who believes police officers working in an extremely dangerous city are grossly undercompensated for the risks they assume might nevertheless take up the badge out of a sense of civic duty to their hometown. * * *

IMPLICIT VALUATION OF LIFE. In his book, *Fatal Tradeoffs* (1992), economist W. Kip Viscusi reviews the body of research that attempts to calculate the dollar value of life implicit in people's choices concerning mortal risk. This research calculates "the risk-dollar tradeoff" involved in such choices. Viscusi believes "it is the risk-dollar tradeoffs of individuals in society that establish the price the government should be willing to pay for greater safety" (p. vii).

Viscusi's review focusses mainly on "labor market" studies, which derive the value of life from the amount of extra pay received by workers in high risk jobs. Also reviewed are studies using "survey" methodology: the surveys ask people what amount of money they would require in exchange for added risk, or would be willing to pay for reduced risk. Viscusi's presentation shows three notable kinds of persistent variability in the results of implicit valuation studies.

First, different studies produce different values of life. Here, arranged by increasing size, are the dollar amounts calculated for life's value in 12 labor market studies reviewed by Viscusi (numbers indicate millions of 1990 dollars): 0.6, 1.5, 2.8, 3.6, 4.6, 5.2, 6.5, 7.8, 9.7, 10.4, 13.5, 16.2. (Table 4–1.) A similar range appears in studies using survey methodology: 0.1, 1.2, 2.7, 3.4, 3.8, 8.8, 9.7, 15.6. (Table 4–4.) Viscusi recognizes that the tradeoff of dollars for risk "varies considerably across data sets and methodologies" (p. 58). He rejects the quest for "a single best value-of-life number" in favor of the idea "that there is a value-of-life range" which policy-makers should consider (pp. 58–9). According to Viscusi, "most of the reasonable estimates of the value of life" based on labor market data for lower income jobs "are clustered in the $3 to $7 million range" (p. 73).

Second, different individuals implicitly value their lives differently. This variance is seen in survey-based studies, where individual valuations are registered. For example, in one large-scale survey study conducted by Viscusi himself, the median value of life was $2.7 million—that is, within the group surveyed, the number who valued their lives at more than $2.7 million was the same as the number who valued their lives at less. But the mean value (arithmetical average) was more than three times higher, $9.7 million, "because the mean figure is pushed upward by some extreme responses at the high end" (p. 69). Viscusi emphasizes that "[t]he value of life is not a universal constant" (p. 58). "Risk-dollar tradeoffs reflect individual preferences that will differ across individuals" (p. 917).

Third, different groups value life differently. In particular, high earners place a higher value on life—implicitly—than low earners. Viscusi emphasizes that valuations of life are "highly responsive to income" (p. 29). "[T]he value of life of workers in typical blue collar risk jobs was on the order of $3 million; and the value of life of individuals in very high-income positions may be $6 million or more" (pp. 264–5). Viscusi comments: "If the evaluation of risks increases with one's wealth, then we should require higher levels of safety for products targeted at higher-income consumers" (p. 7). Then government policies will replicate "the outcomes that would be expected * * * in a market for safety" (p. 29). For example, policies for protection of airline passengers should be more demanding than policies protecting industrial workers. "Recognition of the income elasticity of the value of life will lead to the use of a different value of life depending on the population being protected" (p. 918).

OSHA CANCER POLICY
Identification, Classification and Regulation of Potential Occupational
Carcinogens, 45 Fed.Reg. 5001 (1980).

For cost-benefit analyses of occupational health regulation, an especially serious methodological problem is involved where adverse health outcomes include premature death, because it would be necessary to assign a value to human life.

Attempts to assign economic weights to human life have often assumed a human capital approach, which values an individual's economic contribution to society. Human life valuation is calculated in terms of the present discounted value of future income streams (gross output) or the present discounted value of future income streams minus an individual's consumption (net output). This approach assumes that the only goal of economic policy is to maximize Gross National Product. Human life valuations also depend critically on earnings levels, leading to lower values for the retired, women, and disadvantaged low-wage groups.

Another approach avoids any direct calculations of the loss of potential earnings or spending. Instead, the value of human life is implicitly calculated based on the cost of programs paid for by society that increase or decrease the number of deaths, such as the kidney dialysis program. However, estimates based on these "social" values have been found to differ widely depending on the program.

Another methodology is based on insurance policies. Insurance premiums and death probabilities associated with specific activities have been used to calculate the value that individuals set on their lives. However, this approach is conceptually deficient since life insurance refers only to compensation to others.

Finally, attempts to value life have been based on estimates of wage premiums paid for high-risk occupations, using regression analysis. This methodology is based on the principle that workers in high hazard jobs will demand premiums to compensate them for the additional risks entailed. The annual (hourly wage) premiums required to assume the additional risks are then converted into estimates of the value of human life. The results of this methodology are mixed. Estimates of the value of human life (where risk premiums have been found) vary widely with average figures ranging between $100,000 and $1 million. In addition to technical analytical problems involved in individual studies, the general validity of this methodology rests on the assumption of perfectly competitive labor markets. Hence, this approach requires that workers possess accurate knowledge of risks and make well-informed choices, an unlikely assumption for workplace carcinogens, and that workers can readily move to lower-risk jobs.

Dr. [Lester] Lave, an advocate of cost-benefit analysis [whose testimony was presented by the American Petroleum Institute], pointed out the difficulties of placing a value on life. He stated:

"While dollars are the natural metric of abatement costs, they are alien to the measurement of benefits. As explained above, the notion of explicitly valuing premature death or morbidity in dollars is repugnant. Nonetheless, the refusal [to] do so can be shown to result in grave misallocation of resources and in capricious behavior."

After examining all the evidence in the coke oven proceeding (made part of this Record * * *), where extensive data and arguments were presented on whether it was appropriate to attempt to put a dollar value on life, OSHA concluded:

"that these methodologies do not adequately quantify the value of life. Accordingly we decline [to do] so." (41 FR 48751)

The evidence presented in the Cancer Policy confirms this conclusion. OSHA believes that it is not possible for it to place a value on life and regulate on this basis.

Index

References are to Pages

†